The Ultimate Accountants' Reference, 3rd Edition

Update Service

BECOME A SUBSCRIBER!
Did you purchase this product from a bookstore?

If you did, it's important for you to become a subscriber. John Wiley & Sons, Inc. may publish, on a periodic basis, supplements and new editions to reflect the latest changes in the subject matter that you **need to know** in order to stay competitive in this ever-changing industry. By contacting the Wiley office nearest you, you'll receive any current update at no additional charge. In addition, you'll receive future updates and revised or related volumes on a 30-day examination review.

If you purchased this product directly from John Wiley & Sons, Inc., we have already recorded your subscription for this update service.

To become a subscriber, please call **1-877-762-2974** or send your name, company name (if applicable), address, and the title of the product to:

mailing address: **Supplement Department**
John Wiley & Sons, Inc.
One Wiley Drive
Somerset, NJ 08875

e-mail: **subscriber@wiley.com**
fax: **1-732-302-2300**
online: **www.wiley.com**

For customers outside the United States, please contact the Wiley office nearest you:

Professional & Reference Division
John Wiley & Sons Canada, Ltd.
22 Worcester Road
Etobicoke, Ontario M9W 1L1
CANADA
Phone: 416-236-4433
Phone: 1-800-567-4797
Fax: 416-236-4447
Email: canada@wiley.com

John Wiley & Sons, Ltd.
The Atrium
Southern Gate, Chichester
West Sussex PO 19 8SQ
ENGLAND
Phone: 44-1243-779777
Fax: 44-1243-775878
Email: customer@wiley.co.uk

John Wiley & Sons Australia, Ltd.
33 Park Road
P.O. Box 1226
Milton, Queensland 4064
AUSTRALIA
Phone: 61-7-3859-9755
Fax: 61-7-3859-9715
Email: brisbane@johnwiley.com.au

John Wiley & Sons (Asia) Pte., Ltd.
2 Clementi Loop #02-01
SINGAPORE 129809
Phone: 65-64632400
Fax: 65-64634604/5/6
Customer Service: 65-64604280
Email: enquiry@wiley.com.sg

The Ultimate Accountants' Reference, 3rd Edition

INCLUDING GAAP, IRS AND SEC REGULATIONS, LEASES, AND MORE

STEVEN M. BRAGG

WILEY

JOHN WILEY & SONS, INC.

For general information about our other products and services, please contact our Customer Care Department within the United States at (800) 762-2974, outside the United States at (317) 572-3993 or fax (317) 572-4002.

Wiley also publishes its books in a variety of electronic formats. Some content that appears in print may not be available in electronic books.

For more information about Wiley products, visit our web site at http://www.wiley.com.

Library of Congress Cataloging-in-Publication Data:

ISBN-13   978-0-470-57254-2

Printed in the United States of America

10   9   8   7   6   5   4   3   2   1

CONTENTS

ABOUT THE AUTHOR

Steven Bragg, CPA, has been the chief financial officer or controller of four companies, as well as a consulting manager at Ernst & Young and auditor at Deloitte & Touche. He received a Master's degree in Finance from Bentley College, an MBA from Babson College, and a Bachelor's degree in Economics from the University of Maine. He has been the two-time president of the Colorado Mountain Club, is an avid alpine skier and mountain biker, and is a certified master diver. Mr. Bragg resides in Centennial, Colorado with his wife and two daughters. He has published the following books through John Wiley & Sons:

Accounting and Finance for Your Small Business
Accounting Best Practices
Accounting Control Best Practices
Accounting for Payroll
Billing and Collections Best Practices
Business Ratios and Formulas
Controller's Guide to Costing
Controller's Guide to Planning and Controlling Operations
Controller's Guide: Roles and Responsibilities for the New Controller
Controllership
Cost Accounting
Design and Maintenance of Accounting Manuals
Essentials of Payroll
Fast Close
Financial Analysis
GAAP Guide
GAAP Implementation Guide
GAAS Guide
Inventory Accounting
Inventory Best Practices
Just-in-Time Accounting
Managing Explosive Corporate Growth
Mergers and Acquisitions
Outsourcing
Payroll Best Practices
Sales and Operations for Your Small Business
The Controller's Function
The New CFO Financial Leadership Manual
The Ultimate Accountants' Reference
Treasury Management

Also:

Advanced Accounting Systems (Institute of Internal Auditors)
Run the Rockies (CMC Press)

PREFACE

The Third Edition of *The Ultimate Accountants' Reference* black is designed to give the accountant the answers to all of the most important issues that arise during the typical business day. It provides a comprehensive overview of all aspects of the accounting function, including accounting rules and regulations, transactions, control points, and internal and external reports. It also itemizes a wide range of accounting management issues, such as best practices, budgeting, closing the books, control systems, cost accounting, earnings per share, financial analysis, leases, management information systems, accounting for mergers and acquisitions, initial public offerings, bankruptcy, segment reporting, tax laws, and record keeping. In addition, it covers a number of financial management issues, such as the extension and management of customer credit, financing, cash management, and risk management. The appendices are also rich in detail, describing a sample chart of accounts, itemizing dozens of journal entries, displaying interest rate tables, and listing the most commonly used business ratios. Thus, this Third Edition of *The Ultimate Accountants' Reference* is a true one-stop source of information for the accountant.

The answers to many of the everyday questions posed to the accountant can be answered with the information provided in this book. One can find within these pages the answers to such questions as:

- How is comprehensive income presented?
- How is the statement of cash flows formatted?
- What types of footnotes should be added to the financial statements?
- How do I report on different segments of the business?
- How do I calculate earnings per share?
- How do I report accounting changes or error corrections?
- How do I account for options?
- How do I convert foreign currency transactions for financial reporting purposes?
- How do I set up a perpetual inventory tracking system?
- How do I account for backflushing transactions?
- What types of inventory valuation methods are available?
- What are the rules related to the recognition of revenue?
- How do I account for stock buybacks, dividends, and convertible securities?
- What best practices are most useful to my business?
- How do I account for leases?
- How do I create a budget?
- What techniques can I use to close the books as fast as possible?
- What are the strengths and weaknesses of the various costing systems?
- How do I evaluate a capital project?
- What is my company's cost of capital?
- When do I eliminate unprofitable products?
- How do I set up a cash tracking, reporting, and forecasting system?

- How do I account for hedging transactions?
- How do I manage foreign exchange transactions?
- What are the key risk management issues to be aware of, and how do I mitigate them?
- How does the Initial Public Offering process work?
- What are the current tax laws that address stock options?
- How do I account for a business combination under the purchase method?
- What ratios should I use to monitor corporate cash flows?
- What chart of accounts structure should I use to set up a general ledger?

These and hundreds of other questions are answered in the Third Edition of *The Ultimate Accountants' Reference*.

Centennial, Colorado
January 2010

PART ONE

OVERVIEW OF ACCOUNTING AND ITS ROLE IN THE ORGANIZATION

CHAPTER 1

INTRODUCTION

The intention of this book is to give the accountant the answers to the largest possible number of accounting issues that are likely to arise. Thus, given the wide-ranging scope of this work, the reader should know about its overall structure in order to locate information more easily.

The *Ultimate Accountant's Reference* is divided into seven parts, each of which deals with a different aspect of the accounting function. The first part covers the role of accounting within the modern corporation. Chapter 2, The Role of Accounting, describes the primary tasks for which the accountant is responsible, as well as ethical concerns, and lists the job descriptions of the major positions to be found within the accounting department.

The second part deals with accounting rules and regulations. Chapter 3, Standard-Setting Organizations, describes the origins and responsibilities of the various rule-setting bodies that have created Generally Accepted Accounting Principles (GAAP), not only for United States business entities, but also for government and international organizations. Chapter 4, The Securities and Exchange Commission, gives an overview of the Securities and Exchange Commission (SEC), the EDGAR online reporting system, Staff Accounting Bulletins, and the Acts and SEC regulations that govern the reporting requirements of publicly held corporations. Chapter 5 describes a multitude of Laws that have a direct or indirect impact on accounting.

The third part covers the general format and rules governing the information contained within accounting reports. Chapter 6, The Balance Sheet and Statement of Stockholders' Equity, describe the format of the balance sheet and statement of retained earnings, as well as the definitions of the various categories of assets, liabilities, and equity items that are listed in these reports. Chapter 7, The Income Statement, describes the format of the income statement, as well as the rules governing the presentation of information about discontinued operations, earnings per share, gains and losses, accounting changes, discontinued operations, extraordinary items, other comprehensive income, and prior period adjustments. Chapter 8, The Statement of Cash Flows, describes the format of the statement of cash flows, as well as exemptions from its use and how to handle foreign currency translations when constructing it. Chapter 9, Footnotes, describes a broad range of disclosures that an accountant may be required to attach to the financial statements in the form of footnotes. Chapter 10, Internal Management Reports, departs from the previous chapters in this part, in that it describes reports that are entirely "free form," designed entirely for internal use and not prescribed in format by any accounting pronouncement. These include status, margin, cash, sales and expense, and payroll reports. Chapter 11, Foreign Currency Translation, which covers the proper treatment of foreign currency translation, including the use of the current rate translation method and the remeasurement method, as well as the proper accounting for foreign exchange sale transactions and the recognition of translation adjustments. Chapter 12, Cash, Prepaid Expenses, and Investments, defines cash and investments, describes the different types of marketable securities, derivatives, and long-term investments, and how each one is accounted for.

The fourth part departs from the reporting format of the financial statement and delves into the accounting rules and transactions for each of the asset, liability, equity, and revenue categories. Chapter 13, Inventory, describes the types of inventory, inventory management, how to install an inventory tracking system, the physical inventory counting procedure, and the use of the LIFO, FIFO, average, retail, dollar-value LIFO, and gross margin methods for valuing inventory. The chapter also describes the lower of cost or market rule and the process to follow when allocating overhead costs to inventory. Chapter 14, Accounts Receivable, describes the accounts receivable transaction flow, as well as how to account for factored accounts receivable, sales returns, early payment discounts, long-term accounts receivable, and bad debts. Chapter 15, Fixed Assets, describes the use of a capitalization limit when accounting for newly acquired fixed assets, as well as the proper accounting for newly acquired assets, improvements to existing assets, the disposition of assets, construction in progress, and leasehold improvements. It also covers the various types of depreciation that may be used to account for the gradual reduction in value of fixed assets.

Chapter 16, Current Liabilities and Contingencies, describes the accounts payable transaction flow, and how to account for the period-end cutoff of accounts payable transactions. It also covers the proper accounting for advance payments from customers, accrued expenses, unclaimed wages, interest payable, dividends, termination benefits, estimated product returns, and contingent liabilities. Chapter 17, Debt, describes basic bond transactions and accounting for a bond discount or premium, as well as for non-interest-bearing notes payable. It also covers interest risk management, noncash debt payments, early debt retirement, callable debt, defaulted debt, warrants, sinking funds, bonds converted to equity, and short-term debt that is being refinanced. Chapter 18, Equity, covers the transactions related to common stock, as well as stock options, stock appreciation rights, stock warrants, dividends, stock subscriptions, stock splits, stock retirement, and employee stock ownership plans. Chapter 19, Stock Options, describes the two methods available to account for stock option transactions. Chapter 20, Revenue, covers the multitude of revenue recognition rules, including variations under the accrual method, cash method, installment sales method, completed contract method, percentage of completion method, proportional performance method, production method, and deposit method. It also discusses the special rules related to bill and hold transactions, brokered transactions, appreciation, and initiation fees. Chapter 21, Research and Development, describes the proper accounting for in-house R&D costs, as well as for acquired R&D costs, R&D costs contracted to another party, and the special case of R&D costs in the software industry. Chapter 22, Leases, describes the accounting for both the lessee and lessor, as well as for special situations such as lease extensions, terminations and subleases.

Chapter 23, Earnings per Share, addresses the proper calculation of earnings per share information, as well as its disclosure in the financial statements. Chapter 24, Segment Reporting, describes the rules for determining business segments, as well as how relevant segment information is to be presented in the financial statements. Chapter 25, Interim Reporting, covers the reporting and disclosure requirements for interim periods. Chapter 26, Accounting Changes and Correction of Errors, addresses the types of retroactive reporting changes required when accounting principles are changed or errors are discovered.

The fifth part of the book covers the crucial area of accounting management. This is the core function for many accountants, who can provide value to the organization through the use of better control systems, financial analysis of key investments, and higher levels of departmental efficiency. Chapter 27, Best Practices, covers several dozen of the most common best practices that can improve a company's performance, including the areas of accounts payable, collections, commissions, filing, financial statements, the general ledger, invoicing, management, and payroll. For a thorough treatment of this topic, the reader can also consult the author's *Accounting Best Practices*, 6th Edition (John Wiley & Sons, 2010). Chapter 28, Budgeting, explains the system of interlocking departmental budgets, and presents a sample budget. It also covers a number of budgeting best practices and control systems that assist the accountant in creating a budget in the most efficient manner possible. Chapter 29, Closing the Books, focuses on the various steps required to achieve a fast close, and also describes the steps needed to achieve an instantaneous close. Chapter 30, Control Systems, presents a list of the most essential control points that the accountant should be concerned with, as well as control flowcharts showing where these controls are used. It also discusses the times when it may be appropriate to eliminate controls for efficiency reasons, and covers the various types of fraud that some of these controls are designed to detect and mitigate. Chapter 31, Cost Accounting, focuses on the many types of advanced data collection systems that can be used to compile data for use by cost accounting systems. It also describes the major costing systems that can be used to interpret this data, such as job costing, process costing, standard costing, direct costing, and activity-based costing. It also covers the concepts of throughput accounting, target costing, by-product costing, and cost variances. These topics are covered in more detail in the author's *Cost Accounting* (John Wiley & Sons, 2001). Chapter 32, Financial Analysis, describes how to calculate a company's cost of capital, determine which unprofitable products to eliminate, discount future cash flows, and conduct both breakeven and risk analyses. These topics and more are described in additional detail in the author's *Financial Analysis*, 2nd Edition (John Wiley & Sons, 2007). Finally, Chapter 33, Records Management, deals with the cost of various types of recordkeeping systems, the policies and procedures required for proper record storage, and the types of tax records that must be kept on hand.

The sixth part of the book deals with financial management, which includes customer credit, cash management, long-term financing, and risk management—all topics that are of particular interest to accountants in smaller organizations that do not have separate finance departments. Chapter 34, Customer Credit, describes the types of selling terms that can be extended, how to conduct a credit investigation, and various techniques for collecting overdue accounts receivable. Chapter 35, Financing, describes how to minimize a company's financing needs through proper management, how to deal with banks, and the pros and cons of delaying payments to suppliers. It also addresses the use of factoring and field warehouse financing, floor planning, inventory reduction, leasing, lines of credit, asset-based loans, bonds, bridge loans, preferred stock, sale and leaseback arrangements, and various types of debt in order to deal with a company's financing requirements. Chapter 36, Cash Management, describes the use of a cash-forecasting model and its automation, various cash concentration strategies, and how to invest short-term funds. Chapter 37, Foreign Exchange Management, describes the foreign exchange process and how one can mitigate associated risks. Chapter 38, Risk Management, describes the risk management policies and procedures that can be used to determine and mitigate risks, as well as the types of insurance that are available to reduce any remaining risks. It also describes the claims administration process, claims documentation, and the format of the annual risk management report.

The seventh part of the book deals with four major topics that do not fit easily into any of the preceding categories—mergers and acquisitions, the initial public offering, bankruptcy, and taxation. In Chapter 39, Mergers and Acquisitions, we cover the accounting required to record a business combination under both the purchase and pooling methods of accounting. The chapter also describes how to record investments in a subsidiary by using the cost method, equity method, or consolidation method. It also delves into types of acquisitions, push-down accounting, leveraged buyouts, spin-off transactions, and the proper treatment of goodwill. Chapter 40, The Initial Public Offering, covers the entire IPO process, including preparation, finding an underwriter, registering the IPO, and listing on an exchange. Chapter 41, Going Private, describes the process for taking a public company private. Chapter 42, Bankruptcy, covers the sequence of events in a bankruptcy, as well as the rights of all parties and a variety of special issues. Chapter 43, Taxation, covers over 40 taxation issues, including the Alternative Minimum Tax, partnership taxation, deferred compensation, stock options, and transfer pricing.

The final part of this book is the appendices, which include additional reference information that the accountant is likely to require on a regular basis. Appendix A describes the different types of account code structures that can be used in a chart of accounts, and gives sample charts of accounts for each structure. Appendix B contains a list of nearly all journal entries that an accountant is likely to deal with. Appendix C contains interest rate tables, as well as the formulas used to derive them. These tables cover simple interest, compound interest, the present value of an annuity, and the future amount of an annuity. Appendix D contains more than 40 ratios that can be used to determine a company's financial condition. For more ratios, please consult the author's *Business Ratios and Formulas* 2nd Edition (John Wiley & Sons, 2007). The final appendix includes a complete list of due diligence questions to ask when reviewing a potential acquisition.

In short, *The Ultimate Accountants' Reference* is a complete source of information for the practicing accountant. By using the table of contents, this introduction, and the index to locate information, one can find the answers to most everyday accounting questions in this book.

CHAPTER 2

THE ROLE OF ACCOUNTING

2.1 TASKS OF THE ACCOUNTING FUNCTION

The accounting function has had sole responsibility for processing the bulk of a company's transactions for many years. Chief among these transactions have been the processing of customer billings and supplier invoices. Though these two areas comprise the bulk of the transactions, there has also been a long history of delegating asset tracking to the accounting function. This involves all transactions related to the movement of cash, inventory, and fixed assets. Finally, the accounting staff has been responsible for tracking debt, which can involve a continuous tracking of debt levels by debt instrument, as well as the payments made to reduce them. These have been the transactionbased activities of the accounting staff.

With worldwide barriers to competition crumbling, every company feels the pinch of lower competitive prices and now asks the accounting staff to provide analysis work in addition to the traditional transaction processing. These tasks include margin analysis on existing or projected product lines, geographic sales regions, or individual products. In addition, the accounting staff may even be asked to serve on new product design teams, so that they can determine the projected cost of new products, especially in relation to target costs. Further, the accounting staff must continuously review and report on nonproduct costs, which can range from advertising to utilities. This level of cost review and reporting calls for a different kind of accounting staff than the traditional kind that did nothing but process large volumes of transactionrelated paperwork. It now requires highly trained cost accountants and financial analysts, almost always with college degrees and professional certifications, to conduct the work.

The world of business has become more international. Many companies are doing an increasing volume of business with companies based in other countries. This greatly increases the complexity of accounting, for a company must now determine gains and losses on sales to other countries. There may even be bartering transactions with organizations that do not have ready access to currency. In addition, if there is no separate finance function, the accounting staff may be called on to handle letters of credit and hedging transactions that are designed to reduce the level of risk that goes with foreign dealings. All of these issues call for a level of skill that was not required in the days of simple transaction processing.

In the face of more intensive competition, many companies are also merging or acquiring subsidiaries. This adds a great deal of complexity to the accounting staff's work, for it must now coordinate a multitude of additional tasks in other locations. This includes setting up standard procedures for the processing of receipts, shipments, and cash. Also, closing the financial books at the end of each reporting period becomes much more complex, as the accounting staff must now coordinate the assembly and consolidation of information from multiple subsidiaries. Even if a company decides to consolidate all of its accounting facilities into one central processing location to avoid all this trouble, it still requires the management expertise to bring together the disparate accounting systems into a smoothly operating facility. This is not an easy task. The environment of mergers and acquisitions greatly increases the skill needed by the accounting staff.

The tasks of the accounting function are itemized below. The tasks that belong elsewhere—but are commonly given to the accounting staff in a small company—are noted under a separate heading.

- *Traditional accounting tasks*
  - ○ Accounts payable transaction processing
  - ○ Accounts receivable transaction processing
  - ○ Asset transaction processing
  - ○ Debt transaction processing
- *New accounting tasks*
  - ○ Bartering transactions
  - ○ Coordination and consolidation of accounting at subsidiaries
  - ○ Currency translations
  - ○ Hedge accounting
  - ○ Margin analysis
  - ○ Nonproduct cost analysis
  - ○ Selection, implementation, and operation of accounting software and related systems
  - ○ Target costing
- *New tasks assigned to the accounting function of smaller companies*
  - ○ Computer services systems installation and maintenance
  - ○ Hedging and letter of credit transactions

Given today's highly volatile and ever-changing business environment, the only safe statement to make about the new activities presented in this section is that they will only become more complex, requiring even greater skill by the accounting staff to be accomplished in a manner that is both efficient and effective.

2.2   ROLE OF THE ACCOUNTING FUNCTION

Having noted the expanded number of tasks now undertaken by the modern accounting function, it is important to also note how the role of the accounting staff has changed in relation to the rest of the company.

When the number of accounting tasks was more closely defined around transaction processing, it was common for the accounting staff to be housed in an out-of-the-way corner of a business, where it would work without being impeded by other functions. Now, with a much greater number of tasks, the accounting staff finds itself involved in most major decisions. For example, the cost accountant is expected to serve on product design teams and to let other team members know if new designs will have costs that will meet targeted cost goals. An accounting analyst may be asked by the sales manager to evaluate the profitability of a lease deal being extended to a customer. The controller is frequently asked to sit in on executive committee meetings to give opinions on the cash flow issues for acquisitions or purchases. The accounts receivable clerk may work closely with the sales staff to collect overdue invoices from customers. For these reasons and others, the accounting function now finds itself performing a variety of tasks that make it an integral part of the organization.

A particularly important area in which the role of the accountant has changed is related to processes. When another area of the company changes its operations, which is increasingly common, the accounting staff must devise alterations to the existing systems for processing transactions that will accommodate those changes. For example, if the manufacturing function switches to just-in-time production or computer-integrated manufacturing, this has a profound impact on the way in which the accounting staff pays its bills, invoices customers, monitors job costs, and creates internal reports. Also, if the materials management staff decides to use material requirements planning or integrated distribution management, these new systems will issue information that is of great use to the accounting staff; it should connect its systems to those of the materials management staff to access that information. To alter its processes, the accounting staff must first be aware of these changes, requiring the accounting staff to engage in more interaction with other parts of the company to find out what is going on.

The most historically important role that the accounting staff must change is that of being a brake on other activities. Because most accountants are trained in implementing controls to ensure that assets are not lost, the accounting staff tends to shoot down changes proposed by other departments—the changes will interfere with the controls. The accounting personnel must realize that changes put forward by other functions are not intended to disrupt controls, but to improve the company's position in the marketplace or to increase its efficiency. This means that some controls must be modified, replaced, or eliminated. It is very helpful for the accounting personnel to have an open mind about altering systems, even when the new systems interfere with the accounting staff's system of controls.

In today's increasingly competitive environment, it is very important for companies to develop strong relationships with their key suppliers and customers. These business partners will demand extra services, some of which must be fulfilled by the accounting staff. These changes may include using electronic data interchange transactions, providing special billing formats to customers, or paying suppliers by electronic transfer. If these steps are needed to retain key business partners, then the accounting staff must be willing to do its share of the work. Too frequently, the accounting staff resists these sorts of changes, on the grounds that all transactions must be performed in exactly the same manner. The accounting department must realize that altering its way of doing business is sometimes necessary to support ongoing business relationships.

Altering the focus of the accounting staff from an introverted group that processes paper to one that works with other parts of a company and is willing to alter its systems to accommodate the needs of other departments is required in today's business environment. This is in great contrast to the accounting department of the past, which had a minimal role in other company activities, and which was its conservative anchor.

2.3   IMPACT OF ETHICS ON THE ACCOUNTING ROLE

With the globalization of business, competition has become more intense. It is possible that the ethical foundations to which a company adheres have deteriorated in the face of this pressure. There have been innumerable examples in the press of falsified earnings reports, bribery, kickbacks, and employee thefts. There are vastly more instances of ethical failings that many would perceive to be more minimal, such as employee use of company property for personal use, "smoothing" of financial results to keep them in line with investor expectations, or excessively robust sales or earnings forecasts. The controller and the accounting staff in general play a very large role in a company's ethical orientation, for they control or have some influence over the primary issues that are most subject to ethical problems—reported earnings, cash usage, and control over assets. This section discusses how the accounting function can modify a company's ethical behavior—for good or bad.

The accounting function can have a serious negative impact on a company's ethical standards through nothing more than indifference or lack of caring. For example, if the controller continually acquiesces to management demands to slightly modify the financial statements, this may eventually lead to larger and larger alterations. Once the controller has set a standard for allowing changes to reported earnings, how can the controller define where to draw the line? Another example is when the accounting staff does not enforce control over assets; if it conducts a fixedasset audit and finds that a television has been appropriated by an employee for several months, it can indirectly encourage continuing behavior of this kind simply by taking no action. Other employees will see that there is no penalty for removing assets and will then do the same thing. Yet another example is when the accounting staff does not closely review employee expense reports for inappropriate expenditures. Once again, if employees see that the expense report rules are not being enforced, they will gradually include more expenses in their reports that should not be included. The accounting staff has a significant negative influence over a company's ethical standards simply by not enforcing the rules.

The previous argument can be turned around for an active accounting department. If the controller and the rest of the accounting staff rigidly enforce company policies and procedures and acquire a reputation for no deviations from these standards, the rest of the corporation will be dragged into line. It is especially important that the controller adhere closely to the highest standards, for the rest of the accounting staff will follow the controller's lead. Conversely, if the controller does not maintain a high ethical standard, the rest of the accounting staff will have no ethical leader, and will quickly lapse into apathy. Accordingly, the controller is a company's chief ethics officer, for the position has such a strong influence over ethics. It is a rare week that passes without some kind of ethical quandary finding its way to the controller for resolution.

It is not sufficient to merely say that the accounting staff must uphold high ethical standards, if the standards are not defined. To avoid this problem, the controller should create and enforce a code of ethics. This document may not originate with the controller—many chief executive officers (CEOs) prefer to take on this task. However, the controller can certainly push for an ethical code to be developed higher in the organization. Some illustrative topics to include in a code of ethics are:

- Bidding, negotiating, and performing under government contracts
- Compliance with antitrust laws

- Compliance with securities laws and regulations
- Conflicts of interest
- Cost consciousness
- Employee discrimination on any grounds
- Gifts and payments of money
- Hazardous waste disposal
- International boycotts
- Leave for military or other federal service
- Meals and entertainment
- Political contributions
- Preservation of assets
- Restrictive trade practices
- Standards of conduct
- Use of company assets
- Workplace and product safety

The wide range of ethical topics, some going well beyond the financial arena, make it obvious that the CEO really is the best source of this document, rather than the controller, though the controller can certainly contribute to those portions relating to financial issues.

Once the code of ethics has been created, it must be communicated to all employees. Once again, this is the CEO's job, but the controller should constantly reinforce it with his or her staff. It is especially helpful if the controller visibly refers to the ethical code whenever an ethical issue arises, so that the accounting staff knows that the controller is decisively adhering to the code.

A code of ethics becomes the starting point in the series of judgments a controller must follow when confronted with an ethical issue. The logical series of steps to work through are:

- *Consult the code of ethics.* Having a corporate code of ethics is a great boon to the controller, for he or she can use it as the basis for any ethics-related decision. A senior company officer would have difficulty forcing the controller to adopt a different course of action than what is prescribed by the code of ethics, since this would go against a directive of the Board of Directors. If the controller feels it is necessary to take a course of action contrary to what is stated in the code, then the reasons for doing so should be thoroughly documented. If there is no code, then proceed to the next step.
- *Discuss with immediate supervisor.* The controller's immediate supervisor is probably either the Chief Financial Officer (CFO), Chief Operating Officer (COO), or CEO. These are the most senior positions in the company, occupied by people whose behavior should be at an ethically high standard. Consulting with them for advice is a reasonable second step in the absence of a code of ethics. However, if the supervisor is the one causing the ethical problem, then skip this step and proceed to the next one.
- *Discuss with a trusted peer.* There is usually someone within the company in whom the controller places a great deal of trust. If so, consult with this person in regard

to the proper course of action. Be more circumspect in doing so with a person outside the company, since this runs the risk of spreading information elsewhere, with possible deleterious consequences. If there is no one with whom to discuss the issue, then proceed to the next step.

- *Discuss with the company's ethics committee.* If there is an ethics committee, this is a good forum for discussion. Unfortunately, many companies do not have such a committee, or it meets so infrequently that the immediate needs of the controller may not be met through this approach. In either case, proceed to the next step.

- *Discuss with the Board's audit committee.* Many boards have an audit committee, which should be comprised entirely of independent directors. If so, the controller should take his or her concerns to this group. Keep in mind that this is a serious step, since the controller is now going around the corporate reporting structure, which may have unenviable consequences later on if the controller chose not to tell senior management of this action.

- *Consider leaving the company.* If all these avenues are untenable or result in inadequate advice, the controller should seriously consider leaving the company in the near future. Reaching this final step probably means that the ethical issue is caused by senior management, and also that there are no outside checks on their ethical behavior, such as an audit committee of the Board of Directors.

It is extremely important that the controller issue consistent rulings on ethical issues, so that employees know they are being treated fairly. Though it may seem like a vast increase in paperwork, it may be useful for the controller to record all ethical rulings in a single document, so that there is a good reference source in the event of future ethical problems. This allows the controller to go back and see what judgment was given in previous cases, thereby giving the controller adequate grounds for treating new issues in a similar manner.

In summary, the accounting staff has a large role in enforcing ethical standards throughout a company, since it has such strong influence over several key areas that require ethical judgments, such as the quality of reported earnings, control over assets, and the uses of cash. Accordingly, it is very much in the controller's interests to have a code of ethics that the accounting staff can adhere to in enforcing the appropriate ethical standards.

2.4   ACCOUNTING JOB DESCRIPTIONS

As an accounting department expands, the number of tasks assigned to each position will become more specialized. A larger organization may have specialists in fixed asset accounting, expense reports, or SEC reporting—and these people do nothing else. This section does not attempt to describe the job descriptions of these smaller "niche" positions, but instead provides an overview of the tasks and reporting relationships that one is likely to encounter in an accounting department of moderate size. These descriptions are noted in Exhibits 2.1 through 2.12. Also, the assistant controller job description in Exhibit 2.5 is split into three parts, reflecting the common separation of duties within the department, with one assistant controller being in charge of basic transactions, another of analysis tasks, and a third of financial reporting. These functions may be combined in smaller organizations if there are fewer assistant controllers.

Reports to:	Chief Executive Officer
Responsibilities:	Arrange for equity and debt financing.
	Construct and monitor reliable control systems.
	Develop financial and tax strategies.
	Develop performance measures that support the company's strategic direction.
	Implement operational best practices.
	Invest funds.
	Invest pension funds.
	Maintain appropriate insurance coverage.
	Maintain banking relationships.
	Manage the capital request and budgeting processes.
	Manage the treasury, accounting, investor relations, tax, and human resources departments.
	Monitor financial reports.
	Oversee the issuance of financial information.
	Supervise acquisition due diligence and negotiate acquisitions. Understand and mitigate key elements of the company's risk profile.

EXHIBIT 2.1   CHIEF FINANCIAL OFFICER JOB DESCRIPTION

Reports to:	Chief Financial Officer
Responsibilities:	Approve the accounting department budget.
	Approve the creation of new report formats and reporting systems.
	Assist in the annual audit as required.
	Attend executive committee meetings as required.
	Authorize accounting capital purchases.
	Discuss financial results with senior management.
	Implement auditor recommendations.
	Manage outsourced functions.
	Manage the accounting staff.
	Provide advice to management regarding the impact of acquisitions.

EXHIBIT 2.2   CONTROLLER JOB DESCRIPTION

Reports to:	Chief Financial Officer
Responsibilities:	Advise management on the liquidity aspects of its short- and long-range planning.
	Arrange for equity and debt financing.
	Ensure that sufficient funds are available to meet ongoing operational and capital investment requirements.
	Forecast cash flow positions, related borrowing needs, and available funds for investment.
	Invest funds.
	Invest pension funds.
	Maintain banking relationships.
	Maintain credit rating agency relationships.
	Maintains a system of policies and procedures that impose an adequate level of control over treasury activities.
	Monitor the activities of third parties handling outsourced treasury functions on behalf of the company.
	Oversees the extension of credit to customers.
	Use hedging to mitigate financial risks related to the interest rates on the company's borrowings as well as on its foreign exchange positions.

EXHIBIT 2.3   TREASURER JOB DESCRIPTION

Reports to:	Chief Financial Officer
Responsibilities:	Creates presentations, press releases, and other communication materials for earnings releases, industry events, and presentations to analysts, brokers, and investors.
	Develops and maintains a company investor relations plan.
	Develops and monitors performance metrics for the investor relations function.
	Establishes and maintains relationships with stock exchange representatives.
	Establishes the optimum type and mix of shareholders and creates that mix through a variety of targeting initiatives.
	Manages the investor relations portion of the company Web site.
	Monitors analyst reports and summarizes them for senior management.
	Monitors operational changes through ongoing contacts with company management and develops investor relations messages based on these changes.
	Organizes conferences, road shows, earnings conference calls, and investor meetings.
	Oversees the production of all annual reports, SEC filings, and proxy statements.
	Performs a comprehensive competitive analysis, including financial metrics and differentiation.
	Provides feedback to management regarding the investment community's perception of the company.
	Provides feedback to the management team regarding the impact of stock repurchase programs or dividend changes on the investment community.
	Provides Regulation Fair Disclosure training to all company spokespersons.
	Represents the views of the investor community to the management team in the development of corporate strategy.
	Serves as the key point of contact for the investment community.

EXHIBIT 2.4   INVESTOR RELATIONS OFFICER JOB DESCRIPTION

Reports to:	Controller
Responsibilities: *(Analysis)*	Compile the cash forecast.
	Initiate best practices improvements.
	Issue internal management reports as needed.
	Manage the annual budgeting process.
	Oversee outsourced functions.
	Provide financial analyses as needed.
	Review systems for control weaknesses.
	Supervise cost accounting staff.
	Supervise financial analysis staff.
	Supervise systems analysis staff.
Responsibilities: *(Financial Reporting)*	Initiate best practices improvements.
	Issue timely financial statements.
	Oversee outsourced functions.
	Review capital purchase proposals.
	Supervise general ledger staff.
	Supervise public reporting staff.
	Supervise tax reporting staff.
Responsibilities: *(Transactions)*	Initiate best practices improvements.
	Maintain an orderly accounting filing system.
	Oversee outsourced functions.
	Supervise accounts payable staff.
	Supervise accounts receivable staff.
	Supervise payroll staff.

EXHIBIT 2.5   ASSISTANT CONTROLLER JOB DESCRIPTION

Reports to:	Assistant Controller (Analysis)
Systems tasks:	Audit costing systems.
	Review adequacy of activity-based costing system.
	Review adequacy of data collection systems.
	Review system costs and benefits.
Analysis &	
reporting tasks:	Assist in development of the budget.
	Report on ABC overhead allocations.
	Report on breakeven points by product and division.
	Report on capital budgeting requests.
	Report on margins by product and division.
	Report on periodic variance analyses.
	Report on product target costing.
	Report on special topics as assigned.
Pricing tasks:	Work with marketing staff to update product pricing.

EXHIBIT 2.6   COST ACCOUNTANT JOB DESCRIPTION

Reports to:	Assistant Controller (Transactions)
Responsibilities:	Create a credit scoring model.
	Maintain the corporate credit policy.
	Manage customer credit files.
	Manage relations with credit insurance providers.
	Manage relations with the sales department.
	Manage the application of late fees.
	Manage the corporate financing program.
	Measure department performance.
	Monitor periodic credit reviews.
	Monitor the credit granting and updating process.
	Provide for ongoing training of credit staff.

EXHIBIT 2.7   CREDIT MANAGER JOB DESCRIPTION

Reports to:	Assistant Controller (Transactions)
Responsibilities:	Approve invoice write-offs.
	Ensure that accounts receivable are collected promptly.
	Ensure that customer billings are issued promptly.
	Estimate the bad debt reserve.
	Implement best practices to increase efficiency levels.
	Manage the billings and collections staff.
	Project cash requirements from cash receipts.

EXHIBIT 2.8   BILLINGS AND COLLECTIONS SUPERVISOR JOB DESCRIPTION

Reports to:	Assistant Controller (Transactions)
Responsibilities:	Cross-train the accounts payable staff.
	Ensure that accounts payable are not paid early.
	Ensure that all reasonable discounts are taken on payments.
	Handle supplier payment inquiries.
	Implement best practices to increase efficiency levels.
	Manage the accounts payable staff.
	Project cash requirements from accounts payable.

EXHIBIT 2.9   ACCOUNTS PAYABLE SUPERVISOR JOB DESCRIPTION

Reports to:	Assistant Controller (Transactions)
Responsibilities:	Convert time cards into payroll system entries.
	Create vacation and pay accruals for the periodic financials.
	Cross-train the payroll clerical staff.
	Implement best practices to increase efficiency levels.
	Manage the payroll clerical staff.
	Monitor vacation and sick time taken and available.
	Process payroll in a timely manner.
	Process termination pay within mandated time periods.
	Update pay changes in a timely manner.

EXHIBIT 2.10   PAYROLL SUPERVISOR JOB DESCRIPTION

Reports to:	Assistant Controller (Financial Reporting)
Responsibilities:	Consolidate entries from subsidiary organizations.
	Ensure that monthly bank reconciliations are completed.
	Follow the period-end closing schedule in a timely manner.
	Maintain a standard checklist of period journal entries.
	Maintain detailed backup on all account balances.
	Maintain the chart of accounts.

EXHIBIT 2.11   GENERAL LEDGER ACCOUNTANT JOB DESCRIPTION

Reports to:	Assistant Controller (Financial Reporting)
Responsibilities:	Advise management regarding the tax impact of corporate strategies
	Complete required tax reporting in a timely manner.
	Coordinate audits by various taxation authorities.
	Coordinate outsourced tax preparation work.
	Devise tax strategies to defer tax payments.
	Create tax data collection systems.
	Negotiate with tax authorities over tax payment issues.
	Update the company sales tax database as tax rates change.

EXHIBIT 2.12   TAX ACCOUNTANT JOB DESCRIPTION

2.5 SUMMARY

This chapter has described the expanded role of the accounting department, as well as how it interacts with other parts of the organization, both from the perspective of providing financial information and of controlling the level of ethical integrity. In the next chapter, we will look in more detail at the standard-setting organizations whose output so strongly defines the work of the accountant.

PART TWO

ACCOUNTING RULES AND REGULATIONS

CHAPTER 3

STANDARD-SETTING ORGANIZATIONS

3.1   INTRODUCTION

Who creates the basic rules of accounting that guide the accounting practices of so many accountants? There are several entities that contribute to these basic rules, as will be discussed in this chapter. In addition, the Securities and Exchange Commission (SEC) has a lengthy set of regulations that govern precisely how accounting information is to be presented to the investing public, as discussed in Chapter 4; however, the SEC has chosen to steer clear of the actual accounting rules that govern the profession, choosing instead to strictly focus its attention on the manner of information presentation. The Internal Revenue Service (IRS) also has rules that govern what types of revenue and expense are allowed when compiling an entity's taxable income figure—however, these rules are used in parallel to generally accepted accounting principles (GAAP), and form no part of GAAP. The most common IRS rules are noted in Chapter 43. This chapter focuses strictly on those rule-setting bodies that have gradually compiled the set of rules that we now call GAAP.

3.2   THE COMMITTEE ON ACCOUNTING PROCEDURE

The Committee on Accounting Procedure (CAP) was created in 1939 by the American Institute of Accountants (now known as the American Institute of Public Accountants, or AICPA). It issued a total of 51 Accounting Research Bulletins that responded to specific accounting problems as they arose; this tight focus led to an increasing number of complaints against the CAP over time, because it did not attempt to create an overall accounting framework to which specific accounting pronouncements could then be attached in an orderly manner. Another problem was that it was accused of not conducting a sufficient volume of detailed research to back up the reasoning behind its pronouncements. Yet another issue was the perception that it acted in the interests of the American Institute of Accountants, which was considered a conflict of interest. Furthermore, its pronouncements were not binding on any organizations that issued financial reports. On the plus side, it developed a uniform accounting terminology that was widely used thereafter. Because of the preceding problems, the CAP was eliminated in 1959 in favor of the Accounting Principles Board.

3.3 THE ACCOUNTING PRINCIPLES BOARD

The Accounting Principles Board (APB) was formed in 1958 by the AICPA. Its 18- to 21-member board and supporting staff were quite active in conducting research on accounting issues and promulgating standards. Even though it was phased out in 1973, its APB bulletin numbers 43, 45, 46, and 51, as well as 19 opinions still form a part of GAAP. The APB gained more regulatory force than its predecessor, because the AICPA required its member CPAs to identify and justify any departures from the APB's opinions and statements, while it also gained support from the Securities and Exchange Commission. Nonetheless, it foundered due to its direct support by the AICPA—a more independent organization was needed, which resulted in the Financial Accounting Foundation.

3.4 THE FINANCIAL ACCOUNTING FOUNDATION

The Financial Accounting Foundation (FAF) was founded in 1972. Its 16-member board of trustees is expressly independent from the AICPA, since they come from a number of sponsoring organizations, such as the AICPA, the Financial Executives Institute, the Institute of Management Accountants, the Securities Industry Association, and others. It also has a number of at-large trustees who are not tied to any sponsoring organizations. The FAF does not directly promulgate any accounting standards—rather, it raises funds for the operation of the Financial Accounting Standards Board (FASB) and Government Accounting Standards Board (GASB) that conduct this work, as noted in the following sections. Its fundraising function is enhanced by its being a 501(c)(3) taxable entity, so that contributions to it are tax-deductible. It also exercises general oversight of the FASB and GASB by appointing board members to them, as well as two advisory councils to those entities. It also approves their annual budgets.

3.5 THE FINANCIAL ACCOUNTING STANDARDS BOARD

The successor to the Accounting Principles Board is the Financial Accounting Standards Board (FASB). It was created in 1973. It has a board of seven members, each of whom has a five-year term, and who can be reelected once. It has a staff of about 40 personnel. The organization is funded through the FAF. Its mission is to "establish and improve standards of financial accounting and reporting for the guidance and education of the public, including issuers, auditors, and users of financial information." It maintains a Web site at *www.fasb.org*.

The FASB's authority to issue statements on and interpretations of accounting standards comes from several sources. One is the SEC, which designated it as the source of accounting principles to be used as the basis for financial statements filed with it (as noted in the SEC's Financial Reporting Release No. 1, Section 101). The FASB received similar support from the AICPA through its Rule 203. However, the FASB has no enforcement powers whatsoever—it needs continuing support from the SEC, AICPA, and state boards of accountancy to ensure that its rules are followed.

The FASB works with the Financial Accounting Standards Advisory Council, which is appointed by the FAF. The council's 30 members advise the FASB about technical issues, project priorities, and the selection of task forces to deal with specific accounting issues.

The basic flow of work that the FASB follows when constructing a new accounting pronouncement is:

1. *Admission to agenda.* One of the FASB's criteria for inclusion of an accounting issue in its work schedule is that there is diverse practice in dealing with it that causes varying financial reporting results that can be misleading. There must also be a technically feasible solution, and an expectation that a solution will be generally accepted.

2. *Early deliberations.* The FASB clarifies the issues and obtains opinions regarding each accounting item on its agenda. If a prospective pronouncement appears to be a major project, it will appoint an advisory task force of outside experts to review it, which tends to involve the services of about 15 people. The FASB staff will then write a discussion memorandum with the assistance of this group.

3. *Public hearing.* The FASB will announce a hearing date that is 60 days in advance. Depending upon the issue, these meetings may be very well attended by interested parties.

4. *Tentative resolution.* Two-thirds of the board votes in favor of issuing an exposure draft, which includes a proposed effective date and method of transition to the new accounting rule. This document is not the final one, being rather a draft that is made available for public discussion.

5. *Final deliberations and resolution.* Once responses from the public to the exposure draft have been made, the FASB will make minor adjustments to it and take a final vote. The finalized standard, which includes dissenting views, is then published.

6. *Follow-up interpretations.* There may be some issues related to a new standard that do not become apparent until after it has been in use for a short time. If so, the FASB may clarify or elaborate upon the newly issued statement. These interpretations must also be made available for public comment for at least 30 days before being finalized and published.

The process just noted requires a considerable amount of FASB resources, and so cannot be used to address all accounting issues. To provide more rapid resolution to more urgent or minor issues, it may choose to shift them to its Emerging Issues Task Force (EITF). The EITF is a very active group that is mostly composed of public accounting people who are aware of emerging issues before they become widespread. The chief accountant of the SEC attends its meetings. If it can reach a rapid consensus on an issue, then its findings are published at once and become a basis for GAAP. If there is less consensus, then the issue is shifted to the FASB to be resolved through the more tortuous process just described. The EITF has been criticized because less public discussion is involved in its proceedings than under the more formalized FASB review process.

The FASB also issues technical bulletins when it addresses issues not covered by existing standards, which will not cause a major change in practice, have a minimal perceived implementation cost, and do not result in a unique new accounting practice—in short, technical bulletins address less controversial topics.

A potential problem over the long term is that the SEC, which is a prime sponsor of the FASB, wants it to issue standards that are oriented toward publicly held companies, over which the SEC has reporting control. However, this means that the more onerous reporting requirements intended for larger public companies are also being forced upon smaller private firms that do not have the resources to comply with them. Though there would be great inefficiencies involved in setting up a double accounting standard, one for public and one for private companies, this will be an ongoing cause of tension within the FASB as it continues to churn out pronouncements.

3.6   PUBLIC COMPANY ACCOUNTING OVERSIGHT BOARD (PCAOB)

The PCAOB was formed as part of the Sarbanes-Oxley Act of 2002. This nonprofit organization is administered by five Board members, and has been given considerable control over the public accounting firms that provide auditing services to publicly held companies, particularly in regard to setting auditing standards, registering firms to audit public companies, and ensuring that they comply with the regulations issued by several Acts as well as by government entities.

Public accounting firms must register with the PCAOB before they are allowed to prepare or issue audit reports on U.S. public companies. Though filing fees are modest, many smaller firms have not registered, on the grounds that they will be subject to periodic PCAOB reviews, will need to add specialized staff to conduct control reviews, and will likely incur higher liability insurance expenses. Thus, the net result of mandatory registration has been some degree of concentration of public company auditing with a smaller set of auditing firms.

The PCAOB is authorized to establish auditing and related quality control, ethics, and independence standards that must be adhered to by all registered public accounting firms.

The PCAOB must inspect each registered public accounting firm at least once a year if it provides audit reports for more than 100 public companies, and at least once every three years for audit firms providing audit reports for a lesser number of companies. The result of these reviews is a written report, detailing the PCAOB's assessment of each public accounting firm's compliance with the rules of the Sarbanes-Oxley Act, Securities and Exchange Commission, and itself, as well as their compliance with professional auditing standards and issuance of audit reports.

The PCAOB may also conduct investigations into any acts or omissions by registered public accounting firms that violate any rules of the Sarbanes-Oxley Act or the PCAOB or professional auditing standards, and may impose sanctions to deter any recurrence of the problems uncovered. Sanctions can range from remedial measures, through monetary penalties, and may extend to the barring of a public accounting firm from auditing public companies.

3.7   THE GOVERNMENT ACCOUNTING STANDARDS BOARD

The entity that establishes accounting principles for state and local governments is the Government Accounting Standards Board (GASB), which was created in 1984. It is the successor organization to the National Council on Governmental Accounting, whose standards are still in force unless the GASB has issued specific changes or replacements to them. The GASB's methods of operation (and basic rule-making procedures) are nearly identical to those of the FASB, which is its sister organization. It has seven Board members and a staff of about ten employees. Like the FASB, it works with an advisory council, this one being called the Government Accounting Standards Advisory Council, which is appointed by the FAF. This council consults with the GASB about technical issues, project priorities, and the selection of task forces to deal with specific issues. An interesting variation from the procedures of the FASB's council is that this one periodically conducts an annual membership survey to identify emerging issues.

Its funding comes from the FAF, as is the case for the FASB. The primary source of funding that goes to the FAF is from state and local governments, as well as the General Accounting Office.

The GASB's pronouncements are recognized as authoritative by the AICPA, but there is no entity like the SEC supporting it (which only deals with publicly held companies), and so it tends to have less overall influence than the FASB. Also, since its funding sources are fewer than for the FASB, it has a substantially smaller staff.

3.8   ACCOUNTING STANDARDS EXECUTIVE COMMITTEE (AcSEC)

The Accounting Standards Executive Committee is a volunteer committee of the American Institute of Certified Public Accountants (AICPA). It is considered to be the AICPA's senior technical board, and as such is the only entity allowed to issue accounting opinions on behalf of the AICPA. The committee has 15 members who are selected from the accounting profession, academia, and business in general. The AcSEC focuses its efforts on the development of industry-specific accounting and auditing guidance in areas having unique regulatory or accounting issues. It also attempts to influence the content of accounting pronouncements made by other standard-setting organizations, such as the Financial Accounting Standards Board, Governmental Accounting Standards Board, and the International Accounting Standards Board.

The AcSEC produces a Statement of Position (SOP), which is usually a set of standards for a specialized industry, though some of its earlier statements of position have addressed broader issues, such as the accounting for partnerships, environmental liabilities, and property, plant and equipment. It schedules accounting topics for review if there is no expectation that one of the other standard-setting organizations intends to address it in the near future. The AcSEC agreed in 2002 to restrict itself to industry-specific accounting guidance, so no further broad-based issue coverage is expected.

Given that the AcSEC's members are volunteers and all proposed SOPs must undergo a lengthy public review process as well as a two-thirds affirmative vote by the committee, its findings can require an exceptionally long time to complete. SOPs usually contain considerable guidance, however and are of high quality.

3.9   THE INTERNATIONAL ACCOUNTING STANDARDS BOARD

A large number of organizations now do business in multiple countries and so must deal with different accounting standards within each country where they have subsidiaries. Though a company's headquarters may be located in the United States, which forces the entity as a whole to report under FASB standards, it may be required to make reports, such as loan-related financial statements, at the local level that require different accounting standards. Also, companies that are based abroad but which want to issue securities within the United States must restate their financial results to comply with American accounting rules. In an attempt to standardize the accounting rules of many countries, the International Accounting Standards Board (IASB) was created in April 2001. It is the successor body to the International Accounting Standards Committee (IASC), which in turn was formed in 1973 through an agreement made by the national professional accountancy bodies of Australia, Canada, France, Germany, Japan, Mexico, the Netherlands, the United Kingdom and Ireland, and the United States. The 14 members of its Board serve for a five-year term, which can be renewed once.

The IASB is controlled by a parent organization, which is the IASC Foundation, a Delaware nonprofit corporation. Its role is quite similar to that of the FAF in relation to the FASB and GASB—that is, it provides funding and general oversight to the IASB, while also appointing its members. Meanwhile, the IASB is solely responsible for setting international accounting standards, with the support of the Standards Advisory Council and the Standing Interpretations Committee, both of which are funded and supported by the IASC Foundation.

The IASB's staff works on the development of a single set of international accounting standards, coordinating its efforts with the national standard setting bodies, stock exchanges, and securities regulatory agencies in many countries, as well as such international groups as the United Nations and World Bank. Its accounting standards are issued in the form of International Financial Reporting Standards, which are devised through the same process used by the GASB and FASB.

3.10 THE CONVERGENCE OF U.S. AND INTERNATIONAL ACCOUNTING RULES

The Norwalk Agreement was issued in 2002, committing the FASB and IASB to work toward the convergence of international and U.S. accounting standards. The result has been an exceptionally rapid transition in the direction of convergence. The FASB and IASB have chosen to work closely together, typically with both Boards meeting jointly and even sharing staff on various projects. In addition, the Boards have decided to jointly work on all major accounting projects, and it appears that their new method of operation is to issue both discussion papers and final standards at approximately the same time.

It appears that having both organizations work together has resulted in more political clout, yielding new, high-quality standards affecting politically thorny topics that might have been impossible if either organization had tackled them individually.

Though the long-term convergence goal is laudable, the short-term result is that both the international and U.S. GAAP accounting standards are being changed in order to arrive at a single standard. Consequently, a number of accounting rules are likely to change over the next few years, potentially requiring current and perhaps also retrospective changes in the reported financial results of various business entities.

3.11 SUMMARY

The long chain of standard-setting organizations that began with the Committee on Accounting Procedure in 1939 and that continues today in the form of the IASB, FASB, and GASB has produced a prolific volume of pronouncements that form the primary basis for GAAP. In the meantime, it is an open question whether the current FASB and GASB organizations are the final standard setting organizations that we will see or whether they will begin to mesh their functions with the International Accounting Standards Board. An additional issue is that a powerful backer of the FASB is the SEC, which pushes it in the direction of primarily creating reporting standards for publicly held companies; the difficulty of complying with these standards for smaller, privately held companies may eventually lead to complaints that could bring about a double standard—one rule for public companies and another for private ones. Only time will tell how these issues will be resolved.

CHAPTER 4

THE SECURITIES AND EXCHANGE COMMISSION

4.1 INTRODUCTION

The Securities and Exchange Commission (SEC) exerts a considerable amount of control over the financial reporting activities of publicly held companies, particularly in the areas of new securities issuance and the ongoing release of financial information to the general public (particularly under Regulation FD). Though a complete and detailed review of all SEC requirements is beyond the scope of this chapter, we will review the reasons for the SEC's existence, how it is organized, and the laws under which it gains its authority to issue regulations. An overview of many of its key regulations is provided, but their original text is so detailed and in-depth that the reader is advised to peruse the original text of those regulations that are directly applicable to his or her business.

4.2 OVERVIEW OF THE SEC

The SEC was created as a direct result of the stock market crash of October 1929. Given the massive loss of net worth as a result of the plunge in stock market prices at that time, the federal government felt that a considerable degree of regulation over the securities industry was necessary in order to ensure that the resulting increase in public confidence in the stock market would eventually draw the public back to it.

After a series of hearings to determine what specific forms of regulation would meet this goal, Congress passed the Securities Act and the Securities Exchange Act in 1933 and 1934, respectively. As noted in later sections of this chapter, the two acts were designed to greatly increase the information reported by an entity issuing securities (especially the nature of its business and any associated investment risks), as well as the amount of oversight by the government. The oversight function was centered on the regulation of the markets in which securities were sold, as well as the brokers and investment advisors who worked with investors to buy and sell securities. The reporting of information by securities issuers has blossomed into a key function of the SEC, which requires that timely filings be submitted to it of all material financial information by issuers, which it promptly makes available to the public through its EDGAR online database (see later section).

Congress created the SEC as part of the 1934 Act to administer the new acts. Its powers later increased as other acts were also passed, eventually giving it regulatory authority over public utility holding companies and mutual funds, too. It has a significant amount of enforcement authority to back up its regulatory oversight function, typically bringing about 500 civil enforcement actions per year against any person or business entity that breaks the securities laws. The remaining sections give an overview of the SEC's structure, as well as the laws under which it issues regulations.

4.3 ORGANIZATION OF THE SEC

The SEC is organized around 4 divisions and 18 offices, all of which are described below. Its headquarters is located in Washington, D.C. Its staff is spread across 11 regional and district offices. It is run by five commissioners (one of whom is appointed chairman); all are appointed by the president. The term of each commissioner is five years, with the use of staggered appointments to ensure that only one commissioner is approved each year. Only three of the commissioners are allowed to be members of the same political party, thereby bringing a more neutral flavor to the political leanings of the SEC.

The commissioners have regular meetings at which they amend or interpret existing rules, propose new ones within the guidelines set up under existing congressional laws, and enforce existing regulations. These meetings are generally open to the public, except for those related to some enforcement issues.

The creation of new rules is not a simple process, and the commissioners only see proposed rules after a long series of reviews have been completed. It begins with a *concept release,* in which the SEC's staff describes the problem that it is attempting to address, why it feels there is a problem, and lays out a variety of possible regulatory solutions. The public has an opportunity to comment upon these possible solutions. The resulting text is taken into consideration when the SEC then drafts a *rule proposal*, which is a detailed rule in draft form that is presented to the SEC for approval. The public then has 30 to 60 days to comment on the draft rule proposal; the resulting information is then incorporated into the final rule. The rule proposal will sometimes be the start of the rule creation process, rather than the concept release, if the issue under consideration is not thought to be excessively complicated or controversial. The resulting text of the rule is presented to the full commission for approval. If the rule is considered to be a major one, the additional step of seeking congressional approval may also be taken. In either case, the rule then becomes part of the official set of regulations under which the SEC operates.

The responsibilities of the SEC's various divisions and offices are:

• *Division of Corporate Finance.* This division supervises the corporate disclosure of information to investors. This involves the issuance of information by companies not only when a stock is initially offered to the public, but also on a continuing basis. The basic underlying principle that the division follows is that corporations must make available a complete set of information regarding positive or negative issues that might be relevant to an investor's decisions regarding corporate securities. The division also helps companies with any questions they may have regarding submissions. An example of such assistance is advising a company about the need to register a particular type of security with the SEC. At a more advanced level of inquiry, the division can provide guidance to companies that want to take action in areas that are not clearly governed by existing SEC regulations by writing letters indicating what type of action it would recommend the SEC take if proposed activities were to be taken (a *no-action letter* being an indication that no action would be taken).

Another task is the review of submitted documents for completeness and compliance with its various rules. The primary documents that it reviews are:

○ Annual (10-K) and quarterly (10-Q) filings of financial results.
○ Annual shareholder reports.
○ Merger and acquisition filings.
○ Proxy materials for annual shareholder meetings.
○ Registration statements for new securities.
○ Tender offer documentation.

The division also interprets the laws over which it provides jurisdiction, which are primarily the Securities Act of 1933, the Securities Exchange Act of 1934, and the Trust Indenture Act of 1939 (all of which are described in later sections of this chapter), creating regulations that expand upon the specific requirements listed within these acts. It also provides information and opinions to the Financial Accounting Standards Board, which promulgates accounting principles for professional accountants.

• *Division of Enforcement.* This division investigates instances where securities laws may have been broken, recommends legal action where necessary, and negotiates settlements with violators. Its investigations include private investigative work by its own staff (including interviews and the examination of brokerage records and trading information, using subpoenas if necessary), as well as the collection of information from other sources, such as the securities industry itself, investors, and the media. A sample of the activities that may bring about an investigation by the division are:

○ Insider trading of securities.
○ Manipulating securities prices.
○ Misrepresenting, falsifying, or omitting submitted information about specific securities or a company's financial condition.
○ Sale of securities without prior registration with the SEC.
○ Theft of customer funds by an investment advisor or broker-dealer.
○ Treating customers unfairly.

Legal action is limited to civil cases in federal court or via an administrative law judge, at the discretion of the SEC. If civil action is considered necessary, then the SEC will ask for an injunction from a U.S. District Court to stop whatever activity is violating the law. The court can also authorize penalties or a *disgorgement* (the return of illegally acquired profits). If necessary, the court can prevent an individual from serving as a corporate officer. If an administrative judgment is pursued instead, then the SEC will bring the matter before a judge who works independently from the SEC, and whose decision can be appealed back to the SEC. Penalties can include a censure, monetary payment, disgorgement, disbarment from the securities industry or revocation of one's registration to practice, or a cease-and-desist order. The SEC also provides assistance to various law enforcement agencies if they are working to bring criminal charges in addition to the civil or administrative charges already being brought by the SEC.

- *Division of Market Regulation.* This division creates standards that result in fair and efficient market activities. It regulates the major participants in the securities markets in order to achieve this goal. Its prime targets for regulation are the stock exchanges, clearing agencies (which facilitate the settlement of trades), the Municipal Securities Rulemaking Board, broker-dealer firms, transfer agents (which maintain securities ownership records), and securities information processors. The division's primary responsibilities over these market participants is to conduct an ongoing review of market activities, create and update regulations governing securities market operations, and implement the SEC's broker-dealer financial integrity program. It also oversees a private, nonprofit company called the Securities Investor Protection Corporation (SPIC), which insures the securities and cash of member brokerages in the event of a bankruptcy of one of the brokerages.

- *Division of Investment Management.* This division regulates investment companies through a variety of federal securities laws, with the twin goals of increasing information disclosure without causing the cost of disclosure to be excessive to issuers. Specifically, it reviews enforcement issues involving investment companies, designs new regulations based on existing laws in order to meet changes in the investment environment, reviews filings by investment companies, and responds to requests regarding the need for specific filings. It conducts similar tasks within the utility industry under the authorization of the Public Utility Holding Company Act of 1935, while also conducting periodic audits of utility holding companies.

- *Office of Administrative Law Judges.* The judges in this office administer nonjury hearings regarding allegations of securities law violations brought by the SEC's staff and issue rulings based on the hearings. Parties involved in the hearings can submit to the judge their proposed findings of fact and conclusions of law for consideration alongside other information revealed during the hearings. Judges can then issue initial decisions, which may be appealed to the SEC.

- *Office of Compliance Inspections and Examinations.* As its name implies, this office is responsible for inspecting those activities of organizations registered with the SEC (such as investment companies, broker-dealers, and transfer agents) to ensure that the applicable securities laws are being complied with. It issues a *deficiency letter* to those organizations whose activities require correction, and then returns to monitor the problem areas until they have achieved compliance with the applicable regulations. Major violations are referred to the Division of Enforcement for more vigorous legal attention.

- *Office of Economic Analysis.* This office investigates the economic impact that results from current and proposed SEC regulatory activities. It also reviews any number of market activities required of it by the SEC, and then reports back to the SEC with its findings and advice.

- *Office of Equal Employment Opportunity.* This office focuses primarily on Equal Employment Opportunity (EEO) issues within the SEC, supporting EEO initiatives in the recruitment, training, and compensation of its employees through policy promulgation, audits, and dispute resolutions. It also sponsors diversity and minority forums within the securities industry.

- *Office of External Affairs.* This office is the public relations arm of the SEC. It reviews media coverage of SEC issues and responds to it, while also providing speech material and planning for special events.

- *Office of Filings and Information Services.* This office is responsible for the receipt, custody, and control of all public records filed with the SEC, as well as the records management system used to track them. It also has a Public Reference Branch, which makes documents available to the public that have previously been submitted to the SEC, such as annual and quarterly financial reports. It makes most of these documents available through the Internet at *www.sec.gov*. The information is also available in a somewhat more readable format through a privately managed site called *www.edgar-online.com*. Paper-based documents are also available through the SEC's public reference room in Washington, D.C.

- *Office of the Financial Management.* This office manages the budgeting and financial operations of the SEC, including financial system oversight, resource utilization, cash management, collections, and general accounting operations.

- *Office of Human Resources and Administrative Services.* This office conducts much of the human resources and general management activities of the SEC. Its tasks include security and safety, publications activities, purchasing, property management, recruitment and pay administration, as well as payroll, employee training, and performance reviews.

- *Office of Information Technology.* This office designs, develops, and maintains the SEC's computer systems at both its headquarters and regional locations. It also manages the EDGAR system (see later section), and maintains the SEC's official Web site, which is located at *www.sec.gov*.

- *Office of International Affairs.* This office works with foreign governments to share information regarding regulatory enforcement issues, represents the SEC at international organizations, and also provides technical assistance to the governments of other countries that are creating securities markets.

- *Office of Investor Education and Assistance.* This office handles complaints and questions from individual investors; it cannot actively assist investors with their problems, but can offer advice in regard to how they can proceed with specific issues. It also provides an investor education function by setting up Investors' Town Meetings throughout the country in which office representatives lecture about investment and retirement issues.

- *Office of Risk Assessment.* This group coordinates the SEC's risk manangement program including information analysis & serving as the agency's risk management resources.

- *Office of the Chief Accountant.* The members of this office work with the various domestic and international standard setting bodies, such as the Financial Accounting Standards Board, the American Institute of Certified Public Accountants, and the International Accounting Standards Committee, and auditors to determine the applicability of existing standards and regulations to specific financial reporting situations. It then advises the SEC regarding possible enforcement issues resulting from this analysis.

- *Office of the Executive Director.* This office oversees the budget process, allocation of SEC resources, control systems, administration, and information systems. In short, it is in charge of management policies within the SEC.

- *Office of the General Counsel.* This is the SEC's chief legal officer. In this capacity, the office represents the SEC in various legal proceedings, while also preparing legal briefs and advising the SEC on legal matters. It sometimes enters into and offers advice on interpretations of securities laws that are part of private appellate litigation.

- *Office of the Inspector General.* This office is the internal audit division of the SEC. As such, it investigates control issues within the SEC's operations, with a specific focus on risk identification and mitigation, as well as making recommendations to improve the efficiency and effectiveness of the SEC's overall operations.

- *Office of the Secretary.* This office schedules SEC meetings maintains records of SEC actions; publishes official documents in the *SEC Docket*; in the *Federal Register,* and on the SEC Web site; tracks documents used in administrative proceedings and similar matters; and tracks the status of financial judgments imposed by the SEC as a result of enforcement rulings.

4.4   EDGAR

EDGAR is an acronym for the Electronic Data Gathering, Analysis, and Retrieval system. It is the SEC's primary online tool for automating the collection, validation, indexing, and forwarding of forms filed by companies that are legally required to do so with the SEC. Not only does EDGAR nearly eliminate the paperwork burden on the SEC, but it is also a superior tool for investors and analysts, who have almost immediate online access to the forms being filed. The rules and guidelines under which companies are required to make submissions to EDGAR are codified under the SEC's Regulation S-T.

Official submissions to EDGAR must be in either HTML or ASCII. Anyone who chooses to make a submission in the HTML format is allowed to use hyperlinks between different sections of the same HTML document, and may also include hyperlinks to exhibits that have been included in the same filing. One can also include links to other official filings within the EDGAR database if submissions are made with the new EDGARLink version; however, it is not allowable to include links to documents located outside of the EDGAR database. Hyperlinks are not allowed as a substitute for information that is required to be included in a specific document, even if the required information could be located through a linkage to another document that is also filed through EDGAR.

The SEC does not currently allow video or audio material to be included in submissions to EDGAR, though it is acceptable to include graphic and image material within HTML documents.

It is also possible to make a submission in a PDF (Acrobat) format, but this is considered an unofficial filing that must be accompanied by one of the other two formats. If a PDF file is submitted, only its formatting and graphics may differ from the official filing. Report submissions are made via the Internet to the EDGARFILING Web site.

There are two cases in which a company can plead hardship and avoid making an electronic submission of data. In the first instance, Rule 201 of Regulation S-T allows a temporary exemption for an electronic filer that is having unanticipated trouble in submitting a report, such as in cases where the transmitting computer fails. A paper-based filing, using Form TH (Notification of Reliance on Temporary Hardship Exemption), is still required in this instance, and must be followed within six days by an electronic submission. In the second case, Rule 202 of Regulation S-T allows a permanent exemption for a few cases where the information to be filed is so large that the filer would be caused undue hardship to do so. The first case requires no SEC approval, whereas the second case does.

4.5   THE SECURITIES ACT OF 1933

The Securities Act of 1933 requires companies issuing securities for public purchase to issue financial and other significant information to investors, while also prohibiting fraud or misrepresentations of financial information. The issuance of information is accomplished through the registration of information about the securities with the SEC, which will review submitted information to ensure that disclosure requirements under this act have been met. A key item is that this act is primarily concerned with the issuance of information related to the initial offering of securities only, rather than with ongoing updates to securities-related information (which is covered by the Securities Exchange Act of 1934).

There are a few instances in which the mandated disclosure requirements do not have to be met. If a securities offering is of a limited size, if it is issued by a municipal, state, or federal government, or if the offering is limited to a small number of investors, then it is exempted from registration with the SEC.

The information sent to the SEC provides essential details about (1) the issuing company's properties and business, (2) securities available for sale, (3) the management team, and (4) audited financial statements.

If the information provided by the issuing company can be proven by an investor to be incomplete or inaccurate, then investors may have the right to recover their invested funds from the company.

4.6   THE SECURITIES EXCHANGE ACT OF 1934

This act created the SEC, giving it authority to regulate many players in the securities industry, such as stock exchanges (e.g., the New York Stock Exchange and National Association of Securities Dealers [NASD]), clearing agencies, brokerage firms, and transfer agents. The act requires these market players to register with the SEC, which involves the filing of regularly updated disclosure reports. It prohibits the trading of securities on unregistered exchanges. Also, self-regulatory organizations (such as the NASD) are required to set up rules under which they can ensure that investors are adequately protected while conducting transactions with members of the self-regulatory organizations.

The act requires firms with more than $10 million in assets, and whose securities are held by more than 500 investors, to file both annual reports and a variety of other supplemental reports. The act also applies to anyone who wishes to acquire more than 5% of a company's securities by tender offer or direct purchase to disclose information to the SEC (this provision was added through a 1970 amendment to the act).

The act also creates rules for the types of information included in proxy solicitations that are used to obtain shareholder votes regarding the election of directors and other corporate matters. In brief, the solicitations must disclose all important facts regarding the topics about which the shareholders are being asked to vote. It requires that these solicitations be filed with the SEC prior to their issuance to the shareholders in order to ensure that their content complies with the disclosure rules of the act.

The act also gave the Federal Reserve System's Board of Governors the power to determine the allowable credit limits that could be used to purchase securities through margin trading. It also requires broker-dealers to obtain the written permission of investors before lending any securities carried on the investors' accounts. The intention behind these actions was to avoid the massive loss of wealth that occurred during the 1929 stock market crash, when investors who had purchased heavily on margin lost all of their net worth.

It also prohibits insider trading activities, which occur when a person trades a security based on nonpublic information, particularly when that person has a fiduciary duty to refrain from trading. A 1984 amendment to the act prohibited the officers and directors of a company from short selling the securities issued by their companies. They are also required to report the amount of securities they hold in their companies, and any changes in those holdings, as long as the amount held is more than 10% of the total of registered securities.

The act specifically prohibits market manipulation through such means as giving a false impression of high levels of trading activity in a stock, issuing false information about possible changes in a stock's price, price fixing, and making false statements in regard to a security.

4.7   THE PUBLIC UTILITY HOLDING COMPANY ACT OF 1935

This act authorizes the regulation of interstate holding companies that are engaged in the retail distribution of natural gas or in the electric utility business, with particular attention to perceived abuses by this type of business. A holding company is defined as one that owns at least 10% of a public utility company's voting stock. A holding company is exempted from this act only if it operates within a single state, or is an operating public utility company that operates in a single state or in contiguous ones, is not in the public utility business, is a temporary holding company, or is not a public utility business within the United States.

One intent of the act is to confine each holding company to a single integrated public utility system that would keep each company contained within a single geographic region. Also, to keep this type of company from expanding outside the boundaries of that single public utility system, the act provides that only those nonutility businesses can be bought that are "reasonably incidental or economically necessary or appropriate" to its operations.

The act also provides for the elimination of unnecessary levels of corporate structural complexity, as well as any accumulation of inequitable voting power by certain shareholders. These provisions are designed to keep people with a small number of shares from gaining voting control over a holding company.

The act clearly identifies the types and amounts of securities that a holding company should issue or acquire. Issued securities must correspond to the earning power and capital structure of the holding company. The SEC can only authorize the issuance of securities for a holding company if the proposed issuance has already cleared all hurdles imposed by applicable local state laws.

Also, the act requires holding companies to first obtain the approval of the SEC before acquiring any securities, utility assets, or ownership interest in any other business. This restriction includes obtaining SEC approval before becoming an affiliate of another public utility company. These companies are also not allowed to borrow from each other.

The SEC must also be advised before any sale of assets or securities between holding companies occurs, or any transactions at all between affiliates. In addition, any service or construction contracts that holding companies enter into with each other must be fairly priced, so that there is no undue transfer of assets among companies as a result of the contracts.

In short, this act provides significant restrictions on some types of public utility holding companies in order to forestall the possibility of monopolies being created or an excessive amount of control over this type of company being gathered by a small number of individuals.

4.8   THE TRUST INDENTURE ACT OF 1939

This act applies to debt securities, such as bonds, debentures, and notes that are made available for public sale. These types of securities cannot be offered for sale to the public if there is a trust indenture agreement already in existence between the bond issuer and the bond holder that follows the rules specified by this act. The act also requires that the trustee be a corporation with a minimum amount of capital, that the trustee conforms to high standards of conduct, that the trustee not have conflicting interests that would interfere with its tasks on behalf of the holders of securities, and that the trustee prepare and send reports to security holders.

The act also requires the trustee to maintain a list of securities holders, which must be issued to them at their request. It also provides that the securities issuer provide to the trustee all necessary evidence of compliance with the terms and conditions of the trust indenture agreement.

4.9   THE INVESTMENT COMPANY ACT OF 1940

This act is designed to regulate those entities whose primary occupation is investing in and trading securities, especially those whose securities are made available to investors. The act requires these entities to reveal their investment policies, as well as their financial condition, to investors—both at the initial sale of securities and at regular intervals thereafter. Other information that should be included in these disclosures is the entity's organizational structure, operations, and investment objectives.

The act does not give the SEC authority to supervise these entities or rate the quality of their investments—only to ensure that they are disclosing the required minimum amount of information to investors.

The act goes beyond the basic information reporting requirements to also prohibit investment entities from significantly changing their investment policies or entering into management contracts without shareholder approval. Furthermore, anyone guilty of securities fraud is prohibited from becoming an officer of an investment entity, while brokers, underwriters, and investment bankers are prohibited from forming a majority of its board of directors. Finally, investment entities are prohibited from cross-ownership of each other's securities.

4.10 THE INVESTMENT ADVISERS ACT OF 1940

The Investment Advisers Act of 1940 defines what constitutes an investment adviser, which (in its amended form) is anyone with at least $25 million of assets under management. The act then goes on to require these advisers to register with the SEC, as well as conform to a series of rules that are designed to protect investors, such as maintaining their records in accordance with SEC rules, making those records accessible for SEC audits, and clearly identifying any financial interest they may have in transactions that they have executed for their clients.

Violations of the investment adviser rules fall into the general categories of willful violations of the Securities Act of 1933, the Investment Company Act of 1940, or the Securities Exchange Act of 1934. A violation will also be assumed to have occurred if the adviser has "aided, abetted, counseled, commanded, induced, or procured such a violation by any other person," or has failed to properly supervise another person who has committed these acts. It also counts as a violation the misstatement or omission of key facts related to a securities filing. Penalties assessed are primarily monetary in nature, as well as cease-and-desist orders, though the SEC will sometimes deny, suspend, or revoke an adviser's registration if it feels that such action is in the public interest. Beyond these penalties, the SEC can also recommend criminal action to the Justice Department.

4.11 REGULATION FD

Regulation Fair Disclosure (Regulation FD) is designed to curb the disclosure of material information by companies to selected individuals, such as securities analysts, that is not revealed to the general investing public. The regulation will also supposedly reduce a security analyst's incentive not to disclose this information to the general public (on the grounds that the analyst might no longer be given the privileged information). Imposing Regulation FD may curb the amount of insider trading that has arisen based on the non-public information.

In essence, the regulation requires that an issuer of material information must do so publicly, either by filing the disclosure with the SEC, or by some other broad, non-exclusionary method, such as an Internet Webcast or press release. If material information is disseminated by mistake, then the issuer must act promptly to publicly disclose the information. The regulation does not apply to issuer communications with the press or rating agencies, and communications during the ordinary course of business with business partners, such as customers and suppliers, nor does it apply to any foreign issuers. It does apply to any communications with anyone who is involved with the securities markets on a professional basis, as well as the holders of any securities issued by the company. Also, to keep a company from having to monitor the communications of its entire staff, the regulation only applies to senior management, its investor relations staff, and anyone else who works for the company and who regularly communicates with holders of company securities or anyone involved with the securities markets.

If an issuer violates the regulation, the SEC can initiate an administrative proceeding resulting in a cease-and-desist order, or can go further to seek an injunction or even civil penalties.

4.12   REGULATION M-A

This regulation governs the filing requirements associated with mergers and acquisitions. Information that must be provided to the SEC and securities holders includes:

- *Summary term sheet.* This document itemizes, in bullet point format, the key items of a proposed merger or acquisition transaction such that securities holders can comprehend its importance and key features.
- *Subject company information.* This includes the acquiree's name and address, types of the acquiree's securities to be bought, their trading price, and amount and timing of dividends paid.
- *Identity and background of filing person.* This includes the name, address, and business background of the filer.
- *Terms of the transaction.* This includes the type of securities to be bought, consideration made, expiration date of the offer, and issues related to the transfer of securities to the buyer. If a merger is contemplated, then the reasons for doing so must be given, the need for a vote by securities holders to approve it (if any), the method of accounting used to record the transaction, and its income tax consequences.
- *Past transactions.* This includes a description of the types and amounts of any material transactions in which the parties were engaged in the past two years, as well as any potential conflicts of interest.
- *Purpose of the transaction.* This includes an itemization of the reason for the transaction, what will happen to any acquired securities, and any plans for the sale of assets, dividend changes, or changes to the subject company's organizational structure that will result from the transaction.
- *Amount and source of funds.* This includes an expected amount of funding that will be required to complete the transaction, as well as where the funds are expected to come from, plus key financing terms.
- *Financial statements.* This includes audited financial statements for the past two years, unaudited statements for the most recent quarter, and pro forma statements for the combined entities.
- *Solicitation or recommendation.* This includes a recommendation to securities holders to either accept or reject the transaction, and any recommended alternatives. If the subject company is filing, it can remain neutral in its recommendation.

4.13   REGULATION S-K

This regulation contains the instructions for filing forms with the SEC under the rules set by the Securities Act of 1933, the Securities Exchange Act of 1934, and the Energy Policy and Conservation Act of 1975. It concentrates primarily upon the content of the nonfinancial statements that must be filed, dwelling in particular upon the following topics:

- Description of the general development of the business during the past five years.
- Financial information and a narrative description about individual segments of the business for each of the last three years.
- Financial information about geographic areas for each of the last three years.
- The general types of property owned by the company, as well as where it is located.
- Estimates of oil or gas reserves.

- Any legal proceedings currently under way, either at the company's initiation or to which it is subject.
- The primary markets in which each class of the company's common stock is being traded.
- The approximate number of holders of each type of common stock.
- The amount and timing of the cash dividends declared on each class of common stock for the last two years.
- Description of all securities to be offered for sale.
- Key financial information in a columnar format for the last five years.
- Selected quarterly financial information for the last two years.
- Management's discussion of liquidity, capital resources, and the results of operations.
- Material changes during interim reporting periods.
- Any change in the outside auditing firm in the last two years.
- The market risk associated with trading instruments, as well as how these risks are managed.
- Terms and information about derivative financial instruments.
- The name, age, and position of each company director.
- The name, age, and position of each executive officer.
- The compensation of the CEO and the four most highly paid individuals besides the CEO (but only if their total pay exceeds $100,000). This statement shall separately itemize salary, bonus, option, and pension remuneration.

The regulation also sets forth the reporting requirements for a prospectus, and cross-references a series of industry guides that detail additional, and more specific, reporting requirements. The industry guides are for the oil and gas, bank holding company, real estate limited partnership, property-casualty underwriting, and mining businesses. Regulation S-K provides the foundation for much of the information reporting requirements that publicly held companies must file, and so should be perused in detail by those entities.

4.14   REGULATION S-T

This regulation governs the electronic submission of documents to the SEC. Transmissions may be sent to the SEC, either by dial-up modem or directly through the Internet, on any business day except federal holidays and between the hours of 8 A.M. and 10 P.M., Eastern Standard Time. The following types of documents must be filed in an electronic format:

- Registration statements and prospectuses.
- Statements and applications required by the Trust Indenture Act.
- Statements, reports, and schedules required by the Exchange Act.
- Documents required by the Investment Company Act.
- Documents required by the Public Utility Act.

The following documents must be submitted on paper:

- Confidential treatment requests.
- Supplemental information.

- Shareholder proposals and related correspondence.
- No-action and interpretive letter requests.
- Applications for exemptive relief.
- Promotional and sales material.
- Documents in a foreign language.
- Maps submitted by public utility holding companies.
- Applications for exemption from Exchange Act reporting requirements.
- All first electronic filings, which must also be submitted on paper.

If a company is attempting to meet a filing deadline with the SEC, an electronic submission that is filed on or before 5:30 P.M., Eastern Standard Time, will be presumed to have been filed on that business day, whereas any filing submitted after that time will be presumed to have been filed on the next business day. However, this assumption shifts to 10 P.M. for the filing of registration statements.

If the submitting entity makes an electronic submission that contains errors solely due to errors in the transmission, and if the submitter corrects the errors as soon as possible after becoming aware of the difficulty, then there shall be no liability under the anti-fraud portions of the federal securities laws.

4.15 REGULATION S-X (REQUIREMENTS FOR FINANCIAL STATEMENT REPORTING)

This regulation is the principal one used by the SEC to oversee the form and content of financial statements submitted by the issuers of securities. This is a very important regulation for a publicly held company; to peruse its entire content, one can access it on the SEC's Web site at *www.sec.gov/divisions/corpfin/forms/regsx.htm*. The regulation is composed of the following sections:

- *Article 2: Qualifications and reports of accountants.* The SEC will not recognize as a CPA any person who is not currently registered to practice in the state where his or her home or office is located. It will also not recognize a CPA as being independent if the CPA has a financial interest in the entity being audited, or was a manager or promoter of an auditee at the time of the audit. It requires a CPA's report be dated and manually signed, state that GAAP was followed, state an audit opinion, and clearly itemize any exceptions found.

- *Article 3: General instructions as to financial statements.* Balance sheets must be submitted for the last two year ends, as well as statements of income and cash flow for the preceding three years. If interim financial statements are provided, then standard year-end accruals should also be made for the shorter periods being reported on. Changes in stockholders' equity shall be included in a note or a separate statement. The financial statements of related businesses can be presented to the SEC in a single consolidated format if the companies are under common control and management during the period to which the reports apply. There are a number of tests to determine whether or not consolidated results are required as well as for how many time periods over which the combined financial statements must be reported. If a registrant is inactive (revenues and expenses of less than $100,000, and no material changes in the business or changes in securities) during the period, then its submitted financial statements can be unaudited. There are also special reporting requirements for foreign private issuers, real estate investment trusts, and management investment companies.

- *Article 3a: Consolidated and combined financial statements.* For financial statement reporting purposes, a registrant shall consolidate financial results for business entities that are majority owned, and shall not do so if ownership is in the minority. A consolidated statement is also possible if the year-end dates of the various companies are not more than 93 days apart. Intercompany transactions shall be eliminated from the consolidated reports. If consolidating the results of a foreign subsidiary, then the impact of any exchange restrictions shall be made.

- *Article 4: Rules of general application.* Financial statements not created in accordance with GAAP will be presumed to be misleading or inaccurate. If the submitting entity is foreign based, it may use some other set of accounting standards than GAAP, but a reconciliation between its financial statements and those produced under GAAP must also be submitted. Footnotes to the statements that duplicate each other may be submitted just once, as long as there are sufficient cross-references to the remaining footnote. The amount of income taxes applicable to foreign governments and the United States government shall be shown separately, unless the foreign component is no more than 5% of the total. There must also be a reconciliation between the reported amount of income tax and the amount as computed by multiplying net income by the statutory tax rate. This article also contains an extensive review of the manner in which oil and gas financial results must be reported.

- *Article 5: Commercial and industrial companies.* This article describes the specific line items and related footnotes that shall appear in the financial statements.

  On the balance sheet, this shall include:

  - Cash.
  - Marketable securities.
  - Accounts and notes receivable.
  - Allowance for doubtful accounts.
  - Unearned income.
  - Inventory.
  - Prepaid expenses.
  - Other current expenses.
  - Other investments.
  - Fixed assets and associated accumulated depreciation.
  - Intangible assets and related amortization.
  - Other assets.
  - Accounts and notes payable.
  - Other current liabilities.
  - Long-term debt.
  - Minority interests (footnote only).
  - Redeemable and nonredeemable preferred stock.
  - Common stock.
  - Other stockholder's equity.

On the income statement, this shall include:

- ○ Gross revenues.
- ○ Costs applicable to revenue.
- ○ Other operating costs.
- ○ Selling.
- ○ General and administrative expenses.
- ○ Other general expenses.
- ○ Nonoperating income.
- ○ Interest.
- ○ Nonoperating expenses.
- ○ Income or loss before income taxes.
- ○ Income tax expense.
- ○ Minority interest in income of consolidated subsidiaries.
- ○ Equity in earnings of unconsolidated subsidiaries.
- ○ Income or loss from continuing operations.
- ○ Discontinued operations.
- ○ Income or loss before extraordinary items.
- ○ Extraordinary items.
- ○ Cumulative effect of changes in accounting principles.
- ○ Net income or loss.
- ○ Earnings per share data.

- • *Article 6: Registered investment companies.* This type of company is required to file a balance sheet that contains the following line items:
  - ○ Investments in securities of unaffiliated issuers.
  - ○ Investments in and advances to affiliates.
  - ○ Investments other than securities.
  - ○ Total investments.
  - ○ Cash.
  - ○ Receivables.
  - ○ Deposits for securities sold short and open option contracts.
  - ○ Other assets.
  - ○ Total assets.
  - ○ Accounts payable and accrued liabilities.
  - ○ Deposits for securities loaned.
  - ○ Other liabilities.
  - ○ Notes payable, bonds, and similar debt.
  - ○ Total liabilities.
  - ○ Commitments and contingent liabilities.
  - ○ Units of capital.
  - ○ Accumulated undistributed income or loss.
  - ○ Other elements of capital.
  - ○ Net assets applicable to outstanding units of capital.

The statement of operations for issuers of face-amount certificates shall include the following line items:

- Investment income.
- Investment expenses.
- Interest and amortization of debt discount and expense.
- Provision for certificate reserves.
- Investment income before income tax expense.
- Income tax expense.
- Investment income—net.
- Realized gain or loss on investments—net.
- Net income or loss.

- *Article 6A: Employee stock purchase, savings, and similar plans.* These types of plans must present a statement of financial condition that includes the following line items:
  - Investments in securities of participating employers.
  - Investments in securities of unaffiliated issuers.
  - Investments.
  - Dividends and interest receivable.
  - Cash.
  - Other assets.
  - Liabilities.
  - Reserves and other credits.
  - Plan equity and close of period.

  These plans must include in their statements of income and changes in plan equity the following line items:
  - Net investment income.
  - Realized gain or loss on investments.
  - Unrealized appreciation or depreciation on investments.
  - Realized gain or loss on investments.
  - Contributions and deposits.
  - Plan equity at beginning of period.
  - Plan equity at end of period.

- *Article 7: Insurance companies.* An insurance company must present a balance sheet that includes the following line items:
  - Investments.
  - Cash.
  - Securities and indebtedness of related parties.
  - Accrued investment income.
  - Accounts and notes receivable.
  - Reinsurance recoverable on paid losses.
  - Deferred policy acquisition costs.
  - Property and equipment.
  - Title plant.

- ○ Other assets.
- ○ Assets held in separate accounts.
- ○ Total assets.
- ○ Policy liabilities and accruals.
- ○ Other policyholders' funds.
- ○ Other liabilities.
- ○ Notes payable, bonds, mortgages and similar obligations, including capitalized leases.
- ○ Indebtedness to related parties.
- ○ Liabilities related to separate accounts.
- ○ Commitments and contingent liabilities.
- ○ Minority interests in consolidated subsidiaries.
- ○ Redeemable preferred stock.
- ○ Nonredeemable preferred stock.
- ○ Common stock.
- ○ Other stockholders' equity.
- ○ Total liabilities and stockholders' equity.
- *Article 9: Bank holding companies.* A bank holding company must present a balance sheet that includes the following line items:
  - ○ Cash and cash due from banks.
  - ○ Interest-bearing deposits in other banks.
  - ○ Federal funds sold and securities purchased under resale or similar agreements.
  - ○ Trading account assets.
  - ○ Other short-term investments.
  - ○ Investment securities.
  - ○ Loans.
  - ○ Premises and equipment.
  - ○ Due from customers on acceptances.
  - ○ Other assets.
  - ○ Total assets.
  - ○ Deposits.
  - ○ Short-term borrowing.
  - ○ Bank acceptances outstanding.
  - ○ Other liabilities.
  - ○ Long-term debt.
  - ○ Commitments and contingent liabilities.
  - ○ Minority interest in consolidated subsidiaries.
  - ○ Redeemable preferred stock.
  - ○ Nonredeemable preferred stock.
  - ○ Common stock.
  - ○ Other stockholders' equity.
  - ○ Total liabilities and stockholders' equity.

A bank holding company's income statement must include the following line items:

- ○ Interest and fees on loans.
- ○ Interest and dividends on investment securities.
- ○ Trading account interest.
- ○ Other interest income.
- ○ Total interest income.
- ○ Interest on deposits.
- ○ Interest on short-term borrowings.
- ○ Interest on long-term debt.
- ○ Total interest expense.
- ○ Net interest income.
- ○ Provision for loan losses.
- ○ Net interest income after provision for loan losses.
- ○ Other income.
- ○ Other expenses.
- ○ Income or loss before income tax expense.
- ○ Income tax expense.
- ○ Income or loss before extraordinary items and cumulative effects of changes in accounting principles.
- ○ Extraordinary items.
- ○ Cumulative effects of changes in accounting principles.
- ○ Net income or loss.
- ○ Earnings per share data.

- *Article 10: Interim financial statements.* An interim statement does not have to be audited. Only major line items need be included in the balance sheet, with the exception of inventories, which must be itemized by raw materials, work-in-process, and finished goods either in the balance sheet or in the accompanying notes. Any assets comprising less than 10% of total assets, and that have not changed more than 25% since the end of the preceding fiscal year, may be summarized into a different line item. If any major income statement line item is less than 15% of the amount of net income in any of the preceding three years, and if its amount has not varied by more than 20% since the previous year, it can be merged into another line item. Disclosure must also be made in the accompanying footnotes of any material changes in the business since the last fiscal year end.

- *Article 11: Pro forma financial information.* Pro forma information is required in cases where a business entity has engaged in a business combination or roll-up under the equity method of accounting, or under the purchase or pooling methods of accounting, or if a company's securities are to be used to purchase another business. It is also required if there is a reasonable probability of a spin-off, sale, or abandonment of some part or all of a business. The provided information should consist of a pro forma balance sheet, summary-level statement of income, and explanatory notes. The presented statements shall show financial results on the assumption that the triggering transaction occurred at the beginning of the fiscal year, and shall include a net income or loss figure from continuing operations prior to noting the impact of the transaction.

- *Article 12: Form and content of schedules.* This article describes the format in which additional schedules shall be laid out in submitted information, including layouts for valuation and qualifying accounts. It also itemizes formats for the display of information for management investment companies, which include the following formats: investments in securities of unaffiliated issuers, investments in securities sold short, open option contracts written, investments other than securities, investments in and advances to affiliates, summary of investments, supplementary insurance information, reinsurance, and supplemental information.

4.16   STAFF ACCOUNTING BULLETINS

The SEC requires that public companies report their financial results using generally accepted accounting principles (GAAP), which will change to international financial reporting standards (IFRS) in a few years. However, it also requires the use of more conservative accounting in selected situations, or to fill in gaps in the accounting literature where there is no standard at all, or to impose greater disclosure than would normally be required. The SEC issues its views on these matters through Staff Accounting Bulletins (SABs), which have a question-and-answer format. The SEC describes these Bulletins as follows:

> Staff Accounting Bulletins reflect the Commission staff's views regarding accounting-related disclosure practices. They represent interpretations and policies followed by the Division of Corporation Finance and the Office of the Chief Accountant in administering the disclosure requirements of the federal securities laws.

The following table contains summaries of the more important SABs.

SAB Number	Description
108	A company must quantify the amount of misstatements that were not corrected at the end of the prior-year when quantifying misstatements in the current year's financial statements. This approach is used to avoid the accumulation of significant misstatements on the balance sheet that are deemed immaterial on an annual basis but which are not immaterial when compiled over several years. It is possible that correcting an error in the current year that includes immaterial amounts from previous years could materially misstate the current year's income statement; if so, the correct treatment is to restate the prior-year financial statements, even though such revision is immaterial to the prior-year financial statements. These prior-year corrections do not require the filing of amended reports; instead, the corrections can be made the next time the company files the prior-year financial statements.
107	This Bulletin clarifies SFAS 123(R), without altering it. Key points are that the SEC does not advocate any particular valuation model but does require that the model used encompass all the pertinent factors of an award. If a company chooses to change models, then it should disclose the reasons for the change. The Bulletin also provides guidance on how to compute volatility. Finally, though stock-based compensation must be reported within the same line item used for cash payments, a company can break out the stock-based compensation in the management's discussion and analysis (MD&A) section. The MD&A discussion should also explain whether historical volatility, implied volatility, or a combination of both was used to estimated expected volatility and why its use was appropriate.

SAB Number	Description
104	This Bulletin contains SEC interpretations about a broad range of revenue recognition situations, for which only a sampling of the most common items are noted here. Revenue should not be recognized until it is realized, or realizable and earned. These criteria are met when there is persuasive evidence of an arrangement with the customer, delivery has occurred or services have been rendered, the company's price to the customer is fixed or determinable, *and* collectibility is reasonably assured. Based on these criteria, revenue can be recognized only when any required subsequent approval has been received and risk of ownership has passed to the customer. When an arrangement includes customer acceptance criteria that cannot be tested effectively prior to installation, then revenue recognition is deferred until the criteria are met. Conversely, if the company can test the criteria in advance, or the criteria are based on published specifications for a standard model, then it can recognize revenue upon delivery. In *bill and hold* situations, where a company bills its customer but stores the sold goods on behalf of the customer, revenue can be recognized only if the customer requests this arrangement, has a substantial business purpose for doing so, there is a fixed delivery schedule, and the goods are both segregated and ready for shipment. Finally, revenue recognition can occur when all remaining steps in the revenue recognition process are perfunctory.
100	Restructuring charges that do not relate to the disposal of a discontinued operation cannot be classified as extraordinary items and should be classified as a component of income from continuing operations. Further, if a restructuring charge relates to activities for which the associated revenues and expenses historically have been included in operating income, then the charge should also be recorded as an operating expense. In both cases, there should not be a preceding subtotal showing operating income before restructuring charges. However, the effect of the restructuring charges on the company's results can be discussed in the MD&A section of the quarterly or annual report. This MD&A disclosure should identify major types of restructuring costs and the specific income statement line items to be impacted, disaggregate the costs of multiple exit plans, discuss material revisions to these costs, and note the events and decisions leading to material exit costs.
99	A company should not rely on a rule-of-thumb percentage to determine materiality in cases when items are misstated or omitted. This is because an item should be considered material when the judgment of a reasonable person relying on a financial report would have been changed or influenced by the inclusion or correction of the item—and this action threshold is not necessarily tied to a materiality percentage. Thus, a more complete analysis is required, including a review of the facts in the context of the total mix of available information. For example, a misstatement may: mask a change in a key earnings trend; change a profit to a loss; or hide a failure to meet analyst consensus expectations; affect compliance with loan covenants or regulatory requirements; or trigger a management bonus. If so, it should be considered material, no matter how small it is.
93	Prior to the disposal date of discontinued operations, a company should disclose known trends, events, and uncertainties related to those operations that may materially affect the company. This includes disclosure of contingent liabilities that may remain with the company following disposal of the discontinued operations. If the company retains a financial interest in either the discontinued operations or the buyer of those operations, then it should disclose those issues that can reasonably be expected to affect the amounts the company eventually realizes on the investment.

(Continued)

SAB Number	Description
92	If a company estimates that it will have an environmental remediation or product liability, it should report a liability that is discounted at a rate that will produce an amount at which the liability could be settled in an arm's-length transaction with a third party. It should disclose the discount rate used and expected future payments. Further, the SEC suggests disclosures regarding the judgments and assumptions underlying the recognition and measurement of the liabilities that are sufficient to prevent the financial statements from being misleading. Examples of these disclosures include the terms of cost-sharing arrangements with other potentially responsible parties, the solvency of insurance carriers, and the extent to which contingent losses can be recovered through insurance, indemnification arrangements, and other sources. Further disclosure may be needed for material liabilities for site restoration, postclosure, and monitoring commitments.
74	When an accounting standard has been issued but a company is not yet required to adopt it, the company should disclose the potential effects of adoption, unless the impact on its financial results is not expected to be material. The objectives of the disclosure are to notify the reader that a standard has been issued that the company will adopt in the future and to assist the reader in assessing the impact of the standard on the company's financial statements when adopted.
63	If one company is using funds supplied by other entities for research and development activities, there may be a presumption that the company will repay the funds if there is a significant relationship between the parties. The SEC considers such a relationship to exist when 10 percent or more of the entity providing the funds is owned by related parties, or if there is a lower percentage but a high degree of influence or control over the entity receiving the funds.
54	Purchase transactions resulting in an entity becoming substantially wholly owned establishes a new basis of accounting for the purchased assets and liabilities. This basis of accounting should be the same, regardless of whether the entity continues to exist or is merged into the parent's operations. However, the SEC does not insist on the application of push-down accounting when the acquired entity has a significant minority interest or preferred stock that might impact the parent's ability to control the form of ownership.

4.17   STAFF ACCOUNTING BULLETIN 99: MATERIALITY

The SEC has had some difficulty getting public companies to follow the standard GAAP definition of materiality, which is that an item is material if its inclusion or exclusion from financial statements would change the judgment of a person relying on that information. Since this definition is subject to interpretation, a number of CFOs have stretched the concept to avoid items that may in fact have been material. The SEC issued SAB 99 in order to be more precise in determining the level of an item's materiality.

The SEC staff ruled that misstatements are not necessarily immaterial because they are less than a numerical minimum threshold, and so management must evaluate each one to see if it must be included in the financial statements. Examples of such situations are when:

- It would convert a reported profit into a loss.
- It would drop the earnings level below the consensus earnings expectation.
- It would impact regulatory or loan covenant requirements.
- It allows management to increase the size of its bonus.
- It conceals the presence of an illegal transaction.

- It impacts the reported results of a business segment that management has identified as being important.
- Management is aware that small changes in financial results can trigger significant stock price movements.

Further, auditors are now required to assess the impact on the financial statements of individual misstatements, rather than summarizing them and only evaluating the net result of all such misstatements. Also, a company's auditors must now bring intentional misstatements to the attention of the audit committee, no matter how inconsequential those misstatements may be.

4.18   FORMS TO BE FILED WITH THE SEC

There are a multitude of forms to be filed with the SEC, depending on the types of transactions that a publicly held company initiates. Here are brief descriptions of the most commonly used forms:

- *Form 8-K*. This form is used to report on significant events. The form must be filed if an issuer experiences a change in corporate control, the acquisition or disposition of a significant amount of assets, a change in its public accountant, a director's resignation, or a change in its fiscal year.
- *Form 10-K*. This form is used to report annual financial results under the Securities Exchange Act of 1934. It must be filed within 90 days following the end of a fiscal year.
- *Form 10-Q*. This form is used to report quarterly financial results under the Securities Exchange Act of 1934. It must be filed within 45 days following the end of a quarter, though not for the fourth quarter.
- *Form S-1*. This form is used for the registration of securities under the Securities Act of 1933, though not for securities issued by foreign governments.
- *Form TH*. This form is used to allow an electronic filer using the EDGAR system to temporarily file a paper instead of electronic submission under a temporary hardship claim.

4.19   SUMMARY

This chapter gave a brief overview of the mission of the SEC, how it is organized to meet the requirements of that mission, and the specific laws and regulations under which it operates. If one needs a more complete knowledge of the applicable acts (which are voluminous), one can go to the SEC Web site, which is located at *www.sec.gov*, where additional links will direct one to the appropriate information. Please note that the original acts have been greatly expanded upon by later SEC regulations, so it is best to review the most up-to-date SEC information regarding specific issues.

LAWS IMPACTING ACCOUNTING

5.1 INTRODUCTION

A large number of federal regulations apply to the accounting function. This chapter provides an overview of all the major laws having some impact on it. Given the extremely lengthy nature of some laws, only those portions of the texts that impact the accounting function are summarized here.

The law summaries noted here *generally* describe the original laws, which may have been heavily amended since that time. Consequently, the intent is to provide a general idea of the source of various types of legislation, rather than a precise rendering of the subsequent laws that have been derived from these foundation regulations.

5.2 ETHICS

Continuing problems uncovered in corporate America involving bribery and the deliberate falsification of reported financial information have brought about the acts noted in this section. The Foreign Corrupt Practices Act (FCPA) and the International Anti-Bribery and Fair Competition Act were both designed to stop the bribery of public officials. The Sarbanes-Oxley Act imposed a number of requirements on auditors and the managers of public companies in order to reduce the incidence of falsified financial information being presented to the public. Both the FCPA and Sarbanes-Oxley Act require the use of enhanced control systems in part to achieve their differing objectives.

- *Foreign Corrupt Practices Act of 1977.* This act prohibits all companies from paying bribes to foreign officials, a political party, or a political candidate in order to influence that person in his or her official capacity. Influence means having the person fail to perform his or her official duties or having the person use his or her influence with others in order for the company to obtain or retain business in the foreign country.

---

*The payroll-related laws noted in this chapter have been adapted with permission from *Accounting for Payroll* by Bragg (John Wiley & Sons, 2004).

It also requires issuers of securities to make and keep books, records, and accounts in reasonable detail, that accurately and fairly reflect the transactions and dispositions of assets. This includes devising and maintaining a system of internal accounting controls sufficient to provide reasonable assurances that:

- Transactions are executed in accordance with management's general or specific authorization.
- Transactions are recorded as necessary to permit preparation of financial statements in conformity with generally accepted accounting principles (GAAP).
- Transactions are recorded to maintain accountability for assets.
- Access to assets is permitted only in accordance with management's authorization.
- Asset records are verified with physical assets periodically and appropriate action is taken with respect to any differences.

- *International Anti-Bribery and Fair Competition Act of 1998.* This is an amendment to the Foreign Corrupt Practices Act of 1977. It expands the prohibition on bribery activities to "securing an improper advantage." It also expands the application of the 1977 act to any act of bribery, not just those committed through the mails or interstate commerce. It also extends the penalties of the 1977 act to any foreign company or its representatives engaging in acts of bribery while on U.S. soil. Finally, it expands the application of the 1977 act to international public organizations, which can include such entities as the World Health Organization and the United Nations.

- *Sarbanes-Oxley Act of 2002.* This act includes a number of features that can most broadly be included under the heading of ethics enforcement. It created the Public Company Accounting Oversight Board (PCAOB), designed to oversee the audit firms conducting audits of public companies, and also gives it the power to sanction both companies and individuals for rule violations. It also mandates that audit committees oversee the activities of external auditors, excluding management from the auditing process. Further, it prohibits auditors from offering bookkeeping, investment banking, legal, information technology, actuarial, or internal auditing services to companies they also audit. The law also prohibits an audit firm from selling auditing services to a public company if one of the company's senior officers worked for the audit firm and participated in the audit in the preceding year. In addition, it requires audit partners to rotate off a client at least every five years. The act also sets stiff penalties related to improper maintenance of audit workpapers and the destruction of documents related to a federal or bankruptcy investigation, while also banning personal loans to company executives.

  Chief executive officers (CEOs) and chief financial officers (CFOs) must also attest to the accuracy of quarterly and annual reports filed with the Securities and Exchange Commission (SEC). The act also requires the forfeiture of any profits earned by CEOs and CFOs from equity sales if company financial statements are subsequently restated, thereby giving them no incentive to alter company records to cause a run-up in the stock price. It also gives the SEC authority to issue a lifetime ban on individuals who have committed securities violations from serving on the board of directors of any public company, and also requires the SEC to issue rules requiring a code of ethics for a company's senior financial officers. The act also keeps companies from using off–balance sheet transactions by requiring them to report obligations under lines of credit, leases, guarantees, and significant transactions with unconsolidated entities.

Of particular interest to corporations is the act's emphasis on internal controls. The management team must now have a greater knowledge of the effectiveness of the corporate system of internal controls and make specific representations about their effectiveness, while external auditors must include in their audit reports any significant failings found in the internal control system. This last item requires a great deal of review and documentation of control systems.

Finally, one provision of the act applies not only to public companies but also to private ones. It makes retaliation against whistle-blowers a crime.

5.3 EMPLOYMENT ELIGIBILITY

Employers are required to verify the identity and employment eligibility of any newly hired employees. The Immigration Reform and Control Act required the use of the Form I-9 to control the documentation of this process, while the Illegal Immigration Reform and Immigrant Responsibility Act filled some loopholes in the earlier law. Summaries of the acts are as follows:

- *Illegal Immigration Reform and Immigrant Responsibility Act of 1996 (IIRIRA).* This act shields employers from liability if they have made a good-faith effort to verify a new employee's identity and employment eligibility, and were subsequently found to have committed a technical or procedural error in the identification. If a violation is found, an employer will have 10 business days in which to correct the violation. Noncompliance penalties were greatly increased over those of earlier legislation; in particular, employers can now incur a penalty for each paperwork violation, rather than in total, so the potential fines are much higher.
- *Immigration Reform and Control Act of 1986.* This act requires all employers having at least four employees to verify the identity and employment eligibility of all regular, temporary, casual, and student employees. This is done through a form I-9, which must be completed within three days of an employee's hire date, and retained for the longer of three days from the date of hire or one year following the date of termination.

  The I-9 form includes a complete list of documents that are considered allowable to prove identity and employment eligibility. In brief, those documents proving both identity and employment eligibility include a U.S. passport, a certificate of U.S. citizenship or naturalization, and an Alien Registration Receipt Card, or green card. Those documents proving identity *only* include a driver's license, government ID card, and voter's registration card. Those documents proving work eligibility *only* include a U.S. Social Security card, Certificate of Birth Abroad, and certified birth certificate. One should consult the I-9 form for a complete list.

  If an employer does not comply with this act, penalties can range from $100 to $1,000 per employee hired, plus possible imprisonment if a continuing pattern of noncompliance can be proven. Also, any employee whose identity and employment eligibility has not been proven through the I-9 form must be terminated from employment.

5.4   GARNISHMENTS

Employers are responsible for garnishing the wages of their employees and remitting the resulting funds to various entities in order to reduce the personal debts of the employees. The focus of legislation in this area has been the amount of the deductions that may be made, which jurisdiction shall have precedence in issuing garnishment orders, and how to track the location of employees who switch jobs in order to avoid garnishment orders. The Consumer Credit Protection Act specifies the proportion of total pay that may be garnished, while the Personal Responsibility and Work Opportunity Reconciliation Act addresses the reporting of new hires into a national database. Finally, the Uniform Interstate Family Support Act specifies which jurisdiction shall issue family support-related garnishment orders. Summaries of the acts are as follows:

- *Consumer Credit Protection Act.* This act limits the maximum payroll deduction from an employee's wages for spouse or child support to 60% of his or her disposable earnings, or 50% if the employee is also supporting another spouse or children. Disposable earnings are calculated by subtracting all government-mandated deductions from an employee's gross pay, such as Social Security, Medicare, income taxes of all kinds, and any unemployment or disability insurance. Deductions that are chosen by the employee, such as medical insurance deductions, are *not* included in the disposable earnings calculation.

- *Personal Responsibility and Work Opportunity Reconciliation Act of 1996.* This act requires individual states to provide time-limited assistance to welfare recipients in exchange for work, essentially forcing many people off the welfare roles. The key issue impacting the payroll manager is that each state must now maintain an employer new hire tracking system that rolls up into a Federal Case Registry and National Directory of New Hires. This information is then used to track across state lines parents who are delinquent in making child support payments.

  Employers must report new hires (e.g., any person who is paid wages and is hired to work more than 30 days, including part-time employees) to their state of residence within 20 days of each hire, or at the time of the first regular payroll after the date of hire, whichever is later. The report must be made with a W-4 or equivalent form, which must include the name, address, and Social Security number of the employee, as well as the name, address, and federal tax identification number of the employer.

  States can assess penalties for noncompliance at their option, charging $25 for failing to submit new hire information, and up to $500 if it can be proven that there is a conspiracy between the employer and an employee to avoid reporting this information to the government.

- *Uniform Interstate Family Support Act of 1996 (UIFSA).* This act limits the modification of family support orders to a single state if one party to the dispute resides in that state, thereby eliminating interstate jurisdictional disputes. However, jurisdiction can be shifted to a different state if none of the parents or children continue to reside in the state, or if there is mutual agreement to move the case to another state. This act has been adopted by every state.

  The key results of this act from a payroll perspective are that only one support order can be in effect at one time, and that an income withholding order can be sent to an employer directly from another state. When a withholding order arrives, an employer must follow the rules stated on the order, which will probably specify the address to which payments must be sent, the amount and duration of payments, and possibly the amount of administrative fees that may be withheld.

5.5 HEALTH INSURANCE

Employers can offer health insurance to their employees. If they do so, regulations require them to continue to offer insurance subsequent to employment under certain circumstances, and to offer insurance during employee leaves of absence. The Consolidated Omnibus Budget Reconciliation Act contains the requirements for offering insurance to departed employees, which is expanded upon in the Health Insurance Portability and Accountability Act. The Family and Medical Leave Act contains the rules for offering health insurance to employees who are on leave. Summaries of these acts are as follows:

- *Consolidated Omnibus Budget Reconciliation Act of 1986 (COBRA).* This act allows employees of private sector, state, and local governments who lose their jobs the right to accept continuing health insurance coverage, as long as the former employer had 20 or more employees in the prior year. If an employee is terminated, then he or she can accept coverage for an additional 18 months. If an employee becomes entitled to Medicare coverage or becomes divorced, then the coverage period becomes 36 months. If a spouse or dependent child of an employee loses coverage due to the death of an employee, then they can obtain coverage for up to 36 months. If a dependent child of an employee loses dependent status, then that person can obtain coverage for up to 36 months.

  An employer is required to give notice of potential COBRA coverage to employees when a qualifying event occurs (employees are required to inform the health plan administrator of any divorce, disability, or dependent issues that would bring about qualification for benefits under COBRA). The impacted people then have up to 60 days in which to elect to take COBRA coverage.

  If coverage is chosen, an impacted person can be required to pay up to 102% of the cost of the insurance. If one does not make timely payments under the terms of the insurance plan (within 30 days of the due date), the COBRA coverage can be terminated. COBRA coverage also will end if the employer stops providing medical coverage to its regular employees.

  The penalty to an employer for not complying with the provisions of COBRA is $100 per day for each impacted individual, though the penalty will not be imposed if the employer can prove reasonable cause for the failure and also corrects the situation within 30 days from the point when noncompliance was uncovered.

- *Family and Medical Leave Act of 1993.* This act entitles employees at companies with 50 or more employees to take up to 12 weeks of unpaid leave (which may be taken sporadically) each year for a specified list of family and medical reasons. Only those employees who have worked for the employer for a total of at least 12 months, and worked for the employer for at least 1,250 hours in the last 12 months are covered by the act. A further restriction is that an employee must work at a company location where at least 50 employees are employed within a 75-mile radius of the facility. Valid reasons for taking the leave of absence include the birth of a child, a serious illness, or caring for a family member with a serious illness.

  During the employee's absence, an employer must continue to provide medical insurance coverage if it had been taken by the employee prior to the leave of absence, though the employee can be charged for that portion of the expense that had been deducted from his or her pay prior to the leave. If the employee does not pay this portion of the expense within 30 days, the insurance can be canceled for the remainder of the leave, but must be restored once the employee returns to work.

Upon returning from a leave of absence, an employee must be given the same or equivalent job, with the same level of pay and benefits that he or she had before the leave. In certain cases where job restoration would cause significant economic damage to an employer, key positions will not be restored to returning employees.

This act is enforced by the U.S. Labor Department's Employment Standards Administration, Wage and Hour Division. If violations are not resolved by this entity, the Labor Department can sue employers to compel compliance.

- *Health Insurance Portability and Accountability Act of 1996 (HIPAA).* This act ensures that small (50 or fewer employees) businesses will have access to health insurance, despite the special health status of any employees. Also, insurance carriers must offer coverage renewals in subsequent periods once they have sold coverage to an employer. The key payroll-related aspect of this act is its changes to COBRA regulations. The act entitles anyone who is disabled during the first 60 days of COBRA coverage, as well as that person's family members, to receive up to 29 months of COBRA coverage. Also, COBRA coverage cannot be terminated in cases where a former employee is denied coverage in a new plan due to a preexisting condition, thereby ensuring that the individual will continue to receive medical insurance coverage.

5.6   PENSIONS

Employers may offer participation in pension plans to their employees. If so, government regulations control the documentation and administration of the plans, and also allow ex-military employees to make extra contributions into them. The Employee Retirement Income Security Act covers the documentation and administration of plans, while the Uniformed Services Employment and Reemployment Rights Act governs the additional contribution of funds by ex-military employees into contribution retirement plans. Summaries of these acts are as follows:

- *Employee Retirement Income Security Act of 1974 (ERISA).* This act sets minimum operational and funding standards for employee benefit plans. It covers most private sector employee benefit plans, but does not cover government plans.

  The act requires plan administrators to provide a plan description to any plan participants and to file an annual report about the plan's performance. Plan fiduciaries are required to operate the plan only to the benefit of plan participants, and to act prudently in doing so.

  The Pension and Welfare Benefits Administration of the Department of Labor enforces this act, with the assistance of the Internal Revenue Service for some provisions. The department can bring a civil action to correct law violations, and can bring criminal actions for willful violations. Annual reporting violations can result in a penalty of $1,000 per day.

- *Uniformed Services Employment and Reemployment Rights Act of 1994.* This act encourages people to serve in the armed forces by minimizing the impact on their careers when they return to civilian employment by avoiding discrimination and increasing their opportunities for employment. The primary payroll impact is that an employee returning to a civilian job from the armed forces is allowed to make contributions to his or her 401(k) pension plan up to the amount that would have been allowed if the person had continued employment through the period of service in the armed forces. If the person elects to make these contributions, he or she must do so within a period of three times the service period in the armed forces, up to a maximum of five years.

5.7   TAXES

A number of acts govern the types and amounts of payroll taxes to be withheld from employee paychecks. The Current Tax Payment Act authorizes employer withholding of income taxes from employee pay, while the Social Security Act and Federal Insurance Contributions Act set up Social Security and authorized deductions from pay in order to fund it. The Federal Unemployment Tax Act set up a federal unemployment fund and authorized deductions to pay for it, while the Self-Employment Contributions Act required self-employed parties to pay these taxes themselves. Summaries of the acts are as follows:

- *Current Tax Payment Act of 1943*. This act required employers to withhold income taxes from employee pay, and to remit these deductions to the government on a quarterly basis. This "pay as you go" approach to tax collection surmounted the problem of individuals not having the funds available at year end to pay their income taxes by enforcing incremental payments as wages were initially earned. This act put the onus of tax collection squarely on employers.

- *Federal Insurance Contributions Act of 1935 (FICA)*. This act authorizes the government to collect Social Security and Medicare payroll taxes. These taxes are sometimes referred to as contributions to the Social Security system, since they are eventually returned to taxpayers. Currently, an employer must pay 6.2% of an employee's first $106,800 (which varies each year) in annual earnings, which are matched by the employee. Consequently, the total contribution to Social Security by both parties is 12.4%. The same calculation applies to a 1.45% Medicare tax rate that is based on all taxable pay, with no upper limit. If an employee has multiple employees in a single year, then each one must withhold this tax up to the wage cap of $106,800, even if the grand total employee earnings for the year exceeds that amount.

  The act allows no deductions from the base wage when calculating the total tax due for Social Security or Medicare taxes. Also, a company must retain payroll records for four years from the later of the due date or payment date of these taxes.

- *Federal Unemployment Tax Act (FUTA)*. This act requires employers to pay a tax on the wages paid to their employees, which is then used to create a pool of funds that can be used for unemployment benefits. The tax is based on only the first $7,000 of wages paid to each employee in a calendar year. If an employee has multiple employees in a single year, then each one must withhold this tax up to the wage cap of $7,000, even if the grand total employee earnings for the year exceeds that amount.

  The FUTA tax rate is currently 6.2%, which can then be reduced by the amount of state unemployment taxes paid, usually resulting in a net tax of 0.8% (even though the amount of state unemployment taxes paid may be quite small).

The FUTA tax applies to an employer if it either employs at least one person during each of any 20 weeks in a calendar year, or pays at least $1,500 in wages during any calendar quarter during the current or preceding year. As soon as liability under FUTA is proven, a business is liable for the tax for the full calendar year (even if the test is first applied later in the year), as well as the next calendar year (even if it fails the test in the next calendar year).

- *Racketeer Influenced and Corrupt Organizations (RICO) Act.* This act provides for extended penalties for criminal acts performed as part of a criminal organization. The act allows plaintiffs to sue for triple damages, making this a powerful tool by plaintiffs against employers. It has been used as a countersuit weapon by whistle-blowers who allege ongoing retribution by their employers or former employers, and has been the foundation for recent lawsuits against health maintenance organizations for not passing along cost savings to members, a pharmaceuticals firm for price fixing, and a variety of cases alleging breach of contract.

- *Self-Employment Contributions Act (SECA).* This act requires self-employed business owners to pay the same total tax rates for Social Security and Medicare taxes that are split between employees and employers under the Federal Insurance Contributions Act. One is never forced to pay under both FICA and SECA—only one applies in any given situation.

    The taxes only apply if one's total annual self-employed income is greater than $400, in which case the tax must be applied to *all* income up to a maximum annual limit. Also, some deductions are allowed from business income before the tax is calculated. These deductions include income from interest and dividends, the sale of business property or other assets, and rental income from real estate or personal property (though these deductions do not apply if the generation of these types of income comprises one's core business activity).

- *Social Security Act of 1935.* This groundbreaking act established Old Age and Survivor's Insurance, which was funded by compulsory savings by wage earners. The savings were to be paid back to the wage earners upon their retirement at age 65. The initial payments were 1% of gross wages by both the employee and employer, gradually ramping up to 3% by 1948. Employers were held responsible for withholding this tax from employees' pay. The act also created the Federal Unemployment Trust Fund through additional withholding, which could be reduced by up to 90% if an employee also contributed to a state unemployment fund.

    Originally, only employees engaged in commercial or industrial occupations were covered by this act, though numerous later changes to the act have greatly expanded its coverage.

- *SUTA Dumping Prevention Act of 2004.* SUTA dumping occurs when a business owner shifts employees to an entity that has been granted a lower state unemployment tax rate than another business entity, thereby avoiding the incurrence of state unemployment taxes. Employers obtain lower rating by acquiring such entities, starting a new business that begins with a lower default tax rate, or by essentially manufacturing a low tax rate by only parking long-term staff on an entity's payroll until the lack of unemployment claims has driven down its tax rate. To avoid this situation, the SUTA Dumping Prevention Act bans SUTA dumping, while also requiring state governments to enact legislation preventing employers from inappropriately lowering their unemployment tax rates. The act also imposes "meaningful civil and criminal" penalties on those engaging in SUTA dumping practices.

5.8   WAGES AND OVERTIME

Employers are required to pay their employees at least a minimum wage and overtime rates for work performed in excess of 40 hours per week. These basic issues were originally addressed in the Fair Labor Standards Act (FLSA). The FLSA's provisions were expanded to include contractors working on federal service and construction projects with the Contract Work Hours and Safety Standards Act, and to contractors working on federal construction and repair projects with the Davis-Bacon Act. The McNamara-O'Hara Service Contract Act expanded this coverage to the employees of contractors engaged in federal services contracts, while the Walsh-Healey Public Contracts Act extended coverage to the employees of contractors who sell supplies to the federal government. In addition, the Equal Pay Act required employers to pay both sexes an equal amount for performing the same types of work. Summaries of these acts are as follows:

- *Contract Work Hours and Safety Standards Act.* This act requires federal contractors to pay their "blue collar" workers one and one-half times their basic pay rates for all hours worked over 40 hours during a work week.

  The act applies to all contractors working on federal service and construction projects exceeding $100,000, as well as any federally assisted construction contracts where the government is not the direct contracting agency. Exemptions from the act include contracts for intelligence agencies, transportation, or open market materials purchases. It also does not apply to projects where the government is only guaranteeing a loan or providing insurance.

  The compensation aspects of this act are enforced by the Wage and Hour Division of the Employment Standards Administration. An intentional violation of this act can be punished by a fine of up to $1,000 or six months imprisonment. In addition, a violation of the overtime provisions of the act can result in a $10 penalty per employee for each day that overtime is not paid. The government can ensure that these penalties will be paid by withholding them from the contract payments being made to a contractor. Employees can also sue their employers for any unpaid overtime amounts. In addition, intentional violation of this act can result in the termination of all federal contracts and a contractor's exclusion from receiving future federal contracts for up to three years.

- *Davis-Bacon Act of 1931.* This act provides wage protection to nongovernment workers by requiring businesses engaged in federal construction projects to pay their employees prevailing wages and fringe benefits. Applicable types of federal construction projects include airports, dams, highways, and sewer treatment plants involving either construction or repair work, and exceeding $2,000 in funding.

  The types of employees covered are of the "blue collar" variety, such as mechanics and laborers. Managerial, clerical, and administrative positions are not covered by the act. If an employee is within the correct labor category but is a trainee or apprentice, then that person can receive less than prevailing pay rates if registered as such with the Department of Labor or with a state's apprenticeship agency.

  The "prevailing" wage rates and fringe benefits referred to in the act are the wages and fringe benefits paid to a majority of workers in each labor classification in the geographic region. Alternatively, if there is no majority rate, then the average rate must be paid. These prevailing rates are based on labor information from similar private construction projects in the region, exclusive of other

Davis-Bacon federal projects (unless there are no comparable private projects). If a federal project is based in a rural area, then the prevailing wage data must also be derived from rural regions, while wage data for projects in urban areas must similarly be derived from urban data.

If a contractor violates this act, the agency funding the project can withhold enough funds to pay any underpaid employees of the contractor who fall within the labor categories of the act, while the contractor can be prevented from bidding on federal contracts for three years.

* *Equal Pay Act of 1963.* This act is an extension of the Fair Labor Standards Act, requiring that both sexes receive equal pay in situations where work requires equivalent effort, responsibility, and skills, performed under similar working conditions. Under this act, it is irrelevant if specific individuals of either sex who perform the work have extra skills beyond those needed for designated work. The key issue is whether one can perform those specific skills required for the work. However, wage differentials can exist if they are based on some other factor than sex, such as a piece rate payment system or seniority in a position.

  The Equal Employment Opportunity Commission enforces this act, including the receipt of employee complaints and the conduct of subsequent investigations.

* *Fair Labor Standards Act of 1938.* This important act created standards of overtime pay, minimum wages, and payroll recordkeeping. It applies to any business entity that does at least $500,000 in annual business across interstate lines, as well as all schools and governments. It also covers any domestic service workers who work at least eight hours per week and receive a minimum amount in annual wages. Individual positions that are exempt from its provisions include "white collar" salaried employees, fishermen, newspaper deliverers, farmers, and casual babysitters. Individual positions that are exempt only from its overtime pay provisions include railroad employees, certain broadcasting positions, seamen on American vessels, and news editors (the list is quite detailed, and longer than presented here).

  The act (as amended) requires that covered employees be paid at least the minimum wage of $7.25 per hour, or at least $2.13 to employees who also receive tips. Piece-rate pay is also legal, but the resulting pay must at least match the minimum wage. If an applicable state law requires a higher hourly rate, then the state law will prevail. Overtime pay of one and one-half times the regular rate of pay is also required for all hours worked in excess of 40 in a work week.

  The act prohibits the shipment of goods in interstate commerce that were produced in violation of these provisions. Employees may file a complaint with the Wage and Hour Division of the Department of Labor, or can file suit individually to obtain up to three years of unpaid back pay. The Wage and Hour Division can bring criminal proceedings against a willful violator and issue fines of up to $1,000 per violation.

* *McNamara-O'Hara Service Contract Act of 1965.* This act covers contractors who work on federal government contracts involving services by "service employees." These are nonexempt employees who are not categorized as administrative, professional, or executive. The covered federal contracts do not include services performed outside the geographical boundaries of the United States; for public utilities; for transport contracts involving published tariff rates, construction or building repairs; for employment contracts directly to a government agency; or for services to the communications industry.

Under this act, contractors performing services in excess of $2,500 must pay those employees working on a federal contract at least as much as the wage and benefit levels prevailing locally. If a contract is less than $2,500, then the federal minimum wage rate must be paid. Also, employers must pay overtime at a rate of one and one-half times the regular pay rate for work hours exceeding 40 in a work week. Furthermore, employers must inform those employees working on federal contracts of their pay rates and benefits under this act.

The Wage and Hour Division of the Employment Standards Administration handles complaints related to the wage and benefits provisions of this act. If a violation occurs, the government can withhold sufficient amounts from its contractual payments to a contractor to cover any underpayments to employees, and pursue legal action to recover underpayments, and prevent a contractor from bidding for future federal contracts for up to three years.

- *Walsh-Healey Public Contracts Act of 1936.* This act forces government contractors to comply with the government's minimum wage and hour rules. It applies to those contractors who sell equipment and supplies to the government, as long as the value of contracts is at least $10,000. Under the act, employers must pay their employees one and one-half times their regular rate of pay for overtime hours worked within a work week, and employees must be paid at least the prevailing minimum wage for the same or similar type of work in the region when production is occurring.

  Suppliers in areas that have statutory or regulatory exemptions, such as periodical deliveries, public utilities, and common carriers, are exempted from this act.

  The Wage and Hour Division of the Employment Standards Administration handles complaints related to the wage and benefits provisions of this act. A contractor who does not comply with this act can be liable for damages for the amount of unpaid wages, and can be prevented from receiving government contracts for a three-year period.

5.9 OTHER LAWS IMPACTING ACCOUNTING

A company's credit department will find that it can pursue claims more effectively against individuals under the provisions of the Bankruptcy Abuse Prevention and Consumer Protection Act, while it also stands a better chance of defending its claims against charges of preferential payments by bankrupt customers. The Bank Secrecy Act requires companies to file Form 8300 with the IRS to document cash receipts of $10,000 or more. Summaries of the acts are as follows:

- *Bankruptcy Abuse Prevention and Consumer Protection Act of 2005.* A central component of this act makes it more difficult for individuals to obtain a discharge of debts under Chapter 7 of the bankruptcy code. Creditors can obtain dismissal of a person's bankruptcy case if it can be proved that the bankruptcy filing was an abuse of the Chapter 7 provisions. Abuse is presumed if a debtor's income exceeds the median income of the state in which the debtor resides, and if the debtor either has sufficient net income to repay at least $10,000 over five years, or if between $6,000 and $10,000 of net income is available for repayment over five years and this represents more than 25% of nonproprietary unsecured claims.

  The act also makes it easier for creditors to claim that they did not receive preferential payments from an entity having filed for bankruptcy protection, thereby allowing them to retain payments made by the debtor shortly before its official bankruptcy filing. A creditor can claim lack of preference based on its documented history of payments from the debtor, irrespective of the industry standard for payment terms.

- *Bank Secrecy Act of 1970.* This act was designed to create a paper trail for large financial transactions, thereby giving the government a tool for tracking down money-laundering schemes. The paper trail includes the following reporting requirements:

  - *Currency Transaction Report.* For cash transactions exceeding $10,000 at financial institutions.

  - *Currency Transaction Report by Casinos.* For deposits, withdrawals, or gambling chip exchanges for currency exceeding $10,000 at casinos.

  - *Report of Cash Payments over $10,000 Received in Trade or Business.* For cash received by businesses of at least $10,000. This is filed on IRS Form 8300, requiring information about the identities of the parties, the amounts and types of funds received, and the nature of the transaction.

  - *Suspicious Activity Report.* For the reporting by financial institutions of several suspicious transactions totaling at least $5,000. These transactions include check kiting, check fraud, bribery, counterfeit checks, credit card fraud, embezzlement, and terrorist financing.

  - *Report of International Transportation of Currency or Monetary Instruments.* For the transport of currency or bearer monetary instruments exceeding $10,000 either into or out of the United States.

  - *Report of Foreign Bank and Financial Instruments.* For deposits of at least $10,000 held by U.S. persons in foreign bank accounts.

5.10 SUMMARY

This chapter presented the most important pieces of legislation impacting accounting, including financial reporting, ethics, calculating overtime pay, use of the minimum wage, garnishments, pension plan contributions, employee identification and right to work, Social Security taxes, and unemployment insurance. Though one will not learn about the precise nature of existing regulations by reviewing these legal summaries, they do give a good historical overview of how today's accounting environment was shaped by yesterday's legislation.

PART THREE

ACCOUNTING REPORTS

CHAPTER 6

THE BALANCE SHEET AND STATEMENT OF STOCKHOLDERS' EQUITY

6.1 INTRODUCTION

The balance sheet presents information about an organization's assets, liabilities, and equity at a specific point in time, rather than for a range of dates (as is the case for the income statement, statement of stockholders' equity, and the statement of cash flows). The statement of stockholders' equity reveals equity-related activities for a specified time period. The balance sheet is the more complex of the two statements and so is addressed in greater detail in this chapter, both in terms of its contents and the reasons why different types of costs are used for the various line items contained within it.

6.2 USES OF THE BALANCE SHEET AND STATEMENT OF STOCKHOLDERS' EQUITY

The accountant can use the balance sheet to determine a company's level of liquidity, comparing the amount of current assets to current liabilities, as well as the ability of the entity to pay dividends and interest payments. It can also be used to determine a company's valuation, though the presence of historical costs on the balance sheet may mean that the liquidation value of a company varies considerably from its value as listed on the balance sheet. The statement of stockholders' equity is primarily used to determine the types of equity-related transactions that have occurred during the reporting period.

   The balance sheet is much more useful when combined with the income statement, since the accountant can then compare activity levels in the income statement to the amount of assets and liabilities needed to support them, thereby yielding information about the overall financial health of the enterprise. For example, one can compare the amount of working capital (located on the balance sheet) invested in the business to the sales volume (located on the income statement) to see if the investment is sufficient to adequately support sales levels—if not, the company may fail in short order. As another example, one can compare sales volume to the amount of accounts receivable, accounts payable, or inventory on the balance sheet to see if the turnover levels for these items are high enough to indicate that they are being managed properly.

6.3   THE BALANCE SHEET FORMAT

There is no specifically mandated format associated with the balance sheet. However, it is customary to divide the report into header, assets, liabilities, and stockholders' equity sections. The header should include the name of the company and its legal status, such as "Premier Steaks, Incorporated" or "Buyer & Son, a Limited Liability Partnership." The header should also include a date, which is the snapshot date on which the balance sheet is based. For example, if the report is dated August 31, 2010, then this is the specific date for which information is being presented. It is common to list the report as of the last day of the fiscal period on which the accompanying income statement is also being reported, so that the reader knows that the information in the two reports addresses the same time frame (an entire reporting period in the case of the income statement, and the last day of that period, in the case of the balance sheet). Finally, if the company conducts its accounting on anything but the accrual basis, this should be noted in the header. A typical header is as follows:

Morgenthau Catering, Inc.
Balance Sheet
As of April 30, 2010

The accountant should list the asset section of the balance sheet immediately below the header. An example is shown in Exhibit 6.1. The presented format is intended for the reporting of a single period and so uses separate columns for detailed and summary results. If the accountant were to present side-by-side results for multiple periods, the detailed and summary line items could be merged into a single column in order to make room for the results of the extra periods. Current assets are itemized at the top of the assets section, followed by long-term investments, fixed assets (also called "Property, Plant, and Equipment"), and other assets. The definitions of these categories are described later in the "Asset Definitions" section.

Liabilities are listed after the asset section. An example of this continuation of the balance sheet is noted in Exhibit 6.2. As was the case for assets, current items are listed first—in this case as current liabilities. Following this section are long-term liabilities, and then a grand total for all liabilities. The definitions of the line items shown here are described later in the "Liability Definitions" section.

The final section of the balance sheet, the stockholders' equity section, is itemized last. An example is shown in Exhibit 6.3. This section is divided into categories for capital stock, additional paid-in capital, retained earnings, and other comprehensive income, followed by a grand total. Descriptions of these line items are provided later in the "Stockholders' Equity Definitions" section.

If the accountant is presenting balance sheet information for multiple time periods, he or she should restate the numbers for all time periods to conform to the same reporting structure as the most recent one. For example, accounts receivable from employees cannot be itemized under the "accounts receivable" line item for one period and under "other assets" for another period—it must consistently appear under the same line item in all presented reporting periods, so that the information is comparable.

Current Assets:		
Cash	$1,500,000	
Investments, short-term	3,850,000	
Accounts receivable	7,425,000	
(Allowance for doubtful accounts)	−205,000	
Other accounts receivable	115,000	
Prepaid expenses	50,000	
Inventory		
Raw materials	3,000,000	
Work-in-process	450,000	
Finished goods	1,850,000	
		$18,035,000
Long-Term Investments:		
Investments available for sale	2,000,000	
Investments held to maturity	500,000	
Cash termination value of life insurance	75,000	
		$ 2,575,000
Fixed Assets:		
Computer equipment	4,050,000	
Leasehold improvements	300,000	
Machinery & equipment	3,955,000	
Buildings	6,900,000	
Land	503,000	
Less: accumulated depreciation	−980,000	
		$14,728,000
Other Assets:		
Organizational costs	200,000	
Copyright and patent costs	325,000	
Goodwill	3,750,000	
		$ 4,275,000
Total Assets:		$39,613,000

EXHIBIT 6.1   THE PRESENTATION OF ASSETS IN THE BALANCE SHEET

Current Liabilities:		
Accounts payable	$2,350,000	
Wages payable	450,000	
Taxes payable	175,000	
Current portion of long-term debt	825,000	
Dividends payable	400,000	
Accrued liabilities	265,000	
		$ 4,465,000
Long-Term Liabilities:		
Notes payable	2,575,000	
14% bonds, due in 2025	4,000,000	
Capital lease liabilities	500,000	
Total Long-Term Liabilities:		$ 7,075,000
Total Liabilities:		$11,540,000

EXHIBIT 6.2   THE PRESENTATION OF LIABILITIES IN THE BALANCE SHEET

Capital Stock:		
Common stock, $1 par value,		
1,000,000 shares authorized, 285,000 issued	$ 285,000	
10% preferred stock, $10 par value,		
400,000 shares authorized, 350,000 issued	3,500,000	
		$ 3,785,000
Additional Paid-In Capital:		
From common stock	14,000,000	
From 10% preferred stock	4,000,000	
From expired stock options	100,000	
		$18,100,000
Retained Earnings:		$ 6,525,000
Other Comprehensive Income:		
Unrealized foreign currency translation losses	−280,000	
Unrealized available-for-sale security losses	−57,000	
		−$ 337,000
Total Stockholders' Equity:		$28,073,000

EXHIBIT 6.3 THE PRESENTATION OF EQUITY IN THE BALANCE SHEET

6.4 ASSET DEFINITIONS

To be an asset, a transaction must provide a future economic benefit that will result in cash inflows, the business entity must be able to receive this benefit, and the event that gave the entity the right to the benefit must have already occurred as of the balance sheet date.

In the balance sheet example in Exhibit 6.1, the line items clustered into the current assets section are those assets that the accountant expects to be cash, convertible to cash, or eliminated from the balance sheet within the longer of one year or the company's natural operating cycle. The only exception is any cash that has restrictions on it, such as a borrowing arrangement that requires a company to retain some cash in the lending bank's checking account—in this case, the cash is assumed to be restricted for the term of the loan agreement, and so is classified as a long-term asset until the final year of the loan agreement.

The "cash" line item in the balance sheet can also be entitled "cash and cash equivalents." A cash equivalent is an investment that is highly liquid and within three months of its maturity date. Otherwise, investments are summarized within the "short-term investments" line item, but only for so long as they have maturities of no more than one year, and if the management team is willing to sell them at any time. The accountant can present short-term investments in a single line item, as long as a descriptive footnote describes the types of investments. An alternative is to list the major investment categories in several line items on the balance sheet.

The only accounts receivable that should be contained within the "accounts receivable" line item are those that are acquired during normal business transactions. If there are other accounts receivable, such as those from employees or owners, these should be listed in a separate "other accounts receivable" line item. Also, any allowance for doubtful accounts should be shown separately from the accounts receivable as an offset, so that the reader can easily determine the size of the reserve for bad debts.

Prepaid expenses generally involve transactions in which a payment has been made to a supplier, but the related benefit has not yet been obtained. For example, an early rent payment for the following reporting period or a medical insurance payment that applies to the next period would be listed in this account and charged to expense as soon as the related benefit has been incurred.

There are three main types of inventory that should be separately shown on the balance sheet—raw materials, work-in-process, and finished goods. One can also net them into a single line item and present the detail for the three types of inventory in a footnote. Alternatively, if there is very little inventory, then a single line item with no additional disclosure is acceptable.

Long-term investments are usually listed directly after current assets in the balance sheet. These investments are ones that the company intends to retain for more than one year. Examples of such investments are sinking funds for bond payments or pension funds (for which related payouts may be years in the future).

Fixed assets are listed as a separate category, and can be placed on the balance sheet either before or after long-term investments—but certainly after all current assets. They can also be referred to as "property, plant, and equipment." These are tangible assets that are not used as part of the standard operating process, and that are not used within the operating cycle. Fixed assets are usually grouped into several broad categories, which will vary by the types of assets purchased. The following categories are commonly used:

- Buildings
- Computer equipment
- Furniture and fixtures
- Land
- Leasehold improvements
- Machinery and equipment
- Office equipment
- Software

If a fixed asset has been obtained under a capital lease, it should not be separately identified as a capital lease, but rather should be clustered into the asset category that most nearly describes it. Also, the amount of accumulated depreciation thus far recognized should be listed as an offset to the fixed asset line items. Depreciation can be listed as an offset to each fixed asset line item, but is more commonly presented in total and immediately following all of the fixed assets.

Goodwill is typically presented either as a separate line item or within a separate section near the end of the balance sheet assets section that is entitled "Intangible Assets" and that includes such items as goodwill, copyrights, trademarks, and patents. Goodwill can only be shown on the balance sheet if it has been acquired through a business combination. Costs associated with copyrights, trademarks, and patents can only be those directly incurred by the business, unless they have been marked up as a result of having acquired them through a business combination. The amortization of these assets can be either netted against them or presented on separate line items.

6.5 LIABILITY DEFINITIONS

The format of the liabilities section of the balance sheet was shown earlier in Exhibit 6.2. A liability as recorded on the balance sheet is one that must be settled through the payment of an asset at some point in the future and where the obligation to make the payment has already occurred as of the balance sheet date. Accrued liabilities involve the recognition of liabilities prior to a related transaction being completed. A liability can expire through no action on the part of an organization; for example, an accrued warranty expense can terminate as soon as the warranty period expires that was associated with any sold products or services.

A liability is listed as a current liability if the accountant expects it to be liquidated within the longer of a company's operating cycle or one year. Current liabilities typically include accounts payable, customer deposits (if the associated deliveries to customers will be made within the operating cycle or one year), accrued taxes, accrued wages and vacation pay, and a variety of other accruals associated with current operations. However, all of these items can also be classified as long-term liabilities if one does not expect them to be liquidated within the later of one year or the operating cycle. There can be a split of the same account type between both current and long-term liabilities. For example, there can be accounts payable that are typically due within 30 days and that would be categorized as current liabilities; there may also be accounts payable with very long payment terms and that can therefore be reported under the long-term liabilities section of the balance sheet. Similarly, those capital lease obligations coming due for payment in the short term will be categorized as a current liability, while those portions of the remaining payments coming due at a later date will be listed under the long-term liabilities section of the balance sheet.

Debt is commonly split into short-term and long-term segments in the balance sheet. The portion of debt that is considered to be a current liability is the debt that is expected to be paid off within the longer of one year or the operating cycle. One cannot push debt into the current liabilities section of the balance sheet just because it is the intention of management to pay off the debt in the near term—only the amount of debt specified in the debt agreement for payment in the near term can be itemized as a short-term liability. Also, debt that should clearly be itemized as short term can be shifted into the long-term debt portion of the balance sheet if management intends to refinance it with new debt that is expected to be categorized as long-term debt.

Long-term debt is frequently described in the balance sheet as "Notes Payable" or "Bonds Payable." This is debt that is expected to be paid off in whichever time period is the greater, one year or the operating cycle. This information can be combined with any related discount or premium in a single, summarized line item, or it can be broken out, as in the following example:

Bonds payable $1,000,000
Plus premium   40,000

If summarized into a single line, the same information would be presented as follows:

Bonds payable, plus premium of $40,000 $1,040,000

A deferred income tax liability is recognized on the balance sheet if the reporting entity has experienced temporary differences between net income that it has reported under GAAP and net income as reported under IRS regulations.

6.6   STOCKHOLDERS' EQUITY DEFINITIONS

Stockholders' equity is the residual interest in a business that belongs to its owners after all liabilities are subtracted from assets. It comprises the initial investment by company shareholders, plus retained earnings, less dividends. An example of the layout of this portion of the balance sheet was shown earlier in Exhibit 6.3. It comprises the following categories of equity:

- *Capital stock.* This is the par value of the stock held by shareholders. The balance sheet should enumerate each of the various classes of stock that have been issued, including the par value amount, the number of shares authorized, and the number outstanding. If there is preferred stock outstanding, then additional information for these shares should include their stated interest rate, the callable price point (if any), whether the dividends are cumulative, if the shares give the holder the right to participate in earnings, if they are convertible to common stock, and if so, then at what price they are convertible.
- *Additional paid-in capital.* This is the price at which shares were purchased, less their par value (which was listed in the preceding line item). As was the case for capital stock, additional paid-in capital (APIC) should be listed separately for each type of stock outstanding. There may also be a need for an additional line item to contain cash received from other sources than stock, such as cash from the purchase of warrants that have subsequently expired, from bond conversions at prices greater than the par value of the stock being converted to, or from stock dividends that are recorded at their market price (which is presumably higher than the par value).
- *Treasury stock.* This is any shares that have been repurchased by the corporation, but not canceled.
- *Retained earnings.* This is the cumulative corporate earnings, less any dividends paid out to shareholders.
- *Other comprehensive income.* This is the cumulative change in equity caused by any unrealized gains or losses from foreign currency translation, available-for-sale investments, and the difference between the minimum pension liability and unrecognized previous service costs, if the minimum pension liability is higher.

6.7   THE STATEMENT OF STOCKHOLDERS' EQUITY FORMAT

The statement of stockholders' equity has a relatively undefined format, which gives the accountant a great deal of leeway in designing one that meets his or her reporting needs. In essence, the report is intended to reveal the beginning and ending stockholders' equity for a specific time period, as well as changes in its subsidiary accounts during the period. An example is shown in Exhibit 6.4; this format lists the main components of equity, as well as those equity transactions that arose during the year. A prior period adjustment is also noted in the exhibit, which requires an accompanying footnote to disclose the type of transaction that occurred. Alternatively, it is acceptable to include explanations directly into the report format, though this can result in a lengthy report. If the accompanying financial statements cover multiple years, the accountant can simply repeat this format for as many additional years as are listed in the other statements.

6.8   ACCOUNTING TREATMENT OF OFFSETS
TO ASSETS AND LIABILITIES

Offsetting refers to the netting of assets and liabilities to yield either no line item at all on the balance sheet (if the assets and liabilities exactly offset each other) or a much smaller residual balance. Offsetting is not allowed, except under the most strictly defined

Morgenthau Catering, Inc.
Statement of Stockholders' Equity
for the Year Ended December 31, 2010

	Common Stock	Preferred Stock	Additional Paid-in Capital	Retained Earnings
December 31, 2009	$50,000	$15,000	$85,000	$225,000
Prior period adjustment (Note 1)				−35,000
Sale of 2,500 common shares	2,500		7,500	
Net income				42,500
Dividends				−38,000
December 31, 2010	$52,500	$15,000	$92,500	$194,500

Note 1: The prior period adjustment is related to a correction in the depreciation method used for heavy equipment purchases during the preceding year.

EXHIBIT 6.4   THE PRESENTATION OF THE STATEMENT OF STOCKHOLDERS' EQUITY

circumstances, since the reader of a balance sheet could be misled by the absence of information about potentially large assets or liabilities. Offsetting is only allowed when *all* of the following conditions are met:

- Two parties owe measurable liabilities to each other.
- At least one party has a legally justifiable right to offset its liability against that of its counterpart.
- The party intends to exercise this right.
- The maturity of the party's obligation arrives prior to that of the other entity (since the party with the earliest liability will likely create an offset prior to the other entity and therefore controls the outcome of the transaction).

6.9   CRITIQUE OF THE BALANCE SHEET

Many objections have been raised to the structure and underlying basis of information used to formulate the balance sheet. Here are some of the key issues:

- *Use of historical costs.* In most cases, the information presented in the balance sheet is based on the historical cost of assets and liabilities. This is fine in the case of most current assets, whose valuations are unlikely to change much before they are either used up or paid off. However, inventories in volatile industries, such as computer equipment, can drop in value rapidly, which can give an inventory-laden balance sheet a deceptively large amount of current asset valuation. Similarly, a company that has invested heavily in fixed assets can have a misleading balance sheet if the market value of those assets varies significantly from their historical cost.

  The alternative to the use of historical costs would be their replacement with current costs. The use of current costs would certainly avoid the preceding problems, but takes a considerable amount of time to obtain (thereby delaying the release of the financial statements), and are subject to manipulation. Further, adjustments to historical costs with current costs will require the recognition of some gain or loss on the difference between the two values. Finally, the accountant must put a considerable amount of ongoing effort into the updating of current costs for assets—from a maintenance perspective, it is much easier to record an asset or liability just once at its historical cost and then not have to worry about it again until it is disposed of.

A variation on the use of current costs is the lower of cost or market rule, which is extensively used to reduce the valuation of inventory to its net realizeable value as of the balance sheet date; this approach marks assets *down* to a lower current cost, but does not mark them up to a higher current cost, as would be the case under current costing if the fair market value were higher than the historical cost. Under existing accounting rules, the only circumstance in which an asset's cost is increased to reflect its fair market value is when a gain is realized at the point of sale. Thus, the lower of cost or market rule is a halfway measure that reveals the lowest possible current cost.

- *Use of estimates.* The accountant is required to include in the financial statements estimates for bad debts and inventory obsolescence. These reserves are subject to some degree of manipulation, usually so that reported levels of operating income can be changed to suit management's income targets. For example, an accountant could use a standard formula for determining the amount of bad debt to reserve against, but judgmentally elect to recognize some lesser proportion of the result of the calculation if that would result in the achievement of a specific net income figure. Though an auditor could use a firm's recent history of bad debt experiences to impose a different bad debt reserve, this would only apply to those financial statements that are being audited—all intervening statements would still be subject to manipulation in this area.

- *No adjustment for present value entries.* There are a few situations in which the accountant is required to record a liability at the present value of all readily discernible cash flows at the time when a transaction initially occurs, which uses a discount rate that makes the most sense at the time of the transaction. Though this is a good, rational entry to make at the time of the transaction, the discount rate will change over time as market conditions vary, resulting in an incorrect discounted present value at a later date.

  The obvious solution is to mandate a periodic update of all such transactions with a new discounted present value calculation that is based on the most recent market interest rate. However, this also increases the burden on the accountant, which will also likely delay the release of the financial statements until these calculations can be made.

- *No entry to reflect most intangible assets.* Accounting regulations require the accountant to record only the costs associated with intangible assets, such as the legal fees used to obtain a patent. In some cases, this may grossly understate the actual value of the assets. For example, the Coke formula is worth billions of dollars, but does not appear on that company's balance sheet as a separate line item. Similarly, the market value of many companies, such as Procter & Gamble, Oakley, and Nike are built largely upon the value of the brand names that they have created, but which is not reflected in their balance sheets.

  A possible solution to this dilemma is to have these intangible assets appraised at regular intervals, and noted on the balance sheet, with an adjustment to the equity account to offset the changes in the intangible asset. However, this is also subject to considerable manipulation, because the selection of a tractable appraiser could result in a much higher intangible valuation than a more conservative appraiser might issue.

The primary issue being raised with the information contained in the balance sheet is its use of historical costs. Though certainly a valid point, one must remember that accounting rules are based on the most conservative possible statement of information—that which can be proven through an accounting transaction for which some sort of paperwork exists. Consequently, accounting records tend to be updated only when an asset or liability is procured and later eliminated. If the accounting rules are altered to switch the costs in the balance sheet to the current cost methodology, then the basis of evidence for proving these costs becomes much less solid. Consequently, the legal need to prove where a valuation has come from will probably continue to favor the use of historical costs for most line items in the balance sheet.

6.10 SUMMARY

The content of this chapter focused on the layout of the balance sheet and statement of stockholders' equity. However, there is a great deal of additional information related to this topic. Chapter 9 discusses the footnotes that must accompany the financial statements, while Chapters 12 through 18 cover the proper accounting treatment of every line item in the balance sheet, including cash, investments, inventory, fixed assets, liabilities, and equity.

CHAPTER 7

THE INCOME STATEMENT

7.1 INTRODUCTION

The income statement is perhaps the most commonly studied document that the accounting department produces, since it reveals the results of operations and related activities for a business entity. For this reason, the accountant must be careful to create an income statement that reveals the maximum amount of information to the reader without presenting an overwhelming amount of data. To do so, the income statement must be structured to fit the revenue and expense line items that are most crucial within certain industries—for example, development costs are exceedingly important in the software industry, while they are usually an inconsequential item in a consulting business. Thus, there can be an infinite variety of income statement formats that the accountant can create. However, to be acceptable under GAAP, some activities—such as extraordinary items, accounting changes, and discontinued operations—must be accounted for in a particular manner. Thus, this chapter is designed to give the reader the maximum amount of information about those income statement line items that require specific presentation formats.

7.2 FORMAT OF THE INCOME STATEMENT

The basic format of the income statement begins with the name of the business entity, the name of the report, and the period over which its financial performance is being presented. An example of this is shown in Exhibit 7.1. If the cash basis of accounting is used, this should be noted in the report header, since the reader will otherwise assume that the more common accrual method is being used.

The first set of information presented is the revenue from continuing operations, which consists of those revenues from expected or current cash inflows resulting from a company's regular earnings process. The exact format of revenue reporting used is driven more by custom than by GAAP. In Exhibit 7.1, revenues are reported by product line, but they

Lagerfeld & Son Custom Cabinets
Income Statement
for the month ended July 31, 2010

Revenue:		
Product line A	$12,450	
Product line B	9,250	
Product line C	5,000	
Total Revenue		$26,700
Cost of Goods Sold:		
Materials	$ 4,350	
Direct labor	1,000	
Overhead	3,775	
Commissions	1,350	
Total Cost of Goods Sold		$10,475
Gross Margin		$16,225
Operating Expenses:		
Advertising	$ 500	
Bank charges	100	
Depreciation	2,000	
Insurance	250	
Legal and accounting	350	
Marketing expenses	600	
Outside services	50	
Payroll taxes	300	
Postage and deliveries	275	
Salaries and wages	3,750	
Supplies	450	
Training	50	
Travel and entertainment	825	
Utilities	435	
Miscellaneous expenses	125	
Total Operating Expenses:		$10,060
Gains (losses) on sale of assets	−425	
Other revenues and expenses	175	
Net Income Before Taxes:		$ 5,915
Taxes		$ 2,250
Net Income:		3,665

EXHIBIT 7.1   THE INCOME STATEMENT FORMAT

can just as easily be reported by geographic region, individual products, or subsidiary. They may also be lumped together into a single line item.

The cost of goods sold is described in the next block of information in the income statement. This is described more fully in the next section, but it is customarily assumed to be composed of the materials, labor, and overhead costs included in those products or services that are sold during the reporting period.

The next section of the income statement includes all operating expenses. These are the expenses that are tied to ongoing business transactions and are generally assumed

Results from Discontinued Operations:		
Income from operations—discontinued operations	$ −375	
Gain (loss) from disposition of discontinued operations	−450	
Extraordinary items (less related income taxes of $600):	1,300	
Cumulative effect of a change in accounting principle:	−700	
Net income:		−$3,440

EXHIBIT 7.2   ADDITIONAL ITEMS FOR THE INCOME STATEMENT

to include the sales and marketing, general and administrative, customer support, and engineering departments. These expenses are usually recognized as soon as they are incurred, but may also be allocated over multiple reporting periods if there is some future benefit associated with them. The exact layout of this section is also subject to considerable variation. Some companies prefer to divide it into specific departments, others (as shown in Exhibit 7.1) prefer to describe it by types of expenses, while others itemize it by business location. It is recommended that not too many expenses be lumped into the "miscellaneous expenses" account, since this provides no information to the reader of the report. As a general rule, shift costs into other, more descriptive line items if the amount in this account reaches or exceeds 10% of the total amount of operating expenses. The full format of the income statement is shown in Exhibit 7.1.

As described in the following sections, there are special categories of expense reporting, such as the results from discontinued operations, extraordinary items, and changes in accounting, which must be reported after the results of operations in the income statement. If these items are present, then the "Net Income" line item listed at the bottom of Exhibit 7.1 would be changed to "Net Income before [list additional items to be reported]." A sample format of these extra items is shown in Exhibit 7.2, which is an add-on to Exhibit 7.1.

In addition to the results of operations and the additional items shown in Exhibit 7.2, the income statement must also translate financial results into earnings per share, which is discussed in Section 7.4. Also, comprehensive income must be added to the statement or reported separately; this information is discussed in Section 7.9.

7.3   EXPENSES LISTED IN THE COST OF GOODS SOLD

The traditional expenses that are reported within the cost of goods sold section are direct materials, direct labor, and manufacturing overhead. These are designated as the cost of goods sold more through tradition than any accounting pronouncement. Consequently, the accountant should actively consider adding several other expenses to the cost of goods sold. The primary criterion for adding expenses to this category is that they should vary directly in proportion to revenues. Stated differently, they should only involve those expenses that are required to manufacture or purchase the items that are being sold. For example, salesperson commissions will only be created if a product is sold—this is therefore a perfect cost of goods sold. Another possibility is any royalty that must be paid as a result of a sale. For example, a publisher should include the royalty associated with a manuscript in its cost of goods sold. A close examination of the operating expenses section of the income statement will likely reveal a few costs that vary directly with revenues and so can be more precisely grouped within the cost of goods sold category. A good rule to follow to determine if an expense should be included in the cost of goods sold is whether or not the cost will disappear if a sale is not made. If a sale occurs and a specific expense is therefore incurred, then it should be included in the cost of goods sold.

If the accountant chooses to add extra classifications of expenses to the cost of goods sold, he or she should be sure to revise the financial statements for previous years, so that they are consistently reported within the same expense grouping.

7.4   REPORTING EARNINGS PER SHARE

Basic and diluted earnings per share (EPS) information must be attached to the income statement. *Basic EPS* is the amount of earnings recognized in the reporting period, divided by the average number of shares outstanding during the period. Basic EPS must be shown on the income statement, not only for income from continuing operations, but also for net income. This topic is addressed in more detail in Chapter 23, Earnings per Share.

Diluted earnings per share is also the amount of earnings recognized in the reporting period; however, this is divided not only by the average number of shares outstanding during the period, but also by all potential common shares. Potential shares can include stock options, warrants, convertible securities, employee compensation agreements that involve stock payouts, and vendor agreements that may also involve stock payouts. When calculating diluted EPS, the accountant should add back any interest payments (net of tax effect) made on convertible debt, since the assumption is that all such convertible debt will become common stock for the purposes of the calculation, and so there will be no interest payment made on the debt that presumably no longer exists. An entity with a simple capital structure (that is, one with no additional potential stock) does not need to report diluted EPS on its income statement, since the reported information would be the same as is already shown for basic EPS. However, if there is *any* amount of potential common stock, even if the amount is not material, then diluted EPS must be shown on the income statement.

When determining the number of additional potential shares to include in the diluted EPS calculation, only include those options and warrants for which the average market price for the reporting period is higher than the exercise price—in other words, assume that the holders of these instruments would have no reason to convert them to common stock unless they had a chance to earn a profit on the transaction during the reporting period.

Similarly, if there are shares that will be issued only if certain contingencies are fulfilled, then they are not included in either basic EPS or diluted EPS until the contingencies have actually been fulfilled; they are included in both forms of EPS at that time, even if the shares are not physically issued before the end date of the reporting period.

The EPS calculation for both basic and diluted EPS requires the use of the average number of common shares outstanding during the period. A good way to determine this amount is shown in Exhibit 7.3, where the calculation is shown for a one-quarter reporting period. In the example, stock is both issued and reduced through a number of transactions. For each transaction, the number of share days outstanding is calculated, and then divided by the number of days in the period in order to determine the average number of total shares outstanding for the entire reporting period.

The exhibit shows a total number of share days of 37,750. When we divide this by the total number of days in the quarter, the average number of shares outstanding becomes:

$$\frac{\text{Total number of share days}}{\text{Number of days in the period}} = \frac{37{,}750}{90} = 419 \text{ shares}$$

Description	Transaction Date	Number of Shares	Days Outstanding in Period	Number of Share Days
Beginning shares outstanding	1/1/10	300	90	27,000
Stock bought with options	1/15/10	150	75	11,250
Stock repurchase	2/5/10	–50	55	–2,750
Stock sold to investors	3/1/10	75	30	2,250
Totals	—	575	90	37,750

EXHIBIT 7.3   CALCULATION FOR THE AVERAGE NUMBER OF COMMON SHARES OUTSTANDING

If there is a stock dividend or stock split during the reporting period, the additional shares issued are always assumed to have been issued on the first day of the reporting period. This is done because the total ownership percentages of all shareholders has not changed—it has just been divided into a larger number of shares. Accordingly, a stock split or dividend must be retroactively included in all periods being reported upon, in order to make EPS comparable for all reporting periods.

7.5   TREATMENT OF GAINS AND LOSSES

A gain or loss resulting from a transaction outside of the normal course of operations should be reported as a separate line item in the income statement, as is shown in Exhibit 7.1. Examples of gains and losses of this type are those that result from the sale of assets, a lawsuit judgment, and storm damage to company property. If there is a gain on this type of transaction, then it is only recognized when the related transaction is completed. For example, a gain on sale of machinery is only recognized when the buyer takes possession of the machinery and title is transferred to the new owner. However, a loss is recognized earlier, as soon as the amount of the loss can be reasonably ascertained and it is reasonably certain that the loss will be incurred. Any gain or loss should be reported net of its associated income tax effect.

7.6   TREATMENT OF ACCOUNTING CHANGES

There are several types of accounting changes—in estimate, reporting entity, and principle. *Examples of changes in accounting estimates* can relate to the size of the bad debt reserve, warranty claim reserve, or obsolete inventory reserve, as well as the assumed salvage value of fixed assets and the duration of their useful lives. An example of a *change in reporting entity* is the implementation of a business combination through the pooling of *interests method of accounting. Examples of principle changes* (which is the use of GAAP that is different from the accounting principle previously used, but not for immaterial items) include:

- An accounting change required by a newly promulgated GAAP.
- A change from LIFO to the FIFO method of inventory costing.
- A change from the full cost method in the minerals extraction industry.

An accounting change should be recorded with a cumulative summarization of the change's effect at the beginning of the fiscal year as a line item after extraordinary items on the income statement. This line item should be reported net of the impact of any related income taxes. An example of this reporting structure was shown earlier in Exhibit 7.2. It is also possible to revise earlier income statements with the effect of a change in accounting principle if such a change is specifically mandated by a new accounting principle.

7.7 TREATMENT OF DISCONTINUED OPERATIONS

Discontinued operations refer to a business segment for which there are firm plans for disposition or closure. This would not include a stoppage of production for a single product or ancillary product line, since these are common and ongoing events that represent the incremental changes that businesses regularly make as they modify their operations to meet market demand. Rather, the concept of a discontinued operation refers to a major business division or the sale of a large interest in another unrelated entity.

If a company plans to discontinue some operations, it must recognize any estimated loss related to the discontinuance in the first accounting period in which the management team commits to a disposition plan, and for which costs can be reasonably estimated. If there is a gain from the transaction, then this is reported later, after the disposition transaction has been completed. The disposition plan should include the timing of the disposition, what types of assets are to be eliminated, the method of disposal, and an estimate of the costs and revenues resulting from the transaction.

Losses expected from discontinued operations can include a reduction in the valuation of assets to be disposed of, down to their net realizeable value. However, it is not allowable to allocate general corporate overhead expenses to a discontinued operation, since this might result in the accelerated recognition of expenses that have nothing to do with the disposition. It is also not allowable to include in the loss the cost of asset disposition, such as brokerage fees—these costs are only recognized when incurred.

It is also possible to allocate interest costs to the cost of discontinued operations, but no more than the amount of the interest on debt assumed by the buyer of the discontinued operations (if any), and a reasonable allocation of interest expense that cannot be specified as being attributed to some other part of the remaining organization.

The financial statements should include information about discontinued operations in a separate set of line items immediately following the net income reported from continuing operations in the income statement (as illustrated in Exhibit 7.2). These line items should separately show the gain or loss from the disposition and the partial year operating results of the discontinued operation leading up to the date on which it was discontinued. This information should be shown net of the impact of any related income taxes. The financial results of discontinued operations can also be revealed through a footnote, though this approach is only recommended if the results are immaterial.

If the management team decides to retain operations that had previously been treated as discontinued, then the accountant should reverse the amount of any loss that had previously been recognized; this reversal should occur in the period when the decision to retain the operations is made. If there was an operating loss in the period of initial loss recognition and this loss was included in the initial write-down, then the accountant should allow the operating loss to continue to be recognized in the period of initial loss recognition.

7.8 TREATMENT OF EXTRAORDINARY ITEMS

An extraordinary item must be reported, net of related taxes, after the results from continuing operations on the income statement, though only if it is material. To qualify as an extraordinary item, something must both occur infrequently and be unusual in nature. An event is considered to occur infrequently if company management does not expect it to happen again, while it is considered to be unusual if it is unrelated to ongoing company operations. Examples of extraordinary items are:

- A gain on a troubled debt restructuring.
- A gain or loss on the extinguishment of debt.
- Major casualty losses, due to such causes as floods, earthquakes, and fire.
- The adjustment of an extraordinary item that was reported in a prior period.
- The expropriation of assets.
- The write-off of operating rights of a motor carrier.

Items that are not categorized as extraordinary items include:

- A write-down in the value of assets.
- Changes in the valuation of foreign exchange holdings.
- Costs related to a plant relocation.
- Costs related to a standstill agreement.
- Costs related to environmental damages.
- Costs related to the defense against a takeover attempt.
- Costs related to the settlement of a legal case.
- Gains or losses on the sale of assets.
- Losses caused by a strike.
- The disposal of business segments.

7.9   TREATMENT OF OTHER COMPREHENSIVE INCOME

The net income figure that appears on the income statement does not reveal a small number of changes in assets that are instead reported through the balance sheet. These changes are related to adjustments caused by unrealized foreign currency valuation adjustments, minimum pension liability changes, and unrealized gains or losses on some types of investment securities.

An additional reporting category, called Other Comprehensive Income, is added to the bottom of the income statement (in which case the report is called the Statement of Income and Comprehensive Income), presented separately, or included in the Statement of Changes in Stockholders' Equity. This category includes all of the preceding adjustments that are normally only reported through the balance sheet, so that the reader of the income statement will have a clearer idea of not only the results of company operations, but also of valuation issues that are caused by forces outside of the reporting entity.

Other comprehensive income cannot be reported solely in the footnotes accompanying the financial statements. When reported within the body of the financial statements, the accountant can use any number of formats, since there is no specific format required by GAAP. A possible format is shown in Exhibit 7.4, where each possible adjustment is listed as a separate line item.

7.10   TREATMENT OF PRIOR PERIOD ADJUSTMENTS

There are only two cases where the accountant is allowed to revise the results reported in the income statement of a prior period. The first case is when errors have been discovered

Other Comprehensive Income:	
Minimum pension liability adjustments	−$ 35,000
Unrealized gains/losses on securities	120,500
Foreign currency adjustments	−48,250
Comprehensive Income:	−$68,750

EXHIBIT 7.4   ADDITION TO THE INCOME STATEMENT FOR
COMPREHENSIVE INCOME

in the prior period report that are material enough to require correction. Examples of error corrections include a correction of a computational error, adjustments based on facts that were in existence as of the date of the financial statements being adjusted, and a switch away from an invalid accounting principle to GAAP.

The second case is when material adjustments are required to reflect the realization of income tax benefits caused by the pre-acquisition net operating loss carryforwards of a purchased subsidiary.

In both cases, the impact of the change should be listed both prior to the impact of income taxes and after their effect.

If the accountant is only issuing financial statements that list the results of the current reporting period, then these prior period adjustments can be integrated into the statements simply by modifying the beginning balance of retained earnings. However, if multiple-period results are being reported, then the prior period statements must be restated to reflect these adjustments.

7.11 SUMMARY

The basic format of the income statement is quite simple and easy to understand. Complications arise when the accountant must determine whether or not there are extraordinary items, accounting changes, discontinued operations, prior period adjustments, and the like—all of which require separate presentation in the income statement. There can also be some confusion regarding which expenses should be itemized within the cost of goods sold or operating expenses. The accountant should refer to Chapter 9, Footnotes, for more information about the presentation of additional information about these issues, which should be issued alongside the financial statement.

CHAPTER **8**

THE STATEMENT OF CASH FLOWS

8.1 INTRODUCTION

The statement of cash flows reveals the cash inflows and outflows experienced by an organization during a reporting period. In this respect, it is similar to the income statement, which also covers a specific period of time. The types of cash flows presented are divided into those related to operations, investment activities, and financing activities. This information is intended to give the reader some idea of the ability of an organization to make debt or dividend payments, or to replace needed capital items. It can also be of use in determining whether an organization is issuing more cash in the form of dividends than it is generating from continuing operations, which cannot continue for long. It can also reflect the impact of changes in the management of working capital, since such actions as improved accounts receivable collections or tighter inventory controls will reduce the amount of cash tied up in receivables and inventory (and vice versa, in the case of poor management).

In addition, it presents a clearer picture of cash flows than can be inferred from the income statement or balance sheet, where the use of accruals can make it appear as though an entity is generating large profits, even though it is burning through large quantities of cash. This is of particular concern in rapidly growing companies, where margins from continuing operations may not be sufficient to fund the growth in new sales.

The statement of cash flows is an integral part of the financial statements, and should be presented alongside the balance sheet, income statement, and statement of retained earnings. This is of particular concern if the management team is taking steps to "dress up" the results shown in the statement of cash flows at the expense of a company's long-term financial health, which might be more readily evident through a careful perusal of a complete package of financial statements, rather than just the statement of cash flows. For example, management might not be making a sufficient investment in the replacement of existing fixed assets, thereby making the amount of cash outflows look smaller, even though this will result in more equipment failures and higher maintenance costs that will eventually appear on the income statement.

The following sections itemize the types of cash flows that are to be revealed in each section of the statement of cash flows, as well as its general format, and several special situations. If the reader requires more information about this topic, it is addressed at length in FASB Statement Number 95, with amendments in FASB Statements Number 102 (regarding the exemption of some entities from using it) and 104 (regarding the presentation of deposits and loans in the statement by some types of financial institutions).

8.2   OPERATING ACTIVITIES

The first section of the statement of cash flows contains cash inflows and outflows that are derived from operating activities, which may be defined as any category of cash flows that does not fall into the investing or financing activities in the next two sections of the report. Examples of cash inflows in this category are:

- Collection of interest income or dividends.
- Collection of notes receivable.
- Receipts of sale transactions.

Examples of cash outflows in this category are:

- Interest payments.
- Payments for inventory.
- Payments to suppliers.
- Payroll payments.
- Tax payments.

8.3   INVESTING ACTIVITIES

The second section of the statement of cash flows contains cash inflows and outflows that are derived from investment activities on the part of the organization issuing the report. Examples of cash inflows related to investing activities are:

- Cash received from the sale of assets.
- Loan principal payments by another entity to the reporting entity.
- Sale of another entity's equity securities by the reporting entity.

Examples of cash outflows in this category are:

- Loans made to another entity.
- Purchase of assets.
- Purchases by the reporting entity of another entity's equity securities.

8.4   FINANCING ACTIVITIES

The third section of the statement of cash flows contains cash inflows and outflows that are derived from financing activities on the part of the organization issuing the report. Examples of cash inflows related to financing activities are:

- Proceeds from the sale of the reporting entity's equity securities.
- Proceeds from the issuance of bonds or other types of debt to investors.

Examples of cash outflows in this category are:

- Cash paid for debt issuance costs.
- Debt repayments.

- Dividend payments to the holders of the reporting entity's equity securities.
- Repurchase of the reporting entity's equity securities.

8.5   THE FORMAT OF THE STATEMENT OF CASH FLOWS

The statement of cash flows has no rigidly defined format that the accountant must follow for presentation purposes. Cash flows must be separated into the operating, investing, and financing activities that were just described, but the level of detailed reporting within those categories is up to the accountant's judgment.

The key issue when creating a statement of cash flows is that it contains enough information for the reader to understand where cash flows are occurring and how they vary from the reported net income. The bottom of the report should include a reconciliation that adjusts the net income figure to the net amount of cash provided by operating activities—this is useful for showing the impact of non-cash items, such as depreciation, amortization, and accruals, on the amount of cash provided from operating activities. An example of the statement of cash flows is shown in Exhibit 8.1.

Cash flows from operating activities:		
Cash received from customers	4,507	
Cash paid to suppliers	−3,016	
Cash paid for general & administrative expenses	−1,001	
Cash paid for interest	−89	
Cash paid for income taxes	−160	
Net cash flow from operations:		241
Cash flows from investing activities:		
Purchase of securities	−58	
Sale of securities	128	
Purchase of land	−218	
Purchase of fixed assets	−459	
Net cash used in investing activities:		−607
Cash flows from financing activities:		
Increase in preferred stock	100	
Decrease in customer deposits	−49	
Dividend payment	−125	
Sale of equity securities	500	
Net cash provided by financing activities:		426
Net increase (decrease) in cash:		−181
Reconciliation of Net Income to Net Cash Provided by Operating Activities:		
Net income		206
Reconciling adjustments between net income and net cash from operations:		
Depreciation		39
Change in accounts receivable		200
Change in inventory		138
Change in accounts payable		−275
Change in accrued expenses		−67
Net cash from operations:		241

EXHIBIT 8.1   EXAMPLE OF THE STATEMENT OF CASH FLOWS

8.6   EXEMPTIONS FROM THE STATEMENT OF CASH FLOWS

An investment company is not required to present a statement of cash flows, as long as it falls within the following parameters:

- It has minimal debt.
- It issues a statement of changes in net assets.
- Its investments are carried at market value.
- Nearly all of its investments are highly liquid.

Defined benefit plans and certain other types of employee benefit plans are also not required to issue a statement of cash flows, as long as they follow the guidelines of FASB Statement Number 35, "Accounting and Reporting by Defined Benefit Pension Plans." This statement describes the rules for the annual financial statements associated with a defined benefit pension plan, requiring the inclusion of such information as net assets available for benefits, changes in these benefits, and the present value of plan benefits.

8.7   PRESENTATION OF CONSOLIDATED ENTITIES

When constructing the statement of cash flows as part of a consolidated set of financial statements, all other statements must first be consolidated; this is necessary because information is pulled from the other statements in order to complete the statement of cash flows. Then complete the following consolidation steps:

1. Eliminate all noncash transactions related to the business combination.
2. Eliminate all intercompany operating transactions, such as sales of products between divisions.
3. Eliminate all intercompany investing transactions, such as the purchase of equity securities by different divisions.
4. Eliminate all intercompany financing activities, such as dividend payments between divisions.
5. Add back any income or loss that has been allocated to noncontrolling parties, since this is not an actual cash flow.

8.8   TREATMENT OF FOREIGN CURRENCY TRANSACTIONS

When a company is located in a foreign location, or has a subsidiary located there, a separate statement of cash flows should be created for the foreign entity. This statement is then translated into the reporting currency for the parent company (see Chapter 11, Foreign Currency Translation), using the exchange rate that was current at the time when the cash flows occurred. If the cash flows were spread equably over the entire reporting period, then the exchange rate used can be a weighted average, so long as the final reporting result is essentially the same. The resulting statement of cash flows for the foreign entity may then be consolidated into the statement of cash flows for the entire organization.

8.9   SUMMARY

The statement of cash flows is an extremely useful part of the financial statements, because a financial analyst can determine from it the true state of a business entity's cash flows, which can otherwise be hidden under the accrual method of accounting within the income statement and balance sheet. By using this statement, one can spot situations in which a company appears to be reporting healthy profits and revenue growth, and yet suddenly goes bankrupt due to a lack of cash. Given this and other reasons, the statement should be carefully examined in comparison to the information presented in the income statement and balance sheet in order to gain a clearer picture of the financial health of a business.

FOOTNOTES

9.1 INTRODUCTION

There are a great many circumstances under GAAP rules that require the accountant to report additional information in text form alongside the primary set of financial information, such as the nature of accounting policies being used to derive the statements, contingent liabilities, risks related to derivative instruments, discontinued operations, and error corrections. This chapter covers many of the most common footnotes that must be used. In most cases, examples of footnotes are added in order to clarify the required type of reporting.

9.2   DISCLOSURE OF ACCOUNTING CHANGES

When a company initiates a change in accounting, the accountant must disclose the type of change and describe why the change is being made. In addition, the footnote should list the dollar impact caused by the change for the current and immediately preceding reporting period, as well as the amount of the change in earnings per share. Further, the cumulative effect of the change on retained earnings should be noted. An example is as follows:

> The company switched from the First-in, First-out (FIFO) to the Last-in, First-out (LIFO) inventory valuation method. Its reason for doing so was that a close examination of actual inventory flow practices revealed that the LIFO method more accurately reflected the actual movement of inventory. The net impact of this change in the current period was an increase in the cost of goods sold of $174,000, which resulted in an after-tax reduction in net income of $108,000. This also resulted in a reduction in the reported level of earnings per share of $.02 per share. The same information for the preceding year was a reduction in net income of $42,000 and a reduction in earnings per share of $.01. The cumulative effect of the change on beginning retained earnings for the current period was a reduction of $63,500.

9.3   DISCLOSURE OF ACCOUNTING POLICIES

The financial statements should include a description of the principle accounting policies being followed, such as the method of inventory valuation, the type of depreciation calculation method being followed, and whether or not the lower of cost or market valuation approach is used for inventory costing purposes. Any industry-specific policies should also be disclosed, as well as any unusual variations on the standard GAAP rules. An example is as follows:

> The company calculates the cost of its inventories using the average costing method, and reduces the cost of inventory under the lower of cost or market rule on a regular basis. All fixed assets are depreciated using the sum-of-the-years'-digits method of calculation. Since many of the company's boat-building contracts are multiyear in nature and only involve occasional contractually mandated payments from customers, it consistently uses the percentage of completion method to recognize revenues for these contractual arrangements.

9.4   DISCLOSURE OF ASSET IMPAIRMENTS

If a company writes down the value of assets due to the impairment of their value, the accountant should describe the assets, note which segment of the business is impacted by the loss and disclose the amount of the loss, how fair value was determined, where the loss is reported in the income statement, the remaining cost assigned to the assets, and the date by which the company expects to have disposed of them (if it expects to do so). An example is as follows:

> The company has written down the value of its server farm, on the grounds that this equipment has a vastly reduced resale value as a result of the introduction of a new generation of microprocessor chips. The services of an appraiser were used to obtain a fair market value, net of selling costs, to which their cost was reduced. The resulting loss of $439,500 was charged to

the application service provider segment of the company, and is contained within the "Other Gains and Losses" line item on the income statement. The remaining valuation ascribed to these assets as of the balance sheet date is $2,450,000. There are no immediate expectations to dispose of these assets.

9.5 DISCLOSURE OF BAD DEBT RECOGNITION

The method by which a company derives its bad debt reserves should be noted in a footnote, including the amount of the reserve contained within the balance sheet and its method for recognizing bad debts. Also note any factors influencing the judgment of management in calculating the reserves. An example is as follows:

> The company calculates a bad debt reserve based on a rolling average of actual bad debt losses over the past three months divided by the average amount of accounts receivable outstanding during that period. It calculates separate loss percentages for its government and commercial receivables, since government receivables have a significantly lower loss rate. Given the current recession, management has elected to increase this calculated reserve by an additional 1.5%. As of the balance sheet date, the loss reserve percentage for government receivables was 1.1%, while the reserve for commercial receivables was 2.9%. This resulted in a total loss reserve of $329,000 on outstanding accounts receivable of $18,275,000. The company recognizes all receivables as bad debts that have been unpaid for more than 90 days past their due dates, or earlier upon the joint agreement of management and the collections staff, or immediately if a customer declares bankruptcy.

9.6 DISCLOSURE OF BARTER REVENUE

Barter transactions should be recognized at the fair market value of the assets received in an exchange. The nature of any such transactions should be noted in a footnote, as well as the approximate value of the transactions and how they are recorded in the financial statements. An example is as follows:

> The company provides aerial traffic reports to a number of radio stations, in exchange for which they give air time to the company. The company then obtains advertising to run on these free minutes, from which it collects the proceeds. The company recognizes revenue from these barter transactions only after advertisements have been obtained and have been run on the participating radio stations. No asset is recorded on the company balance sheet when air time is received from radio stations, since there is still significant uncertainty that the company will be able to convert the air time into paid advertisements. In 2010, the revenue recognized from these transactions was $1,745,000.

9.7 DISCLOSURE OF BILL AND HOLD TRANSACTIONS

Bill and hold transactions are generally frowned upon, given the risk of abuse by companies that can use this technique to inflate their revenues. Consequently, if any bill and hold transactions are used, it is best to reveal this information in a footnote, clearly stating that the company follows all GAAP requirements for such transactions, and also noting the dollar amount and percentage of revenues involved and any change in the level of bill and hold revenue from the preceding year. An example is as follows:

> During the past year, the company sold $172,000 worth of stoves to its restaurant customers under "bill and hold" transactions. Under these arrangements, restaurant owners asked the company to retain the stoves in its warehouse facilities until new restaurants had been built to accommodate them. All these customers acknowledged in writing that they had ordered the inventory, that the company was storing the stoves on their behalf, that they had taken on all

risks of ownership, and that the stoves would be delivered in no more than three months. Total bill and hold transactions were $15,000 lower than the $187,000 in similar transactions that had occurred in the preceding year. In both years, bill and hold transactions comprised 14% of total company revenues.

9.8   DISCLOSURE OF BUSINESS COMBINATIONS

If a company enters into a business combination, the accountant should disclose the name of the acquired company and describe its general business operation, the cost of the acquisition, and the number of shares involved in the transaction. If there are contingent payments that are part of the purchase price, then their amount should also be disclosed, as well as the conditions under which the payments will be made. During the accounting period in which the combination is being completed, the accountant should also describe any issues that are still unresolved, as well as the plan for and cost of any major asset dispositions. An example is as follows:

> During the reporting period, the company acquired the OvalMax Corporation, which manufactures disposable gaskets. The transaction was completed under the purchase method of accounting and involved a payment of $52 million in cash, as well as 100,000 shares of common stock. If the OvalMax Corporation can increase its profit level in the upcoming year by 25%, then an additional acquisition payment of $15 million will be paid to its former owners. There are no plans to dispose of any major OvalMax assets, but the majority of its accounting staff will be terminated as part of a plan to merge this function into that of the company. Termination costs associated with this change are expected to be no greater than $2,250,000.

9.9   DISCLOSURE OF CALLABLE OBLIGATIONS

A company may have a long-term liability that can be called if it violates some related covenants. If it has indeed violated some aspect of the covenants, then the accountant must disclose the nature of the violation, how much of the related liability can potentially be called because of the violation, and if a waiver has been obtained from the creditor or if the company has acted to cancel the violation through some action. An example is as follows:

> The company has a long-term loan with a consortium of lenders for which it violated the minimum current ratio covenant during the reporting period. The potential amount callable is one-half of the remaining loan outstanding, which is $5,500,000. However, the consortium granted a waiver of the violation, and also reduced the amount of the current ratio requirement from 2:1 to 1:1 for future periods.

9.10   DISCLOSURE OF CAPITAL STRUCTURE

The financial statements should include a footnote describing the number of shares authorized, issued, and outstanding, their par values, and the rights and privileges associated with each class of stock. A description of these rights and privileges should include dividend preferences and special privileges or unusual voting rights. An example is as follows:

> As of October 31, 2010, the company's capital structure consisted of common stock and Series A preferred stock. There were 10,000,000 shares of common stock authorized and 4.2 million shares outstanding, while there were 1,000,000 shares of preferred stock authorized and 800,000 shares outstanding. Both classes of stock have par values of $0.01 per share. The Series A preferred stockholders are entitled to a full return of their original investments in the event of a liquidation or sale of the company, as well as an additional 100% return, before any distributions are made to common shareholders. These shareholders are also entitled to dividend payments matching any declared for shares of common stock. In addition,

a two-thirds majority of the Series A shareholders must approve any sale of the company or a significant portion of its assets. Also, Series A shareholders are entitled to elect two members of the company's board of directors. Common shareholders are entitled to elect all other members of the board.

9.11 DISCLOSURE OF CASH DEPOSITS IN EXCESS OF FDIC INSURANCE LIMITS

If a company concentrates its cash holdings in accounts exceeding the Federal Deposit Insurance Corporation (FDIC) insurance limit of $100,000, it should disclose the amount exceeding the limit. An example is as follows:

For cash management purposes, the company concentrates its cash holdings in a single account at the Third National Bank of Colorado Springs. The balance in this account may exceed the federally insured limit of $100,000 by the Federal Deposit Insurance Corporation in case of bank failure. At December 31, 2010, the company had $829,000 in excess of the insurance limit at this bank.

9.12 DISCLOSURE OF CASH RESTRICTIONS

If there are restrictions on a company's cash balances caused by compensating balance agreements, a footnote should detail the terms of the agreement as well as the amount of cash restricted by the agreement. An example is as follows:

As part of the company's loan arrangement with the 2nd National Bank of Boise, it must maintain a compensating balance at the bank of no less than $200,000 at all times. The bank segregates this amount and does not allow draw downs from it unless the balance of the associated line of credit is less than $500,000. Also, the bank requires an additional compensating balance of 10% of the loan balance; there is no restriction on use of this additional compensating balance, but the company must pay an additional 2% interest on the loan balance whenever its average cash balance drops below the required compensating balance. During the past year, this resulted in an average 0.4% increase in the average interest rate paid on the line of credit.

9.13 DISCLOSURE OF CHANGE IN REPORTED METHOD OF INVESTMENT

If a company changes from the cost method to the equity method of accounting or vice versa, a footnote should disclose the change in the level of investment that required the change in method. It should also note the general accounting treatment required by each method, as well as the impact of the change on net income and any change in retained earnings resulting from the retroactive application of the new method. An example is as follows:

The company increased its investment in the Alabama Boutiques Company (ABC) in May 2010 from 18% to 35%. Consequently, the company changed from the cost method of accounting for this investment to the equity method. Instead of recording its investment at cost and treating dividends as income, as was the case under the cost method, the company now records its proportionate share of all ABC earnings. The change reduced the company's earnings in 2010 by $109,000, while retained earnings as of the beginning of 2010 were adjusted downward by $128,000 to reflect the retroactive application of the equity method to this investment.

9.14   DISCLOSURE OF CHANGES IN INVESTMENT FAIR VALUE AFTER BALANCE SHEET DATE

If there is a significant change in the value of a company's investments after the balance sheet date but before the issuance of financial statements, the amount of the change should be described in a footnote. Two examples are as follows:

(1) Subsequent to the balance sheet date, the fair value of the company's trading portfolio declined by $98,000, or 17% of the total portfolio value. In addition, the continuing decline of the fair value of the available-for-sale portfolio by an additional $43,000 after the balance sheet date confirms management's opinion that the decline in value of this portfolio has been permanently impaired. For this reason, management recognized a permanent loss of $109,000 in the value of the available-for-sale portfolio subsequent to the balance sheet date.

(2) The fair value of the company's available-for-sale portfolio declined by $89,000 subsequent to the balance sheet date. Because the decline is caused by the expected bankruptcy of an investee, management now considers the investment to be permanently impaired. Fair value declines prior to the balance sheet date had not been considered permanently impaired, since the investee had not announced its bankruptcy intentions at that time. The company plans to record the losses in the Available-for-sale account as permanent impairments in the next quarterly financial statements.

9.15   DISCLOSURE OF COLLATERAL

When accounts receivable are pledged to a lender as collateral on a loan, the terms of the agreement, as well as the carrying amount of the receivables, should be listed in the footnotes. An example is as follows:

The XYZ Scuba Supplies Company has entered into a loan agreement with the International Credit Consortium. Under the terms of the agreement, XYZ has pledged the full amount of its trade receivables as collateral on a revolving line of credit carrying a floating interest rate 2% above the prime rate. The amount loaned cannot exceed 80% of all outstanding accounts receivable billed within the past 90 days. As of the balance sheet date, the total amount of accounts receivable subject to this agreement was $2,500,000.

9.16   DISCLOSURE OF COLLECTIVE BARGAINING AGREEMENTS

If some portion of a company's workforce is unionized, the proportion so organized should be noted, as well as the date when its collective bargaining agreements expire. An example is as follows:

The company has 5,000 employees, of which 100% of its hourly production staff of 2,850 is represented by the International Brotherhood of Electrical Workers. The current collective bargaining agreement with this union expires in June 2011. No other company employees are represented by a union.

9.17   DISCLOSURE OF COMMITMENTS

There are many types of commitments that may require disclosure. For example, there may be a minimum purchase agreement that extends into future reporting periods and which obligates a company to make purchases in amounts that are material. Also, a company may have made guarantees to pay for the debts of other entities, such as a subsidiary.

If these commitments are material, then their nature must be disclosed in the footnotes. The rules are not specific about identifying the exact cost or probability of occurrence of each commitment, so the accountant has some leeway in presenting this information. An example is as follows:

> The company has entered into a contract to purchase a minimum of 500,000 tons of coal per year for the next twenty years at a fixed price of $20.50 per ton, with no price escalation allowed for the duration of the contract. The company's minimum annual payment obligation under this contract is $10,250,000. The price paid under this contract is $1.75 less than the market rate for anthracite coal as of the date of these statements, and had not significantly changed as of the statement issuance date.

9.18 DISCLOSURE OF COMPENSATING BALANCES

A company may have an arrangement with its bank to keep some minimum portion of its cash in an account at the bank; since this cash cannot be drawn down without incurring extra fees, it is essentially not usable for other purposes. If this is a significant amount, it should be split away from the cash balance on the balance sheet and either listed as a separate line item in the current assets section (if the related borrowing agreement expires in the current year) or as a long-term asset (if the related borrowing agreement expires in a later year).

9.19 DISCLOSURE OF CONSIGNMENT REVENUE

Shipments made to a distributor on consignment are not truly sales until sold by the distributor. The exact method of revenue recognition should be clearly stated in a footnote so that readers can be sure that revenue is not recognized too soon in the sales process. Also, inventory may be shipped to a company by its customers on a consignment basis, to be included in custom products that are then sold back to the customers. Only the value added to these custom products should be recognized as revenue. The following footnotes show proper disclosure of these situations.

> (1) The company ships its eyewear products to a number of distributors, having no direct sales function of its own. All shipments to distributors continue to be recorded as inventory by the company until notification of shipment is received from distributors. In selected cases where there has been a problematic payment history by distributors, the company does not record revenue until cash has been received.

> (2) The company produces custom rockets for its payload launch customers. Several customers prefer to supply rocket engines to be incorporated into the company's rockets. Accordingly, these engines are recorded as consignment inventory when received and assigned a zero cost. When the completed rockets are shipped to customers, the price of the consigned engines is not included in the amount billed, thereby reducing the total revenue recognized by the company.

9.20 DISCLOSURE OF CONTINGENT ASSET PURCHASE OBLIGATION

If a company has a contingent liability to purchase an asset, one should disclose the terms of the obligation, as well as the range of costs involved if the obligation comes to pass. An example is as follows:

> The company acquired a below-market lease on its headquarters building in exchange for a contingent liability to purchase the building from the lessor after 15 years for a fixed sum of

$20.7 million. If the company chooses not to exercise this option, it will be contingently liable to the lessor for a nonpurchase penalty of 10% of the market value of the building at that time. A recent appraisal of similar buildings in the area indicates that the current market value of the building is approximately $12 million. When adjusted for probable annual price inflation, the value of the building in 15 years may be approximately $16 million. Thus, the company may be liable for 10% of this amount, or $1.6 million, in 15 years if it chooses not to purchase the building. Since there is a difference of $4.7 million between the eventual purchase price and the expected fair value of the building, the company would only capitalize $16 million if it were to purchase the building, and would charge the remainder of the payment to lease expense. Accordingly, the company must recognize either a penalty of $1.6 million or a lease expense of $4.7 million in 15 years. The company is charging 1/15 of the penalty amount to expense in each of the next 15 years in order to recognize the lesser of the two contingent expenses.

9.21   DISCLOSURE OF CONTINGENT LIABILITIES

A contingent liability is one where a business entity may be required to pay off a liability, but either the amount of the liability cannot reasonably be determined at the report date, or the requirement to pay is uncertain. The most common contingent liability is a lawsuit whose outcome is still pending. If the contingent amount can be reasonably estimated and the outcome is reasonably certain, then a contingent liability must be accrued. However, in any case where the outcome is not so certain, the accountant should describe the nature of the claim in the footnotes. Also, if a lower limit to the range of possible liabilities has been accrued due to the difficulty of deriving a range of possible estimates, then the upper limit of the range should be included in the footnotes. Finally, if a loss contingency arises after the financial statement date but before its release date, then this information should also be disclosed. Two examples are as follows:

(1) The company has one potential contingent liability. It is for an insurance claim related to earthquake damage to the company's California assembly plant. The insurance company is disputing its need to pay for this claim on the grounds that the insurance renewal payment was received by it one day after the policy's expiration date. Company counsel believes that the insurance company's claim is groundless and that it will be required to pay the company the full amount of the claim after arbitration is concluded. The total amount of the claim is $1,285,000.

(2) The company accepted an obligation to increase the purchase price of a newly acquired subsidiary if it met certain earn out goals. Management believes that the subsidiary will match the earn out targets, and so has recognized a contingent liability of $2.3 million and increased the Goodwill account by an identical amount. The liability will be paid subsequent to the completion of an annual audit that will verify the earn out results.

9.22   DISCLOSURE OF CONTINUED EXISTENCE DOUBTS

If there is a significant cause for concern that the business entity being reported upon will not continue in existence, then this information must be included in the footnotes. An example is as follows:

The company has $325,000 of available funds remaining in its line of credit, which it expects to use during the next fiscal year. Thus far, the company has been unable to obtain additional equity or financing to supplement the amount of this line of credit. Given the continuing losses from operations that continue to be caused by a downturn in the chemical production industry, management believes that the company's financing difficulties may result in its having difficulty continuing to exist as an independent business entity.

9.23   DISCLOSURE OF CONTRACT REVENUE RECOGNITION

If a company recognizes revenue based on the percentage of completion method, it should state how it makes this calculation, how it is recorded on the balance sheet, when claims against customers are recognized, and how changes in estimates can impact reported profits or losses on contracts. If there is a change in the method of contract revenue recognition, the reason for doing the change should be revealed, as well as the net effect of the change. Several examples are as follows:

(1) The company recognizes all revenue in its construction division using the percentage of completion method, under which it ascertains the completion percentage by dividing costs incurred to date by total estimated project costs. It revises estimated project costs regularly, which can alter the reported level of project profitability. If project losses are calculated under this method, they are recognized in the current reporting period. Claims against customers are recorded in the period when payment is received. If billings exceed recognized revenue, the difference is recorded as a current liability, while any recognized revenues exceeding billings are recorded as a current asset.

(2) The company recognizes claims against customers when cash receipt is probable, the claim is legally justified, and the amount of the claim can be proven. If any of these factors cannot be reasonably proven, then claims are only recognized upon the receipt of cash. Since claims involve the use of estimates, it is reasonable to record some changes to the initially reported revenue figure upon the eventual receipt of cash, or sooner if there is a firm basis for this information.

(3) The company has switched to the percentage-of-completion method from the completed-contract method for recording the results of its construction projects. Management authorized the change due to the increasingly long-term nature of its contracts, which have increased from single-month to multimonth durations. The net impact of this change was an increase in profits of $218,000 in 2010. The change was carried back to 2009, resulting in a profit increase of $12,000 in that period.

9.24   DISCLOSURE OF CUSTOMERS

If a company has revenues from individual customers that amount to at least 10% of total revenues, then the accountant must report the amount of revenues from each of these customers, as well as the name of the business segment (if any) with which these customers are doing business. An example is as follows:

The company does a significant amount of its total business with two customers. One customer, comprising 15% of total revenues for the entire company, also comprises 52% of the revenues of the Appliances segment. The second customer, comprising 28% of total revenues for the entire company, also comprises 63% of the revenues of the Government segment.

9.25   DISCLOSURE OF DERIVATIVE USE OBJECTIVES

If a company is party to a derivative financial instrument, it should state its objective and related strategies for using such an instrument and what specific risks are being hedged with its use. The following additional disclosures are required for fair value and cash flow hedges:

- *Fair value hedge.* One must disclose the net gain or loss recognized in earnings during the period stemming from the ineffective portion of a fair value hedge, as well as any derivative instrument's gain or loss excluded from the assessment of hedge effectiveness. If a hedged firm commitment no longer qualifies as a fair value hedge, then disclosure must also include the resulting gain or loss shown in earnings.

- *Cash flow hedge.* One must disclose the net gain or loss recognized in earnings during the period stemming from the ineffective portion of a cash flow hedge, as well as any derivative instrument's gain or loss excluded from the assessment of the hedge's effectiveness. Also note the future events that will result in the reclassification of gains or losses from other comprehensive income into earnings, as well as the net amount expected to be reclassified in the next year.

  Further, itemize the maximum time period over which the company hedges its exposure to cash flows from forecasted transactions (if any). Finally, if forecasted transactions are considered unlikely to occur, note the amount of gains or losses shifted from other comprehensive income into earnings as a result of canceling the hedge.

The first footnote sample is for a fair value hedge, while the second addresses a cash flow hedge:

(1) The company designates certain futures contracts as fair value hedges of firm commitments to purchase coal for electricity generation. Changes in the fair value of a derivative that is highly effective and that is designated and qualifies as a fair value hedge, along with the loss or gain on the hedged asset or liability that is attributable to the hedged risk, are recorded in current period earnings. Ineffectiveness results when the change in the fair value of the hedge instruments differs from the change in fair value of the hedged item. Ineffectiveness recorded related to the company's fair value hedges was not significant during fiscal 2010.

(2) If a derivative instrument used by the company in a cash flow hedge is sold, terminated, or exercised, the net gain or loss remains in accumulated other comprehensive income and is reclassified into earnings in the same period when the hedged transaction affects earnings. Accordingly, accumulated other comprehensive income at September 30, 2010 includes $6.5 million of the loss realized upon termination of derivative instruments that will be reclassified into earnings over the original term of the derivative instruments, which extend through December 2014. As of September 30, 2010 the company had entered into contracts for derivative instruments, designated as cash flow hedges, covering 200,000 tons of coal with a floor price of $58 per ton and a ceiling price of $69 per ton, resulting in other current assets of $0.7 million and $0.7 million of accumulated other comprehensive income representing the effective portion of unrealized hedge gains associated with these derivative instruments.

9.26   DISCLOSURE OF DISCONTINUED OPERATIONS

When some company operations are expected to be discontinued, the accountant should identify the discontinued segments at the earliest possible date, as well as the expected date on which the discontinuation will take place. The disclosure should also note the method of disposal, such as sale to a competitor or complete abandonment. If the discontinuation is occurring in the current reporting period, then the accountant should also itemize both the results of operations for the discontinued operation up until the date of disposal and any proceeds from sale of the operations. An example is as follows:

The company has elected to discontinue its Carrier Pigeon Quick Delivery Service. No buyer of this business is expected, so the company expects to shut down the operation no later than February of this year. No significant proceeds are expected from the sale of assets, since most of its assets will be absorbed into other operations of the company.

9.27 DISCLOSURE OF DIVIDENDS

If a company issues a cash dividend, a footnote should reveal the amount of the dividend, the date on which the dividend was declared, the date on which the dividend will be payable, and the date on which shareholders of record will be identified for the distribution. An example is as follows:

> On September 10, 2010, the Board declared a cash dividend of $1.07 per share, payable on November 2, 2010 to shareholders of record on September 25, 2010. This dividend distribution does not violate any covenants associated with the company's existing loans.

If a company chooses to pay shareholders dividends with assets other than cash, a footnote should disclose the nature of the assets being used for payment, the fair market value of the amount distributed, any gain or loss recognized by the company as part of the transaction, and how the transaction was handled in the financial statements. An example is as follows:

> The company distributed inventory dividends to its shareholders of record on April 30, 2010, issuing 10 pounds of its hard candy for every 100 shares of common stock held. The candy had a fair market value of $2,000,000 at the time of the dividend distribution. The company recorded no gain or loss on the transaction. It reduced the inventory asset by the amount of the distribution.

9.28 DISCLOSURE OF EARNINGS PER SHARE

When earnings per share (EPS) data is included in the financial statements, the accountant must also disclose the following information:

- *Omitted securities.* Describe any securities that have been omitted from the diluted earnings per share calculation on the grounds that they are antidilutive, but which could have a dilutive effect in the future.
- *Preferred dividends impact.* Note the impact of dividends on preferred stock when calculating the amount of income available for the basic EPS calculation.
- *Reconcile basic and diluted EPS.* The accountant must present a reconciliation of the numerators and denominators for the calculations used to derive basic and diluted EPS for income related to continuing operations.
- *Subsequent events.* The accountant must describe any event that occurs after the date of the financial statements, but before the date of issuance that would have had a material effect on the number of common shares outstanding if it had occurred during the accounting period being reported upon.

9.29 DISCLOSURE OF EMPLOYEE STOCK OWNERSHIP PLAN

If a company has set up an employee stock ownership plan (ESOP), it should disclose which employees participate in the plan, how dividends received by the plan are used, the formula used to make contributions to the ESOP, how contributed shares are used as collateral on any ESOP debt, how share valuations are assigned to employees, and how the company treats ESOP transactions in its financial reports. The footnote should also disclose any compensation cost recognized during the period. An example is as follows:

> The company makes monthly contributions to its employee stock ownership plan (ESOP) sufficient to make principal and interest payments on its outstanding debt. Shares held by the plan are used as collateral on the debt, but a portion of the shares are released as collateral at

the end of each year in proportion to the amount of debt paid down. At that time, the shares are allocated to qualified employees, who are defined as those working at least 30 hours per week as of year end. Once allocated, shares are included in earnings per share calculations. The company records compensation expense each month based on the market value of the shares expected to be released from collateral at year end. The compensation expense thus recorded in the past year was $189,000. The fair value of shares still held as collateral as of year end was $4,050,000. At year end, the ESOP contained 410,000 shares, of which 270,000 were used as collateral and 140,000 had been released from collateral and recorded as compensation expense.

9.30   DISCLOSURE OF EMPLOYMENT CONTRACT LIABILITIES

A company may enter into a variety of obligations when it agrees to employment contracts, such as a minimum number of years of salary payments, health insurance coverage subsequent to employment termination, and payments for life insurance coverage. If material, the term, potential expense, and descriptions of these agreements should be disclosed in a footnote. It is generally adequate to summarize all employment contract liabilities into a single footnote. An example is as follows:

The company has entered into five-year employment contracts with its CEO, CFO, and CIO, under which they are collectively guaranteed minimum salaries totaling $748,000 in each of the next five years, assuming their continued employment. In addition, the company has guaranteed payment for all of their term life insurance policies payable to their spouses, aggregating $3,000,000, for the five-year period. Since this is a firm liability, the company has recorded the present value of the expense in the current period, totaling $82,500.

9.31   DISCLOSURE OF ERROR CORRECTIONS

When an error correction is made, it is made to the financial results of a prior period. The disclosure is primarily contained within the line items on the face of the financial statements. However, the accompanying footnotes should also describe the nature of the error. An example is as follows:

An error was discovered in the 2010 financial statements, whereby depreciation was incorrectly calculated on the straight-line basis for several major plant installations involving the Watertown cement facility. The double declining balance method should have been used, as per company policy for assets of this nature. Correction of the error resulted in a decrease in the reported net income, net of income taxes, of $147,500.

9.32   DISCLOSURE OF GAIN CONTINGENCIES

When there is a possibility of a potential future gain, one can describe it in a footnote, including the amount of the gain, payment timing, and situation under which the gain arises. However, the wording should include the risks of *not* receiving the gain so that readers are not misled into assigning an incorrectly high probability to the eventual recognition of the gain. Several examples, involving increasing levels of gain probability, are provided:

(1) The company has initiated a suit against ABC Castings in the 4th District Court of Colorado, charging it with the improper design of a casting for a plastic swing sold by the company that has resulted in several million dollars of product warranty costs. The suit seeks recompense for $3.5 million in warranty cost reimbursements. No estimate can be made at this time of the amount of any future gain arising from settlement of this suit.

(2) The company was awarded $2.5 million by a jury trial in the 4th District Court of Colorado in July 2010 in its suit against ABC Castings. ABC has filed an appeal, which could result in

the substantial reduction or elimination of the awarded amount. Accordingly, the company has elected to not record any gain until cash is received from ABC.

(3) The company has reached an out-of-court settlement with ABC Castings, under which ABC has agreed to drop its ongoing appeal of a $2.5 million judgment against it in exchange for an immediate payment of $1.75 million. This payment has been received, so the company has recorded a gain of $1.75 million in the financial statements.

9.33   DISCLOSURE OF GAIN OR LOSS ON AN ASSET SALE

When a company recognizes a material gain or loss on the sale of an asset or a group of assets, it should disclose in a footnote the general transaction, its date, the gross amount of the sale, the amount of the gain or loss, and its presentation in the financial statements. An example is as follows:

The company sold its printing press in August 2010 for $5.3 million as part of a plan to reduce the capacity of its printing facilities in the United States. Net of its original cost, less depreciation and tax effects, this resulted in a net gain of $420,000, which is itemized as a gain on sale of assets in the financial statements.

9.34   DISCLOSURE OF GEOGRAPHIC RISK

If a company's geographic situation renders it more likely to suffer from a future catastrophe based on its geographic location, it can describe this risk in a footnote. Possible situations warranting such disclosure are being located in a floodplain or in a forested area highly subject to wildfires, being near an active earthquake fault line, or being in an area where tornados are common. An example is as follows:

The company's primary chemical processing facility is located directly over the San Andreas fault line, which has a history of producing earthquakes ranging up to 6.9 on the Richter scale. The company has attempted to obtain earthquake insurance, but the nature of its business makes the risk of loss so great for insurers that they will not provide coverage. Accordingly, the company is searching for a new facility in central Nevada and plans to move there within the next three years, shutting down the California facility at that time. In the meantime, the company remains at risk from any earthquake-related incidents, with losses from such an event being potentially large enough to have a material impact on the company's financial results.

9.35   DISCLOSURE OF GOODWILL

If a company elects to immediately write down some or all of the goodwill recorded on its books, there must be disclosure of the reasons for doing so. The footnote should specify why an impairment of goodwill has occurred, the events that have caused the impairment to take place, those portions of the business with which the impaired goodwill is associated, and how the company measured the amount of the loss. Any calculation assumptions used in determining the amount of the write-down should be noted. An example is as follows:

The company has taken a write-down of $1,200,000 in its Goodwill account. This write-down is specifically tied to the increase in competition expected from the approval of a competing patent, given to Westmoreland Steel Company, which will allow it to produce steel much more efficiently than the company's Arbuthnot Foundry, with which the $1,200,000 in goodwill is associated. This write-down is based on the assumption that the Arbuthnot Foundry will not be able to compete with Westmoreland Steel for longer than four years—consequently, the present value of all goodwill that will remain on the company's books four years from the date of these financial statements has been written off.

9.36 DISCLOSURE OF INCOME TAXES

If a company does not recognize a tax liability, then the accountant should disclose the temporary differences, at a summary level, for which no tax liability is recorded, as well as those circumstances under which a liability would be recorded. The accountant should also list any permanent unrecognized tax liabilities related to investments in foreign entities.

The accountant should itemize the amount of any net operating loss carryforwards and related credits, as well as the dates on which they expire. In addition, one should present a reconciliation of the statutory tax rate to the actual rate experienced by the organization during the reporting period, though privately held entities can restrict this reporting to a description of the general types of reconciling items.

The amounts of the following items related to income taxes must be attached to the income statement or reported within it:

- Any investment tax credit.
- Changes in tax assets or liabilities caused by changes in valuation estimates.
- Changes in tax assets or liabilities caused by regulatory changes.
- Net operating loss carryforwards.
- Tax-reducing government grants.
- The current tax expense.
- The deferred tax expense.

9.37 DISCLOSURE OF INCREASE IN VALUE OF A WRITTEN-DOWN HELD-TO-MATURITY INVESTMENT

If a company writes down the value of a held-to-maturity investment, it cannot record any subsequent recovery of the written-down value in the financial statements, but should do so in the footnotes. A disclosure should note the amount of the initial write-down and the amount of any subsequent value recovery. An example is as follows:

> The company wrote down the value of its $850,000 held-to-maturity investment in ABC Corporation in July 2010 by $288,000, based on ABC's bankruptcy filing in that month. Subsequently, ABC emerged from bankruptcy with the commitment to pay off its debt at 92% of face value and on the existing payment schedule. This resulted in an increase in the value of the company's ABC holdings of $220,000, which is not reflected in the attached financial statements.

9.38 DISCLOSURE OF INDUSTRY RISK

If the industry in which a company operates has unique risks related to such factors as intense competition, low barriers to entry, rapidly changing technology, and so on, then a footnote can describe these issues and their potential impact on company operations. An example is as follows:

> The company's primary business is the design, manufacture, and sale of Christmas ornaments. The company's financial results are influenced by the rapidity with which designs are copied by foreign competitors and reproduced at much lower prices, as well as by the company's ability to continue to create new designs that find favor in the marketplace, maintain a large network of distributors, manufacture in sufficient quantities for the Christmas selling season, and dispose of excess inventory without excessive losses. Based on these factors, the company can experience large fluctuations in its future financial results.

9.39   DISCLOSURE OF INSTALLMENT SALES

If installment sales compose a significant proportion of corporate sales, a footnote should disclose the revenue recognition policy used, as well as the amounts of gross profit recognized from the current and prior years, the total amount of deferred gross profit, and its placement on the balance sheet. An example is as follows:

> The company sells kitchen appliances on various installment payment plans. Given the extreme uncertainty associated with the collection of receivables under this plan, the company uses the cost recovery method to recognize profits, under which it recognizes no gross profit until all costs of goods sold have been paid back through cash receipts. In 2010, the company recognized $397,000 of gross profit earned in the current year, as well as $791,000 deferred from prior years. An additional $2,907,000 of deferred gross profits is classified as a current liability in the Unrecognized Gross Profit on Installment sales account.

9.40   DISCLOSURE OF INTANGIBLES

If a company has a material amount of intangible assets on its books, the accountant should describe the types of intangibles, the amortization period and method used to offset their value, and the amount of accumulated amortization. An example is as follows:

> The company has $1,500,000 of intangible assets on its books that is solely composed of the estimated fair market value of patents acquired through the company's acquisition of the R.C. Goodnough Company under the purchase method of accounting. This intangible asset is being amortized over 15 years, which is the remaining term of the acquired patents. The accumulated amortization through the reporting period is $300,000.

9.41   DISCLOSURE OF INVENTORY

If a company uses the LIFO valuation method, it should note the financial impact of any liquidation in LIFO inventory layers. Also, if a company uses other methods of valuation in addition to LIFO, then the extent to which each method is used should be described. Also, irrespective of the type of valuation method used, a company must reveal whether it is using the lower of cost or market adjustment (and the extent of any losses), whether any inventories are recorded at costs above their acquisition costs, whether any inventory is pledged as part of a debt arrangement, and the method of valuation being used. An example is as follows:

> The company uses the LIFO valuation method for approximately 65% of the total dollar value of its inventories, with the FIFO method being used for all remaining inventories. The company experienced a loss of $1.50 per share during the period that was caused by the elimination of LIFO inventory layers. The company also lost $.74 per share during the period as a result of a write-down of inventory costs to market. The company records no inventories above their acquisition costs. As of the balance sheet date, the company had pledged $540,000 of its inventory as part of a line of credit arrangement with the First Federal Industrial Credit Bank.

9.42   DISCLOSURE OF INVESTMENT RESTRICTIONS

If there is a restriction on the ability of a company to access its invested funds, this information should be disclosed, along with the reason for the restriction, the amount restricted, and the duration of the restriction period. An example is as follows:

> The company is required by the terms of its building term loan with the Second National Bank of Milwaukee to restrict all investments related to its loan for the construction of a new

corporate headquarters. Accordingly, the Second National Bank has custody over these funds, which are invested in short-term U.S. Treasury funds yielding approximately 3.25%. The restricted amount is $4,525,000 as of the balance sheet date and is expected to be eliminated as of year end, when the headquarters building will be completed and all contractors paid.

9.43 DISCLOSURE OF INVESTMENTS

If a company holds any investments, the accountant must disclose the existence of any unrealized valuation accounts in the equity section of the balance sheet, as well as any realized gains or losses that have been recognized through the income statement. The classification of any material investments should also be noted (i.e., as available for sale or held to maturity).

If investments are accounted for under the equity method, then the name of the entity in which the investment is made should be noted, as well as the company's percentage of ownership, the total value based on the market price of the shares held, and the total amount of any unrealized appreciation or depreciation, with a discussion of how these amounts are amortized. The amount of any goodwill associated with the investment should be noted, as well as the method and specifications of the related amortization. If this method of accounting is used for an investment in which the company's share of investee ownership is less than 20%, then the reason should be noted; similarly, if the method is not used in cases where the percentage of ownership is greater than 20%, then the reasoning for this should also be discussed. Finally, the accountant should reveal the existence of any contingent issuances of stock by the investee that could result in a material change in the company's share of the investee's reported earnings. The first example gives a general overview of a company's security classification policies. The second entry reveals the breakdown of security types within its available-for-sale portfolio. The third entry describes gains and losses resulting from both the sale of securities and transfers between security portfolios.

(1) The company classifies its investments when purchased and reviews their status at the end of each reporting period. The company classifies those marketable securities bought and intended for sale in the short term as trading securities, and records them at fair market value. The company classifies those debt securities it intends to hold to maturity, and has the intent to do so, as held-to-maturity securities. All remaining securities are classified as available-for-sale securities and are recorded at fair market value. Unrealized gains and losses on trading securities are recognized in earnings, while they are included in comprehensive income for available-for-sale securities.

(2) The company's available-for-sale portfolio is recorded at a total value of $1,150,000, of which $650,000 is equity securities and $500,000 is debt securities. The aggregate fair value of investments in this portfolio is $1,050,000 plus $100,000 of gross unrealized holding losses. The contractual maturity dates of $500,000 in debt securities fall into the following categories:

Maturity Date Range	Debt Reaching Maturity
Less than 1 year	$72,000
1–5 years	109,000
6–10 years	201,000
10+ years	118,000
Totals	$500,000

(3) The company recognized $42,000 in gains from the sale of its securities during the period, which was calculated using the specific identification method. It also recognized a loss

of $36,000 when it transferred securities from its available-for-sale portfolio to its trading portfolio, due to a change in the intent of management to sell the securities in the short term.

(4) The company recorded $1,050,000 of debt securities classified as held to maturity. The following table summarizes the debt by type of issuer and also notes the historical cost at which the debt is recorded on the balance sheet, its fair value, and the gross amount of unrealized gains and losses as of the balance sheet date.

Security Issuer	Historical Cost	Fair Value	Gross Unrealized Gain	Gross Unrealized Loss
U.S. Treasury debt	$450,000	$400,000	—	$50,000
Mortgage-backed loans	275,000	285,000	$10,000	—
Corporate debt	325,000	310,000	—	15,000
Totals	$1,050,000	$995,000	$10,000	$–65,000

The contractual maturities of the $1,050,000 in debt securities recorded in the held-to-maturity portfolio fall into the following date ranges:

Maturity Date Range	Debt Reaching Maturity
Less than 1 year	$275,000
1–5 years	409,000
5–10 years	348,000
10+ years	18,000
Totals	$1,050,000

9.44   DISCLOSURE OF LEASE TERMINATION COSTS

An office or equipment lease agreement typically obligates a company to long-term lease payments with no option to stop those payments even if the company is no longer using the space or equipment. Thus, lease termination costs can be quite high and generally warrant disclosure. A footnote should include disclosure of the pertinent requirements of the lease agreement, the remaining period over which payments are due, and the potential range of costs involved. An example is as follows:

> Due to the downturn in the company's principal asparagus distribution market, it no longer requires its San Francisco transshipment warehouse, for which it has a lease obligation for another six years. The total lease obligation for this facility through the remainder of the lease is $3,025,000. The company is discussing lease termination options with the lessor and is also searching for a sublessee. Given the market conditions, the company does not feel that a sublease can be obtained, and so assumes that a lease termination fee will be required. Accordingly, it has recorded a lease termination charge in the current period of $2,405,000, which is the present value of the total lease obligation.

9.45   DISCLOSURE OF LEASES BY LESSEES

If a company is leasing an asset that is recorded as an operating lease, the accountant must disclose the future minimum lease payments for the next five years, as well as the terms of any purchase, escalation, or renewal options. If an asset lease is being recorded as a capital lease, then the accountant should present the same information, as well as the amount of depreciation already recorded for these assets. Capital lease information should also include a summary, by major asset category, of the gross cost of leased assets. An example is as follows:

The company is leasing a number of copiers, which are all recorded as operating leases. There are no escalation or renewal options associated with these leases. All the leases require the company to pay personal property taxes, maintenance, and return shipping at the end of the leases. There are purchase options at the end of all lease terms that are based on the market price of the copiers at that time. The future minimum lease payments for these leases are as follows:

2010	$195,000
2011	173,000
2012	151,000
2013	145,000
2014	101,000
	$765,000

9.46 DISCLOSURE OF LIFE INSURANCE PROCEEDS

If a company receives a payout from a life insurance policy, it should disclose, in a footnote, the amount of the payout, the event that caused the payout to be earned, and how the transaction was presented in the financial statements. An example is as follows:

The company received a payout of $20,000,000 upon the death of a major shareholder in May 2009. The payout is recognized in the income statement under the Life Insurance Receipts line item. Under the terms of a stock buyback agreement with this shareholder, the company intends to use the proceeds to purchase all company shares held by the shareholder's estate.

9.47 DISCLOSURE OF LITIGATION

Companies are frequently the subject of lawsuits for a variety of alleged situations, such as harassment, patent infringement, and environmental liabilities. One should describe in the footnotes the general nature of each lawsuit, the amount of restitution sought, and the opinion of the company's legal counsel regarding the probable outcome of the suit. If there are many similar suits, they may be summarized for descriptive purposes. If lawsuits would have an immaterial impact on company results, then this can be stated in general terms. Several examples follow:

(1) The company is the target of a class action lawsuit entitled *Smith v. ABC Company*, currently in the 4th District Court of Colorado. In the case, current and previous hourly staff claim nonpayment of overtime pay and seek damages of $20,000,000. The company avers that the case is without merit and continues to vigorously defend its position in the case. It is not possible to determine a probable outcome at this time, and since company management feels a material loss from the suit to be remote, the company has not accrued any related expense.

(2) The company is the target of a sexual harassment lawsuit entitled *Jones v. ABC Company*, currently in the 4th District Court of Colorado. In the suit, a former employee alleges disparaging comments and actions by her immediate supervisor and seeks damages of $1 million. Per the advice of company counsel, the company offered to settle the case for $100,000 and accrued for this expense. However, if the offer is not accepted and the case were to go to trial, the company could be liable for the $1 million sought in the suit.

(3) The company is the target of a variety of legal proceedings as the result of its normal business operations, generally in the area of personal damage claims related to slips and falls in its warehouse facilities. In management's opinion, any liabilities arising from these proceedings would not have a material adverse impact on the company's financial results.

9.48   DISCLOSURE OF LOAN ACCELERATION

If a company cannot maintain the financial covenants called for in a loan document, the lender is usually entitled to require immediate payment of the loan. In such cases, the company should disclose the nature of the covenant violation, the status of any covenant renegotiation, the portion of the debt subject to acceleration, and any reclassification of the debt in the financial statements as a result of this occurrence. An example is as follows:

> The company was unable to meet the current ratio covenant on its debt agreement with the 4th National Bank of Wachovia. The bank has elected not to waive its right to accelerate the maturity of the debt. As a result, the bank can require the company to pay the current loan balance of $3,575,000 at any time. Accordingly, the debt has been reclassified as short-term debt on the balance sheet.

9.49   DISCLOSURE OF LOAN EXTINGUISHMENT

If a company experiences a gain or loss through a debt extinguishment transaction, the accountant should describe the transaction, the amount of debt extinguished, the amount of the gain or loss, the impact on income taxes and earnings per share, and the source of funds used to retire the debt. Three examples follow:

> (1) The company retired all of its callable Series D bonds during the period, totaling $7.2 million. The funds used to retire the bonds were obtained from the issuance of Series A preferred stock during the period. The debt retirement transaction resulted in a gain of $595,000, which had after-tax positive impacts on net income of $369,000 and on per share earnings of $0.29.

> (2) The company used the proceeds from its recent stock sale to retire $2.9 million in debt payable to the 4th National Bank of Wachovia. This debt agreement contained a prepayment penalty clause, so the company recorded a $150,000 expense for this penalty at the time of the prepayment. The company had also been amortizing the loan origination cost of the loan, of which $27,000 had not yet been recognized at the time of the prepayment. The company charged the remaining balance of this cost to expense. These charges, net of income tax benefits, resulted in an extraordinary loss of $124,000 and reduced earnings per share by $0.05.

> (3) In February 2010, the company recorded a loss of $89,000 net of income taxes, related to the write-down of the debt issuance costs for its 9 7/8% bonds. All of these bonds have been called by the company with funds obtained through its recent offering of common stock. The loss is recorded as a loss on debt issuance costs, and will reduce earnings per share by $0.02.

9.50   DISCLOSURE OF LOAN GUARANTEES

If a company is liable for the debt of another entity, a footnote should describe the nature of the indebtedness, the relationship between the two companies, the potential amount of the liability, and the date on which the liability terminates. An example is as follows:

> The company is contingently liable for the outstanding loans of Excelsior Holdings Ltd., in which it owns a 40% interest. The maximum possible loan balance under the guarantee agreement is $4,200,000, of which $3,800,000 is currently outstanding. The loan is a term loan with required periodic principal payments, resulting in complete termination of the loan and the company's loan guarantee as of May 31, 2014.

9.51 DISCLOSURE OF LOAN RESTRUCTURING

If a company restructures its debt, it should disclose any changes in the terms of the debt agreement and changes in income tax liability, as well as any resulting gain or loss. Two examples are as follows:

(1) The company restructured the terms of its $10 million debt with the 4th National Bank of Wachovia to reduce the interest rate from 10% to 7.5%, which included that portion of the accrued interest expense payable for the past two years. This resulted in a one-time gain on interest expense reduction, net of income tax effects, of $350,000. This has been recorded as an extraordinary gain on debt restructuring.

(2) In December 2010, the company redeemed a portion of its 8% bonds payable in 2016, totaling $14.1 million in principal value. In order to redeem the bonds, the company paid a 12% premium to the bondholders, resulting in an extraordinary loss on debt reduction of $1.2 million net of a tax benefit of $508,000. The company paid for the bond redemption with funds obtained through a recent preferred stock offering.

9.52 DISCLOSURE OF LOANS

If a company has entered into a loan agreement as the creditor, the accountant should describe each debt instrument, as well as all maturity dates associated with principal payments, the interest rate, and any circumstances under which the lender can call the loan (usually involving a description of all related covenants). In addition, the existence of any conversion privileges by the lender should be described, and any assets to be used as collateral. Other special disclosures involve the existence of any debt agreements entered into subsequent to the date of the financial statements, related-party debt agreements, and the unused amount of any outstanding letters of credit. An example is as follows:

The company has entered into a line of credit arrangement with the First Federal Commercial Bank, which carries a maximum possible balance of $5,000,000. The loan has a variable interest rate that is 1/2% higher than the bank's prime lending rate. The loan's interest rate as of the date of the financial statements is 8 3/4%. As of the date of the financial statements, the company had drawn down $750,000 of the loan balance. Collateral used to secure the loan is all accounts receivable and fixed assets. The loan must be renegotiated by December 31, 2011, in the meantime, the bank can call the loan if the company's working capital balance falls below $2,000,000 or if its current ratio drops below 1.5 to 1.

9.53 DISCLOSURE OF NONSTANDARD REPORTED METHOD OF INVESTMENT

If a company chooses to account for an investment in a nonstandard manner, such as using the equity method for a minor investment that would normally require the cost method, then it should disclose in a footnote that it exercises a sufficient degree of control over the investee's operating and financial activities to warrant the change (or vice versa for a larger investment recorded under the cost method). Two examples are as follows:

(1) The company owns a 35% interest in the Arkansas Botox Clinics Company (ABC), which would normally be accounted for under the equity method of accounting. However, due to the considerable resistance of the ABC management to the company's investment, the company's management feels that it has minimal control over ABC's financial and operating activities,

and so has chosen to record the investment under the cost method, whereby it records its investment at cost and only records income on the investment when dividends are received.

(2) The company owns a 12% interest in the Alaskan Bear Company (ABC), which would normally be accounted for under the cost method of accounting. However, because the company's CEO is also president of ABC, the company's management feels that it has financial and operating control over ABC, and so has chosen to record the investment under the equity method, whereby it records its proportionate share of ABC's net earnings.

9.54   DISCLOSURE OF PAR VALUE CHANGE

Though rare, companies sometimes will alter their certificates of incorporation to change the par value of their stock. This change is typically in a downward direction, resulting in the shifting of funds from the Stock account to the Additional Paid-in capital account. When this happens, a footnote should include the date and amount of the change, as well as the aggregate amount of funds shifted into or out of the Stock account. An example is as follows:

A majority of the company's shareholders voted on October 10, 2010 to amend the company's certificate of incorporation to reduce the par value of its common stock to $0.01 from $1.00. Due to this change, $990,000 was shifted from the Common Stock account to the Additional Paid-in capital account.

9.55   DISCLOSURE OF POSTEMPLOYMENT BENEFITS

If employees are entitled to benefits subsequent to their employment that are material, then the nature of the transaction, the amount of expense involved, and its treatment in the financial statements should be revealed in a footnote. An example is as follows:

The company's former president, Mr. Smith, was asked to step down by the board on May 5, 2010. As part of the separation agreement, the company agreed to pay Mr. Smith's medical insurance premiums for the next two years and also paid a lump-sum settlement of $2 million. The present value of the entire medical cost was charged to expense in the current period, as was the lump-sum settlement. The medical expense was offset against an Unpaid insurance premiums liability account, which will be gradually reduced as periodic medical insurance payments are made.

9.56   DISCLOSURE OF PRIOR PERIOD ADJUSTMENTS

Prior period adjustments should be itemized for all reporting periods that they impact, both at gross and net of income tax effect. This should be done as line items within the financial statements. However, if the accountant wishes to introduce a greater degree of clarity in relation to any such changes, then also including the information in a footnote would be acceptable. An example is as follows:

The company discovered that the inventory in an outlying warehouse was not counted during the year-end physical inventory count for both of the years reported in the financial statements. The amount of the overlooked inventory in 2009 was $230,000 and in 2010 was $145,000. Retroactive inclusion of these inventory amounts in the financial statements for those years would have resulted in an increase in net income of $142,600 in 2009 and $89,900 in 2010.

9.57   DISCLOSURE OF PURCHASING COMMITMENTS

There may be a minimum purchase agreement extending into future reporting periods and that obligates a company to make purchases in amounts that are material. Also, a company may have made guarantees to pay for the debts of other entities, such as a subsidiary. If these commitments are material, then their nature must be disclosed in the footnotes. The rules are not specific about identifying the exact cost or probability of occurrence of each commitment, so the accountant has some leeway in presenting this information. An example is as follows:

> The company has entered into a contract to purchase a minimum of 500,000 tons of coal per year for the next 20 years at a fixed price of $20.50 per ton, with no price escalation allowed for the duration of the contract. The company's minimum annual payment obligation under this contract is $10,250,000. The price paid under this contract is $1.75 less than the market rate for anthracite coal as of the date of these statements, and had not significantly changed as of the statement issuance date.

9.58   DISCLOSURE OF REDUCTION IN EQUITY METHOD INVESTMENT

If a company's investment in another entity is accounted for under the equity method, any losses recorded under that method should be adequately described in a footnote, which can include the company's percentage ownership in the entity, the amount of any loss by the entity that is recorded on the company's financial records, and the resulting impact on the company's recorded investment in the entity. The footnote should also disclose any requirement for the company to fund further entity losses, if any. If the reported investment has dropped to zero, the footnote should state that the equity method of accounting will not be used in order to avoid recording a negative investment. Three examples follow:

> (1) The company has a 35% interest in the Osaka Electric Company, which operates the power grid in the greater Osaka metropolitan area. This investment has been accounted for under the equity method of accounting since 2009. The company's financial results include a loss of $5.3 million, representing its share of Osaka's loss due to a write-down in goodwill on a failed subsidiary. The loss reduced the company's investment balance in Osaka to $4.0 million. The company has no obligation to fund any additional losses reported by Osaka.

> (2) The company has a 29% interest in the Bogota Power Company, which operates all hydroelectric facilities in Colombia. This investment has been accounted for under the equity method of accounting since 2007. The company's financial results include a loss of $22.8 million, representing its share of Bogota's loss due to reduced maintenance fees paid by the Colombia government. The loss reduced the company's investment balance in Bogota to zero. The company is contractually obligated to provide an additional $100 million in funding if Bogota's losses continue. Given the current regulatory environment, management feels that the additional funds will be required, so a loss contingency of $100 million has been recognized on the balance sheet.

> (3) The company has a 40% investment in the Euclid Power Company. This investment has been accounted for under the equity method of accounting since 2009. The company's financial results include a loss of $21 million, representing its share of Euclid's losses. Recognition of this loss has resulted in a reported investment in Euclid of $0. Since the company cannot report a negative investment in Euclid under the equity method, it will not record its share of future Euclid losses until such time as future Euclid profits offset any subsequent losses that would otherwise have resulted in the reporting of a negative investment by the company.

9.59   DISCLOSURE OF REDUCTION IN THE MARKET VALUE OF EQUITY INVESTMENTS

If management is of the opinion that a permanent decline in an equity investment has occurred, it should note the amount and date of a write-down in the investment valuation, as well as its presentation in the financial statements. An example is as follows:

> The company wrote down the value of several investments in equity instruments held in its available-for-sale portfolio during August 2010 by $193,000. The write-down was based on management's judgment that the equity instruments have experienced a permanent reduction in value. The write-down is itemized as a loss on investments in the operating section of the income statement.

9.60   DISCLOSURE OF RELATED-PARTY LOANS

If a company has issued loans to related parties, it should describe, in a footnote, the nature of the transactions, as well as the amounts involved, interest rates payable, and timing of subsequent payments. Several examples follow:

> (1) The company is owed $2,000,000 in various notes receivable from its executive management team. The notes carry interest rates ranging from 5.25% to 7.5% and will mature within the next 2 to 5 years. The board authorized year-end bonus payments to the executives owing the notes receivable, all of whom chose to forgo payment in exchange for cancellation of their notes payable.

> (2) The company loaned $175,000 to the CEO in 2006 at an interest rate of 6.5%. Neither the principal nor the accrued interest on the note has been paid. The board has elected to forgive $100,000 of the outstanding principal and all associated interest, leaving a balance of $75,000 on which interest has continued to accrue since the loan initiation date in 2010.

> (3) The company has been loaned $350,000 by the CEO. This debt is unsecured, carries an interest rate of 8.2%, and can only be repaid after all bank debt has been retired. The debt is junior to all outstanding bank debt, so the likelihood of debt repayment in the short term is remote. Accordingly, the debt is classified as long-term debt in the financial statements.

9.61   DISCLOSURE OF REVENUE RECOGNITION POLICY

The general principles followed by company management in recognizing revenue should be stated in a footnote. This can include the amount of time over which revenue from maintenance agreements is followed, how the company handles different types of products and services bundled into the same pricing packages, and at what point revenues are recognized in the revenue-generating process. Here are some sample footnotes:

> (1) The company sells maintenance agreements along with its home air-conditioning units. Maintenance revenue is recognized ratably over the term specified within each agreement, which can range from 12 to 60 months. In cases where maintenance agreements are offered to customers at a discount, the company assumes that the discounts really apply to the complete package of air-conditioning products and related maintenance agreements, and so recalculates the discount as a percentage of the entire package. This results in approximately 65% of the discounts being assigned to product sales and the remaining 35% to maintenance sales. The adjusted maintenance revenues are then recognized ratably over the term specified within each agreement. As of the balance sheet date, $1,389,000 of maintenance revenues had not been recognized.

> (2) The company sells electrical appliance monitoring devices to large industrial manufacturers. It charges a nominal amount for each unit sold and takes 5% of the electricity savings generated from the use of each unit for the first three years after which each unit is installed,

up to a maximum of $5,000 per quarter. Given the uncertainty of the savings to be generated from electricity cost savings, the company does not feel that it can reasonably recognize any revenue until after cost savings have been determined at the end of each quarter. Also, since cost savings tend to be disputed by recipients, making cash receipts problematic, management has elected to further delay revenue recognition until after cash has been received from each customer.

In the case of service-related revenues, disclosures should also include information about unearned revenues, such as the amount billed but not earned, and where it is placed on the balance sheet. Related expenses that have been deferred should also be described, including their amount and where they are itemized on the balance sheet. Two examples are as follows:

(1) The company recognizes revenue under the proportional performance method, whereby revenue is recognized based on the hours charged to a project as a percentage of the total hours required to complete the job. Billings occur at quarterly intervals on most contracts, resulting in recognized but unbilled revenue. At the end of 2010, there was $1,895,000 of recognized but unbilled revenue, as compared to $2,905,000 in 2009. This asset is listed in the Unbilled revenue current asset account.

(2) The company recognizes revenue under the specific performance method, whereby revenue is only recognized after specific project milestones have been approved by customers. When costs are incurred prior to a revenue recognition event, they are stored in the Unrecognized project expense current asset account. At the end of 2010, there was $1,505,000 of unrecognized project expense, as compared to $1,759,000 in 2009.

9.62 DISCLOSURE OF ROYALTY PAYMENTS

A royalty agreement involving potentially material payments should be disclosed. The information in the footnote should include a description and the terms of the agreement, as well as the potential amount of the payments. An example is as follows:

The company contracts much of its software game development to third-party developers. These developers receive nonrecoverable advances ranging from $25,000 to $80,000 for each game they create, against which a standard 8% royalty is deducted. Once the full amount of each advance has been earned by a developer, royalty payments are accrued monthly and paid quarterly. All development advances are accounted for as short-term assets in the Development advances account, which currently contains $2,628,000. The company periodically compares product sales to the remaining amount of advances on each product, and writes off those advances for which sales trends indicate that remaining royalties earned will not be sufficient to eliminate the advances. In the past year, the company wrote off $350,000 of development advances for this reason.

9.63 DISCLOSURE OF THE SALE OF HELD-TO-MATURITY INVESTMENTS

If a debt security classified as held to maturity is sold, a footnote should disclose the reason for the sale, as well as the amount of any gains or losses recognized and the amount of any as-yet unamortized premiums or discounts. An example is as follows:

The company liquidated $2,800,000 of its held-to-maturity portfolio in order to pay for an acquisition. The transaction resulted in the recognition of a gain of $145,000. Also, a previously unamortized discount of $16,500 on the original debt purchase was written off as part of the transaction.

9.64 DISCLOSURE OF SALES RETURN ALLOWANCE

There is no specific GAAP requirement that a company state its policy regarding the use of an allowance for sales returns. However, if a reserve has been created, then a footnote should detail how the amount of the reserve was derived. An example is as follows:

> The company recorded an allowance for sales returns of $148,000. This amount is based on a historical average rate of return of 12% of the company's subscription book sale business.

9.65 DISCLOSURE OF SALES WITH SIGNIFICANT RIGHTS OF RETURN

If there is considerable uncertainty regarding the amount of potential sales returns, as may be caused by a new product, potential product obsolescence, or heightened competition, then a company may be forced to not recognize any revenue at all until the right of product return has passed. Since this can cause a substantial reduction in recognized revenue, a footnote describing the reason for the recognition delay would be in order. The information in the following footnotes illustrates a sufficient level of disclosure:

> (1) The company is in the beta testing phase of its new crop-planting system, and so has granted an unconditional right of return to the first 10 customers who have agreed to purchase the product. The right of return privilege extends for six months from the shipment date. Since there is no return history for this new product, the company has recorded the total amount of all 10 sales in an Unearned sales liability account and will not recognize the revenue until the right of return period has expired. The total amount in this account is $328,000. Of this amount, $275,000 will be recognizable in March 2011, and the remaining $53,000 in May 2011, assuming that no products are returned in the interim.

> (2) The company's light saber product is entirely new and is being introduced into a new market, so management feels that it cannot estimate potential levels of product returns. Consequently, the company has not recognized any revenues related to recent shipments of the product until the three-month right of return period has passed. The company plans to reevaluate this policy after a sufficient amount of time has passed for it to make a better estimate of potential sales returns. The initial amount of light saber revenues that would otherwise have been recognized in the first month of shipments was $1,750,000.

9.66 DISCLOSURE OF SEGMENT INFORMATION

If a company is publicly held, the accountant must disclose information about its operating segments in considerable detail, which is described in FASB Statement Number 131. In general, this should include a discussion of the means by which management splits the organization into separate reporting segments. It should also identify the types of products that compose each segment's revenue, the nature of any intercompany transactions between reporting segments, and the reasons for any differences between reported results by segment and consolidated results. A comprehensive disclosure of segment information can be presented in a grid format that itemizes information for each segment in a separate column and that summarizes the total for all segments, net of adjustments, into a consolidated company-wide total.

9.67 DISCLOSURE OF SHIFTS BETWEEN SECURITIES ACCOUNTS

If company management feels that the purpose of various investments have changed, it can shift the funds between its held-to-maturity and available-for-sale categories. If so, it should disclose in a footnote the reason for the change, the aggregate amount of securities shifted between accounts, and any related unrealized gain or loss, net of income taxes. An example is as follows:

> The company shifted approximately half of its securities recorded as held-to-maturity securities to the Held-for-trading account during the last quarter of 2010. These securities had a net carrying value of $42 million at the time of the transfer, including unrealized losses net of income taxes of $2.5 million. Management authorized this change in order to reflect its increased need for additional cash in the short term as part of its general upgrade of production facilities.

9.68   DISCLOSURE OF SIGNIFICANT RISKS

The accountant must disclose in the footnotes that the creation of any financial statement requires the use of some estimates by management. This notation should be accompanied by a list of any significant items in the financial statements that are based on management estimates and that could result in material changes if the estimates prove to be incorrect.

The footnotes should also disclose the existence of any concentrations of revenue with certain customers, as well as concentrations of supplies with certain vendors. In addition, geographic concentrations of business activity should be disclosed, plus the existence of any collective bargaining agreements that cover a significant proportion of the work force. An example is as follows:

> Twenty-three percent of the company's total revenue is with a single customer; there are purchase agreements in place that commit this customer to similar purchase volumes for the next three years. In addition, 10% of company revenues are earned from its Bosnia operation, to which management assigns a high risk of loss if political disturbances in this area continue. Finally, 43% of the company's direct labor force is covered by a collective bargaining agreement with the International Brotherhood of Electrical Workers; the related union agreement is not due to expire for three years.

9.69   DISCLOSURE OF STOCK COMPENSATION

If a company has paid employees or outside entities compensation in the form of stock, the number of shares granted, the effective date of the transaction, and its fair market value should be itemized in a footnote. Several examples follow.

> (1) The board authorized stock compensation to the company's executive team as of July 31, 2010 in the amount of 340,000 shares of common stock. The stock had a fair market value of $14,900,000 on the date of the grant.

> (2) The board authorized the granting of 10,000 shares of common stock with a fair value of $52,000 to the company's legal advisor. The advisor accepted this payment in lieu of a cash payment for ongoing legal services performed.

> (3) The board authorized the granting of 150,000 shares of common stock to a director in exchange for the elimination of $800,000 in accrued interest on a loan the director had extended to the company in 2009.

9.70   DISCLOSURE OF STOCK OPTIONS

If a company has a stock option plan, it must give a general description of the plan, report the number of shares authorized for option grants, and note vesting requirements and maximum option terms. An example of this "header information" is provided in the following footnote:

> The company maintains a stock option plan under which all employees are awarded option grants based on a combination of performance and tenure. All options may be exercised for a period of 10 years following the grant date, after which they expire. All options fully vest after recipients have worked for the company subsequent to the grant date in a full-time capacity for a period of four years. The board has authorized the use of 2,000,000 shares for option grants.

It is not yet required to report the fair value of options granted as compensation expense, though some companies have elected to do so. However, any company choosing not to report this information in its financial statements must still show net income and earnings per share in the accompanying footnotes as though the fair value method had been used to determine the compensation expense associated with option grants.

No matter what compensation expense method is used, a footnote must also describe the range of option exercise prices as of the balance sheet date, as well as the weighted average remaining exercise period for outstanding options, plus the weighted average price at which options were converted during the reporting period.

The first of the following footnotes describes an option plan without any associated compensation expense, while the second includes this information. In the first example, the number of shares authorized for option grants, the total outstanding number of options, and the weighted average exercise price for those options are listed.

(1) The company operates a stock option plan, under which 350,000 options to purchase the company's common stock were granted in 2009. The options fully vest three years from the date of grant and will automatically be canceled if not used within 10 years of the date of grant. The exercise prices of all options granted matched the market price of the stock on the day of grant. Given this matching of exercise prices to market values, there was no compensation expense associated with the options granted, and therefore no compensation expense was recorded. If the company had used the fair value method of option valuation as recommended by SFAS 123, an additional $94,500 in compensation expense would have been recognized, resulting in a reduction in net income, net of income tax changes, of $61,400, as well as a reduction in earnings per share of $.40. As of this date, the following options in aggregate have been granted, exercised, or cancelled since the option plan was created:

	No. of Options	Weighted Average Exercise Price
Options granted	1,890,000	$5.02
Options exercised	−115,000	7.15
Options cancelled	−80,000	8.00
Total outstanding	1,695,000	$4.96

(2) The company recognizes the compensation costs associated with its stock option grants based on their fair market value on the date of grant. The weighted average fair value of options granted during the past year was $11.25, which was calculated using the Black-Scholes option-pricing formula. When using the formula, company management used as inputs a risk-free interest rate of 3.0%, no dividend yield, an expected option life of eight years, and an expected stock volatility of 39%. The immediate recognition of the compensation cost of stock option grants resulted in a reduction during the past year of $329,000 in net income and a reduction in earnings of $0.32 per share.

If option terms are altered, the terms of the change should be noted in a footnote, as well as any financial changes resulting from the modification. An example is as follows:

> The board extended the term of 200,000 options previously granted to the management team. The options had been set to expire at the end of 2009 and were extended to the end of 2010. The option exercise price was compared to the fair market value of company shares on the date when the extension was authorized by the board, resulting in the immediate recognition of $228,000 in compensation expense. There is no deferred compensation expense associated with this transaction, since all extended options had previously been fully vested.

9.71   DISCLOSURE OF A STOCK REPURCHASE PROGRAM

One should describe the date on which a stock repurchase program was authorized by the board of directors, the maximum number of shares to be repurchased, and the current status of the repurchase program. An example is as follows:

> The company's board of directors authorized a stock repurchase program for its Series A preferred stock on June 30, 2010, up to a maximum of two million shares. As of the balance sheet date, the company had repurchased 1,255,000 shares for a total of $58,500,000. The repurchased shares are held in the corporate treasury and cannot be released without board approval.

9.72   DISCLOSURE OF A STOCK SALE

If a company sells stock, a footnote should disclose the type and number of shares sold, the price at which the shares were sold, and the general use of the proceeds. An example is as follows:

> During May 2010, the company sold 4,210,000 shares of its Series B preferred stock at a price of $12 per share, netting $48,500,000 after sale and issuance costs. Management intends to use the proceeds to fund several anticipated acquisitions.

9.73   DISCLOSURE OF STOCK SPLITS

All stock splits and reverse stock splits should be fully documented in a footnote, itemizing the date on which board of directors' approval was granted, the ratio of the stock split, and the date on which the split took effect. The footnote should also contain assurances that all stock-related information in the financial statements has been adjusted to reflect the stock split. Two examples are as follows:

> (1) The company's board of directors authorized a three-for-one reverse stock split on November 15, 2010, to take effect on November 18, 2010. All share and related option information presented in these financial statements and accompanying footnotes has been retroactively adjusted to reflect the reduced number of shares resulting from this action.

> (2) The company's board of directors authorized a three-for-one stock split on November 15, 2010, to take effect on December 20, 2010. Each shareholder of record on November 25, 2010 received two additional shares of common stock for each share held on that date. Additional funds were shifted from the Additional Paid-in capital account to the Common stock account to equal the amount of additional par value represented by the additional shares issued under the stock split. All share and related option information presented in these financial statements and accompanying footnotes has been retroactively adjusted to reflect the increased number of shares resulting from this action.

9.74   DISCLOSURE OF STOCK SUBSCRIPTIONS

If investors have subscribed to company shares, the company should reveal the number of subscribed shares not yet issued. An example is as follows:

> The company offered its common stock for sale to a limited group of investors during the reporting period. The investors subscribed to $4,250,000 of stock at $20.00 per share. Of the amount subscribed, $3,650,000 has been received, resulting in the issuance of 182,500 shares. The share issuance is reflected in all earnings per share information in these financial statements. The unpaid $600,000 of subscriptions will result in the issuance of an additional 30,000 shares when payment is received, which would have reduced earnings per share in the reporting period by $.03 if the subscription payments had been received during the period.

9.75   DISCLOSURE OF SUBSEQUENT EVENTS

If any event occurs subsequent to the date of the financial statements that may have a material impact on the financial statements, then it should be disclosed in the footnotes. The accountant should consider issuing pro forma statements to include a monetary presentation of this information in cases where the amount of the subsequent event significantly changes the organization's financial position. Some examples of subsequent events that should be disclosed are:

- Gains or losses on foreign exchange transactions of a substantial nature.
- Gains or losses on investments of a substantial nature.
- Loans to related parties.
- Loss contingencies.
- Loss of assets to natural disasters.
- Merger or acquisition.
- Receipt of new funds from debt or equity issuances.
- Sale of major assets.
- Settlement of litigation, including the amount of any prospective payments or receipts.

9.76   DISCLOSURE OF TAXATION DISPUTES

A company may be in a variety of stages of investigation by any number of government taxing authorities, ranging from sales and use tax audits to income tax reviews. Disclosure of these reviews can range from a simple statement that an audit is under way through the initial judgment notice to a description of a finalized payment settlement. The following footnotes give examples of several options:

> (1) The company is being reviewed by a California sales tax audit team. Management is of the opinion that this review will not result in any material change in the company's financial results.

> (2) The company has been audited by a California sales tax audit team, which asserts that the company has established nexus in that state and so must remit sales taxes for all sales into California for the past three years, which would total $14 million. Management is of the opinion that there are no grounds for establishing nexus and intends to vigorously contest the issue through the California appeals process, up to and including litigation. Management believes that there is no need to establish any loss accrual related to this matter at this time.

(3) The company has reached agreement with the State of California, under which a payment of $2.5 million for unpaid sales taxes shall be made. The company intends to collect these taxes from its customers, which management believes will substantially reduce the amount of its liability. Accordingly, it has recognized an expense of $600,000 in the current period to cover any sales taxes it cannot collect from customers, and will modify this amount in the future based upon its sales tax collection experience for the amounts due.

9.77   DISCLOSURE OF UNUSED CREDIT FACILITIES

If a company has entered into a credit facility with a lender and some portion of that potential debt is unused, a footnote should disclose the terms of the agreement, the amount of debt outstanding, and the amount available. If there are covenants associated with the facility, the company's ability to meet the covenants should be noted. An example is as follows:

The company has a revolving line of credit with a consortium of banks for a total of $100 million. The debt is secured by the company's accounts receivable and inventory balances, and carries an adjustable interest rate matching the prime rate. The company must meet the terms of several covenants in order to use the facility; it currently meets all covenant requirements. There was $28.5 million outstanding under the line of credit at year end, leaving $71.5 million available for further borrowings.

9.78   DISCLOSURE OF WARRANTS ISSUED

If warrants to purchase stock are issued, a footnote should disclose the reason for the transaction, the number of warrants issued, and the exercise price at which they can be used to purchase shares, as well as the vesting period and expiration date. Two examples are as follows:

(1) The company issued 80,000 warrants to a group of venture capital firms. The warrants allow the firms to purchase the company's common stock at an exercise price of $5.10. There is no vesting period. The warrants expire in 10 years. The warrants were issued as part of the compensation package earned by the firms in assisting the company in the placement of a recent issuance of common stock.

(2) During the year ended 2009, certain holders of warrants to purchase shares of the company's common stock exercised a total of 32,000 warrants to purchase 64,000 shares for a total of $326,400.

9.79   DISCLOSURE OF WARRANTY EXPENSE ALLOWANCE

If there is a history or expectation of significant warranty expenses, one should accrue an appropriate amount when related revenues are recognized. The footnote should describe the basis for the warranty expense calculation, as well as the current amount of the reserve. An example is as follows:

The company recognizes a warranty expense when it recognizes the sale of its amusement park bumper cars. This expense is based on the most recent one year of actual warranty claims, which is currently 1.9% of sales. The current warranty expense reserve, as listed in the Warranty reserve liability account on the balance sheet, is $302,000.

The company has just released a completely reengineered bumper car, containing 90% new parts. Given the large number of changes in this new product, there exists considerable uncertainty in regard to probable future warranty claims, which could be materially larger than the amount previously reserved and which could have a material impact on the company's financial results in the near term.

9.80   DISCLOSURE OF WARRANTY REVENUE RECOGNITION

As is the case with any long-term service revenue contract, the period over which warranty revenues are calculated should be described, if this is a significant proportion of revenues. For many companies, this is a small revenue component not requiring separate disclosure. If it is disclosed, note the term over which warranty revenues are recognized and the amount of unrecognized warranty revenues. An example is as follows:

> The company sells a one-year warranty agreement with its kitchen appliances; warranty revenues compose approximately 8% of total revenues. These revenues are recognized ratably over their service periods, with the unrecognized balance listed as a short-term liability in the Unrecognized warranty revenues account. The unrecognized balance of these sales was $850,000 as of the balance sheet date.

9.81   SUMMARY

The primary focus of the footnote disclosures in this chapter has been on accounting situations that apply to all industries. In addition to the cases noted here, there are also a number of footnote disclosures required for companies operating within specific industries, such as the banking, broadcasting, insurance, motion picture, and software industries.

The reader can find additional information about disclosures in these specialized areas in the *Wiley GAAP Guide 2009.*

CHAPTER 10

INTERNAL MANAGEMENT REPORTS

10.1 INTRODUCTION

Much of the accountant's work must be translated into a report format that is readily un-derstandable to the layman. Some of these reports are the financial statements, the rules for which are laid down in many other chapters of this book in accordance with GAAP. However, there are no rules for internal management reports. The accountant can use any format that results in the greatest comprehension of accounting information. In this chap-ter, we focus on specific examples of internal reports that can be adapted to fulfill this comprehension requirement.

10.2 STATUS REPORTS

Though the financial statements are the primary reporting product of the accountant, they are only issued (at most) once a month, which is too long for many managers to go without information about ongoing company performance. Also, much of the financial information contained within a financial statement is of no use to the typical manager, who is more concerned with operational data. A good alternative to the financial state-ment, both in terms of the frequency of reporting and information presented, is shown in Exhibit 10.1.

This exhibit divides key measurements into three financial areas and three operational areas. The chief financial officer (CFO) and treasurer are most concerned with the first two blocks of measurements, which describe five separate components of company cash flow. The third block notes financial performance information, while the remaining three blocks of measurements are specifically tailored to the needs of the managers of the sales, production, and warehouse departments.

Another status report is the daily financial statement, which can be issued on paper or converted to HTML format and posted to a company's intranet site for general perusal. The example shown in Exhibit 10.2 contains all of the basic financial statement line items. The main difference is that it contains several extra columns that a reader can use to determine the status of the company in reaching its goals. For example, the two columns farthest to the right itemize the actual year-to-date results through the preceding month, which are

| | Current Month | | | | | | | |
	Week 5	Week 4	Week 3	Week 2	Week 1	Apr.	Mar.	Feb.
Cash								
Available Debt (000s)			$1,600	$1,550	$1,500	$1,400	$1,300	$1,200
Overdue Accounts Receivable (000s)			$ 415	$ 400	$ 388	$ 315	$ 312	$ 269
Overdue Accounts Payable (000s)			$ 108	$ 110	$ 114	$ 276	$ 312	$ 401
Working Capital								
Days Accounts Receivable			48	47	46	43	41	51
Days Total Inventory			52	50	49	61	52	46
Financial								
Breakeven, 2 Mo. Rolling (000s)	—	—	—	—	—	$1,430	$1,440	$1,450
Net Profits Before Tax (000s)	—	—	—	—	—	$ 30	($33)	($60)
Sales								
Backlog for Next Month			$1,650	$1,699	$1,724	$1,922	$1,708	$1,651
Backlog for Month after Next			$ 460	$ 450	$ 461	$ 652	$ 505	$ 491
Backlog for Two Months after Next			$ 83	$ 12	$9	$ 296	$ 202	$ 358
Backlog, Total (000s)			$2,193	$2,161	$2,194	$2,870	$2,415	$2,500
Production								
Machine Utilization			74%	77%	80%	70%	67%	66%
% Order Line Items Shipped on Time			82%	80%	83%	79%	73%	64%
% Actual Labor Hrs over Standard			23%	20%	17%	23%	40%	25%
Scrap Dollars (000s)	—	—			—	$46	$51	$54
Warehouse								
$$$ of Total Inventory (000s)			$2,560	$2,565	$2,604	$2,644	$2,352	$2,273
$$$ of Finished Goods (000s)			$ 520	$ 515	$ 536	$ 496	$ 454	$ 668
$$$ of Work-in-Process (000s)			$ 490	$ 510	$ 566	$ 680	$ 555	$ 362
$$$ of Raw Materials (000s)			$1,550	$1,540	$1,502	$1,468	$1,343	$1,243
Inventory Accuracy			64%	60%	56%	68%	80%	71%

EXHIBIT 10.1 KEY COMPANY MEASUREMENTS

May 2010
Daily Flash Report

	Month-to-Date Through 5/3/2010	This Month's Forecast	This Month's Budget	Variance from Budget	Year-to-Date for Prior Months	Average for Prior Months
This Month's Invoicing	**9,424**					
New Business Invoiced	—					
Cash	**926,547**	—	—	—	—	—
Accounts Receivable	**161,311**	—	—	—	—	—
Sales, Month-to-Date	62,203	—	—	—	—	—
Sales, Expected This Month	192,697	—	—	—	—	—
Total Projected Sales	254,900	**254,900**	271,454	(16,554)	804,647	201,162
Cost of Sales		13,846	6,770	6,770	43,709	10,927
Commissions		10,661	19,678	19,678	33,655	8,414
Gross Profit	254,900	230,392	245,006	9,894	727,283	181,821
Gross Profit %	100%	90%	90%	—	90%	90%
Expenses:						
Advertising		1,000	2,500	2,500	485	121
Bank Charges		200	185	185	968	242
Copiers		354	700	700	2,468	617
Depreciation	7,223	7,223	7,875	652	24,992	6,248
Dues & Publications		100	400	400	459	115
GSA Commissions		350	—	—	1,975	494
Insurance		6,869	6,925	6,925	27,477	6,869
Interest Expense	—	—	—	—	4,416	1,104
Legal & Accounting	4,563	4,563	1,500	(3,063)	13,175	3,294
Licenses & Fees		50	150	150	150	38
Marketing		4,500	2,500	2,500	360	90
Meals & Entertainment		1,150	1,500	1,500	4,598	1,150
Outside Services	477	1,055	2,500	2,023	4,221	1,055
Payroll Taxes		10,500	13,119	13,119	39,949	9,987
Postage/Deliveries		550	750	750	2,202	551
Recruiting	1,094	2,000	5,000	3,906	8,469	2,117
Rent	10,788	10,788	10,788	—	43,151	10,788
Reserve for Cancel. Subscr.		6,000	2,032	2,032	21,527	5,382
Salaries		120,000	150,773	150,773	422,280	105,570
Supplies	1,129	4,000	2,500	1,371	39,229	9,807
Telephone	581	2,350	2,800	2,219	7,257	1,814
Training		500	1,250	1,250	5,400	1,350
Trade Shows		1,000	—	—	3,990	998
Travel	41	5,000	6,000	5,959	18,379	4,595
Other Expenses	3,970	4,500	2,265	(1,705)	13,120	3,280
Total Expenses	29,866	194,602	224,012	194,146	710,697	177,674
Profit (Loss)	225,034	35,790	20,994	204,040	16,586	4,147

EXHIBIT 10.2 DAILY FLASH REPORT

then divided by the total number of months in the year thus far to arrive at the average value per month for each line item. This is a useful comparison to the budgeted amount for the current month, which is located in the third column. Yet another source of information is the forecasted result for the month (in the second column), which is the accountant's up-to-the-minute estimate of expected results for the current month. Finally, the first column contains the most recent actual results for the current month, which contains the least complete information until the month is nearly finished. By using four different estimates of financial results for the current month, the reader can draw his or her own conclusions regarding its most likely outcome.

In addition to the monthly information presented in the preceding report, the information in its first few rows details some key accounting measures, such as the volume of invoicing, and the cash and accounts receivable balances. Other measures, such as the total backlog, or the dollar volume of orders completed for the month, can also be added here.

10.3   MARGIN REPORTS

The status reports just described provide a high level of information to the reader. For a more detailed examination of operating results, it is useful to generate several types of margin reports. One option is noted in Exhibit 10.3, which reveals the gross margin of a series of company products, using their standard costs.

This reporting format reveals the gross margin for the sales volumes generated for the year-to-date or month for the listed products. The use of standard costs will reveal accurate margin information, as long as the standard costs are routinely compared to actual costs and adjusted to yield a close approximation to them. By using standards, many computer systems can automatically access all of the listed information and create the report with no human intervention.

Margins can also be presented by customer, as shown in Exhibit 10.4. This format is about the same as the one just shown in Exhibit 10.3, but is summarized by customer. Many accounting systems that are integrated with the production system can automatically provide this information, too. Note, however, that this report does not contain any of the additional sales, packaging, shipping, and customer service costs that are needed to maintain proper relations with customers. These added costs are not normally accessible through a standard costing system, and must be separately derived through an activity-based costing system and then manually added to this report format.

A more complex margin analysis is shown in Exhibit 10.5. This format divides the margins of all customers into high or low margin, with an arbitrary cutoff between the two of 30%. It also splits customers into high or low revenue volume, with an arbitrary cutoff at $100,000 per year. The exact cutoff will vary greatly by company, with the intention being to give management a good feel for which customers provide a combination of the highest margins and volumes (located in the upper right corner) and which are the least profitable ones (in the lower left corner). Also, all of the customers shown in the high-volume categories on the right side of the exhibit have their individual margin percentages listed next to them, for easy reference. Each of the four segments also contains a small block of information that lists the number of customers located within it, the total proportion and dollar amount of sales that they represent, and their combined gross margin. Though this is a labor-intensive report to create, it presents a great deal of information to management regarding which customers to cultivate, which ones to drop, which ones require a price increase, and which ones require additional sales efforts.

Standard Cost of Goods Sold Report
Sorted by Margin %

Item No.	Item Description	Qty Sold	Unit Price	Total Revenue	Unit Cost Material	Unit Cost Labor	Total Cost Material	Total Cost Labor	Margin%	Total Margin $
14003.221	Light Diffuser	3,500	0.025	88	0.002	0.032	9	113	-38.5%	-34
12231	Bolster Arm Cover	3,016	0.8	2,413	0.930	—	2,805	—	-16.3%	-392
12350.001	Cradle Rocker	643	15.64	10,057	14.364	1.077	9,236	692	1.3%	128
12200.7	Baby Bath	65,000	0.141	9,165	0.110	0.024	7,119	1,555	5.4%	491
14003.501	Magnet Cover	5,000	0.116	580	0.066	0.027	329	136	19.8%	115
11706	"Pail, 5 Gallon"	96	1.5	144	1.032	0.109	99	10	24.0%	34
14003.201	Key Pad	7,000	0.075	525	0.023	0.032	158	225	26.9%	141
12320.001	Baby Potty	1,710	7.95	13,595	4.304	1.357	7,360	2,321	28.8%	3,914
14039.02	Ruler, 6"	1,741	0.217	378	0.093	0.054	162	95	32.1%	121
14003.352	Terminal Block	20,000	0.1	2,000	0.040	0.026	795	522	34.1%	683
12006	Food Storage Tray	332,640	0.135	44,906	0.067	0.015	22,230	5,064	39.2%	17,612
14037.01	Remote Control Case	1,150	0.317	365	0.104	0.061	120	70	47.9%	175
14026.1	Medicine Spoon	5,000	0.092	460	0.033	0.015	166	72	48.1%	221
14052.021	Water Bottle	20,000	0.105	2,100	0.034	0.017	684	337	51.4%	1,079
14026.07	Key Case	56,000	0.084	4,704	0.014	0.027	790	1,492	51.5%	2,422
14003.64	Battery Holder	2,500	0.123	308	0.018	0.039	44	98	53.7%	165
14001.03	Battery Case	4,320	2.009	8,679	0.722	0.106	3,120	457	58.8%	5,103
14003.76	Light Pipe	21,000	0.145	3,045	0.015	0.037	316	776	64.1%	1,953
14052.01	Water Bottle Cap	22,000	0.093	2,046	0.024	0.008	529	179	65.4%	1,337
14025.046	"Gasket, 23mm"	106	0.179	19	0.017	0.044	2	5	66.0%	13
14010.096	Retaining Strip	3,000	0.412	1,236	0.054	0.057	161	170	73.3%	905
14025.02	Coin Holder	25,872	0.271	7,011	0.041	0.031	1,063	788	73.6%	5,161
14003.28	"Gasket, 35mm"	2,500	0.09	225	0.006	0.017	16	44	73.6%	166
14003.77	LCD Support Bracket	21,000	0.244	5,124	0.023	0.025	481	525	80.4%	4,118
				1,763,913			861,868	231,180	38.0%	670,866

EXHIBIT 10.3 STANDARD COST OF GOODS SOLD REPORT BY PRODUCT

Standard Margin by Customer Report

Item No.	Item Description	Customer Name	YTD Unit	Unit Price	Std Material Cost	Std Labor Cost	Std Machine Cost	Assembly Overhead Cost	Total Revenue	Total Expense	Total Margin	Direct Std % Margin	Total All Inclusive Margin %
14003	Light Diffuser	Exceptional Child Inc.	2,762	24.830	18.1537	2.0184	3.198	1.457	68,580	68,575	6	19%	0%
12231	Bolster Arm Cover	Exceptional Child Inc.	4,327	25.070	18.1019	2.0184	0.661	1.457	108,478	96,225	12,253	20%	11%
12350	Cradle Rocker	Exceptional Child Inc.	20	0.350	0.0255	0.0435	0.015	0.000	7	2	5	80%	76%
12201	Baby Bath	Exceptional Child Inc.	25	0.250	0.0113	0.0435	0.015	0.000	6	2	4	78%	72%
13250	Mophead	Exceptional Child Inc.	378	56.680	33.2162	5.7876	5.012	4.162	21,425	18,211	3,214	31%	15%
14004	Magnet Cover	Exceptional Child Inc.	17,800	43.600	27.5402	5.7876	5.012	4.162	776,080	756,524	19,556	24%	3%
11706	Pail, 5 Gallon	Anterior Designs	320,869	0.141	0.1095	0.0239	0.052	0.0000	45,243	59,446	(14,203)	5%	−31%
14003	Key Pad	Anterior Designs	45,000	0.230	0.0424	0.0283	0.042	0.0000	10,350	5,074	5,276	69%	51%
12320	Baby Potty	Anterior Designs	53,500	0.250	0.0505	0.0381	0.057	0.0000	13,375	7,769	5,606	65%	42%
13222	Ski Tip	Anterior Designs	3,146	25.670	11.8078	8.1774	2.516	0.202	80,758	71,427	9,331	22%	12%
12300	Diaper Pail	Backman Services	1,022	13.870	7.8078	0.5974	2.516	0.202	14,175	11,369	2,806	39%	20%
14039	Ruler, 6″	Backman Services	3,016	3.970	3.9700	0.0000	—	—	11,974	11,974	—	0%	0%
14003	Terminal Block	Backman Services	3,016	0.800	0.9300	0.0000	—	—	2,413	2,805	(392)	−16%	−16%
13207	Ski Tail	Backman Services	84,090	6.396	3.4643	0.9171	1.769	0.227	537,840	536,270	1,569	31%	0%
12006	Food Storage Tray	Backman Services	10	0.500	0.0671	0.0544	0.019	0.0000	5	1	4	76%	72%
14037	Remote Control Case	Backman Services	127,737	6.019	3.6483	0.6593	1.687	0.328	768,849	807,653	(38,804)	28%	−5%
14026	Medicine Spoon	Diversified Products	7,232	7.290	4.5440	0.6593	1.816	0.328	52,721	53,138	(417)	29%	−1%
14052	Water Bottle	Diversified Products	4,050	7.950	4.3039	1.3573	5.570	0.470	32,199	47,387	(15,188)	29%	−47%
14026	Key Case	Diversified Products	24,614	20.320	13.9105	2.3731	0.947	2.429	500,156	483,908	16,248	20%	3%
14001	Battery Holder	Diversified Products	43,228	6.237	2.5694	0.8685	3.863	0.190	269,591	323,832	(54,241)	45%	−20%
14001	Battery Case	Diversified Products	12	0.200	0.0282	0.0218	0.032	0.0000	2	1	1	75%	59%
14004	Light Pipe	Diversified Products	3,630	15.730	14.3636	1.0766	1.650	0.583	57,100	64,152	(7,052)	2%	−12%
14052	Water Bottle Cap	Diversified Products	25,500	8.915	6.2670	0.4943	0.897	0.291	227,322	202,724	24,599	24%	11%
14025	Gasket, 23mm	Automotive Designs	32,142	7.976	4.6375	0.9292	2.842	0.263	256,365	278,748	(22,383)	30%	−9%
14010	Retaining Strip	Automotive Designs	42,571	5.984	4.4709	0.6200	1.768	0.381	254,753	308,191	(53,438)	15%	−21%
14025	Coin Holder	Automotive Designs	11,881	1.951	0.6697	0.2208	0.431	0.0000	23,180	15,703	7,477	54%	32%
14003	Gasket, 35mm	Automotive Designs	1	13.748	9.3296	1.5807	0.309	0.972	14	12	2	21%	11%
14004	LCD Support	Automotive Designs	3,026	3.017	1.5511	0.3698	0.525	0.0000	9,128	7,400	1,728	36%	19%
									4,142,090	4,238,522	−96,432		−2%

EXHIBIT 10.4 STANDARD COST OF GOODS SOLD REPORT BY CUSTOMER

High Margin — Low Revenue

No. Customers = 30
Percent of Sales = 5%
Annual Sales = $531K
Annual Margin = 47%

AMG Industries
Audobon Park
Boulder Technology
Brindle Corporation
Bucktooth Inc.
Bushmaster Weaponry
Chemical Devices Corp.
Convertible Devices Corp.
Dutch-Made Devices
Englewood Instruments
Great Peaks & Sons
On Top Gourmet Foods
SMC Corp.
Huntington Brickworks
Initial Response Units
International Clearance Co.
Mann's Cutlery
Material Upgrade Company
Newco Pottery
Oliphaunt Fencing
Peak Industries
Quorum Software

High Margin — High Revenue

No. Customers = 10
Percent of Sales = 42%
Annual Sales = $4,313K
Annual Margin = 37%

	Margin %	Annual Dollars
Acme	33%	$ 607,600
Best Western	39%	$ 134,200
Champion	43%	$ 154,900
Estes Door Frames	38%	$ 340,400
Gates and Fencing Int'l	39%	$ 129,800
Hudson River Upholstery	35%	$1,586,200
Killer Kitchen Products	39%	$ 964,400
Monster Equipment	32%	$ 423,300
Sudden Coffee	41%	$ 440,100
Venture Home Foods	41%	$ 139,500
		$4,312,800

Low Margin — Low Revenue

No. Customers = 19
Percent of Sales = 5%
Annual Sales = $493K
Annual Margin = 11%

Aston Davidson Aerospace
Backup Services
Brush Logic
Defensive Innovations
Entirely Upscale Renderings
Fashionable Furniture
Gecko Lawn Furnishings
Halston Oil & Gas
Immediate Response Co.
Jervis Book Binders
Poly Cracker Bird Supply
Primary Rescue Services
Rocky Mountain Oil
Scott Primary Services
Sun Tanning Oil Co.
Tofu Deluxe

Low Margin — High Revenue

No. Customers = 9
Percent of Sales = 48%
Annual Sales = $4,871K
Annual Margin = 22%

	Margin %	Annual Dollars
Anterior Designs	29%	$ 204,000
Bombproof Draperies	14%	$ 130,900
Early Research Corp.	24%	$ 925,000
Engineered Solutions	25%	$ 256,400
Highland Scots	26%	$ 146,500
Kanberra Koala	19%	$1,559,500
Optimum Energy	22%	$ 904,500
Terrible Trouble Kid Stores	16%	$ 548,300
Vertical Drapery Company	24%	$ 196,000
		$4,871,100

Axis labels — Vertical: High Margin / 30% / Low Margin. Horizontal: Low Revenue / $100K / High Revenue.

EXHIBIT 10.5 CUSTOMER MARGIN ANALYSIS

10.4   CASH REPORTS

The standard cash forecast report is discussed in detail in Chapter 12. However, the accountant may wish to obtain additional cash-related information beyond the standard forecasting model. One possibility is to determine the accuracy level of the forecast on a weekly basis, in order to see if the assumptions or data used in the forecast must be changed to make it more accurate. An example of this reporting format is shown in Exhibit 10.6. This report lists the actual cash balance at the end of each week for the last few months, showing alongside each item the cash forecast that had been made one month prior to each actual cash balance. The dollar and percentage amount of each variance are then listed, as well as an explanation of any especially large variances. This can be a most instructive exercise, as the accountant will initially find significant variances between forecasted and actual cash balances; continual examination of the underlying problems that caused the variances is needed in order to eventually arrive at a more accurate cash forecasting system.

The most likely source of large changes in cash requirements tends to come from working capital, simply because of the large investment that is typically required in this area. To see how the main categories of working capital will vary over time, one can set up a combination of numerical and graphical information, as shown in Exhibit 10.7. That not only shows monthly totals for accounts receivable, accounts payable, and inventory, but also the trend line for working capital levels. This is a most useful tool for determining the existence of any problems related to a company's investment in working capital.

Cash Forecasting Accuracy Report
[Explanatory Notes Included if Variance Greater than 5%]

Week	Actual Cash Balance	Forecast 1 Mo. Ago	Variance	Percentage Variance	Explanatory Notes
7-Jan	2,275	2,075	200	9%	DEF customer paid early.
14-Jan	2,150	2,109	41	2%	
21-Jan	2,425	2,581	−156	−6%	ABC customer paid late.
28-Jan	2,725	2,843	−118	−4%	
4-Feb	3,125	3,000	125	4%	
11-Feb	3,225	3,305	−80	−2%	
18-Feb	3,495	3,450	45	1%	
25-Feb	3,445	2,942	503	15%	Bank error in recording check.
4-Mar	3,645	3,751	−106	−3%	
11-Mar	3,555	3,500	55	2%	
18-Mar	3,604	3,209	395	11%	Paid for capital expenditures.
25-Mar	3,704	3,589	115	3%	
1-Apr	3,754	3,604	150	4%	
8-Apr	3,879	3,802	77	2%	
15-Apr	3,939	3,921	18	0%	
22-Apr	3,864	3,900	−36	−1%	
29-Apr	4,264	3,781	483	11%	Customers took 2% early payment discount.
6-May	4,464	4,351	113	3%	
13-May	4,434	4,031	403	9%	Customers took 2% early payment discount.
20-May	4,188	4,000	188	4%	
27-May	4,339	4,503	−164	−4%	

EXHIBIT 10.6   CASH FORECASTING ACCURACY REPORT

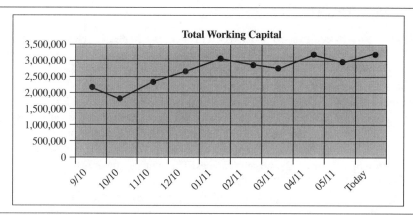

Month	Accounts Receivable	Inventory	Accounts Payable	Total Working Capital
9/10	2,028,000	1,839,000	1,604,000	2,263,000
10/10	1,663,000	1,614,000	1,423,000	1,854,000
11/10	1,498,000	1,784,000	933,000	2,349,000
12/10	1,664,000	1,932,000	942,000	2,654,000
01/11	2,234,000	2,011,000	1,152,000	3,089,000
02/11	2,450,000	2,273,000	1,862,000	2,861,000
03/11	2,042,000	2,419,000	1,671,000	2,790,000
04/11	3,036,000	2,715,000	2,575,000	3,176,000
05/11	2,998,000	2,588,000	2,585,000	3,001,000
Today	2,875,000	2,976,000	2,606,000	3,245,000

Exhibit 10.7   Working Capital Trend Line

10.5   SALES AND EXPENSE REPORTS

When actual sales differ from expectations, the accountant needs a report format that reveals exactly where the variance arose. The format shown in Exhibit 10.8 is a good way to show, customer by customer, the cause of the variance. This report shows both the monthly and year-to-date variance by customer. However, many organizations do not budget their sales by specific customer, unless there are ongoing orders from each one that are easy to predict. If so, this format can be reduced to a smaller number of line items that reveal variances only for specific market segments or groups of customers.

A similar type of format can be used for expense control. By using this approach, the report can be distributed to department managers, who can then issue it to the individuals within their departments who are responsible for specific expense line items. Of particular interest in this report is the last column, which notes the full-year budget for each expense line item. This number is placed next to the year-to-date actual expense and variance numbers, so that managers can see exactly how much allocated funding is still available to them for the rest of the year.

10.6   PAYROLL REPORTS

The largest expense item in many organizations is payroll, which exceeds even the cost of materials. Proper control of this cost requires a detailed report that lists the salary or wage cost of each employee in comparison to the original budget. Such a format is shown in Exhibit 10.9. In the exhibit, employees are grouped by department, with the budgeted

Customer Name	YTD Forecast	YTD Actual	Variance	Month Forecast	Month Actual	Variance
AC Dingo	58,000	73,506	15,506	21,000	8,417	−12,583
Admedix	285,000	738,205	453,205	85,000	178,489	93,489
Best Eastern	32,000	45,886	13,886	15,000	13,041	−1,959
BonaLisa	48,000	44,453	−3,547	8,000	10,868	2,868
Case Western	26,000	74,513	48,513	8,000	13,147	5,147
Champion Systems	24,000	24,493	493	0	11,480	11,480
Easy Go Services	45,000	45,589	589	15,000	17,548	2,548
EMC	1,779,396	2,488,239	708,843	723,878	1,094,675	370,797
Engineered Skating Products	47,000	58,800	11,800	25,000	18,074	−6,926
Estep Industries	26,000	83,858	57,858	12,000	26,539	14,539
Gates Plastics	40,000	42,630	2,630	14,000	12,395	−1,605
Great Plains Software	6,600	2,854	−3,746	2,200		−2,200
Great Deal Foods	0	25,678	25,678	0	25,678	25,678
Hudson & Sons	525,000	409,968	−115,032	300,000	91,459	−208,541
Hunter Stevenson	9,000	38,139	29,139	3,000	6,983	3,983
Innovative Boulder Tech.	22,000	44,970	22,970	14,000	15,001	1,001
Inovonics	9,000	30,173	21,173	3,000	8,386	5,386
Intermediate Diverse Foods	72,000	83,417	11,417	24,000	13,920	−10,080
Kountry Kitchen	350,265	371,051	20,786	138,795	66,964	−71,831
Magma Volcanic Gear	0	4,620	4,620	0	4,620	4,620
Martin Stevenson	9,000	11,647	2,647	3,000	3,975	975
Mile High Sun Systems	80,000	116,002	36,002	30,000	36,457	6,457
Miscellaneous	75,000	2,160	−72,840	25,000		−25,000
Optimus Stoves	390,000	423,465	33,465	120,000	100,274	−19,726
Polyseasonal Designs	27,000	28,063	1,063	5,000	7,244	2,244
Prime Target Company	3,600	1,000	−2,600	1,200	1,000	−200
Product Design Assoc.	5,000	12,348	7,348	5,000	4,020	−980
Progressive Ancillary Co.	25,000	6,402	−18,598	0	5,561	5,561
Ryco Boxes	0	7,387	7,387	0	3,381	3,381
Scott Paper Company	30,000	58,475	28,475	0	36,468	36,468
Sensory Deprivation Co.	0	810	810	0	810	810
Superior Furnishings	210,000	183,743	−26,257	60,000	49,493	−10,507
T. Rex Eatery	8,000	17,197	9,197	0	3,839	3,839
T-Pastry Company	0	2,500	2,500	0	2,500	2,500
Tenerific Kid Toys	0	431	431	0	431	431
Toxonomical Products	4,000	8,348	4,348	0		0
Tranway	9,000		−9,000	3,000		−3,000
Tristar Airways	60,000	10,831	−49,169	20,000	8,244	−11,756
Vendomatic Machinery	41,000	177,399	136,399	20,000	99,641	79,641
Volway Distribution	46,000	118,023	72,023	14,000	27,947	13,947
Westway Oil & Gas	0	2,889	2,889	0	1,445	1,445
Totals	4,426,861	5,920,162	1,493,301	1,718,073	2,030,414	312,341

EXHIBIT 10.8   FORCASTED SALES VERSUS ACTUAL SALES REPORT

salary or wage level for each person noted in bold. Actual pay on an annualized basis is then shown for each successive month of the year. This format gives an extremely detailed view of exactly where a company is investing its payroll dollars. If there are too many employees to make the report easily readable, they can also be summarized by job title within departments, or simply by department, though some of the effectiveness of the report will be lost with the higher degree of summarization.

The report shown in Exhibit 10.9 may not include the overtime pay for nonexempt employees, since this information could skew the annualized payroll information shown. If overtime is a significant proportion of payroll, then it can be shown separately, as in

Name	Department	Budget	Jan	Feb	Mar	Apr	May	Jun
Bowery, Dan	Assembly	28,752	19,524	19,524	19,524	20,267	20,267	20,216
Johnson, Gregory	Assembly	28,752	33,052	33,052	33,052	34,944	32,968	32,272
Monfort, Pat	Assembly	43,260	46,521	46,521	46,521	47,060	47,060	47,060
Zwonter, Steve	Assembly	39,996	47,788	47,788	47,788	47,788	45,019	36,078
Mayes, Dennis	Engineering	48,456	36,504	36,504	36,504	36,504	36,504	38,000
Open	Engineering	48,456	0	0	0	0	0	0
Linger, Lowell	Logistics	25,392	39,750	39,250	39,500	39,000	36,595	41,550
Rose, Jim	Logistics	55,116	53,200	54,990	54,990	54,990	54,990	55,000
Stewart, Thomas	Logistics	25,392	33,058	31,954	32,058	34,359	30,888	29,571
Wallace, Loretha	Logistics	25,392	30,966	30,966	30,966	30,966	24,115	23,870
Delany, Eric	Maintenance	35,880	29,500	29,500	34,320	33,839	34,320	32,020
Henderson, Alex	Maintenance	35,880	49,321	50,721	49,384	51,155	49,348	29,264
Norris, Aaron	Maintenance	35,880	50,960	50,960	50,960	50,960	54,379	67,227
Allen, Mark	Process Tech	40,992	38,972	39,067	38,555	41,574	33,618	44,630
Phorest, Michael	Process Tech	40,992	30,555	30,706	30,541	29,185	31,434	30,145
Short, Bob	Process Tech	None	30,000	32,000	32,000	32,877	32,071	26,018
Anderson, Carl	Production Mgmt	110,000	110,000	110,000	110,000	110,006	110,006	110,000
Graham, Lee	Production Mgmt	42,996	32,000	32,000	34,996	34,996	34,996	35,000
Honest, Darrell	Production Mgmt	70,800	70,798	70,798	70,798	70,798	70,798	70,799
Lawrence, Michael	Production Mgmt	42,996	47,996	47,996	47,996	47,996	47,996	48,000
Summers, Theresa	Production Mgmt	42,996	36,010	36,010	36,010	36,010	36,010	36,000
Bella, Donna	Quality Assurance	24,996	24,031	24,258	24,258	23,465	24,258	22,381
McDonald, Robert	Quality Assurance	24,996	25,386	25,971	25,069	24,063	30,069	27,585
Mills, Alan	Quality Assurance	50,004	49,998	49,998	49,998	49,998	49,998	50,000
Smith, George	Quality Assurance	24,996	18,538	18,538	18,538	18,538	18,528	18,538
Walmsley-Dunnet, Al	Quality Assurance	None	26,000	26,000	26,000	26,000	26,000	26,000
Bossy, Frank	S, G & A	84,456	82,004	82,004	82,004	82,004	82,004	82,000
Gainer, George	S, G & A	124,992	125,008	125,008	125,008	125,008	125,008	125,000
Hammit, Robert	S, G & A	46,056	45,240	45,240	45,240	45,240	45,916	46,000
Spudsit, Jeffrey	S, G & A	75,000	82,550	82,550	82,550	82,550	82,550	89,196
		1,323,872	1,345,230	1,349,874	1,355,128	1,362,140	1,347,713	1,339,420

EXHIBIT 10.9 ANNUALIZED PAY LEVELS REPORT COMPARED TO BUDGET

	1/4	1/18	2/1	2/15	3/01	3/15	3/29	4/12	4/26
Engineering									
Nelson, Mark	23%	6%	15%	10%	18%	15%	0%	6%	18%
Maintenance									
Delatore, Alex	31%	15%	13%	24%	16%	26%	8%	15%	36%
Hansen, Erik	0%	11%	16%	41%	39%	32%	31%	28%	41%
Lage, Laurence	15%	19%	13%	26%	39%	21%	24%	4%	
Mold Shop									
Davidson, Raymond	0%	5%	0%	5%	13%	6%	10%	8%	18%
Miller, Jerry	11%	31%	10%	9%	20%	25%	16%	25%	11%
Stallsworth, Delbert	25%	23%	19%	34%	14%	30%	28%	26%	30%
Process Technicians									
Allen, Aaron	8%	13%	28%	21%	40%	30%	0%	21%	11%
Barron, Alejandro					14%	54%	44%	0%	15%
Estrada, Steve	15%	15%	11%	11%	8%	11%	10%	9%	11%
Michels, Shayne					36%	25%	33%	11%	34%
Reynolds, Mike	0%	0%	11%	0%	11%	34%	11%	14%	10%
Sherman, William					11%	11%	5%	0%	11%
Quality Assurance									
McDonald, Theresa	11%	0%	14%	0%	25%	6%	13%	0%	10%
Reidenbach, Donna	10%	14%	8%	28%	30%	9%	19%	25%	24%
Smith, Jacqueline	0%	13%	13%	13%	13%	13%	13%	0%	13%
Logistics									
Chhoeung, Lin					0%	0%	0%	0%	13%
Gage, Clarence							39%	9%	41%
Jacques, Kum	10%	0%	33%	45%	20%	23%	51%	29%	30%
Stewart, Loretha							26%	53%	46%
Webber, Ricky							0%	1%	0%
SG&A									
Courtney, Debbie	8%	9%	6%	13%	5%	13%	6%	13%	8%
Martin, Beverly	3%	1%	14%	6%	4%	0%	3%	0%	0%
Newby, Ginger	4%	9%	6%	9%	11%	10%	9%	9%	15%
Assembly									
Bowden, Greg					13%	5%	3%	23%	29%	40%
Jackson, Mike					18%	16%	8%	21%	6%	33%
Williams, Rosa					8%	3%	11%	20%	0%	74%
Average of All Overtime	10%	11%	13%	17%	17%	17%	17%	13%	23%

EXHIBIT 10.10   OVERTIME REPORT BY EMPLOYEE

the report format noted in Exhibit 10.10. This report assumes that payrolls are completed once every two weeks, and itemizes the percentage of overtime paid by person within each department. This is most useful if issued to department managers immediately following each payroll, so that they can see who consistently works excessive amounts of overtime.

10.7   GRAPHICAL REPORT LAYOUTS

Many of the preceding reports can be modified to fit into a more easily readable graph format, of which there are many varieties. Six possible graph types are shown in Exhibit 10.11. The formats presented in the exhibit are:

- *Pie chart.* This graph is shown in a three-dimensional format, and can also be presented in a two-dimensional layout (especially when there is more information to pack into the chart). It is best used to show the proportion of parts to the whole

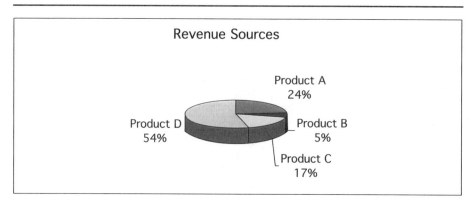

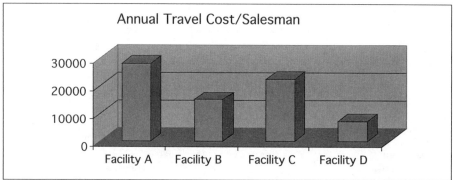

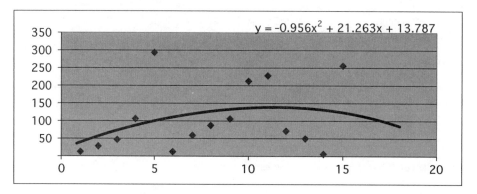

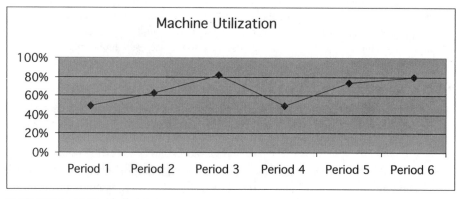

Exhibit 10.11   Examples of Graphical Report Formats

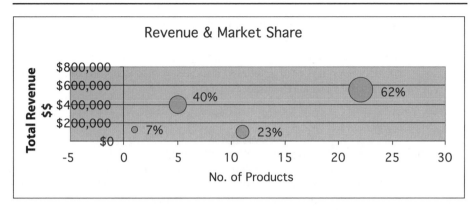

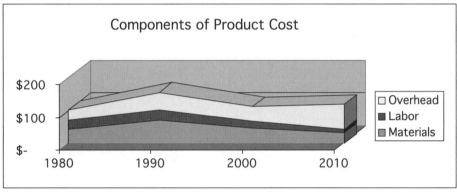

EXHIBIT 10.12   EXAMPLES OF GRAPHICAL REPORT FORMATS (*Continued*)

amount, and cannot be used to show more than a half-dozen items without severely cluttering the graph.

- *Bar chart.* Immediately below the pie chart is a bar chart, also in three-dimensional format. It can be used to compare the amount of a similar item for different entities (in the exhibit, it compares the travel cost for different corporate facilities), and can also be used for a limited amount of trend line analysis. However, similar to the pie chart, it can easily become overloaded if too much data is presented.

- *Scattergraph.* The scattergraph is shown at the bottom of the first page of graphs. It is very useful for pattern analysis, since a large number of data points can be entered into the graph, and then fitted with a trend line that is a "best fit" based on the positions of all data items. As shown in the graph, the slope formula for the line can also be shown.

- *Trend line.* This graph is shown at the top of the second page of graphs. It is heavily used to reveal patterns that occur over time, such as expense levels over multiple periods. It is best not to clutter this graph with too many lines; rather, create a separate graph for each trend in order to more clearly present the data.

- *Bubble chart.* The bubble chart is shown immediately below the trend line graph. This format is more rarely used, since it is designed specifically to reveal market share information.

- *Area chart.* This graph is located at the bottom of the second page of graphs. It resembles a bar chart, in that data can be stacked on top of each other, while also presenting the stacked information over a series of time periods, as is done by a trend line. It is useful for seeing changes in the proportions of revenues or expenses over time. However, it is easily cluttered if too many data items are stacked on top of each other, and so should be used with care.

10.8 SUMMARY

It is evident from the wide array of internal reports presented here that the types and formats of reports available to the accountant are limited only by his or her imagination. None of the reports shown here will precisely fit every organization's needs—on the contrary, the accountant is expected not only to custom-design reports that meet a company's specific informational requirements, but also to continuously modify them as circumstances change over time.

CHAPTER **11**

FOREIGN CURRENCY TRANSLATION

11.1 INTRODUCTION

In today's world of multinational business transactions, even the smallest company may find that it deals with partners in other countries to a large extent. If so, there are a number of transactions, such as accounts receivable and accounts payable, as well as loans and forward exchange contracts, that may be denominated in foreign currencies. Larger organizations may also have foreign subsidiaries that deal primarily in foreign currency transactions. In either case, generally accepted accounting principles state that the transactions must be converted back into U.S. dollars when they are accounted for in a company's financial statements. Since there is some exchange rate risk associated with conducting business in other currencies, this conversion will likely result in the recognition of some gains or losses associated with transactions that are denominated in foreign currencies. In this chapter, we will review how foreign currency translation is accomplished in order to meet the objectives of GAAP.

The key consideration when making foreign currency translations is that when the conversion is complete, we will see the accounting performance in a foreign currency accurately translated into precisely the same performance in U.S. dollars. In other words, a foreign subsidiary whose financial statements have specific current ratios, gross margins, and net profits will see the same results when translated into a report presentation in U.S. dollars.

The current rate method and the remeasurement method are the two techniques used to translate the financial results of a foreign entity's operations into the current rate of its corporate parent. These methods are explained in the following sections.

11.2 THE CURRENT RATE TRANSLATION METHOD

The *current rate translation method* is used when a currency besides the U.S. dollar is determined to be the primary currency used by a subsidiary. This approach is usually selected when a subsidiary's operations are not integrated into those of its United States–based parent, if its financing is primarily in that of the local currency, or if the subsidiary conducts most of its transactions in the local currency.

However, one cannot use this method if the country in which the subsidiary is located suffers from a high rate of inflation, which is defined as a cumulative rate of 100% or more over the most recent three years. In this case, the *remeasurement method* must be used (as described later in this chapter). If the local economy is considered to no longer be inflationary, then the reporting method may be changed back to the current rate method; when this happens, the accounting staff must convert the financial statements of the impacted subsidiary back into the local currency using the exchange rate on the date when the determination is made.

To complete the current rate translation method, the first order of business is to determine the functional currency of the subsidiary. In some locations, a subsidiary may deal with a variety of currencies, which makes this a less-than-obvious decision. It should be the currency in which the bulk of its transactions and financing is used. Next, convert all of the subsidiary's transactions to this functional currency. One should continue to use the same functional currency from year to year in order to provide a reasonable basis of comparison when multiple years of financial results are included in the corporate parent's financial results.

The next step is to convert all assets and liabilities of the subsidiary to U.S. dollars at the current rate of exchange as of the date of the financial statements. The following conversion rules apply:

- Revenues and expenses that have occurred throughout the current fiscal year are converted at a weighted-average rate of exchange for the entire year. A preferable approach is to convert them at the exchange rates in effect on the dates when they occurred, but this is considered too labor-intensive to be practical in most situations.

- Stockholder's equity is converted at the historical rate of exchange. However, changes to retained earnings within the current reporting period are recorded at the weighted average rate of exchange for the year, since they are derived from revenues and expenses that were also recorded at the weighted average rate of exchange.

- Dividends declared during the year are recorded at the exchange rate on the date of declaration.

- Any resulting translation adjustments should be stored in the equity section of the corporate parent's consolidated balance sheet. This account is cumulative, so one should separately report in the footnotes to the financial statements the change in the translation adjustments account as a result of activities in the reporting period.

11.3   EXAMPLE OF THE CURRENT RATE METHOD

A division of the Oregon Clock Company is located in Mexico. This division maintains its books in pesos, borrows pesos from a local bank, and conducts the majority of its operations within Mexico. Accordingly, its functional currency is the peso, which requires the parent's accounting staff to record the division's results using the current rate method.

The peso exchange rate at the beginning of the year is assumed to be .08 to the dollar, while the rate at the end of the year is assumed to be .10 to the dollar. For the purposes of this example, the blended full-year rate of exchange for the peso is assumed to

	Pesos	Exchange Rate	U.S. Dollars
Assets			
Cash	427	.08	34
Accounts Receivable	1,500	.08	120
Inventory	2,078	.08	166
Fixed Assets	3,790	.08	303
Total Assets	7,795		623
Liabilities & Equity			
Accounts Payable	1,003	.08	80
Notes Payable	4,250	.08	340
Common Stock	2,100	.10	210
Additional Paid-in Capital	428	.10	43
Retained Earnings	14	Note 1	0
Translation Adjustments	—	—	–50
Total Liabilities & Equity	7,795		623

Note 1: As noted in the income statement.

Exhibit 11.1   Balance Sheet Conversion Under the Current Rate Method

be .09 to the dollar. The Mexican division's balance sheet is shown in Exhibit 11.1, while its income statement is shown in Exhibit 11.2. Note that the net income figure derived from Exhibit 11.2 is incorporated into the retained earnings statement at the bottom of Exhibit 11.2, and is incorporated from there into the retained earnings line item in Exhibit 11.1. For simplicity, the beginning retained earnings figure in Exhibit 11.2 is assumed to be zero, implying that the company is in its first year of existence.

11.4   THE REMEASUREMENT METHOD

The remeasurement method is used when the U.S. dollar is designated as the primary currency in which transactions are recorded at a foreign location. Another clear indicator of when this method is used is when the subsidiary has close operational integration with its U.S. parent, or when most of its financing, sales, and expenses are denominated in dollars.

Under this method, we translate not only cash, but also any transactions that will be settled in cash (mostly accounts receivable and payable, as well as loans) at the current exchange rate as of the date of the financial statements. All other assets and liabilities

	Pesos	Exchange Rate	U.S. Dollars
Revenue	6,750	.09	608
Expenses	6,736	.09	607
Net Income	14		1
Beginning Retained Earnings	0		0
Add: Net Income	14	.09	0
Ending Retained Earnings	14		0

Exhibit 11.2   Income Statement Conversion Under the Current Rate Method

(such as inventory, prepaid items, fixed assets, trademarks, goodwill, and equity) will be settled at the historical exchange rate on the date when these transactions occurred.

There are a few cases where the income statement is impacted by the items on the balance sheet that have been translated using historical interest rates. For example, the cost of goods sold will be impacted when inventory that has been translated at a historical exchange rate is liquidated. When this happens, the inventory valuation at the historical exchange rate is charged through the income statement. The same approach is used for the depreciation of fixed assets and the amortization of intangible items.

Other income statement items primarily involve transactions that arise throughout the reporting year of the subsidiary. For these items, it would be too labor-intensive to determine the exact exchange rate for each item at the time it occurred. Instead, one can determine the weighted average exchange rate for the entire reporting period, and apply this average to the income statement items that have occurred during that period.

11.5   EXAMPLE OF THE REMEASUREMENT METHOD

A simplified example of a corporate subsidiary's (located in Mexico) balance sheet is shown in Exhibit 11.3 (which is the same balance sheet previously shown in Exhibit 11.1). The peso exchange rate at the beginning of the year is assumed to be .08 to the dollar, while the rate at the end of the year is assumed to be .10 to the dollar. The primary difference in calculation from the current rate method shown earlier in Exhibit 11.1 is that the exchange rate for the inventory and fixed assets accounts have changed from the year-end rate to the rate at which they are assumed to have been originated at an earlier date. Also, there is no translation adjustment account in the equity section, as was the case under the current rate method.

A highly abbreviated income statement is shown in Exhibit 11.4. For the purposes of this exhibit, the blended full-year rate of exchange for the peso is assumed to be .09 to the dollar. Note that the net income figure derived from Exhibit 11.4 is incorporated into the retained earnings statement at the bottom of Exhibit 11.4 and is incorporated from there into the retained earnings line item in Exhibit 11.3.

	Pesos	Exchange Rate	U.S. Dollars
Assets			
Cash	427	.08	34
Accounts Receivable	1,500	.08	120
Inventory	2,078	.10	208
Fixed Assets	3,790	.10	379
Total Assets	7,795		741
Liabilities & Equity			
Accounts Payable	1,003	.08	80
Notes Payable	4,250	.08	340
Common Stock	2,100	.10	210
Additional Paid-in Capital	428	.10	43
Retained Earnings	14	Note 1	68
Total Liabilities & Equity	7,795		741

Note 1: As noted in the income statement.

EXHIBIT 11.3   BALANCE SHEET CONVERSION UNDER THE REMEASUREMENT METHOD

	Pesos	Exchange Rate	U.S. Dollars
Revenue	6,750	.09	608
Goodwill Amortization	500	.08	40
Other Expenses	6,236	.09	561
Remeasurement Gain	—		**61**
Net Income	14		68
Beginning Retained Earnings	0		0
Add: Net Income	14		68
Ending Retained Earnings	14		68

EXHIBIT 11.4   INCOME STATEMENT CONVERSION UNDER THE REMEASUREMENT METHOD

A major issue is that, under the current rate translation method, there was a translation *loss* of $50, while the remeasurement approach resulted in a translation *gain* of $61. This was caused by a difference in the assumptions used in deriving the exchange rate that in turn was used to convert the inventory and fixed asset accounts from pesos into dollars. Consequently, the choice of conversion methods used will have a direct impact on the reported level of profitability.

For smaller companies that only rarely deal with foreign exchange transactions, there is no need to formally recall the details of the preceding translation methods. Instead, if they only participate in an occasional sale transaction, they can simply record the initial sale and related account receivable based on the spot exchange rate on the date when the transaction is initially completed. From that point forward, the amount of the recorded sale will not change—only the related receivable will be altered based on the spot exchange rate as of the date of the balance sheet on which it is reported, adjusting it up or down to reflect the existence of a potential gain or loss at the time of the eventual collection of the receivable. The final gain or loss will be recorded when the receivable is settled, using the spot rate on that date. This procedure will cover the most common transactions that a small business will encounter.

11.6   DECISION TREE

The decision tree shown in Exhibit 11.5 can be used to determine whether one should use the current rate method or remeasurement method when translating the financial statements of a foreign subsidiary into the currency of the corporate parent.

11.7   TRANSLATION OF FOREIGN CURRENCY TRANSACTIONS

The gains and losses resulting from various translation adjustments are treated in different ways, with some initially being stored in the balance sheet and others being recorded at once in the income statement. Here are the key rules to remember:

- If a company is directly engaged in foreign exchange transactions that are denominated in foreign currencies, then any translation adjustments to U.S. dollars that result in gains or losses should be immediately recognized in the income statement. The company can continue to make these adjustments for changes between the last reporting date and the date of the current financial statements, and may continue to do so until the underlying transactions have been concluded.

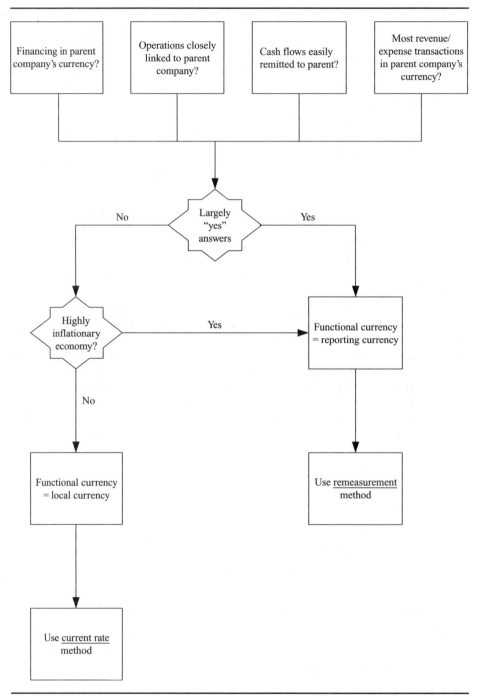

EXHIBIT 11.5   TYPE OF TRANSLATION METHOD DECISION TREE

Example of foreign currency transaction reporting: The Louisiana Backhoe Company (LBC) sells backhoes to a variety of countries in the European Union, all of which are paid for in euros. It sold $200,000 of backhoes to Germany on March 15. The receivable was still outstanding on March 31, which was the date of the quarterly financial statements. As of that date, the exchange rate of the euro has dropped by 1%, so LBC has an unrecognized loss of $2,000. It records this as a loss on foreign currency transactions, and credits its Accounts receivable account to reduce the amount of its receivable asset. When payment on the receivable is made to LBC on April 15, the exchange rate has returned to its level on the sale date of March 15. LBC must now record a gain on its books of $2,000 to offset the loss it had previously recorded.

- Do not report gains or losses on transactions of a long-term nature when accounted for by the equity method. These transactions are defined as those with no settlement date planned in the foreseeable future. Instead, include these transactions in the standard translation procedure used to translate the financial statements of a subsidiary into the currency of its corporate parent.

- If a foreign entity has multiple distinct operations, it is possible that some have different functional currencies. If so, the accountant should regularly review the foreign entity's operations to determine the correct functional currency to use, and translate their financial results accordingly. However, if the results of a selected operation on the financial reports of a foreign entity are insignificant, there is no requirement to break out its financial statements using a different functional currency.

- If there has been a material change in an exchange rate in which a company's obligations or subsidiary results are enumerated, and the change has occurred subsequent to the date of financial statements that are being included in a company's audited results, then the change and its impact on the financial statements should be itemized in a footnote that accompanies the audited results. An example is noted in Chapter 9, Footnotes.

11.8   EXCHANGE RATES USED FOR CALCULATIONS

There can be some confusion regarding the precise exchange rate to be used when conducting foreign currency translations. Here are some guidelines:

- If there is no published foreign exchange rate available on the specific date when a transaction occurred that requires translation, one should use the rate for the date that most immediately follows the date of the transaction.

- If the date of a financial statement that is to be converted from a foreign currency is different from the date of the financial statements into which they are to be converted into U.S. dollars, then use the date of the foreign currency financial statements as the date for the exchange rate to be used as the basis for translation.

- If there is more than one published exchange rate available that can be used as the basis for a translation, use the rate that could have been used as the basis for the exchange of funds that could then be used to remit dividends to shareholders. Alternatively, use the rate at which a settlement of the entire related transaction could have been completed.

11.9   INTERCOMPANY TRANSACTIONS

When the results of a parent company and its subsidiaries are combined for financial statement reporting purposes, the gains or losses resulting from intercompany foreign exchange transactions must be reported in the consolidated statements. This happens when the parent has a receivable denominated in the currency of the subsidiary, or vice versa, and a change in the exchange rate results in a gain or loss. Thus, even though the intercompany transaction is purged from the consolidated financial statement, the associated gain or loss must still be reported. An example of an intercompany transaction is as follows:

> The Seely Furniture Company owns a sawmill in Canada that supplies all of its wood raw materials. The subsidiary holds receivables from the corporate parent that are denominated in U.S. dollars. During the year, there has been a steady increase in the value of the dollar, resulting in a conversion into more Canadian dollars than was the case when each receivable was originally created. By the end of the year, the subsidiary has recorded a gain on currency transactions of $42,000 Canadian dollars. Accordingly, the Seely corporate parent records the gain on its books, denominated in U.S. dollars. Because the year-end exchange rate between the two currencies was $0.73 Canadian per U.S. dollar, the subsidiary's gain is recorded as a gain in U.S. dollars of $30,660 ($42,000 Canadian × 0.73 exchange rate) on the books of the parent.

11.10   SUMMARY

This chapter has described several approaches for converting transactions and financial statements that are denominated in foreign currencies into U.S. dollars. A good knowledge of the rules upon which these conversions are based is essential for determining the correct method of translation. This can have an impact on the recognition or nonrecognition of translation gains and losses.

PART FOUR

ELEMENTS OF THE BALANCE SHEET AND INCOME STATEMENT

CHAPTER 12

CASH, PREPAID EXPENSES, AND INVESTMENTS

12.1 INTRODUCTION

The reporting of cash is one of the easiest parts of the balance sheet to complete, though the same cannot be said for a variety of investments. Accordingly, the bulk of this chapter covers the accounting for available-for-sale, held-to-maturity, and trading securities, as well as fair value, and cash flow. The footnote disclosures required for these items are covered in Chapter 9.

12.2 CASH

If there is a short-term restriction on cash, such as a requirement that it be held in a sinking fund in anticipation of the payment of a corresponding debt within a year, then it should still be itemized as a current asset, but as a separate line item. If there is a long-term restriction on cash, such as a compensating balance agreement that is linked to debt that will not be paid off within the current year, then the cash must be itemized as a long-term asset. Alternatively, if a compensating balance agreement is tied to a loan that matures within the current period, then it may be recorded separately as a current asset.

If a company issues checks for which there are not sufficient funds on hand, it will find itself in a negative cash situation as reported on its balance sheet. Rather than show a negative cash balance there, it is better to shift the amount of the excess checks back into the Accounts Payable liability account, thereby leaving the reported cash balance at or near zero.

Cash held in foreign currencies should be included in the Cash account on the balance sheet, subject to two restrictions. First, it must be converted to U.S. dollars at the prevailing exchange rate as of the balance sheet date. Second, the funds must be readily convertible into U.S. dollars; if not (perhaps due to currency restrictions by the foreign government), the cash cannot properly be classified as a current asset, and instead must be classified as a long-term asset. This later item is a key issue for those organizations that want to report the highest possible current ratio by shifting foreign currency holdings into the Cash account.

12.3 PREPAID EXPENSES

Prepaid expenses are itemized as current assets on the balance sheet and should include early payments on any expenditures that would have been made during the next 12 months. For example, prepayments on key man life insurance, rent, or association fees would be charged to this account. There should be a supporting schedule for this account, detailing each line item charged to it and the amortization schedule over which each item will be ratably charged to expense.

The Prepaid expense account does *not* include deposits, since they are typically not converted back to cash until the end of the agreements requiring their original payment, which may be some years in the future. For example, the usual one-month rent deposit required with a building lease agreement cannot be paid back until the lease term has expired. Instead, deposits are usually recorded in the "Other Assets" or "Deposits" accounts, which are listed as noncurrent assets on the balance sheet.

12.4 ACCOUNTING FOR MARKETABLE EQUITY SECURITIES

Marketable securities are investments that can be easily liquidated through an organized exchange, such as the New York Stock Exchange. If a company also holds securities that are intended for the control of another entity, then these securities should be segregated as a long-term investment. Marketable securities must be grouped into one of the following three categories at the time of purchase and reevaluated periodically to see if they still belong in the designated categories:

- *Available for sale.* This category includes both debt and equity securities. It contains those securities that do not readily fall into either of the following two categories. It can include investments in other companies that constitute less than 20% of total ownership. These securities are reported on the balance sheet at their fair value, while unrealized gains and losses are charged to an equity account and reported in other comprehensive income in the current period. The balance in the equity account is only eliminated upon sale of the underlying securities. If a permanent reduction in the value of an individual security occurs, the unrealized loss is charged against earnings, resulting in a new and lower cost basis in the remaining investment. Any subsequent increase in the value of such an investment above the new cost basis cannot be formally recognized in earnings until the related security is sold, and so the interim gains will be temporarily "parked" in the Unrealized gains account in the equity section of the balance sheet.

  All interest, realized gains or losses, and debt amortization are recognized within the continuing operations section of the income statement. The listing of these securities on the balance sheet under either current or long-term assets is dependent upon their ability to be liquidated in the short term and to be available for disposition within that time frame, unencumbered by any obligations.

- *Held to maturity.* This category only includes debt securities that the company has both the intent and ability to hold until their time of maturity. Their amortized cost is recorded on the balance sheet. These securities are likely to be listed on the balance sheet as long-term assets.

   If marketable securities are shifted into the held-to-maturity category from debt securities in the available-for-sale category, their unrealized holding gain or loss should continue to be stored in the equity section, while being gradually amortized down to zero over the remaining life of each security.

- *Trading securities.* This category includes both debt and equity securities that the company intends to sell in the short term for a profit. It can include investments in other companies constituting less than 20% of total ownership. They are recorded on the balance sheet at their fair value. This type of marketable security is always positioned in the balance sheet as a current asset.

No matter how an investment is categorized, a material decline in its fair value subsequent to the balance sheet date but prior to the release of the financial statements should be disclosed. Further, clear evidence of permanent impairment in the value of available-for-sale securities prior to the release date of the financial statements is grounds for restatement to recognize permanent impairment of the investment.

Examples of available-for-sale transactions: The Arabian Knights Security Company has purchased $100,000 of equity securities, which it does not intend to sell in the short term for profit and therefore designates as available for sale. Its initial entry to record the transaction is as follows:

	Debit	Credit
Investments—available for sale	$100,000	
Cash		$100,000

After a month, the fair market value of the securities drops by $15,000, but management considers the loss to be a temporary decline and so does not record a loss in current earnings. However, it must still alter the value of the investment on the balance sheet to show its fair value and report the loss in Other Comprehensive Income, which requires the following entry:

	Debit	Credit
Unrealized loss on security investment (reported in Other Comprehensive Income)	$15,000	
Investments—available for sale		$15,000

Management then obtains additional information indicating that the loss is likely to be a permanent one, so it then recognizes the loss with the following entry:

	Debit	Credit
Loss on equity securities	$15,000	
Unrealized loss on security investment (reported in Other Comprehensive Income)		$15,000

Another month passes, and the fair value of the investment rises by $3,500. Since this gain exceeds the value of the newly written-down investment, management cannot recognize it, even though the new value of the investment would still be less than its original amount. Instead, the following entry is used to adjust the investment value on the balance sheet:

	Debit	Credit
Investments—available for sale	$3,500	
Unrealized gain on security investment		$3,500
(recorded in Other Comprehensive Income)		

Examples of trading transactions: The Arabian Knights Security Company purchases $50,000 of equity securities that it intends to trade for a profit in the short term. Given its intentions, these securities are added to the corporate portfolio of trading securities with the following entry:

	Debit	Credit
Investments—held for trading	$50,000	
Cash		$50,000

After two months, the fair value of these trading securities declines by $3,500. The company recognizes the change in current earnings with the following entry:

	Debit	Credit
Loss on security investment	$3,500	
Investments—held for trading		$3,500

Later in the year, the fair value of the securities experiences a sudden surge, resulting in a value increase of $5,750. The company records the change with the following entry:

	Debit	Credit
Investments—held for trading	$5,750	
Gain on security investments		$5,750

12.5   TRANSFERS BETWEEN AVAILABLE-FOR-SALE AND TRADING INVESTMENTS

An investment designated as a trading security can be shifted into the available-for-sale portfolio of investments with no recognition of a gain or loss on the value of the investment, since this type of investment should have been adjusted to its fair value in each reporting period already. If a gain or loss has arisen since the last adjustment to fair value, this amount should be recognized at the time of the designation change.

If an investment designated as an available-for-sale security is shifted into the trading portfolio of investments, any gain or loss required to immediately adjust its value to fair value should be made at once. This entry should include an adjustment from any prior write-down in value that may have occurred when securities were classified as available-for-sale. An example of transfer from the trading portfolio to the Available-for-sale portfolio is as follows:

The Arabian Knights Security Company owns $17,500 worth of equity securities that it had originally intended to sell for a profit in the short term, and had so classified the investment in its trading portfolio. Its intent has now changed, and it wishes to hold the securities for a considerably longer period, so it must shift the securities into the Available-for-sale account. It had marked the securities to market one month previously, but now the securities have lost $350 of value. The company records the following entry to reclassify the securities and recognize the additional loss:

	Debit	Credit
Investments—available for sale	$17,150	
Loss on equity securities	350	
Investments—held for trading		$17,500

An example of transfer from the Available-for-sale portfolio to the Trading portfolio is as follows:

The Arabian Knights Security Company finds that it must liquidate $250,000 of its Available-for-sale portfolio in the short term. This investment had previously been marked down to $250,000 from an initial investment value of $275,000, and its value has since risen by $12,000. The incremental gain must now be recognized in current income. The entry is as follows:

	Debit	Credit
Investments—held for trading	$262,000	
Investments—available for sale		$250,000
Gain on security investments		12,000

12.6   ACCOUNTING FOR INVESTMENTS IN DEBT SECURITIES

A debt security can be classified as either held for trading or available for sale (as previously defined for equity securities), or as held to maturity. The held-to-maturity portfolio is intended for any debt securities that a company has the intent and ability to retain for their full term until maturity is reached. An investment held in the held-to-maturity portfolio is recorded at its historical cost, which is not changed at any time during the holding period, unless it is shifted into a different investment portfolio. The only exceptions to this rule are (1) the periodic amortization of any discount or premium from the face value of a debt instrument, depending on the initial purchase price, and (2) clear evidence of a permanent reduction in the value of the investment.

Examples of held-to-maturity transactions: The Arabian Knights Security Company purchases $82,000 of debt securities at face value. The company has both the intent and ability to hold the securities to maturity. Given its intentions, these securities are added to the corporate portfolio of held-to-maturity securities with the following entry:

	Debit	Credit
Investment in debt securities—held to maturity	$82,000	
Cash		$82,000

The fair value of the investment subsequently declines by $11,000. There is no entry to be made, since the investment is recorded at its historical cost. However, the company receives additional information that the debt issuer has filed for bankruptcy and intends to repay debt holders at 50 cents on the dollar. Since management considers this to be a permanent reduction, a charge of $41,000 is recorded in current income with the following entry:

	Debit	Credit
Loss on debt investment	$41,000	
Investment in debt securities—held to maturity		$41,000

The company subsequently learns that the debt issuer is instead able to pay 75 cents on the dollar. This increase in value of $20,500 is not recorded in a journal entry, since it is a recovery of value, but is instead recorded in a footnote accompanying the financial statements.

12.7   TRANSFERS OF DEBT SECURITIES AMONG PORTFOLIOS

The accounting for transfers between debt securities portfolios varies based on the portfolio from which the accounts are being shifted, with the basic principle being that transfers are recorded at the fair market value of the security on the date of the transfer. The treatment of gains or losses on all possible transfers are noted in the table in Exhibit 12.1.

The offsetting entry for any gain or loss reported in the Other Comprehensive Income section of the income statement goes to a contra account, which is used to offset the investment account on the balance sheet, thereby revealing the extent of changes in the trading securities from their purchased cost.

12.8   ACCOUNTING FOR GAINS OR LOSSES ON SECURITIES

The flowchart shown in Exhibit 12.2 shows the decision tree for how gains and losses are handled for different types of securities portfolios. The decision flow begins in the upper-left corner. For example, if a security is designated as available for sale and there is a change in its fair value, then the decision tree moves to the right, asking if there is a permanent value impairment. If so, the proper treatment matches that of a loss for a held-for-trading

"From" Portfolio	"To" Portfolio	Accounting Treatment
Trading	Available for Sale	No entry (assumes gains and losses have already been recorded).
Trading	Held to Maturity	No entry (assumes gains and losses have already been recorded).
Available for sale	Trading	Shift any previously recorded gain or loss shown in Other Comprehensive Income to operating income.
Available for sale	Held to maturity	Amortize to income over the remaining period to debt maturity any previously recorded gain or loss shown in Other Comprehensive Income, using the effective interest method.
Held to maturity	Trading	Record the unrealized gain or loss in operating income.
Held to maturity	Available for sale	Record the unrealized gain or loss in the Other Comprehensive Income section of the income statement.

EXHIBIT 12.1   ACCOUNTING TREATMENT OF DEBT TRANSFERS BETWEEN PORTFOLIOS

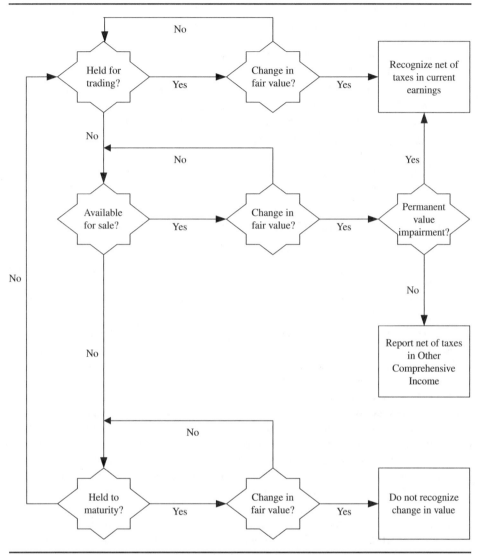

EXHIBIT 12.2   ACCOUNTING FOR GAINS OR LOSSES ON SECURITIES

security; if not, the proper treatment is listed as being reported in the Other Comprehensive Income section of the income statement.

12.9   RECOGNITION OF DEFERRED TAX EFFECTS ON CHANGES IN INVESTMENT VALUATIONS

A deferred tax benefit or tax liability should be recognized alongside the recognition of any change in the fair value of an investment listed in either a trading or available-for-sale portfolio or of a permanent decline in the value of a debt security being held to maturity. The tax impact varies by investment type and is noted as follows:

- *Gains or losses on the trading portfolio.* The deferred tax effect is recognized in the income statement. If there is a loss in value, one should debit the Deferred Tax Benefit account and credit the Provision for income taxes account. If there is a gain in value, one should debit the Provision for income taxes account and credit the Deferred tax liability account.

- *Gains or losses on the available-for-sale portfolio.* Receives the same treatment as noted for gains or losses on the trading portfolio, except that taxes are noted in the Other Comprehensive Income section of the income statement.

- *Gains or losses on the held-to-maturity portfolio.* There is no tax recognition if changes in value are considered to be temporary in nature. If there is a permanent reduction in value, the treatment is identical to the treatment of losses in the trading portfolio, as just noted.

12.10   THE EQUITY METHOD OF INVESTMENT ACCOUNTING

There are three ways to account for an investment. The first is to report the investment at its fair value, the second is to report it under the "equity method," and the third is to fully consolidate the results of the investee in the investing company's financial statements. The rules under which each of these methods is applied are noted in Exhibit 12.3.

The presence of "significant influence" over an investee is assumed if the investor owns at least 20% of its common stock. However, this is not the case if there is clear evidence of not having influence, such as being unable to obtain financial information from the investee, not being able to place a representative on its board of directors, clear opposition to the investor by the investee, loss of voting rights, or proof of a majority voting block that does not include the investor.

Income taxes are only recognized when dividends are received from an investee or the investment is liquidated. Nonetheless, deferred income taxes are recognized when a company records its share of investee income and are then shifted from the Deferred income tax account to income taxes payable when dividends are received. A key issue is the assumed income tax rate used, since it can vary based on an assumption of investment liquidation via dividends (which is at a lower tax rate) or sale of the investment (which is at a higher tax rate).

As just noted in Exhibit 12.3, the equity method of accounting requires one to record the investor's proportionate share of investee earnings, less any dividends received. However, what if the investee records such a large loss that the investor's share of the loss results in a negative investment? When this happens, the correct treatment is to limit the investment to zero and ignore subsequent losses. One should only resume use of the equity method if subsequent investee earnings completely offset the losses that had previously been

Investment Method	Proportion of Ownership	Notes
Fair Value	Less than 20% ownership or no significant influence over investee	Record gains or losses based on fair market value of shares held.
Equity Method	20% to 50% ownership and significant influence over the investee	Record a proportionate share of investee earnings, less dividends received.
Consolidation	50%+ ownership of the investee	Fully consolidate the results of the investor and investee.

EXHIBIT 12.3   ACCOUNTING TREATMENT OF SIGNIFICANT EQUITY INVESTMENTS

ignored. The main exception to this rule is when the investor has committed to fund investee operations or indemnify other creditors or investors for losses incurred. An example of the equity method of accounting is as follows:

The Arabian Knights Security Company purchases 35% of the common stock of the Night Patrollers Security Company for $500,000. At the end of a year, Night Patrollers has earned $80,000 and issued $20,000 in dividends. Under the equity method, Arabian Knights reports a gain in its investment of $28,000 (35% investment × $80,000 in earnings), less dividends of $7,000 (35% investment × $20,000 in dividends) for a total investment change of $21,000. The two entries required to record these changes are as follows:

	Debit	Credit
Investment in Night Patrollers	$28,000	
Equity in Night Patrollers		$28,000
Cash	7,000	
Investment in Night Patrollers		7,000

In addition, Arabian Knight's controller assumes that the investment will eventually be sold, which requires a full corporate tax rate of 34%. Accordingly, the following entry records a deferred income tax on the $28,000 share of Night Patrollers income, while the second entry records the shifting of a portion of this deferred tax to income taxes payable to reflect the company's short-term tax liability for the dividends received (assuming a 34% tax rate for dividend income):

	Debit	Credit
Income tax expense	$9,520	
Deferred taxes		$9,520
Deferred taxes	2,380	
Taxes payable		2,380

It is quite common for the investor to pay a premium over the book value of the investee's common stock. When this happens under the equity method, one should informally (i.e., without the use of journal entries) assign the difference in value to other assets and liabilities of the investee to the extent that the fair value of those assets differs from their net book value. Any changes in these assumed assets should be amortized, resulting in a periodic journal entry to reduce the value of the investor's recorded investment. An example of the amortization of assigned asset valuations is as follows:

To continue with the last example, 35% of the book value of Night Patrollers Security Company was $350,000, as compared to the $500,000 paid by Arabian for 35% of Night Patrollers. Arabian's controller must assign this differential to the excess fair value of any Night Patrollers assets or liabilities over their book value. The only undervalued Night Patrollers asset category is its fixed assets, to which the controller can assign $30,000. The remaining unassigned $120,000 is designated as goodwill. Given the nature of the underlying assets, the $30,000 assigned to fixed assets should be amortized over five years, resulting in a monthly amortization charge of $500. The monthly journal entry is as follows:

	Debit	Credit
Equity in Night Patrollers income	$500	
Investment in Night Patrollers		$500

Any remaining unassigned excess value is considered to be goodwill and is subject to an-nual impairment testing that may result in an additional reduction in the recorded level of investment. An impairment test requires a periodic comparison of the fair value of the in-vestment to the current book value of the investment as recorded by the investor. If the fair value is less than the recorded book value, goodwill is reduced until the recorded invest-ment value matches the new fair value. If the amount of the reduction is greater than the informal goodwill associated with the transaction, then the excess is used to proportionally reduce any amounts previously assigned to the investee's assets. In effect, a large enough reduction in the fair value of its investment will result in an immediate write-down of the recorded investment, rather than a gradual reduction due to amortization. An example of an investment impairment is as follows:

> To continue with the last example, Night Patrollers loses several large security contracts, re-sulting in a significant reduction in the value of the business. Arabian's controller estimates this loss in value to be $130,000, which requires her to eliminate the entire $120,000 good-will portion of the initial investment, as well as $10,000 that had been assigned to the fixed assets category. This later reduction results in a decrease in the monthly amortization charge of $166.66 ($10,000 / 60 months).

If a company *reduces* its investment in an investee to the point where its investment con-stitutes less than 20% of the investee's common stock, it should discontinue use of the equity method of accounting and instead record the investment at its fair value, most likely tracking it as part of the company's available-for-sale portfolio. When the transition occurs from the equity method to the fair value method, no retroactive adjustment in the invest-ment account is required—the investor simply begins using the ending investment balance it had derived under the equity method.

If a company *increases* its investment in an investee to the 20% to 50% range from a lesser figure, it must convert to the equity method of accounting on a retroactive basis. This means that the investor must go back to the initial investment date and recalculate its investment using the equity method of accounting. The offset to any resulting adjustment in the investment account must then be charged to the Retained earnings account as a prior period adjustment. This also requires restatement of prior financial statements in which the fair value method was used to record this investment.

12.11   SUMMARY

Marketable securities require careful attention to the purpose for which they are intended, with the exact categorization resulting in a change in both reported totals on the balance sheet and the treatment of realized and unrealized gains and losses. Finally, investments have different reporting requirements, depending upon a company's intent in regard to their use. Thus, there are a number of rules to be aware of that can alter both the amount and location of investment information in the financial statements.

INVENTORY

13.1 INTRODUCTION

This chapter could also be called "cost flow assumptions," because that is the essence of its content. Cost flows describe the order in which costs are incurred. The reason why cost flows are important is that the cost incurred for an item may change over time so that different costs will appear in the accounting records for the same item. If this occurs, how does the cost accountant handle these costs? Are the earliest costs charged off first, or the later ones? Or is there an alternative approach that avoids the issue? In this chapter, we will look at the specific identification, last-in first-out (LIFO), first-in first-out (FIFO), and weighted-average costing systems, and how each one is used under a different assumption of cost flows. In addition, we will review how to create an inventory tracking system, how to conduct a physical inventory, how to identify and allocate overhead costs, and how the lower of cost or market rule is to be used.

13.2 TYPES OF INVENTORY

Items that may be included in inventory are those that are held for sale, are being produced prior to sale, or are consumed in the production of such items. The main categories of inventory are as follows:

1. *Raw materials.* Any materials that are to be used in the production process and that will become part of a salable product fall into this category.

2. *Work in process.* Any costs from materials, labor, and related overhead used during the production process fall into this category. Raw materials are shifted into this category as soon as they are physically moved to the production process, and the Finished goods account is the recipient of all products leaving this category.

3. *Finished goods.* Any goods that have passed through the production process or that have been purchased for resale fall into this category.

4. *Supplies.* Incidental items that are consumed during the production process may be included in this category. Many organizations choose to charge all supplies to expense in the current period, rather than track them through an inventory account.

5. *Consignment inventory.* Goods held at another location for sale by another party (for example, through a distributor agreement) will fall into this category. Consigned inventory is not owned by the secondary party and should not be listed on its books.

6. *Spare parts.* A company may keep a significant quantity of spare parts on hand, which it then sells to its customers as replacements for worn-out components within the products that it has sold to them in the past. This category can also be rolled into the finished goods category.

13.3 THE INVENTORY TRACKING SYSTEM

A physical inventory count can be eliminated if accurate perpetual inventory records are available. Many steps are required to implement such a system, requiring considerable effort. The accountant should evaluate a company's resources prior to embarking on this process to ensure that they are sufficient to set up and maintain this system. The steps needed to implement an accurate inventory tracking system are as follows:

1. *Select and install inventory tracking software.* The primary requirements for this software are:

    (1) *Track transactions.* The software should list the frequency of product usage, which allows the materials manager to determine what inventory quantities should be changed, as well as to determine which items are obsolete.

    (2) *Update records immediately.* The inventory data must always be up to date, because production planners must know what is in stock, while cycle counters require access to accurate data. Batch updating of the system is not acceptable.

    (3) *Report inventory records by location.* Cycle counters need inventory records that are sorted by location in order to more efficiently locate and count the inventory.

2. *Test inventory tracking software.* Create a set of typical records in the new software, and perform a series of transactions to ensure that the software functions properly. In addition, create a large number of records and perform the transactions again, to

see if the response time of the system drops significantly. If the software appears to function properly, continue to the next step. Otherwise, fix the problems with the software supplier's assistance, or acquire a different software package.

3. *Train the warehouse staff*. The warehouse staff should receive software training immediately before using the system, so that they do not forget how to operate the software. Enter a set of test records into the software, and have the staff simulate all common inventory transactions, such as receipts, picks, and cycle count adjustments.

4. *Revise the rack layout*. It is much easier to move racks prior to installing a perpetual inventory system, because no inventory locations must be changed in the computer system. Create aisles that are wide enough for forklift operation, and cluster small parts racks together for easier parts picking.

5. *Create rack locations*. A typical rack location is, for example, A-01-B-01. This means that this location code is located in Aisle A, Rack 1. Within Rack 1, it is located on Level B (numbered from the bottom to the top). Within Level B, it is located in Partition 1. Many companies skip the use of partitions, on the grounds that an aisle-rack-level numbering system will get a stock picker to within a few feet of an inventory item.

    As one progresses down an aisle, the rack numbers should progress in ascending sequence, with the odd rack numbers on the left and the even numbers on the right. This layout allows a stock picker to move down the center of the aisle, efficiently pulling items from stock based on sequential location codes.

6. *Lock the warehouse*. One of the main causes of record inaccuracy is removal of items from the warehouse by outside staff. To stop this removal, all entrances to the warehouse must be locked. Only warehouse personnel should be allowed access to it. All other personnel entering the warehouse should be accompanied by a member of the warehouse staff to prevent the removal of inventory.

7. *Consolidate parts*. To reduce the labor of counting the same item in multiple locations, group common parts into one place.

8. *Assign part numbers*. Have several experienced personnel verify all part numbers. A mislabeled part is as useless as a missing part, since the computer database will not show that it exists. Mislabeled parts also affect the inventory cost; for example, a mislabeled engine is more expensive than the item represented by its incorrect part number, which may identify it as (for example) a spark plug.

9. *Verify units of measure*. Have several experienced people verify all units of measure. Unless the software allows multiple units of measure to be used, the entire organization must adhere to one unit of measure for each item. For example, the warehouse may desire tape to be counted in rolls, but the engineering department would rather create bills of material with tape measured in inches instead of fractions of rolls.

10. *Pack the parts*. Pack parts into containers, seal the containers, and label them with the part number, unit of measure, and total quantity stored inside. Leave a few parts free for ready use. Only open containers when additional stock is needed. This method allows cycle counters to rapidly verify inventory balances.

11. *Count items*. Count items when there is no significant activity in the warehouse, such as during a weekend. Elaborate cross-checking of the counts, as would be done during a year-end physical inventory count, is not necessary. It is more important

to have the perpetual inventory system operational before the warehouse activity increases again; any errors in the data will quickly be detected during cycle counts and flushed out of the database. The initial counts must include a review of the part number, location, and quantity.

12. *Enter data into the computer.* Have an experienced data entry person input the location, part number, and quantity into the computer. Once the data has been input, another person should cross-check the entered data against the original data for errors.

13. *Quick-check the data.* Scan the data for errors. If all part numbers have the same number of digits, then look for items that are too long or short. Review location codes to see if inventory is stored in nonexistent racks. Look for units of measure that do not match the part being described. For example, is it logical to have a pint of steel in stock? Also, if item costs are available, print a list of extended costs. Excessive costs typically point to incorrect units of measure. For example, a cost of $1 per box of nails will become $500 in the inventory report if nails are incorrectly listed as individual units.

14. *Initiate cycle counts.* Print out a portion of the inventory list, sorted by location. Using this report, have the warehouse staff count blocks of the inventory on a continuous basis. They should look for accurate part numbers, units of measure, locations, and quantities. The counts should concentrate on high-value or high-use items, though the entire stock should be reviewed regularly. The most important part of this step is to examine why mistakes occur. If a cycle counter finds an error, its cause must be investigated and then corrected, so that the mistake will not occur again.

15. *Initiate inventory audits.* The inventory should be audited frequently, perhaps as much as once a week. This allows the accountant to track changes in the inventory accuracy level and initiate changes if the accuracy drops below acceptable levels. In addition, frequent audits are an indirect means of telling the staff that inventory accuracy is important, and must be maintained. The minimum acceptable accuracy level is 95%, with an error being a mistaken part number, unit of measure, quantity, or location. This accuracy level is needed to ensure accurate inventory costing, as well as to assist the materials department in planning future inventory purchases. In addition, establish a tolerance level when calculating the inventory accuracy. For example, if the computer record of a box of screws yields a quantity of 100 and the actual count results in 105 screws, then the record is accurate if the tolerance is at least 5%, but inaccurate if the tolerance is reduced to 1%. The maximum allowable tolerance should be no higher than 5%, with tighter tolerances being used for high-value or high-use items.

16. *Post results.* Inventory accuracy is a team project, and the warehouse staff feels more involved if the audit results are posted against the results of previous audits.

17. *Reward the staff.* Accurate inventories save a company thousands of dollars in many ways. This makes it cost-effective to encourage the staff to maintain and improve the accuracy level with periodic bonuses that are based on the attainment of higher levels of accuracy with tighter tolerances.

The decision tree in Exhibit 13.1 assists in determining which inventory tracking system to install, based on the presence of several items that are required to achieve an accurate perpetual inventory system.

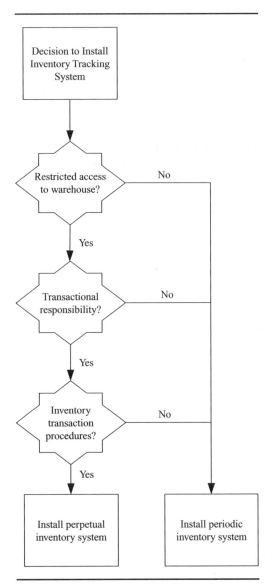

EXHIBIT 13.1   DECISION TREE FOR TYPE OF INVENTORY
TRACKING SYSTEM TO USE

13.4   THE PHYSICAL INVENTORY PROCEDURE

The physical inventory is a manual count of all inventory on hand, and is used to obtain
an inventory valuation for the period-end financial statements. Physical inventories are still
used by many companies; even those that have converted to perpetual systems may find that
sections of the inventory located outside of the warehouse, such as work-in-process, require
a periodic physical count. Companies using such advanced systems as manufacturing cells
may still require a physical count of work-in-process, unless all production is allowed
to flow through the manufacturing process and into finished goods prior to conducting
the count.

Preplanning the physical inventory is critical. The following points will ease the counting process:

- *Use trained personnel.* The inventory counters should all be experienced warehouse personnel, because they are familiar with the parts, as well as their related part numbers and units of measure. The front-office staff has no place in the counting process, because they have no knowledge of these items.
- *Use "dead time."* It is difficult to count while production operations are occurring. Consequently, using weekend or evening time will hasten the counting process.
- *Clean up in advance.* A messy counting area means that the counting team must find the stock before counting it. Save time by organizing the inventory in advance, clearly labeling part numbers and units of measure, and cleaning the counting areas.
- *Train the staff.* The physical inventory teams must be trained in counting procedures, as well as proper cutoff procedures and the completion of forms. The training may require detailed written instructions.
- *Assign the staff.* Allocate inventory locations to specific counting areas.
- *Create an inventory tag form.* This tag is used to record the inventory count for each item, and should include fields for the part number, description, location, unit of measure, counter's signature, and last job performed (if it is a work-in-process item). The tags must be prenumbered.

The actual counting process should include the following steps:

- *Notify the auditors.* The auditors must be notified of the time and place of the physical inventory. An audit team will conduct test counts, observe the procedure generally, and trace the counts to the inventory summary.
- *Assign counting teams to areas.* The following areas should be counted:
  - Central warehouse
  - Receiving inspection
  - Staging areas
  - Finished goods area
  - Work-in-process area
  - Shipping area
  - Outside storage (e.g., in trailer storage or company-owned inventory located at other companies)
  - Rework areas
  - Packaging materials

    The following items should *not* be counted:
  - Consignment inventory
  - Maintenance equipment
  - Material handling containers
  - Office supplies
  - Tools and equipment
  - Written-off inventory
- *Count all areas.* Attach a prenumbered inventory tag to each area that has been counted, in order to prove that the count was completed. The tag should be a

two-part form, so that one copy can be removed and used to summarize the inventory. The count is usually conducted by two-person teams, with one counting and the other recording the information.

- *Review counted areas*. Review the counted areas for missing or duplicate counts, and spot-check counts for correct quantities, part numbers, and units of measure. High dollar–value items should be 100% checked.

- *Control tags*. Collect all tags and look for missing or duplicate tag numbers; resolve any problems before summarizing the information in the next step.

- *Summarize tags*. Input the tag information into the computer, or record it manually on a summary sheet. This sheet should include all of the information contained on the tags. Whether an automated or manual report, the summary should include sufficient space to mark down the market value of each item, so that the cost of each one can be marked to the lower of cost or market for financial statement reporting purposes.

- *Look for discrepancies*. Problems can be unearthed with any of the following techniques:
  - Compare the physical inventory records to perpetual records.
  - Review the extended costs for excessively large dollar amounts. Frequently, incorrect units of measure are the root cause of these problems.
  - Review the unit counts for excessively high counts. Once again, incorrect units of measure may be the culprit.
  - Compare expensive items in the inventory to the summary, to ensure that the correct quantities are recorded and that their costs appear reasonable.

- *Review the cutoff*. Even with an excellent inventory count, the inventory can be severely misstated if inventory is included or excluded without a corresponding sale or liability entry in the accounting records. Review the receiving and shipping records for several days before and after the inventory count, and ensure that an accounting entry exists for each transaction.

13.5 INVENTORY MANAGEMENT

Responsibility for inventory resides with the materials management department, which controls purchasing, manufacturing planning, and warehousing. None of these areas is one over which the controller traditionally exercises control. Nonetheless, the controller should be aware of activities related to inventory management, because they can have a profound impact on the level of funding needed for working capital. The following topics address a number of areas in which inventory decisions impact funding levels.

13.6 INVENTORY PURCHASING

When the purchasing department orders inventory from suppliers, it asks them for the lead time they need to deliver orders and then creates a *safety stock* level to at least match the lead time. For example, if a supplier says that it needs two weeks to deliver goods, and the company uses $100,000 of its inventory per week, then the purchasing department creates a safety stock level of at least $200,000 to keep the company running while it waits for the next delivery. This lead time therefore requires $200,000 of funding. The controller should be aware that extremely distant foreign sourcing, such as to Asia, will drastically lengthen lead times and therefore the amount of safety stock. Conversely, if a company can source its inventory needs from suppliers located very close by, and work with them to reduce their lead times and increase the frequency of their deliveries, this results in lowered safety stock and therefore a reduced need for funding.

Another contributor to long lead times is the manual processing of purchase orders to suppliers. If inventory needs are calculated by hand, then transferred to a purchase order, manually approved, and delivered by mail, a company must retain more safety stock to cover for this additional delay. Conversely, if a company can install a *material requirements planning system* that automatically calculates inventory needs, creates purchase orders, and transmits them to suppliers electronically, then the ordering cycle is significantly reduced and corresponding lead times can be shortened.

The purchasing department orders inventory based on its estimates of what customers are going to buy. No matter how sophisticated, these estimates are bound to be incorrect to some extent, resulting in the purchase of excess inventory. To reduce this forecasting error, a company should attempt to *gain direct access to the inventory planning systems of key customers*. This gives the purchasing staff perfect information about what it, in turn, needs to order from its suppliers and thereby reduces excess inventory levels.

It may also be possible to *shift raw material ownership to suppliers*, so that they own the inventory located on the company's premises. Suppliers may agree to this scenario if the company sole-sources purchases from them. Under this arrangement, the company pays suppliers when it removes inventory from its warehouse, either to sell it or to incorporate it into the manufacture of other goods. The resulting payment delay reduces the need for funding.

All of the preceding changes in purchasing practices can reduce a company's investment in inventory. Conversely, a purchasing practice that contributes to startling increases in funding requirements is the *bulk purchase of inventory*. If the purchasing staff is offered quantity discounts in exchange for large orders, they will be tempted to proclaim large per-unit cost reductions, not realizing that this calls for much more up-front cash and a considerable storage cost and risk of obsolescence.

13.7 INVENTORY RECEIVING

The receiving staff's procedures can have an impact on inventory-related funding. For example, a supplier may ship goods without an authorizing purchase order from the company. If the receiving staff accepts the delivery, then the company is obligated to pay for it. A better practice is to *reject all inbound deliveries that do not have a purchase order authorization*.

Another procedural issue is to require the *immediate entry of all receiving information* into the company's warehouse management system. If this is not done, the risk increases that the receipt will never be recorded, due to lost or misplaced paperwork. The purchasing staff will see that the inventory never arrived and may order additional goods to compensate—which requires more funding. Similarly, a procedure should call for the immediate putaway of inventory items following their receipt, on the grounds that they can become lost in the staging area.

13.8 INVENTORY STORAGE

In a traditional system, inventory arrives from suppliers, is stored in the company warehouse, and is shipped when ordered by customers. The company is funding the inventory for as long as it sits in the warehouse, waiting for a customer order. A better method is to avoid the warehouse entirely by using *drop shipping*. Under this system, a company receives an order from a customer and contacts its supplier with the shipping information, which in turn ships the product directly to the customer. This is a somewhat cumbersome process and may result in longer delivery times, but it completely eliminates the company's investment in inventory and therefore all associated funding needs. This option is available only to inventory resellers.

Another option that severely reduces the amount of inventory retention time is *cross-docking*. Under cross-docking, when an item arrives at the receiving dock, it is immediately moved to a shipping dock for delivery to the customer in a different truck. There is no putaway or picking transaction and no long-term storage, which also reduces the risk of damage to the inventory. Cross-docking works only when there is excellent control over the timing of in-bound deliveries, so the warehouse management system knows when items will arrive. It also requires multiple extra loading docks, since trailers may have to be kept on-site longer than normal while loads are accumulated from several inbound deliveries.

13.9   PRODUCTION ISSUES IMPACTING INVENTORY

The production process is driven by several procedural, policy, and setup issues that strongly impact the amount of inventory and therefore the level of funding.

The traditional manufacturing system is geared toward very long production runs, on the justification that this results in the spreading of fixed costs over a large number of units, which yields the lowest possible cost per unit. The logic is flawed, because such large production runs also yield too much inventory, which then sits in stock and runs the significant risk of obsolescence. To reduce the funding requirement of this excess inventory, a company should produce to demand, which is exemplified by the *just-in-time (JIT) manufacturing system*. A JIT system triggers an authorization to produce if an order only is received from a customer, so there is never any excess inventory on hand. Though a JIT system initially appears to generate higher per-unit costs, the eliminated carrying cost of inventory makes it considerably less expensive. And, from the controller's perspective, a JIT system can release a great deal of cash from inventory.

Another production issue is to *avoid volume-based incentive pay systems*. Some companies pay their employees more if they produce more. Not only does this result in extremely high levels of inventory, but these pay systems tend to yield lower-quality goods, since employees favor higher volume over higher quality. A reasonable alternative is an incentive to meet the production plan exactly. If the plan is derived from a just-in-time system, then employees are only producing to match existing customer orders, which keep funding requirements low.

A related issue is the use of complex, high-capacity machinery. Industrial engineers enjoy these machines, because they feature impressively high-throughput rates. However, they also require immense production volumes in order to justify their initial and ongoing maintenance costs, which once again results in the accumulation of too much inventory. Instead, the controller should favor the *acquisition of smaller, simpler machines having lower maintenance costs*. Such machines can be operated profitably with very small production runs, thereby making it easier to drive down inventory levels.

A simple method for reducing work-in-process inventory is to *use smaller container sizes*. Typically, an employee at a workstation fills a container and then moves it to the next downstream workstation. If the container is a large one, and if there are many workstations using the same size container, then a great deal of work-in-process inventory is being unnecessarily accumulated. By shifting to a smaller container size, the inventory investment is reduced, as is the amount of scrap—because the downstream workstation operator is more likely to spot faults originating in an upstream location more quickly if containers are delivered more frequently.

When a machine requires a substantial amount of time to be switched over to a new configuration for the production of a different part, there is a natural tendency to have very long production runs of the same part in order to spread the cost of the changeover across as many parts as possible. This practice results in too much inventory, so the solution is to *reduce machine setup times* to such an extent that it becomes practicable to have production runs of as little as one unit. Setup reduction can be accomplished by using changeover consultants, process videotaping, quick-release fasteners, color-coded parts, standardized tools, and so forth.

A common arrangement of machines on the shop floor is by functional group, where machines of one type are clustered in one place. By doing so, jobs requiring a specific type of processing can all be routed to the same cluster of machines and loaded into whichever one becomes available for processing next. However, by doing so, there tend to be large batches of work-in-process inventory piling up behind each machine, because this approach calls for the completion of a job at one workstation before the entire job is moved to the next workstation. A better layout is provided by *cellular manufacturing*, where a small cluster of machines are set up in close proximity to one another, each one performing a sequential task in completing a specific type or common set of products. Usually only a few employees work in each cell and walk a single part all the way through the cell before moving on to the next part. By doing so, there is obviously only the most minimal work-in-process inventory in the cell.

13.10   THE BILL OF MATERIALS

A bill of materials is the record of the materials used to construct a product. It is exceedingly worthwhile to examine the bills of material with the objective of reducing inventory. For example, a bill may contain an excess quantity of a part. If so, and the underlying purchase order system automatically places orders for parts, the bill will be used to order too many parts, thereby increasing inventory levels. A *periodic audit of all bills*, where the reviewer compares each bill to a disassembled product, will reveal such errors. For the same reason, the estimated scrap listed in all bills of material should be compared to actual scrap levels; if the estimated scrap level is too high, then the bill will call for too much inventory to be ordered for the next production run.

A significant bill of materials issue from the perspective of inventory reduction is the *substitution of parts*. This may occur when the engineering staff issues an engineering change order, specifying a reconfiguration of the parts that comprise a product. Ideally, the materials management staff should draw down all remaining inventory stocks under the old bill of materials before implementing the new change order. If this is not done, then the company will have a remainder stock of raw materials inventory for which there are no disposition plans.

13.11   PRODUCT DESIGN

A number of design decisions have a considerable impact on the size of a company's investment in inventory. A key factor is the *number of product options* offered. If there are a multitude of options, then a company may find it necessary to stock every variation on the product, which calls for a substantial inventory investment. If, however, it is possible to limit the number of options, then inventory volumes can be reduced substantially. A similar issue is the *number of products* offered. If there is an enormous range of product offerings, it is quite likely that only a small proportion of the total generate a profit; the remainder requires large inventory holdings in return for minimal sales volume.

13.12   CUSTOMER SERVICE

A company may feel that its primary method of competition is to provide excellent customer service, which requires it to never have a stockout condition for any inventory item. This may require an inordinate amount of finished goods inventory. This policy should be reviewed regularly, with an analysis of the inventory cost required to maintain such a high level of order fulfillment.

13.13   INVENTORY DISPOSITION

Even if a company has built up a large proportion of obsolete inventory, continuing attention to an *inventory disposition program* can result in the recovery of a substantial amount of cash. The first step in this program is to create a materials review board, which is comprised of members of the materials management, engineering, and accounting departments. This group is responsible for determining which inventory items can be used in-house and the most cost-effective type of disposition for those items that cannot be used. This may involve sending inventory back to suppliers for a restocking charge, sales to salvage contractors, sales as repair parts through the service department, or even donating them to a nonprofit in exchange for a tax credit. Throwing out inventory is frequently better than keeping it, since retention requires the ongoing use of valuable warehouse space.

13.14   GOODS IN TRANSIT

Inventory that is in transit to the buyer continues to be owned by the seller as long as that entity is responsible for the transportation costs. If the seller is only paying for transportation to a certain point, such as to a third-party shipper, then its ownership stops at that point and is transferred to the buyer.

In reality, companies do not usually track goods in transit, preferring instead to not count them if they have either already left the facility (in the case of the seller) or have not yet arrived at the facility (in the case of the buyer). The reason for avoiding this task is the difficulty in determining the amount of goods in transit that belong to the company, especially when the accounting staff is trying to close the books very quickly and does not want to keep the books open long enough to make a proper determination. This avoidance has minimal impact on the receiving company's recordkeeping, since a missing inventory item would have required both a debit to an inventory account and a credit to a liability account, which cancel each other out. This is more of an issue for the shipping firm, since it is probably recognizing revenue at the point of shipment, rather than at some later point in transit, which can potentially overstate revenue if this occurs near the end of the reporting period.

Examples of different types of transit scenarios: If goods are shipped under a cost, insurance and freight (C&F) contract, the buyer is paying for all delivery costs, and so acquires title to the goods as soon as they leave the seller's location.

If goods are shipped free alongside (FAS), it is paying for delivery of the goods to the side of the ship that will transport the goods to the buyer. If so, it retains ownership of the goods until they are alongside the ship, at which point the buyer acquires title to the goods.

If goods are shipped free on board (FOB) destination, then transport costs are paid by the seller, and ownership will not pass to the buyer until the carrier delivers the goods to the buyer.

As indicated by the name, an ex-ship delivery means that the seller pays for a delivery until it has departed the ship, so it retains title to the goods until that point.

If goods are shipped FOB shipping point, then transport costs are paid by the buyer, and ownership passes to the buyer as soon as the carrier takes possession of the delivery from the seller.

If goods are shipped FOB a specific point, such as Nashville, then the seller retains title until the goods reach Nashville, at which point ownership is transferred to the buyer.

The decision tree in Exhibit 13.2 shows how to determine who owns inventory that is in transit. The "ex-ship" transportation noted in the tree refers to the practice of the seller paying for delivery up to the point when the product is removed from a ship on its way to the buyer.

13.15 ACCOUNTING FOR INVENTORIES

The type and quantity of items stored in inventory can be accounted for on a periodic basis by using the *periodic inventory system*, which requires one to conduct a complete count of the physical inventory in order to obtain a calculation of the inventory cost. A more advanced method that does not require a complete inventory count is the perpetual inventory system; under this approach, one incrementally adds or subtracts inventory transactions to or from a beginning database of inventory records in order to maintain an ongoing balance of inventory quantities. The accuracy of the inventory records under this later approach will likely degrade over time, so an ongoing cycle counting program is needed to maintain its accuracy level.

The *perpetual inventory system* is highly recommended, because it avoids expensive periodic inventory counts, which also tend not to yield accurate results. Also, it allows the purchasing staff to have greater confidence in what inventory is on hand for purchasing planning purposes. Further, accountants can complete period-end financial statements more quickly, without having to guess at ending inventory levels. A perpetual inventory example is as follows:

> A company wishes to install a perpetual inventory system, but it has not established tight control over the warehouse area with fencing or gate control. Accordingly, production employees are able to enter the warehouse and remove items from the shelf for use in the manufacturing process. Because of this issue, inventory balances in the perpetual inventory system are chronically higher than is really the case, since removed items are not being logged out of the system.

> The scenario changes to one where the company has not assigned responsibility for inventory accuracy to anyone in the company, but still creates a perpetual inventory system. As a result, the employees charged with entering inventory transactions into the computer system have no reason to do so, and no one enforces high accuracy levels. In this case, inventory accuracy levels rapidly worsen, especially for those items being used on a regular basis, since they are most subject to transactional inaccuracies. Only the accuracy of slow-moving items remains relatively accurate.

> The scenario changes to one where transactional procedures have not been clearly established, and employees entering inventory transactions have not been properly trained. This results in the worst accuracy levels of the three scenarios, since employees are not even certain if they should be adding or subtracting quantities, what units of measure to enter, or what special transactions call for what types of computer entries.

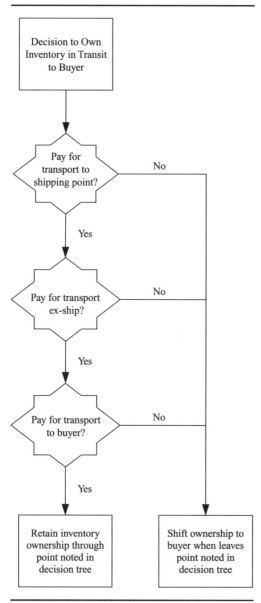

EXHIBIT 13.2   DECISION TREE FOR OWNERSHIP OF
INVENTORY IN TRANSIT

Consigned inventory is any inventory shipped by a company to a reseller, while retaining ownership until the product is sold by the reseller. Until sold, the inventory remains on the books of the originating company and not on the books of the reseller. A common cause of inventory valuation problems is the improper recording of consignment inventory on the books of a reseller. Inventory that has been sold with a *right of return* receives treatment similar to consignment inventory if the amount of future inventory returns cannot be reasonably estimated. Until the probability of returns is unlikely, the inventory must remain on the books of the selling company, even though legal title to the goods has passed to the buyer. An example of right of return is as follows:

> A company has sold a large shipment of refrigerators to a new customer. Included in the sales agreement is a provision allowing the customer to return one-third of the refrigerators within the next 90 days. Since the company has no experience with this customer, it cannot record the full amount of the sale. Instead, it records that portion of the sale associated with the refrigerators for which there is no right of return and waits 90 days until the right of return has expired before recording the remainder of thesale.

13.16   OVERHEAD COSTS ALLOCABLE TO INVENTORY

All costs can be assigned to inventory that are incurred to put goods in a salable condition. For raw materials, this is the purchase price, inbound transportation costs, insurance, and handling costs. If inventory is in the work-in-process or finished goods stages, then an allocation of the overhead costs shown in Exhibit 13.3 must be added.

Allocation of overhead costs can be made by any reasonable measure, but must be consistently applied across reporting periods. Common bases for overhead allocation are direct labor hours or machine hours used during the production of a product. An example of overhead allocation is as follows:

> A company manufactures and sells Product A and Product B. Both require considerable machining to complete, so it is appropriate to allocate overhead costs to them based on total hours of standard machine time used. In March, Product A manufacturing required a total of 4,375 hours of machine time. During the same month, all units of Product B manufactured required 2,615 hours of machine time. Thus, 63% of the overhead cost pool was allocated to Product A and 37% to Product B. This example results in a reasonably accurate allocation of overhead to products, especially if the bulk of expenses in the overhead pool relate to the machining equipment used to complete the products. However, if a significant proportion of expenses in the overhead cost pool could be reasonably assigned to some other allocation measure, then these costs could be stored in a separate cost pool and allocated in a different manner. For example, if Product A were quite bulky and required 90% of the storage space in the warehouse, as opposed to 10% for Product B, then 90% of the warehouse-related overhead costs could be reasonably allocated to Product A.

13.17   LOWER OF COST OR MARKET RULE

A company is required to recognize an additional expense in its cost of goods sold in the current period for any of its inventory whose replacement cost (subject to certain restrictions) has declined below its carrying cost. If the market value of the inventory subsequently rises back to or above its original carrying cost, its recorded value cannot be increased back to the original carrying amount.

Depreciation of factory equipment	Quality control and inspection
Factory administration expenses	Rent, facility and equipment
Indirect labor and production supervisory wages	Repair expenses
Indirect materials and supplies	Rework labor, scrap and spoilage
Maintenance, factory and production equipment	Taxes related to production assets
Officer salaries related to production	Uncapitalized tools and equipment
Production employees' benefits	Utilities

EXHIBIT 13.3   COSTS TO ALLOCATE TO OVERHEAD

More specifically, the lower of cost or market (LCM) calculation means that the cost of inventory cannot be recorded higher than its replacement cost on the open market (the replacement cost is bounded at the high end by its eventual selling price, less costs of disposal), nor can it be recorded lower than that price, less a normal profit percentage. The concept is best demonstrated with the four scenarios listed in the following example:

Item	Selling Price	Completion/ Selling − Cost =	Upper Price Boundary −	Normal Profit =	Lower Price Boundary	Existing Inventory Cost	Replacement Cost (1)	Market Value (2)	LCM
A	$15.00	$4.00	**$11.00**	$2.20	**$ 8.80**	$ 8.00	$12.50	$11.00	**$ 8.00**
B	40.15	6.00	**34.15**	5.75	**28.40**	35.00	34.50	34.15	**34.15**
C	20.00	6.50	**13.50**	3.00	**10.50**	17.00	12.00	12.00	**12.00**
D	10.50	2.35	**8.15**	2.25	**5.90**	8.00	5.25	5.90	**5.90**

(1) The cost at which an inventory item could be purchased on the open market.
(2) Replacement cost, bracketed by the upper and lower price boundaries.

In the example, the numbers in the first six columns are used to derive the upper and lower boundaries of the market values that will be used for the lower of cost or market calculation. By subtracting the completion and selling costs from each product's selling price, we establish the upper price boundary (in bold) of the market cost calculation. By then subtracting the normal profit from the upper cost boundary of each product, we establish the lower price boundary. Using this information, the LCM calculation for each of the listed products is as follows:

- *Product A, replacement cost higher than existing inventory cost.* The market price cannot be higher than the upper boundary of $11.00, which is still higher than the existing inventory cost of $8.00. Thus, the LCM is the same as the existing inventory cost.

- *Product B, replacement cost lower than existing inventory cost, but higher than upper price boundary.* The replacement cost of $34.50 exceeds the upper price boundary of $34.15, so the market value is designated at $34.15. This is lower than the existing inventory cost, so the LCM becomes $34.15.

- *Product C, replacement cost lower than existing inventory cost, and within price boundaries.* The replacement cost of $12.00 is within the upper and lower price boundaries, and so is used as the market value. This is lower than the existing inventory cost of $17.00, so the LCM becomes $12.00.

- *Product D, replacement cost lower than existing inventory cost, but lower than lower price boundary.* The replacement cost of $5.25 is below the lower price boundary of $5.90, so the market value is designated as $5.90. This is lower than the existing inventory cost of $8.00, so the LCM becomes $5.90.

13.18   SPECIFIC IDENTIFICATION INVENTORY VALUATION METHOD

When each individual item of inventory can be clearly identified, it is possible to create inventory costing records for each one, rather than summarizing costs by general inventory type. This approach is rarely used, since the amount of paperwork and effort associated with developing unit costs is far greater than under all other valuation techniques. It is most applicable in businesses such as home construction, where there are very few units of inventory to track, and where each item is truly unique.

13.19   FIRST-IN, FIRST-OUT (FIFO) INVENTORY VALUATION METHOD

A computer manufacturer knows that the component parts it purchases are subject to extremely rapid rates of obsolescence, sometimes rendering a part worthless in a month or two. Accordingly, it will be sure to use up the oldest items in stock first, rather than running the risk of scrapping them a short way into the future. For this type of environment, the first-in, first-out (FIFO) method is the ideal way to deal with the flow of costs. This method assumes that the oldest parts in stock are always used first, which means that their associated old costs are used first, as well.

The concept is best illustrated with an example, which we show in Exhibit 13.4. In the first row, we create a single layer of inventory that results in 50 units of inventory, at a per-unit cost of $10.00. So far, the extended cost of the inventory is the same as we saw under the LIFO, but that will change as we proceed to the second row of data. In this row, we have monthly inventory usage of 350 units, which FIFO assumes will use the entire stock of 50 inventory units that were left over at the end of the preceding month, as well as 300 units that were purchased in the current month. This wipes out the first layer of inventory, leaving us with a single new layer that is composed of 700 units at a cost of $9.58 per unit. In the third row, there is 400 units of usage, which again comes from the first inventory layer, shrinking it down to just 300 units. However, since extra stock was purchased in the same period, we now have an extra inventory layer that comprises 250 units, at a cost of $10.65 per unit. The rest of the exhibit proceeds using the same FIFO layering assumptions.

There are several factors to consider before implementing a FIFO costing system. They are as follows:

- *Fewer inventory layers.* The FIFO system generally results in fewer layers of inventory costs in the inventory database. For example, the LIFO model shown in Exhibit 13.5 contains four layers of costing data, whereas the FIFO model shown in Exhibit 13.4, which used exactly the same data, resulted in no more than two inventory layers. This conclusion generally holds true, because a LIFO system will leave some layers of costs completely untouched for long time periods, if inventory levels do not drop, whereas a FIFO system will continually clear out old layers of costs, so that multiple costing layers do not have a chance to accumulate.

- *Reduces taxes payable in periods of declining costs.* Though it is very unusual to see declining inventory costs, it sometimes occurs in industries where there is either ferocious price competition among suppliers or else extremely high rates of innovation that in turn lead to cost reductions. In such cases, using the earliest costs first will result in the immediate recognition of the highest possible expense, which reduces the reported profit level, and therefore reduces taxes payable.

- *Shows higher profits in periods of rising costs.* Since it charges off the earliest costs first, any very recent increase in costs will be stored in inventory, rather than being immediately recognized. This will result in higher levels of reported profits, though the attendant income tax liability will also be higher.

- *Less risk of outdated costs in inventory.* Because old costs are used first in a FIFO system, there is no way for old and outdated costs to accumulate in inventory. This prevents the management group from having to worry about the adverse impact of inventory reductions on reported levels of profit, either with excessively high or with excessively low charges to the cost of goods sold. This avoids the dilemma noted earlier for LIFO, where just-in-time systems may not be implemented if the result will be a dramatically different cost of goods sold.

FIFO Costing

Part Number BK0043

Column 1	Column 2	Column 3	Column 4	Column 5	Column 6	Column 7	Column 8	Column 9
Date Purchased	Quantity Purchased	Cost per Unit	Monthly Usage	Net Inventory Remaining	Cost of 1st Inventory Layer	Cost of 2nd Inventory Layer	Cost of 3rd Inventory Layer	Extended Inventory Cost
05/03/10	500	$10.00	450	50	(50 × $10.00)	—	—	$500
06/04/10	1,000	$9.58	350	700	(700 × $9.58)	—	—	$6,706
07/11/10	250	$10.65	400	550	(300 × $9.58)	(250 × $10.65)	—	$5,537
08/01/10	475	$10.25	350	675	(200 × $10.65)	(475 × $10.25)	—	$6,999
08/30/10	375	$10.40	400	650	(275 × $10.40)	(375 × $10.40)	—	$6,760
09/09/10	850	$9.50	700	800	(800 × $9.50)	—	—	$7,600
12/12/10	700	$9.75	900	600	(600 × $9.75)	—	—	$5,850
02/08/11	650	$9.85	800	450	(450 × $9.85)	—	—	$4,433
05/07/11	200	$10.80	0	650	(450 × $9.85)	(200 × $10.80)	—	$6,593
09/23/11	600	$9.85	750	500	(500 × $9.85)	—	—	$4,925

EXHIBIT 13.4 FIFO VALUATION EXAMPLE

In short, the FIFO cost layering system tends to result in the storage of the most recently incurred costs in inventory and higher levels of reported profits. It is most useful for those companies whose main concern is reporting high profits rather than reducing income taxes.

13.20   LAST-IN, FIRST-OUT (LIFO) INVENTORY VALUATION METHOD

In a supermarket, the shelves are stocked several rows deep with products. A shopper will walk by and pick products from the front row. If the stocking person is lazy, he will then add products to the front row locations from which products were just taken, rather than shifting the oldest products to the front row and putting new ones in the back. This concept of always taking the newest products first is called last-in, first-out, or LIFO.

The following factors must be considered before implementing a LIFO system:

- *Many layers.* The LIFO cost flow approach can result in a large number of inventory layers, as shown in the exhibit. Though this is not important when a computerized accounting system is used that will automatically track a large number of such layers, it can be burdensome if the cost layers are manually tracked.

- *Alters the inventory valuation.* If there are significant changes in product costs over time, the earliest inventory layers may contain costs that are wildly different from market conditions in the current period, which could result in the recognition of unusually high or low costs if these cost layers are ever accessed. Also, LIFO costs can never be reduced to the lower of cost or market (see the "Lower of Cost or Market Rule" section), thereby perpetuating any unusually high inventory values in the various inventory layers.

- *Reduces taxes payable in periods of rising costs.* In an inflationary environment, costs that are charged off to the cost of goods sold as soon as they are incurred will result in a higher cost of goods sold and a lower level of profitability, which in turn results in a lower tax liability. This is the principle reason why LIFO is used by most companies

- *Requires consistent usage for all reporting.* Under IRS rules, if a company uses LIFO to value its inventory for tax reporting purposes, then it must do the same for its external financial reports. The result of this rule is that a company cannot report lower earnings for tax purposes and higher earnings for all other purposes by using an alternative inventory valuation method. However, it is still possible to mention what profits would have been if some other method had been used, but only in the form of a footnote appended to the financial statements. If financial reports are only generated for internal management consumption, then any valuation method may be used.

- *Interferes with the implementation of just-in-time systems.* As noted in the last bullet point, clearing out the final cost layers of a LIFO system can result in unusual cost of goods sold figures. If these results will cause a significant skewing of reported profitability, company management may be put in the unusual position of opposing the implementation of advanced manufacturing concepts, such as just-in-time systems, that reduce or eliminate inventory levels (with an attendant, and highly favorable, improvement in the amount of working capital requirements).

In short, LIFO is used primarily for reducing a company's income tax liability. This single focus can cause problems, such as too many cost layers, an excessively low inventory valuation, and a fear of inventory reductions due to the recognition of inventory cost layers that may contain very low per-unit costs, which will result in high levels of recognized profit and therefore a higher tax liability. Given these issues, one should carefully consider the utility of tax avoidance before implementing a LIFO cost-layering system. An example of LIFO inventory valuation is as follows:

> The Magic Pen Company has made 10 purchases, which are itemized in Exhibit 13.5. In the exhibit, the company has purchased 500 units of a product with part number BK0043 on May 3, 2010 (as noted in the first row of data), and use 450 units during that month, leaving the company with 50 units. These 50 units were all purchased at a cost of $10.00 each, so they are itemized in Column 6 as the first layer of inventory costs for this product. In the next row of data, an additional 1,000 units were bought on June 4, 2010, of which only 350 units were used. This leaves an additional 650 units at a purchase price of $9.58, which are placed in the second inventory layer, as noted on Column 7. In the third row, there is a net decrease in the amount of inventory, so this reduction comes out of the second (or last) inventory layer in Column 7; the earliest layer, as described in Column 6, remains untouched, since it was the first layer of costs added and will not be used until all other inventory has been eliminated. The exhibit continues through seven more transactions, at one point increasing to four layers of inventory costs.

13.21   DOLLAR VALUE LIFO INVENTORY VALUATION METHOD

This method computes a conversion price index for the year-end inventory in comparison to the base year cost. This index is computed separately for each company business unit. The conversion price index can be computed with the *double-extension method*. Under this approach, the total extended cost of the inventory at both base year prices and the most recent prices are calculated. Then, the total inventory cost at the most recent prices is divided by the total inventory cost at base year prices, resulting in a conversion price percentage, or index. The index represents the change in overall prices between the current year and the base year. This index must be computed and retained for each year in which the LIFO method is used.

There are two problems with the double-extension method. First, it requires a massive volume of calculations if there are many items in inventory. Second, tax regulations require that any new item added to inventory, no matter how many years after the establishment of the base year, have a base year cost included in the LIFO database for purposes of calculating the index. This base year cost is supposed to be the one in existence at the time of the base year, which may require considerable research to determine or estimate. Only if it is impossible to determine a base year cost can the current cost of a new inventory item be used as the base year cost. For these reasons, the double-extension inventory valuation method is not recommended in most cases. An example of double-extension inventory valuation is as follows:

> A company carries a single item of inventory in stock. It has retained the following year-end information about the item for the past four years:

Year	Ending Unit Quantity	Ending Current Price	Extended at Current Year-End Price
1	3,500	$32.00	$112,000
2	7,000	34.50	241,500
3	5,500	36.00	198,000
4	7,250	37.50	271,875

LIFO Costing

Part Number BK0043

Column 1 Date Purchased	Column 2 Quantity Purchased	Column 3 Cost per Unit	Column 4 Monthly Usage	Column 5 Net Inventory Remaining	Column 6 Cost of 1st Inventory Layer	Column 7 Cost of 2nd Inventory Layer	Column 8 Cost of 3rd Inventory Layer	Column 9 Cost of 4th Inventory Layer	Column 10 Extended Inventory Cost
05/03/10	500	$10.00	450	50	(50 × $10.00)	—	—	—	$500
06/04/10	1,000	$9.58	350	700	(50 × $10.00)	(650 × $9.58)	—	—	$6,727
07/11/10	250	$10.65	400	550	(50 × $10.00)	(500 × $9.58)	—	—	$5,290
08/01/10	475	$10.25	350	675	(50 × $10.00)	(500 × $9.58)	(125 × $10.25)	—	$6,571
08/30/10	375	$10.40	400	650	(50 × $10.00)	(500 × $9.58)	(100 × $10.25)	—	$6,315
09/09/10	850	$9.50	700	800	(50 × $10.00)	(500 × $9.58)	(100 × $10.25)	(150 × $9.50)	$7,740
12/12/10	700	$9.75	900	600	(50 × $10.00)	(500 × $9.58)	(50 × $9.58)	—	$5,769
02/08/11	650	$9.85	800	450	(50 × $10.00)	(400 × $9.58)	—	—	$4,332
05/07/11	200	$10.80	0	650	(50 × $10.00)	(400 × $9.58)	(200 × $10.80)	—	$6,492
09/23/11	600	$9.85	750	500	(50 × $10.00)	(400 × $9.58)	(50 × $9.85)	—	$4,825

Exhibit 13.5 LIFO Valuation Example

The first year is the base year upon which the double-extension index will be based in later years. In the second year, we extend the total year-end inventory by both the base year price and the current year price, as follows:

Year-End Quantity	Base Year Cost	Extended at Base Year Cost	Ending Current Price	Extended at Ending Current Price
7,000	$32.00	$224,000	$34.50	$241,500

To arrive at the index between year two and the base year, we divide the extended ending current price of $241,500 by the extended base year cost of $224,000, yielding an index of 107.8%.

The next step is to calculate the incremental amount of inventory added in year two, determine its cost using base year prices, and then multiply this extended amount by our index of 107.8% to arrive at the cost of the incremental year two LIFO layer. The incremental amount of inventory added is the year-end quantity of 7,000 units, less the beginning balance of 3,500 units, which is 3,500 units. When multiplied by the base year cost of $32.00, we arrive at an incremental increase in inventory of $112,000. Finally, we multiply the $112,000 by the price index of 107.8% to determine that the cost of the year two LIFO layer is $120,736.

Thus, at the end of year two, the total double-extension LIFO inventory valuation is the base year valuation of $112,000 plus the year two layer's valuation of $120,736, totaling $232,736.

In year three, the amount of ending inventory has declined from the previous year, so no new layering calculation is required. Instead, we assume that the entire reduction of 1,500 units during that year was taken from the year two inventory layer. To calculate the amount of this reduction, we multiply the remaining amount of the year two layer (5,500 units less the base year amount of 3,500 units, or 2,000 units) times the ending base year price of $32.00 and the year two index of 107.8%. This calculation results in a new year two layer of $68,992.

Thus, at the end of year three, the total double-extension LIFO inventory valuation is the base layer of $112,000 plus the reduced year two layer of $68,992, totaling $180,992.

In year four, there is an increase in inventory, so we can calculate the presence of a new layer using the following table:

Year-End Quantity	Base Year Cost	Extended at Base Year Cost	Ending Current Price	Extended at Ending Current Price
7,250	$32.00	$232,000	$37.50	$271,875

Again, we divide the extended ending current price of $271,875 by the extended base year cost of $232,000, yielding an index of 117.2%. To complete the calculation, we then multiply the incremental increase in inventory over year three of 1,750 units by the base year cost of $32.00/unit, and then multiply the result by our new index of 117.2% to arrive at a year four LIFO layer of $65,632.

Thus, after four years of inventory layering calculations, the double-extension LIFO valuation consists of the following three layers:

Layer Type	Layer Valuation	Layer Index
Base layer	$112,000	0.0%
Year 2 layer	68,992	107.8%
Year 4 layer	65,632	117.2%
Total	$246,624	—

13.22   LINK CHAIN METHOD

Another way to calculate the dollar value LIFO inventory is to use the link chain method. This approach is designed to avoid the problem encountered during double-extension calculations, where one must determine the base year cost of each new item added to inventory. However, tax regulations require that the link chain method only be used for tax reporting purposes if it can be clearly demonstrated that all other dollar value LIFO calculation methods are not applicable due to high rates of churn in the types of items included in inventory.

The link chain method creates inventory layers by comparing year-end prices to prices at the beginning of each year, thereby avoiding the problems associated with comparisons to a base year that may be many years in the past. This results in a rolling cumulative index that is linked (hence the name) to the index derived in the preceding year. Tax regulations allow one to create the index using a representative sample of the total inventory valuation that must comprise at least one-half of the total inventory valuation. In brief, a link chain calculation is derived by extending the cost of inventory at both beginning-of-year and end-of-year prices to arrive at a pricing index within the current year; this index is then multiplied by the ongoing cumulative index from the previous year to arrive at a new cumulative index that is used to price out the new inventory layer for the most recent year. An example of link chain inventory is as follows:

> This example assumes the same inventory information just used for the double-extension example. However, we have also noted the beginning inventory cost for each year and included the extended beginning inventory cost for each year, which facilitates calculations under the link-chain method.

Year	Ending Unit Quantity	Beginning-of-Year Cost/Each	End-of-Year Cost/Each	Extended at Beginning-of-Year Price	Extended at End-of-Year Price
1	3,500	$—	$32.00	$—	$112,000
2	7,000	32.00	34.50	224,000	241,500
3	5,500	34.50	36.00	189,750	198,000
4	7,250	36.00	37.50	261,000	271,875

As was the case for the double-extension method, there is no index for year one, which is the base year. In year two, the index will be the extended year-end price of $241,500 divided by the extended beginning-of-year price of $224,000, or 107.8%. This is the same percentage calculated for year two under the double-extension method, because the beginning of year price is the same as the base price used under the double-extension method.

We then determine the value of the year two inventory layer by first dividing the extended year-end price of $241,500 by the cumulative index of 107.8% to arrive at an inventory valuation restated to the base year cost of $224,026. We then subtract the year one base layer of $112,000 from the $224,026 to arrive at a new layer at the base year cost of $112,026, which we then multiply by the cumulative index of 107.8% to bring it back to current year prices. This results in a year two inventory layer of $120,764. At this point, the inventory layers are as follows:

Layer Type	Base Year Valuation	LIFO Layer Valuation	Cumulative Index
Base layer	$112,000	$112,000	0.0%
Year 2 layer	112,026	120,764	107.8%
Total	$224,026	$232,764	—

In year three, the index will be the extended year-end price of $198,000 divided by the extended beginning-of-year price of $189,750, or 104.3%. Since this is the first year in which the base year was not used to compile beginning-of-year costs, we must first derive the cumulative index, which is calculated by multiplying the preceding year's cumulative index of 107.8% by the new year three index of 104.3%, resulting in a new cumulative index of 112.4%. By dividing year three's extended year-end inventory of $198,000 by this cumulative index, we arrive at inventory priced at base year costs of $176,157.

This is less than the amount recorded in year two, so there will be no inventory layer. Instead, we must reduce the inventory layer recorded for year two. To do so, we subtract the base year layer of $112,000 from the $176,157 to arrive at a reduced year two layer of $64,157 at base year costs. We then multiply the $64,157 by the cumulative index in year two of 107.8% to arrive at an inventory valuation for the year two layer of $69,161. At this point, the inventory layers and associated cumulative indexes are as follows:

Layer Type	Base Year Valuation	LIFO Layer Valuation	Cumulative Index
Base layer	$112,000	$112,000	0.0%
Year 2 layer	64,157	69,161	107.8%
Year 3 layer	—	—	112.4%
Total	$176,157	$181,161	—

In year four, the index will be the extended year-end price of $271,875 divided by the extended beginning of year price of $261,000, or 104.2%. We then derive the new cumulative index by multiplying the preceding year's cumulative index of 112.4% by the year four index of 104.2%, resulting in a new cumulative index of 117.1%. By dividing year four's extended year-end inventory of $271,875 by this cumulative index, we arrive at inventory priced at base year costs of $232,173. We then subtract the preexisting base year inventory valuation for all previous layers of $176,157 from this amount to arrive at the base year valuation of the year four inventory layer, which is $56,016. Finally, we multiply the $56,016 by the cumulative index in year four of 117.1% to arrive at an inventory valuation for the year four layer of $62,575. At this point, the inventory layers and associated cumulative indexes are as follows:

Layer Type	Base Year Valuation	LIFO Layer Valuation	Cumulative Index
Base layer	$112,000	$112,000	0.0%
Year 2 layer	64,157	69,161	107.8%
Year 3 layer	—	—	112.4%
Year 4 layer	56,016	62,575	117.1%
Total	$232,173	$243,736	—

Compare the results of this calculation to those from the double-extension method. The indexes are nearly identical, as are the final LIFO layer valuations. The primary difference between the two methods is the avoidance of a base year cost determination for any new items subsequently added to inventory, for which a current cost is used instead.

13.23   WEIGHTED-AVERAGE INVENTORY VALUATION METHOD

The weighted-average costing method is calculated in exactly in accordance with its name—it is a weighted average of the costs in inventory. It has the singular advantage of not requiring a database that itemizes the many potential layers of inventory at the different costs at which they were acquired. Instead, the weighted average of all units in stock is determined, at which point *all* of the units in stock are accorded that weighted-average value. When parts are used from stock, they are all issued at the same weighted-average cost. If new units are added to stock, then the cost of the additions are added to the weighted average of all existing items in stock, which will result in a new, slightly modified weighted average for *all* of the parts in inventory (both the old and new ones).

This system has no particular advantage in relation to income taxes, since it does not skew the recognition of income based on trends in either increasing or declining costs. This makes it a good choice for those organizations that do not want to deal with tax planning. It is also useful for very small inventory valuations, where there would not be any significant change in the reported level of income even if the LIFO or FIFO methods were to be used. An example of weighted-average inventory valuation is as follows:

Exhibit 13.6 illustrates the weighted-average calculation for inventory valuations, using a series of 10 purchases of inventory. There is a maximum of one purchase per month, with usage (reductions from stock) also occurring in most months. Each of the columns in the exhibit shows how the average cost is calculated after each purchase and usage transaction.

We begin the illustration with the first row of calculations, which shows that we have purchased 500 units of item BK0043 on May 3, 2010. These units cost $10.00 per unit. During the month in which the units were purchased, 450 units were sent to production, leaving 50 units in stock. Since there has only been one purchase thus far, we can easily calculate, as shown in column 7, that the total inventory valuation is $500, by multiplying the unit cost of $10.00 (in column 3) by the number of units left in stock (in column 5). So far, we have a per-unit valuation of $10.00.

Next, we proceed to the second row of the exhibit, where we have purchased another 1,000 units of BK0043 on June 4, 2010. This purchase was less expensive, since the purchasing volume was larger, so the per-unit cost for this purchase is only $9.58. Only 350 units were sent to production during the month, so we now have 700 units in stock, of which 650 were added from the most recent purchase. To determine the new weighted-average cost of the total inventory, we first determine the extended cost of this newest addition to the inventory. As noted in column 7, we arrive at $6,227 by multiplying the value in column 3 by the value in column 6. We then add this amount to the existing total inventory valuation ($6,227 plus $500) to arrive at the new extended inventory cost of $6,727, as noted in column 8. Finally, we divide this new extended cost in column 8 by the total number of units now in stock, as shown in column 5, to arrive at our new per-unit cost of $9.61.

The third row reveals an additional inventory purchase of 250 units on July 11, 2010, but more units are sent to production during that month than were bought, so the total number of units in inventory drops to 550 (column 5). This inventory reduction requires no review of inventory layers, as was the case for the LIFO and FIFO calculations. Instead, we simply charge off the 150 unit reduction at the average per-unit cost of $9.61. As a result, the ending inventory valuation drops to $5,286, with the same per-unit cost of $9.61. Thus, reductions in inventory quantities under the average costing method require little calculation—just charge off the requisite number of units at the current average cost.

The remaining rows of the exhibit repeat the concepts just noted, alternatively adding units to and deleting them from stock. Though there are a number of columns noted in this exhibit that one must examine, it is really a simple concept to understand and work with. The typical computerized accounting system will perform all of these calculations automatically.

13.24   TYPE OF INVENTORY VALUATION SYSTEM TO USE

The decision tree in Exhibit 13.7 assists in determining which inventory valuation system to use, based on the type of inventory, the type of business, and the preferences of management in reporting financial information.

Weighted-Average Costing

Part Number BK0043

Column 1	Column 2	Column 3	Column 4	Column 5	Column 6	Column 7	Column 8	Column 9
Date Purchased	Quantity Purchased	Cost per Unit	Monthly Usage	Net Inventory Remaining	Net Change in Inventory During Period	Extended Cost of New Inventory Layer	Extended Inventory Cost	Average Inventory Cost/Unit
05/03/10	500	$10.00	450	50	50	$500	$500	$10.00
06/04/10	1,000	$9.58	350	700	650	$6,227	$6,727	$9.61
07/11/10	250	$10.65	400	550	−150	$0	$5,286	$9.61
08/01/10	475	$10.25	350	675	125	$1,281	$6,567	$9.73
08/30/10	375	$10.40	400	650	−25	$0	$6,324	$9.73
09/09/10	850	$9.50	700	800	150	$1,425	$7,749	$9.69
12/12/10	700	$9.75	900	600	−200	$0	$5,811	$9.69
02/08/11	650	$9.85	800	450	−150	$0	$4,359	$9.69
05/07/11	200	$10.80	0	650	200	$2,160	$6,519	$10.03
09/23/11	600	$9.85	750	500	−150	$0	$5,014	$10.03

EXHIBIT 13.6 WEIGHTED-AVERAGE COSTING VALUATION EXAMPLE

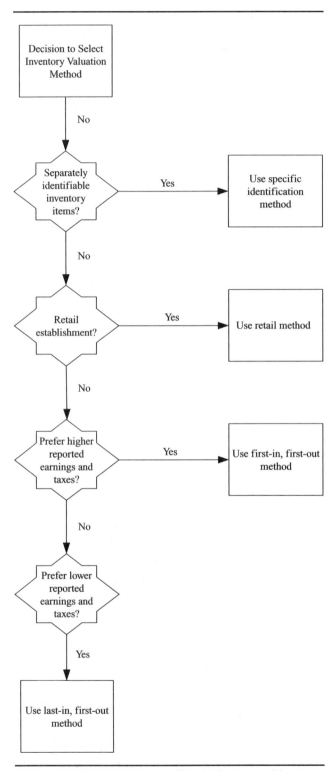

EXHIBIT 13.7   DECISION TREE FOR TYPE OF INVENTORY VALUATION SYSTEM TO USE

13.25   SUMMARY

An examination of a company's flow of costs will result in the decision to value its inventories based on either the specific identification, LIFO, FIFO, dollar-value LIFO, link chain, or weighted-average costing concepts. The LIFO method is the most complex, and results in reduced profit recognition and a lower income tax liability in periods of rising inventory costs. The FIFO method is almost as complex, but tends to result in fewer inventory cost layers; it reports higher profits in periods of rising inventory costs, and so has higher attendant tax liabilities. The dollar-value LIFO and link-chain methods are useful for avoiding the detailed tracking of individual costs for inventory items. The weighted-average costing concept avoids the entire layering issue by creating a rolling average of costs without the use of any cost layers; it tends to provide reported profit figures that are between those that would be described using either the LIFO or FIFO methods. As more companies reduce their inventory levels with advanced manufacturing techniques such as material requirements planning and just-in-time systems, they will find that the reduced amount of inventory left on hand will make the choice of cost flow concept less relevant.

ACCOUNTS RECEIVABLE

14.1 INTRODUCTION

The accounting for accounts receivable appears to be quite straightforward—just convert credit sales into accounts receivable and then cancel them when the corresponding cash is collected. Actually, there are a number of instances where this simple process becomes more complicated—credit card transactions, factoring of receivables, sales returns, early payment discounts, long-term receivables, and bad debts. The following sections discuss the proper accounting steps to take when dealing with these special situations.

14.2 DEFINITION OF ACCOUNTS RECEIVABLE

The Accounts receivable account tends to accumulate a number of transactions that are not strictly accounts receivable, so it is useful to define what should be stored in this account. An account receivable is a claim that is payable in cash and that is in exchange for the services or goods provided by the company. This definition excludes a note payable, which is essentially a return of loaned funds and for which a signed note is usually available as documentary evidence. A note payable should be itemized in the financial statements under a separate account. It also excludes any short-term funds loaned to employees (such as employee advances) or employee loans of any type that may be payable over a longer term. These items may more appropriately be stored in an Other Accounts Receivable or Accounts Receivable from Employees account. Also, an accountant should not create an accrued account receivable to offset an accrued sale transaction (as may occur under the percentage of completion method of recognizing revenue from long-term construction projects); on the contrary, the Accounts receivable account should only contain transactions for which there is a clear, short-term expectation of cash receipt from a customer.

14.3   THE ACCOUNTS RECEIVABLE TRANSACTION FLOW

The typical flow into and out of accounts receivable is quite simple. If there is a sale on credit terms, then the accountant credits the Sales account and debits Accounts receivable. When cash is received in payment from a customer, the Cash account is debited and accounts receivable are credited. Also, there is usually some type of sales tax involved in the transaction, in which case the account receivable is debited for the additional amount of the sales tax and a Sales tax liability account is credited for the same amount. There may be several sales tax liability accounts involved, since the typical sales tax can be broken down into liabilities to city, county, and state governments. These liability accounts are later emptied when sales taxes are remitted to the various government tax collection agencies. Though these steps appear quite simple, they can be complicated by a variety of additional transactions, many of which occur frequently. The following sections outline their treatment.

14.4   CREDIT CARD ACCOUNTS RECEIVABLE

When recording an account receivable that is based on a credit card payment, the accountant may record the receipt of cash at the same time as the credit card transaction; however, the receipt of cash from the credit card provider will actually occur several days later, so this results in an inaccurate representation of cash receipts. This is a particular problem if the credit card transaction is recorded at month end, since the bank reconciliation will show the cash receipt as an unreconciled item that has not really appeared at the bank yet.

A better treatment of credit card accounts receivable is to batch the credit card slips for each credit card provider for each day, and record a single credit to sales and debit to accounts receivable at the time of the credit card transaction for each batch of credit card slips. If the accountant is aware of the credit card processing fee charged by the credit card provider, this should be recorded at once as an offsetting expense. If there is some uncertainty regarding the amount of the fee, then the accountant should expense an estimated amount to a reserve at the time the account receivable is set up, and adjust the reserve when the transaction is settled.

14.5   COLLATERAL, ASSIGNMENTS, AND FACTORING

If a company uses its accounts receivable as *collateral* for a loan, then no accounting entry is required. An *assignment* of accounts receivable, where specific receivables are pledged as collateral on a loan and where customer payments are generally forwarded straight to the lender, also requires no accounting entry. However, if a company directly sells receivables with no continuing involvement in their collection and with no requirement to pay back the creditor in case a customer defaults on payment of a receivable, then this is called *factoring*, and a sale transaction must be recorded (see the "Receivables Ownership Decision" section for more information). Typically, this involves a credit to the Accounts receivable account, a debit to the Cash account for the amount of the buyer's payment, and a Loss on Factoring entry to reflect extra charges made by the factor on the transaction. The amount of cash received from the factor will also be reduced by an interest charge that is based on the amount of cash issued to the company for the period when the factor has not yet received cash from the factored accounts receivable; this results in a debit to the Interest expense account and a credit to the Accounts receivable account.

Account	Debit	Credit
Cash	$15,000	
Accounts Receivable—Factoring Holdback	10,000	
Loss on Factoring	4,800	
Interest Expense	200	
Due from Factoring Arrangement	70,000	
Accounts Receivable		$100,000

EXHIBIT 14.1 SAMPLE FACTORING JOURNAL ENTRY

A variation on this transaction occurs if the company only draws down cash from the factor when needed, rather than at the time when the accounts receivable are sold to the factor. This arrangement results in a smaller interest charge by the factor for the period when it is awaiting payment on the accounts receivable. In this instance, a new receivable is created that can be labeled "Due from Factoring Arrangement."

Another variation occurs when the factor holds back payment on some portion of the accounts receivable, on the grounds that there may be inventory returns from customers that can be charged back to the company. In this case, the proper entry is to offset the account receivable being transferred to the factor with a holdback receivable account. Once all receipt transactions have been cleared by the factor, any amounts left in the holdback account are eliminated with a debit to cash (being paid by the factor) and a credit to the holdback account.

A sample journal entry that includes all of the preceding factoring issues is shown in Exhibit 14.1. In this case, a company has sold $100,000 of accounts receivable to a factor, which requires a 10% holdback provision. The factor also expects to lose $4,800 in bad debts that it must absorb as a result of the transaction and so pays the company $4,800 less than the face value of the accounts receivable, which forces the company to recognize a loss of $4,800 on the transaction. Also, the company does not elect to take delivery of all funds allowed by the factor in order to save interest costs; accordingly, it only takes delivery of $15,000 to meet immediate cash needs. Finally, the factor charges 18% interest for the 30-day period that it is expected to take to collect the factored accounts receivable, which results in an interest charge of $200 on the $15,000 of delivered funds.

If the company factors its accounts receivable, but the factor has recourse against the company for uncollectible amounts (which reduces the factoring fee) or if the company agrees to service the receivables subsequent to the factoring arrangement, then the company still can be construed as having retained control over the receivables. In this case, the factoring arrangement is considered to be a loan, rather than a sale of receivables, resulting in the retention of the accounts receivable on the company's balance sheet, as well as the addition of a loan liability. When receivables are sold with recourse, one should shift the expected amount of bad debts to be incurred from the Allowance for bad debts account to a recourse obligation account, from which bad debts will be subtracted as incurred.

14.6   SALES RETURNS

When a customer returns goods to a company, the accountant should set up an Offsetting sales contra account, rather than backing out the original sale transaction. The resulting transaction would be a credit to the Accounts receivable account and a debit to the Contra account. There are two reasons for using this approach. First, a direct reduction of the original sale would impact the financial reporting in a prior period, if the sale originated in a prior period. Second, a large number of sales returns charged directly against the Sales account would essentially be invisible on the financial statements, with management only seeing a reduced sales volume. Only by using (and reporting) an offsetting Contra account can management gain some knowledge of the extent of any sales returns. If a company ships products on approval (i.e., customers have the right of return) and there is a history of significant returns, then it should create a reserve for sales returns based on historical rates of return. The Offsetting sale returns expense account should be categorized as part of the cost of goods sold. An example of a reserve for sales made on approval is as follows:

> The Dusty Tome Book Company issues new versions of its books to a subscriber list that has purchased previous editions. Historically, it has experienced a 22% rate of return from these sales. In the current month, it shipped $440,000 of books to its subscriber list. Given the historical rate of return, Dusty Tome's controller expects to see $96,800 worth of books returned to the company. Accordingly, she records the following entry:

	Debit	Credit
Sale returns expense	$96,800	
Reserve for sales returns		$96,800

14.7   EARLY PAYMENT DISCOUNTS

Unless a company offers an exceedingly large early payment discount, it is unlikely that the total amount of this discount taken will have a material impact on the financial statements. Consequently, some variation in the allowable treatment of this transaction can be used. The most theoretically accurate approach is to initially record the account receivable at its discounted value, which assumes that all customers will take the early payment discount. Any cash discounts that are not taken will then be recorded as additional revenue. This results in a properly conservative view of the amount of funds that one can expect to receive from the accounts receivable. An alternative that results in a slightly higher initial revenue figure is to record the full, undiscounted amount of each sale in the accounts receivable, and then record any discounts taken in a sales contra account. One objection to this second approach is that the discount taken will only be recognized in an accounting period that is later than the one in which the sale was initially recorded (given the time delay usually associated with accounts receivable payments), which is an inappropriate revenue recognition technique. An alternative approach that avoids this problem is to set up a reserve for cash discounts taken in the period in which the sales occur, and offset actual discounts against it as they occur.

14.8   REPORTING OF LONG-TERM RECEIVABLES

If an account receivable is not due to be collected for more than one year, then it should be discounted at an interest rate that fairly reflects the rate that would have been charged to the debtor under a normal lending situation. An alternative is to use any interest rate that may be noted in the sale agreement. Under no circumstances should the interest rate be one that is less than the prevailing market rate at the time when the receivable was originated. The result of this calculation will be a smaller receivable than is indicated by its face amount. The difference should be gradually accrued as interest income over the life of the receivable. An example of a long-term accounts receivable transaction is as follows:

> The Carolina Furniture Company (CFC) sells a large block of office furniture in exchange for a receivable of $82,000 payable by the customer in two years. There is no stated interest rate on the receivable, so the CFC controller uses the current market rate of 6% to derive a present value discount rate of 0.8900. She multiplies the $82,000 receivable by the discount rate of 0.8900 to arrive at a present value of $72,980, and makes the following entry:

	Debit	Credit
Notes receivable	$82,000	
Furniture revenue		$72,980
Discount on notes receivable		9,020

> In succeeding months, the CFC controller gradually debits the Discount on notes receivable account and credits interest income, so that the discount is entirely eliminated by the time the note receivable is collected. Also, note that the initial debit is to a Notes receivable account, not Accounts receivable, since this is not considered a current asset.

14.9   TREATMENT OF BAD DEBTS

The accountant must recognize a bad debt as soon as it is reasonably certain that a loss is likely to occur, and the amount in question can be estimated with some degree of accuracy. For financial reporting purposes, the only allowable method for recognizing bad debts is to set up a bad debt reserve as a contra account to the Accounts receivable account. Under this approach, one should estimate a long-term average amount of bad debt, debit the bad debt expense (which is most commonly kept in the operating expenses section of the income statement) for this percentage of the period-end accounts receivable balance, and credit the Bad debt reserve contra account. When an actual bad debt is recognized, the accountant credits the Accounts receivable account and debits the reserve. No offset is made to the Sales account. If there is an unusually large bad debt to be recognized that will more than offset the existing bad debt reserve, then the reserve should be sufficiently increased to ensure that the remaining balance in the reserve is not negative.

There are several ways to determine the long-term estimated amount of bad debt for the preceding calculation. One is to determine the historical average bad debt as a proportion of the total credit sales for the past 12 months. Another option that results in a more accurate estimate is to calculate a different historical bad debt percentage based on the relative age of the accounts receivable at the end of the reporting period. For example, accounts aged greater than 90 days may have a historical bad debt experience of 50%, whereas those over 25% have a percentage of 20%, and those below 30 days are at only 4%. This type of experience percentage is more difficult to calculate, but can result in a considerable degree of precision in the size of the bad debt allowance. It is also possible to estimate the bad debt level based on the type of customer. For example, one could make the case that government entities never go out of business and so have a much lower bad debt rate than other types of customers. Whatever approach is used must be backed up quantitatively so that an auditor can trace through the calculations to ensure that a sufficient bad debt reserve has been provided. An example of a bad debt reserve calculation is as follows:

The Granny Clock Company has $120,000 of outstanding accounts receivable. Of that amount, $20,000 is more than 90 days old, while $41,000 is in the 60–90 day category. The company has historically experienced a loss rate of 25% on receivables more than 90 days old, a loss rate of 10% on receivables in the 60–90 day category, and 2% on all other receivables. Based on this information, the controller calculates a reserve of $1,180 on the current receivables ($59,000 × 2%), $41,000 for receivables in the 60–90 day category ($41,000 × 10%), and $5,000 for receivables older than 90 days ($20,000 × 25%), which totals $10,280. The company already has a reserve of $2,000 left over from the previous month, so the new entry is a debit to bad debt expense and a credit to the reserve for bad debts of $8,280 ($10,280 total reserve less the existing balance).

If an account receivable has already been written off as a bad debt and is then collected, the receipt should be charged against the bad debt reserve or to earnings. Incorrect treatment would be to create a new sale and charge the receipt against that, since this would artificially show a higher level of sales than really occurred.

14.10 RECEIVABLES OWNERSHIP DECISION

The main issue involving the use of accounts receivable as collateral or for assignment or factoring is how to treat these activities in the financial statements. The illustration in Exhibit 14.2 may be of some assistance. As shown in the exhibit, if receivables are pledged as collateral on a loan or if they are assigned with recourse or if the company has some means of forcing their return, then the company essentially has control over the receivables and should continue to record them as such on its balance sheet. However, if the receivables purchaser has assumed the risk of loss *and* can pledge the receivables to or exchange the receivables with a third party *and* the company or its creditors can no longer access the receivables for any reason, then the purchaser has control over the assets, and the selling company must record the sale of the receivables and remove them from its balance

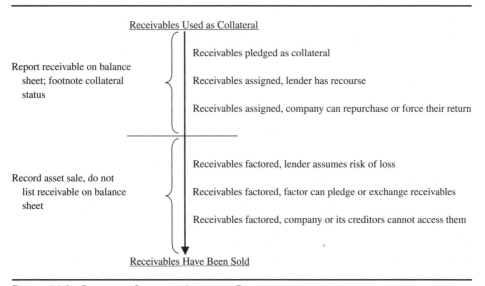

EXHIBIT 14.2 REPORTING STATUS OF ACCOUNTS RECEIVABLE

sheet. Thus, if there is any evidence that the selling company retains any aspect of control over the receivables, they must continue to be recorded on the selling company's balance sheet, with additional footnote disclosure of their status as collateral on a loan.

14.11   SUMMARY

This chapter covered a number of special situations in which the accountant must depart from the standard conversion of sales to accounts receivable to cash. Though some transactions (such as factoring) are relatively uncommon, others (such as bad debt accruals and early payment discounts) occur quite frequently and can have some impact on the reported level of profitability if not handled correctly. Thus, a careful review of these issues is recommended.

FIXED ASSETS

15.1 INTRODUCTION

This chapter covers a wide range of topics related to the types of costs that should be recorded as fixed assets and how they should be depreciated and disposed of. The chapter also covers the treatment of special types of fixed assets, such as construction-in-progress, leasehold improvements, and intangible assets.

15.2 THE CAPITALIZATION LIMIT

A company must set a minimum level of investment in any asset below which it will record the asset as a current-period expense, rather than a long-term asset. This is called the *capitalization limit*. It is imposed from a practicality perspective, since there are a number of potential long-term assets (such as a computer mouse, whose utility will extend over many years) whose costs are so low that they will clutter up a company's asset listings to a great extent. If all potential long-term assets are indeed recorded in the fixed asset register as assets, a company can easily find that its asset tracking and depreciation calculation chore is increased tenfold.

To avoid these problems, a company should have the board of directors approve a capitalization limit below which nothing is capitalized. There are several ways to determine what this limit should be. For example, common usage in the industry may suggest an amount. A company's auditors may suggest an amount based upon what they have seen at other clients. A good alternative is to simply review all transactions for the past few months to see what level of capitalization could potentially be used in order to avoid an excessive amount of record keeping. If this later approach is used, one can use the 80/20 Pareto Rule, selecting a capitalization limit that capitalizes only those 20% of all potential assets that constitute 80% of the dollar volume of all potential assets. A fourth option is to set the capitalization limit at the point where IRS rules recommend items to be capitalized.

15.3 FIXED ASSET PURCHASES

When a company purchases a fixed asset, there are a number of expenditures it is allowed to include in the capitalized cost of the asset. These costs include the sales tax and ownership registration fees (if any). Also, the cost of all freight, insurance, and duties required to bring the asset to the company can be included in the capitalized cost. Further, the cost required to install the asset can be included. Installation costs include the cost to test and break in the asset, which can include the cost of test materials.

If a fixed *asset is acquired for nothing but cash*, then its recorded cost is the amount of cash paid. However, if the asset is acquired by taking on a payable, such as a stream of debt payments (or taking over the payments that were initially to be made by the seller of the asset), then the present value of all future payments yet to be made must also be rolled into the recorded asset cost. If the stream of future payments contains no stated interest rate, then one must be imputed based on market rates when making the present value calculation. If the amount of the payable is not clearly evident at the time of purchase, then it is also admissible to record the asset at its fair market value.

If an *asset is purchased with company stock*, one may assign a value to the assets acquired based on the fair market value of either the stock or the assets, whichever is more easily determinable. An example of an asset acquired with stock is as follows:

> The St. Louis Motor Car Company issues 500 shares of its stock to acquire a sheet metal bender. This is a publicly held company, and on the day of the acquisition its shares were trading for $13.25 each. Since this is an easily determinable value, the cost assigned to the equipment is $6,625 (500 shares times $13.25/share). A year later, the company has taken itself private, and chooses to issue another 750 shares of its stock to acquire a router. In this case, the value of the shares is no longer so easily determined, so the company asks an appraiser to determine the router's fair value, which she sets at $12,000. In the first transaction, the journal entry was a debit of $6,625 to the Fixed asset equipment account and a credit of $6,625 to the Common stock account, while the second transaction was to the same accounts, but for $12,000 instead.

If a company *obtains an asset through an exchange involving a dissimilar asset*, it should record the incoming asset at the fair market value of the asset for which it was exchanged. However, if this fair value is not readily apparent, the fair value of the incoming asset can be used instead. If no fair market value is readily obtainable for either asset, then the net book value of the relinquished asset can be used. An example of an exchange for a dissimilar asset is as follows:

> The Dakota Motor Company swaps a file server for an overhead crane. Its file server has a book value of $12,000 (net of accumulated depreciation of $4,000), while the overhead crane has a fair value of $9,500. The company has no information about the fair value of its file

server, so Dakota uses its net book value instead to establish a value for the swap. Dakota recognizes a loss of $2,500 on the transaction, as noted in the following entry:

	Debit	Credit
Factory equipment	$9,500	
Accumulated depreciation	4,000	
Loss on asset exchange	2,500	
Factory equipment		$16,000

A common transaction is for a company to *trade in an existing asset for a new one, along with an additional payment* that covers the incremental additional cost of the new asset over that of the old one being traded away. The additional payment portion of this transaction is called the "boot." When the boot comprises at least 25% of the exchange's fair value, both entities must record the transaction at the fair value of the assets involved. If the amount of boot is less than 25% of the transaction, the party receiving the boot can recognize a gain in proportion to the amount of boot received. An example of an asset exchange with at least 25% boot is as follows:

The Dakota Motor Company trades in a copier for a new one from the Fair Copy Company, paying an additional $9,000 as part of the deal. The fair value of the copier traded away is $2,000, while the fair value of the new copier being acquired is $11,000 (with a book value of $12,000, net of $3,500 in accumulated depreciation). The book value of the copier being traded away is $2,500, net of $5,000 in accumulated depreciation. Because Dakota has paid a combination of $9,000 in cash and $2,500 in the net book value of its existing copier ($11,500 in total) to acquire a new copier with a fair value of $11,000, it must recognize a loss of $500 on the transaction, as noted in the following entry.

	Debit	Credit
Office equipment (new asset)	$11,000	
Accumulated depreciation	5,000	
Loss on asset exchange	500	
Office equipment (asset traded away)		$7,500
Cash		9,000

On the other side of the transaction, Fair Copy is accepting a copier with a fair value of $2,000 and $9,000 in cash for a replacement copier with a fair value of $11,000, so its journal entry is as follows:

	Debit	Credit
Cash	$9,000	
Office equipment (asset acquired)	2,000	
Accumulated depreciation	3,500	
Loss on sale of asset	1,000	
Office equipment (asset traded away)		$15,500

An example of an asset exchange with less than 25% boot is as follows:

As was the case in the last example, the Dakota Motor Company trades in a copier for a new one, but now it pays $2,000 cash and trades in its old copier, with a fair value of $9,000 and a net book value of $9,500 after $5,000 of accumulated depreciation. Also, the fair value of the copier being traded away by Fair Copy remains at $11,000, but its net book value drops to $10,000 (still net of accumulated depreciation of $3,500). All other information remains the same. In this case, the proportion of boot paid is 18% ($2,000 cash, divided by total consideration paid of $2,000 cash plus the copier fair value of $9,000). As was the case before, Dakota has paid a total of $11,500 (from a different combination of $9,000 in cash and $2,500 in the net book value of its existing copier) to acquire a new copier with a fair value of $11,000, so it must recognize a loss of $500 on the transaction, as noted in the following entry.

	Debit	Credit
Office equipment (new asset)	$11,000	
Accumulated depreciation	5,000	
Loss on asset exchange	500	
Office equipment (asset traded away)		$14,500
Cash		2,000

The main difference is on the other side of the transaction, where Fair Copy is now accepting a copier with a fair value of $9,000 and $2,000 in cash in exchange for a copier with a book value of $10,000, so there is a potential gain of $1,000 on the deal. However, because it receives boot that is less than 25% of the transaction fair value, it recognizes a pro rata gain of $180, which is calculated as the 18% of the deal attributable to the cash payment, multiplied by the $1,000 gain. Fair Copy's journal entry to record the transaction is as follows:

	Debit	Credit
Cash	$2,000	
Office equipment (asset acquired)	8,180	
Accumulated depreciation	3,500	
Office equipment (asset traded away)		$13,500
Gain on asset transfer		180

In this entry, Fair Copy can only recognize a small portion of the gain on the asset transfer, with the remaining portion of the gain being netted against the recorded cost of the acquired asset.

There are a number of ways to handle asset transactions where there is either no exchange of money for the assets or where money is only part of the consideration given. The decision tree in Exhibit 15.1 can be used to determine the correct accounting treatment for the various scenarios.

If a *group of assets is acquired* through a single purchase transaction, the cost should be allocated among the assets in the group based on their proportional share of their total fair market values. The fair market value may be difficult to ascertain in many instances, in which case an appraisal value or tax assessment value can be used. It may also be possible to use the present value of estimated cash flows for each asset as the basis for the allocation, though this measure can be subject to considerable variability in the foundation data, and also requires a great deal of analysis to obtain. An example of a group asset acquisition is as follows:

The Dakota Motor Company acquires three machines for $80,000 as part of the Chapter 7 liquidation auction of a competitor. There is no ready market for the machines. Dakota hires an appraiser to determine their value. She judges machines A and B to be worth $42,000 and $18,000, respectively, but can find no basis of comparison for machine C, and passes on an appraisal for that item. Dakota's production manager thinks the net present value of cash

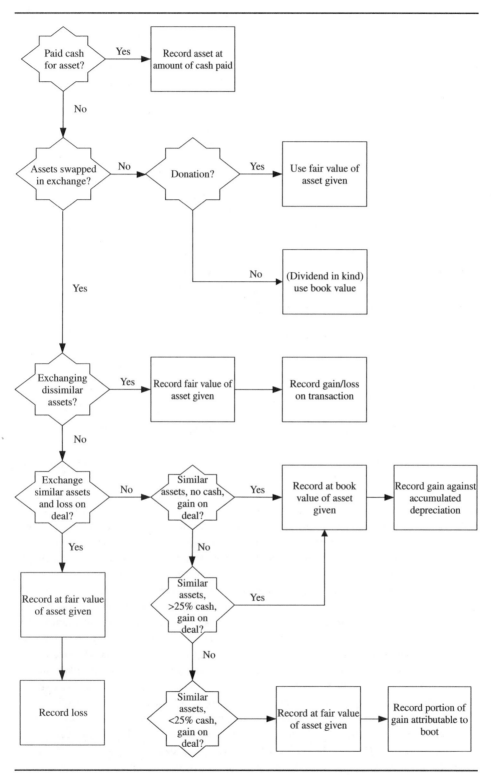

EXHIBIT 15.1   ACCOUNTING FOR NONMONETARY EXCHANGES INVOLVING ASSETS

flows arising from the use of machine C will be about $35,000. Based on this information, the following costs are allocated to the machines:

Machine Description	Value	Proportions	Allocated Costs
Machine A	$42,000	44%	$35,200
Machine B	18,000	23%	18,400
Machine C	35,000	33%	26,400
Totals	$95,000	100%	$80,000

15.4   FIXED ASSET IMPROVEMENTS

Once an asset is put into use, the majority of expenditures related to it must be charged to expense. If expenditures are for basic maintenance, not contributing to an asset's value or extending its usable life, then they must be charged to expense. If expenditures are considerable in amount and increase the asset's value, then they are charged to the Asset capital account, though they will be depreciated only over the predetermined depreciation period. If expenditures are considerable in amount and increase the asset's usable life, then they are charged directly to the Accumulated depreciation account, effectively reducing the amount of depreciation expense incurred.

If an existing equipment installation is moved or rearranged, the cost of doing so is charged to expense if there is no measurable benefit in future periods. If there is a measurable benefit, then the expenditure is capitalized and depreciated over the periods when the increased benefit is expected to occur.

If an asset must be replaced that is part of a larger piece of equipment, one should remove the cost and associated accumulated depreciation for the asset to be replaced from the accounting records and recognize any gain or loss on its disposal. If there is no record of the subsidiary asset's cost, then ignore this step. In addition, the cost of the replacement asset should be capitalized and depreciated over the remaining term of the larger piece of equipment.

An example of current-period expenditures is routine machine maintenance, such as the replacement of worn-out parts. This expenditure will not change the ability of an asset to perform in a future period, and so should be charged to expense within the current period. If repairs are effected in order to repair damage to an asset, this is also a current-period expense. Also, even if an expenditure can be proven to impact future periods, it may still be charged to expense if it is too small to meet the corporate capitalization limit. If a repair cost can be proven to have an impact covering more than one accounting period, but not many additional periods into the future, a company can spread the cost over a few months or all months of a single year by recording the expense in an allowance account that is gradually charged off over the course of the year. In this last case, there may be an ongoing expense accrual throughout the year that will be charged off, even in the absence of any major expenses in the early part of the year—the intention being that the company knows that expenses will be incurred later in the year and chooses to smooth out its expense recognition by recognizing some of the expense prior to it actually being incurred.

If a company incurs costs to avoid or mitigate environmental contamination (usually in response to government regulations), these costs must generally be charged to expense in the current period. The only case in which capitalization is an alternative occurs when the costs incurred can be demonstrated to reduce or prevent future environmental contamination, as well as improve the underlying asset. If so, the asset life associated with these costs should be the period over which environmental contamination is expected to be reduced.

15.5   CAPITALIZATION OF INTEREST

When a company is constructing assets for its own use or as separately identifiable projects intended for sale, it should capitalize as part of the project cost all associated interest expenses. Capitalized interest expenses are calculated based on the interest rate of the debt used to construct the asset or (if there was no new debt) at the weighted-average interest rate that the company pays on its other debt. Interest is not capitalized when its addition would result in no material change in the cost of the resulting asset or when the construction period is quite short (since there is little time over which to accrue interest) or when there is no prospect of completing a project.

The interest rate is multiplied by the average capital expenditures incurred to construct the targeted asset. The amount of interest expense capitalized is limited to an amount less than or equal to the total amount of interest expense actually incurred by the company during the period of asset construction. An example of an interest capitalization transaction is as follows:

> The Carolina Astronautics Corporation (CAC) is constructing a new launch pad for its suborbital rocket–launching business. It pays a contractor $5,000,000 up front and $2,500,000 after the project's completion six months later. At the beginning of the project, it issued $15,000,000 in bonds at 9% interest to finance the project, as well as other capital needs. The calculation of the interest expense to be capitalized is as follows:

Investment Amount	Months to Be Capitalized	Interest Rate	Interest to Be Capitalized
$5,000,000	6	9%/12	$225,000
2,500,000	0	—	0
		Total	$225,000

> There is no interest expense to be capitalized on the final payment of $2,500,000, since it was incurred at the very end of the construction period. CAC accrued $675,000 in total interest expenses during the period when the launch pad was built ($15,000,000 × 9%/12 × 6 months). Since the total expense incurred by the company greatly exceeds the amount of interest to be capitalized for the launch pad, there is no need to reduce the amount of capitalized interest to the level of actual interest expense incurred. Accordingly, CAC's controller makes the following journal entry to record the capitalization of interest:

	Debit	Credit
Assets (Launch Pad)	$225,000	
Interest expense		$225,000

15.6   FIXED ASSET DISPOSITIONS

When a company disposes of a fixed asset, it should completely eliminate all record of it from the fixed asset and related accumulated depreciation accounts. In addition, it should recognize a gain or loss on the difference between the net book value of the asset and the price at which it was sold. For example, Company ABC is selling a machine, which was originally purchased for $10,000 and against which $9,000 of depreciation has been recorded. The sale price of the used machine is $1,500. The proper journal entry is to credit the Fixed asset account for $10,000 (thereby removing the machine from the fixed asset journal), debit the Accumulated depreciation account for $9,000 (thereby removing all related depreciation from the Accumulated depreciation account), debit the Cash account for $1,500 (to reflect the receipt of cash from the asset sale), and credit the "gain on sale of assets" account for $500.

There may be identifiable costs associated with an asset disposition that are required by a legal agreement, known as an *asset retirement obligation* (ARO). For example, a building lease may require the lessee to remove all equipment by the termination date of the lease; the cost of this obligation should be recognized at the time the lease is signed. As another example, the passage of legislation requiring the cleanup of hazardous waste sites would require the recognition of these costs as soon as the legislation is passed.

The amount of ARO recorded is the range of cash flows associated with asset disposition that would be charged by a third party, summarized by their probability weightings. This amount is then discounted at the company's credit-adjusted risk-free interest rate. The risk-free interest rate can be obtained from the rates at which zero-coupon U.S. Treasury instruments are selling.

If there are upward adjustments to the amount of the ARO in subsequent periods, these adjustments are accounted for in the same manner, with the present value for each one being derived from the credit-adjusted risk-free rate at the time of the transaction. These incremental transactions are then recorded separately in the fixed asset register, though their depreciation periods and methods will all match that of the underlying asset. If a reduction in the ARO occurs in any period, this amount should be recognized as a gain in the current period, with the amount being offset pro rata against all layers of ARO recorded in the fixed asset register.

When an ARO situation arises, the amount of the ARO is added to the fixed asset register for the related asset, with the offset to a liability account that will eventually be depleted when the costs associated with the retirement obligation are actually incurred. The amount of the ARO added to the fixed asset is then depreciated under the same method used for the related asset. In subsequent periods, one must also make an entry to accretion expense to reflect ongoing increases in the present value of the ARO, which naturally occurs as the date of the ARO event comes closer to the present date. An example of an ARO transaction is as follows:

> The Ever-Firm Tire Company installs a tire molding machine in a leased facility. The lease expires in three years, and the company has a legal obligation to remove the machine at that time. The controller polls local equipment removal companies and obtains estimates of $40,000 and $60,000 for what it would cost to remove the machine. She suspects the lower estimate to be inaccurate, and so assigns probabilities of 25% and 75% to the two transactions, resulting in the following probability-adjusted estimate:

Cash Flow Estimate	Assigned Probability	Probability-Adjusted Cash Flow
$40,000	25%	$10,000
60,000	75%	45,000
	100%	$55,000

She assumes that inflation will average 4% in each of the next three years and so adjusts the $55,000 amount upward by $6,868 to $61,868 to reflect this estimate. Finally, she estimates the company's credit-adjusted risk-free rate to be 8%, based on the implicit interest rate in its last lease, and uses the 8% figure to arrive at a discount rate of 0.7938. After multiplying this discount rate by the inflation- and probability-adjusted ARO cost of $61,868, she arrives at $49,111 as the figure to add to the Machinery asset account as a debit and the Asset retirement obligation account as a credit.

In the three following years, she must also make entries to increase the Asset retirement obligation account by the amount of increase in the present value of the ARO, which is calculated as follows:

Year	Beginning ARO	Inflation Multiplier	Annual Accretion	Ending ARO
1	$49,111	8%	$3,929	$53,041
2	53,041	8%	4,243	57,285
3	57,285	8%	4,583	61,868

After three years of accretion entries, the balance in the ARO liability account matches the original inflation- and probability-adjusted estimate of the amount of cash flows required to settle the ARO obligation.

15.7   INBOUND FIXED ASSET DONATIONS

If an asset is donated to a company (only common in the case of a not-for-profit corporation), the receiving company can record the asset at its fair market value, which can be derived from market rates on similar assets, an appraisal, or the net present value of its estimated cash flows.

15.8   OUTBOUND FIXED ASSET DONATIONS

When a company donates an asset to another company, it must recognize the fair value of the asset donated, which is netted against its net book value. The difference between the asset's fair value and its net book value is recognized as either a gain or loss. An example of an outbound donation is as follows:

The Nero Fiddle Company has donated to the local orchestra a portable violin repair workbench from its manufacturing department. The workbench was originally purchased for $15,000, and $6,000 of depreciation has since been charged against it. The workbench can be purchased on the eBay auction site for $8,500, which establishes its fair market value. The company uses the following journal entry to record the transaction:

	Debit	Credit
Charitable donations	$8,500	
Accumulated depreciation	6,000	
Loss on property donation	500	
Machinery asset account		$15,000

15.9   CONSTRUCTION IN PROGRESS

If a company constructs its own fixed assets, it should capitalize all direct labor, materials, and overhead costs that are clearly associated with the construction project. In addition, it should charge to the Capital account those fixed overhead costs considered to have "discernible future benefits" related to the project. From a practical perspective, this makes it unlikely that a significant amount of fixed overhead costs should be charged to a capital project.

If a company constructs its own assets, it should compile all costs associated with them into an account or journal, commonly known as the Construction-in-progress (CIP) account. There should be a separate account or journal for each project that is currently under way, so there is no risk of commingling expenses among multiple projects. The costs that can be included in the CIP account include all costs normally associated with the purchase of a fixed asset, as well as the direct materials and direct labor used to construct the asset. In addition, all overhead costs that are reasonably apportioned to the project may be charged to it, as well as the depreciation expense associated with any other assets that are used during the construction process.

One may also charge to the CIP account the interest cost of any funds that have been loaned to the company for the express purpose of completing the project. If this approach is used, one can either use the interest rate associated with a specific loan that was procured to fund the project, or use the weighted-average rate for a number of company loans, all of which are being used for this purpose. The amount of interest charged in any period should be based on the cumulative amount of expenditures thus far incurred for the project. The amount of interest charged to the project should not exceed the amount of interest actually incurred for all associated loans through the same time period.

Once the project has been completed, all costs should be carried over from the CIP account into one of the established fixed asset accounts, where the new asset is recorded on a summary basis. All of the detail-level costs should be stored for future review. The asset should be depreciated beginning on the day when it is officially completed. Under no circumstances should depreciation begin prior to this point.

15.10   ACCOUNTING FOR LAND

Land cannot be depreciated, and so companies tend to avoid charging expenses to this account on the grounds that they cannot recognize taxable depreciation expenses. Nonetheless, those costs reasonably associated with the procurement of land, such as real estate commissions, title examination fees, escrow fees, and accrued property taxes paid by the purchaser should all be charged to the Fixed asset account for land. This should also include the cost of an option to purchase land. In addition, all subsequent costs associated with the improvement of the land, such as draining, clearing, and grading, should be added to the Land account. The cost of interest that is associated with the development of land should also be capitalized. Property taxes incurred during the land development process should also be charged to the Asset account, but should be charged to current expenses once the development process has been completed.

15.11   ACCOUNTING FOR LEASEHOLD IMPROVEMENTS

When a lessee makes improvements to a property that is being leased from another entity, it can still capitalize the cost of the improvements (subject to the amount of the capitalization limit), but the time period over which these costs can be amortized must be limited to the lesser of the useful life of the improvements or the length of the lease.

If the lease has an extension option that would allow the lessee to increase the time period over which it can potentially lease the property, the total period over which the leasehold improvements can be depreciated must still be limited to the initial lease term, on the grounds that there is no certainty that the lessee will accept the lease extension option. This limitation is waived for depreciation purposes only if there is either a bargain renewal option or extensive penalties in the lease contract that would make it highly likely that the lessee would renew the lease.

15.12   THE DEPRECIATION BASE

The basis used for an asset when conducting a depreciation calculation should be its capitalized cost less any salvage value that the company expects to receive at the time when the asset is expected to be taken out of active use. The salvage value can be difficult to determine, for several reasons. First, there may be a removal cost associated with the asset, which will reduce the net salvage value that will be realized (see the earlier ARO discussion). If the equipment is especially large (such as a printing press) or involves environmental hazards (such as any equipment involving the use of radioactive substances), then the removal cost may exceed the salvage value. In this later instance, the salvage value may be negative, in which case it should be ignored for depreciation purposes.

A second reason why salvage value is difficult to determine is that asset obsolescence is so rapid in some industries (especially in relation to computer equipment) that a reasonable appraisal of salvage value at the time an asset is put into service may require drastic revision shortly thereafter. A third reason is the lack of a ready market for the sale of used assets in many instances. A fourth reason is the cost of conducting an appraisal in order to determine a net salvage value, which may be excessive in relation to the cost of the equipment being appraised. For all these reasons, a company should certainly attempt to set a net salvage value in order to arrive at a cost base for depreciation purposes, but it will probably be necessary to make regular revisions to its salvage value estimates in a cost-effective manner in order to reflect the ongoing realities of asset resale values.

In the case of low-cost assets, it is rarely worth the effort to derive salvage values for depreciation purposes; as a result, these items are typically fully depreciated on the assumption that they have no salvage value.

15.13   DEPRECIATION ISSUES

Depreciation is designed to spread an asset's cost over its entire useful service life. Its service life is the period over which it is worn out for any reason, at the end of which it is no longer usable, or not usable without extensive overhaul. Its useful life can also be considered terminated at the point when it no longer has a sufficient productive capacity for ongoing company production needs, rendering it essentially obsolete.

Anything can be depreciated that has a business purpose, has a productive life of more than one year, gradually wears out over time, and has a cost that exceeds the corporate capitalization limit. Since land does not wear out, it cannot be depreciated.

There are a variety of depreciation methods, as outlined in the following sections. Straight-line depreciation provides for a depreciation rate that is the same amount in every year of an asset's life, whereas various accelerated depreciation methods (such as sum of the years digits and double declining balance) are oriented toward the more rapid recognition of depreciation expenses, on the grounds that an asset is used most intensively when it is first acquired. Perhaps the most accurate depreciation methods are those that are tied to actual asset usage (such as the units of production method), though they require much more extensive recordkeeping in relation to units of usage. There are also depreciation methods based on compound interest factors, resulting in delayed depreciation recognition; since these methods are rarely used, they are not presented here.

If an asset is present but is temporarily idle, then its depreciation should be continued using the existing assumptions for the usable life of the asset. Only if it is permanently idled should the accountant review the need to recognize impairment of the asset (see the later section discussing impairment).

An asset is rarely purchased or sold precisely on the first or last day of the fiscal year, which brings up the issue of how depreciation is to be calculated in these first and last partial years of use. There are a number of alternatives available, all of which are valid as long as they are consistently applied. One option is to record a full year of depreciation in the year of acquisition and no depreciation in the year of sale. Another option is to record a half-year of depreciation in the first year and a half-year of depreciation in the last year. One can also prorate the depreciation more precisely, making it accurate to within the nearest month (or even the nearest day) of when an acquisition or sale transaction occurs.

15.14   STRAIGHT-LINE DEPRECIATION

The straight-line depreciation method is the simplest method available and is the most popular one when a company has no particular need to recognize depreciation costs at an accelerated rate (as would be the case when it wanted to match the book value of its depreciation to the accelerated depreciation used for income tax calculation purposes). It is also used for all amortization calculations.

Straight-line depreciation is calculated by subtracting an asset's expected salvage value from its capitalized cost, and then dividing this amount by the estimated life of the asset. For example, a candy wrapper machine has a cost of $40,000 and an expected salvage value of $8,000. It is expected to be in service for eight years. Given these assumptions, its annual depreciation expense is as follows:

$$= \text{(Cost} - \text{salvage value)} \text{ / number of years in service}$$
$$= (\$40,000 - \$8,000) \text{ / 8 years}$$
$$= \$32,000 \text{ / 8 years}$$
$$= \$4,000 \text{ depreciation per year}$$

15.15   DOUBLE DECLINING BALANCE DEPRECIATION

The double declining balance method (DDB) is the most aggressive depreciation method for recognizing the bulk of the expense toward the beginning of an asset's useful life. To calculate it, determine the straight-line depreciation for an asset for its first year (see the previous section for the straight-line depreciation calculation), then double this amount, which yields the depreciation for the first year. Then, subtract the first-year depreciation from the asset cost (using no salvage value deduction), and run the same calculation again for the next year. Continue to use this methodology for the useful life of the asset.

For example, a dry cleaning machine costing $20,000 is estimated to have a useful life of six years. Under the straight-line method, it would have depreciation of $3,333 per year. Consequently, the first year of depreciation under the 200% DDB method would be double that amount, or $6,667. The calculation for all six years of depreciation is noted in the following table:

Year	Beginning Cost Basis	Straight-Line Depreciation	200% DDB Depreciation	Ending Cost Basis
1	$24,000	$3,333	$6,667	$17,333
2	17,333	2,889	5,778	11,555
3	11,555	1,926	3,852	7,703
4	7,703	1,284	2,568	5,135
5	5,135	856	1,712	3,423
6	3,423	571	1,142	2,281

Note that there is still some cost left at the end of the sixth year that has not been depreciated. This is usually handled by converting over from the DDB method to the straight-line method in the year in which the straight-line method would result in a higher amount of depreciation; the straight-line method is then used until all of the available depreciation has been recognized.

15.16 SUM OF THE YEARS DIGITS DEPRECIATION

This depreciation method is designed to recognize the bulk of all depreciation within the first few years of an asset's depreciable period, but does not do so quite as rapidly as the double declining balance method that was described in the last section. Its calculation can be surmised from its name. For the first year of depreciation, one adds up the number of years over which an asset is scheduled to be depreciated and then divides this into the total number of years remaining. The resulting percentage is used as the depreciation rate. In succeeding years, simply divide the reduced number of years left into the total number of years remaining.

For example, a punch press costing $24,000 is scheduled to be depreciated over five years. The sum of the years' digits is 15 (Year 1 + Year 2 + Year 3 + Year 4 + Year 5). The depreciation calculation in each of the five years is as follows:

1. Year 1 = (5/15) * $24,000 = $ 8,000
2. Year 2 = (4/15) * $24,000 = $ 6,400
3. Year 3 = (3/15) * $24,000 = $ 4,800
4. Year 4 = (2/15) * $24,000 = $ 3,200
5. Year 5 = (1/15) * $24,000 = $ 1,600
$24,000

15.17 UNITS OF PRODUCTION DEPRECIATION METHOD

The units of production depreciation method can result in the most accurate matching of actual asset usage to the related amount of depreciation that is recognized in the accounting records. Its use is limited to those assets to which some estimate of production can be attached. It is a particular favorite of those who use activity-based costing systems, since it closely relates asset cost to actual activity.

To calculate it, one should first estimate the total number of units of production that are likely to result from the use of an asset. Next, divide the total capitalized asset cost (less salvage value, if this is known) by the total estimated production to arrive at the depreci-ation cost per unit of production. Then, derive the depreciation recognized by multiplying the number of units of actual production during the period by the depreciation cost per unit. If there is a significant divergence of actual production activity from the original estimate, the depreciation cost per unit of production can be altered from time to time to reflect the realities of actual production volumes.

As an example of this method's use, an oil derrick is constructed at a cost of $350,000. It is expected to be used in the extraction of 1,000,000 barrels of oil, which results in an anticipated depreciation rate of $0.35 per barrel. During the first month, 23,500 barrels of oil are extracted. Under this method, the resulting depreciation cost is:

$$= \text{(cost per unit of production)} \times \text{(number of units of production)}$$
$$= (\$0.35 \text{ per barrel}) \times (23{,}500 \text{ barrels})$$
$$= \$8{,}225$$

This calculation can also be used with service hours as its basis, rather than units of production. When used in this manner, the method can be applied to a larger number of assets for which production volumes would not otherwise be available.

15.18 ASSET IMPAIRMENT

A company is allowed to write down its remaining investment in an asset if it can be proven that the asset is impaired. Impairment can be proven if an asset's net book value is greater than the sum of the undiscounted cash flows (including proceeds from its sale) expected to be generated by it in the future. Having an asset's net book value be greater than its fair value is not a valid reason for an asset write-down, since the asset may still have considerable utility within the company, no matter what its market value may be.

There is no requirement for the periodic testing of asset impairment. Instead, it should be done if there is a major drop in asset usage or a downgrading of its physical condition, or if government regulations or business conditions will likely result in a major drop in usage. For example, if new government regulations are imposed that are likely to signif-icantly reduce a company's ability to use the asset, as may be the case for a coal-fired electricity-generating facility that is subject to pollution controls, then an asset impairment test would be necessary. The test can also be conducted if there are major cost overruns during the construction of an asset or if there is a history or future expectation of operating losses associated with an asset. An expectation of early asset disposition can also trigger the test.

To calculate an impairment loss, determine an asset's fair value, either from market quotes or by determining the expected present value of its future cash flows. Then, write off the difference between its net book value and its fair value. This action may also result in a change in the method or duration of depreciation. For example, if an asset impairment write-down is made because an asset's life is expected to be shortened by five years, then the period over which its associated depreciation will be calculated should also be reduced by five years. If asset impairment is being calculated for a group of assets (such as an entire assembly line or production facility), then the amount of the asset impairment is allocated to the assets within the group based on their proportional net book values (though not below the separately identifiable fair value of any asset within the group).

If an asset is no longer in use, and there is no prospect for it to be used at any point in the future, then it must be written down to its expected salvage value. Since there will then be no remaining asset value to depreciate, all depreciation stops at the time of the write-down.

15.19   INTANGIBLE ASSETS

When an intangible asset is purchased, it should be capitalized on the company books at the amount of cash for which it was paid. If some other asset was used in exchange for the intangible, then the cost should be set at the fair market value of the asset given up. A third alternative for costing is the present value of any liability that is assumed in exchange for the intangible asset. It is also possible to create an intangible asset internally (such as the creation of a customer list), as long as the detail for all costs incurred in the creation of the intangible asset is adequately tracked and summarized.

If an intangible asset has an indefinite life, as demonstrated by clearly traceable cash flows well into the future, then it is not amortized. Instead, it is subject to an annual impairment test, resulting in the recognition of an impairment loss if its net book value exceeds its fair value. If an intangible asset in this category were to no longer have a demonstrably indefinite life, then it would convert to a normal amortization schedule based on its newly defined economic life.

If any intangible asset's usefulness is declining or evidently impaired, then its remaining value should be written down to no lower than the present value of its remaining future cash flows.

When a company acquires another company or its assets, any excess of the purchase price over the fair value of tangible assets should be allocated to intangible assets to the greatest degree possible. Examples of such assets are customer lists, patents, trademarks, and brand names. When some value is assigned to these intangible assets, they will then be amortized over a reasonable time period. If the excess purchase price cannot be fully allocated to intangible assets, the remainder is added to the Goodwill account.

Goodwill cannot be amortized. Instead, it is subject to annual impairment testing, or more frequently if circumstances indicate that impairment is likely. The impairment test is based on the lowest level of business entity to which the goodwill can be assigned. For example, if Company A purchases another business and renames it as an operating division of Company A, then the impairment test will only be conducted on the results of that division. Alternatively, if the purchased business is merged into the operations of Company A in such a manner that its operating results can no longer be tracked, then the impairment test will be conducted on the results of all of Company A.

Goodwill impairment testing is conducted by comparing the net book value (including goodwill) of the subject business unit to its fair value. If the fair value figure is greater, then no adjustment is required. However, if the fair value figure is lower than the net book value, take the following steps:

1. Determine the fair value of the subject business unit.
2. Determine the fair value of the individual assets and liabilities, excluding goodwill, within the business unit.
3. Subtract the fair value of the individual assets and liabilities determined in Step 2 from the fair value of the subject business unit determined in Step 1 to arrive at the carrying value of the goodwill.
4. Subtract the goodwill carrying value from the amount at which it is recorded on the company books. Write off any excess goodwill amount remaining on the company books.

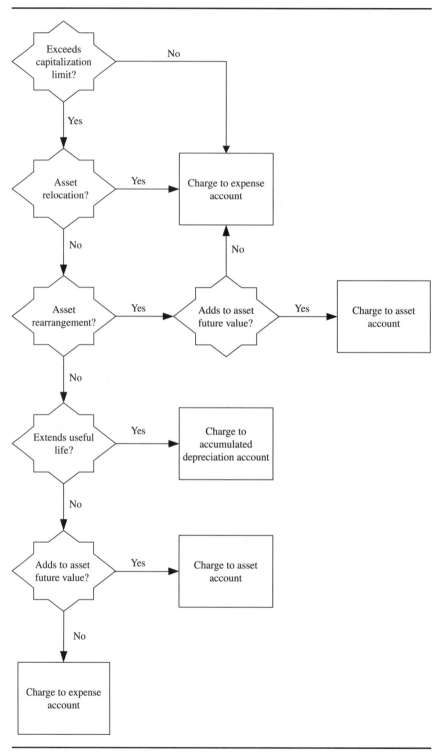

EXHIBIT 15.2   ASSET ACQUISITION CAPITALIZATION OR EXPENSE DECISION

If there is any subsequent increase in the fair value of the subject business unit, the impairment amount already written off cannot be recovered. An example of intangible amortization is as follows:

> Mr. Mel Smith purchases cab license #512 from the city of St. Paul for $20,000. The license term is for five years, after which he can renew it with no anticipated difficulties. The cash flows from the cab license can reasonably be shown to extend into the indefinite future, so there is no amortization requirement. However, the city council then changes the renewal process to a lottery where the odds of obtaining a renewal are poor. Mr. Smith must now assume that the economic life of his cab license will end in five years, so he initiates amortization to coincide with the license renewal date.

An example of an intangible asset purchase is as follows:

> An acquirer spends $1 million more to purchase a competitor than its book value. The acquirer decides to assign $400,000 of this excess amount to a patent formerly owned by the competitor, which it then amortizes over the remaining life of the patent. If the acquirer assigns the remaining $600,000 to a customer list asset, and the customer loss rate is 20% per year, then it can reasonably amortize the $600,000 over five years to match the gradual reduction in value of the customer list asset.

15.20   THE ASSET ACQUISITION CAPITALIZATION OR EXPENSE DECISION

There are a variety of decision points involved in the determination of how to treat an expenditure related to a fixed asset. The decision tree shown in Exhibit 15.2 can be used to determine the correct accounting treatment of these expenditures. There may be some uncertainly about whether an expenditure adds to an asset's future value or extends its useful life, which result in different treatments, as indicated at the bottom of the decision tree. When this situation arises, choose the decision point corresponding to the most dominant impact of the expenditure. For example, switching to a concrete roof from a wooden one may extend the life of a structure, but its dominant impact is to increase the building's future value.

15.21   SUMMARY

This chapter has presented a number of rules regarding the proper costing of incoming assets, the recognition of gains or losses on their disposition, how to calculate the proper depreciable basis for a new asset, what types of costs may be added to the capitalized cost of an existing asset, and what types of depreciation calculation can be applied to an asset. The key factor to consider when using this information is that one should establish a firm set of guidelines for the consistent treatment of all assets, so that there is no long-term inconsistency in the method of recording asset-related transactions.

CHAPTER 16

CURRENT LIABILITIES
AND CONTINGENCIES

16.1 INTRODUCTION

The treatment of accounts payable is somewhat more complicated than that of its counterpart on the balance sheet, accounts receivable. This is so because the underlying transaction is more complex, and also because of the wide range of accruals that may potentially be required for the accountant to fairly represent the state of current liabilities on the balance sheet. This chapter describes a wide range of current liabilities and contingencies, and how they should be accounted for.

16.2 THE ACCOUNTS PAYABLE TRANSACTION FLOW

The typical transaction flow for the accounts payable process is for the purchasing department to release a purchase order to a supplier, after which the supplier ships to the company whatever was ordered. The shipping manifest delivered with the product contains the purchase order number that authorizes the transaction. The receiving staff compares the delivery to the referenced purchase order, and accepts the delivery if it matches the purchase order. The receiving staff then sends a copy of the receiving documentation to the accounts payable department. Meanwhile, the supplier issues an invoice to the company's accounting department. Once the accounting staff receives the invoice, they match it to the initiating purchase order as well as the receiving documentation, thereby establishing proof that the invoice was both authorized and received. If everything cross-checks properly, then the invoice is entered into the accounting system for payment, with a debit going to either an expense account or an asset account, and a credit going to the Accounts payable account. Once the invoice is due for payment, a check is printed, and a credit is made to the Cash account and a debit to the Accounts payable account.

A variation on this transaction is for the accounting staff to initially record an account payable at an amount net of its early payment discount. However, this requires one to apportion the amount of the discount over all line items being billed on the supplier invoice. Also, since taking or avoiding the early payment discount can also be viewed as an unrelated financing decision, this would lead one to record each invoice at its gross amount and then to record the discount separately if the decision is made to take it.

The accounts payable transaction flow is one requiring a number of types of paperwork to be assembled from three different departments, which tends to lead to a great deal of confusion and missing paperwork. Frequently, the delay is so excessive that the accounting staff cannot process the paperwork in time to meet the deadlines by which early payment discounts can be taken. Accordingly, there are several alternatives to the basic process flow that can alleviate its poor level of efficiency:

- *Pay without approval.* Invoices may be entered into the system immediately upon receipt and paid, irrespective of where they may stand in the approval process. This approach ensures that all early payment discounts are taken, but tends to result in some payments for unauthorized shipments.

- *Pay from the purchase order.* A much simpler variation of the traditional approach just described is to require that all deliveries be authorized by a purchase order and that the receiving staff have access to this information online at the receiving dock, so that they can check off receipts as soon as they appear. The computer system then automatically schedules payment to the supplier, based on the price per unit listed in the purchase order and the quantity recorded at the receiving dock. This approach requires considerable interaction with suppliers to ensure that the resulting payments are acceptable.

- *Pay from completed production.* The most streamlined approach to the payment of accounts payable is that used by just-in-time manufacturing systems, under which suppliers are precertified as to the quality of their products, which therefore require no inspection by a company's receiving staff at all. Instead, the suppliers deliver directly to the production workstations where the parts are immediately needed, avoiding all receiving paperwork. Once the company completes its production process, it determines the number of finished goods completed, and the number of units of parts from each supplier that were included in those completed finished goods. It then pays the suppliers based on this standard number of parts. This system requires a high degree of accuracy in production tracking, as well as a separate scrap tracking system that accumulates all parts thrown out or destroyed during the production process (since suppliers must also be reimbursed for these parts).

Many invoices are also received that have nothing to do with the production process, such as utility, subscription, and rent billings. These should first be entered in the accounts payable system for processing, and then routed to the applicable managers for approval.

In many cases, the accounts payable staff is authorized to approve these invoices up to the amount of the periodic budget, with further inspection required if the budget is exceeded.

16.3   ACCOUNTING FOR THE PERIOD-END CUTOFF

If an accountant were to issue financial statements immediately after the end of a reporting period, it is quite likely that the resulting financial statements would underreport the amount of accounts payable. The reason is that the company may have received inventory items prior to period end and have recorded them as an increase in the level of inventory (thereby reducing the cost of goods sold), without having recorded the corresponding supplier invoice, which may have been delayed by the postal service until a few days following the end of the period.

Proper attention to the period-end cutoff issue can resolve this problem. The key activity for the accountant is to compare the receiving department's receiving log for the few days near period end to the supplier invoices logged into that period, to see if there are any receipts for which there are no supplier invoices. If so, the accountant can accrue the missing invoice at the per-unit rate shown on the originating purchase order, or else used the cost noted on an earlier invoice for the same item.

Similarly, there will be a number of other types of invoices that will arrive several days after the end of the period, such as maintenance billings and telephone bills. The accountant can anticipate their arrival by accruing for them based on a checklist of invoices that are typically late in arriving and for which an estimate can be made that is based on invoices from previous reporting periods.

Proper attention to the cutoff issue is extremely important, since ignoring it can lead to wide gyrations in reported income from period to period, as invoices are continually recorded in the wrong period.

16.4   CURRENT LIABILITIES—PRESENTATION

If a company has a long-term payable that is approaching its termination date, then any amount due under its payment provisions within the next year must be recorded as a current liability. If only a portion of total payments due under the liability is expected to fall within that time frame, then only that portion of the liability should be reported as a current liability. A common situation in which this issue arises is a copier leasing arrangement, where the most recent payments due under the agreement are split away from the other copier lease payments that are not due until after one year. This situation commonly arises for many types of long-term equipment and property rentals.

16.5   CURRENT LIABILITIES—ADVANCES

If a customer makes a payment for which the company has not made a corresponding delivery of goods or services, then the accountant must record the cash receipt as a customer advance, which is a liability. This situation commonly arises when a customer order is so large or specialized that the company is justified in demanding cash in advance of the order. Another common situation occurs when customers are required to make a deposit, for example to a property rental company that requires one month's rent as a damage deposit. This may be recorded as a current liability if the corresponding delivery of goods or services is expected to occur within the next year. However, if the offset is expected to be further in the future, then it should be recorded as a long-term liability.

16.6   CURRENT LIABILITIES—BONUSES

Rather than waiting until bonuses are fully earned and payable to recognize them, one should accrue some proportion of the bonuses in each reporting period if there is a reasonable expectation that they will be earned and that the eventual amount of the bonus can be approximately determined.

16.7   CURRENT LIABILITIES—COMMISSIONS

The amount of commissions due to the sales staff may not be precisely ascertainable at the end of the reporting period, since they may be subject to later changes based on the precise terms of the commission agreement with the sales staff, such as subsequent reductions if customers do not pay for their delivered goods or services. In this case, commissions should be accrued based on the maximum possible commission payment, minus a reduction for later eventualities; the reduction can reasonably be based on historical experience with actual commission rates paid.

16.8   CURRENT LIABILITIES—COMPENSATED ABSENCES

A company is required to accrue an expense for compensated absences, such as vacation time, when employees have already earned the compensated absence, the right has been vested, the payment amount can be estimated, and payment is probable. If a company is required to pay for earned compensation absences, then vesting has occurred. A key issue is any "use it or lose it" provision in the company employee manual, which has a dramatic effect on the amount of compensated absences to be accrued. If such a policy exists, then the accrual is limited to the maximum amount of the carry-forward. If not, the accrual can be substantial if the vested amount has built up over many years. The payment amount is typically based on the most recent level of pay for accrual calculation purposes, rather than any estimate of future pay levels at the time when the absence is actually compensated. An example of a vacation accrual is as follows:

> Mr. Harold Jones has earned 450 hours of vacation time, none of which has been used. He currently earns $28.50 per hour. His employer should maintain an accrued vacation expense of $12,825 (450 hours × $28.50/hour) to reflect this liability. However, if the company has a "use it or lose it" policy that allows only an 80 hour carry-forward at the end of each year, then the accrual is only $2,280 (80 hours × $28.50/hour).

The amount of sick time allowed to employees is usually so small that there is no discernible impact on the financial statements whether they are accrued or not. This is particularly true if unused sick time cannot be carried forward into future years as an ongoing residual employee benefit that may be paid out at some future date. If these restrictions are not the case, then the accounting treatment of sick time is the same as for vacation time.

16.9   CURRENT LIABILITIES—DEBT

There are a number of circumstances under which a company's debt must be recorded as current debt on the balance sheet. They are as follows:

- If the debt must be repaid entirely within the current operating cycle.
- If the debt is payable over a longer term, but it is also due on demand at the option of the lender.

- If the company is in violation of any loan covenants and the lender has not waived the requirement.
- If the company is in violation of any loan covenants, the lender has issued a short-term waiver, but it is unlikely that the company can cure the violation problem during the waiver period.
- If the debt agreement contains a subjective acceleration clause, and there is a strong likelihood that the clause will be activated.

If only a portion of a company's debt falls under the preceding criteria, then only that portion impacted by the rules must be recorded as current debt, with the remainder recorded as long-term debt.

If a company intends to refinance current debt with long-term debt, it can classify this debt as long-term on the balance sheet, but only if the refinancing occurs or a refinancing agreement is signed after the balance sheet date but before the issuance date. If this approach is taken, the amount of current debt that can be reclassified as long-term debt cannot exceed the amount of debt to be refinanced, and is also limited by the amount of new debt that can be acquired without violating existing loan covenants.

16.10   CURRENT LIABILITIES—EMPLOYEE TERMINATIONS

If company management has formally approved of a termination plan designed to reduce headcount, the expenses associated with the plan should be recognized at once if the accountant can reasonably estimate the associated costs. The *first requirement* after plan approval is that the plan clearly outline the benefits to be granted. This information usually specifies a fixed dollar payout based on the amount of time that an employee has been with the company. The *second requirement* is that the plan must specify the general categories and numbers of employees to be let go, since the accountant needs this information to extend the per-person benefit costs specified in the first requirement. Further significant changes to the plan should be unlikely; this locks in the range of possible costs that are likely to occur as a result of the plan, rendering the benefit cost accrual more accurate. An example of accrual for termination benefits is as follows:

> The Arabian Knights Security Company plans to close its Albuquerque branch office and terminate the employment of all people working there. The action is scheduled for three months in the future. The company's employee manual states that all employees are entitled to one week of severance pay for each year worked for the company. The average number of weeks of severance under this policy is 3.5 for the group to be terminated, and the average pay for the 29 employees affected is $39,500. Thus, the company must immediately accrue a termination expense of $77,101 (29 employees × $39,500 average pay / 52 weeks × 3.5 weeks).

16.11   CURRENT LIABILITIES—PROPERTY TAXES

A company should accrue the monthly portion of its property tax liability based on its assessed property tax liability during the fiscal year of the taxing authority. An example of a property tax accrual is as follows:

> The Arabian Knights Security Company owns property in Arapahoe County, Colorado. Arabian operates under a calendar year, while Arapahoe's fiscal year ends on June 30. Arapahoe sends a notice to Arabian that Arabian's property tax assessment will be $33,600 in the current fiscal year, payable in March of the following year. Accordingly, Arabian's controller begins

to accrue 1/12 of the assessment in each month of Arapahoe's fiscal year, beginning in July. The entry is:

	Debit	Credit
Property tax expense	$2,800	
Property tax payable		$2,800

When Arabian pays the assessment in March of the following year, it makes the following entry:

	Debit	Credit
Property tax payable	$33,600	
Cash		$33,600

Since property taxes are typically paid prior to the end of the taxing authority's fiscal year, this series of transactions will likely result in a debit balance in the Property tax payable account for the last few months of the fiscal year, since the company will not have recorded the entire property tax expense until that time.

16.12 CURRENT LIABILITIES—ROYALTIES

If a company is obligated to pay a periodic royalty to a supplier of goods or services that it uses or resells, then it must accrue an expense if the amount is reasonably determinable.

16.13 CURRENT LIABILITIES—WAGES

Even if a company times its payroll period-end dates to correspond with the end of each reporting period, this will only ensure that no accrual is needed for those employees who receive salaries (since they are usually paid through the payroll period ending date). The same is not usually true for those who receive an hourly wage. In their case, the pay period may end as much as a week prior to the actual payment date. Consequently, the accountant must accrue the wage expense for the period between the pay period end date and the end of the reporting period. This can be estimated on a person-by-person basis, but an easier approach is to accrue based on an historical hourly rate that includes average overtime percentages. One must also include the company's share of all payroll taxes in this accrual. An example of an unpaid wage accrual form is shown later in the "Forms and Reports" section.

16.14 CURRENT LIABILITIES—WARRANTY CLAIMS

If a company has a warranty policy on its products or services, and it can reasonably estimate the amount of any warranty claims, it should accrue an expense for anticipated claims. One can also use industry information if in-house warranty claim data is not available. For warranty claims not expected to be received in the current operating cycle, the accrued expense can be split into current and long-term liabilities. An example of warranty claims is as follows:

The Halloway Marine Company produces outboard motors for the sport fishing industry. It has historically experienced a warranty expense of 1.5% of its revenues, and so records a warranty expense based on that information. However, it has just developed a jet-powered engine for which it has no warranty experience. The engine has fewer moving parts than a traditional engine, and so should theoretically have a low warranty claim rate. No other companies in the industry offer a jet engine, so no comparable information is available. The controller chooses to use the 4.8% warranty claim rate applicable to its prior new-engine introductions as the basis for an accrual, since this is the only valid warrant information pertaining to the new product. The controller makes a note to review this accrual regularly to see if the trend of warranty expenses changes after the engine has been on the market for some time.

16.15   CONTINGENCIES

A *contingent liability* is one that will occur if a future event comes to pass and that is based on a current situation. For example, a company may be engaged in a lawsuit; if it loses the suit, it will be liable for damages. Other situations that may give rise to a contingent liability are a standby letter of credit (if the primary creditor cannot pay a liability, then the company's standby letter of credit will be accessed by the creditor), a guarantee of indebtedness, an expropriation threat, a risk of damage to company property, or any potential obligations associated with product warranties or defects.

If any of these potential events exists, then the accountant is under no obligation to accrue for any potential loss until the associated events come to pass, but should disclose them in a footnote. However, if the conditional events are *probable* and the amount of the loss can be reasonably estimated, then the accountant must accrue a loss against current income. The amount of the contingent liability must be reasonably determinable or at least be stated within a high-low range of likely outcomes. If the liability can only be stated within a probable range, then the accountant should accrue for the most likely outcome. If there is no most likely outcome, then the minimum amount in the range should be accrued. If the probable amount of a loss changes, then an adjustment should be made in the current period to reflect this change in estimate.

There is a wide range of possible contingent liabilities for which footnote disclosure is appropriate. A number of examples are shown in Chapter 9.

16.16   CONTINGENCIES—DEBT COVENANT VIOLATION

If a company violates a debt covenant on long-term debt, it must reclassify the debt as short-term. However, if the lender waives its right to call the debt, the company can leave the existing debt classification alone. The only exception is if the lender retains the right to require compliance with the covenant in the future, and the company is unlikely to be able to comply with the debt covenants on an ongoing basis. In this last instance, the debt must still be classified as short-term.

16.17   CONTINGENCIES—DEBT GUARANTEES

If a company has guaranteed the debt of a third party, it does not have to record a contingent liability unless there is a reasonable probability that the primary debt holder will be unable to repay the debt. If an ongoing assessment of this probability results in an estimate that the company will be required to cover the debt, a contingent liability should be recorded at that time.

16.18   CONTINGENCIES—GUARANTEED MINIMUM OPTION PRICE

If a company grants stock options that include a minimum payment if the value of the options does not exceed a minimum level, then the amount of this minimum payment should be recognized as a compensation expense, to be ratably recognized over the option service period. If the employee forfeits the options prior to completion of the service period, the compensation expense can be reversed.

16.19 SUMMARY

There are a number of situations applying to current liabilities that require differing accounting treatment—unclaimed payroll checks, warranties, contingent liabilities, and the like. In addition, there are a number of ways to handle the accounts payable process flow that will result in varying degrees of efficiency and accuracy. Best practices related to the accounts payable function can be explored in greater detail in *Accounting Best Practices,* 6th Edition (Bragg, John Wiley & Sons, 2010).

DEBT

17.1 INTRODUCTION

There are a number of issues related to debt that the accountant is likely to face. For example, how should one account for the early retirement of debt, a change in the terms of a debt agreement, or the presence of a discount or premium on the sale of bonds, or the use of warrants? These common issues, as well as others related to defaulted debt, callable debt, sinking funds, debt that has been converted to equity, debt refinancings, and noncash debt payments, are all addressed in this chapter.

17.2 OVERVIEW OF BONDS

The typical bond is a long-term (1 to 30 year) obligation to pay a creditor, which may be secured by company assets. A traditional bond agreement calls for a semiannual interest payment, while the principal amount is paid in a lump sum at the termination date of the bond. The issuing company may issue periodic interest payments directly to bondholders, though only if they are registered; another alternative is to send the entire amount of interest payable to a trustee, who exchanges bond coupons from bondholders for money from the deposited funds.

The issuing company frequently creates a sinking fund well in advance of the bond payoff date, so that it will have sufficient funds available to make the final balloon payment (or buy back bonds on an ongoing basis). The bond agreement may contain a number of restrictive covenants that the company must observe, or else the bondholders will be allowed a greater degree of control over the company or allowed to accelerate the payment date of their bonds.

A bond will be issued at a stated face value interest rate. If this rate does not equate to the market rate on the date of issuance, then investors will either bid up the price of the bond (if its stated rate is higher than the market rate) or bid down the price (if its stated rate is lower than the market rate). The after-market price of a bond may subsequently vary considerably if the market rate of interest varies substantially from the stated rate of the bond.

Some bonds are issued with no interest rate at all. These *zero-coupon bonds* are sold at a deep discount and are redeemed at their face value at the termination date of the bond. They are of particular interest to those companies that do not want to be under the obligation of making fixed interest payments during the term of a bond.

The interest earned on a bond is subject to income taxes, except for those bonds issued by government entities. These bonds, known as *municipal bonds*, pay tax-free interest. For this reason, they can be competitively sold at lower actual interest rates than the bonds offered by commercial companies.

The *serial bond* does not have a fixed termination date for the entire issuance of bonds. Instead, the company is entitled to buy back a certain number of bonds at regular intervals, so that the total number of outstanding bonds declines over time.

An alternative is the use of attached warrants, which allow the bondholder to buy shares of company stock at a prespecified price. If the warrants are publicly traded, then their value can be separated from that of the bond, so that each portion of the package is recognized separately in a company's balance sheet.

Though some corporations issue their own bonds directly to investors, it is much more common to engage the services of an investment banker, who not only lines up investors for the company, but who may also invest a substantial amount of its own funds in the company's bonds. In either case, the board of directors must approve any new bonds, after which a trustee is appointed to control the bond issuance, certificates are printed and signed, and delivery is made either to the investment banking firm or directly to investors in exchange for cash.

17.3 DEBT CLASSIFICATION

It is generally not allowable to reclassify a debt that is coming due in the short term as a long-term liability on the grounds that it is about to be refinanced as a long-term debt. This treatment would likely result in no debt ever appearing in the current liabilities portion of the balance sheet. This treatment is only allowable if the company has the intention to refinance the debt on a long-term basis, rather than simply rolling over the debt into another short-term debt instrument that will, in turn, become due and payable in the next accounting year. Also, there must be firm evidence of this roll-over into a long-term debt instrument, such as the presence of a debt agreement or an actual conversion to long-term debt subsequent to the balance sheet date.

If a debt can be called by the creditor, then it must be classified as a current liability. However, if the period during which the creditor can call the debt is at some point subsequent to one year, then it may still be classified as a long-term debt. Also, if the call option only applies if the company defaults on some performance measure related to the debt, then the debt only needs to be classified as a current liability if the company cannot cure the problem with the performance measure within whatever period is specified under the terms of the debt. Further, if a debt agreement contains a call provision that is likely to be activated under the circumstances present as of the balance sheet date, then the debt should be classified as a current liability; conversely, if the probability of the call provision being invoked is remote, then the debt does not have to be so classified. Finally, if only a portion of the debt can be called, then only that portion need be classified as a current liability.

17.4   INTEREST RISK MANAGEMENT

Interest rate risk is the possibility of a change in interest rates that has a negative impact on a company's profits. A company incurs interest rate risk whenever it borrows or extends credit. This is a serious issue for companies with large amounts of outstanding debt, since a small hike in their interest expense could not only have a large negative impact on their profits but possibly also violate several loan covenants, such as the interest coverage ratio. A less critical issue is when a company forecasts a certain amount of available cash in the coming year that will be available for investment purposes but cannot reliably forecast the return on investment beyond the first few months of the year. In this situation, the company is forced to budget for some amount of interest income, but it has no way of knowing if the forecasted interest rate will be available throughout the year. In the first case, interest rate volatility can cause serious cash flow problems, and in the second case, it can cause a company to miss its budgeted interest income.

Before delving into specific risk management techniques, a controller must determine the overall level of risk that the company is willing to accept. At the most conservative level of *full-cover hedging*, a company enters into hedging positions that completely eliminate all exposure. *Selective hedging* leaves room for some hedging activity, usually by the predetermined setting of minimum and maximum risk levels. The minimum amount of risk management is none at all, known as a *naked position*. A naked position may be intentional, based on management's assessment that hedging is not necessary, or through simple ignorance of how hedging can be used. Conversely, a company can engage in *speculative positions*, where they essentially reverse the underlying exposure. A speculative position is not recommended, since a company can place itself at considerable risk by doing so; also, this strategy establishes the presumption that the company is earning profits from its financing activities, rather than from its operations. Normally, financial activities are considered to be in support of operations and therefore should never place those operations at risk.

The primary strategies for interest risk management are the use of forwards, futures, and options, and are described in the following subsections.

Forwards

A *forward rate agreement* (FRA) is an agreement between two parties to lock in an interest rate for a predetermined period of time. Under the FRA agreement, a borrower wants to guard against the cost of rising interest rates, while the counterparty is wishes to protect against declining interest rates. The counterparty is usually a bank.

When a buyer engages in an FRA, and if interest rates rise, then it will be paid by the counterparty for the amount by which actual interest rates exceed the *reference rate*

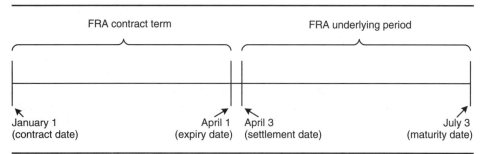

FRA contract term   FRA underlying period

January 1   April 1   April 3   July 3
(contract date)   (expiry date) (settlement date)   (maturity date)

EXHIBIT 17.1 FRA TIMELINE

(typically based on an interbank rate such as LIBOR or Euribor) specified in the FRA. Assuming that the buyer was using the FRA to hedge the interest rate on its borrowings, it then pays its lender the increased interest rate and offsets this added cost with the payment from the counterparty. Conversely, if interest rates decline, then the buyer pays the counterparty the difference between the reduced interest rate and the reference rate specified in the FRA and adds this cost to the reduced interest rate that it pays its lender. Thus, the FRA buyer has locked in a fixed interest rate, irrespective of the direction in which actual interest rates subsequently move.

A number of date conventions are used in an FRA. The *contract date* is the start date of the agreement. The next sequential date in the agreement is the *expiry date*, which is when the difference between the market rate and the reference rate is determined. The *settlement date* is when the interest differential is paid; this is also the first day of the underlying period. Finally, the *maturity date* is the last day of the underlying FRA period. These dates are shown in the timeline example in Exhibit 17.1. In the exhibit, the FRA contract term is three months, running from January 1 to April 1. The underlying period is three months, from April 3 to July 3.

On the settlement date, one party pays the other, using a three-step process. First, it compares the contract interest rate on the contract date to the reference rate on the expiry date of the FRA. Second, it determines the difference between the two interest rates for the underlying period, multiplied by the notional amount of the contract. Thus, the parties take a *notional position* only, which means that one party pays the other only for the *incremental* change in interest rates. The formula under which incremental interest payments are made under an FRA is shown in Exhibit 17.2. Finally, the paying party discounts the amount of the payment against the reference rate and pays this amount to the other party. The formula for discounting the payment to its net discounted present value is shown in Exhibit 17.3.

There are a broad range of time periods over which an FRA can be used. It is possible to enter into a FRA (for example) that begins in nine months and expires in 12 months, or which begins in one year and expires in two years. Standard descriptive notation for

---

Payment = Notional amount × (Day count fraction) × (Reference rate − FRA rate)

Note: The day count fraction is the portion of a year over which rates are calculated, which is 360 days in Europe and the United States, although 365 days may be used elsewhere.

EXHIBIT 17.2 FRA INTEREST PAYMENT FORMULA

$$\text{Payment} = \frac{\text{Settlement amount}}{1 + (\text{days in FRA underlying period}/360 \text{ days})}$$

EXHIBIT 17.3   PAYMENT DISCOUNTING FORMULA

the terms of a variety of possible FRAs is shown in Exhibit 17.4. In essence, the notation sets the effective (beginning) and termination dates of the FRA, with each date being the number of months from the present month.

A controller can also combine a sequential group of FRAs into an *FRA strip*, which provides a hedge for a longer interval.

> Gulf Coast Petrochemical expects to borrow $25 million in one year's time to finance a new offshore drilling platform, and will need the funds for a period of one year. The current market interest rate is 5.00%, and Gulf Coast's controller anticipates that the rate will rise to 6.00% by the time the company needs the money. To lock in the 5.00% rate, he enters into a 12 × 24 FRA at 5.00%, where the reference rate is the LIBOR rate. The settlement amount of the FRA will depend on the 12-month LIBOR in 12 months. At that time, the reference rate has risen to 5.80%. Accordingly, the bank that was the counterparty to the FRA determines that (prior to discounting) it must pay $200,000 to Gulf Coast, which it calculates as:
>
> **$200,000** = $25,000,000 × (360 days in contract/360 days in year)
>
> × (.058 reference rate − .050 contract rate)
>
> The final step in the process is for the bank to calculate its discounted payment to Gulf Coast. The discounted payment is **$189,035.92**, which is calculated as $200,000/(1 + (360/360 × 5.80%)), in accordance with the formula in Exhibit 17.3, and using the 5.80% reference rate.
>
> The controller of Abbott Software wants to buy an FRA to hedge the risk of an interest rate increase in $30 million of debt that he plans to borrow in one month, extending for nine months. He plans to use a strip of consecutive three-month FRAs to construct this longer-term hedge. The FRA terms and rates are as follows:

FRA Term	FRA Rate
1 × 4 months	4.00%
5 × 7 months	4.20%
8 × 10 months	4.40%

> The FRA rate gradually increases over time, since it is based on the yield curve which is usually upward-sloping. The controller buys the FRAs; the resulting reference (actual) rates

FRA Term	Expanded Text of FRA Term	Effective Term
1 × 3	Effective 1 month from now, terminates 2 months from now	2 months
1 × 7	Effective 1 month from now, terminates 7 months from now	6 months
3 × 6	Effective 3 months from now, terminates 6 months from now	3 months
3 × 9	Effective 3 months from now, terminates 9 months from now	6 months
6 × 12	Effective 6 months from now, terminates 12 months from now	6 months
12 × 18	Effective 12 months from now, terminates 18 months from now	6 months

EXHIBIT 17.4   TERM NOTATION FOR A FORWARD RATE AGREEMENT

are shown in the following table, along with the variance between the FRA and reference rates for each of the three FRAs.

FRA Term	Contract Rate	Reference Rate	Variance
1 × 4 months	4.00%	3.90%	−0.10%
5 × 7 months	4.20%	4.25%	0.05%
8 × 10 months	4.40%	4.50%	0.10%

For the 1 × 4 FRA, ABC pays the other party $7,500, which is calculated as:

$$-\textbf{\$7,500} = \$30,000,000 \times (90/360)\,(.0390 - .0400)$$

Abbott's discounted payment to the other party is **$7,427.58**, which is calculated as $7,500/ (1 + (90/360 × 3.90%)), in accordance with the formula in Exhibit 17.3, and using the 3.90% reference rate for the 1 × 4 FRA.

For the 5 × 7 FRA, the other party pays Abbott $3,750, which is calculated as:

$$\textbf{\$3,750} = \$30,000,000 \times (90/360) \times (.0425 - .0420)$$

Its discounted payment is **$3,710.58**, which is calculated as $3,750/(1 + (90/360 × 4.25%)), in accordance with the formula in Exhibit 17.3, and using the 4.25% reference rate for the 5 × 7 FRA.

For the 8 × 10 FRA, the other party pays ABC $7,500, which is calculated as:

$$\textbf{\$7,500} = \$30,000,000 \times (90/360) \times (.0450 - .0440)$$

Its discounted payment is **$7,416.56**, which is calculated as $7,500/(1 + (90/360 × 4.50%)), in accordance with the formula in Exhibit 17.3, and using the 4.40% reference rate for the 8 × 10 FRA.

Thus, over the nine-month period, Abbott is paid a net total of $3,699.56 from its hedging activity, which it then uses to offset its increased borrowing cost.

Futures

An interest rate future is an exchange-traded forward contract that allows a company to lock in an interest rate for a future time period. Interest rate futures trade on the Chicago Mercantile Exchange, or CME (www.cmegroup.com). The standard futures contract is in Eurodollars, which are bank deposits comprised of U.S. dollars and held outside the United States. However, the CME also offers futures contracts in a variety of other interest rate products, including 30-day federal funds, one-month LIBOR, and even Euroyen TIBOR (Tokyo Interbank Offered Rate). Most trading volume is in Eurodollar contracts. Eurodollar contracts are available for as much as 10 years into the future, though trading volumes drop off substantially after the first 3 years.

A Eurodollar futures contract allows the buyer to lock in the interest rate on $1 million; if the buyer wishes to lock in the interest rate on a larger amount, then he must purchase additional contracts in $1 million increments. The quoted prices are derived from a base-line index of 100, and decline in amount for periods further in the future. The difference between the baseline index and the quoted price is the interest rate on the contract. For example, recent Eurodollar rates traded on the CME were:

March	99.050	September	97.255
June	97.500	December	96.990

A company can buy a futures contract through a broker. The broker will charge a fee on the transaction, and also imposes margin requirements on the company that are used to ensure that the buyer or seller fulfills the futures contract's obligations. The initial margin requirement is calculated on the basis of the maximum likely volatility for one day. The initial margin varies from a low of 1/16th of a percent of the contract amount for three-month contracts, to 2% for 10-year treasury bonds.

The futures position represented by a contract is *marked to market* (valued at market rates) every day; if the most recent valuation results in an incremental loss, then the margin account is reduced, and a *margin call* requires the contract holder to add more funds to the margin account to bring it up to the maintenance level. If the contract holder does not respond to the margin call, the broker can close out the futures position by offsetting the contract (at the contract holder's cost). Thus, the margin account keeps unrealized losses from accumulating, which might otherwise result in a contract default.

On the final day of the contract, the exchange prices the contract, and makes a final cash settlement of the profit or loss due to or from the company.

An interest rate future is a standard contract, with a standard value, term, and under-lying instrument; thus, its terms may vary somewhat from the amount of a company's borrowings. This means that there is likely to be an imperfect hedge, which means that the company utilizing a futures contract still must carry some amount of risk.

The controller of Gulf Coast Petroleum decides to sell a three-month future with a contract term of six months. The current three-month LIBOR is 4.50%, and the 6 × 9 forward rate is 4.85%. Since the controller wishes to hedge a principal amount of $25 million, he sells 25 contracts of $1 million each. The future is now listed as 95.15, which is calculated as 100 minus the 4.85% forward rate. The future expires after six months; at that time, the forward rate has declined to 4.35%, which means that the future is now listed as 95.65 (derived from 100 minus the 4.35% forward rate). This means that Gulf Coast has earned a profit of $31,250, which is derived as follows:

$$\textbf{\$31,250} = \$25,000,000 \times (90/360) \times (.9565 \text{ ending price} - .9515 \text{ beginning price})$$

Interest Rate Swaps

The *interest rate swap* is an agreement between two parties (where one party is almost always a bank) to exchange interest payments in the same currency over a defined time period, which normally ranges from 1 to 10 years. One of the parties is paying a fixed rate of interest while the other is paying a variable rate. The variable interest rate is paid whenever a new coupon is set, which typically is once a quarter. Fixed interest usually is paid at the end of each year.

By engaging in a swap, a company can shift from fixed to variable payments, or vice versa. Thus, if a company uses a swap to shift from variable to fixed interest payments, it can better forecast its financing costs and avoid increased payments, but it loses the chance of reduced interest payments if rates were to decline. If it takes the opposite position and swaps fixed rates for variable rates, then it is essentially betting that it will benefit from a future decline in interest rates. An interest rate swap is especially useful for a company with a weak credit rating, since such entities must pay a premium to obtain fixed rate debt. They may find it less expensive to obtain variable rate debt, and then engage in an interest rate swap to secure what is essentially a fixed rate payment schedule.

The parties to an interest rate swap deal directly with each other rather than using a standard product that is traded over an exchange. They customarily use the standard master agreement that is maintained by the International Swaps and Derivatives Association (*www.isda.org*). The ISDA represents participants in the privately negotiated derivatives industry and maintains standard contracts for derivatives transactions. The parties commonly modify a variety of features within the agreement to suit their needs.

ABC Company borrows $10 million. Under the terms of the agreement, ABC must make quarterly interest payments for the next three years that are based on the London Interbank Offered Rate (LIBOR), which is reset once a quarter under the terms of the borrowing agreement. Since the interest payments are variable, the company will experience reduced interest payments if LIBOR declines but will pay more if LIBOR increases. ABC's management is more concerned about the risk of LIBOR increasing, so it eliminates this risk by entering into an interest rate swap in which it agrees to pay interest for three years on $10 million at a fixed rate while its counterparty agrees to make floating interest rate payments for three years on $10 million to ABC. The first-year payment stream for the transaction is shown in the following table, where the counterparty makes quarterly payments to ABC, which vary based on changes in LIBOR. ABC makes a single fixed interest rate payment to the counterparty at the end of year 1. The result of these transactions is that ABC experiences a net reduction in its interest expense of $20,000 in the first year of the swap agreement.

Payment Date	Loan Fixed Rate	Applicable LIBOR Quarterly Rate	Payments from the Counterparty to ABC Company	Payments from ABC Company to the Counterparty
March 31	—	4.20%	$105,000	
June 30	—	4.35%	108,750	
September 30	—	4.60%	115,000	
December 31	4.25%	4.65%	116,250	$425,000
Totals			**$445,000**	**$425,000**

The controller should arrange for payments under an interest swap agreement to be as closely aligned as possible with the payment terms of the underlying debt agreement. Thus, it is not useful if a counterparty's payment to the company is scheduled to arrive several weeks after the company is scheduled to pay its bank under a loan agreement. Instead, the counterparty's payment should be scheduled to arrive just prior to the due date specified in the loan agreement, thereby better aligning the company's cash flows.

Another strategy is to use an *interest rate cap option*. The cap option allows a company to limit the extent of interest rate increases while still retaining some of the benefit if interest rates subsequently decline. However, the cost of the rate cap will increase a company's borrowing cost incrementally. The cost of a rate cap option can be reduced by acquiring a more tailored solution called a *knockout cap*. Such a cap limits a company's debt service cost only so long as the baseline interest rate measurement does not exceed a certain interest rate. If the actual rate exceeds the upper boundary of the cap, then the company receives no protection at all.

To use the same example, ABC Company buys a 6.00% interest rate cap, which keeps ABC's potential interest rate liability from exceeding 6.00%. Thus, if the interest rate were to actually reach 6.50%, the cap seller would pay ABC 0.50%, while ABC would pay its bank 6.50% interest on the loan, yielding a net interest rate of 6.00%.

Now let us alter the example to assume that ABC's controller considers it likely that interest rates will only rise slightly. He wants to save on the cost of the interest rate cap, so he purchases a knockout cap that provides protection only up to 6.50%. The actual LIBOR rate jumps to 6.60%, thereby triggering the knockout. ABC must now pay the entire 6.60% interest on the loan, while the cap seller has no obligation to pay ABC.

Interest rate swaps only work if there are counterparties available who are willing to take on the company's perceived risk. However, when there is a general consensus that interest rates will increase, a greater volume of market participants will want to lock in their low borrowing rates with fixed interest rates, which tends to force the cost of a swap higher. The reverse situation arises when there is a general consensus that rates will decline; more companies shift into variable-rate debt in expectation of benefiting from lower rates, which makes it less expensive to create a swap for a fixed rate.

ABC Company wants to exchange its variable rate payments for fixed rate payments for a period of three years. The benchmark government fixed rate yield for that time period is 5.50%, and a spread of 0.30% is added to the benchmark, which incorporates the supply and demand for a fixed rate swap. Thus, ABC must pay a fixed rate of 5.80% if it chooses to engage in an interest rate swap transaction.

If the parties to a swap agreement choose to terminate it prior to the contractual termination date, they determine the net present value of future payment obligations by each party. They then net the payments together to determine the net incremental payment to be made, which goes to whichever party is disadvantaged by terminating the swap. A variation on this approach is the *blend and extend*, where the close-out cost of the original swap agreement is incorporated into a new swap agreement.

It is also possible to assign the swap agreement to a third party, which is then obligated to make and receive payments until the contract maturity date. As part of the contract assignment, whichever party is assigning the swap will either pay to the new counterparty or receive from it a payment reflecting the net present value of cash flows remaining under the swap agreement.

One more alternative is to acquire a new swap agreement that offsets the payment streams of the original swap agreement.

There are several risks to be aware of when entering into swap agreements. They are:

- *Basis risk*. This is caused by the mismatch between the cash flows involved in a swap. For example, the reference rate may be tied to LIBOR while the interest rate on a company's borrowing may be tied to some other index, such as an index of money market funds. Thus, if LIBOR increased by 0.5% and the basis for a company's debt increased by 0.6%, the payments it receives through a swap arrangement still would leave the company with an unhedged 0.1% interest rate increase.

- *Counterparty risk*. One of the parties to a swap agreement may not meet its financial obligations. Accordingly, it is important for the counterparty to have excellent credit quality. If a bank or broker is acting as the intermediary between two parties, then it may assume the counterparty risk by charging a fee to both parties to the swap.

- *Legal risk*. One of the parties to an over-the-counter transaction may have incorrectly or incompletely filled out a contract, or the signer of it may not have been authorized to do so.

Debt Call Provisions

If a company is issuing its own debt, it can include a *call provision* in the debt instrument that allows the company to retire the debt at a predetermined price. A controller would take advantage of this provision if market rates were to decline subsequent to issuance of the debt and could then refinance at a lower interest rate. The call provision typically incorporates higher prices for earlier calls, which gradually decline closer to par pricing farther into the future. This higher initial price point compensates investors for the interest income they otherwise would have earned if the company had not called the debt. Also, a call provision limits a bond's potential price appreciation to the amount of its call price, since the issuer will then call the bond. Consequently, the call provision is useful to a company by allowing it to buy back expensive debt and reissue at lower rates, but only if the savings from doing so exceed the amount of the call price.

For example, ABC Company could issue bonds with a call provision that allows it to buy back the bonds at 105% of par value after two years, then again at 103% of par value after six years, and then at their par value after eight years.

Options

An options contract is a trade that gives the buyer the right to buy or sell an amount of futures contracts at some date in the future. The cost of this right is the *options premium*, and it is paid to the counterparty at the beginning of the contract. This cost will vary based on such factors as the remaining term of an option, the strike price, and the volatility of the reference interest rate. If the option is entered into through an exchange, the exchange will ask for a deposit, which is refundable when the deal is completed.

In the options market, the party buying an option wants to reduce its risk while the party selling an option is willing to be paid to accept the risk. Thus, the cost of an option is based on the comparative level of perceived risk. The options premium increases the borrowing cost of the party wishing to reduce its interest rate risk, so if the option is priced too high, a prospective hedger may elect to retain the risk.

A *call option* on interest rates protects the option buyer from rising interest rates while a *put option* protects the option buyer from declining rates. Both types of options are benchmarked against a reference rate that is set forth in the option contract. Thus, if the reference rate is 5.00%, subsequent changes in the interest rate are measured in terms of their variation from 5.00% in determining potential benefits to option buyers. An interest rate option contract includes the following key components:

- A benchmark reference rate, as just described.
- A strike price, which is the interest rate at which the option buyer can borrow or lend funds.
- The amount of funds that can be borrowed or loaned.
- How the contract can be settled, such as by cash payment or by delivery of the underlying asset.
- The contract expiry date.

It is possible to modify these features to meet a company's specific needs by dealing in the over-the-counter market.

An interest rate option can be modified to include a *cap*; the buyer pays a premium in order to be protected from higher interest rates above the cap strike rate. At the expiry date of the option, the seller reimburses the buyer if the reference rate is above the cap strike rate and pays nothing if the reference rate is below the strike rate.

ABC Company has $5 million of variable rate debt that resets every three months. ABC's controller buys a 3×6 interest rate cap with a strike price of 6.00% to cover its debt. The reference rate is the Euribor rate on the reset date. Subsequently, the reference rate increases to 6.30%. The seller must reimburse ABC for the difference between the cap strike price and the reference rate. The calculation of the payment is:

$$\mathbf{\$3,750} = \frac{\$5,000,000 \times (0.0630 - 0.0600) \times 90 \text{ days}}{360 \text{ days}}$$

In order to determine ABC Company's true savings, the cost of the option must be offset against the $3,750 payment from the option seller, so the net amount of the hedge does not entirely cover ABC's increased interest rate payment.

A company can engage in a longer-term cap by purchasing a strip of options with consecutive expiry dates and the same strike price for all options. The following table shows an option strip covering an 18-month period, where the principal was $1 million. The first few months are not included in the table, since the option for that period would expire at the beginning of the period, yielding a zero payout.

Option	Term	Strike Price	3-Month LIBOR Rate	(A) Payout Rate	(B) Principal	A × B × (90/360) Payment Calculation
1	3×6	4.50%	4.35%	0.00%	$1,000,000	—
2	6×9	4.50%	4.45%	0.00%	1,000,000	—
3	9×12	4.50%	4.55%	0.05%	1,000,000	$125
4	12×15	4.50%	4.60%	0.10%	1,000,000	250
5	15×18	4.50%	4.70%	0.20%	1,000,000	500
					Total	**$875**

In the example, the strike price at the expiry date of the first two options is higher than the reference rate, so the company does not trigger the option; this is not a concern to the controller, since the underlying debt payments that he is most concerned about have not increased, either. However, the reference rate is higher for the remaining three option periods, which triggers three payments to the company totaling $875. The controller then uses the payments from these options to offset the increased cost of his debt during the same time periods.

If a controller considers the cost of a cap to be too expensive, an alternative is to purchase a *collar* from a bank. This is comprised of a purchased cap and a sold floor. The option that the controller sells (the floor) is used to take any profits from favorable interest rates and use them to pay for the cap. For this cost-offset method to work, the controller must align the time periods, reference rates, and exercise details of the cap and floor. If an option expires with the reference rate between the cap and floor rates, then neither side of the collar is exercised.

The controller of the Alaskan Barrel Company anticipates that interest rates will fluctuate between 4.5% and 6.5% over the next two years and is comfortable incurring interest expenses anywhere within that range. To avoid paying interest greater than 6.5%, she purchases a 6.5% cap and sells a 4.5% floor. If the interest rate stays between 4.5% and 6.5%, then neither the cap nor the floor is triggered. However, if interest rates rise to 7.0%, then the cap will pay for the 0.5% excess over the 6.5% cap. Also, if the interest rate falls below 4.5%, Alaskan must pay the difference between the reference rate and the floor of 4.5%, thereby effectively limiting its lowest possible interest rate to 4.5%.

Swaptions

A *swaption* is an option on an interest rate swap. The buyer of a swaption has the right, but not an obligation, to enter into an interest rate swap with predefined terms at the expiration of the option. In exchange for a premium payment, the buyer of a swaption can lock in either a fixed or a variable interest rate. Thus, if a controller believes that interest rates will rise, he can enter into a swaption agreement, which he can later convert into an interest rate swap if interest rates do indeed go up.

> The Shapiro Pool Company needs to finance its construction of the pool complex for the Summer Olympic Games. It expects to do so at the floating LIBOR rate plus 1.5% in six months, with a duration of three years. To protect itself from rates increasing above 7.0%, Shapiro buys a swaption. The swaption agreement gives Shapiro the right, but not the obligation, to enter into an interest rate swap where it pays a fixed rate of 7.0% and receives LIBOR plus 1.5%. If the reference rate in nine months is above 7.0%, then Shapiro should exercise the option to enter into the swap.

A swaption can be a risky endeavor for a swaption seller, since the seller is taking on potentially substantial risk in exchange for a premium. Thus, the swaption buyer should carefully examine the credit risk of the swaption seller, both at the initiation of the transaction and throughout its term.

Counterparty Limits

There is a limit to the amount of the risk management strategies outlined here that a company can employ. The counterparty to FRAs, swaps, and collars are usually banks, and they will reduce their risk by setting up counterparty limits for each company doing business with them. Every time a company enters into one of these agreements with a bank, the bank reduces the available amount of the limit assigned to that company. Thus, it is possible that some of the risk strategies outlined here will not be available beyond a certain level of activity.

Summary of Interest Risk Management Strategies

Of the strategies presented here, forwards and futures are the most inflexible, because they do no more than lock a company into a set rate and present an opportunity loss if rates turn in the opposite direction from the constructed hedge. Options are more flexible, since they can be tailored to provide payoffs that closely match a company's exposure while also yielding benefits from a favorable market move.

A comparison of the various interest rate risk management strategies is shown in Exhibit 17.5.

17.5   BONDS SOLD AT A DISCOUNT OR PREMIUM TO THEIR FACE VALUE

When bonds are initially sold, the entry is a debit to cash and a credit to bonds payable. However, this only occurs when the price paid by investors exactly matches the face amount

	Forward Rate Agreements	Futures	Interest Rate Swaps	Options
Notional payments	Yes	Yes	Not necessarily	Yes
Agreement type	Customized	Standard	Customized	Standard or customized
Collateral requirement	None	Initial margin and margin calls	None	Initial margin and margin calls if originated on an exchange
Counterparty	Bank	Exchange	Bank	Bank or exchange
Counterparty limits imposed	Yes	No	Yes	Yes
Method of exchange	Over the counter	Exchange traded	Over the counter	Exchange traded or over the counter
Settlement frequency	At expiry date	Daily	On coupon dates	Either daily or at expiry date

EXHIBIT 17.5   INTEREST RISK MANAGEMENT STRATEGY COMPARISON

of the bond. A more common occurrence is that the market interest rate varies somewhat from the stated interest rate on the bond, so investors pay a different price in order to achieve an effective interest rate matching the market rate. For example, if the market rate were 8% and the stated rate were 7%, investors would pay less than the face amount of the bond so that the 7% interest they later receive will equate to an 8% interest rate on their reduced investment. Alternatively, if the rates were reversed, with a 7% market rate and 8% stated rate, investors would pay more for the bond, thereby driving down the stated interest rate to match the market rate. If the bonds are sold at a discount, the entry will include a debit to a Discount on bonds payable account. For example, if $10,000 of bonds are sold at a discount of $1,500, the entry would be:

	Debit	Credit
Cash	$8,500	
Discount on bonds payable	1,500	
Bonds payable		$10,000

If the same transaction were to occur, except that a premium on sale of the bonds occurs, then the entry would be:

	Debit	Credit
Cash	$11,500	
Premium on bonds payable		$1,500
Bonds payable		10,000

An example of a discount calculation is as follows:

The Arabian Knights Security Company issues $1,000,000 of bonds at a stated rate of 8% in a market where similar issuances are being bought at 11%. The bonds pay interest once a year and are to be paid off in 10 years. Investors purchase these bonds at a discount in order to earn an effective yield on their investment of 11%. The discount calculation requires one to determine the present value of 10 interest payments at 11% interest, as well as the present value of $1,000,000, discounted at 11% for 10 years. The result is as follows:

Present value of 10 payments of $80,000 = $80,000 × 5.8892	=	$ 471,136
Present value of $1,000,000	= $1,000,000 × .3522 =	$ 352,200
		$ 823,336
Less: stated bond price		1,000,000
Discount on bond		$ 176,664

In this example, the entry would be a debit to Cash for $823,336, a credit to Bonds Payable for $1,000,000, and a debit to Discount on Bonds Payable for $176,664. If the calculation had resulted in a premium (which would only have occurred if the market rate of interest was less than the stated interest rate on the bonds), then a credit to Premium on Bonds Payable would be in order.

17.6   EFFECTIVE INTEREST METHOD

The amount of a discount or premium should be gradually written off to the Interest expense account over the life of the bond. The only acceptable method for writing off these amounts is through the *effective interest method*, which allows one to charge off the difference between the market and stated rate of interest to the existing Discount or Premium account, gradually reducing the balance in the Discount or Premium account over the life of the bond. If interest payment dates do not coincide with the end of financial reporting periods, a journal entry must be made to show the amount of interest expense and related discount or premium amortization that would have occurred during the days following the last interest payment date and the end of the reporting period. An example of the effective interest method is as follows:

To continue with our example, the interest method holds that, in the first year of interest payments, the Arabian Knights Security Company's accountant would determine that the market interest expense for the first year would be $90,567 (bond stated price of $1,000,000 minus discount of $176,664, multiplied by the market interest rate of 11%). The resulting journal entry would be:

	Debit	Credit
Interest expense	$90,567	
Discount on bonds payable		$10,567
Cash		80,000

The reason why only $80,000 is listed as a reduction in cash is that the company only has an obligation to pay an 8% interest rate on the $1,000,000 face value of the bonds, which is $80,000. The difference is netted against the existing Discount on bonds payable account. The following table shows the calculation of the discount to be charged to expense each year for the full 10-year period of the bond, where the annual amortization of the discount is added back to the bond present value, eventually resulting in a bond present value of $1,000,000 by the time principal payment is due, while the discount has dropped to zero.

Year	Beginning Bond Present Value (4)	Unamortized Discount	Interest Expense (1)	Cash Payment (2)	Credit to Discount (3)
1	$823,336	$176,664	$90,567	$80,000	$10,567
2	$833,903	$166,097	$91,729	$80,000	$11,729
3	$845,632	$154,368	$93,020	$80,000	$13,020
4	$858,652	$141,348	$94,452	$80,000	$14,452
5	$873,104	$126,896	$96,041	$80,000	$16,041
6	$889,145	$110,855	$97,806	$80,000	$17,806
7	$906,951	$93,049	$99,765	$80,000	$19,765
8	$926,716	$73,284	$101,939	$80,000	$21,939
9	$948,655	$51,346	$104,352	$80,000	$24,352
10	$973,007	$26,994	$107,031	$80,000	$26,994
	$1,000,000	$0			

(1) = Bond present value multiplied by the market rate of 11%
(2) = Required cash payment of 8% stated rate multiplied by face value of $1,000,000
(3) = Interest expense reduced by cash payment
(4) = Beginning present value of the bond plus annual reduction in the discount

17.7 DEBT ISSUED WITH NO STATED INTEREST RATE

If a company issues debt that has no stated rate of interest, then the accountant must create an interest rate for it that approximates the rate that the company would likely obtain, given its credit rating, on the open market on the date when the debt was issued. The accountant then uses this rate to discount the face amount of the debt down to its present value, and then records the difference between this present value and the loan's face value as the loan balance. For example, if a company issued debt with a face amount of $1,000,000, payable in five years and at no stated interest rate, and the market rate for interest at the time of issuance was 9%, then the discount factor to be applied to the debt would be 0.6499. This would give the debt a present value of $649,900. The difference between the face amount of $1,000,000 and the present value of $649,900 should be recorded as a discount on the note, as shown in the following entry:

	Debit	Credit
Cash	$649,900	
Discount on note payable	350,100	
Notes payable		$1,000,000

17.8 DEBT ISSUANCE COSTS

The costs associated with issuing bonds can be substantial. These include the legal costs of creating the bond documents, printing the bond certificates and (especially) the underwriting costs of the investment banker. Since these costs are directly associated with the procurement of funds that the company can be expected to use for a number of years (until the bonds are paid off), the related bond issuance costs should be recorded as an asset and then written off on a straight-line basis over the period during which the bonds are expected to be used by the company. This entry is a debit to a Bond issuance asset account and a credit to cash. However, if the bonds associated with these costs are subsequently paid off earlier than anticipated, one can reasonably argue that the associated remaining bond issuance costs should be charged to expense at the same time.

17.9   NOTES ISSUED WITH ATTACHED RIGHTS

An issuing company can grant additional benefits to the other party, such as exclusive distribution rights on its products, discounts on product sales, and so on—the range of possibilities is endless. In these cases, one should consider the difference between the present value and face value of the debt to be the value of the additional consideration. When this occurs, the difference is debited to the Discount on note payable account and is amortized using the *effective interest method* that was described earlier. The offsetting credit can be credited to a variety of accounts, depending on the nature of the transaction. The credited account is typically written off either ratably (if the attached benefit is equally spread over many accounting periods) or in conjunction with specific events (such as the shipment of discounted products to the holder of the debt). Though less common, it is also possible to issue debt at an above-market rate in order to obtain additional benefits from the debt holder. In this case, the entry is reversed, with a credit to the Premium on note payable account and the offsetting debit to a number of possible accounts related to the specific consideration given. An example of a note issued with attached rights is as follows:

The Arabian Knights Security Company has issued a new note for $2,500,000 at 4% interest to a customer, the Alaskan Pipeline Company. Under the terms of the five-year note, Alaskan obtains a 20% discount on all security services it purchases from Arabian during the term of the note. The market rate for similar debt was 9% on the date the loan documents were signed.

The present value of the note at the 9% market rate of interest over a five-year term is $1,624,750, while the present value of the note at its stated rate of 4% is $2,054,750. The difference between the two present value figures is $430,000, which is the value of the attached right to discounted security services granted to Alaskan. Arabian should make the following entry to record the loan:

	Debit	Credit
Cash	$2,500,000	
Discount on note payable	430,000	
Note payable		$2,500,000
Unearned revenue		430,000

The unearned revenue of $430,000 can either be recognized incrementally as part of each invoice billed to Alaskan, or it can be recognized ratably over the term of the debt. Since Arabian does not know the exact amount of the security services that will be contracted for by Alaskan during the term of the five-year note, the better approach is to recognize the unearned revenue ratably over the note term. The first month's entry would be as follows, where the amount recognized is 1/60 of the beginning balance of unearned revenue:

	Debit	Credit
Unearned revenue	$7,166.67	
Services revenue		$7,166.67

17.10   NOTES ISSUED FOR PROPERTY

When a note is issued in exchange for some type of property, the stated interest rate on the note is used to value the debt for reporting purposes unless the rate is not considered to be "fair." If it is not fair, then the transaction should be recorded at either the fair market value of the property or the note, whichever can be more clearly determined. An example of a debt with an unfair interest rate, exchanged for property, is as follows:

> The Arabian Knights Security Company exchanges a $50,000 note for a set of motion detection equipment from the Eye Spy Company. The equipment is custom-built for Arabian, so there is no way to assign a fair market value to it. The note has a stated interest rate of 3% and is payable in three years. The 3% rate appears to be quite low, especially since Arabian just secured similar financing from a local lender at a 7% interest rate. The 3% rate can thus be considered not fair for the purposes of valuing the debt, so Arabian's controller elects to use the 7% rate instead.
>
> The discount rate for debt due in three years at 7% interest is 0.8163. After multiplying the $50,000 face value of the note by 0.8163, the controller arrives at a net present value for the debt of $40,815, which is recorded in the following entry as the value of the motion detection equipment, along with a discount that shall be amortized to interest expense over the life of the loan.

	Debit	Credit
Motion detection equipment	$40,815	
Discount on notes payable	9,185	
Notes payable		$50,000

17.11   EXTINGUISHMENT OF DEBT

A company may find it advisable to repurchase its bonds prior to their maturity date, perhaps because market interest rates have dropped so far below the stated rate on the bonds that the company can profitably refinance at a lower interest rate. Whatever the reason may be, the resulting transaction should recognize any gain or loss on the transaction, as well as recognize the transactional cost of the retirement and any proportion of the outstanding discount, premium, or bond issuance costs relating to the original bond issuance. An example of debt extinguishment is as follows:

> To return to our earlier example, if the Arabian Knights Security Company were to buy back $200,000 of its $1,000,000 bond issuance at a premium of 5%, and were to do so with $125,000 of the original bond discount still on its books, it would record a loss of $10,000 on the bond retirement ($200,000 × 5%), while also recognizing 1/5 of the remaining discount, which is $25,000 ($125,000 × 1/5). The entry would be as follows:

	Debit	Credit
Bonds payable	$200,000	
Loss on bond retirement	10,000	
Discount on bonds payable		$ 25,000
Cash		185,000

If the issuing company finds itself in the position of being unable to pay either interest or principle to its bondholders, there are two directions the accountant can take in reflecting the problem in the accounting records. In the first case, the company may only temporarily be in default and attempting to work out a payment solution with the bondholders. Under this scenario, the amortization of discounts or premiums, as well as of bond issuance costs and interest expense, should continue as they have in the past. However, if there is no chance of payment, then the amortization of discounts or premiums, as well as of bond issuance costs, should be accelerated, being recognized in full in the current period. This action is taken on the grounds that the underlying accounting transaction that specified the period over which the amortizations occurred has now disappeared, requiring the accountant to recognize all remaining expenses.

If the issuing company has not defaulted on a debt, but rather has restructured its terms, then the accountant must determine the present value of the new stream of cash flows and compare it to the original carrying value of the debt arrangement. In the likely event that the new present value of the debt is less than the original present value, the difference should be recognized in the current period as a gain.

Alternatively, if the present value of the restructured debt agreement is *more* than the carrying value of the original agreement, then a loss is *not* recognized on the difference—instead, the effective interest rate on the new stream of debt payments is reduced to the point where the resulting present value of the restructured debt matches the carrying value of the original agreement. This will result in a reduced amount of interest expense being accrued for all future periods during which the debt is outstanding.

In some cases where the issuing company is unable to pay bondholders, it gives them other company assets in exchange for the interest or principal payments owed to them. When this occurs, the issuing company first records a gain or loss on the initial revaluation of the asset being transferred to its fair market value. Next, it records a gain or loss on the transaction if there is a difference between the carrying value of the debt being paid off and the fair market value of the asset being transferred to the bondholder. An example of an asset transfer to eliminate debt is as follows:

The Arabian Knights Security Company is unable to pay off its loan from a local lender. The lender agrees to cancel the debt, with a remaining face value of $35,000, in exchange for a company truck having a book value of $26,000 and a fair market value of $29,000. There is also $2,500 of accrued but unpaid interest expense associated with the debt. Arabian's controller first revalues the truck to its fair market value and then records a gain on the debt settlement transaction. The entries are as follows:

	Debit	Credit
Vehicles	$ 3,000	
Gain on asset transfer		$ 3,000
Note payable	$35,000	
Interest payable	2,500	
Vehicles		$29,000
Gain on debt settlement		8,500

If convertible debt (see the "Convertible Debt" section) is issued with a conversion feature that is already in the money, then the intrinsic value of that equity component should have been recorded as a credit to the Additional paid-in capital account. If so, the intrinsic value must be remeasured as of the debt retirement date and then removed from the Additional paid-in capital account. This may result in the recognition of a gain or loss, depending on the difference between the original and final intrinsic value calculations.

17.12   SCHEDULED BOND RETIREMENT

A bond agreement may contain specific requirements to either create a sinking fund that is used at the maturity date to buy back all bonds, or else to gradually buy back bonds on a regular schedule, usually through a trustee. In either case, the intention is to ensure that the company is not suddenly faced with a large repayment requirement at the maturity date. In this situation, the company usually forwards funds to a trustee at regular intervals, who in turn uses it to buy back bonds. The resulting accounting is identical to that noted under the "Extinguishment of Debt" section. In addition, if the company forwards interest payments to the trustee for bonds that the trustee now has in its possession, these payments are used to purchase additional bonds (since there is no one to whom the interest can be paid). In this case, the journal entry that would normally record this transaction as interest expense is converted into an entry that reduces the principal balance of the bonds outstanding.

17.13   CONVERTIBLE DEBT

The *convertible bond* contains a feature allowing the holder to turn in the bond in exchange for stock when a preset strike price for the stock is reached, sometimes after a specific date. This involves a specific conversion price per share, which is typically set at a point that makes the transaction uneconomical unless the share price rises at some point in the future.

To account for this transaction under the popular *book value method*, the principal amount of the bond is moved to an equity account, with a portion being allocated to the Capital account at par value and the remainder going to the Additional paid-in capital account. A portion of the discount or premium associated with the bond issuance is also retired, based on the proportion of bonds converted to equity. If the *market value method* is used instead, the conversion price is based on the number of shares issued to former bondholders, multiplied by the market price of the shares on the conversion date. This will likely create a gain or loss as compared to the book value of the converted bonds. An example of debt conversion using the book value method is as follows:

A bondholder owns $50,000 of bonds and wishes to convert them to 1,000 shares of company stock that has a par value of $5. The total amount of the premium associated with the original bond issuance was $42,000, and the amount of bonds to be converted to stock represents 18% of the total amount of bonds outstanding. In this case, the amount of premium to be recognized will be $7,560 ($42,000 × 18%), while the amount of funds shifted to the Capital stock at par value account will be $5,000 (1,000 shares × $5). The entry is as follows:

	Debit	Credit
Bonds payable	$50,000	
Premium on bonds payable	7,560	
Capital stock at par value		$ 5,000
Additional paid-in capital		52,560

An example of bond conversion using the market value method is as follows:

Use the same assumptions as the last example, except that the fair market value of the shares acquired by the former bondholder is $5.50 each. This creates a loss on the bond conversion of $5,000, which is added to the Additional paid-in capital account. The entry is as follows:

	Debit	Credit
Bonds payable	$50,000	
Loss on bond conversion	5,000	
Premium on bonds payable	7,560	
Capital stock at par value		$ 5,000
Additional paid-in capital		57,560

17.14 CONVERTIBLE DEBT ISSUED IN THE MONEY

The situation becomes more complicated if convertible bonds are issued with a stock conversion strike price that is already lower than the market price of the stock. In this case, the related journal entry must assign a value to the shares that is based on the potential number of convertible shares multiplied by the difference between the strike price and the market value of the stock. If there are a series of strike prices for different future dates in the bond agreement, then the lowest strike price should be used to determine the intrinsic value of the deal. If bonds are issued with a strike price that is in the money, but contingent upon a future event, then any recognition of the intrinsic value of the equity element is delayed until the contingent event has occurred.

(1) Example of bond issuance when the strike price is in the money: An investor purchases $50,000 of bonds that are convertible into 10,000 shares of common stock at a conversion price of $5. At the time of issuance, the stock had a fair market value of $6.50. The intrinsic value of the conversion feature at the time of issuance is $15,000, based on the difference between the fair market value of $6.50 and the conversion price of $5.00, multiplied by the 10,000 shares that would be issued if a full conversion were to take place. The entry would be as follows:

	Debit	Credit
Cash	$50,000	
Bonds payable		$35,000
Additional paid-in capital		15,000

(2) Example of bond issuance when a sequence of strike prices are in the money: Use the same information as the last example, except that the bond agreement contains a lower strike price of $4.50 after three years have passed. Since this later strike price results in a greater intrinsic value being assigned to equity than the initial strike price, the later price is used for the valuation calculation. The calculation is 11,111 shares ($50,000 divided by a strike price of $4.50), multiplied by the $2 difference between the strike price and the fair market value, resulting in a debit to cash of $50,000, a credit to Bonds Payable of $27,778, and a credit to Additional Paid-in Capital of $22,222.

(3) Example of bond issuance when the strike price is in the money but is dependent on a contingent event: Use the same information as was used for the first example, except that conversion cannot take place until the stock of all Series. A preferred shareholders has been bought back by the company. The initial journal entry is a simple debit to Cash of $50,000 and a credit to Bonds Payable of $50,000, since there is no intrinsic value to the equity component at this time. Once the Series A shareholders are bought out, the intrinsic value of the equity is recognized by debiting the Discount on bonds payable account and crediting the Additional paid-in capital accounts for $15,000.

17.15   CONVERTIBLE DEBT—ACCRUED BUT UNPAID INTEREST ON CONVERTED DEBT

If a convertible debt agreement's terms state that a bondholder shall forfeit any accrued interest at the time the bondholder converts to equity, the company must recognize the accrued interest expense anyway, net of income taxes. The offset to the expense is a credit to the Capital account. An example of unpaid accrued interest on converted debt is as follows:

> Mr. Abraham Smith owns $25,000 of the North Dakota Railroad's convertible debt. He elects to convert it to the railroad's common stock and forfeits the accrued $520 of interest expense that was not yet paid as of the conversion date. The railroad debits the Interest expense account and credits the Capital account for $520.

17.16   CONVERTIBLE DEBT—SUBSEQUENT CHANGE IN OFFERING TO INDUCE CONVERSION

If a company induces its bondholders to convert their holdings to equity by subsequently improving the conversion feature of the bond agreement, it must record an expense for the difference between the consideration given to induce the conversion and the consideration originally noted in the bond agreement. An example of subsequent change in conversion terms is as follows:

> Mr. Abraham Smith owns $25,000 of the North Dakota Railroad's convertible debt. The bonds were originally issued with a conversion price of $50 per share, which the railroad has subsequently lowered to $40 to induce conversion. The shares have a market value of $38 and a par value of $1. Mr. Smith elects to convert to stock, resulting in the following calculation:

	Before Change in Terms	After Change in Terms
Face amount of bonds	$25,000	$25,000
Conversion price	50	40
Total shares converted	500	625
Fair value per share	38	38
Value of converted stock	$19,000	$23,750

The difference between the total values of converted stock before and after the change in terms is $4,750, resulting in the following entry to record the entire conversion transaction:

	Debit	Credit
Bonds payable	$25,000	
Debt conversion expense	4,750	
Capital account, par value		$ 625
Additional paid-in capital		29,125

17.17   DEBT ISSUED WITH STOCK WARRANTS

A company may attach warrants to its bonds in order to sell the bonds to investors more easily. A warrant gives an investor the right to buy a specific number of shares of company stock at a set price for a given time interval.

To account for the presence of a warrant, the accountant must determine its value if it were sold separately from the bond, determine the proportion of the total bond price to allocate to it, and then credit this proportional amount into the Additional paid-in capital account. An example of bonds issued with attached warrants is as follows:

A bond/warrant combination is purchased by an investor for $1,100. The investment banker handling the transaction estimates that the value of the warrant is $150, while the bond (with a face value of $1,000) begins trading at $975. Accordingly, the value the accountant assigns to the warrant is $146.67, which is calculated as follows:

$$\frac{\text{Warrant value}}{\text{Bond value} + \text{Warrant value}} \times \text{Purchase price} = \text{Price assigned to warrant}$$

$$\frac{\$150}{\$975 + \$150} \times \$1,100 = \$146.67$$

The accountant then credits the $146.67 assigned to the warrant value to the Additional Paid-in capital account, since this is a form of equity funding, rather than debt funding, for which the investor has paid. The Discount on bonds payable represents the difference between the $1,000 face value of the bond and its assigned value of $953.33. The journal entry is as follows:

	Debit	Credit
Cash	$1,100.00	
Discount on bonds payable	46.67	
Bonds payable		$1,000.00
Additional paid-in capital		146.67

17.18   ACCOUNTING FOR INTEREST RISK MANAGEMENT ACTIVITIES

The following discussion of accounting is targeted at derivative financial instruments, of which the two main forms of derivatives are option contracts and forward contracts. Within these main categories are interest rate caps and floors, forward interest rate agreements, interest rate collars, futures, swaps, and swaptions.

Derivatives represent rights and obligations, and must be reported as assets and liabilities at their fair value. A gain or loss on a derivative that is not designated as a hedge must be recognized in earnings. If a derivative is designated as a hedge, then the accounting for it varies depending on whether it an effective hedge or an ineffective hedge.

A *fair value hedge* primarily relates to the hedging of fixed interest balance sheet items, while *cash flow hedges* mean hedges against the risk associated with future interest payments from a variable interest balance sheet transaction. Since risk mitigation generally is associated with variable interest payments, the appropriate type of accounting is the cash flow hedge. Thus, the remainder of this section discusses the accounting for a cash flow hedge only.

To establish a valid cash flow hedge, one must document the relationship between the hedging instrument and an asset, liability, or forecasted transaction (including expected date of occurrence and amount). The documentation must also describe the hedging strategy, risk management objectives, and how the effectiveness of the transaction shall be measured. The method for effectiveness assessment must be defined at the time of hedge designation and must be maintained consistently throughout the hedge period. Further, similar types of hedges should be documented and treated in the same manner, unless a different method can be reasonably justified.

In addition, the hedging relationship must be expected to be highly effective in producing offsetting cash flows and evaluated at least quarterly to ensure that this is the case.

One must discontinue a cash flow hedge when the hedge criteria are no longer met, the hedging designation is cancelled, or the derivative instruments used in the hedge are terminated. If any of these circumstances arise, a new hedging relationship can be documented with a different derivative instrument.

When reporting derivative gains and losses for a cash flow hedge, the effective portion of the gain or loss is reported in other comprehensive income while any gains or losses attributable to the ineffective portion of the hedge are reported in earnings. For example, any differences in the key terms between a hedged item and the hedging instrument, such as notional amounts, maturities, quantities, or delivery dates, would cause some amount of ineffectiveness, and the amount of that ineffective portion of the hedge would be included in earnings.

Whenever one expects a net loss from the hedging transaction, the amount not expected to be recovered must be shifted in the current period from other comprehensive income to earnings. Also, if a hedging relationship is established for a forecasted cash flow transaction and the transaction is deemed unlikely to occur, any gain or loss thus far recorded in other comprehensive income must be shifted to earnings in the current period.

Accounting for an Interest Rate Swap

On July 1, 2009, Abbott Corp. borrows $5 million with a fixed maturity (no prepayment option) of June 30, 2013, carrying interest at prime + 1/2%. Interest is due only semiannually. At the same date, it enters into a plain vanilla–type swap arrangement, calling for fixed payments at 8% and receipt of prime + 1/2%, on a notional amount of $5 million. At that date prime is 7.5%, and there is no premium due on the swap arrangement.

This swap qualifies as a cash flow hedge, and it is appropriate to assume no ineffectiveness, since it fulfills all GAAP criteria.

NOTE: These criteria are: the notional amount of the swap and the principal amount of the debt are equal; the fair value of the swap at inception is zero; the formula for computing net settlements under the swap is constant during its term; the debt may not be prepaid; all interest payments on the debt are designated as being hedged and no payments beyond the term of the swap are so designated; there is no floor or cap on the variable rate of the debt that is not likewise designated for the swap; the repricing dates of the swap match those of the variable rate debt; and the same index is designated for the hedging instrument and the underlying obligation.

Accordingly, as rates change over the term of the debt and of the swap arrangement, changes in the value of the swap are reflected in other comprehensive income, and the swap will appear on the balance sheet as an asset or liability at fair value. As the maturity of the debt approaches, the value of the swap will converge on zero. Periodic interest expense in the income statement will be at the effective rate of 8%.

Assume that the prime rate over the four-year term of the loan, as of each interest payment date, is as follows, along with the fair value of the remaining term of the interest rate swap at those dates:

Date	Prime rate (%)	Fair value of swap*
December 31, 2009	6.5	$ −150,051
June 30, 2010	6.0	−196,580
December 31, 2010	6.5	−111,296
June 30, 2011	7.0	−45,374
December 31, 2011	7.5	0
June 30, 2012	8.0	23,576
December 31, 2012	8.5	24,038
June 30, 2013	8.0	0

*Fair values are determined as the present values of future cash flows resulting from expected interest rate differentials, based on the current prime rate, discounted at 8%.

Regarding the fair values presented in the previous table, it should be assumed that the fair values are precisely equal to the present value, at each valuation date (assumed to be the interest payment dates), of the differential future cash flows resulting from utilization of the swap. Future variable interest rates (prime + 1/2%) are assumed to be the same as the existing rates at each valuation date (i.e., there is no basis for any expectation of rate changes, and therefore the best estimate is that the current rate will persist over time). The discount rate, 8%, is assumed to be constant over time.

Thus, for example, the fair value of the swap at December 31, 2009, would be the present value of an annuity of seven payments (the number of remaining semiannual interest payments due) of $25,000 each (pay 8%, receive 7%, based on then-existing prime rate of 6.5%) to be made to the swap counterparty, discounted at an annual rate of 8% (using 4% for the semiannual discounting, which is a slight simplification). This computation yields a present value of a stream of seven $25,000 payments to the swap counterparty amounting to $150,051 at December 31, 2009, which is a liability to be reported by the entity at that date. The offset is a debit to other comprehensive income, since the hedge is (presumably) judged to be 100% effective in this case. Semiannual accounting entries will be as follows:

December 31, 2009

Interest expense	175,000	
Accrued interest (or cash)		175,000

To accrue or pay semiannual interest on the debt at the variable rate of prime + 1/2% (7.0%)

Interest expense	25,000	
Accrued interest (or cash)		25,000

To record net settlement on swap arrangement [8.0 − 7.0%]

Other comprehensive income	150,051	
Swap contract		150,051

To record the fair value of the swap contract as of this date (a net liability because fixed rate payable to counterparty of 8% exceeds floating rate receivable from counterparty of 7%)

June 30, 2010

Interest expense	162,500	
Accrued interest (or cash)		162,500

To accrue or pay semiannual interest on the debt at the variable rate of prime + 1/2% (6.5%)

Interest expense	37,500	
Accrued interest (or cash)		37,500

To record net settlement on swap arrangement [8.0 − 6.5%]

Other comprehensive income	46,529	
Swap contract		46,529

To record the fair value of the swap contract as of this date (increase in obligation because of further decline in prime rate)

December 31, 2010

Interest expense	175,000	
Accrued interest (or cash)		175,000

To accrue or pay semiannual interest on the debt at the variable rate of prime + 1/2% (7.0%)

Interest expense	25,000	
Accrued interest (or cash)		25,000

To record net settlement on swap arrangement [8.0 − 7.0%]

Other comprehensive income	150,051	
Swap contract		150,051

To record the fair value of the swap contract as of this date (decrease in obligation due to increase in prime rate)

(Continued)

June 30, 2011

Interest expense	187,500	
Accrued interest (or cash)		187,500

To accrue or pay semiannual interest on the debt at the variable rate of prime + 1/2% (7.5%)

Interest expense	12,500	
Accrued interest (or cash)		12,500

To record net settlement on swap arrangement [8.0 – 7.5%]

Swap contract	65,922	
Other comprehensive income		65,922

To record the fair value of the swap contract as of this date (decrease in obligation due to further increase in prime rate)

December 31, 2011

Interest expense	200,000	
Accrued interest (or cash)		200,000

To accrue or pay semiannual interest on the debt at the variable rate of prime + 1/2% (8.0%)

Interest expense	0	
Accrued interest (or cash)		0

To record net settlement on swap arrangement [8.0 – 8.0%]

Swap contract	45,374	
Other comprehensive income		45,374

To record the fair value of the swap contract as of this date (further increase in prime rate to the original rate of inception of the hedge eliminates fair value of the derivative)

June 30, 2012

Interest expense	212,500	
Accrued interest (or cash)		212,500

To accrue or pay semiannual interest on the debt at the variable rate of prime + 1/2% (8.5%)

Receivable from counterparty (or cash)	12,500	
Interest expense		12,500

To record net settlement on swap arrangement [8.0 – 8.5%], counterparty remits settlement

Swap contract	23,576	
Other comprehensive income		23,576

To record the fair value of the swap contract as of this date (increase in prime rate creates net asset position for derivative)

December 31, 2012

Interest expense	225,000	
Accrued interest (or cash)		225,000

To accrue or pay semiannual interest on the debt at the variable rate of prime + 1/2% (9.0%)

Receivable from counterparty (or cash)	25,000	
Interest expense		25,000

To record net settlement on swap arrangement [8.0 – 9.0%], counterparty remits settlement

Swap contract	462	
Other comprehensive income		462

To record the fair value of the swap contract as of this date (increase in asset value due to further rise in prime rate)

June 30, 2013 (Maturity)

Interest expense	212,500	
Accrued interest (or cash)		212,500

To accrue or pay semiannual interest on the debt at the variable rate of prime + 1/2% (8.5%)

Receivable from counterparty (or cash)	12,500	
Interest expense		12,500
Other comprehensive income	24,038	
Swap contract		24,038

To record the fair value of the swap contract as of this date (value declines to zero as expiration date approaches)

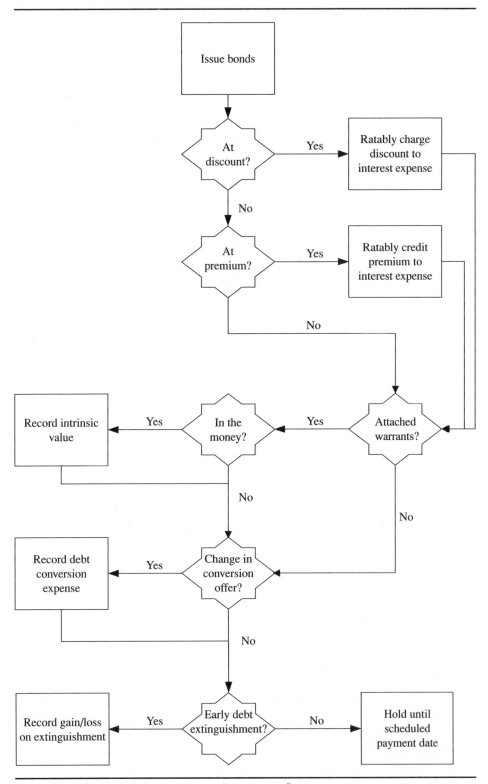

EXHIBIT 17.6 DECISION POINTS DURING THE LIFETIME OF A BOND

17.19 DECISION POINTS DURING THE LIFETIME OF A BOND

The decision tree shown in Exhibit 17.6 shows the general set of decisions to be made during the life of a bond, beginning with the treatment of discounts or premiums on the initial sale price and proceeding through the presence of attached warrants and early debt extinguishment. The decisions in the top third of the tree will impact nearly all bonds, since it is unusual *not* to have a discount or premium. The middle third only impacts attached warrants, with most of the action items involving "in the money" warrants.

17.20 SUMMARY

Among all the preceding topics, a few key issues arise. First, debt must always be recorded at the market interest rate, which may involve the use of present value discounting or the use of discounts or premiums from the stated face value of a bond; this principle is designed to give the reader of a financial statement a clear idea of the true cost of a company's debt. Second, any debt origination costs associated with a debt should be amortized over the life of the debt, so that the cost is matched to the underlying benefit—that of having obtained the debt. Third, if there is a reasonable expectation that a debt may be due and payable within one year, then it must be listed as a current liability—this clearly identifies the risk that debt may be payable in the short term, which may potentially result in a cash flow problem. Finally, any change in the terms of a debt agreement resulting in a gain or loss should be recognized at once, either through monetary recognition or footnotes, so that one can readily see its long-term financial impact. Thus, the key issues involving debt are the clear presentation of the cost and timing of debt liabilities.

CHAPTER **18**

EQUITY

18.1 INTRODUCTION

A small company will start with nothing more than the issuance of common stock to create its equity. However, as the organization grows and its funding and compensation needs proliferate, a wide range of additional equity-related stratagems will arise—stock splits, stock subscriptions, warrants, and stock appreciation rights are some of the topics that one should address. In this chapter, we review all of these items and more, with particular attention to the journal entries required to record each transaction. Stock options are described in the next chapter.

18.2 LEGAL CAPITAL AND CAPITAL STOCK

The owners of common stock are the true owners of the corporation. Through their share ownership, they have the right to receive dividend distributions, to vote on various issues presented to them by the board of directors, to elect members of the board of directors, and to share in any residual funds left if the corporation is liquidated. If the company is liquidated, they will not receive any distribution from its proceeds until all creditor claims have been satisfied, as well as the claims of holders of all other classes of stock. There may be several classes of common stock, which typically have different voting rights attached to them; the presence of multiple types of common stock generally indicates that some shareholders are attempting some degree of preferential control over a company through their type of common stock.

Most types of stock contain a par value, which is a minimum price below which the stock cannot be sold. The original intent for using par value was to ensure that a residual amount of funding was contributed to the company and could not be removed from it until dissolution of the corporate entity. In reality, most common stock now has a par value that is so low (typically anywhere from a penny to a dollar) that its original intent no longer works. Thus, though the accountant still tracks par value separately in the accounting records, it has little meaning.

If an investor purchases a share of stock at a price greater than its par value, the difference is credited to an Additional paid-in capital account. For example, if an investor buys one share of common stock at a price of $82, and the stock's par value is $1, then the entry would be:

	Debit	Credit
Cash	$82	
Common stock—par value		$ 1
Common stock—additional paid-in capital		81

When a company initially issues stock, there will be a number of costs associated with it, such as the printing of stock certificates, legal fees, investment banker fees, and security registration fees. These costs can be charged against the proceeds of the stock sale, rather than be recognized as expenses within the current period.

If a company accepts property or services in exchange for stock, the amount listed on the books as the value of stock issued should be based on the fair market value of the property or services received. If this cannot easily be determined, then the current market price of the shares issued should be used. If neither is available, then the value assigned by the board of directors at the time of issuance is assumed to be the fair market value.

Preferred stock comes in many flavors, but essentially is stock that has fewer (or none) of the rights conferred upon common stock, but that provides a variety of incentives, such as guaranteed dividend payments and preferential distributions over common stock, to convince investors to buy it. The dividends can also be preconfigured to increase to a higher level at a later date, which is called *increasing rate preferred stock*. This is an expensive form of funds for a company, since the dividends paid to investors are not tax-deductible as interest expense.

The dividends provided for in a preferred stock agreement can only be distributed after the approval of the board of directors (as is the case for dividends from common stock), and so may be withheld. If the preferred stock has a cumulative provision, then any dividends not paid to the holders of preferred shares in preceding years must be paid prior to dividend payments for any other types of shares. Also, some preferred stock will give its owners voting rights in the event of one or more missed dividend payments.

Because this stock is so expensive, many companies issue it with a call feature stating the price at which the company will buy back the shares. The call price must be high enough to give investors a reasonable return over their purchase price, or else no one will initially invest in the share.

18.3   CONVERTIBLE PREFERRED STOCK

Preferred stock may also be converted by the shareholder into common stock at a preset ratio, if the preferred stock agreement specifies that this option is available. If this conversion occurs, the accountant must reduce the par value and Additional paid-in capital accounts for the preferred stock by the amount at which the preferred stock was purchased and then shift these funds into the same common stock funds. An example of a preferred stock conversion to common stock is as follows:

If a shareholder of preferred stock were to convert one share of the Grinch Toy Removal Company's preferred stock into five shares of its common stock, the journal entry would be as follows, on the assumption that the preferred stock was bought for $145, and that the par value of the preferred stock is $50 and the par value of the common stock is $1:

	Debit	Credit
Preferred stock—par value	$50	
Preferred stock—additional paid-in capital	95	
Common stock—par value		$ 5
Common stock—additional paid-in capital		140

In the journal entry, the Par value account for the common stock reflects the purchase of five shares, since the par value of five individual shares (i.e., $5) has been recorded, with the remaining excess funds from the preferred stock being recorded in the additional Paid-in capital account. However, if the par value of the common stock were to be greater than the entire purchase price of the preferred stock, the journal entry would change to bring in extra funds from the Retained earnings account in order to make up the difference. If this were to occur with the previous assumptions, except with a common stock par value of $40, the journal entry would be:

	Debit	Credit
Preferred stock—par value	$50	
Preferred stock—additional paid-in capital	95	
Retained earnings	55	
Common stock—par value		$200

18.4 STOCK SPLITS

A stock split involves the issuance of a multiple of the current number of shares outstanding to current shareholders. For example, a one-for-two split of shares when there are currently 125,000 shares outstanding will result in a new amount outstanding of 250,000. This is done to reduce the market price on a per-share basis. In addition, by dropping the price into a lower range, it can have the effect of making it more affordable to small investors, who may then bid up the price to a point where the split stock is cumulatively more valuable than the unsplit stock.

A stock split is typically accompanied by a proportional reduction in the par value of the stock. For example, if a share with a par value of $20 were to be split on a two-for-one basis, then the par value of the split stock would be $10 per share. This transaction requires no entry on a company's books. However, if the split occurs without a change in the par value, then funds must be shifted from the Additional paid-in capital account to the Par value account.

A reverse split may also be accomplished if a company wishes to proportionally increase the market price of its stock. For example, if a company's common stock sells for $2.35 per share and management wishes to see the price trade above the $20 price point, then it can conduct a ten-for-one reverse split, which will raise the market price to $23.50 per share, while reducing the number of outstanding shares by 90%. In this case, the par value per share would be increased proportionally, so that no funds were ever removed from the Par value account. An example of a stock split with no change in par value is as follows:

If 250,000 shares were to be split on a one-for-three basis, creating a new pool of 750,000 shares, and the existing par value per share of $2 were not changed, then the accountant would have to transfer $1,000,000 (the number of newly created shares times the par value of $2) from the Additional paid-in capital account to the Par value account to ensure that the legally mandated amount of par value per share was stored there.

18.5   STOCK SUBSCRIPTIONS

Stock subscriptions allow investors or employees to pay in a consistent amount over time and receive shares of stock in exchange. When such an arrangement occurs, a receivable is set up for the full amount expected, with an offset to a Common stock subscription account and the Additional paid-in capital account (for the par value of the subscribed shares). When the cash is collected and the stock is issued, the funds are deducted from these accounts and shifted to the standard Common stock account. An example of a stock subscription is as follows:

> If the Slo-Mo Molasses Company sets up a stock subscription system for its employees, and they choose to purchase 10,000 shares of common stock with a par value of $1 for a total of $50,000, the entry would be as follows:

	Debit	Credit
Stock subscriptions receivable	$50,000	
Common stock subscribed		$40,000
Additional paid-in capital		10,000

> When the $50,000 cash payment is received, the Stock subscriptions receivable account will be offset, while funds stored in the Common stock subscribed account are shifted to the Common stock account, as noted in the following entry:

	Debit	Credit
Cash	$50,000	
Stock subscriptions receivable		$50,000
Common stock subscribed	50,000	
Common stock		50,000

18.6   RETAINED EARNINGS

Retained earnings are that portion of equity not encompassed by the various Par value or Additional paid-in capital accounts. It is increased by profits and decreased by distributions to shareholders and several types of stock transactions.

Retained earnings can be impacted if the accountant makes a prior period adjustment that results from an error in the prior financial statements; the offset to this adjustment will be the Retained earnings account, and will appear as an adjustment to the opening balance in the Retained earnings account. A financial statement error would be one that involved a mathematical error or the incorrect application of accounting rules to accounting entries. A change in accounting *estimate* is not an accounting error, and so should not be charged against retained earnings.

Retained earnings can be restricted through the terms of lending agreements. For example, a lender may require the company to restrict some portion of its retained earnings through the term of the loan, thereby giving the lender some assurance that funds will be available to pay off the loan. Such a restriction would keep the company from issuing dividends in amounts that cut into the restricted retained earnings.

18.7   STOCK WARRANTS

A stock warrant is a legal document giving the holder the right to buy a company's shares at a specific price, and usually for a specific time period, after which it becomes invalid. It is used as a form of compensation instead of cash for services performed by other entities for the company, and may also be attached to debt instruments in order to make them appear more attractive investments to buyers.

If the warrant attached to a debt instrument cannot be detached and sold separately from the debt, then it should not be separately accounted for. However, if it can be sold separately by the debt holder, then the fair market value of each item (the warrant and the debt instrument) should be determined, and then the accountant should apportion the price at which the combined items were sold between the two, based on their fair market values. An example of value allocation to warrants is as follows:

For example, if the fair market value of a warrant is $63.50, the fair market value of a bond to which it was attached is $950, and the price at which the two items were sold was $1,005, then an entry should be made to an Additional paid-in capital account for $62.97 to account for the warrants, while the remaining $942.03 is accounted for as debt. The apportionment of the actual sale price of $1,005 to warrants is calculated as follows:

$$\frac{\text{Fair market value of warrant}}{\text{Fair market value of warrant} + \text{Fair market value of bond}} \times \text{Price of combined instruments}$$

or,

$$\frac{\$63.50}{(\$63.50 + \$950.00)} \times \$1,005 = \$62.97$$

If a warrant expires, then the funds are shifted from the Outstanding warrants account to an Additional paid-in capital account. To continue with the last example, this would require the following entry:

	Debit	Credit
Additional paid-in capital—warrants	$62.97	
Additional paid-in capital—expired warrants		$62.97

If a warrant is subsequently used to purchase a share of stock, then the value allocated to the warrant in the accounting records should be shifted to the common stock accounts. To use the preceding example, if the warrant valued at $62.97 is used to purchase a share of common stock at a price of $10.00, and the common stock has a par value of $25, then the Par value account is credited with $25 (since it is mandatory that the par value be recorded), and the remainder of the funds are recorded in the Additional paid-in capital account. The entry is as follows:

	Debit	Credit
Cash	$10.00	
Additional paid-in capital–warrants	$62.97	
Common stock—par value		25.00
Common stock—additional paid-in capital		47.97

18.8 DIVIDENDS

Dividends must be authorized for distribution by the board of directors. They are not allowed to make such a distribution if the company is insolvent or would become insolvent as a result of the transaction.

When the board of directors votes to issue dividends, this is the *declaration date*. At this time, by the board's action, the company has incurred a liability to issue a dividend. Unless the dividend is a stock dividend, the accountant must record a dividend payable at this time, and debit the Retained earnings account to indicate the eventual source of the dividend payment.

The dividend will be paid as of a *record date*. This date is of considerable importance to shareholders, since the entity holding a share on that date will be entitled to receive the dividend. If a share is sold the day before the record date, then the old shareholder forgoes the dividend and the new one receives it. As of the payment date, the company issues dividends, thereby debiting the Dividends payable account and crediting the Cash account (or the account of whatever asset is distributed as a dividend).

On rare occasions, a company will choose to issue a *property dividend* to its shareholders. Under this scenario, the assets being distributed must be recorded at their fair market value, which usually triggers the recognition of either a gain or loss in the current income statement. An example of a property dividend is as follows:

> The Burly Book Binders Company declares a property dividend for its shareholders of a rare set of books, which have a fair market value of $500 each. The 75 shareholders receive one book each, which represents a total fair market value of $37,500. The books were originally obtained by the company at a cost of $200 each, or $15,000 in total. Consequently, a gain of $22,500 ($37,500 minus $15,000) must be recognized. To do so, the accountant debits the Retained earnings account for $37,500, credits the Gain on property disposal account for $22,500, and credits its Dividends payable account for $15,000. Once the books are distributed to the shareholder, the accountant debits the Dividends payable account for $15,000 and credits the Inventory account for $15,000 in order to eliminate the dividend liability and reflect the reduction in book inventory.

A dividend may also take the form of a *stock dividend*. This allows a company to shift funds out of the Retained earnings account and into the Par value and Additional paid-in capital accounts, which reduces the amount of funding that the Internal Revenue Service would see when reviewing the company for an excessive amount of retained earnings (which can be taxed). These distributions are also not taxable to the recipient. If the amount of a stock dividend represents less than one-quarter of the total number of shares currently outstanding, then this is considered to be a distribution that will not greatly impact the price of existing shares through dilution; accordingly, the accountant records the fair market value of these shares in the Par value and Additional paid-in capital accounts, and takes the offsetting funds out of the Retained earnings account. An example of a small stock dividend is as follows:

> If the Bobber Fishing Equipment Company wished to issue a stock dividend of 10,000 shares, and their fair market value were $32 per share, with a par value of $1, then the entry would be:

	Debit	Credit
Retained earnings	$320,000	
Common stock—par value		$ 32,000
Additional paid-in capital		288,000

If more than one-quarter of the total amount of outstanding shares is to be distributed through a stock dividend, then we assume that the value of the shares will be watered down through such a large distribution. In this case, funds are shifted from retained earnings only to cover the amount of the par value for the shares to be distributed. An example of a large stock dividend is as follows:

Using the preceding example (and assuming that 10,000 shares were more than 25% of the total outstanding), the entry would change to the following:

	Debit	Credit
Retained earnings	$32,000	
Common stock—par value		$32,000

If there are not sufficient funds in the Retained earnings account to make these entries, then the number of shares issued through the stock dividend must be reduced. However, given the small size of the par values that many companies have elected to use for their stock, the amount of retained earnings required may actually be less for a very large stock dividend than for a small one, since only the par value of the stock must be covered in the event of a large distribution.

A *liquidating dividend* is used to return capital to investors; thus, it is not strictly a dividend, which is intended to be a distribution of earnings. This transaction is impacted by the laws of the state of incorporation for each organization and so cannot be readily summarized here. However, the general entry in most cases is to credit cash and debit the Additional paid-in capital account.

The decision tree shown in Exhibit 18.1 itemizes the journal entry required for each of the various types of dividends as of the declaration date.

18.9   TREASURY STOCK

If the board of directors elects to have the company buy back shares from shareholders, the stock that is bought in-house is called *treasury stock*. A corporation's purchase of its own stock is normally accounted for under the *cost method*. Under this approach, the cost at which shares are bought back is listed in a Treasury stock account. When the shares are subsequently sold again, any sale amounts exceeding the repurchase cost are credited to the Additional paid-in capital account, while any shortfalls are first charged to any remaining additional paid-in capital remaining from previous treasury stock transactions, and then to retained earnings if there is no additional paid-in capital of this type remaining. For example, if a company chooses to buy back 500 shares at $60 per share, the transaction would be:

	Debit	Credit
Treasury stock	$30,000	
Cash		$30,000

If management later decides to permanently retire treasury stock that was originally recorded under the cost method, then it backs out the original par value and additional paid-in capital associated with the initial stock sale, and charges any remaining difference to the Retained earnings account. To continue with the previous example, if the 500 shares

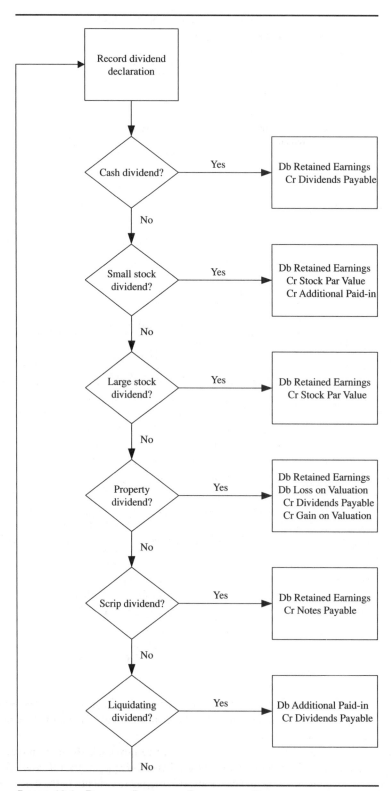

EXHIBIT 18.1   DIVIDEND ENTRIES ON DECLARATION DATE

had a par value of $1 each, had originally been sold for $25,000 and all were to be retired, the entry would be as follows:

	Debit	Credit
Common stock—par value	$ 500	
Additional paid-in capital	24,500	
Retained earnings	5,000	
Treasury stock		$30,000

If instead the company subsequently chooses to sell the shares back to investors at a price of $80 per share, the transaction is:

	Debit	Credit
Cash	$40,000	
Treasury stock		$30,000
Additional paid-in capital		10,000

If treasury stock is subsequently sold for more than it was originally purchased, the excess amount may also be recorded in an Additional paid-in capital account that is specifically used for treasury stock transactions; the reason for this segregation is that any subsequent sales of treasury stock for less than the original buyback price require the accountant to make up the difference from any gains recorded in this account; if the account is emptied and there is still a difference, then the shortage is made up from the Additional paid-in capital account for the same class of stock, and then from retained earnings.

In the less common case where there is no intention of ever reselling treasury stock, it is accounted for at the point of purchase from shareholders under the *constructive retirement method*. Under this approach, the stock is assumed to be retired, and so the original common stock and Additional paid-in capital accounts will be reversed, with any loss on the purchase being charged to the Retained earnings account, and any gain being credited to the Additional paid-in capital account. For example, if a company were to buy back 500 shares at $60 per share and the original issuance price was $52 (par value of $1), then the transaction would be:

	Debit	Credit
Common stock—par value	$ 500	
Additional paid-in capital	25,500	
Retained earnings	4,000	
Cash		$30,000

Note that under the constructive retirement approach, no treasury account is used, since the assumption is that the shares are immediately retired from use, rather than being parked in a Treasury stock holding account.

A special case arises when a company is forced to buy back shares at above-market prices under the threat of a corporate takeover. When this happens, the difference between the repurchase price and the market price must be charged to expense in the current period.

18.10   STOCK APPRECIATION RIGHTS

Sometimes the management team chooses not to issue stock options to employees, perhaps because employees do not have the funds to purchase shares or because no stock is available for an option plan. If so, an alternative is the stock appreciation right (SAR). Under this approach, the company essentially grants an employee a fake stock option and issues compensation to the employee at a future date if the price of company stock has risen from the date of grant to the date at which the compensation is calculated. The amount of compensation paid is the difference between the two stock prices.

To account for a SAR, the accountant must determine the amount of any change in company stock during the reporting period and charge the amount to an accrued compensation expense account. If there is a decline in the stock price, then the Accrued expense account can be reduced. If an employee cancels the SAR agreement (perhaps by leaving the company), then the entire amount of accrued compensation expense related to that individual should be reversed in the current period.

If the company pays the recipients of SAR compensation in stock, then it usually grants shares on the payment date based on the number of shares at their fair market value that will eliminate the amount of the accrued compensation expense. The journal entry required is a debit to the Accrued compensation liability account, and a credit to the Stock rights outstanding account.

If a service period is required before a SAR can be exercised, the amount of the compensation expense should be recognized ratably over the service period. An example of an SAR transaction is as follows:

> The Big Fat Pen Company decides to grant 2,500 SARs to its chief pen designer. The stock price at the grant date is $10. After one year, the stock price has increased to $12. After the second year, the stock price has dropped to $11. After the third year, the price increases to $15, at which point the chief pen designer chooses to cash in his SARs and receive payment. The related transactions would be:

End of Year 1:	Debit	Credit
Compensation expense ($2 net gain × 2,500 shares)	$ 5,000	
SAR liability		$ 5,000
End of Year 2:		
SAR liability	$ 2,500	
Compensation expense ($1 net loss × 2,500 shares)		$ 2,500
End of Year 3:		
Compensation expense ($4 net gain × 2,500 shares)	$10,000	
SAR liability		$10,000
SAR liability (payment of employee)	$12,500	
Cash		$12,500

18.11   EMPLOYEE STOCK OWNERSHIP PLANS

An Employee Stock Ownership Plan (ESOP) is one where employees receive additional compensation in the form of stock that is purchased by the ESOP from the corporation. Since the company usually has a legal obligation to provide shares or contributions to the ESOP (which are then used to buy its stock), the ESOP should be considered an extension of the company for accounting purposes. This means that if the ESOP obligates itself to a bank loan in order to buy shares from the company, the company should record this liability on its books even if the company is not a guarantor of the loan. The entry would be a debit to cash and a credit to loans payable. However, a loan from the company to the ESOP does not require an accounting entry, since the company is essentially making a loan to itself.

In addition, if the company has obligated itself to a series of future contributions of stock or cash to the ESOP, it should recognize this obligation by recording a journal entry that debits the full amount of the obligation to an Unearned ESOP shares account (this is reported as a contra-equity account) and crediting the Common stock account.

When the company makes a contribution to the plan, the funds are usually shifted to the lender who issued a loan to pay for the initial purchase of stock. Accordingly, the note payable and related interest expense accounts are both debited, while a second entry also debits a compensation expense account and credits the Additional paid-in capital and unearned ESOP shares accounts to reflect the coincident allocation of shares to ESOP participants. Of particular interest is the treatment of dividends issued by the sponsoring company. When declared, a compensation expense must be recognized for all shares in the ESOP that have *not* been allocated to ESOP participants, rather than the usual charge to retained earnings. This tends to be a disincentive for the board of directors to declare a dividend, since the declaration immediately triggers an expense recognition. Examples of ESOP transactions are as follows:

The Arabian Knights Security Company establishes an ESOP for its employees. The ESOP arranges for a bank loan of $100,000 and uses it to purchase 10,000 shares of no par value stock. The entry is:

	Debit	Credit
Cash	$100,000	
Notes payable		$100,000
Unearned ESOP shares	$100,000	
Common stock		$100,000

Arabian then contributes $10,000 to the plan, which is used to pay down both the principal and interest components of the debt. The entry is:

	Debit	Credit
Interest expense	$2,000	
Notes payable	8,000	
Cash		$10,000

The ESOP plan requires an allocation of shares to plan participants at the end of each calendar year. For the current year, 2,000 shares are allocated. On the date of allocation, the fair market value of the shares is $13. Since the fair value is $3 higher than the original share purchase price of $10, the difference is credited to the Additional paid-in capital account. The entry is:

	Debit	Credit
Compensation expense	$26,000	
Additional paid-in capital		$ 6,000
Unearned ESOP shares		20,000

Arabian then declares a dividend of $0.50 per share. The dividend applied to the 8,000 remaining unallocated shares is charged to a Compensation expense account, while the dividend applied to the 2,000 allocated shares is charged to the Retained earnings account. The entry is:

	Debit	Credit
Retained earnings	$8,000	
Compensation expense	2,000	
Dividend payable		$10,000

18.12   SUMMARY

Many of the topics addressed in this chapter are designed to assist a company in bringing in more funds or acquiring funds at a lower cost. These include stock splits (which can increase a firm's overall capitalization by making individual shares of stock more affordable), stock subscriptions (which bring in a steady stream of new capital), and warrants (which reduce the cost of any debt instruments to which they are attached). Other topics are more oriented toward innovative ways to compensate employees, such as stock options, stock appreciation rights, and employee stock ownership plans. Though it is a rare organization that will make use of all these concepts, one should be aware of the information presented here for each item, in order to understand which ones would work best for an organization. Several of the topics covered, such as options, stock appreciation rights, and ESOPs, involve highly technical accounting and legal rules that call for the active participation of specialists to ensure that they are set up and administered properly.

CHAPTER 19

STOCK OPTIONS

19.1 INTRODUCTION

The accounting treatment of stock options has garnered a considerable amount of commentary within the accounting profession of late, so it has been split off from the preceding equity chapter for more detailed treatment. This chapter includes a technical discussion of the only approved method of accounting for options, as well as specific accounting procedures for implementing it, and commentary on associated recordkeeping issues.

19.2 OPTION ACCOUNTING

An option is an agreement between a company and another entity (frequently an employee) that allows the entity to purchase shares in the company at a specific price within a specified date range. The assumption is that the options will only be exercised if the fixed purchase price is lower than the market price so that the buyer can turn around and sell the stock on the open market for a profit. Options are accounted for under the *fair value method* promulgated in SFAS 123(R).

Under the SFAS 123(R) approach, compensation expense must be recognized for options granted, even if there is no difference between the current market price of the stock and the price at which the recipient can purchase the stock under the terms of the option. A compensation expense arises because the holder of an option does not actually pay for any stock until the date when the option is exercised, and so can earn interest by investing the money elsewhere until that time. This ability to invest elsewhere has a value and is measured by using the risk-free interest rate (usually derived from the current interest rate on U.S. government securities). The present value of these interest earnings is based on the expected term of the option (i.e., the time period extending to the point when one would reasonably expect them to be used) and is reduced by the present value of any stream of dividend payments that the stock might be expected to yield during the interval between the present time and the point when the stock is expected to be purchased, since this is income forgone by the buyer.

The prospective volatility of the stock is also factored into the equation. If a stock has a history of considerable volatility, an option holder can wait to exercise his options until the stock price spikes, which creates more value to the option holder than if the underlying shares had minimal volatility. The difference between the discounted price of the stock and the exercise price is then recognized as compensation expense. Stock price volatility is easily measured if a company's stock is publicly held. However, if a company is privately held, SFAS 123(R) mandates that a modified fair value model be used, where the volatility of an industry sector index is used as a surrogate for the company's stock.

Any fair value model used to determine the value of stock options must account for all of the following factors, each of which has an impact on valuation:

- Option exercise price
- Current price of share to be purchased with the option
- Expected option term
- Expected share price volatility
- Expected share dividends
- Expected risk-free interest rate over the option term

The most commonly used model for fair value calculations is the Black-Scholes model. It computes a call price based on the factors noted above; expected share price volatility is typically derived based on the standard deviation of recent historical stock prices. The problem with this model is that the preceding list of variables cannot be altered from period to period, so that the model's results are less likely to be accurate over time. Also, the model is inherently complex; when there are a number of different option grants to calculate, it is best to acquire Black-Scholes calculation software into which the various options and related variables can be entered, and let the software conduct the valuation calculations.

An alternative fair value model is the lattice model. This model involves the construction of a tree diagram in which different possible stock prices are estimated, along with probabilities of occurrence, for a broad range of future time periods. When combined with expected stock price volatility, dividends, and the risk-free interest rate at each node on the lattice, a better representation of option fair value can be derived than is the case with the Black-Scholes model. An example is shown in Exhibit 19.1.

In the example, the Arabian Knights Security Company issues 100,000 options to its employees when the market price is $25. The options will expire in two years. Dividends are expected to be $1 per year, the option exercise price is $30, and the risk-free rate is 5%. Arabian's employees have historically proven to be risk-averse, with 80% of options being exercised after one year if the stock price exceeds the exercise price. The remaining 20% are expected to exercise their options after the second year, with no options being forfeited as long as the exercise price is exceeded. There is an equal probability that the stock price will increase or decline by $10 during the first year, with the same pattern likely to hold for the second year, based on the price at the end of the first year.

The cost of the options using the lattice model is derived by computing the sum of the probability-weighted outcomes, discounted to their present value using the risk-free rate. In the exhibit, there are two scenarios under which the option holders will exercise their options, which are as follows:

- *Scenario one.* At the end of year one, if the stock price has increased to $35, then 80% of the option holders will exercise their options for a gain of $5 per option, less the $1 of dividend forgone, or $4 per option. When discounted using the 5% risk-free rate, the gain is $3.81 ($4.00 × 0.9524). When further reduced by the 50%

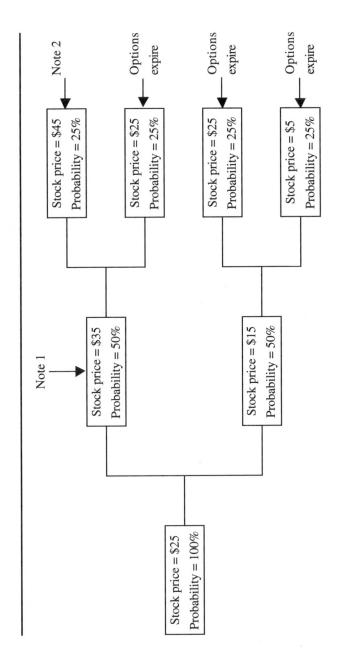

Note: Option exercise price = $30

Note 1: Options exercised for $5 gain per share, less $1.00 dividend
Note 2: Options exercised for $15 gain, per share less $2.00 dividend

Exhibit 19.1   Lattice Model for Option Valuations

253

probability that this stock price will be achieved and that only 80% of the option holders will exercise at this time, the gain is reduced to:

$1.52 = ($3.81 present value of gain) × (50% probability of stock price reaching $35)

   × (80% of option holders exercising)

- *Scenario two.* At the end of year two, if the stock price has increased to $45, then the remaining 20% of the option holders will exercise their options for a gain of $15 per option, less the $2 of dividends forgone over two years, or $13 per option. When discounted using the 5% risk-free rate, the gain is $11.79 ($13.00 × 0.9070). When further reduced by the 25% probability that this stock price will be achieved and that 20% of the option holders will exercise at this time, the gain is reduced to:

$0.59 = ($11.79 present value of gain) × (25% probability of stock price reaching $45)

   × (20% of option holders exercising)

The sum of the two scenarios resulted in an estimated fair value of $2.11 per option (scenario one valuation of $1.52 + scenario two valuation of $0.59).

The calculations required to determine the present value of options are complex and typically require the use of a computer program.

Assuming that a computer model has been used to derive the fair value of options using either the Black-Scholes or lattice models, what accounting is then used to record this information? The following examples clarify the situation.

- *Initial option issuance with vesting.* ABC Company issues 1,000 options to its employees, entitling them to purchase $1 par value shares at $30 each. The options have a fair value of $5 each, and vest over two years. Forfeitures are expected to be 10% in each of the two years. The proportion of shares expected to vest will therefore be 0.81 (90% in year one × 90% in year two). The total compensation expense will be $4,050 (1,000 options × 81% expected to vest × $5 fair value). Since vesting occurs over two years, the following entry is needed in each of the two years in order to recognize the full $4,050 of compensation expense:

	Debit	Credit
Compensation expense	2,025	
Additional paid-in capital		2,025

- *Adjustment of forfeiture rate.* To continue with the preceding example, the actual forfeiture rate during the first year is 12% rather than the original estimate of 10%. The company elects to use the 12% rate for the entire vesting period. This results in a revised vesting percentage of 0.77 (88% in year one × 88% in year two). The total compensation expense now declines to $3,850 (1,000 options × 77% expected to vest × $5 fair value). This requires a $200 reduction in the compensation expense from the previous amount of $4,050, which is reflected in the following entry:

	Debit	Credit
Additional paid-in capital	200	
Compensation expense		200

- *Exercise of options.* To continue with the preceding two examples, the vesting period is completed and 770 options are exercised. Option holders pay ABC Company $30 for each option, resulting in cash receipts of $23,100. Since the stock has a par value of $1, $770 is credited to the Common stock account. The additional paid-in capital associated with the compensation expense is reversed, and the remaining balance is credited to the Additional paid-in capital account.

	Debit	Credit
Cash	23,100	
Additional paid-in capital	3,850	
Common stock		770
Additional paid-in capital		26,180

The use of present value calculations under SFAS 123(R) means that financial estimates are being used to determine the most likely scenario that will eventually occur. One of the key estimates to consider is that not all stock options will eventually be exercised—some may lapse due to employees leaving the company, for example. One should include these estimates when calculating the total amount of accrued compensation expense so that actual results do not depart significantly from the initial estimates. However, despite the best possible estimates, the accountant will find that actual option use will inevitably vary from original estimates. When these estimates change, one should account for them in the current period as a change of accounting estimate.

If a company elects to cancel options by purchasing them from an option holder, and the price paid is higher than the value of the options as calculated under the fair value method, then the difference is fully recognized as compensation expense at once, since any vesting period has been accelerated to the payment date.

19.3 COMPENSATION EXPENSE RECOGNITION

Compensation expense should be recognized ratably over the vesting period. If there is "cliff vesting," where all options fully vest only after a set time period has passed, then the calculation is to ratably spread the expense over the entire vesting period. An example of compensation expense recognition with cliff vested options is as follows:

The Arabian Knights Security Company issues 9,000 options to its president. The compensation expense associated with the options is $50,000. The option plan calls for cliff vesting after three years, so the company's controller records a monthly charge to compensation expense of $1,388.89 ($50,000 divided by 36 months).

The situation becomes more complex if the vesting schedule calls for vesting of portions of the option grant at set intervals. When this happens, the compensation expense associated with each block of vested options is recognized ratably over the period leading up to the vesting. For example, the compensation associated with a block of options that vest in one year must be recognized as expense entirely within that year, while the compensation associated with a block of options that vest in two years must be recognized as expense over the two years leading up to the vesting date. The net impact of this approach is significantly higher compensation expense recognition in the early years of an option plan that allows incremental vesting over multiple years. An example of compensation expense recognition with incremental vesting is as follows:

Assume the same information as the last example, except that the president's options vest in equal proportions at the end of years 1, 2, and 3. The following table shows that 61% of the total compensation expense recognition is now shifted into the first year of the vesting period.

	1st Year Vesting	2nd Year Vesting	3rd Year Vesting
1st 3,000 options	100%		
2nd 3,000 options	50%	50%	
3rd 3,000 options	33%	33%	33%
Percent of total	61%	28%	11%
Expense recognition	$30,500	$14,000	$5,500

A complication to the preceding example is that SFAS 123(R) also requires that expense recognition be adjusted as the rate of anticipated option forfeiture changes over time, not as forfeitures actually occur. This means that the initial compensation expense calculation must be adjusted downward for the proportion of options expected to be forfeited. Thus, some forfeiture estimation must be made on a regular basis, perhaps based on a combination of the historical forfeiture rate, the current forfeiture rate, and the impact of future changes in stock prices on this rate. Whatever method is used, it should be thoroughly documented and consistently applied.

As a further complication to the preceding example, the fair value of the options must be remeasured at fair value in each reporting period, with adjustments made against earnings in the current period. Thus, ongoing changes in estimated forfeitures and fair value can considerably complicate the compensation expense recognition picture.

If the terms of an option grant are modified, such as by repricing, extending the option life, or changing vesting conditions, then the fair value of the options before and after the terms change must be measured, with the difference being recognized as compensation expense if the fair value has increased as a result of the change.

19.4   OPTIONS—MEASUREMENT USING SFAS 123 REQUIREMENTS

Use this procedure to calculate the initial compensation expense when options are first granted, using the guidelines of SFAS 123 (R).

1. Obtain the signed options agreement.
2. Verify that the option grant has been authorized under a board-approved option program.
3. Obtain software that calculates the value of options using the Black-Scholes pricing model.
4. Input the exercise price of the options, as listed in the signed options agreement.
5. Input the number of options granted.

6. Input the expected term of the options, based on the most recent rolling three-year history of exercised options.

7. Input the expected percentage of forfeited options, based on the most recent rolling three-year history of forfeited options.

8. Input the risk-free interest rate, using the rate on the most recent issuance of U.S. Treasury 90-day notes.

9. Input the stock volatility percentage, using the measured volatility for the most recent rolling three-year period. Ignore this step if the company is privately held.

10. Subtract the total exercise price for the options from the option valuation derived from the computer model to arrive at the compensation expense to be recorded.

11. Record the compensation expense ratably over the vesting period of the options granted.

19.5   STOCK OPTION RECORDKEEPING

If there are many option grants to a large number of employees, it is necessary to maintain a report listing the number of options granted, the exercise price for each grant, and the expiration date of each set of options. The report shown in Exhibit 19.2 shows this information for one sample employee, as well as the number of options vested and the prospective purchase price (good for equity planning) if each block of options were to be purchased.

If a company expenses its stock option grants, it should fully document the inputs to its use of the Black-Scholes option valuation model, which is used to calculate the compensation expense associated with the option grants. This information is likely to be carefully reviewed by auditors, as well as by analysts and investors, since changes in the assumptions can be used to alter reported profit levels. For example, if a company has reduced the vesting period for its stock options, this is reasonable evidence for a reduction in the option life assumption in the Black-Scholes model, so a listing of the reduced option vesting periods and the authorizing board motion should be attached to the journal entry as supporting evidence.

When a company recognizes the compensation expense associated with its option grants, it should document the method under which it ratably spreads the expense over time. There are two techniques available, yielding significantly different expense recognition amounts (as discussed earlier in the "Option Accounting" section), so this information should be attached to the journal entries used to record the expense.

Date Granted	Options Granted	Exercise Price	Options Vested	Purchase Price	Expiration Date
Clay, Alfred					
02/01/10	1,317	0.6800	878	$ 597.04	01/31/20
04/03/10	2,633	0.8200	1,755	$ 1,439.10	04/02/20
12/01/10	2,633	0.9000	878	$ 790.20	11/30/20
09/01/11	5,266	0.9800	5,266	$ 5,160.68	08/31/21
12/31/11	1,317	1.0300	1,317	$ 1,356.51	12/30/21
03/08/12	2,633	1.0800	2,633	$ 2,843.64	03/07/22
Totals	15,799		12,727	$12,187.17	

EXHIBIT 19.2   STOCK OPTION DETAIL REPORT

19.6 SUMMARY

Additional information on stock options is available elsewhere in this book. Please refer to the *Wiley GAAP Guide 2009* for references to FASB source documents concerning options, as well as to Chapter 43, Taxation, in this book, for a discussion of the tax treatment of options.

CHAPTER **20**

REVENUE

20.1 INTRODUCTION

When considering revenue, the accountant typically assumes that there is only one point at which revenue is recognized, which is when the completed product or service is delivered to the customer. However, this chapter will cover 10 revenue recognition methods, all of which can be used under specific circumstances, and few of which precisely conform to this accounting rule. Consequently, the accountant should be aware of which of the revenue recognition scenarios presented in this chapter are most applicable to his or her situation, and report revenues accordingly.

20.2 REVENUE RECOGNITION CONCEPTS

The accountant should not recognize revenue until it has been earned. There are a number of rules regarding exactly when revenue can be recognized, but the key point is that revenue occurs at the point when substantially all services and deliveries related to the sale transaction have been completed. Within this broad requirement, here are a number of more precise rules regarding revenue recognition:

- *Recognition at point of delivery.* One should recognize revenue when the product is delivered to the customer. For example, revenue is recognized in a retail store when a customer pays for a product and walks out of the store with it in hand. Alternatively, a manufacturer recognizes revenue when its products are placed onboard a conveyance owned by a common carrier for delivery to a customer; however, this point of delivery can change if the company owns the method of conveyance, since the product is still under company control until it reaches the customer's receiving dock.

- *Recognition at time of payment.* If payment by the customer is not assured, even after delivery of the product or service has been completed, then the most appropriate time to recognize revenue is upon receipt of cash. For example, if a book publisher issues new editions of books to the buyers of the last edition without any indication that they will accept the new shipments, then waiting for the receipt of cash is the most prudent approach to the recognition of revenue.

- *Other rules.* In addition to the preceding rules, there are a few others that are applicable in all instances. The first is that the seller should have no obligation to assist the buyer in reselling the product to a third party; if this were the case, it would imply that the initial sale had not yet been completed. The second is that any damage to the product subsequent to the point of sale will have no impact on the buyer's obligation to pay the seller for the full price of the product; if this were the case, one would reasonably assume that at least some portion of the sale price either includes a paid warranty that should be separated from the initial sale price and recognized at some later date, or that the sale cannot be recognized until the implied warranty period has been completed. The third rule is that the buying and selling entities cannot be the same entity, or so closely related that the transaction might be construed as an intercompany sale; if this were the case, the intercompany sale would have to be eliminated from the financial statements of both the buyer and the seller for reporting purposes, since the presumption would be that no sale had occurred.

20.3 REVENUE RECOGNITION SCENARIOS

The most common revenue recognition system is based on the *accrual method*. Under this approach, if the revenue recognition rules presented in the last section have been met, then revenue may be recognized in full. In addition, expenses related to that revenue, even if supplier invoices have not yet been received, should be recognized and matched against the revenue. An example of revenue recognition is as follows:

If the High Pressure Dive Company sells a set of face masks for $500 and recognizes the revenue at the point of shipment, then it must also recognize at the same time the $325 cost of those masks, even if it has not yet received a billing from the supplier that sold it the masks. In the absence of the billing, the cost can be accrued based on a purchase order value, market value, or supplier price list.

The *installment method* is used when there is a long string of expected payments from a customer that are related to a sale, and for which the level of collectibility of individual payments cannot be reasonably estimated. This approach is particularly applicable in the case of multiyear payments by a customer. Under this approach, revenue is recognized only in the amount of each cash receipt, and for as long as cash is received. Expenses can be proportionally recognized to match the amount of each cash receipt, creating a small profit or loss at the time of each receipt.

An alternative approach, called the *cost recovery method*, uses the same revenue recognition criterion as the installment sales method, but the amount of revenue recognized is exactly offset by the cost of the product or service until all related costs have been recognized; all remaining revenues then have no offsetting cost, which effectively pushes all profit recognition out until near the end of the installment sale contract.

It is generally not allowable to record inventory at market prices at the time when production has been completed. However, this is allowed in the few cases where the item produced is a commodity, has a ready market, and can be easily sold at the market price. Examples of such items are gold, silver, and wheat. In these cases, the producer can mark up the cost of the item to the market rate at the point when production has been completed. However, this amount must then be reduced by the estimated amount of any remaining selling costs, such as those required to transport the commodity to market. In practice, most companies prefer to recognize revenue at the point of sale. Consequently, this practice tends to be limited to those companies that produce commodities, but that have difficulty in calculating an internal cost at which they can record the cost of their production (and so are forced to use the market price instead).

When property is sold on a conditional basis, where the buyer has the right to cancel the contract and receive a refund up until a prespecified date, the seller cannot recognize any revenue until the date when cancellation is no longer allowed. Until that time, all funds are recorded as a deposit liability. If only portions of the contract can be canceled by the buyer, then revenue can be recognized at once by the seller for just those portions not subject to cancellation.

20.4   BILL AND HOLD REVENUE TRANSACTIONS

When a company is striving to reach difficult revenue goals, it will sometimes resort to bill and hold transactions, under which it completes a product and bills the customer, but then stores the product rather than sending it to the customer (who may not want it yet). Though there are a limited number of situations where this treatment is legitimate (perhaps the customer has no storage space available), there have also been a number of cases where bill and hold transactions have subsequently been proven to be a fraudulent method for recognizing revenue. Consequently, the following rules must now be met before a bill and hold transaction will be considered valid:

- *Completion.* The product being stored under the agreement must be ready for shipment. This means that the seller cannot have production staff in the storage area making changes to the product subsequent to the billing date.
- *Delivery schedule.* The products cannot be stored indefinitely. Instead, there must be a schedule in place for the eventual delivery of the goods to the customer.
- *Documentation.* The buyer must have signed a document in advance clearly stating that it is buying the products being stored by the seller.
- *Origination.* The buyer must have requested that the bill and hold transaction be completed, and have a good reason for doing so.
- *Ownership.* The buyer must have taken on all risks of ownership, so the seller is now simply the provider of storage space.
- *Performance.* The terms of the sales agreement must not state that there are any unfulfilled obligations on the part of the seller at the time when revenue is recognized.
- *Segregation.* The products involved in the transaction must have been split away from all other inventory and stored separately. They must also not be made available for the filling of orders from other customers.

20.5   RECORDING REVENUES AT GROSS OR NET

Some companies that act as brokers will over-report their revenue by recognizing not just the commission they earn on brokered sales, but also the revenue earned by their clients. For example, if a brokered transaction for an airline ticket involves a $1,000 ticket and a $20 brokerage fee, the company will claim that it has earned revenue of $1,000, rather than the $20 commission. This results in the appearance of enormous revenue (albeit with very small gross margins), which can be quite misleading. Consequently, one should apply the following rules to see if the full amount of brokered sales can be recognized as revenue:

- *Principal.* The broker must act as the principal who is originating the transaction.
- *Risks.* The broker must take on the risks of ownership, such as bearing the risk of loss on product delivery, returns, and bad debts from customers.
- *Title.* The broker must obtain title to the product being sold at some point during the sale transaction.

There are several key indicators in a transaction that reveal whether it should be recorded at gross or net. It should be recorded at gross if the following indicators are present:

- The company adds value to products sold, perhaps through alteration or added services.
- The company can establish a selling price to the customer.
- The company is responsible to the customer for order fulfillment.
- The company takes title to inventory before shipping it to the customer.

The transaction should be recorded at net if the answer to any of the preceding indicators is "no." In addition, it should be recorded at net if the following indicators are present:

- The company earns a fixed fee (such as a commission payment) from a transaction.
- The company only has one source of supplier for the product it sells.
- The supplier cannot obtain payment from the company if the customer does not pay.

If a specific transaction contains indicators pointing in either direction, the decision to record at gross or net should be based on the preponderance of evidence pointing in a particular direction.

Given the large company valuations that can be achieved by recording the largest possible amount of revenue, it is no surprise that companies have a tendency to record revenue even when they are only acting as brokers, rather than the initiators of revenue transactions. The decision tree in Exhibit 20.1 is designed to show the criteria that a company must pass before it can record revenue at the gross amount; all three criteria must be satisfied; otherwise, only the commission or broker fee associated with the sale can be recorded as revenue.

An example of recording revenues at gross or net is as follows:

The Aboriginal Travel Agency (ATA), which sells trips to Australia, purchases blocks of tickets from the airlines and resells them to customers as part of its package deals. If it cannot find purchasers for the tickets, it must absorb the cost of the tickets. In this case, ATA should record as revenues the entire amount of the airline tickets, since it has taken title to the tickets, bears the risk of loss, and is originating the transaction.

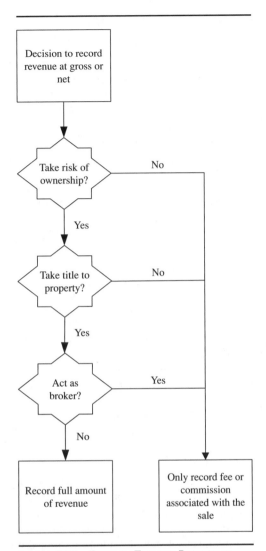

EXHIBIT 20.1 DECISION TREE FOR RECORDING REVENUE AT GROSS OR NET

ATA also reserves airlines seats on behalf of its clients, charging a $30 fee for this service. Since it is only acting as an agent for these transactions, it can only record the $30 fee as revenue, not the price of the airline tickets.

20.6 REDUCING REVENUE BY CASH PAID TO CUSTOMERS

If a company pays cash consideration to its customers, this is presumed to be a reduction in the company's revenue. The only exception is when a clearly identifiable benefit is being passed from the customer to the company, and the fair value of that benefit can be estimated. If the fair value of the benefit is less than the amount of cash paid, the difference must be deducted from revenue. This approach is designed to keep companies from inflating their reported revenue levels through delayed cash-back payments to customers as part of sales deals. Alternatively, if the company pays its customers with goods or services, the transaction should be recorded as an expense. An example of revenue reduction based on cash payments to customers is as follows:

> An international customer of the ABC Widget Company has operations in a country that has imposed foreign exchange controls. As part of an agreement to sell widgets to this customer, ABC agrees to overbill the customer by 10% and rebate this amount to a customer location in a third country. Whenever this transaction occurs, ABC should credit its Cash account and debit its Revenue account by the amount of the overbilling.

An example of expense incurrence based on noncash payments to customers is as follows:

> The XYZ Technology Company sells a variety of software packages to its customers, and offers free training classes at its in-house university to purchasers. In a recent sale, the company promised 10 days of free training, which equated to 20 days of instructor time at a payroll cost of $7,000. Accordingly, this cost was shifted from the training department's payroll expense and charged to the sale as a cost of goods sold.

20.7 LONG-TERM CONSTRUCTION CONTRACTS

In the construction industry, one option for revenue recognition is to wait until a construction project has been completed in all respects before recognizing any related revenue. This is called the *completed contract method*. It makes the most sense when the costs and revenues associated with a project cannot be reasonably tracked, or when there is some uncertainty regarding either the addition of costs to the project or the receipt of payments from the customer. However, this approach does not reveal the earning of any revenue on the financial statements of a construction company until its projects are substantially complete, which gives the reader of its financial statements very poor information about its ability to generate a continuing stream of revenues (except for projects of such short duration that they will be initiated and completed within the same accounting period). Consequently, the percentage of completion method is to be preferred when costs and revenues can be reasonably estimated.

The *percentage of completion method* is most commonly used in the construction industry, where very long-term construction projects would otherwise keep a company from revealing any revenues on its financial statements until its projects are completed, which might occur only at long intervals. Under this approach, the accounting staff creates a new asset account for each project, in which it accumulates all related expenses. At the end of each reporting period, the budgeted gross margin associated with each project is added to the total expenses accumulated in each account, and subtracted from the accumulated billings to date. If the amount of expenses and gross profit exceeds the billings figure, then the company recognizes revenue matching the difference between the two figures. If the expenses and gross profit figure are less than the amount of billings, the difference is stored in a liability account. An example of the percentage of completion method is as follows:

> The ABC Construction Company is constructing a log cabin–style office building for a company specializing in rustic furniture. Thus far, it has accumulated $810,000 in expenses on the project and billed the customer $1,000,000. The estimated gross margin on the project is 28%. The total of expenses and estimated gross profit is therefore $1,125,000, which is calculated as $810,000 divided by $(1 - 0.28)$. Since this figure exceeds the billings to date of $1,000,000,

the company can recognize additional revenue of $125,000. The resulting journal entry would be:

	Debit	Credit
Unbilled contract receivables	$125,000	
Contract revenues earned		$125,000

Under an alternative scenario, ABC Construction has billed the customer $1,200,000, while all other information remains the same. In this case, the amount of revenue earned is $1,125,000, which is $75,000 less than the amount billed. Consequently, the company must record a $75,000 liability for the incremental amount of work it must still complete before it can recognize the remaining revenue that has already been billed. The resulting journal entry would be:

	Debit	Credit
Contract revenues earned	$75,000	
Billings exceeding projects costs and margin		$75,000

An alternative approach for measuring the percentage of completion is the *cost-to-cost method*. Under this approach, we measure the percentage of completion by dividing the total amount of expenses incurred to date by the total estimated project cost. This method only works well if the total estimated project cost is regularly revised to reflect the most accurate expense information. Also, it tends to result in proportionately greater amounts of revenue recognition early in a project, since this is when most of the materials-related costs are incurred. A more accurate way to calculate the percentage of completion when there are large up-front materials costs is to only include the materials costs when the aspects of the project in which they are used are completed.

An example of the cost-to-cost method is as follows:

The ABC Construction Company is building a hotel, and has elected to purchase the materials for the air-conditioning system, costing $200,000, at the beginning of the project. The total estimated project cost is $2,000,000, and the amount billable to the customer is $2,500,000. After one month, ABC has incurred a total of $400,000 in costs, including the air-conditioning equipment. This is 20% of the total project cost, and would entitle ABC to recognize $500,000 of revenue (20% of $2,500,000). However, because the air-conditioning equipment has not yet been installed, a more accurate approach would be to exclude the cost of this equipment from the calculation, resulting in a project completion percentage of 10% and recognizable revenue of $250,000.

The trouble with these methods is that one must have good cost tracking and project planning systems in order to ensure that all related costs are being properly accumulated for each project and that cost overruns are accounted for when deriving the percentage of completion. For example, if poor management results in a doubling of the costs incurred at the halfway point of a construction project, from $5,000 up to $10,000, this means that the total estimated cost for the entire project (of $10,000) would already have been reached when half of the project had not yet been completed. In such a case, one should review the remaining costs left to be incurred and change this estimate to ensure that the resulting percentage of completion is accurate.

If the percentage of completion calculation appears suspect when based on costs incurred, one can also use a percentage of completion that is based on a Gantt chart or some other planning tool that reveals how much of the project has actually been completed. For example, if a Microsoft Project plan reveals that a construction project has reached the 60% milestone, then one can reasonably assume that 60% of the project has been completed, even if the proportion of costs incurred may result in a different calculation.

Costs that may be included in the Construction-in-progress account include direct labor, materials, and overhead related to the project. Expenses included in overhead should be consistently applied across multiple projects, as should be the method of applying overhead to jobs; this keeps one from arbitrarily shifting overhead expenses between project accounts.

If the estimate of costs left to be incurred plus actual costs already incurred exceeds the total revenue to be expected from a contract, then the full amount of the difference should be recognized in the current period as a loss, and presented on the balance sheet as a current liability. If the percentage of completion method has been used on the project, then the amount recognized will be the total estimated loss on the project plus all project profits previously recognized. If, after the loss estimate has been made, the actual loss turns out to be a smaller number, the difference can be recognized in the current period as a gain. An example of project loss recognition is as follows:

> The ABC Construction Company's cost accountant has determined that its construction of a military barracks building will probably result in a loss of $80,000, based on his most recent cost estimates. The company uses the percentage of completion method, under which it had previously recorded gross profits of $35,000 for the project. Thus, the company must record a loss of $115,000 in the current period, both to record the total estimated loss and to back out the formerly recognized profit. The entry is as follows:

	Debit	Credit
Loss on uncompleted project	$115,000	
Estimated loss on uncompleted contract		$115,000

If costs are incurred prior to the signing of a project contract, these costs must be charged to expense at once, rather than storing them in the Construction-in-progress account as an asset. It is not allowable to retroactively shift these costs from an expense account into the Construction-in-progress account.

20.8   SERVICE REVENUES

Service revenues differ from product sales in that revenue recognition is generally based on the performance of specific activities rather than on the shipment of a product. There are four ways in which service revenues can be recognized. They are presented as follows, in ascending order from the most conservative to the most liberal approaches:

1. *Collection method.* Used when there is significant uncertainty about the collection of payment from customers.

2. *Completed performance method.* Used when the primary service goal is not achieved until the end of a contract, or if there are no intermediate milestones upon which revenue calculations can be based.

3. *Specific performance method.* Used when revenue is tied to the completion of a specific act.

4. *Proportional performance method.* Used when a number of specific and clearly identifiable actions are taken as part of an overall service to a customer. Rather than waiting until all services have been performed to recognize any revenue, this approach allows one to proportionally recognize revenue as each individual action is completed. The amount of revenue recognized is based on the proportional amount of direct costs incurred for each action to the estimated total amount of direct costs required to complete the entire service. However, if the service involves many identical actions (such as delivering the newspaper for a year), then revenue can be based on the proportion of actions completed thus far under the contract. Alternatively, if the service period is fixed but the amount of service provided cannot be determined (such as annual customer support for a software package), then service revenue can be ratably recognized over the service period.

Exhibit 20.2 shows the criteria under which one should use either the collection, completed performance, specific performance, or proportional performance methods. The flowchart is designed to show that, unless various revenue-related problems exist in a service contract, the proportional performance method is the default revenue recording method.

An example of the proportional performance method using direct costs is as follows:

If a service contract for $100,000 involved the completion of a single step that required $8,000 of direct costs to complete, and the total direct cost estimate for the entire job were $52,000, then the amount of revenue that could be recognized at the completion of that one action would be $15,385 (calculated as $8,000/$52,000) × $100,000).

An example of the proportional performance method using a fixed period is as follows:

A software company sells annual support agreements along with its software packages. A typical support agreement costs $2,400 per year. The company has no obligation other than to respond to customer calls, whose timing, duration, and frequency cannot be predicted. Accordingly, it ratably recognizes $200 of revenue per month for each agreement, which is 1/12 of the total amount.

Costs related to service contracts should generally be charged to expense when incurred. The exception is for direct costs, which are stored in a Prepaid expenses account until revenue is recognized, at which point they are charged to expense. This treatment of direct costs is complicated somewhat under the proportional performance method, where costs are only charged to expense in proportion to the amount of revenue being recognized.

20.9 RECOGNITION OF LOSSES ON SERVICE CONTRACTS

If the amount of direct costs incurred on a services project plus the estimate of remaining costs to be incurred exceeds the net revenue estimate for a project, the excess cost should be charged to expense, with the offsetting credit first being used to eliminate any deferred costs and any remainder being stored in a liability account. An example of loss recognition on a services contract is as follows:

The ABC Software Development Company expects to earn $100,000 in revenues from the sale of a new computer game it is developing. Unfortunately, its incurred direct expenses of $64,000 and estimated remaining costs of $50,000 exceed projected revenues by $14,000.

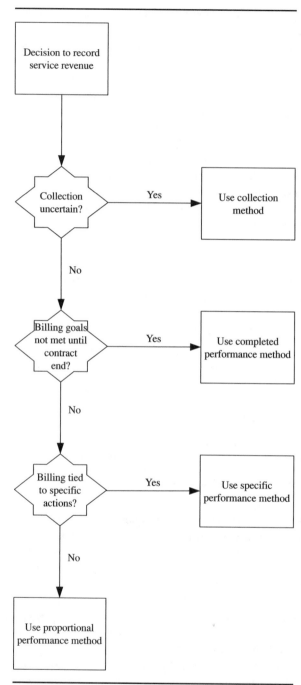

EXHIBIT 20.2   DECISION TREE FOR RECORDING SERVICE REVENUES

The company had stored an additional $3,500 of incurred costs related to the project in an asset account. The following entry records the initial loss transaction:

	Debit	Credit
Loss on service contract	$14,000	
Unrecognized contract costs		$3,500
Estimated loss on service contracts		$10,500

As actual losses are incurred in later periods, the Estimated loss on service contracts account is debited to reduce the outstanding liability.

20.10   RECORDING INITIATION FEES AS SERVICE REVENUE

A company may charge an initiation fee as part of a service contract, such as the up-front fee that many health clubs charge to new members. This fee should only be recognized immediately as revenue if there is a discernible value associated with it that can be separated from the services provided from ongoing fees that may be charged at a later date. However, if the initiation fee does not yield any specific value to the purchaser, then revenue from it can only be recognized over the term of the agreement to which the fee is attached. For example, if a health club membership agreement were to last for two years, then the revenue associated with the initiation fee should be spread over two years.

20.11   RECORDING OUT-OF-POCKET EXPENSE REIMBURSEMENTS

It is a common occurrence for service companies to bill their customers for any out-of-pocket expenses incurred, such as photocopying and delivery charges. It is not acceptable to record customer reimbursement of these expenses as a reduction in expenses. Instead, revenue must be credited for the amount of any reimbursements made. An example of treatment of out-of-pocket expense reimbursements is as follows:

> The ABC Legal Services LLP entity charges a client for $552.00 in document delivery charges. It incorporates this charge into its standard monthly customer billing, crediting revenues for $552.00 and debiting receivables for $552.00.

20.12   SALES WHEN COLLECTION IS UNCERTAIN

There are two methods used to record sales when the collection of those sales is uncertain. The first approach is the *installment method*, under which both revenue and the associated cost of goods sold are recognized at the time of the initial sale, but gross profit recognition is deferred until cash payments are received. This method requires one to track the gross margin percentage for each reporting period, so the correct percentage can be recognized when the associated cash receipts arrive at a later date. The second approach is the *cost recovery method*, under which the recognition of all gross profit is delayed until cash payments have been received that equal the entire cost of goods sold. The cost recovery method is the more conservative method, and should only be used when the collection of sales is highly uncertain.

For both recognition methods, installment accounts receivable are recognized as current assets, since the full term of the installment sale represents the normal operating cycle of the company. However, if installment sales are not a part of normal company operations, then the receivables are classified as long-term assets. In either case, installment accounts receivable should be itemized on the balance sheet by year. For example, all outstanding receivables due for payment in 2010 would be listed next to the title "Installment Receivables Due in 2010" in the balance sheet.

A typical component of installment sales is interest income, which is included in the periodic installment payments. Since installment payments are typically designed to be equal amounts, the interest income component of these billings will constitute a gradually decreasing amount as more of the installment receivable is paid off. In order to properly account for the interest income component of installment sales, interest income must be stripped out of each payment made and credited to the Interest income account, leaving the remaining balance of the payment subject to accounting under either the installment or cost recovery method. For the cost recovery method, interest income related to any long-term installment sales increase the unrecognized gross profit until the aggregate customer payments exceed the asset cost, after which the interest income is recognized. An example of the installment method is as follows:

The Gershwin Music Company sells musical instruments in bulk to school districts. Under one recent deal, it sold $10,000 of instruments to a district in Indiana at a gross profit of 30%. The district paid for the instruments in four annual installments that included 8% interest. The following table illustrates the recognition of both interest income and gross profit under the deal. Equal cash payments of $3,019.21 were made at the end of each year (column 1), from which interest income was separated and recognized (column 2), leaving an annual net receivable reduction (column 3). The gross profit on the deal (column 5) was recognized in proportion to the amount of accounts receivable reduction each year, which was 30% of column 3.

	(1)	(2)	(3)	(4)	(5)
Date	Cash Payment	Interest @ 8%	Receivable Reduction	Receivable Balance	Profit Realized
1/1/2009				$10,000.00	
12/31/2009	$3,019.21	$800.00	$2,219.21	$7,780.79	$665.76
12/31/2009	$3,019.21	$622.46	$2,396.75	$5,384.04	$719.02
12/31/2010	$3,019.21	$430.72	$2,588.49	$2,795.56	$776.55
12/31/2011	$3,019.20	$223.64	$2,795.56	$0.00	$838.67
		$2,076.83			$3,000.00

In short, Gershwin recognized 30% of the deferred gross profit contained within each cash payment, net of interest income. As an example of the journal entry made with each cash receipt, the company made the following entry to record the cash payment received on 12/31/2009:

	Debit	Credit
Cash	$3,019.21	
Interest income		$800.00
Accounts receivable		$2,219.21
Deferred gross profit	$665.76	
Recognized gross profit		$665.76

An example of the cost recovery method is as follows:

We use the same assumptions for the Gershwin Music Company under the cost recovery method. Cash payments are the same, as are the interest charges and beginning balance. However, no gross profit or interest income is realized until all $7,000 of product costs have been recovered through cash payments net of interest income. Instead, interest income is shifted to a deferred account. To reflect these changes, column 5 shows a declining balance of unrecovered costs that are eliminated when the third periodic payment arrives. This allows Gershwin's controller to recognize a small amount of deferred interest income in the third year, representing the net amount of cash payment left over after all costs have been recovered. In the final year, all remaining deferred interest income can be recognized, leaving the deferred gross margin as the last item to be recognized.

	(1)	(2)	(3)	(4)	(5)	(6)	(7)
Date	Cash Payment	Interest @ 8%	Receivable Reduction	Receivable Balance	Unrecovered Cost	Profit Realized	Interest Realized
1/1/2009				$10,000.00	$7,000.00		
12/31/2009	$3,019.21	$800.00	$2,219.21	$7,780.79	$4,780.79		
12/31/2010	$3,019.21	$622.46	$2,396.75	$5,384.04	$2,384.04		
12/31/2011	$3,019.21	$430.72	$2,588.49	$2,795.56	$—		$204.43
12/31/2012	$3,019.20	$223.64	$2,795.56	$0.00	$—	$3,000.00	$1,872.40
		$2,076.83				$3,000.00	$2,076.83

20.13   REPOSSESSION OF GOODS UNDER INSTALLMENT SALES

It is acceptable to only recognize bad debts under installment sales, since the seller can usually repossess the underlying goods. However, when the goods are repossessed, their value must be adjusted to their fair market value, which in most cases calls for the recognition of a loss. An example of goods repossession is as follows:

The Hudson's Bay Trailer Company has repossessed a construction trailer, for which $40,000 of accounts receivable is still outstanding, as well as $10,000 of deferred gross profit. The trailer has a fair market value of $28,000, so the company records the following entry to eliminate the receivable and deferred gross profit, while recognizing a loss of $2,000 on the write-down of the construction trailer:

	Debit	Credit
Deferred gross margin	$10,000	
Finished goods inventory	$28,000	
Loss on inventory write-down	$2,000	
Accounts receivable		$40,000

20.14   REVENUE RECOGNITION WHEN RIGHT OF RETURN EXISTS

If a sale transaction allows the buyer to return goods to the seller within a stated time period, then the transaction should only be recognized when one can reasonably estimate the amount of returns. If so, a sales return allowance should be established at the time of the sale and coincident with the recognition of the sale. In practice, many companies do not record a returns allowance because the amount of sales returns is so small.

If the amount of sales returns cannot be reasonably estimated, then revenue recognition must be delayed until the expiration date of the return privilege has passed.

20.15   REVENUE RECOGNITION FOR ACCRETION AND APPRECIATION

Some company assets will grow in quantity over time, such as the timber stands owned by a lumber company. A case could be made that this accretion is a form of revenue, against which some company costs can be charged that are related to the accretion. However, this accretion in value is *not* one that can be recognized in a company's financial reports. The reason is that no sale transaction has occurred that shifts ownership in the asset to a buyer.

Some company assets, such as property or investments, will appreciate in value over time. Once again, a case could be made that the financial statements should reflect this increase in value. However, as was the case with accretion, accounting rules do not allow one to record revenue from appreciation in advance of a sale transaction that shifts the asset to a buyer.

For both accretion and appreciation, it is not allowable to record an unrealized gain in the financial statements; instead, the gain can only appear at the time of a sale transaction. The current accounting treatment tends to understate a company's assets, since it restricts the recorded valuation to the original purchase price; however, the use of estimates to reflect increases in asset value could be so easily skewed by corporate officers striving to improve reported level of profitability or company valuation that there would not necessarily be any improvement in the accuracy of reported information if the accretion or appreciation methods were to be used.

20.16   SUMMARY

Despite the large number of revenue recognition scenarios presented in this chapter, the accountant will probably only use the accrual method in most situations. The other revenue recognition methods noted here are designed to fit into niche situations where the circumstances of an industry require other solutions to be found. There are also very specific revenue recognition rules that apply to some industries, such as the broadcasting, software development, motion picture, and oil and gas industries; for more detailed information about revenue recognition in these cases, please refer to *Wiley Revenue Recognition* (Bragg, 2007), published by John Wiley & Sons.

CHAPTER **21**

RESEARCH AND DEVELOPMENT

21.1 INTRODUCTION

Research and development (R&D) costs are a growing portion of the expenses recognized by companies. Given this, accountants are increasingly concerned with the impact of these costs on the financial statements. In this chapter, we will review the definition of R&D and how it is reported if conducted in-house or if purchased, and do this from the perspective of a contract R&D organization. We conclude with a discussion of R&D costs as they relate to software development.

21.2 DEFINITION OF RESEARCH AND DEVELOPMENT

The definition of R&D is broken into two parts. *Research* is the planned search for the discovery of new knowledge. Obviously, the intent of research is that it will result in either an improvement in an existing product or process, or the creation of a new one. However, there is no assurance that this will happen, so the primary definition of research is the *search* for new knowledge.

Development is the enhancement of existing products or processes, or the creation of entirely new ones. This process does not have to be the direct outgrowth of in-house research efforts, for the knowledge gained from new research can be acquired from any source. Paragraph 8 of SFAS No. 2 states that development "includes the conceptual formulation, design, and testing of product alternatives, construction of prototypes, and operation of pilot plants. It does not include routine or periodic alterations to existing products, production lines, manufacturing processes, and other ongoing operations even though these operations may represent improvements, and it does not include market research or market testing activities." Thus, development is essentially the application of knowledge for specific business purposes.

Both research and development activities can be conducted by an in-house department, or they can be bought from another company, perhaps as part of an ongoing research contract or through the outright purchase of another business. It is also possible for a company to be formed for the sole purpose of conducting research and development activities, followed by the transference of any new knowledge, products, or processes to another entity that has sponsored the work.

21.3 ACCOUNTING FOR IN-HOUSE R&D COSTS

Any R&D costs incurred by a company must be charged to expense in the current period, unless they have alternative future uses (such as fixed assets). R&D costs cannot be included in an overhead cost pool, since these costs might then be deferred into a future period. The total amount of R&D expense must be reported in the financial statements. The following list includes the R&D costs that must be expensed:

- *Contract services.* R&D work performed by an outside entity on behalf of the company, and for which the company pays, must be charged to expense as an R&D cost.
- *Indirect costs.* Any costs that can be reasonably allocated to R&D activities through a consistently applied cost allocation system shall be charged to R&D expense.
- *Intangibles purchased from others.* See the next section.
- *Materials, equipment, and facilities.* Any of these costs that are acquired for R&D work and that have no alternative future value must be expensed. If they do have an alternative future value, then they must be capitalized and depreciated over time as a cost of R&D.
- *Personnel.* Any personnel costs, such as salaries, wages, benefits, and payroll taxes that are associated with personnel engaged in R&D work, shall be charged as an R&D expense.

This rule covers all research, plus testing and modification of product alternatives, proto-types and models, the design of new tools and dies, pilot plants not commercially feasible, or any engineering work conducted prior to being ready for manufacture.

There are also a number of costs that are not to be included in the R&D expense category. They are nearly always costs that must be expensed as incurred, rather than capitalized, and so are not different from R&D costs in terms of their treatment. However, companies would artificially increase their reported R&D expense (which is a separate line item in the financial statements) if they were to include these items in the R&D category, which might give investors an artificial impression of the size of funding being directed toward R&D activities. The costs not to be included in R&D are:

- *Engineering costs.* These include efforts to make minor incremental enhancements to existing products or to make minor customized adjustments to products for existing customers, as well as the design of tools and dies on a routine basis.
- *Facility costs.* These include the start-up cost of new facilities that are not intended for use as R&D facilities.
- *Legal costs.* These include the cost of patent applications, the cost of litigation to support them, and the costs associated with their licensing to or from other parties.
- *Production costs.* These include industrial engineering, quality assurance, and troubleshooting work engaged in during the commercial production of a product.

21.4 ACCOUNTING FOR ACQUIRED R&D COSTS

If a company purchases its R&D work from some other entity, then the cost of this work to the company must be expensed in the period incurred. However, if a company acquires intangibles that may be used in R&D activities (such as through a corporate acquisition), and which have alternative future uses, the intangibles must be amortized over time. For example, if a company were to purchase another entity, then under the purchase method of accounting, it could assign intangible costs to identifiable assets that are related to R&D, such as patents, formulas, and new product designs, as well as to more concrete items, such as equipment used in R&D experiments.

This latter case has given rise to inconsistent accounting treatment, because acquiring companies sometimes make the assumption that some acquired intangibles are directly associated with R&D costs (rather than being capitalized under the assumption that they have alternative future uses) and are using this assumption as the basis for writing them off at once, rather than amortizing their cost over a number of years. Under this scenario, if there is any doubt regarding the proper treatment of intangibles associated with R&D, it is best to amortize the cost.

21.5 ACCOUNTING FOR R&D COSTS CONTRACTED TO ANOTHER PARTY

If a company specializes in the provision of R&D to other businesses, the accounting for these costs will essentially be determined by the contents of each R&D contract signed. For example, if a contract states that R&D work will be billed to a client on a time and materials basis, then the expense can easily be recorded in conjunction with any associated billings. A more common case is that the R&D organization receives a large amount of initial funding; if there is no obligation to return the funds, they may be recorded at once as revenue. However, if there is a requirement that the funds be used for specific R&D work or else be returned, then the funds must be recorded as a liability that will gradually be drawn down as offsetting R&D costs are incurred.

21.6 R&D COSTS IN THE SOFTWARE INDUSTRY

The basic rule regarding the recognition of R&D expenses for software development (for software to be sold to customers, as opposed to software developed strictly for in-house use) is that development is considered to be R&D (and therefore to be expensed at once) until the point is reached when technological feasibility has been demonstrated. All costs incurred from the point when that demonstration occurs to the time when commercial products are delivered can be capitalized and amortized over time (which is the period over which some economic benefit is expected from the sale of the software).

This is a somewhat more liberal treatment than under the traditional R&D rules, since there is a short time period during which some costs can be deferred through capitalization. However, the point at which technological feasibility is most easily demonstrated is the release of a beta test version of the software, which may be so close to the commercial release date (usually a matter of months) that the amount of costs that can be capitalized during this short period is relatively small. A more aggressive approach is available if a company uses detailed program designs, which allows it to prove technological feasibility at an earlier point in the software development process. Under this approach, feasibility occurs when the product design is complete, when the design has been traced back to initial product specifications, *and* when it can be proved that all high-risk elements in the product design have been investigated and resolved through coding and testing.

If a company is developing software strictly for internal use, a different set of rules applies. In this case, all costs associated with the development work can be capitalized. However, it must not be the intention of management at the time of development to externally market the software (in which case the preceding rule applies). If management subsequently decides to market software that was originally intended solely for internal use, then any profits received will first be offset against the carrying value of the software; once the carrying value is reduced to zero, subsequent profits may be recognized as such.

The only costs that cannot be capitalized under this approach are those associated with the conceptual formulation of the software, the review and testing of alternative systems, and any overhead and training costs associated with the project. In particular, if the total price of a purchased software package includes the cost of training and maintenance, then the training cost must be split out and expensed as training is incurred, while the maintenance fee must be spread equally over the period to which it applies.

Costs that can be capitalized for internal software projects are all those incurred during the coding and system implementation phases of the project; these costs typically include the salaries of all personnel involved in the project, as well as their related payroll tax and benefit costs, plus the cost of outside services required to assist with the project (such as consultants). This capitalization rule also applies to the internal cost required to modify purchased software that is intended for internal use. Amortization of these costs must begin at the point when essentially all testing has been completed, even if there is no one currently using the system. If an internal development project appears to be in danger of not being completed (as defined by lack of completion funding, significant programming difficulties, major cost overruns, or lack of profits within the sponsoring business unit), then all related costs that have thus far been capitalized must be expensed in the current period.

21.7 SUMMARY

In brief, R&D costs must be expensed in the current period unless there is some future alternative use to which the items generating the costs can be put, which then relegates the R&D costs to a lifetime of amortization. Of some concern to the accountant is which costs are to be included in the R&D category for financial statement reporting purposes, since this line item can be greatly increased by incorrectly including a number of ongoing expenses that are more properly related to commercial production activities (and that would artificially reduce the cost of goods sold at the same time). There are some limited cases in which R&D costs for software firms can be capitalized, thereby increasing their short-term reported level of income, but the restrictions placed on this option do not allow for a large amount of capitalization, except for software that is developed strictly for internal use.

LEASES

22.1 INTRODUCTION

The accounting for leases is subject to a considerable number of rules, which vary for the lessee and lessor, and which fall into the categories of operating leases, capital leases, sales-type leases, direct financing leases, and leveraged leases. There are also special rules for lease terminations and extensions, subleases, and sale-leaseback transactions. Given the number of variations, this chapter presents clear guidelines for determining which type of lease accounting to use and presents examples of each major lease transaction.

22.2 ACCOUNTING FOR LEASES—LESSEE

A typical lease is recorded by the lessee as an *operating lease*. The lessee must record a lease as a *capital lease* if the lease agreement contains any one of the following four clauses:

- A bargain purchase option, whereby the lessee can purchase the asset from the lessor at the end of the lease term at a price substantially lower than its expected residual value at that time.
- Transfer of asset ownership to the lessee at the end of the lease term.
- A lease term so long that it equals or exceeds 75% of the asset's anticipated economic life.
- The present value of the minimum lease payments is at least 90% of the asset's fair value.

The lessee accounts for an operating lease by charging lease payments directly to expense. There is no balance sheet recognition of the leased asset at all. If the schedule of lease payments varies in terms of either timing or amount, the lessee should consistently charge the same rental amount to expense in each period, which may result in some variation between the lease payment made and the recorded expense. However, if there is a demonstrable change in the asset being leased that justifies a change in the lease payment being made, there is no need to use straight-line recognition of the expense. An example of accounting for changing lease payments is as follows:

> The Alabama Botox Clinics (ABC) Company has leased a group of operating room equipment under a five-year operating lease arrangement. The monthly lease cost is $1,000 for the first 30 months and $1,500 for the second 30 months. There is no change in the equipment being leased at any time during the lease period. The correct accounting is to charge the average monthly lease rate of $1,250 to expense during every month of the lease. For the first 30 months, the monthly entry will be:

	Debit	Credit
Equipment rent expense	$1,250	
Accounts payable		$1,000
Accrued lease liability		250

> During the final 30 months, the monthly entry will be:

	Debit	Credit
Equipment rent expense	$1,250	
Accrued lease liability	250	
Accounts payable		$1,500

The lessee accounts for a *capital lease* by recording as an asset the lower of its fair value or the present value of its minimum (i.e., excluding taxes and executory costs) lease payments (less the present value of any guaranteed residual asset value). When calculating the present value of minimum lease payments, use the lesser of the lessee's incremental borrowing rate or the implicit rate used by the lessor. The time period used for the present value calculation should include not only the initial lease term, but also additional periods where nonrenewal will result in a penalty to the lessee, or where lease renewal is at the option of the lessor.

If the lessee treats a leased asset as a capital lease because the lease agreement results in an actual or likely transfer of ownership to the lessee by the end of the lease term, then it is depreciated over the full expected life of the asset. However, if a leased asset is being treated as a capital lease when the lessor is still likely to retain ownership of the asset after the end of the lease term, then it is only depreciated for the period of the lease. An example of a capital lease transaction is as follows:

> The Arkansas Barrel Company (ABC) leases a woodworking machine under a five-year lease that has a one-year extension clause at the option of the lessor, as well as a guaranteed residual value of $15,000. ABC's incremental borrowing rate is 7%. The machine is estimated to have a life of seven years, a current fair value of $90,000, and a residual value (not the guaranteed residual value) of $5,000. Annual lease payments are $16,000.

> The first step in accounting for this lease is to determine if it is a capital or operating lease. If it is a capital lease, one must calculate its present value, then use the effective interest method to determine the allocation of payments between interest expense and reduction of the lease obligation, and then determine the depreciation schedule for the asset. Later, there will be a closeout journal entry to record the lease termination. The steps are as follows:

> **1.** *Determine the lease type.* The woodworking machine is considered to have a life of seven years; since the lease period (including the extra year at the option of the lessor)

covers more than 75% of the machine's useful life, the lease is designated a capital lease.

2. *Calculate asset present value.* The machine's present value is a combination of the present value of the $15,000 residual payment due in six years and the present value of annual payments of $16,000 per year for six years. Using the company incremental borrowing rate of 7%, the present value multiplier for $1 due in six years is 0.6663; when multiplied by the guaranteed residual value of $15,000, this results in a present value of $9,995. Using the same interest rate, the present value multiplier for an ordinary annuity of $1 for six years is 4.7665; when multiplied by the annual lease payments of $16,000, this results in a present value of $76,264. After combining the two present values, we arrive at a total lease present value of $86,259. The initial journal entry to record the lease is as follows:

	Debit	Credit
Leased equipment	$86,259	
Lease liability		$86,259

Allocate payments between interest expense and reduction of lease liability. ABC's controller then uses the effective interest method to allocate the annual lease payments between the lease's interest expense and reductions in the lease obligation. The interest calculation is based on the beginning balance of the lease obligation. The calculation for each year of the lease is as follows:

Year	Annual Payment	Interest Expense	Reduction in Lease Obligation	Remaining Lease Obligation
0				$86,259
1	$16,000	$6,038	$ 9,962	76,297
2	16,000	5,341	10,659	65,638
3	16,000	4,595	11,405	54,233
4	16,000	3,796	12,204	42,029
5	16,000	2,942	13,058	28,991
6	16,000	2,009	13,991	15,000

1. *Create depreciation schedule.* Though the asset has an estimated life of seven years, the lease term is for only six years, after which the lessor expects the asset to be returned. Accordingly, the asset will be depreciated only over the lease term of six years. Also, the amount of depreciation will only cover the asset's present value of $86,259 minus the residual value of $5,000. Therefore, the annual depreciation will be $13,543 ($86,259 present value—$5,000 residual value/6 years lease term).

2. *Record lease termination.* Once the lease is completed, a journal entry must record the removal of the asset and its related depreciation from the fixed assets register, as well as the payment to the lessor of the difference between the $15,000 guaranteed residual value and the actual $5,000 residual value, or $10,000. That entry is as follows:

	Debit	Credit
Lease liability	$15,000	
Accumulated depreciation	81,259	
Cash		$10,000
Leased equipment		86,259

22.3 ACCOUNTING FOR LEASES—LESSOR

From the perspective of the lessor, if none of the four criteria previously noted for a lessee lease are met, a lease must be treated as an operating lease. If at least one of the four criteria is met and (1) lease payments are reasonably collectible, and (2) there are minimal uncertainties about future lessor unreimbursable costs, then the lessor must treat a lease as one of the following three lease types:

- *Sales-type lease.* When the lessor will earn both a profit and interest income on a lease transaction.
- *Direct financing lease.* When the lessor will earn only interest income on a lease transaction.
- *Leveraged lease.* The same as a direct financing lease, but the financing is provided by a third-party creditor.

22.4 ACCOUNTING FOR OPERATING LEASES—LESSOR

If the lessor treats a lease as an operating lease, it records any payments received from the lessee as rent revenue. As was the case for the lessee, if there is an unjustified change in the lease rate over the lease term, the average revenue amount should be recognized on a straight-line basis in each reporting period. Any assets being leased are recorded in a separate Investment in Leased Property account in the fixed assets portion of the balance sheet, and are depreciated in accordance with standard company policy for similar assets. If the lessor extends incentives (such as a month of no lease payments) or incurs costs associated with the lease (such as legal fees), they should be recognized over the lease term.

22.5 ACCOUNTING FOR SALES-TYPE LEASES—LESSOR

If the lessor treats a lease as a *sales-type lease*, the initial transaction bears some similarity to a standard sale transaction, except that there is an unearned interest component to the entry. A description of the required entry is contained in the following table, which shows all debits and credits.

Debit	Credit	Explanation
Lease receivable		The sum of all minimum lease payments, minus executory costs, plus the actual residual value
Cost of goods sold		The asset cost, plus initial direct costs, minus the present value* of the actual residual value.
	Revenue	The present value* of all minimum lease payments
	Leased asset	The book value of the asset
	Accounts payable	Any initial direct costs associated with the lease
	Unearned interest	The lease receivable, minus the present value* of both the minimum lease payments and actual residual value.

*The present value multiplier is based on the lease term and implicit interest rate.

Once payments are received, an entry is needed to record the receipt of cash and corresponding reduction in the lease receivable, as well as a second entry to recognize a portion of the unearned interest as interest revenue, based on the effective interest method.

At least annually during the lease term, the lessor should record any permanent reductions in the estimated residual value of the leased asset. It cannot record any increases in the estimated residual value.

When the asset is returned to the lessor at the end of the lease term, a closing entry eliminates the lease receivable associated with the actual residual value, with an offsetting debit to the Fixed asset account. An example of a sales-type lease transaction is as follows:

The Albany Boat Company (ABC) has issued a seven-year lease to the Adventure Yachting Company (AYC) on a boat for its yacht rental business. The boat cost ABC $450,000 to build and should have a residual value of $75,000 at the end of the lease. Annual lease payments are $77,000. ABC's implicit interest rate is 8%. The present value multiplier for an ordinary annuity of $1 for seven years at 8% interest is 5.2064. The present value multiplier for $1 due in seven years at 8% interest is 0.5835. We construct the initial journal entry with the following calculations:

- ○ *Lease receivable.* This is the sum of all minimum lease payments, which is $539,000 ($77,000/year × 7 years), plus the actual residual value of $75,000, for a total lease receivable of $614,000.
- ○ *Cost of goods sold.* This is the asset cost of $450,000, minus the present value of the residual value, which is $43,763 ($75,000 residual value × present value multiplier of 0.5835).
- ○ *Revenue.* This is the present value of all minimum lease payments, or $400,893 ($77,000/year × present value multiplier of 5.2064).
- ○ *Inventory.* ABC's book value for the yacht is $450,000, which is used to record a reduction in its Inventory account.
- ○ *Unearned interest.* This is the lease receivable of $614,000, minus the present value of the minimum lease payments of $400,893, minus the present value of the residual value of $43,763, which yields $169,344.

Based on these calculations, the initial journal entry is as follows:

	Debit	Credit
Lease receivable	$614,000	
Cost of goods sold	406,237	
Revenue		$400,893
Boat asset		450,000
Unearned interest		169,344

The next step in the example is to determine the allocation of lease payments between interest income and reduction of the lease principle, which is accomplished through the following effective interest table:

Year	Annual Payment	Interest Revenue	Reduction in Lease Obligation	Remaining Lease Obligation
0				$444,656
1	$77,000	$35,572	$41,428	403,228
2	77,000	32,258	44,742	358,486
3	77,000	28,679	48,321	310,165
4	77,000	24,813	52,187	257,978
5	77,000	20,638	56,362	201,616
6	77,000	16,129	60,871	140,745
7	77,000	11,255	65,745	75,000

The interest expense shown in the effective interest table can then be used to record the allocation of each lease payment between interest revenue and principal reduction. For example, the entries recorded for Year 4 of the lease are as follows:

	Debit	Credit
Cash	$77,000	
Lease receivable		$77,000
Unearned interest	24,813	
Interest revenue		24,813

Once the lease expires and the boat is returned to ABC, the final entry to close out the lease transaction is as follows:

	Debit	Credit
Boat asset	$75,000	
Lease receivable		$75,000

22.6   ACCOUNTING FOR DIRECT FINANCING LEASES—LESSOR

If the lessor treats a lease as a *direct financing lease*, it will only recognize interest income from the transaction; there will be no additional profit from the implicit sale of the underlying asset to the lessee. This treatment arises when the lessor purchases an asset specifically to lease it to the lessee. The other difference between a direct financing lease and a sales-type lease is that any direct costs incurred when a lease is originated must be amortized over the life of the lease, which reduces the implicit interest rate used to allocate lease payments between interest revenue and a reduction of the lease principal.

A description of the required entry is contained in the following table, which shows all debits and credits.

Debit	Credit	Explanation
Lease receivable		The sum of all minimum lease payments, plus the actual residual value
	Leased asset	The book value of the asset
	Unearned interest	The lease receivable minus the asset book value

At least annually during the lease term, the lessor should record any permanent reductions in the estimated residual value of the leased asset. It cannot record any increases in the estimated residual value. An example of a direct financing lease transaction is as follows:

The Albany Leasing Company (ALC) purchases a boat from a third party for $700,000 and intends to lease it to the Adventure Yachting Company for six years at an annual lease rate of $140,093. The boat should have a residual value of $120,000 at the end of the lease term. Also, there is $18,000 of initial direct costs associated with the lease. ALC's implicit interest rate is 9%. The present value multiplier for an ordinary annuity of $1 for six years at 9% interest is 4.4859. The present value multiplier for $1 due in six years at 9% interest is 0.5963. We construct the initial journal entry with the following calculations:

- *Lease receivable.* This is the sum of all minimum lease payments, which is $840,558 ($140,093/year × 6 years), plus the residual value of $120,000, for a total lease receivable of $960,558.
- *Leased asset.* This is the asset cost of $700,000.
- *Unearned interest.* This is the lease receivable of $942,558, minus the asset book value of $700,000, which yields $260,558.

Based on these calculations, the initial journal entry is as follows:

	Debit	Credit
Lease receivable	$960,558	
Initial direct costs	18,000	
Leased asset		$700,000
Unearned interest		260,558
Cash		18,000

Next, ALC's controller must determine the implicit interest rate associated with the transaction. Though ALC intended the rate to be 9%, she must add to the lease receivable the initial direct costs of $18,000, resulting in a final gross investment of $978,558 and a net investment (net of unearned interest income of $260,558) of $718,000. The determination of the implicit interest rate with this additional information is most easily derived through an electronic spreadsheet. For example, the IRR function in Microsoft Excel will automatically create the new implicit interest rate, which is 8.2215%.

With the revised implicit interest rate completed, the next step in the example is to determine the allocation of lease payments between interest income, a reduction of initial direct costs, and a reduction of the lease principal, which is accomplished through the following effective interest table:

Year	Annual Payment	Unearned Interest Reduction	Interest Revenue	Reduction of Initial Direct Costs	Reduction in Lease Obligation	Remaining Lease Obligation	Remaining Lease Obligation
0						$718,000	$700,000
1	$140,093	$63,000	$59,031	$3,969	$81,062	636,938	622,907
2	140,093	56,062	52,366	3,696	87,727	549,211	538,876
3	140,093	48,499	45,154	3,345	94,939	454,271	447,281
4	140,093	40,255	37,348	2,907	102,745	351,526	347,444
5	140,093	31,270	28,901	2,369	111,192	240,334	238,621
6	140,093	21,476	19,759	1,717	120,334	120,000	120,000*
	Totals	260,558*		18,000*			

*Rounded

The calculations used in the table are as follows:

- *Annual payment.* The annual cash payment due to the lessor.
- *Unearned interest reduction.* The original implicit interest rate of 9% multiplied by the beginning balance in the Remaining Lease Obligation (2) column, which does not include the initial direct lease cost. The total at the bottom of the column equals the unearned interest liability that will be eliminated over the course of the lease.

○ *Interest revenue.* The revised implicit interest rate of 8.2215% multiplied by the beginning balance in the Remaining Lease Obligation (1) column, which includes the initial direct lease costs.

○ *Reduction of initial direct costs.* The amount in the Unearned Interest Reduction column minus the amount in the Interest Revenue column, which is used to reduce the balance of the initial direct costs incurred. The total at the bottom of the column equals the initial direct costs incurred at the beginning of the lease.

○ *Reduction in lease obligation.* The Annual Payment minus the Interest Revenue.

○ *Remaining lease obligation.* The beginning lease obligation (including initial direct costs) less the principal portion of the annual payment.

○ *Remaining lease obligation.* The beginning lease obligation, not including initial direct costs, less the principal portion of the annual payment.

Based on the calculations in the effective interest table, the journal entry at the end of the first year would show the receipt of cash and a reduction in the lease receivable. Another entry would reduce the unearned interest balance, while offsetting the initial direct costs and recognizing interest revenue. The first-year entries are as follows:

	Debit	Credit
Cash	$140,093	
Lease receivable		$140,093
Unearned interest	63,000	
Interest revenue		59,031
Initial direct costs		3,969

22.7   LEASE TERMINATIONS

On the date that a lessee notifies the lessor that it intends to terminate a lease, the lessee must recognize a liability for the fair value of the termination costs, which include any continuing lease payments, less prepaid rent, plus deferred rent, minus the amount of any sublease payments. Changes in these estimates are recorded immediately in the income statement.

If the lessor has recorded a lease as a sales-type or direct financing lease, it records the underlying leased asset at the lower of its current net book value, present value, or original cost, with any resulting adjustment being recorded in current earnings. At the time of termination notice, the lessor records a receivable in the amount of any termination payments yet to be made, with an offsetting credit to a Deferred rent liability account. The lessor then recognizes any remaining rental payments on a straight-line basis over the revised period during which the payments are to be received.

22.8   LEASE EXTENSIONS

If a *lessee* extends an operating lease and the extension is also classified as an operating lease, then the lessee continues to treat the extension in the same manner it has used for the existing lease. If the lease extension requires payment amounts differing from those required under the initial agreement but the asset received does not change, then the lessee should consistently charge the same rental amount to expense in each period, which may result in some variation between the lease payment made and the recorded expense.

If a *lessee* extends an existing capital lease but the lease structure now requires the extension to be recorded as an operating lease, the lessee writes off the existing asset, as well as all associated accumulated depreciation, and recognizes either a gain or loss on the transaction. Payments made under the lease extension are handled in accordance with the rules of a standard operating lease.

If a *lessee* extends an existing capital lease, and the structure of the extension agreement requires the lease to continue to be recorded as a capital lease, the lessee changes the asset valuation and related lease liability by the difference between the present value of the new series of future minimum lease payments and the existing balance. The present value calculation must use the interest rate used for the same calculation at the inception of the original lease.

When a lease extension occurs and the *lessor* classifies the extension as a direct financing lease, the lease receivable and estimated residual value (downward only) are adjusted to match the new lease terms, with any adjustment going to unearned income. When a lease extension occurs and the *lessor* classifies an existing direct financing or sales-type lease as an operating lease, the lessor writes off the remaining lease investment and instead records the asset at the lower of its current net book value, original cost, or present value. The change in value from the original net investment is recorded against income in the period when the lease extension date occurs.

22.9 SUBLEASES

A sublease arises when leased property is leased by the original lessee to a third party. When this happens, the original lessee accounts for the sublease as though it were the original lessor. This means that it can account for the lease as an operating, direct sales, or sales-type lease. The original lessee continues to account for its ongoing lease payments to the original lessor as though the sublease did not exist.

22.10 SALE-LEASEBACK TRANSACTIONS

A sale-leaseback transaction arises when a property owner sells the property to another entity, which leases the property back to the original owner. If the transaction results in a loss, then the lessee recognizes it fully in the current period.

If the present value of the rental payments is at least 90% of the property's fair value, the lessee is considered to have retained substantially all rights to use the property. Under this scenario, there are two ways to account for the transaction:

1. If the lease qualifies as a capital lease, the lessee accounts for it as such and recognizes any profits on the initial property sale over the lease term in proportion to the asset amortization schedule.

2. If the lease qualifies as an operating lease, the lessee accounts for it as such and recognizes any profits on the initial property sale over the lease term in proportion to the lease payments.

If the present value of the rental payments is less than 10% of the property's fair value, the lessee should recognize all gains from the transaction fully in the current period. If the rental payments under the transaction appear unreasonable based on market prices at the time of lease inception, the payments are adjusted to make them "reasonable." The difference between the adjusted and existing lease rates is amortized over the life of the asset (if a capital lease) or the life of the lease (if an operating lease).

If the present value of the rental payments is more than 10% but less than 90% of the property's fair value, any excess profit on the asset sale can be recognized by the lessee on the sale date. If the lease is treated as a capital lease, excess profit is calculated as the difference between the asset's sale price and the recorded value of the leased asset. If the lease is treated as an operating lease, excess profit is calculated as the difference between the asset's sale price and the present value of the minimum lease payments, using the lower of the lessor's implicit lease rate or the lessee's incremental borrowing rate.

22.11   SUMMARY

Besides the detailed accounting transactions shown in the chapter, please refer to the *Wiley GAAP Guide 2009* to view primary FASB source documents related to leases, as well as Chapter 9, Footnotes, to view sample lease-related footnotes. There are also a number of sample leasing journal entries located in Appendix B.

CHAPTER **23**

EARNINGS PER SHARE

23.1 INTRODUCTION

Earnings per share (EPS) is one of the most commonly used metrics for determining the impact of a company's operational results on the share value of individual shareholders. The basic EPS calculation is to divide a company's net income or loss by the total number of shares of common stock outstanding, which is discussed at more length in the "Earnings per Share for a Simple Capital Structure" section. However, the presence of a variety of convertible securities that can alter the number of shares outstanding results in a significantly more complex EPS calculation, as addressed in the "Diluted Earnings per Share" and subsequent sections. The reporting requirements for EPS are outlined in the following section.

23.2 EARNINGS PER SHARE PRESENTATION REQUIREMENTS

All EPS presentation requirements noted below apply to publicly held companies. If a privately held company chooses to present EPS information, then it must use the presentation requirements and calculation methodologies described in this chapter.

If a company has only issued capital stock and has no securities that can be converted into stock (i.e., a simple capital structure), then it must present EPS for both income from continuing operations and net income on the income statement. If a company has a more complex capital structure, it must present basic *and* diluted EPS for both income from continuing operations and net income on the income statement.

If a company reports a discontinued operation, an extraordinary item, or the cumulative effect of an accounting change, then it must also present the basic and diluted EPS for each of these items either on the financial statements or in their attached footnotes.

If a company chooses to present additional per-share amounts that are not required, it should reveal them in the attached footnotes, not on the income statement itself.

A company must present EPS information as part of the income statement for all periods it is reporting. Also, if diluted EPS is presented for any one period of a multiperiod financial statement presentation, it must be reported for all of the periods presented.

23.3 EARNINGS PER SHARE FOR A SIMPLE CAPITAL STRUCTURE

A company reporting EPS under a simple capital structure format will only have common stock, and no securities that can potentially dilute EPS, such as options, warrants, or convertible bonds.

The essence of the calculation used for EPS in a simple capital structure is to divide income available to common shareholders by the weighted-average number of common shares outstanding during the period. The income available to common shareholders is defined as total income minus any preferential claims against the income by other securities (usually declared dividends on preferred stock). Any dividends in arrears are not deducted from income from the purposes of this calculation, since they were deducted in previous periods. The calculation of the weighted-average number of common shares outstanding during the period is impacted by the following factors:

- *Treasury stock.* If stock is acquired by the company, these shares are excluded from the EPS calculation as of the date of acquisition.
- *New issuances.* If stock is issued during the measurement period, these shares are included in the EPS calculation as of the date of issuance.
- *Conversion into common stock.* If securities are converted into common stock during the measurement period, these shares are included in the EPS calculation as of the date of conversion.
- *Stock dividend or split.* A change in the number of shares resulting from a dividend, split, or reverse split is to be recognized retroactively for the entire period over which EPS calculations are presented. This rule applies even if the dividend or split occurs after the end of the reporting period but before the release of financial statements.
- *Issuance as part of a business combination.* If shares are issued as part of a business combination, the issuance is assumed to occur as of the date of the combination.

The following example illustrates the concepts of an EPS calculation for a simple capital structure, using these events during the reporting year:

- $250,000 of net income
- $28,000 of declared dividends on preferred stock
- 1,000,000 shares of common stock outstanding at the beginning of the calendar year
- 20,000 shares acquired on February 1
- 50,000 shares sold to the public on June 1
- 150,000 shares issued as part of a business combination on September 1
- 25% stock dividend declared on November 1, totaling 297,500 shares

We will first calculate the numerator portion of the EPS calculation, as follows:

$$\frac{(\$250,000 \text{ net income}) - (\$28,000 \text{ declared dividends})}{\text{Common shares outstanding}}$$

$$= \frac{\$222,000 \text{ net income}}{\text{Common shares outstanding}}$$

The calculation of the denominator is shown in the following table:

Transaction Description	Actual Shares	Retroactive Effect of Stock Dividend	Subtotal	Portion of Year Outstanding	Weighted-Average Shares Outstanding
Shares at beginning of year	1,000,000	250,000	1,250,000	12/12	1,250,000
Shares acquired on February 1	(20,000)	—	(20,000)	11/12	−18,333
Shares sold on June 1	50,000	12,500	62,500	7/12	36,458
Shares issued on September 1	150,000	37,500	187,500	4/12	62,500
		Totals	1,480,000		**1,330,625**

We now include the weighted-average number of common shares outstanding, as just derived, into the EPS calculation:

$$= \frac{\$222,000 \text{ net income}}{1,330,625 \text{ common shares}}$$

$$= \underline{\$0.17} \text{ earnings per share}$$

A scenario sometimes arises where declared dividends on preferred stock may be payable as either cash or common stock, or apportioned among both forms of payment. If so, the amount of the declared dividend must still be subtracted from net income, irrespective of the form of payment. However, if some shares of common stock are issued as part of the preferred stock dividend, then the denominator must be adjusted for the number of shares issued, using the weighted average calculation just noted in the preceding table.

23.4   DILUTED EARNINGS PER SHARE

A company reporting EPS under a complex capital structure will have securities that can potentially be converted into common stock. Examples of these securities are options, warrants, convertible preferred stock, contingent shares, and convertible bonds. An option or warrant grants the right to obtain common stock at specific price points over a predefined time period. Both convertible preferred stock and convertible bonds contain an option for the holder to convert the stock or bonds into common stock. Contingent shares are shares that will be issued subject to the occurrence of some future event. Contingent shares are considered to be fully issued for the entire reporting period if they are contingent upon the maintenance of current earnings levels.

The diluted EPS calculation includes all securities whose effect will dilute EPS (e.g., dilutive), while excluding all securities whose effect would not reduce EPS (e.g., antidilutive). The intent of this calculation is to show investors the highest possible level of EPS dilution. By presenting it alongside the basic EPS figure in the financial statements, investors can see the current EPS situation as well as the worst-case scenario. The diluted EPS calculation can be conducted using the treasury stock method or the if-converted method, which are covered in the next two sections.

23.5   TREASURY STOCK METHOD

The treasury stock method is primarily used to calculate diluted EPS for options and warrants. It assumes that all options and warrants are exercised at the beginning of the reporting period or actual date of issuance (if later in the year), and that funds obtained from the exercise are used to repurchase the shares at the average market price for the reporting period. Since the market price is assumed to be higher than the exercise price (otherwise the option holder would have no incentive to exercise the option), this means that the company will not repurchase all of the shares acquired by the option holder, resulting in more shares outstanding. The calculation using the treasury stock method is as follows:

Net dilution = (Shares issued) − (Proceeds received/Average market price per share)

The following is an example of how the treasury stock method is calculated:

The Edgerton Steel Company has net income of $1,500,000 and 100,000 common shares outstanding. In addition, 25,000 options were outstanding during the year, all with exercise prices of $5, and the average market price for the stock was $12 during that time. The following calculation determines how many additional shares to add to the denominator of the diluted EPS calculation:

Proceeds if all 25,000 options are exercised at $7	=	$175,000
Number of shares issued	=	25,000
Number of shares to be reacquired at $12 market price	=	14,583
($175,000 proceeds divided by $12 market price)		
Number of shares issued and not reacquired	=	10,417
(25,000 shares issued − 14,583 shares reacquired)		

Edgerton Steel's basic and diluted EPS are as follows:

Basic EPS	Diluted EPS
$\dfrac{\$1,500,000 \text{ net income}}{100,000 \text{ common shares}} = \$15.00 \text{ EPS}$	$\dfrac{\$1,500,000 \text{ net income}}{110,417 \text{ common shares}} = \$13.58 \text{ diluted EPS}$

23.6   IF-CONVERTED METHOD

The if-converted method is primarily used to calculate diluted EPS for convertible securities. It assumes that all securities convertible into common stock are converted into common stock at the beginning of the year or actual date of issuance (if later in the year). However, since converted securities are no longer able to participate in any preferential dividends, the dividends or interest expense (less income tax effect) related to these convertible securities are no longer subtracted from net income in the numerator of the EPS calculation.

The following is an example of how the if-converted method is calculated:

The Chesapeake Coal Company has net income of $750,000 and 100,000 common shares outstanding. In addition, it has 1,000 bonds outstanding, each at a 6% interest rate and convertible into 25 shares of common stock. They were issued at a par value of $1,000, have been outstanding since the beginning of the year, and none were converted to common stock during the year. Chesapeake's incremental tax rate is 40%.

To calculate diluted EPS, we assume that all the bonds are converted to common stock as of the beginning of the year, which would add 25,000 shares to the denominator of the diluted EPS calculation (1,000 bonds × 25 shares converted in exchange for each bond). Also, net income is increased by the amount of interest expense saved (net of applicable income taxes), in accordance with the following formula:

$$(\$750,000 \text{ net income}) + (6\% \text{ interest} \times 1,000 \text{ bonds} \times \$1,000 \text{ par value} \times (1 - 40\% \text{ tax}))$$

$$= \$750,000 \text{ net income} + \$36,000 \text{ interest savings net of tax}$$

$$= \$786,000 \text{ adjusted net income}$$

This results in the following EPS and diluted EPS calculations:

Basic EPS	Diluted EPS
$\dfrac{\$750,000 \text{ net income}}{100,000 \text{ common shares}} = \$7.50 \text{ EPS}$	$\dfrac{\$786,000 \text{ net income}}{125,000 \text{ common shares}} = \$6.29 \text{ diluted EPS}$

If the diluted EPS calculation had resulted in an EPS number higher than that of the basic EPS, then the impact of the convertible bonds would have been considered nondilutive, and they would not have been included in the diluted EPS calculation.

23.7   EARNINGS PER SHARE DISCLOSURES

The following disclosures are required for EPS, and should be included in the footnotes accompanying the financial statements:

- *Reconciliation.* For each period reported in the financial statements, a reconciliation must be presented of the differences between the basic and diluted EPS calculations, including the individual impact on both net income and share amounts for each type of security.
- *Impact of preferred dividends.* The effect of preferred dividends on the net income figure in the numerator of the basic EPS calculation must be disclosed.
- *Dividend nonpayment.* If a company has declared dividends on preferred stock but not paid them, then the amount in arrears must be disclosed.
- *Antidilutive securities.* An itemization must be provided of all securities not included in the diluted EPS calculation on the grounds that they would have had an antidilutive effect.
- *Subsequent events.* A description must be provided of any transactions occurring between the end of the reporting period and the issuance of the financial statements that would have materially changed the number of common shares or potential common shares if the transactions had occurred during the reporting period.

23.8   SUMMARY

The intent behind the disclosure of basic and diluted EPS information is to ensure that investors have a full knowledge of the impact of operational earnings on their shares, both from the perspective of current shares outstanding and a worst-case full-dilution scenario (however unlikely that may be). The calculation of both types of EPS is a highly mechanical process, involving no variation from a limited set of calculation options. Thus, there is no room for management modification of EPS information without running afoul of the EPS rules.

SEGMENT REPORTING

24.1 INTRODUCTION

Segment reporting is the disclosure of financial information about the major components of a company's various lines of business. The requirement for segment reporting was brought about by the presence of conglomerates that only report summarized results, thereby giving investors no information about the financial condition of their component lines of business. Thus, segment reporting is designed to improve the clarity of reported financial information. Segment reporting requirements apply solely to publicly held businesses; not-for-profit and nonpublic businesses are only encouraged to provide the information outlined in this chapter.

24.2 SEGMENT REPORTING REQUIREMENTS

One of the main concerns in segment reporting is the definition of a business segment. It is defined as an entity within a company that is engaging in business activities from which it may earn revenues and incur expenses (or even those solely incurring expenses), for which separate financial information is produced internally, and whose operating results are regularly reviewed by the company's chief operating decision maker. Entities within a company *not* considered segments include the corporate headquarters, its pension plan, and functional departments. This definition is useful from the perspective of a company's organization of financial information in the chart of accounts, since it is probably already collecting and storing information in the manner required for segment reporting. Even if a company has no discernible business segments, it must still disclose some information outlined later in the "Segment-Related Disclosures" section, covering revenues and selected additional information for major customers, geographic areas, and products and services.

When creating segment reporting, a company can choose from several reporting options. It can report segment results by types of products or services, by geographic region, by legal entity, or by type of customer. For whichever segment reporting methodology selected, the company must report each segment's revenue, profit or loss, and its assets. The following information must also be reported if they are included in the segment information provided to the company's chief operating decision maker:

- Revenues from external customers
- Intercompany revenues
- Interest revenue
- Interest expense
- Depreciation, depletion, and amortization expense
- Equity in the net income of investees accounted for by the equity method
- Income taxes
- Extraordinary items
- Significant non-cash expenses

Further, the segment information reported must reconcile to the company's consolidated financial results. In addition, the company must provide commentary on how it determined the composition of each segment, as well as differences in measurement practices between segments and between reporting periods.

A significant difficulty for companies presenting financial information for multiple periods is that they must restate prior-year segment reporting information (including interim periods) whenever recent changes in their internal structure mandate a change in the currently reported segments, unless it is impractical to do so (as would be the case if the information is not available or would be too expensive to accumulate).

24.3   TESTING FOR REPORTABLE SEGMENTS

A company must report segment information if a segment is considered significant under any one of the following three tests:

- *Revenues test*. The revenue of a segment comprises at least 10% of total consolidated revenue.
- *Profit and loss test*. The absolute amount of a segment's profit or loss is at least 10% of the greater of the combined profits of all operating segments reporting a profit, or at least 10% of the combined losses of all operating segments reporting a loss.
- *Assets test*. Segment assets are at least 10% of the combined assets of all operating segments. This test does not include any assets reserved for corporate use.

Even if a segment fails these tests, it is still considered a reportable segment if it has passed one of the tests in the past and is expected to do so again in the future. Using the same logic, a segment does not have to be reported if it only passes one or more of the tests due to an unusual event, and is not expected to pass the tests again.

In addition, segment reporting must encompass at least 75% of all company operations, or else additional segments must be designated as reportable until the 75% target is met.

The following example illustrates these concepts:

The ABC Company internally reports on the results of five segments, which are listed below as segments A through E:

Segment	Revenue (000s)	Profit (000s)	Loss (000s)	Assets
A	$ 280	$ 61		$ 200
B	412		$(35)	90
C	100	20		150
D	82	10		60
E	365	84		510
	$1,239	**$175**	**$(35)**	**$1,010**

Because the total profit of $175 is higher than the total reported loss of $35, the $175 profit is used for the 10% profit and loss test. The results of the testing are shown below, where an "X" next to a segment indicates that it has passed a 10% test, and must be reported:

Segment	Revenues Test (1)	Profit and Loss Test (2)	Assets Test (3)	75% of Revenues Test
A	X	X	X	$ 280
B	X			412
C		X	X	100
D				
E	X	X	X	365
		Reportable segment revenue		$1,157
		75% of total revenue of $1,239		929
		Excess revenue reported through segments		$ 228

(1) 10% × $1,239 total revenues = $124 minimum segment revenue
(2) 10% × $175 total profits = $18 minimum segment profit
(3) 10% × $1,010 total assets = $101 minimum segment assets

Thus, only segment D does not have sufficient revenue, profits, or assets to be included in the ABC Company's segment reporting. The other four segments easily provide a sufficient level of reportable revenue to meet the 75% revenue test.

In addition, other segments that fail the preceding tests can still be reported if management feels that information about these segments would be useful to those reading the financial statements. Further, a segment for which reporting was required in the immediately preceding period but which now fails the preceding tests must still be separately reported.

For all remaining segments that are not reportable under the preceding tests, their information must be summarized into an "all other" category and reported separately, including the sources of their revenue.

24.4   SEGMENT AGGREGATION

A company is allowed to aggregate the reporting of multiple segments if they have similar economic characteristics and are similar in each of these areas:

- Their products and services
- Their production processes
- Their types of customers
- Their methods of distribution or provision of services
- The regulatory environments under which they operate

A company having difficulty meeting the 75% test can aggregate information for smaller segments in order to arrive at a reportable segment, but only if the segments share a majority of the five characteristics noted in the preceding bullet points.

A conglomerate can easily have so many segments that the reporting of this information can become overwhelming. Accordingly, a general guideline is to aggregate the reporting results of closely related segments if the number of segments reported would otherwise exceed 10.

24.5   COST AND ASSET ALLOCATION ISSUES

Though segment reporting is designed to reveal the operating results of individual reporting entities within the company, it is allowable to allocate common costs to the segments as long as these allocations are also performed for internal reporting purposes, and are normally used by the corporate decision maker to evaluate segment profits or losses. However, the costs being allocated must demonstrably benefit the segments to which they are being allocated; this cannot be corporate overhead costs that only benefit the corporation as a whole.

The rules applied to cost allocation also apply to asset allocation. If an asset is assigned or allocated to a segment for internal reporting purposes, then it should be assigned or allocated in a similar manner for external segment reporting.

24.6   SEGMENT-RELATED DISCLOSURES

The following categories of disclosures are needed if a company reports segment information:

- General segment information:
  - *Change in segments.* Disclosure is required if a company is presenting financial information for multiple years, and changes to its internal structure mandate a change in the segments being reported. In the year of change to the revised segment reporting, the company must disclose segment information using both the old and new basis of segmentation.
  - *Major customers.* Disclosure is required if corporate sales to a single customer or group of customers under common control exceeds 10%. If so, it must disclose the total revenue from each of these customers, as well as the segment(s) earning this revenue. It does not need to report the identity of these customers. For disclosure purposes, the entire federal government is considered a single customer, as would be all divisions of a foreign, state, or local government.
  - *Products and services.* Unless considered impractical, the company is to disclose revenue from each product or service, or grouping thereof.
  - *Geographic areas.* Disclosure is required for the breakdown between international sales and domestic sales, as well as for all long-lived assets, where domestic sales are defined as those operations in its home country that generate revenues. If a company operates in multiple foreign countries and revenues or long-lived assets in an individual foreign country are material, then those revenues and assets should be separately disclosed, as well as the basis under which revenues were attributed to each country reported. Though not required, a company can also provide the same information for groups of countries.

- Segment-specific disclosure:
  - *Overview.* Disclosure is required of the method used to identify segments, the types of product and service revenues included in each segment's revenue, and the presence of any segment aggregation.
  - *Basis of measurement.* Disclosure is required for the basis of accounting for transactions between reportable segments, and the reason for any differences between the measurement of segment profitability or assets and the company's consolidated profitability or assets. The nature of any changes in measurement methods from prior periods must also be explained.
  - *Reconciliation.* Disclosure is required for the reconciliation of all segment amounts reported to the same consolidated information. This should at least include revenues, profit or loss prior to income taxes, extraordinary items, and discontinued operations, and assets. It should also be done for every other significant item of information disclosed. All significant reconciling items must be individually described.
  - *Interim reporting.* When interim financial statements are issued, segment reporting is more limited. It should include for each reportable segment the revenue from external customers, intersegment revenue, profit or loss, total assets (though only if there has been a significant change from the amount reported in the most recent annual financial statements), a description of any changes in the system of measurement used or the system used to determine segments, and a reconciliation of all segment amounts reported to the same consolidated information.

24.7 SUMMARY

While working though the various rules and tests noted in this chapter for segment reporting, it is useful to remember the overriding objective of segment reporting, which is to provide information about the different types of businesses in which a company operates, so that users of the financial statements can more easily understand its performance. With that objective in mind, it may be easier to determine which segments to report, aggregate, or ignore.

INTERIM REPORTING

25.1 INTRODUCTION

Interim reporting refers to the reporting of financial information by business entities for periods of less than one year. The key concept of interim reporting is the reporting of annual expenses in these reports in a manner apportioned fairly across all interim periods by some reasonable measure of activity. If the measure of activity used as the basis of expense allocation proves to be incorrect, then the expenses in subsequent interim reports are to be adjusted to reflect the estimation errors. By using this approach to expense allocation, the revenues and expenses shown in each interim report should avoid an excessive degree of misleading fluctuations in reported financial results.

25.2 REQUIREMENTS FOR INTERIM REPORTING

There is no requirement under U.S. GAAP to issue interim financial reports; no company is required to issue more than annual financial statements. However, the Securities and Exchange Commission requires publicly held companies to issue quarterly financial results, known as 10-Q or 10-QSB reports. Also, it is common practice for most organizations to issue monthly financial statements in order to keep track of performance; given the rapid pace of change and high levels of competition, it would be imprudent for a company to only measure its level of revenue and profitability just once a year. In many instances, lenders require monthly financial statements for so long as any loan agreements are outstanding. Thus, nonpublic firms, which make up the vast majority of all companies, do not have to issue interim reports, but there are many reasons why it is still common practice to do so.

25.3 INTERIM REPORTING GUIDELINES

If a company issues interim financial reports, it should follow the standards set forth in the following bullet points:

- *Revenue.* The treatment of revenue recognition for interim reporting is identical to how it is handled for annual financial reporting for product and service sales, as well as for long-term construction contracts.

- *Cost of goods sold.* It is acceptable to use the gross profit method to estimate the cost of goods sold and ending inventory. Under this approach, purchases during the reporting period are added to the physical inventory count from the end of the last reporting period, less sales during the current period to arrive at an estimate of ending inventory and the cost of goods sold. The trouble with this approach is that it assumes only an average rate of production scrap, as built into the bill of materials, but does not address excess scrap or obsolescence, nor any change in the assumed margin on sales from the historical rate. Thus, this estimating approach can result in incorrect interim results that must be corrected once a physical inventory count has been completed.

- *Lower of cost or market valuation.* If the market value of inventory declines below its cost during an interim reporting period, but there is substantial evidence that the decline will be reversed before the fiscal year-end, then there is no need to record the difference between the market value and cost as an expense. However, this exception to the lower of cost or market rule is considered by the Emerging Issues Task Force (EITF) to essentially only apply to seasonal price fluctuations. Also, if a loss on a lower of cost or market situation is recorded in an interim report and the market value subsequently increases during a following interim period, then the amount of the loss can be reversed and recorded as a gain.

- *LIFO inventory layers.* If a company values its inventory using the last in, first out (LIFO) method and it liquidates a portion of a base period layer during an interim reporting period, but there is an expectation that the layer will be replaced before the fiscal year-end, then the expected cost to replace the inventory should be added to the interim period's cost of sales. Conversely, if the liquidation occurs and there is no expectation that the layer will be replaced before the fiscal year-end, then the full extent of the liquidation is recognized in the interim reporting period in which it occurs.

- *Standard costing variances.* If a company uses a standard costing system to value its inventory and there are purchase price or volume variances during the interim period, these variances need not be recorded if they are expected to be absorbed by the fiscal year-end. If this is not the case, then the variances should be recognized within the current interim reporting period.

- *Expenses benefiting more than one interim period.* If an expense is incurred that clearly benefits more than one interim reporting period, then the expense should be spread across all impacted reporting periods. For example, annual property taxes may be recognized in each interim reporting period of the year, though it is only paid once a year. The type of expense allocation should be appropriate to the type of expense, reasonably matching the recognition of expense to the benefits derived. Other examples of expenses that may be reasonably recognized across multiple interim reporting periods include advertising, bonuses, major maintenance, and quantity discounts to customers.

For example, the Arkansas BirdBath Company (ABC) has a bonus plan for its employees that rewards them with a total of $240,000 in bonuses if they attain sales of $2 million by the end of the calendar year. There is no bonus if the $2 million figure is not reached. ABC has historically sold 20% of its products in the first quarter, 60% in the second quarter, and 20% in the third quarter. It has had no material sales in the fourth quarter. Its actual sales in the current year are as follows:

	1st Quarter	2nd Quarter	3rd Quarter	4th Quarter	Total
Actual sales	$410,000	$1,190,000	$ 350,000	$0	$ 1,950,000
Budget	400,000	1,200,000	400,000	0	2,000,0000
Bonus recognized	$ 49,200	$ 142,800	$(192,000)	0	$ 0

At the end of the first quarter, ABC's sales are ahead of plan, so it appears reasonable that the staff will be paid its bonus. Accordingly, the controller recognizes 20.5% of the total bonus, which represents the proportion of sales to the goal amount thus far attained ($410,000/$2,000,000). At the end of the second quarter, year-to-date sales are still on pace to attain the $2,000,000 target, so the controller records another $142,800, which represents 80% of the total bonus, less the portion recognized in the first quarter. However, revenues are too low in the third quarter. With no expectation of any further sales in the fourth quarter, it is evident that the bonus will not be issued, so the controller reverses the entire bonus accrual at the end of the third quarter.

- *Extraordinary expenses.* If an extraordinary item occurs during an interim period, then report its entire effect separately in that period if the impact is material. Materiality is based on estimated income for the full fiscal year. If the impact of the item is immaterial based on this benchmark, then do not report it separately from operational results.

- *Discontinued operations and unusual events.* If a company operation is discontinued during an interim period or some other unusual event occurs, then report its entire effect separately in that period if the impact is material. Materiality is based on estimated income for the interim period. If the impact of the item is immaterial based on this benchmark, then do not report it separately from operational results.

- *Income taxes.* If a company were to estimate its income tax expense using its results just for an interim period, it may result in a tax rate lower than the final full-year rate, which is based on presumably higher full-year profits. Thus, interim reports should always record the income tax expense based on the expected tax rate for the full year, assuming the use of all credits and tax planning techniques during the full year.

- *Accounting changes.* If there is a change in accounting principle, then previous interim financial statements should be retroactively restated to reflect the change. If the accounting change involves the recognition of a cumulative effect, then the cumulative change is recognized in the first quarter of the current fiscal year; if the company has already issued subsequent interim reports, then they must be restated to incorporate this recognition in the first quarter.

- *Legal settlements.* If a company agrees to a legal settlement during an interim period, its amount can be reasonably estimated, and the settlement amount is material, then the portion of the settlement directly related to the current interim period is recognized within that period, previous interim periods within the same fiscal year are restated to recognize that portion of the settlement directly related to those periods, and the remaining amount directly related to prior years is recognized in the first interim period of the current fiscal year.

For example, the ChopUp Weeder Company has just settled a lawsuit during its third quarter. Under the terms of the settlement, ChopUp must pay the holder of a patent a 2% royalty on its premier SliceUp Weeder machine, which must also be applied to all historical sales of the product. Sales of the SliceUp product are noted in the following table, as well as the royalty expense to be added to the restated quarterly results for the first and second quarters, and the royalty expense related to sales in prior years, which must be recognized in the first quarter:

	Prior Years	1st Quarter	2nd Quarter	3rd Quarter
SliceUp Weeder sales	$2,250,000	$100,000	280,000	310,000
2% Royalty expense	45,000	2,000	5,600	6,200
Expense recognition during period	—	$ 47,000	$ 5,600	$ 6,200

- *Earnings per share.* The calculation of earnings per share for interim reporting is identical to how it is handled for annual financial reporting.

25.4 INTERIM-PERIOD DISCLOSURES

If a cumulative-type accounting change occurs during an interim reporting period, a company must disclose the following information about the change in its interim financial report:

- The nature of the change and the justification for it.
- The impact of the change on both income from continuing operations and net income for the interim period in which the change is recorded.
- The impact of the change on both income from continuing operations and net income for subsequent interim reporting periods for which reports were already issued prior to adoption of the cumulative-type accounting change.
- The impact of the change on both income from continuing operations and net income for all post-change interim reporting periods within the same fiscal year.
- The impact of the change on both income from continuing operations and net income for the interim period of the preceding fiscal year covering the same period as the interim period in which the change is recorded.

If a company is subject to significant seasonal variation, then it should disclose the seasonal nature of its operations. Further, it should consider issuing a supplement to each interim report with information for the 12-month period ending at the interim date for the current interim reporting period. By presenting this additional 12-month information, the company is essentially presenting information that cancels the impact of seasonality on its interim reports.

If a company is publicly held, it must disclose the following information as an attachment to its quarterly financial statements, and must include the current year-to-date and comparable information for the preceding year:

- Basic and diluted earnings per share
- Seasonal revenues and expenses

- Significant changes in estimates or provisions for income tax estimates
- Discontinued operations
- Extraordinary, unusual, or infrequent items
- Contingent items
- Effect of changes in accounting principles or estimates
- Significant changes in financial position

If a publicly held company does not separately report the results of its fourth quarter (i.e., annual results are reported instead), the company must still separately disclose any impact on fourth-quarter results of activities occurring during that quarter, including: accounting changes, extraordinary or unusual items, and business disposals. Disclosure must also be made of the aggregate effect of year-end adjustments that have a material impact on the results of that quarter.

If a company is publicly held, it must also disclose the following information regarding interim activities on the Form 8-K within four business days of the incurrence of the event:

- *Assets.* The acquisition or disposition of significant amounts of assets, as well as the costs required to complete exit or asset disposal actions, must be described. Also, the material impairment of assets must be disclosed.
- *Governance.* Any change in corporate control must be disclosed, as well as changes in corporate directors and officers. Also, changes to the articles of incorporation, bylaws, or code of ethics must be noted.
- *Legal standing.* The company must disclose if it has filed for bankruptcy, whether it has received a delisting notice or notice of failure to satisfy a listing rule, or the transfer of its stock listing.
- *Obligations.* The initiation or termination of any material definitive agreement resulting in rights or obligations material to the company must be disclosed. Also, any off–balance sheet arrangements creating a direct financial obligation must be noted, as well as events triggering such obligations.
- *Other disclosures.* The following additional disclosures are required:
  - Material nonpublic information about a prior fiscal year or quarter
  - The unregistered sale of equity securities
  - The material modification of the rights of security holders
  - A change in the company's auditor
  - A change in the corporate fiscal year

25.5 SUMMARY

The interim reporting requirements expressed in this chapter have been supported by U.S. GAAP standards for a long time. However, due to the ongoing drive toward the convergence of U.S. GAAP and international standards, there is a possibility that these standards will be modified to some extent in the near future. The result could be some modification in favor of current international standards, which recognize annual operating expenses in the interim period incurred, rather than being spread over all interim periods.

CHAPTER 26

ACCOUNTING CHANGES AND CORRECTION OF ERRORS

26.1 INTRODUCTION

The discussion of accounting changes and correction of errors in this chapter is based on the FASB's Statement of Financial Accounting Standards (SFAS) Number 154, which was issued in 2005. This statement overruled the previous accounting principles as outlined in APB Opinion Number 20 and SFAS Number 3, which had governed this area of accounting for many years. The reason for the change was to achieve convergence between U.S. and international accounting standards.

26.2 DEFINITIONS

Given the technical nature of the discussion in this chapter, it is useful to know precisely what different types of accounting changes involve. Accordingly, definitions are provided as follows:

- *Accounting change.* A change in accounting principle, estimate, or reporting entity.
- *Change in accounting principle.* A change from one to another generally accepted accounting principle (GAAP) when more than one GAAP applies to a situation, or when the former GAAP is being phased out. Changing the method of GAAP application is also considered a change in accounting principle. For example, a change from the LIFO to the FIFO inventory valuation method is a change in accounting principle.
- *Change in accounting estimate.* A change in the assessment of the present status and future benefits or obligations of assets or liabilities. For example, changes in reserves, service lives, salvage values, and warranty obligations are changes in accounting estimate.
- *Change in reporting entity.* Either a change in reporting for an individual company to consolidated reporting results, or a change in the subsidiaries or entities

making up consolidated reporting results. A business combination is not considered a change in reporting entity.

- *Error in financial statements.* A mathematical mistake, oversight or misuse of facts, or incorrect application of GAAP resulting in the incorrect presentation or disclosure of information in financial statements.

26.3 CHANGES IN ACCOUNTING PRINCIPLE

A change in accounting principle should be allowed only if the change is mandatory as a result of a new accounting pronouncement, or if the use of the replacement principle is clearly preferable to the principle previously used. A change in accounting estimate is allowable if it justifiably involves a change in the estimated period to be benefited by an asset.

A change in accounting principle calls for retrospective application of the change, unless there are specific transition requirements associated with the accounting principle. This does not apply if the accounting principle is being initially adopted due to events occurring for the first time, or which were previously immaterial, or if the change is impracticable. The change shall be considered impracticable if it cannot be performed after every reasonable effort has been made to do so, or if it requires assumptions about the intent of management in prior periods that cannot be affirmed, or it if requires significant estimates for which information was not available when the statements were originally produced. A change in principle is not allowed if it was originally adopted for a single, nonrecurring event.

Retrospective application of the principle calls for the following changes:

- Calculate the cumulative effect of the change, including related income tax effects, on periods prior to those shown in the financial statements, and include it in the assets, liabilities, and retained earnings of the beginning of the first period presented.
- Calculate the period-specific effects of the change, including related income tax effects, on all periods presented in the financial statements and adjust the statements for each period to reflect the change.
- If it is impractical to calculate the period-specific effects of the change for all periods shown in the financial statements, then include the cumulative effect of the change on all periods in the assets, liabilities, and retained earnings of the beginning of the first period presented.
- If it is impractical to determine the cumulative effect of a change, then apply it as of the earliest possible date.
- If the change is made in an interim reporting period, then it shall apply to all preceding interim periods being reported.

26.4 CHANGES IN ACCOUNTING ESTIMATE

If there is a change in accounting estimate, the change must be accounted for either in the period in which the change occurs (if it affects only that period) or in both the period in which the change occurs and subsequent periods (if it impacts both periods). A change in accounting estimate does not require a retrospective change to earlier financial statements.

A change in accounting estimate shall take effect only if it is preferable to the existing estimate. For example, the usage pattern of an asset may have altered over time, so that a revised estimate of its depreciable life more accurately reflects the usage pattern of the asset than the existing depreciation interval.

26.5   CHANGES IN REPORTING ENTITY

When an accounting change results in the issuance of financial statements that are essentially the results of a different business entity, the effect of the change must be retroactively applied to all other preceding annual and interim reporting periods shown on the financial statements.

26.6   CORRECTION OF ERRORS

If an error is discovered in the financial statements for a previous reporting period, then the statements must be reissued. The cumulative amount of the error on reporting periods preceding those presented in the financial statements shall be included in the beginning of the first period presented. Depending on the type of correction, the adjustment is likely to include a change in the beginning balance of retained earnings, in addition to other entries. In addition, the change must be retroactively made to each subsequent reporting period presented in the financial statements.

26.7   DISCLOSURE OF ACCOUNTING CHANGES AND CORRECTION OF ERRORS

A company making accounting changes must make the following disclosures in the footnotes accompanying its financial statements in the period in which these changes occur:

- *Effects of change.* The effect of the change for the current and any affected prior periods on the following items:
  - ○ Income from continuing operations
  - ○ Net income
  - ○ Other affected financial statement line items
  - ○ Any affected per-share amounts
  - ○ Cumulative effect on retained earnings as of the beginning of the earliest presented period
- *Fourth-quarter reporting.* If an entity fails to separately report its fourth quarter interim results from its annual financial results and there was an accounting change during the fourth quarter, then it must disclose the effects of the change on the fourth quarter.
- *Impracticability of prior change.* If retrospective application is impractical, then disclose the reason why the application is considered impracticable, and how the change is being reported.
- *Reason for change.* An explanation for any change in accounting principle, including why it is preferable to the principle previously being used.

If there is an error correction, then the reporting entity must disclose that its financial statements have been restated, including a description of the nature of the error. In addition, the following disclosures must be made:

- *Cumulative impact on prior periods.* If the error correction calls for a cumulative change to the beginning balance of the earliest period presented, the cumulative amount of the change on each impacted line item must be stated.

- *Impact of error.* The effect of the correction on each line item must be disclosed, including per-share information for each prior period included in the financial statements.

Disclosure of a change in estimate is not necessary unless the effect of the change is material.

26.8 SUMMARY

The issuance of SFAS 154 simplified the treatment of the reporting of accounting changes and errors, while converging with international standards. As outlined in this chapter, SFAS 154 has increased the number of instances in which accounting changes and errors must be applied retroactively.

PART FIVE

ACCOUNTING MANAGEMENT

BEST PRACTICES

27.1 INTRODUCTION

All accounting processes can be improved in some manner in order to increase the overall efficiency and effectiveness of the accounting department. Such improvements are known as best practices. They can range from such simple expedients as the creation of a signature stamp to increase the speed of check signing to the installation of advanced document management systems that allow one to avoid most records management issues. The full range of best practices would encompass an entire book, and does: for a full treatment of this topic, please refer to Bragg, *Accounting Best Practices*, 6th Edition (John Wiley & Sons, 2010) as well as Bragg, *Inventory Best Practices* (John Wiley & Sons 2004); Bragg, *Billing and Collections Best Practices* (John Wiley & Sons, 2004); Bragg, *Payroll Best Practices* (John Wiley & Sons, 2005); and Bragg, *Accounting Controls Best Practices* (John Wiley & Sons, 2006). This chapter contains a number of the more common best practices, listed in alphabetical order by functional area, as well as a graphical representation of the approximate cost and implementation time needed to install each one. Any best practice that requires a high cost has a notation of three stacks of money, while those best practices requiring fewer funds have a correspondingly smaller number of stacks. Similarly, a best practice requiring a lengthy installation time has a notation containing three alarm clocks, while those with shorter installation times have a smaller number of clocks.

Seven process flowcharts are also included as a separate section. These process flows show the most efficient manner in which a number of common accounting-related processes can be handled, incorporating a large number of best practices. Flowcharts are provided for accounts payable, credit and collections, inventory, payroll, cash management, cost accounting, and internal auditing.

The body of knowledge for accounting best practices is constantly increasing. To obtain up-to-date information in this area, periodically access the author's *www. accountingtools.com* Web site for more information.

27.2 BEST PRACTICES

- *Accounts payable: audit expense reports.* Rather than review every line item on every expense report submitted, the accounting manager can schedule a random audit of a small number of expense reports, which will be indicative of any problems that may be present in other, unaudited reports. If so, either the scope of the audit can be expanded, or else the accounting staff can focus on just those issues that are uncovered in a broader sample of expense reports. Also, if the audits of certain employees continue to reveal ongoing problems, those individuals can be scheduled for full reviews of all expense reports submitted. By taking this approach, a company can still spot the majority of expense report exceptions, while expending much less effort in finding them.

Cost:

Installation time:

- *Accounts payable: automate recurring payments.* A few payments, such as space rental, copier lease, and subscription billings, are the same every month, and are likely to last for some time into the future. To avoid the repetitive entry of these items into the accounts payable database, many off-the-shelf accounting packages allow one to set up automatically recurring payments that must only be entered in the system one time. This option should only be used if it allows for a termination date, since automated payments may otherwise inadvertently pass well beyond their actual termination dates.

Cost:

Installation time:

- *Accounts payable: automate supplier query responses.* The accounts payable staff can spend a large part of its time answering queries from suppliers who want to know when they will be paid. The staff time devoted to this activity can be sharply reduced by installing a computerized phone linkage system that steps suppliers through a menu of queries so that they can find out the status of payments directly from the computer system. It is also possible to do this through an Internet site. Some employee interaction with suppliers will still be necessary, since there will be cases where invoices are not recorded in the system at all, and so will require manual intervention to fix.

Cost:

Installation time:

- *Accounts payable: automate three-way matching.* The most labor-intensive effort by the accounts payable staff is to manually compare receiving documents to supplier invoices and internal purchase orders to ensure that all payments made to suppliers are both authorized and received in full. To avoid much of this work, a number of high-end computerized accounting systems will conduct the comparison automatically and warn the staff when they find inconsistencies. However, this means that the purchasing staff must enter its purchase orders into the system, as well as the receiving staff, which requires extra coordination with these departments.

Cost:

Installation time:

- *Accounts payable: create an online purchasing catalog.* Employee purchases of office supplies and maintenance items constitute a large part of the purchases made by most companies, as well as a correspondingly large part of the accounts payable transactions that it must handle. To avoid this payable work, an online purchasing catalog can be created that itemizes all company-approved items; employees can select items directly from this catalog and place an online order. These orders will be batched by the computer system and automatically sent to suppliers, who will ship directly to the ordering personnel. Suppliers will then issue summarized invoices to the company, which greatly reduces the paperwork of the accounting staff. It will also reduce a large part of the work of the purchasing staff. However, setting up the system and coordinating its installation with suppliers results in a very lengthy installation interval.

Cost:

Installation time:

- *Accounts payable: eliminate manual check payments.* There are some instances when checks are needed on such short notice that they cannot be included in the scheduled check runs of the accounting staff. Instead, someone must obtain approval on short notice, cut a manual check, have it signed, and log it into the computer system. To avoid these time-consuming steps, one can promulgate a general prohibition on issuing this sort of payment, and can increase the use of petty cash if this will allow the accounting staff to replace manual check payments with cash payments.

Cost:

Installation time: 🕐

- *Accounts payable: issue payments based on purchase order approval only.* The typical company payment requires multiple approvals: on the purchase requisition, the purchase order, supplier invoice, and check. A much simpler approach is to require a single approval on the purchase order and ignore all other required approvals. By doing so, the amount of time required to complete accounting transactions can be substantially reduced, since documents must no longer be sent to managers for approval and sit in their "in" boxes. However, this means that the controls over purchase order approvals must be iron-clad, so that there is no chance of a supplier payment being sent out without some sort of authorized approval.

Cost:

Installation time:

- *Accounts payable: issue payments based on receipts only.* As noted in a preceding best practice, one of the most time-consuming aspects of the accounts payable function is the matching of receiving documents to purchase orders and supplier invoices. To avoid this entire approach, a company can have the receiving staff access purchase orders through a computer terminal, and approve received items on the spot through the terminal. The company then issues payments to suppliers based on the prices listed on the purchase orders, rather than waiting for a supplier invoice to arrive. This completely eliminates the matching process. However, this approach requires a great deal of computer software customization, t he integration of sales tax tables into the software, and the cooperation of suppliers in accepting payments from the system. This should be considered an advanced best practice that requires great expertise to install.

Cost:

Installation time:

- *Accounts payable: issue standard adjustment letters to suppliers.* When the accounts payable staff has a valid reason for making a deduction from a payment to a supplier, this can result in a prolonged series of complaints from the supplier, who is wondering why a short payment was made. The adjustment will appear on the next monthly statement of unpaid invoices from the supplier, and will likely end with a series of irate collection calls. At some point, the accounting staff may feel that the cost savings from taking the deduction was not worth the effort required to convince the supplier of the reasoning behind it. This issue can be solved by checking off a box on a standard adjustment letter and mailing the letter to the supplier. The letter should note the invoice number that is at issue, as well as a series of common problems that caused the short payment to be made. The accounting staff can quickly check off the appropriate box and mail it out, using far less time than would be required to construct a formal, customized letter of notification. The letter should contain space for a free-form written description of the issue, in case it is a unique one not covered by any of the standard explanations already listed on the letter.

Cost:

Installation time:

- *Accounts payable: pay via automated clearinghouse transactions.* The check payment transaction involves printing checks, attaching backup materials to the checks, sending them out for signatures, then attaching check stubs to supporting documents and filing them away, while the checks are mailed. A much simpler approach that avoids all of these steps is to obtain the bank routing numbers and account numbers from all suppliers and then send payments directly to these accounts with automated clearinghouse transactions. This can be accomplished with customized accounting software, but is much easier if the software already contains this feature; it is normally only found on more expensive packages.

Cost:

Installation time:

- *Accounts payable: pay with purchasing cards.* The bulk of all paperwork dealt with by the accounts payable staff is for small-dollar items. Many of these purchases can be consolidated by distributing purchasing cards (for example, credit cards) to those employees who most frequently make purchases. By doing so, a company can reduce the amount of paperwork to a single supplier statement each month. Furthermore, some cards can be set to only allow a certain dollar amount of purchases per day, to allow purchases from only certain types of stores, and even to show daily purchases on an Internet site, where a supervisor can immediately restrict purchasing levels if spending habits appear to be a problem. On the downside, it can be difficult to report use taxes based on purchasing card receipts, which may lead to slightly higher use tax remittances.

Cost:

Installation time:

- *Accounts payable: send supplier invoices to an EDI data entry shop.* When a company creates the capability to accept online invoices from suppliers via EDI transmissions, it will find that it must still maintain a clerical staff in order to conduct data entry on those paper invoices still being mailed to the company by some suppliers. It can avoid this expense by remailing the invoices to a data entry outsourcing shop that will reenter the invoices into an EDI format and transmit them to the company, thereby ensuring that 100% of all invoices will be received in the EDI format. A good way to avoid the time delay associated with remailing invoices to the data entry supplier is to have all suppliers (those not using EDI) send their invoices to a lockbox that is accessed directly by the supplier. It may also be possible to charge suppliers a small fee if they do not use EDI, thereby covering the cost of the data entry work.

Cost:

Installation time:

- *Accounts payable: sign checks with a signature stamp.* One of the slowest parts of the check creation process is finding an authorized check signer and waiting for that person to sign the checks (which could be days if the person is busy). A better approach is to purchase a signature stamp and have someone on the accounting staff stamp the checks. However, the stamp must be kept locked up in a secure location, so that no unauthorized check signing occurs. Also, since there will no longer be a review of checks before they are sent out, there must be a strong control over payments earlier in the process, by requiring purchase order authorizations before any goods or services are ordered from suppliers.

Cost:

Installation time:

- *Accounts payable: use negative assurance for invoice approvals.* One of the largest problems for the accounts payable staff is the continuing delay in receiving approvals of supplier invoices from authorized employees throughout the company. Invoices tend to sit on employee desks as low-priority items, resulting in constant reminders by the accounting staff to turn in documents, resulting in late payments and missed early payment discounts. This universal problem can be avoided through the use of negative assurance. Under this approval system, invoice copies are sent to authorizing employees, and are automatically paid when due unless the employees tell the accounts payable staff *not* to issue payment. By focusing only on those invoices that may be incorrect, the accounting staff can process the vast majority of all submitted invoices without cajoling anyone to submit an approved document. The process can be streamlined even further by digitizing an incoming invoice and e-mailing it to the authorizing employee. By doing so, employees can be reached even when they are off-site, as long as they check their e-mail on a regular basis. By linking these transmissions to workflow software, the accounting staff can designate how long an invoice can wait in a recipient's e-mail box before it is automatically routed to another authorized person, thereby ensuring that *someone* will see every invoice and raise a red flag if a potential problem exists.

Cost:

Installation time:

- *Collections: approve customer credit prior to sales.* The accounting or finance staff will sometimes find that it is put under considerable pressure by the sales staff to give credit approval to sales already made to prospective customers. Since the sales staff will earn a commission on these sales, the pressure to approve credit can be quite intense, even if the customer does not have a sufficient credit history to deserve it. This can result in an excessive amount of bad debt write-offs. To avoid this situation, the sales and accounting departments can work together to create a list of sales prospects and determine credit levels for them, based on publicly available credit information, before the prospects are ever contacted. However, this is not a cost-effective solution if new customers are of the walk-in variety or if average per-customer sales are so low that the cost of conducting credit checks makes this best practice too expensive to implement.

Cost:

Installation time:

- *Collections: authorize small balance write-offs with no management approval.* Customers will occasionally pay for slightly less than the amount of an account receivable, leaving a small balance cluttering up the accounts receivable database. It can be quite time-consuming to create a permission form for signature by an accounting manager that will lead to the elimination of these small balances. A better approach is to create a policy that allows the collections staff to write off small balances without any permission from management personnel.

Cost:

Installation time:

- *Collections: automate fax delivery of dunning letters.* A computer can be attached to the accounting computer system that is dedicated to sending faxes. This machine is quite useful if it is linked to the collections database so that reminder faxes can be sent to those customers whose payments are overdue. The severity of the wording on these faxes can increase over time as the number of days late increases. Faxes can even be sent slightly prior to payment due dates to jog the memory of customers in regard to payment. However, this can be a very expensive option if a customized software linkage must be created between the collections database and the automated faxing system.

Cost:

Installation time:

- *Collections: automate fax delivery of overdue invoices.* The preceding best practice for faxing dunning letters can be expanded to also send customers copies of their overdue invoices. In addition, it can be used by the collections staff to only send invoices to those customers to whom collection calls have been made, and who do not have the invoice in hand already. The same software customization issues apply to this best practice as the last one.

Cost:

Installation time:

- *Collections: e-mail invoices in Acrobat format.* It can be extremely difficult to obtain payment for some invoices. This usually arises when the approval of a specific individual at a customer is required, and that person is either rarely available or so disorganized that the paperwork invariably disappears. Adobe's Acrobat software has eliminated these problems by creating a perfect copy of an invoice as printed by any accounting system into a PDF file that can be attached to an e-mail and forwarded straight to a customer's accounting department where it can be opened, printed, and paid. By using this approach, one can create a completely electronic methodology for obtaining approval of invoices by customers.

Implementing the conversion of invoices into the Acrobat format is quite simple. First go to the Adobe Web site (*www.adobe.com*) to order the Acrobat software. Once received and installed, go to your accounting software package and prepare to print an invoice. When the printing screen appears, change the assigned printer to the PDF format, which will appear as one of the available printers. The software will ask you where to store the resulting file and what to name it. After a few seconds, the conversion of the invoice into a picture-perfect PDF file will be complete. The resulting PDF file can be easily incorporated into an e-mail message as a file attachment.

Cost:

Installation time:

- *Collections: print separate invoices for each line item billed.* Sometimes, customers will take issue with one line item on an invoice and refuse to pay the entire invoice until the pricing on that one line item has been resolved, which lengthens the overall interval for collections. To avoid this problem, a company can consider issuing a separate invoice for each line item, rather than clustering them onto a single invoice. This will reduce the average collection period, but may not be cost-effective if the average price for each line item is quite small. It can be a very effective approach, however, for large-dollar line items.

Cost:

Installation time:

- *Collections: send out repeating invoices before the scheduled date.* If a company has a database of prices that it knows it will charge customers on set dates, such as those for subscriptions or ongoing standard maintenance fees, it can create and mail the invoices a few days prior to the dates on which they are scheduled to be sent. By creating invoices early, the receiving companies have more time to route the invoices through their internal approval processes, resulting in slightly earlier payments to the issuing company. This is a very inexpensive way to improve the speed of cash flow.

Cost:

Installation time:

- *Collections: stratify required collection calls.* There can be an overwhelming number of potential collection calls to make and not enough employees to make the calls. In this situation, one should sort the overdue invoices by dollar size and target the largest ones for the bulk of all calls. This means that the collections staff will focus its efforts on those invoices with the greatest potential dollar return in exchange for the effort put into the calls. This does not mean that small dollar invoices will be ignored, but the related calls may be delayed or fewer in number.

Cost:

Installation time:

- *Commissions: automate commission calculations.* The calculation of commissions can be a painful process of ascertaining the latest commission deals struck by the sales manager, combing through all of the invoices from the latest month to calculate the preliminary calculation, sending the resulting commission reports to the sales staff, and then dealing with irate sales personnel who think that they have not been fully compensated. A better approach is to first standardize the commission calculation system so that it can be automated through the accounting computer system. Doing so will result in far fewer complaints from the sales staff about supposedly incorrect commission calculations, no chance of the accounting staff making calculation errors (since the computer is now doing it for them), and a much faster completion of this key step in the month-end closing process.

Cost:

Installation time:

- *Commissions: simplify and standardize the commission payment structure.* As noted earlier in the "automate commission calculations" best practice, a company's commission structure can be extremely complex and difficult to calculate, and can take a considerable amount of practice to calculate properly. Even if automation of the process is considered too difficult, one can still work with the sales manager to improve the simplicity of calculations. This results in much less review time for the calculations, as well as a more understandable system about which the sales staff will be less likely to make inquiries.

Cost:

Installation time:

- *Filing: create a document archiving and destruction system.* The operations of the accounting department can be significantly slowed if there is either some difficulty with finding documents or if there are so many stored in the department that it is difficult to rapidly locate the correct items amid the proliferation of paper. As noted in Chapter 33, the accounting department can set up and follow a detailed set of policies and procedures that are designed to codify and streamline the storage of documents. Such a system can also ensure that stored documents are tagged with destruction dates, per a standard document retention policy, so that they can be removed from storage on the predetermined dates, thereby creating more room for the accounting department.

Cost:

Installation time:

- *Filing: install a document imaging system.* The problems that a company experiences with missing documents, excessive amounts of space devoted to document storage, and attendant filing costs can largely be eliminated by installing a document imaging system. This involves digitizing documents through a scanner and storing them in a high-capacity storage device on a computer network, so that employees can call up images of the documents online. This eliminates the risk of lost documents and vastly reduces the amount of required document storage space. However, there may still be a need for off-site storage of some documents if there is a legal requirement for their retention. Also, this system can be very expensive, especially if employees requiring access to it do not already have computer terminals for access to the image database and must be so equipped.

Cost:

Installation time:

- *Filing: stop attaching payment information to checks.* The review of payment information associated with checks by an authorized check signer is considered a key control over the proper disbursement of funds. However, many check signers sign checks with no review at all, considering this step to be a nuisance. If so, an alternative that streamlines the check creation process is to require approval of expenditures earlier in the process, thereby eliminating the need for a check signer (see the previous best practice related to the use of a signature stamp). If there is no check signer, then there is no need to attach related paperwork to checks. An alternative is to have check signers request additional paperwork for only those checks that they wish to inquire more closely about, which relieves the accounts payable staff of the chore of attaching paperwork to the vast majority of all checks.

Cost:

Installation time:

- *Filing: stop storing computer reports.* It is common practice to store paper copies of all computer reports, even when the information is still available either in the computer system or on archiving tapes. One can greatly reduce the amount of required document storage space by only printing out reports for archiving purposes when the related computer files are about to be deleted. Also, there should be a standardized list of reports whose paper copies must be archived—by doing so, a number of unnecessary reports will be kept out of the archives. To make this best practice work properly, there must be sufficient control over the deletion of computer files to ensure that information is not deleted before related reports that are required for archiving have been printed.

Cost:

Installation time:

- *Filing: store records for more time periods in the computer system.* The typical packaged accounting computer system allows for the online storage of information for the current and immediately preceding years. The detailed information pertaining to all years prior to these dates will be eliminated, which means that this information must be converted to a paper format and archived. To avoid the associated cost of storing these files, some accounting packages are now offering the option to store records for more accounting periods online. Though there can be a considerable additional storage cost associated with this activity, plus a slower computer access speed, this can greatly reduce the need to store archived paper documents. An additional benefit is that accounting reports can be created that will automatically generate comparison reports from many years of online data, which eliminates the need to do so manually with information gleaned from paper documents.

Cost:

Installation time:

- *Financial statements: automate recurring journal entries.* Some journal entries that are created each month as part of the financial statement production process are unlikely to change from month to month. For example, a standard amortization or depreciation expense will not change from period to period unless the underlying amount of assets is altered. Rather than manually reentering these journal entries in each accounting period, one can use a common feature in most accounting software packages that provides for the repetitive automatic creation of selected journal entries for as far into the future as specified. This reduces the labor associated with the closing process, and also ensures that recurring entries will not accidentally be skipped.

Cost:

Installation time:

- *Financial statements: conduct an online bank reconciliation.* Some of the larger national and superregional banks have created either dial-up or Internet access to detailed bank account information for their customers. This is a considerable benefit from the perspective of completing the monthly bank reconciliation, since the accounting staff can now review the bank's detailed records as frequently as each day and conduct an ongoing bank reconciliation. This will not only ensure that company records exactly match bank records at all times, but also eliminates the need to wait for the formal bank statement to be mailed to the company at the end of the month before the closing process is completed, thereby speeding up the production of accurate financial statements.

Cost:

Installation time:

- *Financial statements: create a closing itinerary.* The production of financial statements in an orderly manner requires a tightly scheduled process that interlinks the activities of a number of people. It is very difficult to manage this process without a formal document that itemizes each step in the process, who is responsible for each step, and when each step should be completed. The steps required for the closing process are described in Chapter 29. One should also regularly revise the closing itinerary to reflect ongoing changes in the closing process that are improving its speed and accuracy.

Cost:

Installation time:

- *Financial statements: reduce the number of accruals.* An accounting staff that is excessively focused on achieving perfect accuracy in its financial statements can create a large number of accruals. However, accruals can take a great deal of research to prepare, and interfere with the timely closing of the accounting records. It is better to ignore those smaller accruals that will have only a minimal impact on the financial statements, and concentrate on completing a smaller number of key accruals, thereby improving the overall speed of closing.

Cost:

Installation time:

- *Financial statements: reduce the number of variances investigated.* Whenever a preliminary version of the financial statements is completed, there will be a large number of possible variances from the budget or historical records that the accounting staff could investigate before closing the accounting books. Such investigation takes a great deal of time, so pursuing all possible variance analyses will interfere with the timely closing of the books. To avoid this trouble, the accounting manager should create a rule that forbids all variance analysis if variances fall below a standard dollar or percentage amount. If there still appears to be reason for further review of smaller variances, this can be done *after* the financial statements have been produced, with any resulting changes being recorded in the next accounting period.

Cost:

Installation time:

- *Financial statements: use standardized journal entries.* The majority of journal entries that are made each month are similar in format to those made in previous months; they involve the same account numbers, and may even use the same debits and credits, though the dollar figures may change. Recreating these entries every month requires time, and one runs the risk of making an error. To avoid these problems, one can create either automated or paper-based standard journal entry forms that are cross-referenced in the closing checklist. By doing so, the accounting staff can verify that all required journal entries have been completed, and that the same journal entry format is used during every closing process.

Cost:

Installation time:

- *General ledger: copy the chart of accounts for all subsidiaries.* The consolidation of accounting results for all corporate subsidiaries can be quite a chore if each one uses a different chart of accounts. A mapping table is needed to convert each subsidiary's results into the format used by the corporate parent. Though the mapping table can be incorporated into a reasonably advanced computerized general ledger, it is much simpler to require all subsidiaries to use the same chart of accounts. However, this best practice requires a considerable amount of time to implement, since all subsidiaries must have input into the account structure used; just because the corporate parent prefers to use a particular format does not mean that the businesses it owns can easily dovetail the results of their operations into the same format.

Cost:

Installation time:

- *General ledger: eliminate small-balance accounts.* Over time, there is a tendency to add accounts to the general ledger in order to track special types of expenses. However, many of these expenses are so small in amount that the resulting information does not justify the added cost of tracking the additional account. Consequently, it is best to periodically review the amount of funds being stored in all accounts, and eliminate those that are too small.

Cost:

Installation time:

- *General ledger: reduce the number of line items in the chart of accounts.* As noted in the preceding best practice, one can regularly eliminate accounts that experience excessively small amounts of activity. This process can be taken a step further by merging larger accounts together if there is no good reason for separating the information contained within the accounts. For example, there may be a dozen different types of work-in-process inventory that are recorded in different accounts, but the separated information is not used by anyone. Consequently, a general ongoing best practice is to continually examine the chart of accounts with the objective of shrinking it down to only those accounts that are necessary for significant reporting purposes.

Cost:

Installation time:

- *General ledger: store operating data in the general ledger.* When financial statements are produced, they frequently contain operating data, such as headcount, sales backlog dollars, and production capacity. To ensure that this information is reliably stored and readily accessible, extra fields can be created in many general ledger software packages that allow for the storage of alphanumeric information. One can then store operating data in these fields. This is an inexpensive form of data warehouse.

Cost:

Installation time:

- *Invoicing: delivery person creates the invoice.* Invoices sent to customers may require subsequent correction with credits if the customer disagrees with the quantity delivered or rejects some items based on quality issues. Since it takes a great deal of time for the accounting staff to complete these corrections, a better approach is to have the delivery person create an invoice at the point of delivery that contains the quantities to which the customer has already agreed. This eliminates the need for subsequent adjustments. However, this best practice requires a company to have its own employees make deliveries, and also calls for a portable computer and printer for the use of each delivery person. There can also be control problems, since the delivery person may collude with the recipient to bill for a smaller quantity than is actually delivered.

Cost:

Installation time:

- *Invoicing: issue electronic data interchange invoices.* Sending a paper invoice through the mail introduces a time lag before it reaches the recipient. In addition, it may be lost in the mail or misrouted once it arrives at the target company, or some data on it may be incorrectly keyed into the customer's accounts payable system. To avoid all of these problems, one can issue invoices by EDI, which involves filling out a standardized transaction form and e-mailing it either directly to the customer or to a third party organization that maintains an electronic mailbox on behalf of the customer. This approach ensures that invoices will reach customers at once, and can be verified by the return transmission of an acknowledgment of receipt. This method works best when EDI transmission software is directly linked to the billing system so that invoices will be issued automatically.

Cost:

Installation time:

- *Invoicing: issue single-period invoices.* When a company sells products at very low prices, such as nuts and bolts, the cost of the invoice to the customer may be more than the cost of the products. In these instances, it makes more sense to only issue a single invoice at the end of each month, rather than a series of small invoices. Though this saves on invoicing costs, it will shift cash flows from accounts receivable farther into the future, due to the delay in billings. To avoid this problem, one should also look into shortening the payment terms listed on the invoices.

Cost:

Installation time:

- *Invoicing: reduce the number of invoice parts printed.* When invoices are printed, there may be several copies that go to the customer, another that is filed alphabetically, another that is filed numerically, and yet another that is sent to the collections staff. This requires an expensive multipart form, as well as greater filing costs and a virtual blizzard of paperwork within the accounting department. It is better to reduce the number of invoice parts to the absolute minimum required. This may include sending just one invoice copy to the customer, and retaining one other copy for internal reference purposes.

Cost:

Installation time:

- *Management: create a policies and procedures manual.* Though a highly experienced accounting staff may know its tasks by heart and require no written manual, this is not the case when new employees are added to the department or tasks are swapped within the existing staff. When this happens, there is no documentation available that can be used as a basis for training, resulting in slow improvements in knowledge and lots of mistakes in the interim. A policies and procedures manual also improves the level of transactional consistency between the accounting operations of multiple subsidiaries, since their procedures would otherwise tend to diverge over time. It is also possible to issue the manual over the company intranet, which greatly reduces the cost of distribution and the frequency of updates.

Cost:

Installation time:

- *Management: create a staff training schedule.* When new employees are hired into the accounting department, they are typically given enough training to perform their jobs and nothing more. Instead, a training schedule should be tailored to the needs of each employee, so that each is cross-trained in the tasks of other employees, and also learns about process improvement to constantly enhance the transactions for which they are already responsible. This does not mean that all employees require extensive funding to take college courses, but rather that a company develop a mix of seminars, readings, and outside courses that will meet its own particular training needs.

Cost:

Installation time:

- *Management: issue a monthly schedule of activities.* The accounting staff is driven by a specific schedule of activities to an extent greater than that of any other department—it must pay taxes on certain dates, process payroll on other dates, issue financial statements on still other dates, and so on. It is a rare case when all of these dates can be memorized, and so some items will occasionally not be completed on time. To avoid this situation, there should be a standard calendar of activities that is updated at the end of each month and issued to the entire accounting staff, with the due dates of each recipient highlighted on it. This requires constant updating as requirements change.

Cost:

Installation time:

- *Management: measure key departmental performance items.* The accounting manager does not have any idea whether the performance of the accounting department is improving or degrading over time unless there is a set of measurements that can be used to create a trend line of performance. This may involve meeting due dates .earlier, such as issuing financial statements in two days instead of three, or creating fewer transactional errors. The measurement list should be relatively short, so that attention can be focused on just those few issues that are most crucial to departmental performance. Other measures can be added over time, as original measurement targets are met or exceeded. This can also be a useful tool for setting up performance-based pay changes for employees.

Cost:

Installation time:

- *Management: outsource selected functions.* Some accounting functions are of such a technical nature, or are so prone to error, that it may be easier to let an experienced supplier handle them instead. A commonly outsourced function is payroll, which can be shifted to a supplier that will not only calculate payroll and issue checks, but also issue management reports related to payroll, as well as pay various governing authorities all associated payroll taxes. Other functions that can be outsourced include collections, accounts payable, the production of financial statements, and local, state, and federal taxes. The downside to these services is that they cost more than they would if they were handled internally, and they require some oversight by the accounting manager to ensure that they are handled properly.

Cost:

Installation time:

- *Management: review process flows.* Most processes are altered over time as variations occur in the way a company does business. The result is a patchwork of inefficient steps that increase both the time and cost of doing business. This can be avoided by flowcharting the process behind each accounting transaction and then reviewing it over time to see if it can be streamlined. Though this requires some skill in examining process flows, the result can be significant reductions in the cost of transaction processing.

Cost:

Installation time:

- *Payroll: automate vacation accruals.* Accruing and tracking vacation time for employees can be full of errors, for each employee may have been awarded a different vacation period, become employed at a different date during the year, or have some vacation be carried forward from the previous year. To avoid these problems, some payroll outsourcing companies and most high-end payroll software packages contain features that allow one to set up standard vacation accruals for each employee. They can factor in vacation carryforwards as well as individual employee start dates. The only trouble with this best practice is that a company must still manually accumulate and deduct vacation time taken, so that employees can see their net vacation time available. This information will typically be added to their pay stubs.

Cost:

Installation time:

- *Payroll: collect time worked data through an automated time clock.* The collection of hours worked by hourly employees for the purposes of paying them and tracking hours charged to specific jobs is among the most time-consuming and error-filled transactions in the accounting profession. These problems are caused by the manual timecard entries that must be interpreted by payroll clerks into hours worked for each employee—frequently involving missing, false, or unreadable entries. To avoid these problems, a company can invest in electronic time clocks. Under this system, employees are issued bar-coded or magnetic stripe cards, which they slide through a slot on the clock when they are clocking in or out. This action triggers a time entry that is sent to a central payroll computer, where the time entries are stored. Missing scans are noted on management reports, so that they can be fixed before the payroll processing date. Using this approach, there is only a minimal need for data correction, thereby eliminating much of the work by payroll clerks. However, these clocks can cost $2,000 each, and so can only be justified if there are currently many payroll errors or a large staff of payroll clerks that can be eliminated.

Cost: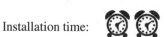

Installation time:

- *Payroll: eliminate deductions from paychecks for employee purchases.* Employees sometimes buy products for themselves through the company's purchasing department in order to take advantage of the lower prices offered to the company. When this happens, they may ask that the cost of the purchased items be gradually deducted from their paychecks. This means that the accounting staff must determine the amount of periodic deductions, as well as when the deductions must stop—all of which takes up valuable accounting time. It is better to create a policy that no employee purchases will be allowed (or at least that employees must pay for all purchases themselves, without deductions), thereby keeping extra deduction-related work away from the payroll staff.

Cost:

Installation time:

- *Payroll: minimize payroll deductions.* A company can offer a large number of benefits to its employees, many of which require some sort of deduction from payroll. For example, a company can set up deductions for employee medical, dental, life, and supplemental life insurance, as well as cafeteria plan deductions for medical insurance or child care payments, as well as 401(k) deductions and 401(k) loan deductions. If there are many employees and many deduction types, the payroll staff can be snowed under at payroll processing time by the volume of changes continually occurring in this area. Also, whenever there is a change in the underlying cost of insurance provided to the company, the company commonly passes along some portion of these costs to the employees, resulting in a massive updating of deductions for all employees who take that particular type of insurance. This not only takes time away from other, more value-added accounting tasks, but also is subject to error, so that adjustments must later be made to correct the errors, which requires even more staff time.

  There are several ways to address this problem. One is to eliminate the employee-paid portion of some types of insurance. For example, if the cost to the company for monthly dental insurance is $20 per employee and the related deduction is only $2 per person, management can elect to pay for the entire cost, rather than burden the accounting staff with the tracking of this trivial sum. Another alternative is to eliminate certain types of benefits, such as supplemental life insurance or 401(k) loans, in order to eliminate the related deductions. Yet another alternative is to create a policy that limits employee changes to any benefit plans so that they can only make a small number of changes per year. This eliminates the continual changing of deduction amounts in favor of just a few large bursts of activity at prescheduled times during the year. A very good alternative is to create a benefit package for all employees that requires a single deduction of the same amount for everyone, or for a group (such as one deduction for single employees and another for employees with families); employees can then pick and choose the exact amount of each type of benefit they want within the boundaries of each benefit package, without altering the amount of the underlying deduction. This last alternative has the unique advantage of consolidating all deductions into a single item, which is much simpler to administer. Any of these approaches to the problem will reduce the number or timing of deduction changes, thereby reducing the workload of the payroll staff.

Cost:

Installation time:

- *Payroll: pay employees with direct deposit.* There is no significant difference in efficiencies when a company pays its employees with a check or direct deposit, since the company must still deliver to each employee either a paper check or a deposit advice. Direct deposit may even be slightly more expensive, since there may be a small ACH transfer fee associated with each deposit. Nonetheless, the use of direct deposit is generally welcomed by employees, who appreciate not having to physically travel to a bank to deposit payments. It is particularly useful for employees who travel, since they may not be in a position to cash their checks until well after pay dates, and no longer have to worry about cash shortages when direct deposits are used.

Cost:

Installation time:

- *Payroll: post forms on an intranet site.* Employees frequently come to the accounting department to ask for any of the variety of forms required for changes to their payroll status, such as the IRS's W-4 form, address changes, cafeteria plan sign-up or change forms, and so on. These constant interruptions interfere with the orderly flow of accounting work, especially when the department runs out of a form and must scramble to replenish its supplies. This problem is neatly solved by converting all forms to Adobe Acrobat's PDF format and posting them on a company intranet site for downloading by all employees. Using this approach, no one ever has to approach the accounting staff for the latest copy of a form. Also, employees can download the required form from anywhere, rather than having to wait until they are near the accounting location to physically pick one up. Further, the accounting staff can regularly update the PDF forms on the intranet site, so there is no risk of someone using an old and outmoded form.

Cost:

Installation time:

- *Payroll: reduce the number of payrolls per year.* Every time that a payroll cycle is processed, the payroll staff must accumulate all hours worked, deduction information, and other payroll data, summarize it into either an in-house payroll system or send it to a supplier, and then issue checks to employees. This effort can be reduced by shrinking the number of payrolls that are processed each year. The best alternatives are to process either 24 or 26 payrolls per year. Twenty-six payrolls tend to work better if there are a number of hourly employees, since payrolls will correspond to their weekly timekeeping system. If there are mostly salaried employees, then 24 payrolls can be used, since processing dates will correspond to the end of each month, making it unnecessary to create a salary accrual for hours worked but not paid at the end of each month.

Cost:

Installation time:

- *Payroll: restrict prepayments.* Some employees who travel will request an advance on their paychecks prior to taking trips, so that they will have enough funds to pay for travel costs. This requires that the accounting staff track the amount of all advances, as well as their later deduction from expense reports. It is a system that is highly subject to abuse, since employee advances may never be deducted from expense reports, or employees may leave without reimbursing the company. The same problem arises when employees request advances on their paychecks for personal reasons. To avoid these problems, a policy can be created that forbids the use of prepayments. Instead, company purchasing cards can be issued to employees who travel, so that all travel charges are paid directly by the company. If employees want advances on their pay, the company can direct them to a local finance company.

Cost:

Installation time:

27.3   BEST PRACTICES PROCESS FLOWCHARTS

This section contains seven process flowcharts for some of the more common accounting-related processes, each one incorporating a large number of best practices. The reader can use each process flowchart as the source document for significant system improvements. The following discussions include key aspects of each of the process flows.

The first best practice process flowchart addresses accounts payable, and is shown in Exhibit 27.1. In the flowchart, the initiation of a purchase is typically founded on the issuance of a purchase order, without which any deliveries will be rejected by the receiving department. Alternative ordering systems that bypass the need for a purchase order include the use of an online purchasing catalog and procurement cards.

There are several techniques available for entering supplier invoices into the computer system for matching purposes, including electronic data interchange (EDI) entry. Once entered, the computer system determines if there is a completed W-9 form on hand, and requires each supplier to complete one prior to issuing payment. The system also allows for the direct entry of employee expense reports, with built-in error-checking and audit flagging routines to improve the odds of locating improper expense submissions. After all entries are loaded into the computer system, it automatically schedules payments to suppliers and employees, and issues an electronic payment to each one.

There are a number of ways to improve the issuance of credit and subsequent collection of invoices, as shown in Exhibit 27.2. The foundation for improved results in the credit granting area is the consistent use of a credit policy, which is modified for products having unusually high or low margins (loose credit for high-margin items and tighter credit for low-margin items), or for items declared to be obsolete (loose credit). The initial credit risk can also be reduced through the use of credit insurance. The odds of obtaining payment can also be improved through the adoption of a simplified pricing structure that is more understandable to customers. Once the invoice is issued, the credit department can contact customers to explain the company's payment terms. Once an invoice becomes overdue, the collections staff has a large number of collection tools at its disposal. Some are fully automated—the issuance of dunning letters and faxing of overdue invoices are examples. To make the most efficient use of the collection staff's time, the bulk of collection calls should be made to those customers having the largest overdue balances, while a payment deduction investigation system should be used to determine if customers are withholding payment for a valid reason.

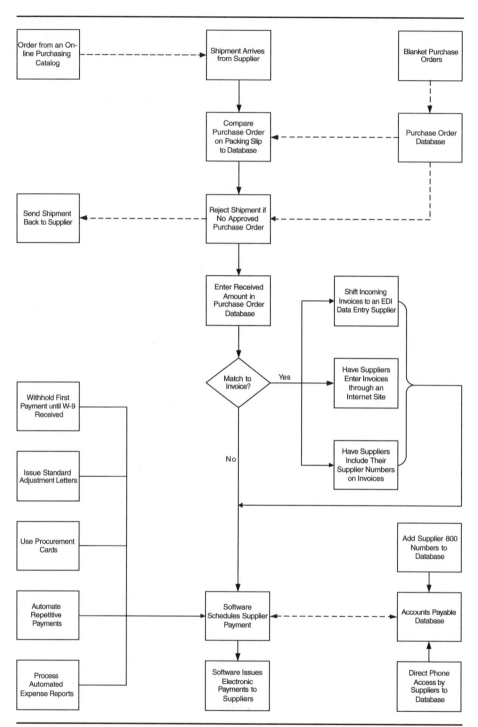

EXHIBIT 27.1   ACCOUNTS PAYABLE PROCESS FLOWCHART

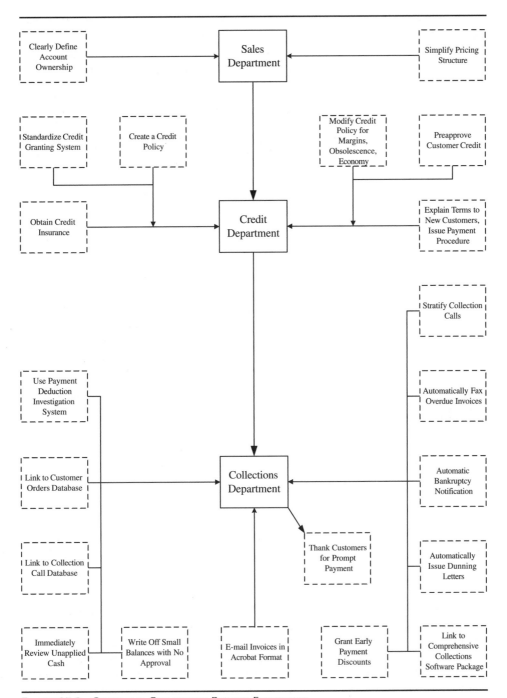

EXHIBIT 27.2 CREDIT AND COLLECTIONS PROCESS FLOWCHART

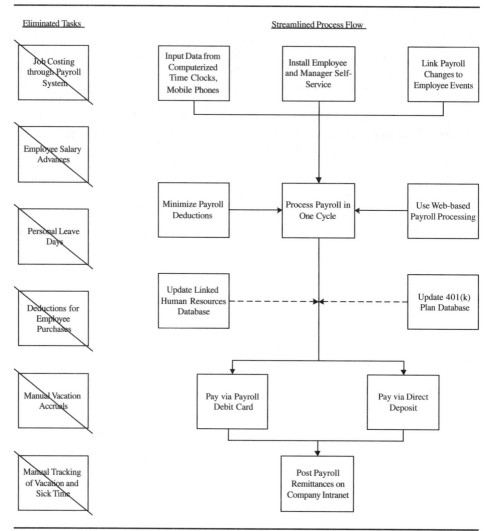

EXHIBIT 27.3   PAYROLL PROCESS FLOWCHART

The payroll flowchart shown in Exhibit 27.3 is notable in that it describes a number of practices that should *not* be done, since they contribute to a reduced level of efficiency within the payroll department. These items are all noted down the left side of the flowchart with a diagonal line through them, and share the characteristic of requiring manual intervention in the payroll process. For example, giving an employee a salary advance requires cutting a manual paycheck, recording it in the payroll software, and then deducting this payment from the next official payroll cycle—all non-value-added activities!

The flowchart also shows that the payroll process is subject to a great deal of automation, through the use of several computerized timekeeping input devices, online self-service for both employees and managers, and electronic payments using debit cards and direct deposit. Thus, payroll is one of the most fruitful areas in which to implement best practice improvements.

27.4   SUMMARY

There are thousands of best practices that a company can use to enhance its accounting operations. The best practices noted here are only some of the more common ones currently in use. The most concentrated source of additional accounting best practices information is the author's series of best practices books, as noted in the introduction to this chapter. Another approach is to attend seminars that deal specifically with this issue. Another source of information is accounting periodicals, which sometimes contain articles about how other companies have implemented improvements to their systems. This source is particularly useful because the articles may include information about how to reach the author, so that additional information can be gleaned about specific best practices. Also, local accounting organizations may sometimes sponsor presentations from members at other companies who have installed system enhancements. Finally, a multidivision company may contain a number of accounting departments, any of which may have unique best practices that would be useful. Thus, one must tap into a number of data resources in order to obtain information about additional best practices

BUDGETING

28.1 INTRODUCTION

Budgeting is one of the most important activities that an accountant can engage in, for it provides the basis for the orderly management of activities within a company. A properly created budget will funnel funding into those activities that a company has determined to be most essential, as defined in its strategic plan. Furthermore, it provides a bridge between strategy and tactics by itemizing the precise tactical events that will be funded, such as the hiring of personnel or acquisition of equipment in a key department. Once the budget has been approved, it also acts as the primary control point over expenditures, since it should be compared to purchase requisitions prior to purchases being made, so that the level of allowed funding can be ascertained. In addition, the results of specific departments can be compared to their budgets, which is an excellent tool for determining the performance of department managers. For all of these reasons, a comprehensive knowledge of the budgeting process is crucial for the accountant.

In this chapter, we will look at the system of budgets and how they are linked together, review a sample budget, cover the key elements of flex budgeting, address the processes required to construct a budget, and finish with coverage of the control systems that can be used if a budget is available.

28.2 THE SYSTEM OF INTERLOCKING BUDGETS

A properly designed budget is a complex web of spreadsheets that account for the activities of virtually all areas within a company. As noted in Exhibit 28.1, the budget begins in two places, with both the revenue budget and research and development budget. The revenue budget contains the revenue figures that the company believes it can achieve for each upcoming reporting period. These estimates come partially from the sales staff, which is responsible for estimates of sales levels for existing products within their current territories. Estimates for the sales of new products that have not yet been released and for existing products in new markets will come from a combination of the sales and marketing staffs, who will use their experience with related product sales to derive estimates. The greatest

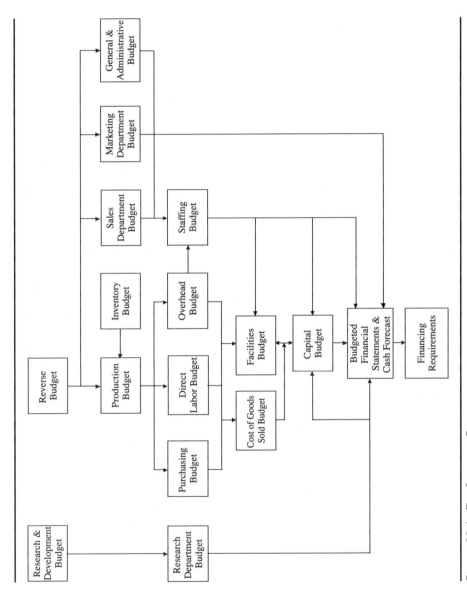

EXHIBIT 28.1 THE SYSTEM OF BUDGETS

335

fallacy in any budget is to impose a revenue budget from the top management level without any input from the sales staff, since this can result in a company-wide budget that is geared toward a sales level that is most unlikely to be reached.

A revenue budget requires prior consideration of a number of issues. For example, a general market share target will drive several other items within the budget, since greater market share may come at the cost of lower unit prices or higher credit costs. Another issue is the compensation strategy for the sales staff, since a shift to higher or lower commissions for specific products or regions will be a strong incentive for the sales staff to alter their selling behavior, resulting in some changes in estimated sales levels. Yet another consideration is which sales territories are to be entered during the budget period—those with high target populations may yield very high sales per hour of sales effort, while the reverse will be true if the remaining untapped regions have smaller target populations. It is also necessary to review the price points that will be offered during the budget period, especially in relation to the pricing strategies that are anticipated from competitors. If there is a strategy to increase market share as well as to raise unit prices, then the budget may fail due to conflicting activities. Another major factor is the terms of sale, which can be extended, along with easy credit, to attract more marginal customers; conversely, they can be retracted in order to reduce credit costs and focus company resources on a few key customers. A final point is that the budget should address any changes in the type of customer to whom sales will be made. If an entirely new type of customer will be added to the range of sales targets during the budget period, then the revenue budget should reflect a gradual ramp-up that will be required for the sales staff to work through the sales cycle of the new customers.

Once all of these factors have been ruminated upon and combined to create a preliminary budget, the sales staff should also compare the budgeted sales level per person to the actual sales level that has been experienced in the recent past to see if the company has the existing capability to make the budgeted sales. If not, the revenue budget should be ramped up to reflect the time it will take to hire and train additional sales staff. The same cross-check can be conducted for the amount of sales budgeted per customer, to see if historical experience validates the sales levels noted in the new budget.

Another budget that initiates other activities within the system of budgets is the research and development budget. This is not related to the sales level at all (as opposed to most other budgets), but instead is a discretionary budget that is based on the company's strategy to derive new or improved products. The decision to fund a certain amount of project-related activity in this area will drive a departmental staffing and capital budget that is, for the most part, completely unrelated to the activity conducted by the rest of the company. However, there can be a feedback loop between this budget and the cash budget, since financing limitations may require management to prune some projects from this area. If so, the management team must work with the research and development manager to determine the correct mix of projects with both short-range and long-range pay-offs that will still be funded. This is as much an art as a science, though the process can be helped along by a capital budgeting evaluation, as described in Chapter 35, Financial Analysis.

The production budget is largely driven by the sales estimates contained within the revenue budget. However, it is also driven by the inventory-level assumptions in the inventory budget. The inventory budget contains estimates by the materials management supervisor regarding the inventory levels that will be required for the upcoming budget period. For example, a new goal may be to reduce the level of finished goods inventory from 10 turns per year to 15. If so, some of the products required by the revenue budget can be bled off from the existing finished goods inventory stock, requiring smaller production require-ments during the budget period. Alternatively, if there is a strong focus on improving the level of customer service, then it may be necessary to keep more finished goods in stock, which will require more production than is strictly called for by the revenue budget. This concept can also be extended to work-in-process (WIP) inventory, where the installation of advanced production planning systems, such as manufacturing resources planning or just-in-time [manufacturing systems], can be used to reduce the level of required inventory. Also, just-in-time purchasing techniques can be used to reduce the amount of raw materi-als inventory that is kept on hand. All of these assumptions should be clearly delineated in the inventory budget, so that the management team is clear about what systemic changes will be required in order to effect altered inventory turnover levels. Also, one should be aware that any advanced production planning system takes a considerable amount of time to install and tune, so it is best if the inventory budget contains a gradual ramp-up to dif-ferent planned levels of inventory.

Given this input from the inventory budget, the production budget is used to derive the unit quantity of required products that must be manufactured in order to meet revenue tar-gets for each budget period. This involves a number of interrelated factors, such as the availability of sufficient capacity for production needs. Of particular concern should be the amount of capacity at the bottleneck operation. Since this tends to be the most expensive capital item, it is important to budget a sufficient quantity of funding to ensure that this operation includes enough equipment to meet the targeted production goals. If the bot-tleneck operation involves skilled labor, rather than equipment, then the human resources staff should be consulted regarding its ability to bring in the necessary personnel in time to improve the bottleneck's capacity in a timely manner.

Another factor that drives the budgeted costs contained within the production budget is the anticipated size of production batches. If the batch size is expected to decrease, then more overhead costs should be budgeted in the production scheduling, materials handling, and machine setup staffing areas. If longer batch sizes are planned, then there may be a pos-sibility of proportionally reducing overhead costs in these areas. This is a key consideration that is frequently overlooked, but which can have an outsized impact on overhead costs. If management attempts to contain overhead costs in this area while still using smaller batch sizes, then it will likely run into larger scrap quantities and quality issues that are caused by rushed batch setups and the allocation of incorrect materials to production jobs.

Step costing is also an important consideration when creating the production budget. Costs will increase in large increments when certain capacity levels are reached. The man-agement team should be fully aware of when these capacity levels will be reached, so that it can plan appropriately for the incurrence of added costs. For example, the addition of a second shift to the production area will call for added costs in the areas of supervisory staff, an increased pay rate, and higher maintenance costs. The inverse of this condition can also occur, where step costs can decline suddenly if capacity levels fall below a specific point.

Production levels may also be affected by any lengthy tooling setups or changeovers to replacement equipment. These changes may halt all production for extended periods, and so must be carefully planned for. This is the responsibility of the industrial engineering staff. The accountant would do well to review the company's history of actual equipment setup times to see if the current engineering estimates are sufficiently lengthy, based on past history.

The expense items included in the production budget should be driven by a set of sub-sidiary budgets, which are the purchasing, direct labor, and overhead budgets. These bud-gets can simply be included in the production budget, but they typically involve such a large proportion of company costs that it is best to lay them out separately in greater detail in separate budgets. Specific comments on these budgets are:

- *Purchasing budget.* The purchasing budget is driven by several factors, first of which is the bill of materials that composes the products that are planned for production during the budget period. These bills must be accurate, or else the purchasing budget can include seriously incorrect information. In addition, there should be a plan for controlling material costs, perhaps through the use of concentrated buying through few suppliers, or perhaps through the use of long-term contracts. If materials are highly subject to market pressures, constitute a large proportion of total product costs, and have a history of sharp price swings, then a best-case and worst-case costing scenario should be added to the budget, so that managers can review the impact of costing issues in this area. If a just-in-time delivery system from suppliers is contemplated, then the purchasing budget should reflect a possible increase in material costs caused by the increased number of deliveries from suppliers. It is also worthwhile to budget for a raw material scrap and obsolescence expense; there should be a history of costs in these areas that can be extrapolated based on projected purchasing volumes.

- *Direct labor budget.* One should not make the mistake of budgeting for direct labor as a fully variable cost. The production volume from day to day tends to be relatively fixed and requires a set number of direct labor personnel on a continuing basis to operate production equipment and manually assemble products. Further, the production manager will realize much greater production efficiencies by holding onto an experienced production staff, rather than letting them go as soon as production volumes make small incremental drops. Accordingly, it is better to budget based on reality, which is that direct labor personnel are usually retained, even if there are ongoing fluctuations in the level of production. Thus, direct labor should be shown in the budget as a fixed cost of production, within certain production volume parameters.

  Also, this budget should describe staffing levels by type of direct labor position; this is driven by labor routings, which are documents that describe the exact type and quantity of staffing needed to produce a product. When multiplied by the unit volumes located in the production budget, this results in an expected level of staffing by direct labor position. This information is most useful for the human resources staff, which is responsible for staffing the positions.

  The direct labor budget should also account for any contractually mandated changes in hourly rates, which may be itemized in a union agreement. Such an agreement may also have restrictions on layoffs, which should be accounted for in the budget if this will keep labor levels from dropping in proportion budgeted reductions in production levels. Such an agreement may also require that layoffs be conducted in order of seniority, which may force higher-paid employees into positions that would normally be budgeted for less expensive laborers. Thus, the presence of a union contract can result in a much more complex direct labor budget than would normally be the case.

  The direct labor budget may also contain features related to changes in the efficiency of employees and any resulting changes in pay. For example, one possible pay arrangement is to pay employees based on a piece rate, which directly ties their performance to the level of production achieved. If so, this will probably only apply to portions of the workforce, so the direct labor budget may involve pay rates based on both piece rates and hourly pay. Another issue is that any drastic increases in the budgeted level of direct labor personnel will likely result in some initial declines in labor efficiency, since it takes time for new employees to learn their tasks. If this is the case, the budget should reflect a low level of initial efficiency, with a ramp-up over time to higher levels that will result in greater initial direct labor costs. Finally, efficiency improvements may be rewarded with staff bonuses from time to time; if so, these bonuses should be included in the budget.

- *Overhead budget.* The overhead budget can be a simple one to create if there are no significant changes in production volume from the preceding year, because this involves a large quantity of static costs that will not vary much over time. Included in this category are machine maintenance; utilities; supervisory salaries; wages for the materials management, production scheduling, and quality assurance personnel; facilities maintenance; and depreciation expenses. Under the no-change scenario, the most likely budgetary alterations will be to machinery or facilities maintenance, which is dependent on the condition and level of usage of company property.

  If there is a significant change in the expected level of production volume, or if new production lines are to be added, then one should examine this budget in great detail, for the underlying production volumes may cause a ripple effect that results in wholesale changes to many areas of the overhead budget. Of particular concern is the number of overhead-related personnel who must be either laid off or added when capacity levels reach certain critical points, such as the addition or subtraction of extra work shifts. Costs also tend to rise substantially when a facility is operating at very close to 100% capacity, because maintaining a high level of capacity on an ongoing basis tends to call for an inordinate amount of effort.

The purchasing, direct labor, and overhead budgets can then be summarized into a cost of goods sold budget. This budget should incorporate, as a single line item, the total amount of revenue, so that all manufacturing costs can be deducted from it to yield a gross profit margin on the same document. This budget is referred to constantly during the budget creation process, since it tells management whether its budgeting assumptions are yielding an acceptable gross margin result. Since it is a summary-level budget for the production side of the budgeting process, this is also a good place to itemize any production-related statistics, such as the average hourly cost of direct labor, inventory turnover rates, and the amount of revenue dollars per production person.

Thus far, we have reviewed the series of budgets that descend in turn from the revenue budget through the production budget. However, there are other expenses that are unrelated to production. These are categories in a separate set of budgets. The first is the sales department budget. This includes the expenses that the sales staff must incur in order to achieve the revenue budget, such as travel and entertainment, as well as sales training. Of particular concern in this budget is the amount of budgeted headcount that is required to meet the sales target. It is essential that the actual sales per salesperson from the most recent completed year of operations be compared to the same calculation in the budget to ensure that there is a sufficiently large budget available for an adequate number of sales personnel. This is a common problem, for companies will make the false assumption that the existing sales staff can make heroic efforts to wildly exceed its previous-year sales efforts. Furthermore, the budget must account for a sufficient time period in which new sales personnel can be trained and form an adequate base of customer contacts to create a meaningful stream of revenue for the company. In some industries, this learning curve may be only a few days, but it can be the better part of a year if considerable technical knowledge is required to make a sale. If the latter situation is the case, it is likely that the procurement and retention of qualified sales staff is the key element of success for a company, which makes the sales department budget one of the most important elements of the entire budget.

The marketing budget is also closely tied to the revenue budget, for it contains all of the funding required to roll out new products, merchandise them properly, advertise for them, test new products, and so on. A key issue here is to ensure that the marketing budget is fully funded to support any increases in sales noted in the revenue budget. It may be necessary to increase this budget by a disproportionate amount if one is trying to create a new brand, issue a new product, or distribute an existing product in a new market. These costs can easily exceed any associated revenues for some time. A common budgeting problem is failing to provide sufficient funding in these instances, leading to a significant drop in expected revenues.

Another nonproduction budget that is integral to the success of the corporation is the general and administrative budget. This contains the cost of the corporate management staff, plus all accounting, finance, and human resources personnel. Since this is a cost center, the general inclination is to reduce these costs to the bare minimum. However, in order to do so, there must be a significant investment in technology to achieve reductions in the manual labor usually required to process transactions; thus, there must be some provision in the capital budget for this area.

There is a feedback loop between the staffing and direct labor budgets and the general and administrative budget, because the human resources department must staff itself based on the amount of hiring or layoffs that are anticipated elsewhere in the company. Similarly, a major change in the revenue volume will alter the budget for the accounting department, since many of the activities in this area are driven by the volume of sales transactions. Furthermore, a major increase in the capital budget, especially for items requiring prolonged construction activities, will require an investment in additional cost accounting personnel, who will track these expenditures. Thus, the general and administrative budget generally requires a number of iterations in response to changes in many other parts of the budget.

Though salaries and wages should be listed in each of the departmental budgets, it is useful to list the total headcount for each position through all budget periods in a separate staffing budget. This allows the human resources staff to tell when specific positions must be filled so that they can time their recruiting efforts most appropriately. This budget also provides good information for the person responsible for the facilities budget, since he or she can use it to determine the timing and amount of square footage requirements for office space. Rather than being a standalone budget, the staffing budget tends to be one whose formulas are closely intertwined with those of all other departmental budgets, so that a change in headcount information on this budget will automatically translate into a change in the salaries expense on other budgets. It is also a good place to store the average pay rates, overtime percentages, and average benefit costs for all positions. By centralizing this cost information, the human resources staff can more easily update budget information. Since salary-related costs tend to constitute the highest proportion of costs in a company (excluding materials costs), this tends to be a heavily used budget.

The facilities budget is based on the level of activity that is estimated in many of the budgets just described. For this reason, it is one of the last budgets to be completed. This budget is closely linked to the capital budget, since expenditures for additional facilities will require more maintenance expenses in the facilities budget. This budget typically contains expense line items for building insurance, maintenance, repairs, janitorial services, utilities, and the salaries of the maintenance personnel employed in this function. It is crucial to estimate the need for any upcoming major repairs to facilities when constructing this budget, since these can greatly amplify the total budgeted expense.

Another budget that includes input from virtually all areas of a company is the capital budget. This should comprise either a summary listing of all main fixed asset categories for which purchases are anticipated or else a detailed listing of the same information; the latter case is only recommended if there are comparatively few items to be purchased. The capital budget is of great importance to the calculation of corporate financing requirements, since it can involve the expenditure of sums far beyond those that are normally encountered through daily cash flows. The contents of the capital budget should be carefully examined to determine if it has an impact on a company's bottleneck operation. All too often, expenditures are made that make other operations more efficient, but that do not increase its ability to produce more product by increasing the capacity of the bottleneck operation. For more information about this topic, please refer to the throughput accounting chapter in Bragg, *Cost Accounting* (John Wiley & Sons, 2001).It is also necessary to ensure that capital items are scheduled for procurement sufficiently far in advance of related projects that they will be fully installed and operational before the scheduled first activity date of the project. For example, a budget should not itemize revenue from a printing press for the same month in which the press is scheduled to be purchased, for it may take months to set up the press. A final item is that capital purchases may be tied to the pet projects of senior managers, rather than to the strategic or tactical goals of the company. Consequently, it may be useful to review all capital items in the budget to ensure that they are all needed in order to meet these goals.

The end result of all budgets just described is a set of financial statements that reflect the impact on the company of the upcoming budget. At a minimum, these statements should include the income statement and cash flow statement, since these are the best evidence of fiscal health during the budget period. The balance sheet is less necessary, since the key factors upon which it reports are related to cash, and that information is already contained within the cash flow statement. These reports should be directly linked to all the other budgets, so that any changes to the budgets will immediately appear in the financial statements. The management team will closely examine these statements and make numerous adjustments to the budgets in order to arrive at a satisfactory financial result.

The budget-linked financial statements are also a good place to store related operational and financial ratios, so that the management team can review this information and revise the budgets in order to alter the ratios to match benchmarking or industry standards that may have been set as goals. Typical measurements in this area can include revenue and income per person, inventory turnover ratios, and gross margin percentages. This type of information is also useful for lenders, who may have required minimum financial performance results as part of loan agreements, such as a minimum current ratio or debt-to-equity ratio.

The cash forecast is of exceptional importance, for it tells company managers whether the proposed budget model will be feasible. If cash projects result in major cash needs that cannot be met by any possible financing, then the model must be changed. The assumptions that go into the cash forecast should be based on strictly historical fact, rather than the wishes of managers. This stricture is particularly important in the case of cash receipts from accounts receivable. If the assumptions are changed in the model to reflect an advanced rate of cash receipts that exceeds anything that the company has heretofore experienced, then it is very unlikely that it will be achieved during the budget period. Instead, it is better to use proven collection periods as assumptions and alter other parts of the budget to ensure that cash flows remain positive.

The cash forecast is a particularly good area in which to spot the impact of changes in credit policy. For example, if a company wishes to expand its share of the market by allowing easy credit to marginal customers, then it should lengthen the assumed collection period in the cash forecast to see if there is a significant downgrading of the resulting cash flows.

The other key factor in the cash forecast is the use of delays in budgeted accounts payable payments. It is common for managers to budget for extended payment terms in order to fund other cash flow needs, but several problems can result from this policy. One is the possible loss of key suppliers who will not tolerate late payments. Another is the risk of being charged interest on late payments to suppliers. A third problem is that suppliers may relegate a company to a lower level on their lists of shipment priorities, since they are being paid late. Finally, suppliers may simply raise their prices in order to absorb the cost of the late payments. Consequently, the late payment strategy must be followed with great care, only using it on those suppliers who do not appear to notice, and otherwise only doing it after prior negotiation with targeted suppliers to make the changed terms part of the standard buying agreement.

The last document in the system of budgets is the discussion of financing alternatives. This is not strictly a budget, though it will contain a single line item, derived from the cash forecast, which itemizes funding needs during each period itemized in the budget. In all other respects, it is simply a discussion of financing alternatives, which can be quite varied. This may involve a mix of debt, supplier financing, preferred stock, common stock, or some other, more innovative approach. The document should contain a discussion of the cost of each form of financing, the ability of the company to obtain it, and when it can be obtained. Managers may find that there are so few financing alternatives available, or that the cost of financing is so high, that the entire budget must be restructured in order to avoid the negative cash flow that calls for the financing. There may also be a need for feedback from this document back into the budgeted financial statements in order to account for the cost of obtaining the funding, as well as any related interest costs.

In the next section, we will review an example of the budgets that have just been described, to see how they are formatted and linked together to result in a cohesive set of budgets that can be used to conduct a business's future oper ations.

28.3   A SAMPLE BUDGET

In this section, we will review several variations on how a budget can be constructed, using a number of examples. The first budget covered is the revenue budget, which is shown in Exhibit 28.2. The exhibit uses quarterly revenue figures for a budget year rather than monthly figures in order to conserve space. It contains revenue estimates for three different product lines that are designated as Alpha, Beta, and Charlie.

The Alpha product line uses a budgeting format that identifies the specific quantities that are expected to be sold in each quarter, as well as the average price per unit sold. This format is most useful when there are not so many products that such a detailed delineation would create an excessively lengthy budget. It is a very useful format, for the sales staff can go into the budget model and alter unit volumes and prices quite easily. An alternative format is to only reveal this level of detail for the most important products, and to lump the revenue from other products into a single line item, as is the case for the Beta product line.

The most common budgeting format is used for the Beta product line, where we avoid the use of detailed unit volumes and prices in favor of a single lump-sum revenue total for each reporting period. This format is used when there are multiple products within each

REVENUE BUDGET
FOR THE FISCAL YEAR ENDED XX/XX/10

	Quarter 1	Quarter 2	Quarter 3	Quarter 4	Totals
Product Line Alpha:					
Unit price	$ 15.00	$ 14.85	$ 14.80	$ 14.75	—
Unit volume	14,000	21,000	25,000	31,000	91,000
Revenue subtotal	$ 210,000	$ 311,850	$ 370,000	$ 457,250	$1,349,100
Product Line Beta:					
Revenue subtotal	$1,048,000	$1,057,000	$1,061,000	$1,053,000	$4,219,000
Product Line Charlie:					
Region 1	$ 123,000	$ 95,000	$ 82,000	$ 70,000	$ 370,000
Region 2	$ 80,000	$ 89,000	$ 95,000	$ 101,000	$ 365,000
Region 3	$ 95,000	$ 95,000	$ 65,000	$ 16,000	$ 271,000
Region 4	$ 265,000	$ 265,000	$ 320,000	$ 375,000	$1,225,000
Revenue subtotal	$ 563,000	$ 544,000	$ 562,000	$ 562,000	$2,231,000
Revenue grand total	$1,821,000	$1,912,850	$1,993,000	$2,072,250	$7,799,100
Quarterly revenue proportion	23%	24.5%	25.6%	26.6%	100.0%
Statistics:					
Product line proportion:					
Alpha	11.5%	16.3%	18.6%	22.1%	17.3%
Beta	57.6%	55.3%	53.2%	50.8%	54.1%
Charlie	30.9%	28.4%	28.2%	27.1%	28.6%
Product line total	100.0%	100.0%	100.0%	100.0%	100.0%

EXHIBIT 28.2   THE REVENUE BUDGET

product line, making it cumbersome to create a detailed list of individual products. However, this format is the least informative and gives no easy way to update the supporting information.

Yet another budgeting format is shown for the Charlie product line, where projected sales are grouped by region. This format is most useful when there are many sales personnel, each of whom has been assigned a specific territory in which to operate. This budget can then be used to judge the ongoing performance of each salesperson.

These revenue reporting formats can also be combined, so that the product line detail for the Alpha product can be used as underlying detail for the sales regions used for the Charlie product line—though this will result in a very lengthy budget document.

There is also a statistics section at the bottom of the revenue budget that itemizes the proportion of total sales that occurs in each quarter, plus the proportion of product line sales within each quarter. Though it is not necessary to use these exact measurements, it is useful to include some type of measure that informs the reader of any variations in sales from period to period.

Both the production and inventory budgets are shown in Exhibit 28.3. The inventory budget is itemized at the top of the exhibit, where we itemize the amount of planned inventory turnover in all three inventory categories. There is a considerable ramp-up in work-in-process inventory turnover, indicating the planned installation of a manufacturing planning system of some kind that will control the flow of materials through the facility.

The production budget for just the Alpha product line is shown directly below the inventory goals. This budget is not concerned with the cost of production, but rather with the number of units that will be produced. In this instance, we begin with an on-hand

		PRODUCTION AND INVENTORY BUDGET FOR THE FISCAL YEAR ENDED XX/XX/10			
	Quarter 1	Quarter 2	Quarter 3	Quarter 4	Totals
Inventory Turnover Goals:					
Raw Materials Turnover	4.0	4.5	5.0	5.5	4.8
W-I-P Turnover	12.0	15.0	18.0	21.0	16.5
Finished Goods Turnover	6.0	6.0	9.0	9.0	7.5
Product Line Alpha Production:					
Beginning Inventory Units	15,000	21,000	20,000	15,000	—
Unit Sales Budget	14,000	21,000	25,000	31,000	91,000
Planned Production	20,000	20,000	20,000	27,375	87,375
Ending Inventory Units	21,000	20,000	15,000	11,375←	
Bottleneck Unit Capacity	20,000	20,000	20,000	40,000	
Bottleneck Utilization	100%	100%	100%	68%	
Planned Finished Goods Turnover	15,167	15,167	11,375	11,375←	

EXHIBIT 28.3   THE PRODUCTION AND INVENTORY BUDGET

inventory of 15,000 units, and try to keep enough units on hand through the remainder of the budget year to meet both the finished goods inventory goal at the top of the exhibit and the number of required units to be sold, which is referenced from the revenue budget. The main problem is that the maximum capacity of the bottleneck operation is 20,000 units per quarter. In order to meet the revenue target, we must run that operation at full bore through the first three quarters, irrespective of the inventory turnover target. This is especially important because the budget indicates a jump in bottleneck capacity in the fourth quarter from 20,000 to 40,000 units—this will occur when the bottleneck operation is stopped for a short time while additional equipment is added to it. During this stoppage, there must be enough excess inventory on hand to cover any sales that will arise. Consequently, production is planned for 20,000 units per quarter for the first three quarters, followed by a more precisely derived figure in the fourth quarter that will result in inventory turns of 9.0 at the end of the year, exactly as planned.

The production budget can be enhanced with the incorporation of planned machine downtime for maintenance, as well as for the planned loss of production units to scrap. It is also useful to plan for the capacity needs of nonbottleneck work centers, since these areas will require varying levels of staffing, depending upon the number of production shifts needed.

The purchasing budget is shown in Exhibit 28.4. It contains several different formats for planning budgeted purchases for the Alpha product line. The first option summarizes the planned production for each quarter; this information is brought forward from the production budget. We then multiply this by the standard unit cost of materials to arrive at the total amount of purchases that must be made in order to adequately support sales. The second option identifies the specific cost of each component of the product, so that management can see where cost increases are expected to occur. Though this version provides more information, it occupies a great deal of space on the budget if there are many components in each product, or many products. A third option shown at the bottom of the exhibit summarizes all purchases by commodity type. This format is most useful for the company's buyers, who usually specialize in certain commodity types.

The purchasing budget can be enhanced by adding a scrap factor for budgeted production, which will result in slightly higher quantities to buy, thereby leaving less chance of

PURCHASING BUDGET
FOR THE FISCAL YEAR ENDED XX/XX/10

	Quarter 1	Quarter 2	Quarter 3	Quarter 4	Totals
Inventory Turnover Goals:					
Raw Materials Turnover	4.0	4.5	5.0	5.5	4.8
Product Line Alpha Purchasing (Option 1):					
Planned Production	20,000	20,000	20,000	27,375	
Standard Material Cost/Unit	$ 5.42	$ 5.42	$ 5.67	$ 5.67	
Total Material Cost	$108,400	$108,400	$113,400	$155,216	$485,416
Product Line Alpha Purchasing (Option 2):					
Planned Production	20,000	20,000	20,000	27,375	
Molded Part	$ 4.62	$ 4.62	$ 4.85	$ 4.85	
Labels	$ 0.42	$ 0.42	$ 0.42	$ 0.42	
Fittings & Fasteners	$ 0.38	$ 0.38	$ 0.40	$ 0.40	
Total Cost of Components	$ 5.42	$ 5.42	$ 5.67	$ 5.67	
Product Line Alpha Purchasing (Option 3):					
Plastic Commodities					
Molded Part Units	20,000	20,000	20,000	27,375	
Molded Part Cost	$ 4.62	$ 4.62	$ 4.85	$ 4.85	
Adhesives Commodity					
Labels Units	20,000	20,000	20,000	27,375	
Labels Cost	$ 0.42	$ 0.42	$ 0.42	$ 0.42	
Fasteners Commodity					
Fasteners Units	20,000	20,000	20,000	27,375	
Fasteners Cost	$ 0.38	$ 0.38	$ 0.40	$ 0.40	
Statistics:					
Materials as Percent of Revenue	36%	36%	38%	38%	

EXHIBIT 28.4   THE PURCHASING BUDGET

running out of raw materials. Another upgrade to the exhibit would be to schedule purchases for planned production some time in advance of the actual manufacturing date, so that the purchasing staff will be assured of having the parts on hand when manufacturing begins. A third enhancement is to round off the purchasing volumes for each item into the actual buying volumes that can be obtained on the open market. For example, it may only be possible to buy the required labels in volumes of 100,000 at a time, which would result in a planned purchase at the beginning of the year that would be large enough to cover all production needs through the end of the year.

The direct labor budget is shown in Exhibit 28.5. This budget assumes that only one labor category will vary directly with revenue volume—that category is the final assembly department, where a percentage in the far right column indicates that the cost in this area will be budgeted at a fixed 3.5% of total revenues. In all other cases, there are assumptions for a fixed number of personnel in each position within each production department. All of the wage figures for each department (except for final assembly) are derived from the planned hourly rates and headcount figures noted at the bottom of the page. This budget can be enhanced with the addition of separate line items for payroll tax percentages, benefits, shift differential payments, and overtime expenses. The cost of the final assembly

DIRECT LABOR BUDGET

FOR THE FISCAL YEAR ENDED XX/XX/10

	Quarter 1	Quarter 2	Quarter 3	Quarter 4	Totals	Notes
Machining Department:						
Sr. Machine Operator	$ 15,120	$ 15,372	$ 23,058	$ 23,058	$ 76,608	
Machining Apprentice	$ 4,914	$ 4,964	$ 9,929	$ 9,929	$ 29,736	
Expense subtotal	$ 20,034	$ 20,336	$ 32,987	$ 32,987	$106,344	
Paint Department:						
Sr. Paint Shop Staff	$ 15,876	$ 16,128	$ 16,128	$ 16,128	$ 64,260	
Painter Apprentice	$ 5,065	$ 5,216	$ 5,216	$ 5,216	$ 20,714	
Expense subtotal	$ 20,941	$ 21,344	$ 21,344	$ 21,344	$ 84,974	
Polishing Department:						
Sr. Polishing Staff	$ 16,632	$ 11,844	$ 11,844	$ 11,844	$ 52,164	
Polishing Apprentice	$ 4,360	$ 4,511	$ 4,511	$ 4,511	$ 17,892	
Expense subtotal	$ 20,992	$ 16,355	$ 16,355	$ 16,355	$ 70,056	
Final Assembly Department:						
General Laborer	$ 63,735	$ 66,950	$ 69,755	$ 72,529	$272,968	3.5%
Expense subtotal	$ 63,735	$ 66,950	$ 69,755	$ 72,529	$272,968	
Expense grand total	$125,702	$124,985	$140,441	$143,215	$534,343	
Statistics:						
Union Hourly Rates:						
Sr. Machine Operator	$15.00	$15.25	$15.25	$15.25		
Machining Apprentice	$ 9.75	$ 9.85	$ 9.85	$ 9.85		
Sr. Paint Shop Staff	$15.75	$16.00	$16.00	$16.00		
Painter Apprentice	$10.05	$10.35	$10.35	$10.35		
Sr. Polishing Staff	$11.00	$11.75	$11.75	$11.75		
Polishing Apprentice	$ 8.65	$ 8.95	$ 8.95	$ 8.95		
Headcount by Position:						
Sr. Machine Operator	2	2	3	3		
Machining Apprentice	1	1	2	2		
Sr. Paint Shop Staff	2	2	2	2		
Painter Apprentice	1	1	1	1		
Sr. Polishing Staff	3	2	2	2		
Polishing Apprentice	1	1	1	1		

EXHIBIT 28.5   THE DIRECT LABOR BUDGET

department can also be adjusted to account for worker efficiency, which will be lower during production ramp-up periods when new, untrained employees are added to the workforce.

A sample of the overhead budget is shown in Exhibit 28.6. In this exhibit, we see that the overhead budget is really made up of a number of subsidiary departments, such as maintenance, materials management, and quality assurance. If the budgets of any of these departments are large enough, it makes a great deal of sense to split them off into a separate budget, so that the managers of those departments can see their budgeted expectations more clearly. Of particular interest in this exhibit is the valid capacity range noted on the far right side of the exhibit. This signifies the production activity level within which the budgeted overhead costs are accurate. If the actual capacity utilization were to fall outside of this range, either high or low, a separate overhead budget should be constructed with costs that are expected to be incurred within those ranges.

OVERHEAD BUDGET
FOR THE FISCAL YEAR ENDED xx/xx/1o

	Quarter 1	Quarter 2	Quarter 3	Quarter 4	Totals	Valid Capacity Range
Supervision:						
Production Manager Salary	$ 16,250	$ 16,250	$ 16,250	$ 16,250	$ 65,000	—
Shift Manager Salaries	$ 22,000	$ 22,000	$ 23,500	$ 23,500	$ 91,000	40%–70%
Expense subtotal	$ 38,250	$ 38,250	$ 39,750	$ 39,750	$ 156,000	
Maintenance Department:						
Equipment Maint. Staff	$ 54,000	$ 56,500	$ 58,000	$ 60,250	$ 228,750	40%–70%
Facilities Maint. Staff	$ 8,250	$ 8,250	$ 8,500	$ 8,500	$ 33,500	40%–70%
Equipment Repairs	$225,000	$225,000	$275,000	$225,000	$ 950,000	40%–70%
Facility Repairs	$ 78,000	$ 29,000	$ 12,000	$ 54,000	$ 173,000	40%–70%
Expense subtotal	$365,250	$318,750	$353,500	$347,750	$1,385,250	
Materials Management Department:						
Manager Salary	$ 18,750	$ 18,750	$ 18,750	$ 18,750	$ 75,000	—
Purchasing Staff	$ 28,125	$ 18,750	$ 18,750	$ 18,750	$ 84,375	40%–70%
Materials Mgmt Staff	$ 28,000	$ 35,000	$ 35,000	$ 35,000	$ 133,000	40%–70%
Production Control Staff	$ 11,250	$ 11,250	$ 11,250	$ 11,250	$ 45,000	40%–70%
Expense subtotal	$ 86,125	$ 83,750	$ 83,750	$ 83,750	$ 337,375	
Quality Department:						
Manager Salary	$ 13,750	$ 13,750	$ 13,750	$ 13,750	$ 55,000	—
Quality Staff	$ 16,250	$ 16,250	$ 16,250	$ 24,375	$ 73,125	40%–70%
Lab Testing Supplies	$ 5,000	$ 4,500	$ 4,500	$ 4,500	$ 18,500	40%–70%
Expense subtotal	$ 35,000	$ 34,500	$ 34,500	$ 42,625	$ 146,625	
Other Expenses:						
Depreciation	$ 14,000	$ 15,750	$ 15,750	$ 15,750	$ 61,250	—
Utilities	$ 60,000	$ 55,000	$ 55,000	$ 60,000	$ 230,000	40%–70%
Boiler Insurance	$ 3,200	$ 3,200	$ 3,200	$ 3,200	$ 12,800	—
Expense Subtotal	$ 77,200	$ 73,950	$ 73,950	$ 78,950	$ 304,050	
Expense Grand Total	$601,825	$549,200	$585,450	$592,825	$2,329,300	

EXHIBIT 28.6 THE OVERHEAD BUDGET

COST OF GOODS SOLD BUDGET
FOR THE FISCAL YEAR ENDED XX/XX/10

	Quarter 1	Quarter 2	Quarter 3	Quarter 4	Totals
Product Line Alpha:					
Revenue	$ 210,000	$ 311,850	$ 370,000	$ 457,250	$1,349,100
Materials Expense	$ 108,400	$ 108,400	$ 113,400	$ 155,216	$ 485,416
Contribution Margin $$	$ 101,600	$ 203,450	$ 256,600	$ 302,034	$ 863,684
Contribution Margin %	48%	65%	69%	66%	64%
Product Line Beta:					
Revenue	$1,048,000	$1,057,000	$1,061,000	$1,053,000	$4,219,000
Materials Expense	$ 12,000	$ 14,000	$ 15,000	$ 13,250	$ 54,250
Contribution Margin $$	$1,036,000	$1,043,000	$1,046,000	$1,039,750	$4,164,750
Contribution Margin %	99%	99%	99%	99%	99%
Revenue—Product Line Charlie:					
Revenue	$ 563,000	$ 544,000	$ 562,000	$ 562,000	$2,231,000
Materials Expense	$ 268,000	$ 200,000	$ 220,000	$ 230,000	$ 918,000
Contribution Margin $$	$ 295,000	$ 344,000	$ 342,000	$ 332,000	$1,313,000
Contribution Margin %	52%	63%	61%	59%	59%
Total Contribution Margin $$	$1,432,600	$1,590,450	$1,644,600	$1,673,784	$6,341,434
Total Contribution Margin %	79%	83%	83%	81%	81%
Direct Labor Expense:	$ 125,702	$ 124,985	$ 140,441	$ 143,215	$ 534,343
Overhead Expense:	$ 601,825	$ 549,200	$ 585,450	$ 592,825	$2,329,300
Total Gross Margin $$	$ 705,073	$ 916,265	$ 918,709	$ 937,744	$3,477,791
Total Gross Margin %	39%	48%	46%	45%	44%
Statistics:					
No. of Production Staff*	23	22	22	23	
Avg. Annual Revenue per Production Employee	$ 316,696	$ 347,791	$ 362,364	$ 360,391	

* Not including general assembly staff.

EXHIBIT 28.7   THE COST OF GOODS SOLD BUDGET

A sample cost of goods sold budget is shown in Exhibit 28.7. This format splits out each of the product lines noted in the revenue budget for reporting purposes, and subtracts from each one the materials costs that are noted in the purchases budget. This results in a contribution margin for each product line that is the clearest representation of the impact of direct costs (that is, material costs) on each one. We then summarize these individual contribution margins into a summary-level contribution margin, and then subtract the total direct labor and overhead costs (as referenced from the direct labor and overhead budgets) to arrive at a total gross margin. The statistics section also notes the number of production personnel budgeted for each quarterly reporting period, plus the average annual revenue per production employee—these statistics can be replaced with any operational information that management wants to see at a summary level for the production function, such as efficiency levels, capacity utilization, or inventory turnover.

The sales department budget is shown in Exhibit 28.8. This budget shows several different ways in which to organize the budget information. At the top of the budget is a block of line items that lists the expenses for those overhead costs within the department that cannot be specifically linked to a salesperson or region. In cases where the number of sales staff is quite small, *all* of the department's costs may be listed in this area.

	Quarter 1	Quarter 2	Quarter 3	Quarter 4	Totals
	SALES DEPARTMENT BUDGET				
	FOR THE FISCAL YEAR ENDED XX/XX/10				
Departmental Overhead:					
Depreciation	$ 500	$ 500	$ 500	$ 500	$ 2,000
Office Supplies	$ 750	$ 600	$ 650	$ 600	$ 2,600
Payroll Taxes	$ 2,945	$ 5,240	$ 5,240	$ 8,186	$ 21,611
Salaries	$ 38,500	$ 68,500	$ 68,500	$107,000	$ 282,500
Travel & Entertainment	$ 1,500	$ 1,500	$ 1,500	$ 2,000	$ 6,500
Expense subtotal	$ 44,195	$ 76,340	$ 76,390	$118,286	$ 315,211
Product Line Alpha:	$ 32,000	$ 18,000	$ 0	$ 21,000	$ 71,000
Expenses by Salesperson:					
Jones, Milbert	$ 14,000	$ 16,500	$ 17,000	$ 12,000	$ 59,500
Smidley, Jefferson	$ 1,000	$ 9,000	$ 8,000	$ 12,000	$ 30,000
Verity, Jonas	$ 7,000	$ 9,000	$ 14,000	$ 12,000	$ 42,000
Expense subtotal	$ 22,000	$ 34,500	$ 39,000	$ 36,000	$ 131,500
Expenses by Region:					
East Coast	$ 52,000	$ 71,000	$ 15,000	$ 0	$ 138,000
Midwest Coast	$ 8,000	$ 14,000	$ 6,000	$ 12,000	$ 40,000
West Coast	$ 11,000	$ 10,000	$ 12,000	$ 24,000	$ 57,000
Expense subtotal	$ 71,000	$ 95,000	$ 33,000	$ 36,000	$ 235,000
Expense grand total	$137,195	$205,840	$148,390	$190,286	$ 681,711
Statistics:					
Revenue per salesperson	$607,000	$637,617	$664,333	$690,750	$2,599,700
T&E per salesperson	$ 500	$ 500	$ 500	$ 667	$ 2,167

EXHIBIT 28.8   THE SALES DEPARTMENT BUDGET

Another alternative is shown in the second block of expense line items in the middle of the sales department budget, where all of the sales costs for an entire product line are lumped together into a single line item. If each person on the sales staff is exclusively assigned to a single product line, then it may make sense to break down the budget into separate budget pages for each product line, and list all of the expenses associated with each product line on a separate page.

A third alternative is shown next in Exhibit 28.8, where we list a summary of expenses for each salesperson. This format works well when combined with the departmental overhead expenses at the top of the budget, since this accounts for all of the departmental costs. However, this format brings up a confidentiality issue, since the compensation of each salesperson can be inferred from the report. Also, this format would include the commission expense paid to each salesperson—since commissions a re a variable cost that is directly associated with each incremental dollar of sales, they should be itemized as a separate line item within the cost of goods sold.

A final option listed at the bottom of the example is to itemize expenses by sales region. This format works best when there are a number of sales personnel within the department who are clustered into a number of clearly identifiable regions. If there were no obvious regions or if there were only one salesperson per region, then the better format would be to list expenses by salesperson.

At the bottom of the budget is the usual statistics section. The sales department budget is only concerned with making sales, so it should be no surprise that revenue per salesperson

MARKETING BUDGET
FOR THE FISCAL YEAR ENDED XX/XX/10

	Quarter 1	Quarter 2	Quarter 3	Quarter 4	Totals
Departmental Overhead:					
Depreciation	$ 650	$ 750	$ 850	$ 1,000	$ 3,250
Office Supplies	$ 200	$ 200	$ 200	$ 200	$ 800
Payroll Taxes	$ 4,265	$ 4,265	$ 4,265	$ 4,265	$ 17,060
Salaries	$ 55,750	$ 55,750	$ 55,750	$55,750	$223,000
Travel & Entertainment	$ 5,000	$ 6,500	$ 7,250	$ 7,250	$ 26,000
Expense subtotal	$ 65,865	$ 67,465	$ 68,315	$68,465	$270,110
Campaign-Specific Expenses:					
Product Line Alpha	$ 14,000	$ 26,000	$ 30,000	$ 0	$ 70,000
Product Line Beta	$ 18,000	$ 0	$ 0	$24,000	$ 42,000
Product Line Charlie					$ 0
Advertising	$ 10,000	$ 0	$ 20,000	$ 0	$ 30,000
Promotional Tour	$ 5,000	$ 25,000	$ 2,000	$ 0	$ 32,000
Coupon Redemption	$ 2,000	$ 4,000	$ 4,500	$ 1,200	$ 11,700
Product Samples	$ 2,750	$ 5,250	$ 1,250	$ 0	$ 9,250
Expense subtotal	$ 51,750	$ 60,250	$ 57,750	$25,200	$194,950
Expense grand total	$117,615	$127,715	$126,065	$93,665	$465,060
Statistics:					
Expense as percent of total sales	6.5%	6.7%	6.3%	4.5%	6.0%
Expense proportion by quarter	25.3%	27.5%	27.1%	20.1%	100.0%

EXHIBIT 28.9   THE MARKETING DEPARTMENT BUDGET

is the first item listed. Also, since the primary sales cost associated with this department is usually travel costs, the other statistical item is the travel and entertainment cost per person.

Exhibit 28.9 shows a sample marketing budget. As was the case for the sales department, this one also itemizes departmental overhead costs at the top, which leaves space in the middle for the itemization of campaign-specific costs. The campaign-specific costs can be lumped together for individual product lines, as is the case for product lines Alpha and Beta in the exhibit, or with subsidiary line items, as is shown for product line Charlie. A third possible format, which is to itemize marketing costs by marketing tool (for example, advertising, promotional tour, coupon redemption, etc.) is generally not recommended if there is more than one product line, since there is no way for an analyst to determine the impact of individual marketing costs on specific product lines. The statistics at the bottom of the page attempt to compare marketing costs to sales; however, this should only be treated as an approximation, since marketing efforts will usually not result in immediate sales, but rather will result in sales that build over time. Thus, there is a time lag after incurring a marketing cost that makes it difficult to determine the efficacy of marketing activities.

A sample general and administrative budget is shown in Exhibit 28.10. This budget can be quite lengthy, including such additional line items as postage, copier leases, and office repair. Many of these extra expenses have been pruned from the exhibit in order to provide a compressed view of the general format to be used. The exhibit does not lump together the costs of the various departments that are typically included in this budget, but rather identifies each one in separate blocks; this format is most useful when there are separate managers for the accounting and human resources functions, so that they will have a better

GENERAL AND ADMINISTRATIVE BUDGET
FOR THE FISCAL YEAR ENDED XX/XX/10

	Quarter 1	Quarter 2	Quarter 3	Quarter 4	Totals	Notes
Accounting Department:						
Depreciation	$ 4,000	$ 4,000	$ 4,250	$ 4,250	$ 16,500	
Office Supplies	$ 650	$ 650	$ 750	$ 750	$ 2,800	
Payroll Taxes	$ 4,973	$ 4,973	$ 4,973	$ 4,973	$ 19,890	
Salaries	$ 65,000	$ 65,000	$ 65,000	$ 65,000	$260,000	
Training	$ 500	$ 2,500	$ 7,500	$ 0	$ 10,500	
Travel & Entertainment	$ 0	$ 750	$ 4,500	$ 500	$ 5,750	
Expense subtotal	$ 75,123	$ 77,873	$ 86,973	$ 75,473	$315,440	
Corporate Expenses:						
Depreciation	$ 450	$ 500	$ 550	$ 600	$ 2,100	
Office Supplies	$ 1,000	$ 850	$ 750	$ 1,250	$ 3,850	
Payroll Taxes	$ 6,598	$ 6,598	$ 6,598	$ 6,598	$ 26,392	
Salaries	$ 86,250	$ 86,250	$ 86,250	$ 86,250	$345,000	
Insurance, Business	$ 4,500	$ 4,500	$ 4,500	$ 4,500	$ 18,000	
Training	$ 5,000	$ 0	$ 0	$ 0	$ 5,000	
Travel & Entertainment	$ 2,000	$ 500	$ 500	$ 0	$ 3,000	
Expense subtotal	$105,798	$ 99,198	$ 99,148	$ 99,198	$403,342	
Human Resources Department:						
Benefits Programs	$ 7,284	$ 7,651	$ 7,972	$ 8,289	$ 31,196	**0.4%**
Depreciation	$ 500	$ 500	$ 500	$ 500	$ 2,000	
Office Supplies	$ 450	$ 8,000	$ 450	$ 450	$ 9,350	
Payroll Taxes	$ 2,869	$ 2,869	$ 2,869	$ 2,869	$ 11,475	
Salaries	$ 37,500	$ 37,500	$ 37,500	$ 37,500	$150,000	
Training	$ 5,000	$ 0	$ 7,500	$ 0	$ 12,500	
Travel & Entertainment	$ 2,000	$ 1,000	$ 3,500	$ 1,000	$ 7,500	
Expense subtotal	$ 55,603	$ 57,520	$ 60,291	$ 50,608	$224,021	
Expense grand total	$236,523	$234,591	$246,411	$225,278	$942,804	
Statistics:						
Expense as proportion of revenue	13.0%	12.3%	12.4%	10.9%	12.1%	
Benchmark comparison	11.5%	11.5%	11.5%	11.5%	11.5%	

EXHIBIT 28.10   THE GENERAL AND ADMINISTRATIVE BUDGET

understanding of their budgets. The statistics section at the bottom of the page itemizes a benchmark target of the total general and administrative cost as a proportion of revenue. This is a particularly useful statistic to track, since the general and administrative function is a cost center and requires such a comparison in order to inform management that these costs are being held in check.

A staffing budget is shown in Exhibit 28.11. This itemizes the expected headcount in every department by major job category. It does not attempt to identify individual positions, since that can lead to an excessively lengthy list. Also, because there may be multiple positions identified within each job category, the *average* salary for each cluster of jobs is identified. If a position is subject to overtime pay, its expected overtime percentage is identified on the right side of the budget. Many sections of the budget should have linkages to this page, so that any changes in headcount here will be automatically reflected in the other sections. This budget may have to be restricted from general access, since it contains salary information that may be considered confidential information.

	Quarter 1	Quarter 2	Quarter 3	Quarter 4	Average Salary	Overtime Percent
Sales Department:						
Regional Sales Manager	1	2	2	3	$120,000	0%
Salesperson	2	4	4	6	$ 65,000	0%
Sales Support Staff	1	1	1	2	$ 34,000	6%
Marketing Department:						
Marketing Manager	1	1	1	1	$ 85,000	0%
Marketing Researcher	2	2	2	2	$ 52,000	0%
Secretary	1	1	1	1	$ 34,000	6%
General & Administrative:						
President	1	1	1	1	$175,000	0%
Chief Operating Officer	1	1	1	1	$125,000	0%
Chief Financial Officer	1	1	1	1	$100,000	0%
Human Resources Mgr.	1	1	1	1	$ 80,000	0%
Accounting Staff	4	4	4	4	$ 40,000	10%
Human Resources Staff	2	2	2	2	$ 35,000	8%
Executive Secretary	1	1	1	1	$ 45,000	6%
Research Department:						
Chief Scientist	1	1	1	1	$100,000	0%
Senior Engineer Staff	3	3	3	4	$ 80,000	0%
Junior Engineer Staff	3	3	3	3	$ 60,000	0%
Overhead Budget:						
Production Manager	1	1	1	1	$ 65,000	0%
Quality Manager	1	1	1	1	$ 55,000	0%
Materials Manager	1	1	1	1	$ 75,000	0%
Production Scheduler	1	1	1	1	$ 45,000	0%
Quality Assurance Staff	2	2	2	3	$ 32,500	8%
Purchasing Staff	3	2	2	2	$ 37,500	8%
Materials Mgmt Staff	4	5	5	5	$ 28,000	8%
Total Headcount	39	42	42	48		

STAFFING BUDGET
FOR THE FISCAL YEAR ENDED xx/xx/10

EXHIBIT 28.11   THE STAFFING BUDGET

The facilities budget tends to have the largest number of expense line items. A sample of this format is shown in Exhibit 28.12. These expenses may be offset by some rental or sublease revenues if a portion of the company facilities is rented out to other organizations. However, this revenue is only shown in this budget if the revenue amount is small; otherwise, it is more commonly found as an "other revenue" line item on the revenue budget. A statistics section is found at the bottom of this budget; it refers to the total amount of square feet occupied by the facility. A very effective statistic is the amount of unused square footage, which can be used to conduct an ongoing program of selling off, renting, or consolidating company facilities.

The research department's budget is shown in Exhibit 28.13. It is most common to segregate the department-specific overhead that cannot be attributed to a specific project at the top of the budget, and then cluster costs by project below that. By doing so, the management team can see precisely how much money is being allocated to each project. This may be of use in determining which projects must be canceled or delayed as part of the budget review process. The statistics section at the bottom of the budget notes the

FACILITIES BUDGET
FOR THE FISCAL YEAR ENDED XX/XX/10

	Quarter 1	Quarter 2	Quarter 3	Quarter 4	Totals
Facility Expenses:					
Contracted Services	$ 5,500	$ 5,400	$ 5,000	$ 4,500	$ 20,400
Depreciation	$29,000	$29,000	$28,000	$28,000	$114,000
Electricity Charges	$ 4,500	$ 3,500	$ 3,500	$ 4,500	$ 16,000
Inspection Fees	$ 500	$ 0	$ 0	$ 500	$ 1,000
Insurance	$ 8,000	$ 0	$ 0	$ 0	$ 8,000
Maintenance Supplies	$ 3,000	$ 3,000	$ 3,000	$ 3,000	$ 12,000
Payroll Taxes	$ 1,148	$ 1,148	$ 1,148	$ 1,186	$ 4,628
Property Taxes	$ 0	$ 5,000	$ 0	$ 0	$ 5,000
Repairs	$15,000	$ 0	$29,000	$ 0	$ 44,000
Sewage Charges	$ 250	$ 250	$ 250	$ 250	$ 1,000
Trash Disposal	$ 3,000	$ 3,000	$ 3,000	$ 3,000	$ 12,000
Wages—Janitorial	$ 5,000	$ 5,000	$ 5,000	$ 5,500	$ 20,500
Wages—Maintenance	$10,000	$10,000	$10,000	$10,000	$ 40,000
Water Charges	$ 1,000	$ 1,000	$ 1,000	$ 1,000	$ 4,000
Expense grand total	$85,898	$66,298	$88,898	$61,436	$302,528
Statistics:					
Total Square Feet	52,000	52,000	78,000	78,000	
Square Feet/Employee	839	813	1,219	1,099	
Unused Square Footage	1,200	1,200	12,500	12,500	

EXHIBIT 28.12   THE FACILITIES BUDGET

proportion of planned expenses in the categories of overhead, research, and development. These proportions can be examined to see if the company is allocating funds to the right balance of projects that most effectively meets its product development goals.

The capital budget is shown in Exhibit 28.14. This format clusters capital expenditures by a number of categories. For example, the first category, entitled "bottleneck-related expenditures," clearly focuses attention on those outgoing payments that will increase the company's key productive capacity. The payments in the third quarter under this heading are directly related to the increase in bottleneck capacity that was shown in the production budget (Exhibit 28.3) for the fourth quarter. The budget also contains an automatic assumption of $7,000 in capital expenditures for any net increase in indirect labor headcount, which encompasses the cost of computer equipment and office furniture for each person. If the company's capitalization limit is set too high to list these expenditures on the capital budget, then a similar line item should be inserted into the general and administrative budget, so that the expense can be recognized under the office supplies or some similar account.

The capital budget also includes a category for profit-related expenditures. Any projects listed in this category should be subject to an intensive expenditure review, using cash flow discounting techniques (as described in Chapter 32, "Financial Analysis") to ensure that they return a sufficient cash flow to make their acquisition profitable to the company. Other categories in the budget cover expenditures for safety or required items, which tend to be purchased with no cash flow discounting review. An alternative to this grouping system is to only list the sum total of all capital expenditures in each category, which is most frequently used when there are far too many separate purchases to list on the budget. Another variation is to only list the largest expenditures on separate budget lines, and cluster

RESEARCH DEPARTMENT BUDGET
FOR THE FISCAL YEAR ENDED XX/XX/10

	Quarter 1	Quarter 2	Quarter 3	Quarter 4	Totals
Departmental Overhead:					
Depreciation	$ 500	$ 500	$ 400	$ 400	$ 1,800
Office Supplies	$ 750	$ 2,000	$ 1,500	$ 1,250	$ 5,500
Payroll Taxes	$ 9,945	$ 9,945	$ 9,945	$ 11,475	$ 41,310
Salaries	$130,000	$130,000	$130,000	$150,000	$ 540,000
Travel & Entertainment	$ 0	$ 0	$ 0	$ 0	$ 0
Expense subtotal	$141,195	$142,445	$141,845	$163,125	$ 588,610
Research-Specific Expenses:					
Gamma Project	$ 20,000	$ 43,500	$ 35,000	$ 12,500	$ 111,000
Omega Project	$ 5,000	$ 6,000	$ 7,500	$ 9,000	$ 27,500
Pi Project	$ 14,000	$ 7,000	$ 7,500	$ 4,500	$ 33,000
Upsilon Project	$ 500	$ 2,500	$ 5,000	$ 0	$ 8,000
Expense subtotal	$ 39,500	$ 59,000	$ 55,000	$ 26,000	$ 179,500
Development-Specific Expenses:					
Latin Project	$ 28,000	$ 29,000	$ 30,000	$ 15,000	$ 102,000
Greek Project	$ 14,000	$ 14,500	$ 15,000	$ 7,500	$ 51,000
Mabinogian Project	$ 20,000	$ 25,000	$ 15,000	$ 10,000	$ 70,000
Old English Project	$ 6,250	$ 12,500	$ 25,000	$ 50,000	$ 93,750
Expense subtotal	$ 68,250	$ 81,000	$ 85,000	$ 82,500	$ 316,750
Expense grand total	$248,945	$282,445	$281,845	$271,625	$1,084,860
Statistics:					
Budgeted number of patent applications filed	2	0	1	1	4
Proportion of expenses:					
Overhead	56.7%	50.4%	50.3%	60.1%	217.5%
Research	15.9%	20.9%	19.5%	9.6%	65.8%
Development	27.4%	28.7%	30.2%	30.4%	116.5%
Total Expenses	100.0%	100.0%	100.0%	100.0%	400.0%

EXHIBIT 28.13   THE RESEARCH DEPARTMENT BUDGET

together all smaller ones. The level of capital purchasing activity will determine the type of format used.

All of the preceding budgets roll up into the budgeted income and cash flow statement, which is noted in Exhibit 28.15. This format lists the grand totals from each of the preceding pages of the budget in order to arrive at a profit or loss for each budget quarter. In the example, we see that a large initial loss in the first quarter is gradually offset by smaller gains in later quarters to arrive at a small profit for the year. However, the presentation continues with a cash flow statement that has less positive results. It begins with the net profit figure for each quarter, adds back the depreciation expense for all departments, and subtracts out all planned capital expenditures from the capital budget to arrive at cash flow needs for the year. This tells us that the company will experience a maximum cash shortfall in the third quarter. This format can be made more precise by adding in time lag factors for the payment of accounts payable and the collection of accounts receivable.

The final document in the budget is an itemization of the finances needed to ensure that the rest of the budget can be achieved. An example is shown in Exhibit 28.16, which

CAPITAL BUDGET
FOR THE FISCAL YEAR ENDED xx/xx/10

	Quarter 1	Quarter 2	Quarter 3	Quarter 4	Totals
Bottleneck-Related Expenditures:					
Stamping Machine			$150,000		$150,000
Facility for Machine			$ 72,000		$ 72,000
Headcount-Related Expenditures:					
Headcount Change 3					
$7,000 Added Staff	$ 0	$ 21,000	$ 0	$42,000	$ 63,000
Profit-Related Expenditures:					
Blending Machine		$ 50,000			$ 50,000
Polishing Machine		$ 27,000			$ 27,000
Safety-Related Expenditures:					
Machine Shielding		$ 3,000	$ 3,000		$ 6,000
Handicapped Walkways	$8,000	$ 5,000			$ 13,000
Required Expenditures:					
Clean Air Scrubber			$ 42,000		$ 42,000
Other Expenditures:					
Tool Crib Expansion				$18,500	$ 18,500
Total expenditures	$8,000	$106,000	$267,000	$60,500	$441,500

EXHIBIT 28.14   THE CAPITAL BUDGET

carries forward the final cash position at the end of each quarter that was the product of the preceding cash flow statement. This line shows that there will be a maximum shortfall of $223,727 by the end of the third quarter. The next section of the budget outlines several possible options for obtaining the required funds (which are rounded up to $225,000)—debt, preferred stock, or common stock. The financing cost of each one is noted in the far right column, where we see that the interest cost on debt is 9.5%, the dividend on preferred stock is 8%, and the expected return by common stockholders is 18%.

The third section on the page lists the existing capital structure, its cost, and the net cost of capital. This is quite important, for anyone reviewing this document can see what impact the financing options will have on the capital structure if any of them are selected. For example, the management team may prefer the low cost of debt, but can also use the existing capital structure presentation to see that this will result in a very high proportion of debt to equity, which increases the risk that the company would not be able to repay the debt to the lender.

The fourth and final part of the budget calculates any changes in the cost of capital that will arise if any of the three financing options are selected. A footnote points out the incremental corporate tax rate—this is of importance to the calculation of the cost of capital, because the interest cost of debt can be deducted as an expense, thereby reducing its net cost. In the exhibit, selecting additional debt as the preferred form of financing will result in a reduction in the cost of capital to 10.7%, whereas a selection of high-cost common stock will result in an increase in the cost of capital, to 12.9%. These changes can have an impact on what types of capital projects are accepted in the future, for the cash flows associated with them must be discounted by the cost of capital in order to see if they result in positive cash flows. Accordingly, a reduction in the cost of capital will mean that

BUDGETED INCOME AND CASH FLOW STATEMENT
FOR THE FISCAL YEAR ENDED XX/XX/10

	Quarter 1	Quarter 2	Quarter 3	Quarter 4	Totals
Revenue:	$1,821,000	$1,912,850	$1,993,000	$2,072,250	$7,799,100
Cost of Goods Sold:					
Materials	$ 388,400	$ 322,400	$ 348,400	$ 398,466	$1,457,666
Direct Labor	$ 125,702	$ 124,985	$ 140,441	$ 143,215	$ 534,343
Overhead					
Supervision	$ 38,250	$ 38,250	$ 39,750	$ 39,750	$ 156,000
Maintenance Department	$ 365,250	$ 318,750	$ 353,500	$ 347,750	$1,385,250
Materials Management	$ 86,125	$ 83,750	$ 83,750	$ 83,750	$ 337,375
Quality Department	$ 35,000	$ 34,500	$ 34,500	$ 42,625	$ 146,625
Other Expenses	$ 77,200	$ 73,950	$ 73,950	$ 78,950	$ 304,050
Total Cost of Goods Sold	$1,115,927	$ 996,585	$1,074,291	$1,134,506	$4,321,309
Gross Margin	$ 705,073	$ 916,265	$ 918,709	$ 937,744	$3,477,791
Operating Expenses:					
Sales Department	$ 137,195	$ 205,840	$ 148,390	$ 190,286	$ 681,711
General & Admin. Dept.					
Accounting	$ 75,123	$ 77,873	$ 86,973	$ 75,473	$ 315,440
Corporate	$ 105,798	$ 99,198	$ 99,148	$ 99,198	$ 403,343
Human Resources	$ 55,603	$ 57,520	$ 60,291	$ 50,608	$ 224,021
Marketing Department	$ 117,615	$ 127,715	$ 126,065	$ 93,665	$ 465,060
Facilities Department	$ 85,898	$ 66,298	$ 88,898	$ 61,436	$ 302,528
Research Department	$ 248,945	$ 282,445	$ 281,845	$ 271,625	$1,084,860
Total Operating Expenses	$ 826,176	$ 916,888	$ 891,609	$ 842,290	$3,476,963
Net Profit (Loss)	−$ 121,103	−$ 624	$ 27,100	$ 95,455	$ 828

	Quarter 1	Quarter 2	Quarter 3	Quarter 4	Totals
Cash Flow:					
Beginning Cash	$ 100,000	$ 20,497	−$ 34,627	−$ 223,727	
Net Profit (Loss)	−$ 121,103	−$ 624	$ 27,100	$ 95,455	$ 828
Add Depreciation	$ 49,600	$ 51,500	$ 50,800	$ 51,000	$ 202,900
Minus Capital Purchases	−$ 8,000	−$ 106,000	−$ 267,000	−$ 60,500	−$ 441,500
Ending Cash	$ 20,497	−$ 34,627	−$ 223,727	−$ 137,772	

EXHIBIT 28.15   THE BUDGETED INCOME AND CASH FLOW STATEMENT

projects with marginal cash flows will become more acceptable, while the reverse will be true for a higher cost of capital.

The budgeting examples shown here can be used as the format for a real-life corporate budget. However, it must be adjusted to include a company's chart of accounts and departmental structure, so that it more accurately reflects actual operations. Also, it should include a detailed benefits and payroll tax calculation page, which will itemize the cost of Social Security taxes, Medicare, unemployment insurance, workers' compensation insurance, medical insurance, and so on. These costs are a substantial part of a company's budget, and yet are commonly lumped together into a simplistic budget model that does not accurately reflect their true cost.

Though the budget model presented here may seem excessively large, it is necessary to provide detailed coverage of all aspects of the corporation, so that prospective changes to it can be accurately modeled through the budget. Thus, a detailed format is strongly recommended over a simple, summarized model.

FINANCING BUDGET
FOR THE FISCAL YEAR ENDED XX/XX/10

	Quarter 1	Quarter 2	Quarter 3	Quarter 4	Financing Cost
Cash Position:	$ 20,497	−$ 34,627	−$223,727	−$137,772	
Financing Option One:					
Additional Debt		$225,000			9.5%
Financing Option Two:					
Additional Preferred Stock	$225,000				8.0%
Financing Option Three:					
Additional Common Stock	$225,000				18.0%
Existing Capital Structure:					
Debt	$400,000				9.0%
Preferred Stock	$150,000				7.5%
Common Stock	$500,000				18.0%
Existing Cost of Capital	11.8%				
Revised Cost of Capital:					
Financing Option One	10.7%				
Financing Option Two	11.2%				
Financing Option Three	12.9%				

Note: Tax rate equals 38%.

EXHIBIT 28.16   THE FINANCING BUDGET

28.4   THE FLEX BUDGET

One problem with the budget model shown in the last section is that many of the expenses listed in it are directly tied to the revenue level. If the actual revenue incurred is significantly different from the budgeted figure, then so many expenses will also shift in association with the revenue that the comparison of budgeted to actual expenses will not be valid. For example, if budgeted revenues are $1 million and budgeted material costs are $450,000, one would expect a corresponding drop in the actual cost of materials incurred if actual revenues drop to $800,000. A budget-to-actual comparison would then show a significant difference in the cost of materials, which would in turn cause a difference in the gross margin and net profit. This issue also arises for a number of other variable or semivariable expenses, such as salesperson commissions, production supplies, and maintenance costs. Also, if there are really large differences between actual and budgeted revenue levels, other costs that are more fixed in nature will also change, such as the salaries, office supplies, and even facilities maintenance (because facilities may be sold off or added to, depending on which direction actual revenues have gone). These represent large step cost changes that will skew actual expenses so far away from the budget that it is difficult to conduct any meaningful comparison between the two.

A good way to resolve this problem is to create a flexible budget, or "flex" budget, that itemizes different expense levels depending upon changes in the amount of actual revenue. In its simplest form, the flex budget will use percentages of revenue for certain expenses, rather than the usual fixed numbers. This allows for an infinite series of changes in budgeted expenses that are directly tied to revenue volume. However, this approach ignores changes to other costs that do not change in accordance with small revenue variations. Consequently, a more sophisticated format will also incorporate changes to many additional expenses when certain larger revenue changes occur, thereby accounting for step costs. By making these changes to the budget, a company will have a tool for comparing actual to budgeted performance at many levels of activity.

Though the flex budget is a good tool, it can be difficult to formulate and administer. One problem with its formulation is that many costs are not fully variable, instead having a fixed cost component that must be included in the flex budget formula. Another issue is that a great deal of time can be spent developing step costs, which is more time than the typical accounting staff has available, especially when in the midst of creating the standard budget. Consequently, the flex budget tends to include only a small number of step costs, as well as variable costs whose fixed cost components are not fully recognized.

Implementation of the flex budget is also a problem, for very few accounting software packages incorporate any features that allow one to load in multiple versions of a budget that can be used at different revenue levels. Instead, some include the option to store a few additional budgets, which the user can then incorporate into the standard budget-to-actual comparison reports. This option does not yield the full benefits of a flex budget, since it only allows for a few changes in expenses based on a small number of revenue changes, rather than a set of expenses that will automatically change in proportion to actual revenue levels incurred. Furthermore, the option to enter several different budgets means that someone must enter this additional information into the accounting software, which can be a considerable chore if the number of budget line items is large. For these reasons, it is more common to see a flex budget incorporated into an electronic spreadsheet, with actual results being manually posted to it from other accounting reports.

28.5   CAPITAL BUDGETING—TRADITIONAL METHOD

Capital Purchase Evaluations

When evaluating whether or not one should invest a considerable amount of funds in capital projects, the accountant has a number of tools available, such as the hurdle rate, payback period, net present value, and internal rate of return—all of which are covered in this section.

The hurdle rate, with some variations, is a company's cost of capital, which we covered in the last section. Most capital projects must generate a stream of cash flows that, when discounted at the hurdle rate, will generate a positive cash balance. If this were not the case, then a company would be investing funds at a rate of return less than the cost of the capital it would be using to pay for the project. However, there are cases where the hurdle rate will diverge from the cost of capital. For instance, if a project is perceived to have an extremely high level of risk (such as investments in unproven technology), then the rate may be increased substantially. Another example is a government-mandated enhancement to the air "scrubbers" in a coal-fired electrical generating plant, which must be installed irrespective of the hurdle rate. Thus, there can be justifiable variations between the hurdle rate and the cost of capital.

The hurdle rate is used to discount the stream of cash flows spun off by a capital project, so that the cash flows are translated into their current-period value. To do so, we use a discounting factor that is listed in the "Compound Interest (Present Value of 1 Due in N

Year	Description	Cash Flow	Discount Factor	Present Value
0	Initial capital purchase	−$250,000	1.000	−$250,000
0	Working capital requirement	−175,000	1.000	−175,000
1	Gross margin on product sales	+45,000	.9346	+42,057
1	Project maintenance costs	−10,000	.9346	−9,346
2	Gross margin on product sales	+85,000	.8734	+74,239
2	Project maintenance costs	−15,000	.8734	−13,101
3	Gross margin on product sales	+120,000	.8163	+97,956
3	Project maintenance costs	−20,000	.8163	−16,326
4	Gross margin on product sales	+120,000	.7629	+91,548
4	Project maintenance costs	−25,000	.7629	−19,073
5	Gross margin on product sales	+60,000	.7130	+42,780
5	Project maintenance costs	−27,500	.7130	−19,608
5	Release of working capital	+175,000	.7130	+124,775
5	Sale of capital equipment	+60,000	.7130	+42,780
	Present value of cash flows	—	—	13,681

EXHIBIT 28.17   DISCOUNTED CASH FLOWS FROM A CAPITAL PROJECT

Periods)" table in Appendix C to discount a cash flow estimated to occur in a future period back to the present period, using the hurdle rate as the discount rate. For example, if we have a cash flow of $100,000 occurring in Year Four, and assume a hurdle rate of 9%, then we will use a discount rate of .7084 to determine that the current value of this cash flow is $70,840. In case one's assumptions fall outside of the table in Appendix C, the formula to use is:

$$\frac{1}{(1 + \text{discount rate})^{\text{numbers of years}}}$$

If one is using Microsoft Excel to derive the calculation, then the formula in that electronic spreadsheet is:

$$= 1/((1 + [\text{enter the discount rate}])\,\hat{}\,[\text{enter the number of years}])$$

Virtually all cash flows caused by a capital project should be subject to cash discounting. For example, Exhibit 28.17 shows a stream of cash flows for a capital project that are spread over a five-year period. They relate to the initial capital and working capital cost, ongoing maintenance costs, annual gross margin on sale of products created by the capital item (net of income taxes), and the sale of equipment and release of working capital at the end of the project. Each cash flow is assigned a discounting factor that is based on the year in which it occurs, based on an assigned hurdle rate of 7%.

The exhibit shows a stream of cash flows that results in a slight positive cash flow, and so should be approved. A more comprehensive review would also include the positive tax impact of depreciation costs on the cash flows, and any personnel or other overhead costs associated with the project. This summation of all discounted cash flows is called the "net present value" method (NPV) and is a commonly used technique for evaluating capital investments.

Another evaluation method that relies on discounting is the "internal rate of return" method (IRR). This approach alters the discount rate until the stream of discounted cash flows equals zero. By doing so, one can see if the adjusted discount rate is relatively close to the standard corporate hurdle rate, and so may require only minor changes to the cash flow estimates to bring them up to or in excess of the hurdle rate. It is also useful when the management team wants to compare the rates of return on different projects, usually when there is only limited funding available and it wants to invest in those projects with the highest possible rate of return. It is determined manually with a "high-low" approach of calculating discounted cash flows that gradually brings the accountant to the correct IRR value. It is more easily calculated with an electronic spreadsheet, such as Microsoft Excel. If that software is used, the calculation would be:

$$= ([\text{range of values}], [\text{guess as to the value of the IRR}])$$

The NPV and IRR methods are quantitatively valid ways to either justify or cancel proposed capital investments. However, they involve estimates of cash flows that may be well into the future, and calculations using discount rates that may also be subject to some degree of dispute. In cases where these issues make the use of NPV or IRR somewhat questionable, one can fall back on the old technique of "payback." Under the payback approach, we ignore the time value of money and instead create a simple calculation that estimates the earliest date on which the initial investment in a capital project is paid back to the company. If the payback period is quite short, then the company's risk of loss on investment is minimal. Unfortunately, this technique does not focus on the potential for substantial cash flows from a project some years into the future, and may result in investments only in projects with rapid returns, which is not a way to run a business with a long-range view of its prospects.

To calculate a project's payback, one can divide the total investment in it by its average annual cash flows. For example, a project with an initial investment of $500,000 and average annual returns of $175,000 would have a payback period of 2.86 years ($500,000/$175,000). However, this approach may yield flawed results if the cash flows vary widely from year to year. This concept is illustrated in Exhibit 28.18, where we see that the cash flows resulting from the $500,000 investment are skewed well into the future, even though their average annual cash flow is $175,000, resulting in a payback that does not actually occur until 4.0 years have passed. Consequently, it is safer to calculate payback on a year-by-year basis.

The accountant is likely to not only evaluate capital proposals with the preceding evaluation methods, but also to handle much of the application paperwork associated with them. A sample of a capital request form is shown in Exhibit 28.19. This form contains the fields needed to conduct a discounted cash flow analysis, for it requires a detailed list of expected cash flows by year, by using a number of key revenue and expense categories. The "type of project" section is also of importance, for it tells the reviewer if a project is subject to a different hurdle rate. For example, a project that is being implemented to resolve a safety issue will probably be approved, irrespective of the hurdle rate or the presence of any positive cash flows at all. The bottom section of the form is crucial for the approval process. It notes the range of approval signatures that must be obtained before the proposal will be

Year	Net Cash Flow	Net Unreturned Investment
0	−$500,000	−$500,000
1	0	−500,000
2	0	−500,000
3	200,000	−300,000
4	300,000	0
5	375,000	+375,000

EXHIBIT 28.18 PAYBACK CALCULATION ON A YEAR-BY-YEAR BASIS

completed, with the number of approvals rising with the level of proposed investment in the project. This form should be issued to the sponsors of capital projects with a sample form and instructions, so they can easily see how it is to be filled out.

After a capital proposal has been approved, the accountant should continue to track actual cash flows and compare them to budgeted levels, so that the management team can see if some project sponsors have a history of incorrectly estimating cash flows in order to obtain project approvals. The postapproval review will also spot any control issues that may arise with the capital approval process, so that the process can subsequently be enhanced for future capital investments.

Capital Budgeting—Throughput Based

The traditional capital budgeting approach involves having the management team review a series of unrelated requests from throughout the company, each one asking for funding for various projects. Management decides whether to fund each request based on the discounted cash flows projected for each one. If there are not sufficient funds available for all requests having positive discounted cash flows, then those with the largest cash flows or highest percentage returns usually are accepted first, until the funds run out.

There are several problems with this type of capital budgeting:

1. Most important, there is no consideration of how each requested project fits into the entire system of production; instead, most requests involve the local optimization of specific work centers that may not contribute to the total throughput of the company.
2. There is no consideration of the constrained resource, so managers cannot tell which funding requests will result in an improvement to the efficiency of that operation.
3. Managers tend to engage in a great deal of speculation regarding the budgeted cash flows resulting from their requests, resulting in inaccurate discounted cash flow projections. Since many requests involve unverifiable cash flow estimates, it is impossible to discern which projects are better than others.

A greater reliance on throughput accounting concepts eliminates most of these problems. First, the priority for funding should be placed squarely on any projects that can improve the capacity of the constrained resource, based on a comparison of the incremental additional throughput created to the incremental operating expenses and investment incurred.

Second, any investment requests not involving the constrained resource should be subject to an intensive critical review, likely resulting in their rejection. Since they do not impact the constrained resource, these investments cannot impact system throughput in any way, so their sole remaining justification must be the reduction of operating expenses or the mitigation of some type of risk.

The one exception to investing in nonconstraint resources is when there is so little excess capacity in a work center that it has difficulty recovering from downtime. This can be a major problem if the lack of capacity constantly causes holes in the inventory buffer and places the constrained resource in danger of running out of work. In this case, a good investment alternative is to invest in a sufficient amount of additional sprint capacity to ensure that the system can recover rapidly from a reasonable level of downtime. If a manager is applying for a capital investment based on this reasoning, she should attach to the proposal

Capital Investment Proposal Form

Name of Project Sponsor: *H. Henderson*　　　　　　**Submission Date:** *09/09/10*

Investment Description:
Additional press for newsprint.

Cash Flows:

Year	Equipment	Working Capital	Maintenance	Tax Effect of Annual Depreciation	Salvage Value	Revenue	Taxes	Total
0	−5,000,000	−400,000		800,000				−5,400,000
1			−100,000	320,000		1,650,000	−700,000	1,170,000
2			−100,000	320,000		1,650,000	−700,000	1,170,000
3			−100,000	320,000		1,650,000	−700,000	1,170,000
4			−100,000	320,000		1,650,000	−700,000	1,170,000
5		400,000	−100,000	320,000	1,000,000	1,650,000	−700,000	2,570,000
Totals	−5,000,000	0	−500,000	2,400,000	1,000,000	8,250,000		1,850,000

Tax Rate:	**40%**
Hurdle Rate:	**10%**
Payback Period:	4.28
Net Present Value:	(86,809)
Internal Rate of Return:	9.4%

362

Type of Project (check one):

Legal requirement   ____

New product-related   ____

Old product extension   _Yes_

Repair/replacement   ____

Safety issue   ____

Approvals:

Amount	Approver	Signature
<$5,000	Supervisor	____
$5–19,999	General Mgr	____
$20–49,999	President	____
$50,000+	Board	____

Reproduced with permission: Bragg, *Financial Analysis: A Controller Guide*, John Wiley & Sons, 2000, p. 24.

EXHIBIT 28.19 CAPITAL REQUEST FORM

a chart showing the capacity level at which the targeted resource has been operating over the past few months as well as the severity of holes in the buffer caused by that operation.

At what point should a company invest in more of the constrained resource? In many cases, the company has specifically designated a resource to be its constraint, because it is so expensive to add additional capacity, so this decision is not to be taken lightly. The decision process is to review the impact on the incremental change in throughput caused by the added investment, less any changes in operating expenses. Because this type of investment represents a considerable step cost (where costs and/or the investment will jump considerably as a result of the decision), management usually must make its decision based on the perceived level of long-term throughput changes rather than on smaller expected short-term throughput increases.

The issues just above have been addressed in the summary-level capital budgeting form shown in Exhibit 28.20. *This* form splits capital budgeting requests into three categories: (1) constraint related, (2) risk related, (3) non–constraint related. The risk-related category covers all capital purchases for which the company must meet a legal requirement or for which there is a perception that the company is subject to an undue amount of risk if it does *not* invest in an asset. All remaining requests that do not clearly call into the constraint-related or risk-related categories drops into a catch-all category at the bottom of the form. The intent of this format is to clearly differentiate between different types of approval requests, with each one requiring different types of analysis and management approval.

The approval levels vary significantly in the throughput-based capital request form. Approvals for constraint-related investments include a process analyst (who verifies that the request actually will impact the constraint) as well as generally higher-dollar approval levels for lower-level managers—the intent is to make it easier to approve capital requests that will improve the constrained resource. Approvals for risk-related projects first require the joint approval of the corporate attorney and chief risk officer, with added approvals for large expenditures. Finally, the approvals for non–constraint-related purchases involve lower-dollar approval levels, so the approval process intentionally is made more difficult.

28.6 THE BUDGETING PROCESS

The budgeting process is usually rife with delays, which are caused by several factors. One is that information must be input to the budget model from all parts of the company—some of which may not put a high priority on the submission of budgeting information. Another reason is that the budgeting process is highly iterative, sometimes requiring dozens of budget recalculations and changes in assumptions before the desired results are achieved. The typical budgeting process is represented in Exhibit 28.21, where we see that there is a sequential process that requires the completion of the revenue plan before the production plan can be completed, which in turn must be finished before the departmental expense budgets can be finished, which then yields a financing plan. If the results do not meet expectations, then the process starts over again at the top of the exhibit. This process is so time-consuming that the budget may not be completed before the budget period has already begun.

There are a number of best practices that can be used to create a more streamlined budgeting process. Here are some of the more common ones:

- *Reduce the number of accounts.* The number of accounts included in the budget should be reduced, thereby greatly reducing the amount of time needed to enter and update data in the budget model.

Capital Request Form

Project name: _____

Name of project sponsor: _____

Submission date: _____   Project number: _____

☐ **Constraint-Related Project**	<u>Approvals</u>
Initial expenditure: $ _____	All _____ Process Analyst
Additional annual expenditure: $ _____	
Impact on throughput: $ _____	$100,000 _____ Supervisor
Impact on operating expenses: $ _____	$100,001 - _____ $1,000,000 President
Impact on ROI: $ _____	
(Attach calculations)	$1,000,000+ _____ Board of Directors

☐ **Risk-Related Project**	<u>Approvals</u>
Initial expenditure: $ _____	_____ Corporate Attorney
Additional annual expenditure: $ _____	< $50,000 ⎰
Description of legal requirement fulfilled or risk issue mitigated (attach description as needed):	_____ Chief Risk Officer
_____	$50,001 + _____ President
_____	$1,000,000+ _____ Board of Directors

☐ **Non-Constraint-Related Project**	<u>Approvals</u>
Initial expenditure: $ _____	All _____ Process Analyst
Additional annual expenditure: $ _____	
☐ Improves sprint capacity? Attach justification of sprint capacity increase	<$10,000 _____ Supervisor
	$10,001 - _____ $100,000 President
☐ Other request Attach justification for other request type	$100,000+ _____ Board of Directors

Exhibit 28.20 Throughput-Based Capital Request Form

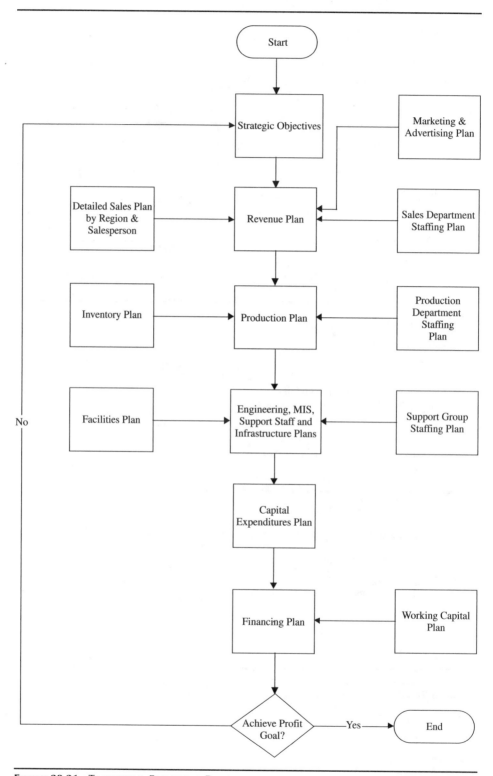

EXHIBIT 28.21 TRADITIONAL BUDGETING PROCESS

- *Reduce the number of reporting periods.* One can consolidate the 12 months shown in the typical budget into quarterly information, thereby eliminating two-thirds of the information in the budget. If the budget must later be reentered into the accounting system in order to provide budget-to-actual comparisons, then a simple formula can be used to divide the quarterly budget back into its monthly components—which is still much less work than maintaining 12 full months of budget information.

- *Use percentages for variable cost updates.* When key activities, such as revenues, are changed in the budget model, one must peruse the entire budget in order to determine what related expenses must change in concert with the key activities. A much easier approach is to use percentage-based calculations for variable costs in the budget model so that these expenses will be updated automatically. They should also be color-coded in the budget model, so that they will not be mistaken for items that are manually changed.

- *Report on variables in one place.* A number of key variables will impact the typical budget model, such as the assumed rate of inflation in wages or purchased parts, tax rates for income, payroll, and workers' compensation, medical insurance rates, and so on. These variables are much easier to find if they are set up in a cluster within the budget, so that one can easily reference and alter them. Under this arrangement, it is also useful to show key results (such as net profits) on the same page with the variables, so that one can make alterations to the variables and immediately see their impact without having to search through the budget model to find the information.

- *Use a budget procedure and timetable.* The budget process is plagued by many iterations, since the first results will nearly always yield profits or losses that do not meet a company's expectations. Furthermore, it requires input from all parts of a company, some of which may lag in sending in information in a timely manner. Accordingly, it is best to construct a budgeting procedure that specifically identifies what job positions must send budgeting information to the budget coordinator, what information is required of each person, and when that information is due. Furthermore, there should be a clear timetable of events that is carefully adhered to, so that plenty of time is left at the end of the budgeting process for the calculation of multiple iterations of the budget.

In addition to these efficiency-improvement issues, there are other ways to modify the budgeting process so that it can be completed much more quickly. The following changes should be considered:

- *Itemize the corporate strategy.* The strategy and related tactical goals that the company is trying to achieve should be listed at the beginning of the budget model. All too frequently, management loses sight of its predetermined strategy when going through the many iterations that are needed to develop a realistic budget. By itemizing the corporate strategy in the budget document, it is much less likely that the final budget model will deviate significantly from the company's strategic direction.

- *Identify step-costing change points.* The budget model should have notations incorporated into it that specify the capacity levels at which expenses are valid. For example, if the production level for Product A exceeds 100,000 per year, then a warning flag should be generated by the budget model that informs the budget manager of the need to add an extra shift to accommodate the increased production requirements. Another example is to have the model generate a warning flag when the average revenue per salesperson exceeds $1,000,000, since this may be the maximum expectation for sales productivity and will require the addition of more sales personnel to the budget. These flags can be clustered at the front of the budget model, so that problems will be readily apparent to the reader.

- *Specify maximum amounts of available funding.* One of the warning flags just noted should include the maximum level of funding that the company can obtain. If an iteration of the budget model results in excessively high cash requirements, then the flag will immediately point out the problem. It may be useful to note next to the warning flag the amount by which the maximum funding has been exceeded so that this information is readily available for the next budget iteration.

- *Base expense changes on cost drivers.* Many expenses in the budget will vary in accordance with changes in various activities within the firm. As noted earlier in this section, expenses can be listed in the budget model as formulas so that they vary in direct proportion to changes in budgeted revenue. This same concept can be taken a step further by listing other types of activities that drive cost behavior, and linking still other expenses to them with formulas. For example, the amount of telephone expense is directly related to the number of employees, so it can be linked to the total number of employees on the staffing budget. Another example is the number of machine setup personnel, which will change based on the planned number of production batches to be run during the year. This level of automation requires a significant degree of knowledge of how selected expenses interact with various activities within the company.

- *Budget by groups of staff positions.* A budget can rapidly become unwieldy if every position in the company is individually identified—especially if the names of all employees are listed. This format requires constant updating as the budget progresses through multiple iterations. A better approach is to itemize by job title, which allows one to vastly reduce the number of job positions listed in the budget.

- *Rank projects.* A more complex budget model can incorporate a ranking of all capital projects, so that any projects with a low ranking will be automatically eliminated by the model if the available amount of cash drops below the point where they could be funded. However, this variation requires that great attention be paid to the ranking of projects, since there may be some interrelationship between projects—if one is dropped but others are retained, then the ones retained may not be functional without the missing project.

- *Issue a summary-level model for use by senior management.* The senior management team is primarily concerned with the summary results of each department, product line, or operating division, and does not have time to wade through the details of individual revenue and expense accounts. Further, it may require an increased level of explanation from the budgeting staff if they do choose to examine these details. Accordingly, the speed of the iteration process can be enhanced by producing a summary-level budget that is directly linked to the main budget, so that all fields in it are updated automatically. The senior management team can more easily review this document, yielding faster updates to the model.

- *Link a bonus sliding scale to the budget.* A reasonably progressive budgeting model will include a direct link into the corporate bonus plan, with staff being paid bonuses based on their achievement of certain goals. Though the intention is good —to create incentives to achieve the budget—it actually tends to create more problems than it solves. One problem is that, if employees realize that they will fall short of their bonus targets, they will be more likely to hoard their resources or possible sales for the next period, when they will have a better opportunity to achieve better performance and be paid a bonus. The result is wild swings in corporate performance from period to period as employees cycle through the hoard-to-splurge cycle. Another problem is that, if the bonus target cannot be attained by normal means, employees will stretch or break the accounting rules in a variety of ways to achieve the target. The solution is to link the budget to a sliding performance scale that contains no "hard" performance goals. The best example of the sliding bonus scale is what it is *not*: There are no specific goals at which the bonus target suddenly increases in size. Instead, the bonus is a constant percentage of the goal, such as 1% of sales or 5% of net after-tax profits. Also, there should be no upper boundary to the sliding scale, which would present employees with the disincentive to stop performing once they have reached a maximum bonus level. Similarly, theoretically there should be no lower limit to the bonus either, though it is more common to see a baseline level that is derived from the corporate breakeven point, on the grounds that employees must at least ensure that the company does not lose money. The sliding scale approach also makes it much easier to budget for the bonus expense at various activity levels rather than trying to budget for the more common all-or-nothing bonus payment.

As a result of these improvements, the budgeting process will change to the format shown in Exhibit 28.22, where the emphasis changes away from many modeling iterations toward the incorporation of a considerable level of automation and streamlining into the structure of the budget model. Following this approach, produces a budget that will require much less manual updating and that will sail through the smaller number of required iterations with much greater speed.

28.7 BUDGETARY CONTROL SYSTEMS

There are several ways in which a budget can be used to enhance a company's control systems, so that objectives are met more easily and it is more difficult for costs to stray from approved levels.

One of the best methods for controlling costs is to link the budget for each expense within each department to the purchasing system. This results in a computer system that will automatically accumulate the total amount of purchase orders that have been issued thus far against a specific account, and will refuse any further purchase orders when the budgeted expense total has been reached. This approach can involve the comparison of the monthly budget to monthly costs, or compare costs to annual budgeted totals. The latter approach can cause difficulty for the inattentive manager, since actual expenses may be running well ahead of the budget for most of the year, but the system will not automatically flag the problem until the entire year's budget has been depleted. Alternatively, a comparison to monthly budgeted figures may result in so many warning flags on so many accounts that the purchasing staff is unable to purchase many items. One workaround for this problem is to use a fixed overage percentage by which purchases are allowed to exceed the budget; another possibility is to only compare cumulative expenses to quarterly budget totals, which reduces the total number of system warning flags.

Another budgetary control system is to compare actual to budgeted results for the specific purpose of evaluating the performance of employees. For example, the warehouse

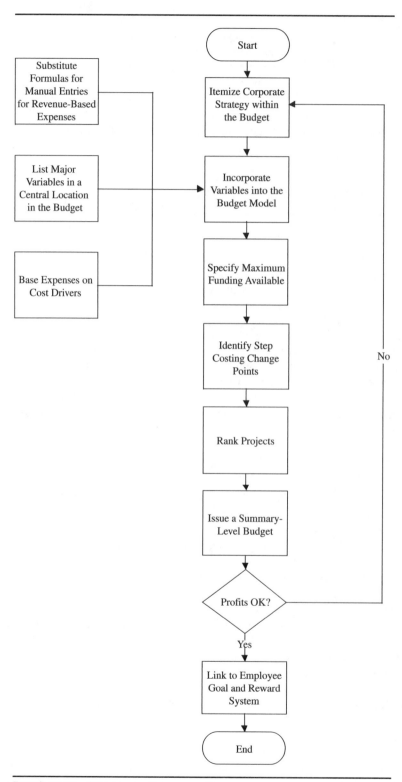

EXHIBIT 28.22 STREAMLINED BUDGETING PROCESS

Account No.	Description	Actual Results	Budgeted Results	Variance
4500-010	Arizona Revenue	$43,529	$51,000	−$7,471

EXHIBIT 28.23 LINE ITEM BUDGET REPORTING FOR SPECIFIC EMPLOYEES

manager may be judged based on actual inventory turnover of 12X, which compares unfavorably to a budgeted turnover rate of 15X. Similarly, the manager of a cost center may receive a favorable review if the total monthly cost of her cost center averages no more than $152,000. This also works for the sales staff, who can be assigned sales quotas that match the budgeted sales levels for their sales territories. In this manner, a large number of employees can have their compensation levels directly tied to the achievement of budgeted goals. This is a highly effective way to ensure that the budget becomes a fixture in the lives of employees.

Yet another budgetary control system is to use it as a feedback loop to employees. This can be done by issuing a series of reports at the end of each reporting period that are specifically designed to match the responsibilities of each employee. For example, Exhibit 28.23 shows a single revenue line item that is reported to a salesperson for a single territory. The salesperson does not need to see any other detailed comparison to the budget, because he is not responsible for anything besides the specific line item that is reported to him. This reporting approach focuses the attention of many employees on just those segments of the budget that they have control over. Though this approach can result in the creation of dozens or even hundreds of reports by the accounting department, they can be automated on most packaged accounting software systems, so that only the initial report creation will take up much accounting time.

An additional control use for the budget is to detect fraud. The budget is usually based upon several years of actual operating results, so unless there are major changes in activity levels, actual expense results should be fairly close to budgeted expectations. If not, variance analysis is frequently used to find out what happened. This process is an excellent means for discovering fraud, since this activity will usually result in a sudden surge in expense levels, which the resulting variance analysis will detect. The two instances in which this control will not work is when the fraud has been in existence for a long time (and so is incorporated into the budgeted expense numbers already) or the amount of fraud is so low that it will not create a variance large enough to warrant investigation.

28.8 SUMMARY

The budget should not be treated as a chore that must be completed at the end of each fiscal year and then ignored, but rather as the foundation for all activities to be completed during the upcoming budget period. It drives the planning for capital expenditures, sales efforts, hiring, marketing campaigns, and research efforts. Due to its comprehensive nature, the accountant should use the budget as both a planning tool and a subsequent control over activities throughout the organization. The budget explanations, examples, and processes shown in this chapter will assist the accountant in achieving these goals.

CHAPTER **29**

CLOSING THE BOOKS

29.1 INTRODUCTION

One of the primary tasks faced by any accountant is either some participation in, or the management of, the periodic delivery of financial statements. When poorly managed, this can result in the late delivery of the statements, as well as inconsistent treatment of recurring accounting issues from period to period, incorrect information, and minimal supporting commentary. In this chapter, we will cover the steps needed not only to properly organize the financial statement production process, but also how to close the books quite rapidly. The concept of closing the books is addressed in considerably more detail in the author's book *Fast Close*, 2nd ed. (John Wiley & Sons, 2009).

Speed of closure is an important goal, for it shifts the focus of the accounting department away from the production of the statements for a large part of the following month, which leaves more time for other activities, such as process improvement of accounting transactions, creating new data collection systems, or providing better financial analysis to the management team. This also results in better morale within the department, since the accounting staff can take pride in knowing that they are part of an efficient and effective process that results in a quality deliverable. Also, a key element in the organization of the financial statement production process is the ongoing and in-depth review of all accounting transactions that feed into the statements, so that errors can be eliminated from them before they reach the financial statements. This ongoing review process leads to considerable efficiencies in operations throughout the accounting department. Consequently, rapidly producing accurate financial statements should be considered an important goal for the accounting department.

29.2 THE CURRENT STATE OF THE FINANCIAL STATEMENTS

Before discussing how to improve the closing process, it is useful to first determine the current state of the closing process, which requires a multitude of steps and requires many days to complete. A representative view of the situation is illustrated in Exhibit 29.1 where the closing process is broken down into activities related to payroll, invoicing, payables, inventory, cash, and final closing activities.

In the exhibit, closing activities are spread out over 11 business days after the end of the month, with activities assigned a minimum time frame of four hours each. Closing activities are as follows:

- *Payroll activities.* These activities require two days, and relate primarily to the accumulation of hours worked for expense accruals and hours that can be billed to customers.

- *Invoicing activities.* Invoicing activities require substantially more time to complete, due to delays in receiving billing information from the shipping department and especially because employees are typically late in submitting expense reports containing expenses that are re-billable to customers. Further, commissions cannot be completed until after final invoices are issued, which adds another time block onto the end of the closing process.

- *Payables activities.* The largest bottleneck is accounts payable, because the controller typically waits up to a week to ensure that all supplier invoices have arrived before attempting to accrue for any additional expenses. The fixed assets register is updated only after payables have been closed, to ensure that all supplier billings for fixed assets have been received, while depreciation cannot be completed until after the fixed assets have been added. Thus, a series of sequential events lengthen the duration of payables-related activities.

- *Inventory activities.* The physical counting and valuation of inventory is represented in the flowchart as requiring nearly six days, but can extend far longer, since the accuracy of the inventory records drives the duration of this process. A considerable degree of inaccuracy can lead to multiple inventory recounts.

- *Cash activities.* The primary delay built into the closing of cash activities is waiting for the month-end bank statement to arrive in the mail. If there are multiple bank statements, then this can become a logjam of reconciliation work several days after month-end.

- *Final closing activities.* Once all the transaction-related work has been completed, a number of final closing activities can extend the close for an additional week. This period is especially prolonged if subsidiaries are sending in accounting information that must be mapped to the corporate chart of accounts, and for which intercompany transactions must be identified and eliminated. Also, since a variety of errors may be present in the financial statements, there is typically a process of several days during which the statements are created, reviewed, and adjusted through several iterations.

Thus, it is evident that there are a number of bottlenecks in the closing process that cumulatively result in a lengthy close. Only multiple improvements, as outlined in the remainder of this chapter, will result in a more compressed closing period.

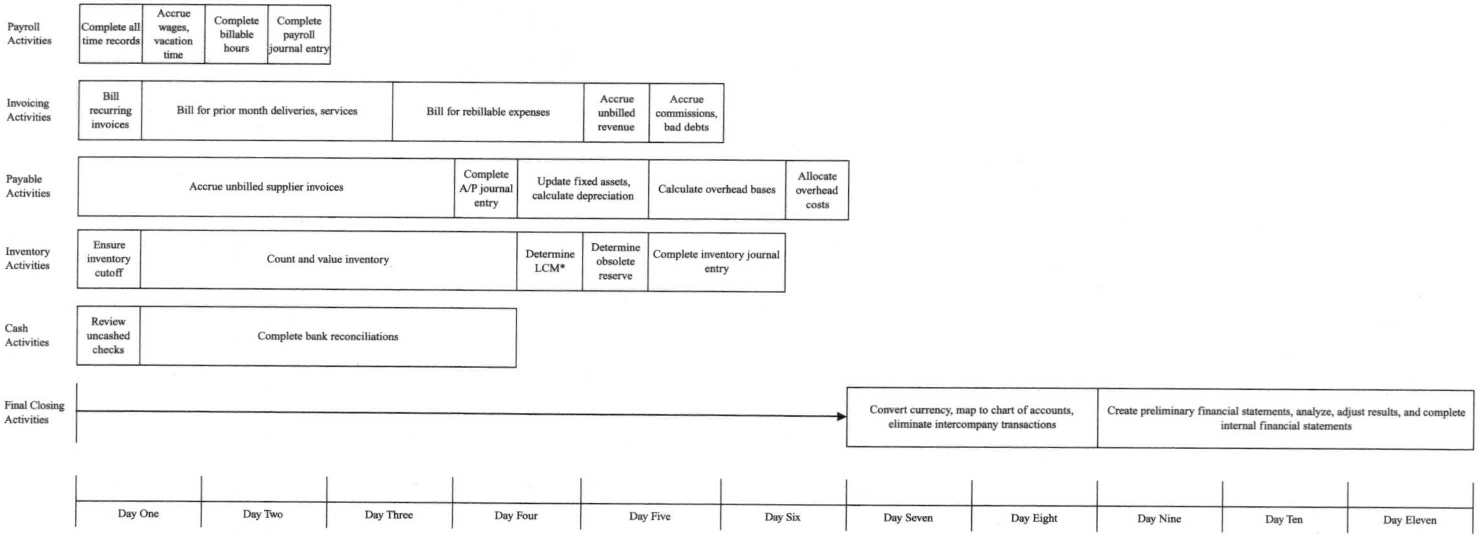

Payroll Activities

Complete all time records | Accrue wages, vacation time | Complete billable hours | Complete payroll journal entry

Invoicing Activities

Bill recurring invoices | Bill for prior month deliveries, services | Bill for rebillable expenses | Accrue unbilled revenue | Accrue commissions, bad debts

Payable Activities

Accrue unbilled supplier invoices | Complete A/P journal entry | Update fixed assets, calculate depreciation | Calculate overhead bases | Allocate overhead costs

Inventory Activities

Ensure inventory cutoff | Count and value inventory | Determine LCM* | Determine obsolete reserve | Complete inventory journal entry

Cash Activities

Review uncashed checks | Complete bank reconciliations

Final Closing Activities

Convert currency, map to chart of accounts, eliminate intercompany transactions | Create preliminary financial statements, analyze, adjust results, and complete internal financial statements

Day One | Day Two | Day Three | Day Four | Day Five | Day Six | Day Seven | Day Eight | Day Nine | Day Ten | Day Eleven

* LCM = Lower of cost or market

EXHIBIT 29.1 UNMODIFIED CLOSING PROCESS

29.3 INTERIM REPORTS

One of the best ways to satisfy financial report recipients with information is to query them about what types of information they need to see as soon as possible, and then report on this information apart from the financial statements. For example, if they need to see revenue figures for the full month as soon as possible, it may make sense to issue daily or weekly summaries instead, as well as an estimated revenue figure just before the end of the reporting period. With this approach, the management team gets to see what it wants at regular intervals, and has less need to see the full set of financial statements, which the accounting staff can then complete and issue a few days later, with no pressure being exerted by anyone because they want to see the information. Other examples of the types of information that report recipients might want to see in advance of the financial statements are both revenue and margins by salesperson, product, or region; cash flow; capital expenditures; and specific performance measurements, such as the days of accounts receivable on hand.

If this approach is taken, then it is very important to build especially strong control systems around the information that is reported early. The main reason for doing this is that the recipients have already established that this is the most important information that they want to see, so it has to be as accurate as possible when issued. Since the time of issuance will be prior to the release of the full financial statements, there will be little time to cross check the underlying data for accuracy. Consequently, the control systems used to collect and summarize the data must be good enough to spot any errors at once and warn the accounting staff that there is a problem.

The use of interim reports is an effective way to issue only the most crucial information as early and frequently as possible, resulting in better information for recipients and less pressure on the accounting staff to complete the financial statements in short order.

29.4 GENERAL IMPROVEMENTS FOR CLOSING THE BOOKS

There are several general activities that will contribute to the speedy and orderly closing of the financial records. One of the most important is to create an expectation with the management team that it will take some time before the speed of closure will improve. The process described in the next few sections is a highly iterative one that can drive the closing process down to as little as one day, but it may be a year or more before this goal is attained. Pointing out the gradual nature of this process will eliminate any expectation that a sudden leap in closure speed will occur.

Another general improvement is to place rigid controls over the types of preclosure information being released by the accounting department. When information is handed out before it has been checked for accuracy, the accounting staff will find itself in the uncomfortable position later on of having to waste time issuing revised reports and explaining why the original information was incorrect. These activities will take place right in the middle of the closing process and so contribute to a much slower release of financial statements. However, management may insist on receiving some types of information as soon as possible; if so, the best approach is to create extra controls over the data that goes into the reported information, so that there is little risk of its inaccuracy. Thus, it is crucial to avoid releasing inaccurate information prior to the issuance of the financial statements.

Another general activity is to document the existing process that is used to create financial statements. This should include a listing of which employees perform certain tasks, the dates on which those tasks are to be completed, and their sequential order. This information forms the basis upon which changes will be made. Writing down the process will likely increase the speed of closure, since the accounting manager can then use it as a checklist to monitor the progress of the closing process.

The standardization of the chart of accounts throughout the organization is a very useful activity, for it reduces the work required to consolidate the financial statements. With a common account structure, there is no need to create a detailed system for mapping accounts from various subsidiaries into a master chart of accounts. Though this can be a difficult and prolonged task to accomplish, the result will be a much smoother closing process.

Yet another general activity is to organize the resources of the department so that it is fully staffed during the periods when financial statements are being compiled. This means that vacations should not be allowed for those employees who are expected to work on the statements during the days when the closing process is under way. If there will be periods when the workload is expected to exceed the available capacity of the staff, then overtime hours should be scheduled well in advance. It also means that any other activities within the accounting area, such as meetings, the preparation of other reports, or training sessions, should be routinely shifted to some other dates that will not conflict with the closing process.

A final general activity is to include a class on the closing process in the mix of departmental training activities. By doing so, the accounting staff can learn about the entire process, so that they will realize how their individual activities affect it. They can also learn about the various techniques available for documenting and analyzing process flows, with a particular focus on reducing cycle times. This knowledge is of great value when the accounting department works on the reduction of time needed to close the books. This training can be extended to include additional personnel, so that the department is fully cross-trained in all of the tasks associated with producing financial statements; by doing so, the department will still be able to complete financial statements on time, even if a few employees are not available to work on them during the closing period.

29.5   CLOSING ACTIVITIES PRIOR TO PERIOD-END

The days prior to the end of the accounting period can be used to complete a large quantity of activities related to the close. This is a prime area for improvements, since many accounting organizations seem to think that the closing process does not begin until the accounting period is complete. In reality, a properly managed closing process will have very few tasks to complete *after* the end of the accounting period. In this section, we will review many of these activities.

In terms of slowing down the production of financial statements, one of the worst offenders is the bank reconciliation. It does not usually arrive from the bank until a week after the account period has closed, and then it requires a rush effort to complete. To avoid this problem, several of the larger national and superregional banks now offer online access to detailed banking records, which allows one to conduct an ongoing bank reconciliation throughout the month. As a result, all adjusting entries for the bank reconciliation will have been made well before the end of the accounting period, so that there is no further work to be done in this area after the period end.

Another activity is the ongoing review of key account balances during the accounting period, or at least a single review several days prior to the period end. This allows the accounting staff to see if there are any unusually high or low account balances that require investigation. This review may involve a comparison to budgeted levels or a trend line of balances from previous periods. By checking balances a few days early, the accounting staff can spot and correct problems that would otherwise require examination during the "crunch period" immediately following the end of the accounting period, when there are few resources available for such activities.

It is also possible to complete all depreciation and amortization calculations prior to period-end. Though it is quite likely that a few assets arriving close to the period end will not be recorded in these calculations, they will be picked up for the following period's financial statements, and so will have a minimal impact on reported results. If this method is used, there should be an additional waiting period at the end of the fiscal year, so that *all* assets can be recorded for auditing purposes.

Another possibility is to create a bad debt reserve in advance of the period end that is based on a historical trend line of bad debt experiences. This accrual can be adjusted every quarter or so in order to reflect actual bad debt experience. As long as there is a reasonably well-founded history of bad debts upon which to rely, there is no reason to conduct a painstaking review of this reserve at the end of each reporting period.

One can also reduce the time needed to produce the written financial statements by creating boilerplate footnotes in advance to accompany the statements. The footnotes can have blank spots in the few areas that require adjustments based on the period-end figures, while the remaining verbiage is reviewed in advance to verify that it is still applicable to the financial situation.

Another report-related activity is to review the format and content of the previous period's financial statements with the management team to see if they need all of the information that was presented. If not, then these items can be eliminated, which reduces the amount of data gathering and summarization that would otherwise be required.

Cost allocations are a prime target for advance work. The bases upon which overhead allocations are typically made are carefully recalculated after every period-end, even though the percentage changes in the bases tend to be quite small. A better approach is to allocate costs using bases that are developed from the financial and operational results of the last few reporting periods, which ignores the results of the current period. Doing so allows the allocation bases to be developed at any time during the current accounting period, and they can then be quickly multiplied by period-end costs to determine actual allocations.

Another possibility is to create and partially populate journal entry forms in advance. For example, forms can be created in advance for all of the following entries, including account numbers and descriptions:

- Amortization
- Audit fee
- Bad debt
- Depreciation
- Insurance
- Interest income
- Interest expense
- Property taxes
- Royalties
- Salaries and wages accrual
- Vacation accrual
- Bank reconciliation

Some accruals, such as for salaries and wages, can also be completed in advance using estimations. For example, the accounting staff can approximate the number of people who will be working during the period between the last pay day and the end of the accounting period, and create an accrual for this amount. These entries tend to be slightly inaccurate, but can be improved upon by diligent reviews of variances between estimates and actual results.

A small number of accruals will involve the exact same amount of money in every accounting period. If so, these can be converted into automatically recurring entries (assuming that the accounting software will allow this) and so can be entered once and then avoided, save for an occasional review to see if the entry is still valid.

The number of possible activities that one can engage in prior to the period end makes it clear that the closing process is one that can be conducted in a continuous manner, rather than in a rush, and so is more conducive to smooth scheduling of accounting staff time.

29.6 CLOSING ACTIVITIES SUBSEQUENT TO PERIOD-END

Once the accounting period has ended, the primary focus should be on the remaining activities needed to complete the close that are bottleneck operations. In other words, all management attention should focus on those few items that require the largest amount of staff time to complete. There are only a few items in this category. The worst one used to be the bank reconciliation, but in the last section we learned how to shift the bulk of the work associated with that activity into the prior period. One of the other bottlenecks is the completion of invoicing from activities at the end of the prior period. The completion of this activity is dependent upon the forwarding of shipping documentation by the shipping staff, so it is helpful to send the accounting staff to that area to assist in the completion of paperwork, which they can then hand-carry back to the accounting department. This activity can also be automated, as noted in the next section.

Another bottleneck operation is the completion of accounts payable. One could wait a week for all supplier invoices to arrive in the mail and then enter them into the computer system, but this introduces a one-week delay into the closing process. A better approach is to compile a list of recurring invoices that always arrive late, and accrue an estimated balance for each one, rather than wait for the actual invoice to arrive. Also, if purchase orders are used, any open ones can be compared to the receiving log to see if the associated purchases have arrived, even if the supplier invoice has not, and then accrue for the amount of the purchase order. This process can also be automated, as noted in the next section.

Another bottleneck operation is the investigation and resolution of variances. This step tends to occur last, after the financial statements have been produced, but are clearly not showing accurate results. As noted in the last section, some variance analysis can be conducted in the prior period, based on partial results. However, some variances will still arise. One way to reduce the workload is to only review items that exceed a minimum variance threshold percentage, and leave all other variances for investigation after the statements have been released. Though this defers some likely transactional corrections, they will be so small that they would not have made a significant alteration in the reported financial results.

A final bottleneck is the accumulation of quantity and costing information for the period-end inventory. If a manual inventory count is conducted at the end of each period, then several days and many hours of staff time must be devoted to this activity, resulting in significant delays in the closing. To combat this, the inventory system should be shifted to a perpetual one, where ongoing inventory balances are constantly updated. This allows one to avoid period-end inventory counts and focus instead on cycle counts, which are small ongoing counts that constantly review different parts of the inventory area. These steps avoid all period-end activities related to inventory.

Even with the bottleneck-related problems being systematically addressed and reduced in size, there are a number of other activities that can be improved upon, though their impact will not be as great. One is to avoid the creation of small accruals. In too many instances, an overly zealous accounting manager requires the staff to calculate and create accruals for every conceivable expense, even though their net impact is minimal. This results in a barely discernible impact on the financial statements, but a considerable workload on the staff. To avoid the problem, there should be a minimum accrual size below which accruals will not be created.

There can also be a problem with an overabundance of journal entries that are made during this period, possibly conflicting with each other. The problem arises because multiple employees have the ability to enter journal entries. A better approach is to funnel all journal entries through a small group of authorized personnel, so that these employees can track what entries are made, compare them to a standard set of entries, and verify that the correct entries are made, in the correct amounts, and to the correct accounts.

It is also possible to analyze the post period-end processing flow and revise it so that activities are accomplished in parallel, rather than serially. For example, a processing flow may be arranged so that the first task must be completed before the next task is addressed, which in turn feeds into yet another task. This process flow incorporates a great deal of wait time between activities, and therefore tends to greatly extend the time required to complete the final task at the end of the chain of activities. It is better to split apart these processes into smaller groups so that the number of dependencies is reduced. This allows one to complete the closing much more quickly.

A final item is related to management of the process—the accounting manager should schedule a daily meeting with the accounting staff to go over the tasks that need to be completed in order to close the books. These meetings should always include a handout that specifies the exact tasks required of each person on the team, when the tasks must be completed, and whether or not they have been done. If the closing process is a highly accelerated one, it may even be necessary to hold more than one meeting per day to ensure that tasks are being properly completed. This task cannot be overemphasized—proper management has a major positive impact on the efficiency and effectiveness of the closing process.

29.7 CLOSING ACTIVITIES SUBSEQUENT TO STATEMENT ISSUANCE

During the issuance of financial statements, it is quite likely that several problems will be encountered, such as errors in a few transactions that required manual correction by the accounting staff, or perhaps a failure in the closing schedule that resulted in some wasted time and delayed issuance of the statements. If these problems crop up once, they will very likely do so again, unless prompt action is taken to resolve them before the next set of financial statements must be issued. Consequently, it is important to call a meeting immediately after the financial statements have been completed, so that all participants in the process can categorize the problems encountered and prioritize them for resolution. Responsibility for completion of the most critical items can then be handed out, with follow-up meetings scheduled by the accounting manager to ensure that progress is made in resolving the issues.

These meetings do not have to focus on just the problems that were encountered. Another major topic of discussion can be streamlining methods that further reduce the time needed before the statements can be issued. This may involve changes in who does some portions of the work, or perhaps the reduced use of some accounting controls that are interfering with the processing time. This may also include an ongoing analysis of the critical path used by the accounting team, with particular attention being paid to the time required for the completion of certain processing steps, as well as wait times for key activities. The number of potential topics is quite large, and should keep an accounting team busy on an ongoing basis with a continual stream of prospective improvements to be considered.

Another valuable activity is to utilize the services of the internal audit department in arriving at solutions to systemic problems that are interfering with the production of financial statements. Specifically, if the accounting staff finds recurring transactional problems that are originating outside of the accounting department, then it should call for an audit to ascertain the root cause of the problem, as well as recommendations for how to resolve it. The only problem is that the internal audit staff may have a long backlog of requested audits, and cannot address the requested issues for some time. Consequently, it is important to list all issues to be handed over to the internal audit staff as soon as they are discovered, rather than burying them in a long list of problems to be addressed at a later date.

29.8   THE CLOSING CHECKLIST

The result of the discussion in the preceding sections should be a closing schedule such as the one shown in Exhibit 29.2. This schedule itemizes the various activities to be completed as part of the standard period-end close. Individual companies can likely add more specific

---

In Advance:

- Accrue Bad Debt Reserve
- Accrue Interest Expense
- Accrue Subscriptions
- Accrue Unpaid Hourly Wages
- Accrue Unused Vacation Time
- Allocate Rent
- Complete Bank Reconciliations, Interest Income (Prev. Statement)
- Record Depreciation
- Review Billable Hours in Timekeeping System
- Fund the Flexible Spending Account (FSA) Bank Account
- Enter Commissions through Current Date
- Review Department Financials for Errors
- Reconcile Prepaid Assets Account

During:

- Accrue Royalties
- Accrue Bonuses
- Accrue Revenue for Unbilled Projects
- Complete Billable Hours Invoicing
- Finalize and Accrue Commissions
- Record Income Tax Liability
- Tie Detail to Balance Sheet
- Convert Financials to PDF Format and Issue

After:

- Update Procedures
- Request New Programming
- Lock Prior Timesheet Periods

EXHIBIT 29.2   CLOSING SCHEDULE

tasks to this basic list and may want to consider assigning task completions to specific dates, rather than "in advance" of the close, "during" closing day, and "after" closing day, as is used in the exhibit. If many people are involved in the closing processing, this schedule can also be subdivided into numerous smaller schedules that are precisely tailored to the responsibilities of each person, with only the controller or an assistant controller having overall responsibility for the entire closing operation.

29.9   RESULTS OF CLOSING IMPROVEMENTS

If all of the preceding improvement suggestions were to be implemented, the timing of the revised closing process would be similar to the process flow shown in Exhibit 29.3, where most of the closing activities have been shifted into the period prior to the end of the month, leaving only one day to actually close the books. Comments regarding the changes in timing are as follows:

- *Payroll activities.* Since payroll is usually processed before the end of the month, the only activity that must be delayed until after month-end is the verification of hours entered in the timekeeping system for the period from the end of the last pay period to the end of the month.
- *Invoicing activities.* Though final billing still represents the most labor-intensive activity following month-end, a number of preliminary steps can be taken to reduce the labor involved, including preliminary commission calculations and the early billing of recurring invoices.
- *Payables activities.* By relying more on purchase orders and accruals, it is possible to entirely eliminate the waiting period for late supplier invoices, which allows multiple downstream activities to be shifted into the period before month-end.
- *Inventory activities.* A high level of inventory record accuracy allows one to rapidly create the inventory valuation, which changes the inventory close from a long-term, error-prone series of activities to a nonevent.
- *Cash activities.* By conducting a daily bank reconciliation using the bank's online bank statement capability, there is no need to have any cash-related events extend past month-end.
- *Final closing activities.* By centralizing accounting and using a single chart of accounts, as well as a reduced set of core financial statements, it is possible to complete an internal set of financial statements by the end of the first day following month-end.

Thus, a careful restructuring of closing activities, coupled with a high level of inventory record accuracy and more centralization of the accounting function, can lead to an error-free close in a minimum amount of time.

29.10   THE INSTANTANEOUS CLOSE

A few companies are now touting their achievement of an instantaneous close. In its ultimate form, this means that one can request a financial statement from the computer system at the stroke of midnight on the last day of the accounting period and expect to see an accurate set of financial statements.

To achieve this extraordinary level of promptness and accuracy requires correspondingly extraordinary attention to all of the systems that feed into the financial statements.

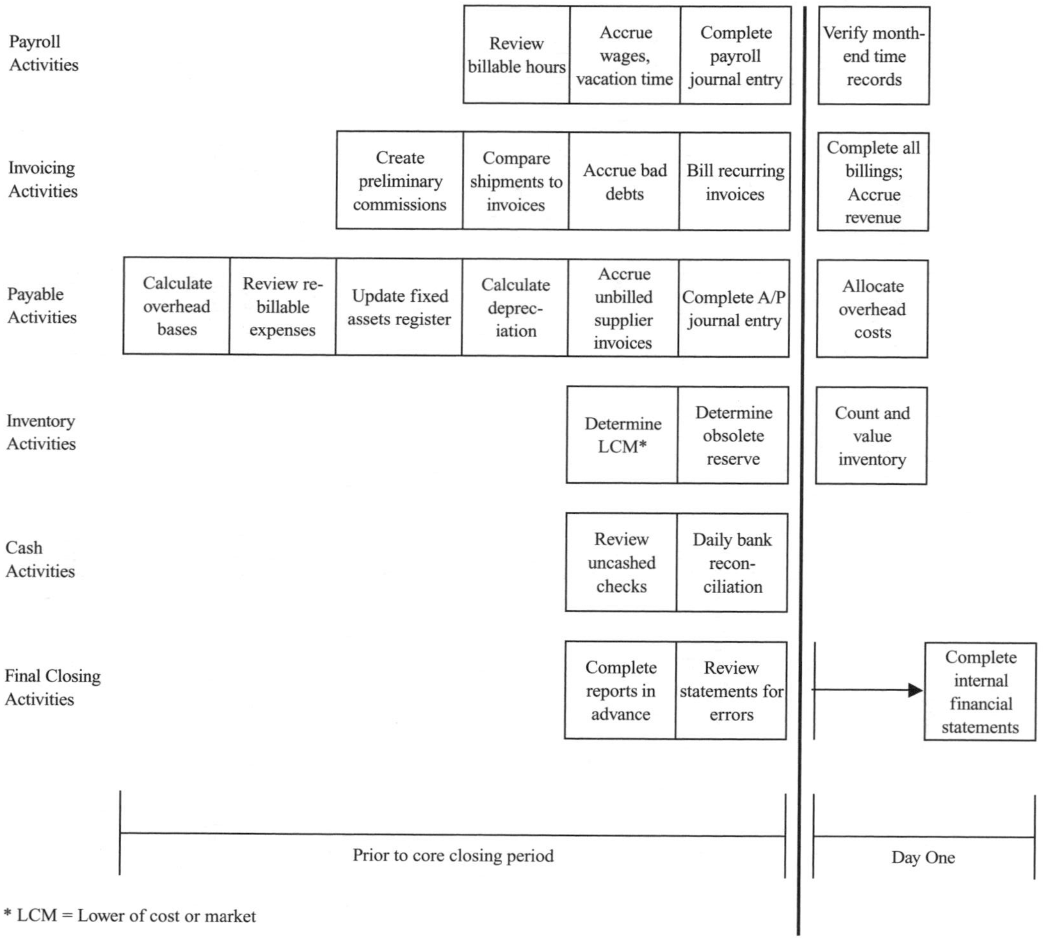

Payroll
Activities

Invoicing
Activities

Payable
Activities

Inventory
Activities

Cash
Activities

Final Closing
Activities

Calculate overhead bases	Review re-billable expenses	Create preliminary commissions	Review billable hours	Accrue wages, vacation time	Complete payroll journal entry	Verify month-end time records
		Create preliminary commissions	Compare shipments to invoices	Accrue bad debts	Bill recurring invoices	Complete all billings; Accrue revenue
		Update fixed assets register	Calculate depreciation	Accrue unbilled supplier invoices	Complete A/P journal entry	Allocate overhead costs
				Determine LCM*	Determine obsolete reserve	Count and value inventory
				Review uncashed checks	Daily bank reconciliation	
				Complete reports in advance	Review statements for errors	Complete internal financial statements

Prior to core closing period | Day One

* LCM = Lower of cost or market

EXHIBIT 29.3 COMPRESSED CLOSING PROCESS

There should be minimal manual data entry or intervention of any sort, as well as such a small number of transactional errors that their incurrence results in no discernible difference in the accuracy of the financial statements. Here are some of the areas in which significant changes must be made in order to achieve the instantaneous close:

- *Accurate perpetual inventory system.* There can be no problems with the perpetual inventory system in terms of inventory identification, location codes, quantities, or units of measure. To achieve such a high degree of accuracy calls for a very highly trained warehouse staff, as well as constant cycle counts of the inventory and immediate follow-up of any issues found during the counts. Furthermore, the perpetual inventory records must be linked to the accounting database so that the data can be immediately pulled into the financial statements.

- *Automated bank reconciliations.* To avoid the lengthy delays typically associated with bank reconciliations, a company must arrange with its bank for a direct electronic linkage to its banking records so that it can electronically compare its book records to the bank records. The result will be a small number of reconciling items that can be quickly reviewed and fixed by the accounting staff.

- *Automatic accrual calculations.* Accruals can be automated if there are linkages to supporting databases. For example, the payroll database should contain a record of how many hours have been reported by all hourly employees, right up to the last day of the accounting period; a program can multiply these hours worked by employee pay rates, including shift differentials and overtime, to arrive at quite an accurate wage accrual. The salary accrual calculation can also be automated by linking it to the payroll database, which allows a program to determine a salary accrual in a similar manner. This approach will also work for the vacation accrual (by a linkage to the payroll database) and the bad debt accrual (by a linkage to the collections history database, along with some collection assumptions).

- *Automatic commission calculations.* There is no time to manually review all invoices completed during the past accounting period, calculate commission splits, overrides, and bonuses, and still meet the financial statement issuance deadline. Instead, the commission structure must be converted into a comprehensible and standardized structure that can be programmed into the accounting system, resulting in the automatic calculation of commissions. It is even better to post commissions for the sales staff to review over the course of the accounting period, so that they can talk to the accounting staff if they see any errors in the calculations.

- *Automatic depreciation calculations and posting.* When an account payable that is coded for a fixed asset is entered, the computer system must be able to automatically pull the entered data into a fixed asset program that will calculate depreciation and post the information to the accounting records. This will require some programming work to allow for additional data entry up front that will sufficiently identify each asset, as well as the asset class in which it should be recorded.

- *Automatic invoice generation.* A common delay in the financial statement completion process is the transfer of shipping data from the shipping department to the accounting staff, which bills it to customers. This is a highly manual process. To get around it, the receiving staff must create bills of lading through a computer that is linked to product price tables, which in turn can be used to automatically create invoices. Even better, the invoices can be replaced by electronic data interchange transactions that are automatically sent to customers. This process is more difficult for services companies, since they must collect information from employees regarding hours worked during the period, as well as the tasks on which they worked. This issue can be alleviated by having employees enter their information through a company Intranet site, which in turn is linked to an invoicing program within the accounting system. This tends to be a lengthy process to accomplish.

- *Automatic payables posting.* Financial statements can be seriously delayed if a company is waiting for a few remaining supplier invoices to arrive—which may take one or two extra weeks. To avoid this, a company can revert to the use of purchase orders for all purchases of any significant size; if a product has been received from a supplier by the end of the accounting period, but not its associated invoice, then the company can use the underlying purchase order information to accrue for the cost of the received item, thereby avoiding the need for the supplier invoice to create an accurate set of financial statements. In addition, there can be a considerable delay associated with the comparison of purchase orders to supplier invoices and receiving documentation before accounts payable will be entered into the accounting database. To avoid this trouble, the receiving staff can check off receipts at a computer terminal in the receiving area that are authorized through a purchase order, which in turn can trigger an automatic payment to the supplier. This avoids the entire document-matching process, thereby eliminating a hindrance to the creation of instantaneous financial statements.

Though the word "automatic" occurs a great deal in the preceding list of capabilities, it is not really necessary to have a fully automated system in order to achieve an instantaneous close. Any activity that can be completed before the end of an accounting period, such as estimated accruals or online bank reconciliations, can still be performed manually, since it will have no impact on the release date for the financial statements.

It is also possible to take the concept of the instantaneous close a step further and close the books at any time during the reporting period, so that one can see an accurate picture of the company's financial results. This capability requires somewhat more work to become perfectly accurate, since the system must incorporate incremental journal entries that itemize costs for a partial period that would normally only be entered at the end of the period. The most common issues here are accrued salaries and wages, as well as depreciation. For example, salaries are normally paid just a few times per month, and are only recorded in the accounting records at those intervals. This means that anyone trying to create financial statements just prior to the date when salary information is entered into the system will see financial results that are deficient in the amount of salary expense. A reasonable way to avoid this problem for salary expenses is to link the accounting database to the human resources database so that a computer program can make a reasonable estimate of the daily salary expense based on the number of employees and create an entry in the general ledger that reflects this estimate. The computer system must also be able to reverse out these daily entries whenever actual salary costs are entered, in order to avoid double counting of salary expenses. This level of sophistication calls for a great deal of programming expertise, as well as a more cluttered general ledger that will contain many daily accruals and related accrual reversals.

An alternative approach to the use of automated daily accruals is to have the accounting staff manually determine the amount of the daily accruals in advance, set them up into a single journal entry, and make the journal entry every morning, so that anyone accessing the company's financial information after that time will be able to see reasonably accurate daily financial information. This is a much less expensive way to handle daily accruals.

However, the accounting staff must frequently update its standard daily journal entry to ensure that the accrual is as close to actual results as possible.

The instantaneous close, as well as its more advanced cousin, the daily close, require extraordinarily accurate underlying accounting information in order to yield accurate results. This means that the accounting staff must labor to clean up the processes for all of the transactions that flow into the financial statements, which can take a very long time to achieve. In addition, the accounting computer systems must be modified to achieve higher levels of automation than is normally found in a standard off-the-shelf accounting package. Accordingly, this level of achievement is only found in companies with a great devotion to transactional excellence and a large budget for computer system customizations.

29.11 CLOSING THE BOOKS OF A PUBLIC COMPANY

A publicly held company must take one additional step in the issuance of its financial statements, which is to file those statements with the Securities and Exchange Commission (SEC). Unfortunately, the filing process requires the involvement of several outside parties, which makes it impossible to close the books in a single day. In fact, closing in a month can be considered a respectable accomplishment. In this section, we will note the extra steps required to file financial statements with the SEC, who is involved in the process, and what steps can be taken to shorten the time period.

Constructing the SEC Filing

Financial statements and supporting disclosures must be filed by publicly held companies with the SEC on a quarterly basis. Those statements issued for the first, second, and third quarters of a company's fiscal year are called 10Q reports, while the year-end report is called a 10K report.

The 10Q and 10K reports include a company's basic financial statements as well as a number of additional disclosures that greatly exceed the size of the statements. While a company may be accustomed to producing the financial statements in short order, the other parts of the SEC filings can require a considerable amount of additional time to complete. Exhibit 29.4 shows a sampling of the additional contents of a 10K report, as well as the likely timing of when each item can be completed.

It is apparent from the "timing" discussion in Exhibit 29.4 that all disclosures in a 10K report can, to some extent, be completed prior to the end of the reporting period, with the notable exceptions of the MD&A section and some financial statement footnotes.

The items described in the table are general SEC requirements that apply to all public companies. Companies in specialized industries, such as insurance or banking, must make extensive additional industry-specific disclosures in the financial statement footnotes. Also, certain activities require additional footnote disclosures, such as stock options, business combinations, pensions, and the use of variable interest entities. The sum total of these disclosures can result in SEC filings having the approximate size of a small book.

Some smaller companies with minimal accounting support outsource the 10Q and 10K reports to SEC specialists who create the entire reports. This solution works best for companies with small accounting staffs and relatively simple operations that require minimal disclosures. However, an SEC specialist is going to be flooded with work from multiple clients during quarterly reporting periods, so it can be difficult to obtain a completed report in a timely manner. If this is a company's best alternative for constructing an SEC filing, it should reserve a block of the specialist's time well in advance and be absolutely certain

Item Header	Description	Timing
Description of the business	Describes the company's general purpose; its history, business segments, customers, suppliers, sales and marketing operations, customer support, intellectual property, competition, and employees. It is designed to give the reader a grounding in what the company does and the business environment in which it operates.	Should be completed well before the financial statements, since the information it contains is general in nature and is not dependent on any financial results.
Risk factors	An exhaustive compilation of all risks to which the company is subjected. Serves as a general warning to investors of what actions might negatively impact their investments in the company.	Should be completed well in advance, typically in cooperation with the company's general counsel.
Description of property	Describes the company's leased or owned facilities, including square footage, lease termination dates, and lease amounts paid per month.	All of this information can be readily compiled well in advance of the financial statements.
Legal proceedings	Describes current legal proceedings involving the company and the company's estimate of the likely outcome of those proceedings.	Can complete an initial description of all legal proceedings before the end of the reporting period and have the general counsel update it just prior to final issuance.
Market for company stock	Notes where the company's stock trades, the number of holders of record, and high and low closing prices per share, by quarter.	Most of the high-low bid prices require no updates, other than to drop the oldest quarter and add the newest. The number of shareholders of record requires input from the stock transfer agent, which should be available one day after the period-end.
Management's discussion and analysis (MD&A)	Involves multiple areas of required commentary, including opportunities, challenges, risks, trends, key performance indicators, future plans, and changes in revenues, cost of goods sold, other expenses, assets, and liabilities.	Requires much of the 10K preparation time. Key performance indicators can include operational information, which may not be available until several days after the period-end. Also, the description of changes in accounts requires a detailed variance analysis that may not be practicable until after the financial statements have been completed. Thus, the variance analysis is a bottleneck.
Footnotes to the financial statements	Includes all disclosures required by generally accepted accounting principles (GAAP), including descriptions of acquisitions, discontinued operations, fixed assets, accrued liabilities, related party transactions, income taxes, stock options, segment information, and many other possibilities, depending on the nature of a company's transactions.	Some GAAP disclosures change little between periods and can be updated easily with a brief review prior to period-end. Other disclosures require some detail, such as fixed assets and accrued liabilities, and so are completed late in the 10K preparation process.

EXHIBIT 29.4   SAMPLING OF 10K REPORT CONTENTS

Item Header	Description	Timing
Controls and procedures	A statement generally describing the company's system of internal controls, testing of controls, changes in controls, and management's conclusions regarding the effectiveness of controls.	This information is not contingent on completion of the financial statements, so it can be completed well in advance of most of other parts of the 10K.
Identification of control persons	Identifies executive officers, directors, promoters, and control persons.	Can be deferred and included in the annual proxy statement.
Executive compensation	Itemizes various types of compensation received by company executives.	Can be deferred and included in the annual proxy statement.
Security ownership of control persons and management	Notes the number of shares of all types owned or controlled by certain beneficial owners and management.	Can be deferred and included in the annual proxy statement.

EXHIBIT 29.4   SAMPLING OF 10K REPORT CONTENTS (*Continued*)

to provide the person with all necessary items as of that date (usually the trial balance and an array of supporting documents, such as a calculation of earnings per share, the number of shares outstanding, any customers with sales exceeding 10% of total sales, etc.). Also, the specialist is not as familiar with the company's operations as an insider would be, so the controller must carefully review the resulting 10Q or 10K report to ensure that no discussion items are incorrect or misleading.

Given the many additional items of information needed, it can take a number of days to complete the 10Q and 10K report, especially if the company must wait in line for the services of an outside specialist to write them.

Quarterly Auditor Reviews and Audits

The company's external auditors must conduct a review of the 10Q reports and a full audit of the 10K report. (Henceforth, we will describe both reviews and audits as "audits.") These audits represent the longest block of time between creating the initial set of financial statements and filing reports with the SEC, so they are worth considerable attention from the perspective of a fast close. The goal is to shrink the length of the audit work.

The duration of an audit will depend on the complexity of the company's financial records, the strength of its control systems, the manpower assigned to the work by both the company and its auditors, testing work already completed by the auditors, the accuracy of the 10Q or 10K report, and the accuracy of the underlying records. The following bullet points note ways to alter these variables to achieve the shortest possible audit:

- *Maximize auditor manpower.* Auditors must complete a clearly defined series of review or audit steps that require a specific amount of time. Usually it is not possible to reduce the total number of work hours involved, but it may be possible to influence the auditors to assign the maximum number of their staff to the work, in order to compress more work into fewer days. This concept can only be taken so far—assigning 100 auditors to a review that requires 100 hours does *not* mean that the review will be completed in one hour! The countervailing pressure from the auditors is that, if they have multiple publicly held clients, they must spread a limited number of auditors over multiple companies. However, if the company's audit committee is willing to apply pressure on the auditors, this can at least result in a fully staffed audit. If the auditor agrees to maximize staffing, this will only be for a limited amount of time that is carefully scheduled, so the company must have its records completely ready for an audit on the scheduled audit start date.

- *Retain experienced auditors.* A key factor in the efficiency of an audit is the experience level of the auditors assigned to work on the company's audit. This does not mean that the company should insist on having no one below the level of partner conduct its audits. However, the controller should have a considerable interest in seeing the same auditors return time and again. An auditor who has a long history of reviewing a company's controls and records is much more efficient than someone who has no knowledge of the company. Thus, the company should express continuing interest in retaining existing auditors on an ongoing basis. In addition, if a new auditor is assigned to the next audit, volunteer to give him a training session before the period-end close, which can involve a tour of the facilities, meetings with key accounting personnel, preliminary transaction tests, and the like. The goal is to increase new auditor familiarity with the company before the audit begins.

- *Maximize audit support by the company.* If the auditors are willing to maximize their staffing of an audit, then the company should do so as well. There is a significant amount of audit support work to be done, such as completing analytical reviews, pulling underlying files from records, and assisting with receivable confirmations. If anything, the controller should assign too many staff to support the auditors, to ensure that these tasks are completed promptly. Ultimately, the goal of overstaffing is to ensure that the auditors complete their work within the scheduled time period, so that no auditors have to be released from the company's audit and sent to their next scheduled audit, thereby prolonging the completion of the company's audit.

- *Encourage preliminary testing.* There are a number of tests that auditors can complete prior to the year-end audit; for example, they can review debt, equity, and fixed asset detail records a month or so in advance of the audit, which leaves them with minimal roll-forward work to complete during the actual audit. The company should encourage this preliminary testing, since it reduces the length of the audit. This solution is of minimal value for quarterly reviews, since auditors are not conducting such extensive testing during those times.

- *Delay the audit.* The entire SEC filing process actually may be completed sooner if the audit is delayed a few days. This is because, as just noted, the auditors can assign a maximum number of staff to an audit only for a limited period of time—and if the company has not had sufficient time to prepare materials for the auditors, then audit staff time will be wasted, thereby prolonging the audit. Thus, despite the seemingly reverse logic of delaying the start of the audit, it actually can reduce the total length of the filing process.

- *Increase control strength.* If audit testing determines that there are errors in the underlying accounting records, the auditors must spend more time reviewing an even larger sample of accounting records. This requires more time by both the auditors (who are the scarce resource) and the company's staff, who must pull the additional records for the auditors to review. Consequently, it pays off in reduced audit time if the company installs the strongest possible controls over accounting transactions. In particular, if the audit team finds errors in a particular set of transactions, then the controller should be absolutely certain that new controls have eliminated the bulk of those errors by the time of the next audit. Increasing control strength may require significant in-house staffing, so the controller must weigh the incremental cost of new controls against the corresponding reduction in audit duration.

- *Double-check the 10Q or 10K report.* Auditors do not like to waste time reviewing multiple versions of SEC reports, since it turns them into high-priced document reviewers and also extends the duration of the audit. Instead, once the first draft of a document is prepared, have a second person review it in great detail. In particular, verify that historical information matches what was reported in earlier SEC filings. If the reviewer finds multiple errors, it make sense to have yet another person conduct an additional review, to ensure that *all* mistakes are rooted out before the auditors see a draft.

- *Complete supporting documentation for footnotes.* Besides the financial statements, the 10Q and 10K reports contain extensive discussions of the company's financial results in the management's discussion and analysis section. The auditors will review the MD&A section in considerable detail and will want proof of various assertions made by the company. For example, if the company states that its consulting segment comprises 75% of total company revenues, then the company should have a spreadsheet prepared that proves this. By creating a standard package of supporting documentation for the auditors, a company can shave some additional time from its audit.

Even if a company implements *all* of the preceding recommendations, there is still a limit on how short the audit process can become. It is scheduled by a third party who faces conflicting priorities with multiple clients, there will be auditor shortages, and most of the audit work must be conducted by the auditors. For all of these reasons, and despite all the work a controller may complete to initially prepare financial statements in a single day, auditing the results may not be completed for weeks thereafter.

Audit Committee Approval

The company's audit committee must also give its formal approval of the 10Q and 10K filings. The committee may consent to approving an early version of either report, but by far the most common scenario is to send them the final version, after all changes have been made. This is a reasonable request by the audit committee, since it does not want to approve reports that may subsequently be changed. Because this approval stands as a discrete step between the auditor review and EDGARizing (as discussed next), it is a bottleneck that lengthens the filing time.

The audit committee approval meeting must be set multiple days in advance, in order to coordinate the schedules of the committee members. The committee generally wants to see the 10Q or 10K report at least 24 hours before the meeting, so it has sufficient time for a proper review. The group then discusses the report during a conference call, the controller or an assistant notes all recommendations made during the meeting, and the accounting staff then creates an updated version of the report after the call.

It is extremely difficult to reduce the audit committee's timeline, but there are a few ways to achieve minor time reductions. One possibility is to issue a disclosure memo to the committee members well before they see the financial statements. A disclosure memo itemizes the accounting issues that the company is addressing in the current financial statements, such as a change in accounting method. If the committee members are aware of these issues in advance, they will be less likely to address them again during the committee meeting and even less likely to request changes in the financial statements.

Another possibility is to issue the financial statements to the committee members before the supporting footnotes and disclosures are released. The financial statements usually are complete several days earlier, so the committee can see them as soon as possible. Again, this leaves less material for discussion during the formal audit committee meeting.

Finally, the committee members can be encouraged to contact the controller prior to the committee meeting to discuss any changes they would like to see in the financial statements. This reduces the length of the committee meeting and also allows the accounting staff sufficient time to update the reports at their leisure before the meeting.

While these improvements can incrementally reduce the length of the audit committee's approval process, the main issue is the formal committee meeting itself: It must be scheduled well in advance and is difficult to change, so it is a bottleneck in the SEC filing process.

EDGARizing

The SEC accepts 10Q and 10K filings through its Electronic Data Gathering, Analysis, and Retrieval (EDGAR) system. The reports can be submitted to the system in various formats, of which HyperText Markup Language (HTML) is the most common, and eXtensible Markup Language (XML) is soon to be required. Companies filing their reports with the SEC almost always forward them to a firm specializing in the conversion of their reports into HTML or XML (known as EDGARizing); the specialist converts the statements to the required format and then files them with the SEC on behalf of the company.

A company's auditors usually insist on reviewing its EDGARized reports prior to filing and in fact will not allow the statements to be filed at all until this review has taken place. This can result in several rounds of corrections, as the auditors require changes that the EDGARizing firm must make. These extra iterations are expensive, both in terms of auditor and EDGARizing fees and the extra time required to file the reports with the SEC. Thus, it is well worth the effort to conduct a detailed review of the 10Q or 10K report before forwarding it to the EDGARizing firm.

Quarterly and annual filings usually arrive at an EDGARizing firm from multiple companies at about the same time, which can create a considerable backlog and lengthens the time required to file. The best way around this problem is to file well before the SEC-mandated due dates, so that there are fewer competing filings. Another option is to retain the services of a smaller local EDGARizing firm, which will be more likely to put greater emphasis on completing a company's filings in a timely manner.

29.12 SUMMARY

Filingfinancial statements with the Securities and Exchange Commission in one day is impossible. In fact, filing within a month may be difficult to achieve. This vast expansion of the one-day goal is caused primarily by the mandatory auditor review at the end of each quarter and the full audit at the end of each fiscal year. These reviews and audits are under the control of an outside audit firm, which has ultimate control over the speed of the process. Though we have noted numerous methods for reducing the filing process somewhat, the involvement of outside auditors presents a significant hurdle that cannot be avoided.

This chapter has pointed out a number of activities that can be of great assistance in reducing the time frame needed to close the accounting books and issue financial statements. Doing so properly requires three key elements: an intense focus on the improvement of all processes that feed into the production of financial statements, an accounting supervisor who can effectively manage the entire process, and (for those companies looking to achieve an extremely fast close) the transfer of nearly all manual accounting functions to a computer system that automatically completes all but the most complicated transactions. With all of these components in place, a company can achieve not only very fast closing times, but also an exceptionally efficient accounting department.

CONTROL SYSTEMS

30.1   INTRODUCTION

One of the chief roles of the accountant is to examine each process that involves financial transactions to see where there is a risk of losing assets and to install control points that will prevent those losses from occurring. For example, a major potential weakness in the billing process is that the shipping department may never inform the accounting staff of a shipment, resulting in no invoice being sent to a customer. In this chapter, we review the need for control systems, discuss the types of fraudulent activities that make the use of controls particularly important, cover the controls used in 13 key transactions, and describe many other controls that can be added to the typical accounting system.

Since controls frequently have a cost associated with them, it is also possible to take them *out of* an accounting system in order to save money; we will discuss the process of spotting these controls and evaluating their usefulness prior to removing them.

For additional information about controls, please refer to *Accounting Controls Best Practices* (Bragg, John Wiley & Sons, 2006), which details over 400 controls used in several dozen accounting processes.

30.2   THE NEED FOR CONTROL SYSTEMS

The most common situation in which a control point is needed is when an innocent error is made in the processing of a transaction. For example, an accounts payable clerk neglects to compare the price on a supplier's invoice to the price listed on the authorizing purchase order, which results in the company paying more than it should. Similarly, the warehouse staff decides to accept a supplier's shipment, despite a lack of approving purchasing documentation, resulting in the company being obligated to pay for something that it does not need. These types of actions may occur as a result of poor employee training, inattention, or a special set of circumstances that were unforeseen when the accounting processes were originally constructed. There can be an extraordinary number of reasons why a transactional error arises, which can result in errors that are not caught, and which in turn lead to the loss of corporate assets.

Controls act as review points at those places in a process where these types of errors have a habit of arising. The potential for some errors will be evident when a process flow expert reviews a flowchart that describes a process, simply based on his or her knowledge of where errors in similar processes have a habit of arising. Other errors will be specific to a certain industry—for example, the casino industry deals with enormous quantities of cash and so has a potential for much higher monetary loss through its cash-handling processes than do similar processes in other industries. Also, highly specific circumstances within a company may generate errors in unlikely places. For example, a manufacturing company that employs mostly foreign workers who do not speak English will experience extra errors in any processes where these people are required to fill out paperwork, simply due to a reduced level of comprehension of what they are writing. Consequently, the typical process can be laced with areas in which a company has the potential for loss of assets.

Many potential areas of asset loss will involve such minor or infrequent errors that accountants can safely ignore them and avoid the construction of any offsetting controls. Others have the potential for a very high risk of loss and so are shored up with not only one control point, but a whole series of multilayered cross-checks that are designed to keep all but the most unusual problems from arising or being spotted at once.

The need for controls is also driven by the impact of their cost and interference in the smooth functioning of a process. If a control requires the hiring of an extra person, then a careful analysis of the resulting risk mitigation is likely to occur. Similarly, if a highly efficient process is about to have a large and labor-intensive control point plunked down into the middle of it, it is quite likely that an alternative approach should be found that provides a similar level of control, but from outside the process.

The controls installed can be of the preventive variety, which are designed to spot problems as they are occurring (such as online pricing verification for the customer order data entry staff) or of the detective variety, which spot problems after they occur, so that the accounting staff can research the associated problems and fix them after the fact (such as a bank reconciliation). The former type of control is the best, since it prevents errors from ever being completed, whereas the second type results in much more labor by the accounting staff to research each error and correct it. Consequently, the type of control point installed should be evaluated based on the cost of subsequent error correction.

All of these factors—perceived risk, cost, and efficiency—will have an impact on a company's need for control systems, as well as the preventive or detective type of each control that is contemplated.

30.3   TYPES OF FRAUD

The vast majority of transactional problems that controls guard against are innocent errors that are caused by employee errors. These tend to be easy to spot and correct, when the proper control points are in place. However, the most feared potential loss of assets is not through these mistakes, but through deliberate fraud on the part of employees, since these transactions are deliberately masked, making it much more difficult to spot them. Here are the most common types of fraud that are perpetrated:

- *Cash and investment theft.* The theft of cash is the most publicized type of fraud, and yet the amount stolen is usually quite small when compared to the byzantine layers of controls that are typically installed to prevent such an occurrence. The real problem in this area is the theft of investments, when someone sidesteps existing controls to clean out a company's entire investment account. Accordingly, the accountant should spend the most time designing controls over the movement of invested funds.

- *Expense account abuse.* Employees can use fake expense receipts, apply for reimbursement of unapproved items, or apply multiple times for reimbursement through their expense reports. Many of these items are so small that they are barely worth the cost of detecting, while others, such as the duplicate billing to the company of airline tickets, can add up to very large amounts. Controls in this area tend to be costly and time-consuming.

- *Financial reporting misrepresentation.* Though no assets appear to be stolen, the deliberate falsification of financial information is still fraud, because it impacts a company's stock price by misleading investors about financial results. Controls in this area should involve internal audits to ensure that processes are set up correctly, as well as full audits (not reviews or compilations) by external auditors.

- *Fixed assets theft.* Though the term "fixed assets" implies that every asset is big enough to be immovable, many items—particularly computers—can be easily stolen and then resold by employees. In many instances, there is simply no way to prevent the loss of assets without the use of security guards and surveillance equipment. Given that many organizations do not want to go that far, the most common control is the purchase of insurance with a minimal deductible, so that losses can be readily reimbursed.

- *Inventory and supplies theft.* The easiest theft for an employee is to remove inventory or supplies from a storage shelf and walk away with them. Inventory controls can be enhanced through the use of fencing and limiting access to the warehouse, but employees can still hand inventory out through the shipping and receiving gates. The level of controls installed in this area will depend upon the existing level of pilferage and the value of inventory and supplies.

- *Nonpayment of advances.* The employees who need advances, either on their pay or for travel, are typically those who have few financial resources. Consequently, they may not pay back advances unless specifically requested to do so. This requires detailed tracking of all outstanding advances.

- *Purchases for personal use.* Employees with access to company credit cards can make purchases of items that are diverted to their homes. Controls are needed that require one to have detailed records of all credit card purchases, rather than relying on a cursory scan and approval of an incoming credit card statement.

- *Supplier kickbacks.* Members of the purchasing staff can arrange with suppliers to source purchases through them in exchange for kickback payments directly to the purchasing staff. This usually results in a company paying more than the market rate for those items. This is a difficult type of fraud to detect, since it requires an ongoing review of prices paid as compared to a survey of market rates.

Fraud problems are heightened in some organizations, because the environment is such that fraud is easier to commit. For example, a rigorous emphasis on increasing profits by top management may lead to false financial reporting in order to "make the numbers." Problems can also arise if the management team is unwilling to pay for controls or for a sufficient number of supervisory personnel, if it is dominated by one or two people who can override existing controls, or if it has high turnover so that new managers have a poor grasp of existing controls. Fraud is also common when the organizational structure is very complex or the company is growing quite rapidly, since both situations tend to result in fewer controls that create opportunities to remove assets. Consequently, fraud is much more likely if there are unrealistic growth objectives, there are problems within the management ranks, or if controls are not keeping pace with changes in the organizational structure.

30.4 ORDER ENTRY AND CREDIT CONTROLS

If a company records all of its order entry and credit review tasks on paper, then a significant amount of paperwork is required to ensure that there is a sufficient degree of control over the system, as shown in Exhibit 30.1 (where controls are listed next to black diamonds). The basic issue is that a combination of the sales order and bill of lading are needed by multiple departments as the principal tools for credit review, inventory picking, and billing, so they must be created using multipart forms and distributed through many departments.

As shown in the exhibit, the order entry process begins with the receipt of a customer purchase order, which the order entry staff uses to verify if the buyer has previously been approved by the credit department. They also verify if the price listed on the customer purchase order is an approved price as listed in the corporate price book. If either control point results in a problem, then they contact the customer to resolve the problem. Next, the order entry staff creates a five-part sales order that is based on the information in the customer purchase order. Another control is to then verify that the information in the two documents matches, and to correct any problems uncovered. The sales order is then distributed, with one copy going to the customer (effectively creating another control, since the customer may also compare it to the original purchase order for accuracy), to the billing department (which now has notice that a billing will eventually need to be invoiced to the customer), and to the credit department.

The credit department conducts a credit review to ensure that the customer has sufficient good credit to justify releasing the order, and stamps and initials its approval on one copy of the sales order if this is the case. A copy of the approved sales order then goes to the shipping department, which is not allowed to make a shipment unless the credit stamp appears on the sales order. Once they ship the order, the shipping staff creates a three-part bill of lading, of which one copy accompanies the shipment, and one copy goes to the billing department, serving as notification that the customer order can now be billed.

When the order entry and credit review system is converted to a computerized system, there is no longer a need for a sales order at all, since the information shown on the order is now distributed through the computer. Also, the number of copies of the bill of lading is reduced, though a hard copy is still sent to the customer with the shipment.

As shown in Exhibit 30.2 (where controls are listed next to black diamonds), the order entry staff must still verify that a customer submitting a purchase order is an approved buyer, but then varies from the paper-based process by entering the customer purchase order into the computer system's order entry module. The order entry staff can then conduct an immediate check of the inventory status of each item ordered to see if there are any stockout conditions, and notify the customer of this condition in case they would prefer to order an alternative item. The computer then conducts an automatic comparison of the purchase order price to the standard corporate price file, and notifies the order entry staff if the price is incorrect. This is also a good time to enter nonstandard billing terms

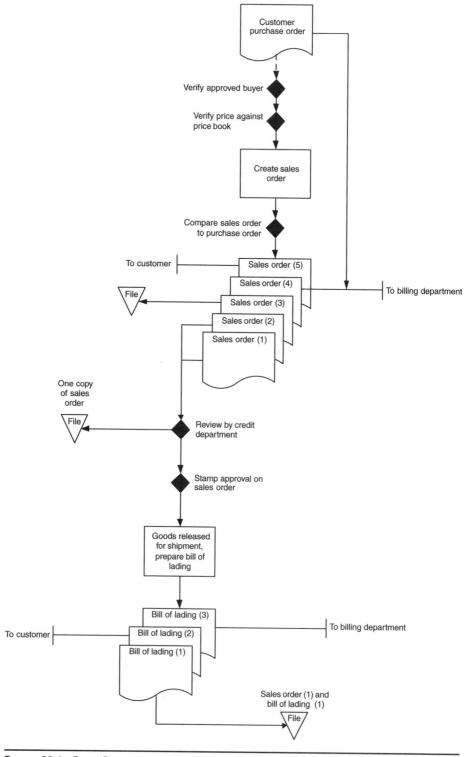

EXHIBIT 30.1   BASIC ORDER ENTRY AND CREDIT CONTROL SYSTEM

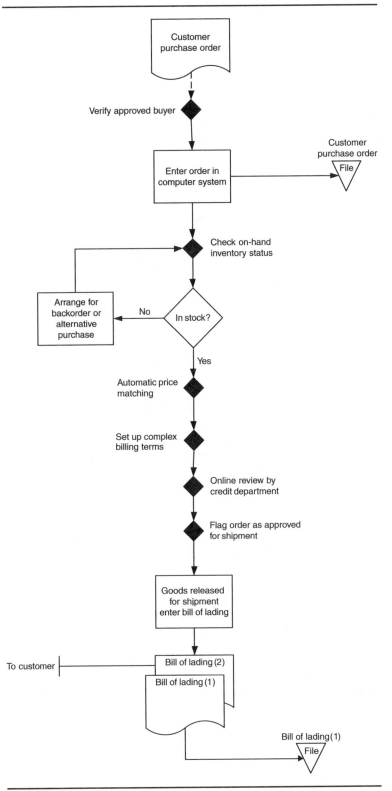

EXHIBIT 30.2 COMPUTERIZED ORDER ENTRY AND CREDIT CONTROL SYSTEMS

in the computer system, thereby providing early notice to the billing department. The computer system then routes the order to the credit department, which conducts an online credit review and clicks on a flag in the computer record if it is approved for shipment. The system then routes the approved order to the shipping department, where the system prints out a picking ticket and a subsequent bill of lading. Finally, the computer system automatically notifies the billing department that the order has shipped.

The control system for order entry and credit review becomes more simplified if orders are received electronically from the customer, as shown in Exhibit 30.3 (where controls are listed next to black diamonds). As noted in the exhibit, there are two ways for electronic orders to enter the computer system: one approach is for customers to place orders through an electronic form, in which case they will probably pay up-front with a credit card, thereby eliminating any further need for a credit review; the alternative is for a customer to send an electronic data interchange (EDI) message. If an EDI message is being used, then the customer already has a significant relationship with the company (since EDI linkages are typically only created between long-term trading partners), and therefore probably has a significant amount of credit with the company. The computer automatically compares the amount of the EDI order to the customer's available credit balance, and then flags the order as approved for shipment. The computer system then automatically checks inventory status and communicates any expected delays to the customer. The computer system then routes the order to the warehouse for shipment. There is no need for human intervention through this entire process, unless an exception condition arises; if so, the system will route the order to a staff person for resolution.

30.5   INVENTORY CONTROLS

The purchasing of inventory in a noncomputerized environment involves the use of multipart requisition and purchase order forms, as shown in Exhibit 30.4 (where controls are listed next to black diamonds). To begin the purchase transaction, the warehouse staff conducts an inventory review, determines which items require replenishment, and fills out a requisition form. The form must be prenumbered, so the warehouse and purchasing departments can track the sequence of requisition numbers that have resulted in purchase orders, thereby telling them if any requisitions have been lost. Upon receipt of the requisition in the purchasing department, the purchasing staff creates a multipart purchase order (also prenumbered for the same reason). One copy goes back to the warehouse, where it is matched against the initiating requisition to ensure that the purchase order is correct. Another copy goes to the accounts payable department, where it will eventually be matched to the supplier invoice and a receiving document, to be used as authorization to pay the customer. A third copy goes to the receiving department, where it will be used as authorization for receipt of the incoming delivery from the supplier (and to reject deliveries for which there is no authorizing purchase order). A second copy goes to the supplier, authorizing it to ship the goods to the company, while the purchasing staff retains the final copy. Once the goods are received, a copy of the receiving report goes to the purchasing department, where it is matched against its file of open purchase orders, so the purchasing staff can not only track late deliveries, but also cancel residual undelivered amounts.

Another key item in the warehouse is to ensure that inventory quantity records are kept properly updated through the use of perpetual inventory tracking system, which continually updates the current balance of on-hand inventory. The controls for such a system,

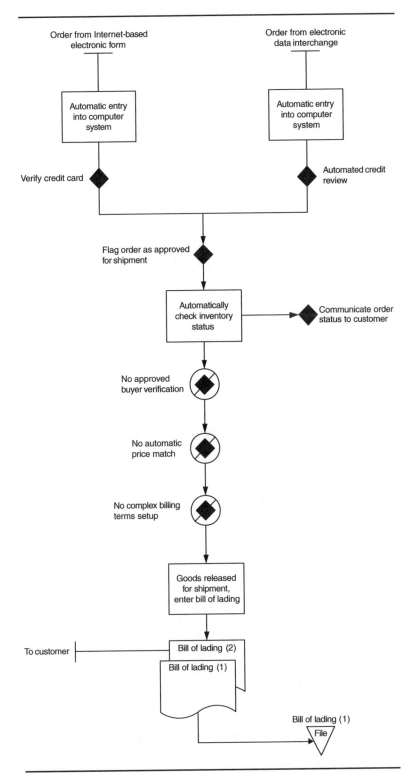

EXHIBIT 30.3 ORDER ENTRY AND CREDIT CONTROLS WITH ELECTRONIC ORDERING

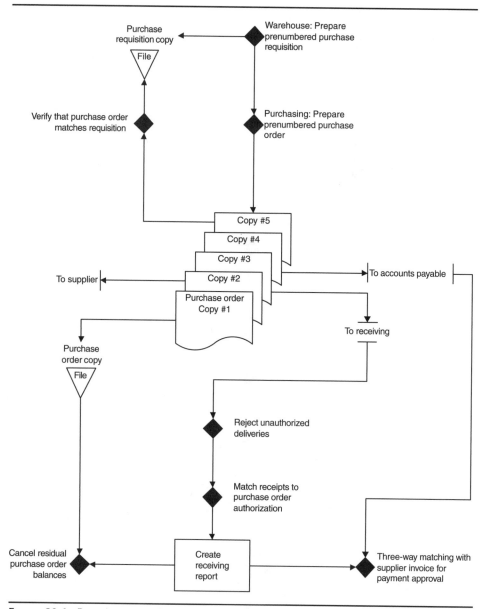

EXHIBIT 30.4   BASIC INVENTORY PURCHASING CONTROL SYSTEM

assuming no computerization of the process, are shown in Exhibit 30.5 (where the controls are listed next to black diamonds). On the flowchart, a recordkeeping transaction is initiated whenever any inventory movement occurs, such as the receipt, movement, or picking of inventory. The warehouse staff records each of these transactions on a separate move ticket, which is given to a warehouse clerk who updates the record file. One control over these move tickets is that they are prenumbered, so the warehouse clerk can track which move tickets have not been recorded. Second, blocks of move tickets should be assigned to specific warehouse staff, so if a move ticket is never submitted, the warehouse clerk will know which staff person has the ticket, and can more easily track it down.

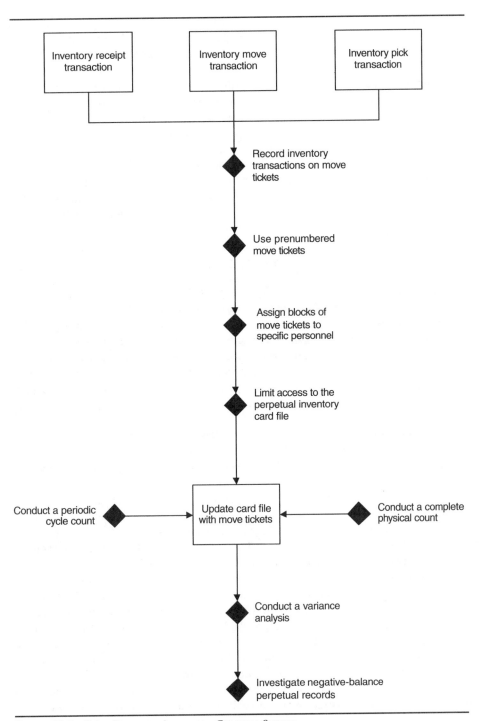

EXHIBIT 30.5   BASIC PERPETUAL INVENTORY CONTROL SYSTEM

The warehouse clerk is assigned sole responsibility over the updating of the perpetual inventory card file, thereby eliminating the risk that access by multiple people could result in duplicate or missing entries, and also keeps other warehouse staff from stealing inventory and then recording the theft in the card file as a valid transaction.

In addition to the basic move ticket tracking process, the perpetual inventory system can be supplemented with other controls. The most important is the use of a cycle counting system, whereby small sections of the inventory are counted and corrected every day on a rolling basis, with the reasons for any record errors being investigated and causes corrected. Of less use is a more infrequent physical count of the entire inventory; it is intended to correct the balances shown in the perpetual records, rather than to correct underlying causes, and so contributes less to long-term record accuracy than cycle counting. Also, the warehouse staff should regularly review the perpetual records for negative inventory balances and investigate the reasons for this error, much as they would for any cycle counting error.

30.6 ACCOUNTS PAYABLE CONTROLS

The manual accounts payable process flow is one of the key processes used today, especially by smaller businesses. The control aspects of the system are shown in Exhibit 30.6 (where the controls are listed next to black diamonds). The key control in this process flow is to manually compare the quantities and pricing on the authorizing purchase order received from the purchasing staff, the invoice received from the supplier, and the receiving documentation from the receiving department (commonly called a three-way match). If the pricing information on the purchase order and supplier invoice is the same, and the quantity information on all three documents is the same, then the supplier invoice is approved for payment.

In addition to the three-way match, the payables staff also conducts a review for duplicate supplier invoices in order to avoid paying any invoices twice. They then store the payables by due date in order to pay them in accordance with the terms listed on the supplier invoice.

The next step is to prepare checks to pay the supplier invoices. Check stock is always kept in locked storage to avoid theft. Once prepared, the voucher package of supporting materials is attached to each check and sent to an authorized check signer, so the signer can review the underlying basis for each check prior to signing it. Once signed, the voucher package is perforated, so it cannot be used as supporting material for a subsequent check.

The manual accounts payable system can be considerably streamlined with the use of a computerized payables system, as shown in Exhibit 30.7 (where the controls are listed next to black diamonds). Under this approach, purchase orders have been entered into the accounting database by the purchasing staff, as well as receiving information by the receiving department, so most of the information needed for three-way matching can be conducted by the computer, which reports exceptions to the accounting staff for investigation. Further, the computer automatically checks for duplicate invoice numbers, so the potential for duplicate invoicing is only a problem for supplier invoices that contain no invoice number. The payables staff pays for invoices based on a computer report that lists when each invoice is due, so there is no longer a need to sort the invoices by due date.

When checks are printed, there is no longer a need for a carbon copy of each check, as noted earlier in Exhibit 30.6, because checks are usually printed as a single document on a laser printer, with a duplicate remittance advice being printed on the page. The remainder of the payables process is similar to the manual approach, except that the computer

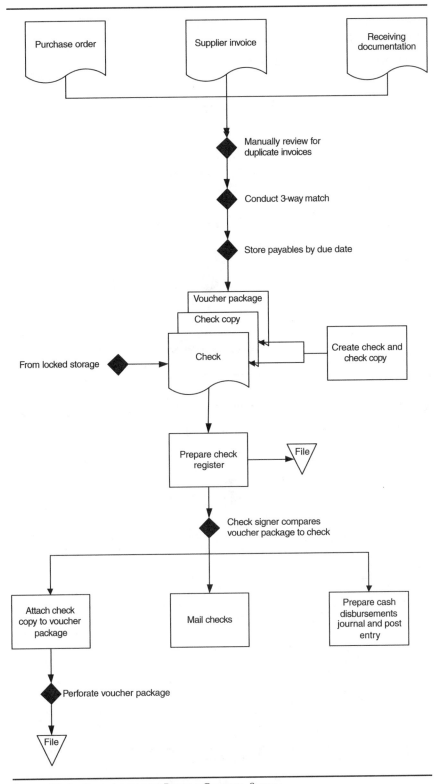

EXHIBIT 30.6   BASIC ACCOUNTS PAYABLE CONTROL SYSTEM

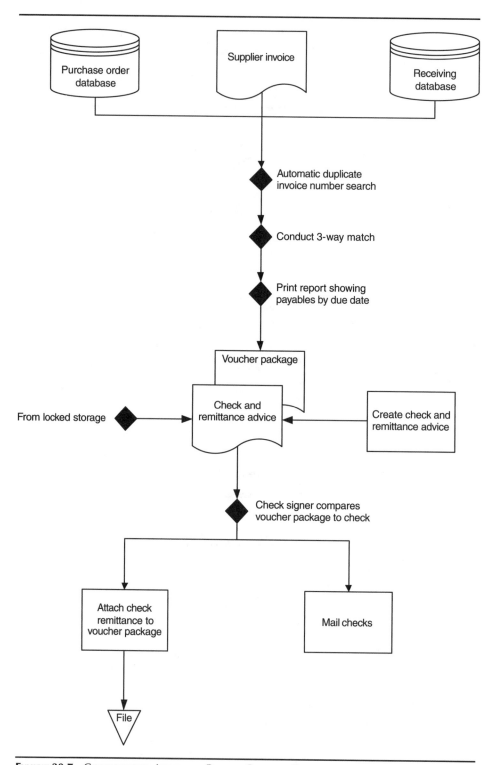

EXHIBIT 30.7   COMPUTERIZED ACCOUNTS PAYABLE CONTROL SYSTEM

system automatically updates all journals—there is no need for manual posting of purchasing information.

30.7   BILLING CONTROLS

The essential elements of the manual billing process are shown in Exhibit 30.8 (where the controls are listed next to black diamonds). The billing department first accumulates a copy of the sales order, customer purchase order, and bill of lading (which is necessary to ensure that billing only takes place following shipment). Once received, they review the sales order to ensure that it contains a credit approval stamp from the credit department. If not, there has been a control breach earlier in the shipment process, so the payables staff must notify the controller and credit department of the problem. The billing staff then creates the invoice in triplicate, using the pricing on the sales order and quantities on the bill of lading.

Once each invoice is completed, it should be proofread for errors by someone other than the original preparer (since a second party is more likely to thoroughly search for errors). Also, all invoice forms should be prenumbered, and a tracking system should ensure that all invoices are accounted for. Two of the invoice copies are then retained internally, while the final copy is sent to the customer. The outside of the envelope should be stamped with "address correction requested" to ensure that customer addresses are updated in a timely manner.

There are two scenarios under which the billing function can be computerized, and both are shown in Exhibit 30.9. Under scenario A, the accounting department has computer software to assist it with the billing function, but all other systems leading up to billing are manual. Under this system, the billing staff must still wait for a copy of the sales order, bill of lading, and customer purchase order to arrive from other departments, and then input this information into the computer to create an invoice. Under this scenario, there is not a great deal of efficiency gained over a manual billing process, except that the computer can conduct automated error checking as the invoice is created, and all account postings are handled automatically.

The more efficient approach is shown in scenario B in Exhibit 30.9, where all order entry and shipping information has already been entered into the computer. Under this system, the primary control is to print a preview report to ensure that each invoice is accurate. Aside from the entry of miscellaneous charges, such as freight, there is no need for any data entry.

30.8   CASH RECEIPTS CONTROLS

The manual cash receipts process involves a number of controls and handling by different people, as shown in Exhibit 30.10 (where the controls are listed next to black diamonds). Though the process could be substantially more streamlined, cash is the most easily stolen asset, and so requires more separation of responsibility to ensure a higher level of control.

Under a completely manual system, when checks arrive in the mailroom, the mailroom staff prepares a check pre-list on which they itemize each check. By doing so, they are creating an initial record of cash receipts against which the final deposit can be compared to see if any checks were subsequently removed. The mailroom staff also stamps each check "for deposit only" to the company bank account, which makes it more difficult for anyone to later alter the endorsement to shift the payment to some other account. The checks are then sent to the cashier, who enters them in the cash receipts journal and prepares the daily bank deposit. A different clerk compares the deposit to the check pre-list to ensure that

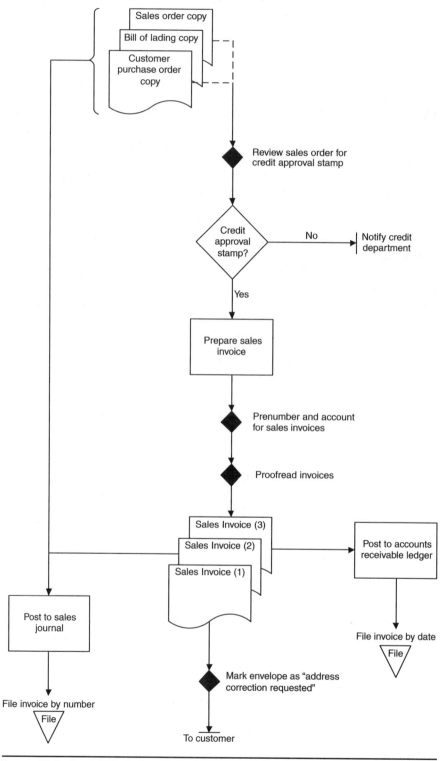

EXHIBIT 30.8   BASIC BILLING CONTROL SYSTEM

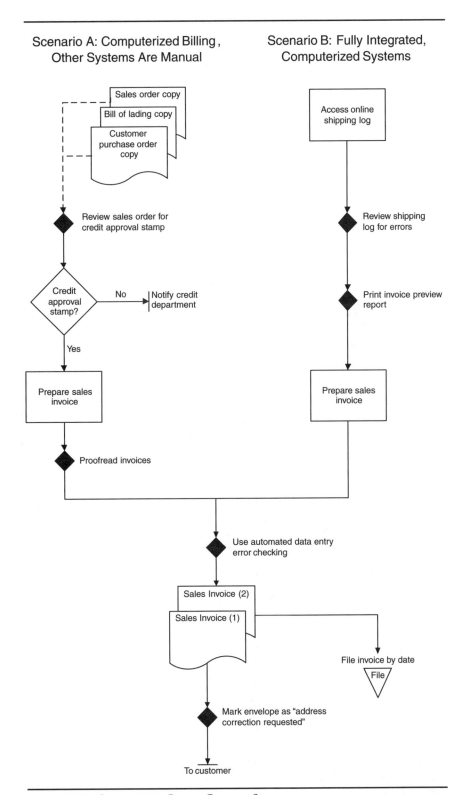

Scenario A: Computerized Billing, Other Systems Are Manual

Sales order copy

Bill of lading copy

Customer purchase order copy

Review sales order for credit approval stamp

Credit approval stamp? — No → Notify credit department

Yes

Prepare sales invoice

Proofread invoices

Scenario B: Fully Integrated, Computerized Systems

Access online shipping log

Review shipping log for errors

Print invoice preview report

Prepare sales invoice

Use automated data entry error checking

Sales Invoice (2)

Sales Invoice (1)

File invoice by date

File

Mark envelope as "address correction requested"

To customer

EXHIBIT 30.9   COMPUTERIZED BILLING CONTROL SYSTEM

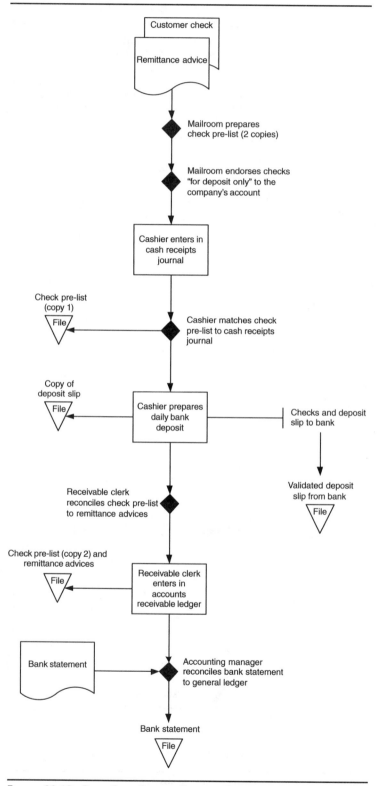

EXHIBIT 30.10   BASIC CASH RECEIPTS CONTROL SYSTEM

the amounts are the same. Once the deposit is made, the second clerk also matches the validated bank deposit slip to the original deposit slip and check pre-list to ensure that the check delivery was fully deposited. Once the bank statement arrives at month-end, the accounting manager reconciles it to the general ledger and investigates any variances. Thus, control is improved by separating tasks among four parties in this process—the mailroom staff, the cashier, a second clerk, and the accounting manager.

The cash receipts process flow becomes only slightly less convoluted when a computer is introduced, as shown in Exhibit 30.11. Under this system, a significant change is the cashier's posting of cash receipts directly into the computer, which automatically updates the cash receipts journal and related accounts receivable records.

If a lockbox is used, then this process flow becomes substantially more streamlined, since there is no cash on the premises. The mailroom staff is no longer involved in preparing a check pre-list, though it may be asked to mail any residual cash receipts to the lockbox. Also, there is no longer a need for a daily bank deposit or matching of validated deposit slips, since the cash is already at the bank .

30.9   PAYROLL CONTROLS

Payroll is a complex process involving multiple steps into which errors can easily creep. In addition, there is a significant risk of payroll fraud. Given both of these factors, it is necessary to build a number of controls into the system, especially one involving manual payroll processing (where the error rate is especially high).

The manual payroll process flow is shown in Exhibit 30.12 (where the controls are listed next to black diamonds). The first problem in this process is ensuring that all employee timecards have been collected, so the payroll staff must compare timecards received to the employee master list, and locate the missing timecards. Next, all regular and overtime hours worked must be approved by employee supervisors to ensure that no false time reporting occurs. The payroll staff then verifies that all special payroll authorizations received, such as pay deductions, raises, and vacation requests, have been properly authorized. Finally, the payroll staff incorporates all of this information into a manual calculation of gross wages earned, deductions, and taxes due. Given the complexity of this task, a second party should always review the calculations for errors.

Once the payroll calculations are verified, the payroll staff creates paychecks and issues them directly to recipients, preferably requiring some form of legal identification prior to doing so; this ensures that paychecks falsely made out to "ghost" employees are not intercepted and cashed. Each check recipient should sign a receipt form to prove that they have received their check. Since employees are not always on hand on payday, the person distributing checks should retain all unclaimed checks in a secure location, and regularly attempt to distribute them to the proper recipients.

Other payroll activities include depositing withheld and matching taxes on the appropriate dates, as well as posting payroll information to the payroll register.

When a company advances to the use of a computer to calculate payroll, this eliminates some payroll tasks, but there are still a number of manual processes surrounding it, as shown in Exhibit 30.13. In this flowchart, the payroll staff must still accumulate timecards, but now enters this information directly into the computer, which matches it against a list of valid employees and informs the payroll staff if there are any missing timecards. To ensure that timecard data entry has been accurate, a new control is required to match timecard totals to the amounts entered in the computer.

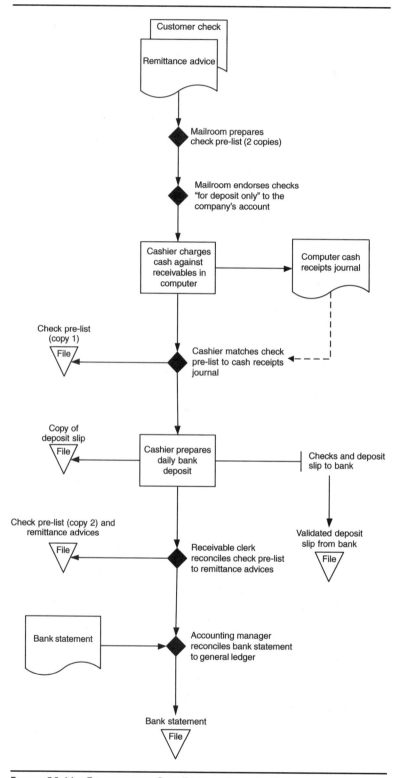

EXHIBIT 30.11   COMPUTERIZED CASH RECEIPTS CONTROL SYSTEM

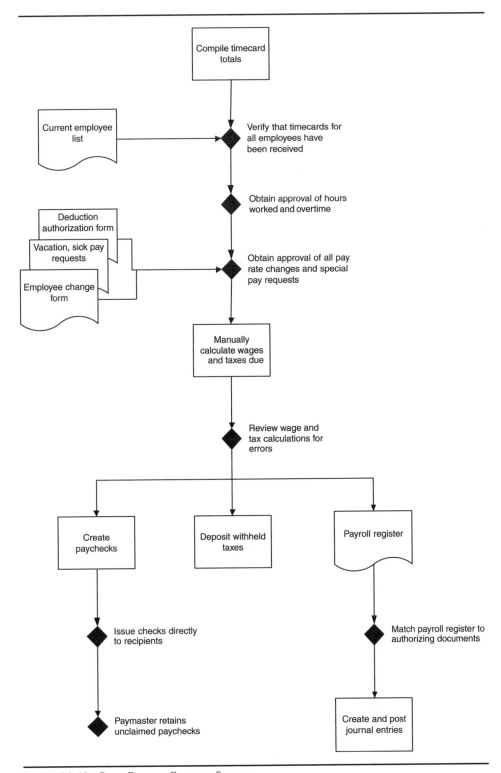

EXHIBIT 30.12   BASIC PAYROLL CONTROL SYSTEMS

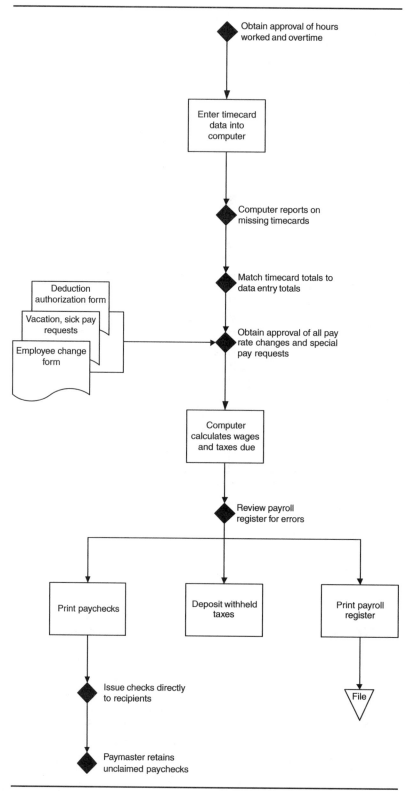

EXHIBIT 30.13   COMPUTERIZED PAYROLL CONTROL SYSTEMS

Following the initial data entry, the payroll staff must still verify the authorization of pay changes and then enter this information into the computer, which automatically calculates gross and net pay, deductions, and taxes. This information must still be reviewed for errors. The remaining steps in the payroll process are similar to those for a manual system, except that the computer system automatically posts the results of the payroll to the payroll register and general ledger.

The controls noted here for a computerized payroll system do not include a number of additional enhancements, such as employee and manager self-service, automated time-keeping systems, and direct deposit. When these additional systems are layered onto the core computerized payroll system, the payroll staff no longer has any data entry chores, and instead spends its time solely on such overview tasks as control and error monitoring.

30.10   CLOSING CONTROLS

The general financial statement closing process does not vary much by company and generally follows the process flow shown in Exhibit 30.14. Public companies must endure a number of additional steps, including a quarterly audit review, approval of the audit committee, and conversion of the financial statements into a format readable by the SEC's EDGAR filing system. These extra steps can add weeks to the closing process and several additional controls.

The controls noted in the flowchart are described at greater length next, in sequence from the top of the flowchart to the bottom.

- *Use a closing checklist.* It is mandatory to follow a closing checklist when closing the books. Given the complexity of the closing process, this is the only way to ensure that every closing step has been completed. In addition, the financial statement preparer should initial each closing step as completed. Further, a supervisor should then review the checklist and all underlying journal entries to ensure that the close has been properly completed, and also initial the checklist.

- *Prepare supporting documentation for all complex manual entries.* Any journal entry that requires a complex calculation, such as an obsolescence reserve or an overhead allocation, must be supported by extensive written documentation.

- *Require approval for key entries.* Key journal entries are those that are at the highest risk of error or that have a significant monetary impact on the financial statements. These entries should be carefully reviewed and approved by a supervisor, who should initial the closing checklist.

- *Reconcile all significant balance sheet accounts.* Categorize all balance sheet accounts by risk that they may contain errors and by size of potential errors. Higher-risk accounts typically involve manual entries and complex transactions. Those accounts scoring highest must be fully reconciled before the financial statements are issued. Accounts with lower scores can be completed prior to the end of the reporting period, even if this means that additional entries will be added to the accounts subsequent to the reconciliation. This review process should require the use of a checklist of accounts to be reconciled and a formal review of the reconciliations by a second person.

- *Conduct an analytical review of the balance sheet, income statement, and cash flow statement.* This is a spreadsheet-based comparison of the balance in an account as compared to the same balance in a previous period, to see if the change is reasonable. For example, it can include a comparison of the first quarter of this

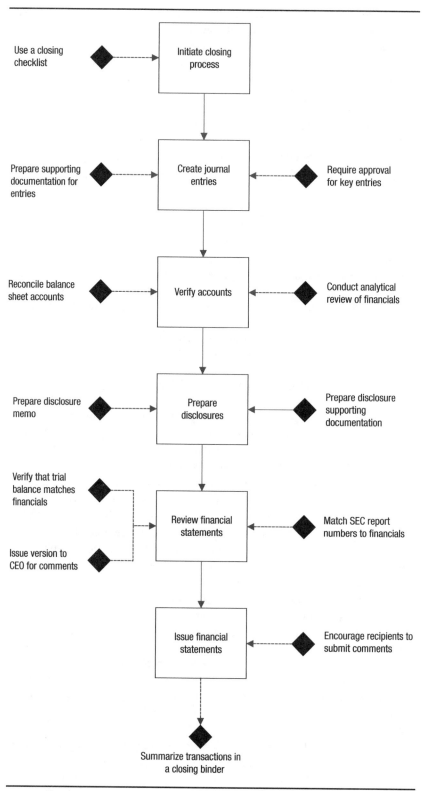

EXHIBIT 30.14   SYSTEM OF CONTROLS FOR FINANCIAL REPORTING

	Quarter 2	Quarter 1	% Change	$ Change	Explanation
Customer Analysis					
IBM	$10,500	$10,100	+4%	+$300	Not applicable
Interior Department	15,900	23,500	−32%	+7,600	23 additional billable staff
Lockheed Martin	28,500	19,500	−46%	−900	ABC project was cancelled
Balance Sheet Analysis					
Accounts receivable	$42,000	$36,000	+17%	+$6,000	In line with sales increase
Fixed assets	14,500	10,000	+45%	+4,500	Acquired airplane
Accounts payable	10,000	9,500	5%	+500	Not applicable
Notes payable	8,000	3,500	129%	+4,500	Acquired airplane
Income Statement Analysis					
Sales—consulting	$85,000	$73,000	+16%	+$12,000	Net increase in IRS project
Employee benefits	2,500	2,000	+25%	+500	Health insurance increase
Marketing	700	2,100	−67%	−1,400	Trade show in first quarter
Salaries	43,000	42,000	+2%	+1,000	Not applicable
Travel	250	950	−74%	−700	Travel to/from trade show

EXHIBIT 30.15   ANALYTICAL REVIEW EXAMPLES

year to the first quarter of last year, with a detailed explanation required for all variances greater than 10% and $25,000. Another option is to annualize the current partial-year results and compare them to the preceding full-year results. Examples of analytical reviews by customer and by account are shown in Exhibit 30.15. Note how "not applicable" is used as an explanation whenever the period-over-period analysis is too small to be worthy of any investigatory time.

- *Prepare a disclosure memo to the disclosure committee.* It is useful to have a group of experts in financial disclosures review key accounting issues once a quarter. An excellent vehicle for this review is a disclosure memo, in which the controller itemizes key accounting issues for their review. The disclosure committee should include an SEC expert, corporate counsel, and the CEO. It may also be useful to send a copy to the company's audit manager. A highly abbreviated disclosure memo is shown in Exhibit 30.16.

- *Prepare supporting documentation for all footnote disclosures.* Footnote disclosures that are read by the public put the company at risk if they are inaccurate, so have a complete set of supporting documents that show exactly how the information in each disclosure was derived.

- *Verify that the trial balance matches the financial statements.* It is entirely possible that a late journal entry will alter the trial balance, which can be a major problem if the financial statements have already been printed. Accordingly, this control should be used near the end of the financial statement process. Before issuing any statements, make sure that the trial balance still matches the financial statements. This can be a particular problem when the accounting staff has recently altered the format of the financials, since the new format may inadvertently not include some accounts or include some accounts more than once.

- *Issue preliminary version of financial statements to the chief executive officer (CEO) for comments.* The CEO is required to sign off on financial statements that are included in SEC filings. Given this person's vested interest in the financial statements, it makes sense to issue a preliminary copy to him well before the financials are ready for issuance, so that any concerns can be addressed well in advance. This is also a weak control, since the CEO may spot an accounting problem or (more likely) an inaccurate disclosure.

This memo notes the accounting treatment used for a variety of items in the third-quarter 10Q filing. The memo is being sent to you, because our internal controls procedure requires that you review it *and respond back* by e-mail that you have received and reviewed it. Key accounting disclosures are:

1. *Intangible asset/goodwill impairment.* We test for goodwill impairment at the subsidiary level, which we must do at least annually, as well as whenever an impairment event occurs. The goodwill assigned to each subsidiary and its annual testing date are as follows:
    -   Subsidiary A, $1.3 million, 4th quarter
    -   Subsidiary B, $1.9 million, 4th quarter
    -   Subsidiary C, $4.2 million, 4th quarter

    All impairment tests fall into the next quarter. Given current cash flows, there is no evidence of impairment at this time.

2. *Revenue accruals.* Subsidiary A has a number of fixed-fee contracts, for which it has historically used the percentage-of-completion method to record revenue. However, the SEC has stipulated that public companies must use the proportional method instead (which is based on milestones achieved). We have reviewed the proportional method with our auditors following the last year-end audit and documented a standard procedure for revenue recognition.

3. *MD&A topics.* Since we are acquiring companies with few material assets, a considerable proportion of the prices we pay must be allocated to intangible assets. This allocation is provided to us by third-party valuation firms. These firms are slow in providing final reports, so we are forced to initially estimate the amount of the purchase price allocated between goodwill and intangible assets and then create a second (adjusting) entry once the valuation report is received. This can result in some inaccuracy in the amount of amortization reported for a short interval.

    Subsidiary B has just brought up the risk of high fuel prices on the operation of its airplanes and the resulting decline in profitability of its data collection activities. The subsidiary's staff is preparing a risk disclosure concerning this issue.

4. *Assessment and evaluation of operational or legal risks.* A former business partner of Subsidiary C has filed suit against the company, related to alleged amounts owed to it from a deal several years ago and seeking relief of $1,000,000. Since the case has been thrown out of court twice before, we do not assign any probability to a monetary settlement.

EXHIBIT 30.16 DISCLOSURE MEMO EXAMPLE

-   *Match all SEC report numbers to the financial statements.* A person besides the preparer of the quarterly or annual SEC report should carefully compare all numbers in the document to the underlying trial balance and other supporting materials. In addition, this reviewer should compare the prior period comparisons in the SEC report to the actual prior period reports. By doing so, the company should catch and correct the bulk of all errors, thereby, it is hoped, yielding a clean review of the document by the auditors.

-   *Encourage financial statement recipients to submit comments.* The company managers who receive the financial statements may have particular insights into company operations that the accounting staff is not aware of. If so, it makes sense when issuing financial statements to these people to append a note requesting that they provide comments on any issues that appear to be incorrect or questionable. Though not a strong control, occasionally it may provide warning of a reporting problem.

-   *Summarize all supporting transactions in a closing binder.* It is not acceptable to prepare a detailed justification for a journal entry and then lose the justification. Instead, collect all supporting documentation for all entries made during a reporting period and organize them into a closing binder. Ideally, each page of the binder should be indexed back to a table of contents, so that anyone can easily locate materials within the binder.

The controls just noted must be used for the quarterly filings of public companies, since these entities are most concerned with avoiding errors. There may be some opportunity to reduce the level of control over the other months of the year, since these other financial statements are generally only used internally.

The controls just discussed form the core controls for financial statement preparation; also consider occasionally using the following two controls, which are related to spreadsheets:

1. *Lock and archive spreadsheets used for journal entries.* There is a considerable risk within the accounting department that any spreadsheets used to derive journal entries will simply be wiped clean in the following month and used again, which eliminates any evidence (besides printed matter) of how journal entries were derived. To avoid this issue, have the accounting staff copy formulas into a new spreadsheet for each month and lock the old spreadsheets to avoid reuse.

2. *Periodically review the structure of supporting spreadsheets.* Electronic spreadsheets are highly subject to errors and must be reviewed regularly to ensure that they still operate as intended. Accordingly, there should be at least an annual review of all spreadsheets used to compile the financial statements. This review should encompass a verification of all calculations used, references to other spreadsheets, and the ranges used to summarize data.

30.11 KEY CONTROLS

There are thousands of possible controls that can be used to ensure that a company maintains proper control over its assets. The following list represents the most common controls found in most organizations. These can be supplemented by additional controls in cases where the potential for loss of assets is considered to be exceptionally high, with the reverse being true in other instances. Examples of additional controls can be found in Bragg, *Accounting Controls Best Practices* 2nd Edition (John Wiley & Sons, 2009). The controls are as follows:

1. *Cash.* The handling of cash is considered to be rife with control issues, resulting in perhaps an excessive use of controls. Though many potential controls are listed below, one should attempt to create a mix of controls that balances their cost against incremental gains in the level of control achieved. They are as follows:

   ○ *Compare check register to actual check number sequence.* The computer's list of checks printed should exactly match the checks that have actually been used. If not, this can be evidence that someone has removed a check from the check stock in hopes that it will not be noticed. This irregularity is most common for laser check stock, since these checks are stored as separate sheets, rather than as a continuous roll of check stock, and so can be more easily pilfered.

   ○ *Conduct spot audits of petty cash.* It is possible to misrepresent the contents of a petty cash box through the use of miscellaneous receipts and IOU vouchers. By making unscheduled audits, one can sometimes spot these irregularities.

○ *Control check stock.* The check stock cannot be stored in the supply closet along with the pencils and paper, because anyone can remove a check from the stack and then be only a forged signature away from stealing funds from the company. Instead, the check stock should be locked in a secure cabinet, to which only authorized personnel have access.

○ *Control signature plates.* If anyone can access the company's signature plates, then it is not only possible to forge checks, but also to stamp authorized signatures on all sorts of legal documents. Accordingly, these plates should always be kept in the company safe.

○ *Create a checklist in the mail room.* If there is any chance that someone in the accounting department is removing customer checks before they are included in the daily deposit records, then the mail room staff can be asked to create a separate list, which can later be compared to the deposit slip list to see if there are any differences.

○ *Deposit all checks daily.* If checks are kept on hand for several days, there is an increased likelihood that someone will gain access to them and cash them into his or her own account. Consequently, bank deposits should be made every day.

○ *Divert incoming cash to a lockbox.* If cash or checks from customers never reach a company, then a host of control problems related to the potential misuse of that cash goes away. To do this, a lockbox can be set up that is controlled by the company's bank, and customers can be asked to send their payments to the lockbox address. Some payments will inevitably still be mailed directly to the company, but the proportion of these payments will drop if customers are promptly asked to send future payments to the lockbox address.

○ *Fill in empty spaces on checks.* If the line on a check that lists the amount of cash to be paid is left partially blank, a forger can insert extra numbers or words that will result in a much larger check payment. This can be avoided by having the software that prints checks insert a line or series of characters in the spaces.

○ *Limit petty cash reserves.* If there is little money in a petty cash box, then there is less incentive for anyone to steal the box. If there is a large amount of cash volume flowing through the box, then a useful alternative is procurement cards.

○ *Reconcile petty cash.* There tends to be a high incidence of fraud related to petty cash boxes, since money can be more easily removed from them. To reduce the incidence of these occurrences, unscheduled petty cash box reconciliations can be initiated, which may catch perpetrators before they have covered their actions with a false paper trail. This control can be strengthened by targeting those petty cash boxes that have experienced unusually high levels of cash replenishment requests.

○ *Require that petty cash vouchers be filled out in ink.* Anyone maintaining a petty cash box can easily alter a voucher previously submitted as part of a legitimate transaction, and remove cash from the petty cash box to match the altered voucher. To avoid this, one should require that all vouchers be completed in ink. To be extra careful, one can even require users to write the amount of any cash transactions on vouchers in words instead of numbers (e.g., "fifty-two dollars" instead of "52.00"), since numbers can be more easily modified.

○ *Mutilate voided checks.* A voided check can be retrieved and cashed. To keep this from happening, a stamping device that cuts the word "void" into the surface of the check should be used, thereby sufficiently mutilating it that it cannot be used again.

○ *Perform bank reconciliations.* This is one of the most important controls anywhere in a company, for it reveals all possible cash inflows and outflows. The bank statement's list of checks cashed should be carefully compared to the company's internal records to ensure that checks have not been altered once they leave the company or that the books have not been altered to disguise the amount of the checks. It is also necessary to compare the bank's deposit records to the books to see if there are discrepancies that may have been caused by someone taking checks or cash out of the batched bank deposits. Further, one should compare the records of all company bank accounts to see if any check kiting is taking place. In addition, it is absolutely fundamental that the bank reconciliation be completed by someone who is unassociated with the accounts payable, accounts receivable, or cash receipts functions, so that there is no way for anyone to conceal their wrongdoings by altering the bank reconciliation. Finally, it is now possible to call up online bank records through the Internet so that a reconciliation can be conducted every day. This is a useful approach, since irregularities can be spotted and corrected much more quickly.

○ *Review uncashed checks.* If checks have not been cashed, it is possible that they were created through some flaw in the accounts payable system that sent a check to a nonexistent supplier. An attempt should be made to contact these suppliers to see if there is a problem.

○ *Update signature cards.* A company's bank will have on file a list of check signatories that it has authorized to sign checks. If one of these people leaves the company for any reason, he or she still has the ability to sign company checks. To void this control problem, the bank's signature card should be updated as soon as a check signer leaves the company.

○ *Separate responsibility for the cash receipt and cash disbursement functions.* If a person has access to both the cash receipt and disbursement functions, it is much easier for that person to commit fraud by altering the amount of incoming receipts, and then pocket the difference. To avoid this, each function should be handled by different people within the organization.

○ *Stamp incoming checks with "deposit to account number . . ."* It is possible that employees with access to customer checks will try to cash them, as might anyone with access to the mail once it has left the company. This can be made more difficult by stamping the back of the check with "deposit to account number *xxxxx,*" so that they would have to deface this stamp in order to cash the check.

○ *Verify amount of cash discounts taken.* A cash receipts person can falsely report that customers are taking the maximum amount of early payment discounts when they have not actually done so, and pocket the amount of the false discount. This can be detected by requiring that photocopies of all incoming checks be made and then tracing payments on which discounts have been taken back to the copies of the checks. This is a less common problem area, since it requires a perpetrator to have access to both the receipts and payments aspects of the accounting operation, and so is a less necessary control point.

2. *Investments.* The shifting of investment funds is the area in which a person has the best chance for stealing large quantities of company funds or of placing them in

inappropriate investments that have a high risk of loss. The following controls are designed to contain these risks:

- *Impose investment limits.* When investing its excess funds, a company should have a policy that requires it to only invest certain amounts in particular investment categories or vehicles. For example, only the first $100,000 of funds are insured through a bank account, so excess funding beyond this amount can be shifted elsewhere. As another example, the board of directors may feel that there is too much risk in junk bond investments, and so will place a general prohibition on this type of investment. These sorts of policies can be programmed into a treasury workstation, so that the system will automatically flag investments that fall outside a company's preset investment parameters.

- *Require authorizations to shift funds among accounts.* A person who is attempting to fraudulently shift funds out of a company's accounts must have approval authorization on file with one of the company's investment banks to transfer money out to a noncompany account. This type of authorization can be strictly controlled through signatory agreements with the banks. It is also possible to impose strict controls over the transfer of funds *between* company accounts, since a fraudulent person may uncover a loophole in the control system whereby a particular bank has not been warned *not* to allow fund transfers outside of a preset range of company accounts, and then shift all funds to that account and thence to an outside account.

- *Require board approval of substantial changes in investment account designations.* Management can modify the amount of reported gains or losses on investments by shifting investment designations from the "available-for-sale" investment portfolio to the "trading" portfolio. If the gain or loss on such a change in designation is significant, the board of directors should be notified in advance of the reason for the change and its impact on the level of earnings.

- *Verify consistent use of the same income tax rate for equity method transactions.* GAAP allows the assumed use of tax rates for either dividend payments or capital gains to record gains from equity method transactions. This can result in improperly switching between different tax rates on successive equity method transactions in order to meet short-term profitability goals. A simple control over this problem is to periodically review the calculation of journal entries in the Income tax expense account to see if tax rate usage has been consistent.

- *Require approval of the assumed tax rate used for equity method transactions.* As noted in the preceding control, GAAP allows one to use a range of possible tax rates for equity method transactions, which can result in improperly altering tax rates to meet profitability goals. To avoid this problem, the general ledger accountant should be required to obtain management approval of any journal entries involving the Income tax expense account.

3. *Accounts receivable.* Controls are needed in the accounts receivable area to ensure that employees do not take payments from customers and then hide the malfeasance by altering customer receivable records. Here are the most common controls:

- *Compare checks received to applications made against accounts receivable.* It is possible for an accounts receivable clerk with the dual responsibility of cash application to cash a check to his or her personal account and then hide evidence of the stolen funds by continually applying subsequent cash received against the oldest accounts receivable. This can be spotted by conducting an occasional comparison of checks listed on the deposit slip for a given day to the accounts against which the funds were credited.

○ *Confirm payment terms with customers.* Receivable collections can be particularly difficult when the sales staff has established side agreements with customers that alter payment terms—especially when the sales staff does not communicate these new terms to the collections department. One can discover the existence of these deals by confirming payment terms at the time of invoice creation with selected customers, and then working with the sales manager to reprimand those sales staff who have authorized special terms without notifying anyone else in the company.

○ *Confirm receivables balances.* If an employee is falsely applying cash from customers to different accounts in order to hide the loss of some cash that he or she has extracted from the company, it is possible to detect this problem by periodically sending out a confirmation form to customers to verify what they say they have paid to the company.

○ *Match invoiced quantities to the shipping log.* It is useful to spot-check the quantities invoiced to the quantities listed on the shipping log. By doing so, one can detect fraud in the billing department caused by invoicing for too many units, with the accounting staff pocketing the difference when it arrives. This is a rare form of fraud, since it generally requires collaboration between the billing and cash receipts staff, and so the control is only needed where the fraud risk clearly exists.

○ *Require approval of bad debt expenses.* A manager should approve any bad debt write-offs from the accounts receivable listing. Otherwise, it is possible for someone to receive a check from a customer, cash it into their own account, and write off the corresponding account receivable as a bad debt. This control can be greatly enhanced by splitting the cash receipts function away from the collections function, so that it would require collusion to make this type of fraud work.

○ *Require approval of credits.* It is possible for someone in the accounts receivable area to grant a credit to a customer in exchange for a kickback from the customer. This can be prevented through the use of approval forms for all credits granted, as well as a periodic comparison of credits granted to related approval forms. It is acceptable to allow the accounting staff to grant very small credits in order to clean up miscellaneous amounts on the accounts receivable listing, but these should be watched periodically to see if particular customers are accumulating large numbers of small credits.

○ *Verify invoice pricing.* The billing department can commit fraud by issuing fake invoices to customers at improperly high prices and then pocketing the difference between the regular and inflated prices when the customer's check arrives. Having someone compare the pricing on invoices to a standard price list before invoices are mailed can spot this issue. As was the case for the last control, this form of fraud is only possible when there is collaboration between the billing and cash receipts staff, so the control is only needed when the fraud risk is present.

4. *Inventory.* A company's inventory can be so large and complex that extensive controls are needed simply to give it any degree of accuracy at all. Consequently,

virtually all of the following controls are recommended to achieve a high level of inventory record accuracy:

o *Audit shipment terms.* Certain types of shipment terms will require that a company shipping goods retain inventory on its books for some period of time after the goods have physically left the company, or that a receiving company record inventory on its books prior to its arrival at the receiving dock. Though in practice most companies will record inventory only when it is physically present, this is technically incorrect under certain shipment terms. Consequently, a company should perform a periodic audit of shipment terms used to see if there are any deliveries requiring different inventory treatment. The simplest approach is to mandate no delivery terms under which a company is financially responsible for transportation costs.

o *Audit the receiving dock.* A significant problem from a recordkeeping perspective is that the receiving staff may not have time to enter a newly received delivery into the corporate computer system, so the accounting and purchasing staffs have no idea that the items have been received. Accordingly, one should regularly compare items sitting in the receiving area to the inventory database to see if they have been recorded. One can also compare supplier billings to the inventory database to see if items billed by suppliers are not listed as having been received.

o *Conduct inventory audits.* If no one ever checks the accuracy of the inventory, it will gradually vary from the book inventory as an accumulation of errors builds up over time. To counteract this problem, one can either schedule a complete recount of the inventory from time to time or else an ongoing cycle count of small portions of the inventory each day. Whichever method is used, it is important to conduct research in regard to why errors are occurring, and attempt to fix the underlying problems.

o *Control access to bill of material and inventory records.* The security levels assigned to the files containing bill of material and inventory records should allow access to only a very small number of well-trained employees. By doing so, the risk of inadvertent or deliberate changes to these valuable records will be minimized. The security system should also store the keystrokes and user access codes for anyone who has accessed these records, in case evidence is needed to prove that fraudulent activities have occurred.

o *Keep bill of material accuracy levels at a minimum of 98%.* The bills of material are critical for determining the value of inventory as it moves through the work-in-process stages of production and eventually arrives in the finished goods area, since they itemize every possible component that comprises each product. These records should be regularly compared to actual product components to verify that they are correct, and their accuracy should be tracked.

o *Pick from stock based on bills of material.* An excellent control over material costs is to require the use of bills of material for each item manufactured and then require that parts be picked from the raw materials stock for the production of these items based on the quantities listed in the bills of material. By doing so, a reviewer can hone in on those warehouse issuances that were *not* authorized through a bill of material, since there is no objective reason why these issuances should have taken place.

○ *Require approval to sign out inventory beyond amounts on pick list.* If there is a standard pick list used to take raw materials from the warehouse for production purposes, then this should be the standard authorization for inventory removal. If the production staff requires any additional inventory, they should go to the warehouse gate and request it, and the resulting distribution should be logged out of the warehouse. Furthermore, any inventory that is left over after production is completed should be sent back to the warehouse and logged in. By using this approach, the cost accountant can tell if there are errors in the bills of material that are used to create pick lists, since any extra inventory requisitions or warehouse returns probably represent errors in the bills.

○ *Require transaction forms for scrap and rework transactions.* A startling amount of materials and associated direct labor can be lost through the scrapping of production or its occasional rework. This tends to be a difficult item to control, since scrap and rework can occur at many points in the production process. Nonetheless, the manufacturing staff should be well trained in the use of transaction forms that record these actions, so that the inventory records will remain accurate.

○ *Restrict warehouse access to designated personnel.* Without access restrictions, the company warehouse is like a large store with no prices—just take all you want. This does not necessarily mean that employees are taking items from stock for personal use, but they may be removing excessive inventory quantities for production purposes, which leads to a cluttered production floor. Also, this leaves the purchasing staff with the almost impossible chore of trying to determine what is in stock and what needs to be bought for immediate manufacturing needs. Consequently, a mandatory control over inventory is to fence it in and closely restrict access to it.

○ *Review inventory for obsolete items.* The single largest cause of inventory valuation errors is the presence of large amounts of obsolete inventory. To avoid this problem, periodically print a report that lists which inventory items have *not* been used recently, including the extended cost of these items. A more accurate variation is to print a report itemizing all inventory items for which there are no current production requirements (only possible if a material requirements planning system is in place). Alternatively, one can use a report that compares the amount of inventory on hand to annual historical usage of each item. With this information in hand, one should then schedule regular meetings with the materials manager to determine what inventory items should be scrapped, sold off, or returned to suppliers.

○ *Review the condition of returned inventory.* Sales returns tend not to be in pristine condition, so a company must record a write-down to their fair value at the time of the return. However, the warehouse staff tends to place them back in stock without any consideration of condition, resulting in the overstatement of finished goods inventory. A good control is to have all sales returns set to one side for review, after which they are either shifted back to stock at full value, thrown away, donated, or reclassified as used stock and assigned a reduced inventory value.

○ *Segregate customer-owned inventory.* If customers supply a company with some parts that are used when constructing products for them, it becomes very easy for this inventory to be mingled with the company's own inventory, resulting in a false increase in its inventory valuation. Though it is certainly possible to assign customer-specific inventory codes to these inventory items in order to clearly identify them, a more easily discernible control is to physically segregate these goods in a different part of the warehouse.

5. *Prepaid expenses.* The largest problem with prepaid expenses is that they tend to turn into a holding area for payments that should have been converted into expenses at some point in the past. There is also a potential for advances to be parked in this area that should have been collected. The following controls address these problems:

   ○ *Reconcile all prepaid expense accounts as part of the month-end closing process.* By conducting a careful review of all prepaid accounts once a month, it becomes readily apparent which prepaid items should now be converted to an expense. The result of this review should be a spreadsheet that itemizes the nature of each prepaid item in each account. Since this can be a time-consuming process involving some investigative work, it is best to review prepaid expense accounts shortly before the end of the month so that a thorough review can be conducted without being cut short by the time pressures imposed by the usual closing process.

   ○ *Review all employee advances with the payroll and payables staffs at least once a month.* A common occurrence is for an employee to claim hardship prior to a company-required trip, and request a travel advance. Alternatively, an advance may be paid when an employee claims that he or she cannot make it to the next payroll check. For whatever the reason, these advances will be recorded in an employee advances account, where they can sometimes be forgotten. The best way to ensure repayment is a continual periodic review, either with the accounts payable staff who process employee expense reports (against which travel advances should be netted) or the payroll staff (which deducts pay advances from future paychecks).

   ○ *Require approval of all advance payments to employees.* The simplest way to reduce the burden of tracking employee advances is not to make them in the first place. The best approach is to require management approval of any advances, no matter how small they may be.

6. *Employee advances.* Employees may ask for advances on their next paycheck or to cover the cost of their next trip on the company's behalf. In either case, it is easy to lose track of the advance. The following controls are needed to ensure that an advance is eventually paid back.

   ○ *Continually review all outstanding advances.* When advances are paid to employees, it is necessary to continually review and follow up on the status of these advances. Employees who require advances are sometimes in a precarious financial position and must be issued constant reminders to ensure that the funds are paid back in a timely manner. A simple control point is to have a policy that requires the company to automatically deduct all advances from the next employee paycheck, thereby greatly reducing the work of tracking advances.

   ○ *Require approval of all advance payments to employees.* When employees request an advance for any reason—as a draw on the next paycheck or as funding for a company trip—this should always require formal signed approval from their immediate supervisors. The reason is that an advance is essentially a small short-term loan, which would also require management approval. The accounts payable supervisor or staff should only be allowed to authorize advances when they are in very small amounts.

7. *Fixed assets.* The purchase and sale of fixed assets require special controls to ensure that proper authorization has been obtained to conduct either transaction, and also to ensure that the funds associated with fixed assets are properly accounted for. All of the following controls should be implemented to ensure that these goals are achieved.

   ○ *Compare capital investment projections to actual results.* Managers have been known to make overly optimistic projections in order to make favorable cases for asset acquisitions. This issue can be mitigated by conducting regular reviews of the results of asset acquisitions in comparison to initial predictions and then tracing these findings back to the initiating managers. This approach can also be used at various milestones during the asset construction to ensure that costs incurred match original projections.

   ○ *Ensure that capital construction projects are not delayed for accounting reasons.* Accounting rules require one to capitalize the interest expense associated with the construction of certain types of assets. By artificially delaying the completion date of an asset, or by delaying the official completion date for accounting purposes, one can improperly extend the time period over which interest expense can be ascribed to a project and capitalized as part of its cost, thereby reducing the overall corporate interest expense and increasing profits. This problem can be avoided by personally reviewing the physical status of construction projects in relation to planning documents, such as Gantt charts, and determining the validity of reasons for delays in completion.

   ○ *Ensure that fixed asset purchases have appropriate prior authorization.* A company with a capital-intensive infrastructure may find that its most important controls are over the authorization of funds for new or replacement capital projects. Depending upon the potential amount of funding involved, these controls may include a complete net present value (NPV) review of the cash flows associated with each prospective investment, as well as multilayered approvals that reach all the way up to the board of directors. A truly comprehensive control system will also include a postcompletion review that compares the original cash flow estimates to those actually achieved, not only to see if a better estimation process can be used in the future, but also to see if any deliberate misrepresentation of estimates was initially made.

   ○ *Test for asset impairment.* There are a variety of circumstances under which the net book value of an asset should be reduced to its fair value, which can result in significant reductions in the recorded value of an asset. This test requires a significant knowledge of the types of markets in which a company operates, the regulations to which it is subject, and the need for its products within those markets. Consequently, only a knowledgeable person who is at least at the level of a controller should be relied upon to detect the presence of assets whose values are likely to have been impaired.

   ○ *Verify that all changes in asset retirement obligation assumptions are authorized.* A company can artificially increase its short-term profitability by altering the assumed amount of future cash flows associated with its asset retirement obligations. Since downward revisions to these assumptions will be reflected in the current period's income statement as a gain, any changes to these assumptions should be approved prior to implementation.

○ *Verify that correct depreciation calculations are being made.* Though there is no potential loss of assets if incorrect depreciation calculations are being made, this can result in an embarrassing adjustment to the previously reported financial results at some point in the future. This control should include a comparison of capitalized items to the official corporate capitalization limit, in order to ensure that items are not being inappropriately capitalized and depreciated. The control should also include a review of the asset categories in which each individual asset has been recorded, in order to ensure that an asset has not been misclassified, and therefore incorrectly depreciated.

○ *Verify that fixed asset disposals are properly authorized.* A company does not want to have a fire sale of its assets taking place without any member of the management team knowing about it. Consequently, the sale of assets should be properly authorized prior to any sale transaction being initiated, if only to ensure that the eventual price paid by the buyer is verified as being a reasonable one.

○ *Verify that cash receipts from asset sales are properly handled.* Employees may sell a company's assets, pocket the proceeds, and report to the company that the asset was actually scrapped. This control issue can be reduced by requiring that a bill of sale or receipt from a scrapping company accompany the file for every asset that has been disposed of.

○ *Verify the fair value assumptions on dissimilar asset exchanges.* Accounting rules allow one to record a gain or loss on the exchange of dissimilar assets. Since this calculation is based on the fair value of the assets involved (which is not already clearly stated in the accounting records), the possibility exists for someone to artificially create an asset fair value that will result in a gain or loss. This situation can be avoided by having an outside appraiser review the fair value assumptions used in this type of transaction.

○ *Verify that fixed assets are being utilized.* Many fixed assets are parked in a corner and neglected, with no thought to their being profitably sold off. To see if this problem is occurring, the accounting staff should conduct a periodic review of all fixed assets, which should include a visual inspection and discussion with employees to see if assets are no longer in use.

8. *Accounts payable.* This is one of the most common areas in which the misuse of assets will arise, as well as the one where transactional errors are most likely to occur. Nonetheless, an excessive use of controls in this area can result in a significant downgrading in the performance of the accounts payable staff, so a judiciously applied blend of controls should be used.

○ *Audit credit card statements.* When employees are issued company credit cards, there will be some risk that the cards will be used for noncompany expenses. To avoid this, one can spot-check a few line items on every credit card statement, if not conduct a complete review of every statement received. For those employees who have a history of making inappropriate purchases, but for whom a credit card is still supplied, it is also possible to review their purchases online (depending upon what services are offered by the supplying bank) on the same day that purchases are made, and alter credit limits at the same time, thereby keeping tighter control over credit card usage.

- ○ *Compare payments made to the receiving log.* With the exception of payments for services or recurring payments, all payments made through the accounts payable system should have a corresponding record of receipt in the receiving log. If not, there should be grounds for investigation into why a payment was made. This can be a difficult control to implement if there is not an automated three-way matching system already in place, since a great deal of manual cross-checking will be needed.

- ○ *Compare the invoice numbers of supplier invoices received.* When suppliers are not paid promptly, they will probably send another copy of an invoice to the company on the grounds that the first one must have been lost. If the first invoice is just being processed for payment, there is a good chance that the company will pay for both the original invoice and its copy. Consequently, the accounting software should automatically compare the invoice numbers of all invoices received, to see if there are duplications.

- ○ *Impose limitations on credit card purchases.* When credit cards are issued to employees, a company has a number of possible restrictions it can place on the cards that will help to keep employee spending within certain predefined limits. For example, if the card is issued by a specific store, then purchases can be limited to that entity. However, since this can result in a large number of credit card types, a more popular alternative is the procurement (or purchasing) card. This is a credit card for which a number of additional limits are imposed. This can include a maximum dollar amount for individual transactions, or be limited to maximum amounts per day, or be restricted to stores that have a certain SIC code. Depending on the level of service offered through the procurement card, the monthly charge statement can also list the general category of product purchased.

- ○ *Require approval of all invoices that lack an associated purchase order.* If the purchasing department has not given its approval to an invoice, then the accounting staff must send it to the supervisor of the department to whom it will be charged so that this person can review and approve it.

- ○ *Require supervisory review and approval of credit card statements.* Even with the restrictions just noted for procurement cards, it is still possible for purchases to be made that are not authorized. If it seems necessary to verify employee spending habits, then copies of credit card statements can be sent to employee supervisors for review. This does not have to be for payment approval, but at least to ensure that supervisors are aware of the types of charges being made.

- ○ *Verify authorizations with a three-way match.* Though extremely labor-intensive, it is important to compare a supplier's invoice to the authorizing purchase order to ensure that the details of each one match, while also matching the billed amount to the receiving documentation to ensure that the company is only paying for the amount received. Some computer systems can automate this matching process. An alternative is to have the receiving staff approve the amounts received from suppliers by comparing them to purchase orders, which then allows the accounting staff to pay suppliers from the authorizing purchase order, rather than the supplier invoice.

9. *Current liabilities.* The general area of current liabilities is one in which items can inadvertently build up over time when they should be charged to expense. The

following controls impose close monitoring over the most common current liability accounts.

○ *Include an accrual review in the closing procedure for bonuses, commissions, property taxes, royalties, sick time, vacation time, unpaid wages, and warranty claims.* There are many possible expenses for which an accrual is needed, given their size and repetitive nature. This control is designed to force a continual review of every possible current liability as part of the standard monthly closing procedure so that no key accruals are missed.

○ *Review accrual accounts for unreversed entries.* Some accruals, such as unpaid wage accruals and commission accruals, are supposed to be reversed in the following period, when the actual expense is incurred. However, if an accountant forgets to properly set up a journal entry for automatic reversal in the next period, a company will find itself having recorded too large an expense. A simple control is to include in the period-end closing procedure a review of all accounts in which accrual entries are made, to ensure that all reversals have been completed.

○ *Create standard entries for reversing journal entries.* As a continuation of the last control point, an easy way to avoid problems with accrual journal entries that are supposed to be reversed is to create boilerplate journal entry formats in the accounting system that are preconfigured to be automatically reversed in the next period. As long as these standard formats are used, there will never be an unreversed journal entry.

○ *Include a standard review of customer advances in the closing procedure.* If a company regularly deals with a large number of customer deposits, there is a significant risk that the deposits will not be recognized as revenue in conjunction with the completion of any related services or product sales. This problem can be avoided by requiring a periodic review of the status of each deposit as part of the period-end closing procedure.

○ *Include an accrual review in the closing procedure for income taxes payable.* A common practice is to only accrue for income taxes on a quarterly basis, when estimated taxes are due. The trouble is that this is a substantial expense being excluded from all monthly financial statements not falling at the end of each reporting quarter and so tends to skew the reported results of those months. By including in the closing procedure a line item requiring the accrual of an income tax liability, the accounting staff is forced to address this issue every time financial statements are issued.

○ *Maintain historical expense information about warranty claims both for ongoing product sales and new product introductions.* If a company creates a warranty expense accrual for a new product based on its standard claim rate for existing products, the warranty expense will probably be underaccrued for the initial introductory period of the product, since more product problems will arise early in a product launch that are corrected in later models. A good control over this underreporting is to track warranty expenses separately for new model introductions and ongoing sales, so a reasonable basis of information can be used for each type of accrual.

○ *Match the final monthly payroll pay date to the last day of the month.* The unpaid wage accrual can be significant when employee pay dates differ substantially from the last day of the reporting period. This problem can be partially resolved by setting the last (or only) pay date of the month on the last day of the month and paying employees through that date, which eliminates the need for any wage accrual. This control is most effective for salaried employees, who are typically paid through the pay date. There is usually a cutoff for hourly employees that is several days prior to the pay date, so some wage accrual would still be necessary for these employees.

○ *Automate the period-end cutoff.* A common closing activity is to compare the receiving department's receiving log for the few days near period end to the supplier invoices logged in during that period, to see if there are any receipts for which there are no supplier invoices. This is a slow and error-prone activity. A good alternative is to use the computer system to automatically locate missing invoices. The key requirements are a purchase order system covering all significant purchases, as well as rapid updating of the inventory database by the warehouse staff when items are received. If these features exist, a batch program can be written linking the purchase order, inventory, and accounting databases, and that compares inventory receipts to received invoices. If no invoice exists, the program calculates the price of the missing invoice based on the purchase order. It then creates a report for the accounting staff itemizing all receipts for which there are no invoices and calculating the price of the missing invoices. This report can be used as the basis for a journal entry at month end to record missing invoices.

○ *Create a standard checklist of recurring supplier invoices to include in the month-end cutoff.* A number of invoices arrive after month end that are related to services and for which an accrual should be made. The easiest way to be assured of making these accruals is to create a list of recurring invoices, with their approximate amounts, and use it as a check-off list during the closing process. If the invoice has not yet arrived, then accrue for the standard amount shown on the list.

○ *Automate or sidestep the matching process.* The most common way to establish the need for a payment to a supplier is to compare an incoming supplier invoice to the authorizing purchase order, as well as receiving documentation to ensure that the item billed has been accepted. If both these sources of information agree with the invoice, then the accounts payable staff can proceed with payment. The trouble is that this process is terribly inefficient and highly error prone. There are three ways to improve this critical control point:

• *Use matching automation software.* Most high-end accounting software packages offer an automated matching system that automatically compares all three documents and highlights mismatches for further review. The trouble is that this software is expensive, requires linked computer databases for accounting, purchasing, and the warehouse, and also still requires manual labor to reconcile any mismatches it locates.

• *Authorize payments at the receiving point.* This advanced concept requires the presence of a computer terminal at the receiving dock. Upon receipt of a shipment, the receiving staff authorizes payment by accessing the purchase order in the computer system that relates to the receipt and checking off those items received. The computer system then schedules a payment without any supplier invoice. This approach is theoretically the most efficient way to control the payables process, but requires considerable custom programming as well as training of the receiving staff.

- *Shift payments to procurement cards.* A large proportion of all purchases are too small to require any matching process, since the labor expended exceeds the value of the control. Instead, create a procurement card system and encourage employees to make purchases with the cards, up to a maximum limit. This program greatly reduces the number of transactions requiring matching, thereby focusing the attention of the accounts payable staff on just those transactions most likely to contain errors of a significant dollar value.

10. *Notes payable.* The acquisition of new debt is usually a major event that is closely watched by the chief financial officer, and so requires few controls. Nonetheless, the following control points are recommended as general corporate policies.

   ○ *Gain management approval of the initial debt entry related to debt issued in exchange for property.* It is quite possible that the stated interest rate on any debt issued in exchange for property will not match the fair market rate at the time of the transaction. Since the stated rate can be used to value the debt transaction unless the rate is not considered to be fair, this can lead to some abuse in asset valuation. For example, if the stated rate is below the market rate and is still used to record the property acquisition transaction, the present value of the debt will be higher, resulting in a larger asset valuation. If the asset is depreciated over a longer period than would the interest expense that would otherwise be recognized if the higher market interest were used, then a company has effectively shifted expense recognition into the future and increased its profits in the short term. Consequently, management approval of the interest rate used to value the acquisition should be obtained, while a justification for the interest rate used should be attached to the journal entry.

   ○ *Include a task for debt issuance cost capitalization in the bond establishment procedure.* There should be a standard procedure describing each step in the recording of an initial bond issuance. The procedure should include a requirement to capitalize and ratably amortize all debt issuance costs. Otherwise, these costs will be expensed at the beginning of the debt issuance, rather than being linked to the benefits of the incurred debt over the life of the debt.

   ○ *Include in the debt procedure a line item to charge unamortized discounts or premiums to expense proportionate to the amount of any extinguished debt.* The general ledger accountant may not remember to write off any unamortized discount or premium when debt is extinguished, so the debt extinguishment procedure should include a line item requiring that this task be addressed. Otherwise, expense recognition could potentially be delayed until the original payment date of the debt, which may be many years in the future.

   ○ *Include in the month-end closing procedure a task to record interest expense on any bonds for which interest payments do not correspond to the closing date.* The payment of interest to bond holders is a natural trigger for the recording of interest expense, but there is no such trigger when there is no payment. To enforce the proper recording not only of unpaid interest expense but also of any amortization on related bond discounts or premiums, a specific task should be included in the closing procedure, as well as a required sign-off on the task.

- ○ *Report to the board of directors the repayment status of all debt.* GAAP requires that all unamortized discounts and premiums be recognized in the current period if there is no reasonable chance that the debt will be repaid. Since this acceleration has a significant impact on reported earnings in the current period, there may be some unwillingness to classify debt as unable to be paid. By requiring a standard report to the board of directors regarding the status of debt repayments at each of its meetings, the board can decide on its own when amortization must be accelerated, and can force management to do so.

- ○ *Require approval of the terms of all new borrowing agreements.* A senior corporate manager should be assigned the task of reviewing all prospective debt instruments to verify that their interest rate, collateral, and other requirements are not excessively onerous or conflict with the terms of existing debt agreements. It may also be useful from time to time to see if a lending institution has inappropriate ties to the company, such as partial or full ownership in its stock by the person responsible for obtaining debt agreements.

- ○ *Require evidence of intent and ability to recategorize debt from short term to long term.* If a company shifts the classification of its short-term debt to the long-term debt category, this can mislead investors and creditors in regard to the company's short-term obligations. A good control is to require evidence supporting the reporting shift, such as a board motion to take on replacement long-term debt, plus a signed long-term loan to pay off the short-term debt. This documentation should be attached to the journal entry that shifts short-term debt into the long-term debt category.

- ○ *Require supervisory approval of all borrowings and repayments.* As was the case with the preceding control point, high-level supervisory approval is required for all debt instruments—except that this time it is for final approval of each debt commitment. If the debt to be acquired is extremely large, it may be useful to have a policy requiring approval by the board of directors, just to be sure that there is full agreement at all levels of the organization regarding the nature of the debt commitment. To be a more useful control, this signing requirement should be communicated to the lender, so that it does not inadvertently accept a debt agreement that has not been signed by the proper person.

- ○ *Require written and approved justification for the interest rate used to value debt.* When the stated interest rate on debt varies significantly from the market rate of interest, GAAP requires that the debt be valued using the market rate. However, the exact amount of this market rate is subject to interpretation, which has an impact on the amount of interest expense recognized. Requiring justification for and approval of the rate used introduces some rigor to the process.

11. *Equity.* The following controls ensure the application of consistent calculations for the recording of equity grants and options, as well as the avoidance of financial statement manipulation in the issuance of dividends.

- ○ *Include stock appreciation rights (SAR) compensation expense accruals in the standard closing procedure.* A company could delay or ignore any changes in the value of SAR grants to its employees, thereby avoiding the recognition of any associated compensation expense. This problem can be avoided by including the accrual as a standard action item in the monthly closing procedure. The issue can also be highlighted by including it as a footnote attached to the financial statements, thereby requiring periodic updating of the footnote information.

○ *Use a standard stock valuation form when calculating SAR compensation expense.* A company can use a variety of methods for determining the market value of company stock as part of its recognition of compensation expense, especially when the shares are not publicly traded. This can give rise to different methods being used over time, depending on which one results in the smallest compensation expense recognition. The best way to avoid this problem is to create a standard calculation form, which forces the use of a single calculation format for all SAR-related compensation expense calculations.

○ *Independent substantiation must be obtained to verify the valuation of stock issued in exchange for goods and services received.* When stock is swapped for goods or services, the stock is valued at the fair value of the goods or services. Since the offsetting debit is to an expense, the amount of this valuation can have a major impact on reported profit levels. This control is designed to force the accounting staff to go through the steps of obtaining outside verification of the fair value at which they have chosen to record the transaction.

○ *Obtain board approval of a specific date range within which dividends are to be declared each year.* This control is designed to keep the board of directors from deliberately altering reported financial results through the timing of dividend declarations. For example, the board can declare either property or scrip dividends on specific dates that are designed to result in gains or losses (for property dividends) or changes in debt levels (for scrip dividends). The same problem applies when dividends are declared for ESOP shares, since the dividends for unallocated ESOP shares are charged to compensation expense in the current period.

○ *Require board approval of the fair value justification for all assets used in property dividends.* Since the recognition of the difference between the fair and book value of assets being distributed can have a major impact on reported earning levels, the board should be made fully aware of the justification for any asset fair values departing significantly from book value, and the impact the resulting gain or loss will have on reported earnings.

○ *Review the assumptions used to determine the compensation cost for options.* The most common formula used to develop the compensation cost associated with stock option grants under the SFAS 123 approach is the Black-Scholes formula, which requires the input of a number of assumptions in order to generate a compensation cost. Even small changes in these assumptions can result in a significant change in compensation costs, so there is a risk of formula manipulation in order to alter reported financial results. In particular, compensation expenses can be reduced by reducing the assumed stock volatility or the assumed life of an option, or by increasing the assumed risk-free interest rate or dividend yield. A periodic review of these assumptions, particularly in comparison to the assumptions used for prior calculations, can spot significant or clearly incorrect assumptions.

○ *Verify that option grant extensions are measured on the date of authorization.* When the term of an option grant is extended, one must recognize compensation expense under the terms of APB 25 (if that approach is being used) on the extension date if there is an unrecognized difference between the market and exercise prices of the stock. This rule can give rise to some variation in the date on which the measurement is made, in the hope that the market price of the stock will drop, thereby resulting in a lower compensation expense. By creating a procedure that clearly requires the calculation to be made on the date of authorization, this problem can be eliminated.

- ○ *Use a consistent fair market value estimation method.* If a company is using the terms of APB 25 as the basis for recognizing compensation expense, then it must compare the fair market value of the stock on the option grant date to the exercise price, and charge the difference to compensation expense if the exercise price is lower than the market price. If a company is privately held, it may be difficult to determine the fair market value of the stock, which can result in reduced fair value estimates in order to avoid recognizing any compensation expense. One should require a consistent valuation estimation methodology so a company does not alter its valuation formula every time options are granted .

12. *Revenues.* The key controls concern related to revenues is that all shipments be invoiced in a timely manner. A controls failure in this area can lead to a major revenue shortfall and threaten overall company liquidity.

- ○ *Compare all billings to the shipping log.* There should be a continual comparison of billings to the shipment log, not only to ensure that everything shipped is billed, but also to guard against illicit shipments that involve collusion between outside parties and the shipping staff. Someone who is handing out products at the shipping dock will rarely be obliging enough to record this transaction in the shipping log, so the additional step of carefully comparing finished goods inventory levels to physical inventory counts and reviewing all transactions for each item must be used to determine where inventory shrinkage appears to be occurring.

- ○ *Compare customer-requested delivery dates to actual shipment dates.* If customer order information is loaded into the accounting computer system, run a comparison of the dates on which customers have requested delivery to the dates on which orders were actually shipped. If there is an ongoing tendency to make shipments substantially early, there may be a problem with trying to create revenue by making early shipments. Of particular interest is the situation that occurs when there is a surge of early shipments in months when revenues would otherwise have been low, indicating a clear intention to increase revenues by avoiding customer-mandated shipment dates. It may be possible to program the computer system to not allow the recording of deliveries if the entered delivery date is prior to the customer-requested delivery date, thereby effectively blocking early revenue recognition.

- ○ *Compare declared percentage of completion to estimated work required to complete projects.* A very common way to record excessive revenue on a construction project is to falsely state that the percentage of completion is greater than the actual figure, thereby allowing the company to record a greater proportion of revenues in the current period. Though difficult to verify with any precision, a reasonable control is to match the declared percentage of completion to a percentage of the actual hours worked, divided by the total estimated number of hours worked. The two percentages should match.

- ○ *Compare discounts taken to return authorizations granted.* Customers will sometimes take deductions when paying company invoices, on the grounds that they have returned some products to the company. The problem is that the company may never have authorized the returns, much less received them.

A comparison of the returns authorization log to the list of discounts taken in the cash receipts journal will provide evidence that a customer is not paying for its obligations.

○ *Compare invoice dates to the recurring revenue database.* In cases where a company obtains a recurring revenue stream by billing customers periodically for maintenance or subscription services, there can be a temptation to create early billings in order to record revenue somewhat sooner. For example, a billing on a 12-month subscription could be issued after 11 months, thereby accelerating revenue recognition by one month. This issue can be spotted by comparing the total of recurring billings in a month to the total amount of recurring revenue for that period as compiled from the corporate database of customers with recurring revenue. Alternatively, one can compare the recurring billing dates for a small sample of customers to the dates on which invoices were actually issued.

○ *Compare related company addresses and names to customer list.* By comparing the list of company subsidiaries to the customer list, one can determine if any intercompany sales have occurred, and if these transactions have all been appropriately backed out of the financial statements. Since employees at one subsidiary may conceal this relationship by using a false company name or address, one can verify the same information at all the other subsidiaries by matching subsidiary names and addresses to their supplier lists, since it is possible that the receiving companies are *not* trying to hide the intercompany sales information.

○ *Identify shipments of product samples in the shipping log.* A product that is shipped with no intention of being billed is probably a product sample being sent to a prospective customer, marketing agency, and so forth. These should be noted as product samples in the shipping log, and the internal audit staff should verify that each of them was properly authorized, preferably with a signed document.

○ *Investigate all journal entries increasing the size of revenue.* Any time a journal entry is used to increase a sales account, this should be a "red flag" indicating the potential presence of revenues that were not created through a normal sales journal transaction. These transactions can be legitimate cases of incremental revenue recognition associated with prepaid services, but can also be barter swap transactions or fake transactions whose sole purpose is to increase revenues. It is especially important to review all sales transactions where the offsetting debit to the sales credit is *not* accounts receivable or cash. This is a prime indicator of unusual transactions that may not really qualify as sales. For example, a gain on an asset sale or an extraordinary gain may be incorrectly credited to a sales account that would mislead the reader of a company's financial statements that its operating revenues have increased.

○ *Issue financial statements within one day of the period end.* By eliminating the gap between the end of the reporting period and the issuance of financial statements, it is impossible for anyone to create additional invoices for goods shipping subsequent to the period end, thereby automatically eliminating any cutoff problems.

○ *Require a written business case for all barter transactions.* Require the creation of a business case detailing why a barter transaction is required and what type of accounting should be used for it. The case should be approved by a senior-level manager before any associated entry is made in the general ledger. The case should be attached to the associated journal entry and filed. This approach makes it less likely that sham barter swap transactions will be created.

○ *Watch for expense loading on cost-plus contracts.* When a company is guaranteed by the customer to pay for all expenses incurred, there exists a temptation to load extra expenses into an account. These expense additions can be spotted by looking for charges from suppliers whose costs are not normally charged to a specific type of contract, as well as by looking for expense types that increase significantly over expenses incurred in previous periods, and by investigating any journal entries that increase expense levels.

13. *Cost of goods sold.* There are many ways in which a company can lose control over its costs in the cost of goods sold area, since it involves many personnel and the largest proportion of company costs. The application of the following suggested controls to a production environment will rely heavily on the perceived gain that will be experienced from using them versus the extent to which they will interfere with the smooth functioning of the production department.

○ *Audit inventory material costs.* Inventory costs are usually either assigned through a standard costing procedure or as part of some inventory layering concept, such as LIFO or FIFO. In the case of standard costs, one should regularly compare assigned costs to the actual cost of materials purchased to see if any standard costs should be updated to bring them more in line with actual costs incurred. If it is company policy to only update standard costs at lengthy intervals, then one should verify that the variance between actual and standard costs is being written off to the cost of goods sold.

○ *Audit production setup cost calculations.* If production setup costs are included in inventory unit costs, there is a possibility of substantial costing errors if the assumed number of units produced in a production run is incorrect. For example, if the cost of a production setup is $1,000 and the production run is 1,000 units, then the setup cost should be $1 per unit. However, if someone wanted to artificially increase the cost of inventory in order to create a jump in profits, the assumed production run size could be reduced. In the example, if the production run assumption were dropped to 100 units, the cost per unit would increase ten-fold to $10. A reasonable control over this problem is to regularly review setup cost calculations. An early warning indicator of this problem is to run a report comparing setup costs over time for each product to see if there are any sudden changes in costs. Also, access to the computer file storing this information should be strictly limited.

○ *Compare the cost of all completed jobs to budgeted costs.* A company can suffer from major drops in its gross margin if it does not keep an eagle eye on the costs incurred to complete jobs. To do so, the cost accountant should compare a complete list of all costs incurred for a job to the initial budget or quote and determine exactly which actual costs are higher than expected. This review should result in a list of problems that caused the cost overruns, which in turn can be addressed by the management team so that they do not arise again. This process should also be performed while jobs are in process (especially if the jobs are of long duration) so that these problems can be found and fixed before job completion.

○ *Compare projected manning needs to actual direct labor staffing.* The production manager will have a tendency to overstaff the production area if he or she is solely responsible for meeting the requirements of the production plan, since an excess of labor will help to ensure that products are completed on time. This tendency can be spotted and quantified by using labor routings to determine the amount of labor that should have been used and then comparing this standard to the actual labor cost incurred.

○ *Compare unextended product costs to those for prior periods.* Product costs of all types can change for a variety of reasons. An easy way to spot these changes is to create and regularly review a report that compares the unextended cost of each product to its cost in a prior period. Any significant changes can then be traced back to the underlying costing information to see exactly what caused each change. The main problem with this control is that many less-expensive accounting systems do not retain historical inventory records. If so, the information should be exported to an electronic spreadsheet or separate database once a month, where historical records can then be kept.

○ *Pick from stock based on bills of material.* An excellent control over material costs is to require the use of bills of material for each item manufactured and then require that parts be picked from the raw materials stock for the production of these items based on the quantities listed in the bills of material. By doing so, a reviewer can hone in on those warehouse issuances that were *not* authorized through a bill of material, since there is no objective reason why these issuances should have taken place.

○ *Purchase based on blanket purchase orders and related releases.* The purchasing staff is already doing its job if all purchases are authorized through purchase orders. However, they will be doing this work more efficiently if repeating purchase orders can be summarized into blanket purchase orders, against which releases are authorized from time to time. The internal audit staff should periodically determine if there are opportunities for the use of additional blanket purchase orders, if current ones are being used properly, and if the minimum quantity commitments listed on existing blanket orders are being met, thereby keeping the company from paying penalties for missing minimum order totals.

○ *Reject all purchases that are not preapproved.* A major flaw in the purchasing systems of many companies is that all supplier deliveries are accepted at the receiving dock, irrespective of the presence of authorizing paperwork. Many of these deliveries are verbally authorized orders from employees throughout the company, many of whom are not authorized to make such purchases or who are not aware that they are buying items at high prices. This problem can be eliminated by enforcing a rule that all items received must have a corresponding purchase order on file that has been authorized by the purchasing department. By doing so, the purchasing staff can verify that there is a need for each item requisitioned and that it is bought at a reasonable price from a certified supplier.

○ *Review inventory layering calculations.* Most inventory layering systems are automatically maintained through a computer system and cannot be altered. In these cases, there is no need to verify the layering calculations. However, if the layering information is manually maintained, one should schedule periodic reviews of the underlying calculations to ensure proper cost layering. This usually involves tracing costs back to specific supplier invoices. However, one should also trace supplier invoices forward to the layering calculations, since it is quite possible that invoices have been excluded from the calculations. Also verify consistency in the allocation of freight costs to inventory items in the layering calculations.

- ○ *Review a sorted list of extended product costs in declining dollar order.* This report is more commonly available than the historical tracking report noted in the last bullet point, but contains less information. The report lists the extended cost of all inventory on hand for each inventory item, sorted in declining order of cost. By scanning the report, one can readily spot items that have unusually large or small valuations. However, finding these items requires some knowledge of what costs were in previous periods. Also, a lengthy inventory list makes it difficult to efficiently locate costing problems. Thus, this report is inferior to the unextended historical cost comparison report from a control perspective.

- ○ *Verify the calculation and allocation of overhead cost pools.* Overhead costs are usually assigned to inventory as the result of a manually derived summarization and allocation of overhead costs. This can be a lengthy calculation, subject to error. The best control over this process is a standard procedure that clearly defines which costs to include in the pools and precisely how these costs are to be allocated. In addition, one should regularly review the types of costs included in the calculations, verify that the correct proportions of these costs are included, and ensure that the costs are being correctly allocated to inventory. A further control is to track the total amount of overhead accumulated in each reporting period—any sudden change in the amount may indicate an error in the overhead cost summarization .

14. *Travel and entertainment expenses.* Employee expense reports can involve dozens of line items of requested expense reimbursements, a few of which may conflict with a company's stated reimbursement policies. In order to ensure that these "gray area" expense line items are caught, many accountants will apply a disproportionate amount of clerical time to the minute examination of expense reports. The need for this level of control will depend upon the accountant's perception of the amount of expenses that will be reduced through its use. In reality, some lesser form of control, such as expense report audits, are generally sufficient to keep expense reports "honest."

- ○ *Audit expense reports at random.* Employees may be more inclined to pass through expense items on their expense reports if they do not think that the company is reviewing their expenses. This issue can be resolved fairly inexpensively by conducting a few random audits of expense reports and following up with offending employees regarding any unauthorized expense submissions. Word of these activities will get around, resulting in better employee self-monitoring of their expense reports. Also, if there is evidence of repeat offenders, the random audits can be made less random by requiring recurring audits for specific employees.

- ○ *Issue policies concerning allowable expenses.* Employees may submit inappropriate expenses for reimbursement simply because they have not been told that the expenses are inappropriate. This problem can be resolved by issuing a detailed set of policies and procedures regarding travel. The concept can be made more available to employees by posting the information on a corporate intranet site. Also, if there is an online expense report submission system in place, these rules can be incorporated directly into the underlying software, so that the system will warn employees regarding inappropriate reimbursement submissions.

   ○ *Require supervisory approval of all expense reports.* If there are continuing problems with expense reimbursement submissions from employees, it may be necessary to require supervisory approval of all expense reports. This has the advantage of involving someone who presumably knows why an employee is submitting a reimbursement form, and who can tell if the company should pay for it. The downside is that expense reports tend to sit on manager's desks for a long time, which increases the time period needed before an employee will receive payment.

15. *Payroll expenses.* The controls used for payroll cover two areas—the avoidance of excessive amounts of pay to employees and the avoidance of fraud related to the creation of paychecks for nonexistent employees. Both types of controls are addressed here.

   ○ *Require approval of all overtime hours worked by hourly personnel.* One of the simplest forms of fraud is to come back to the company after hours and clock out at a later time, or have another employee do it on one's behalf, thereby creating false overtime hours. This can be resolved by requiring supervisory approval of all overtime hours worked. A more advanced approach is to use a computerized time clock that categorizes each employee by a specific work period, so that any hours worked after his or her standard time period will be automatically flagged by the computer for supervisory approval. They may not even allow an employee to clock out after a specific time of day without a supervisory code first being entered into the computer.

   ○ *Require approval of all pay changes.* Pay changes can be made quite easily through the payroll system if there is collusion between a payroll clerk and any other employee. This can be spotted through regular comparisons of pay rates *paid* to the approved pay rates *stored* in employee folders. It is best to require the approval of a high-level manager for all pay changes, which should include that person's signature on a standard pay change form. It is also useful to audit the deductions taken from employee paychecks, since these can be altered downwards to effectively yield an increased rate of pay. This audit should include a review of the amount and timing of garnishment payments, to ensure that these deductions are being made as required by court orders.

   ○ *Issue checks directly to recipients.* A common type of fraud is for the payroll staff to either create employees in the payroll system, or to carry on the pay of employees who have left the company, and then pocket the resulting paychecks. This practice can be stopped by ensuring that every paycheck is handed to an employee who can prove his or her identity.

   ○ *Issue lists of paychecks issued to department supervisors.* It is quite useful to give supervisors a list of paychecks issued to everyone in their departments from time to time, because they may be able to spot payments being made to employees who are no longer working there. This is a particular problem in larger companies, where any delay in processing termination paperwork can result in continuing payments to ex-employees. It is also a good control over any payroll clerk who may be trying to defraud the company by delaying termination paperwork and then pocketing the paychecks produced in the interim.

- *Compare the addresses on employee paychecks.* If the payroll staff is creating additional fake employees and having the resulting paychecks mailed to their home addresses, then a simple comparison of addresses for all check recipients will reveal duplicate addresses (though employees can get around this problem by having checks sent to post office boxes—this control issue can be stopped by creating a policy to prohibit payments to post office boxes).

16. *Occupancy expenses.* Though a relatively minor item, the following control is intended to ensure that employees are prudent in their acquisition of furnishings for company offices.

    - *Compare the cost of employee furnishings to company policy.* Employees may obtain furnishings at a cost that is well beyond what would be obtained by a prudent manager. This issue can be addressed by promulgating a policy that outlines the maximum cost of furnishings per employee and by enforcing it with occasional internal audits of costs incurred. Another means of enforcement is to authorize a standard set of furnishings for the purchasing staff to procure, with any furnishings outside this list requiring special approval.

17. *Hedging.* Hedging involves strictly mandated recognition of losses under certain circumstances. Most of the following controls involve the use of recurring hedge transaction reviews and documentation to ensure that losses are promptly recognized:

    - *Include in the hedging procedure a requirement for full documentation of each hedge.* Hedging transactions are only allowed under GAAP if they are fully documented at the inception of the hedge. One can ensure compliance by including the documentation requirement in an accounting procedure for creating hedges.

    - *Include in the closing procedure a requirement to review the effectiveness of any fair value hedges.* GAAP requires that hedging transactions only be accounted for as fair value hedges if a hedging relationship regularly produces offsets to fair value changes. Since this review must be conducted on at least a quarterly basis and every time financial statements are issued, including the requirement in the closing procedure is an effective way to ensure compliance with GAAP.

    - *Compare hedging effectiveness assessments to the corporate policy setting forth effectiveness ranges.* GAAP does not specify the exact amount by which hedging instruments and hedged items must offset each other in order to be deemed highly effective, so a corporate policy should be established (see the Policies section) to create such a standard. This control is intended to ensure that the policy is followed when making effectiveness assessments. Comparison to the corporate policy should be included in the assessment procedure.

    - *Include in the monthly financial statement procedure a review of the recoverability of cash flow hedge losses.* GAAP requires that a nonrecoverable cash flow hedge loss be shifted in the current period from other comprehensive income to earnings. Since this can only result in a reduced level of earnings, accounting personnel tend not to conduct the review. Including the step in the monthly procedure is a good way to ensure prompt loss recognition.

    - *Include in the monthly financial statement procedure a review of the likely occurrence of forecasted cash flow transactions.* GAAP requires that any accumulated gain or loss recorded in other comprehensive income be shifted into

earnings as soon as it becomes probable that the forecasted cash flow transaction will not take place. Including a standard periodic review of forecasted
transactions in the monthly procedure is a good way to ensure prompt inclusion
of accumulated gains or losses in earnings.

18. *Foreign currency translations.* The following control should be used to ensure that
translation methods are not arbitrarily switched in order to show or avoid translation
gains or losses.

○ *Gain external auditor approval of any changes in translation method.* A key
difference between the current rate and remeasurement methods of translation
is that translation adjustments under the current rate method are placed in the
balance sheet, whereas adjustments under the remeasurement method are recognized on the income statement as gains or losses. The accounting staff could
be tempted to shift between the two methods in order to show specific financial
results on the corporate income statement. For example, if there were a translation gain, one would be more likely to use the remeasurement method in order
to recognize it on the income statement. This problem is especially likely when
the criteria for using one method over the other could be construed either way.
The best way to avoid this problem is to have a disinterested third party (i.e., the
auditors) approve any change in method over what was used in the preceding
year.

○ *Require management approval of calculations for the status of inflationary
economies.* It is possible to alter the translation method based on the inflationary status of a foreign economy, possibly resulting in the recognition (or not) of
translation gains or losses on the income statement. If one were inclined to shift
the translation method, a defensible basis for doing so would be the inflationary
status of the economy in which a foreign entity does business. The inflationary status could be altered by using either incorrect inflation data or shifting
the beginning and ending dates of the calculation to correspond to inflation data
more in line with one's required result. This issue can be resolved by requiring
management or internal audit reviews of these calculations, especially when a
change in inflationary status has recently occurred.

19. *General.* A few continuing payments to suppliers are based on long-term contracts.
Most of the following controls are associated with having a complete knowledge
of the terms of these contracts, so that a company does not make incorrect payment
amounts.

○ *Monitor changes in contractual costs.* This is a large source of potential expense reductions. Suppliers may alter the prices charged to the company on their
invoices from the rates specified on either purchase orders, blanket purchase orders, or long-term contracts, in hopes that no one at the receiving company will
notice the change in prices. Of particular concern should be prices that the supplier can contractually change in accordance with some underlying cost basis,
such as the price of oil, or the consumer price index—suppliers will promptly
increase prices based on these escalator clauses, but will be much less prompt
in reducing prices in accordance with the same underlying factors. The internal
audit team can review these prices from time to time, or the accounting computer system can automatically compare invoice prices to a database of contract
terms. Another alternative is to only pay suppliers based on the price listed in
the purchase order, which entirely negates the need for this control.

○ *Monitor when contracts are due for renewal.* A company may find itself temporarily paying much higher prices to a supplier if it inadvertently lets expire a long-term contract containing advantageous price terms. To avoid this difficulty, a good control is to set up a master file of all contracts that includes the contract expiration date, so that there will be fair warning of when contract renegotiations must be initiated.

○ *Require approval for various levels of contractually-based monetary commitment.* There should be a company policy that itemizes the levels of monetary commitment at which additional levels of management approval are required. Though this may not help the company to disavow signed contracts, it is a useful prevention tool for keeping managers from signing off on contracts that represent large or long-term monetary commitments.

○ *Obtain bonds for employees in financial sensitive positions.* If there is some residual risk that, despite all the foregoing controls, corporate assets will still be lost due to the activities of employees, it is useful to obtain bonds on either specific employees or for entire departments, so that the company can be reimbursed in the event of fraudulent activities.

The preceding set of recommended controls only encompasses the most common ones. These should be supplemented by reviewing the process flows used by a company to see if there is a need for additional (or fewer) controls, depending upon how the processes are structured. Controls will vary considerably by industry, as well—for example, the casino industry imposes multilayered controls over cash collection, since it is a cash business. Thus, these controls should only be considered the foundation for a comprehensive set of controls that must be tailored to each company's specific needs.

30.12 WHEN TO ELIMINATE CONTROLS

Despite the lengthy list of controls noted in the last section, there are times when one can safely take controls away. By doing so, one can frequently eliminate extra clerical costs, or at least streamline the various accounting processes. To see if a control is eligible for removal, the following steps should be used:

1. *Flowchart the process.* The first step is to create a picture of every step in the entire process in which a control fits by creating a flowchart. This is needed in order to determine where other controls are located in the process flow. With a knowledge of redundant control points or evidence that there are no other controls available, one can then make a rational decision regarding the need for a specific control.

2. *Determine the cost of a control point.* Having used a flowchart to find controls that may no longer be needed, we must then determine their cost. This can be a complex calculation, for it may not just involve a certain amount of labor, material, or overhead costs that will be reduced. It is also possible that the control is situated in the midst of a bottleneck operation, so that the presence of the control is directly decreasing the capacity of the process, thereby resulting in reduced profits. In this instance, the incremental drop in profits must be added to the incremental cost of operating the control in order to determine its total cost.

3. *Determine the criticality of the control.* If a control point is merely a supporting one that backs up another control, then taking it away may not have a significant impact on the ability of the company to retain control over its assets. However, if

its removal can only be counteracted by a number of weaker controls, it may be better to keep it in operation.

4. *Calculate the control's cost/benefit.* The preceding two points can be compared to see if a control point's cost is outweighed by its criticality, or if the current mix of controls will allow it to be eliminated with no significant change in risk, while stopping the incurrence of its cost.

5. *Verify the use of controls targeted for elimination.* Even when there is a clear-cut case for the elimination of a control point, it is useful to notify everyone who is involved with the process in which it is imbedded in order to ascertain if there is some other purpose for which it is being used. For example, a control that measures the cycle time of a manufacturing machine may no longer be needed as a control point, but may be an excellent source of information for someone who is tracking the percentage utilization of the equipment. In these cases, it is best to determine the value of the control to the alternate user of the control before eliminating it. It may be necessary to work around the alternate use before the control point can be removed.

This control evaluation process should be repeated whenever there is a significant change to a process flow. Even if there has not been a clear change for some time, it is likely that a large number of small changes have been made to a process, whose cumulative impact will necessitate a controls review. The period of time between these reviews will vary by industry, since some have seen little process change in many years, while others are constantly shifting their business models, which inherently requires changes to their supporting processes.

If there are any significant changes to a business model, such as the addition of any kind of technology, entry into new markets, or the addition of new product lines, a complete review of all associated process flows should be conducted both prior to and immediately after the changes, so that unneeded controls can be promptly removed or weak controls enhanced .

30.13 SUMMARY

The main focus of this chapter has been on the specific control points that can be attached to an accounting system in order to reduce the risk of loss. The selection of these controls should be contingent upon an evaluation of the risks to which an accounting system is subject, as well as the cost of each control point and its impact on the overall efficiency of each accounting process. In a larger organization, the continuing examination, selection, and installation of control points can easily become a full-time job for a highly trained process expert. Smaller organizations that cannot afford the services of such a person will likely call upon the in-house accounting staff to provide such control reviews, which should be conducted on a fixed schedule in order to ensure that ongoing incremental changes to processes are adequately supported by the correct controls.

COST ACCOUNTING

31.1   INTRODUCTION

Cost accounting is one of the most crucial aspects of the accounting profession, for it is the primary means by which the accounting department transmits company-related performance information to the management team. A properly organized cost accounting function can give valuable feedback regarding the impact of product pricing, cost trends, the performance of cost and profit centers, and production and personnel capacity, and can even contribute to some degree to the formulation of company strategy. Despite this wide array of uses, many accountants rarely give due consideration to the multitude of uses to which cost accounting can be put. Instead, they only think of how cost accounting will feed information into the financial statements. This orientation comes from a strong tendency in business schools to train students in generally accepted accounting principles (GAAP) and how they are used to create financial statements.

In this chapter, we will depart from the strong orientation toward GAAP that is observed in much of the remainder of this book and instead focus on how one can collect data, summarize it, and report it to management with the goal of helping the management team to run the business. For this function, we care much less about the proper reporting of accounting information and more about how information can be presented in a format that yields the greatest possible level of utility to the recipient. For issues regarding the proper valuation of inventory in accordance with GAAP, please refer to Chapter 13.

31.2   THE PURPOSE OF COST ACCOUNTING INFORMATION

The purpose of cost accounting differs from that of many other topics discussed in this book. It is primarily concerned with helping the management team to understand the company's operations. This is in opposition to many other accounting topics, which are more concerned with the proper observance of very precise accounting rules and regulations, as laid down by various accounting oversight entities, to ensure that reported results meet certain standards.

The cost accounting function works best without any oversight rules and regulations, because, in accordance with its stated purpose of assisting management, it tends to result in hybrid systems that are custom-designed to meet specific company needs. For example, a company may find that a major requirement is to determine the incremental cost that it incurs for each additional unit of production so that it can make accurate decisions regarding the price of incremental units sold (possibly at prices very close to the direct cost). If it were to use accounting standards, it would be constrained to use only a costing system that allocated a portion of overhead costs to product costs—even though these are not incremental costs. Accordingly, the cost accounting system used for this specific purpose will operate in contravention of GAAP, because following GAAP would yield results that do not assist management.

Because there are many different management decisions for which the cost accounting profession can provide valuable information, it is quite common to have several costing systems in place, each of which may use different costing guidelines. To extend the previous example, the incremental costing system used for incremental pricing decisions may not be adequate for a different problem, which is creating profit centers that are used to judge the performance of individual managers. For this purpose, a second costing system must be devised that allocates costs from internal service centers to the various profit centers; in this instance, we are adding an allocation function to the incremental costing system that was already in place. Even more systems may be required for other applications, such as transfer pricing between company divisions and the costing of inventory for external financial reporting purposes (which does require attention to GAAP guidelines). Consequently, cost accounting frequently results in a multitude of costing systems, which may only follow GAAP guidelines by accident. The cost accountant's primary concern is whether or not the information resulting from each system adequately meets the needs of the recipients.

Any cost accounting system is comprised of three functional areas: the collection of raw data, the processing of this data in accordance with a costing methodology, and the reporting of the resulting information to management in the most understandable format. The remainder of this chapter is split into sections that address each of these three functional areas. The area that receives the most coverage is the processing function, for there are a number of different methodologies available, each of which applies to different situations. For example, job costing is used for situations where specifically identifiable goods are produced in batches, while direct costing is most applicable in situations in which management does not want to see any overhead allocation attached to the directly identifiable costs of a product. The large number of processing methodologies presented here is indicative of the broad range of options available to the cost accountant for processing raw data into various types of reports for management use.

31.3 INPUT: DATA COLLECTION SYSTEMS

The first step in setting up a data collection system is to determine what *types* of data to gather. One can simply collect every conceivable type of data available, but this will result in immensely detailed and cumbersome collection systems that are expensive and require a great deal of employee time to collect and record. A better approach is to determine what types of outputs are required, which can then be used to ascertain the specific data items needed to create those outputs. This allows the controller to ignore many types of data, simply because no one needs them. However, the process of determining data requirements from projected outputs must be revisited on a regular basis, for changes in the business will require changes in the required cost accounting reports, and therefore changes in the types of data collected.

The process of backtracking from a required output to a set of required data elements is best illustrated with an example. If a company is manufacturing a set of products whose components and assembly are entirely outsourced, then it is logical to create management reports that focus on the prices being charged to the company by its suppliers, rather than creating an elaborate time recording system for the small number of quality inspectors who are responsible for reviewing completed goods before they are shipped out to customers. In this case, the bulk of the data used by the costing system will come out of the accounts payable and purchasing records. Another example is a software company, where the costing focus is on the labor time charged to specific development projects and the ability of project managers to meet their deadlines, rather than on the minor cost of purchasing compact disks, packaging, and training materials that are shipped to customers. In this case, most of the cost accounting data will come from the timekeeping and project-tracking databases. Thus, the nature of the business will drive the decision to collect certain types of data.

Once the cost accountant knows what data to collect, there is still the issue of creating a data accumulation system. There are several factors that will influence this decision. One is *cost;* if there are many employees who will be recording information continuously, then the unit cost of the data collection device cannot be too expensive, or else its total cost will exceed the utility of the collected data. Another issue is *data accuracy;* if the data collected absolutely, positively must be correct, then a more elaborate solution, such as bar code scanning, which is designed to yield completely accurate results, should be the preferred solution. However, if the level of required accuracy is lower, then perhaps manual keypunch entry or handwritten data sheets would be acceptable. Another factor is the *employees* who will use the data collection systems; if they are highly trained, then they can be relied on to use complex keypunching systems, whereas a poorly trained workforce that has no idea of what data it is collecting or why it is being used, should be allowed to collect only data that will be heavily cross-checked for errors. Of additional concern is the *timeliness* of the data collected. If there is a need for up-to-the-minute transmission of data to managers, then the only solution will be some form of automated data gathering. On the other hand, only an occasional report to management may require a slower manual data-gathering approach. Another factor to consider is the *existing level of automation* within the company. For example, if there is a clear production path for all products that sends every completed item down a specific conveyor belt, then the installation of a fixed bar code scanner on that conveyor is a reasonable approach for recording data about production quantities. However, this would be a poor solution if products were being hand-carried away from a multitude of production processes to the warehouse, since many of the items created would never pass by the bar code scanner. A final consideration is the *production methodology* currently in use. If it is a lean manufacturing system, such as a just-in-time system, there will be a strong orientation away from requiring employees to conduct any data entry work, since extremely focused and efficient workflows are the key to success in this environment—which is interrupted if data entry tasks are included. In these cases, one should avoid any type of manual data entry, focusing instead on more automated approaches.

Given the previous parameters, it is clear that the controller must devise a wide array of data collection tools in order to collect data in the most appropriate manner. The following bullet points describe a number of the more common (and upcoming) data collection tools:

- *Punch clocks.* A data collection tool that is proving to have a great deal of longevity is the punch clock. This is used by hourly employees to record the times when they arrive for work and leave at the end of the day. The process is a simple one; take your time card from a storage rack, insert it into the top of the clock, which stamps the time on it, and return your card to the storage rack. The payroll staff then uses these cards to calculate payroll. The greatest advantage of this approach is that a time clock is very inexpensive. However, it requires conversion of the time card data by the payroll staff into another format before it can be used, which introduces the likelihood of computational errors. Also, it is difficult to use for recording time worked on specific jobs.

- *Electronic time clocks.* This clock allows employees to swipe a badge through a reader on the side or top of the clock. This results in a computer entry for the time of the scan, which is also associated with the employee code that is embedded in the card, through the use of either a bar code or a magnetic stripe. A more advanced version uses the biometric measurement of the outlines of one's hand to determine the identity of the employee (thereby eliminating the need for an employee badge, which might otherwise be lost or used to make a scan for someone who is not on the premises). This represents a significant advance over the punch clock, because there is no need for secondary calculations that might result in an error. It also yields greater control over the time-recording process, since it gives immediate feedback to supervisors regarding missed or late scans. An additional benefit is that employees can enter job numbers as part of the scanning process, so that time is charged to specific jobs. However, the electronic time clock costs up to $2,000 each, and so is usually restricted to high-volume applications where there are many employees—punch clocks are therefore only used in high-volume locations, where they are more cost-effective.

- *Bar code scanners.* A bar code scanner is a device that reads bar code labels with either a fixed or rapidly rotating laser beam, and converts the bar code symbology into a character-based format that is then stored in the computer system. These scanners come in many shapes and sizes, ranging from a $100 fixed-beam scanner that looks like a pen (but which may require a number of scans to read a bar code) to a $10,000 fixed-position scanner that is bolted to a conveyor belt and which emits 30 scans per second as bar-coded packages move past it. There are also portable scanners, which are heavily used in warehousing operations, that can store scanned information in local RAM memory for later uploading to a computer, or that contain direct radio frequency access to the company computer and can therefore transmit the data immediately. The type of scanner purchased will depend on the level of automation required and the budget available for this purpose. Bar code scanning is highly recommended for repetitive data entry situations where the *same* data is collected many times. On the other hand, it is of less use where the data collected changes constantly or involves a large quantity of text that would require an extremely large bar code. Nonetheless, some portion of most data entry applications can involve the use of bar code scanning.

- *Terminal data entry.* An increasingly common form of data entry is to not use any new data collection devices—instead, one just buys lots more computer terminals and makes them available to users throughout the company. Employees can then be given direct access to the computer screens that require input from them and can enter information directly into the computer system. This avoids the middleman data entry person, as well as the risk that the data entry staff might misinterpret the data on an employee's form and type in the wrong information. The process can be facilitated by the use of error-checking protocols within the computer software, so that users will be flagged if they make entries that are clearly outside of a narrow band of expected responses. Also, computer screens can be devised for individual users that are designed to assist them in entering only the data they have access to, and in the most efficient manner. However, it can be expensive to rig all locations in a company with computer terminals and all linking wiring, while some employees may move around so much that having them use a fixed terminal is not a viable option. Consequently, this approach may have limited applicability, depending on the situation.

- *Paper-based data entry.* Despite all of the other forms of advanced data entry noted here, the most common method for collecting data is still from a paper document. This approach is inexpensive, requires no web of interlinked electronic devices throughout a facility, and is familiar to all employees as a method of data capture. However, it does not result in a fast flow of data through an organization, since it may be days or weeks before the information contained on a form is rekeyed into the computer system. Also, it is easy to lose forms, especially when they are being used throughout a facility and there is no rigid tracking of individual forms to ensure that none are lost. Furthermore, this approach requires the services of an expensive data entry person to interpret the data on the forms (sometimes incorrectly) and type the results into the computer system. Given these problems, it is no surprise that the proportion of data gathering that uses this approach is shrinking—nonetheless, it still constitutes the majority of all data gathering techniques in most organizations.

Thus, there are a wide range of data entry systems available. In most instances, the controller who is designing a data collection system will need to use a mix of these options to ensure that the correct mix of high data accuracy and low collection cost is achieved.

31.4 PROCESSING: DATA SUMMARIZATION SYSTEMS

Having covered the data collection portion of cost accounting, we now move to the various costing methodologies that are available for processing the raw data into a format that is most useful for management consumption. The primary advantages and disadvantages of the systems whose functions are noted in the following sections are:

- *Job costing.* This is a commonly used system that is primarily targeted at production situations where customized goods are produced for specific customers. It is very useful for tracking the exact cost of individual products, and is the only valid technique for accumulating costs for cost-plus contractual arrangements. It can also yield accurate results about the ongoing costs of a current job, which is useful for monitoring purposes. However, this system requires a large quantity of detailed data collection and data entry, which is expensive. It also runs the risk of including some inaccurate data, which requires expensive control systems to minimize.

Furthermore, there may be a significant allocation of overhead costs to each job, which may be inaccurately applied.

- *Process costing.* This is also a heavily used system and is most common in situations where large quantities of exactly the same product are created. Costs are collected in bulk for entire time periods and then allocated out to the volume of entire production runs during that period. This results in a fair degree of accuracy when costs are averaged out and assigned to individual units. However, some degree of estimation is required when determining total production quantities completed, since some units may be only partially completed at the end of the production period. Consequently, there is some room for variation in final production costs. This method requires much less data collection than job costing, but the level of information accuracy is correspondingly lower.

- *Standard costing.* This methodology has been installed in many companies as an adjunct to both the job-costing and process-costing systems. It is designed to set standard costs for all material and labor costs incurred by a company, against which actual results can be compared through variance analysis. This can result in excellent control over company costs, but only if the accounting staff is diligent in uncovering the reasons for variances from costing standards, and the management team is helpful in correcting the discovered problems. It is also useful for budgeting, setting prices, and closing the financial books in a rapid manner. However, it is also time-consuming to set and maintain standards; in environments where this maintenance function is not performed, standards can be so far away from actual results that variance analysis is no longer useful for management purposes. Also, a company that has adopted continuous process improvement principles will find that any standards adopted will almost immediately become obsolete, requiring constant correction. Furthermore, most standards are set at the product level, rather than at the batch level, so there is no basis of comparison when using this method for cost control over production batches. Another problem is that comparisons to actual costs tend to focus management attention on labor variances, which have historically been a large part of the cost accounting report package, even though these costs comprise only a small proportion of total production costs in most manufacturing environments. Finally, it tends to perpetuate inefficiencies, if personnel use the current standard cost as a baseline for behavior; they will have no incentive to improve costs to a point that is substantially better than the preset standard, resulting in languishing efficiency levels. For these reasons, standard costing is now used in a more limited role that in previous years.

- *Direct costing.* This is a favorite methodology for those managers who are constantly confronted with incremental costing and pricing decisions where the inclusion of overhead costs in a product's total cost will yield inaccurate information. Thus, direct costing is an ideal approach for determining the lowest possible price at which to sell incremental units. However, it yields inaccurate results when used for long-term pricing, since it takes no account of overhead costs that must be included in a company's standard prices if it is to assure itself of long-term profitability. It is also not allowed for inventory valuation purposes by GAAP, which requires the inclusion of allocated overhead costs.

- *Throughput accounting.* A variation on direct costing is throughput costing. This methodology holds that the only direct cost is direct materials, with even direct labor costs being thrown out when making most cost-related management decisions. The main tenet of throughput accounting is that a company must carefully manage the bottleneck operation in its production facility, so that the largest possible contribution margin is created. The main advantage of throughput accounting is that it yields the best short-term incremental profits if it is religiously followed when making production decisions. However, this can result in production mixes that seriously delay the completion of jobs for some customers, which is not good for customer relations.

- *Activity-based costing (ABC).* The ABC methodology is a much more accurate way to associate overhead costs with specific activities, which in turn can be assigned to product costs. Its main advantage is that it builds a direct correlation between the occurrence of an activity and related overhead costs, so that changes in the activity can be reliably expected to result in corresponding changes in the overhead costs. This results in valuable information for the management team, which uses it not only to gain some measure of control over its overhead costs, but also to gain an understanding of which products use more activities (and therefore overhead costs) than others. The downside of this methodology is that it requires a great deal of costing knowledge, time, and management commitment before a functioning ABC system becomes operational, and will henceforth require considerable upkeep to maintain. It also requires the construction of an ABC database that is separate from the general ledger, which can be an expensive proposition to both create and maintain. It is not really necessary in situations where there are few products, obvious process flows, and minimal machine setups, because a less complex cost accumulation system will still result in reasonably accurate product costs.

- *Target costing.* This costing methodology is the most proactive of all the methodologies, for it involves the direct intervention of the cost accounting staff in the product design process, with the express intent of creating products that meet preset cost and gross margin goals. This is opposed to the usual practice of accumulating costs after products have been designed and manufactured, so that managers will find out what a product costs after it is too late to make any changes to the design. This costing system is highly recommended to any company that designs its own products, since it can result in significant reductions in product costs before they are "locked in" when the design is completed. This technique usually requires a great deal of cost accounting staff time and can lengthen the product development process, but is well worth the effort.

- *By-product and joint product costing.* This type of costing involves using some rational means for allocating costs to products for which there is no clearly attributable cost. The various methods for conducting these allocations are primarily used for valuing inventory for external reporting purposes. It is generally unwise to use this information for any management purpose, since decisions based on allocated costs, with the intention of changing those costs, will usually fail. Consequently, by-product and joint product costing is not recommended for anything other than inventory valuation.

This brief review of the advantages and disadvantages of each costing methodology should make it clear not only that they are wildly different from each other in concept, but also that they are all designed to deal with different situations, several of which may be found within the same company. Accordingly, a controller must become accustomed to slipping in and out of a methodology when the circumstances warrant the change, and will very likely use a combination of these systems at the same time, if demanded by the circumstances.

In the following sections, we will review the workings of each of these costing methodologies.

31.5 PROCESSING: JOB COSTING

Job costing involves a series of transactions that accumulate the costs of materials, labor, and overhead (of which there are two different calculations) to a specific job. For each of these costing categories, costs are accumulated through a series of transactions before they are finally charged to a specific job. In this section, we will trace the journal entries used for all of these costs.

The basic flow of journal entries required for direct materials is noted in Exhibit 31.1 which itemizes the general format of each sequential transaction. When raw materials are purchased, they are rarely charged to a particular job upon receipt. Instead, they are stored

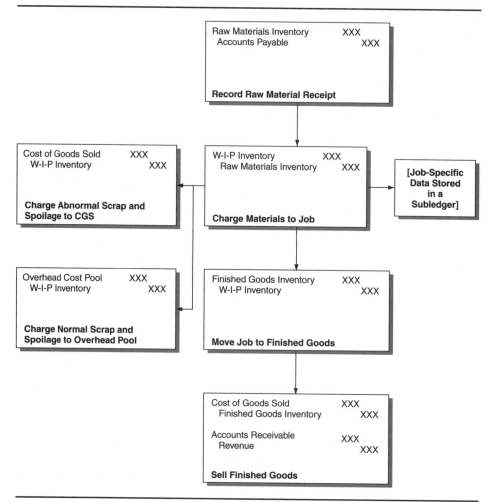

EXHIBIT 31.1 JOB COSTING TRANSACTIONS FOR DIRECT MATERIALS

in the warehouse, so there is a debit to the raw materials inventory and a credit to accounts payable. Once production is scheduled, the raw materials will be sent to the production floor, which triggers another transaction, to be created by the warehouse staff—a debit to the work-in-process inventory account and a credit to the raw materials inventory account.

During the production process, it is quite likely that some portion of the materials will be destroyed as part of the normal production process; if so, another entry will be required that creates a debit to the overhead cost pool and a credit to remove the cost from the work-in-process inventory account. This normal amount of scrap will then be allocated through the overhead cost pool back to product costs—we will deal with this issue shortly, when we talk about the cost flow for overhead costs. If there are excessive amounts of scrap, then these will be instead charged directly to the cost of goods sold with a debit, while the work-in-process account is reduced with a credit.

Once the production process has been completed (which may be a few moments for simple products, and months for complex ones), it is shifted back to the warehouse in the form of finished goods. To record this transaction, we use a debit to the finished goods inventory account and a credit to work-in-process inventory. Once the goods are sold from stock, a final entry relieves the finished goods inventory account with a credit and charges the cost to the cost of goods sold with a debit.

One of the numerous benefits of a just-in-time system is that materials are in the production process for such a short period of time that there is no point in creating transactions that move their cost in and out of work-in-process inventory. Instead, a single transaction shifts raw material costs from the raw materials inventory account to cost of goods sold (though there may be an extra entry to record the cost in finished goods inventory if completed products are not immediately sold). This greatly reduces the number of potential problems that can arise with the recording of transactions.

The recording of labor costs follows a slightly different path than what is typically seen for material costs. Instead of taking a direct route into the work-in-process inventory account, labor costs either can be charged at once to the overhead cost pool or go into work-in-process inventory. The charge to an overhead cost pool is done if there is no direct relationship between the incurrence of the labor cost and the creation of a product—this results in a debit to the overhead cost pool and a credit to the wages expense account. However, if there is a direct tie between the incurrence of labor costs and the production of specific products, then the debit is instead to the work-in-process inventory (or a separate labor) account. These cost flows are shown in Exhibit 31.2.

If the wages have flowed into an overhead cost pool, these costs will be summarized at the end of the accounting period and charged to specific products based on any number of allocation methodologies. The allocation calculation will result in another transaction that shifts the overhead costs to product costs, which can occur both at the work-in-process and finished goods stages of production. Meanwhile, labor costs that have been charged directly to work-in-process inventory will then be shifted to finished goods inventory and later to the cost of goods sold in the same manner as for materials costs.

As was the case for material costs, there are a large number of labor transactions that are required to track the flow of labor costs through the production process under the job-costing methodology. There is a high risk that transactional errors will arise, just because of the large number of transactions, so control systems must be created that keep errors from occurring and verify that completed transactions are correct.

The final job-costing process under the job-costing system is the allocation of costs to products. There are two ways to do this—either with the actual costs incurred during the production process, or else with standard costs that are later adjusted to match actual

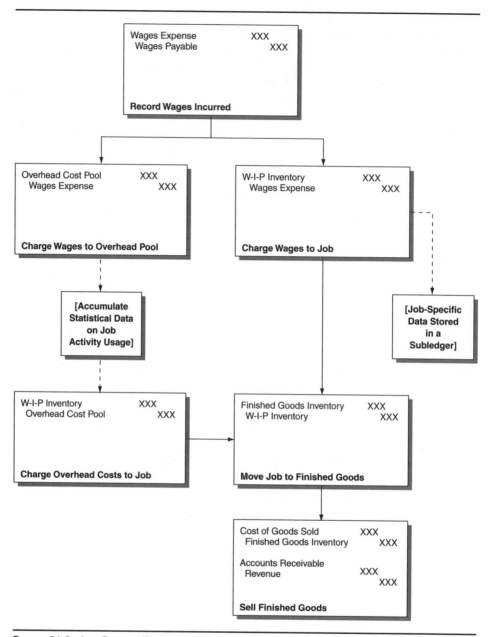

EXHIBIT 31.2   JOB COSTING TRANSACTIONS FOR LABOR

costing experience. The first of these approaches is called actual cost overhead allocation, while the latter is called normal cost overhead allocation. We will address the actual cost overhead allocation first.

Under actual costing, there are several sources of costs that will flow into an overhead cost pool. As shown in Exhibit 31.3, all production supplies that cannot be traced to a specific product will be debited to the overhead account and credited to accounts payable (the credit may also be charged to raw materials inventory or supplies expense, if supplies were

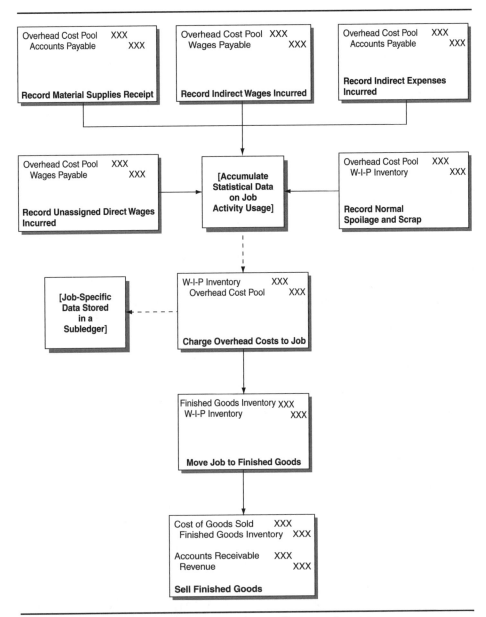

EXHIBIT 31.3   JOB COSTING TRANSACTIONS FOR ACTUAL OVERHEAD ALLOCATIONS

first charged to either of these accounts). As already noted, some labor costs will also be charged to the overhead account. Also, and as previously noted under the materials costing flow, normal amounts of production scrap and spoilage will be charged to overhead. Indirect wages and other indirect costs will also flow into the overhead cost pool. At the end of the accounting period, the cost pool is charged out to various products based on a variety of possible allocation calculations, which are addressed in the activity-based costing section later in this chapter. Once overhead costs have been assigned to specific products, they follow the usual pattern of being moved to the finished goods inventory while their associated completed products are held in storage, and from there to the cost of goods sold upon sale of the product.

The allocation of costs to specific jobs can be delayed for some time under the actual cost overhead allocation method, because some costs can be compiled only at the end of the month, or perhaps not until several weeks thereafter. This is a problem for those companies that want more immediate costing information. We use normal overhead cost allocations to resolve this problem. Normal costing means that a company charges out costs in the short term using a historical average for its overhead costs, rather than actual costs. This process is shown in Exhibit 31.4. This allows costs to be charged to jobs at once. To ensure that the historical average being used for allocations does not stray too far from actual results, it is periodically compared to actual costs (which must still be accumulated) and adjusted as necessary.

When actual and normal costs are compared, there should be a small variance, which can be disposed of in several ways. One approach is to charge off the entire variance to the cost of goods sold, though this can create an unusually high or low cost of goods sold. Another approach is to spread the variance among the cost of goods sold, work-in-process inventory, and finished goods inventory, based on the total balances remaining in each account at the end of the reporting period. A final approach is to retroactively charge the variance to every job. These three options require an increasing amount of work to accomplish, in the order described. For that reason, the first option is the most commonly used, while allocation to individual jobs is a rarity.

The very large number of transactions required in a job-costing system makes it a very inefficient costing methodology from the perspective of the accounting department, which must verify that all of the transactions entered are correct. It can also call for the purchase of large quantities of data collection equipment, such as automated time clocks and bar code scanners, which can be quite expensive. Furthermore, this system requires some participation by production personnel in the data collection process, which detracts from their primary mission of manufacturing products. However, given the need for job-costing information, a company may find that there is no reasonable alternative to using this system. If so, the controller should carefully review the need for each type of data that can be potentially produced by the system, and collect only those that will result in valuable information—this will create a more efficient data collection environment that focuses only on the key cost elements.

31.6   PROCESSING: PROCESS COSTING

Process costing is used in those situations when it is impossible to clearly differentiate the cost of individual units of production. For example, it is a prime candidate for use in an oil refinery, where it is impossible to track the cost of an individual gallon of diesel fuel.

The most common method for calculating process costs on a per-unit basis is to accumulate all production-related costs during the accounting period and calculate a weighted average per-unit cost based on these totals and the amount of production that was completed during the period, or which is currently still in process. An example of this calculation is shown in Exhibit 31.5.

In the exhibit, there are three blocks of calculations, each one segregated by a horizontal line. The top block contains a conversion calculation, which converts the amount of completed and work-in-process units into units to which materials and other costs can be allocated. The first column of numbers contains the calculation for the allocation of direct materials costs, while the final column of numbers calculates the allocation of all other production costs. For the purposes of this calculation, we assume that there are two types

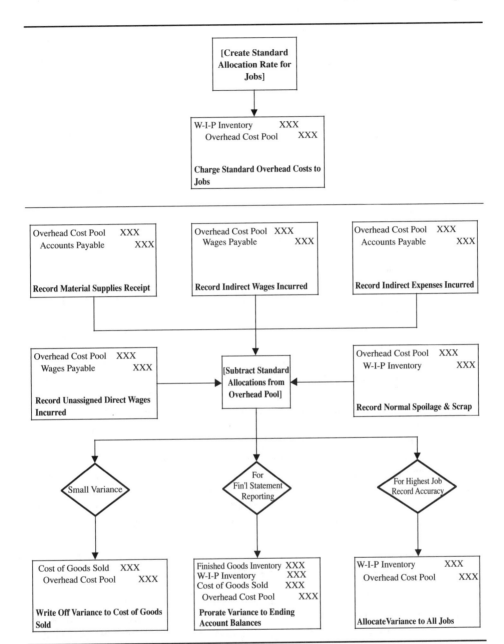

EXHIBIT 31.4 JOB COSTING TRANSACTIONS FOR NORMAL OVERHEAD COST ALLOCATIONS

of costs—direct materials, which are typically added at the beginning of the production process, and all other costs, which can be added at a multitude of other points during the manufacturing sequence.

Since materials costs are assumed to occur at the earliest stage of production, the calculation of equivalent units for direct material cost allocation is quite easy—just use the number of finished goods completed (1,000) and the number of units in work-in-process inventory (350). However, for the purposes of allocating all other production costs, we must reduce the amount of work-in-process inventory by an estimate of their aggregate

Units Summary	Direct Material Units	Conversion Factor	Conversion Cost Units	
Completed Units	1,000		1,000	
Ending Units in Process	350	60%	210	
Unit Totals	1,350		1,210	

Unit Cost Calculation	Direct Materials		Conversion Costs	Totals
Beginning Work-in-Process Cost	$20,000		$15,000	$35,000
Current Period Costs	$28,000		$21,500	$49,500
Total Costs	$48,000		$36,500	$84,500
Unit Totals(see above)	1,350		1,210	
Cost per Unit	$35.556		$30.165	

Unit Cost Allocation	Direct Materials		Conversion Costs	Totals
Cost of Completed Units	$35,556		$30,165	$65,721
Cost of Ending WIP Units	$12,444		$ 6,335	$18,779
Totals	$48,000		$36,500	$84,500

EXHIBIT 31.5 WEIGHTED AVERAGE PROCESS-COSTING CALCULATION

level of completion, which in the example is 60%. This results in total converted units of production of 1,210.

In the middle block of calculations, we accumulate the total cost of production and divide it by the equivalent number of units of production to determine the cost per unit. This calculation includes the costs that had been carried over in the work-in-process inventory from the preceding accounting reporting period, totaling $35,000. We add to this the current cost of production, which is $49,500, to yield a total cost of $84,500 that must be allocated to units of production. When divided by the slightly different units of production being used for direct material costs and all other production costs, we arrive at a direct material cost per unit of $35.556 and all other costs per unit of $30.165.

The lowermost block of calculations requires us to multiply the cost per unit (as determined in the middle block) by the total number of units (as determined in the top block). The calculation is identified with arrows. The result is $48,000 in direct material costs, of which $35,556 are charged to completed units and the remainder to work-in-process units. Total other production costs are $36,500, of which $30,165 are charged to completed units and the remainder to work-in-process. As a cross-check, we can see that the total allocated is $84,500, which matches the total amount of funds that were to be allocated, as noted on the far-right side of the middle block.

This method is a simple one that requires very little data collection. However, some companies like to make the task even easier by avoiding the collection and interpretation of actual costs at the end of each accounting period. Instead, they prefer to use standard unit costs for their calculations, which allows them to calculate total costs more frequently and with no related data collection costs. This type of calculation is shown in Exhibit 31.6.

In the exhibit, the first block of calculations does not change—we still assume that a conversion factor must be applied to the ending work-in-process inventory for the purposes of assigning other production costs than direct materials. The difference arises in the second block, where we use only a standard cost per unit, rather than a summarization of actual costs. This cost is then carried forward into the third block of calculations, where

Units Summary	Direct Material Units	Conversion Factor	Conversion Cost Units
Completed Units	1,000		1,000
Ending Units in Process	350	60%	210
Unit Totals	1,350		1,210

Unit Cost Calculation	Direct Materials		Conversion Costs
Standard Unit Cost	$32,000		$31,500

Unit Cost Allocation	Direct Materials	Conversion Costs	Totals
Standard Cost of Completed Units	$32,000	$31,500	$63,500
Standard Cost of Ending WIP Units	$11,200	$ 6,615	$17,815
Standard Cost Totals	$43,200	$38,115	$81,315

Period Variance			
Beginning Standard Work-in-ProcessCost	$20,000	$15,000	$35,000
Current Period Actual Costs	$28,000	$21,500	$49,500
Total Period Costs	$48,000	$36,500	$84,500
Standard Cost Totals	$43,200	$38,115	$81,315
Cost Variance	$ 4,800	$(1,615)	$ 3,185

EXHIBIT 31.6   PROCESS-COSTING CALCULATION USING STANDARD COSTS

we see that a total of $81,315 has been allocated to the ending finished goods and work-in-process inventory. However, this ending figure varies from the $84,500 that resulted from the preceding actual costing calculation in Exhibit 31.5. The difference of $3,185 was caused by a slight variance between the preset standard cost and the actual cost. The presence of this variance causes us to add a fourth block of calculations at the bottom of the exhibit, in which we compare the actual costs incurred during the period to the standard costs, which shows that more costs than expected were incurred in the direct materials column, while fewer costs were incurred under the other production costs column.

The main issue for the controller is what to do with this variance. If negligible, it can be charged off to the cost of goods sold. If it is so large that expensing the difference will result in an appreciable impact on reported earnings, then a more accurate approach is to apportion the variance among the cost of goods sold, work-in-process inventory, and finished goods inventory.

The data collection and calculations required for a process-costing system are substantially simpler than what is required for a job-costing system, and so process costing is a favorite approach for those who wish to pare their data collection costs or who produce such large volumes of similar products that there is no point in attempting to track the costs of individual products.

31.7   PROCESSING: STANDARD COSTING

The first step in the creation of a standard-costing system is to create a set of standard costs in a variety of different areas. The industrial engineering staff is assigned the task of creating direct labor standard costs, while the purchasing staff is most typically assigned the chore of creating standard costs for purchased goods, and the controller is called on to coordinate the development of a set of standard overhead costs. If there are subproducts created during the production process that may be valued at the end of each accounting reporting period, then the industrial engineering staff will calculate these standards. It is also possible to reduce the areas in which standard costs are used, with actual costs being accumulated in other areas. This mix of costing types can arise when there is some concern that reasonably accurate standard costs cannot be constructed or if existing actual costing systems already produce reasonably accurate results.

Another issue to settle as soon in the standard cost development process as possible is the timing of changes to these standards. This can be done quite infrequently, perhaps once every few years, or as rapidly as once a month (which results in standard costs that are nearly indistinguishable from actual costs). The key determinant influencing the pace of change is the perceived pace at which actual costs are changing. If there are minimal changes to a manufacturing process, then there is certainly no reason to constantly review the process and set new standards. Conversely, a company that has installed an aggressive continuous improvement strategy will find that its standard costs are constantly falling behind changes in actual costs, which requires constant revisions to standards.

The assumptions used to create standard costs must also be addressed. For example, an industrial engineer must make some assumptions about the speed of efficiency improvements being realized by the production staff (known as the learning curve) in order to determine the future standard cost that roughly matches these expected changes in efficiency. Similarly, a standard cost must be matched to the expected production equipment configuration to be used, since this has a considerable impact on the overhead costs that can be assigned to a product. Another key assumption is the volume of production, since a large assumed production run will spread its setup cost over many units, whereas a short production run will result in higher setup costs on a per-unit basis. Yet another factor is the assumed condition of the equipment to be used in the manufacturing process, since poorly maintained or old equipment will be in operation for fewer hours than would otherwise be the case. The production system being used, such as just-in-time or manufacturing resource planning, will also have a significant impact on standard costs, since different systems result in the incurrence of different types of costs in such areas as machine setup time, equipment depreciation, materials handling costs, and inventory investment costs. An issue that is particular to direct labor is the anticipated result of union negotiations, since these directly and immediately impact hourly wage rates. A final issue to consider is the presence and quality of work instructions for the production staff; the absence of detailed and accurate instructions can have a profound and deleterious impact on costs incurred. Given the large number of issues involved in the setting of accurate standard costs, it is no surprise that this task can require the ongoing services of an experienced group of professionals, the cost of which must be considered when making the decision to use a standard-costing system.

A final factor to consider when creating standard costs is the level of attainability of the costs. One option is to devise an *attainable standard,* which is a cost that does not depart very much from the existing actual cost. This results in reasonable cost targets that employees know they can probably meet. Another alternative is to use *historical costs* as the basis for a standard cost. This is generally not recommended, for the resulting costs are no different from a company's existing actual cost structure, and so gives employees no incentive to attempt to reduce costs. The diametrically opposite approach is to create a set of *theoretical standards,* which are based on costs that can only be achieved if the manufacturing process runs absolutely perfectly. Since employees cannot possibly meet these cost goals for anything but very short periods of time, it tends to result in lower employee morale. Thus, of the potential range of standard costs that can be set, the best approach is to set moderate stretch goals that are achievable.

Finally, we are ready to begin using standard costs. But for what purpose do we use them? One common usage is in budgeting. By creating detailed standard costs for all budgeting line items, company managers can be presented with financial statements that compare actual results to standard costs, so that they can see where actual results are falling behind expectations. However, this is a simple approach that requires little real attention to the setting of standards at the product level.

Another reason for using standards is to create benchmarks for inclusion in a manufacturing resources planning (MRP II) production system. This commonly used system multiplies a production forecast by a detailed set of product labor, materials, and capacity requirements to determine how many direct labor personnel and specific materials and how much machine capacity will be needed. This system requires extremely detailed and accurate standards to be successful. The standards needed by MRP II are for units of labor, materials, and capacity, rather than their costs. In other words, a direct labor standard for an MRP II system may be 12 minutes of labor, rather than its cost for those 12 minutes of $4.58.

Yet another use for standards is in product pricing. The company sales staff frequently asks the engineering staff to provide it with cost estimates for new product configurations, many of which are only slightly different from existing products. However, the engineering staff may take days or weeks to provide the sales personnel with this information—which may be too long to satisfy an impatient customer. By using standard costs, the sales staff can compile product costs very quickly with only a brief approval review from the engineering staff. Or, if the engineering staff is still in charge of creating new product cost estimates, then they can also use standard costs to more rapidly arrive at their estimates. In either case, customers will receive reliable price quotes much more rapidly than was previously the case.

A very common use for standard costs is for the valuation of inventory. Many companies do not want to be bothered with the time-consuming accumulation of actual inventory costs at the end of each accounting period, and so they create standard costs for valuation purposes, which they occasionally compare to actual costs to ensure that the inventory valuation is accurate. It is not worth the effort to create standard costs for this purpose if a company's inventory levels are extremely low, or if a just-in-time manufacturing system is in use, since the amount of time that will be saved in valuing inventory is small, given the minor quantities of stock that will be kept in the warehouse. However, manufacturers with large inventory balances will find that this is still an effective way to rapidly determine the value of inventory.

Unfortunately, the use of standard costs for inventory valuation is also subject to control problems, for deliberate manipulation of standards can result in large changes in the value of inventory, which in turn impacts the reported level of company profits. For example, the standard cost for a finished goods item can include an assumption for the amount of production setup costs allocated to each item, which is heavily influenced by the assumed number of units produced in a manufacturing run. By shifting the assumed length of the production run downward, the amount of cost allocated to each unit goes up. This type of interference with standard costs can result in wildly inaccurate reported financial results.

If standard costs are used for inventory valuation, the accounting staff will periodically compare standard to actual costs to ensure that there are not excessively large differences between the two. If a company is audited at year end, then the auditors will require a comparison to actual costs, and a write-off of the difference to the cost of goods sold (if standard costs are higher than actual costs) or an increase in the inventory balance (if actual costs are higher than standard costs). Since a significant difference between the two types of costs can result in a startling change in the reported level of income during the period when this adjustment is made, it is wise to review some of the large-cost items on a regular basis in order to ensure that there will be no surprises at the time of reconciliation to actual costs.

Consequently, we can see that there are still several areas in which standard costs can be used to create greater efficiencies in selected areas of activity. However, the number of viable applications has fallen with the advent of new computer systems and production methodologies, so one should carefully review the proposed applications for standard costs before conducting an implementation.

31.8   PROCESSING: DIRECT COSTING

A direct cost is a cost that is directly associated with changes in production volume. This usually restricts the definition of direct costs to direct materials and direct labor (and a strong case can be made for *not* using direct labor, since this cost tends to be present even when production volumes vary). For example, the materials used to create a product are a direct cost, whereas the machine used to convert the materials into a finished product is not a direct cost, because it is still going to be sitting on the factory floor, irrespective of any changes in production volume. The use of direct costing results in a slightly different income statement, as shown in Exhibit 31.7.

The only difference between the income statement shown in Exhibit 31.7 and a more traditional format is that all indirect costs have been shifted below the gross margin line and into the production department's costs. Though this seems like a subtle change, it focuses the attention of the management team on the incremental changes in the cost of goods sold that are usually masked by a large and relatively fixed amount of overhead costs.

By focusing solely on the direct cost of a product or activity, a controller can provide valuable information to management regarding prospective changes in costs that will arise as a result of some management action. For example, if a change to a more efficient type of processing equipment is contemplated, then the direct cost of a product may be lowered

Revenue		$1,000,000
Cost of Goods Sold		
Direct Materials	$320,000	
Direct Labor	170,000	
Total Direct Costs		$ 490,000
Gross Margin		
Operating Expenses		
Production Department	325,000	
General and Administrative	115,000	
Total Operating Expenses		$ 440,000
Net Profit		$ 50,000

EXHIBIT 31.7   INCOME STATEMENT FORMATTED FOR DIRECT COSTING

if this will result in less material usage. This may also result in less direct labor cost if the machine takes over some tasks previously performed by employees—this will cut direct costs, but may increase overhead costs if the cost of the machine is higher than that of the machine it is replacing. Yet another example is when a customer wants the lowest possible price for a product, and the company has some free capacity available for producing what the customer needs; the use of direct costing will reveal the lowest possible cost that must be covered by the price charged to the customer in order to break even. Direct costing can also be used to determine which customers are the most profitable, by subtracting the direct cost of their purchases from the prices paid, which yields the amount they are contributing toward the company's coverage of overhead costs and profit. Another very good use for direct costing is to include the concept in the budgeting system, where it is used to change budgeted variable costs to match the actual sales volumes achieved; this approach achieves a much closer match between the budgeted and actual cost of goods sold, because the budget now flexes with the actual volume level experienced. For all of these reasons, direct costing is a highly recommended costing system.

However, there are a number of situations in which direct costing should *not* be used, and in which it will yield incorrect information. Its single largest problem is that it completely ignores all indirect costs, which make up the bulk of all costs incurred by today's companies. This is a real problem when dealing with long-term costing and pricing decisions, since direct costing will likely yield results that do not achieve long-term profitability. For example, a direct-costing system may calculate a minimum product price of $10.00 for a widget that is indeed higher than all direct costs, but which is lower than the additional overhead costs that are associated with the product line. If the company continues to use the $10.00 price for all product sales for well into the future, then the company will experience losses because overhead costs are not being covered by the price. The best way to address this problem is to build strict boundaries around the circumstances where incremental prices derived from a direct-costing system are used.

Another problem with direct costing is that it assumes a steady level of unit costs for the incremental costing and pricing decisions for which it is most often used. For example, a company receives an offer from a customer to buy 5,000 units of product X at a fixed price. The cost accounting staff may determine that the proposed price will indeed yield a profit, based on the direct cost per unit, and so recommends that the deal be approved. However, because the staff has focused only on direct costs, it has missed the fact that the company is operating at near full-capacity levels and that to process the entire 5,000-unit order will require the addition of some costly machinery, the acquisition of which will make the proposed deal a very expensive one indeed. To avoid this problem, anyone using a direct-costing system must have access to company capacity information and should coordinate with the production scheduling staff to ensure that capacity levels will permit their incremental pricing and costing scenarios to be achieved.

A subtle issue that many users of direct-costing systems miss is that the types of costs that fall within the direct costing definition will increase as the volume of units in a direct costing decision goes up. For example, the only direct cost involved with a single unit of production is the direct materials used to build it, whereas a larger production volume will likely involve some change in the related number of manufacturing employees needed on the production line; these are well-accepted concepts. However controllers frequently forget that additional direct costs will be included when the production volume rises to even higher levels. For example, if the direct-costing decision involves an entire production line, then all of the equipment and supervisory costs that are tied to that production line are now also influenced by the decision to produce or not produce, and so should be included in the direct-costing system. At an even larger level, the decision to use the production of an entire facility should include every cost needed to run that facility, which may include utilities, rent, and insurance—costs that are not normally included in smaller-volume production decisions. Consequently, direct-costing analysis must be conducted within narrowly defined volume ranges, with careful attention to what costs are likely to vary with the volumes that are under review.

Direct costing cannot be used for inventory valuation, because it is disallowed by GAAP. The reason for this is that under a direct-costing system, all costs besides direct costs are charged to the current period. There is no provision for capitalizing overhead costs and associating them with inventory that will be sold off in future periods. This results in an imbalance between the reported level of profitability in each period and the amount of production that occurred. For example, a manufacturer of Christmas ornaments with a direct-costing system may sell all of its output in one month of the year, but be forced to recognize all of its indirect production costs in every month of the year, which will result in reported losses for 11 months of the year. Under GAAP, these indirect costs would be capitalized into inventory and recognized only when the inventory is sold, thereby more closely matching reported revenues and expenses. Given the wide disparity between the reported results, it is no surprise that GAAP bans the use of direct costing for inventory valuation.

31.9 PROCESSING: THROUGHPUT COSTING

A costing methodology that focuses on capacity utilization is called throughput accounting. It assumes that there is always one bottleneck operation in a production process that commands the speed with which products or services can be completed. This operation becomes the defining issue in determining what products should be manufactured first, since this in turn results in differing levels of profitability.

The basic calculation used for throughput accounting is shown in Exhibit 31.8. This format is a simplified version of the layout used by Thomas Corbett on page 44 of *Throughput Accounting* (North River Press, Great Barrington, MA: 1998), though all of the numbers contained within the example have been changed.

The exhibit shows a series of electronic devices that a company can choose from for its near-term production requirements. The second column describes the amount of throughput that each of the products generates per minute in the bottleneck operation; "throughput" is the amount of margin left after all direct material costs have been subtracted from revenue. For example, the 19″ Color Television produces $81.10 of throughput, but requires ten minutes of processing time in the bottleneck operation, resulting in throughput per minute of $8.11. The various electronic devices are sorted in the exhibit from top to bottom in order of largest throughput per minute. This ordering tells the user how much of the most profitable products can be produced before the total amount of available time in the bottleneck (which is 62,200 minutes, as noted at the top of the exhibit) is used up. The calculation for bottleneck utilization is shown in the "Unit Demand/Actual Production" column. In that column, the 19″ color Television has a current demand for 1,000 units, which requires 10,000 minutes of bottleneck time (as shown in the following column). This allocation of bottleneck time progresses downward through the various products until we come to the 50″ High-Definition TV at the bottom of the list, for which there is only enough bottleneck time left to manufacture 1,700 units.

By multiplying the dollars of throughput per minute times the number of minutes of production time, we arrive at the cumulative throughput dollars resulting from the manufacture

	Maximum Constraint Time:	**62,200**			

Product	Throughput $$/Minute of Constraint	Required Constraint Usage (min.)	Unit Demand/ Actual Production	Cumulative Constraint Utilization	Cumulative Throughput Product
19″ Color Television	$8.11	10	1,000/1,000	10,000	$ 81,100
100-Watt Stereo	$7.50	8	2,800/2,800	22,400	$ 168,000
5″ LCD Television	$6.21	12	500/500	6,000	$ 37,260
50″ High-Definition TV	$5.00	14	3,800/1,700	23,800	$ 119,000

Throughput Total	$ 405,360
Operating Expense Total	$ 375,000
Profit	$ 30,360
Profit Percentage	7.5%
Investment	$ 500,000
Return on Investment	6.1%

EXHIBIT 31.8   THE THROUGHPUT ACCOUNTING MODEL

(and presumed sale) of each product, which yields a total throughput of $405,360. We then add up all other expenses, totaling $375,000, and subtract them from the total throughput, which gives us a profit of $30,360. These calculations comprise the basic throughput accounting analysis model.

Now let us reexamine the model based on a rejuggling of the priority of orders. If the cost accounting manager were to examine each of the products based on the addition of allocated overhead and direct labor costs to the direct materials that were used as the foundation for the throughput dollar calculations, she may arrive at the conclusion that, when fully burdened, the 50″ High-Definition TV is actually the most profitable, while the 19″ Color Television is the least profitable. Accordingly, she recommends that the order of production be changed to reflect these "realities," which gives us the new throughput report shown in Exhibit 31.9.

The result is a significant loss, rather than the increase in profits that had been expected. Why the change? The trouble is that allocated overhead costs have no bearing on throughput, because allocated costs will not change in accordance with incremental production decisions, such as which product will be manufactured first. Instead, the overhead cost pool will exist, irrespective of any modest changes in activity levels. Consequently, it makes no sense to apply allocated costs to the production scheduling decision, when the only issue that matters is how much throughput per minute a product can generate.

Capital budgeting is an area in which throughput costing analysis can be applied with excellent results. The trouble with most corporate capital budgeting systems is that they do not take into consideration the fact that the only valid investment is one that will have a positive impact on the amount of throughput that can be pushed through a bottleneck operation. Any other investment will result in greater production capacity in other areas of the company that still cannot produce any additional quantities, since the bottleneck operation controls the total amount of completed production. For example, the throughput model in Exhibit 31.10 shows the result of an investment of $28,500 in new equipment

			Maximum Constraint Time:	**62,200**	

Product	Throughput $$/Minute of Constraint	Required Constraint Usage (min.)	Unit Demand/ Actual Production	Cumulative Constraint Utilization	Cumulative Throughput Product
50″ High Definition TV	$5.00	14	3,800/3,800	53,200	$ 266,000
100-Watt Stereo	7.50	8	2,800/1,125	9,000	$ 67,500
5″ LCD Television	6.21	12	500/0	0	$ 0
19″ Color Television	8.11	10	1,000/0	0	$ 0

Throughput Total	$ 333,500
Operating Expense Total	375,000
Profit	−41,500
Profit Percentage	−12.4%
Investment	500,000
Return on Investment	−8.3%

EXHIBIT 31.9   A REVISED THROUGHPUT ANALYSIS BASED ON ALLOCATED COSTS

that is added later in the production process than the bottleneck operation. The result is an increase in the total investment, to $528,500, and absolutely no impact on profitability, which yields a reduced return on investment of 5.7%.

A more profitable solution would have been to invest in anything that would increase the productivity of the bottleneck operation, which could be either a direct investment in

			Maximum Constraint Time:	**62,200**	

Product	Throughput $$/Minute of Constraint	Required Constraint Usage (min.)	Unit Demand/ Actual Production	Cumulative Constraint Utilization	Cumulative Throughput Product
19″ Color Television	$8.11	10	1,000/1,000	10,000	$ 81,100
100-Watt Stereo	7.50	8	2,800/2,800	22,400	168,000
5″ LCD Television	6.21	12	500/500	6,000	37,260
50″ High-Definition TV	5.00	14	3,800/1,700	23,800	119,000

Throughput Total	$ 405,360
Operating Expense Total	375,000
Profit	30,360
Profit Percentage	7.5%
Investment	528,500
Return on Investment	5.7%

EXHIBIT 31.10   A REVISED THROUGHPUT ANALYSIS BASED ON ADDITIONAL INVESTMENT

			Maximum Constraint Time:	**62,200**	
Product	Throughput $$/Minute of Constraint	Required Constraint Usage (min.)	Unit Demand/ Actual Production	Cumulative Constraint Utilization	Cumulative Throughput Product
19″ Color Television	$8.11	10	1,000/1,000	10,000	$ 81,100
100-Watt Stereo	7.50	8	2,800/2,800	22,400	168,000
5″ LCD Television	6.21	12	500/500	6,000	37,260
			Throughput Total		$286,360
			Operating Expense Total		375,000
			Profit		−88,640
			Profit Percentage		−30.9%
			Investment		500,000
			Return on Investment		−17.7%

EXHIBIT 31.11   A REVISED THROUGHPUT ANALYSIS WITH ONE LESS PRODUCT

that operation, or an investment in an upstream operation that will reduce the amount of processing required for a product by the bottleneck operation.

As another example, the cost accounting staff has conducted a lengthy activity-based costing analysis, which has determined that a much higher amount of overhead cost must be allocated to the high-definition television, which results in a loss on that product. Accordingly, the product is removed from the list of viable products, which reduces the number of products in the mix of production activity, as shown in Exhibit 31.11.

The result is a reduction in profits. The reason is that the cost accounting staff has made the incorrect assumption that, by eliminating a product, all of the associated overhead cost will be eliminated, too. Though a small amount of overhead might be eliminated when the production of a single product is stopped, the bulk of it will still be incurred.

Throughput accounting does a very good job of tightly focusing attention on the priority of production in situations where there is a choice of products that can be manufactured. It can also have an impact on a number of other decisions, such as whether to grant volume discounts, outsource manufacturing, stop the creation of a product, or invest in new capital items. Given this wide range of activities, it should find a place in the mix of costing methodologies at many companies. We now shift to a discussion of activity-based costing (ABC), whose emphasis is the complete reverse of throughput accounting—it focuses on the proper allocation of overhead.

31.10   PROCESSING: ACTIVITY-BASED COSTING

An ABC system is designed to match overhead costs as closely as possible with company activities. By doing so, overhead costs can be reasonably associated with products, departments, customers, or other users of activities, which tells managers where overhead costs are being used within a company. This results in much better control over overhead costs.

There are several ways to allocate overhead costs. Some overhead costs, such as utilities, are associated with specific machines. For example, a machine may require ten cents of electricity per minute. If so, this overhead cost can be charged out to those products that are run through the machine, based on the time spent being worked upon it. Other overhead costs are associated with a specific product line, and can reasonably be allocated to the activities performed within that product line.

For example, there is typically a supervisor who is assigned to a single product line. If so, the fully burdened salary of this person can be charged to such related activities as production and maintenance scheduling. Still other overhead costs may be grouped by commodity used in the production process. For example, each member of the purchasing staff may be responsible for the procurement of a specific commodity. If so, this overhead cost can be distributed to individual products based on their usage of the commodity. Clearly, there are many valid ways to allocate overhead costs to various activities, and from there to users of those costs. An ABC system creates a structured approach to the accumulation, storage, and allocation of overhead costs using many of these activity measures.

An ABC system is a difficult and complex one to create, because of the wide variety of costs that must be accumulated, tracked in relation to different types of activities, and charged off. Here are the primary steps involved in creating such a system:

1. *Determine the scope of the system.* A fully developed ABC system that encompasses all costs throughout a company is a massive undertaking that may not yield any results for several years. A better approach is to conduct a gradual rollout of the system that produces results more quickly. Accordingly, a key factor is limiting each incremental rollout of the system to a carefully defined segment of the business. The determination of scope should also include a review of the level of detailed analysis that the system is to produce, since an excessive focus on detail may result in a system that is too expensive in relation to the utility of the information produced.

2. *Set aside direct costs.* There will be several direct costs that can be clearly and indisputably traced to specific products. These costs should be identified early in the design phase, so that they will not be erroneously added to the ABC allocation system.

3. *Locate costs in the general ledger.* The next step is to identify each of the overhead costs in the general ledger that will be allocated by the ABC system. This can be a difficult undertaking, for the required costs may be lumped together in the ledger, and must be segregated through a new data collection system that involves the creation of a new general ledger account number. Alternatively, the split may be achieved less accurately by allocating a percentage of the cost in a single general ledger account to several overhead cost items that will then be allocated.

4. *Store costs in cost pools.* All of the costs that have been identified within the general ledger must now be stored in a series of cost pools. Each cost pool accumulates costs that are similar to each other. For example, a building cost pool will include the costs of insurance and maintenance for a building, whereas a product line cost pool may include the marketing and supervisory costs that can be traced to a specific product line. A third type of cost pool is one that is related to a specific production batch, and can include such costs as production control labor, tooling, materials handling, and quality control. The total number of cost pools used will have a direct impact on the maintenance costs of an ABC system, so the design team must

balance the increased allocation accuracy associated with more cost pools with the extra labor needed to maintain them.

5. *Determine activity drivers.* Having summarized overhead costs into a set of cost pools, we must now allocate them, which we do with an activity driver—this is a variable that reasonably explains the consumption of costs from a cost pool. For example, some accounts payable costs are closely associated with the number of checks printed and mailed, while some engineering costs vary directly with the number of design changes added to a product. Examples of other activity drivers are the number of machine setups, the number of maintenance work orders, the number of purchase orders, and the number of customer orders processed. Whichever activity driver is chosen as the basis for cost pool allocation should be easy to calculate, require minimal data collection, and have a reasonably close cause-and-effect relationship with a cost pool.

6. *Spread costs from secondary to primary cost pools.* Some of the cost pools include costs that are, in turn, distributed to other cost pools. These costs are usually for internal company services, such as management information systems services that are provided to other departments. These secondary cost pools must be allocated to primary cost pools.

7. *Calculate the overhead cost per activity unit.* We then divide the total number of occurrences of each activity driver into the total amount of costs in the primary cost pools for the accounting period, which results in a dollar figure per unit of activity.

8. *Assign activity costs to cost objects.* The final step is to calculate the usage of each activity driver by a cost object (which is anything that uses activities, such as products or customers). For example, if a product requires the creation of two purchase orders (which are activity drivers) and the ABC system has determined that each purchase order requires $32.15 to create, then the amount of overhead charged to the product will be $64.30.

In brief, the ABC process involves taking costs out of the general ledger and assigning them to either secondary or primary cost pools, which are then distributed to cost objects through the use of activity drivers. The overall process is shown in Exhibit 31.12.

31.11   PROCESSING: TARGET COSTING

Most of the costing methodologies described in this chapter are primarily concerned with the interpretation of costing data after it has already been incurred. Target costing differs from them in that it describes the costs that are expected to be incurred, and how this will impact product profitability levels. By describing costs in a proactive and future-oriented manner, managers can determine how they should alter product designs before they enter the manufacturing process in order to ensure that the company earns a reasonable profit on all new products.

To use this methodology, a cost accountant is assigned to a new product design team, and asked to continually compile the projected cost of a product as it moves through the design process. Managers will use this information not only to make product alterations, but also to drop a product design if it cannot meet its cost targets.

There are four basic steps involved in target costing. First, the design team conducts market research to determine the price points that a company is most likely to achieve if it creates a product with a certain set of features. The research should include information

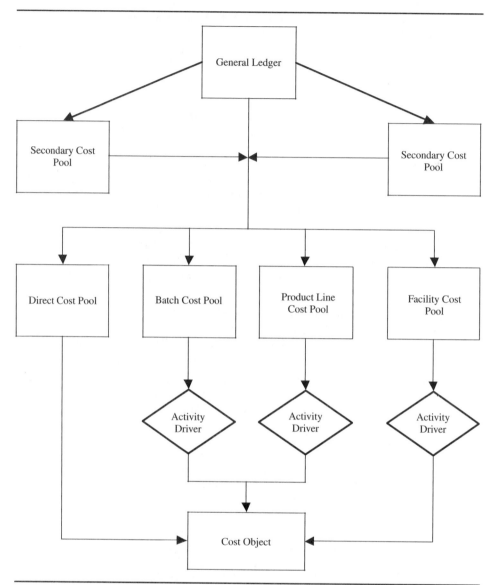

Exhibit 31.12 The ABC Process Flow

about the perceived value of certain features on a product, so that the design team can add or subtract features from the design with a full knowledge of what these changes probably will do to the final price at which the product will be sold. The second step is to subtract from the prospective product price a gross margin that must be earned on the product; this can be a standard company-wide margin that must be earned on all new products, or perhaps a more specific one that management has imposed based on the perceived risk of the project. By subtracting the required margin from the expected price, we arrive at the maximum amount that the product can cost. This total cost figure drives the next step.

The design team then uses value engineering to drive down the cost of the product until it meets its overall cost target. Value engineering requires considerable attention to the elimination of production functions, a product design that is cheaper to manufacture, a planned reduction of product durability in order to cut costs, a reduced number of product features, less expensive component parts, and so on—in short, any activity that will lead to a reduced product cost. This process also requires the team to confirm costs with the suppliers of raw materials and outsourced parts, as well as the processing costs that will be incurred internally. The controller plays a key role at this stage, regularly summarizing costing information and relaying it not only to the team members, but to the managers who are reviewing the team's progress. A standard procedure at this point is to force the team to come within a set percentage of its cost target at various milestones (such as being within 12% of the target after three months of design work, 6% after four months, and on target after five months); if the team cannot meet increasingly tighter costing targets, then the project will be canceled.

Once these design steps have been completed and a product has met its targeted cost level, the target costing effort is shifted into a different activity, which is follow-on activities that will reduce costs even further after the product has entered its production phase. This final step is used to create some excess gross margin over time, which allows the company to reduce the price of the product to respond to presumed increases in the level of competition. The sources of these cost reductions can be either through planned supplier cost reductions or through waste reductions in the production process (known as kaizen costing). The concepts of value engineering and kaizen costing can be used repeatedly to gradually reduce the cost of a product over time, as shown in Exhibit 31.13. In the exhibit, we see that the market price of a product follows a steady downward trend, which is caused by ongoing competitive pressure as the market for the product matures. To meet this pricing pressure with corresponding reductions in costs, the company initially creates product A, and uses value engineering to design a preset cost into the product. Once the design is released for production, kaizen costing is used to further reduce costs in multiple stages until there are few additional reductions left to squeeze out of the original design. At this point, the design team uses value engineering to create a replacement product B that incorporates additional cost savings (likely including the cost reduction experience gleaned from the kaizen costing stages used for product A) that result in an even lower initial cost. Kaizen costing is then used once again to further reduce the cost of product B, thereby keeping the cost reduction process moving in an ever-downward direction. The entire target costing process, incorporating all of the preceding steps, is shown in Exhibit 31.14.

31.12 PROCESSING: BY-PRODUCT AND JOINT PRODUCT COSTING

There are a few situations in which multiple salable products are created as part of a production process, and for which there are no demonstrably clear-cut costs beyond those incurred for the main production process. When this happens, the cost accountant must determine a reasonable method for allocating these costs.

The first step in this allocation process is to determine the "split-off" point, which is the last point in the production process where one still cannot determine the final product. For example, a batch of sugar, water, and corn syrup can be converted into any of a number of hard candy products, up until the point where the slurry is shifted to a slicing machine that cuts up the work-in-process into a final and clearly identifiable product. From this point onward in the production process, we can either have a main product and an incidental side product (known as a "by-product"), or several major products (which are known as "joint" products). The accounting for these different types of final products is somewhat different.

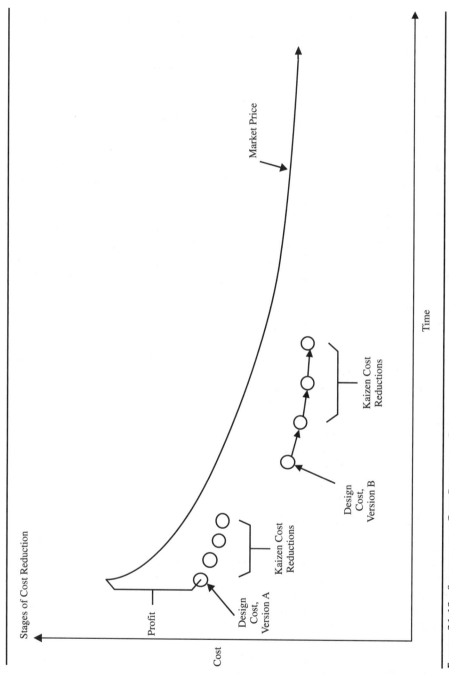

EXHIBIT 31.13 STAGES IN THE COST REDUCTION PROCESS

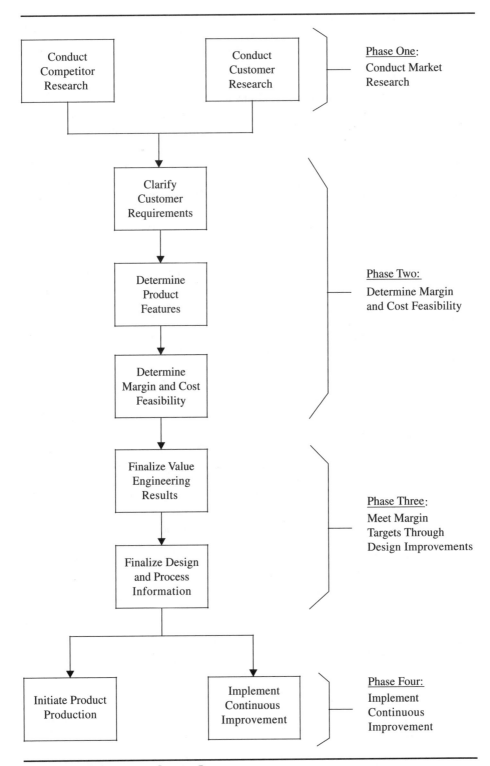

EXHIBIT 31.14 THE TARGET COSTING PROCESS

The simplest cost allocation method is to determine the proportion of total revenue that each product coming from a joint production process will generate, and then apportion all joint costs based on the relative proportions of revenue that are to be earned by each product. For example, if Product A earns $10 and Product B earns $5, then two thirds of the total joint cost will be allocated to Product A and one third of the total joint cost will be allocated to Product B. By-products are assumed to have such a minor incidental impact on revenues that it is simpler to apportion no costs to them at all; instead, any revenues gained from the sale of by-products will be credited to the cost of goods sold.

This assumption that by-products have minimal value can be flawed in some circumstances. For example, the metal scrap that arises from a stamping operation may be accumulated for several months, at which point enough has been accumulated that a reasonable amount of revenue is realized. Because no cost has been assigned to the metal scrap, there is no cost to offset this modest surge in revenues, which therefore creates an unexpected jump in gross margins in the period when the sale of scrap occurs. This can be a particular problem if a company designates a by-product as being anything resulting in a moderately large proportion of total production, such as 5% to 10%; the revenue to be gained from such a large quantity of by-product, against which no costs are charged, can cause quite a dramatic change in the reported gross margin level. To avoid this problem, it is best to charge some cost to *all* products coming from a joint manufacturing process, even if they are by-products.

An alternative calculation for joint costs is to estimate the final gross margin of each joint product, which is based on the final sale price less the amount of costs incurred by each product between the split-off point and the point of sale. This is a more complicated approach to the allocation problem, and can be especially difficult to calculate if the costs incurred after the split-off point are so variable that they are difficult to estimate in advance. Consequently, the simpler method of basing joint cost allocations only on revenues earned by each joint product is the preferred approach.

An example of the two joint cost allocation methods is shown in Exhibit 31.15. The calculation that is based solely on revenues is shown on the left side of the exhibit. For this calculation, we see that $250.00 of production costs have been incurred up to the split-off point; this cost is split based on the final revenues to be gained from the sale of Product A and Product B. There is no allocation to Product C, since it is not estimated to have any revenue. The result is an allocation of $148.15 in costs to Product A and $101.85 to Product B. The greater complexity of the second allocation method is shown on the right side of the exhibit. This calculation requires us to not only determine the final per-unit revenues expected from each product, but also to summarize the costs that will accrue to each product after the split-off point. The calculation then subtracts these incremental costs from the final revenues for each product to arrive at a gross margin figure. The allocated cost of $250.00 is then allocated to each product based on the proportional size of each product's gross margin. The result is substantially different from the first calculation. Thus, we can see that a shift from one allocation calculation to another can have a substantial impact on the reported profitability of each product that comes out of a joint production process.

A key issue related to joint and by-product pricing is how to set prices for products that contain some allocated joint costs. The main point is not to base prices on allocated costs at all, since these costs have no direct bearing on the incremental cost of each product. For example, if one were to alter the method of allocation for Product A in the last exhibit from the revenue-based model to the gross-margin based model, the allocated cost would change from $148.15 to $97.22—the price should not change to match the cost decrease,

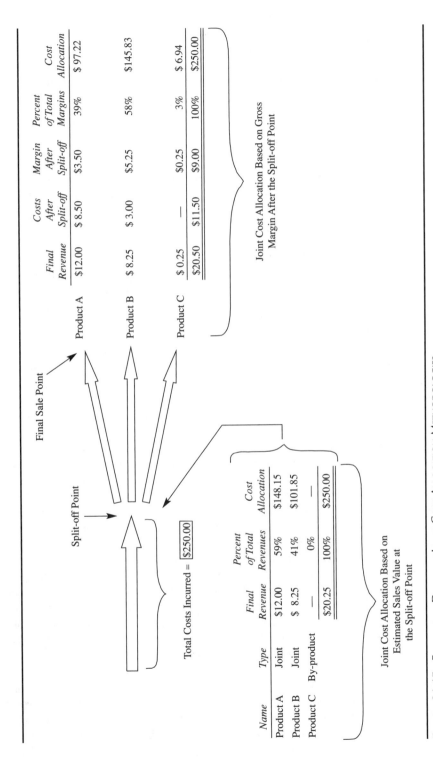

Name	Type	Final Revenue	Percent of Total Revenues	Cost Allocation
Product A	Joint	$12.00	59%	$148.15
Product B	Joint	$ 8.25	41%	$101.85
Product C	By-product	—	0%	—
		$20.25	100%	$250.00

Joint Cost Allocation Based on Estimated Sales Value at the Split-off Point

	Final Revenue	Costs After Split-off	Margin After Split-off	Percent of Total Margins	Cost Allocation
Product A	$12.00	$ 8.50	$3.50	39%	$ 97.22
Product B	$ 8.25	$ 3.00	$5.25	58%	$145.83
Product C	$ 0.25	—	$0.25	3%	$ 6.94
	$20.50	$11.50	$9.00	100%	$250.00

Joint Cost Allocation Based on Gross Margin After the Split-off Point

Final Sale Point

Split-off Point

Product A

Product B

Product C

Total Costs Incurred = $250.00

EXHIBIT 31.15 EXAMPLE OF DIFFERENT JOINT COST ALLOCATION METHODOLOGIES

just because someone inside the company has decided to alter the allocation calculation. A better approach is to determine the cost of each product after the split-off point, since these costs are directly associated with individual products; the total of these costs should constitute the minimum acceptable price at which a company is willing to sell its products, since this price would allow it to cover the clearly identifiable costs associated with each of its products. Of course, this minimum price does not allow for a profit, so the actual price should be at a higher level that will cover all joint costs when the sale of all resulting joint products occurs.

31.13   OUTPUTS: COST VARIANCES

A costing methodology of any type is not of much use if there is no output from it that gives valuable information to the management team. One of the primary outputs that is expected is a listing of costing variances, which are actual costs that depart from expectations. There are a number of standard variance calculations that can be summarized into a report, and which we will cover in this section.

Variances fall into three categories. The first is a price variance, and is the difference between the standard purchase cost of an item and the actual cost at which it was purchased, multiplied by the actual number of units purchased. It can be used to describe the variances in the general cost categories of purchased parts, direct labor, and overhead, and so is seen in three different places on cost variance reports.

The second type of variance is the efficiency variance. This is the difference between the actual quantity of resources needed to manufacture something, less the standard quantity, multiplied by its standard cost. This variance can also be broken down into three subvariances: a direct labor efficiency variance, a yield variance that relates to materials usage, and a variable overhead efficiency variance. There is no efficiency variance related to fixed overhead costs, since they are not expected to change with volume, and so have no targeted level of efficiency against which to compare.

The final variance is the volume variance. It applies to only one cost type, as opposed to the other variances; this is fixed overhead costs. Fixed overhead costs are charged to the cost of goods sold, or other parts of the income statement, as a fixed amount per accounting period, rather than as a percentage of the volume of production. Because of this difference in the method of cost allocation, a change in the actual production volume from the level that was expected when the allocation was set will result in a volume variance. It is calculated by multiplying the fixed overhead portion of the overhead rate by the number of units produced, and then subtracting this amount from the total fixed overhead cost pool.

An example of these variances, and the calculations used to derive them, is shown in Exhibit 31.16. In the upper-left corner of the variance report, we see that there is a total variance of $61,725. The block of costs immediately below this shows the cost categories in which the variance arose, which sum to $61,725. Below and to the side of these variances are subsidiary variances that are linked back to the four major cost categories. For instance, the materials price variance in the upper-right corner reveals that the price paid for materials is $1.25 higher than expected, while the material yield variance located directly below it shows that 1,500 more units of materials were used for production than had been anticipated. The total variance from these two calculations is $26,000, which traces back to the total direct materials variance on the left side of the report. All of the variances trace back through the report in a similar manner. This is a good format for showing how variance calculations are derived, and how they flow through the accounting reporting system.

Product Line 400GL3
Cost Variance Report

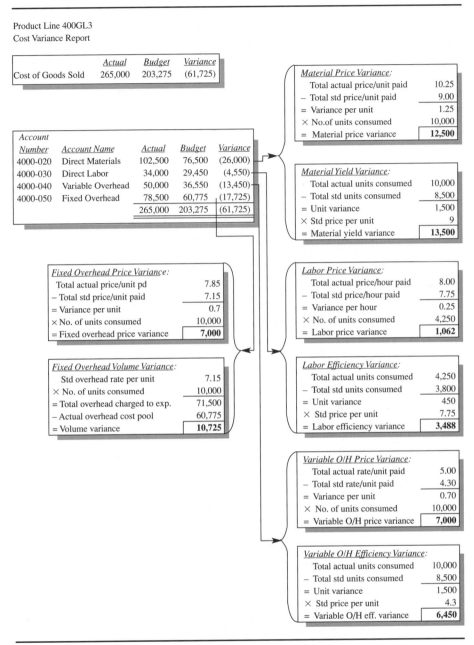

	Actual	Budget	Variance
Cost of Goods Sold	265,000	203,275	(61,725)

Account Number	Account Name	Actual	Budget	Variance
4000-020	Direct Materials	102,500	76,500	(26,000)
4000-030	Direct Labor	34,000	29,450	(4,550)
4000-040	Variable Overhead	50,000	36,550	(13,450)
4000-050	Fixed Overhead	78,500	60,775	(17,725)
		265,000	203,275	(61,725)

Material Price Variance:
Total actual price/unit paid	10.25
– Total std price/unit paid	9.00
= Variance per unit	1.25
× No.of units consumed	10,000
= Material price variance	**12,500**

Material Yield Variance:
Total actual units consumed	10,000
– Total std units consumed	8,500
= Unit variance	1,500
× Std price per unit	9
= Material yield variance	**13,500**

Fixed Overhead Price Variance:
Total actual price/unit pd	7.85
– Total std price/unit paid	7.15
= Variance per unit	0.7
× No. of units consumed	10,000
= Fixed overhead price variance	**7,000**

Labor Price Variance:
Total actual price/hour paid	8.00
– Total std price/hour paid	7.75
= Variance per hour	0.25
× No. of units consumed	4,250
= Labor price variance	**1,062**

Fixed Overhead Volume Variance:
Std overhead rate per unit	7.15
× No. of units consumed	10,000
= Total overhead charged to exp.	71,500
– Actual overhead cost pool	60,775
= Volume variance	**10,725**

Labor Efficiency Variance:
Total actual units consumed	4,250
– Total std units consumed	3,800
= Unit variance	450
× Std price per unit	7.75
= Labor efficiency variance	**3,488**

Variable O/H Price Variance:
Total actual rate/unit paid	5.00
– Total std rate/unit paid	4.30
= Variance per unit	0.70
× No. of units consumed	10,000
= Variable O/H price variance	**7,000**

Variable O/H Efficiency Variance:
Total actual units consumed	10,000
– Total std units consumed	8,500
= Unit variance	1,500
× Std price per unit	4.3
= Variable O/H eff. variance	**6,450**

EXHIBIT 31.16   COST VARIANCE REPORT

A company may not choose to report on all of these variances, since the detailed investigation of each one can be extremely time consuming. Thus, the variance for the direct labor price may not be reported on the grounds that management has little control over it when pricing is ruled by a formal agreement with a labor union. Similarly, the fixed overhead volume variance may not be reported because it relates more to ongoing production volumes than to management's ability to control the size of the overhead cost pool. Variances that are more commonly reported on are the material price variance and all types of efficiency variances; the material price variance is used to monitor the performance of the purchasing staff, while efficiency variances are used to oversee the entire manufacturing process.

Some variances are not worthy of regular reporting, because they require an inordinate amount of data collection work in exchange for information that is not of much use to management. For example, a detailed scrap variance that itemizes every item that was thrown out during a reporting period, alongside the reasons for each one, calls for a very large amount of investigative effort. The resulting report will contain information that may result in some long-term savings, but probably not enough to justify the work required to create the report. Thus, report compilation work should be considered when reporting on variances.

Once the cost variance report has been completed, the accounting staff either will be asked to conduct an investigation into the causes of specific variances, or should do so on its own. If so, it is useful to know in advance what types of problems are most likely to cause variances, so that investigative work can be first targeted at these items. The most common causes of each major variance are:

- *Fixed overhead spending variance*
  - Suppliers have increased their prices for products and services that fall into this expense category. Review related supplier contracts for scheduled price increases.
  - The company has increased its usage of the products or services recorded in this category. If so, the costs may actually be variable, and should be shifted to a variable overhead account.
- *Labor price variance*
  - The standard rate has not been altered to match changes in the union's labor contract.
  - The standard does not include extra charges, such as shift premiums, bonuses, or overtime.
  - The people actually conducting work are at different pay rates than those that were assumed to be doing the work when the labor standards were created.
- *Material price variance*
  - The actual price paid is based on a different purchasing volume than what was assumed when the price standard was originally set.
  - The standard price was erroneously copied from a similar product that has a significantly different price.
  - The purchasing staff is now buying replacement parts that have a different price than the parts that were the basis for the standard.
- *Selling price variance*
  - Products were sold with different options than the products used to set selling price standards.
  - Customers have ordered in different unit volumes than those used to determine the standard price.
  - Customers have paid prices different from the invoiced prices (which will require investigation to resolve).
  - Customers were given promotional discounts on prices paid.

- *Variable overhead spending variance*
  - The supplier has changed its per-unit pricing. Look for a contractually mandated change in the per-unit price.
  - The company is purchasing in different volumes, which alters the per-unit price paid.
  - There are misclassifications in costs between the variable overhead and other accounts.

Though there are certainly other causes for variances, these are among the most common ones, and so should be investigated first. Also, the accounting staff will find that the same causes are likely to crop up over and over again, so it is useful to develop and continually update a list of variances caused from previous reporting periods. This becomes the accounting staff's "short list" of variance causes that can be used to track down similar problems in the future.

31.14   SUMMARY

This chapter has covered the variety of methods that can be used for data collection purposes, what types of costing methodologies can be utilized to process this incoming data, and how the results can be reported to management. Of the three areas covered, the most important is the proper use of the correct costing methodology, for this has a major impact on the type of information reported to management. There are many ways to reshuffle the incoming data, using systems as diverse as activity-based costing and throughput accounting (which emphasize entirely different information), so the cost accountant must have an excellent knowledge of what each system does and how it can be used. A key issue to remember is that a single costing system will not meet all of a company's reporting needs. The result should be a mix of systems that are selected for specific purposes, and that can be changed to meet different information reporting requirements.

FINANCIAL ANALYSIS

32.1 INTRODUCTION

The accountant must be concerned with more than the proper handling and reporting of transactions. It is becoming increasingly common for the accounting staff to be asked to review the data behind key financial decisions and to make recommendations to management. In this chapter, we cover the topics that are most commonly seen by the accountant—the cost of capital, capital budgeting, breakeven, risk analysis, and business cycle forecasting. A basic grounding in these topics is becoming a necessary skill for the accountant.

32.2 THE COST OF CAPITAL

The accountant is sometimes called upon to render an opinion about the wisdom of investing in new assets. The basis for any such opinion is a knowledge of a firm's cost of capital. If the return from any asset investment will be less than the cost of capital, then the accountant's opinion should be to forgo the investment. Consequently, it is crucial to know the amount of a company's cost of capital and under what circumstances it may vary.

The cost of capital is composed of three forms of funding—debt, preferred stock, and common stock. There are other forms of funding, such as convertible stock, but these are all variations on one of the three primary types of funding. Descriptions of each type of funding are:

- *Debt*. This includes any arrangement by a company to accept cash in exchange for a future return of principal as well as interest. It is the least expensive form of funding, because the interest charged by lenders can be deducted as a business expense for tax purposes, which can result in an extremely low net cost of funds.

- *Preferred stock*. This includes any stock issuance in which shareholders are entitled to some form of dividend, while the company has no obligation to return the underlying funds contributed by the shareholders. Because these payments take the form of dividends, rather than interest, they are not tax deductible, and so result in a higher cost of funds. It can be difficult to place a value on the exact cost of preferred stock, because the company may have the right to delay dividend payments (which reduces their cost) and preferred shareholders may have the right to convert their shares to common stock (which increases the cost of funds).

- *Common stock.* This type of stock carries with it no direct requirement by the company to pay back shareholders in any way, though the board of directors can authorize dividend distributions to them. Investors rely instead on stock appreciation and the eventual sale of their stock to realize a return. Because of the greater risk of this type of investment, common stock will have the greatest assumed return to the investor, and so has the highest cost of funds.

A few calculations will show how these three types of funding can be combined to create a cost of capital. We will calculate the cost of each funding type in turn, and then combine them into a weighted average. To calculate the cost of debt, we first determine the after-tax cost of the interest expense, which is one minus the tax rate, multiplied by the interest expense; we then multiply this by the total amount of debt outstanding, which results in the total interest expense. We then divide this by the total amount of debt, which is decreased by any discount or increased by any premium that occurred on the initial issuance of the debt to buyers. For example, if we issued \$1,000,000 of debt at a discount of 5%, had an incremental corporate income tax rate of 38%, and paid an interest rate of 8%, the formula for the cost of debt would look like this:

$$\text{After-tax cost of debt} = \frac{((\text{Interest percentage}) \times (1 - \text{incremental tax rate})) \times \text{total debt}}{(\text{Total debt}) - (\text{discount on sale of debt})}$$

$$\text{After-tax cost of debt} = \frac{((8\%) \times (1 - 38\%)) \times \$1,000,000}{(\$1,000,000) - (\$50,000)}$$

$$\text{After-tax cost of debt} = \underline{5.221\%}$$

Determining the cost of preferred stock is much simpler than was the case for debt, since the interest paid on this type of "mixed" equity is not tax deductible. Consequently, if the stated interest rate for preferred stock is 12%, then that is its actual cost to the company—the impact of income taxes does enter into the equation. However, there may be instances where the holder of a preferred share is allowed the option to convert the share to common stock (which has a higher cost to the company, as we shall discuss shortly). If so, should the cost of capital incorporate the potential conversion to common stock, or use the cost of the existing share? The answer depends upon the exact terms under which the preferred shareholder will convert to common stock. Usually, there is a conversion ratio or strike price at which the conversion can take place, and that will only be cost-beneficial to the holder of the preferred stock under certain circumstances. For example, a preferred share may be convertible to common stock once the price of the common stock on the open market reaches \$18.00, or it may have a fixed conversion ratio of one share of preferred stock for 1/2 share of common stock. Given these conversion options, it will be apparent to the preferred stock shareholder when it becomes economically viable to convert the share to common stock. It will be equally apparent to the person who is deriving the cost of capital; this person should include in the cost of capital the cost of preferred stock until such time as conditions make it feasible for preferred shareholders to switch to common stock and then alter the cost of capital calculation accordingly. This is in opposition to the view that one should convert all preferred stock to common stock under the terms of any conversion formula, on the grounds that it yields the most expensive cost of capital. On the contrary, the cost of capital should reflect all funding costs at the current time, which should include preferred stock that will not be converted to common stock.

The cost of common stock is more difficult to determine. To calculate it, we start with the rate of return that investors are historically achieving with similar stocks, which requires the assembly of a market basket of similar stocks and then taking an average of the group. This calculation is subject to some interpretation, both in terms of which stocks to include in the market basket and what historical period to use to determine the average rate of return. Then we subtract from this average the standard rate of return that one can achieve by purchasing any risk-free security, such as U.S. government securities. The difference is an incremental amount that investors expect to earn above the risk-free rate of return. In addition, the specific common stock under examination may vary more or less than the average market rate of variance, depending upon the cyclicality of its industry, the degree of financial leverage that it uses, and other factors. This variability, known as its "beta," is calculated by many stock monitoring services. The beta should be multiplied by the incremental rate of return above the risk-free return, with the result being added back to the risk-free return in order to derive the cost of capital for common stock. The formula is:

> Cost of capital
> for common stock = Risk-free + (beta × (average return minus risk-free return))

For example, a company with a beta of .85 would have a cost of common stock of 12.9625% if the risk-free rate of return, as evidenced by U.S. Treasuries, was 4.25% and a market basket of similar stocks yielded an average return of 14.5%. The calculation is:

> Cost of capital
> for common stock = 4.25% + (.85 × (14.5% minus 4.25%))

Though we have reviewed the costing calculations for each component of the cost of capital, we must still combine them into a blended rate. This is done using a weighted average, based on the amount of funding obtained from each source. If we were to use the $1,000,000 of debt (less a discount of $50,000) that was used as an example earlier in this section, plus $500,000 of preferred stock and $2,500,000 of common stock at the costing levels just noted, we would arrive at the weighted average cost of capital noted in Exhibit 32.1.

In the exhibit, there is a large proportion of high-cost common stock to debt and preferred stock, which gives the company a minimal risk of not meeting its fixed interest payments. If a company's management were inclined to reduce the cost of capital, it could do so by obtaining more debt and using it to buy back common stock. This would certainly eliminate some high-cost common stock, but at the price of increasing the size of interest payments, which in turn would increase the amount of fixed costs, and therefore raise the

Funding Source	Total Funding	×	Percentage Cost of Funding	=	Dollar Cost of Funding
Debt	$ 950,000	×	5.221%		$ 49,600
Preferred stock	500,000	×	12.000%		60,000
Common stock	2,500,000	×	12.963%		324,075
Totals	$ 3,950,00	×	10.979%		$433,675

EXHIBIT 32.1   WEIGHTED AVERAGE COST OF CAPITAL

breakeven point for the company, which can be risky if it is already operating at close to the breakeven level. Thus, there is an increased risk of business failure for those companies that attempt to reduce their cost of capital by transferring their sources of funding from equity to debt.

Though we have just reviewed the calculations for determining a company's existing cost of capital, this does not necessarily mean that it is the cost that should be applied to the valuation of all prospective capital projects. There are two issues that may require one to use a different cost of capital. The first is that the company may have to alter its capital structure in order to obtain any additional funding. For example, lenders may have informed the company that no more debt will be available unless more equity is added to its capital base. In this instance, the cost of capital to be applied to a new capital purchase should be the incremental cost of funds that will specifically apply to the next investment. The second issue is that the cost of capital just calculated was for the existing blend of debt and equity, whose costs may very well have changed on the open market since the date when it was obtained. Debt costs will vary on the open market, as will investor expectations for returns on stock. Consequently, it may be advisable to periodically recalculate the cost of capital not only to reflect current market conditions for new funding, but also on an incremental basis, which can then be applied to a review of new capital investments. The only case where these strictures would not apply is when the amount of new capital investments is so small that there is little likelihood that obtaining funds for them will require a significant change in the existing capital structure.

If there are too many possible capital investments for the amount of funding available, one can keep increasing the cost of capital that is used to discount the cash flows from each project (as noted in the next section) in order to see which projects have the highest discounted cash flows. However, capital investments that are only based on discounted cash flow will ignore other issues that should have a bearing on the investment decision. One such factor is the risk of the project; it will be higher if the investment is in a new market, as opposed to one that is an extension of an existing market. Also, if there is a history of good returns on investment in a particular area, then there is a lower risk of loss on future investments in the same area. Further, the risk of heightened competition in some areas should be factored into the investment decision. Consequently, it is better to use the cost of capital to throw out only those capital investments that are clearly incapable of achieving a minimum return, and then further narrow the field of potential investment candidates by carefully reviewing other strategic and tactical factors related to each project.

One must also be aware of changes in the cost of capital that may arise in various subsidiaries of a conglomerate, where there may be significantly different levels of business risk in each one. One of the reasons why conglomerates are assembled is to combine the varying levels of business risk in each component business, so that the average level of risk, as defined by the probability of achieving an even stream of cash flows, is maximized. The problem with using a blended cost of capital that is based on a multitude of disparate businesses is that the rate may be applied to individual businesses whose levels of risk would normally involve a much higher cost of capital, while other businesses operating in mature industries with predictable results may be constrained by the use of a cost of capital that is too high. One way to avoid this problem is to derive a cost of capital that is based on the debt and equity structure of other companies that are located solely in the industries within which specific subsidiaries operate. This yields a cost of capital for the subsidiary, which may be a more accurate measure for determining the discounted return on various capital projects. However, there may be some companies within the industry that have excessively aggressive or conservative capital structures, which may result in a range of possible costs of capital.

32.3 BREAKEVEN ANALYSIS

Every accountant should be aware of a company's breakeven point, for this tells management what revenue level it must maintain in order to achieve a profit. The formula for breakeven is simple enough—just add up all fixed costs for the period, divide by the gross margin percentage, and the result will be the total revenue level to be achieved in order to yield a profit of exactly zero. For example, a company with fixed costs of $3,700,000 and gross margins of 33% must sell more than $11,212,121 to earn a profit.

It can be of use to translate the breakeven formula into a graphical representation, such as the one noted in Exhibit 32.2. This graph contains a horizontal line that represents the level of fixed costs, such as salaries, rent, and leases, that will be incurred irrespective of the revenue level. The slanted line that connects at the x-intercept with the fixed cost line represents variable costs, such as the materials used to manufacture products. The slanted line beginning at the x-y intercept represents the revenue to be recognized at various levels of production volume. According to the exhibit, the company will begin to generate a profit at an approximate capacity utilization level of 40%. Above the noted breakeven point, income taxes will be subtracted from profits, which are shown in the upper right corner of the graph.

The breakeven chart shown in Exhibit 32.2 is a very simple one, because it assumes that there are no changes in costs at any volume level. In reality, additional fixed costs must

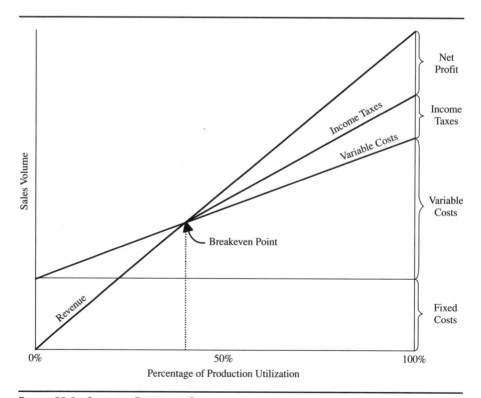

EXHIBIT 32.2 SIMPLIFIED BREAKEVEN CHART

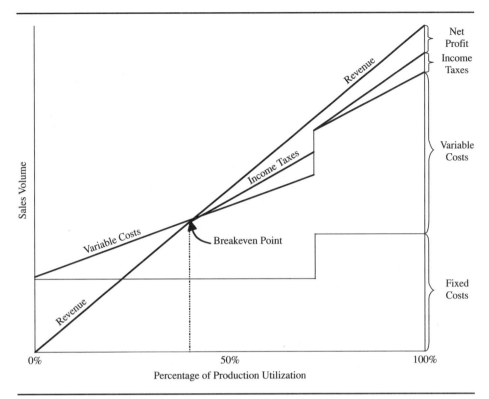

EXHIBIT 32.3   BREAKEVEN CHART INCLUDING IMPACT OF STEP COSTING

be incurred as production volumes increase. For example, there will come a point where production capacity for one eight-hour shift cannot be expanded; only by hiring additional supervisors, production planners, maintenance staff, and materials management personnel for the second and third shifts can capacity be increased. All of these costs are shown in Exhibit 32.3, where there is a large jump in the level of fixed costs at about the time when production capacity reaches the 70% level. Because of this significant increase, the exhibit shows that the point at which profits are maximized is just prior to the jump in fixed costs. The accountant should be aware of the points where costs will step up in this manner, and advise management of the resulting changes in profits.

The breakeven graph is of particular use in determining the inherent risk in a business forecast. A well-designed forecast will contain high, median, and low revenue and cost levels that bracket the full range of expected company performance for the upcoming year. By adding the full range of these estimates to a breakeven graph, as shown in Exhibit 32.4, one can see if there is any risk of loss during the forecasted period. In the exhibit, the lowest level of projected revenue will result in a loss; this issue should be communicated back to management as part of the forecasting process, so that it can alter its budget to avoid the potential loss.

Other situations in which the breakeven graph can be used are to determine the impact of a changed product mix on overall profits, changes in per-unit selling prices, the range of potential profits to be expected, production volumes needed to offset various per-unit prices, and the level of revenue needed to cover the cost of a capital acquisition. Thus, breakeven analysis is an essential tool for financial analysis.

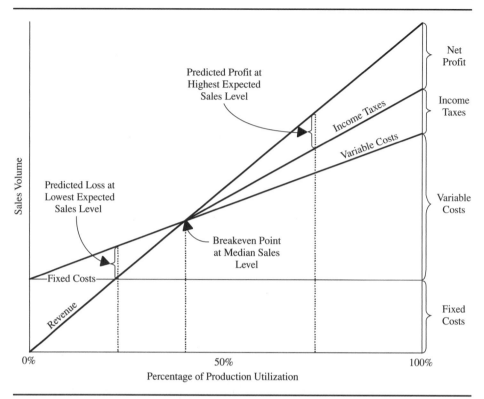

EXHIBIT 32.4   RISK ANALYSIS OF A BUSINESS FORECAST

32.4   ELIMINATING UNPROFITABLE PRODUCTS

Pareto analysis holds that 80% of the activity in a given situation is caused by 20% of the population. This rule is strongly applicable to the profitability of a company's products, where 80% of the total profit is generated by 20% of the products. Of the remaining 80% of the product population, it is reasonable to assume that some make no profit at all. Consequently, financial analysis should encompass the regularly scheduled review of all company product offerings to determine which products should be withdrawn from the marketplace. This is a valuable analysis for the following reasons:

- *Complexity.* In general, too many products lead to an excessive degree of system complexity within a company in order to support those products.
- *Excessive inventory.* Each inventory item usually contains some unique parts, which require additional storage space in the warehouse as well as a working capital investment in those parts and the risk of eventual obsolescence. Further, the presence of unique parts in a product may be the sole reason why the purchasing department continues to deal with a supplier; canceling the product allows the company to reduce the number of suppliers it uses, thereby gaining greater volume discounts with the remaining suppliers.
- *Engineering time.* If there are changes to products, the engineering staff must update the bill of material and labor routing records, all of which takes time.

- *Marketing literature.* The marketing department usually maintains a unique set of literature for each product, which requires periodic updating and reprinting.
- *Servicing cost.* The customer support staff must be trained in the unique features of each product, so they can answer customer questions adequately.
- *Warranty cost.* Some products have a considerable warranty cost, possibly due to design flaws or inadequate materials that require sizable warranty reserves.

When conducting a product withdrawal analysis, care must be taken not to assume that some expenses will be eliminated along with a product. Instead, an expense may have been allocated to a product but still will remain once the product is gone. For example, the servicing cost of the customer support staff is unlikely to result in the actual elimination of a customer support position just because a single product has been cancelled. Instead, customer support overhead will now be assigned to the smaller remaining pool of products. Thus, it is extremely important to include only direct costs in a product withdrawal analysis and to exclude any overhead allocations. To be certain that a product cancellation is not merely shifting overhead costs elsewhere, it is useful to develop before-and-after pro forma financial statements to see if an improvement in profitability really results from the cancellation.

As just noted, only direct costs should be used in calculating the profitability of a product for purposes of the cancellation decision. This results in the following formula:

$$
\begin{array}{rl}
 & \underline{\text{Standard list price (1)}} \\
- & \underline{\text{Commission (2)}} \\
- & \text{Buyer discounts (3)} \\
- & \text{Material cost (4)} \\
- & \text{Scrap cost (5)} \\
- & \text{Outsourced processing (6)} \\
- & \text{Inventory carrying cost (7)} \\
- & \text{Packaging cost (8)} \\
- & \text{Unreimbursed shipping cost (9)} \\
- & \underline{\text{Warranty cost (10)}} \\
= & \underline{\text{Profit (loss)}}
\end{array}
$$

Comments regarding the formula follow and match the numbers next to each line item in the formula:

1. *Standard list price.* If a product has a number of prices based on volume discounts or other criteria, it may be necessary to create a model using the costs itemized in the model to determine the breakeven price below which no profit is earned. The result may be a decision not necessarily to cancel the product but rather to not sell it at less than a certain discounted price, below which it makes no profit.

2. *Commission.* Salespeople sometimes earn a commission on product sales. If these commissions are clearly identifiable with a specific product and will not be earned if the product is not sold, then include the commission in the product cost.

3. *Buyer discounts.* The inclusion of buyer discounts in the calculation calls for some judgment. It should not be included if discounts are a rare event and comprise only a small dollar amount. If discounts are common, then calculate an average discount amount and deduct it from the standard list price.

4. *Material cost.* This is the cost of any materials included in the manufacture of a product.

5. *Scrap cost.* If a standard amount of scrap can be expected as part of the production process that is specifically identifiable with a product, then include this cost in the profitability calculation.

6. *Outsourced processing.* If any production work related to the product is completed by an outside entity, then the cost of this work should be included in the calculation on the grounds that the entire cost of the outsourced processing will be eliminated along with the product.

7. *Inventory carrying cost.* This should be only the incremental inventory carrying cost, which is usually only the interest cost of the company's investment in inventory specifically related to the product. It should not include the cost of warehouse storage space or insurance, since both of these costs are fixed in the short term and are very unlikely to change as a result of the elimination of a single product. For example, a company may lease a warehouse and is obligated to make monthly lease payments irrespective of the amount of storage space being taken by inventory used for a specific product.

8. *Packaging cost.* Include the cost of any packaging materials used to contain and ship the product, but only if those materials cannot be used for other products.

9. *Unreimbursed shipping cost.* If the company is absorbing the cost of shipments to customers, then include this cost, net of volume discounts from the shipper.

10. *Warranty cost.* Though normally a small expense on a per unit basis, an improperly designed product or one that includes low-quality parts may have an extremely high average warranty cost. If significant, this cost should be included in the profitability analysis.

In addition, please note that production labor costs are *not* included in the preceding calculation. The reason is that production labor rarely varies directly with the level of production; instead, a fixed number of workers will be in the production area every day, irrespective of the level of work performed. Thus, the cancellation of a product will not impact the number of workers employed. If a product cancellation will result in the verifiable and immediate elimination of labor positions, however, then the incremental cost of the eliminated labor should be included in the calculation.

In some cases, financial analysis reveals that some products are unprofitable, but management chooses to keep the products for a limited period of time in order to use up remaining stocks of inventory. If so, it is useful to include the prospective effect of the cancellation in the upcoming budgeting period, as of the date on which cancellation is anticipated. To ensure that planned product withdrawals are included in any new budgets, consider including in the budgeting procedure a formal step to investigate any pending product cancellations.

Another consideration is that an unprofitable product may be of critical importance to customers. If so, it may be useful to offer an upgrade path to another (presumably more profitable) product that provides them with the required level of functionality. If there is no obvious replacement, the product cancellation process is likely to be greatly prolonged until a new upgrade product can be readied for service.

Even if a product is clearly unprofitable, it may be needed by a key customer who orders other, more profitable products from the company. If so, combine the profits of all sales made to that customer to ensure that the net combined profit is sufficiently high to warrant the retention of the unprofitable product. If this is not the case, consider cancelling the unprofitable product and negotiating with the customer for a price reduction on other products in order to retain the customer.

Another cancellation issue is the presence of dependent products. There may be ancillary products that are supplements to the main product and that provide additional profits to the overall product line. For example, the profit margin on a cell phone may be negative, but there may be a sufficiently high profit level on extra cell phone batteries, car chargers, headsets, and phone covers to more than offset the loss on the initial product sale. In these cases, the margins on all ancillary products should be included in the profitability analysis.

Finally, the frequency of product profitability reviews will be greatly dependent on product life cycles. If products have very short life cycles, sales levels will drop rapidly once products enter the decline phase of their life cycles, potentially leaving the company with large stocks of excess inventory. In these situations, it is critical to conduct frequent reviews in order to keep a company's investment in working capital from becoming excessive.

There are also two nonfinancial reasons for retaining unprofitable products that must be considered before cancelling a product.

1. A company may want to offer to customers a full range of product offerings, so they can purchase anything they need from the company, without having to go to a competitor. This may require the retention of a product whose absence would otherwise create a hole in the corporate product line.

2. It may be necessary to offer a product in a specific market niche in order to keep competitors from entering a market that the company considers to be crucial to its ongoing viability.

32.5   RISK ANALYSIS

The preceding forms of analysis all assume that the data being used as input to the various calculations is accurate. If not, then the results of each analysis may be incorrect, and lead to bad business decisions. There are several ways to improve the accuracy of data used, as well as quantify the level of risk associated with it.

The primary area in which there is a high risk of inaccuracy is in forecasts of any kind. The information used for a forecast is frequently based on the opinions of a small number of people, who may have biases that skew their forecasts away from actual results. The accuracy of forecasts can be improved by a number of means, such as calling upon outside experts for independent analysis and review, using an internal review board that discusses the data and recommends changes where needed, or calling upon the sales staff (those with the best knowledge of market conditions) for an opinion. It is also useful to compare actual results against forecasts by person, to see who is consistently making the best (and worst) forecasts.

Once all estimates have been received, the accountant should determine their range of values. If they are broadly dispersed, then there is a strong likelihood that using the median of all estimates as the basis for financial analysis will not include many of the estimates, which may be far higher or lower than the median. When there is a great deal of dispersion in the data, it is best to calculate its amount, and report this information alongside any resulting financial analysis, so that the reader can form an opinion regarding the level of risk for which the resulting analysis is not accurate. Dispersion can be determined with the standard deviation calculation. This measures the average scatter of data about the mean by arriving at a figure that represents the average distance of every data item from the midpoint. A large standard deviation means that the range of data is quite varied. In such cases, one should be wary of any resulting summarization of the data, since there are many possible outcomes that vary substantially from each other.

The standard deviation can be converted into the coefficient of variation by dividing the standard deviation by the mean of the data. The coefficient of variation is a more useful number, because it restates the standard deviation in terms of a percentage. For example, a standard deviation may be 152.7, but one cannot tell if this is good or bad until it is converted into the coefficient of variation, where one then finds out that it represents only a 5% standard deviation from the mean, which therefore gives one good reliance on the underlying data.

There is always a chance that the data used to make financial projections will be incorrect. This risk can be related to the reader of a financial report in terms of a quantification, such as the coefficient of variation, or in relation to the relative level of inaccuracy that has occurred in projections in the past, or in a narrative format; in this last case, it is up to the reader of the report to judge how much risk is included in the presented information.

32.6   BUSINESS CYCLE FORECASTING

Business cycles tend to be of very long duration, involving gradual expansions and contractions of the national and international economies. They are influenced by an enormous array of issues—raw material availability, wars, earthquakes, monetary policy, and so on. At this level, the typical corporation will rely upon large banks, investment houses, or forecasting specialists to give it information about expected changes in the economy, for it simply does not have the time, money, expertise, or inclination to undertake such a task by itself.

However, every company operates within one or more much smaller niches within the national economy, and these niches may be influenced by a sufficiently small number of variables that it is worthwhile for a company to maintain its own forecasting function that addresses those variables. For example, United Airlines operates within the air travel segment of the economy, while the Ford Motor Company operates within the motor vehicles segment. The level of business activity that United will experience within its niche is heavily influenced by the cost of jet fuel, since this cost is typically passed along to the consumer through ticket prices. Similarly, Ford is also influenced by the cost of fuel, because demand for its fuel-efficient cars will rise and demand for its "gas hog" cars will fall in association with long-term gas price increases.

If the accountant becomes involved in business cycle forecasting, there are a number of forecasting models that may be of use. One is the anticipation survey. This approach holds that the best determinant of future conditions is to poll the most experienced and knowledgeable people in the industry and summarize their opinions regarding future conditions. Another approach is to construct a time series model that extends historical trend lines into the future; this approach can be reasonably accurate in the very short term, but is similar to driving a car by peering closely into the rearview mirror. A third alternative is to use econometric models, which are complex formulations that depend upon the interaction of hundreds of variables; these are too expensive for a single company to maintain, but can be managed by well-funded industry trade groups or more commonly by specialist forecasting firms. A fourth approach is to use leading indicators to forecast economic changes. These are activities that have a history of changing prior to changes in the economy, such as the number of new business formations, unemployment insurance claims, and capacity utilization. If a small number of leading indicators are tracked that have a specific bearing upon the conditions within one's industry, it is possible to obtain a general idea of near-term economic conditions.

What approach should the accountant use in creating forecasts? One alternative is to use the national forecasts that are published in the major business magazines on a regular basis. However, these apply to the economy as a whole, and may have little applicability to a specific market niche. A more accurate, but more expensive, approach is to hire a forecasting firm that can develop a forecast for a specific subset of the economy. Finally, one can develop an in-house forecasting capability. Under this scenario, it is best to work with the management team to develop a small set of key variables that they believe has the largest impact on the business cycle within the company's industry. Then collect data about these variables for as many years in the past as possible, and compare them to actual business conditions over time to see if they are correlated. If so, initiate a system for collecting the variables on a regular basis, and then develop a simplified spreadsheet model into which they can be loaded for forecasting purposes. Before sharing the results of this model with the management team, be sure to summarize the variables and key assumptions used in the development of the model, so that management will have a general understanding of its formulation. Finally, the actual business cycle results should be compared to predicted results to see if the model works properly, and adjusted as necessary to bring it into closer alignment with actual results. This last approach to forecasting is clearly the most time-consuming one to implement, but can result in the best information, especially if a great deal of time goes into its creation, data collection, and ongoing maintenance.

32.7 SUMMARY

The accountant will be called upon to provide financial analyses on nearly any topic imaginable—whether to invest in different types of securities, select a price point for a new product, replace manual labor with automation, and so on. There is no way to prepare the accountant for every possible situation that may arise, so this chapter has focused solely on those key concepts that are most likely to arise on the most frequent basis. These are the cost of capital, product elimination, breakeven analysis, risk analysis, and business cycle forecasting. The concepts included within them can be combined and built upon to derive financial analyses for more topics than those presented here.

RECORDS MANAGEMENT

33.1   INTRODUCTION

The accountant is put in change of records management in most companies, except those organizations that are so large that this function can be shifted to a full-time staff. The accountant must keep several counterbalancing goals in mind when setting up a records management system. One issue is to minimize the cost of recordkeeping; however, this goal will conflict with the opposing goals of having ready access to necessary information, as well as of retaining documents for periods much longer than is economically the most efficient. Consequently, this is an area that should be governed by a strict set of policies and procedures that are carefully designed to balance the conflicting goals of the function. The accountant's optimum solution then becomes following those policies and procedures in the most effective and efficient manner possible.

In this chapter, we will itemize the various costs that are incurred by a recordkeeping system, so that the significant costs associated with this function are clearly understood. We will then proceed to a discussion of the policies and procedures that are necessary for recordkeeping, and finish with a short discussion of computerized records management systems.

33.2   RECORDKEEPING COSTS

The costs associated with recordkeeping are much higher than most people realize. There are not only the clearly quantifiable costs of storage, but also the subjective ones related to lawsuits that are lost for lack of proper recordkeeping, as well as any forensic accounting needed to reconstruct lost information. Particularly in the case of lost lawsuits, the potential cost of recordkeeping can be startlingly high. Consequently, a clear understanding of these costs is necessary in order to point out the need for top-notch record management systems, as are described in the following sections.

The following bullet points note the most common quantifiable costs of record storage, as well as how they should be calculated:

- *Space rental.* Any space taken up by filing cabinets or boxes represents either a direct lease cost or else an opportunity cost for space that could more profitably be put to use for other activities. This is a particularly high cost if records are kept on site, as opposed to a lower-cost warehousing facility. To determine this cost, summarize not only the space directly taken up by stored records, but also the width of all walkways around them that cannot otherwise be used due to the potential for reduced access to the records. If the facility is entirely company-owned and there is no clear-cut way to sell off the storage space, then the cost of storage can be calculated by determining the costs that would not be incurred if other facilities could be consolidated into the storage space.

- *Storage equipment.* Storage equipment may be as minimal as cardboard boxes, or extend to the use of fireproof safes, storage cabinets, or forklifts. The expense associated with these investments should be added to the overall cost of storage. Be sure to tie the depreciation rate on capital items to their actual usage period (subject to standard depreciation period restrictions).

- *Fire suppression systems.* The local fire warden may require special fire suppression systems for storage areas, which may extend to the use of expensive sprinkler or Halon systems. The cost of these items should also include the periodic cost of system inspections, testing, and maintenance.

- *Transportation.* If files are stored in other facilities, it will be necessary to move them back to the company's premises whenever needed. This cost of transport should be easy to calculate if movement is done by a third party, since there will be a billing for each move. If the transport function is kept within the company, then some portion of the moving staff's wages should be charged to this activity.

- *Insurance.* A modest amount of insurance is required to protect a company from loss of its records. However, there may be additional insurance required that protects the company from the increased fire hazard represented by stored records.

- *Clerical costs.* There is a significant cost associated with the personnel who are engaged in filing documents, retrieving them, shifting them to ff-site locations, and bringing them back from time to time. If there is a great deal of "churn" in the amount of paperwork that is moved in and out of storage, this can be the largest cost associated with record storage.

- *Computer systems.* Those companies that have shifted over to electronic storage must account for the capital cost of computer acquisitions, as well as ongoing equipment replacement and maintenance costs. This cost should include an apportionment of the time required by the computer services staff to maintain the system.

By summarizing all of the preceding costs, many accountants will find that the cost of record management is very high. Consequently, there is a positive cost-benefit associated with the formalized recordkeeping systems noted in the following sections, so that the cost of this activity is minimized.

33.3   RECORDKEEPING POLICIES AND PROCEDURES

There are an enormous number of document types that flow through a corporation every year, many of which will be reviewed repeatedly for a number of years thereafter. Without a proper recordkeeping system, a company will incur substantially higher costs in the areas noted in the preceding section. The best way to ensure that these costs are minimized is to set up and follow a system of policies and procedures. The following policies should serve as the groundwork for a complete set of related procedures:

- *Document retention policy.* All too often, there is no criterion for how long a record is to be retained, and so documents will tend to pile up in a disorderly manner. To avoid this trouble, there should be a policy that carefully itemizes the number of years that each type of document will be stored before it is destroyed. The number of years for which various types of documents must be retained will, to some extent, be determined by local or federal government regulations. For a detailed listing of recommended storage intervals for documents, one can consult the *Guide to Record Retention Requirements,* which is published by the U.S. Government Printing Office. If there is some expectation or history of lawsuits in certain areas of company operations, it may also be necessary to retain selected documents to serve as a possible future legal defense, in which case the statute of limitations will serve as the proper guideline for the date of document destruction. Accordingly, the legal staff should be consulted when this schedule is constructed. If there are contractual agreements with other entities that might result in audits of company records, then the retention period for any related documents should be tied to the termination dates of the contracts; for example, a cost-plus government construction job may require a company to retain all job-costing records for a period of three years after the completion date of the contract. The records most likely to fall into this category are those related to billings, fixed assets, inventory, and manufacturing costs. There will also be a number of documents that should be kept for as long as the company is in existence. These documents include blueprints, formulas, copyrights, patents, trademarks, leases, the certificate of incorporation, bylaws and constitution, and the board minute book. If there are other documents for which there are no governmental or legal reasons for retention, then the basis for determining a retention period should be the time period after which there is no reasonable expectation that they will be used. An example of a policy that incorporates these guidelines is shown in Exhibit 33.1. The time periods noted in the table are examples only, and should not be used for an actual document retention policy without first being reviewed by legal counsel. Any ongoing changes to this table should be authorized by legal counsel as well as the chief accounting position in the company.

- *Storage area policy.* Most records storage areas are located in spare rooms for which no other use can currently be found. No consideration is given to the safety or future condition of the records that will result from such storage. To avoid this problem, there should be a policy that specifies the condition of the designated storage area. This should include criteria for fireproofing, flood proofing, allowable minimum and maximum temperatures and humidity levels, and records fumigation.

- *Responsibility for recordkeeping policy.* The preceding policies involve tasks that will cut across the responsibilities of virtually all major company departments, which makes them very difficult policies to administer. Accordingly, a policy should be created that concentrates responsibility for these policies, as well as all attendant procedures, with a specific job position. The policy should describe the position's responsibilities in general terms, as well as its reporting relationship.

With these three policies in place, we now know which documents to retain, how long to do so, where to store them, and who will manage the process. However, this still leaves a number of unanswered questions at a more detailed level, such as how documents are to be identified, indexed, retrieved, and destroyed. The following procedures should be created so that guidelines will be available for these tasks:

- *Box-indexing procedure.* A procedure is needed that will use a standard indexing system to identify each box of records. One possibility is to start an index number

Type of Record	Retention Period (years)
Advertising, original artwork	10
Advertising, research reports	2
Advertising, tear sheets and proofs	Permanent
Articles of incorporation	Permanent
Audit report, external	Permanent
Audit report, internal	10
Audit workpapers, internal	4
Bank reconciliation	6
Bank statement	6
Bond, fidelity	10
Budget	5
Check, dividend (canceled)	6
Check, payable (canceled)	6
Check, payroll (canceled)	3
Collection notes	While customer is active
Contract document	5 years after termination
Copyright application	Permanent
Cost estimates	5
Credit application, customer	While customer is active
Customs paperwork	5
Debit/credit memo	5
Deposit slip	6
Expense reports	5
Financial statements	Permanent
Forecasts	5
Franchise record	5 years after termination
Guarantees	5
Insurance claim, other than employee	3 years after completion
Insurance claim, workers' compensation	3 years after completion
Inventory, cost record	3
Inventory, count sheet	3
Invoice, company	5
Invoice, supplier	5
Journal entry	10
Lease document	5 years after termination
Ledger, general	Permanent
Ledger, subsidiary	Permanent
License, business	10
Litigation record	5 years after termination
Minute book	Permanent
Mortgage	5 years after termination
Note payable	5 years after termination
Note receivable	5 years after termination
Overhead allocation calculations	5
Patent application	Permanent
Plan, annual	5
Plan, long-range	5
Proxy	6
Purchase order	5
Receiving record	5
Report, to shareholders	Permanent
Royalty record	10
Security registration	Review after 5 years
Shareholder list	6
Trademark application	Permanent

EXHIBIT 33.1   DOCUMENT RETENTION TABLE

with the year to which the records pertain, and then add a sequential number that identifies the specific box for that year. For example, the 13th box of records for the year 2001 would be "2001-13." An indexing file could then be compiled that itemizes each document stored within each of these box numbers. However, a problem with this method is that when the time arrives to destroy records, the entire box may be destroyed, even though some of the records within the box may be scheduled for earlier or later destruction. One way around this problem is to separate documents that are to be kept in a permanent file, and store them elsewhere (given their nature, these documents should be stored in the highest security environment, and so deserve special handling in any case). Another possibility is to use the same indexing system just noted, but to use the year of document *destruction* as part of the index, rather than the year of document *creation*. This makes it much less likely that documents will be destroyed at the wrong time.

- *Box identification procedure.* In those instances where documents are kept in storage boxes, there should be a procedure that establishes a standardized type of identification, as well as common storage of similarly identified boxes. For example, the procedure should clarify the exact spot on the box where an identifying index number will be recorded, which should be the end of the box that will be readily apparent to the casual observer if the boxes are palletized, with only one side showing. Otherwise, labels attached to other sides of a box will not be visible, requiring the dismantlement of an entire pallet to ascertain the index number of each box. Another procedural issue is how the index number is to be marked on the box. If a label is used, it may fall off over time. A better approach is to mark the box with indelible ink, even if this means that the box will not be usable for some other purpose at a later date.

- *Confidential document storage procedure.* When most records are filed away for storage, they are kept in open areas that are readily accessible for many employees. However, if the records are of a sensitive nature, such as payroll or legal documents, then a procedure is needed that will segregate these records at once and ensure that they are stored in the most secure location. The procedure should specify, in detail, the documents or document categories that are to be handled in this manner. If there are many documents from a specific area, such as human resources, that will fall into the confidential category, then it may be easier for the procedure to state that all documents from this area will be confidential, unless specifically stated otherwise. The procedure should also note the minimum levels of security and document handling that will be required, as well as who is responsible for their safety. For example, the procedure may require off-site storage in containers that are proof against fire damage up to a specific temperature and for a specified time period, with access requiring the approval of stated company positions.

- *Document destruction procedure.* The destruction of documents requires special controls, for a company may have to defend this practice in court if there is an appearance of unscheduled document destruction whose use in court might otherwise be damaging to the company. Consequently, a procedure should require the use of a document destruction certificate, which specifies which documents are to be destroyed, a cross-reference to the company policy that itemizes the duration of document retention prior to destruction, approval signatures, and the signature of at least one person who witnesses the actual document destruction.

- *Document retrieval procedure.* If the corporate staff is allowed full access to all on-site records, it is very likely that the quality of recordkeeping will decline in short order, for only a trained clerk who is responsible for the records will have any reason to preserve order as documents are pulled and returned, and boxes are shifted about. Consequently, a procedure should specify how documents are to be requested from an authorized clerical staff, which will in turn retrieve the requested records, log them out, and turn them over to requesting employees. This procedure should include the use of a request form, a logout form, and a report that itemizes all withdrawn documents.

- *Document transfer-to-storage procedure.* Documents tend to be sent to long-term record storage by dumping them into storage boxes at the end of the fiscal year and carting them off. This makes it more likely that different types of documents with different storage requirements will be lumped together, which leads to the risk of their being destroyed after incorrect time periods. To avoid this problem, a procedure should identify how current documents should be segregated and reviewed before they are to be sent to long-term storage. This should include a formal sign-off on the contents of each shipping carton.

- *Storage area layout procedure.* The storage area should not become a large pile of disorganized boxes. Instead, a procedure should be created that outlines how different types of records are to be stored within the area. This may include separate storage for permanent files and confidential documents, separate storage by the year of document creation, the most recently filed documents in the most accessible area, or some other variations. The procedure may also make some provision for the labeling scheme to be used to identify aisles and bins in a logical manner.

The creation of the policies and procedures outlined in this section should be partially based on a cost-benefit analysis. This analysis should compare the expected risk that documents will be needed at some future date to the cost of retaining them. The result of this review may well be a reduction in the storage requirements or locations for some types of records, so that only the most critical documents are retained for long periods in the safest and most secure environment. This cost-benefit review should be conducted periodically, and especially as the nature of the business changes, to see if the perceived risk level for document retention has changed, and with it the need for changes in records management policies and procedures.

33.4 REQUIRED TAX RECORDS

Because of the propensity of various government entities to hand out penalties and interest charges when tax filings are incorrect or late, it behooves the accountant to maintain an especially high level of control over all tax records. Of particular importance is a calendar that itemizes all of the dates when tax forms are due for filing, when payments must be made, and when tax auditors are scheduled to arrive. An example of a tax calendar is shown in Exhibit 33.2.

A more advanced format for the tax calendar is to store it in a central database, so that the information contained within it can be readily updated and reviewed by all users who are involved with tax information. With such a system, it may also be possible to have the computer automatically issue e-mails to targeted employees, warning them of upcoming due dates.

	Jan	Feb	Mar	Apr	May	Jun	Jul	Aug	Sep	Oct	Nov	Dec
Federal (consolidated)												
Estimated payments for calendar year 2010				15		15			15			15
Tax return for year-end 2010			15*			15*			15 (Final)			
Mail tax packages to subsidiaries and divisions for year-end 2010	15											
Preliminary analysis of liability account for financial statements	31											
Discuss retirement, 5500 etc. package to be completed		28										
Final analysis of liability account for year-end 2010		28										
Form 599-1099**										X		
Federal use tax—highway vehicles***							31					
Federal use tax—commercial vehicles***							31					
Federal excise quarterly return	31			30			31			31		
Federal excise monthly payment (2nd)	31	28	31	30	31	30	31	31	30	31	30	31
Federal excise monthly payment (1st)	15	15	15	15	15	15	15	15	15	15	15	15

EXHIBIT 33.2 TAX CALENDAR

* May extend—not extension of time to pay total tax liability, only extension of time to file final return.
** Tax organization will file federal, New York, Massachusetts, Washington, D.C., and North Dakota.
***Whenever applicable during tax year.

Required Information	Colorado Personal Property Tax
Locations for which reporting required	Facilities in Centennial, Englewood, and Lone Tree
Tax form addressee	Douglas County Tax Assessor's Office, Colorado
Form name/number	Personal Property Declaration Form (92A)
Form due date	2/28/XX
Data sources for form completion	Fixed asset and asset addition/disposal records
General ledger source account	XX-1400 through XX-1650
Storage index location	Tax permanent file #12

EXHIBIT 33.3   TAX SUMMARY TABLE

Recordkeeping must also be maintained in great detail for all taxes for which a company must file a return. Failure to do so on the dates required can result in significant penalties and interest charges. In a few cases, a missing tax form can even lead to the suspension of a company's legal right to do business. Consequently, a tax summary table, such as the one shown in Exhibit 33.3, should be constructed. This table should include summary-level information about each type of tax form that a company must complete, including the company locations for which reporting is required, the type of form needed, filing due dates, data sources, and related file storage locations. It may also be useful to note the size of potential tax penalties if a form is not filed in a timely manner, so that the tax preparation staff can categorize tax form preparations based on which ones could cost the company the most money. As a result, when the tax calendar previously shown in Exhibit 33.2 reveals that a form must be filed in the near future, someone on the tax staff can access the tax summary table for the specified tax, and have ready access to all of the key information needed to prepare the form.

The summary-level information associated with tax forms is by no means stable, so a company should assign someone the task of periodically updating these forms with the most recent information. If there is no staff time available for this, the tasks can also be outsourced to a competent tax review organization, which will send form updates to the company as tax-related changes arise.

Recordkeeping also extends to the working papers created during the process of completing tax forms. Since these documents may be called upon if taxing authorities question a company's submitted tax forms, there should be a system for organizing these workpapers. At a minimum, each set of working papers should include a copy of the completed tax form, as well as reference notes on the copy that refers back to those portions of the working papers that were used to compile the tax form. If tax research was conducted as part of the tax form preparation, then a copy of the research notes, containing lists of all referenced authorities, should be included in the working papers. If there is any related correspondence with taxing authorities, these letters should also be included in the file. The complete set of documentation should also be numbered sequentially and indexed, so that it will be obvious if any of the pages are subsequently removed from the file. Once each file of working papers is complete, it should be referenced in a master taxation index and stored in a secure location. Since there is some chance of paying additional taxes if a company's tax position is challenged and it cannot produce the underlying working papers to defend itself, the level of storage security provided must be of the highest order.

A final recordkeeping issue related to taxes is the proper structure of the chart of accounts (COA). If the COA is not properly designed to accumulate information that will feed into specific line items in various tax forms, the taxation staff must spend an inordinate amount of time in separately compiling the required information. Such information may be incorrect, since it is manually compiled, and is likely to contain errors. It is also difficult to recompile if lost, which makes recordkeeping for it a particularly difficult task. A better alternative is to construct the COA with the advice of the tax staff, so that it can be properly structured to assist in accumulating tax-related information.

33.5 SUMMARY

Record management is a task that is frequently assigned to the accounting staff. To accomplish this task, the accounting staff must work with legal counsel to determine the best records retention policy that offsets the cost of record storage against the risk that documents will be needed at some point in the future. The resulting policy can then be used to set up procedures for a record management system.

PART SIX

FINANCIAL MANAGEMENT

CUSTOMER CREDIT

34.1 INTRODUCTION

A company may have many customers—perhaps thousands of them. It must decide, for each one, how much credit it will extend, the time period before which each payment is due, and the size and nature of any discounts given. This can be a monumental task, and must be done properly, or else the organization may suffer from bad debts so large that its cash reserves are drained. Alternatively, an excessively restrictive credit policy can result in lost sales that interfere with corporate growth. Given the critical nature of customer credit, we will review in this chapter the types of credit and credit terms most commonly used, how to conduct a credit evaluation of a customer, and how to collect overdue funds. We will see that a proper credit policy, when combined with credit extension and collection systems, can add to a company's profitability.

34.2 TYPES OF CREDIT

There are a wide array of credit types that can be extended to a customer, though merchandise credit and letters of credit tend to be used in all but a few situations. Accordingly, we will concentrate on these two categories of credit.

Merchandise credit is used when products are sold to a customer against a promise by the customer of future payment, in accordance with a predetermined set of payment terms. Though merchandise credit can be extended on an order-by-order basis, it is more common to set up a customer with a predetermined maximum amount of credit, beyond which shipments will not be made until the existing amount of unpaid invoices has been reduced. The decision to grant merchandise credit to a customer is usually made by the credit department, which is part of the treasurer's staff. In a smaller company, this chore will fall within the purview of the accounting department. The techniques used to derive the amount of credit are described in the "Credit Examination" section of this chapter.

If merchandise credit is not available, or if there is difficulty in collecting on such credit, a company can work with its customer to create a promissory note, under which the customer agrees to pay the company a fixed amount, at a fixed or variable interest rate, and in accordance with a fixed schedule of payments. Promissory notes can usually be sold to a third party, and so are a reasonably liquid form of repayment. However, it can take a great deal of time to negotiate one.

A simpler variation on the promissory note is to factor one's accounts receivable through a third party, which generates immediate cash at the price of a transaction fee. It is also common for the factoring organization to have recourse against the company if it cannot collect on an account receivable, so the risk of bad debt loss is still with the company. Though this is an expensive form of credit, it can dramatically accelerate a company's cash flow.

The letter of credit (LOC) is used almost entirely for international sales, since it gives the seller assurance that a shipment to another country will be paid for in full, without any credit problems arising. It is a major tool for the ongoing development of international trade, and so its terms are well protected by many court cases that consistently rule in its favor.

The LOC is a document under which an entity can draw upon the credit of the bank that has issued the LOC for a specific amount, subject to a set of detailed performance conditions noted in the LOC. For example, Alpha Company wishes to purchase goods from Beta Company, which is located in a different country. Beta insists that the transaction be handled through an LOC. To do so, Alpha goes to its local bank and requests an LOC. The bank shifts money from Alpha's bank account into an escrow account, where it will be held until drawn down by Beta. Alpha's bank then sends the LOC document to its correspondent bank in Beta's country. When Beta has shipped the goods itemized on the LOC to Alpha, it takes its proof of delivery to the correspondent bank. Alpha's bank then sends the money to its correspondent bank, which pays Beta. In essence, this is an elaborate form of cash payment at the time of shipment, and can be construed as cash in advance, since many banks would require Alpha Company to hand over the full amount of cash listed on the LOC prior to their sending the documentation to the correspondent bank. Given the high level of probability that cash will be paid if the terms of the LOC are met, the LOC is sometimes used domestically.

An LOC is called "irrevocable" if the bank issuing it cannot cancel it until its stated expiration date. If the LOC is called "confirmed," then both the originating and correspondent banks have guaranteed its payment. These are standard features.

A modification on most types of credit is to have the parent company of a customer or an individual within it guarantee payment of any credit issued. By doing so, the company has two sources from which it can demand repayment. Customers will not normally agree to this provision, but can be forced to do so if their credit options are limited or if the company is the sole source of a particular service or product.

Another credit option is to sell on consignment, so that the goods sent to a customer are still the legal property of the company, and therefore can be taken back if the customer does not pay for them subsequent to their sale. However, the usual terms of such an agreement are that the company cannot expect payment until the point of sale by the customer, which may mean that it is funding a large amount of finished goods inventory for a long period of time.

The type of credit granted will be highly dependent upon the type of credit strategy adopted by a company. If its goal is to keep bad debt losses to an absolute minimum, then it will keep credit levels low, or only accept cash payments. However, if company managers want to greatly increase the rate of corporate growth, one approach is to offer credit to many more customers, and in larger quantities. By doing so, it can steal business away from competitors who have more restrictive credit policies, though at the cost of a higher level of bad debt. It may also want to loosen credit terms if it wishes to clear out an excessive amount of on-hand inventory, or to shut down a product line entirely. If the gross margin on a product sale is very high, then the associated credit terms can be loosened considerably, since the company stands to lose very little of its costs if the customer reneges on its payment. Whatever the mix of selling terms may be, the most appropriate level of credit granted to customers is the point at which increased margins from the sale of merchandise on relaxed credit terms is exactly offset by the increased cost of delayed payments and bad debts.

34.3   SELLING TERMS

There are a number of selling terms that can be used, as well as formats in which they are presented. The key factors in a set of selling terms are the time to maturity and the cash discount. The time to maturity is the number of days from the date of the invoice to the day when payment is required. For example, if the invoice date is March 1 and the terms are "net 30," then it is due for payment on March 30. The cash discount is the percentage that a customer can deduct from a payment if it pays before a preset date, which is useful for accelerating cash flows. The cash discount is not normally of much use for collections from customers with a history of payment delinquency, since they may not have enough cash on hand to take advantage of the discounts. An example of a cash discount is "2%/10," which means that the customer can take a 2% discount if it pays within 10 days of the invoice date. When the time to maturity and cash discount terms are combined from the previous examples, they would appear on an invoice as "2%/10 Net 30" or "2/10 N 30."

Some customers will take a cash discount even when they are not paying early (and may pay quite late). If so, the customer has abrogated the payment terms, so it is reasonable to charge back the customer for the amount of the discount taken. At a minimum, the general ledger should be arranged so that all discounts taken are stored in a separate account, with a notation regarding the name of the customer and whether or not it was incorrectly taken. By collecting this information, the accountant can inform the purchasing staff of problem customers, which they can use to increase prices to a point that will compensate for the improper discounts.

A much less common form of selling term is to specify the number of days after month-end when the payment is due. For example, the terms could be "10 EOM" or "Net 10 PROX," which means that the payment is due 10 days after the end of the month (hence the "EOM," for "end of month"). The PROX is an abbreviation for proximo, which is an old commercial term that refers to the next month. This selling term was more commonly used when computer systems were not available, since collection employees would not have to keep track of a wide range of invoice due dates, but instead knew that all invoices were due on the same day of each month, and could conduct collection activities in accordance with that information. This selling term assumes that some customers will be required to pay a little late, and others a little early, so that the average receivable period should be the same as under any other selling terms methodology; however, slow-paying customers who are invoiced near the end of the month will still pay late, which results in a net days' receivable figure that is somewhat longer under this system.

Seasonal dating can also be included in the selling terms. This is used when a company wants to sell goods that are out-of-season, both in order to clear out its warehouse and also to record some revenue during the slow part of the selling season. To do so, it guarantees its customers that they will not have to pay invoices until a specific date has been reached (usually well into the main part of the selling season), no matter when they took delivery. An example of such terms is "5 days, April 1," or "5 April 1," which means that the invoice is due five days after April 1.

There may also be a trade discount listed on an invoice, which is a discount given in exchange for either an especially large-volume order, or because the customer has agreed to purchase goods outside of the normal selling season. This discount is typically listed separately from the time to maturity and cash discount percentage.

An invoice may also state that an interest rate will be charged for payments that exceed a certain late date. Any notation regarding interest rates is typically added as a footnote to the bottom of the invoice. The upper range of this interest rate is bounded by each state's interest rate cap laws. Commonly, the interest rate will begin to apply after a grace period of at least 10 days has passed after the maturity date of the invoice. The interest rate is calculated automatically by the accounting software, which will generate invoices containing the interest rate at the end of each month. The accountant should be prepared to write off the majority of these interest rate charges, since most customers will refuse to pay them. Nonetheless, it can be an effective tool for reminding customers to pay on time.

In situations where customers have a poor credit history, or if the company has an immediate need for cash, its terms will be cash on delivery (COD). Under this arrangement, the company retains title to the shipped goods until payment is made by the customer to the delivery company at the point of shipment delivery. However, this form of selling terms is expensive, since the delivery company charges a fee for collecting the funds, while the company is also liable for the freight on any returned goods if the customer decides not to pay.

The COD concept can be accelerated even more to include either cash in advance for an entire order or progress payments that are doled out by the customer as its order reaches various milestones of completion at the company. These terms are typically used when the product being ordered is a custom one that the company cannot otherwise sell if the customer cancels its order, or if the completion date is so far in the future that the company needs cash in advance in order to have sufficient working capital to complete the order.

34.4   CREDIT EXAMINATION

It can be quite difficult to determine an appropriate credit level for a customer, since the amount of investigation required to develop an accurate picture of a potential customer's financial situation may exceed the time available to the credit department. Accordingly, there are a number of shortcuts discussed in this section that yield good results while requiring less investigative effort. If the amount of credit contemplated is quite high, however, a full and detailed credit review is necessary. The contents of that review are also noted here.

If the amount of credit needed by a customer is quite low, then the credit department can authorize it by default, with no further investigation. However, in order to counterbalance this credit with the risk of loss, the amount given is usually very small. In order to authorize a larger amount of credit, the customer should be asked to fill out a credit form, on which is itemized the contact name of the customer's banker, as well as at least three of its trade references. If these references are acceptable, then the level of credit granted can be increased to a modest level. However, it is a simple matter for a customer in difficult financial straits to influence the credit "picture" that it is presenting to the company, by making sure that all of its trade references are paid on time, even at the expense of its other suppliers, who are paid quite late.

To avoid this difficulty, the credit department can invest in a credit report from one of the credit reporting agencies, such as Dun & Bradstreet. The price can vary from $20 to $70 per report, depending upon the type of information requested and the number of reports ordered (the credit services strongly encourage prepayment in exchange for volume discounts). These services collect payment information from many companies, as well as loan information from public records, financial information from a variety of sources, and on-site visits. The resulting reports give a more balanced view of a customer than its more sanitized trade references list.

Part of the credit report itemizes the average credit granted to the customer by its other trading partners. By averaging this figure, one can arrive at a reasonable credit level for the company to grant it, too. The report will also itemize the average days that it takes the customer to pay its bills. If this period is excessively long, then the credit department can reduce the average credit level granted by some factor, in accordance with the average number of days over which the customer pays its bills. For example, if the average outstanding credit is $1,000, and the customer has a record of paying its bills 10 days late, then the credit department can use the average credit of $1,000 as its basis, and then reduce it by 5% for every day over which its payments are delayed. This would result in the company granting credit of $500 to the customer.

However, credit reports can be manipulated by customers, resulting in misleading or missing information. For example, a privately held firm can withhold information about its financial situation from the credit reporting agency. Also, if it knows that there are some poor payment records listed in its credit report, it can pay the credit agency to contact a specific set of additional suppliers (presumably with a better payment history from the customer), whose results will then be included in the credit report. Also, the information in the average credit report may not be updated very frequently, so the company purchasing the information may be looking at information that is so dated that it no longer relates to the customer's current financial situation.

If the amount of credit requested is much higher than a company is comfortable with granting based on a credit report, then it should ask for audited financial statements from the customer on an annual basis, and subject them to a review that includes the following key items:

- *Age of receivables.* If a customer has trouble receiving its invoices, then it will have less cash available to pay its suppliers. To determine receivables turnover, divide annualized net sales by the average balance of accounts receivable. In order to convert this into the number of days of receivables outstanding, multiply the average accounts receivable figure by 360 and divide the result by annualized net sales.

- *Size and proportion of the allowance for doubtful accounts.* If the customer is reserving an appropriate amount for its expected bad debts, then by comparing the amount of the allowance for doubtful accounts to the total receivable balance, one can see if the customer has overcommitted itself on credit arrangements with its own customers. However, many organizations will not admit (even to themselves) the extent of their bad debt problems, so this figure may be underestimated.

- *Inventory turnover.* A major drain on a company's cash is its inventory. By calculating a customer's inventory turnover (annualized cost of goods sold divided by the average inventory), one can see if it has invested in an excessive quantity of inventory, which may impair its ability to pay its bills.

- *Current and quick ratios.* By comparing the total of all current assets to the total of current liabilities, one can see if a customer has the ability to pay for its debts with currently available resources. If this ratio is below 1:1, then it can be considered a credit risk, though this may be a faulty conclusion if the customer has a large, untapped credit line that it can use to pay off its obligations. A more accurate measure is the quick ratio (cash plus accounts receivable, divided by current liabilities). This ratio does not include inventory, which is not always so easily liquidated, and so provides a better picture of corporate liquidity. Of particular concern when reviewing these ratios is *overtrading*. This is a situation in which the current ratio is poor and debt levels are high, which indicates that the customer is operating with a minimum level of cash reserves, and so is likely to fail in short order. This type of customer tends to have a good payment history up until the point where it completely runs out of available debt to fund its operations and abruptly goes bankrupt.

- *Ratio of depreciation to fixed assets.* If a customer has little available cash, it tends not to replace aging fixed assets. The evidence of this condition lies on the balance sheet, where the proportion of accumulated depreciation to total fixed assets will be very high.

- *Age of payables.* If a customer has little cash, its accounts payable balance will be quite high. To test this, compare the total accounts payable on the balance sheet to total nonpayroll expenses and the cost of goods sold to see if more than one month of expenses is stored in the payables balance.

- *Short-term debt payments.* If a customer cannot pay for its short-term debt requirements, then it certainly cannot pay its suppliers. To check on the level of debt repayment, go to the audited financial statements and review the itemization of minimum debt payments located in the footnotes. This should be compared to the cash flow report to see if there is enough cash to pay for upcoming debt requirements.

- *Amount of equity.* If the amount of equity is negative, then warning bells should be ringing. The customer is essentially operating from debt and supplier credit at this point, and should not be considered a candidate for any credit without the presence of a guarantee or security.

- *Debt/equity ratio.* If investors are unwilling to put in more money as equity, then a customer must fund itself through debt, which requires fixed payments that may interfere with its cash flow. If the proportion of debt to equity is greater than 1:1, then calculate the times interest earned, which is a proportion of the interest expense to cash flow, to see if the company is at risk of defaulting on payments.

- *Gross margin and net profit percentage.* Compare both the gross margin and net profit percentages to industry averages to see if the company is operating within normal profit ranges. The net profit figure can be modified by the customer through the innovative use of standard accounting rules, and so can be somewhat misleading.

- *Cash flow.* If the customer has a negative cash flow from operations, then it is in serious trouble. If, on the other hand, it is on a growth spurt and has negative cash flow because of its investments in working capital and facilities, and has sufficient available cash to fund this growth, then the presence of a strong cash outflow is not necessarily a problem.

The key factor to consider when using any of the preceding credit review items is that the information presented is only a snapshot of the customer's condition at a single point in time. For a better understanding of the situation, the credit department should maintain a trend line of the key financial information for all customers to whom large lines of credit have been extended, so that any deleterious changes will be obvious.

If the financial statements are based on one time of year when the seasonality of sales may be affecting the reported accuracy of a company's financial condition, it may be better to request copies of statements from different periods of the year. For example, the calendar year-to-date June financial statements for a company with large Christmas sales will reveal very large inventory and minimal revenue, which does not accurately reflect its full-year condition.

The presence of potential credit problems will typically appear in just one or two areas, since the customer may be trying to hide the evidence from its suppliers. Fortunately, other sources of information can be used to confirm any suspicions aroused by a review of a customer's financial statements. For example, the sales staff can be asked for an opinion about the visible condition of the customer; if it appears run down, this is strong evidence that there is not enough money available to keep up its appearance.

Also, if the customer is a publicly held entity, a great deal of information is available about it through EDGAR On-line, which carries the last few years' worth of mandatory filings by the customer to the Securities and Exchange Commission. This information can be used to supplement and compare any information provided directly to the company by the customer.

It is critical that the financial information provided by a customer for review is fully audited, and not the result of a review or compilation. These lesser reviews do not ensure that the customer's books have been thoroughly reviewed and approved by an independent auditor, and so may potentially contain incorrect information that could mislead the credit department into issuing too much credit to the customer.

34.5   COLLECTION TECHNIQUES

The collection of overdue accounts receivable can be a messy and prolonged affair that results in irate customers and poor collection results. However, when properly organized, it can result in better customer relations, greatly improved cash flow, and fewer bad debts. To achieve this condition, the underlying collection methodology must be changed, as well as the methods used for contacting and dealing with customers.

The first step in improving the collection function is to reorganize the system that tracks overdue accounts. One approach is to purchase a collections software package that can be custom-designed to link to the existing accounting system. These packages contain a number of features that are most useful for the collections person, such as assigning certain overdue accounts to specific collections employees so that they only see the accounts of customers assigned to them. The software also tracks contact information, stores notes about the most recent conversations with customers, and issues automatic reminders on the dates when customers should be called (even prioritized by time zone, so that calls will only be made during a customer's business hours). These systems can automatically issue dunning letters by fax or e-mail. The end result is a much more organized approach to collections than is normally the case.

If a company cannot afford to invest in such an automated system, it is still possible to create a simplified paper-based system that provides some of the same functionality, though not with the same degree of efficiency. For example, customers can be allocated to specific collections personnel and the accounts receivable aging report sorted in accordance with that allocation, so that subsets of the report are given to each collections person. Also, many aging reports include information about the contact name and phone number for each customer, so these reports can be used as the basis for collection calls. In order to create a history of contact information, each collections person can maintain a binder that includes for each customer a list of alternate contact names throughout their organizations, as well as the resolution of preceding collection problems.

Here are some of the techniques one can use to contact and deal with customers that can greatly improve the amount of money collected, as well as the speed with which it arrives:

- *Approve credit levels in advance.* Before the sales staff makes a sales call, they should first contact the credit department to see what level of credit will be granted. By doing so, the credit department's staff is not placed in the uncomfortable position of approving credit after an order has been received. However, this approach is not of much use if there is limited customer information available, or if the dollar volume of each sale is so small that there would not be much risk of exceeding the credit level.

- *Show respect.* Overriding all collection actions taken, it is critical to treat customers with the proper degree of respect. In the vast majority of cases, customers are not trying to actively defraud a company, but rather are trying to work through a short-term cash shortfall or perhaps have mislaid the payment paperwork. In these cases, shouting at a customer in order to obtain payment will probably have the reverse effect of being paid later in retaliation for the poor treatment.

- *Increase the level of contact.* In keeping with the first point, the level and intensity of contact should gradually increase as the delinquency period extends. For example, the accounting system can automatically send out a reminder e-mail or fax just prior to the due date on an invoice, which may be sufficient for someone at the customer to verify that the paperwork is in order and ready for payment. Then, if a payment is slightly overdue, a collections person can send a polite, nonconfrontational fax to the customer. The next level of contact would be a friendly reminder call that follows up on the information in the fax. If subsequent calls do not rapidly result in resolution, then the level of contact increases by shifting to the manager of the accounts payable staff or some higher accounting position, possibly extending up to the owner or president. Only after these attempts have failed should the intensity of contact become more stern, progressing through more strident dunning letters, shifting to a letter from the corporate attorney, and finally being moved to a collection agency. By taking this approach, the vast majority of all contacts are made in a low-key and nonconfrontational manner, which sets the stage for good long-term collection relations with a customer.

- *Involve the sales staff.* The salesperson who initially sold the product to a customer will have different contacts within that organization than those used by the collections person. By asking the salesperson to assist in collecting funds, a larger number of people can be brought into the payment decision at the customer location. This is particularly effective when salesperson commissions are tied to cash received, rather than invoices issued. Also, if the sales staff is aware of credit problems, they will be less inclined to exacerbate the situation by selling more products to the customer.

- *Contact in advance for large amounts.* If a company has extended a large amount of credit to a customer for a specific order, it makes sense to contact the customer prior to the due date of the invoice, just to make sure that all related paperwork in the accounts payable area is in order, thereby ensuring that the invoice will be paid on time.

- *Document all contacts.* If there is no record of whom a collections person talked to, or when the discussion took place, then it is very difficult to follow up with the correct person after the previously agreed-upon number of days, which results in very inefficient collections work. Instead, each collections person must diligently maintain a log of all activities. If possible, the accounting system should also generate a trend line of payments, so that a collections person can see if there are any developing cash flow problems at a customer.

- *Agree to and enforce a payment plan if necessary.* If a customer simply has no cash available with which to pay off an account receivable, it is reasonable to accept a payment plan under which portions are paid off over time, though one should attempt to obtain payment for the cost of the product as early as possible, so that only the profit margin is delayed. This keeps a company's own cash position from deteriorating, so that it can continue to pay its own bills. If a payment plan is used, the collections person should send a letter by overnight mail to the customer, confirming the terms of the agreement, and then contact the customer immediately if a scheduled payment is late by even one day so that there is no question in the customer's mind that the company takes the collection process seriously and will hold it to the terms of the agreement.

- *Obtain return of goods if customer cannot pay.* There will be a few instances in which the customer has no ability to pay the company at all. When this happens, try to persuade the customer to return the products to the company, even agreeing to pay for return freight if necessary. By doing so, the company can resell the goods and earn its profits elsewhere. This concept does not apply if the goods were custom-made, if freight costs are excessive, if the selling season is over, or if the goods may have sustained some damage.

- *Alter credit terms for problem customers.* If it is apparent that a customer is having ongoing trouble in paying for invoices, then its credit terms must be restricted. This can range from a minor reduction in the dollar total allowed it, or can extend to the use of cash on delivery or even cash in advance terms. This is also an effective collection tool, for the imposition of onerous terms can make a customer more likely to pay for outstanding invoices if there is the prospect of easier terms once the invoices are paid.

- *Block shipments to problem customers.* If a customer has additional orders in process within the company, the collections person should be able to block their shipment until payments have been received on existing invoices. This action is made easier in some enterprise resources planning (ERP) systems, where one can freeze customer orders in the computer system by resetting a flag field in the accounting database.

The preceding recommendations will still allow some bad debts to occur, but the frequency of their incidence and their size will be reduced through the continuing attention to problem accounts that have been outlined here.

34.6   SUMMARY

This chapter has shown that there is a variety of ways in which a company can creatively extend credit to its customers, as well as different terms under which that credit can be paid back. A variety of analytical tools can also be used to determine the most appropriate level of credit that should be granted to a customer, while the collections function can be organized in such a way that bad debt losses are kept to a minimum. The key factor running through all of these tasks is that the customer credit function requires constant vigilance and careful management to ensure that credit losses are reduced, consistent with corporate credit policies.

FINANCING

35.1 INTRODUCTION

A business of any size is likely to require extra funding at some point during its history that exceeds the amount of cash flow that is generated from ongoing operations. This may be caused by a sudden growth spurt that requires a large amount of working capital, an expansion in capacity that calls for the addition of fixed assets, a sudden downturn in the business that requires extra cash to cover overhead costs, or perhaps a seasonal business that calls for extra cash during the off-season. Different types of cash shortages will call for different types of funding, of which this chapter will show that there are many types. In the following sections, we will briefly describe each type of financing and the circumstances under which each one can be used, as well as the management of financing issues and bank relations.

35.2 MANAGEMENT OF FINANCING ISSUES

The procurement of financing should never be conducted in an unanticipated rush, with the management team running around town begging for cash to meet its next cash need. A reasonable degree of planning will make it much easier to not only tell *when* additional cash will be needed, but also *how much*, and what means can be used to obtain it.

To achieve this level of organization, the first step is to construct a cash forecast, which is covered in detail in Chapter 36, Cash Management. With this information in hand, one can determine the approximate amounts of financing that will be needed, as well as the duration of that need. This information is of great value in structuring the correct financing deal. For example, if the company is expanding into a new region and needs working capital for the sales season in that area, then it can plan to apply for a short-term loan, perhaps one that is secured by the accounts receivable and inventory purchased for the store in that region. Alternatively, if the company is planning to expand its production capacity through the purchase of a major new fixed asset, it may do better to negotiate a capital lease for its purchase, thereby only using the new equipment as collateral and leaving all other assets available to serve as collateral for future financing arrangements.

Besides this advanced level of cash flow planning, a company can engage in all of the following activities in order to more properly control its cash requirements and sources of potential financing:

- *Maximize the amount of loans using the borrowing base.* Loans that use a company's assets as collateral will offer lower interest rates, since the risk to the lender is much reduced. The accountant should be very careful about allowing a lender to attach all company assets, especially for a relatively small loan, since this leaves no collateral for use by other lenders. A better approach is to persuade a lender to accept the smallest possible amount of collateral, preferably involving specific assets rather than entire asset categories. The effectiveness of this strategy can be tracked by calculating the percentage of the available borrowing base that has been committed to existing lenders. Also, if the borrowing base has not yet been completely used as collateral, then a useful measurement is to determine the date on which it is likely to be fully collateralized, so that the planning for additional financing after that point will include a likely increase in interest costs.

- *Line up investors and lenders in advance.* Even if the level of cash planning is sufficient for spotting shortages months in advance, it may take that long to find lenders willing to advance funds. Accordingly, the accountant should engage in a search for lenders or investors as early as possible. If this task is not handled early on, then a company may find itself accepting less favorable terms at the last minute. The effectiveness of this strategy can be quantified by tracking the average interest rate for all forms of financing.

- *Minimize working capital requirements.* The best form of financing is to eliminate the need for funds internally, so that the financing is never needed. This is best done through the reduction of working capital, as is described later in the sections devoted to accounts receivable, accounts payable, and inventory reduction in this chapter.

- *Sweep cash accounts.* If a company has multiple locations and at least one bank account for each location, then it is possible that a considerable amount of money is lingering unused in those accounts. By working with its bank, a company can automatically sweep the contents of those accounts into a single account every day, thereby making the best use of all on-hand cash and keeping financing requirements to a minimum.

35.3   BANK RELATIONS

Part of the process of obtaining financing involves the proper care and feeding of one's banking officer. Since one of the main sources of financing is the bank with which one does business, it is exceedingly important to keep one's assigned banking officer fully informed of company activities and ongoing financial results. This should involve issuing at least quarterly financial information to the banking officer, as well as a follow-up call to discuss the results, even if the company is not currently borrowing any funds from the bank. The reasoning behind this approach is that the banking officer needs to become comfortable with the business's officers and also gain an understanding of how the company functions.

Besides establishing this personal relationship with the banking officer, it is also important to centralize as many banking functions as possible with the bank, such as checking, payroll, and savings accounts, sweep accounts, zero balance accounts, and all related services, such as lockboxes and online banking. By doing so, the bank officer will realize that the company is paying the bank a respectable amount of money in fees, and so is deserving of attention when it asks for assistance with its financing problems.

Company managers should also be aware of the types of performance measurements that bankers will see when they conduct a loan review, so that they can work on improving these measurements in advance. For example, the lender will likely review a company's quick and current ratios, debt/equity ratio, profitability, net working capital, and number of days on hand of accounts receivable, accounts payable, and inventory. The banking officer may be willing to advise a company in advance on what types of measurements the bank will examine, as well as the preferred minimum amounts of each one. For example, it may require a current ratio of 2:1, a debt/equity ratio of no worse than 40:1, and days of inventory of no worse than 70. By obtaining this information, a company can restructure itself prior to a loan application in order to ensure that its application will be approved.

Even by taking all of these steps to ensure the approval of financing, company management needs to be aware that the lender may impose a number of restrictions on the company, such as the ongoing maintenance of minimum performance ratios, the halting of all dividends until the loan is paid off, restrictions on stock buybacks and investments in other entities, and (in particular) the establishment of the lender in a senior position for all company collateral. By being aware of these issues in advance, it is sometimes possible to negotiate with the lender to reduce the amount or duration of some of the restrictions.

In short, a company's banking relationships are extremely important, and must be cultivated with great care. However, this is a two-way street that requires the presence of an understanding banking officer at the lending institution. If the current banking officer is not receptive, then it is quite acceptable to request a new one, or to switch banks in order to establish a better relationship.

The remaining sections describe different types of financing that a company can potentially obtain, including the reduction of working capital in order to avoid the need for financing.

35.4   ACCOUNTS PAYABLE PAYMENT DELAY

Though not considered a standard financing technique, since it involves internal processes, one can deliberately lengthen the time periods over which accounts payable are paid. For example, if a payables balance of $1,000,000 is delayed for an extra month, then the company has just obtained a rolling, interest-free loan for that amount, financed by its suppliers.

Though this approach may initially appear to result in free debt, it has a number of serious repercussions. One is that suppliers will catch on to the delayed payments in short order, and begin to require cash in advance or on delivery for all future payments, which will forcibly tell the company when it has stretched its payments too far. Even if it can stay just inside of the time period when these payment conditions will be imposed, suppliers will begin to accord the company a lesser degree of priority in shipments, given its payment treatment of them, and may also increase their prices to it in order to offset the cost of the funds that they are informally extending to the company. Also, if suppliers are reporting payment information to a credit reporting bureau, the late payments will be posted for all to see, which may give new company suppliers reason to cut back on any open credit that they would otherwise grant it.

A further consideration that argues against this practice is that suppliers who are not paid will send the company copies of invoices that are overdue. These invoices may very well find their way into the payment process and be paid alongside the original invoice copies (unless there are controls in place that watch for duplicate invoice numbers or amounts). As a result, the company will pay multiple times for the same invoice, thereby incurring an extra cost.

The only situation in which this approach is a valid one is when the purchasing staff contacts suppliers and negotiates longer payment terms, perhaps in exchange for higher prices or larger purchasing volumes. If this can be done, then the other problems just noted will no longer be issues.

Thus, unless payment delays are formally negotiated with suppliers, the best use of this financing option is for those organizations with no valid financing alternatives, that essentially are reduced to the option of irritating their suppliers or going out of business.

35.5 ACCOUNTS RECEIVABLE COLLECTION ACCELERATION

A great deal of corporate cash can be tied up in accounts receivable for a variety of reasons. A company may have injudiciously expanded its revenues by reducing its credit restrictions on new customers, or it may have extended too much credit to an existing customer that it has no way of repaying in the short term, or it may have sold products during the off-season by promising customers lengthy payment terms, or perhaps it is in an industry where the customary repayment period is quite long. Given the extent of the problem, a company can rapidly find itself in need of extra financing in order to support the amount of unpaid receivables.

This problem can be dealt with in a number of ways. One approach is to offer customers a credit card payment option, which accelerates payments down to just a few days. Another alternative is to review the financing cost and increased bad debt levels associated with the extension of credit to high-risk customers, and eliminate those customers who are not worth the trouble. A third alternative is to increase the intensity with which the collections function is operated, using automated dunning letter (and fax) generation software, collections software that interacts with the accounts receivable files, and ensuring that enough personnel are assigned to the collections task. Finally, it may be possible to reduce the number of days in the standard payment terms, though this can be a problem for existing customers who are used to longer payment terms.

The reduction of accounts receivable should be considered one of the best forms of financing available, since it requires the acquisition of no debt from an outside source.

35.6 CREDIT CARDS

A large company certainly cannot rely upon credit cards as a source of long-term financing, since they are liable to be canceled by the issuing bank at any time, nor are they inexpensive, because credit card rates consistently approach the legal interest limits in each state. Furthermore, they may require someone's personal guarantee. Nonetheless, the business literature occasionally describes accounts by small business owners who have used a large number of credit cards to finance the beginnings of their businesses, sometimes using cash advances from one card to pay off the minimum required payment amounts on other cards. Given the cost of these cards and the small amount of financing typically available through them, this is not a financing method that is recommended for any but the most risk-tolerant and cash-hungry businesses.

35.7   EMPLOYEE TRADEOFFS

In rare cases, it is possible to trade off employee pay cuts in exchange for grants of stock or a share in company profits. However, a company in severe financial straits is unlikely to be able to convince employees to switch from the certainty of a paycheck to the uncertainty of capital gains or a share in profits from a company that is not performing well. If this type of change is forced upon employees, then it is much more likely that the best employees will leave the organization in search of higher compensation elsewhere. Another shortfall of this approach is that a significant distribution of stock to employees may result in employees (or their representatives) sitting on the board of directors.

In short, this option is not recommended as a viable form of financing.

35.8   EQUITY

When a company issues its stock to investors, it may be required to register the stock with the Securities and Exchange Commission (SEC). This is a laborious, expensive, and prolonged process. A better alternative is to use an exemption from the SEC regulations, which allows for a more streamlined equity sale.

One such exemption is available under a Regulation D offering. Under this approach, securities can be sold only to an *accredited investor*. An accredited investor is one whom the issuing company reasonably believes falls within any of these categories at the time of the securities sale:

1. A bank, broker-dealer, insurance company, investment company, or employee benefit plan;
2. A director, executive officer, or general partner of the issuing company;
3. A person whose individual net worth (or joint net worth with a spouse) exceeds $1 million;
4. A person having individual income exceeding $200,000 or joint income with a spouse exceeding $300,000 in each of the last two years, with a reasonable expectation for reaching the same income level in the current year; and
5. Any trust with total assets exceeding $5 million.

Securities sold under a Regulation D offering cannot be resold without registration, so investors can be expected to demand *piggyback rights*, whereby they will be included in the company's next registration document.

Another exemption is available under Regulation A, which allows exemption from registration if an offering is no larger than $5 million in aggregate per year. The exemption is restricted to American and Canadian companies, and it is not available to investment and development-stage (such as blank-check companies) companies. Anyone using this exemption must also create an offering circular, similar to the one that would be required for a registered offering.

There are three critical advantages to the exemption provided under Regulation A.

1. There is no limit on the number of investors, nor must they pass any kind of qualification test (as would be the case under Regulation D).

2. There are no restrictions on the resale of any securities sold under the regulation.

3. The key difference between a Regulation A offering and a registered offering is the absence of any periodic reporting requirements. This is a major reduction in costs to the company and is the most attractive aspect of the exemption.

35.9   FACTORING

Under a factoring arrangement, a finance company agrees to take over a company's accounts receivable collections and keep the money from those collections in exchange for an immediate cash payment to the company. This process typically involves having customers mail their payments to a lockbox that appears to be operated by the company, but which is actually controlled by the finance company. Under a true factoring arrangement, the finance company takes over the risk of loss on any bad debts, though it will have the right to pick which types of receivables it will accept in order to reduce its risk of loss. A finance company is more interested in this type of deal when the size of each receivable is fairly large, since this reduces its per-transaction cost of collection. If each receivable is quite small, the finance company may still be interested in a factoring arrangement, but it will charge the company extra for its increased processing work. The lender will charge an interest rate, as well as a transaction fee for processing each invoice as it is received. There may also be a minimum total fee charged, in order to cover the origination fee for the factoring arrangement in the event that few receivables are actually handed to the lender. A company working under this arrangement can be paid by the factor at once, or can wait until the invoice due date before payment is sent. The latter arrangement reduces the interest expense that a company would have to pay the factor, but tends to go against the reason why the factoring arrangement was established, which is to get money back to the company as rapidly as possible.

A similar arrangement is accounts receivable financing, under which a lender uses the accounts receivable as collateral for a loan, and takes direct receipt of payments from customers, rather than waiting for periodic loan payments from the company. A lender will typically only loan a maximum of 80% of the accounts receivable balance to a company, and only against those accounts that are less than 90 days old. Also, if an invoice against which a loan has been made is not paid within the required 90-day time period, then the lender will require the company to pay back the loan associated with that invoice.

Though both variations on the factoring concept will accelerate a company's cash flow dramatically, it is an expensive financing option, and so is not considered a viable long-term approach to funding a company's operations. It is better for short-term growth situations, where money is in short supply, to fund a sudden need for working capital. Also, a company's business partners may look askance at such an arrangement, since it is an approach associated with organizations that have severe cash flow problems.

35.10   FIELD WAREHOUSE FINANCING

Under a field warehousing arrangement, a finance company (usually one that specializes in this type of arrangement) will segregate a portion of a company's warehouse area with a fence. All inventory within it is collateral for a loan from the finance company to the company. The finance company will pay for more raw materials as they are needed, and is paid back directly from accounts receivable as soon as customer payments are received. If a strict inventory control system is in place, the finance company will also employ someone who will record all additions to and withdrawals from the secured warehouse. If not, then the company will be required to frequently count all items within the secure area and report this information back to the finance company. If the level of inventory drops below the amount of the loan, then the company must pay back the finance company the difference between the outstanding loan amount and the total inventory valuation. The company is also required under state lien laws to post signs around the secured area, stating that a lien is in place on its contents.

Field warehousing is highly transaction intensive, especially when the finance company employs an on-site warehouse clerk, and so is a very expensive way to obtain funds. This approach is only recommended for those companies that have exhausted all other less-expensive forms of financing.

35.11 FLOOR PLANNING

Some lenders will directly pay for large assets that are being procured by a distributor or retailer (such as kitchen appliances or automobiles) and be paid back when the assets are sold to a consumer. In order to protect itself, the lender may require that the price of all assets sold be no lower than the price the lender originally paid for them on behalf of the distributor or retailer. Since the lender's basis for lending is strictly on the underlying collateral (as opposed to its faith in a business plan or general corporate cash flows), it will undertake very frequent recounts of the assets, and compare them to its list of assets originally purchased for the distributor or retailer. If there is a shortfall in the expected number of assets, the lender will require payment for the missing items. The lender may also require liquidation of the loan after a specific time period, especially if the underlying assets run the risk of becoming outdated in the near term.

This financing option is a good one for smaller or underfunded distributors or retailers, since the interest rate is not excessive (due to the presence of collateral).

35.12 INVENTORY REDUCTION

A terrific drain on cash is the amount of inventory kept on hand. The best way to reduce it, and therefore shrink the amount of financing needed, is to install a manufacturing planning system, for which many software packages are available. The most basic is the material requirements planning system (MRP), which multiplies the quantities planned for future production by the individual components required for each product to be created, resulting in a schedule of material quantities to be purchased. In its most advanced form, MRP can schedule component deliveries from suppliers down to a time frame of just a few hours on specific dates. If its shop floor planning component is installed, it can also control the flow of materials through the work-in-process area, which reduces work-in-process inventory levels by avoiding the accumulation of partially completed products at bottleneck operations. Understandably, such a system can make great inroads into a company's existing inventory stocks. A more advanced system, called manufacturing resources planning (MRP II), adds the capabilities of capacity and labor planning, but does not have a direct impact on inventory levels.

The just-in-time (JIT) manufacturing system blends a number of requirements to nearly eliminate inventory. It focuses on short equipment setup times, which therefore justifies the use of very short production runs, which in turn keeps excessive amounts of inventory from being created through the use of *long* production runs. In addition, the system requires that suppliers make small and frequent deliveries of raw materials, preferably bypassing the receiving area and taking them straight to the production workstations where they are needed. Furthermore, the production floor is rearranged into work cells, so that a single worker can walk a single unit of production through several production steps, which not only prevents work-in-process from building up between workstations, but also ensures that quality levels are higher, thereby cutting the cost of scrapped products. The key result of this system is a manufacturing process with very high inventory turnover levels.

The use of inventory planning systems to reduce inventory levels and hence financing requirements is an excellent choice for those organizations already suffering from a large investment in inventory, and that have the money and the time to install such systems. The use of MRP, MRP II, and JIT systems will not be of much help in alleviating short-term cash flow problems, since they can require the better part of a year to implement, and several more years to finetune.

35.13 LEASE

A lease covers the purchase of a specific asset, which is usually paid for by the lease provider on the company's behalf. In exchange, the company pays a fixed rate, which includes interest and principal, to the leasing company. It may also be charged for personal property taxes on the asset purchased. The lease may be defined as an operating lease, under the terms of which the lessor carries the asset on its books and records a depreciation expense, while the lessee records the lease payments as an expense on its books. This type of lease typically does not cover the full life of the asset, nor does the buyer have a small-dollar buyout option at the end of the lease. The reverse situation arises for a capital lease, where the lessee records it as an asset and is entitled to record all related depreciation as an expense. In this latter case, the lease payments are split into their interest and principal portions, and recorded on the lessee's books as such.

The cost of a lease can be reduced by clumping together the purchases of multiple items under one lease, which greatly reduces the paperwork cost of the lender. If there are multiple leases currently in existence, they can be paid off and released through a larger single lease, thereby obtaining a lower financing cost.

The leasing option is most useful for those companies that only want to establish collateral agreements for specific assets, thereby leaving their remaining assets available as a borrowing base for other loans. Leases can be arranged for all but the most financially shaky companies, since lenders can always use the underlying assets as collateral. However, unscrupulous lenders can hide or obscure the interest rate charged on leases, so that less financially knowledgeable companies will pay exorbitant rates.

35.14 LEASE, SYNTHETIC

A synthetic lease has the same accounting treatment as a regular lease, but is treated as a loan for tax purposes, giving the lessee both interest and depreciation expense deductions. Also, given the structure of the lease, the underlying asset being leased does not appear on the company's balance sheet, giving the company the appearance of greater financial stability (especially since neither the related loan interest expense or depreciation are recorded). Further, the company has complete control over the asset, which is not usually the case when leasing from a third party.

In essence, either the company or a third-party lender creates a special-purpose entity (SPE), which obtains a loan to purchase the property, which the SPE then leases to the company. The company's lease payments to the SPE only need to be sufficiently large to cover the SPE's interest payments on the loan. Interest costs tend to be low, since the SPE is separated from the bankruptcy liabilities of the company and the SPE's own operating documents make it difficult to seek bankruptcy protection, which makes it an attractive borrower to lenders.

The main problem with synthetic leases is the cost to create them, which typically makes them a viable alternative only when the asset to be leased costs at least $10 million. Also, the lease is noncancelable, and the company must both manage the property and accept responsibility for any reduction in the property's value by the end of the lease. However, the terms of most synthetic leases allow the company to purchase the asset from the SPE and sell it, thereby eliminating the company's lease liability.

35.15 LINE OF CREDIT

A line of credit is a commitment from a lender to pay a company whenever it needs cash, up to a preset maximum level. It is generally secured by company assets, and for that reason bears an interest rate not far above the prime rate. The bank will typically charge an annual maintenance fee, irrespective of the amount of funds drawn down on the loan, on the grounds that it has invested in the completion of paperwork for the loan. The bank will also likely require an annual audit of key accounts and asset balances to verify that the company's financial situation is in line with the bank's assumptions. One problem with a line of credit is that the bank can cancel the line or refuse to allow extra funds to be drawn down from it if the bank feels that the company is no longer a good credit risk.

The line of credit is most useful for situations in which there may be only short-term cash shortfalls or seasonal needs that result in the line being drawn down to zero at some point during the year. If one's cash requirements are expected to be longer term, then a term note or bond is a more appropriate form of financing.

35.16 LOAN, ASSET-BASED

A loan that uses fixed assets or inventory as its collateral is a common form of financing by banks. The bank will use the resale value of fixed assets (as determined through an annual appraisal) and/or inventory to determine the maximum amount of available funds for a loan. If inventory is used as the basis for the loan, a prudent lender will typically not lend more than 50% of the value of the raw materials and 80% of the value of the finished goods, on the grounds that it may have to sell the inventory in the event of a foreclosure, and may not obtain full prices at the time of sale. Lenders will be much less likely to accept inventory as collateral if it has a short shelf life, is so seasonal that its value drops significantly at certain times of the year, or is subject to rapid obsolescence.

Given the presence of collateral, this type of loan tends to involve a lower interest rate. However, the cost of an annual appraisal of fixed assets or annual audit by the bank (which will be charged to the company) should be factored into the total cost of this form of financing.

35.17   LOAN, BOND

A bond is a fixed obligation to pay, usually at a stated rate of $1,000 per bond, that is issued by a corporation to investors. It may be a *registered bond*, in which case the company maintains a list of owners of each bond. The company then periodically sends interest payments, as well as the final principal payment, to the investor of record. It may also be a *coupon bond*, for which the company does not maintain a standard list of bondholders. Instead, each bond contains interest coupons that the bondholders clip and send to the company on the dates when interest payments are due. The coupon bond is more easily transferable between investors, but the ease of transferability makes them more susceptible to loss.

A bond is generally issued with a fixed interest rate. However, if the rate is excessively low in the current market, then investors will pay less for the face value of the bond, thereby driving up the net interest rate paid by the company. Similarly, if the rate is too high, then investors will pay extra for the bond, thereby driving down the net interest rate paid.

A number of features may be added to a bond in order to make it more attractive for investors. For example, its terms may include a requirement by the company to set up a sinking fund into which it contributes funds periodically, thereby ensuring that there will be enough cash on hand at the termination date of the bond to pay off all bondholders. There may also be a conversion feature that allows a bondholder to turn in his or her bonds in exchange for stock; this feature usually sets the conversion ratio of bonds to stock at a level that will keep an investor from making the conversion until the stock price has changed from its level at the time of bond issuance, in order to avoid watering down the ownership percentages of existing shareholders. A bond offering can also be backed by any real estate owned by the company (called a real property mortgage bond), by company-owned equipment (called an equipment bond), or by all assets (called a general mortgage bond). In rare instances, bonds may even be backed by personal guarantees or by a corporate parent.

There are also features that bondholders may be less pleased about. For example, a bond may contain a call feature that allows the company to buy back bonds at a set price within certain future time frames. This feature may limit the amount of money that a bondholder would otherwise be able to earn by holding the bond. The company may also impose a staggered buyback feature, under which it can buy back some fixed proportion of all bonds at regular intervals. When this feature is activated, investors will be paid back much sooner than the stated payback date listed on the bond, thereby requiring them to find a new home for their cash, possibly at a time when interest rates are much lower than what they would otherwise have earned by retaining the bond. The bondholder may also be positioned last among all creditors for repayment in the event of a liquidation (called a subordinated debenture), which allows the company to use its assets as collateral for other forms of debt; however, it may have to pay a higher interest rate to investors in order to offset their perceived higher degree of risk. The typical bond offering will contain a mix of these features that impact investors from both a positive and negative perspective, depending upon its perceived level of difficulty in attracting investors, its expected future cash flows, and its need to reserve assets as collateral for other types of debt.

Bonds are highly recommended for those organizations large enough to attract a group of investors willing to purchase them, since the bonds can be structured to precisely fit a company's financing needs. Bonds are also issued directly to investors, so there are no financial intermediaries, such as banks, to whom transactional fees must be paid. Also, a company can issue long-maturity bonds at times of low interest rates, thereby locking in modest financing costs for a longer period than would normally be possible with other forms of financing. Consequently, bonds can be one of the lowest-cost forms of financing.

35.18 LOAN, BRIDGE

A bridge loan is a form of short-term loan that is granted by a lending institution on the understanding that the company will obtain longer-term financing shortly that will pay off the bridge loan. This option is commonly used when a company is seeking to replace a construction loan with a long-term note that it expects to gradually pay down over many years. This type of loan is usually secured by facilities or fixtures in order to obtain a modest interest rate.

35.19 LOAN, ECONOMIC DEVELOPMENT AUTHORITY

Various agencies of state governments are empowered to guarantee bank loans to organizations that need funds in geographic areas where it is perceived that social improvement goals can be attained. For example, projects that will result in increased employment or the employment of minorities in specific areas may warrant an application for this type of loan. It is usually extended to finance a company's immediate working capital needs. Given these restrictions, an economic development authority loan is only applicable in special situations.

35.20 LOAN, LONG-TERM

There are several forms of long-term debt. One is a long-term loan issued by a lending institution. These loans tend to be made to smaller companies that do not have the means to issue bonds or commercial paper. To reduce the risk to the lender, these loans typically require the company to grant the lender senior status over all other creditors in the event of liquidation. This is a standard requirement, because the lender is at much greater risk of default over the multiyear term of the loan, when business conditions may change dramatically. If there is no way for a lender to take a senior position on collateral, then the company should expect to pay a much higher interest rate in exchange for dropping the lender into a junior position in comparison to other creditors. If the lender also wants to protect itself from changes in long-term interest rates, it may attempt to impose a variable interest rate on the company. However, if the lender simply creates the loan and then sells it to a third party, it may be less concerned with future changes in the interest rate.

A long-term loan nearly always involves the use of fixed payments on a fixed repayment schedule, which will involve either the gradual repayment of principal, or else the gradual repayment of interest, with the bulk of the principal being due at the end of the loan as a balloon payment. In the latter case, a company may have no intention of paying back the principal, but instead will roll over the debt into a new loan and carry it forward once again. If this is the case, the company treasurer may review the trend of interest rates and choose to roll over the debt to a new loan instrument at an earlier date than the scheduled loan termination date, when interest rates are at their lowest possible levels.

Commercial paper is debt that is issued directly by a company, typically in denominations of $25,000. It is generally unsecured and can be sold in a public market, since it is not registered to a specific buyer. Commercial paper is not an option for smaller companies, since the cost of placing the paper, as well as its level of acceptance in the public markets, will limit its use to only the largest organizations.

In summary, long-term debt is a highly desirable form of financing, since a company can lock in a favorable interest rate for a long time, which keeps it from having to repeatedly apply for shorter-term loans during the intervening years, when business conditions may result in less favorable debt terms.

35.21 LOAN, SHORT-TERM

The most common type of business loan extended by banks is the short-term loan. It is intended to be repaid within one year. The short time frame reduces the risk to the bank, which can be reasonably certain that the business's fortunes will not decline so far within such a short time period that it cannot repay the loan, while the bank will also be protected from long-term variations in the interest rate.

The short-term loan is intended to cover seasonal business needs, so that the cash is used to finance inventory and accounts receivable build-up through the main selling season, and is then repaid immediately after sales levels drop off and accounts receivable are collected. It can also be used for short-term projects, such as for the financing of the production requirements for a customer project that will be repaid as soon as the customer pays for the completed work. For these reasons, the timing of repayment on the loan should be right after the related business activity has been completed.

In some cases, a company may obtain such a loan if it really needs a long-term loan, but feels that it will obtain lower interest rates on long-term debt if it waits for interest rates to come down. However, this strategy can backfire if interest rates are on an upward trend, since a company will be at risk of large changes in interest rates every time that it pays off a short-term debt instrument and rolls the funds over into a new short-term loan.

35.22 PRIVATE INVESTMENT IN PUBLIC EQUITY

A private investment in public equity (PIPE) involves the sale of a public company's equity to accredited private investors, usually at a discount of about 10% to 20% below the market price. Because a PIPE is a private investment, it does not require registration with the SEC, can be completed quickly, and involves less administrative expense than would be the case for a large public offering. Since stock is sold in large blocks under this method, a company tends to gain larger, more long-term investors, especially if the issuing company sells the shares directly, and so can select which investors it wants.

However, some PIPE agreements also require a company to pay out additional shares if its stock price falls within a certain time period, which can result in a considerable level of ownership dilution for other investors. It may also be necessary to sweeten the PIPE deal with warrants or a variety of conversion options that are highly favorable to the investor. Another problem arises when an investment bank is used to find investors, since the company no longer has control over who is buying its shares, which may result in an investor pool with short-term cash-out expectations. This last problem can be handled to some extent by forcing investors to sign lock-up agreements under which they will not sell their shares for a certain period of time.

The worst-case scenario when a PIPE is used is when the PIPE agreement grants more shares to investors when the common stock price declines. When manipulated by short selling, a company may find that its share price declines precipitously, requiring more stock to be issued, followed by more short selling, and so on, until the company's ownership shifts to the PIPE investors. This is known as a death spiral PIPE. To avoid this problem, the PIPE agreement should specify a floor price below which no further shares of compensatory stock will be issued to investors.

35.23   PREFERRED STOCK

Preferred stock contains elements of both equity and debt, since it generally pays interest on the amount of funding paid in. However, the interest may be withheld on a cumulative basis by order of the board of directors, the shares do not have to be repaid, and they may be convertible to common stock. Also, the interest on preferred stock is considered a dividend under the tax laws, and so is not tax-deductible. As a result, the cost of preferred stock tends to be higher than other forms of debt, and, if the stock is convertible, shareholders may find that their ownership has been diluted by the preferred shareholders who have converted their shares to common stock.

Preferred stock is a good solution for those organizations that are looking for a long-term source of funds without a requirement to make fixed interest payments on *specific* dates (since preferred stock dividends can be deferred). It is also useful for companies that are being forced by their lending institutions to improve their debt/equity ratios, but that do not want to reduce the ownership percentages of their existing common stockholders through the infusion of new equity (only an option if the preferred shares are not convertible to common stock).

35.24   SALE AND LEASEBACK

Under this arrangement, a company sells one of its assets to a lender and then immediately leases it back for a guaranteed minimum time period. By doing so, the company obtains cash from the sale of the asset that it may be able to more profitably use elsewhere, while the leasing company handling the deal obtains a guaranteed lessee for a time period that will allow it to turn a profit on the financing arrangement. A sale and leaseback is most commonly used for the sale of a corporate building, but can also be arranged for other large assets, such as production machinery.

A sale and leaseback is useful for companies in any type of financial condition, for a financially healthy organization can use the resulting cash to buy back shares and prop up its stock price, while a faltering organization can use the cash to fund operations. Obviously, it is only an option for those organizations that have substantial assets available for sale.

35.25   SUMMARY

The previous discussion shows that there is a large array of approaches available to solve the problem of obtaining financing. The best ones by far involve the reduction of a company's working capital needs through internal management and process-oriented streamlining techniques, thereby reducing or eliminating the need for any financing. Once this approach has been maximized, a company that properly forecasts its cash needs and then makes long-range plans for the procurement of financing in the required amounts will be in a much better position to obtain the lowest-cost financing, as opposed to those organizations that must scramble for funding at the last minute.

CASH MANAGEMENT

36.1 INTRODUCTION

Cash management is absolutely crucial to the operation of any but the most wealthy organizations. If there is ever a cash shortfall, payroll cannot be met, suppliers are not paid, scheduled loan payments will not be made, and investors will not receive dividend checks. Any one of these factors can either bring down a business or ensure a change in its management in short order.

In order to avoid these problems, this chapter covers how to construct a cash forecast and automate the creation of some of the information contained within it, as well as how to create a feedback loop for gradually increasing the accuracy of the forecast. We also describe a number of methods for concentrating cash flows as well as how to invest excess funds.

36.2 THE CASH FORECASTING MODEL

The core of any cash management system is the cash forecast. It is imperative for the management team to be fully apprised of any cash problems with as much lead time as possible. The sample model shown in Exhibit 36.1 is a good way to provide this information.

The cash forecast in the exhibit lists all cash activity on a weekly basis for the next nine weeks, which is approximately two months. These are followed by a partial month, which is needed in case the month that falls after the first nine weeks is also contained within the nine weeks. In the exhibit, the first week of May is listed, so the remaining three weeks of that month are described within a partial month column. There are also two more full months listed in the last two columns. By using this columnar format, the reader can see the expected cash flows for the next one-third of a year. The final two months on the

Cash Forecast

Date Last Updated	**3/9/10**									(partial)		
					For the Week Beginning on							
	3/9/10	3/16/10	3/23/10	3/30/10	4/6/10	4/13/10	4/20/10	4/27/10	5/4/10	May-10	Jun-10	Jul-10
Beginning Cash Balance	$1,037,191	$1,034,369	$968,336	$967,918	$918,082	$932,850	$918,747	$829,959	$834,924	$754,124	$808,592	$798,554
Receipts from Sales Projections:												
Coal Bed Drilling Corp.								$12,965		$16,937		$174,525
Oil Patch Kids Corp.										$48,521		$28,775
Overfault & Sons Inc.									$2,500		$129,000	
Platte River Drillers									$3,000	$53,000		
Powder River Supplies Inc.											$18,500	$14,500
Submersible Drillers Ltd.									$8,700	$2,500	$16,250	$16,250
Commercial, Various											$25,000	$25,000
Uncollected Invoices:												
Canadian Drillers Ltd.			$9,975									
Coastal Mudlogging Co.			$6,686									
Dept. of the Interior		$1,823		$11,629						$18,510		
Drill Tip Repair Corp.				$5,575		$2,897						
Overfault & Sons Inc.			$9,229									
Submersible Drillers Ltd.				$4,245								
U.S. Forest Service	$	$2,967	$812	$8,715								
Cash, Minor Invoices	$2,355	—	$3,668	—	$21,768							
Total Cash In	$4,178	$2,967	$30,370	$30,164	$21,768	$2,897	—	$12,965	$14,200	$139,468	$188,750	$259,050

EXHIBIT 36.1 SAMPLE CASH FORECAST

Cash Forecast

Date Last Updated	3/9/10											
				For the Week Beginning on							(partial)	
	3/9/10	3/16/10	3/23/10	3/30/10	4/6/10	4/13/10	4/20/10	4/27/10	5/4/10	May-10	Jun-10	Jul-10
Cash Out:												
Payroll + Payroll Taxes		$ 62,000		$ 65,000			$ 68,000		$ 71,000	$ 71,000	$ 138,000	$ 138,000
Commissions				$ 7,000					$ 7,000		$ 8,000	$ 9,000
Rent			$ 10,788				$ 10,788			$ 10,788	$ 10,788	$ 10,788
Capital Purchases			$ 10,000		$ 10,000				$ 10,000		$ 10,000	$ 10,000
Other Expenses	$ 7,000	$ 7,000	$ 10,000	$ 8,000	$ 7,000	$ 7,000	$ 10,000	$ 8,000	$ 7,000	$ 14,000	$ 32,000	$ 32,000
Total Cash Out:	$ 7,000	$ 69,000	$ 30,788	$ 80,000	$ 17,000	$ 7,000	$ 88,788	$ 8,000	$ 95,000	$ 85,000	$ 198,788	$ 199,788
Net Change in Cash	$ (2,822)	$ (66,033)	$ (418)	$ (49,836)	$ 14,768	$ (14,103)	$ (88,788)	$ 4,965	$ (80,800)	$ 54,468	$ (10,038)	$ 59,262
Ending Cash:	$ 1,034,369	$ 968,336	$ 967,918	$ 918,082	$ 932,850	$ 918,747	$ 829,959	$ 834,924	$ 754,124	$ 808,592	$ 798,554	$ 857,816
Budgeted Cash Balance:			897,636					833,352		800,439	815,040	857,113

EXHIBIT 36.1 SAMPLE CASH FORECAST (*Continued*)

forecast will tend to be much less accurate than the first two, but are still useful for making estimates about likely cash positions.

The top row on the report in the exhibit lists the date when the cash report was last updated. This is crucial information, for some companies will update this report every day, and the management team does not want to confuse itself with information on old reports. The next row contains the beginning cash balance. The leftmost cell in the row is encircled by heavy lines, indicating that the person responsible for the report should update this cell with the actual cash balance as of the first day of the report. The remaining cells in the row are updated from the ending cash balance for each period that is listed at the bottom of the preceding column. The next block of rows contains the expected receipt dates for sales that have not yet occurred. It is useful to break these down by specific customer and type of sale, rather than summarizing them into a single row, so that the sales staff can be held responsible for this information. The sales staff should review this information regularly to see if the timing and amount of each expected cash receipt is still correct.

The next block of rows in the exhibit shows the specific weeks within which accounts receivable are expected to be collected. This section can become quite large and difficult to maintain if there are many accounts receivable, so it is better to only list the largest items by customer, and then lump all others into a minor invoices row, as is the case in the exhibit. The input of the collections staff should be sought when updating these rows, since they will have the best insights into collection problems. The sum of all the rows thus far described is then listed in the "Total Cash In" row.

The next block of rows in the exhibit shows the various uses for cash. A service company is being used in this forecast, so the largest single use of cash is payroll, rather than the cost of goods sold, as would be the case in a manufacturing company. Other key cash outflows, such as monthly commission and rental payments, as well as capital purchases, are shown in the following rows. Being a service business, there are few other expenses, so they are lumped together in an "other expenses" row. In this case, cash payments have a slight tendency to be toward the beginning of the month, so the cash flows are adjusted accordingly. If the cost of goods sold had been a major component of the forecast, then it would have either been listed in aggregate and based on a percentage of total sales, or else split into a different cash outflow for each product line. The latter case is more useful when the gross margin is significantly different for each product line, and when the sales by product line vary considerably over time.

There are a few other rows that could be added to the model, depending upon the type of payments that a company makes. For example, there could be an annual dividend payment, quarterly income tax payment, or monthly principal and interest payments to lenders. These and other items can be added to enhance the basic model, if needed. However, the model requires considerable effort to update, so one should carefully consider the extra workload needed before adding more information requirements to it.

The bottom of the exhibit summarizes the end-of-period cash position, while also comparing it to the budgeted cash balance for the end of each month. The comparison is important, for it tells management if actual results are departing significantly from expectations.

The exhibit assumes a high degree of manual data entry, rather than automation, but it is certainly possible to use additional formulas in the model in order to reduce the work required to update it. For example, an aggregate assumption can be made regarding the days of receivables that are generally outstanding, and have the model determine the total amount of cash receipts from existing invoices based on that assumption. However, if the total amount of accounts receivable is skewed in favor of a few large invoices, any changes in the timing of cash receipts for those few invoices can significantly alter the aggregate assumption for the number of days outstanding. Similarly, a day of inventory assumption is generally acceptable for deriving a cash usage figure for inventory purchases, but this is highly dependent upon the ability of the production department to manufacture exactly in accordance with the production schedule so that actual inventory levels stay near their planned levels, while the purchasing staff only buys components in the quantities itemized by the manufacturing planning system.

36.3   MEASURING CASH FORECAST ACCURACY

A cash forecast is useless unless it can be relied upon to yield accurate forecasts. There are a number of ways to improve the forecast, all involving the continuing comparison of past forecasts to actual results and correcting the system to ensure that better information is provided for future forecasts.

A key area in which the cash forecast can be wildly incorrect is in receipts from sales forecasts. A detailed review of this area will reveal that some salespersons do not want to forecast any sales, because then they will be held accountable for their predictions. This problem requires constant feedback with the sales staff to correct, and may require reinforcement by including the sales forecasting function in the annual review and compensation plan for them.

Another problem is in the accounts payable area, where actual cash outflows will typically exceed forecast cash outflows. This imbalance is caused by a faulty accounts payable data entry process, whereby invoices are initially mailed by suppliers to people outside of the accounts payable department, or because invoices are sent out for approval before they are logged into the accounting system, thereby resulting in their late appearance in the forecast, usually just before they need to be paid. These problems can be solved by asking suppliers to send invoices straight to the accounting department, and by entering all invoices into the accounting system before sending them out for approval. It is also possible to review open purchase orders to see if there are any missing invoices that are supposed to be currently payable, thereby proactively starting a search for the missing invoices.

A major cash flow variance will arise if a fixed asset is suddenly purchased that was not included in the cash forecast. This problem is best resolved by giving the accounting staff complete access to the capital budgeting process so that it can tell what capital requests are in queue for approval and when they are likely to require cash payments to obtain.

In short, the accuracy of the cash forecast requires great attention to processes that provide its source data. The accounting staff should regularly compare forecasted to actual results and work their way back through the underlying systems to determine what issues caused the error—and then correct them.

36.4   CASH FORECASTING AUTOMATION

The steps just noted to create a cash forecast can be quite cumbersome to accumulate, especially if there are multiple departments or subsidiaries spread out across many locations. When the cash forecast is generated on a regular basis, the required workload can be extraordinarily high. Automation can be used to avoid some of the most time-consuming steps.

Many off-the-shelf accounting software packages contain standard reports that itemize the daily or weekly time buckets in which payments are scheduled to be made, based on each supplier invoice date and the number of days before they are due for payment, including any requirements for early payment in order to take advantage of early payment discounts. The cash flow information provided by this report is quite reliable, but tends to be less accurate for the time period several weeks into the future, because of delays in the entry of supplier invoice information into the accounting system. This delay is usually caused by the divergence of incoming invoices to managers for approval. By first entering the invoice information and *then* sending the invoices out for approval, this time delay can be avoided, thereby improving the accuracy of the automated accounts payable payment timing report.

If there is a well-managed purchase order system in place that is stored in a purchasing database, then the accounts payable report format can be stretched further into the future with some accuracy. Since purchase orders may be issued for some months into the future, and involve specific delivery dates, this information can be compiled into a report that reveals when the payments to suppliers based on these purchase orders will be sent out. It is also useful for the purchase of fixed assets, since these orders are so large that suppliers will not normally process an order in the absence of a signed purchase order. However, a large asset purchase may require an up-front payment that will not become apparent until the purchase order is entered into the accounting system, which will result in the sudden appearance of a large cash requirement on the report in the near future.

There are some instances in which invoice payments can be predicted for well into the future even in the absence of a purchase order. These are typically recurring payments in a constant amount, such as facility lease payments or maintenance payments that are prespecified under a long-term contract. If these payments are listed in the accounts payable system as recurring invoices, then the accounts payable payment timing report will include them.

The same report is available in many accounting software packages for accounts receivable, itemizing the day or week buckets in which invoice payments are scheduled to be received, based on their original issuance dates and the number of days before customers are required to pay for them. However, this report tends to be much less accurate, for any overdue invoice payments are scheduled for immediate payment in the current period, when in fact there may be collection problems that will delay receipt for quite some time. Also, the report does not account for the average delay in payments that varies by each customer, in accordance with each one's timeliness in making payments. Consequently, this report should be manually modified, especially for the largest outstanding invoices, to reflect the accounting staff's best estimates of when payments will actually be received.

In a few cases, software packages will also extend current payroll payments into the future, by assuming that the existing salaries for current employees will continue at the same rates and that hourly employees will be paid for a regular work week for all future reporting periods. This is not a viable option for those companies that outsource their payroll, since the in-house software will not have any way to predict cash flows if it does not contain any information about payroll.

The preceding discussion shows that there are numerous ways in which elements of the cash forecast can be automated. However, there are so many variables, such as uncertain receipt dates for accounts receivable, changes in payroll levels, and the sudden purchase of fixed assets, that any automatically generated reports should be adjusted by the accounting staff's knowledge of special situations that will throw off the results of the reports. Also, the basis for automated reports is primarily very short-term accounts receivable and payable information that will rapidly become inaccurate for periods much greater than a month, so manual adjustments to the cash forecast will become increasingly necessary for later time periods.

36.5 CASH MANAGEMENT CONTROLS

Once a cash forecasting system is in place, one can tell if there will be cash flow difficulties coming up in the short term and take steps to ensure that the problems are minimized. In this section, we look at a variety of methods for controlling the flow of cash, which involves not only a speeding up of the cash handling process, but also an increased focus on reducing a company's cash requirements in all operational areas. The specific items are:

- *Avoid early payments.* Though it seems obvious, the accounts payable department will pay suppliers early from time to time. This can occur because the accounting staff has already input a default payment interval into the accounting computer, and is not regularly reviewing supplier invoices to see if the payment terms have changed. It is also possible that only a few check runs are being printed per month, which results in some invoices being paid slightly early, simply because the next check run is not scheduled for some time; this can be avoided through the use of either more check runs or the implementation of a policy to only pay on or after the payment due date, thereby shifting these checks to a later check run.

- *Avoid engineering design changes.* If minor modifications are allowed to be made to products currently in production, this probably means that some parts that were included in the old design will no longer fit in the new design. Unless great care is taken to use up all of the old parts prior to switching to the modified product, there will be a gradual build-up of parts in the warehouse that can no longer be used, thereby increasing the company's investment in raw materials inventory. For this reason, the value received from design changes must be clearly proven to outweigh their added inventory cost.

- *Avoid stuffing the distribution pipeline.* One way to manufacture abnormally high sales is to offer especially good deals to one's customers, thereby dumping on them an excessive quantity of goods. However, doing so will eventually backfire on the company, since customers will not need to purchase from the company again for some time, resulting in reduced future sales. For the purposes of this discussion, the issue is particularly important if the deal offered to customers is delayed payment in exchange for their accepting goods immediately. By doing so, a company greatly increases the amount of cash that is needed to fund a much larger accounts receivable balance.

- *Conduct a prompt bank reconciliation.* The management team can find itself scrambling for cash if the bank's and the company's cash records diverge significantly, due to delays in completing a bank reconciliation. To avoid this, it is possible to conduct a bank reconciliation every day through an online connection to the bank's database, or at least by immediately completing the reconciliation as soon as the report is received from the bank.

- *Eliminate excess checking accounts.* Most checking accounts do not earn interest on the funds stored within them, so the presence of more than one account means that an excess volume of cash is being spread out in too many accounts. By evaluating the need for each checking account and consolidating as many as possible, one can reduce the amount of unused cash in the system. For a further refinement to this approach, see the later comment in this section about zero balance accounts.

- *Eliminate invoicing errors.* An invoicing error of any type can result in a greatly delayed customer payment, while the problem is identified and corrected. To avoid this problem, the accounting department should keep a log of all errors encountered, and assign a task force to the chore of altering the invoicing process in order to eliminate the errors in the future.

- *Improve sales forecast accuracy.* If the forecasts upon which the production schedule is based are inaccurate, then there is a strong chance that there will be some production overages, which will result in excess inventory that must be funded for a long time, until the inventory can be sold off. This forecasting error can be improved upon by obtaining direct access to the forecasts of the company's customers, so that the production scheduling staff can see exactly what the demand levels are likely to be. It is also possible to switch to a just-in-time manufacturing system, where the focus is on producing to order, rather than to a forecast (though by no means always achievable). At a minimum, one should compare sales forecasts to historical sales records at both the customer and product level to see if the forecasts have any basis in historical fact, and investigate those with the greatest variances.

- *Install lockboxes.* Most banks offer the service of opening one's mail, extracting customer payments, and depositing them directly into one's account, which can shave anywhere from one to three days off the transit time required to move cash into one's account. The savings is especially great if lockboxes are distributed throughout the country, so that customers are directed to send their payments to those lockboxes located nearest to them. This requires the company to contact all customers and request them to shift their payments to the lockbox address, which will be a post office box number. In exchange for this service, the bank will charge a small monthly service fee, plus a fee for each check processed. During the processing of cash, the bank will photocopy each incoming check and mail it to the company so that the accounts receivable staff can record the cash receipt in the accounting computer system.

- *Install zero balance accounts.* The concentration of all available cash can be heightened not only through the use of lockboxes, but also by keeping the resulting cash in investment accounts and then shifting the cash automatically to the checking accounts only when checks are drawn against them. This type of checking account is called a zero balance account. It can also be used for a payroll account.

- *Lengthen supplier payment terms.* If a few key suppliers have required the company to pay on very short terms, then this can greatly reduce the amount of cash that a company has available. The purchasing staff should be asked to negotiate with these suppliers to lengthen terms, perhaps at the cost of committing to larger purchasing volumes or slightly higher prices. When this change takes place, the purchasing staff must notify the accounting department, or else it will continue to pay on the original shorter terms, which are already listed in the accounts payable system, and will automatically be used for all future payments unless manually changed.

- *Outsource cash-intensive functions.* Some activities, such as computer services, require considerable investments in capital equipment. To avoid this expenditure, those departments can be outsourced to a supplier, thereby not only avoiding additional asset investments, but also allowing the company to sell off any existing assets, perhaps to the supplier that takes over the function. This tends to be a longer-term solution, since shifting any function outside a company requires a great deal of transitional planning.

- *Reduce purchasing overages.* An overly efficient purchasing department can buy greater quantities of items than are strictly needed in the short term, on the grounds that it does not want to issue a number of purchase orders for small quantities when a single order would have sufficed, thereby saving it a great deal of personnel time. These large purchases can lead to a considerable excess use of cash. A good way to avoid this problem is to invest in a materials management system, such as material requirements planning (MRP), under which the system specifies exactly what materials to buy, and can even issue the required purchase orders. The purchasing staff can also be evaluated based on the number of raw material inventory turns, which will focus them away from making unnecessarily large purchases.

- *Sell fixed assets.* The accounting department should regularly review the complete list of fixed assets to see if there are any that are no longer in use, and so can be sold. Though this task should be left up to the department managers, cash conservation is not one of their primary tasks, and so they tend to ignore old assets. One way around this performance problem is to measure department managers based on their return on assets; by doing so, they will constantly work to reduce the asset base for which they are responsible, which will lead to the increased conversion of old assets into cash.

- *Sell obsolete inventory.* The accounting staff should create a report that shows which inventory items have not been used recently, or which items are stocked in such excessive quantities that they will not be drawn down for a long time. With this information, the purchasing department can contact suppliers to sell back the inventory or obtain credits against future purchases. If neither approach will work, the company may still be able to obtain a tax deduction by donating the inventory to a nonprofit organization.

- *Tighten customer credit.* If the accounts receivable balance appears to be disproportionately high or if the proportion of overdue accounts receivable is excessive, then reduce the amount of credit extended to selected customers. However, this can interfere with the corporate growth rate if the strategy involves increasing sales through the use of easy credit.

- *Tighten the process flow that results in cash.* The entire process of taking a customer order, building the product, delivering it, sending an invoice, and receiving payment can be an extraordinarily involved and lengthy one. If it is handled improperly, the inflow of cash once a customer order has been received will be greatly delayed. In order to avoid this problem, one should periodically reexamine the entire process with the objective of minimizing the time required to receive cash at the end of the process. For example, one can avoid queue times when orders are waiting in the "in" boxes of employees by concentrating as many steps in the hands of one employee as possible (called process centering). Another possibility is to replace portions of the existing system with new technology, such as the use of lockboxes to accelerate the receipt of cash, or the use of a centralized ordering database that tracks the flow of orders through the system. For information about tightening the process, please refer to Bragg, *Just-in-Time Accounting*, 3rd Edition (John Wiley & Sons, 2009).

- *Use a manufacturing planning system.* Any production planning system will greatly streamline the flow of materials through a manufacturing facility. Accordingly, any company engaged in production should invest in a material requirements planning (MRP), manufacturing resources planning (MRP II), or just-in-time (JIT)

If Paid On:	1/10, N 30	2/10, N 30
Day 10	0%	0%
Day 20	36.9%	73.8%
Day 30	18.5%	36.9%
Day 40	12.3%	24.6%

EXHIBIT 36.2   ANNUAL INTEREST COST OF NOT TAKING A CASH DISCOUNT

system. Though all have different underlying concepts and methods of operation, they will all result in reduced inventory levels. When properly installed, the JIT system is particularly effective in achieving this result.

- *Verify times when cash discounts are applicable.* Though it is standard practice to always take discounts in exchange for early payments to suppliers whenever they are offered, one should verify that the discounts taken are worth their cost. As noted in Exhibit 36.2, there are situations in which it does not make sense to take the discount. For example, the second column of the exhibit shows that an invoice paid on regular terms of 30 days, rather than at a discount of 1% after 10 days have passed, will have a net annualized interest cost to the company of 18.5%. We derive the 18% figure from the 1% interest cost that the company is incurring to wait an extra 20 days to make a payment; since there are roughly eighteen 20-day periods in a year, the annualized interest rate is about 18 times 1%, or 18%. To take the example a step further, if cash is in such short supply that the company cannot pay for the early discount, and in fact can only pay after 40 days have passed, its cost of funds will have dropped to 12.3%, which may be quite close to its existing cost of funds, and so may appear to be a reasonable alternative to paying early.

A key issue in the preceding bullet points is that the opportunity to manage cash lies in all areas of a company, for the points covered include the finance, accounting, production, sales, distribution, and engineering departments. Thus, the management of cash should not be considered the sole responsibility of the finance and accounting departments.

36.6   THE BENEFITS OF CASH CONCENTRATION

The typical company has a number of bank accounts, each containing either a credit balance or a debit balance that is being covered by a bank overdraft. At a small-company level, and in the absence of a formal controller position, these balances probably are monitored by an assistant controller, with occasional cash transfers to cover debit balances. Interest income is probably minimal.

As the company becomes larger and the number of its bank accounts expands, the total volume of idle cash balances becomes too great to ignore. At this stage, the company hires a controller to manage the cash. The controller likely will advance the following list of benefits related to aggregating the cash in all of those bank accounts:

- *Elimination of idle cash.* The controller's best argument will be that cash idling in a multitude of accounts can be aggregated into interest-earning investments.
- *Improved investment returns.* If the company's cash can be aggregated, then it is easier to allocate the cash into short-term, low-yield investments and

Scenario without Cash Concentration

	Overdraft Interest Rate	Credit Balance Interest Rate	Cash Balance in Account	Annual Interest
Subsidiary 1	8%	3%	$ 100,000	$ 3,000
Subsidiary 2	8%	3%	(50,000)	(4,000)
Subsidiary 3	8%	3%	(35,000)	(2,800)
Subsidiary 4	8%	3%	75,000	2,250
		Totals	$ 90,000	$ (1,550)

Scenario with Cash Concentration

	Overdraft Interest Rate	Credit Balance Interest Rate	Cash Balance in Account	Annual Interest
Subsidiary 1	8%	3%	-	-
Subsidiary 2	8%	3%	-	-
Subsidiary 3	8%	3%	-	-
Subsidiary 4	8%	3%	-	-
		Total	$ 90,000	$ 2,700

EXHIBIT 36.3 CHANGE IN INTEREST INCOME FROM CASH CONCENTRATION BANKING

higher-yield, longer-term investments. The overall results should be an improved return on investment.

- *More cost-effective oversight of accounts.* When an automated sweeping arrangement is used to concentrate cash, there is no need to review subsidiary account balances manually. This can yield a significant reduction in labor costs.
- *Internal funding of debit balances.* Where a company is grappling with ongoing debit balance problems in multiple accounts, the avoidance of high-cost bank overdraft charges alone may be a sufficient incentive to use cash concentration. An example of the change in costs is shown in Exhibit 36.3. In the first part of the exhibit, ABC Company has bank accounts at four of its subsidiaries. Each of the accounts earns the same 3% interest rate on credit balances while the banks all charge the same 8% rate on debit balances (overdrafts). In the second part of the exhibit, ABC shifts all of its funds into a cash concentration account, thereby avoiding the 8% overdraft charge, and realizing a significant improvement in its interest income.

In the exhibit, interest income improves by $4,250, which makes cash concentration cost effective as long as the sweeping fee charged by the bank is less than that amount.

36.7 CASH CONCENTRATION STRATEGIES

A company having multiple locations can pursue a variety of cash concentration strategies, which tend to bring larger benefits with greater centralization. The five strategies are:

1. *Complete decentralization.* Every subsidiary or branch office with its own bank account manages its own cash position. This is fine if balances are small, so that there is little synergy to be gained by concentrating cash in a single account. However, if large cash balances are languishing in some accounts or other accounts are incurring overdraft charges, then a more centralized approach is called for. A more

advanced version of this strategy is to centralize accounts in the country of currency (e.g., dollars are kept in the United States and yen are kept in Japan). This alternative is transactionally efficient but does not centralize cash sufficiently for investment purposes.

2. *Centralized payments, decentralized liquidity management.* A company can implement a centralized payment factory that handles all payables for all company subsidiaries but issues payments from local accounts. This method improves the overall planning for cash outflows but does not improve the management of excess cash balances, for which local managers are still responsible. Also, if investments are managed at the local level, there is a greater risk that the corporate investment policy will not be followed.

3. *Centralized liquidity management, decentralized payments.* The accounting staff centralizes cash into a concentration account (either through sweeps or notional pooling) and has responsibility for investments. However, local managers are still responsible for disbursements.

4. *All functions centralized.* The accounting staff pools all cash into a concentration account, invests it, and manages disbursements. This is an excellent structure for optimizing investment income and also gives the controller considerable control over the accounts payable portion of the company's working capital. Larger companies usually follow this strategy but may not carry it through to cross-border centralization. Instead, they may centrally manage key currencies, such as euros and dollars, while allowing regional control over other currencies.

   In cases where cash is invested from a central location and multiple currencies are involved, it may be necessary for the accounting staff to invest funds locally (i.e., in the home country of the currency), because of legal or foreign exchange restrictions.

The most centralized of these strategies is the most efficient approach for cash concentration, but it may not be the most cost effective. If a company has relatively few subsidiaries with low account balances, creating a central accounting staff to manage the cash may add more overhead than will be offset by increased interest income or reduced interest expense.

36.8 POOLING CONCEPTS

Cash concentration requires that a company create a *cash pool.* This is comprised of a cluster of subsidiary bank accounts and a concentration account. Funds physically flow from the subsidiary accounts into the concentration account under a *physical sweeping* method. Alternatively, cash balances in the subsidiary accounts can be concentrated in the master account only within the bank's records, with the cash remaining in the subsidiary accounts. This later method is called *notional pooling.*

If a pooling arrangement includes accounts located in more than one country, this is known as a *cross-border cash pool.* A company may elect to pool cash within the home country of each currency (e.g., U.S. dollars are pooled in the United States), which is known as the *single currency–center* model. If a company pools all of its foreign currency accounts in a single location, this is a *multi–currency center* arrangement. Multi–currency centers are generally easier to manage, but transactions are more expensive than under the single currency–center model.

36.9 PHYSICAL SWEEPING

When a company sets up a *zero-balance account*, its bank automatically moves cash from that account into a concentration account, usually within the same bank. The cash balance in the zero-balance account (as the name implies) is reduced to zero whenever a sweep occurs. If the account has a debit balance at the time of the sweep, then money is shifted from the concentration account back into the account having the debit balance. An example is shown in Exhibit 36.4.

In the example, two of three subsidiary accounts initially contain credit (positive) balances, and Account C contains a debit (negative) balance. In the first stage of the sweep transaction, the cash in the two accounts having credit balances are swept into the concentration account. In the next stage of the sweep, sufficient funds are transferred from the concentration account to offset the debit balance in Account C. At the end of the sweep, then, there are no credit or debit balances in the zero-balance accounts.

It is also possible to use *constant balancing* to maintain a predetermined minimum balance in a subsidiary account, which involves sweeping only those cash levels above the minimum balance and reverse sweeping cash into the subsidiary account if the balance drops below the minimum balance.

Daily sweeping may not be necessary outside of a company's designated core currencies. This is especially likely when non–core currency account balances are relatively low. If so, it may be more cost effective to sweep them less frequently or to implement *trigger balances*. A trigger balance is an account balance level above which excess funds are swept out of the account.

Some concentration banks can also monitor a company's account balances at third-party banks using SWIFT (Society for Worldwide Interbank Financial Telecommunication) messages and create transfer requests to move excess cash to the concentration bank. The key point with account sweeping is to fully automate it; the effort involved in manually tracking account balances and shifting funds on a daily basis is not only expensive but also likely to cause errors.

In most sweeping transactions, the sweeps occur on an *intraday* basis, which means that balances are transferred to the concentration account before the end of the day. Consequently, some cash may be left behind in subsidiary accounts rather than being centralized. This occurs when cash arrives in an account after execution of the daily sweep. The cash will remain in the subsidiary account overnight and be included in the following day's sweep. If a bank can accomplish true *end-of-day* sweeps, then no cash will be left behind in local accounts. If a company is not dealing with such a bank, then a proactive approach to depositing checks before cut-off times is the best way to avoid unused cash.

There may be a need to track the amounts of cash swept from each zero-balance account into the concentration account; if so, the company records an intercompany loan from the subsidiary to the corporate parent in the amount of the cash transferred through the cash concentration process. Here are four reasons for doing so:

1. *Subsidiary-level financial reporting requirements.* A subsidiary may have an outstanding loan, for which a bank requires the periodic production of a balance sheet. Since account sweeping shifts cash away from a subsidiary's balance sheet, detailed sweep tracking is needed to put the cash back on the subsidiary's balance sheet for reporting purposes. This can be done by recording an intercompany loan from the subsidiary to the corporate parent in exchange for any swept cash, which can then be reversed to place the cash back on the subsidiary's balance sheet.

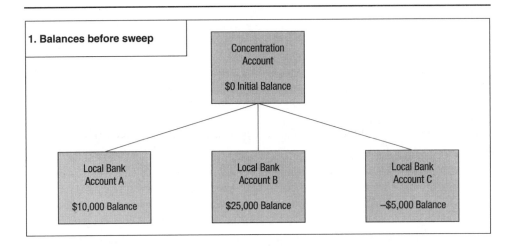

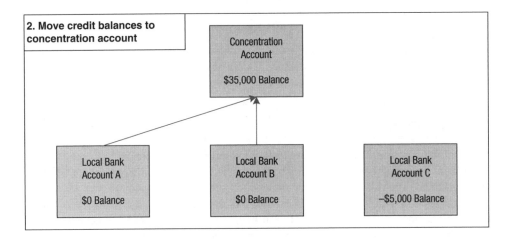

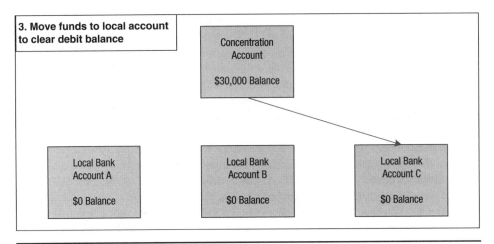

EXHIBIT 36.4   ZERO-BALANCE SWEEP TRANSACTION

2. *Interest income allocation.* A company may elect to allocate the interest earned at the concentration account level back to the subsidiaries whose accounts contributed cash to the concentration account. Some countries require that this interest allocation be done to keep a company from locating the concentration account in a low-tax jurisdiction, where the tax on interest income is minimized. Thus, the amounts of cash swept into and out of a subsidiary account must be tracked in order to properly allocate the correct proportion of interest income to that account.

3. *Interest expense allocation.* Some tax jurisdictions may require the parent company to record interest expense on intercompany loans associated with the transfer of cash in a physical sweeping arrangement. If so, the company must track the intercompany loan balances outstanding per day, the amount of which then is used as the principal for the calculation of interest expense. The interest rate used for these calculations should be the market rate; any other rate can be construed by local tax authorities to be transfer pricing designed to shift income into low-tax regions.

4. *Central bank reporting.* Some central banks require that they be sent reports on transfers between resident and nonresident accounts. This may be handled by the company's bank but still can increase the administrative burden associated with the sweep.

Some banks have the capability to track the amount of balance sweeps from each subsidiary account on an ongoing basis, which a company can use as its record of intercompany loans.

36.10 NOTIONAL POOLING

Notional pooling is a mechanism for calculating interest on the combined credit and debit balances of accounts that a corporate parent chooses to cluster together, without actually transferring any funds. This approach allows each subsidiary company to take advantage of a single, centralized liquidity position while still retaining daily cash management privileges. Also, since it avoids the use of cash transfers to a central pooling account, there is no need to create or monitor intercompany loans, nor are there any bank fees related to cash transfers (since there are no transfers). In addition, notional pooling largely eliminates the need to arrange overdraft lines with local banks. Further, interest earnings tend to be higher than if investments were made separately for the smaller individual accounts. Also, it offers a solution for partially owned subsidiaries whose other owners may balk at the prospect of physically transferring funds to an account controlled by another entity. And finally, the use of notional pooling is not a long-term commitment; on the contrary, it is relatively easy to back out of the arrangement.

Where global notional pooling is offered (usually where all participating accounts are held within a single bank), the pool offsets credit and debit balances on a multicurrency basis without the need to engage in any foreign exchange transactions. An additional benefit of global notional pooling lies in the area of intercompany cash flows; for example, if there are charges for administrative services, the transaction can be accomplished with no net movement of cash.

Once a company earns interest on the funds in a notional account, interest income usually is allocated back to each of the accounts comprising the pool. For tax management reasons, it may be useful for the corporate parent to charge the subsidiaries participating in the pool for some cash concentration administration expenses related to management of the pool. This scenario works best if the corporate subsidiaries are located in high-tax regions where reduced reportable income will result in reduced taxes.

The main downside of notional pooling is that it is not allowed in some countries, especially in portions of Africa, Asia, and Latin America (though it is very common in Europe). In these excluded areas, physical cash sweeping is the most common alternative. Also, the precise form of the notional pooling arrangement will vary according to local laws; some countries allow cross-border pooling while others do not.

In addition to the prohibition against notional pooling in some countries, it is difficult to find anything but a large multinational bank that offers cross-currency notional pooling. Instead, it is most common to have a separate notional cash pool for each currency area.

36.11 INVESTMENT CRITERIA

When considering various forms of cash investment, the controller should first consider the *safety of the principal* being invested. It would not do to invest company funds in a risky investment in order to earn extraordinarily high returns if there is a chance that any portion of the principal will be lost. Accordingly, a company policy should limit investments to a specific set of low-risk investment types. Also, some consideration should be given to the *maturity* and *marketability* of an investment. For example, if an investment in a block of apartment houses appears to generate a reasonably risk-free return and a good rate of return, it is still a poor investment from a cash management perspective, because the investment probably cannot be converted to cash on short notice. Accordingly, it is best to make investments only where there is a robust market available for their immediate resale. The final consideration when making an investment is its *yield*—and this is truly the last consideration after the previous items have already been reviewed. Within the boundaries of appropriate levels of risk, maturity, and marketability, the controller can then pick the investment with the highest yield. Since these criteria tend to limit one to very low-risk investments, the yield will also likely be quite low.

The investment criteria for a company that finds itself in a rapid-growth situation are more circumscribed. It typically burns through its cash reserves quite rapidly, so the liquidity of its investments must be extremely high in order to allow rapid access to the funds. Unfortunately, high liquidity is commonly associated with low investment returns, so the controller is forced to invest in low-yield investments. In addition, the company cannot risk loss on its investments, because it is critically important to keep cash available to feed the company's growth engine. Since risk is also associated with return, the controller must, once again, favor low-yield investments for minimal risk.

36.12 INVESTMENT OPTIONS

Within the investment boundaries just noted, there are a number of investment options available. Here are the most common ones that have low risk levels, short maturity dates, and high levels of marketability:

- *Bankers' acceptances.* Banks sometimes guarantee (or *accept*) corporate debt, usually when they issue a loan to a corporate customer, and then sell the debt to investors. Because of the bank guarantee, this debt is viewed as an obligation of the bank.
- *Bonds near maturity dates.* A corporate bond may not mature for many years, but one always can purchase a bond that is close to its maturity date. There tends to be

a minimal risk of loss (or gain) on the principal amount of this investment, since there is a low risk that interest rates will change so much in the short time period left before the maturity date of the bond that its value will be impacted. A variation on this type of investment is the municipal bond, for which there is no tax on the interest income; however, in consideration of this reduced liability, its yield also tends to be somewhat lower than on other types of bonds.

- *Certificates of deposit (CDs).* These certificates are essentially term bank deposits, typically having durations of up to two years. They usually pay a fixed interest rate upon maturity, though some variable-rate CDs are available. There is a perception that they are more secure than commercial paper, since CDs are issued by banks, which are more closely regulated than companies. There is up to $100,000 of Federal Deposit Insurance Corporation (FDIC) insurance coverage of this investment. The secondary market for CDs can vary and calls for some review prior to making an investment. A more restrictive CD may require an early-withdrawal penalty.

- *Commercial paper.* Larger corporations issue short-term notes that carry higher yields than those on government debt issuances. There is also an active secondary market for them, so there is usually no problem with liquidity. Commercial paper is generally not secured; however, staying with the commercial paper issued by "blue chip" organizations minimizes the risk of default. Most commercial paper matures in 30 days or less and rarely matures in greater than 270 days, in order to avoid the registration requirements of the Securities and Exchange Commission. Commercial paper is issued at a discount, with the face value being paid at maturity.

- *Money market fund.* This is a package of government instruments, usually comprised of Treasury bills, notes, and bonds, that is assembled by a fund management company. The investment is highly liquid, with many investors putting in funds for as little as a day. There are varying levels of risk between different money market funds, since some funds are more active in trying to outperform the market (with an attendant increase in risk).

- *Repurchase agreement.* This is a package of securities (frequently government debt) that an investor buys from a financial institution, under the agreement that the institution will buy it back at a specific price on a specific date. It is most commonly used for the overnight investment of excess cash from a company's cash concentration account, which can be handled automatically by the company's primary bank. The typical interest rate earned on this investment is equal to or less than the money market rate, since the financial institution takes a transaction fee that cuts into the rate earned.

- *U.S. Treasury issuances.* The United States government issues a variety of notes with maturity dates that range from less than a year (U.S. Treasury certificates) through several years (notes) to more than five years (bonds). The wide range of maturity dates gives one a broad range of investment options. Also, there is a strong secondary market for these issuances, so they can be liquidated in short order. U.S. government debts of all types are considered to be risk free and thus have lower yields than other forms of investment. At times, the demand for these issuances has been so strong that yields have been essentially zero.

The summary table in Exhibit 36.5 shows the key features of each of the preceding types of investments.

Investment Type	Maturity	Issued By	Interest Rate	Interest Paid	Secured	Capital Access Prior to Maturity
Bankers' acceptances	Less than 1 year	Banks	Fixed	Discount to face value	Yes	Secondary market available
Bonds near maturity date	Multiyear	Corporations and governments	Fixed	Coupon	No	Secondary market available
Certificates of deposit	1 day to 2 years	Banks	Mostly fixed, variable available	On maturity	FDIC only	Secondary market available
Commercial paper	Overnight to 270 days	Corporations	Fixed	Discount to face value	No	Secondary market available
Money market fund	Weighted average of 90 days or less	Assemblage of federal government issuances	Variable	Periodic	No	Secondary market available
Repurchase agreement	Negotiable	Corporations and banks	Negotiable	On maturity	Yes	Negotiable
U.S. Treasury issuances	Varies	Federal government	Fixed	On maturity	No	Secondary market available

EXHIBIT 36.5 INVESTMENT COMPARISON

When any of the preceding investments are initially issued to an investor or dealer, this is considered a *primary market transaction*. It is quite likely that many of these investments will be resold subsequently to a series of investors, depending on the duration of the investment. These subsequent transactions are considered to be trading in the *secondary market*.

Many of the secondary market transactions pass through the hands of dealers, who add a small markup to the price of each investment that they then sell to an investor. However, it is possible to deal directly with the United States Treasury to buy government debt. The government has set up the *www.publicdebt.treas.gov* Web site. A company can use the site to create a TreasuryDirect account for making electronic purchases of debt. Though the intent of the site is to sell debt that is held to maturity, one can request a debt sale through the Federal Reserve Bank of Chicago via the Treasury's Sell Direct system; the government will then sell one's debt investments on the open market in exchange for a small fee per security sold. The usual investment will be in Treasury bills, since they have the shortest term to maturity and therefore can liquidate prior to any need for a commissionable sale to a broker or reseller. More information about this service is available by downloading the Treasury Direct Investor Kit from the aforementioned Web site.

36.13 INVESTMENT STRATEGIES

The controller should develop a standard methodology for investing funds. This goes beyond the selection of a type of investment and enters the realm of strategies that can range from being passive (and requiring no attention) to those that are quite active and call for continuing decision making. This section describes a range of possible investment strategies.

At the most minimal level of investment strategy, the controller can do nothing and leave idle balances in the corporate bank accounts. This is essentially an *earnings credit strategy*, since the bank uses the earnings from these idle balances to offset its service fees. If a company has minimal cash balances, then this is not an entirely bad strategy—the earnings credit can be the equivalent of a modest rate of return, and if there is not enough cash to plan for more substantive investments, leaving the cash alone is a reasonable alternative.

A *matching strategy* simply matches the maturity date of an investment to the cash flow availability dates listed on the cash forecast. For example, ABC Company's cash forecast indicates that $80,000 will be available for investment immediately but must be used in two months for a capital project. The controller can invest the funds in a two-month instrument, such that its maturity date is just prior to when the funds will be needed. This is a very simple investment strategy that is more concerned with short-term liquidity than return on investment and is used most commonly by firms having minimal excess cash.

A *laddering strategy* involves creating a set of investments that have a series of consecutive maturity dates. For example, ABC Company's cash forecast indicates that $150,000 of excess cash will be available for the foreseeable future, and its investment policy forbids any investments having a duration of greater than three months. The controller could invest the entire amount in a three-month instrument, since this takes advantage of the presumably somewhat higher interest rates that are available on longer-term investments. However, there is always a risk that some portion of the cash will be needed sooner. In order to keep the investment more liquid while still taking advantage of the higher interest rates available through longer-term investments, the controller breaks the available cash into thirds and invests $50,000 in a one-month instrument, another $50,000 in a two-month instrument, and the final $50,000 in a three-month instrument. As each investment matures, the controller reinvests it into a three-month instrument. By doing so, ABC always has $50,000 of the invested amount coming due within one month or less. This improves liquidity while still taking advantage of longer-term interest rates.

A *tranched cash flow strategy* requires the controller to determine what cash is available for short-, medium-, and long-term investment and then to adopt different investment criteria for each of these investment tranches. The exact investment criteria will vary based on a company's individual needs, but here are three examples of how the tranches might be arranged:

1. The short-term tranche is treated as cash that may be needed for operational requirements on a moment's notice. This means that cash flows into and out of this tranche can be strongly positive or negative. Thus, return on investment is not a key criterion; instead, the controller focuses on very high levels of liquidity. The return should be the lowest of the three tranches but should also be relatively steady.

2. The medium-term tranche includes cash that may be required for use within the next 3 to 12 months, and usually only for highly predictable events, such as periodic tax or dividend payments or capital expenditures that can be planned well in advance. Given the much higher level of predictability in this tranche, the controller can accept longer-term maturities with moderate levels of volatility that have somewhat higher returns on investment.

3. The long-term tranche includes cash for which there is no planned operational use and that the controller feels can be safely invested for at least one year. The priority for this tranche shifts more in favor of a higher return on investment, with an attendant potential for higher levels of volatility and perhaps short-term capital loss, with a reduction in the level of liquidity.

Portrayed graphically, the tranches would appear as noted in Exhibit 36.6. The corporate cash balance should rarely decline into the long-term tranche, with occasional forays into the medium-term tranche while the cash level will vary considerably within the short-term tranche.

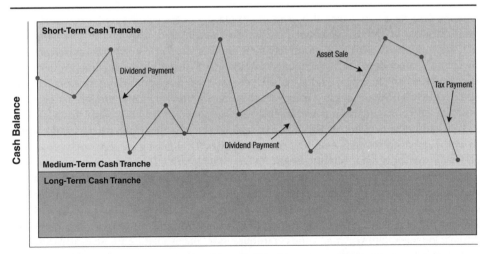

EXHIBIT 36.6 INVESTMENTS BY CASH FLOW TRANCHES

	Baseline Return	+	Additional Basis Points	Percent of Portfolio	Return Enhancement
Short-term tranche	1 month Treasuries	+	0	50%	0 bps
Medium-term tranche	1 month Treasuries	+	15	40%	+6 bps
Long-term tranche	1 month Treasuries	+	60	10%	+6 bps
			Total Incremental Return		+12 bps

EXHIBIT 36.7   RETURNS FROM TRANCHED CASH FLOW STRATEGY

An example of the numerical result of a tranched cash flow strategy is shown in Exhibit 36.7, which assumes a baseline return to be the return on one-month Treasuries, with a target of increased basis points (bps) above that standard for the medium-term and long-term tranches.

To engage in the tranched cash flow strategy, the controller should review the cash forecast regularly and adjust the amounts of cash needed in each of the three tranches. Inattention to these adjustments could result in an unanticipated cash requirement when the cash in the company's long-term tranche is tied up in excessively long illiquid investments.

36.14   RISK REDUCTION STRATEGIES

A simple risk reduction strategy is to avoid investments in the securities of any single entity in favor of investments solely in one or more money market funds. These funds provide instant diversification across a multitude of issuers, with the attendant risk being constantly reviewed by a staff of risk management professionals. The use of money market funds is especially cost effective for smaller accounting departments that cannot afford the services of an in-house investment manager.

The Federal Deposit Insurance Corporation insures a bank customer's deposits at the bank against the failure of the bank, up to a maximum reimbursement of $100,000; types of deposits covered by the insurance include certificates of deposit, checking accounts, and money market accounts. This protection is minimal for the deposits of all but the smallest companies; however, it is possible to place a much larger amount of funds with the Certificate of Deposit Account Registry Service (located at *www.cdars.com*), which maintains the FDIC coverage on up to $50 million of deposits. It achieves this coverage by splitting larger deposits into amounts of just under $100,000 and spreading the deposits over a network of more than 2,000 banks. Under this system, customers select a single bank in the network as their primary bank, which in turn issues them a statement listing each holding. There is no depositor fee for this service, although network banks pay CDARS to be listed in the network. A possible risk with CDARS is that, if the primary bank were to fail, a depositor's funds could be tied up by the FDIC during its recovery period. Of course, a controller could simply shop for a large number of CDs with different banks and manually track the investments, but the CDARS system is simpler to administer.

In order to invest funds, cash must be physically shifted out of a company's cash concentration account and into the investment. This physical shift is required by the Federal Reserve's Regulation Q, which prohibits banks from paying interest on demand deposits. A common method to circumvent this restriction is to create a *sweep account*, where funds are automatically swept out of the concentration account at the end of each business day and moved into an interest-earning account. The interest earned is less than what may be available from other investments, since the bank charges a sweeping fee. However, a sweep is still a good option for smaller amounts of cash that would not otherwise be actively managed.

The overnight sweep can be set up as a *one-to-one sweep*, where the company's funds are used to buy a specific asset. An alternative is for the bank to pool funds from multiple customers and buy an asset in the bank's name, which it liquidates in the morning and apportions back to its customers. This is called a *one-to-many sweep*. The one-to-one sweep is safer for the company if its bank enters bankruptcy, since the asset was purchased in the company's name, and the company therefore has title to the asset. The one-to-many sweep is more risky in the event of a bankruptcy, since the asset was purchased in the name of the bank, which leaves the company having a claim to the asset, along with all other creditors.

This section noted three risk-reduction strategies. Using the inherent diversification of money market funds is the simplest means for reducing risk. Setting up a CDARS account can greatly improve the amount of FDIC insurance coverage of a company's investments, while the use of one-to-one sweeps provides extra protection in the event of a bank's bankruptcy.

36.15 SUMMARY

The cash management function is an important one that deserves the utmost attention from the accountant, since a cash shortfall can bring a company's operations to an abrupt halt in short order. The cash management process is based upon a foundation of detailed and ongoing cash forecasting, which should be regularly compared to actual results in order to review and improve the accuracy of the overall process. Only by doing so can a company predict the amount and timing of cash problems, and work to correct them in a timely manner.

CHAPTER 37

FOREIGN EXCHANGE MANAGEMENT

37.1   INTRODUCTION

When a company accepts foreign currency in payment for its goods or services, it accepts some level of foreign exchange risk, since the value of that currency in comparison to the company's home currency may fluctuate enough between the beginning of the contract and receipt of funds to seriously erode the underlying profit on the sale. This subject is becoming more of an issue over time, because global competition is making it more likely that a company *must* accept payment in a foreign currency.

When dealing in foreign currencies, a company must determine its level of exposure, create a plan for how to mitigate that risk, engage in daily activities to implement the plan, and properly account for each transaction. Each of these steps is covered in the following sections.

37.2   FOREIGN EXCHANGE QUOTE TERMINOLOGY

Before delving into foreign exchange risk, it is useful to understand the terminology used in the foreign exchange quotation process. When comparing the price of one currency to another, the *base currency* is the unit of currency that does not fluctuate in amount while the *quoted currency* or *price currency* does fluctuate. The U.S. dollar is most commonly used as the base currency. For example, if the dollar is the base currency and $1.00 is worth 0.7194 euros, this quote is called the *indirect quote* of presenting a quote for euros. However, if the euro is used as the base currency, the same quote becomes $1.39 per euro (and is calculated as 1/0.7194) and is referred to as a *direct quote*. The direct quote is the inverse of the indirect quote. If neither the base currency nor the quoted currency is the U.S. dollar, then the exchange rate between the two currencies is called a *cross rate*.

As an example of an indirect quote, the U.S. dollar is listed first and the currency it is being paired with is listed second. Thus, a USD/EUR quote (dollars/euros) means that $1.00 equals 0.7194 euros. Conversely, a EUR/USD (euros/dollars) quote is a direct quote and means that €1 equals $1.3900. The key factor to remember with any quote pairing is that the first currency referenced always has a unit value of 1.

Most exchange rates are quoted to four decimals, since the sums involved in currency transactions are so large that the extra few decimals can have a meaningful impact on payments. A *point* is a change of one digit at the fourth decimal place of a quote.

A foreign exchange dealer will quote both *bid* and *offer* foreign exchange prices. The bid price is the price at which the dealer will purchase a currency; the ask price is the price at which the dealer will sell a currency.

The current exchange rate between any two currencies is known as the *spot rate*. When two parties to a foreign exchange transaction exchange funds, this occurs on the *delivery date* or *value date*. When a company requires foreign exchange immediately, it engages in a *spot settlement*, though there actually is a one- to two-day delay in final settlement of the transaction.

Toledo Toolmakers learns from its bank on June 1 that it has just received €50,000. Toledo's controller wants to convert these funds into dollars and so calls its bank and requests the U.S. dollar exchange rate in euros. The bank quotes an exchange rate of $1.3900 per €1. The controller immediately sells the euros at the rate of $1.3900. Settlement is completed two working days later, on the delivery date of June 3, when Toledo will receive $35,971.

37.3 THE NATURE OF FOREIGN EXCHANGE RISK

We will assume that a company's home currency is the U.S. dollar. If, during the interval when a customer is obligated to pay the company, the dollar appreciates against the customer's currency, then the customer is paying with a reduced-value currency, which causes the company to record a foreign exchange loss once it is paid.

Toledo Toolmakers sells goods to an Italian company for €100,000. At the time of sale, €1 is worth $1.39079 at the spot rate, which is a total sale price of $139,079. The customer is not obligated to pay until 90 days have passed; upon receipt of the euro payment in 90 days, the value in dollars will be based on the spot rate at the time of receipt. On the day when payment is received, the spot rate has dropped to $1.3630, which reduces the value of the payment to $136,300, resulting in a decline of $2,779, or 2%. Toledo must record this reduction as a loss.

There is also a possibility that exchange rates will move in the opposite direction, which creates a gain for the selling company. Smaller firms that do not engage in much foreign currency trade are more likely to accept the gains and losses from changes in the spot rate. However, this can cause wild swings in the profitability of larger firms with substantial multicountry trading activity. These firms are more likely to seek a solution that reduces their earnings volatility. Hedging is the solution. A broad array of possible solutions will be covered later in this chapter.

Before considering hedging solutions, a controller needs to know if there is any currency risk that requires such a solution—and that is not always a simple matter to determine. The next section discusses this problem.

37.4 DATA COLLECTION FOR FOREIGN EXCHANGE
RISK MANAGEMENT

Determining the extent of a company's currency risk can be a frustrating exercise for the foreign exchange specialist, who is often at the receiving end of a flood of disorganized information arriving from the accounting, budgeting, tax, and treasury departments.

The specialist must somehow aggregate this information, not only into a current statement of currency positions but also into a reliable forecast of where currency positions are expected to be in the near to medium term. This information is then used as the foundation for a hedging strategy.

A large firm with an enterprise resources planning (ERP) system can accumulate its existing net currency exposures from the ERP system automatically, but such is not the case for a company with more distributed accounting systems; its staff will likely accumulate the information manually from each subsidiary, then load it into an electronic spreadsheet in order to net out the positions of each subsidiary and determine the level of currency exposure. Obviously, companies with an ERP system have a significant advantage in determining the amount of this *booked exposure*.

The currency forecast can be unusually difficult to formulate, because a company may have many subsidiaries, each of which has some level of exposure in multiple currencies that varies continually. Ideally, there should be a forecast for each currency, which can result in a multitude of forecasts. To manage the forecasting workload, the foreign exchange specialist usually constructs forecasts for only those currencies in which the company is most heavily committed and ignores currencies where the company generally has minimal currency positions. The resulting *forecasted exposure* estimates the most likely size of currency transactions that will occur in the near and medium term, so that hedging plans can be made to mitigate these exposures.

Booked exposure, especially when derived from ERP information, should be quite accurate. However, forecasted exposure is only moderately accurate in the near term, and its accuracy declines rapidly within a year. This reduced accuracy strongly impacts the amount of hedging that a company may be willing to engage in, as discussed in the next section.

37.5 FOREIGN EXCHANGE HEDGING STRATEGIES

A variety of foreign exchange hedging strategies are noted in this section. The three main strategy groupings are:

1. To not hedge the exposure
2. To hedge the exposure through business practices
3. To hedge the exposure with a derivative

Also, within the third category, a controller must decide on what level of exposure to hedge. One possible strategy could be to hedge 100% of booked exposures, 50% of forecasted exposures over the next rolling 12-month period, and 25% of forecasted exposures over the following 12-month period. This gradually declining *benchmark hedge ratio* for longer forecast periods is justifiable on the assumption that the level of forecast accuracy declines over time, so that one should hedge against the minimum amount of exposure that will almost certainly occur.

The controller of Toledo Toolmakers compares her trailing 6-month stream of euro-denominated cash flows (in thousands) to the original forecast, which appears in Exhibit 37.1.

The forecasted cash flow is consistently higher than the actual cash flow by 5% to 10%, which is a very high level of forecasting accuracy and is indicative of mature and stable cash flows. In this case, the controller can safely adopt a 90% benchmark hedge ratio, which should hedge nearly all of the forecasted exposure. However, what if a company has more difficulty in predicting its cash flows? Exhibit 37.2 reveals a considerably more variable cash flow situation.

	Jan	Feb	Mar	Apr	May	Jun
Forecast	€3,051	€3,293	€4,011	€3,982	€3,854	€3,702
Actual	2,715	3,015	3,742	3,800	3,750	3,509
€ Variance	–336	–278	–269	–182	–104	–193
% Variance	–11%	–8%	–7%	–5%	–3%	–5%

EXHIBIT 37.1   SAMPLE FORECASTED AND ACTUAL CASH FLOW STREAM (STABLE)

In this more difficult forecasting environment, the average variance of actual cash flows from the forecast is 21%, but also lower than the forecast by 41% in half of the reporting periods. In this case, the controller may well feel justified in adopting a benchmark hedge ratio of only 60%, in order to hedge only that portion of cash flows that is most likely to occur.

The benchmark hedge ratio does not need to be consistent across the entire currency portfolio. There may be significant differences in the level of forecasting accuracy by currency, so a high-confidence currency forecast with little expected volatility can be matched with a higher benchmark hedge ratio, while a questionable forecast may justify a much lower ratio. Introducing this higher degree of granularity into the hedging strategy allows for better matching of hedging activity to foreign exchange risk.

The benchmark hedge ratio is also important from the perspective of the availability of hedge accounting. If the benchmark hedge ratio can be proven to cause a "high probability" of hedging effectiveness, then hedge accounting (which can delay the recognition of hedging gains and losses) can be used. Consequently, an ongoing analysis of the most appropriate benchmark hedge ratio would leave open the option of using hedge accounting.

Accept the Risk

Not hedging the exposure is the simplest strategy of all. A company can accept the foreign exchange risk and record any gains or losses on changes in the spot rate as they occur. The size of a company's currency exposure may dictate whether to hedge or not. For a smaller currency position, the expense associated with setting up and monitoring a hedge may be greater than any likely loss from a decline in the spot rate. Conversely, as a company's currency positions increase in size, the risk also increases and makes this strategy less appealing.

The next strategies are all internal business practices that reduce currency exposure.

Insist on Home Currency Payment

It is possible to insist on being paid in the company's home currency, so that the foreign exchange risk shifts entirely to the customer. This is a likely strategy for a company that is dominant in its industry and that therefore can impose terms on its customers.

	Jan	Feb	Mar	Apr	May	Jun
Forecast	€3,051	€3,293	€4,011	€3,982	€3,854	€3,702
Actual	2,142	3,409	4,000	1,862	3,915	2,274
€ Variance	–909	116	–11	–2,120	61	–1,428
% Variance	–30%	4%	0%	–53%	2%	–39%

EXHIBIT 37.2   SAMPLE FORECASTED AND ACTUAL CASH FLOW STREAM (UNSTABLE)

However, smaller firms will find that they have a modest competitive advantage if they allow customers to pay in their own currencies.

The worst option is to offer a customer a choice of currencies in which to make a payment, since it invariably will use the one having the more favorable exchange rate; the company essentially bears the downside risk in this scenario, with no upside potential.

Currency Surcharges

If a customer will not pay in a company's home currency, a related option is to bill the customer a currency surcharge if the company incurs a foreign exchange loss between the time of billing and payment. The surcharge may not be billed for minor changes in the exchange rate (to avoid paperwork) but is triggered by a significant decline in the exchange rate. Customers are rarely happy about this, since they are taking on the foreign exchange risk, and they cannot budget for the amount of the surcharge. It is also hardly a competitive advantage for a company to impose this practice on its customers.

Get Paid on Time

When a company deals with a counterparty in another country, the payment terms may be quite long, due to longer delivery schedules or border-crossing delays, or simply because of longer customary payment intervals in the other country. If a payment period is unusually prolonged, then the company is exposed to changes in the spot rate to a much greater extent than would be the case if the payment interval were compressed. Consequently, it behooves a company's sales staff to strive constantly toward sales agreements with shorter payment terms; likewise, the collections staff should be unusually aggressive in collecting from foreign customers.

Foreign Currency Loans

It is possible to offset a foreign currency risk exposure by creating a counter liability, such as a loan. To do so, a company can borrow an amount of money in the foreign currency that matches the amount of the receivable. When the customer pays off the receivable, the company uses the proceeds to pay off the loan—all in the same currency. This is an especially attractive option if foreign interest rates on debt are low or if there are tax advantages specific to the foreign tax location of which the company can take advantage.

Sourcing Changes

If a large amount of foreign currency cash flows are coming from a specific country, one way to hedge this risk is to start using suppliers located in the same country. By doing so, the company can find a ready use for the incoming currency, by turning it around and sending it right back to the same country. A more permanent possibility is to either buy or build a facility in that country, which will require currency not only for the initial capital investment but also to fund continuing operations. This is a particularly favorable option if local government subsidies give the company additional cost savings. However, local sourcing is not a good option if it will interrupt a smoothly operating supply chain.

Foreign Currency Accounts

If a company regularly receives and pays out funds in a particular foreign currency, it may make sense to open a foreign exchange account, in which it maintains a sufficient currency balance to meet its operational needs. This approach can be cost effective, because the company otherwise would have to buy the foreign currency in order to pay those suppliers requiring payment in that currency and then separately sell the same currency upon receipt of customer payments. While the company still is accepting the risk of loss on fluctuations in the exchange rate, it is eliminating the cost of continually buying and selling the currency.

Such a bank account does not necessarily have to be held in the country where the currency originates. It is also possible, and likely more efficient, to maintain a variety of currency accounts in a single major currency center, such as New York, London, or Amsterdam.

Unilateral, Bilateral and Multilateral Netting Arrangements

A company that regularly conducts business in multiple countries must spend a considerable amount of time settling foreign exchange transactions. It may buy and sell the same currencies many times over as it processes individual payables and receivables. There are three ways to reduce the volume of these transactions, depending on the number of parties involved. They are:

1. *Unilateral netting.* A company can aggregate the cash flows among its various subsidiaries, to determine if any foreign exchange payments between the subsidiaries can be netted, with only the (presumably) smaller residual balances being physically shifted. This reduces the volume of foreign exchange cash flows and therefore the associated foreign exchange risk.

2. *Bilateral spreadsheet netting.* If two companies located in different countries transact a great deal of business with each other, then they can track the payables owed to each other and net out the balances at the end of each month. One party pays the other the net remaining balance.

3. *Multilateral centralized netting.* When there are multiple parties wishing to net transactions, it becomes much too complex to manage with a spreadsheet. Instead, the common approach is to net transactions through a centralized exchange, such as Arizona-based EuroNetting (*www.euronetting.com*). Under a centralized netting system, each participant enters its payables into a centralized database through an Internet browser or some other file upload system. The netting service converts each participant's net cash flows to an equivalent amount in each participant's base currency and then uses actual traded exchange rates to determine the final net position of each participant. The exchange operator then pays or receives each participant's net position and uses the proceeds to offset the required foreign exchange trades.

Each type of netting arrangement can involve a broad array of payment types, covering such areas as products, services, royalties, dividends, interest, loans, and hedging contracts.

When bilateral or multilateral netting is used, the parties usually sign a master agreement that itemizes the types of netting to be performed as well as which contracts or purchase orders are to be included in the arrangement.

Although netting can be a highly effective way to reduce foreign exchange transaction costs, some governments do not recognize the enforceability of netting arrangements, because they can undermine the payment rights of third-party creditors. Consequently, consult a qualified attorney prior to entering into a netting arrangement.

The remaining strategies in this section involve the use of derivatives to hedge foreign exchange risk.

Forward Exchange Contracts

Under a forward exchange contract, which is the most commonly used foreign exchange hedge, a company agrees to purchase a fixed amount of a foreign currency on a specific date, and at a predetermined rate. Doing this allows the company to lock in the rate of exchange up front for settlement at a specified date in the future. The counterparty is typically a bank, which requires a deposit to secure the contract, with a final payment due in time to be cleared by the settlement date. If the company has a credit facility with the bank acting as its counterparty, then the bank can allocate a portion of that line to any outstanding forward exchange contracts and release the allocation once the contracts have been settled. The forward exchange contract is considered to be an over-the-counter transaction, because there is no centralized trading location, and customized transactions are created directly between parties.

> Toledo Toolmakers, has a €100,000 receivable at a spot rate of $1.39079. Toledo can enter into a forward foreign exchange (FX) contract with a bank for €100,000 at a forward rate of $1.3900, so that Toledo receives a fixed amount of $139,000 on the maturity date of the receivable. When Toledo receives the €100,000 payment, it transfers the funds to the bank acting as counterparty on the forward FX contract and receives $139,000 from the bank. Thus, Toledo has achieved its original receivable amount of $139,000, even if the spot rate has declined during the interval.

The price of a currency on the maturity date (its forward price) is comprised of the spot price, plus a transaction fee, plus or minus points that represent the interest rate differential between the two currencies. The combination of the spot rate and the forward points is known as the *all-in forward rate*. The interest rate differential is calculated in accordance with these two rules:

1. The currency of the country having a higher interest rate trades at a discount.
2. The currency of the country having a lower interest rate trades at a premium.

For example, if the domestic interest rate is higher than that of the foreign currency, then forward points are deducted from the spot rate, which makes the foreign currency less expensive in the forward market. The result of this pricing is that the forward price should make the buyer indifferent to taking delivery immediately or at some future date. Thus, if the spot price of euros per dollar were €0.7194 and there was a discount of 40 points for forwards having a one-year maturity, then the all-in forward rate would be €0.7154.

The calculation of the discount or premium points follows this formula:

$$\text{Premium/discount} = \text{Exchange rate} \times \text{interest rate differential} \times \frac{\text{Days of contract duration}}{360}$$

> The six-month U.S. dollar money market rate is 2.50% and the six-month euro money market rate is 3.75%. The USD/EUR exchange rate is 0.7194. The number of days in the forward exchange contract is 181. Because the euro interest rate exceeds the dollar interest rate, the dollar is at a premium to the euro. Thus, the USD/EUR forward exchange rate exceeds the spot rate. The premium is calculated as:
>
> 0.7194 spot rate × .0125 interest differential × (181/365 days) = .0045 premium
>
> The premium is therefore 45 points, which results in a USD/EUR forward exchange rate of 0.7194 + 0.0045, or 0.7239.

There are a few problems with forward exchange contracts to be aware of. First, because they are special transactions between two parties, it can be difficult to sell them to a third party. Also, the transaction premium offered may not be competitive.

Another problem is that the arrangement relies on the customer paying the company on or before the date when the forward FX contract matures. To continue using Toledo Toolmakers in an example, its terms to a European Union customer may require payment in 60 days, so it enters into a forward contract to expire in 63 days, which factors in an allowance of three extra days for the customer to pay. If the customer does not pay within 63 days, then Toledo still has to deliver euros on that date to fulfill its side of the forward contract.

It is possible to mitigate this problem with the variability of customer payments by entering into a *forward window contract*. This contract has a range of settlement dates during which the company can settle the outstanding contract at the currency rate noted in the contract. This contract is slightly more expensive than a standard forward exchange contract but makes it much easier to match incoming customer payments to the terms of the contract.

A related problem is when a company enters into a forward exchange contract to hedge an anticipated cash flow, but the cash never appears at all, perhaps because a sale was cancelled. In this case, the controller can enter into an offsetting forward exchange contract to negate the initial contract.

Toledo Toolmakers learns on July 15 that a Belgian customer has financial difficulties, and has defaulted on a payment of €250,000 that Toledo expected to receive on October 15. Unfortunately, Toledo already sold this amount through a forward exchange contract having a EUR/USD exchange rate of 1.3900, with a settlement date of October 15. Since it now has an obligation to deliver currency that will not be available on October 15, it needs to enter into an offsetting agreement to buy €250,000 on the same date.

Since the date of the original contract, the exchange rate has worsened, so that Toledo now enters into a three-month forward exchange contract having a EUR/USD rate of 1.3850. On the settlement date, Toledo buys €250,000 for $346,250 (250,000 × $1.3850) and sells them for $347,500 (250,000 × $1.3900), thereby incurring a loss of $1,250.

A variation on the forward contract is the *nondeliverable forward*. Under this arrangement, the only payment made between the parties is the difference between the spot rate and the forward rate. This net-cash solution can greatly reduce the total gross amount of funds being transferred.

Currency Futures

A currency future is the same as a forward exchange contract, except that it trades on an exchange. Each contract has a standardized size, expiry date, and settlement rules. The primary currency futures center with substantial volume is the Chicago Mercantile Exchange (CME). The CME offers futures trading between the major currencies as well as some of the emerging market currencies; however, the volume of contracts in the emerging market currencies is quite low.

These contracts normally are handled through a broker, who charges a commission. There is also a margin requirement, so that the buyer may be called on to submit additional funds over time if the underlying futures contract declines in value. Part of this margin is an initial deposit whose size is based on the contract size and the type of position being acquired. All futures contracts are marked to market daily, with the underlying margin accounts being credited or debited with the day's gains or losses. If the balance of the margin account drops too far, then the contract buyer must contribute more funds to the margin account. If the buyer does not update the margin account as required, it is possible that the position will be closed out.

Since currency futures have standard sizes and expiry dates, it is quite likely that a futures hedging strategy will not exactly match the underlying currency activity. For example, if a company needs to hedge a projected receipt of €375,000, and the related futures contract trades only in units of €100,000, then the company has the choice of selling either three or four contracts, totaling €300,000 and €400,000, respectively. Further, if the projected currency receipt date varies from the standard futures contract expiry date, then the company will be subject to some foreign exchange risk for a few days. Thus, the standardized nature of currency futures contracts result in an imperfect hedge for users.

> Toledo Toolmakers ships product to a German customer in February and expects to receive a payment of €425,000 on June 12. Toledo's controller elects to hedge the transaction by selling a futures contract on the CME. The standard contract size for the EUR/USD pairing is €100,000, so Toledo sells four contracts to hedge its expected receipt of €425,000. This contract always expires on Fridays; the nearest Friday following the expected receipt date of the euros is on June 15, so Toledo enters into contracts having that expiry date. Because the standardized futures contracts do not exactly fit Toledo's transaction, Toledo is electing not to hedge €25,000 of the expected receipt, and it will also retain the risk of exchange rate fluctuations between its currency receipt date of June 12 and its currency sale date of June 15.

Currency Options

A foreign currency option requires the payment of a premium in exchange for a right to use one currency to buy another currency at a specified price on or before a specified date. A *call option* permits the buyer to buy the underlying currency at the strike price while a *put option* allows the buyer to sell the underlying currency at the strike price.

An option is easier to manage than a forward exchange contract, because a company can choose not to exercise its option to sell currency if a customer does not pay it. Not exercising an option is also useful when it becomes apparent that a company can realize a gain on changes in the exchange rate that would not have been the case if it were tied into a forward exchange contract.

Options are especially useful for those companies interested in bidding on contracts that will be paid in a foreign currency. If they do not win the bid, they can simply let the option expire, without any obligation to purchase currency. If they win the bid, then they have the option of taking advantage of the exchange rate that they locked in at the time they formulated the bid. Thus, options allow a company to realize the original margin that they quoted to a customer rather than potentially having the margin erode due to exchange risk.

In an option agreement, the cost to the buyer is fixed up front, while the cost to the seller is potentially unlimited—which tends to increase the cost of the option to the point where the seller is willing to take on the risk associated with the contract. From the seller's perspective, the amount of an option premium is based on the strike price, time to expiration, and the volatility of the underlying currency. If the currency is highly volatile, then it is more likely that the buyer will exercise the option, which increases the risk for the seller. Thus, an option for a nonvolatile currency is less expensive, since it is unlikely to be exercised.

Currency options are available both over the counter and on exchanges. Those traded on exchanges are known as *listed options*. The contract value, term, and strike price of a listed option is standardized, whereas these terms are customized for an over-the-counter option.

Within an option agreement, the *strike price* states the exchange rate at which the underlying currency can be bought or sold, the *notional contract amount* is the amount of currency that can be bought or sold at the option of the buyer, and the *expiry date* is the date when the contract will expire, if not previously exercised. If the option is *in the money*, then the buyer can exercise it at a better price than the current exchange rate. If the option is *at-the-money*, then the buyer can exercise it at the current market price, while it is considered to be *out of the money* if the buyer can exercise it only at an exchange rate that is worse than the market rate. A *European-style option* is exercisable only on the expiry date; an *American-style option* can be exercised at any time prior to and including the expiry date.

The problem with an option is that it requires the payment of an up-front premium to purchase ut, so not exercising the option means that the fee is lost. This may be fine if a gain from currency appreciation offsets the fee, but it is an outright loss if the nonexercise was caused by the customer not paying on time.

> Toledo Toolmakers buys a 90-day option to buy €100,000 at $1.3900 for a fee of $4,000, which it plans to use as a hedge against a €100,000 payment from a customer that is due in 90 days. At the end of the option contract, the spot rate is $1.4350. Toledo elects to not exercise the option, thereby receiving €100,000 from its customer that can be exchanged at the spot price of $1.4350 for a total of $143,500. Thus, Toledo has gained $4,500 on the differential in the spot price, less $4,000 for the cost of the option, for a net profit of $500.

A more complicated version of the option is the *foreign exchange collar*. Under this strategy, a company buys one option and sells another at the same time, using the same expiry date and the same currencies. Doing so establishes an exchange rate range for a company. The upper limit of the exchange rate is established by the option the company buys; the lower limit is established by the option that the company sells. If the exchange rate remains within the upper and lower price points of the collar, then neither option is exercised. By accepting a moderate range of acceptable prices, a company can offset the cost of the premium paid for the purchased option with the premium from the option that is sold. The options are usually European style, so they are exercised only on the expiry date.

> Toledo Toolmakers is contractually obligated to pay a French supplier €500,000 in three months. The current EUR/USD exchange rate is 1.3900. Toledo's controller does not want to pay an option premium. The three-month EUR/USD forward exchange rate is 1.3950, and the controller is willing to accept a variation of 0.02 both above and below this rate, which means that the acceptable currency range is from 1.3750 to 1.4150. The option premium for selling euros at 1.4150 is 0.10, while Toledo can also earn the same premium for buying euros at 1.3750. Thus, the cost of one option is exactly offset by the earnings from the other option, resulting in a net option cost of zero.
>
> The actual exchange rate on the settlement date is 1.4300, so the controller exercises the option to sell €500,000 at 1.4150, thereby avoiding an incremental loss of $7,500, which Toledo otherwise would have incurred if it had been forced to sell euros at 1.4300.

Another issue with options is that they must be marked to market at the end of every reporting period, with the gain or loss recorded in the company's financial statements.

Currency Swaps

A currency swap is a spot transaction on the over-the-counter market that is executed at the same time as a forward transaction, with currencies being exchanged at both the spot date and the forward date. One currency is bought at the spot rate and date; the transaction is reversed at the forward date and rate. Thus, once the swap expires, both parties return to their original positions. The currency swap acts as an investment in one currency and a loan in another. The amount of a foreign exchange swap usually begins at $5 million, so this is not an option for smaller foreign exchange cash positions.

The exchange rates of both transactions are set at the time of the initial transaction, so the difference between the two rates is caused by the interest differential between the two currencies over the duration of the swap.

> Toledo Toolmakers has excess euros that it will need in nine months to pay for a capital project in Europe. In the interim, its controller wants to invest the euros in a short-term instrument while also obtaining use of the funds in U.S. dollars to cover its operating cash flow needs. To do so, Toledo engages in a foreign exchange swap with its bank under which it buys $10 million at a 0.7194 USD/EUR exchange rate and sells €7,194,000. Simultaneously, Toledo agrees to sell back $10 million of U.S. dollars in nine months at a rate of 0.7163 and buy back €7,163,000. The difference between the spot rate and forward rate of 0.0031 represents the interest rate differential between euros and U.S. dollars over the nine months spanned by the swap agreement, or $31,000. Toledo earns the extra interest, because it has chosen to invest in the currency having the higher interest rate.

The currency swap is useful when a company forecasts a short-term liquidity shortfall in a specific currency and has sufficient funds in a different currency to effect a swap into the currency where funds are needed. In addition, the company offsets what is likely to be a high interest rate on the short-term debt with the lower interest rate that it was earning on funds in a different currency.

> Toledo Toolmakers has a short-term negative euro account balance of €500,000, which it expects will continue for the next six months. During that time, Toledo must pay its bank London Interbank Offered Rate (LIBOR) plus 2% for the current account deficit. At the current LIBOR rate of 3.5% and EUR/USD spot rate of 1.3900, this represents an interest expense of $19,113, which is calculated as follows:
>
> $19,113 = 500,000 \times 1.3900$ exchange rate $\times 5.5\%$ interest rate $\times (180/360$ days$)$
>
> Toledo has several million U.S. dollars available, so it engages in a six-month swap of dollars for euros, thereby eliminating the negative account balance. The interest rates in Europe and the United States are identical, so there is no premium or discount between the currencies. Toledo was earning the LIBOR rate on its short-term investments. The interest income that it gave up by engaging in the swap was $12,163, which is calculated as follows:
>
> $12,163 = 500,000 \times 1.3900$ exchange rate $\times 3.5\%$ interest rate $\times (180/360$ days$)$
>
> Thus, by using a swap to use low-interest investments to offset higher-cost debt, Toledo saves $6,950.

The currency swap is also useful when a foreign currency cash flow is delayed, and a company normally would be obligated to sell the currency on the expected receipt date, as per the terms of a forward exchange contract. To meet this contractually obligated payment, a company can swap its other currency reserves into the currency that must be sold and reverse the transaction later, when the expected cash flow eventually arrives.

Proxy Hedging

If a company elects to receive a currency that is not actively traded, it may have a difficult time locating a hedge in the same currency. However, changes in the value of the currencies of a large economic area, such as Southeast Asia, tend to be closely correlated with each other. If the controller feels that this correlation will continue, then it may make sense to instead hedge through a highly correlated currency. However, just because the respective values of a currency pair were highly correlated in the past does not mean that they will continue to be correlated in the future, since a multitude of political and economic issues can break the correlation.

Summary of Strategies

Forward exchange contracts are the most heavily used form of hedging, for two reasons.

1. They are very inexpensive, having a modest transactional cost.
2. They are an over-the-counter product and therefore can be precisely tailored to a company's individual needs.

However, they firmly lock a company into the current spot rate, giving it no opportunity to participate in any future favorable price movements. While a company could use partial hedging to give itself some upside potential, this is also a two-way street, with increased risk of loss if exchange rates move in the wrong direction.

Currency futures are more easily entered into and sold off, since they are standardized products that trade through a formal exchange system. However, these conveniences also present a problem, since a company's hedging requirements cannot precisely fit the amount or timing of available futures contracts. Futures also suffer from the same problem as forward exchange contracts—they leave no room to participate in any future favorable price movements.

Currency options have a clear advantage over the preceding two strategies in that they allow a buyer to exercise an option or let it lapse, thereby allowing a controller to take advantage of favorable price movements. Against this major benefit is ranged the biggest problem with options—the premium imposed by the option seller. In practice, controllers tend to buy options that are relatively far out of the money, since these options are less expensive, but doing so means that they must retain some foreign exchange risk. Because of the premium, options appear to be the most expensive alternative; however, one must also factor in the opportunity cost of using forward exchange contracts or currency futures where one cannot take advantage of favorable price swings. When netted against the option premium, the cost of options does not appear to be so prohibitive. Options also require closer monitoring than other strategies, since one must judge exactly when to exercise them.

In summary, forward exchange contracts and currency futures are easier and less expensive to engage in than options, and so are favored by organizations with simpler treasury operations and conservative risk profiles. Options are more expensive in the short-term and require closer monitoring but can be financially rewarding.

37.6 HEDGE ACCOUNTING[1]

There are complex hedging rules that permit a company to elect to obtain special accounting treatment relative to foreign currency risks. These rules include the establishment, at inception, of criteria for measuring hedge effectiveness and ineffectiveness. Periodically, each hedge must be evaluated for effectiveness, using the pre-established criteria, and the gains or losses associated with hedge ineffectiveness must be reported currently in earnings, and not deferred to future periods.

In the instance of foreign currency hedges, companies must exclude from their assessments of hedge effectiveness the portions of the fair value of forward contracts attributable to spot-forward differences (i.e., differences between the spot exchange rate and the forward exchange rate).

In practice, this means that companies must estimate the cash flows on forecasted transactions based on the current spot exchange rate, appropriately discounted for time value.

---

[1] Adapted with permission from the *Wiley GAAP Guide 2009* (John Wiley & Sons, 2009), Chapter 23.

Effectiveness is then assessed by comparing the changes in fair values of the forward contracts attributable to changes in the dollar spot price of the pertinent foreign currency to the changes in the present values of the forecasted cash flows based on the current spot exchange rate(s).

On October 1, 2009, Toledo Toolmakers orders from its European supplier, Gemutlichkeit GmbH, a machine that is to be delivered and paid for on March 31, 2010. The price, denominated in euros, is €4,000,000. Although Toledo will not make the payment until the planned delivery date, it has immediately entered into a firm commitment to make this purchase and to pay €4,000,000 upon delivery. This creates a euro liability exposure to foreign exchange risk; thus, if the euro appreciates over the intervening six months, the dollar cost of the equipment will increase.

To reduce or eliminate this uncertainty, Toledo desires to lock in the purchase cost in euros by entering into a six-month forward contract to purchase euros on the date when the purchase order is issued to and accepted by Gemutlichkeit. The spot rate on October 1, 2009, is $1.40 per euro, and the forward rate for March 31, 2010 settlement is $1.44 per euro. Toledo enters into a forward contract on October 1, 2009, with the First Intergalactic Bank to pay US $5,760,000 in exchange for the receipt of €4,000,000 on March 31, 2010, which can then be used to pay Gemutlichkeit. No premium is received or paid at the inception of this forward contract.

Assume the relevant time value of money is measured at 1/2% per month (a nominal 6% annual rate). The spot rate for euros at December 31, 2009, is $1.45, and at March 31, 2010, it is $1.48. The forward rate as of December 31 for March 31 settlement is $1.46.

Entries to reflect the foregoing scenario are as follows:

10/1/09	*No entries, since neither the forward contract nor the firm commitment have value on this date*		
12/31/09	Forward currency contract	78,818	
	Gain on forward contract		78,818
	To record present value (at 1/2% monthly rate) of change in value of forward contract [= change in forward rate (1.46 − 1.44) × €4,000,000 = $80,000 to be received in three months, discounted at 6% per annum]		
	Loss on firm purchase commitment	197,044	
	Firm commitment obligation		197,044
	To record present value (at 1/2% monthly rate) of change in amount of firm commitment [= change in spot rate (1.45 − 1.40) × €4,000,000 = $200,000 to be paid in three months, discounted at 6% per annum]		
	Gain on forward contract	78,818	
	Loss on firm purchase commitment		197,044
	P&L summary (then to retained earnings)	118,226	
	To close the gain and loss accounts to net income and thus to retained earnings		
3/31/10	Forward currency contract	81,182	
	Gain on forward contract		81,182
	To record change in value of forward contract {[= (1.48 − 1.44) × €4,000,000 = $160,000] − gain previously recognized ($78,818)}		
	Loss on firm commitment	122,956	
	Firm commitment obligation		122,956

To record change in amount of firm commitment {[=
(1.48 – 1.40) × €4,000,000] less loss previously
recognized ($197,044)}

Firm commitment obligation	320,000	
Machinery and equipment	5,600,000	
Cash		5,920,000

To record purchase of machinery based on spot
exchange rate as of date of contractual commitment
(1.40) and close out the firm commitment obligation
(representing effect of change in spot rate during
commitment period)

Cash	160,000	
Forward contract		160,000

To record collection of cash on net settlement of
forward contract [= (1.48 – 1.44) × €4,000,000]

Gain on forward contract	81,182	
P&L summary (then to retained earnings)	41,774	
Loss on firm purchase commitment		122,956

To close the gain and loss accounts to net income
and thus to retained earnings

With respect to fair value hedges of firm purchase commitments denominated in a foreign currency, the change in value of the contract related to the changes in the differences between the spot price and the forward or futures price would be excluded from the assessment of hedge effectiveness. As applied to the foregoing example, therefore, the net credit to income in 2009 ($118,226) can be further analyzed into two constituent elements: the amount arising from the change in the difference between the spot price and the forward price, and the amount resulting from hedge ineffectiveness.

The former item, not attributed to ineffectiveness, arose because the spread between spot and forward price at hedge inception, $(1.44 – 1.40) = .04$, fell to $(1.46 – 1.45) = .01$ by December 31, for an impact amounting to $(.04 –.01) = .03 \times €4,000,000 = \$120,000$, which, reduced to present value terms, equaled $118,227. The net credit to earnings in December 2009, $(\$78,818 + 118,226) = \$197,044$, relates to the spread between the spot and forward rates on December 31 and is identifiable with hedge ineffectiveness.

Forward Exchange Contract Accounting

Foreign currency transaction gains and losses on assets and liabilities that are denominated in a currency other than the home currency can be hedged if a U.S. company enters into a forward exchange contract. The following example shows how a forward exchange contract can be used as a hedge, first against a firm commitment and then, following delivery date, against a recognized liability.

A general rule for estimating the fair value of forward exchange rates is to use the changes in the forward exchange rates and discount those estimated future cash flows to a present-value basis. An entity will need to consider the time value of money if significant in the circumstances for these contracts. The following example does not apply discounting of the future cash flows from the forward contracts, in order to focus on the relationships between the forward contract and the foreign currency denominated payable.

Toledo Toolmakers enters into a firm commitment with Dempsey Inc., Inc., of Germany, on October 1, 2009, to purchase a computerized robotic system for €6,000,000. The system will be delivered on March 1, 2010, with payment due 60 days after delivery (April 30, 2010). Toledo decides to hedge this foreign currency firm commitment and enters into a forward exchange contract on the firm commitment date to receive €6,000,000 on the payment date. The applicable exchange rates are shown in the table.

Date	Spot Rates	Forward Rates for April 30, 2009
October 1, 2009	€1 = $1.55	€1 = $1.570
December 31, 2009	€1 = $1.58	€1 = $1.589
March 1, 2010	€1 = $1.58	€1 = $1.585
April 30, 2010	€1 = $1.60	

The example continues in Exhibit 37.3 and separately presents both the forward contract receivable and the dollars payable liability in order to show all aspects of the forward contract. For financial reporting purposes, most companies present just the net fair value of the forward contract that would be the difference between the current value of the forward contract receivable and the dollars payable liability. Note that the foreign currency hedges in the illustration are not perfectly effective. However, for this example, the degree of ineffectiveness is not deemed to be sufficient to trigger income statement recognition.

The transactions that reflect the forward exchange contract, the firm commitment, and the acquisition of the asset and retirement of the related liability appear next. The net fair value of the forward contract is shown below each set of entries for the forward exchange contract.

Foreign Currency Investment Hedge Accounting

A company can invest in a subsidiary located in another country and issue a loan to act as a hedge against the investment in the subsidiary. This loan can be designated as a hedge. The gain or loss from the designated hedge to the extent that it is effective is reported as a translation adjustment.

Toledo Toolmakers has invested $15 million in a subsidiary in Germany, for which the euro is the functional currency. The initial exchange rate is €1.2:$1, so the initial investment is worth €18 million. Toledo issues a debt instrument for €12 million and designates it as a hedge of the German investment. Toledo's strategy is that any change in the fair value of the loan attributable to foreign exchange risk should offset any translation gain or loss on two-thirds of Toledo's German investment.

At the end of the year, the exchange rate changes to €0.8:$1. Toledo uses the following calculation to determine the translation gain on its net investment:

€18,000,000/$0.8 = $22,500,000 − €18,000,000/$1.2 = $15,000,000 = $7,500,000

Toledo uses the following calculation to determine the translation loss on its euro-denominated debt:

€12,000,000/$0.8 = $15,000,000 − €12,000,000/$1.2 = $10,000,000 = $5,000,000

Toledo creates the following entries to record changes in the value of the translation gain on its investment and translation loss in its debt, respectively:

Investment in subsidiary	7,500,000	
Cumulative translation adjustment (equity)		7,500,000
Cumulative translation adjustment (equity)	5,000,000	
Euro-denominated debt		5,000,000

Forward Contract Entries

(1) 10/1/08 (forward rate for 4/30/09 €1 = $1.57)

Forward contract receivable	9,420,000	
Dollars payable		9,420,000

This entry recognizes the existence of the forward exchange contract using the gross method. Under the net method, this entry would not appear at all, since the fair value of the forward contract is zero when the contract is initiated. The amount is calculated using the 10/1/08 forward rate for 4/30/09 (€6,000,000 × $1.57 = $9,420,000).

Net fair value of the forward contract = $0

Note that the net fair value of the forward exchange contact on 10/1/08 is zero because there is an exact amount offset of the forward contract receivable of $9,420,000 with the dollars payable liability of $9,420,000. Many companies present only the net fair value of the forward contract on their balance sheets, and therefore, they would have no net amount reported for the forward contract at its inception.

(2) 12/31/08 (forward rate for 4/30/09 €1 = $1.589)

Forward contract receivable	114,000	
Gain on hedge activity		114,000

The dollar values for this entry reflect, among other things, the change in the forward rate from 10/1/08 to 12/31/08. However, the actual amount recorded as gain or loss (gain in this case) is determined by all market factors.

Net increase in fair value of the forward contract = (1.589 − 1.57 = .019 × €6,000,000 = $114,000).

The increase in the net fair value of the forward exchange contract on 12/31/08 is $114,000 for the difference between the $7,134,000 ($7,020,000 plus $114,000) in the forward contract receivable and the $7,020,000 for the dollars payable liability. Many companies present only the net fair value on their balance sheet, in this case as an asset. And this $114,000 is the amount that would be discounted to present value, if interest is significant, to recognize the time value of the future cash flow from the forward contract.

(4) 3/1/09 (forward rate for 4/30/09 €1 = $1.585)

Loss on hedge activity	24,000	
Forward contract receivable		24,000

Hedge Against Firm Commitment Entries

(3) 12/31/08

Loss on hedge activity	114,000	
Firm commitment		114,000

The dollar values for this entry are identical to those in entry (2), reflecting the fact that the hedge is highly effective (100%) and also the fact that the market recognizes the same factors in this transaction as for entry (2). This entry reflects the first use of the firm commitment account, a temporary liability account pending the receipt of the asset against which the firm commitment has been hedged.

(5) 3/1/09

Firm commitment	24,000	
Gain on hedge activity		24,000

These entries again will be driven by market factors, and they are calculated the same way as entries (2) and (3). Note that the decline in the forward rate from 12/31/08 to 3/1/09 resulted in a loss against the forward contract receivable and a gain against the firm commitment [1.585 − 1.589 = (.004) × €6,000,000 = ($24,000)].

Exhibit 37.3 Net Fair Value of the Forward Contract

Forward Contract Entries	Hedge Against Firm Commitment Entries

Forward Contract Entries

Net fair value of the forward contract = $90,000

The net fair value of the forward exchange contract on 3/1/09 is $90,000 for the difference between the $9,510,000 ($9,420,000 + 114,000 − $24,000) in the forward contract receivable and the $9,420,000 for the dollars payable liability. Another way of computing the net fair value is to determine the change in the forward contract rate from the initial date of the contract, 10/1/08, which is $1.585 − $1.57 = $.015 × €6,000,000 = $90,000. Also note that the amount in the firm commitment temporary liability account is equal to the net fair value of the forward contract on the date the equipment is received.

(7) 4/30/09 (spot rate €1 = $1.60)

Forward contract receivable 90,000

    Gain on forward contract 90,000

The gain or loss (gain in this case) on the forward contract is calculated using the change in the forward to the spot rate from 3/1/09 to 4/30/09 [€6,000,000 × ($1.60 − $1.585) = $90,000] Net fair value of the forward contract = $180,000

The net fair value of the forward exchange contract on 4/30/09 is $180,000 for the difference between the $9,600,000 ($9,510,000 + $90,000) in the forward contract receivable and the $9,420,000 for the dollars payable liability. The net fair value of the forward contract at its terminal date of 4/30/09 is based on the difference between the contract forward rate of €1 = $1.57 and the spot rate on 4/30/09 of €1 = $1.60. The forward contract receivable has reached its maturity and the contract is completed on this date at the forward rate of €1 = $1.57 as contracted on 10/1/08. If the entity recognizes an interest factor in the forward contract over the life of the contract, then interest is recognized at this time on the forward contract, but no separate accrual of interest is required for the accounts payable in euros.

(9) 4/30/09

Dollars payable 9,420,000

Foreign currency units (€) 9,600,000

    Cash 9,420,000

    Forward contract receivable 9,600,000

This entry reflects the settlement of the forward contract at the 10/1/08 contracted forward rate (€6,000,000 × $1.17 = $7,020,000) and the receipt of foreign currency units valued at the spot rate (€6,000,000 × $1.20 = $7,200,000).

Hedge Against Firm Commitment Entries

(6) 3/1/09 (spot rate €1 = $1.58)

Equipment 9,390,000

Firm commitment 90,000

    Accounts payable (€) 9,480,000

This entry records the receipt of the equipment, the elimination of the temporary liability account (firm commitment), and the recognition of the payable, calculated using the spot rate on the date of receipt (€6,000,000 × $1.58 = $9,480,000).

(8) 4/30/09

Transaction loss 120,000

    Accounts payable (€) 120,000

The transaction loss related to the accounts payable reflects only the change in the spot rates and ignores the accrual of interest. [€6,000,000 × ($1.60 − $1.58) = $120,000]

(10) 4/30/09

Accounts payable (€) 9,600,000

    Foreign currency units (€) 9,600,000

This entry reflects the use of the foreign currency units to retire the account payable.

EXHIBIT 37.3 NET FAIR VALUE OF THE FORWARD CONTRACT (*Continued*)

The net effect of these translation adjustments is a net increase in Toledo's investment of $2.5 million. In the following year, the exchange rates do not change, and Toledo sells its subsidiary for $17.5 million. Toledo's tax rate is 30%. Its reporting annual gains and losses follow.

	Year 1	Year 2
Net income:		
Gain on sale of investment in ABC Company		$2,500,000
Income tax expense		(750,000)
Net gain realized in net income		1,750,000
Other comprehensive income:		
Foreign currency translation adjustment, net of tax	$1,750,000	
Reclassification adjustment, net of tax		(1,750,000)
Other comprehensive income net gain/(loss)	$1,750,000	$(1,750,000)

If a company is hedging only its booked exposure, it may make sense from a paperwork perspective not to attempt to use hedge accounting, since its positions are necessarily short and will not benefit from any recognition deferral. However, if a company chooses to hedge its forecasted position, which may cover a considerably longer time period, then its primary challenge is to prove that the hedge can be matched to a pool of exposures having the same time horizon as the hedge. A simple way to do this is to hedge only a portion of the total exposure, so that the full amount of the hedge always can be matched against some portion of the exposure.

37.7   FOREIGN EXCHANGE HEDGE CONTROLS

There are a variety of controls that the accounting department can implement in order to reduce the risk profile of its hedging activities. These controls are divided into ones related to hedging authorizations, contracts, hedge accounting, and risk assessment.

Authorization Controls

- *Define dealing responsibilities.* Management should define the authorizations and responsibilities of all accounting staff engaged in foreign exchange transactions, including the position titles authorized to deal, the instruments they are allowed to deal in, and limits on open positions.
- *Issue an updated signatory list to counterparties at least once a year.* Schedule a periodic distribution of the company's authorized derivative contract signers to all counterparties, to keep unauthorized transactions from taking place, as well as whenever someone is dropped from the list. This should be a written notification, followed by a call to verify receipt.
- *Centralize foreign exchange trading operations.* Centralization makes it easier to maintain control over a company's trading activities.

Contractual Controls

- *Verify contract terms and signatory.* It is possible that a company may have difficulty forcing a counterparty to pay for its obligations under an over-the-counter contract if the counterparty did not fill out the contract correctly, or if the signatory to the agreement was not authorized to do so. The company's legal department can follow up on these issues whenever a new contract is signed.

- *Confirm all hedging transactions.* As soon as a hedging deal is concluded, a person different from the transaction originator should confirm the details of the deal. This should be a matching of the company's transaction details to those of the counterparty or exchange, which may involve a written or electronic message (such as an e-mail or SWIFT MT300).

- *Use standardized master agreements.* By using the master agreements provided by such organizations as the International Swaps and Derivatives Association, a company can avoid entering into contracts having inadequate coverage that may leave it at risk.

Hedge Accounting Controls

- *Include in the hedging procedure a requirement for full documentation of each hedge.* Hedging transactions are allowed under generally accepted accounting principles (GAAP) only if they are fully documented at the inception of the hedge. One can ensure compliance by including the documentation requirement in an accounting procedure for creating hedges.

General Risk Assessment Controls

- *Determine counterparty creditworthiness.* In cases where a company expects to deal directly with a counterparty through an over-the-counter hedging transaction (as opposed to deal with an exchange), the controller should determine the creditworthiness of the counterparty prior to entering into the contract. Otherwise, the company could be taking on a significant risk that the counterparty cannot meet its obligations under the contract. This control can be expanded to include specific procedures to follow in the event of a counterparty credit downgrade.

- *Full-risk modeling.* The accounting staff should periodically conduct full-risk modeling of its foreign exchange positions to determine both the potential risk inherent in its unhedged portfolio and what the company's gain or loss would have been on a rolling historical basis if it had not engaged in hedging transactions.

- *Audit spreadsheet calculations and contents.* If a company is compiling its currency cash flows in spreadsheets, then there is a significant risk of spreadsheet error. A qualified auditor should review the spreadsheets at least annually, with a particular examination of formula ranges and totals. It is also possible that entire cash accounts or entities may not be included in the spreadsheets, so the auditor should be ognizant of missing information.

37.8 FOREIGN EXCHANGE HEDGE POLICIES

The policies noted next are divided into ones that introduce consistency into the accounting for hedges, create boundaries around the amounts and durations of hedging activities, and authorizations to engage in hedging.

Accounting Consistency Policies

- *The determination of hedge effectiveness shall always use the same method for similar types of hedges.* GAAP allows one to use different assessment techniques in determining whether a hedge is highly effective. However, changing methods, even when justified, allows the accounting staff room to alter effectiveness designations, which can yield variations in the level of reported earnings. Consequently, creating and consistently using a standard assessment method for each type of hedge eliminates the risk of assessment manipulation.

- *A hedge shall be considered highly effective if the fair values of the hedging instrument and hedged item are at least __% offset.* GAAP does not quantitatively specify what constitutes a highly effective hedge, so a company should create a policy defining the number. A different hedging range can be used for different types of hedges.

Deal Boundaries

- *The benchmark hedge ratio shall be __% for booked exposures, __% for forecasted exposures over the next 12-month period, and __% of forecasted exposures for the following __month period.* This staggered benchmark hedging policy gives the accounting staff firm guidance regarding the amount of hedging activity to engage in. The benchmark hedge ratio should decline over the three periods noted in the policy, to reflect the increased uncertainty of cash flows further in the future.

- *Review benchmark hedge ratio.* The accounting staff should periodically compare forecasted foreign currency cash flows to actual results, by currency, and determine if the benchmark hedge ratio is appropriate, based on the company's forecasting ability.

- *All derivative transactions shall be limited to a time horizon of __ months, and involve no more than $_____ in aggregate and $_____ individually.* This policy is designed to put general boundaries around the use of derivatives and can be expanded to include the authorized types of derivatives, and who can bind the company in derivatives transactions. It can even include the compensation for foreign exchange trader performance, since an excessive bonus plan can lead to risky trading behavior. If implemented, this policy must be updated regularly, since ongoing changes in a company's business may mandate different types of transactions or volumes.

Authorization Policies

- *The controller is authorized to discontinue hedging transactions with those counterparties with whom the company has experienced ongoing or significant operational problems.* This policy is deliberately vague, giving the controller authority to stop doing business with a counterparty for any number of reasons, such as improper contract completion, incorrect contract signatories, or difficulty in settling accounts.

- *Authorization to deal in foreign exchange hedging transactions shall be issued solely by the board of directors.* Not only does this policy tend to reduce the number of people authorized to deal in hedging transactions, but it is also a requirement of many banks that deal in such transactions.

- *All sales contracts not denominated in U.S. dollars must be approved in advance by the accounting department.* This policy not only gives the accounting staff advance notice of a forthcoming sale for which a hedge may be required but may also give them some leverage to force a contract change, so that it is denominated in the company's home currency.

37.9   RECORDKEEPING FOR FOREIGN EXCHANGE HEDGING ACTIVITIES

At the inception of a fair value hedge, GAAP requires documentation of the relationship between the hedging instrument and the hedged item, the risk management objectives of the hedging transaction, how the hedge is to be undertaken, the method to be used for gain or loss recognition, identification of the instrument used for the hedge, and how the effectiveness calculation is measured. Since hedge accounting cannot be used unless this documentation exists, it is important to store a complete set of documentation for each hedge for the duration not only of the hedge but also through the audit following the hedge termination. It can then be included in the archives with accounting documentation for the year in which the transaction terminated.

37.10   SUMMARY

Foreign exchange risk management can be used to reduce the volatility of a company's cash flows and earnings. If currency options are used aggressively by a well-trained and experienced accounting team, it can even generate additional profits. A controller should at least maximize the use of all internal hedging strategies, such as internal netting, sourcing changes, and prompt payment, which are all zero-cost alternatives. The next step up is to use a selection of forward exchange contracts, currency futures, or currency options to hedge any remaining foreign exchange risk.

This may seem to require a considerable amount of monitoring by the accounting staff. However, most multinational companies are not so far-flung that they need to track more than a dozen currencies. For such organizations, it is quite practical to aggregate currency positions across a relatively small number of subsidiaries and then engage in one forward trade per month for each currency. Only companies trading in dozens of currencies need a more comprehensive and automated system to aggregate and forecast information as well as a larger accounting team to measure risk and conduct trading activities.

The accounting for hedging is complex, requiring considerable documentation and a large volume of entries to record each transaction. Given the short-term nature of many currency hedging transactions, it may make more sense to ignore hedge accounting entirely and simply record hedging gains and losses as they occur. For longer-term hedges, a controller is more likely to opt for hedge accounting.

RISK MANAGEMENT

38.1 INTRODUCTION

Some well-managed companies have fallen because they did not pay attention to risk. For example, it is difficult to recover from a fire that destroys a data center or production facility, or from the theft of all one's securities and cash. Though rare, these occurrences can be so catastrophic that it is not possible to recover. An otherwise healthy organization is destroyed, throwing many people out of work and eliminating the equity stake of the owners.

On a lesser scale and much more common are the lawsuits that nearly every company must face from time to time. These may relate to employee injuries, customer or supplier claims regarding contracts, or perhaps sexual harassment or some form of discrimination. These lawsuits do not normally end a company's existence, but they can cripple it if awards are excessive or the company is not in a solid financial position to begin with.

This chapter covers the risk management policies and procedures that keep a company from being seriously injured by these and other types of risk-related problems. In addition, it notes the role of the risk manager in mitigating a company's risk by modifying internal systems as well as by purchasing insurance. The types of insurance that a company can buy are also discussed, as well as how to select a broker or underwriter to help service a company's needs. The chapter concludes with coverage of how to administer insurance claims and how to write a risk management report that clearly identifies a company's risks and how they are being addressed.

38.2 RISK MANAGEMENT POLICIES

A company must determine the amount of risk that it is willing to undertake. When the board of directors attempts to quantify this, it frequently finds that it is uncomfortable with the level of risk that it currently has, and mandates more action, through new policies, that reduce the level of risk. The policies can include a number of risk management issues, such as the financial limits for risk assumption or retention, self-insurance parameters, the financial condition of insurance providers, and captive insurance companies. The policies

1. ABC Company will obtain insurance only from companies with an A.M. Best rating of at least B++.
2. All self-insurance plans will be covered by an umbrella policy that covers all losses exceeding $50,000.
3. No insurance may be obtained from captive insurance companies.
4. The company must always have current insurance for the following categories, and in the stated amounts:
   - Director's and officer's insurance, $5 million.
   - General liability insurance, $10 million.
   - Commercial property insurance that matches the replacement cost of all structures and inventory.
   - Business interruption insurance, sufficient for four months of operations.

EXHIBIT 38.1   A COMPREHENSIVE POLICY FOR RISK MANAGEMENT

do not have to cover some issues that are already required by law, such as workers' compensation insurance. An example of a comprehensive insurance policy is noted in Exhibit 38.1.

There are several key points to consider in the exhibit. First, a company may be tempted to purchase very inexpensive insurance, which typically comes from an insurance provider that is in poor financial condition. If the company subsequently files a claim on this insurance, it may find that the provider is not in a position to pay it. Consequently, the first policy item defines the minimum financial rating that an insurance provider must attain before the company will purchase insurance from it. Another is that a company wants to put a cap on the maximum amount of all risks that it is willing to tolerate, so that it cannot be blindsided by a large loss that is not covered by insurance. The second policy point, which requires a cap on self-insured risks, covers this problem. Finally, the board may feel more comfortable defining the precise amount of insurance coverage needed in specific areas. Though the policy shows a few specific insurance amounts, it is usually better to define a formula for calculating the appropriate amount of insurance, such as commercial property insurance, that will cover the replacement cost of structures and inventory. This keeps the amount defined on the policy from becoming outdated due to changing business conditions. These are some of the most important insurance issues that a risk management policy should cover.

38.3   MANAGER OF RISK MANAGEMENT

In most large companies, the risk management function is assigned to a manager, who reports to the chief financial officer, treasurer, or controller. This executive is charged with the responsibility of implementing procedures consistent with the corporate risk management policy (as noted in Exhibit 38.1). This person works closely with other functional areas, such as engineering, safety and health, personnel and industrial relations, production, plant security, legal, and accounting. It is important that this person have a thorough knowledge of the company's operations, products, and services, as well as its risk history, so that he or she can evaluate risks and exposure properly. Within these constraints, the job description of the typical risk manager is:

- Ascertain and appraise all corporate risks.
- Estimate the probability of loss due to these risks.

- Ensure compliance with state, federal, and local requirements regarding insurance.
- Select the optimum method for protecting against losses, such as changes to internal procedures or by acquiring insurance.
- Work with insurance agents, brokers, consultants, and insurance company representatives.
- Supervise a loss prevention program, including planning to minimize losses from anticipated crises.
- Maintain appropriate records for all aspects of insurance administration.
- Continually evaluate and keep abreast of all changes in company operations.
- Stay current on new techniques being developed in the risk management field.
- Conduct a periodic audit of the risk management program to ensure that all risks have been identified and covered.

38.4   RISK MANAGEMENT PROCEDURES

Once the risk management policies have been defined, it is necessary to determine a number of underlying procedures to support them. These guide the actions of the risk manager in ensuring that a company has taken sufficient steps to ensure that risks are kept at a minimum. The procedures follow a logical sequence of exploring the extent of risk issues, finding ways to mitigate those risks internally, and then using insurance to cover any risks that cannot otherwise be reduced. In more detail, the five procedures are:

1. *Locate risk areas.* Determine all hazards to which the company is subject by performing a complete review of all properties and operations. This should include a review of not only the physical plant but also of contractual obligations, leasehold requirements, and government regulations. The review can be completed with insurable hazard checklists that are provided by most insurance companies, with the aid of a consultant, or by reviewing historical loss data provided by the company's current insurance firm. However, the person conducting this review must guard against the FUD Principle (fear, uncertainty, and doubt) that is cheerfully practiced by all insurance companies. That is, they tend to hone in on every conceivable risk and amplify the chance of its occurrence, so that a company will purchase lots of unnecessary insurance. The best way to avoid this problem is to employ an extremely experienced risk manager who knows which potential risks can be safely ignored. The following areas, at a minimum, should be reviewed:
   - *Buildings and equipment.* The risk manager should list the type of construction, location, and hazards to which each item is exposed. Each structure and major piece of equipment should be listed separately. The current condition of each item should be determined and its replacement cost evaluated.
   - *Business interruption.* The risk manager should determine the amount of lost profits and continuing expenses resulting from a business shutdown as the result of a specific hazard.
   - *Liabilities to other parties.* The risk manager should determine the risk of loss or damage to other parties by reason of company products, services, operations, or the acts of employees. This analysis should include a review of all contracts, sales orders, purchase orders, leases, and applicable laws to determine what commitments have been undertaken and what exposures exist.

○ *Other assets.* The risk manager should review cash, inventory, and accounts receivable to determine the possible exposure to losses by fire, flood, theft, or other hazards.

2. *Determine the risk reduction method.* Match each risk area with a method for dealing with it. The possible options for each risk area include avoidance, reduction of the hazard, retaining the hazard (that is, self insurance), or transferring the risk to an insurance company. Note that only the last option in this list includes the purchase of insurance, for there are many procedures that a company can implement to reduce a risk without resorting to insurance. The selection of a best option is based on a cost-benefit analysis that offsets the cost of each hazard against the cost of avoiding it, factoring in the probability of the hazard's occurrence. The general categories of risk reduction are:

○ *Duplicate.* A company can retain multiple copies of records to guard against the destruction of critical information. In addition, key systems such as local area networks, telephone systems, and voice mail storage can be replicated at off-site locations to avoid a shutdown caused by damage to the primary site. For example, airlines maintain elaborate backup systems for their seat reservation databases.

○ *Prevent.* A company can institute programs to reduce the likelihood and severity of losses. For example, some companies invite the Occupational Safety and Health Administration (OSHA) to inspect their premises and report on unsafe conditions; the companies then correct the issues to reduce their risk of loss. If a company requires employees to wear hardhats in construction areas, then a falling brick may still cause an accident, but the hardhat will reduce the incident's severity. Examples of prevention techniques include improving lighting, installing protective devices on machinery, and enforcing safety rules.

○ *Segregate.* A company can split up key assets such as inventory and distribute it to multiple locations (for example, warehouses). For example, the military maintains alternate command centers in case of war.

3. *Implement internal changes to reduce risks.* Once the types of risk avoidance have been determined, it is time to implement them. This usually involves new procedures or installations, such as fire suppression systems in the computer processing facility, or altered cash tracking procedures that will discourage an employee from stealing money. Changes to procedures can be a lengthy process, for they include working with the staff of each functional area to create a new procedure that is acceptable to all users, as well as following up with periodic audits to ensure that the procedures are still being followed.

4. *Select a broker.* Every company will require some insurance, unless it takes the hazardous approach of self-insuring virtually every risk. It is necessary to select a broker who can assist the company in procuring the best possible insurance. The right broker can be of great help in this process, not just in picking the least expensive insurance, but also in selecting the correct types of coverage, determining the financial strength of insurers, postloss service, and general knowledge of the company's business and of the types of risk that are most likely to occur in that environment. Unfortunately, many companies look for new brokers every few years on the principle that a long-term broker will eventually raise prices and gouge the company. In reality, a long-term relationship should be encouraged, since the broker will gain a greater knowledge of the company's risks as problems occur and

claims are received, giving it a valuable insight into company operations that a new broker does not have.

5. *Determine the types of insurance to be purchased.* Once the broker has been selected, the risk manager can show the preliminary results of the insurance review to the broker, and they can then mutually determine the types of insurance that are needed to supplement the actions already taken internally to mitigate risk. The types of insurance include the following:

    ○ *Boiler and machinery.* Covers damage to the boilers and machinery, as well as payments for injuries caused by the equipment. Providers of this insurance also review the company's equipment and issue a report recommending safety improvements.

    ○ *Business interruption.* Allows a company to pay for its continuing expenses and in some cases will pay for all or part of its anticipated profits.

    ○ *Commercial property.* The minimum "basic form" of this insurance covers losses from fires, explosions, wind storms, hail, vandalism, and other perils. The "broad form," which is an expanded version, covers everything in the basic form plus damage from falling objects, the weight of snow, water damage, and some causes of building collapse. Optional coverage includes an inflation escalator clause, replacement of destroyed structures at the actual replacement cost, and coverage of finished goods at their selling price (instead of at their cost).

    ○ *Comprehensive auto liability.* This coverage is usually mandatory and requires a minimum level of coverage for bodily injury and property damage.

    ○ *Comprehensive crime.* Covers property theft, robbery, safe and premises burglary, and employee dishonesty; in the case of employee dishonesty, the company purchases a fidelity bond, which can cover a named individual, a specific position, or all employees. Some policies will also cover ransom payments.

    ○ *Directors and officers.* Provides liability coverage to corporate managers for actions taken while acting as an officer or director of the corporation.

    ○ *General liability.* Covers claims involving accidents on company premises, as well as by its products, services, agents, or contractors. An umbrella policy usually applies to liability insurance and provides extra coverage after the primary coverage is exhausted. An umbrella policy has few exclusions.

    ○ *Group life, health, and disability.* There are several types of life insurance: *split-dollar life insurance* covers an employee, and its cost is split between the company and the employee; *key person insurance* covers the financial loss to the company in case an employee dies; and a *cross-purchase plan* allows the co-owners of a business to buy out the share of an owner who dies. *Health insurance* typically covers the areas of hospital, medical, surgical, and dental expenses. Disability insurance provides income to an individual who cannot work due to an injury or illness. The disability insurance category is subdivided into *short-term disability* (payments made while someone is recovering his or her health following an injury or illness) and *long-term disability* (continuing payments with no anticipation of a return to work).

    ○ *Inland marine.* Covers company property that is being transported. Examples of covered items include trade show displays and finished goods being shipped.

    ○ *Ocean marine and air cargo.* Covers the transporting vehicle (including loss of income due to loss of the vehicle), liability claims against the vehicle's owner or operator, and the cargo.

○ *Workers' compensation.* Provides medical and disability coverage to workers who are injured while performing duties related to their jobs. The insurance is mandatory, the employer pays all costs, and no legal recourse is permitted against the employer. There are wide variations in each state's coverage of workers' compensation, including levels of compensation, types of occupations that are not considered, and the allowability of negligence lawsuits.

These steps allow a risk manager to determine the types and potential severity of a company's risks, as well as how to reduce those risks, either through internal changes or by purchasing various types of insurance coverage.

38.5   TYPES OF INSURANCE COMPANIES

There are several types of insurance companies. Each one may serve a company's insurance needs very well, but there are significant differences between them that a company should be aware of before purchasing an insurance contract. The types of insurance companies include:

- *Captive insurance company.* This is a stock insurance company that is formed to underwrite the risks of its parent company or in some cases a sponsoring group or association.
- *Lloyds of London.* This is an underwriter operating under the special authority of the English Parliament. It may write insurance coverage of a nature that other insurance companies will not underwrite, usually because of high risks or special needs not covered by a standard insurance form. It also provides the usual types of insurance coverage.
- *Mutual.* This is a company in which each policyholder is an owner, and where earnings are distributed as dividends. If a net loss results, policyholders may be subject to extra assessments. In most cases, however, nonassessable policies are issued.
- *Reciprocal organization.* This is an association of insured companies that is independently operated by a manager. Advance deposits are made, against which are charged the proportionate costs of operations.
- *Stock company.* This is an insurance company that behaves like a normal corporation—earnings not retained in the business are distributed to shareholders as dividends and not to policyholders.

Another way to categorize insurance companies is by the type of service offered. For example, a *monoline* company provides only one type of insurance coverage, while a *multiple line* company provides more than one kind of insurance. A *financial services company* provides not only insurance but also financial services to customers.

A company can also use *self-insurance* when it deliberately plans to cover losses from its own resources rather than through those of an insurer. It can be appropriate in any of the following cases:

- When the administrative loss of using an insurer exceeds the amount of the loss.
- When a company has sufficient excess resources available to cover even the largest claim.
- When excessive premium payments are the only alternative.
- When insurance is not available at any price.

A form of partial self-insurance is to use large deductibles on insurance policies, so that a company pays for all but the very largest claims. Finally, a company can create a *captive insurer* that provides insurance to the parent company. Captive insurers can provide coverage that is tailored to the parent organization and can provide less dependence on the vagaries of the commercial insurance market. A variation on the captive insurer concept is a *fronting program*, in which a parent company buys insurance from an independent insurance company, which then reinsures the exposure with a captive of the parent company. This technique is used to avoid licensing the captive insurer in every state where the parent company does business, though the captive insurer must still be authorized to accept reinsurance. Fronting also allows the parent company to obtain local service from the independent insurance company while shifting the exposure to the captive company. No matter what form the self-insurance may take, the risk manager should work with the controller to determine the amount of loss reserves to set aside to pay for claims as they arise.

In some states, a company can become a self-insurer for workers' compensation. To do this, a company must qualify under state law as a self-insurer, purchase umbrella coverage to guard against catastrophic claims, post a surety bond, and create a claims administration department to handle claims. The advantages of doing this are lower costs (by eliminating the insurer's profit) and better cash flow (because there are no up-front insurance payments). The disadvantages of this approach are extra administrative costs as well as the cost of qualifying the company in each state in which the company operates.

These are some of the variations that a company can consider when purchasing insurance, either through a third party or a controlled subsidiary, or by providing its own coverage.

38.6   CLAIMS ADMINISTRATION

Some insurance companies take an extremely long time to respond to claims and may reject them if they are not reported in a specific format. To avoid these problems, thereby receiving the full amount of claims as quickly as possible, the risk manager must implement a strict claims administration process, as described in this section.

The risk manager should assemble a summary of information to review whenever a claim is filed. By having this information in one place, the risk manager avoids missing any steps that might interfere with the prompt settlement of a claim. The summary should include:

- *Instructions for itemizing damaged items.* Be sure to compile a complete list of all damaged items, including their inventory values, estimates, appraisals, and replacement costs. This assists the claims adjusters in determining the price they will pay to compensate for any claims.
- *Claims representatives.* There should be a list of the names, addresses, and phone numbers of the claims adjusters who handle each line of insurance. This usually requires a fair amount of updating, since there may be a number of changes to this information every year, especially if a company uses a large number of insurance companies for its various types of risk coverage.
- *Key internal personnel.* Company policy may require that the risk manager notify internal personnel if claims have been filed or payments received on those claims. For example, the accountant may want to know if payment for a large claim has been received, so that an entry can be made in the accounting records.

- *Underlying problems.* The risk manager should have a standard group of follow-up steps to review whenever a claim occurs so that there is a clear understanding of why a claim occurred, as well as how the underlying problem that caused the claim can be avoided in the future. Without these instructions, it is possible that a company will repeat the problem over and over again, resulting in many claims and a vastly increased insurance premium.

- *Instructions for safeguarding damaged items.* If material has been damaged, it is the responsibility of the company to ensure that it is not damaged further, which would result in a larger claim. For example, a company must protect the materials in a warehouse from further damage as soon as it discovers that the roof has leaked and destroyed some items. If it does not take this action, the insurer can rightly claim that it will only pay for the damage that occurred up to the point when the company could have taken corrective action.

The above information is necessary for the filing of every insurance claim. In addition, there are two steps related to claims administration that the risk manager should attend to on an ongoing basis:

1. *Accounting techniques.* The risk manager should work with the accountant to develop a standard set of accounting entries that are used for insurance claims as well as to summarize the cost of risk management. These relate to accumulating cost information for each claim so that the risk manager can easily summarize the appropriate information related to each claim and use it to file for reimbursement. This information should include the costs of claims preparation, security and property protection, cleanup, repair costs, property identification, and storage costs.

2. *Audit program.* No matter how good the procedures may be for the claims administration process, it is common for the claims administration staff to forget or sidestep some procedures. This is especially common when there is frequent employee turnover in this area, with poor training of the replacement staff. To identify procedural problems, it is useful to conduct a periodic review of the claims administration process. To ensure consistency in this audit, there should be a standard audit program that forms the minimum set of audit instructions (to be expanded upon as needed) for use in conducting each audit.

It can be cost-effective to have some claims administered by outside service companies, quite often by the insurance carrier itself. Usually high-volume, low-cost-per-unit items such as medical claims are in this category. When outside services are used, the accountant must establish with the provider the controls to be followed and the reports to be prepared. Periodic audits of the outside claims processing operation should be made by the company to ensure that claims are being handled in a controlled and effective manner.

38.7 INSURANCE FILES

Insurance recordkeeping is vital to ascertain that adequate insurance coverage has been obtained and is being administered properly. The primary risks that this recordkeeping avoids are inadvertently dropping insurance through lack of renewal and having inadequate insurance given a company's actual claims record. The layout of insurance records described in this section helps a company to avoid these problems.

There are several main categories of insurance records. The first section identifies each policy. The next section is a tickler file that lists key due dates for each policy. This is useful for ensuring that all policy payments are made on time, so that they do not lapse. The next section is the activity file, which describes the claim history and open claims for each policy. Finally, there is the value file, which itemizes the insurable values covered by each policy. The activity and value files are needed to determine the size of claims or the value being covered, so the risk manager can see if each policy provides a sufficient amount of coverage. When properly maintained, these files give the risk manager a basis for sound management of his or her function. The contents of each type of file are:

- *Identification file*. Lists key information on each policy:
  - Abstract of coverage, showing exclusions
  - Broker
  - Effective dates
  - Insurer
  - Policy number
  - Rates, premiums, and refunds
  - Type of insurance coverage
- *Tickler file*. Lists key dates for each policy:
  - Inspection dates
  - Policy expiration date
  - Premium payment dates
  - Reporting dates
- *Activity file*. Describes the claim history and open claims for each policy:
  - Historical comparison of premiums to losses
  - History file on closed claims
  - Reserves established
  - Status of each claim
  - Support and documentation of each claim
- *Value file*. Itemizes the insurable values covered by each policy:
  - Detail of actual cash value of each item covered by a policy
  - Detail of replacement cost of each item covered by a policy
  - Summary of insurable values listed on each policy

38.8 ANNUAL RISK MANAGEMENT REPORT

The risk manager should issue a risk management report to the board of directors every year. This document reviews all perceived risks to which a company is subject and then describes the steps taken to mitigate those risks. It is of great value to the board, because it needs to know the extent of potential risks and how they can impact company operations. Unfortunately, not many controllers or chief financial officers are aware of what should go into the annual risk management report. This presents a problem if the board asks either of these managers, to whom the risk manager usually reports, about the contents of this document. To avoid this problem, the contents of a typical risk management report are described in this section, including an example based on an organization that provides training in high-risk outdoor activities.

Section II: Review of Risks
- *Risk related to education:*
  1. Risk of school equipment failing
  2. Risk of accidents due to improper instruction

Section III: Ways to Cover Risks
- *Risk of school equipment failing.* School equipment is reviewed and replaced by the school governing committees on a regular basis. Instructors are also authorized to immediately remove equipment from use if they spot unusual damage that may result in equipment failure.
- *Risk of accidents due to improper supervision.* School instructors must first serve as assistant instructors under the supervision of a more experienced instructor, who evaluates their skills and recommends advancement to full instructor status. The typical instructor has previously completed all prerequisite courses, and has considerable outdoor experience. All instructors must have taken a mountain-oriented first aid class within the last year.

Section IV: Supplemental Insurance Coverage
- *Risk of school equipment failing.* The general liability policy covers this risk for the first $500,000 of payments to a claimant. The umbrella policy covers this risk for an additional $5 million after the coverage provided by the general liability policy is exhausted.
- *Risk of accidents due to improper instruction.* Same insurance coverage as for the risk of school equipment failing.

EXHIBIT 38.2   EXAMPLE OF A RISK MANAGEMENT REPORT

The risk management report contains four sections. The first is an overview that describes the contents of the report, the timing of when it is issued, and to whom it is delivered. The second section itemizes all risks that are perceived to be significant. If every possible risk were to be listed, the document might be too voluminous for easy reading. These risks should be grouped with subheadings, rather than appearing as an enormous list that is difficult for the reader to digest. The third section notes the ways to cover those risks, excluding insurance (which is addressed in the fourth section). These are operational changes such as altered procedures or processes, or additional training. Finally, the fourth section notes the insurance that has been purchased to provide additional coverage to those risk areas that cannot be adequately covered by internal changes. These four sections give the board an adequate knowledge of a company's efforts in the risk management area.

The example in Exhibit 38.2 presents an extract from the risk management report of an organization that provides outdoor training classes. The example skips the overview section and proceeds straight to the enumeration of risks, how they are covered, and what types of insurance are also needed. This is a good example of the format that an accountant should look for in a risk management report.

38.9 SUMMARY

In a larger company, there is usually a risk manager who identifies and finds ways to mitigate risk, either through internal changes or by purchasing insurance. Because this manager frequently reports to either the controller or CFO, it is important for these people to have an overall knowledge of how risk management works. This chapter answered the need by describing the policies and procedures used by a risk manager, and that person's job description. The types of insurance companies, the paperwork handled by the risk manager, and the annual risk management report were also described.

PART SEVEN

OTHER ACCOUNTING TOPICS

MERGERS AND ACQUISITIONS

39.1 INTRODUCTION

There are many situations in which a company merely makes a small investment in another company, rather than making an outright purchase. This requires three possible types of accounting, depending upon the size of the investment and the degree of control attained over the subject company—all three methods, which are the cost, equity, and consolidation methods, are described here.

We also delve into special topics associated with mergers and acquisitions, including push-down accounting, leveraged buyouts, spin-off transactions, and the proper treatment of goodwill.

When reading this text, one should keep in mind that the terms "merger" and "acquisition" are not the same thing. An *acquisition* is a transaction in which both the acquiring and acquired company are still left standing as separate entities at the end of the transaction. A *merger* results in the legal dissolution of one of the companies, and a *consolidation* dissolves both of the parties and creates a new one, into which the previous entities are merged.

39.2 EVALUATING ACQUISITION TARGETS

The analysis of an acquisition is like no other type of financial analysis—not because the analysis itself is different, but because of the logistics of the situation. Typically, a potential acquisition situation arises suddenly, requires the fullest attention of the accounting staff for a short time, and then subsides, either because the acquisition is judged to be not a good one or because the deal is completed and management takes over the activities of melding the organizations together. In either case, the controller is ensconced in the front end of the process, rendering opinions on any possible corporate purchase that the chief executive officer (CEO) sees fit to investigate.

Because of the suddenness of an acquisition evaluation, the controller must be fully prepared to switch from any current activities into a full-bore analysis mode. This chapter includes the bulk of analyses that one should pursue in order to determine if the condition of an acquiree is as its purports to be. However, much more than a checklist is required. A controller and his or her staff have other duties, and cannot let them lie in order to conduct an investigation. Accordingly, the capacity of the accounting department to complete a potentially massive analysis chore may not exist if the department is still to operate in anything close to a normal and efficient manner. Accordingly, a controller has three choices to make. First, if there are very few acquisition evaluations to make and the potential acquirees are small ones, then it may be possible to accept some degree of disruption in the accounting ranks and perform all the work with the existing staff. A second alternative is to form an acquisition analysis group that does nothing but evaluate potential candidates on a full-time basis. This is an excellent approach if a company is embarked on the path of growth by acquisition, and is willing to buy as many corporations as possible. The third alternative is to hire an outside auditing firm to conduct the financial analysis on behalf of the company. This is a good alternative if the in-house staff does not have the time or training to conduct the work, and if there are not enough acquisitions to justify hiring a full-time team of analysts. However, using outside auditors can be an expensive proposition, and one must be careful to ensure that the audit staff used is of a high enough level of training and experience to conduct a thorough review. Thus, the number of potential acquisitions and the ability of the internal accounting staff to complete acquisition analysis work will dictate the method a controller uses to obtain sufficient analysis assistance.

With the acquisition analysis team in place, a controller can proceed through the remainder of this section to determine the precise sets of analysis questions to answer in order to ensure that the type of acquisition being contemplated is fully analyzed—without wasting time on any additional analysis work. The main analysis areas are as follows:

- *Personnel*. If a company has need of employees with great experience or skill, it can fill the need by buying a company that employs them. This is a rare circumstance when only a few people are involved, since it is easier to hire them away with employment offers. However, if a potential acquiree has one or more departments that are justly famous for their work, then buying the company may be worthwhile in order to obtain those specific departments. This situation arises most frequently with engineering or research firms. The main analysis needed here is to determine the current compensation levels of the people being acquired, as well as how these pay levels compare to both internal and industry pay standards, and the presence of any long-term compensation agreements and their net present value.

- *Patents*. A target company may possess one or more valuable patents, especially ones that can be used to enhance the value of the acquiring company's products. This approach is most common with research and drug firms. In this case, the primary analysis focuses on the cost of maintaining those patents, the number of years remaining prior to expiration, and (especially) the expected cash flows to be obtained from them prior to their expiration.

- *Brands*. A brand name is immensely valuable if it has been carefully maintained for many years, has been strongly supported with proper marketing, and represents excellent products. This is a good reason to acquire a target company, and this is most common in the consumer goods field. The analysis for this type of acquisition focuses on the incremental profits to be gained by use of the brand name in relation to the cost of maintaining the brand.

- *Capacity*. If a company is faced with a long lead time or technological challenges to acquire greater production capacity, it may be worthwhile to purchase a production facility from another company. The analysis for this type of acquisition focuses on the age and usefulness of the machinery and facility purchased.

- *Assets and liabilities.* When an entire company is purchased, the acquiring organization is taking over virtually all assets, as well as all associated risks. In this instance, a comprehensive review of all balance sheet line items is mandatory.
- *Profitability.* A company may be bought because it has a greater percentage of profitability than the acquiring company, which increases the acquiring company's combined profitability. For this acquisition, a close review of the income statement and balance sheet is necessary.
- *Cash flow.* If a company has a large store of cash or continuing cash flows, it is a prime target for purchase by companies that need the cash, possibly to fund further acquisitions. For this type of acquisition, an intensive review of the balance sheet, income statement, and funds flow statement is necessary.

If a company is involved in a friendly acquisition, then the target company is generally willing to open its accounting books for inspection. The exception to the rule is that, if the target company is a direct competitor to the acquiring organization, then it will resist discussions of trade secrets or processes that will allow it to continue to effectively compete against the acquiring company in case the acquisition does not occur. Also, if an acquisition is of the unfriendly variety, then the opposing company will be quite active in denying access to any information whatever. This is an especially serious problem when a company is privately held, since very little information will be publicly available. In these situations where information is not readily obtainable, how can a controller find a sufficient amount of information to conduct an analysis?

The first step is to dredge up all possible sources of information. One possibility is the target company's credit report, which may list a recent financial statement (though, since it is usually supplied by the target company, which may not interested in publicly displaying its financial health, it may not be remotely accurate). Another source is articles in trade journals about the organization, as well as a simple review of the facility. By counting the number of cars in the parking lot, one can make a rough estimate, based on the industry average of sales per employee, of the amount of company sales. It may also be possible to talk to former or current employees about the company, as well as its customers or suppliers. Another option is to talk to local recruiters about the positions for which they have been asked to recruit, which may indicate problems that have resulted in employee turnover. Also, the credit report will list all assets against which lenders have filed security claims, which shows the degree to which the target company is using financial leverage to fund its operations. It may also be possible to hire an investigative agency to acquire more information. Finally, reviewing public records about lawsuit filings will reveal if there is any outstanding litigation against the firm. Here is a list of additional outside information sources that may be of use in compiling a comprehensive set of data for a prospective acquisition:

- *Stock transfer agent.* This entity can verify the target company's outstanding capitalization.
- *Title search company.* These organizations, of which Dun & Bradstreet is the best known, will review all public records for the existence of liens on the assets of the target company. The list of liens should be compared to any outstanding debt schedules provided to the buyer to see if there are any discrepancies.

- *Patent/trademark search company.* This type of company reviews all legal filings to see if there are infringement lawsuits against the patents or trademarks of the target company, and it can also obtain copies of the original patents or trademarks.
- *Appraisal companies.* An appraisal company can provide a list of the appraised value of a target company's assets, though it will not reveal this information without the prior approval of the target company.

If the target company is diligent in blocking attempts at obtaining information about it, and this results in a significant loss of information, the controller will not be able to complete a full analysis of the situation. If so, it is very useful to make a list of what information has *not* been obtained and what the risk may be of not obtaining it. For example, if there is no information available about a company's gross margin, then there is a risk of making too large an offer for a company that does not have the margins to support the price. Once all these risks are assembled into a list, one should determine the level of risk the company is willing to bear by not having the information, or in deciding to invest the time and money to obtain the information. This will be an iterative process, as the number of questions posed by the controller gradually decreases, and the cost and time needed to find the answers to the remaining questions goes up. At some point, the CEO will decide that enough information is available to proceed with making an offer or that the work required is excessive and stop any further investigative efforts and proceed to the investigation of other target companies for whom information is easier to obtain.

If the main reason for acquiring a target company is to hire away a specific person or group of people who are deemed to have valuable skills, a controller has one of two analysis options to pursue. The first is that, if the company has chosen to purchase the entire target company, then a full-blown analysis of all assets, liabilities, controls, and legal issues must be conducted. The analysis for those categories are noted under the following sections of this chapter. However, if the company has persuaded the target company to accept payment in exchange for the transfer of some smaller portion of the company that includes the targeted employees, then the analysis work becomes much more specific.

An example of a partial purchase to obtain employees occurs when a target company decides to eliminate one of its lines of business, and sells the related customer list and assets to the acquiring company. As part of the transaction, the target company lays off its employees that were associated with the line of business that is being transferred to the new company. The acquiring company obtains a list of these employees from the selling company and contacts them to offer them jobs. Because of the nature of this transaction, there is essentially nothing more than a transfer of assets, which greatly reduces the amount of analysis required of the controller. Only the following analyses should be conducted that are specifically targeted at the employees to be hired, with an emphasis on their quality, cost, and turnover:

- *Investigate employee names listed on patents.* If individual employees are named on patents or patent applications filed by the target company, then it is a good bet that those employees may be in a revenue-sharing agreement with the company employing them. If so, the controller must research further to determine the amounts paid to the employees for use of the patents, such as a fee per unit sold or an annual payment. These patent payments must be added to the employee salaries to determine the true cost of bringing in the new personnel.
- *Interview customers and suppliers about employees.* If there are problems with the desired employees, the target company is almost certainly not going to reveal this

information, since it is trying to obtain payment for "selling" them to the acquiring company. Accordingly, it may be necessary to call the target company's suppliers or customers to see if they have had dealings with the people under consideration, and what their opinions may be.

- *Compare employee pay levels to industry and internal averages.* Obtain the pay rates for the entire department to be acquired, and determine the distribution of pay through the group to see if there are any inordinately highly paid people. Then compare these rates not only to the industry average, but also the acquiring company's average, to determine the difference between the pay levels about to be brought in and the existing rates. If there is a major difference between the two pay rates, then an additional cost of the acquisition may be to bring the pay levels of the in-house staff up to match those of the incoming personnel, in order avoid turmoil caused by the pay differential.

- *Determine the current turnover rate in the targeted department.* If there is a high turnover rate in the department being acquired, then the cost of acquisition may not be worthwhile if there is a high risk of losing the entire group.

- *Review long-term compensation agreements.* If a target company has obtained the services of a number of exceptional employees, it is quite possible that it has done so by offering them expensive, long-term employment contracts. The controller should review them not only for the projected payment amounts, increases, and net present value, but also for golden parachute clauses that pay these employees exorbitant amounts if the target company is purchased.

The upshot of what a controller is looking for when reviewing the acquisition of personnel is the actual cost of those employees and the potential impact on their counterparts. The first item is purely financial in nature, while the second is a matter for conjecture regarding the impact of a group of higher-paid employees on the existing, in-house group that is paid less. The controller can only provide the information regarding pay disparities to the CEO and human resources director and let them determine what to do to boost the morale of the existing staff when they learn about the higher wages being paid to the newly arriving personnel. An example of the analysis report that the controller should issue for an acquisition based on personnel is shown in Exhibit 39.1.

Description	Additional Information	Summary Costs
Total cost of incoming staff (15 staff)		$1,237,500
Average cost of incoming staff	$82,500	
Average cost of in-house staff	73,000	
Prior year employee turnover level	10%	
Additional cost to match in-house salaries to incoming salaries (13 staff)		123,500
Net present value of projected patent payments to employees		420,000
Cost of employment contract buyouts		250,000
Total cost of employee acquisition		**$2,031,000**
Total cost per employee acquired (15 staff)		**$ 135,400**
Industry average pay rate per person		**$ 80,000**
Percentage premium over market rate		**69%**

EXHIBIT 39.1 ANALYSIS REPORT FOR ACQUISITION OF PERSONNEL

Note that the cost of acquisition has been converted at the bottom of the example into a cost per employee, which is then compared to the average market rate. The premium to be paid over the market rate gives management its best idea of the true cost of the staff it is acquiring, and whether or not it is a good idea to proceed with the acquisition.

If a company wants to acquire a patent from another company, it does not usually go to the extreme of buying the whole company. Instead, it negotiates for the patent itself, which makes the analysis work substantially easier for the controller. There are few measures to investigate, with an emphasis on the existing costs and revenues currently experienced by the holder of the patent. Management may require additional analysis to include the estimated additional revenues and costs that will subsequently be incurred by its use of the patent, which may vary from the use to which it has been put by the current patent owner. The primary analyses are as follows:

- *Determine annual patent renewal costs.* Annual patent costs are quite minimal, but should be included in any patent analysis, such as the one noted in Exhibit 39.2, in order to present a comprehensive set of cost information.
- *Determine current patent-related revenue stream.* This information is needed to determine the amount of money that the company is willing to pay for a patent; however, if the company wants to shift the focus of the patent to a different application, then this number is less useful. Without cooperation from the target company, this can be a very difficult number to determine, since the only alternative is to contact those companies who are licensed to use the patent and see if they will reveal the per-unit payment they are required to make to the target company for use of their patent. If the target company is willing to reveal this information, then also obtain it for the last few years, to see if there is an upward or downward trend line for the revenues; if the trend is downward, then the revenue stream for which the company is paying is worth less.
- *Ascertain extent of current litigation to support patent.* A major issue for any patent holder is the amount of money it must spend to keep other entities from encroaching on the patent with parallel patents or just issuing products that illegally use technology based on the patent. These legal costs can be enormous. If a company wants to take over a patent, it must be aware of the extent of encroachment and the cost of legally pursuing the encroachers.

An example of the analysis report that the controller should issue for a patent purchase is shown in Exhibit 39.2.

The bottom line of the patent acquisition analysis report is the net present value of all cash flows, which the CEO and controller can use as the highest recommended amount to

Description	Additional Information	Summary Revenues & Costs
Years left prior to patent expiration	10 years	
Net present value of cash inflows		$1,200,000
Discounted cost of remaining filing costs		−42,000
Discounted cost of expected annual legal fees		−375,000
Net present value of patent		$ 783,000

EXHIBIT 39.2 ANALYSIS REPORT FOR PATENT ACQUISITION

pay for the patent. However, given alternative uses for the patent that they may be contemplating, they may anticipate a higher cash inflow that will allow them to pay a higher price for the patent.

The analyses needed to review a brand name are relatively simple from the financial perspective, though somewhat more involved from the legal side, since one must conduct research to ensure that there is a clear title to the trademark, as well as ascertain the extent of possible infringements on the brand name, and the extent and recent history of litigation needed to support the brand. The primary analyses are as follows:

- *Determine the amount of annual trademark fees.* This is a very minor item, but can grow to considerable proportions if the trademark is being maintained worldwide, which requires filings and maintenance fees in a multitude of jurisdictions.

- *Determine clear title to the brand name.* This is not just a matter of paying for a small amount of research by a legal firm to determine the existence of any countervailing trademarks, but also requires a search in multiple jurisdictions if the buying company wants to expand the brand to other countries.

- *Ascertain the amount and trend of any current cash inflows from the brand name.* The two best analysis options are to either measure just that portion of sales that are specifically due to licensing agreements (and therefore easily traceable) or by measuring the incremental difference in cash flows from all products under the brand name, in comparison to those of the industry average or specific competitors.

- *Note the amount and trend of any legal fees needed to stop encroachment.* A quality brand frequently attracts a number of companies that build inexpensive knockoffs, and illegally sell them for vastly reduced prices. Given the reduced quality and prices, the net impact of these fake goods is to cheapen the brand's image. Consequently, constant legal pursuit of these companies is the only way to keep imitating products off the market. The controller should estimate the cost of current lawsuits, roughly estimated by reviewing all current lawsuits that are public record, or by asking the target company. If the acquiring company wants to maintain the brand image, it must be willing to continue to use legal alternatives, so the current legal cost can be used as a reasonable benchmark of future cost as well.

- *Note any challenges to use of the brand name.* Yet another legal issue is that there may be lawsuits pending that claim the trademark of another person or corporation supersedes the one about to be purchased. If so, a search of all open lawsuits should reveal this information. Once again, if the company contemplates worldwide usage of the brand name, then a much more extensive search for competing trademarks in other locations is necessary. If there are cases where someone else has filed for the right to use the brand name in another country, then the controller should calculate the estimated cost of acquiring the rights to that name.

In Exhibit 39.3, we itemize the financial analysis associated with a brand name acquisition that a controller should expect to issue to management.

When a company purchases a specific manufacturing facility from another company, it is usually doing so to increase its capacity. With this end in mind, the key analyses revolve around the condition and cost of the facility, so that one can determine the amount of replacement machinery to install, as well as the actual production capacity percentage, the cost per percent of capacity, and the facility's overhead cost. For many of the analyses, the information the controller assembles must cover three activity levels—minimum, normal, and maximum capacity levels. The reason for the threefold format (as also shown in

Description	Additional Information	Summary Revenues & Costs
Net present value of current cash inflows		$ 500,000
Discounted cost of annual trademark fees		−65,000
Cost of trademark search (for clear title)		−175,000
Discounted cost of annual legal fees		−780,000
Cost to purchase competing brand names	See note	−2,250,000
Total net cost of brand name		**$−2,770,000**

Note: A competing trademark has already been filed by company XYZ in all countries of the European Community and Japan. The cost required to purchase this trademark is included in the analysis.

EXHIBIT 39.3   ANALYSIS REPORT FOR BRAND ACQUISITION

Exhibit 39.4) is that management may not use the facility as much as it anticipates, in which case it must be aware of the minimum costs that will still be incurred, as well as the extra costs that must be covered if the facility runs at the highest possible rate of production. The primary analyses are as follows:

- *Determine the facility overhead cost required for minimum, standard, and maximum capacity.* Any facility requires a minimum cost to maintain, even if it is not running. Such costs include taxes, security, insurance, and building maintenance. Management must know this minimum cost level, in case it does not use the facility, but must still pay for the upkeep. Also, current accounting records will reveal the overhead needed to run the facility at a normal level, while the industrial engineering or production personnel can estimate the additional costs needed to run the plant at full capacity.

- *Ascertain the amount of capital replacements needed.* Some machinery will be so worn out or outdated that it must be replaced. This information is beyond the knowledge of a controller, but not of an industrial engineer or production manager, who can walk through the facility and determine the condition of the equipment. If this is not readily apparent, then perusing the maintenance records will reveal which machines require so much continuing work that a complete replacement is a more efficient alternative.

Description	Costs at Minimum Capacity Usage	Costs at Normal Capacity Usage	Costs at Maximum Capacity Usage
Facility overhead cost	$1,000,000	$3,500,000	$5,000,000
Capital replacement cost*	0	0	400,000
Equipment maintenance cost	0	450,000	600,000
Cost of environmental damage insurance	50,000	50,000	50,000
Cost to investigate possible environmental damage	100,000	100,000	100,000
Facility modification costs	0	0	700,000
Total costs	**$1,150,000**	**$4,100,000**	**$6,850,000**
Percent capacity level	0%	50%	85%
Cost per percent of capacity	**N/A**	**$ 82,000**	**$ 81,000**

*Represents the depreciation on capital replacement items.

EXHIBIT 39.4   ANALYSIS REPORT FOR CAPACITY ACQUISITIONS

- *Find out the periodic maintenance cost of existing equipment.* Even if equipment does not require replacement, it must still be maintained, which can be a considerable cost. This information should be obtained for the normal run rate, and estimated for the maximum capacity level.

- *Determine the maximum production capacity.* The industrial engineering staff must estimate the maximum capacity level at which the facility can run, subject to expenditures for equipment replacements and facility modifications.

- *Investigate any environmental liabilities.* Sometimes, the target company is more than willing to get rid of a facility if it suspects there is environmental damage that must be fixed. This can be an extraordinarily expensive item, and can sometimes exceed the cost of the entire facility. To guard against this problem, a controller should determine the cost of conducting an environment investigation, as well as the cost of insurance to provide coverage in case such damage is discovered after the purchase date.

- *Determine the cost of modifications needed to increase the capacity of the facility.* Unless a facility has been very carefully laid out in the beginning for the highest possible maximization of throughput, it is likely that it can use a significant overhaul of its layout. To do this, the industrial engineering staff must review the current situation and recommend the shifting of equipment and installation of additional materials movement capabilities.

The preceding analyses are summarized in the sample capacity analysis report shown in Exhibit 39.4, which includes low-medium-high categories for costs that are based on projected capacity utilization levels. At the bottom of the example, all costs are converted into a dollar amount for each percent of capacity used. Note that there is no utilization listed for the minimum level, since the facility is shuttered under this assumption.

A company will sometimes acquire just the assets of another organization. This is most common when there is some risk associated with the liabilities of the target company, such as lawsuits or environmental problems or an excessive amount of debt. When assets are purchased, the buyer can be quite selective in buying only those assets that are of the most value, such as patents, brands, or personnel, which have been covered in previous subsections. At this point, we note only the following additional analyses needed to ensure that all other assets are properly reviewed prior to an acquisition:

- *Conduct a fixed asset audit.* Before paying for an asset, make sure that the asset is there. The fixed asset records of some companies are in such poor condition that assets still on the books may have been disposed of years before. An appraiser or an internal audit team can conduct this review.

- *Appraise the value of fixed assets.* Even if an asset exists, it may have far less value than the amount listed in the fixed asset database. To be sure of the current value of all assets, have an appraiser review them and determine their value. The final appraisal report should contain two values for each asset—the rush liquidation value and a higher value based on a more careful liquidation approach. These two values can be the focus of a great deal of negotiating between the buyer and the target company, since the buyer will want to pay based on the rush liquidation value, and the target company will prefer to sell at the price indicated by the slower liquidation approach.

- *Ascertain the existence of liens against assets.* A company should not purchase an asset if there is a lien against it. This usually occurs when the target company has used the assets as collateral for loans or has used leases to finance the purchase of specific assets. The standard procedure in an acquisition is to have lenders remove liens prior to the completion of an acquisition, which frequently requires paying off those lenders with a new "bridge" loan that covers the period of a few weeks or days between the removal of liens and the transfer of payment from the buyer to the target company, which is then used to pay off the bridge loan.

- *Determine the collectibility of accounts receivable.* If the purchase includes all current accounts receivable, then trace the largest invoices back to specific shipments, and confirm them with the customers to whom the invoices were sent. Also, be sure to trace the history of bad debt write-offs to determine an appropriate average amount that will reflect the amount of the current accounts receivable that will become bad debt.

- *Verify the bank reconciliation for all bank accounts.* For any checking or investment account, verify the amount of cash at the bank and reconcile it to the amount listed in the corporate accounting records. Also, investigate any reconciling items to ensure that they are appropriate.

- *Audit the existence and valuation of remaining assets.* There are usually a number of smaller-dollar assets on the books, such as the payoff value of life insurance, deposits on rentals and leases, and loans to employees or officers. All of these items must be audited, both through investigation of the original contracts on which they are based and through confirmations from those entities who owe the target company money.

- *Determine the value of any tax loss carryforward.* If the buyer is acquiring a tax loss carryforward from the target company, it can use this to reduce its own tax burden. The controller should use either the corporate tax staff or outside auditors to review the validity of the target company's tax returns to ensure that the reported loss on which the carryforward is based is valid, as well as to review the (ever changing) tax laws to ensure that the company is qualified to use the loss carryforward (which under current laws can only be recognized over a very long time period).

A sample of an analysis report for assets is noted in Exhibit 39.5.

In Exhibit 39.5, only the appraised rapid liquidation value of the assets to be purchased is listed in the "Valuation Summary" column, whereas two other forms of asset valuation are noted in the "Additional Information" column. The reason for this treatment of asset values is that the controller is presenting to management the lowest possible asset value,

Description	Additional Information	Valuation Summary
Appraised value of assets (rapid liquidation)		$16,000,000
Appraised value of assets (slow liquidation)	$18,500,000	
Book value of assets	19,000,000	
Book value of assets with outstanding liens	19,000,000	
Book value of accounts receivable		5,500,000
Recommended bad debt reserve		−150,000
Value of cash and investments		750,000
Net present value of remaining assets	Discount rate is 13%	629,500
Net present value of tax loss carryforwards	Discount rate is 13%	2,575,000
Total asset valuation		**$25,304,500**

EXHIBIT 39.5   ANALYSIS REPORT FOR ASSETS

which it will use to determine its lowest offering price for the purchase of the target company's assets. The other higher asset values are included as notations, in case management wants to bid a higher dollar amount and needs to determine its upper boundaries for a reasonable offer price. In addition, the value of remaining assets and the tax loss carryforward are both listed at their net present values. The reason for using discounting for these two items is that they may not be readily liquidated in the short term. For example, other assets may include loans to employees or officers that will take several years to collect, while only a portion of a tax loss carryforward can usually be used in each year. Accordingly, the discount rate for the net present value calculation for each of these line items is noted in the "additional information" column in the example. Also, the bad debt deduction from the accounts receivable is not the one used by the target company, but rather the one compiled by the controller's staff, following its review of the history of bad debt write-offs and the risk of bad debt occurrences for the current group of accounts receivable.

If a company decides to purchase a target company as a complete entity, rather than buying pieces of it, then the liabilities side of the balance sheet will also be part of the purchase, and will require analysis by the controller. The main liability analyses are as follows:

- *Reconcile unpaid debt to lender balances.* There may be a difference between the amount recorded on the company's books as being the debt liability and the lender's version of the amount still payable. If there is some doubt regarding whose version is correct, one should always use the amount noted by the lender, since this entity will not release its lien on company assets until it believes itself to be fully paid.

- *Look for unrecorded debt.* A target company may have incorrectly reported a capital lease as an operating lease or be recording some other form of debt payment as an expense, without recording the underlying debt liability. One can review the target company's stream of payments to see if there are any continuing payments, most likely in the same amount from period to period, that indicate the presence of a debt pay down.

- *Audit accounts payable.* One should also verify that all accounts payable listed on the target company's books are actual expenses and not duplications of earlier payments. Also, one should investigate the unvouchered accounts payable to see if these are all approved and binding expenses, and if there are additional receipts for which there are no existing accounts payable listed in the accounting records.

- *Audit accrued liabilities.* A target company that wants to obtain the highest possible selling price will downplay these expenses, so one must be careful to verify the existence of all possible accrued expenses, and then recalculate how the accruals were derived, to ensure that the underlying expenses that these accruals will eventually offset are accurate. The following accruals are among the more common ones:
  - Income taxes
  - Payroll taxes
  - Personal property taxes
  - Warranty costs
  - Product recalls

Description	Additional Information	Summary Revenues & Costs
Book balance of debt		$3,750,000
Add: Additional lender balance due	See Note 1	15,000
Add: Unrecorded capital leases	See Note 2	175,000
Book balance of accounts payable		2,200,000
Add: Unrecorded accounts payable	See Note 3	28,000
Subtract: Duplicate accounts payable	See Note 4	−2,000
Book balance of accrued liabilities		450,000
Add: Additional accrual for property taxes	See Note 5	80,000
Add: Accrual for workers' compensation insurance	See Note 6	15,000
Total liabilities valuation		**$6,711,000**

Note 1: Company recorded $15,000 in late interest payments as a debt reduction.
Note 2: Capital leases for six forklifts recorded as expenses.
Note 3: No supplier invoice recorded for maintenance supplies received on last day of the month.
Note 4: Supplier invoices for in-house construction work recorded under both vouchered and unvouchered accounts payable.
Note 5: Original accrual did not reflect an increase of 2.3% in the tax rate.
Note 6: Original accrual based on a payroll level that is 15% lower than the actual payroll amount.

EXHIBIT 39.6   ANALYSIS REPORT FOR LIABILITIES

All of the preceding analyses are summarized into the sample analysis report for liabilities, which is described in Exhibit 39.6. Of particular interest are the line items for reconciliation problems, such as extra debt and accounts payable, as well as corrections to the accrued expenses. All of these adjustments are used to negotiate a lower price for the target company, since the higher liabilities reduce its net value.

There are several methods that a controller should use when reviewing the profitability of a target company. One is to track the trends in several key variables, since these will indicate worsening profit situations. Also, it is important to segment costs and profits by customer, so that one can see if certain customers soak up an inordinate proportion of the expenses. Further, it may be possible to determine the head count associated with each major transaction, so that one can determine the possibility of reducing expenses by imposing transaction-related efficiencies that have worked for the acquiring company. The intent of these analyses is to quickly determine the current state and trend of a target company's profits, as well as to pinpoint those customers and costs that are associated with the majority of profits and losses. The main analyses are as follows:

- *Review a trend line of revenues.* If there has been a decline in the rate of growth or an overall decline in revenues, then review the company's percentage of the total market to see if the cause might be a shrinkage in the overall market. If not, then review sales by product and customer to determine the exact cause of the problem.

- *Review a trend line of bad debt expense.* As a market matures and additional sales are harder to come by, a company's management may loosen its credit terms, which allows it to increase sales but at the cost of a higher level of bad debt, which may exceed the additional gross margin earned from the incremental sales that were added. To see if a target company has resorted to this approach to increasing sales, review the trend line of bad debt expense to see if there has been a significant increase. Also, review the current accounts receivable for old invoices that have not yet been written off as bad debt, and also see if there are sales credits that are actually bad debts. The sum of these items constitute the true bad debt expense.

- *Review a trend line of sales discounts.* As a follow-up to the last item, management may offer discounts to customers in advance for additional sales, or add customers who are in the habit of taking discounts, whether approved or not. These issues are most common when a company's sales are no longer trending upward, and management is looking for a new approach to spur sales, even at the cost of reduced margins due to the discounts. These discounts may be stored in a separate account for sales discounts, or mixed in with sales credits of other kinds.

- *Review a trend line of material costs.* For most organizations outside of the service sector, this is the largest cost, and so requires a reasonable degree of attention. The controller cannot hope to delve into all possible aspects of material costs during a due diligence review, such as variances for scrap, purchase prices, or cycle counting adjustments. However, it is easy to run a trend line of material costs for the last few years, just to see if these costs are changing as a proportion of sales. A small increase in costs here can relate to the entire cost of a department in other areas of the company, due to the large overall cost of materials, so a change of as little as one percent in this expense category is a cause for concern.

- *Review a trend line of direct labor costs.* One should review the trend line of direct labor costs in much the same manner as for material costs. Though this is usually a much smaller cost than for materials, it is still sufficiently large to be a cause for concern if there is a significant trend line of increasing expenses.

- *Review a trend line of gross margins.* This measure is worthy of comparison to industry averages or to the gross margins of specific competitors, so the acquiring company can gain some idea of the production efficiencies of the company it is attempting to purchase.

- *Review a trend line of net margins.* If the gross margin looks reasonable, then proceed to a trend line analysis of net margins. If there is a declining trend here that was not apparent in the preceding gross margin analysis, then one can focus on the sales, general, and administrative expense areas to see where the cost increase has occurred.

- *Ascertain the gross profit by product.* Review the gross profit for each product at the direct cost level, to determine which ones have excessively low profit levels and are targets either for withdrawal from the market or a price increase. If possible, also determine the cost of fixed assets that are associated with each product (i.e., product-specific production equipment), so that the buyer can budget for an asset reduction alongside any product terminations.

- *Review a trend line of overhead personnel per major customer.* One can determine the overhead needed to support a profitable base of customers with a ratio of overhead personnel to the number of major customers. This review can extend much more deeply to determine which customers require inordinate amounts of time by the support staff, though this information is rarely available.

- *Review a trend line of overhead personnel per transaction.* Determine the number of personnel involved in all major transactions, such as accounts payable, accounts receivable, receiving, and purchasing, and divide this number into the annual total of all these transactions. If there appears to be an excessive number of employees per transaction, then the acquirer may be able to reduce personnel costs in these areas.

Type of Analysis Conducted	Notes
Review a trend line of revenues	Percentage rate of growth has declined in last two years.
Review a trend line of bad debt expense	Bad debt expense has increased, due to relaxation of credit standards.
Review a trend line of sales discounts	80% of the newest customers have all been given sales discounts of 10%–15%.
Review a trend line of material costs	No significant change.
Review a trend line of direct labor costs	No significant change.
Review a trend line of gross margins	The gross margin has dropped 13% in the last two years, entirely due to increased bad debts and sales discounts.
Review a trend line of net margins	Slightly worse reduction than indicated by the gross margin trend line analysis.
Ascertain the gross profit by product	All products experienced a reduction in gross profit in the last two years.
Ascertain the gross profit by customer	Sales to older customers have retained their gross margin levels, but newer customers have substantially lower margins.
Review a trend line of overhead personnel per major customer	There has been a slight increase in the collections staffing level in the last two years, due to the difficulty of collecting from newer customers.
Review a trend line of overhead personnel per transaction	No significant change.

Conclusions and recommendations: The target company has experienced flattening sales and so has shifted new sales efforts to low-end customers who cannot pay on time and will only accept lower priced-products, which also increases the overhead needed to service these accounts. Recommend dropping all low-margin, low-credit customers, as well as all associated overhead costs to increase profits.

EXHIBIT 39.7   ANALYSIS REPORT FOR PROFITABILITY

As part of a due diligence analysis, these measures and trend lines will tell a controller where to focus the bulk of the analysis team's attention in determining the extent of problem areas and their impact on profitability. In the example analysis report shown in Exhibit 39.7, a qualitative review of each analysis area is noted, since this review is intended to find further problems, not to devise a valuation for the target company.

The analysis of a target company's cash flows is a critical item if the entire organization is to be purchased. If a controller were to miss this item, the buying company could find itself paying for an organization that must be supported with a massive additional infusion of cash. The key cash flow analyses to focus on are as follows:

- *Review trend line of net cash flow before debt and interest payments.* Begin with the cash flows shown on the statement of cash flows. Then ignore the impact of debt and interest payments, since inordinately high cash flows to pay for these two items may mask a perfectly good underlying business. If there is a pronounced additional requirement for more cash to fund either the acquisition of fixed assets or working capital, then identify the culprit and proceed with the following cash flow analyses. This first trend line, then, was to determine the existence of a problem, and to more precisely define it.

- *Review trend line of working capital.* Poor customer credit review policies or inadequate collection efforts will lead to an increased investment in accounts receivable, while excessive production or product obsolescence will increase the inventory investment. Also, a reduction in the days of credit before payments are made to suppliers will reduce the free credit that a company receives from them. To see if there is a problem in this area, add the total accounts receivable to inventory and subtract the accounts payable balance to arrive at the total working capital amount. Then, plot this information on a trend line that extends back for at least a year. If there is a steady increase in total working capital, determine which of the three components have caused the problem.

- *Segment working capital investment by customer and product.* One should focus on the accounts receivable and finished goods inventory investments to see if there is a specific customer who is responsible for a working capital increase, or review just the inventory investment to see if a specific product is the cause. This information should be cross-referenced against analyses for profitability by customer and product to see if there are any combinations of low-profit, high investment customers or products that are obvious targets for termination.

- *Review trend line of capital purchases.* This is a simple matter to investigate by general fixed asset category, since this information is reported on the balance sheet. However, there may be good reasons for large increases in fixed asset investments, such as automation, the addition of new facilities, or a general level of competitiveness in the industry that requires constant capital improvements. Only by being certain of the underlying reasons for cash usage in this area can one suggest that cash can be saved here by reducing the volume of asset purchases.

The report that a controller issues as part of the cash flow analysis is primarily composed of judgments regarding the need for historical cash flows, estimates of future cash flows, and the ways that the acquiring company can alter these flows through specific management actions. A sample of such a report is shown in Exhibit 39.8.

Besides purely financial issues, there is a wide array of legal issues that one's legal staff must peruse. In most cases, the analysis issues noted here are related to various kinds of

Type of Analysis Conducted	Notes
Review trend line of net cash flow before debt and interest payments	The target company is experiencing a massive cash outflow in both the working capital and fixed assets areas.
Review trend line of working capital	There is a severe cash outflow, due to $2,000,000 in accounts receivable invested in the Gidget Company, as well as a large investment in five distribution warehouses for its Auto-Klean product, each of which requires $1,500,000 in inventory.
Segment working capital investment by customer and product	The main cash outflows are due to the Gidget Company customer and the Auto-Klean product.
Review trend line of capital purchases	Has purchased $10,000,000 of automation equipment to improve margins on its sales to the Gidget Company.

Conclusions and recommendations: There is a major investment in sales to the Gidget Company, which is not justified by the 5% return on sales to that customer. The receivable investment of $2,000,000 can be eliminated by stopping sales to this customer, while $5,000,000 can be realized from the sale of automation equipment used for the production of items for sale to it. Also, the number of distribution warehouses for the Auto-Klean product can be reduced by two, which will decrease the inventory investment by $3,000,000. The amount of cash investment that can be eliminated as a result of these actions is $10,000,000.

EXHIBIT 39.8 ANALYSIS REPORT FOR CASH FLOW

contracts. When these arise, a key analysis point is to see if they can be dissolved in the event of a corporate change of control. Many contracts contain this feature, so that onerous agreements will not cause a potentially high-priced purchase to fall apart. Key legal reviews are as follows:

- *Bylaws.* This document will include any "poison pill" provisions that are intended to make a change of control very expensive.
- *Certificate of incorporation, including name changes.* This is used to find the list of all names under which the target company operates, which is needed for real estate title searches.
- *Employment contracts.* Key employees may be guaranteed high pay levels for a number of years, or a "golden parachute" clause that guarantees them a large payment if the company is sold.
- *Engineering reports.* These documents will note any structural weaknesses in corporate buildings that may require expensive repairs.
- *Environmental exposure.* Review all literature received from the Environmental Protection Agency, as well as the Occupational Safety and Health Administration, and conduct environmental hazard testing around all company premises to ascertain the extent of potential environmental litigation.
- *Insurance policies.* Verify that the existing insurance policies cover all significant risks that are not otherwise covered by internal safety policies. Also, compare these policies to those held by the buyer to see if there can be savings by consolidating the policies for both companies.
- *Labor union agreements.* If the target company is a union shop, the union contract may contain unfavorable provisions related to work rules, guaranteed pay increases, payouts or guaranteed retraining funds in the event of a plant closure, or onerous benefit payments.
- *Leases.* Creating a schedule of all current leases tells a buyer the extent of commitments to pay for leased assets, as well as interest rates and any fees for early lease terminations.
- *Licenses.* A license for a target company to do business, usually granted by a local government, but possibly also by another company for whom it is the distributor or franchisee, may not be transferable if there is a change of ownership. This can be quite a surprise to a buyer that now finds that it cannot use the company it has just bought.
- *Litigation.* This is a broad area that requires a considerable amount of review before legal counsel can be reasonably satisfied as to the extent and potential liability associated with current and potential litigation. This review should encompass an investigation of all civil suits and criminal actions that may include contract disputes, fraud, discrimination, breach of employment contract, wrongful termination, inadequate disclosure issues, deceptive trade practices, antitrust suits, or other issues. It should also include tax claims and notices of potential litigation received from any of the following government agencies:
  - Department of Justice
  - Department of Labor
  - Equal Employment Opportunity Commission
  - Federal Trade Commission

Description	Additional Information	Summary of Costs
Poison pill payout provision	Bylaws section 2, clause 14	$12,500,000
Golden parachute provision	For all officers	3,250,000
Discounted cost of all lease provisions	Copiers, forklifts	320,000
Discounted pension plan funding requirements		4,750,000
Discounted cost of sponsorship agreement		220,000
Termination payment for long-term supplier contracts		540,000
Total cost of contractual and legal issues		**$21,580,000**

EXHIBIT 39.9   ANALYSIS REPORT FOR CONTRACTUAL AND LEGAL ISSUES

- o Internal Revenue Service
- o Securities and Exchange Commission (applies only to a publicly held entity)
- *Marketing materials.* The target company's advertising of its product capabilities can be a source of potential litigation, if the publicized product claims are overstated.
- *Pension plans.* Determine the size of the employer-funded portion of the pension plan. This will require the services of an actuary to verify the current cost of required future funding.
- *Product warranty agreements.* Review the published warranty that is issued alongside each product to verify its term, as well as what specific features it will replace in the event of product failure.
- *Sponsorship agreements.* A target company may have a long-term commitment to sponsor an event that will require a significant expenditure to maintain or terminate.
- *Supplier or customer contracts.* A target company may be locked into a long-term agreement with one or more of its suppliers or customers, possibly guaranteeing unfavorable terms that will noticeably impact profits if the buyer purchases the company.

Though the preceding nonfinancial issues are primarily related to the legal liabilities of a corporate entity, there are a few cases where the controller may be called upon to provide an estimate of possible attendant costs. For example, one can quantify the extra cost required to fulfill any "poison pill" provisions. One can also determine the net present value of all employment, labor union, and lease provisions that require a specified minimum set of payments for a designated time period. An example of the format used to summarize these expenses is shown in Exhibit 39.9.

39.3 VALUING AN ACQUISITION TARGET

Once a buyer has identified a prospective target, it needs to establish an initial valuation for it. In this section, we describe a variety of valuation methods, the concept of the control premium, the discounted cash flow model, a variety of qualitative factors that can influence the valuation, and reasons for using different forms of payment.

Alternative Valuation Methods

There are a number of ways to value a target company. Although the most common method is discounted cash flow, it is best to evaluate a number of alternative methods, and compare their results to see if several approaches arrive at approximately the same general valuation. This gives the buyer solid grounds for making its offer.

Using a variety of methods is especially important for valuing newer target companies with minimal historical results, and especially for those growing quickly; all of their cash is being used for growth, so cash flow is an inadequate basis for valuation.

If the target company is publicly held, then the buyer can simply base its valuation on the *current market price per share*, multiplied by the number of shares outstanding. The current trading price of a company's stock is not a good valuation tool if the stock is thinly traded. In this case, a small number of trades can alter the market price to a substantial extent, so that the buyer's estimate is far off from the value it would normally assign to the target. Most target companies do not issue publicly traded stock, so other methods must be used to derive their valuation.

When a private company wants to be valued using a market price, it can adopt the unusual ploy of filing for an initial public offering while also being courted by the buyer. By doing so, the buyer is forced to make an offer that is near the market valuation at which the target expects its stock to be traded. If the buyer declines to bid that high, then the target still has the option of going public and realizing value by selling shares to the general public. However, given the expensive control measures mandated by the Sarbanes-Oxley Act and the stock lockup periods required for many new public companies, a target's shareholders usually are more than willing to accept a buyout offer if the price is reasonably close to the target's expected market value.

Another option is to use a *revenue multiple* or *earnings before interest, taxes, depreciation, and amortization (EBITDA) multiple*. It is quite easy to look up the market capitalizations and financial information for thousands of publicly held companies. The buyer then converts this information into a multiples table, such as the one shown in Exhibit 39.10, which itemizes a selection of valuations within the consulting industry. The table should be restricted to comparable companies in the same industry as that of the seller and of roughly the same market capitalization. If some of the information for other companies is unusually high or low, then eliminate these outlying values in order to obtain a median value for the company's size range. Also, it is better to use a multiday average of market prices, since these figures are subject to significant daily fluctuation.

The buyer can then use this table to derive an approximation of the price to be paid for a target company. For example, if a target has sales of $100 million and the market capitalization for several public companies in the same revenue range is 1.4 times revenue, then the buyer could value the target at $140 million. This method is most useful for a turn-around situation or a fast-growth company, where there are few profits (if any). However, the revenue multiple method pays attention only to the first line of the income statement and completely ignores profitability. To avoid the risk of paying too much based on a revenue multiple, it is also possible to compile an EBITDA multiple for the same group of comparable public companies and use that information to value the target.

Better yet, use both the revenue multiple and the EBITDA multiple in concert. If the revenue multiple reveals a high valuation and the EBITDA multiple a low one, it is entirely possible that the target is essentially buying revenues with low-margin products or services or extending credit to financially weak customers. Conversely, if the revenue multiple yields a lower valuation than the EBITDA multiple, this is more indicative of a late-stage company that is essentially a cash cow or one where management is cutting costs to increase profits, but possibly at the expense of harming revenue growth.

The revenue and EBITDA multiples just noted are not the only ones available. The table can be expanded to include the *price/earnings ratio* for a public company's traded stock.

	($ Millions)			EBITDA*	Revenue	EBITDA*
Large Caps (> $5 billion)	Market Capitalization	Revenue	EBITDA*	Percentage	Multiple	Multiple
Electronic Data Systems	$ 9,720	$22,134	$ 1,132	5%	0.4	8.6
General Dynamics	$ 36,220	$27,240	$ 3,113	11%	1.3	11.6
Lockheed Martin	$ 43,020	$41,862	$ 4,527	11%	1.0	9.5
Northrop Grumman	$ 25,350	$32,018	$ 3,006	9%	0.8	8.4
Medium Caps (< $5 billion)						
ManTech International	$ 1,630	$ 1,448	$ 114	8%	1.1	14.3
Perot Systems	$ 1,850	$ 2,612	$ 184	7%	0.7	10.1
SAIC, Inc.	$ 3,640	$ 8,935	$ 666	7%	0.4	5.5
SRA International	$ 1,540	$ 1,269	$ 93	7%	1.2	16.6
Small Caps (< $1.5 billion)						
CACI, Inc.	$ 1,470	$ 1,938	$ 146	8%	0.8	10.1
ICF International	$ 258	$ 727	$ 71	10%	0.4	3.6
SI International	$ 299	$ 511	$ 39	8%	0.6	7.7
Stanley, Inc.	$ 570	$ 409	$ 25	6%	1.4	22.8
Micro Caps (< $250 million)						
Dynamics Research Corp.	$ 92	$ 230	$ 13	6%	0.4	7.1
Keynote Systems	$ 210	$ 68	$ (5)	-7%	3.1	(42.0)
NCI, Inc.	$ 249	$ 304	$ 22	7%	0.8	11.3
Tier Technologies	$ 152	$ 111	$ (22)	-20%	1.4	(6.9)
Averages by Capitalization						
Large caps	$ 28,578	$30,814	$ 2,945	10%	0.9	9.7
Medium caps	$ 2,165	$ 3,566	$ 264	7%	0.6	8.2
Small caps	$ 649	$ 896	$ 70	8%	0.7	9.2
Micro caps	$ 176	$ 178	$ 2	1%	1.0	87.9

* EBITDA = Earnings before interest, taxes, depreciation and amortization

EXHIBIT 39.10   COMPARABLE VALUATIONS TABLE

Also, if the comparable company provides one-year projections, then the revenue multiple can be renamed a *trailing multiple* (for historical 12-month revenue), and the forecast can be used as the basis for a *forward multiple* (for projected 12-month revenue). The forward multiple gives a better estimate of value because it incorporates expectations about the future. The forward multiple should be used only if the forecast comes from guidance that is issued by a public company. The company knows that its stock price will drop if it does not achieve its forecast, so the forecast is unlikely to be aggressive.

Revenue multiples are the best technique for valuing high-growth companies, since these entities usually are pouring resources into their growth and have minimal profits to report. Such companies clearly have a great deal of value, but it is not revealed through their profitability numbers.

However, multiples can be misleading. When acquisitions occur within an industry, the best financial performers with the fewest underlying problems are the choicest acquisition targets and therefore will be acquired first. When other companies in the same area put themselves up for sale later, they will use the earlier multiples to justify similarly high prices. However, because they may have lower market shares, higher cost structures, older products, and the like, the multiples may not be valid. Thus, it is useful to know some of the underlying characteristics of the companies that were previously sold to see if the comparable multiple should be applied to the current target company.

Another possibility is to replace the market capitalization figure in the table with *enterprise value*. The enterprise value is a company's market capitalization, plus its total debt outstanding, minus any cash on hand. In essence, it is a company's theoretical takeover price, because the buyer would have to buy all of the stock and pay off existing debt while pocketing any remaining cash.

Another way to value an acquisition is to use a *database of comparable transactions* to determine what was paid for other recent acquisitions. Investment bankers have access to this information through a variety of private databases, and while a great deal of information can be collected online through public filings or press releases.

The buyer can also derive a valuation based on a target's *underlying real estate values*. This method works only in those isolated cases where the target has a substantial real estate portfolio. For example, in the retail industry, where some chains own the property on which their stores are situated, the value of the real estate is greater than the cash flow generated by the stores themselves. In cases where the business is financially troubled, it is entirely possible that the purchase price is based entirely on the underlying real estate, with the operations of the business itself being valued at essentially zero. The buyer then uses the value of the real estate as the primary reason for completing the deal. In some situations, the prospective buyer has no real estate experience and so is more likely to heavily discount the potential value of any real estate when making an offer. If the seller wishes to increase its price, it could consider selling the real estate prior to the sale transaction. By doing so, it converts a *potential* real estate sale price (which might otherwise be discounted by the buyer) into an achieved sale with cash in the bank and may also record a one-time gain on its books based on the asset sale, which may have a positive impact on its sale price.

An acquiree's real estate may even be the means for an acquirer to finance the deal. For example, if the acquiree owns property, it may be possible to enter into a sale-and-leaseback transaction that generates enough cash to pay for the acquisition. Another possibility is to look for property leases held by the acquiree that are below current market rates and sublease them for a profit. Finally, it may be possible to consolidate acquiree locations and sell any remaining properties that are no longer needed.

If a target has products that the buyer could develop in-house, then an alternative valuation method is to compare the *cost of in-house development* to the cost of acquiring the completed product through the target. This type of valuation is especially important if the market is expanding rapidly right now and the buyer will otherwise forgo sales if it takes the time to pursue an in-house development path. In this case, the proper valuation technique is to combine the cost of an in-house development effort with the present value of profits forgone by waiting to complete the in-house project. Interestingly, this is the only valuation technique where most of the source material comes from the buyer's financial statements rather than those of the seller.

The most conservative valuation method of all is the *liquidation value* method. This is an analysis of what the selling entity would be worth if all of its assets were to be sold off. This method assumes that the ongoing value of the company as a business entity is eliminated, leaving the individual auction prices at which its fixed assets, properties, and other assets can be sold off, less any outstanding liabilities. It is useful for the buyer to at least estimate this number, so that it can determine its downside risk in case it completes the acquisition but the acquired business then fails utterly.

The *replacement value* method yields a somewhat higher valuation than the liquidation value method. Under this approach, the buyer calculates what it would cost to duplicate the target company. The analysis addresses the replacement of the seller's key infrastructure. This can yield surprising results if the seller owns infrastructure that originally required lengthy regulatory approval. For example, if the seller owns a chain of mountain huts that are located on government property, it is essentially impossible to replace them at all, or only at vast expense. An additional factor in this analysis is the time required to replace the target. If the time period for replacement is considerable, the buyer may be forced to pay a premium in order to gain quick access to a key market.

It is also possible to create a *hybrid valuation model* that mixes several of the preceding methods. For example, the buyer could calculate the liquidation value of a target and then add to that number the next two or three years of free cash flow. This method yields a conservative valuation that the buyer would be hard put *not* to realize and that might form the basis for a minimum bid.

Although all of these methods can be used for valuation, they usually supplement the primary method—the discounted cash flow (DCF) method—which will be addressed shortly.

The Control Premium

Why does a buyer offer to pay more for a target than the price at which the target's shares currently trade? One reason is certainly to keep other potential bidders from entering the fray with their own bids. However, the real reason is that shares trade based on their value to individual shareholders, who have no control over the business; thus, a share price is based only on the prospective financial return that a shareholder expects to achieve. However, if a buyer wishes to obtain control over the target, then it should expect to pay a control premium over the current stock price. By doing so, it has complete control over the potential size and timing of cash flows. Historically, this has made the control premium worth somewhere in the range of 35% to 50% of a target's freely traded stock value. Recent control premiums for the purchase of publicly traded companies can be found in the annual *Control Premium Study* that is published by Mergerstat (located at *www.mergerstat.com*).

Synergy Gains

If the buyer pays the full share value of a target as well as a control premium, how does it expect to earn a return? The target's existing shareholders appear to be receiving all of the value inherent in the business. There are certainly cases where the target's stock price may be unusually low, such as when industry is at the low point of a business cycle, where profits are minimized. In such cases, the buyer snaps up deals based on timing. However, these are isolated instances. In most cases, the buyer is depending on the realization of synergies between its own company and the target, which may be considerable.

A buyer with expert knowledge of potential synergy gains can earn substantial amounts that comfortably exceed the purchase price. However, a buyer may run into an experienced seller who wants a share of those synergy gains. If the seller wants payment for an excessive portion of the expected gains, the buyer must walk away from the deal; there is simply no way to earn a profit from the transaction.

Synergies are realized only by strategic buyers, not financial buyers. A financial buyer simply buys a business in order to hold it and gain appreciation value from its internal growth over time. A strategic buyer, however, is willing to pay a higher price in the knowledge that it can squeeze out extra value. Thus, the strategic buyer may be willing to pay a higher price than a financial buyer, perhaps in the range of a 5% to 20% premium over what a financial buyer would pay.

A canny seller will court strategic buyers in order to maximize the price paid but must be aware that it must leave a generous amount of the potential synergies to the buyer, in order to make the acquisition sufficiently tempting.

The Discounted Cash Flow Model

The best possible reason to buy a company is for the cash that it can generate. The discounted cash flow (DCF) model is designed to reveal the *free cash flow* that is available for distribution to investors at the end of each year shown in the model. This means that the model must not only reveal the cash generated by ongoing operations but also subtract out all planned capital expenditures and tax payments, so that completely unrestricted cash surpluses or shortfalls are revealed for each year in the model.

The typical DCF model includes a projection of the target's cash flows for the next five years, plus a terminal value for what the target theoretically can be sold for at the end of that time period (which is based on prices currently being obtained for comparable companies). An example of a DCF is shown in Exhibit 39.11.

The buyer should beware of models where the terminal value is by far the largest component of the model; the terminal value is the least predictable part of the valuation, because it is the farthest into the future and assumes a specific sale price that is very difficult to justify. If the terminal value comprises the bulk of the DCF, the buyer will need to supplement the DCF analysis with other forms of valuation analysis.

A major part of the DCF analysis is the interest rate that is used for discounting the value of future cash flows to the current period. This interest rate is equivalent to the buyer's incremental cost of capital. The cost of capital is the weighted average cost of the buyer's debt, preferred stock, and equity. The cost of equity is the most difficult to determine but usually involves the capital asset pricing model. On an extremely simplified basis, the cost

	Year 1	Year 2	Year 3	Year 4	Year 5	Terminal Value
+ Revenues	$ 438	$ 473	$ 511	$ 552	$ 596	
- Cost of goods sold	$ 175	$ 189	$ 204	$ 221	$ 238	
= Gross margin	$ 263	$ 284	$ 307	$ 331	$ 358	
- General and administrative	$ 171	$ 184	$ 199	$ 215	$ 232	
= Earnings before interest and taxes	$ 92	$ 99	$ 107	$ 116	$ 125	
- Interest	$ 5	$ 5	$ 5	$ 5	$ 5	
- Taxes	$ 33	$ 35	$ 38	$ 41	$ 44	
- Incremental working capital change	$ 22	$ 24	$ 26	$ 30	$ 33	
- Incremental fixed asset change	$ 15	$ 16	$ 18	$ 19	$ 20	
+ Depreciation	$ 14	$ 15	$ 17	$ 18	$ 19	
= Cash flow	$ 31	$ 34	$ 37	$ 39	$ 42	$ 120
Discount rate	10%	10%	10%	10%	10%	
Annual discount rate	0.90909	0.82645	0.75131	0.68301	0.62092	0.56447
Discounted cash flows	$ 28	$ 28	$ 28	$ 26	$ 26	$ 68
Net present value	$ 204					

EXHIBIT 39.11 DISCOUNTED CASH FLOW MODEL

Capital Type	Amount Outstanding	Interest Rate	Cost
Debt	$25,000,000	7%	$1,750,000
Preferred stock	10,000,000	10%	1,000,000
Equity	30,000,000	14%	4,200,000
Totals	$65,000,000	**10.7%**	$6,950,000

EXHIBIT 39.12   WEIGHTED AVERAGE COST OF CAPITAL CALCULATION

of equity is at least 5% to 7% higher than the current interest rate on U.S. government treasury notes and can be substantially higher. As an example, the table in Exhibit 39.12 shows the dollar amount of the three components of a company's cost of capital, yielding a weighted average cost of capital of 10.7%.

It is preferable to use the *incremental* cost of capital, which incorporates the buyer's most recent cost of debt. The incremental rate is better, because that is the rate at which the buyer will need to obtain funding to pay for the target.

It is also possible to adjust the cost of capital for the perceived risk of the target company. For example, if the target is a well-established one with predictable cash flows, the buyer can simply use its cost of capital as the discount rate. However, if the target's cash flows are more uncertain, the buyer can add a risk percentage to its discount rate. By doing so, cash flows that are farther in the future will be worth less in the DCF, resulting in a lower valuation for the target.

The buyer may also adjust the discount rate downward for any especially valuable characteristics that the seller may have, such as subject-matter experts or patents on key technology. However, this is an entirely subjective reduction. The buyer would do better to attempt to quantify these characteristics of the seller elsewhere in the model, such as an increase in revenues from company-wide use of the seller's patented products.

The interest rate used in the debt portion of the cost of capital can vary considerably, resulting in significant changes in the value of the target company. For example, if interest rates increase, the buyer's cost of capital also increases. When the buyer uses this increased cost of capital as its discount factor in the DCF model, target company valuations will decline. Conversely, if interest rates drop, then target values increase. Thus, external economic factors driving interest rates are directly related to acquisition prices.

Also, the size of the target can alter the buyer's cost of capital. For example, if the prospective deal would require a large amount of financing by the buyer, it is likely that its incremental debt cost will increase, which in turn impacts its cost of capital. If this is the case, then the projected increase in the cost of capital is the most appropriate discount rate in the DCF model; using this will make the acquisition look less attractive.

The DCF is the most reliable method for valuing a mature, slow-growth company with established cash flows. It is not used so frequently for high-growth entities that are using all available cash to support their increasing working capital needs. Instead, buyers tend to use comparable valuations for these targets. However, it is always of some value to also run a DCF, because it reveals a reliable minimum valuation for the target. The buyer can also create a variety of cash flow projections for the target that are farther out in the future than the usual five years used for the model to get some idea of what the target's cash flows will be like once its high-growth period is over.

Constructing Cash Flow Scenarios

Where does the buyer obtain the information needed to construct a cash flow analysis? The seller will prefer to show estimates of future sales, which inevitably reveal an optimistic "hockey stick" of sudden growth in "just a few more months." If the buyer were to use just these projected numbers, it would likely arrive at a valuation that is too high and overpay for the seller. A better method is to create multiple scenarios, where the seller's estimates are reserved for the most optimistic version. Another most likely estimate should be based on the seller's most recent historical results while a conservative version assumes that the seller's historical results worsen significantly.

Although the use of three cash flow scenarios certainly shows some valuation prudence, it can hide unsupported assumptions within the scenarios. For example, an analyst might assume a simplistic revenue decline of 10% in the conservative version, which is not based on any concrete risk analysis. Instead, use documented changes in specific variables in the three versions. For example, if there appears to be a risk of soft pricing in the market, use the conservative scenario to specifically model price declines of various sizes. Similarly, if there is a risk of supplier bottlenecks, model the impact of price increases for key materials. Also, if the target must match research expenditures elsewhere in the industry, review percentage changes in these expenditures. By taking the time to document these more detailed analyses, a buyer can determine the price points, volume levels, and cost structures at which a target breaks even and when the target can potentially earn a great deal of money.

Another factor to consider in one or more of the valuation scenarios is the presence or absence of seller risk guarantees. For example, if the seller is guaranteeing to pay for any undocumented lawsuits or payouts related to documented lawsuits, the buyer can eliminate this factor from its conservative scenario. In essence, the more risks the seller guarantees, the lower the expenses shown in the model and the higher the valuation that the buyer can offer to the seller.

Once these cash flow versions are constructed, the buyer should multiply each one by a weighting factor and not simply average them. The most likely scenario should receive the bulk of the weighting, such as 60% or 70%, with the outlying conservative and optimistic versions receiving the remainder. Thus, a 20-60-20 or 15-70-15 weighting essentially assumes that the seller's most recent historical results are most likely to continue into the future.

A more conservative method of cash flow analysis is to construct an estimate based entirely on historical results, with a weighting system that favors the most recent year. For example, if the buyer wants to model the target's past five years of results, it can multiply the target's cash flows by five for the most recent year, by four for the immediately preceding year, and so on. Once all five years have been added together, divide by 15 to arrive at the weighted cash flow for the five-year period. The resulting 5, 4, 3, 2, 1 weighting system gives some credence to relatively old cash flows and great merit to recent results. This method is not recommended, since it is based entirely on prior results and gives no weighting at all to a target's future prospects.

Cash Flow Adjusting Factors

The buyer cannot simply run a DCF of a target's existing operations and consider itself done. Doing this would imply that the buyer intends to make virtually no changes to the target once it has completed the acquisition. In reality, there are multiple changes to be considered, many of which should be included in the projected cash flow.

In many acquisitions, the buyer assumes that the combined entities will be able to increase revenues beyond what the companies were achieving separately. However, revenue synergies are notoriously difficult to achieve, because they require the cooperation of a third party (customers). An experienced buyer usually reduces or even eliminates any revenue synergies in the cash flow model. Instead, it focuses on cost reductions, which are entirely within its control.

Not only should the buyer *not* budget for revenue gains, but it should strongly consider modeling for a modest revenue *decline* at the target that is caused by some degradation in its customer base. This is caused by any changes in service levels, salespeople, or products that customers may experience as a result of the acquisition. Also, competitors will likely be circling the target's customers like sharks, hoping to pick off a few. Further, if the buyer is planning to acquire only a single division of a larger company, the target may lose some customers simply because the associated services or products of its parent company will no longer be sold, or not as a package. Thus, a reasonable modeling technique is to incorporate a modest decline in the target's customer base, especially during the initial year of the acquisition. A common reduction in the customer base is in the range of 2% to 5%.

The buyer must also assume a variety of acquisition expenses, including legal fees, valuation services, appraisals, environmental audits, and financial audits. If the buyer has engaged in a number of acquisitions, it can easily compile a database of what these costs have been in the past and use it to estimate such costs in a prospective valuation. If the buyer anticipates diverting a substantial amount of management time toward the integration of the target's operations into its own, it can also estimate the impact of this "soft" cost on the entire business.

One likely cost control scenario is that some employees will be let go. If so, there will be some cost savings by eliminating their positions, but there will also be a short-term additional cost associated with severance pay. If the buyer is taking on this obligation, it must factor severance pay into its cash flow assumptions.

A special case is adjustments to the cash flows associated with a target's defined benefit pension plan. These costs can vary substantially over time, so an analyst should intensively review the actuarial assumptions underlying any such plans. For example, if the buyer believes that the plan is underfunded, it has reasonable grounds for demanding a reduction in the purchase price, so that it can offset the imminent funding liability. Conversely, if the plan is overfunded, the seller can bargain for a purchase price increase, which effectively pays it back for the amount of the overfunding. The funding status is by no means obvious, since it is driven by the future interest rate assumption used by the plan actuary; the higher the rate, the fewer existing assets are needed to offset projected plan liabilities. Consequently, arguments over the correct interest rate assumption will alter the purchase price and will result in changes to the DCF.

Another issue is the cyclicality of the industry in which the target is located. If there are strong historical cycles, the buyer should assume that there will be a recurrence. This requires that the cash flow model assume the presence of both the upside and downside of that cycle, using historical information for both the duration and size of the cycle. This method gives the buyer a reasonable idea of how cash flows will change over time. In many instances, highly variable cyclical results will force the buyer to abandon a deal because the downside of the cycle eliminates or reverses the profits generated during other years.

An area missed by many cash flow models is the immediate sale of some assets following the acquisition. Either party may have duplicate or obsolete assets that can be dispositioned for immediate cash. If the buyer can presell some assets before a purchase agreement even closes, this is a "hard" cash inflow to include in the cash flow model.

The buyer should also be aware of the seller's fixed asset replacement cycle. It is entirely possible that the buyer has delayed key asset purchases in order to give the appearance of having excellent cash flow. However, its equipment and facilities may now be so run down that the buyer must expend significant amounts over multiple years to replace the assets. The dollar value of the replacement amounts should be gleaned during the due diligence stage and entered into the DCF.

The buyer should also include in the DCF the impact of any cost escalation clauses in the seller's contracts with its suppliers. For example, there may be a series of scheduled annual increases in a building lease or a price increase in a raw materials contract. As was the case with fixed asset replacements, these costs are not readily apparent and must be found during the due diligence process.

Finally, the buyer may have some concern about the accuracy of the financial statements it is using to compile a cash forecast, if the target cannot provide audited financial statements. If there has never been an audit, and especially if the buyer's due diligence indicates some issues with the presented financial information, the buyer may have to adjust cash projections downward or base a valuation on only the most conservative scenario. To avoid this, the target should have its books audited for the past year (and preferably two years) in order to qualify for high cash flow assumptions in the buyer's valuation model.

The Earnout

There are times when the buyer and the seller have entirely different concepts of the valuation to be used for the acquisition, usually because the buyer is basing its valuation on the seller's historical performance while the seller is using a much higher forward-looking view of its prospective performance. The *earnout* frequently is used to bridge the valuation perception gap between the two parties. Under an earnout, the seller's shareholders will be paid an additional amount by the buyer if it can achieve specific performance targets (usually the same ones it has already claimed it will achieve during the acquisition negotiations).

The earnout is also a useful tool for the buyer, because the seller's management team has a strong incentive to grow the business for the next few years. In addition, the buyer can shift a portion of its purchase price into a future liability that likely can be paid from cash earned in the future by the seller. It is also useful for the seller's shareholders, since it defers income taxes on the payment.

However, many earnouts also result in lawsuits, because the buyer merges the acquiree into another business unit, charges corporate overhead to it, or shifts key staff elsewhere in the company—all factors that make it extremely difficult for the acquiree's management team to earn the additional payment or even to determine what its performance has become. Even if there are no lawsuits, the acquiree's management team may be so focused on achieving their earnout that they do not assist the rest of the buying entity with other matters, so that corporate-level goals are not reached. Also, if the earnout award is based strictly on the achievement of revenue rather than profit, then the acquiree's management team may pursue unprofitable sales in order to meet their earnout goals.

The problems with earnouts can be mitigated by continuing to track the acquiree's performance separately in the financial statements, carefully defining the earnout calculation in the original acquisition document, requiring earnouts to be based solely on net income achieved, and adding an additional layer of compensation based on working more closely with the rest of the buying company, such as commissions for cross-selling. Also, to keep the acquiree happy, do not institute a "cliff" goal, where no bonus is paid unless the entire target is reached. Instead, use a sliding scale, so that some bonus is paid even if only a portion of the performance target is achieved.

Qualitative Factors

Thus far, the valuation discussion has centered entirely on a quantitative analysis of how much to pay for the selling entity. Although quantitative analysis certainly forms the core of a valuation, the buyer must also consider a broad array of qualitative factors. A sampling of the more common ones are as follows:

- *Difficulty of duplication.* If a buyer perceives that the barriers to entering a seller's field of operations are high, or if the cost of duplicating the seller's operations is excessive, the buyer may be more inclined to pay a premium for the business. For example, a proprietary database may take so long to duplicate that a buyer will value the seller just based on the cost it would otherwise incur to create the database from scratch.

- *Risk of expiring contracts.* A seller whose revenues are tied to short-term sales, without immediate prospects for renewing the backlog, will be perceived to have a lower valuation than an entity possessing a strong backlog and clear evidence of long-term sales agreements with its customers.

- *Management.* A seller's cost structure, perception in the marketplace, and customer relations are driven in large part by the quality of its management team. If this group is perceived to be first class, it can increase the corporate valuation, since these people typically have exceptional skill in growing businesses and in anticipating and overcoming operational problems.

- *Client base.* A significant factor in determining valuation is the size, type, and distribution of clients. For example, a seller with a single client will be perceived to be at great risk of losing all of its sales if the client is dissatisfied. Alternatively, a broad mix of clients, particularly those large enough to support multiple sales, will reduce the perceived risk of sales loss.

- *Inherent risk.* A seller whose financial performance can be impacted dramatically by adverse situations will have a comparatively lower valuation. For example, farm businesses can be severely impacted by drought conditions.

- *Disaster analysis.* Even beyond the inherent risk just noted, the buyer should closely review the characteristics of the seller's business to see if there is any risk of a truly catastrophic failure, such as a facility being destroyed because it is situated on an earthquake fault line. Even if the probability of a disaster is low, the consequences may be so large that the buyer must either walk away from the deal or find a mitigating action to offset the risk.

- *Lawsuits.* Nothing will drive a buyer away faster than an unresolved lawsuit, especially one with a demand for a large settlement. Even if there is no lawsuit, the prospect of one, as evidenced by lawsuits targeted at others in the same industry, can have a negative impact on valuation.

- *Patents.* If a seller has established key patents or processes that give it a clear competitive advantage, this can increase its valuation level.

- *Branding.* If a seller has invested a great deal of time and effort in creating brands for its products or services, this can give it a significant boost in valuation.

However, if the seller has not continued to invest in its brand, there is a risk of brand degradation that will require years to rebuild.

It is best to wait until the quantitative analysis has been completed and then adjust the baseline quantitative results with estimates of the additional impact of the items just noted.

Which Valuation Method Is Best?

The buyer should use a number of different valuation models. By doing so, it can obtain a high-low range of estimates that gives it the general boundaries for a valuation. The best valuation estimate usually begins with a DCF analysis, adjusted for comparable transaction multiples. For example, a standard DCF analysis may reveal that a target is worth $15 million, which is approximately 8 times its most recently reported EBITDA. However, because the target is located in a "hot" industry, with unusually high multiples of 12 times EBITDA, the buyer should consider increasing the size of its offer to match the going rate. Its alternative is to wait until such time as the industry valuation gradually declines, at which point the DCF results and comparables are in closer alignment.

An example of what a range of values could look like is shown in Exhibit 39.13, where several methods are used that were discussed earlier in the "Alternative Valuation Methods" subsection. In the example, note that the revenue multiple method yields a clearly outsized valuation while the real estate values method results in an excessively low one. Since these valuations are clearly beyond what the other methods are indicating, the high-low valuation extremes are excluded from the likely valuation range.

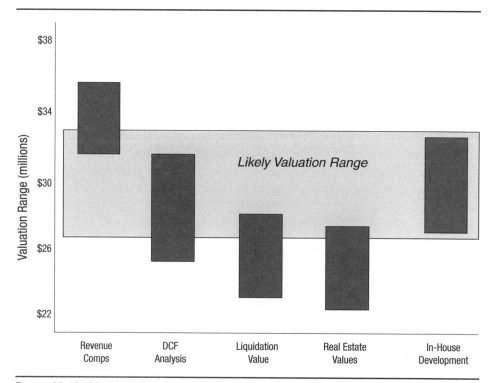

EXHIBIT 39.13 VALUATION RANGE ANALYSIS

The buyer should also create a hard cap on the valuation, beyond which it will not go under any circumstances. To derive it, the buyer should have a higher-level executive review all of the valuation models and use them to set a price ceiling. This executive should not be directly involved in the prospective acquisition and should nave no personal interest in whether the buyer acquires the target. The resulting price cap is the absolute maximum that the buyer will pay. By establishing such a cap, the buyer can avoid overbidding in the heat of negotiations.

Also, although initially it may seem odd to do so, the buyer should consider establishing a floor price. By establishing a price that is reasonably fair to the seller, there is less risk that the seller will back out at the last moment and court other bidders. Also, the seller is more cooperative with subsequent integration efforts if it believes it was paid a fair amount. Of course, if the seller is in desperate straits and wants to sell at any price, then the buyer should hardly balk at paying too little.

The Method of Payment

The buyer can pay the seller in cash, debt, or stock. If the seller accepts *cash*, then it must immediately pay income taxes on its gain. However, the seller also obtains an entirely liquid asset and is no longer tied to the future results of its business. Generally speaking, the buyer is willing to pay less if the payment is in cash, since the buyer will have to dip into its capital resources to obtain the funds, rendering it less able to deal with other issues that may require cash funding. If the buyer goes on to achieve significant synergy gains, then its shareholders will receive the entire benefit of the gains while the seller's shareholders will receive no gain. Finally, the buyer may want to pay cash simply because it can, and other bidders cannot. If the buyer is cash rich and interest rates are so high that the cost of debt is prohibitive for other bidders, it can make an offer that the seller literally cannot refuse.

If the buyer pays in *stock*, the seller gains tax-deferred status on the payment. If the seller is in no immediate need of cash, this might make a stock payment a reasonable form of compensation. The other consideration in a stock payment is the buyer's expectation that it will create sufficient synergies to improve the value of its stock. By paying the seller in stock, the buyer's shareholders are forgoing some of the synergy gains to be achieved and giving them to the seller. Conversely, if the seller suspects that it cannot achieve sufficient synergies, it can offload some of the risk to the seller by issuing stock. Finally, if the buyer is a private company, the seller has no clear path to eventually liquidating any shares paid to it, which makes this option extremely unacceptable.

The buyer's payment behavior is also driven by its perception of how fairly the market is currently valuing its stock. If the buyer feels that its stock price is currently trading at a maximum level, it will be more inclined to use its stock for acquisitions; it will act in the reverse manner if its stock is trading at a low price. If the buyer consistently uses its stock to acquire multiple companies in succession, the market may feel that this is a sign that the buyer's management believes the stock has reached a maximum valuation and so will tend to trade down its price.

If the buyer pays with *debt*, the seller is in the worst position of all three payment scenarios. The seller's shareholders do not obtain any liquid assets in the short term, they do not share in any upside potential caused by synergy gains that would have been realized by stock ownership, and they are totally dependent on the buyer's management team to create enough cash flow to pay them. If the seller has collateralized the assets of the sold business, this is still not adequate, since the buyer may have stripped the entity of assets by the time the seller obtains possession of it.

In short, the seller prefers cash for its liquidity value but forgoes the opportunity to share in any synergy gains that stock ownership would have provided. The buyer prefers a cash payment if it is sure of its ability to achieve significant synergies, which it wants to retain through stock ownership. A debt payment is the worst-case scenario for the seller, which obtains neither liquidity nor appreciation value. Although these choices frequently are driven solely by the financing available to the buyer, this is not always the case. If the buyer has the option of paying in stock or cash but pays in cash, this is a significant indicator that it believes it can reserve significant synergy gains for its shareholders. If the buyer has the same option but pays in stock, it may be more concerned with its ability to achieve synergy gains and so is offloading some of the risk onto the seller.

The buyer can model its payment options with a pro forma spreadsheet, such as the one shown in Exhibit 39.14. The exhibit contains an example of a 100% stock payment, followed by a 100% cash payment. The key financial information for the buyer and seller is identical in both scenarios. In the stock payment scenario, the buyer plans to achieve $535,000 in savings through various cost reductions. However, because it plans to pay in stock, it is passing some of the gains over to the selling shareholders, as reflected in the earnings per share figure. In the cash payment scenario, the buyer plans to achieve the same savings but must also incur the interest cost of a loan that it uses to pay cash to the seller's shareholders. Although the added interest burden drags down the net earnings of the combined entities, the existing buyer shareholders receive the entire synergy gains, resulting in an impressive earnings per share boost.

Summary

There are multiple ways to create a valuation for a target company, and the buyer should consider using several of them to do so. This results in a range of possible values, usually yielding a relatively narrow range of prices within which the buyer should place a bid. While there are a number of qualitative factors that can result in significant changes to the values, the buyer should be wary of unsupported changes yielding substantial boosts in the valuation. When these additional factors are introduced, the buyer will likely find itself paying too much, and never achieving an adequate return on its investment.

The buyer should track performance information on its acquisitions, to see how the projected valuations actually turned out. If there were significant differences between the model and reality, then the buyer should be willing to constantly adjust the model to bring it closer to reality. This feedback loop is extremely valuable for obtaining more accurate valuations in the future.

39.4 TYPES OF ACQUISITIONS

In an acquisition, the overriding issue for the seller is to avoid paying income taxes. In order to avoid doing so, the form of reorganization must comply with several key sections of the Internal Revenue Code (IRC), specifically sections 354-358 and 367-368. These sections define the various types of permissible tax-free acquisitions and the conditions under which they apply. This section addresses the various types of acquisitions and their tax (and other) implications for the participants.

Stock Payment Scenario	Buyer	Seller	Adjustment	Adjustment Notes	Combined Results
Revenues	$24,000	$3,000			$27,000
Cost of sales	$16,000	$2,000	-$360	(1)	$17,640
Administrative	$6,000	$500	-$175	(2)	$6,325
Interest	$100	$50			$150
Income before tax	$1,900	$450			$2,885
Income tax at 34%	$646	$153			$981
Net income	$1,254	$297			$1,904
Outstanding shares	400	100			
Seller shares retired			-100		
Buyer shares issued			150	(3)	550
Earnings per share	$ 3.14	$ 2.97			$ 3.46

Cash Payment Scenario	Buyer	Seller	Adjustment	Adjustment Notes	Combined Results
Revenues	$24,000	$3,000			$27,000
Cost of sales	$16,000	$2,000	-$360	(1)	$17,640
Administrative	$6,000	$500	-$175	(2)	$6,325
Interest	$100	$50	$180	(4)	$330
Income before tax	$1,900	$450			$2,705
Income tax at 34%	$646	$153			$920
Net income	$1,254	$297			$1,785
Outstanding shares	400	100			
Seller shares retired			-100		
Buyer shares issued					400
Earnings per share	$ 3.14	$ 2.97			$ 4.46

(1) 2% reduction in purchasing costs for the combined entities
(2) Overlapping administrative costs eliminated
(3) Share exchange is 1.5 buyer shares for each seller share
(4) Sale price is 1x revenues, financed with 6% loan

EXHIBIT 39.14 PAYMENT SCENARIOS

Tax Implications of an Acquisition

When determining the proper structure of an acquisition, the taxability of the transaction to the seller plays a key role. It is possible that the seller may want to pay income taxes immediately rather than delaying the recognition of a gain. This scenario arises when their tax basis in the acquiree is more than the price being paid for it, resulting in the complete avoidance of taxes. However, it is far more likely that the seller will have a minimal tax basis in the acquiree and so wishes to avoid the immediate recognition of a gain. To avoid gain recognition, the Internal Revenue Service (IRS) has stipulated that the following requirements be met:

- The transaction must have a bona fide business purpose other than tax avoidance.
- There must be a *continuity of interest*, where the ownership interests of the selling stockholders continue into the acquiring entity. This is achieved by having the buyer pay a substantial portion of the purchase price in its own stock. The IRS considers a "substantial portion" of the purchase price to be at least 50%. Some transactions

are structured to pay sellers preferred stock rather than common stock, so that they still meet the requirements of the continuity of interest rule, but also give the sellers rights to additional payments, as would be the case with debt.

- There must be a *continuity of business enterprise*, where the buyer must either continue the seller's historic business or use a significant proportion of the acquired assets in a business.

The IRS has incorporated these requirements into four types of legal reorganization, which are commonly described as Type A, B, C, or D reorganizations. The letter designations come from the paragraph letters in the IRC under which they are described. All four types of reorganizations, as well as several variations, are described in greater detail later in this chapter.

In an acquisition, the buyer generally recognizes no gain or loss. Instead, its primary tax concern is the tax basis and holding period of the assets it acquires. Ideally, it wants to restate the assets to their fair market values (FMVs), on the assumption that the FMV is higher than the tax basis of the seller. If the FMV is indeed higher, then the buyer can record a larger amount of asset depreciation, which reduces its future tax liability. The buyer can restate assets to their FMV only if it acquires them through an asset acquisition (see next subsection). Otherwise, it will retain the assets' tax basis and holding period. However, retaining the original tax basis and holding period may be acceptable if the purchase price of the assets is less than their carry forward basis, since the buyer can recognize more depreciation expense than if it were to restate the assets to their FMV.

There is one scenario where the buyer can complete a nontaxable reorganization and still record the acquired assets at their FMVs. This is possible under Section 338 of the IRC, which allows this treatment if the buyer acquires at least 80% of the total voting power and 80% of the total value of the seller's stock within a 12-month period. However, Section 338 is laced with a variety of restrictions that reduce its applicability.

In short, the primary driver of the type of acquisition used is the seller's need to defer taxes. The buyer's interests involve a far smaller tax impact than that experienced by the seller, so the seller's wishes generally determine the method used.

Asset Acquisition

The only type of acquisition that is *not* addressed by the IRC is the asset acquisition, because this is a taxable transaction.

In an asset acquisition, the buyer acquires either all or a selection of the seller's assets and liabilities. This transaction is most favorable to the buyer, which can record the acquired assets at their FMV (which is usually an increase from the seller's tax basis), thereby yielding more depreciation to use as a tax shield. This also results in a smaller gain if the buyer subsequently sells the assets. However, the buyer must also obtain legal title to each asset it acquires, which can require a considerable amount of paperwork. Also, depending on the circumstances, the seller may have to notify its creditors of the impending transaction. For example, if the buyer intends to acquire a seller's below-market asset lease agreement, the lessor may agree to the sale only if it can increase its lease rate.

An asset sale is not tax efficient for the seller. Of primary importance is that the seller must pay income taxes on the difference between the consideration received and the seller's basis in the entity. The situation is more dire if the selling entity is a "C" corporation, due to a dual taxation scenario. First, the "C" corporation must pay taxes to the extent that the total consideration received exceeds its adjusted basis in the assets sold. In addition, assuming that the "C" corporation intends to distribute its remaining assets to stockholders and dissolve, the stockholders must pay taxes to the extent that the distributions received exceed their cost basis in the stock.

Also, if the seller previously had claimed an investment tax credit on an asset that it is now selling, the credit may be recaptured, thereby increasing its income taxes.

An asset acquisition can be used to avoid acquiring unknown or contingent liabilities. For example, if the selling entity is the subject of a lawsuit and the buyer wishes to avoid any liability related to the lawsuit, it can selectively purchase assets, leaving the selling entity with responsibility for any legal settlement. However, some environmental laws stipulate that the liability for future hazardous waste cleanups can attach to assets. Consequently, the buyer of real estate assets should go to considerable lengths to verify the extent of any environmental contamination prior to purchase.

An asset acquisition is also useful for the partial sale of a business that has multiple products or product lines. For example, a buyer may want to purchase only a single product in order to fill out its product line, leaving the seller with most of its original business intact. Although it is also possible to spin off such assets into a separate legal entity, it is often easier simply to conduct an asset sale.

The form of the purchase agreement varies from that used for an entity purchase. Instead, the parties use a general assignment and bill of sale, with an attached schedule that itemizes each asset or liability being transferred.

Depending on the proportion of assets sold to the buyer, this transaction can require the direct approval of at least a majority of the seller's stockholders. The selling entity remains in existence and continues to be owned by the same stockholders. However, if most or all of its assets are sold, then the seller's stockholders normally liquidate the entity.

Type A Reorganization

A Type A reorganization is governed by paragraph A of Section 368(a)(1) of the IRC, which simply states that a reorganization is "a statutory merger or consolidation." To expand on this limited definition, a statutory merger involves the transfer of all seller assets and liabilities to the buyer in exchange for the buyer's stock while a statutory consolidation involves the transfers of the assets of two companies into a new entity in exchange for the stock of the new entity. In both cases, the selling entities are then liquidated.

An additional requirement of a Type A reorganization is to have a continuity of interest, as explained earlier in the "Tax Implications of a Reorganization" subsection. In order to meet this rule, the buyer should issue at least 50% of its stock as part of the purchase price. The transaction must also meet the continuity of business enterprise rule.

This transaction allows for tax deferral by the seller for that portion of the purchase price paid with the buyer's stock. The buyer must assume all of the seller's assets and liabilities.

The boards of both entities must approve the transaction, as do at least a majority of the stockholders of the selling entity. Since the selling entity's board of directors must approve the transaction, this is not a suitable vehicle for a hostile takeover.

The principal difference between the Type A and B reorganizations is that other consideration besides stock can be paid under a Type A, whereas the price paid under a Type B must be solely for stock. Also, the selling entity is dissolved in a Type A but can be retained in a Type B reorganization.

The Type A reorganization is not commonly used when valuable contracts are associated with the selling entity, because they may be terminated at the option of the business partners when the selling entity is liquidated at the end of the reorganization.

In summary, the Type A reorganization is primarily of benefit to the seller, which can obtain some cash, debt, or preferred stock as part of the purchase price while still retaining tax-deferred status on the purchase price that is paid with the buyer's stock. It is less useful for the buyer, which runs the risk of losing contracts associated with the selling entity.

Type B Reorganization

A Type B reorganization is governed by paragraph B of Section 368(a)(1) of the IRC. The paragraph is as follows:

> The acquisition by one corporation, in exchange solely for all or a part of its voting stock (or in exchange solely for all or a part of the voting stock of a corporation which is in control of the acquiring corporation), of stock of another corporation if, immediately after the acquisition, the acquiring corporation has control of such other corporation (whether or not such acquiring corporation had control immediately before the acquisition).

In essence, the buyer exchanges nothing but its stock for the stock of the seller, resulting in the selling entity becoming a subsidiary of the buyer. The IRS has clarified the basic definition to state that only *voting* stock can be used in the transaction. For example, if the buyer issues any preferred or nonvoting stock as part of the deal, then it no longer qualifies as a Type B reorganization. Also, the seller cannot give the selling entity's stockholders the option of being paid with cash instead of stock.

In addition, the buyer must gain immediate control over the seller, which the IRS defines as the buyer receiving at least 80% of the stock of the selling entity. However, it is allowable to gain *creeping control* over the seller, where the buyer gains control over a period of no more than 12 months. Creeping control is allowable only if the buyer has a plan for gaining control during this time period.

Finally, this transaction is subject to the IRS's continuity of interest and continuity of business enterprise requirements.

In summary, the Type B reorganization is most useful when the selling entity must be retained, usually because it has valuable contracts that would otherwise be terminated if the entity were to be liquidated.

Type C Reorganization

A Type C reorganization is governed by paragraph C of Section 368(a)(1) of the IRC. The paragraph is as follows:

> The acquisition by one corporation, in exchange solely for all or a part of its voting stock (or in exchange solely for all or a part of the voting stock of a corporation which is in control of the acquiring corporation), of substantially all of the properties of another corporation, but in determining whether the exchange is solely for stock the assumption by the acquiring corporation of a liability of the other shall be disregarded.

In order to be a nontaxable transaction, paragraph C requires that the seller transfer essentially all of its assets in exchange for the buyer's voting stock. Further, those assets transferred must be critical to the continuation of the business, which is an element of the continuity of interest requirement discussed earlier. Also, the continuity of business enterprise requirement must be fulfilled. Finally, the stock paid for the transaction must be entirely the seller's *voting* stock, and the selling entity must liquidate itself.

To qualify under the asset transfer requirement of the Type C reorganization, the seller must transfer to the buyer at least 90% of its net assets, including all of those assets considered critical to the ongoing operations of the business.

It is possible for the buyer to pay some cash as part of this transaction. However, at least 80% of the FMV of the assets purchased must be solely for stock, so only the remaining asset value can be paid for with cash. The seller must pay income taxes on any portion of the purchase that is not paid for with the buyer's stock.

Any dissenting shareholders may have the right to have their ownership positions appraised and then paid in cash. The extent of these cash payments will increase the total proportion of nonstock payment made, which can affect the nontaxable nature of the entire transaction. Thus, a significant proportion of dissenting shareholders can prevent the C reorganization from being used.

In summary, the Type C reorganization is most useful when the seller is willing to accept mostly stock in payment and the buyer does not need the selling entity, which is liquidated. The buyer can also record the acquired assets at their FMV, which is generally higher than the tax basis that otherwise would be inherited from the seller.

Type D Reorganization

A Type D reorganization is governed by paragraph D of Section 368(a)(1) of the Internal Revenue Code. The paragraph is as follows:

> A transfer by a corporation of all or a part of its assets to another corporation if immediately after the transfer the transferor, or one or more of its shareholders (including persons who were shareholders immediately before the transfer), or any combination thereof, is in control of the corporation to which the assets are transferred; but only if, in pursuance of the plan, stock or securities of the corporation to which the assets are transferred are distributed in a [qualifying transaction].

Type D reorganizations can be either *acquisitive* or *divisive*. An *acquisitive* reorganization is when the seller transfers substantially all of its assets to the buyer in exchange for at least 80% of the buyer's voting and nonvoting stock. This is also known as a reverse merger.

A divisive Type D reorganization is when a single entity separates into two or more separate entities. The division occurs in two steps: First, a company transfers some of its assets to a corporation in exchange for voting control of that entity. Then it transfers the acquired control to its own stockholders. There are three types of divisive reorganizations, all of which are tax-free:

1. *Spin-off*. Stockholders end up with shares of both the original and new entities.
2. *Split-off*. Some stockholders retain their shares in the original entity while others swap their stock in the original entity for shares of the new entity. This approach is most useful if there is a difference of opinion among the stockholders regarding the future direction of the original entity, since they now have a choice regarding which entity to own.
3. *Split-up*. The original entity creates two new entities, transfers its assets to them, and then liquidates. Stockholders end up with shares in the surviving entities. As was the case with a split-off, this approach is also useful for separating internal factions who disagree about how the company is being managed.

All of the variations noted here are also subject to four requirements.

1. The original entity must distribute the stock of the new entity to its stockholders, resulting in their control of it.
2. The original entity can distribute the stock of the new entity only to its stockholders.
3. Subsequent to the transaction, both entities must be actively engaged in business.

4. The transaction cannot be intended to avoid tax payments.

A Type D reorganization is intended primarily to govern the tax-free division of a company into smaller entities rather than to acquire another entity.

Triangular Merger

A triangular merger is a reorganization in which a subsidiary owned by the buyer merges with the seller, with the selling entity then liquidating. Being a merger rather than an acquisition, the transaction will eliminate all minority stockholders, since they are legally required to accept the buyer's purchase price. Also, the approval of only the selling entity's board of directors is needed, not the selling stockholders.

For a triangular transaction to be nontaxable, the buyer must have at least 80% control over its subsidiary and must acquire at least 90% of the FMV of the buyer's net assets. Also, the transaction between the subsidiary and the selling entity must satisfy the requirements noted earlier for a Type A reorganization, which include the presence of a continuity of interest and a continuity of business enterprise.

Reverse Triangular Merger

A reverse triangular merger is a reorganization in which a subsidiary owned by the buyer merges into the seller, with the subsidiary then liquidating. The buying parent company's voting stock is then transferred to the selling stockholders in exchange for their stock in the selling entity. Being a merger rather than an acquisition, the transaction will eliminate all minority shareholders, since they are legally required to accept the buyer's purchase price. Also, the approval of only the selling entity's board of directors is needed, not the selling stockholders.

For a reverse triangular merger to be nontaxable, the selling entity must acquire substantially all of the assets of the buyer's subsidiary, and the buyer must obtain at least 80% control of the selling entity. Also, the buyer must acquire at least 90% of the FMV of the buyer's net assets.

The reverse triangular merger is used most commonly when the selling entity has valuable contracts that would otherwise be cancelled if the selling entity were not to survive the acquisition transaction. It is also used when the selling entity's stock is too widely held to make a direct stock purchase practicable, or where there may be a significant proportion of dissenting stockholders.

Sellers tend to be less enthralled with a reverse triangular merger, because this type of reorganization severely limits the amount of cash they can receive. Because the selling entity must give up at least 80% of its stock for the stock of the buyer's subsidiary, this leaves no more than 20% of the total purchase price available for payment in cash. Nonetheless, this is one of the most common types of reorganization in use.

All-Cash Acquisition

What if a seller has no interest in deferring any taxable gains arising from the sale of the business? This is most likely when an owner wishes to cash out of a business and retire. If so, the seller is most likely to insist on selling the entire entity and not just its assets, thereby avoiding all potential liabilities. Given this transfer of risk to the buyer, and the difficulty of obtaining sufficient cash for the deal, the buyer is more likely to insist on a lower purchase price.

The result for the seller is an entirely taxable transaction. The seller will pay income tax on the difference between the cash paid and his basis in the entity being sold. Conversely, the buyer will step up the basis of the acquiree's assets to their FMV, thereby gaining more depreciation to offset against future gains.

If the buyer intends to acquire the seller's legal entity, then the approval for an all-cash transaction generally is limited to the seller's board of directors. If the intent is to acquire only selected assets, then the approval process usually extends to the shareholders too.

Appraisal Rights

If a shareholder of a selling entity does not approve of an acquisition, he can exercise appraisal rights, under which the buyer must offer alternative consideration (typically cash) for their shares, which is based on the appraised value of the selling entity. This can be a real problem in a Type B reorganization, where virtually all of the consideration must be in stock.

Appraisal rights are less of an issue when both entities are publicly held. For example, if a company is incorporated in Delaware, the Delaware court does not give appraisal rights to the stockholders of a public company when the consideration is the stock of another public company.

Summary

There are many types of reorganizations available for use. The type selected is subject to many factors, of which the most important is the taxability of the transaction to the seller. Next in importance is the buyer's ability to retain valuable contracts controlled by the selling entity, followed by the buyer being able to record the selling entity's assets at their fair market values. Also of concern is the potential for a dissenting stockholder of the selling entity to exercise appraisal rights, which would eliminate the use of the popular Type B reorganization. The following table summarizes the key options available under most of the reorganization methods described here.

	Asset Sale	Type A	Type B	Type C	Pure Cash
Business enterprise rule	N/A	Yes	Yes	Yes	N/A
Continuity of interest rule	N/A	Yes	Yes	Yes	N/A
Maximum cash payment	N/A	50%	None	20%	100%
Selling entity liquidated?	No	Yes	No	Yes	N/A
Appraisal rights allowed?	No	Yes	Yes	Yes	N/A
Taxable to sellers?	Yes	Only cash portion	No	Only cash portion	Yes
Selling shareholder approval needed?	Yes	Yes	No	Yes	No
Buyer basis in acquired assets?	FMV	Carryover	Carryover	FMV	FMV

The type of reorganization selected is critical to both parties to an acquisition, especially the seller. Thus, the seller should carefully explore the available options with an attorney experienced in such transactions rather than accepting whatever form of reorganization is initially proposed by the buyer.

39.5 THE PURCHASE METHOD

In brief, this approach to accounting for a business combination assumes that the acquiring company spreads the acquisition price over the assets being bought at their fair market value, with any remaining portion of the acquisition price being recorded in a goodwill account. The company being purchased can be bought with any form of consideration, such as stock, cash, or property.

There are three primary steps involved in accounting for a purchase transaction. The first is to determine the purchase price, the second is to allocate this price among the various assets of the company being purchased, and the third is to account for the first-year partial results of the purchased entity on the buyer's financial statements. The issue with the first step is that the purchase price is based on the fair market value of the consideration given to the seller. For example, if the purchase is made with stock, the stock must be valued at its fair market value. If treasury stock is used as part of the consideration, then this must also be valued at its fair market value. If the buyer's stock is thinly traded or closely held, then it may be necessary to obtain the services of an investment banker or appraiser, who can use various valuation models and industry surveys to derive a price per share.

The second step in the purchase method is to allocate the purchase price among the acquired company's assets and liabilities, which are then recorded in the buyer's accounting records. The method of valuation varies by line item on the acquired company's balance sheet. Here are the key valuation rules:

- *Accounts receivable.* Record this asset at its present value, less the allowance for bad debts. Given the exceedingly short time frame over which this asset is outstanding, there is generally no need to discount this valuation, unless there are receivables with very long collection terms. Also, since the acquisition transaction is generally not completed until several months after the acquisition date (given the effort required to make the accounting entry), the amount of the allowance for bad debts can be very precisely determined as of the acquisition date.

- *Marketable securities.* These assets should be recorded at their fair market value. This is an opportunity for the buyer to mark up a security to its fair market value (if such is the case), since GAAP normally only allows for the recognition of reductions in market value. For this reason, this is an area in which there is some opportunity to allocate an additional portion of the purchase price beyond the original cost of the asset. However, since most companies only invest in short-term, highly liquid securities, it is unlikely that there will be a large amount of potential appreciation in the securities.

- *Inventory—raw materials.* These assets should be recorded at their replacement cost. This can be a problem if the acquiree is in an industry, such as computer hardware, where inventory costs drop at a rapid pace as new products rapidly come into the marketplace. Consequently, the buyer may find itself with a significantly lower inventory valuation as a result of the purchase transaction than originally appeared on the accounting records of the acquiree.

- *Inventory—finished goods.* These assets should be recorded at their selling prices, less their average profit margin and disposition costs. This can be a difficult calculation to make if the finished goods have variable prices depending upon where or in what quantities they are sold; in such cases, the determination of selling price should be based on a history of the most common sales transactions. For example, if 80% of all units sold are in purchase quantities that result in a per-unit price of $1.50, then this is the most appropriate price to use. This rule can be avoided, however, if the acquiree has firm sales contracts as of the date of the acquisition with specific customers that can be used to clearly determine the prices at which the finished goods will actually be sold.

If the acquirer had been using a last-in, first out (LIFO) inventory valuation system, then the newly derived valuation for the finished goods inventory shall be used as the LIFO base layer for all inventory obtained through the purchase transaction.

- *Inventory—work-in-process.* These assets receive the same valuation treatment as finished goods, except that the cost of conversion into finished goods must also be subtracted from their eventual sale price.
- *Property, plant, and equipment (PP&E).* These assets should be recorded at their replacement cost. This can be a difficult task that lengthens the interval before the acquisition journal entry is completed, because some assets may be so old that there is no equivalent product currently on the market, or equipment may be so specialized that it is difficult to find a reasonable alternative on the market. This valuation step frequently calls for the services of an appraiser.
- *Property, plant, and equipment (PP&E) to be sold.* If the buyer intends to sell off assets as of the acquisition date, then these assets should be recorded at their fair market value. This most accurately reflects their disposal value as of the acquisition date.
- *Capital leases.* If the acquiree possesses assets that were purchased with capital leases, then the accountant should value the asset at its fair market value, while valuing the associated lease at its net present value.
- *Research and development (R&D) assets.* If any assets associated with specific R&D projects are part of the acquiree, the accountant should charge these assets off to expense if there is no expectation that they will have an alternative future use once the current R&D project has been completed. The precise allocation of assets to expense or asset accounts can be difficult, since the existing projects may be expected to last well into the future, or the future use of the assets may not be easy to determine. Consequently, one should carefully document the reasons for the treatment of R&D assets.
- *Intangible assets.* These assets are to be recorded at their appraised values. If the buyer cannot reasonably assign a cost to them or identify them, then no cost should be assigned.
- *Accounts and notes payable.* Accounts payable can typically be recorded at their current amounts as listed on the books of the acquiree. However, if the accounts payable are not to be paid for some time, then they should be recorded at their discounted present values. The same logic applies to notes payable; since all but the shortest-lived notes will have a significantly different present value, they should be discounted and recorded as such. This treatment is used on the assumption that the buyer would otherwise be purchasing these liabilities on the date of the acquisition, not on a variety of dates stretching out into the future, and so must be discounted to show their value on the acquisition date.
- *Accruals.* These liabilities are typically very short-term ones that will be reversed shortly after the current accounting period. Accordingly, they are to be valued at their present value; discounting is rarely necessary.

- *Pension liability.* If there is an unfunded pension liability, even if not recognized on the books of the acquiree, it must be recognized by the buyer as part of the purchase transaction.
- *Stock option plan.* If the buyer decides to take over an existing stock option plan of the acquiree, then it must allocate part of the purchase price to the incremental difference between the price at which shares may be purchased under the plan and the market price for the stock as of the date of the acquisition. However, if the buyer forced the acquiree to settle all claims under the option plan prior to the acquisition, then this becomes a compensation expense that is recorded on the books of the acquiree.

If the acquiring company (Charleston Corporation) buys the acquiree's (Denton Corporation) stock with $500,000 of cash, the entry on Charleston's books would be:

	Debit	Credit
Investment in Denton Corporation	$500,000	
Cash		$500,000

Alternatively, if Charleston were to make the purchase using a mix of 20% cash and 80% for a note, the entry would be:

	Debit	Credit
Investment in Denton Corporation	$500,000	
Cash		$100,000
Note payable		400,000

Another approach would be to exchange 5,000 shares of Charleston's $1 par value stock for that of Denton as a form of payment. Under this method, the entry would be:

	Debit	Credit
Investment in Denton Corporation	$500,000	
Common stock—par value		$5,000
Common stock—additional paid-in capital		495,000

The result of all the preceding valuation rules is shown in Exhibit 39.15, where we show the calculation that would be required to adjust the books of an acquiree in order to then consolidate it with the results of the acquiring company. The exhibit shows the initial book cost of each account on the acquiree's balance sheet, followed by a listing of the required valuation of each account under the purchase method, the adjustment required, and the new account valuation. The new account valuation on the right side of the table can then be combined directly into the records of the acquiring company. Under the "Purchase Method Valuation" column, a designation of "NPV" means that the net present value of the line item is shown, a designation of "FMV" means that the fair market value is shown (less any costs required to sell the item, if applicable), "RC" designates the use of replacement cost, "SLM" designates the use of sale price less the gross margin, and "AV" designates an asset's appraised value.

Account	Acquiree Records	Purchase Method Valuation	Required Adjustment	Adjusted Acquiree Records
Assets				
Cash	$ 1,413	$ 1,413	$ 0	$1,413
Receivables	4,000	4,000	0	4,000
Receivables, long term	1,072	(NPV) 808	(CR) 264	808
Marketable securities	503	(FMV) 490	(CR) 13	490
Inventory—raw materials	921	(RC) 918	(CR) 3	918
Inventory—WIP	395	(SLM) 429	(DB) 34	429
Inventory—finished goods	871	(SLM) 950	(DB) 79	950
Property, plant, & equipment	6,005	(RC) 7,495	(DB) 1,490	7,495
Equipment for sale	803	(FMV) 745	(CR) 58	745
Capital lease assets	462	(FMV) 500	(DB) 38	500
Goodwill	0	0	(DB) 4,677	4,677
Investment in acquiree	0	0	(CR) 14,600	−15,000
Intangibles	593	(AV) 650	(DB) 57	650
Total assets	$17,038	$18,398	(CR) $8,563	$8,075
Liabilities				
Accounts payable	$ 3,992	$ 3,992	$ 0	$3,992
Notes payable, long term	3,300	(NPV) 2,950	(DB) 350	2,950
Accrued liabilities	325	325	0	325
Capital lease liabilities	450	(NPV) 400	(DB) 50	400
Pension liability	408	408	0	408
Total liabilities	$ 8,475	$ 8,075	(DB) $ 400	$8,075
Shareholder's equity				
Common stock	4,586	—	(DB) 4,586	$0
Paid-in capital	100	—	(DB) 100	0
Retained earnings	3,877	—	(DB) 3,877	0
Total equity	$ 8,563	—	(DB) $8,563	$0
Total liabilities & equity	$17,038	—	(DB) $8,963	$8,075

EXHIBIT 39.15   ADJUSTMENTS TO THE ACQUIREE'S BOOKS FOR A PURCHASE CONSOLIDATION

In the exhibit, debits and credits are specified for each adjusting entry listed in the "Required Adjustment" column. The amount of goodwill shown in the "Required Adjustment" column is derived by subtracting the purchase price of $15,000 from the total of all fair market and other valuations shown in the "Purchase Method Valuation" column. In this case, we have a fair market valuation of $18,398 for all assets, less a fair market valuation of $8,075 for all liabilities, which yields a net fair market value for the acquiree of $10,323. When this fair market value is subtracted from the purchase price of $15,000, we end up with a residual of $4,677, which is listed in the goodwill account. Please note that the "Adjusted Acquiree Records" column on the right side of the exhibit still must be added to the acquirer's records to arrive at a consolidated financial statement for the combined entities.

The third step in the acquisition process is to account for the first year partial results of the acquired company on its books. Only the income of the acquiree that falls within its current fiscal year, but after the date of the acquisition, should be added to the buyer's accounting records. In addition, the buyer must charge all costs associated with the acquisition to current expense—they *cannot* be capitalized. These acquisition costs should be almost entirely for outside services, since any internal costs charged to the acquisition would likely have been incurred anyway, even in the absence of the acquisition. The only variation from this rule is the costs associated with issuing equity to pay for the acquisition; these costs can be recorded as an offset to the additional Paid-in capital account. An additional item is that a liability should be recognized at the time of the acquisition for any plant closings or losses on the dispositions of assets that are planned as of that date; this is not an expense that is recognized at a later date, since we assume that the buyer was aware at the purchase date that some asset dispositions would be required.

If the acquirer chooses to report its financial results for multiple years prior to the acquisition, it does *not* report the combined results of the two entities for years prior to the acquisition.

A *reverse acquisition* is one in which the company issuing its shares or other payment is actually the acquiree, because the acquiring company's shareholders do not own a majority of the stock after the acquisition is completed. Though rare, this approach is sometimes used when a shell company with available funding buys an operating company, or when a publicly held shell company is used to buy a nonpublic company, thereby avoiding the need to go through an initial public offering (IPO) by the nonpublic company. In this case, the assets and liabilities of the shell corporation are revalued to their fair market value and then recorded on the books of the company being bought.

39.6 THE COST METHOD

The cost method is used to account for the purchase of another company's stock when the buyer obtains less than 20% of the other company's shares and when it does not have management control over it. The buyer does not have control if it cannot obtain financial results from the other company that it needs to create entries under the equity method (see next section) or if it fails to obtain representation on the board of directors, is forced to relinquish significant shareholder rights, or the concentration of voting power is clearly in evidence among a different group of shareholders.

Under this method, the investing company records the initial investment at cost on its books. It then recognizes as income any dividends distributed by the investee after the investment date.

39.7 THE EQUITY METHOD

The equity method of accounting for an investment in another company is used when the investor owns more than 20% of the investee's stock or less than 20% but with evidence of some degree of management control over the investee, such as control over some portion of the investee's board of directors, involvement in its management activities, or the exchange of management personnel between companies. The method is only used when the investee is a corporation, partnership, or joint venture, and when both organizations remain separate legal entities.

Under the equity method, the acquirer records its initial investment in the investee at cost. For example, if the initial investment in Company ABC were $1,000,000 in exchange for ownership of 40% of its common stock, then the entry on the books of the investor would be:

	Debit	Credit
Investment in Company ABC	$1,000,000	
Cash		$1,000,000

After the initial entry, the investor records its proportional share of the investee's income against current income. For example, if the investee has a gain of $120,000, the investor can recognize its 40% share of this income, which is $48,000. The entry would be:

	Debit	Credit
Investment in Company ABC	$48,000	
Investment income		$48,000

The credit in the last journal entry can more precisely be made to an undistributed investment income account, since the funds from the investee's income have not actually been distributed to the investor.

The investor should also record a deferred income tax expense based on any income attributed to the investee. To continue with the preceding example, if the incremental tax rate for the investor is 38%, then it would record the following entry that is based on its $48,000 of Company ABC's income:

	Debit	Credit
Income tax expense	$18,240	
Deferred taxes		$18,240

If the investee issues dividends, then these are recorded as an offset to the investment account and a debit to cash. Dividends are not recorded as income, since income was already accounted for as a portion of the investee's income, even though it may not have been received. For example, if dividends of $25,000 are received from Company ABC, the entry would be:

	Debit	Credit
Cash	$25,000	
Investment in Company ABC		$25,000

If the market price of the investor's shares in the investee drops below its investment cost, there are not normally any grounds for reducing the amount of the investment. However, if the loss in market value appears to be permanent, then a loss can be recognized and charged against current earnings. Evidence of a permanent loss in market value would be a long-term drop in market value that is substantially below the investment cost, or repeated and substantial reported losses by the investee, with no prospects for an improvement in reported earnings. For example, if the market price of the stock in

Company ABC necessitated a downward adjustment in the investor's valuation, the entry would be:

	Debit	Credit
Loss on investments		$50,000
Investment in Company ABC	$50,000	

If, after making a downward adjustment in its investment, the investor finds that the market price has subsequently increased, it cannot return the carrying amount of the investment to its original level. The new basis for the investment is the amount to which it has been written down. This will increase the size of any gain that is eventually recognized upon sale of the investment.

If the investee experiences an extraordinary gain or loss, the investor should record its proportional share of this amount as well. However, it is recorded separately from the usual investment accounts. For example, if Company ABC were to experience an extraordinary loss of $15,000, the entry would be:

	Debit	Credit
Undistributed extraordinary loss	$15,000	
Investment in Company ABC		$15,000

If the investee experiences such large losses that the investor's investment is reduced to zero, the investor should stop recording any transactions related to the investment, in order to avoid recording a negative investment. If the investee eventually records a sufficient amount of income to offset the intervening losses, then the investor can resume use of the equity method in reporting its investment.

If the investor loses control over the investee, then it should switch to the cost method of reporting its investment. When it does this, its cost basis should be the amount in the investment account as of the date of change. However, the same rule does not apply if the investor switches from the cost method to the equity method—in this case, the investor must restate its investment account to reflect the equity method of accounting from the date on which it made its initial investment in the investee.

When reporting the results of its investment in another company under the equity method, the investor should list the investment in a single investment in subsidiary line item on its balance sheet and in an investment income line item on its income statement.

39.8   THE CONSOLIDATION METHOD

When a company buys more than 50% of the voting stock of another company, but allows it to remain as a separate legal entity, then the financial results of both companies should be combined in a consolidated set of financial statements. However, if the companies are involved in entirely different lines of business, it may still be appropriate to use the equity method; otherwise, the combined results of the two enterprises could lead to misleading financial results. For example, if a software company with 90% gross margins combines with a steel rolling facility whose gross margins are in the 25% range (both being typical margins for their industries), the blended gross margin presents a misleading view of the gross margins of both entities.

Another case in which a 50%+ level of ownership might not result in the use of a consolidation is when the investing company only expects to have temporary control over the acquiree (perhaps because it is reselling the acquiree) or if the buyer does not have control over the acquiree (perhaps because control is exercised through a small amount of restricted voting stock). In either case, the equity method should be used.

When constructing consolidated financial statements, the preacquisition results of the acquiree should be excluded from the financial statements. If there is a year of divestiture, the financial results of the acquiree in that year should only be consolidated up until the date of divestiture.

39.9   PUSH-DOWN ACCOUNTING

Push-down accounting is the inclusion of acquisition accounting adjustments in the books of the acquired company. These may be recorded separately in a worksheet that is used to create financial statements or directly in the accounting records of the acquiree. The use of worksheet adjustments, rather than direct changes to the acquiree's accounting records, is preferable when the historical records are needed either for tax-reporting purposes or to determine the amount of a minority interest share in the acquiree.

When push-down accounting is used, the acquiree can alter the valuation of all of its assets and liabilities to reflect those made by its corporate parent as part of the purchase method of accounting used to account for the consolidation. This will also result in a change in depreciation expense to reflect any changed fixed asset valuations (and possible changes in the expected useful lives of some assets). There may also be goodwill amortization to reflect the gradual reduction of a goodwill asset recognized as part of the purchase transaction.

There are several objections to push-down accounting. One is that it eliminates the use of the historical basis of accounting for transactions, which is one of the foundations of accounting theory. Another problem is that, in cases where an acquirer gradually buys an acquiree through a series of stock purchases, the use of push-down accounting would result in a series of revaluations that would create multiple changes in the financial statements of the acquiree. Given that the AICPA has not given authoritative guidance on this issue, *privately* held companies may use it or not, as they so choose.

Push-down accounting is strongly favored by the SEC for *publicly* held companies that have concluded acquisitions under the purchase method of accounting that result in wholly owned subsidiaries. The SEC requires that the subsidiary also include in its financial statements the cost of any debt used by the acquirer to purchase it if the acquiree guarantees the debt or plans a debt or equity offering to retire the existing debt, or if there are plans for the subsidiary to assume the debt.

If there are minority interests in the acquiree or if there is outstanding public debt or preferred stock issued by the subsidiary, then the SEC does not insist on the use of push-down accounting.

39.10   LEVERAGED BUYOUTS

A leveraged buyout occurs when funding, which is largely based on debt that is secured by the assets of the acquiree, is used to buy the acquiree. In such cases, it is useful to form a holding company, which buys the stock of the acquiree and becomes its corporate parent. A holding company is particularly useful if the acquiree is publicly held, since it can become the repository for any shares tendered by shareholders of the acquiree in the event of a tender offer.

The acquiree's management team is frequently part of the leveraged buyout, either because it has initiated the buyout itself or because the investors buying the acquiree realize the importance of keeping the management team in place and offer it either shares or stock options as an incentive to stay. If the management team already owns stock in the acquiree, it can avoid taxes by exchanging this stock for the stock of the holding company that is conducting the buyout.

Of particular concern to whoever is initiating a leveraged buyout is the type of accounting basis that it will be allowed to use when recording the transaction. If there is a change in voting control (which is governed by exceedingly complex rules), then the buyout must be recorded under the purchase method of accounting (see earlier section); this approach results in the recording of all acquiree assets and liabilities at their fair market values, with any remaining unallocated purchase price being recorded as goodwill, which must then be gradually written off. If there is a lesser degree of change in the amount of voting control (common enough when the management team is simply increasing its level of ownership), the buyout is considered to be a financial restructuring; in this case, there is no change in the accounting basis. The latter case has the advantage of resulting in no goodwill amortization over many future years, as would be the case under the purchase method, and so yields better financial results in later years.

39.11 SPIN-OFF TRANSACTIONS

A company may find it necessary to transfer an operating division directly to company shareholders as a separate entity. If so, it should be transferred at the book values of all assets and liabilities related to the division as of the date of transfer. If the net amount of all assets and liabilities to be transferred is a positive book value, then this amount is to be offset against the company's Retained earnings account. Alternatively, if the division being transferred has a negative book value, then the offset (which will be an increase) is to the Additional paid-in capital account; the change in account is based on the assumption that investors have essentially paid the company to take the negative net worth division off the company's hands, so they are contributing capital to the company for this privilege.

If the company only owns a small minority interest in the division, then the transaction should be considered a property dividend. Under this concept, the company's share in the division must be transferred at its fair market value, rather than its book value.

Another consideration is that the corporate parent must continue to track the financial results of the division being spun off up until the date of spin-off, and record the results of the division's operations through that date on its books.

39.12 SUMMARY

This chapter described the complete range of activities related to a merger or acquisition: conducting an evaluation of a prospective acquiree, assigning it a value, and accounting for the resulting transaction. It also covered a number of related specialty topics, such as push-down accounting, leveraged buyouts, and spin-off transactions. Nonetheless, the M&A area is an enormous one and this chapter cannot provide adequate coverage of the topic without taking over most of the book. Consequently, for more in-depth coverage, please consult *Mergers and Acquisitions* (Bragg, John Wiley & Sons, 2008).

THE INITIAL PUBLIC OFFERING

40.1 INTRODUCTION

The initial public offering (IPO) is considered by many business owners to be the true sign of success—they have grown a business to the point where its revenue volume and profitability are large enough to warrant public ownership. However, the road to an IPO is both expensive and time-consuming, and requires significant changes to a company. This chapter describes the pluses and minuses of being public, as well as the steps required and costs to be incurred in order to achieve that goal.

40.2 REASONS TO GO PUBLIC

Though a management team may not say it, a major reason for going public is certainly to create a market for the shares they already own. Though these shares may not be available for sale for some time after the IPO (see the "Restrictions on Stock in a Publicly Traded Company" section), they will eventually be able to cash in their shares and options, potentially generating considerable profits from doing so. This reason is not publicized to the public, since they will be less likely to invest if they think that the management team is simply cashing in and then leaving the business.

A slight variation on the wealth creation theme is that, by having a broad public market for their shares, original shareholders are likely to see a rise in the value of their shares, even if they have no intention of selling the shares. The reason is that there is no longer a penalty for not having a ready market for the shares, which adds a premium to what the shares would have been worth if the company had remained privately held.

The same logic can be used as a tool for employee retention. A private company can issue options to its employees, but they are worth little to the employees unless there is a market in which they can sell the shares. By going public, a company may experience increased employee retention, since the employees wish to wait until their options vest so that they can cash in the resulting shares for a profit.

Going public is also useful from the estate-planning perspective. If the owner of a private company dies, his or her heirs are frequently forced to sell the entire business in order to pay estate taxes (though with proper planning, life insurance payouts can be used instead). By taking the company public, the heirs are only forced to sell a portion of the company to pay estate taxes, at least leaving them some portion of the business as a residual.

From an operating perspective, going public gives a company a large pot of cash, which it can use to increase its competitiveness by increasing its asset base, improving marketing, hiring qualified staff, funding more product research, and so on. This can be such a competitive advantage that other companies in the same market segment may be forced to go public as well, just to raise enough funds to survive against their newly funded competitor.

Along the same lines, having publicly held shares allows a company to more readily include its shares in the purchase price of an acquisition. The acquiree is much more willing to accept this form of compensation, since it can sell the shares for cash to other investors. This is a powerful tool for some companies, who use it as the primary method for consolidating a group of smaller, privately held organizations within an industry.

From a financing perspective, going public lowers a company's cost of capital. The main reason is that investors are willing to pay a higher price for a company's stock than if the shares had been privately issued, since they can easily sell the shares. This premium can reduce the cost of capital by several percent. In addition, issuing shares to the public reduces the power that private investors previously may have had over the business, which could have included restrictions on operations, guaranteed dividend payments, or their prior approval of a potential sale of the business. Also, by being publicly held, it is much less time-consuming and less expensive to raise funds through subsequent rounds of financing.

Another financing reason to go public is that new equity drastically lowers the proportion of debt to equity that is recorded on the corporate balance sheet, which is looked upon with great favor by lenders. With the new equity in hand, a company can then ask lenders for a larger amount of debt, which they will be likely to lend until the amount handed over results in a significantly higher debt/equity ratio.

Thus, there are excellent wealth-creating, operating, and financing reasons to pursue an IPO. However, there are just as many reasons for *not* doing so, which are itemized in the next section.

40.3 REASONS NOT TO GO PUBLIC

One of the best reasons for not going public is its cost. These costs are detailed in the following section, while the fees for trading on an exchange are listed later in the "Listing on an Exchange" section. In brief, a small company will be fortunate indeed to incur less than a half-million dollars in up-front fees as part of an IPO. A large company can expect to pay many times these base level expenses. Also, a company conducting a small offering will find that the proportional cost of obtaining equity funding is extremely high, since the underwriter will charge a higher fee as a percentage of the amount raised in order to cover its costs and still earn a profit on the transaction.

Besides the initial cost of going public, there will be incremental increases in ongoing expenses. Most obviously, additional staff must be hired into the accounting department, whose job will be to keep up with all reports required by the SEC. In addition, the cost of director's and officer's insurance (D&O) will skyrocket from what would have been paid when a company was privately held, assuming that the insurance can be obtained at all. The reason for this increase is the vastly increased pool of investors who may be tempted to sue the company on the grounds of material misstatements in its public comments (such as its registration statement for the IPO) in the event that the stock price drops. One can reasonably expect the cost of this insurance to increase by a factor of at least ten.

Another problem is that a smaller company with a modest market capitalization will have difficulty establishing a market for its stock. If it is too small, institutional investors (who like to buy and sell in large blocks of stock) will have minimal interest in making an investment. Because of this small market, a company's stock will be more likely to be subject to manipulation by a small number of investors, who can short sell it to drive the stock down and then purchase large blocks of stock at a reduced price in order to gain some measure of control over the company.

Loss of control is quite possible, unless the owner has retained a large proportion of corporate stock, or unless a separate class of super-voting-stock has been established that gives the owners additional votes at shareholder meetings. Otherwise, outside investors can either buy up shares to create large voting blocks or band together to create the same result.

Information disclosure is yet another problem. In addition to the expense of having additional accounting staff to organize and report this information, there is the problem of disclosing information to a company's competitors, who only need to access the SEC's Web site to access all required reports filed by the company. Though many pundits claim that the types of information disclosed will not harm the competitive posture of a public company, competitors can tell from its financial statements when it has put itself out on a financial limb by obtaining too much debt, and can easily start a price war at this point that could cause the company to miss debt payments and therefore possibly go into bankruptcy.

A serious concern is the risk of shareholder class action lawsuits. These arise when there is a drop in the stock price that shareholders claim was the result of material misstatements in the registration statement or in any other information releases thereafter. These lawsuits are the reason for much more expensive D&O insurance. They will be targeted at the company as a whole, the corporate directors, whomever signed the registration statement, any experts who have given statements on behalf of the company, and its underwriters. The threat of lawsuits is one of the main reasons why IPO prices are frequently set somewhat low—there is less chance that the price will drop further, giving investors no reason to sue.

Another issue is the constant pressure from investors and analysts to show improved results every quarter. If a company is private, it can easily stand lower profits for a year or so while it ramps up new products and markets, but being public makes this completely practical approach to growing a business more difficult to implement. Investors can attempt to unseat the management team by approving a different board of directors if they feel that growth rates are below their expectations. This issue can only be dealt with by continually informing the investing public of management's intentions for corporate growth, so that investors will adopt a longer-term perspective.

Finally, the management team must understand that it now exists not to serve itself, but to serve the investing public. This major shift in focus calls for the elimination of unusually high compensation packages to the managers, as well as a commitment to increasing shareholder value over other objectives that may have been in vogue at the company prior to going public. Management may be uncomfortable with this paradigm shift, resulting in investor unhappiness with a perceived lack of attention to their needs by management.

There are so many negatives to going public that the managements of many perfectly good private companies have elected to stay away from the public markets. In addition, a great many companies that have gone public find these issues to be so burdensome that they have elected to take themselves private once again.

40.4   THE COST OF AN IPO

Even a small company should expect to pay a minimum of a half-million dollars to complete an IPO. This expense comprises a number of fees. Accounting and legal fees will consume the largest proportion of the total. Expect to pay at least $250,000 in legal fees. Audit fees will vary, depending on the size and complexity of the company, but certainly expect to pay at least three times the cost of a normal audit. This figure will increase if there are weak internal control systems that require the auditors to conduct more extensive audit tests. Further, printing costs for the prospectus will exceed $100,000 for all but the most "plain Jane" documents, which will increase if a large number of revisions to the registration statement are required prior to printing. Also, initial filing fees with a number of government and regulatory bodies will likely consume a minimum of another $25,000.

In addition to these professional fees, the underwriter requires a significant payment that is based on the percentage of capital raised. The usual fee is in the range of 6% to 7% if an offering exceeds $20 million, with the percentage gradually increasing to as much as 15% of the total offering if it is quite small (in the $1 to $3 million range). This cost can be reduced if a company accepts "best efforts" marketing by the underwriter, whereby it does not guarantee a full sale of the entire stock offering. In this case, the percentage fee will drop by 2% to 3%.

To make the situation worse, with the exception of the underwriter fee, most of these costs are incurred prior to the sale of any stock, so a company will be charged with the full expense of an IPO even if it is never completed. If the company withdraws from the IPO process, it must pay the fees incurred to that point by its underwriter, though this obligation is not usually required when the underwriter withdraws. Furthermore, if the IPO is merely delayed, many of the costs must be incurred again, since the underlying operational and financial information upon which the original offering was contemplated will have changed and must be reexamined by the lawyers and accountants.

40.5   PREPARING FOR THE IPO

Preparing for an IPO begins years before the actual event, because the company must "clean up" prior to being presented to the investing public as a quality investment. This house cleaning involves the following steps:

- *Increase the competence of the management team.* The single greatest driver of corporate value is the quality of the management team. The owners must evaluate each management position and replace anyone who is not a team player, who does not drive efficiency and effectiveness throughout his or her department, and who does not have a tight strategic vision. Obtaining a manager who is well known at a national level can have a startling positive impact on the perceived value of the company as a whole. A key point is that a management team is not a one-man show. Investors need to see a competent supporting team that can readily take over the business in the event that one key manager dies or leaves the company.
- *Create a reward system that is tied to strategy.* With the assistance of a compensation expert, design a reward system not only for the management team but also for the entire company that gives them incentive to focus their activities on those areas of the business that must be improved prior to the IPO (as described in all the points in this section). A key area is in the use of stock options, which can be issued several years prior to the IPO, when the company's value is substantially lower,

resulting in significant gains for the recipients after the company goes public. To do this, one should set aside a large pool of stock for option conversions, and do so well in advance of the IPO, in order to avoid having the new shareholders vote to create it.

- *Obtain audited financials.* A reputable audit firm, and preferably one with a national presence, should audit the financial statements for the three years prior to the IPO. A review or compilation is not acceptable—these less-expensive and less-thorough forms of an audit will be rejected by the underwriter and the SEC when the registration statement is filed.

- *Obtain a top securities law firm.* Though there may be little perceived need for a law firm well in advance of an IPO, it is useful to have such a firm examine the legal structure of the business and recommend changes that will properly position the company for the IPO. The need for this firm will rise dramatically during the IPO filing period, when its lawyers will review the company's prospectus and registration statement to ensure its completeness in accordance with SEC regulations. The lawyers will also channel all communications to and from the SEC in regard to both the initial registration and filings subsequent to the IPO.

- *Strip out personal transactions.* The owners of a private business typically mesh their personal affairs with those of the company to a considerable extent. This can include keeping personal servants on the company payroll, having the company guarantee personal loans, loaning company money to their other businesses, and giving themselves inordinate levels of compensation. Stopping these practices can be quite difficult for an owner, whose overall level of compensation may drop substantially as a result.

- *Show 25% annual growth.* Potential investors want to invest in companies with a record of strong growth, preferably at least 25% for each of the last few years. To create a business in line with these expectations, the business owner must close down or sell off those portions of the business that have no reasonable near-term prospect for growth, or (worse) those areas that are not only *not* growing, but which also require substantial cash infusions that could be better applied to higher-growth business segments.

- *At least show breakeven profitability.* Investors understand that extra expenses must be incurred in order to ramp up sales, so they are not looking for inordinate profit levels in addition to high sales growth rates. However, there should be no losses appearing on the income statement for the past few years, since this would imply an inability by management to control costs, which brings into question the viability of the entire business model. This may also require a business to switch away from some tax reduction strategies that it may have pursued as a private company in order to reduce its tax liability, in favor of ensuring that some degree of profitability appears in the financial statements. Another alternative for ensuring some profitability is a tighter focus on cost controls, perhaps through the use of benchmarking or best practices implementations that are recommended by consultants.

- *Fill the product pipeline.* Investors want to see a company that has established a clear competitive differentiation in the market place. This can be done through the advance funding of research and development projects that lead to the creation of a stream of new products. Since it takes a long time to create new products, the investment in this activity should begin far in advance of the IPO. It is particularly important not to appear like a "one-hit wonder," with only a single winning product—be sure to create a process that reliably generates a continuing stream of products.

- *Achieve critical mass.* In order to attract the attention of institutional investors, a company must have a market capitalization of at least $100 million. At this point, their participation will yield an active market for the stock, which can help to drive up the stock price. To reach this capitalization level, a company requires substantial revenue volume. Though roughly a quarter of all public companies have revenues of less than $10 million, a much higher level is required to reach the crucial $100 million capitalization level. In order to do this, company management may need to concentrate on making acquisitions in the years leading up to the IPO, with the objective of building enough critical mass for the IPO.

- *Expand high-growth segments.* Investors want to see a high rate of growth in areas where other public companies have been rewarded with high price-earnings (P/E) multiples. To do this, the management team should be aware of P/E multiples for all companies in its market segment, and allocate funding to those areas of the business that will reward the company with a high P/E multiple when it goes public. This capital allocation process is a difficult one, for the market can increase or decrease P/E multiples in a very short time period, depending on its perception of how "hot" a market segment may be.

- *Pick an independent board.* Investors want a majority of the board of directors to be independent from the management team, in order to place investor interests ahead of those of the management team. Though this group can be selected just prior to the IPO, it is better to do so at least a year in advance, in order to give this group time to settle into their roles and learn about company operations.

- *Protect owner wealth.* The owner of a company that has just gone public, and who has sold some proportion of his or her shares to the public, should expect to be paying a large amount of taxes. To reduce this tax burden, the owner can spend the previous few years gifting company stock to heirs, which can be given tax-free in blocks of $10,000 per year to each recipient (or $20,000 if the owner is married). In addition, if there are potential capital losses on any investments, this is the year in which they should be recognized in order to offset the gains from the IPO.

The main point of this section is to impress upon the CFO the need for advance planning for an IPO, preferably beginning a minimum of three years prior to it. Only by taking this long view to going public can a company position itself properly to achieve the maximum value for its shareholders, while minimizing the tax impact for its original owners.

40.6 FINDING AN UNDERWRITER

The process of becoming a public company begins with the search for a qualified underwriter who can lead the company through the maze of steps needed to go public. An underwriter is an entity that sells company shares either directly to individual investors or to institutional buyers, such as mutual fund managers. The largest underwriters operate on an international scale, while others have a regional focus or only concentrate their attention on specific market niches in which they have built up a considerable degree of expertise. A major underwriter may have built up a large retail brokerage operation, as well as have significant institutional sales capacity, though some of these underwriters have elected to focus more on one of the two sales channels over the other.

It is better to use underwriters with an established reputation, despite their higher cost, because investors tend to trust them more, which can result in a higher stock price. Conversely, using an underwriter with a poor reputation (i.e., for drumming up the price of stocks that later crash) is much more likely to result in unhappy investors, potential investor lawsuits, and a thinly traded stock. It is also important to use an underwriter with a strong research capability and a commitment to use this resource to distribute information about the company and its industry to investors. A good way to determine who has the best analyst coverage of an industry is to ask investors and other brokerage houses whose reports they feel are the most complete and accurate.

Underwriters have a tendency to sell shares to institutional investors, because these are sophisticated investors who buy in large volumes, thereby reducing the sales efforts of the underwriters. This can be a problem if a large percentage of the company's shares are being sold to the public, because institutional investors are much more likely to gain control over the company or at least gain a formidable block of voting stock that can be used to influence the company's direction.

If an IPO is a small one, an underwriter may handle the entire issuance by itself. However, it more commonly leads a team of underwriters as the managing underwriter if there is a substantial amount of stock to be sold to the public. It creates this syndication not only to spread its own risk in the transaction, but also to ensure that shares are sold to a wide cross-section of the investing public, which is critical for creating a strong market for the company's stock.

A larger company with a strong track record will attract the attention of a number of underwriters who are eager to take it public. When selecting from among this group, one should look for a business with a strong reputation for successfully bringing new offerings to market, which can be easily discerned by reviewing the business press for the last few years. Another key factor should be its distribution capacity, since the company will want a broad range of investors, rather than a small number of powerful institutional investors. The underwriter should also be able to commit to the creation of a strong aftermarket in the company's stock, which can be verified by making reference calls to the CFOs of other companies that it has already taken public as the managing underwriter. These reference calls should include queries about the level of service provided, the level of underwriter expertise, the breadth of share placement among investors, and subsequent promotion through research reports. If the underwriter already employs an analyst for the company's industry, this is a strong indicator of the underwriter's commitment to an aftermarket. Further, one should ask if the analyst plans to issue regular research reports to the underwriter's clients about the company. Of particular concern should be the underwriter's history of bringing companies public as the *managing* underwriter, rather than as one of a large syndicate. If the underwriter has primarily been a syndicate member, this is a strong indication that it lacks experience in managing the IPO process.

Unfortunately, most companies are too small to attract a flurry of underwriter interest. Instead, they must work hard to attract the attention of just one or two. To do so, the owner should have already achieved all of the long-range targets noted in the last section. In addition, the management team should construct a detailed business plan that dovetails with prior company results, while also showing exactly how it plans to use the cash received from the stock offering to achieve future growth and profitability. The plan should most certainly *not* describe any intent by management to sell off its shares, since this tells underwriters that they want to cash out of the company, potentially leaving investors to shift for themselves. This document should include a detailed description of all key members of the management team, since underwriters are well aware of the importance of a strong team. Further, the plan should itemize all risk areas and explain how the company plans to hedge those risks while pursuing its growth plans. Above all, the plan must present a compelling story that will attract a high-quality underwriter.

If an underwriter is sufficiently interested in the company, it will conduct an exhaustive due diligence process to verify that what the company says about itself is true. This is likely to include interviews throughout the company, a detailed analysis of all operations, company tours, and reference calls to company suppliers and customers. In particular, the underwriter will investigate the background of each key executive in detail, so be sure that their published resumes are accurate. The underwriter must conduct this level of detailed review in order to protect itself in case problems arise after the IPO that it should have seen prior to the stock offering. If there is even a hint of the company trying to mislead the underwriter about material issues, the underwriter will walk away, so be certain to verify all information in the business plan prior to releasing it to the underwriter.

If the underwriter remains interested in the company after the due diligence phase, it will sign a letter of intent with the company. This letter outlines the following issues:

- *Type of agreement*. The letter will state if the arrangement with the underwriter will be a "firm commitment" deal or a "best efforts" deal. The firm commitment approach is used by most large underwriters, and requires them to purchase a fixed number of shares from the company at a fixed price, which is discounted from the price at which they will then sell the shares to investors. This is the preferred approach, since a company will be guaranteed a fixed amount of cash. The alternative is a best efforts deal, under which the underwriter merely tries to sell as many shares as it can and takes a commission on those shares it sells. This alternative does not guarantee a company any cash, while still requiring it to meet with the various requirements of being a publicly held entity, and so is much less preferable. A best efforts deal is most common when a company's prospects are considered sufficiently risky that the underwriter is uncomfortable purchasing the entire stock offering, thereby putting itself at risk of being unable to resell them.

- *Expenses*. The underwriter will outline the expenses it expects to charge the company. The largest portion of these costs will be a percentage of the stock offering. More information about this is listed in the earlier "The Cost of an IPO" section. This is a good time for the CFO to consider swapping an issuance of warrants with the underwriter in exchange for a lower commission rate. Another significant cost listed in the agreement will be the legal expenses incurred by the underwriter for its legal counsel to review state "blue sky" laws to see how they apply to the offering. The CFO should insist on a cap on these expenses, which can be substantial. The underwriter may also require the company to pay for any out-of-pocket expenses incurred by the underwriter if the company withdraws from the IPO—if so, be sure to insert a maximum expense cap in the agreement. There should be no expense reimbursement requirement if the underwriter is the party who withdraws from the offering.

- *Overallotment option*. This option is another manner in which the underwriter can profit from a potentially lucrative stock offering. It allows the underwriter to purchase additional shares from the company, up to a specified maximum amount, within a short time period following the IPO date. If the underwriter feels that it can sell additional shares at a high price, it will buy the extra shares from the company, sell them to investors, and pocket the difference. The overallotment option is usually acceptable to company management, unless the additional shares sold might potentially interfere with their control of the company.

- *Expected stock price.* The agreement will list a price at which the underwriter expects to sell the company's shares, though this is strictly a preliminary number that can vary considerably, depending on market fluctuations and the receptiveness of institutional investors to the proposed price during the subsequent road show.

During the period between the time that the company engages the services of an underwriter and 25 days after its securities begin trading, the company is in a so-called "quiet period," when it should not issue any marketing statements or materials that could be construed as an attempt to promote the stock. For example, no projections about expected company performance should be issued. To avoid any chance of breaking the SEC's quiet period regulations, any company communications during this period should be cleared by legal counsel prior to release.

Once the letter of intent is signed by both parties, they jointly move forward into the IPO registration process, which is described in the next section.

40.7 REGISTERING FOR AND COMPLETING THE IPO

Registering for and completing the IPO process usually takes three to four months. The basic steps in the process are due diligence investigations of a company's operations and finances, followed by the creation of a registration statement, whose contents are then updated based on SEC comments. This is followed by a road show, final pricing of the stock, filing of the final prospectus with the SEC, and then closing the deal with the underwriter. The following discussion is based on a firm commitment deal with an underwriter. A best efforts deal differs from this discussion primarily in the length of time required to obtain payment from the underwriter, which may require two to three extra months following the registration effective date.

The due diligence process is conducted by the underwriter and is a vastly expanded version of the due diligence it went through when it was initially investigating the company. In this case, it will require outside auditors to comb the company's financial records at a level of detail significantly greater than a standard audit and then issue a "comfort letter" to the underwriter, stating the additional procedures that it completed at the request of the underwriter. These procedures usually relate to unaudited financial information that is included in the registration statement. The auditors send the comfort letter to the underwriter once the initial registration statement has been filed.

The registration statement comprises a prospectus and additional information required by the SEC. The statement is the SEC's Form S-1. The prospectus portion of the statement is an overview of the company's operations and finances, and is carefully designed to be a balance of marketing language intended to bolster the stock and a tedious itemization of every conceivable risk to which the company is or may be subject, with the intent of avoiding liability in case the company's prospects sour after it goes public. It also includes all standard financial reports, such as the balance sheet, income statement, statement of cash flows, and shareholders' equity. It will also include interim financial statements if the registration statement is declared effective (more on that shortly) more than 134 days subsequent to the company's fiscal year end. The registration statement is a complex document, so the CFO should expect 30 to 60 days to pass before the initial version is ready for review by the SEC.

The registration statement is then forwarded to the SEC, which usually takes about one month to review it, after which it issues a letter of comment, which contains required changes that must be added to the statement in order to bring it into compliance with SEC regulations. Their comments can include such issues as an expansion of risk disclosures, cross-referencing information within the prospectus, questions about the use of certain accounting policies, and adding information to support claims made. Once these changes are made in an amended filing, the SEC has the right to continue reviewing the document until it declares the statement to be effective.

The company must also submit the registration statement to the National Association of Securities Dealers (NASD), which wants to ensure that the underwriter's compensation is not excessive. The statement must also be sent to each state in which the company plans to offer its shares for sale, so they can verify that the offering meets individual state reporting requirements.

The prospectus portion of the registration statement is then sent to prospective investors. This "red herring" version of the statement may not yet have been approved by the SEC, and will not include a final stock price, but will list a range within which the final price will fall. This version is used to educate investors in advance about the offering, but is not used to solicit the sale of stock. It is also sent to the syndicate of other underwriters that the primary, or "managing," underwriter will assemble to help sell the stock.

After filing the registration statement and prior to its effective date, the CEO and CFO (sometimes accompanied by other members of management) go on a road show to visit a number of key institutional investors and analysts, where they make a sales pitch about the company, but do not attempt to sell any shares. This is a physically exhausting process that typically lasts about two weeks. As an example of just one day in a typical road show circuit, the CEO of a Silicon Valley company boarded a private jet in San Francisco at 5 A.M. and flew to five cities across the United States, stopping for a one-hour presentation in each city (several being on the East Coast), before flying back to San Francisco—the same day. He did this for nine days in a two-week period. Preparing for the road show also requires long hours, frequently including training by speech coaches and even etiquette consultants.

While the management team is conducting the road show, its legal counsel will file an application with the stock exchange on which it wishes to be listed, while also selecting a registrar (who tracks all stock, pays out dividends of various types, and mails reports to shareholders) and a transfer agent (who handles the transfer of shares between parties) to handle subsequent stock-related issues. It will also submit filings in accordance with the securities laws of all states in which the company expects to sell shares.

Once the SEC is satisfied with all changes made to the registration statement, company management meets with the underwriter to set the final price of the stock. Price setting is part science and part art form. Ostensibly, the price should be based on a quantitative measure, such as the existing price/earnings multiple or price/revenue multiple for similar companies. Other operational issues may also be considered that will modify the price to some extent, such as backorder volume, sales trends, the proportion of expenses to sales, the quality of management, the outlook for the entire industry, the severity of current or potential competition, pending pollution issues, or the presence of valuable patents. However, the comments of institutional investors who were contacted during the road show will have a strong bearing on the final price. They are usually relied upon to purchase a significant proportion of the company's stock, and if they show resistance to purchasing stock at a specific price, then the underwriter will recommend a price reduction. In addition, the underwriter will underprice the issuance slightly in order to ensure a complete sale of all shares offered to the public, while also giving it some grounds for avoiding a lawsuit in case the stock price later declines, and investors claim that the initial price was too high. The extent of the underpricing tends to be greater during the IPO in comparison to secondary offerings, so management may want to consider selling slightly fewer shares at this time in order to avoid dilution.

Underwriters like to price IPO shares in the range of $10 to $20, on the grounds that this avoids penny stock status (which is $5 or less) and the perception that investors will be less likely to buy shares priced above $25. To achieve this range, the company may have to conduct either a stock split or a reverse stock split. For example, if the underwriter decides that a company's total valuation is $50,000,000 and that the stock price will be $20, then there should be 2,500,000 shares outstanding in order to achieve the designated price per share. If the company actually has 10,000,000 shares outstanding, then it must conduct a four-for-one reverse stock split in order to bring the number of outstanding shares down to the required 2,500,000 level.

The underwriter will also want to sell in excess of one million shares during the IPO, not only to create an active trading market for the stock, but also to meet the minimum outstanding shares rules of the stock exchanges (as noted further in the "Listing on an Exchange" section).

Once all parties agree to the stock price, this is included in the registration statement as an amendment, along with the net proceeds by the company resulting from the offering and the underwriter's commission. The company then asks the SEC to declare the registration statement "effective." This request is typically accompanied by a request to accelerate the SEC's standard 20-day waiting period between the filing date of the last amendment and the date when the registration is declared effective, which the SEC generally agrees to as long as the prospectus has already been sufficiently widely circulated to prospective investors in its "red herring" format. After the registration is declared effective, the company issues the prospectus to the investors who previously received the "red herring," as well as any others who wish to review it.

The underwriter and the company will then sign a "lockup agreement," under which management restricts itself from selling any company shares it owns for a minimum period, usually of at least a half-year.

Finally, at a closing meeting that usually takes place about one week after the registration effective date, the underwriter hands over payment for all shares proffered under the IPO offering in exchange for the share certificates. This delay of a few days is needed for the underwriter to collect cash from its investors, who will then receive the stock from the underwriter. The company is now officially a public entity.

40.8 ALTERNATIVES FOR SELLING SECURITIES

A traditional IPO may not be available to a company for a variety of reasons. Potential underwriters may feel that a company's underlying technological prowess is too unproven to make a convincing case to potential shareholders. The same reasoning may apply to its rate of growth or the perceived quality of its management team. Or, the market may be saturated with other IPOs, so there is no room for another one without accepting an unreasonably low price. If any of these circumstances applies, a company may consider using the options listed in this section—an "OpenIPO" offering, the purchase of a shell corporation, or a SCOR offering.

One alternative to the traditional sale of stock through an underwriter is to use an "OpenIPO" auction. Under this approach, potential investors download a prospectus over the Internet from an underwriter that specializes in this type of offering. If investors wish to bid on the shares, they open an account with the underwriter, select a bid price and the number of shares desired, and send the underwriter a check for that amount. This bid can be withdrawn at any time prior to the offering date. Based on the range of bids received, the underwriter then creates a public offering price at which share purchases will be accepted (which matches the price of the lowest bid received, below which all other bids exceed the number of shares to be offered). All investors bidding above this price will be issued their full share allocations, while those whose bids were below the price will be refunded their money. Those investors bidding the exact amount of the public offering price will receive some portion of their requested number of shares, depending upon how many other investors requested shares at that price and how many shares are still available for sale. This approach tends to result in higher share prices, resulting in either more proceeds flowing to the company or fewer shares being sold (resulting in more control by the original shareholders).

For example, a company wishes to sell one million shares to the public. Investors bid for 500,000 shares at $14 each, while bids are also received for 300,000 shares at $13.50 and 600,000 at $12.00. Since the entire offering can be sold at a price of $12, this becomes the public offering price. All investors bidding at prices of $14 and $13.50 per share will receive their full allocations of shares, and will pay $12 per share. Of the 600,000 shares bid at $12, investors will receive only one-third of their requested amounts, since this will result in one million shares being sold, which was the original target.

Another option for selling securities is to first merge with a publicly held shell corporation and then commence stock sales through that shell. A shell is a corporate entity for which there is no substantial business activity; it typically arises when the underlying business fails or is sold off, leaving a legal entity that is still authorized to sell shares to the public. Under this approach, one can purchase a shell for a relatively small amount (though it can increase if the shell still holds substantial assets) and may also take advantage of any net operating loss carryforwards contained within the shell (a common occurrence), though only a small proportion of these losses can be used for tax purposes if there has been a change in control of the shell corporation. On the downside, shell corporations are famous for having undisclosed liabilities that will haunt the newly merged firm, as well as for being promoted by shady stock brokers who manipulate the stock to their own advantage. Consequently, it is extremely important to investigate anyone who is promoting the sale of a shell, as well as all financial, legal, and operating aspects of the shell.

Another alternative is to file for a small corporate offering registration (SCOR). This is a simplified registration used by companies that want to raise up to $1 million within a 12-month period. One must complete the 50-question Form U-7 and file it with the state securities commission for the state in which the company operates. The form requires no review by the SEC, but must be reviewed by the state securities commission. This form can then be used as a prospectus by the company in its search for investors (since this approach does not normally involve an underwriter). This approach can be taken by any entity incorporated in either the United States or Canada, except for investment or public companies.

The SCOR approach falls under the restrictions of Rule 504 of the SEC's Regulation D, which governs private and limited stock offerings. Rule 504 allows a company to sell shares to an unlimited number of investors, who do not have to meet any accreditation standards. It also allows the company to advertise the stock offering, and does not restrict the resale of stock in any way. In short, the SEC is unusually liberal in its regulation of small stock offerings in the size range of a SCOR.

Though the SCOR approach is far less expensive than an IPO, it carries other risks and uncertainties. First, a company using this approach may try to avoid expenses by not using legal counsel. This approach may lay it open to potential shareholder lawsuits due to some unexpected oversight in the registration and solicitation process. The obvious mitigation approach to this risk is to bring the best legal counsel into the SCOR filing process as soon as possible and to solicit its advice at every step of the offering. Also, the management team must sell the shares to investors, an activity that may not fall within its range of expertise. Finally, due to the lack of an underwriter, there will not be a ready market for subsequent sales of the stock, making investment liquidations a chancy affair for investors.

40.9   LISTING ON AN EXCHANGE

Though a company has successfully completed an IPO, its stock is not yet traded on a stock exchange. If a company is not listed on an exchange, its securities will be designated as over-the-counter (OTC) stocks, and will most likely appear in the Pink Sheets. The "pink sheet" name is derived from the color of stock price sheets that were distributed by the National Quotation Bureau starting in 1904, and which served as a pricing reference for stock trades through local stock dealers. The paper-based service recently expanded into the Internet-based "Electronic Quotation Service," which provides real-time price quotes for over-the-counter securities to market makers and brokers. This market is a dangerous one for investors, who must conduct their own research into prospective investments, and who are at considerable risk of losing their entire investments in companies that may be in distressed circumstances, or whose stocks are so thinly traded that they are subject to large price swings. Consequently, avoiding OTC status by enrolling in a stock exchange is considered highly advantageous.

This section discusses the listing process as well as the listing requirements, fees, advantages and disadvantages of the three major stock exchanges: the American Stock Exchange (Amex), NASDAQ, and New York Stock Exchange (NYSE). The original listing fees and annual listing fees for these exchanges are consolidated for comparison purposes at the end of the section.

The Listing Process

The listing process is similar for all three exchanges. The first step is for a company to file a listing application with the exchange of its choice, along with a filing fee. The introductory application includes an itemization of the amounts and types of stock that the company wishes to list on the exchange, the size and composition of its shareholder base, and identification of its directors and officers. The exchange then follows up with more detailed questions, which generally inquire about any outstanding lawsuits, the availability of financing arrangements, recent SEC comment letters, recent private placements, investor relations consulting agreements, and research reports and investor newsletters about the company. The exchanges are also very particular about having a company conform its by-laws to their requirements, particularly in regard to the structure and composition of its audit, nominating, and compensation committees.

The exchange then reviews the application to ensure that the applicant is in compliance with the exchange's listing qualifications. The review typically consists of two stages, with a staff person conducting the initial review and summarizing the application for a supervisor, who then passes judgment on the application. If there are issues, the exchange sends a comment letter to the company, describing what must be changed before it will approve the company for listing. The exchange also reserves a ticker symbol for the company at this time. The applicant then sends back a response letter, detailing the actions it has taken to comply with the exchange's requirements. There may be several iterations of questions and answers between the exchange and the company, and they usually require multiple months to complete.

If the exchange approves the applicant for listing, then the company and the exchange mutually agree on an initial trading date. Depending on the exchange, the company's chief executive officer (CEO) may be invited to ring the opening bell on the initial trading date. Also, for the American and New York Stock Exchanges, the company will select a specialist who is responsible for making a market in its stock.

American Stock Exchange

The Amex targets smaller companies with modest market capitalizations. It is easily the most aggressive of the three exchanges in attracting new listings. Its staff regularly scans new stock registrations that are filed with the SEC and contacts registrants about listing with the Amex. It also sends staff out to prospects to discuss the advantages of listing. Thus, a micro-cap company is far more likely to be petitioned by the Amex than by any other exchange.

The Amex provides a number of services to each listing company:

- *Specialist.* The key Amex benefit is an assigned trading specialist. The specialist is obliged, to the extent reasonably practical, to purchase and sell a listed company's securities for its own account in order to help maintain an orderly market, with minimal price changes between transactions. Listed companies have direct access to their specialist, who can tell them about the market activity in their shares.
- *Liaison.* The Amex assigns a liaison, called an Amex Issuer Services Director (ISD), to every listed company. The ISD assists each company in obtaining services provided by the Amex.
- *Amex Online Web site.* This Web site allows listed companies to conduct peer analysis comparisons and historical charting, locate analyst ratings, research contact information for analysts and investment management firms, and view a complete calendar of earnings releases and conference calls.
- *Strategy seminars.* The Amex makes available a pair of strategy seminars each year to listed companies. These seminars focus on topics in investor relations, investment banking, corporate governance, equity trading, and regulatory issues.
- *CEO dinners.* The Amex coordinates a series of CEO dinners throughout the country that allow CEOs to network with their counterparts in other Amex-listed companies.
- *Investor relations audit.* The Amex conducts a review of a listed company's communication materials, develops an investor fact sheet, and provides buy side and sell side contacts.

The Amex's listing requirements are designed to attract smaller companies with relatively small floats. A company can qualify under any one of the four standards shown in Exhibit 40.1 in order to be accepted for listing on the Amex.

In addition, there are stock distribution guidelines, which are intended to ensure that a sufficiently broad array of investors own a company's stock. They are shown in Exhibit 40.2.

Requirements	Standard 1	Standard 2	Standard 3	Standard 4
Pretax income	$750,000			
Market capitalization			$50 million	$75 million or
Total assets				$75 million and
Total revenue				$75 million
Market value of public float	$3 million	$15 million	$15 million	$20 million
Minimum price	$3	$3	$2	$3
Operating history		2 years		
Stockholders' equity	$4 million	$4 million	$4 million	

EXHIBIT 40.1   AMERICAN STOCK EXCHANGE INITIAL LISTING GUIDELINES

A close reading of these listing guidelines reveals that the Amex is amenable to listing almost any company, and it has created many variations on its acceptance criteria in order to attract the largest possible number of companies. For example, only Standard 1 even requires reported income; in all other cases, the Amex does not require evidence of profitability. Also, three of the standards do not require an operating history, so short-lived entities can very quickly become listed. Standard 4 was specially designed for telecommunications companies, which rarely report profits but which have considerable revenue and assets. The only area in which the Amex has significant requirements across all standards is the market value of a company's public float. Thus, as long as a company has a sufficient volume of tradable stock, the Amex is interested in listing it.

Of some interest, the official Amex guidelines are literally "guidelines." The Amex has been known to waive some listing requirements, so it is best to make inquiries rather than simply to assume that certain initial listing standards are unattainable.

On an ongoing basis, a listed company must maintain a $1 million market value of public float. In addition, it must maintain $2 million in stockholders' equity if it has had losses in two of the most recent three years, or $4 million if it has had losses in three of the most recent four years, or $6 million if it has had losses in the five most recent fiscal years. If a company cannot satisfy these equity requirements, it can still remain on the Amex if it has a market capitalization of at least $50 million or total assets and revenue of $50 million each. The Amex does not have an ongoing minimum stock price requirement.

Public stockholders	Option A: 800
	Option B: 400
	Option C: 400
Public float (shares)*	Option A: 500,000
	Option B: 1,000,000
	Option C: 500,000
Average daily volume	Option C: 2,000

Public float is all shares not held directly or indirectly by any officer or director of a listed company, or by any other person who is the beneficial owner of more than 10% of the total shares outstanding.

EXHIBIT 40.2   AMERICAN STOCK EXCHANGE STOCK DISTRIBUTION
GUIDELINES

Requirements	Standard 1	Standard 2	Standard 3
Stockholders' equity	$5 million	$4 million	$4 million
Market value of publicly held shares	$15 million	$15 million	$5 million
Operating history	2 years		
Market value of listed securities		$50 million	
Net income from continuing operations (in the latest fiscal year or in two of the last three fiscal years)			$750,000
Publicly held shares	1 million	1 million	1 million
Bid price	$4	$4	$4
Round-lot shareholders	300	300	300
Market makers	3	3	3

EXHIBIT 40.3 NASDAQ CAPITAL MARKET INITIAL LISTING STANDARDS

In short, the Amex is ideal for listing by smaller companies. Its main competition is the NASDAQ's Capital Market, which similarly caters to smaller entities.

Overview of the NASDAQ

The NASDAQ acronym stands for the National Association of Securities Dealers Automated Quotation. In brief, it is the largest electronic stock market in the United States. Being entirely electronic, it executes orders faster and at lower cost than most other stock exchanges. However, there is no assigned specialist who makes a market in a company's stock. This can result in somewhat greater stock volatility as well as a larger relative spread.

The NASDAQ operates the Market Intelligence Desk (MID), which monitors the activity of a listed company's stock. The controller can contact the MID for updates about recent stock activity. This contact is through an MID Director, who is a predetermined point of contact for each company. In isolated instances, the MID may contact the controller by phone or e-mail if there is unusual market activity.

The MID Director arranges for additional services to its listing companies. These include a full-service corporate insurance broker, a research report service, and investor relations services. However, in most cases, a listed company will incur extra fees for these services.

NASDAQ Capital Market

The NASDAQ operates a stock exchange for smaller companies, called the NASDAQ Capital Market. This exchange competes with the American Stock Exchange.

A company can qualify under any one of the three standards shown in Exhibit 40.3 in order to be accepted for listing on the NASDAQ Capital Market.

On an ongoing basis, a company must exceed one of the three standards shown in Exhibit 40.4 to continue to be listed on the exchange:

As was the case with the Amex, the NASDAQ Capital Market substantially reduces its continued listing requirements from the initial listing requirements so that it is relatively easy to remain on the exchange.

NASDAQ Global Market

The NASDAQ operates a stock exchange for larger companies, called the NASDAQ Global Market. This exchange competes with the New York Stock Exchange.

Requirements	Standard 1	Standard 2	Standard 3
Stockholders' equity	$2.5 million		
Market value of listed securities		$35 million	
Net income from continuing operations (in the latest fiscal year or in two of the last three fiscal years)			$500,000
Publicly held shares	500,000	500,000	500,000
Market value of publicly held securities	$1 million	$1 million	$1 million
Bid price	$1	$1	$1
Round-lot shareholders	300	300	300
Market makers	2	2	2

EXHIBIT 40.4   NASDAQ CAPITAL MARKET CONTINUED LISTING STANDARDS

A company can qualify under any one of the three standards shown in Exhibit 40.5 in order to be accepted for listing on the NASDAQ Global Market.

In addition, an applicant must have either 450 round-lot stockholders, or a total of 2,200 stockholders, and 1,250,000 publicly held shares.

On an ongoing basis, a company must exceed one of the two standards shown in Exhibit 40.6 to continue to be listed on the exchange.

New York Stock Exchange

The NYSE specifically caters to the largest and wealthiest public companies in the world. It is considered prestigious to be listed on the NYSE. To keep this club exclusive, the NYSE has the toughest initial and continued listing standards of any exchange. Besides prestige, the main advantage of a NYSE listing is that some fund managers are allowed to invest only in NYSE-listed companies, so the pool of potential investors is quite large.

The NYSE hosts a number of virtual investor forums, which are web conferences designed to provide investors with direct access to executives from companies listed on the NYSE. It also hosts industry-specific conferences, which the executives of NYSE-listed companies can attend.

Requirements	Standard 1	Standard 2	Standard 3
Pretax earnings	Aggregate $11 million in past three years, and $2.2 million in each of the past two fiscal years, and $0+ in past three years		
Cash flows		Aggregate $27.5 million in past three years, and $0+ in each of the prior three fiscal years	
Market capitalization (average over prior 12 months		$550 million	$850 million
Revenue (previous fiscal year)		$110 million	$90 million
Bid price	$5	$5	$5
Market makers	3	3	3

EXHIBIT 40.5   NASDAQ GLOBAL MARKET INITIAL LISTING STANDARDS

Requirements	Standard 1	Standard 2
Stockholders' equity	$10 million	
Market value or Total assets/total revenue		$50 million or $50 million/$50 million
Publicly held shares	750,000	1.1 million
Market value of publicly held shares	$5 million	$15 million
Bid price	$1	$1
Round lot stockholders	400	400
Market makers	2	4

EXHIBIT 40.6   NASDAQ GLOBAL MARKET CONTINUED LISTING STANDARDS

The NYSE also assigns a client service team to each listed company, which fulfills the same role as the Amex's Issuer Services Director and the NASDAQ's Market Intelligence Desk Director. Also, as was the case with the Amex, a newly listed company selects a specialist who is responsible for making a market in the company's stock.

The NYSE's listing requirements are designed to attract larger companies with significant market capitalizations and operating results. It requires minimum standards in two areas, which are stock distribution and financial results. Its stock distribution requirements are:

1.   400 round-lot stockholders, or

2.   2,200 total stockholders and average monthly trading volume for the last six months of 100,000 shares, or

3.   500 total stockholders and average monthly trading volume for the last 12 months of 1,000,000 shares.

An additional stock distribution requirement is to have 1.1 million public shares outstanding, with a market value of $100 million.

The NYSE also has multiple variations on its initial listing requirements relating to financial results. They are:

1.   Aggregate pretax earnings over the past three years of $10 million, and a minimum of $2 million in each of the two most recent years, or

2.   Aggregate operating cash flow of $25 million over the last three years (applicable only for companies with at least a $500 million market cap and $100 million revenues during the most recent 12 months), or

3.   Revenues for the most recent fiscal year of at least $75 million and a market capitalization of at least $750 million.

On an ongoing basis, a listed company must maintain performance under one of three standards outlined in Exhibit 40.7. This is a simplified version of the complex NYSE standards; see the *www.nyse.com* Web site for a complete set of continued listing standards.

Comparing the Stock Exchanges

There are significant differences in the fees charged by the various stock exchanges. Exhibit 40.8 presents the initial listing fees for the exchanges, showing the lowest and highest possible prices. For companies having in excess of 50 million shares, the maximum fees will apply.

Requirements	Earnings Standard	Cash Flow Standard	Pure Valuation Standard
Average closing price over a 30-day trading period	$1	$1	$1
Average market capitalization over a 30-day trading period	$75 million and	$250 million and	$375 million and
Total stockholders' equity	$75 million or		
Average market capitalization over a 30-day trading period	$25 million		
Total revenues for most recent 12 months		$20 million	
Total revenues for the most recent fiscal year			$15 million

EXHIBIT 40.7   NEW YORK STOCK EXCHANGE CONTINUED LISTING STANDARDS

The Amex has positioned itself to be slightly less expensive than the NASDAQ Capital Market, though the pricing difference is minor. Similarly, the NASDAQ Global Market has positioned its prices to be clearly below those of the NYSE. However, for companies with the resources to list on the NYSE, its higher fees are probably not a significant factor.

In addition, each exchange charges an annual listing fee, which is shown in Exhibit 40.9. Again, rather than showing the full range of prices, the table reveals the lowest and highest possible prices. The maximum annual listing fee for the NYSE is misleading, since it applies only to a very high share volume. Accordingly, an additional row is included for 50 million shares, to give some indication of pricing for a midrange share volume.

The differences between the annual fees charged by the Amex and the NASDAQ Capital Market are insignificant. If a very large company lists on the NYSE, its annual fees can substantially exceed those it would incur if it listed on the NASDAQ Global Market.

The number of required round-lot stockholders does not vary significantly among the exchanges, with the usual requirement varying between 300 and 500 round-lot stockholders. Once a company has been trading on an exchange for a few months, it usually exceeds these figures by a substantial amount.

All of the exchanges allow a company to be listed even if it does not report pretax income by requiring a higher float, cash flow, or market capitalization. These alternative requirements are easier to meet on the Amex and NASDAQ Capital Market and more difficult to meet on the NASDAQ Global Market and NYSE.

The continued listing requirements are much lower than the initial listing requirements for all of the exchanges. For example, the Amex has no minimum stock bid price for a continued listing while the NASDAQ Capital Market's bid price requirement drops from an initial listing requirement of $4 to $1; the NASDAQ Global Market's requirement drops from $5 to $1.

Shares	Amex	NASDAQ Capital Market	NASDAQ Global Market	NYSE
Up to 5 million	$45,000	$50,000	$100,000	$150,000
50+ million	70,000	75,000	150,000	250,000

EXHIBIT 40.8   COMPARISON OF STOCK EXCHANGE INITIAL LISTING FEES

Shares	Amex	NASDAQ Capital Market	NASDAQ Global Market	NYSE
Up to 5 million	$16,500	$27,500	$30,000	$38,000
50 million	32,500	27,500	45,000	46,500
Maximum	34,000	27,500	95,000	500,000

EXHIBIT 40.9   COMPARISON OF STOCK EXCHANGE ANNUAL LISTING FEES

The Amex has issued a study claiming that the average relative spread of its listed stocks is somewhat lower than the same spread on the NASDAQ. The relative spread is the difference between a stock's quoted bid and ask price relative to the stock price, with a small relative spread indicating a high degree of stock liquidity. As the study is internally generated, it is impossible to say if the Amex's findings are accurate. However, an item of note is that the study also reveals a relative spread for over-the-counter stocks of nearly triple the Amex and NASDAQ spreads. This shows a high level of illiquidity in the over-the-counter market, which is an excellent reason for a company to step up to a major stock exchange listing as soon as possible.

Of more importance is that Amex directors do not sell products or services to their assigned companies, whereas a NASDAQ director's compensation is based partially on his or her ability to sell products and services to assigned companies. A company may not experience any real difference in costs because of these differences, but there is certainly more selling pressure in the NASDAQ environment.

All of the exchanges require compliance with a variety of governance standards, such as a majority of independent directors, audit committees, and codes of conduct. There are no significant differences between the governance standards required by the various exchanges.

Summary

Being listed on a stock exchange is a key corporate goal. The usual track is for a company to list initially on either the Amex or NASDAQ Capital Market, and then move up to either the NYSE or the NASDAQ Global Market when it increases in size. By moving up to a higher-end exchange, a public company becomes eligible for trading by more funds. This increases a stock's trading volume; reduces its volatility, it is hoped; and may positively influence its price because of increased demand.

40.10   RESTRICTIONS ON STOCK IN A PUBLICLY TRADED COMPANY

When an investor acquires restricted securities, the SEC requires that the securities be registered before the investor can sell them to another party. Restricted securities are typically issued through a private stock placement, Regulation D offering, or through an employee stock benefit plan. Also, if unrestricted securities are sold by a "control" person (one with the ability to either directly or indirectly influence management decisions), the securities become restricted once sold. These securities (except those issued by a control person) bear a restrictive legend, stating that the securities may not be resold unless they are registered with the SEC or exempt from its registration requirements.

Since resale of a security is critical to an investor's eventual liquidity, registration is an extremely important goal. However, registration can be both an expensive and prolonged task that many public companies avoid. Fortunately for investors, Rule 144 presents a possible exemption from the SEC's registration requirement.

Rule 144 allows for the resale of restricted securities if a number of conditions are met, which primarily involve the passage of time. They are:

1. *Holding period.* If the securities issuer is subject to the periodic reporting requirements of the Securities Exchange Act of 1934 (e.g., issues 10Q, 10K, and other periodic reports), then the securities holder must hold the securities for at least six months. If the securities issuer is not reporting under the Exchange Act, then the holding period is one year.

2. *Adequate current information.* The securities issuer must be current in its reporting under the Exchange Act.

3. *Trading volume formula.* If the securities holder is an affiliate of the company (i.e., one who is in a control position), then the number of securities available for sale during any three-month period cannot exceed the greater of 1% of the outstanding shares of the same class being sold, or if the class is listed on a stock exchange or the NASDAQ, the greater of 1% of the average reported weekly trading volume during the four weeks preceding the investor's filing of a notice of sale using a Form 144. If the securities issuer's stock is only traded over-the-counter, then only the 1% rule applies.

4. *Ordinary brokerage transactions.* If the securities holder is an affiliate, the securities sale must be handled as a routine trading transaction, where the broker cannot receive more than a normal commission. The seller and broker cannot solicit orders to buy the securities, other than to respond to various types of unsolicited inquiries.

5. *File a notice of proposed sale.* If the securities holder is an affiliate, the proposed sale must be filed with the SEC on a Form 144 if the sale involves more than 5,000 shares or the aggregate dollar amount is greater than $50,000 in any three-month period. The completed form shall be filed concurrently with either the placing with a broker of a sale order or the execution with a market maker of such a sale. The sale must take place within three months of filing the form, or else an amended notice must be filed. If the securities are admitted for trading on a national securities exchange, then one copy of the completed form must also be transmitted to the exchange.

If a securities holder has held the restricted securities for at least one year, and has not been a company affiliate for at least the past three months, then the securities can be resold without regard to the preceding conditions. If the company is fulfilling its reporting requirements under the Exchange Act, then the holding period is reduced to six months.

Once these conditions are met, the securities holder must have the restrictive legend removed before the securities can be sold. Legend removal must be done by the company's stock transfer agent, which will only do so with the written approval of the issuing company's counsel. This written approval is in the form of an opinion letter.

40.11   SUMMARY

The objective of many successful business owners is to take their companies public so that they can eventually sell off some portion of their shares in the business and retire. However, this reasoning does not always work out in practice, because of the considerable expense of the IPO, the ongoing cost of reporting to the public and of ongoing exchange listing fees, potential investor lawsuits, and the risk of loss of control of the business. Consequently, one should carefully consider the reasoning behind an IPO before proceeding.

CHAPTER **41**

GOING PRIVATE

41.1 INTRODUCTION

Many companies find that the cost and liability of operating a publicly owned business is not worth the hassle and elect to remove themselves from public trading. This is possible only if a company has fewer than 300 shareholders. Reducing the shareholder count to this level involves the filing of a lengthy schedule with the Securities and Exchange Commission (SEC), which is described in this chapter.

41.2 THE GOING-PRIVATE TRANSACTION

If a publicly held company wishes to reduces the number of its shareholders in order to go private, it must disclose information that is itemized under the SEC's Rule 13e-3, which is located in the Securities Exchange Act of 1934. This rule applies to situations where a company plans to buy back its securities, as described in the next section.

The information required under these circumstances must be filed on Schedule 13E-3, to which amendments must be added if there are material changes to the information presented on it. The primary information listed on the schedule includes complete company financial statements and various financial information on a per-share basis. The company must also include information regarding the identity of the persons filing the schedule, terms of the arrangement, future plans, the reason for going private, and the source and financing terms for the funding required to complete the transaction. A key goal of this filing (from the perspective of the SEC) is to force the company to describe the impact of the going-private event on unaffiliated security holders.

41.3 RULE 13E-3

The SEC's Rule 13e-3 applies to any transaction where equity securities are being purchased by the issuing company, or when a tender offer for those securities is being made by the issuing company or an affiliate. Such a transaction must result in having less than 300 people hold the equity security or the removal of that class of equity securities from being listed on a national exchange.

When an equity security is withdrawn from circulation by the issuing company, the rule also states that information about the withdrawal shall not be misleading or attempt to defraud a security holder.

The rule requires the issuing company to file Schedule 13E-3 prior to withdrawing a class of securities as well as to file amendments to it to reflect any material changes in the information itemized in the original filing. These amendments will be concluded with an amendment reporting the final results of the withdrawal transaction.

The rule further requires that the issuing company disclose to security holders the following information:

- A summary term sheet.
- The purposes, alternatives, reasons for and effects of the transaction.
- Fairness of the transaction to the security holder.
- Reports, opinions, appraisals and negotiations related to the transaction.
- Information concerning the rights of the security holders to conduct appraisals.
- All other information listed in Schedule 13E-3, except for exhibits. A "fair and adequate summary" can be substituted for this information.

If there are changes to the information offered to security holders, then the rule requires that these changes be promptly reported to them. In any event, the original set of disclosures must be issued to the security holders no later than 10 business days prior to any withdrawal transaction. If securities are held in trust for securities holders by a broker/dealer, then the issuer must forward these information materials to the broker/dealer, with instructions to forward it to the security holders.

These reporting requirements are not required if the issuer offers security holders another equity security in exchange for the one being retired, but only if the replacement security has essentially the same rights as the old security, including voting, dividends, redemption and liquidation rights, or if common stock is offered. The reporting is also not required if the security withdrawal is already allowed under the specific provisions itemized in the instrument creating or governing that class of securities.

41.4   SHAREHOLDER COUNT MANIPULATION

A crucial factor in reducing the shareholder count to fewer than 300 is that this must be fewer than 300 *shareholders of record*. Thus, if a number of shareholders place their shares with a broker, then the broker counts as just one shareholder, and the shareholders do not count at all. By asking shareholders to shift their shares to designated brokers, it is possible for a company to experience a substantial drop in its shareholder count. However, if a broker learns that a company has gone private, it may send the shares that it has been retaining on a custodial basis back to the shareholders; this is called a *broker kick-out*. If a broker kick-out occurs, then a company may find itself once again with more than 300 shareholders and be subject to SEC reporting requirements.

41.5   FILLING OUT SCHEDULE 13E-3

Schedule 13E-3 must be filed with the SEC prior to the withdrawal of securities by the issuing company. Some elements of this schedule may also be sent to the security holders, as noted in the last section. This schedule is essentially a full and complete disclosure of the withdrawal transaction.

The lead page of the schedule requires one to note the name of the issuing company, the name of the person filing the statement, and the title of the class of securities to be withdrawn under the terms contained within the schedule. The 16 remaining sections of the report are as follows:

1. *Summary term sheet.* This term sheet must describe the primary terms of the proposed transaction, yielding sufficient information for security holders to understand the basic structure and terms of it. All information in this summary should reference a more detailed discussion in a separate disclosure statement that is sent to the security holders.

2. *Subject company information.* State the name and address of the company. In addition, note the exact title and number of shares outstanding in the security class to be retired. Further, describe the market in which the securities are traded as well as their high-low sale prices for each quarter in the past two years. Point out the frequency and amount of any dividends paid during the past two years as well as any restrictions on the company's ability to pay dividends. Also, note the date and size of any public offering of the securities to be retired, if they occurred within the past three years. Finally, mention any prior purchases of the subject security within the past two years, including the amount and range of prices paid.

3. *Identity and background of filing person.* State the name and contact information for the person filing the schedule. Also list the person's current occupation and the name of his or her place of employment as well as this information for the past five years. Finally, state whether the person was convicted of a criminal activity in the past five years, and, if so, when and where the court proceedings took place. This includes any judgment blocking the person from future activities subject to federal or state securities laws.

4. *Terms of the transaction.* List the primary terms of the proposed purchase transaction, which should include the total number and class of securities that the company wishes to buy, the price offered for them, and the expiration date of the offer. Also, note if the offering period will be repeated or extended, and the date ranges when current security owners can withdraw from sale any securities they have tendered under the terms of this agreement. Further, describe the procedures to be used by security holders for tendering and withdrawing securities. If the company intends to purchase only some of the outstanding securities, then describe how purchases will be made on a pro rata basis as well as what will happen in the event of an over subscription. In addition, point out any material accounting treatment or income tax consequences as a result of the transaction. Also, list any variations on the standard set of purchase terms if they differ by security holder. For those security holders who may object to the transaction, itemize any appraisal rights they may have. Finally, if other securities are being offered as a trade for the subject securities, describe any arrangements the company may have to offer them for public trading.

5. *Past contacts, transactions, negotiations, and agreements.* List any transaction occurring in the past two years between the filing person and the company if they comprise more than 1% of the company's revenue, or between the filing person and an officer of the company if they comprise more than $60,000. Also, describe any transactions or discussions between the filing person and the company during

the past two years that addressed any merger or acquisition, tender offers, director elections, or significant asset sales. Finally, as a blanket disclosure, note any other arrangements between the filing person and any other person regarding the company's securities, which can include security transfers, security votes, joint ventures, loan arrangements, and loan or loss guarantees. This notation should include securities that are pledged in any manner, such that a different person could obtain security voting rights.

6. *Purposes of the transaction and plans or proposals.* Describe how any acquired securities will be treated, such as retirement or being held in treasury. Also, cover any plans for the company's subsequent merger, liquidation, or sale of major assets, as well as any prospective changes in the company's dividend policy, debt level, or capitalization. Further, note any planned changes in the size or structure of the board of directors as well as any changes in the management team or its employment contracts. Finally, as a blanket disclosure, note any other prospective material changes to the company's structure or business.

7. *Purposes, alternatives, reasons and effects.* Describe the underlying reason for the transaction as well as any alternatives to it that were considered and why they were rejected in favor of the proposed transaction. Further, note the impact of the transaction on the company, which should include its federal tax consequences.

8. *Fairness of the transaction.* State whether the company thinks the proposed transaction is fair or not to those security holders not affiliated with the company as well as the factors considered in determining fairness. If any company director either abstained from or rejected the vote for this transaction, list that person's name and the reason for his or her vote. In addition, state if the transaction was approved by a majority of the unaffiliated directors. Further, note whether the unaffiliated directors have retained an unaffiliated person who represents the interests of the unaffiliated security holders in constructing the terms of the transaction. Also point out if the transaction requires the approval of a majority of the security holders.

9. *Reports, opinions, appraisals, and negotiations.* State whether the company has received an outside party's appraisal of the proposed transaction; if so, list the appraiser's name, as well as his or her qualifications, and any material relationship between the appraiser and the company, either in the past or prospectively. Also, describe the method used to select the appraiser and if the appraiser recommended the amount of consideration to be paid as part of the transaction. Further, summarize the contents of the appraisal report, including the procedures followed, its findings and recommendations, and any limitations imposed on the appraiser by the company. Finally, state that the full appraisal report is available for review by security holders.

10. *Source and amounts of funds or other consideration.* Note the source and amount of funds that will be used in the proposed transaction as well as any material conditions that will be imposed on the company in order to obtain the required funds. Also, describe any alternative financing plans that have been arranged in case the primary source does not work. If the required funds are coming from a borrowing arrangement, then summarize the loan agreement. Further, describe all costs to be incurred as part of the transaction, such as legal, accounting, and appraisal costs.

11. *Interest in securities of the subject company.* List the number and percentage of the subject securities owned by each company officer or director. Also, describe all

transactions involving the subject securities within the past 60 days, including the persons involved, the transaction dates, the amounts of securities involved, and the price per share.

12. *The solicitation or recommendation.* State if any company officer or director intends to sell securities owned by that person as well as how each of these people intends to vote their securities in regard to this transaction. Also, state if any person listed in this section has made a recommendation in regard to this transaction and the reasons therefore.

13. *Financial statements.* If this information is sent to security holders, one can instead include summarized financial information. If so, instructions must be included in the schedule for how the security holders can obtain more detailed financial information.

14. *Persons/assets, retained, employed, compensated, or used.* List all people who will make solicitations related to the proposed transaction, including the terms of their employment and compensation. This should include any company officers or employees working on the transaction.

15. *Additional information.* Provide any additional material information that will keep the information contained in the schedule from being misleading to the reader.

16. *Exhibits.* There are a number of exhibits to be attached to the schedule. They should include any additional disclosure materials issued to the security holders, such as going-private disclosure documents, related loan agreements, appraisals, and a detailed discussion of security holder appraisal rights.

The statement must be signed by the filing person or that person's representative (including the representative's authorization to sign). Once completed, file eight copies of the schedule with the SEC.

41.6 FORM 15

The Schedule 13e-3 is required only if a company engages in a transaction that will reduce the number of its security holders prior to going private. If a company already has fewer than 300 shareholders, then there is no need to file the Schedule 13e-3. Instead, the only notification to the SEC is the one-page Form 15. This is an extremely simple document, and essentially notifies the SEC that the company intends to stop filing reports. If the company has already completed a Schedule 13e-3 transaction and now has fewer than 300 shareholders, then it must also file a Form 15 to complete its going-private transaction.

41.7 SUMMARY

Filling out the Schedule 13e-3 described in this section is a time-consuming process. The Internal Revenue Service estimates that an appropriate interval for doing so is 150 hours, so be well advised to use a project team to work through this lengthy document. Also, be sure to have legal counsel review it and also subject it to accuracy reviews, so that security holders cannot later claim there are any inaccuracies in the schedule that give them a reason to sue for damages of any kind. If completed properly, the schedule is the foundation document for a successful withdrawal of securities from public ownership, so a company can go private.

BANKRUPTCY

42.1 INTRODUCTION

Though no controller ever wants to be involved in a corporate bankruptcy, circumstances may dictate otherwise. The road through the bankruptcy process absolutely requires the best possible legal counsel; this person can advise on a wide range of possible strategies to take in dealing with creditors and the bankruptcy court, and the myriad of claims and counterclaims that can arise over the (sometimes) multiyear course of a bankruptcy case. Before calling in legal counsel, the controller should read this chapter to gain a basic understanding of the main players in the bankruptcy drama, how the bankruptcy process works, creditor priorities, tax issues, and other related issues.

42.2 APPLICABLE BANKRUPTCY LAWS

All applicable laws related to bankruptcy are issued by the federal government, and are contained within Title 11 of the U.S. Code, referred to as the Bankruptcy Code. Chapter 3 of the Code describes how to file for bankruptcy, while Chapter 5 covers debtor and creditor relations, Chapter 7 describes a corporate liquidation, and Chapter 11 itemizes the steps involved in a corporate reorganization.

A Chapter 7 liquidation is a relatively passive affair for the controller, who essentially watches while a court-appointed trustee sells off business assets and distributes the resulting cash to creditors and stockholders in a carefully prescribed order of payment (see the "Creditor and Shareholder Payment Priorities" section). A Chapter 11 reorganization generally allows management to remain in control while the company negotiates with its creditors to settle outstanding claims.

The code allows any company to file for bankruptcy at any time. There is no requirement to have a negative net worth, only that a company have a place of business in the United States. The decision to voluntarily enter bankruptcy is the board of director's. This group must approve a motion, such as the one noted in Exhibit 42.1, which should be retained in the corporate minute book. Alternatively, any group of creditors can jointly

WHEREAS, the Board of Directors of the Corporation has determined that the Corporation must file a voluntary Chapter 11 petition in bankruptcy court;

BE IT RESOLVED, that the Corporation's officers and any member of its law firm _____ are hereby authorized and directed to deliver all documents needed to effect the filing of a Chapter 11 petition on behalf of the Corporation;

RESOLVED IN ADDITION, that the Corporation's officers are hereby authorized and directed to represent the Corporation in all bankruptcy proceedings, and take all necessary actions on behalf of the Corporation in connection with this petition;

RESOLVED IN ADDITION, that any actions taken by the Corporation's officers prior to the date of this resolution in regard to the bankruptcy petition are hereby approved by the Corporation;

RESOLVED IN ADDITION, that this consent, when signed by the Board members, shall be effective as of [date].

EXHIBIT 42.1   EXAMPLE OF A BOARD'S BANKRUPTCY RESOLUTION

file an involuntary bankruptcy petition, thereby forcing a company into bankruptcy against its will.

42.3 PLAYERS IN THE BANKRUPTCY DRAMA

A company files a bankruptcy petition with the local *bankruptcy court*. This court is a division of the U.S. District Court, so there is at least one bankruptcy court in each state to mirror the organizational structure of the district court system. There are no juries in the bankruptcy court—instead, all decisions are made by the *bankruptcy judge*. The judge is appointed to a 14-year renewable term. Though bankruptcy cases are assigned to individual judges on a random basis, certain district courts have a reputation for containing a high proportion of business-friendly judges, so companies may attempt to file for bankruptcy in those districts in order to increase their odds of being assigned a "good" judge.

An *examiner* may be assigned by the bankruptcy court to conduct an investigation of a company's finances. This is usually an outside audit firm that does not have previous ties to the company. An examiner must be appointed if the total amount of company debt exceeds $5 million, and is frequently appointed if there is evidence of extensive insider transactions, fraud, or incompetence.

If the company files for liquidation under Chapter 7 of the Code, the court will assign a *trustee* to oversee the liquidation. A trustee is usually not assigned to a Chapter 11 reorganization, since the current management team is assumed to be running the reorganization process. However, a trustee will be assigned to a Chapter 11 reorganization if there is proof of fraud or gross incompetence by the existing management team. The trustee's fees are paid from the assets of the bankrupt company.

If a trustee is not assigned to a Chapter 11 reorganization, then the *existing management team* is assigned to manage the bankruptcy. At this point, the role of the management team shifts from attaining a high return on equity for shareholders to ensuring that creditors are paid back to the greatest extent possible—essentially, the management team's boss has changed to a new group of entities. If the management team continues to make decisions that place shareholders ahead of creditors, they stand a good chance of being replaced by the bankruptcy court with a trustee. The management team is obligated to work with creditors to devise a repayment plan that is acceptable to all key parties, while also keeping the bankruptcy court informed of its progress with monthly operating reports.

The *secured creditors* and the *unsecured creditors committee* must work with the management team or trustee in devising a plan of reorganization. The secured creditors will be primarily interested in obtaining the full value from any collateral that has been assigned to them. Usually, only the seven largest unsecured creditors are included in the unsecured creditors committee, since the inclusion of all creditors would make for a most unwieldy group. Members of this committee are supposed to represent all other unsecured creditors before the bankruptcy court.

Finally, there are a number of advisors that a company or the bankruptcy court may employ. *Lawyers* who specialize in bankruptcy proceedings should be asked to advise on the timing, location, and structure of the bankruptcy filing at the earliest possible date. As previously noted, *auditors* may be called in by the court to examine the corporate books, while *accountants* may be hired by the company to prepare for the auditor's arrival. It is also useful to hire a *public relations* firm that can put a favorable spin on the bankruptcy proceedings with a company's business partners. If creditors are wary of the management team's ability to return a company to solvency, they may insist on the hiring of a *turnaround specialist*, who either fills the president's position or becomes an advisor to that person. *Appraisers* may also be employed to determine the market value of secured creditor collateral, as well as the overall value of the company as a going concern. Finally, in a worst-case scenario, an *auction house* may be brought in to liquidate all corporate assets.

42.4   CREDITOR AND SHAREHOLDER PAYMENT PRIORITIES

The Bankruptcy Code lists a specific order in which bankruptcy claims will be paid, which is as follows:

1. *Secured claims.* A creditor who has obtained collateral against a company liability will be paid up to the liquidation value of the collateral. Any excess amount owed will then be shifted to the unsecured creditor claims category.

2. *Administration costs related to the bankruptcy.* Any legal, trustee, or other advisory fees related to the bankruptcy.

3. *Employee payroll.* Unpaid wage and salary expenses incurred within 90 days of the bankruptcy filing date.

4. *Taxes.* Any unpaid taxes owed to government entities, which can include corporate income, sales, payroll, and personal property taxes.

5. *Unsecured creditor claims.* All claims not previously specified that are not secured by any form of collateral. This tends to compose the bulk of creditor claims in a bankruptcy. Distributions to this group are made on a pro rata basis if there are not sufficient funds available to pay off 100% of all claims.

6. *Shareholders.* Any equity holder will only be paid if the claims of all entities previously noted on this list have been satisfied, which frequently leaves nothing at all Also, any shareholder who obtains a favorable court judgment in relation to a securities fraud claim will have the amount of the judgment clustered into this category—which means that the judgment may never be paid.

42.5   THE BANKRUPTCY SEQUENCE OF EVENTS

If a company decides to enter Chapter 11 bankruptcy, it must complete a petition to the bankruptcy court that is accompanied by a board-approved bankruptcy resolution (as described earlier in Exhibit 42.1). The first order of business when filing this petition is determining the best court to which it should be submitted. Though all bankruptcy judges operate under the same guidelines and therefore should issue the same opinions when presented with the same facts, this is not quite the case. Some bankruptcy judges are considered to be more friendly to debtors, while others may be swayed by the potential loss of jobs if a company has a large number of employees working near the court. Thus, a company incorporated in Delaware may elect to file for bankruptcy there, due to the business-friendly reputation of its judges, but could instead file for bankruptcy in the district where its largest base of employees is located. Other reasons for picking a specific venue are the familiarity of the company's counsel with a specific court, or simply the expense of having to frequently travel to a distant venue for bankruptcy hearings.

The filing itself requires a great deal of manual labor, though some of its components can be delayed a number of days after the initial bankruptcy filing. The most labor-intensive parts of the filing are as follows:

- *Schedules of Assets and Liabilities.* This is essentially a very detailed balance sheet that itemizes all types of property (such as individual accounts receivable and all fixed assets), as well as listings of all creditors having secured and unsecured claims, and the amounts of those claims. It is very important to note whether each claim is disputed, uncertain in amount, or contingent upon some event. By doing so, all possible creditors will be added to the court's notification list of bankruptcy actions, so they cannot claim they were never notified. This keeps the company from dealing with additional undocumented claims once it departs bankruptcy protection. These schedules also include lists of unexpired contracts and codebtors. A company will almost certainly never arrive at a complete list of all assets and liabilities upon its first filing of these schedules with the bankruptcy court, but it can file updated schedules at a later date as more information becomes available.

- *Statement of Financial Affairs.* This is a very detailed. income statement for the year to date and the two preceding years. Of particular interest is an additional schedule detailing all payments to creditors in the 90 days immediately preceding the bankruptcy filing, which is used to determine if the company is entitled to retrieve payments made to creditors. Another schedule itemizes all gifts paid out within the past year, which can be used to find any fraudulent transfers that may be recovered by the company.

The company is officially in bankruptcy as of the time when the filing is date-stamped by a clerk of the court. As of this date and time, creditors are barred from taking further action against the company to collect funds or other assets owed to them, which includes collection calls, taking possession of collateral, lien enforcement, canceling insurance, withholding tax refunds, initiating lawsuits, or setting off outstanding debtor debts against debts by them to the company. However, outside entities can still proceed with criminal prosecution, and landlords can evict debtors if the terms of their leases expired prior to the bankruptcy filing.

The company must also file a petition for the retention of professionals to assist it in the bankruptcy case. This can include lawyers, accountants, special managers to assist in operations, appraisers, and a public relations firm. The petition may include a provision to pay these professionals for any assistance already given to the company prior to the bankruptcy petition.

Once the bankruptcy petition has been filed, the first order of business is to apply for *first-day orders*. These are court orders for the company to pay preexisting claims by employees (primarily wages and salaries) and key suppliers, so there is no significant short-term disruption in company business in the early days of the bankruptcy. Though employee wages and salaries are routinely allowed in first day orders, supplier payments will only be allowed if the suppliers are difficult to replace or would cause major disruption to the business.

The court must also confirm the result of negotiations the company will undertake with any utilities. A utility is required by law to continue providing services to a bankrupt company for only the first 20 days of its bankruptcy, after which it can cut off service if the company cannot provide additional assurance of payment, such as a large deposit. Given the need for continued service by such suppliers, the court is typically most willing to approve of any reasonable arrangements that will provide utilities with some assurance of payment.

The court may also confirm retention bonuses to key personnel, which are especially important for those who have key business knowledge or contacts, and whose departure might result in a major business disruption. Courts may also confirm modest severance packages for key personnel, but are unlikely to do so for exorbitant "golden parachute" deals.

The next key step in the bankruptcy process is to secure sufficient financing to keep the company operating. Though it may be possible to carefully manage working capital to such an extent that no other financing is needed, a company should at least obtain a line of credit to tide it over any unforeseen cash flow dips. The simplest approach is to continue an existing line of credit, though this will certainly require additional negotiations with the lender, who may want additional collateral, frequent operational reports, periodic loan payments, and considerable input into an operating budget. If a new lender must be found to extend a line of credit, then the company can offer it collateral, as well as a "super priority" over other administrative expenses, so that the lender will be paid in full prior to any other administrative expense claims. In rare cases, it is also possible to offer "super priority" to a lender on assets that have been already encumbered by other liens. This last approach only works if the company can prove that the amount of collateral encumbered by existing creditors exceeds the value of their claims, in which case the difference can be offered (with court approval) to the new lender.

With financing taken care of, the company must then stabilize its operations. A key area to address is maintaining reasonable credit terms with suppliers, whose first knee-jerk reaction to the bankruptcy filing will be to switch over to cash on delivery payment terms. This can be done by keeping suppliers appraised of the progress of the bankruptcy case, as well as by following through on payment commitments on an ongoing basis. A good approach is to negotiate good payment terms with suppliers subsequent to the bankruptcy filing in exchange for attempting to convince the court that the suppliers should be paid in full as part of the first day orders. Even if a supplier does switch to cash on delivery terms, the controller can attempt to reestablish credit in small amounts and on short payment intervals, and then gradually improve these terms by proving the company's ability to follow through on the reduced terms.

Operational stabilization activities do not require court approval, though management can have its collective hand slapped by the court if it engages in activities that fall outside the bounds of normal business activities, such as the sale of assets or any activity that can be perceived as paying off a creditor's prebankruptcy claims. The unsecured creditors committee will be rightfully concerned about the amount of asset sales, since they are a source of funds that can be used to pay off the creditor's claims. The court will want to obtain the best possible price for any assets that management wants to sell, so it may require considerable shopping among potential buyers in order to secure a good sale price.

As the company proceeds through the various stages of the bankruptcy, it must also file a monthly operating report with the bankruptcy court. This report is generally due 15 days after the end of the month and should include detailed financial statements, as well as such supporting documents as bank statements and accounts receivable and accounts payable aging reports. The standard contents of such a report are as follows:

- Current month receipts and disbursements matrix, by bank account.
- Accounts receivable aging.
- Accounts payable aging.
- Cash disbursements report.
- Balance sheet matrix, by subsidiary.
- Postpetition income statement, by subsidiary.
- Year-to-date income statement, prepetition by subsidiary.
- Year-to-date income statement, postpetition by subsidiary.
- Schedule of additions to and deletions from fixed assets.
- Schedule of payments to insiders and professionals.
- Schedule of changes in employee headcount.
- Schedule of current insurance policies and periods of coverage.
- Discussion of progress toward the filing of a plan of reorganization.

Relatively early in the bankruptcy process, the company should ask the court to issue a *bar date order*. This order states that creditors must file a claim by a specific date or be unable to file a claim thereafter. By publicizing this court order extensively with all creditors (a good idea is to send it to everyone in the supplier address database, even if there is no evidence of a claim), a company can ensure that it is at minimal risk of having any additional claims arise after the bankruptcy case has been completed.

If a company is publicly held, it must also notify the Securities and Exchange Commission (SEC) of the intended filing, as well as of the progress of the bankruptcy case at regular intervals. These regular notifications may be accompanied by ongoing discussions with the SEC about the potential delisting of the company's stock and securities. Also, the SEC may wish to conduct its own investigation into the reasons for the bankruptcy filing, since there may be charges of fraud from investors to which it may wish to respond, or it may wish to file charges of its own.

In addition to the SEC, a publicly held company may find itself negotiating with the stock exchange where its shares are listed for sale. An exchange usually has a rule that a company's stock will be delisted if its price drops below one dollar for a period of at least 90 days, though the exchanges typically offer prolonged grace periods while companies find a way to increase the price (such as through a reverse stock split).

A key benefit to a bankrupt entity is its legal right to review all executory contracts and unexpired leases, and either accept or reject them. An executory contract is one where there is enough unfinished activity related to the contract by both parties that if either party were to halt its activities, the other party could claim a breach of contract. A lease is any series of ongoing payments in exchange for the use of property, such as a copier, vehicle, or facility. These two contract definitions will address many types of contracts, leaving a company with an exceptional ability to reconsider a large proportion of its legal agreements, which can result in a significant reduction in its liabilities.

Though a company has the right to accept or reject these types of contracts, it should take its time in doing so, until it is certain of having a viable business plan that can reasonably be expected to take it out of bankruptcy. Otherwise, all payments under an accepted contract will fall into the administrative expense category, where they will be ranked ahead of unsecured creditor claims (which is why the unsecured creditors committee tends to protest contract acceptances). The only downside of waiting to confirm a contract is that the company is still obligated to make payments under the contract's terms while the decision is being made. In short, it is best to string along any contracts that management is fairly sure it *will* confirm, and cancel any that it clearly *does not* want.

If management chooses to reject a contract, the remaining payments under the contract do not disappear—instead, they are shifted into unsecured creditor claims, where they may have a significantly lower chance of being paid. Since some leases have extremely long terms, the total amount of these rejected payments can be so large that they are a substantial proportion of all unsecured claims, thereby reducing the value of all other claims in cases where the amount of eventual payout by the company is limited. To prevent a lessor from being in such a dominant payment position, the bankruptcy law restricts lease claims to the lesser of 15% of all remaining rent payments or one year's rent.

If management chooses to accept a contract, the other party may choose to breach it, using the bankruptcy as an excuse. If so, management can offer to place a large deposit with the other party or take some other similar action in order to give it assurances of being able to complete the contract.

Company management is allowed four months from the bankruptcy petition date to come up with a plan of reorganization and another two months to have it approved by the court. These time intervals can be extended, sometimes for many additional months, as long as the management team is clearly attempting in good faith to complete a plan. If it does not do so, other parties are allowed to file reorganization plans instead, essentially working around the company.

Devising a reorganization plan can be exceedingly difficult, and certainly time-consuming, because the company must work with the various creditor groups and equity holders in order to gain general agreement to the plan. The cause of the difficulty is the differing objectives of the various groups. For example, secured creditors are primarily concerned with retaining the full value of their collateral and thereby gaining full payment of their claims. Alternatively, "vulture" investors who have bought the company's debt at a steep discount are more likely to want a portion of company stock, so they can gain operating control. Unsecured creditors generally want a cash payment, even if only for a small percentage of their claims, while shareholders are happy to retain even a small amount of equity. Clearly, gaining any sort of agreement from this diverse group can be quite a chore, and usually only occurs after negotiations have gone on for many months.

The reorganization plan is likely be a variation on one or a combination of several payment options, which are as follows:

- *Long-term cash payments.* Secured lenders are the. chief beneficiaries, since it may be years before the company can generate enough cash to pay them off and finally get to the unsecured creditor group. Shareholders can do well under this approach, and may team with the secured shareholders in approving it.
- *Asset liquidation.* Though not necessarily a complete liquidation of. the business, this approach is designed to pay off creditors in the near term, leaving a much

smaller company. Both the secured and unsecured creditors are likely to support this approach.

- *Debt or capital infusion.* This approach works where there is a general recognition that the company will be of the most value to all parties if it continues to exist to pay off its debts. However, adding equity will dilute the shareholders, and adding debt will introduce new secured creditors, so this approach is not highly favored by anyone.
- *Convert debt to equity.* This approach is used when. there is no source of cash with which to pay off creditors. Shareholders may be diluted in the extreme, so they will not vote for it. Creditors only use this option as a last resort, since they will not receive any cash payment.

No matter what form of payment is used to satisfy creditors, the plan will follow the same general structure. First, the plan will describe how the various creditors are classified in voting blocks. Similar types of claims are clustered together for voting purposes, so a secured creditor might be grouped into a secured creditor voting block, and also in an unsecured creditor voting block to the extent that any of its claim is not supported by collateral. The next section describes how each class of creditor will be treated. For example, secured creditors will be paid in full, while unsecured creditors will receive a quarter of the amount owed to them. The plan next describes exactly how the management team proposes to accomplish this payout, which may include a complete operational budget, as well as an organizational restructuring, securing new loans, merging with another entity, and so on. There is also a section that specifies exactly which leases and contracts the company has decided to either accept or reject, so there is a formal record in the event that another party brings suit over the issue at a later date.

Next, the management team creates an executive summary of the reorganization plan, called a disclosure statement. This statement is issued to creditors and is used to convince them to vote in favor of the reorganization plan.

Following approval by the court of the disclosure statement, the company then sends it, along with a voting ballot, to those creditors whose claims are impaired (i.e., their claims are unlikely to be paid off in full). The package is not sent to anyone whose claims will be paid in full (e.g., a secured creditor), since the court assumes that they will approve the plan. Creditors will be divided into classes for voting purposes. A class is construed as a group of creditors whose claims will be paid off in the same manner. For example, one group may be offered 30 cents on the dollar, while another group may be offered stock in the company in exchange for the amounts owed to them. In order for the plan to be approved by the creditors, at least one half of all voting creditors in each class must vote in favor of it, as well as two-thirds of the dollar value of all claims being voted within that class. This is called the *one-half/two-thirds requirement*. For example, if there are 50 creditors within a class and only eight of them vote, then the one-half/two-thirds rule will only apply to those eight votes. Thus, a very small fraction of just one class of creditors could potentially have control over whether a plan is accepted.

With the voting completed, the plan will then go to the court for final approval. There are a number of regulatory tests that the court will apply to the plan prior to final approval. Of particular interest to the management team is a "best interests of creditors" test, which must show that the creditors will be better off through the approval of the presented plan than they would be if the company simply liquidated. The management team must have this concept firmly in mind when it first drafts the reorganization plan, so the plan is not ultimately rejected by the court.

If all creditor classes have approved of the plan and all regulatory hurdles have been passed, then the court is likely to approve the plan of reorganization. However, if a creditor class has rejected the plan, the management team has the option of requesting that the plan be accepted by the court anyway, which is called a "cramdown." Under this scenario, at least one creditor class must have approved of the plan, and the management team must provide for full payment of the claims of the creditor classes that have rejected it. This typically means that the claims of any classes having a lower priority than those of the rejecting class will not be paid. In particular, equity holders, who have the lowest priority, will almost certainly receive nothing. In short, a cramdown can only be accomplished by probably eliminating the equity stakes of the original shareholders.

Once the plan is approved, the court officially discharges the company from all the debts that the reorganization plan does not require it to pay. If the company later goes into bankruptcy again, it will only owe creditors for the reduced amount of the debts that were itemized in the reorganization plan.

Given the large number of steps required for a company to complete before a discharge can be obtained from a bankruptcy court, it is obvious that the cost of professional fees through this lengthy process will be substantial and may consume a large proportion of the estate. Consequently, the management team should be careful not to wait too long before entering bankruptcy protection, when it still has enough funds on hand to pay the professionals and still have some money left over to see it through the process. This means that entering bankruptcy is not a last-minute affair, but rather one that is discussed well in advance with legal counsel regarding the appropriate timing of the event.

42.6   TAX LIABILITIES IN A BANKRUPTCY

Taxes are not usually discharged as a result of a bankruptcy filing. Most prepetition tax debts are classified for payment purposes within the creditor and shareholder payment priority list. They are as follows:

- Income taxes for years prior to the bankruptcy.
- Income taxes assessed within 240 days prior to the bankruptcy filing.
- Income taxes not assessed, but assessable as of the petition date.
- Withholding taxes for which the company is liable.
- The employer's share of employment taxes on wages.
- Excise taxes on any transactions occurring prior to the bankruptcy date.

If a company files for liquidation under Chapter 7 of the bankruptcy law, then these taxes will be paid out of whatever company assets are left, once the claims of creditors with a higher priority have been fulfilled. If the entity is under Chapter 11 bankruptcy protection, then it can pay these taxes to the IRS over six years; this will include an interest assessment. Any taxes that arise during the period when a company is in bankruptcy are considered to be ongoing administrative expenses, and so will be paid at once.

If a company is late in paying the state unemployment tax, it is normally restricted to making a 90% deduction of the amount paid into the federal unemployment fund against the state tax. However, this penalty is waived in the case of a bankrupt company, so that the full amount of the federal unemployment payment can still be taken against the state unemployment tax.

In some cases, the amount of debt canceled while in bankruptcy is considered to be taxable income to the bankrupt entity. If so, the amount of the debt reduction can be used to reduce the basis of any depreciable property (but not more than the total basis of property held, less total liabilities held directly after the debt cancellation). As an alternative, it can be used to (1) offset any net operating loss for the year in which the debt cancellation took place, (2) offset any carryovers of amounts normally used to calculate the general business credit, (3) offset any minimum tax credit, (4) offset any net capital loss and any capital loss carryover, and then (5) offset any passive activity losses. These offsets can be dollar-for-dollar for canceled debt, except for the reduction of *credit* carryovers, which can be reduced at the rate of 33 1/3 cents for every dollar of canceled debt.

A special concern to corporate officers is the payment of payroll withholding taxes. These taxes are held in trust by the company until they are turned over to the government, and so are not considered to be part of the bankrupt company and must still be paid in full even after the bankruptcy filing. The government can bypass the company and collect these funds from the company's officers (which can include anyone who signs the payroll checks, even though this person may not be an officer!). Thus, to avoid personal liability, officers must be sure to remit withheld taxes when due, both before and during a bankruptcy pro ceeding.

42.7 SPECIAL BANKRUPTCY RULES

A company is authorized (and required) to collect payments made to creditors in the 90 days prior to the bankruptcy filing that constitute a larger payment than the creditor would have received if it had been reimbursed with other unsecured creditors subsequent to the bankruptcy. An unsecured creditor who is sued for repayment in this manner then has its claim clumped in with all other unsecured creditors and will be paid on a pro rata basis along with the others. This rule does not include secured creditors, since they would have been paid the same amount if they had waited until after the bankruptcy for reimbursement. The 90-day period used for this rule is extended to a full year for cases where payments were made to company insiders.

Part of the process of operational stabilization is a review of all liens on company property. If a creditor has publicly registered a notice with a state official, such as the Secretary of State, that it has a lien on company property, then the company is obligated to acknowledge the lien and categorize the creditor as a secured creditor. This person is much more likely to receive full reimbursement for all collateralized debts. However, if the creditor has not publicly registered such a notice, then any lien it has on company property will be stripped away, leaving the creditor no better off for reimbursement purposes than the other unsecured creditors. This rule applies even if company management *knows* that the creditor has a lien on company assets.

One crucial instance where creditors are not barred from further collection activity is when a secured creditor claims that further use by the company of its collateral will gradually diminish the amount of its security interest. For example, a loan that is collateralized by a company's inventory will gradually become more at risk of not being repaid if the level of inventory drops subsequent to the bankruptcy filing. In this case, the creditor can require the company to replace the diminished collateral with other forms of collateral, by cash payments that reduce the amount of debt, or by some other negotiated solution.

42.8 ALTERNATIVES TO BANKRUPTCY

Bankruptcy is an exceedingly expensive undertaking, so the controller may want to consider alternatives prior to taking the plunge. One option is to ask creditors for *extensions* on payments. Creditors who grant this request may ask for collateral in return, which may cause a chain reaction of additional negotiations with other entities that already have senior collateral positions on assets. The controller may wish to deal with creditors individually in regard to extensions, in case some can be persuaded to accept longer payment terms than others. If creditors band together into a creditor's committee, then a standard repayment period is the more likely result.

A slightly more drastic alternative (for creditors) is for the controller to approach them about a *composition*, which is their acceptance of partial payment on debts owed. Though creditors will obviously not be paid in full, they may accept this alternative over the company's bankruptcy, on the grounds that they will gain a greater distribution than would be the case in bankruptcy. This approach is least acceptable to secured creditors, who may stand to gain full payment on debts owed if they wait for bankruptcy proceedings, on the assumption that the resale value of their attached collateral at least matches the amounts owed to them.

Creditors may require some representation in management affairs or on the board of directors in exchange for these reductions or delays in payments. Though the controller may experience some loss of control, this is typically well worth the reduction in expenses associated with a bankruptcy.

42.9 SUMMARY

The controller should come away from this chapter having learned two key points. First, bankruptcy can be very expensive, due to the number of bankruptcy professionals who must be employed. Second, the number of steps and outside parties involved in a bankruptcy make this a very long process to successfully conclude. For both of these reasons, it is critically important that a company enter bankruptcy with enough cash to see it through the process. This means that a bankruptcy should be planned well in advance, perhaps as one of a variety of strategic alternatives, and entered as soon as it becomes the most viable approach to resolving business issues. Conversely, the worst way to enter bankruptcy is after having unsuccessfully tried all other alternatives, used up all cash, and obtained (and exhausted) every possible form of credit. This later approach nearly always results in a company's eventual liquidation, rather than its successful emergence from bankruptcy at some point in the future.

CHAPTER 43

TAXATION

43.1 INTRODUCTION

The issue of taxation is one that confronts the accountant on a regular basis and in relation to a wide array of issues. This may include the proper treatment of overpayments to employees, the correct handling of personal property tax reporting, the tax impact of consignment revenue, and a broad array of other, highly specific items. The tax laws related to many of these issues change regularly, and so require the most up-to-date information. This chapter provides information that is current as of its publication date, but one should consult a taxation professional if there is any indication that the tax laws may have changed since that time.

The approach that a company should take to taxation issues is based upon its taxation strategy, which is noted in the first section. The remainder of the chapter lists nearly 46 taxation topics in alphabetical order, from the Accumulated Earnings Tax to the recognition of warranty expenses. If the reader does not see a specific topic in a section header, please refer to the index, since it may be included within another section or under a different section title.

43.2   THE STRATEGY OF TAX PLANNING

The obvious objective of tax planning is to minimize the amount of cash paid out for taxes. However, this directly conflicts with the general desire to report as much income as possible to shareholders. Only in the case of privately owned firms do these conflicting problems go away, since the owners have no need to impress anyone with their reported level of earnings and would simply prefer to retain as much cash in the company as possible by avoiding the payment of taxes.

For those organizations that are intent on reducing their tax burdens, there are four primary goals to include in their tax strategies, all of which involve increasing the number of differences between the book and tax records, so that reportable income for tax purposes is reduced. The four items are:

1. *Accelerate deductions.* By recognizing expenses sooner, one can force expenses into the current reporting year that would otherwise be deferred. The primary deduction acceleration involves deprecation, for which a company typically uses MACRS (an accelerated depreciation methodology acceptable for tax reporting purposes), and straight-line depreciation, which results in a higher level of reported earnings for other purposes.

2. *Take all available tax credits.* A credit results in a permanent reduction in taxes, and so is highly desirable. Unfortunately, credits are increasingly difficult to find, though one might qualify for the research and experimental tax credit (see later section). There are more tax credits available at the local level, where they are offered to those businesses willing to operate in economic development zones, or as part of specialized relocation deals (normally only available to larger companies).

3. *Avoid nonallowable expenses.* There are a few expenses, most notably meals and entertainment, that are completely or at least partially not allowed for purposes of computing taxable income. A key company strategy is to reduce these types of expenses to the bare minimum, thereby avoiding any lost benefits from nonallowable expenses.

4. *Increase tax deferrals.* There are a number of situations in which taxes can be shifted into the future, such as payments in stock for acquisitions, or the deferral of revenue received until all related services have been performed. This can shift a large part of the tax liability into the future, where the time value of money results in a smaller present value of the tax liability than would otherwise be the case.

One should refer back to these four basic tax goals when reading through the various tax issues noted in the following sections, in order to see how they fit into a company's overall tax strategy.

43.3 ACCUMULATED EARNINGS TAX

There is a double tax associated with a company's payment of dividends to investors, because it must first pay an income tax from which dividends *cannot* be deducted as an expense, and then investors must pay income tax on the dividends received. Understandably, closely held companies prefer not to issue dividends in order to avoid the double taxation issue. However, this can result in a large amount of capital accumulating within a company. The IRS addresses this issue by imposing an accumulated earnings tax on what it considers to be an excessive amount of earnings that have not been distributed to shareholders.

The IRS considers accumulated earnings of less than $150,000 to be sufficient for the working needs of service businesses, such as accounting, engineering, architecture, and consulting firms. It considers accumulations of anything under $250,000 to be sufficient for most other types of businesses. A company can argue that it needs a substantially larger amount of accumulated earnings if it can prove that it has specific, definite, and feasible plans that will require the use of the funds within the business. Another valid argument is that a company needs a sufficient amount of accumulated earnings to buy back the company's stock that is held by a deceased shareholder's estate.

If these conditions are not apparent, then the IRS will declare the accumulated earnings to be taxable at a rate of 15%. Also, interest payments to the IRS will be due from the date when the corporation's annual return was originally due. The severity of this tax is designed to encourage organizations to issue dividends on a regular basis to their shareholders so that the IRS can tax the shareholders for this form of income.

43.4 ALTERNATIVE MINIMUM TAX

The Alternative Minimum Tax (AMT) is a separate tax system that is designed to ensure that one does not completely avoid the payment of taxes through a variety of income tax shelters. The AMT must be calculated alongside the usual income tax forms. If the amount payable under the AMT calculation is higher than under the regular tax calculation, then the AMT amount must be paid. The AMT does not apply to any company that is reporting its first tax year in existence or if its average annual gross receipts for the preceding three years did not exceed $7.5 million. The AMT must be calculated for all other business entities.

The IRS form for the AMT is Form 4626. The differences from the typical tax system lie in the adjustments (generally reductions in reported expenses) and preferences (generally increases in reported revenue), which are itemized in a number of subcategories under line two, the most commonly used being:

- *Depletion.* Depletion deductions for mines, wells, and other natural deposits are limited to the property's adjusted basis at the end of the year, unless the corporation is an independent producer or royalty owner claiming percentage depletion for oil and gas wells.
- *Depreciation.* The depreciation expense must be recalculated under AMT, which stipulates that any depreciation that had been calculated using the 200% declining balance method must now be calculated using the 150% declining balance method, switching to the straight-line method in the first year in which this yields a larger deduction. The period over which depreciation is calculated is not changed under the AMT calculation.

- *Installment sales.* The installment sale method cannot be used for AMT calculation purposes for any nondealer property dispositions.
- *Long-term contracts.* The percentage of completion method must be used for AMT to calculate the taxable income from any long-term contract (with the exception of home construction contracts).
- *Passive activities.* All passive activity gains or losses for a closely held or personal service company must take into account the corporation's AMT adjustments, preferences, and AMT prior year unallowed losses.

In practice, the AMT is one of the most difficult tax calculations to accurately complete, and requires the services of an experienced tax expert. Also, separate records should be kept for the AMT for a number of years, since some of the net operating losses and related deductions may be applicable to the tax returns filed in later years.

43.5 BARTER

Barter occurs when a company receives goods or services in exchange for its own goods and services; cash is not exchanged as part of the transaction. When barter occurs, one must recognize income for the incremental gain in the fair market value of the products or services received over one's cost basis in the products or services given up.

The tax treatment of a barter transaction is more difficult if personal services are involved. For example, if an electrician performs services on a doctor's house in exchange for medical services from the doctor, both parties are providing services that have no cost basis, and so must be recorded at their full fair market value by both parties.

The tax treatment is somewhat different in the case of barter exchanges. A barter exchange occurs when a third party encourages the use of barter transactions by partially converting individual transactions into a form of money, giving each party a credit in exchange for its services that can then be used to "buy" the services of some other entity that is also listed on the exchange. The barter exchange must report to the IRS the fair market value of all transactions passing through it. There are certain instances when backup withholding on transactions conducted through a barter exchange will be required by the IRS.

43.6 BONUSES AND AWARDS

If a company gives its employees bonuses or cash awards of any type, these are taxable income and must be recorded on employee W-2 forms. If a noncash award is given, then the fair market value of this award must also be recorded on the W-2 form as taxable income.

If an award is given that is based on achievement, such as a safety or length of service achievement, then the cumulative cost to the employer of up to $400 can be excluded from employee pay during the course of each calendar year. If these awards are given under a written award program, then the annual amount excluded per employee is increased to $1,600. This type of award cannot be a disguised pay supplement: to ensure that these payments are truly rewards for unique achievements, the IRS has imposed safeguard rules that disallow length of service awards if they are awarded for fewer than five years of service. Similarly, safety awards are considered taxable income to the recipient if they are given to a supervisor or other professional employee, or if more than 10% of all qualified employees receive such awards during the year. Finally, all such awards must be awarded as part of a meaningful presentation.

In addition to being excluded from the receiving employee's taxable income, any employee achievement awards that fall within the preceding guidelines are also excludable for employment tax purposes as well as from the Social Security benefit base.

43.7   CASH METHOD OF ACCOUNTING

The normal method for reporting a company's financial results is the accrual basis of accounting, under which expenses are matched to revenues within a reporting period. However, for tax purposes, it is sometimes possible to report income under the cash method of accounting. Under this approach, revenue is not recognized until payment for invoices is received, while expenses are not recognized until paid.

The cash basis of accounting can result in a great deal of manipulation from the perspective of the IRS, which discourages its use, but does not prohibit it. As an example of income manipulation, a company may realize that it will have a large amount of income to report in the current year, and will probably have less in the following year. Accordingly, it prepays a number of supplier invoices at the end of the year, so that it recognizes them at once under the cash method of accounting as expenses in the current year. The IRS prohibits this type of behavior under the rule that cash payments recognized in the current period can only relate to current-year expenses. Nonetheless, it is a difficult issue for the IRS to police. The same degree of manipulation can be applied to the recognition of revenue, simply by delaying billings to customers near the end of the tax year. Also, in situations where there is a sudden surge of business at the end of the tax year, possibly due to seasonality, the cash method of accounting will not reveal the sales until the following year, since payment on the invoices from customers will not arrive until the next year. Consequently, the cash method tends to underreport taxable income.

In order to limit the use of this method, the IRS prohibits it if a company has any inventories on hand at the end of the year. The reason for this is that expenditures for inventory can be so large and subject to manipulation at year end that a company could theoretically alter its reported level of taxable income to an enormous extent. The cash basis is also not allowable for any "C" corporation, partnership that has a "C" corporation for a partner, or a tax shelter. However, within these restrictions, it is allowable for an entity with average annual gross receipts of $5 million or less for the three tax years ending with the prior tax year, as well as for any personal service corporation that provides at least 95% of its activities in the services arena.

The IRS imposes some accrual accounting concepts on a cash-basis organization in order to avoid some of the more blatant forms of income avoidance. For example, if a cash-basis company receives a check at the end of its tax year, it may be tempted not to cash the check until the beginning of the next tax year, since this would push the revenue associated with that check into the next year. To avoid this problem, the IRS uses the concept of *constructive receipt*, which requires one to record the receipt when it is made available to one without restriction (whether or not it is actually recorded on the company's books at that time). Besides the just-noted example, this would also require a company to record the interest on a bond that comes due prior to the end of the tax year, even if the associated coupon is not sent to the issuer until the next year.

There are some differences between the financial statements that a company reports under the accrual and cash methods. For instance, there are no accounts receivable or payable listed on the books of a cash-method business, which can be disconcerting for one who is attempting to determine the extent of an organization's true assets and liabilities. Also, there are no period-end accruals, such as would normally be found for salaries and wages, taxes, royalties, commissions, and other expenses. Furthermore, the receipt of property or services must be accounted for at their fair market value when reporting taxable income. Consequently, the use of the cash method of accounting for a company's other financial reporting needs is considered unsatisfactory from a purely informational perspective, thereby forcing a company to either maintain two sets of books, or to maintain just one using either basis of accounting, and then make adjustments to determine its results under the alternative basis of accounting.

"C" Corporations. The "C" corporation is the most common type of corporation, because its form allows for the broadest range of organizational structure. It can have an unlimited number of shareholders, which may include other corporations. It can also have different classes of stock, so that some shareholders can have different voting or dividend rights than the holders of other types of shares. It also has the ability to switch its organizational structure to an "S" corporation, but it cannot use any residual net operating loss carryforwards if it does so.

The main problem with the "C" corporation is that it must pay income taxes. Consequently, if the corporation pays income taxes and then issues dividends to its shareholders (who then pay taxes on the dividends), then shareholders are essentially paying taxes twice.

43.8 CHANGE OF ACCOUNTING METHOD

It is acceptable to choose any permitted accounting method when a company files its first tax return. However, once the company elects to change its method of accounting, the IRS's approval must be obtained. The reason for this is that switching methods can result in a timing difference in the recognition of taxable income for a company; the IRS must see evidence that there is a nontax reason for changing accounting methods before it will approve such a change. The application for a change of accounting method is Form 3115.

Any requested changes that are not already identified in the form will require the attachment of a note that itemizes the reason for the requested change, an explanation for its legal basis (including applicable statutes, references, published rulings, and court cases), as well as a thorough description of the company's main line of business. It is useful not to make a regular habit of requesting changes in accounting methods, since the IRS will determine if there is a history of changes that has a pattern of reducing a company's tax liability. Also, when one perceives that there may be difficulty in obtaining approval of the change listed in a Form 3115, a request for a conference can be filed along with the form, which will be arranged before the IRS formally replies to the change in accounting method.

It is necessary to obtain IRS approval if there is a change from the cash method to the accrual method, or vice versa, or a change in the method used to value inventory (which requires a considerable amount of reporting on Form 3115), or a change in the methodology for calculating depreciation expense.

Any calculation errors, even if their correction results in a change in a company's reported level of taxable earnings, do not require IRS approval to fix.

43.9 CHANGE OF TAX YEAR

It may be necessary to change to a different tax year from the one that a business entity originally used when it was created. A good reason is that the nature of the business results in a great deal of transactional volume at the same time that the company is attempting to close its books for the year, which can be quite difficult to do. For example, many retailers prefer to have a fiscal year that terminates at the end of January, so that they will have processed all of the sales associated with the Christmas holiday and will now have minimal inventories left to count for their year ends.

To apply to the IRS for a change in the tax year, use Form 1128, which is available online at the IRS Web site. The form requires one to itemize the current overall method of accounting (that is, cash basis, accrual basis, or a hybrid method), and also to describe the general nature of the business. The IRS will also want to know if you have requested a change in the tax year at any time in the past three years, as well as the amount of the taxable gain or loss in those years, plus an estimate of the gain or loss during the short year that will be a byproduct of the changeover to a new year.

The form will also require information about the business organization's relationship to any special types of organizations, such as a controlled foreign corporation, a passive foreign investment company, a foreign sales corporation, an "S" corporation, or a partnership, or if it is the beneficiary of an estate.

One must also attach a written explanation of the reason for the request to change the tax year. If this explanation is not included, then the request will automatically be denied. If the requesting organization is an "S" corporation or a partnership and already has a tax year that is not a fiscal year, then one must explain how permission for this change was obtained (since the IRS requires a calendar year for these entities, unless special permission has been granted). Finally, if a foreign-controlled corporation is requesting the change, a complete list of all shareholders in it, as well as their addresses and ownership shares, must be provided.

43.10 CLUB DUES

The IRS does not recognize as a valid business expense any payments to clubs, including initiation fees or dues, that provide entertainment activities to its members or guests. This ban includes country clubs, airline clubs, and athletic clubs. If an employee submits an expense report to a company that contains these nondeductible expenses and the company chooses to reimburse the employee for them, then these are to be considered income to the employee and must be included in his or her W-2 form.

This restriction does not apply to any expenses incurred to attend a trade association or professional association meeting, or to initiate or maintain one's membership in such organizations, though the meetings must be related to the industry in which one does business or one's professional area of interest.

43.11 CONSIGNMENT REVENUE

A company should not report shipments to dealers or distributors under consignment sales as taxable revenue (or as reportable revenue under generally accepted accounting principles). The sale should not be recognized until a sale of the goods has been made by the consignee. Even if title to the goods has transferred to the buyer, it should still be considered a consignment sale if the buyer has the right to return the product and the buyer does not have to pay until the buyer resells the product, or the seller must repurchase the goods at the buyer's request (which includes the cost of the buyer's storage).

43.12 DEFERRED COMPENSATION

There are a variety of deferred compensation plans used by employers who attempt to lock in their employees as far into the future as possible. Under any of these plans, an employee's tax objective is to only pay a tax when the compensation is actually received, while the employer wants to receive a full expense deduction for any amounts paid—and the sooner, the better.

If a plan meets enough criteria to be classified as an *exempt trust* or *qualified plan*, then a company can immediately recognize the expense of payments made into it, even though the employees being compensated will not be paid until some future tax year. Also, the value of funds or stock in the trust can grow on a tax-deferred basis, while participants in the plan will not be taxed until they are paid from it. In addition, the funds paid from such a plan may be eligible for rollover into an IRA, which results in an additional delay in the recognition of taxable income. While the funds are held in trust, they are also beyond the reach of any company creditors.

In order to become a qualified plan, it must meet a number of IRS requirements, such as a minimum level of coverage across the company-wide pool of employees, the prohibition of benefits under the plan for highly compensated employees to the exclusion of other employees, and restrictions on the amount of benefits that can be issued under the plan. Since many employers are only interested in creating deferred compensation plans in order to retain a small number of key employees, they will instead turn to a *nonqualified plan*, which avoids the requirement of having to offer the plan to a large number of employees.

If the plan is nonqualified, then the employer can only record the compensation expense at the same time that the employees are compensated. A company that only wants to extend deferred compensation agreements to a few select employees will tend to use this type of plan, since it does not require payments to a large number of employees, and it allows the company to increase the amount of per-person compensation well beyond the restricted levels required under a qualified plan.

A useful variation on the nonqualified plan concept is the *rabbi trust*, which is an irrevocable trust that is used to fund deferred compensation for key employees. Under this approach, a company contributes stock to a third-party trustee, such as a bank or trust company, with the stock being designated for eventual payment to a few key employees. Employee vesting can take seven years or even longer in a few instances, which gives companies an excellent tool to lock in key employees over long periods of time. Employees can be paid from the trust either in stock or cash, and will recognize income at the time of receipt. The company can recognize an expense at the same time that the employee recognizes income; however, if the employee gradually vests in the plan, the expense can be proportionally recognized by the company at the time of vesting. If the payments made into the trust are in the form of company stock, then the company must only record as an expense the value of the stock at the time of grant, and can ignore any subsequent changes in the stock's value. A company that uses a rabbi trust does not have to make extensive reports to the government under ERISA rules; instead, it is only necessary to make a one-time disclosure of the plan within four months of its inception. It is also necessary to initiate the plan prior to the start of any services to which the payments apply, or at least include in the plan a forfeiture clause that is active throughout the term of the deferred compensation agreement.

The terms of a rabbi trust must also state that a key employee's benefits from the plan cannot be shifted to a third party. It must also state that the trust be an unfunded one for the purposes of both taxes and Title I of ERISA. Further, the plan must define the timing of future payments, or the events that will trigger payments, as well as the amount of payments to be made to recipients.

A key consideration for any company contemplating the creation of a rabbi trust is that the plan assets must be unsecured, and cannot unconditionally vest in the employees who are beneficiaries of the plan. This requirement is founded on the economic benefit doctrine, which holds that the avoidance of taxation can only occur if the receipt of funds is subject to a substantial risk of forfeiture. To this end, the plan document must state that plan participants are classed with general unsecured creditors in terms of their right to receive funds from the plan. The contractual obligation to pay employees from the plan cannot be secured by any type of note, since this defeats the purpose of having the assets be available to general creditors. However, just because the funds can be claimed by general creditors does not mean that they are available for other company uses—payment obligations to targeted employees must be made before any funds may be extracted for other company uses.

The unsecured status of a rabbi trust can be a cause of great concern for the employees who are being paid under its terms. Not only are the funds contributed to the trust at risk of being claimed by general creditors, but so too are all salary deferrals made by the targeted employees into the trust. This is a particular problem in the event of corporate bankruptcy, since secured creditors will be paid in full before the key employees can claim any remaining funds from the trust, which may result in a small payment or none at all. When a bankruptcy occurs or seems likely, the company is required to notify the trustee, which must halt all subsequent scheduled payments to plan participants and hold all remaining funds for distribution to secured creditors. Further, a change in control may result in a new management team that is not inclined to honor the terms of a deferred compensation agreement that require additional payments into the trust, in which case the recipients under the plan may sue the company for the missing benefits. There is some protection for key employees in this case, however, because the terms of the deferred compensation agreement will require the third-party trustee to make payments to employees as they become due; the main problem is that the funds for these payments will only continue to be available if the company pays funds into the trust.

If the perceived risk to plan participants outweighs the advantages of having a rabbi trust, it is also possible to create a *secular trust*. Under this approach, plan participants will have their assets protected in the event of corporate insolvency, but the reduced level of risk is offset by current taxation of the deferred compensation, which defeats the purpose of having the plan. A combined version of the two plans, called a *rabbicular trust*, starts as a rabbi trust, but then converts to a secular trust if the company funding the plan approaches bankruptcy. However, this approach will still result in the immediate recognition of all income at the time of conversion to a secular trust.

Though the rabbi trust concept can result in substantial benefits to both an employer and key employees, it is not allowed in some states, or is allowed only in a modified form. Also, rabbicular trusts must be carefully written to comply with all deferred compensation laws at both the state and federal levels. Consequently, the assistance of a qualified taxation professional should be obtained before setting up either type of deferred compensati on plan.

43.13 DEPRECIATION

The depreciation calculation that the IRS allows for the calculation of taxable income requires the use of the Modified Accelerated Cost Recovery System (MACRS) in nearly all cases. MACRS consists of two depreciation systems, one being the General Depreciation System (GDS) and the other being the Alternative Depreciation System (ADS).

The ADS depreciation system uses straight-line depreciation calculations and a longer recovery period than is required for GDS. One must use ADS for tangible property that is used mostly outside of the United States, as well as any tax-exempt use property, or tax-exempt bond-financed property. These are rare cases, so many businesses will never run an ADS calculation, though they can elect to use ADS instead of GDS. Given the reduced amount of up-front depreciation that is recognized under this approach, few companies choose to do so.

The much more common depreciation method is GDS, which uses the declining balance method for depreciation calculations and has a shorter recovery period. Under GDS, property can be placed into eight property classes, each of which has a different recovery period. The six main property classes (3-year, 5-year, 7-year, 10-year, 15-year, and 20-year) are shown in Exhibit 43.1; where the percentage of original depreciable basis that can be taken in each successive taxable year is shown. The remaining two property classes that are not shown are for nonresidential real property and residential rental property.

The cumulative total amount of depreciation for each of the property classes is shown in Exhibit 43.2, rather than the annual depreciation percentage that was shown in Exhibit 43.1.

The most common types of property allowed under the 5-year GDS category are computers, office equipment, automobiles and light trucks, appliances, and carpets. If ADS were to be used, the depreciation period would lengthen to six years for office equipment and nine years for appliances and carpets. The types of assets that fall into the 7-year GDS category are office furniture, as well as any property that has not been designated as falling into a different category. For ADS calculation purposes, office furniture is depreciated over 10 years, while default assets are depreciated over 12 years. The type of assets that fall into the 15-year GDS category are fences, roads, and shrubbery (all of which are depreciated over 20 years under ADS).

When calculating depreciation under the GDS system, different conventions are used for the amount of depreciation recognition allowed in the first year. Generally, the IRS

Year of Recovery	200% Declining Balance				150% Declining Balance	
	3-Year Class	5-Year Class	7-Year Class	10-Year Class	15-Year Class	20-Year Class
1	33.33	20.00	14.29	10.00	5.00	3.750
2	44.45	32.00	24.49	18.00	9.50	7.219
3	14.81	19.20	17.49	14.40	8.55	6.677
4	7.41	11.52	12.49	11.52	7.70	6.177
5		11.52	8.93	9.22	6.93	5.713
6		5.76	8.92	7.37	6.23	5.285
7			8.93	6.55	5.90	4.888
8			4.46	6.55	5.90	4.522
9				6.56	5.91	4.462
10				6.55	5.90	4.461
11				3.28	5.91	4.462
12					5.90	4.461
13					5.91	4.462
14					5.90	4.461
15					5.91	4.462
16					2.95	4.461
17						4.462
18						4.461
19						4.462
20						4.461
21						2.231

EXHIBIT 43.1   PERCENTAGE OF DEPRECIABLE BASIS BY TAX YEAR AND PROPERTY CLASS

Year of Recovery	200% Declining Balance				150% Declining Balance	
	3-Year Class	5-Year Class	7-Year Class	10-Year Class	15-Year Class	20-Year Class
1	33.33	20.0	14.29	10.00	5.00	3.75
2	77.78	52.0	38.78	28.00	14.50	10.97
3	92.59	71.20	56.27	42.40	23.05	17.65
4	100.00	82.72	68.76	53.92	30.75	23.82
5		94.24	77.69	63.14	37.68	29.54
6		100.00	86.61	70.51	43.91	34.82
7			95.54	77.06	49.81	39.71
8			100.00	83.61	55.71	44.23
9				90.17	61.62	48.69
10				96.72	67.52	53.15
11				100.00	73.43	57.62
12					79.33	62.08
13					85.24	66.54
14					91.14	71.00
15					97.05	75.46
16					100.00	79.92
17						84.39
18						88.85
19						93.31
20						97.77
21						100.00

EXHIBIT 43.2   CUMULATIVE DEPRECIATION PERCENT BY TAX YEAR AND PROPERTY CLASS

prefers to see a half-year convention used, under which property purchased at any point during the first year receives as much depreciation expense as if it had been purchased at the mid-point of the year. A mid-month convention is also used for all nonresidential real property (which is land or improvements to land) and residential rental property. A mid-quarter convention is also sometimes used if the dollar amount of the property placed in service during the last three months of the tax year constitutes more than 40% of the total base of all property placed in service for the entire year; this calculation does not include the cost of property that was bought and sold within the same year.

There are a few cases where MACRS cannot be used. Specifically, it cannot be used to depreciate intangible property, motion picture film or videotape, or sound recordings.

It is allowable in some situations to use a different depreciation method besides MACRS, as long as it is not based on the number of years that have elapsed. For example, the units of production method depreciates a fixed asset based upon the number of units of production that have passed through it. If it is estimated that a total of 500,000 units of production can be completed by a machine, and 124,500 units were actually produced in a year, then 124,500/500,000, or 24.9% of the total cost of the machine can be depreciated in that year.

A small amount of asset purchases in each year can be charged off to expense at once under IRS rules, rather than depreciating them, thereby reducing the amount of taxable income reported. This situation is described under Section 179 of the Internal Revenue Code. The maximum Section 179 deduction allowed for 2005 was $105,000.

The Section 179 deduction is allowable for any tangible personal property (such as machinery and equipment), other tangible property used as an integral part of a manufacturing or extraction (mining) operation, or for use by utilities. There is also a special application for property used in the production or distribution of petroleum products. It is allowable to use the deduction if the acquired property is used at least 50% for business purposes; if there is some proportion of usage that is less than 100%, one can arrive at the correct deduction by multiplying the item's cost by the percentage of business usage. Also, if an asset is partially purchased with cash and partially with some other asset as a trade-in, then only the cash portion of the payment can be deducted under Section 179.

There are also a few instances where no Section 179 deduction can be made. It cannot be used if assets are acquired from a related party, or if acquired by one member of a controlled group (that is, subsidiary) from another member of the same controlled group.

Section 179 deductions cannot be used to create a taxable loss for a business, though they can be used to offset other sources of business income to arrive at a reduced level of reported taxable income. Given these restrictions, the Section 179 deduction is of minor interest to large corporations, but can be a useful way to delay tax payments for smaller businesses with modest amounts of reported taxable income.

43.14   DISTRIBUTIONS

This section describes a variety of distributions to the shareholders or partners in "C" and "S" corporations, as well as partnerships, and their varying treatment under the tax laws.

A return of capital to shareholders in a "C" corporation is first offset against the shareholders' basis in their stock, resulting in no taxable gain. If the return of capital exceeds the shareholders' basis, then the excess amount is taxed as a capital gain. If the distribution is part of a corporate liquidation, and the amount returned is less than the shareholders' basis, then the difference can be claimed as a capital loss.

If a corporation issues a dividend to its shareholders, it must be recorded as ordinary income by the shareholders, on the grounds that it is the result of earnings within the short term, and so has no reason to be considered a long-term capital gain. If the company also has a dividend reinvestment plan available under which shareholders can purchase more shares with their dividends, then any discount on the purchase of additional dividends must be reported as ordinary taxable income in the current period.

If an entity sells stock prior to the payment date of a dividend but after the date when it was declared, then the entity to whom the dividend check is addressed must include the amount of dividend in its taxable income.

A company may distribute a stock dividend to its shareholders. If so, there is no immediate taxable income to the recipient. However, the shareholder must allocate his or her basis in the existing stock between it and the newly acquired stock dividend in direct proportion to the fair market value of each one on the date when the stock dividend was issued.

If an "S" corporation distributes its current or retained earnings to shareholders, it is treated as a nontaxable reduction in one's basis in the stock. Distributions in excess of one's basis are treated as a gain. All current-year income or loss experienced by an "S" corporation is passed directly through to its shareholders, and must be reported by them in proportion to their ownership shares in the business. One's current-year share of income in an "S" corporation will increase one's basis in the corporation.

Mutual funds and real estate investment trusts are allowed to make capital gain distributions to their shareholders, which will be taxed under the reduced long-term capital gains tax.

If a distribution is made to a partner in a partnership in the form of marketable securities, the partner need only recognize taxable income to the extent that the current market value of the securities on the day of the distribution exceeds the basis of the partner's interest (which is the money and adjusted basis of any property that the partner originally contributed to the partnership).

43.15 ESTIMATED TAXES

Corporations are required to pay to the IRS an estimated quarterly income tax. It is clearly not to a company's advantage to estimate too high and have the government hold its money until its final Form 1120 has been completed, so one should be aware of the rules regarding minimum estimated tax payments.

The IRS cannot levy a penalty for underpayment of estimated taxes if the full-year corporate tax is estimated to be less than $500. The same rule applies if a company remits four equal estimated payments that total at least 100% of the prior year corporate tax liability, except in cases where the company did not file a return in the previous year (since the estimated tax would always be zero), if there was no tax liability in the previous year, or if the prior tax year was less than 12 months (which happens when a company switches to a new tax year). A different rule applies to corporations with at least $1 million of taxable income in any one of the immediately preceding three tax years; they can use the prior year tax liability as the basis for the first quarterly estimated tax payment of the new tax year, but must then use an estimate of current year results to make payments for the final three quarters of the year.

If a company has a tax year that matches the calendar year, then its estimated tax payments are due on April 15th, June 15th, September 15th, and December 15th. If the tax year covers any other time period, then the four payments are sequentially due on the 15th day of the fourth, sixth, ninth, and twelfth months of the tax year. If any of these days fall on a weekend or legal holiday, then payments remitted on the following day will still be counted as being paid on time.

In the event that an estimated tax payment was higher than the actual result, a corporation can file for a quick refund, using Form 4466, which is the Corporation Application for Quick Refund of Overpayment of Estimated Tax. The form must be filed after a corporation's tax year end and before the 16th day of the third month after the tax year, but in advance of its filing its annual income tax return. The quick refund is only available to those corporations having made estimated payments that exceed their expected liability by at least 10% and by at least $500.

43.16 FINANCIAL REPORTING OF TAX LIABILITIES

The proper reporting of tax liabilities is covered by statement number 109 of the Financial Account Standards Board (FASB). In it, the FASB outlines the proper reporting standards for the effects of income taxes resulting from a company's activities. The primary objectives of these standards are to recognize not only the amount of taxes payable for the current reporting year, but also any deferred tax liabilities and assets for the future tax consequences of events that have already been reported on in the company's financial statements or tax returns.

The standards set forth in FASB 109 are based on a few key principles. First, a current asset or liability account is recognized to the extent that there are current year taxes payable or refundable. Second, a company must recognize a deferred tax liability or asset in the amount of any estimated future taxes that can be reasonably attributed to temporary tax differences or carryforwards. Third, the recognition of any deferred tax assets is to be reduced by any tax assets that are not reasonably expected to be realized.

If there is a difference between the amount of recognized income or loss in a given year that is allowed by tax laws, as opposed to financial reporting standards, then these temporary differences must be recognized on the financial statements as deferred tax assets or liabilities. These accounts will be gradually drawn down over time as the deferred impact of the reporting differences are gradually recognized. For example, revenue may be recognized in the current year under generally accepted accounting principles (GAAP), but deferred under applicable tax laws, which will result in a deferment in the recognition of taxable income to later years; in this case, a tax liability will be created in the amount of the applicable tax that has been deferred. On the other hand, an increase in the deferred asset account for taxes will occur if the tax laws require a company to defer the recognition of expenses that have already been recognized under GAAP, since these can be used at a later date to reduce the amount of taxable income.

There are also differences between taxable and GAAP reporting that are permanent differences—that is, the differences between the two reporting methods will never be reconciled. An example is the interest income on municipal bonds, which is recognized in the financial records, but is permanently excluded from reportable income on the tax records. When permanent differences are involved, no asset or liability is recorded on the financial records, since there is no prospect of the differences ever being recognized.

The first step in calculating deferred tax assets and liabilities is to itemize the nature and amount of each type of loss and tax credit carryforward, as well as the remaining time period over which each carryforward is expected to extend. Next, we separately summarize the total deferred tax liability for all temporary differences and the total deferred asset related to all carryforwards. The final step is to ascertain the amount (if any) of a valuation allowance needed to offset the deferred tax asset. This allowance can be necessary if there is evidence that some proportion of the deferred tax asset may not be recognized. For example, there may be an expectation that the full amount of a credit carryforward cannot be offset against a sufficient amount of income during the upcoming time period during which the tax laws allow a company to use the credit. The estimates used to create the allowance will require a great deal of judgment, so the FASB has added some guidelines that take away some of the uncertainty. It requires one to review several sources of likely future income against which the carryforwards can be offset, which are the (1) future reversal of temporary tax differences, (2) future taxable income that will arise, exclusive of the reversal of any temporary tax differences, (3) tax planning strategies, and (4) existing taxable income for which carrybacks are permitted. If there is a reasonable basis for a taxable source of revenue income from any one or a combination of these four items, then there is no need for a valuation allowance.

Also, all reasonable forms of evidence regarding future expectations for taxable income should be included in the review. It is also possible to take into account during the review the presence of any tax strategies that a prudent company would consider in order to take advantage of and use any tax assets in the future. As a result of the review, a valuation allowance should be set up if it is more likely than not that there will not be sufficient taxable income in the future to offset any tax assets. However, it is not allowable to set up a valuation allowance when there is no clear need for one.

When these calculations are completed, it is necessary to separately report the deferred liability, deferred asset, and valuation allowance for the deferred asset on the balance sheet. In the first year when this entry is made, a company can include the entire adjustment in net income as of the beginning of the year of adoption of the FASB 109 rules, or it can restate the financial results of prior years to include the changes, which yields a better year-to-year comparison of financial results.

After the correct entries are booked, the accountant's job is still not complete, for the entries may require periodic updates to reflect changes in the tax rates that apply to the company. The tax rate at which a tax liability or asset is computed for financial statement reporting purposes is either the maximum tax rate to which the business is generally subject (assuming that its income is always so high that it exceeds any graduated rates) or else an average rate for the general range of tax rates within which its taxable income usually carries it. If there is a change in the tax laws that results in a different income tax rate structure, then the journal entries used to record the tax liabilities and assets must be altered to more appropriately reflect the new tax rates. For example, if a company has a tax asset, an increase in the tax rate will result in an increase in the recorded asset. This change to the financial records should take place as of the day when the new tax rates take effect. The entire effect of a change in tax rates on the reporting of deferred tax assets or liabilities is recorded in the period when the tax rate change occurs.

43.17 FOREIGN EARNED INCOME

The foreign earned income (FEI) tax is only applicable to individuals, not to a corporation. Nonetheless, it is mentioned here because it applies to any employee posted outside of the United States.

Under FEI, employees living abroad could exclude up to $87,600 of their foreign earned income from taxation in 2009. The only type of revenue that can be excluded with this exemption is that which is earned from personal services (which includes one's salary, bonuses, commissions, housing and automobile allowance, and cost of living allowance); it does not include dividends, capital gains, interest, and income from rental properties.

If a person is only out of the country for part of the tax year, then the amount of the exclusion must be prorated to cover only that portion of his or her time that was spent outside of the country.

An individual qualifies for this exclusion if he or she has a tax home in a foreign country, is a United States citizen, and either has been outside of the country for 330 days within a consecutive 12-month period, or passes a foreign residency test that is based on the permanence of the foreign dwelling occupied, the type and duration of the visa under which one is working within the foreign country, and the status of any dwelling being maintained within the United States at the same time.

43.18 GIFTS (BUSINESS)

The IRS imposes a maximum deduction of just $25 for every gift that a company gives directly or indirectly to another person. For example, if a company gives a $25 gift to each of ten people, then $250 is deductible. However, if a company gives ten $25 gifts to one person, then only $25 is deductible. This restriction does not include any incidental costs, such as the shipping and handling associated with the shipment of gifts.

The limitation does not apply to any gift that costs $4 or less, has the company name clearly imprinted on it, and is part of a mass distribution of the gift (such as an imprinted company pen or calendar). Under this variation, a company could give any number of gifts to a person, and could deduct the cost of all the gifts handed out.

There is some flexibility in categorizing a cost as a gift or an entertainment expense, depending upon one's participation in the gift. For example, if the company has tickets to a sporting event, and an employee takes a customer to the game, then the cost of the tickets can be expensed as either a gift (which is subject to the $25 limitation) or an entertainment expense. However, if the tickets are simply given to the customer and no employee accompanies the person to the game, then the tickets are categorized as a gift.

43.19   GOODWILL AND OTHER INTANGIBLES

The tax treatment of intangible expenses falls under the category of Section 197 of the IRS regulations. Expenses can only be included in this category if they are related to a significant change in the ownership or use of a company, such as a startup or the acquisition of another business or a substantial part of its assets. Goodwill is the excess of the purchase price of an acquisition over the cost of the assets acquired. Any expenses that fall into this category will be amortized on a straight-line basis over 15 years. The following expenses can be amortized under Section 197:

- *Workforce in place.* This includes the cost of buying out an existing employee contract as part of an acquisition, or workforce-related costs that are strictly based upon the circumstances of an acquisition.
- *Business books and records.* This includes the cost of customer lists, subscription lists, and lists of advertisers and clients, as well as the intangible value of technical and training manuals that are being acquired.
- *Customer-based intangibles.* This includes that portion of an acquisition purchase price that relates to a customer or circulation base or any customer relationship resulting in the provision of future goods and services.
- *Government licensing cost.* This includes the cost to apply for any government-granted license, such as a liquor license.
- *Patents, copyrights, franchises, and trademarks.* This includes the purchase price of any acquired legal rights, as well as the legal cost of applying for patents, copyrights, and trademarks. It also includes the purchase price of a franchise (though not of a sports franchise).
- *Supplier-based intangible.* This includes that portion of an acquisition purchase price that relates to favorable supply contracts or relations with distributors.

To keep companies from claiming a loss on an intangible expense that has been capitalized under Section 197 (if it has become worthless), one must allocate the remaining unamortized expense among all other types of intangibles acquired through the same transaction, thereby continuing to amortize the expense.

To keep companies from using Section 197 to an excessive degree, there are antichurning rules in place that prevent amortization from being used in cases where a change of ownership is really caused by the shifting of property among related parties. The rules governing antichurning are quite lengthy, but essentially state that churning cannot take place when property passes between family members, between companies that are owned by the same parent organization, or if there is any provable degree of common control over both entities involved in a transfer of property.

43.20   HYBRID METHODS OF ACCOUNTING

The IRS allows a combination of cash, accrual, and special methods of accounting as long as the resulting system clearly shows taxable income, and if the system is used consistently. However, hybrid systems must factor in the following systemic requirements:

- *Accrual method.* If the accrual method of accounting is used to record expenses, then it must also be used to record revenue.
- *Cash method usage.* If the cash method of accounting is used to record revenue, then it must also be used consistently for the recording of all expense items.

- *Inventory.* If inventory is present, then the accrual method must be used for recording purchases and sales, though the cash method can be used for recording other items appearing on the income statement.

Though these restrictions may appear to severely hamper the use of any hybrid system, it is still possible to create one where the accrual method is only used to record revenue, or where the cash method is only used to record expenses.

43.21 IMPUTED INTEREST EXPENSE

The amount of interest income that a company receives is considered by the IRS to be fully taxable ordinary income, which falls into the highest tax bracket. For that reason, the IRS uses the imputed interest concept to make sure that all interest income is recognized. Under this concept, a company must record interest income (or expense, if it is paying for the associated debt) at the current market rate at the time a debt instrument is initiated. If not, the IRS will assume (or impute) a higher interest rate that is 110% of the interest rate paid on whatever type of Treasury debt has approximately the same number of years to maturity as the debt instrument in question. This higher rate is called the *Applicable Federal Rate*.

This rule also applies to installment sales, so the interest portion of these payments must also be broken out if the total amount of a series of installment payments exceeds $3,000. The general rule to see if an installment sale requires the calculation of imputed interest if the total of all payments due more than six months after the date when the sale occurred is greater than the present value of the payments, plus the present value of any interest charges noted in the installment sale contract.

Another variation on the imputed interest concept is the *Original Issue Discount* (OID). This applies to situations when an investor buys a bond, note, or other long-term debt instrument at a price that is lower than its eventual redemption price. The difference between its purchase price and the final redemption price at maturity is the OID. The IRS requires the investor to recognize the income from the OID as it accrues over time, irrespective of the presence of any interest income actually received from the issuer of the debt.

43.22 INSTALLMENT SALES

Under an installment sale, the sale of an asset becomes an installment sale if the contract states that at least one payment is made in a tax year later than the one in which the sale took place. When this happens, many entities that are on the accrual basis of accounting are allowed to use what is essentially an income recognition method under the cash basis of accounting to recognize the gross profit from the sale over the years in which payments are made.

Under the installment sale rules, such a sale is essentially an exchange of the seller's property for the buyer's promise to pay at some later time through the use of a debt instrument, which becomes an exchange of assets rather than the payment of cash for the seller's asset. Under the normal tax rules for an exchange of property, the increase in value over the fair market value of the item sold is to be recognized at once as income, but the installment sale rule varies from this approach in assuming that income is not considered to have been received until the cash associated with the buyer's debt instrument is received. In essence, tax recognition under an installment sale is designed to let a seller pay taxes only when the cash is available with which to pay the taxes.

The installment sales method cannot be used to report a gain from the sale of stock or securities traded on an established securities market, nor does it apply to those businesses that regularly sell the same type of property on an installment plan (such as a car dealership). It also cannot be used if the installment sale results in a loss. In this case, it can only be deducted in the tax year in which the transfer of property occurs.

In order to calculate the amount of gain to recognize in each year, it is necessary to split the payments received into their interest income component (see the "Imputed Interest" section), a gain on sale of the property, and a return on the taxpayer's adjusted basis in the property (which is increased by any associated selling expenses). The portion of each payment that is ascribed to interest income will be taxed as ordinary income, while the gain may be taxed as a long-term capital gain (depending on the circumstances), and the return on the taxpayer's adjusted basis will be tax-free. This means that the taxpayer will be taxed on that portion of the gross profit recognized each year, which spreads out the amount of the total tax payment over the full term of the installment sale agreement.

If the total selling price is reduced prior to the completion of all payments on an installment sale, the gross profit on the sale will also change, and therefore the amount of tax due. One must then recalculate the gross profit percentage for the remaining payments with the reduced sale price and then subtract the gain already reported in previous tax years. The remaining gain can be spread over the remaining future installment payments.

Form 6252 is used to report installment sales to the IRS. This form should not be filed by an accrual basis taxpayer who "elects out" of using the installment method, recognizes the entire gain from a sale of property, and pays the associated tax at once. Any entity that chooses to use the installment method by filing Form 6252 does not have the option to switch back to a full and immediate recognition of income under the accrual basis of accounting, unless an amended return is filed no more than six months after the due date of the return, excluding extensions.

43.23 INVENTORY VALUATION

When inventory is used to support the sale of goods, the type of accounting method used to determine what is included in inventory and how its cost is established is crucial to the development of an accurate amount of reported taxable income.

From the perspective of the IRS, the types of items that should be included in a company's inventory are the same as those authorized under generally accepted accounting principles—that is, raw materials, work-in-process, finished goods, and supplies that are integrated into the finished product. A company that wants to avoid tax payments will likely attempt to narrowly define what is included in inventory so that all items falling outside that definition will be charged to expense, thereby reducing the level of taxable income.

The area in which large shifts in the level of inventory are most likely to occur is in the definition and recognition of the point at which a company obtains title to inventory, and when this title is transferred to another entity. For example, once a company pays for raw materials or merchandise, that inventory should be recorded on the company's books, even though it may very well be still in transit to the company. At the other end of the sales cycle, goods should no longer be included in inventory once they have been handed over to a third-party freight company for delivery to a customer, except for the case in which the shipping terms specify that the company retains title to the goods until they reach the customer's receiving dock. This latter instance is similar to a cash on delivery (COD) arrangement, where the company should continue to record an item as being in stock until it is paid for by the customer at the time of delivery. If goods have been sent to a distributor under a consignment agreement, then the company retains title to the products until sold, and so those items must continue to be recorded in inventory. If the company is the distributor and is receiving consigned goods, then of course the reverse situation applies, and it should not record the inventory as its own asset. Additionally, any inventory used for marketing purposes, such as display items, should also be recorded in inventory.

Once the quantity of inventory on hand has been firmly established, the next issue is to properly determine its cost in a manner that is acceptable to the IRS. The most approved method for doing so is the *specific identification method*, under which a company tracks the exact cost of each item in stock. This is easiest to do if each unit of stock is clearly identifiable, but in most cases this is not practical, especially when there are large quantities of each item running through the warehouse. In this latter case, the IRS prefers that either the FIFO or LIFO method be used.

Under the FIFO method, the assumption is that the first product purchased will also be the first one to be used, and so the earliest cost at which a product was purchased will be the first one applied to the sale of a product. This tends to result in a higher level of ending inventory dollars, on the assumption that inventory costs are constantly rising (as is generally the case in an inflationary economy). The opposite philosophy is true under the LIFO assumption, which assumes that the last item purchased will be the first one used. This method tends to result in a lower ending inventory valuation, since the most recent (and higher) costs will have been charged to the cost of goods sold. Companies that are trying to avoid paying income taxes will have a preference for the LIFO method, since it yields a lower level of reported earnings.

A company can convert to the LIFO method by filing Form 970, Application to Use LIFO Inventory Method, with the IRS.

It is also possible to use the *retail method* for valuing inventory for tax purposes. This method is most commonly applied to the inventories of retailers or distributors, who have nothing but finished goods in stock. To derive costs under the retail method, the total selling price of goods in stock is reduced by the average markup originally applied to the inventory, thereby yielding a close approximation to the original cost. The first step in this process is to determine the markup percentage. To do so, add together the total retail price of all goods in the beginning inventory and the total retail price of all items purchased subsequently. Then subtract the total cost of goods sold contained within the beginning inventory and the cost of all items subsequently purchased from the total price just calculated. Finally, divide the result, which is the total markup dollars, by the total selling price that was initially calculated. With the markup percentage in hand, we can now multiply it by the total retail price of the ending inventory, which results in the total markup dollars in the ending inventory. By subtracting this amount from the total retail price of the ending inventory, we arrive at the cost of the ending inventory. Since there may be different markup percentages for different classes of product, it is more accurate to cluster together products with similar markup percentages into groups, and calculate the cost of each inventory group separately.

If a company uses the retail method in conjunction with the LIFO valuation method, then it must adjust its ending retail selling prices so that they factor in the impact of price markdowns and markups. If the retail method is used without the LIFO valuation method, then the ending retail selling prices can only be adjusted for markups, not markdowns.

It is not acceptable under IRS rules to apply the direct costing method to inventory. Under this practice, all costs not directly associated with a product (such as most overhead costs) are charged directly to the cost of goods sold during the current period, rather than being allocated to ending inventory. If this method were allowable, a company could charge off a larger part of its costs in the current period, thereby reducing the amount of taxable income.

No matter which method (specific identification method, FIFO, LIFO, or retail method) is used, there is still the issue of what costs to allocate to the cost of each inventory item. For example, if a company buys raw materials under a volume purchasing discount, it cannot charge to inventory the list price, but rather only the price paid, which is net of the volume discount. On the other hand, the amount of any cash discount taken in exchange does not have to be factored into the inventory valuation (but whatever method chosen must be used consistently).

A company should not artificially inflate the value of any inventory on hand, so one should periodically reduce the inventory valuation by comparing the current market price that can be obtained for each inventory item to its cost, and adjust its recorded cost down to the lower of cost or market. This is also in accordance with generally accepted accounting principles. This rule does not apply for tax purposes if the inventory being reviewed is to be sold to a customer under a firm fixed price contract, nor does it apply to any inventory that is accounted for under the LIFO valuation method.

There will also be cases in which a company has second-hand or damaged goods in stock that it cannot sell at full price. Though it may be tempting to write off the total value of these items, thereby increasing the cost of goods sold and reducing the level of reported income, the IRS prefers that a company never value them at less than their scrap value, and preferably at their estimated sale price (less the cost of disposition); by requiring this higher valuation, the IRS ensures that the amount of taxable income reported will be higher than if the value of these items were simply eliminated from the inventory valuation.

It is allowable to value a company's inventory using one method for book purposes and another for tax purposes, except in the case of the LIFO inventory valuation method. In this case, the tax advantages to be gained from the use of LIFO are so significant that the IRS requires a user to employ it for both book and tax purposes. Furthermore, if LIFO is used in any one of a group of financially related companies, the entire group is assumed to be a single entity for tax reporting purposes, which means that they must all use the LIFO valuation approach for both book and tax reporting. This rule was engendered in order to stop the practice of having LIFO-valuation companies roll their results into a parent company that used some other method of reporting, thereby giving astute companies high levels of reportable income and lower levels of taxable income at the same time.

43.24   LIFE INSURANCE

It is common practice for a company to provide group term life insurance to its employees as part of a standard benefit package. This requires some extra reporting from a tax perspective, however. If the amount of the life insurance benefit exceeds $50,000, the company must report the incremental cost of the life insurance over $50,000 (to the extent that the employee is not paying for the additional insurance) on the employee's W-2 form as taxable income. In the less common case where the company provides life insurance that results in some amount of cash surrender value, then the cost of this permanent benefit to the employee must also be included in the employee's W-2 form. The only case in which these costs are not included on an employee's W-2 form is when the company is the beneficiary of the policy, rather than the employee. The opposite situation arises if the company is providing life insurance only to a few key employees, rather than to all employees; in this case, the entire cost of the insurance must be reported on the employee's W-2 form as taxable income.

43.25   LIKE-KIND EXCHANGES

Under Section 1031, if one exchanges business or investment property solely for business or investment property of a like kind, then no gain or loss is recognized on the transaction. To be acceptable to the IRS, the assets exchanged must be of a similar nature (such as an office building for an office building), and the owner must use both assets for the same purpose. If other types of property or payment are received as part of the transaction, then these other items are recognized as a taxable gain on the transaction, though the rest of the transaction still qualifies as a like-kind exchange. The like-kind exchange rule does not apply to exchanges of inventory, securities, or partnership interests, nor does it apply to exchanges of real property located inside the United States for property located outside the United States.

It is also possible to have a deferred exchange even when there is a delay in the time when one asset is sold and another is bought. It is typically called a *1031 tax-deferred exchange*, or a *Starker*, which is named after the first person to be challenged by the IRS over this transaction. For this exchange to qualify as a like-kind exchange, the replacement property must be identified within 45 days of the transfer of the asset given up and the earlier of the receipt of the replacement property (no later than 180 days after the date of transfer) or the due date of the tax return for the year of initial asset transfer. In the interim, a third party, such as a title company, holds the proceeds from the first sale in escrow and then purchases the new property on the behalf of the original seller and transfers it to that entity.

43.26   LOSSES

A net operating loss (NOL) may be carried back and applied against profits recorded in the two preceding years, with any remaining amount being carried forward for the next 20 years, when it can be offset against any reported income. If there is still an NOL left after the 20 years have expired, then the remaining amount can no longer be used. One can also irrevocably choose to ignore the carryback option and only use it for carryforward purposes. The standard procedure is to apply all of the NOL against the income reported in the earliest year, with the remainder carrying forward to each subsequent year in succession until the remaining NOL has been exhausted.

The number of carryback years can be extended to three years from the standard two years if the NOL was caused by a casualty or theft, or if it was attributable to a disaster, as declared by the president, and the company is a qualified small business (which is a sole proprietorship or partnership that has average annual revenue of $5 million or less during the three-year period ending with the tax year of the NOL). A farming business is allowed to use a five-year carryback.

If an NOL has been incurred in each of multiple years, then the NOLs should be applied against reported income (in either prior or later years) in order of the first NOL incurred. This rule is used because of the 20-year limitation on an NOL, so that an NOL incurred in an earlier year can be used before it expires.

The quickest way to receive cash back as a result of an NOL carryback is to file a Form 1045 (Application for Tentative Refund), but there is a shorter time period available in which to file it. It must be filed on or after the date when the tax return identifying the NOL is filed, but no later than one year after the NOL year.

The NOL is a valuable asset, since it can be used for many years to offset future earnings. A company buying another entity that has an NOL will certainly place a high value on the NOL, and may even buy the entity strictly in order to use its NOL. To curtail this type of behavior, the IRS has created the Section 382 limitation, under which there is a limitation on its use if there is at least a 50% change in the ownership of an entity that has an unused NOL. The limitation is derived through a complex formula that essentially multiplies the acquired corporation's stock times the long-term tax-exempt bond rate. The Section 382 rules can also limit the NOL recognition of a company that has not changed its ownership, simply because of the manner in which a change in ownership is defined under the Section. To avoid these problems, a company with an unused NOL that is seeking to expand its equity should consider issuing straight preferred stock (no voting rights, no conversion privileges, and no participation in future earnings) in order to avoid any chance that the extra equity will be construed as a change in ownership.

If a company has incurred an NOL in a short tax year, it must deduct the NOL over a period of six years, starting with the first tax year after the short tax year. This limitation does not apply if the NOL is for $10,000 or less, or if the NOL is the result of a short tax year that is at least nine months long, and is less than the NOL for a full 12-month tax year beginning with the first day of the short tax year. This special NOL rule was designed to keep companies from deliberately changing their tax years in order to create an NOL within a short tax year. This situation is quite possible in a seasonal business where there are losses in all but a few months. Under such a scenario, a company would otherwise be able to declare an NOL during its short tax year, carry back the NOL to apply it against the previous two years of operations, and receive a rebate from the IRS.

43.27 NEXUS

A company may have to complete many more tax forms than it would like, as well as remit taxes to more government entities, if it can be established that it has nexus within a government's area of jurisdiction. Consequently, it is very important to understand how nexus is established.

The rules vary by state, but nexus is generally considered to have occurred if a company maintains a facility of any kind within a state, or if it pays the wages of someone within that state. In some locales, the definition is expanded to include the transport of goods to customers within the state on company-owned vehicles (though nexus is not considered to have occurred if the shipment is made by a third-party freight carrier). A more liberal interpretation of the nexus rule is that a company has nexus if it sends sales personnel into the state on sales calls or training personnel there to educate customers, even though they are not permanently based there. To gain a precise understanding of how the nexus rules are interpreted by each state, it is best to contact the department of revenue of each state government.

A recent issue that is still being debated in the courts is that Internet sales may be considered to have occurred within a state if the server used to process orders or store data is kept within that state, even if the server is only rented from an Internet hosting service.

If nexus has been established, a company must file to do business within the state, which requires a small fee and a refiling once every few years. In addition, it must withhold sales taxes on all sales within the state. This is the most laborious issue related to nexus, since sales taxes may be different for every city and county within each state, necessitating a company to keep track of potentially thousands of different sales tax rates. Also, some states may require the remittance of sales taxes every month, though this can be reduced to as little as once a year if the company predicts that it will have minimal sales taxes to remit, as noted on its initial application for a sales tax license.

Some states or local governments will also subject a company to property or personal property taxes on all assets based within their jurisdictions, which necessitates even more paperwork.

Though the amount of additional taxes paid may not be that great, the key issue related to the nexus concept is that the additional time required to track tax liabilities and file forms with the various governments may very well require additional personnel in the accounting department. This can be a major problem for those organizations in multiple states, and should be a key planning issue when determining the capacity of the accounting department to process tax-related transactions. Some organizations with a number of subsidiaries will avoid a portion of the tax filing work by only accepting the nexus concept for those subsidiaries that are clearly established within each governmental jurisdiction, thereby avoiding the tax filing problems for all other legal entities controlled by the parent corporation.

43.28   ORGANIZATIONAL EXPENSES

When setting up a business, some costs can be capitalized and then amortized over at least 60 months. These organizational costs fall into the following three categories:

1. *Business start-up costs.* A cost falls into this category if it is incurred prior to the first day of business, or if it is incurred in order to operate an existing business. Examples of this type of cost are market surveys, fees for such professionals as accountants and lawyers who are working on the incorporation of the business, travel costs to set up business arrangements with suppliers and customers, the salaries of employees while they are being trained to perform services for the company, and advertisements related to the initial start-up of the business. However, costs incurred in order to research and purchase a specific business entity cannot be amortized as organization expenses.

2. *Corporation organization costs.* A cost falls into this category if it is incurred within a corporation's first tax year, and includes organizational meetings for directors and shareholders, incorporation fees, and accounting and legal fees related to the start-up (such as the creation of a corporate charter, bylaws, minutes of meetings, and the formulation of the terms to be included on original stock certificates). Costs incurred to create or issue stock certificates cannot be amortized as organizational costs, nor can the cost of transferring assets to the corporation.

3. *Partnership organization costs.* The same costs can be included in this category as for corporate organization costs. The cost of admitting or removing partners is not included, nor are the costs of syndication fees for marketing or issuing interests in the partnership.

The amortization period begins during the first month in which business operations are started. Any remaining costs yet to be amortized at the point when a business is sold can be deducted at the time of sale.

43.29   PARTNERSHIP TAXATION

A group of two or more people carrying on any sort of business without becoming incorporated is considered to be a partnership. An entity with these characteristics cannot be termed a partnership if it is an insurance company, a real estate investment trust, or a tax-exempt organization, or is owned by a local or regional government.

If the partnership takes the form of a *general partnership*, in which all of the partners are active, then each partner is liable for the negligence of any and all other partners, as well as for the liabilities of the partnership. To get around this significant problem, it is possible to create a *limited partnership*, in which limited partners are only liable for the funds they have invested as capital in the business, while a general partner, who operates the partnership on their behalf, is liable for all activities and losses. A limited partnership is subject to the IRS regulations governing passive activities (see the "Passive Activity Losses" section), which keeps the partnership from recognizing passive losses that exceed the income derived from any passive activities. Also, if the partnership has losses so large that they exceed the capital contributions of the partners (for example, the amount they have at risk in the business), then IRS rules will prohibit the recognition of any losses that exceed the amount that the partners have at risk.

A variation on the partnership concept is a *limited liability company*; this is an entity that files articles of incorporation, and whose members are not personally liable for the organization's liabilities.

A partnership is governed by a partnership agreement, which specifies how the ownership percentages of the partnership are determined, and under what circumstances and payment plans partners can be bought out by the remaining partners. The partnership agreement can specify preferential returns for some of the partners. If the partnership agreement is not clear about how income is to be distributed, then it will be based on the partners' relative contributions to the partnership. If there are variations in the proportional share of each partner during the tax year, perhaps due to additional contributions to the partnership, then the average share of each partner must be calculated and used to determine the proportional distribution of income among the partners at the end of the tax year; however, alternative arrangements for preferential returns, if specified in the partnership agreement, will override this calculation.

Every partnership must file an information return on Form 1065 that specifies its taxable income at the end of the year, as well as the identity of each partner and the amount of the income that is attributable to each one. The partnership must issue Schedule K-1 of Form 1065 to all partners on a timely basis, or else a penalty will be charged against the partnership for each K-1 form not issued. The K-1 form is used by each partner as a source of income or loss from the business that is then included in his or her personal income tax return. If the partnership does not file a tax return in a timely manner, then it can be assessed a penalty of $50 per partner for each month in which the return is late, up to a maximum of five months.

Even if the profits from a partnership are not distributed to its partners, the profits are still taxable income to the partners. This generally results in a minimum distribution to the partners each year, which allows them to pay their taxes, and which also keeps large amounts of money from accumulating within the business. If any funds are retained in the business rather than being distributed, they increase the capital contribution of the partners for tax purposes.

If a partnership experiences a loss, the share distributed to each partner will only be allowable to the extent that it offsets the adjusted basis in each partner's partnership interest. If the amount of the loss exceeds the adjusted basis, then it cannot be deducted in that year, but may be carried forward for potential offsets against future increases in the interests of the partners. This principle is based on the concept that a partner cannot lose more than his or her total interest in the partnership.

Partners may have to make estimated tax payments during the course of the tax year as a result of income from a partnership. If so, the estimated tax must, at a minimum, be the smaller of 90% of the expected partnership income for the year, or 100% of the total tax paid in the preceding year. Also, partners are not counted as employees of a partnership, and so must pay a self-employment tax.

A partnership can make a number of elections regarding the reporting of income. For example, it can choose among the accounting, cash, and hybrid methods of accounting. It can also choose between two types of MACRS depreciation, various types of revenue recognition, and different approaches for recognizing organizational expenses. These issues are dealt with throughout this chapter. The main point is that the accounting methodology choices available to a partnership are the same as those available to a corporation.

If a partner contributes money to a partnership, followed by a distribution to the partner from the partnership, the two transactions will be netted and treated as a sale of property, especially if the contribution is contingent upon the later distribution, and if the partner's right to the distribution is not impacted by the success of partnership operations. However, if the contribution and later distribution occur more than two years apart, then it is presumed that the transactions are separate and unrelated.

Distributions can be made to partners up to the amount of their adjusted basis in the company. The partnership will not recognize any gain or loss as a result of a distribution to its partners, since this is a flow-through of accumulated capital to them. If a distribution of property is made to the partners, they will not recognize a gain or loss on the transaction until they later dispose of it.

43.30 PASSIVE ACTIVITY LOSSES

Many individuals and some businesses passively participate in business activities that result in income or losses. They can claim passive activity losses on their tax returns based on these financial results. Passive participation is defined as having a trade or business activity in which one does not materially participate during the tax year, or participating in a rental activity (even if there is evidence of a substantial level of activity in the venture). One is considered to be an active investor if any of the following tests is true:

- One annually expends more than 500 hours of participation in the activity.
- One's participation comprises essentially all of the activity for a business.
- More than 100 hours of annual participation, which was at least as much as that of any other participant in the business.
- Materially participated in the business in any five of the last 10 tax years.
- Materially participated in a personal service business for any three previous tax years.

A limited partner is generally not considered to be materially involved in a business. A closely held corporation or a personal service corporation is considered to materially participate in a business if shareholders owning more than 50% of the corporation's shares materially engage in the business. Also, an investing entity is considered to be materially engaged in a business if it has an interest in an oil or gas well that is held directly or through an entity that does not reduce its liability.

Passive activity losses can only be claimed by individuals, estates, trusts, personal service corporations, and closely held "C" corporations. Conversely, passive activity losses cannot be claimed by grantor trusts, partnerships, and "S" corporations.

If passive activity losses have occurred, they can only be offset against passive activity gains. Activities that are defined by the IRS as *not* passive are gains on the sale of property that has not been used in a passive activity, investment income, and personal services income. If there is an excess credit from a passive loss after all offsets have been made against passive income, then the credit can be carried forward to the next tax year for a later offset. However, all passive losses that are carried forward can be recognized at the time when the passive investor liquidates the investment.

The total amount of a passive loss will be limited to the total amount for which a passive investor is at risk. For example, if an entity invests $1,000 in a business venture, then it is only at risk for $1,000, and cannot deduct more than that amount under any circumstances as a passive loss.

43.31 PROPERTY TAXES

Local governments use property tax assessments as one of their primary forms of tax receipt. Personal property taxes are assessed based on a company's level of reported fixed assets in the preceding year, and typically are paid once a year. In order to minimize this tax, the accounting department should regularly review the fixed asset list to see which items can be disposed of, thereby shrinking the taxable base of assets. Also, by increasing the capitalization limit, fewer items will be classified as assets, and so will also not be taxed.

Local taxing authorities can also impose a tax based on any real property owned by a business. The buildings and land that fall into this category will be appraised by the local assessor, with the resulting assessment being multiplied by a tax rate that is determined by the local government. The assessment can be challenged. If a recent assessment change results in a significant boost in the reported value of a business's real property, it is certainly worthwhile to engage the services of a private assessor to see if the new valuation can be reduced.

If a business rents its property, the tax on real property can either be absorbed by the landlord or passed through to the business, depending upon the terms of the lease. If subleasing from another business, the property tax can either be absorbed by that entity or passed through to the business, again depending on the terms of the lease.

43.32 RETIREMENT PLANS

There is an enormous variety of retirement plans available, each of which has a slightly different treatment under the tax laws, resulting in varying levels of investment risk to the employee or different levels of administrative activity. In this section, we will give a brief overview of each type of retirement plan.

A *qualified retirement* plan is one that is designed to observe all of the requirements of the Employee Retirement Income Security Act (ERISA), as well as all related IRS rulings. By observing these requirements, an employer can immediately deduct allowable contributions to the plan on behalf of plan participants. Also, income earned by the plan is not taxable to the plan. In addition, participants can exclude from taxable income any contributions they make to the plan, until such time as they choose to withdraw the funds from the plan. Finally, distributions to participants can, in some cases, be rolled over into an Individual Retirement Account (IRA), thereby prolonging the deferral of taxable income. The two types of qualified retirement plan are:

1. *Defined contribution plan.* This is a plan in which the employer is liable for a payment into the plan of a specific size, but not for the size of the resulting payments from the plan to participants. Thus, the participant bears the risk of the results of investment of the monies that have been deposited into the plan. The participant can mitigate or increase this risk by having control over a number of different investment options. The annual combined contribution to this type of plan by both the participant and employer is limited to the lesser of $49,000 or 100% of a participant's compensation (though this is restricted in several cases—see the following specific plan types). Funds received by participants in a steady income stream are taxed at ordinary income tax rates and cannot be rolled over into an IRA, whereas a lump sum payment can be rolled into an IRA. Some of the more common defined contribution plans are as follows:

   ○ *401(k) plan.* This is a plan set up by an employer, into which employees can contribute the lesser of $16,500 or 100% of their pay, which is excluded from taxation until such time as they remove the funds from the account. All earnings of the funds while held in the plan will also not be taxed until removed from the account. Employers can also match the funds contributed to the plan by employees, and also contribute the results of a profit-sharing plan to the employees' 401(k) accounts. The plan typically allows employees to invest the funds in their accounts in a number of different investment options, ranging from conservative money market funds to more speculative small cap or international stock funds; the employee holds the risk of how well or poorly an investment will perform—the employer has no liability for the performance of investments. Withdrawals from a 401(k) are intended to be upon retirement or the attainment of age 59 1/2, but can also be distributed as a loan (if the specific plan document permits it), or in the event of disability or death.

   ○ *403(b) plan.* This plan is similar to a 401(k) plan, except that it is designed specifically for charitable, religious, and educational organizations that fall under the tax-exempt status of 501(c)(3) regulations. It varies from a 401(k) plan in that participants can only invest in mutual funds and annuities, and also in that contributions can exceed the limit imposed under a 401(k) plan to the extent that participants can catch up on contributions that were below the maximum threshold in previous years.

   ○ *Employee stock ownership plan (ESOP).* The bulk of the contributions made to this type of plan are in the stock of the employing company. The employer calculates the amount of its contribution to the plan based on a proportion of total employee compensation, and uses the result to buy an equivalent amount of stock and deposit it in the ESOP. When an employee leaves the company, he or she will receive either company stock or the cash equivalent of the stock in payment of his or her vested interest.

   ○ *Money purchase plan.* The employer must make a payment into each employee's account in each year that is typically based on a percentage of total compensation paid to each participant. The payments must be made, irrespective of company profits (see next item).

○ *Profit sharing plan.* Contributions to this type of plan are intended to be funded from company profits, which is an incentive for employees to extend their efforts to ensure that profits will occur. However, many employers will make contributions to the plan even in the absence of profits. This plan is frequently linked to a 401(k) plan, so that participants can also make contributions to the plan.

2. *Defined benefit plan.* This plan itemizes a specific dollar amount that participants will receive, based on a set of rules that typically combine the number of years of employment and wages paid over the time period when each employee worked for the company. An additional factor may be the age of the participant at the time of retirement. Funds received by participants in a steady income stream are taxed at ordinary income tax rates, and cannot be rolled over into an IRA, whereas a lump sum payment can be rolled into an IRA. This type of plan is not favorable to the company, which guarantees the fixed payments made to retirees, and so bears the risk of unfavorable investment returns that may require additional payments into the plan in order to meet the fixed payment obligations. Some of the more common defined benefit plans are:

○ *Cash balance plan.* The employer contributes a *pay credit* (usually based on a proportion of that person's annual compensation) and an *interest credit* (usually linked to a publicly available interest rate index or well-known high-grade investment such as a U.S. government security) to each participant's account within the plan. Changes in plan value based on these credits do not impact the fixed benefit amounts to which participants are entitled.

○ *Target benefit plan.* Under this approach, the employer makes annual contributions into the plan based on the actuarial assumption at that time regarding the amount of funding needed to achieve a targeted benefit level (hence the name of the plan). However, there is no guarantee that the amount of the actual benefit paid will match the estimate upon which the contributions were based, since the return on invested amounts in the plan may vary from the estimated level at the time when the contributions were made.

The preceding plans all fall under the category of qualified retirement plans. However, if a company does not choose to follow ERISA and IRS guidelines, it can create a *nonqualified retirement plan*. By doing so, it can discriminate in favor of paying key personnel more than other participants or to the exclusion of other employees. All contributions to the plan and any earnings by the deposited funds will remain untaxed as long as they stay within the trust. However, the downside of this approach is that any contribution made to the plan by the company cannot be recorded as a taxable expense until the contribution is eventually paid out of the trust into which it was deposited and to the plan participant (which may be years in the future). Proceeds from the plan are taxable as ordinary income to the recipient and cannot be rolled over into an IRA. For more information about nonqualified retirement plans, see the "Deferred Compensation" section in this chapter.

An example of a nonqualified retirement plan is the 457 plan, which allows participants to defer up to $16,500 of their wages per year. It is restricted to the use of government and tax-exempt entities. Distributions from the plan are usually at retirement, but can also be at the point of the employee's departure from the organization, or a withdrawal can be requested on an emergency basis. A key difference between the 457 plan and the qualified retirement plans is that the funds deposited in the trust by the employer can be claimed by creditors, unless the employer is a government entity.

A plan that can fall into either the defined contribution or defined benefit plan category is the Keogh plan. It is available to self-employed people, partnerships, and owners of unincorporated businesses. When created, a Keogh plan can be defined as either a defined contribution or defined benefit plan. If the Keogh plan is set up as a defined contribution plan, the annual contribution is restricted to the lesser of 100% of the participant's annual compensation or $49,000. If the plan is set up as a defined benefit plan, the annual contribution is restricted to the lesser of 100% of the participant's average compensation for his or her highest three consecutive years, or $195,000 (as of 2009). It is not allowable to issue loans against a Keogh plan, but distributions from it can be rolled over into an IRA. Premature withdrawal penalties are similar to those for an IRA.

An employer may want neither to deal with the complex reporting requirements of a qualified retirement plan, nor set up a nonqualified plan. A very simple alternative is the *personal retirement account* (PRA), of which the most common is the individual retirement arrangement. The primary types of PRAs are:

- *Individual retirement arrangement (IRA).* This is a savings account that is set up for the specific use of one person who is less than 70 1/2 years old. Contributions to an IRA are limited to the lesser of $5,000 per year (or $6,000 if the person is more than 50 years old) or a person's total taxable compensation (which can be wages, tips, bonuses, commissions, and taxable alimony). There is no required minimum payment into an IRA. Contributions to an IRA are not tax deductible if the contributor also participates in an employer's qualified retirement plan, and his or her adjusted gross income is greater than $53,000 if single filer, $85,000 if filing a joint return. If a working spouse is not covered by an employer's qualified retirement plan, then he or she may make a fully deductible contribution of up to $5,000/$6,000 per year to the IRA, even if the other spouse has such coverage. However, this deduction is eliminated when a couple's adjusted gross income reaches $169,000, and begins to decline at $159,000. Earnings within the plan are shielded from taxation until distributed from it.

  It is mandatory to begin withdrawals from an IRA as of age 70 1/2; if distributions do not occur, then a penalty of 50% will be charged against the amount that was not distributed. When funds are withdrawn from an IRA prior to age 59 1/2 they will be taxed at ordinary income tax rates and will also be subject to a 10% excise tax. However, the excise tax will be waived if the participant dies, is disabled, is buying a home for the first time, or is paying for some types of higher education costs or medical insurance costs that exceed 7 1/2% of the participant's adjusted gross income (as well as any medical insurance premiums following at least one-quarter year of receiving unemployment benefits). The following list reveals the wide range of IRA accounts that can be set up:

  ○ *Education Savings Account.* This type of IRA is established for the express purpose of providing education to the beneficiary. Though contributions to this IRA are not exempt from taxable income, any earnings during the period when funds are stored in the savings account will be tax-free at the time when they are used to pay for the cost of education. The annual contribution limit into this account is $2,000, and it is limited to the time period prior to the beneficiary reaching the age of 18. The amount in this IRA can be moved to a different family member if the new beneficiary is less than 30 years old. The amount in the IRA must be distributed once the beneficiary reaches the age of 30. If a distribution is not for the express purpose of offsetting education expenses, then the distribution is taxable as ordinary income, and will also be charged a 10% excise tax.

○ *Inherited IRA.* This is either a Roth or traditional IRA that has been inherited from its deceased owner, with the recipient not being the deceased owner's spouse. After the owner's death, no more than five years can pass before the beneficiary receives a distribution, or an annuity can be arranged that empties the IRA no later than the beneficiary's life expectancy. This IRA is not intended to be a vehicle for ongoing contributions from the new beneficiary, so tax deductions are not allowed for any contributions made into it. Also, the funds in this IRA cannot be shifted into a rollover IRA, since this action would circumvent the preceding requirement to distribute the funds within five years.

○ *Rollover IRA.* This is an IRA that an individual sets up for the express purpose of receiving funds from a qualified retirement plan. There are no annual contribution limits for this type of IRA, since its purpose is to transfer a preexisting block of funds that could be quite large. Funds deposited in this account, as well as any earnings accumulating in the accounts, are exempt from taxation until removed from it. Rollover funds can also be transferred (tax-free) into another qualified retirement plan. A common use of the rollover account is to "park" funds from the qualified plan of a former employer until the individual qualifies for participation in the plan of a new employer, at which point the funds are transferred into the new employer's plan.

○ *Roth IRA.* Under this IRA, there are offsetting costs and benefits. On the one hand, any contribution to the IRA is not deductible; however, withdrawals from the account (including earnings) are not taxable at all, as long as the recipient is at least 59 1/2 years old, is disabled, uses the funds to buy a first-time home, or is made a beneficiary following the death of the IRA participant. Contributions are limited to $5,000 per year, and can be continued indefinitely, irrespective of the participant's age. However, no contribution is allowed once the participant's adjusted gross income reaches $176,000 for a joint filer, or $120,000 for a single filer, and will gradually decline beginning at $166,000 and $105,000, respectively.

○ *Savings incentive match plan for employees (SIMPLE).* Under this IRA format, an employer with no other retirement plan and who employs fewer than 100 employees can set up IRA accounts for its employees, into which employees can contribute up to $11,500 per year (or up to $14,000 if over 50 years old). The employee commits to make a matching contribution of up to 3% of the employee's pay, depending upon how much the employee has chosen to contribute. The employer also has the option of reducing its contribution percentage in two years out of every five consecutive years, or can commit to a standard 2% contribution for all eligible employees, even if they choose not to contribute to the plan. Vesting in the plan is immediate. The downside to this plan from an employee's perspective is that the excise tax assessment for a withdrawal within the first two years of participation is 25%, rather than the usual 10% that is assessed for other types of IRA accounts.

○ *Simplified employee pension.* This plan is available primarily for self-employed persons and partnerships, but is available to all types of business entities. It can only be established if no qualified retirement plan is already in use. The maximum contribution that a self-employed person can make is 20% of net earnings. The maximum contribution that an employer can make is the lesser of 25% of an employee's compensation, or $49,000. The amount paid is up to the discretion of the employer. The contribution is sent at once to an IRA that has been set up in the name of each employee and that is owned by the employee. Once the money arrives in the IRA, it falls under all of the previously noted rules for an IRA.

43.33 S CORPORATIONS

An "S" corporation has unique taxation and legal protection aspects that make it an ideal way to structure a business if there are a small number of shareholders. Specifically, it can only be created if there are no more than 75 shareholders, if only one class of stock is issued, and if all shareholders agree to the "S" corporation status. All of its shareholders must be either citizens or residents of the United States. Shareholders are also limited to individuals, estates, and some types of trusts and charities. Conversely, this means that "C" corporations and partnerships cannot be shareholders in an "S" corporation. The requirement for a single class of stock may prevent some organizations from organizing in this manner, for it does not allow for preferential returns or special voting rights by some shareholders.

The "S" corporation generally does not pay taxes. Instead, it passes reported earnings through to its shareholders, who report the income on their tax returns. This avoids the double taxation that arises in a "C" corporation, where a company's income is taxed, and then the dividends it issues to its shareholders are taxed as income to them a second time. An "S" corporation's reported income is passed through to shareholders on Schedule K-1 of Form 1120S. The amount of income is allocated to each shareholder on a simple per-share basis. If a shareholder has held stock in the corporation for less than a full year, then the allocation is on a per-share, per-day basis. The per-day part of this calculation assumes that a shareholder still holds the stock through and including the day when the stock is disposed of, while a deceased shareholder will be assumed to retain ownership through and including the day when he or she dies.

An "S" corporation is required to file a tax return, no matter how small its reported profit or loss may be, until it is completely dissolved. The required filing date is the 15th day of the month following the close of an "S" corporation's tax year, though it can be extended for an additional six months. If a tax payment is late (in the few instances where an "S" corporation owes a tax), then a late filing penalty equal to 5% of the tax owed per month may be imposed, up to a limit of 25%. There is also a penalty of $50 per shareholder if the "S" corporation fails to provide K-1 forms to the shareholders, which they need to report their proportional share of the corporation's income.

There are a few cases where an "S" corporation can owe taxes. For example, it can be taxed if it has accumulated earnings and profits from an earlier existence as a "C" corporation and its passive income (see the "Passive Activity Losses" section) is more than 25% of total gross receipts. It can also be liable for taxes on a few types of capital gains, recapture of the old investment tax credit, and LIFO recapture. If any of these taxes applies, then the "S" corporation must make quarterly estimated income tax payments. On the other hand, an "S" corporation is not subject to the alternative minimum tax.

If the management team of an "S" corporation wants to terminate its "S" status, the written consent of more than 50% of the shareholders is required, as well as a statement from the corporation to that effect. If the corporation wants to become an "S" corporation at a later date, there is a five-year waiting period from the last time before it can do so again, unless it obtains special permission from the IRS.

43.34   SALES AND USE TAXES

Sales taxes are imposed at the state, county, and city level—frequently by all three at once. It is also possible for a special tax to be added to the sales tax and applied to a unique region, such as for the construction of a baseball stadium or to support a regional mass transit system. The sales tax is multiplied by the price paid on goods and services on transactions occurring within the taxing area. However, the definition of goods and services that are required to be taxed will vary by state (not usually at the county or city level), and so must be researched at the local level to determine the precise basis of calculation. For example, some states do not tax food sales, on the grounds that this is a necessity whose cost should be reduced as much as possible, while other states include it in their required list of items to be taxed.

A company is required to charge sales taxes to its customers and remit the resulting receipts to the local state government, which will split out the portions due to the local county and city governments and remit these taxes on the company's behalf to those entities. If the company does not charge its customers for these taxes, it is still liable for them, and must pay the unbilled amounts to the state government, though it has the right to attempt to bill its customers after the fact for the missing sales taxes. This can be a difficult collection chore, especially if sales are primarily over the counter, where there are few transaction records that identify the customer. Also, a company is obligated to keep abreast of all changes in sales tax rates and charge its customers for the correct amount; if it does not do so, then it is liable to the government for the difference between what it actually charged and the statutory rate. If a company overcharges its customers, the excess must also be remitted to the government.

The state in which a company is collecting sales taxes can decide how frequently it wants the company to remit taxes. If there are only modest sales, the state may decide that the cost of paperwork exceeds the value of the remittances, and will only require an annual remittance. It is more common to have quarterly or monthly remittances. The state will review the dollar amount of remittances from time to time and adjust the required remittance frequency based on this information.

All government entities have the right to audit a company's books to see if the proper sales taxes are being charged, and so a company can theoretically be subject to three sales tax audits per year—one each from the city, county, and state revenue departments. Also, since these audits can come from any taxing jurisdiction in which a company does business, there could literally be thousands of potential audits.

The obligation to collect sales taxes is based on the concept of *nexus*, which is covered in the "Nexus" section of this chapter. If nexus exists, then sales taxes must be collected by the seller. If not, the recipient of purchased goods instead has an obligation to compile a list of items purchased and remit a use tax to the appropriate authority. The use tax is in the same amount as the sales tax. The only difference is that the remitting party is the buyer instead of the seller. Use taxes are also subject to audits by all taxing jurisdictions.

If the buyer of a company's products is including them in its own products for resale to another entity, then the buyer does not have to pay a sales tax to the seller. Instead, the buyer will charge a sales tax to the buyer of *its* final product. This approach is used under the theory that a sales tax should only be charged one time on the sale of a product. However, it can be a difficult chore to explain the lack of sales tax billings during an audit, so sales taxes should only be halted if a buyer sends a sales tax exemption form to the company, which should then be kept on file. The sales tax exemption certificate can be named a resale certificate instead, depending upon the issuing authority. It can also be issued to government entities, which are generally exempt from sales and use taxes. As a general rule, sales taxes should always be charged unless there is a sales tax exemption certificate on file—otherwise, the company will still be liable for the remittance of sales taxes in the event of an audit.

43.35 SALES RETURNS/BAD DEBTS

A company can reduce the amount of its gross revenue for tax reporting purposes based on the amount of returned goods from customers at the point when it has accepted liability for the returned goods. This means that any items that are still in dispute with customers at the end of the tax year cannot yet be removed from gross revenue.

There are two ways to reduce gross revenue by the amount of bad debts. The first is called the *specific charge-off method*, and is the most commonly used approach for tax purposes. Under this method, a company can deduct that portion of a specific bad debt that is uncollectible. The proof of uncollectibility is that the company must have taken reasonable steps to collect the debt or receivable. Good evidence of a bad debt is the bankruptcy of the debtor, though in this case the amount of the debt must be reduced by the amount of any asset distribution from the bankruptcy proceedings. Also, if a debtor has paid for part of its debt by transferring property to the company, then the amount of the debt should be reduced by the fair market value of the received property as of the date when the property was received (not the date when the property was later converted to cash).

Under the specific charge-off method, a company is limited in its deduction to that portion of a bad debt that the company also wrote off on its financial records during the tax year, which prevents a company from manipulating its tax records to achieve a lower tax liability than is indicated by its financial results. If the IRS audits a company's books and disallows a partial deduction for a bad debt, and the bad debt becomes fully worthless in a later year, then the company can still deduct the full amount in the tax year when it became fully worthless. A bad debt cannot be deducted in a year after the one in which it became worthless and was recorded as such in the company's financial records. Instead, a company must file for a refund by the later of seven years after the date when the original return was due, or two years from the date when it paid the tax for the year when the bad debt became worthless. If the refund is for a partially worthless debt, then the time frame in which to file for a refund drops to the later of three years from the date when an original return was due or two years from the date when the tax was paid.

The *nonaccrual experience method* can also be used to recognize bad debts for tax purposes, but only if a company uses the accrual method of accounting, and if the bad debt is related to the performance of services, and does not involve a debt on which interest or a penalty is charged for late payment. Under this method, a company does not accrue income that it expects to be uncollectible, thereby avoiding the need for a specific charge-off of bad debts.

If a company uses the cash method of accounting, it is not possible to ever take any bad debt deduction, since the related revenue is only recognized at the time of cash receipt, which never occurs if the billing is a bad debt.

43.36 SOCIAL SECURITY TAX

The standard tax rate that is not only withheld from employee pay, but also matched by employers, is 6.20% of gross pay. For a self-employed person, the rate is 12.40%. The maximum amount of wages and tips subject to the Social Security tax is $106,800; this figure is increased regularly, so be sure to review it each year.

43.37 STOCK APPRECIATION RIGHTS

A stock appreciation right (SAR) is a form of compensation that rewards an employee if there is an increase in the value of a company's stock, without actually owning the stock. For example, an employee is given 1,000 SARs at the company's current stock price. When the stock price later increases, the employee exercises the SARs at his or her option, resulting in a cash payment by the company to the employee for the net amount of the increase. No stock actually changes hands.

The employee recognizes no income and the company no expense at the time the SARs are granted. Tax recognition only occurs for both parties once the employee chooses to exercise the SARs and the company issues a payment for them. The company will treat this cost as a salary or bonus expense.

43.38 STOCK OPTIONS

A stock option gives an employee the right to buy stock at a specific price within a specific time period. Stock options come in two varieties: the *incentive stock option* (ISO) and the *nonqualified stock option* (NSO).

Incentive stock options are taxable to the employee neither at the time they are granted, nor at the time when the employee eventually exercises the option to buy stock. If the employee does not dispose of the stock within two years of the date of the option grant or within one year of the date when the option is exercised, then any resulting gain will be taxed as a long-term capital gain. However, if the employee sells the stock within one year of the exercise date, then any gain is taxed as ordinary income. An ISO plan typically requires an employee to exercise any vested stock options within 90 days of that person's voluntary or involuntary termination of employment.

The reduced tax impact associated with waiting until two years have passed from the date of option grant presents a risk to the employee that the value of the related stock will decline in the interim, thereby offsetting the reduced long-term capital gain tax rate achieved at the end of this period. To mitigate the potential loss in stock value, one can make a Section 83(b) election to recognize taxable income on the purchase price of the stock within 30 days following the date when an option is exercised, and withhold taxes at the ordinary income tax rate at that time. The employee will not recognize any additional income with respect to the purchased shares until they are sold or otherwise transferred in a taxable transaction, and the additional gain recognized at that time will be taxed at the long-term capital gains rate. It is reasonable to make the Section 83(b) election if the amount of income reported at the time of the election is small and the potential price growth of the stock is significant. On the other hand, it is not reasonable to take the election if there is a combination of high reportable income at the time of election (resulting in a large tax payment) and a minimal chance of growth in the stock price, or if the company can forfeit the options. The Section 83(b) election is not available to holders of options under an NSO plan.

The alternative minimum tax (AMT) must also be considered when dealing with an ISO plan. In essence, the AMT requires that an employee pay tax on the difference between the exercise price and the stock price at the time when an option is exercised, even if the stock is not sold at that time. This can result in a severe cash shortfall for the employee, who may only be able to pay the related taxes by selling the stock. This is a particular problem if the value of the shares subsequently drops, since there is now no source of high-priced stock that can be converted into cash in order to pay the required taxes. This problem arises frequently in cases where a company has just gone public, but employees are restricted from selling their shares for some time after the IPO date and run the risk of losing stock value during that interval. Establishing the amount of the gain reportable under AMT rules is especially difficult if a company's stock is not publicly held, since there is no clear consensus on the value of the stock. In this case, the IRS will use the value of the per-share price at which the last round of funding was concluded. When the stock is eventually sold, an AMT credit can be charged against the reported gain, but there can be a significant cash shortfall in the meantime. In order to avoid this situation, a employee could choose to exercise options at the point when the estimated value of company shares is quite low, thereby reducing the AMT payment; however, the employee must now find the cash to pay for the stock that he or she has just purchased, and also runs the risk that the shares will not increase in value and may become worthless.

An ISO plan is only valid if it follows these rules:

- Incentive stock options can only be issued to employees. A person must have been working for the employer at all times during the period that begins on the date of grant and ends on the day three months before the date when the option is exercised.

- The option term cannot exceed 10 years from the date of grant. The option term is only five years in the case of an option granted to an employee who, at the time the option is granted, owns stock that has more than 10% of the total combined voting power of all classes of stock of the employer.

- The option price at the time it is granted is not less than the fair market value of the stock. However, it must be 110% of the fair market value in the case of an option granted to an employee who, at the time the option is granted, owns stock that has more than 10% of the total combined voting power of all classes of stock of the employer.

- The total value of all options that can be exercised by any one employee in one year is limited to $100,000. Any amounts exercised that exceed $100,000 will be treated as a nonqualified stock option (to be covered shortly).

- The option cannot be transferred by the employee and can only be exercised during the employee's lifetime.

If the options granted do not include these provisions, or are granted to individuals who are not employees under the preceding definition, then the options must be characterized as nonqualified stock options.

A *nonqualified stock option* is not given any favorable tax treatment under the Internal Revenue Code (hence the name). It is also referred to as a *nonstatutory stock option*. The recipient of an NSO does not owe any tax on the date when options are granted, unless the options are traded on a public exchange. In that case, the options can be traded at once for value, and so tax will be recognized on the fair market value of the options on the public exchange as of the grant date. An NSO option will be taxed when it is exercised, based on the difference between the option price and the fair market value of the stock on that day. The resulting gain will be taxed as ordinary income. If the stock appreciates in value after the exercise date, then the incremental gain is taxable at the capital gains rate.

There are no rules governing an NSO, so the option price can be lower than the fair market value of the stock on the grant date. The option price can also be set substantially higher than the current fair market value at the grant date, which is called a *premium grant*. It is also possible to issue *escalating price options*, which use a sliding scale for the option price that changes in concert with a peer group index, thereby stripping away the impact of broad changes in the stock market and forcing the company to outperform the stock market in order to achieve any profit from granted stock options. Also, a *heavenly parachute* stock option can be created that allows a deceased option holder's estate up to three years in which to exercise his or her options.

Company management should be aware of the impact of both ISO and NSO plans on the company, not just employees. A company receives no tax deduction on a stock option transaction if it uses an ISO plan. However, if it uses an NSO plan, the company will receive a tax deduction equal to the amount of the income that the employee must recognize. If a company does not expect to have any taxable income during the stock option period, then it will receive no immediate value from having a tax deduction (though the deduction can be carried forward to offset income in future years), and so would be more inclined to use an ISO plan. This is a particularly common approach for companies that have not yet gone public. On the other hand, publicly held companies, which are generally more profitable and so must search for tax deductions, will be more inclined to sponsor an NSO plan. Research has shown that most employees who are granted either type of option will exercise it as soon as possible, which essentially converts the tax impact of the ISO plan into an NSO plan. For this reason also, many companies prefer to use NSO plans.

43.39   TAX RATE, CORPORATE

Exhibit 43.3 shows the tax rate schedule that should be used for determining a corporation's tax due on its 1120 form.

A qualified personal service corporation is taxed at a flat rate of 35% on taxable income. This situation arises when a corporation performs substantially all of its work on personal services, and at least 95% of the corporation's stock is owned by its employees, retired employees, or the estate of a deceased employee.

43.40   TAX YEAR

A company reports its taxable income to the IRS based on a tax year, which is determined at the time a company files its first tax return. This determination must be made by the due date when an entity's tax return is due following the end of the tax year. For a "C" corporation or "S" corporation, the due date is the 15th day of the third month following

Over	But Not Over	The Tax Is (Base Amount)		Percentage	Of the Amount Over:
$ 0	$ 50,000	—		15%	$ 0
50,000	75,000	$ 7,500	+	25%	50,000
75,000	100,000	13,750	+	34%	75,000
100,000	335,000	22,250	+	39%	100,000
335,000	10,000,000	113,900	+	34%	335,000
10,000,000	15,000,000	3,400,000	+	35%	10,000,000
15,000,000	18,333,333	5,150,000	+	38%	15,000,000
18,333,333	—	—		35%	0

Exhibit 43.3   IRS Corporate Tax Rate Schedule

the end of the tax year, while the due date for individuals, participants in a partnership, and shareholders in an "S" corporation is the 15th day of the fourth month after the end of the tax year.

The default period to use for a tax year is the calendar year, which is January 1 through December 31. Unless special permission is given, the calendar year must be used as the tax year for a sole proprietor, a shareholder in an "S" corporation, or a personal service corporation. A personal service corporation is a "C" corporation, primarily performs personal services (as defined by compensation costs for personal services activities being at least 50% of all compensation costs), and the owners are primarily owners who not only perform much of the services work, but who also own more than 10% of the company's stock. Personal services include activities in the areas of consulting, the performing arts, actuarial work, accounting, architecture, health and veterinary services, law, and engineering.

The rule for setting the tax year of a partnership is more complex; if one or multiple partners having the same tax year own a majority interest in the partnership, then the partnership must use their tax year; if there is no single tax year used by the majority partners, then the partnership must use the tax year of all its principal partners (those with a stake of at least 5%); if the partners do not share the same tax year, then the tax year used must be the one that results in the smallest amount of deferred partner income. This is calculated by determining the number of months remaining in each partner's tax year (using as the basis of calculation the earliest tax year-end among the partners), and multiplying this amount by the percentage share in partnership earnings for each partner. Then add up this calculation for all partners, and determine the tax year-end that will result in the smallest possible number. The result will generally be the earliest tax year-end among the partners that follows the existing partnership year-end.

The use of the calendar year as the tax year is also required if one does not keep sufficiently accurate tax-related records, use an annual accounting period, or if one's present tax year does not qualify as a fiscal year (which the IRS defines as 12 consecutive months ending on the last day of any month except December).

It is also possible to file for a 52- to 53-week tax year, as long as the fiscal year is maintained on the same basis. The 52- to 53-week year always ends on the same day of the week, which one can select. This can result in tax years that end on days other than the last day of the month. In order to file for this type of tax year with the IRS, one should include a statement with the first annual tax return that notes the month and day of the week on which its tax year will always end, and the date on which the tax year ends. It is possible to change to a 52- to 53-week tax year without IRS approval, as long as the new tax year still falls within the same month under which an entity currently has its tax year end, and a statement announcing the change is attached to the tax return for the year in which the change takes place.

The 52- to 53-week tax year presents a problem for the IRS, since it is more difficult to determine the exact date on which changes to its tax rules will apply to any entity that uses it. To standardize the date of the tax year-end for these entities, the IRS assumes that a 52- to 53-week tax year begins on the first day of the calendar month closest to the first day of its tax year, and ends on the last day of the calendar month closest to the last day of its tax year.

A company can apply to the IRS to have its tax year changed if there is a valid business purpose for doing so. When reviewing an application for this change, the IRS is primarily concerned with any possible distortion of income that will have an impact on taxable income. For example, a cause for concern would be shifting revenues into the following tax year, as would be the case if a company switched to a tax year that ended just prior to the main part of its selling season, thereby shifting much of its revenue (and taxable income) to a future period. To use the same example, this might also cause a major net operating loss during the short tax year that would result from the change, since much of the revenue would be removed from the year. In cases such as this, the IRS would not be inclined to approve a change in the tax year. If the IRS sees that the change will result in a neutral or positive change in reported income, then it will more favorably review any business reasons for supporting the change, such as timing the year-end to correspond with the conclusion of most business activities for the year (such as the use of January as a year-end for many retailing firms). Thus, the prime consideration for the IRS when reviewing a proposed change of tax year will always be its potential impact on tax receipts.

The one case in which the IRS will automatically approve a change in the tax year is the 25% test. Under this test, a company calculates the proportion of total sales for the last two months of the proposed tax year as compared to total revenues for the entire year. If this proportion is 25% or greater for all of the last three years, then the IRS will grant a change in the tax year to the requested year-end date. If a company does not yet have at least 47 months of reportable revenues upon which to base the calculation, then it cannot use this approach to apply for a change in its tax year.

A tax year must fall under the rules just stated, or else it is considered to be improper, and must be changed with IRS approval. For example, if a company were founded on the 13th day of the month, and the owner assumes that the fiscal and tax year will end exactly one year from that point (on the 12th day of the same month in the next year), this is an improper tax year, because it does not end on the last day of the month, nor does it fall under the rules governing a 52- to 53-week year. In such cases, a company must file an amended income tax return that is based on the calendar year and then get IRS approval to change to a tax year other than the calendar year (if the calendar year is not considered appropriate for some reason).

When a company either changes to a new tax year or is just starting operations, it is quite likely that it will initially have a short tax year. If so, it must report taxable income for that short period beginning on the first day after the end of the old tax year (or the start date of the organization, if it is a new one) and ending on the day before the first day of the new tax year. The key issue when reporting taxable income for a short tax year is that the amount subject to tax is not the reported net income for the short year, but rather the annualized amount. The annualized figure is used because it may place the company in a higher tax bracket. For example, if the Hawser Company has a short tax year of six months and has taxable income for that period of $50,000, it must first annualize the $50,000, bringing full-year taxable income to $100,000. The tax percentage is higher on $100,000 than on $50,000, resulting in a tax of $22,500 on the annualized figure. The Hawser Company then pays only that portion of the tax that would have accrued during its short tax year, which is half of the $22,500 annualized tax, or $11,250.

The tax calculation method for a short tax year can cause problems for those organizations that have highly seasonal revenue patterns, since they may have a very high level of income only during a few months of the year, and losses during the remaining months. If the short tax year falls into this high-revenue period, the company will find that by annualizing its income as per the tax rules, it will fall into a much higher tax bracket than would normally be the case, and pay considerably more taxes. This issue can be addressed in the following year by filing for a rebate. However, in case an uncomfortable cash shortfall occurs that may not be alleviated for some months, one should be aware of this problem in advance and attempt to plan the timing of the short tax year around it.

If a company wishes to change its tax year, it must obtain approval (with a few exceptions) from the IRS. To do so, complete and mail IRS Form 1128 by the 15th day of the second calendar month following the close of the short tax year. Do not actually change tax years until formal approval from the IRS has been received.

43.41 TRANSFER PRICING

Transfer pricing is a key tax consideration, because it can result in the permanent reduction of an organization's tax liability. The permanent reduction is caused by the recognition of income in different taxing jurisdictions that may have different tax rates.

The basic concept behind the use of transfer pricing to reduce one's overall taxes is that a company transfers its products to a division in another country at the lowest possible price if the income tax rate is lower in the other country, or at the highest possible price if the tax rate is higher. By selling to the division at a low price, the company will report a very high profit on the final sale of products in the other country, which is where that income will be taxed at a presumably lower income tax rate.

For example, Exhibit 43.4 shows a situation in which a company with a location in countries Alpha and Beta has the choice of selling goods either in Alpha or transferring them to Beta and selling them there. The company is faced with a corporate income tax rate of 40% in country Alpha. To permanently avoid some of this income tax, the company sells its products to another subsidiary in country Beta, where the corporate income tax rate is only 25%. By doing so, the company still earns a profit ($60,000) in Country Alpha, but the bulk of the profit ($125,000) now appears in country Beta. The net result is a consolidated income tax rate of just 28%.

	Country Alpha Location	Country Beta Location
Sales to subsidiary:		
Revenue	$1,000,000	
Cost of goods sold	$ 850,000	
Profit	$ 150,000	
Profit percentage	15%	
Sales outside of company:		
Revenue		$1,500,000
Cost of goods sold		$1,000,000
Profit		$ 500,000
Profit percentage		33%
Income tax percentage	40%	25%
Income tax	$ 60,000	$ 125,000
Consolidated income tax	$ 185,000	
Consolidated income tax percentage	28%	

EXHIBIT 43.4 INCOME TAX SAVINGS FROM TRANSFER PRICING

The IRS is well aware of this tax avoidance strategy and has developed tax rules that do not eliminate it, but that will reduce the leeway that an accountant has in altering reportable income. Under Section 482 of the IRS code, the IRS's preferred approach for developing transfer prices is to use the market rate as its basis. However, very few products can be reliably and consistently compared to the market rate, with the exception of commodities, because there are costing differences between them. Also, in many cases, products are so specialized (especially components that are custom-designed to fit into a larger product) that there is no market rate against which they can be compared. Even if there is some basis of comparison between a product and the average market prices for similar products, the accountant still has some leeway in which to alter transfer prices, because the IRS will allow one to add special charges that are based on the cost of transferring the products, or extra fees, such as royalty or licensing fees that are imposed for the subsidiary's use of the parent company's patents or trademarks, or for administrative charges related to the preparation of any documentation required to move products between countries. It is also possible to slightly alter the interest rates charged to subsidiaries (though not too far from market rates) for the use of funds sent to them from the parent organization.

If there is no basis upon which to create prices based on market rates, then the IRS's next most favored approach is to calculate the prices based upon the *work back method*. Under this approach, one begins at the end of the sales cycle by determining the price at which a product is sold to an outside customer, and then subtracts the subsidiary's standard markup percentage and its added cost of materials, labor, and overhead, which results in the theoretical transfer price. The work back method can result in a wide array of transfer prices, since a number of different costs can be subtracted from the final sale price, such as standard costs, actual costs, overhead costs based on different allocation measures, and overhead costs based on cost pools that contain different types of costs.

If that approach does not work, then the IRS's third most favored approach is the cost plus method. As the name implies, this approach begins at the other end of the production process and compiles costs from a product's initiation point. After all costs are added before the point of transfer, one then adds a profit margin to the product, thereby arriving at a transfer cost that is acceptable by the IRS. However, once again, the costs that are included in a product are subject to the same points of variation that were noted for the work back method. In addition, the profit margin added should be the standard margin added for any other company customer, but can be quite difficult to determine if there are a multitude of volume discounts, seasonal discounts, and so on. Consequently, the profit margin added to a product's initial costs can be subject to a great deal of negotiation.

An overriding issue to consider, no matter what approach is used to derive transfer prices, is that taxing authorities can become highly irritated if a company continually pushes the outer limits of acceptable transfer pricing rules in order to maximize its tax savings. When this happens, a company can expect continual audits and penalties on disputed items, as well as less favorable judgments related to any taxation issues. Consequently, it makes a great deal of sense to consistently adopt pricing policies that result in reasonable tax savings, are fully justifiable to the taxing authorities of all involved countries, and do not push the boundaries of acceptable pricing behavior.

Another transfer pricing issue that can modify a company's pricing strategy is the presence of any restrictions on cash flows out of a country in which it has a subsidiary. In these instances, it may be necessary to report the minimum possible amount of taxable income at the subsidiary, irrespective of the local tax rate. The reason is that the only way for a company to retrieve funds from the country is through the medium of an account receivable, which must be maximized by billing the subsidiary the highest possible amount for transferred goods. In this case, tax planning takes a back seat to cash flow planning.

Yet another issue that may drive a company to set pricing levels that do not result in reduced income taxes is that a subsidiary may have to report high levels of income in order to qualify for a loan from a local credit institution. This is especially important if the country in which the subsidiary is located has restrictions on the movement of cash, so that the parent company would be unable to withdraw loans that it makes to the subsidiary. As was the case for the last item, cash flow planning is likely to be more important than income tax reduction.

A final transfer pricing issue to be aware of is that the method for calculating taxable income may vary in other countries. This may falsely lead one to believe that another country has a lower tax rate. A closer examination of how taxable income is calculated might reveal that some expenses are restricted or not allowed at all, resulting in an actual tax rate that is much higher than originally expected. Consultation with a tax expert for the country in question prior to setting up any transfer pricing arrangements is the best way to avoid this problem.

43.42 UNEMPLOYMENT TAXES

Both the state and federal governments will charge a company a fixed percentage of its payroll each year for the expense of unemployment funds that are used to pay former employees who have been released from employment. The state governments administer the distribution of these funds and will compile an experience rating on each company, based on the number of employees it has laid off in the recent past. Based on this experience rating, it can require a company to submit larger or smaller amounts to the state unemployment fund in future years. This can become a considerable burden if a company has a long history of layoffs. Consequently, one should consider the use of temporary employees or outsourcing if this will give a firm the ability to retain a small number of key employees and avoid layoffs while still handling seasonal changes in workloads. Also, if a company is planning to acquire another entity, but plans to lay off a large number of the acquiree's staff once the acquisition is completed, it may make more sense to only acquire the acquiree's assets and selectively hire a few of its employees, thereby retaining a pristine unemployment experience rating with the local state government.

The federal unemployment tax is imposed on a company if it has paid employees at least $1,500 in any calendar quarter, or had at least one employee for some portion of a day within at least 20 weeks of the year. In short, nearly all companies will be required to remit federal unemployment taxes. For the 2009 calendar year, the tax rate was 6.2% of the first $7,000 paid to each employee; this tends to concentrate most federal unemployment tax remittances into the first quarter of the calendar year. In many states, one can take a credit against the federal unemployment tax for up to 5.4% of taxable wages, which results in a net federal unemployment tax of only .8%. This tax should be computed and remitted on a quarterly basis—if the quarterly total is $100 or less, it may be carried forward to the next quarter rather than be remitted.

If a company is shifting to a new legal entity, perhaps because of a shift from a partnership to a corporation, or from an "S" corporation to a "C" corporation, it will probably have to set itself up with a new unemployment tax identification number with the local state authorities. This is a problem if the organization being closed down had an unusually good experience rating, since the company will be assigned a poorer one until a new experience rating can be built up over time, which will result in higher unemployment taxes in the short term. To avoid this problem, one should contact the local unemployment taxation office to request that the old company's experience rating be shifted to the new one.

43.43 WARRANTY EXPENSES

An accountant may be tempted to reduce the amount of taxable income by increasing the reserve for warranty costs, or to manipulate the reserve over time in order to report "managed" income figures. The IRS has foreseen this issue by banning the recording of a warranty reserve for the purposes of calculating taxable income. Instead, warranty costs can only be recognized as they are incurred, thereby avoiding the temptation to manipulate taxable income in this area.

43.44 SUMMARY

The key goal when dealing with any of the preceding tax issues is to steer a course that minimizes or delays a company's tax liability, preferably without also reducing the level of income listed on its financial statements.

Using a questionable approach to reporting taxable income can result in fines and penalties so large that the savings one was trying to achieve are thoroughly reversed. It is therefore highly recommended that a company work with a professional tax accountant or lawyer to determine the best course of action when dealing with each of the tax issues noted in this chapter, in order to adopt a course of action that meets the company's tax goals while also staying within the intent of the tax law.

THE CHART OF ACCOUNTS

This appendix describes the types of account numbering formats that can be used to construct a chart of accounts and also lists sample charts of accounts that use each of the formats. All of the charts of accounts shown in this appendix follow the same general sequence of account coding, which itemizes the accounts in the balance sheet first and the income statement second. That sequence looks like this:

Current assets

Fixed assets

Other assets

Current liabilities

Long-term liabilities

Equity accounts

Revenue

Cost of goods sold

Selling, general and administrative expenses

Income taxes

Extraordinary items

A.1 THREE-DIGIT ACCOUNT CODE STRUCTURE

A three-digit account code structure allows one to create a numerical sequence of accounts that contains up to 1,000 potential accounts. It is useful for small businesses that have no predefined departments or divisions that must be broken out separately. A sample chart of accounts using this format follows.

Account Number	Description
010	Cash
020	Petty cash
030	Accounts receivable

(Continued)

Account Number	Description
040	Reserve for bad debts
050	Marketable securities
060	Raw materials inventory
070	Work-in-process inventory
080	Finished goods inventory
090	Reserve for obsolete inventory
100	Fixed assets—Computer equipment
110	Fixed assets—Computer software
120	Fixed assets—Furniture and fixtures
130	Fixed assets—Leasehold improvements
140	Fixed assets—Machinery
150	Accumulated depreciation—Computer equipment
160	Accumulated depreciation—Computer software
170	Accumulated depreciation—Furniture and fixtures
180	Accumulated depreciation—Leasehold improvements
190	Accumulated depreciation—Machinery
200	Other assets
300	Accounts payable
310	Accrued payroll liability
320	Accrued vacation liability
330	Accrued expenses liability—Other
340	Unremitted sales taxes
350	Unremitted pension payments
360	Short-term notes payable
370	Other short-term liabilities
400	Long-term notes payable
500	Capital stock
510	Retained earnings
600	Revenue
700	Cost of goods sold—Materials
710	Cost of goods sold—Direct labor
720	Cost of goods sold—Manufacturing supplies
730	Cost of goods sold—Applied overhead
800	Bank charges
805	Benefits
810	Depreciation
815	Insurance
825	Office supplies
830	Salaries and wages
835	Telephones
840	Training
845	Travel and entertainment
850	Utilities
855	Other expenses
860	Interest expense
900	Extraordinary items

Notice how each clearly definable block of accounts begins with a different set of account numbers. For example, current liabilities begin with "300," revenues begin with "600," and cost of goods sold items begin with "700." This not only makes it easier to navigate through the chart of accounts, but is also mandated by many computerized accounting software packages.

A.2   FIVE-DIGIT ACCOUNT CODE STRUCTURE

A five-digit account code structure is designed for those organizations with clearly defined departments, each of which is tracked with a separate income statement. This format uses the same account codes for the balance sheet accounts that we just saw for three-digit account codes, but replicates at least the operating expenses for each department (and sometimes for the revenue accounts, too). An example of this format is as follows, using the engineering and sales departments to illustrate the duplication of accounts.

Account Number	Department	Description
00-010	xxx	Cash
00-020	xxx	Petty cash
00-030	xxx	Accounts receivable
00-040	xxx	Reserve for bad debts
00-050	xxx	Marketable securities
00-060	xxx	Raw materials inventory
00-070	xxx	Work-in-process inventory
00-080	xxx	Finished goods inventory
00-090	xxx	Reserve for obsolete inventory
00-100	xxx	Fixed assets—Computer equipment
00-110	xxx	Fixed assets—Computer software
00-120	xxx	Fixed assets—Furniture and fixtures
00-130	xxx	Fixed assets—Leasehold improvements
00-140	xxx	Fixed assets—Machinery
00-150	xxx	Accumulated depreciation—Computer equipment
00-160	xxx	Accumulated depreciation—Computer software
00-170	xxx	Accumulated depreciation—Furniture and fixtures
00-180	xxx	Accumulated depreciation—Leasehold improvements
00-190	xxx	Accumulated depreciation—Machinery
00-200	xxx	Other assets
00-300	xxx	Accounts payable
00-310	xxx	Accrued payroll liability
00-320	xxx	Accrued vacation liability
00-330	xxx	Accrued expenses liability—Other
00-340	xxx	Unremitted sales taxes
00-350	xxx	Unremitted pension payments
00-360	xxx	Short-term notes payable
00-370	xxx	Other short-term liabilities
00-400	xxx	Long-term notes payable
00-500	xxx	Capital stock
00-510	xxx	Retained earnings
00-600	xxx	Revenue
00-700	xxx	Cost of goods sold—Materials
00-710	xxx	Cost of goods sold—Direct labor
00-720	xxx	Cost of goods sold—Manufacturing supplies
00-730	xxx	Cost of goods sold—Applied overhead
10-800	Engineering	Bank charges
10-805	Engineering	Benefits
10-810	Engineering	Depreciation
10-815	Engineering	Insurance
10-825	Engineering	Office supplies
10-830	Engineering	Salaries and wages
10-835	Engineering	Telephones
10-840	Engineering	Training
10-845	Engineering	Travel and entertainment

(Continued)

Account Number	Department	Description
10-850	Engineering	Utilities
10-855	Engineering	Other expenses
10-860	Engineering	Interest expense
20-800	Sales	Bank charges
20-805	Sales	Benefits
20-810	Sales	Depreciation
20-815	Sales	Insurance
20-825	Sales	Office supplies
20-830	Sales	Salaries and wages
20-835	Sales	Telephones
20-840	Sales	Training
20-845	Sales	Travel and entertainment
20-850	Sales	Utilities
20-855	Sales	Other expenses
20-860	Sales	Interest expense
00-900	xxx	Extraordinary items

In this example, all expense accounts are replicated for every department. This does not mean, however, that all accounts must be *used* for every department. For example, it is most unlikely that bank charges will be ascribed to either the engineering or sales departments. Accordingly, those accounts that are not to be used can be rendered inactive in the accounting system, so that they never appear in the general ledger.

A.3   SEVEN-DIGIT ACCOUNT CODE STRUCTURE

A seven-digit account code structure is used by those companies that not only have multiple departments, but also multiple divisions or locations, for each of which the management team wants to record separate accounting information. This requires the same coding structure used for the five-digit system, except that two digits are placed in front of the code to signify a company division. These new digits also apply to balance sheet accounts, since most organizations will want to track assets and liabilities by division. The following chart of accounts, which identifies accounts for divisions in Atlanta and Seattle, and which continues to use the engineering and sales departments, is an example of how the seven-digit account code structure is compiled.

Account No.	Division	Department	Description
10-00-010	Atlanta	xxx	Cash
10-00-020	Atlanta	xxx	Petty cash
10-00-030	Atlanta	xxx	Accounts receivable
10-00-040	Atlanta	xxx	Reserve for bad debts
10-00-050	Atlanta	xxx	Marketable securities
10-00-060	Atlanta	xxx	Raw materials inventory
10-00-070	Atlanta	xxx	Work-in-process inventory
10-00-080	Atlanta	xxx	Finished goods inventory
10-00-090	Atlanta	xxx	Reserve for obsolete inventory
10-00-100	Atlanta	xxx	Fixed assets—Computer equipment
10-00-110	Atlanta	xxx	Fixed assets—Computer software
10-00-120	Atlanta	xxx	Fixed assets—Furniture and fixtures
10-00-130	Atlanta	xxx	Fixed assets—Leasehold improvements
10-00-140	Atlanta	xxx	Fixed assets—Machinery

(Continued)

Account No.	Division	Department	Description
10-00-150	Atlanta	xxx	Accumulated depreciation—Computer equipment
10-00-160	Atlanta	xxx	Accumulated depreciation—Computer software
10-00-170	Atlanta	xxx	Accumulated depreciation—Furniture and fixtures
10-00-180	Atlanta	xxx	Accumulated depreciation—Leasehold improvements
10-00-190	Atlanta	xxx	Accumulated depreciation—Machinery
10-00-200	Atlanta	xxx	Other assets
10-00-300	Atlanta	xxx	Accounts payable
10-00-310	Atlanta	xxx	Accrued payroll liability
10-00-320	Atlanta	xxx	Accrued vacation liability
10-00-330	Atlanta	xxx	Accrued expenses liability—other
10-00-340	Atlanta	xxx	Unremitted sales taxes
10-00-350	Atlanta	xxx	Unremitted pension payments
10-00-360	Atlanta	xxx	Short-term notes payable
10-00-370	Atlanta	xxx	Other short-term liabilities
10-00-400	Atlanta	xxx	Long-term notes payable
10-00-500	Atlanta	xxx	Capital stock
10-00-510	Atlanta	xxx	Retained earnings
10-00-600	Atlanta	xxx	Revenue
10-00-700	Atlanta	xxx	Cost of goods sold—Materials
10-00-710	Atlanta	xxx	Cost of goods sold—Direct labor
10-00-720	Atlanta	xxx	Cost of goods sold—Manufacturing supplies
10-00-730	Atlanta	xxx	Cost of goods sold—Applied overhead
10-10-800	Atlanta	Engineering	Bank charges
10-10-805	Atlanta	Engineering	Benefits
10-10-810	Atlanta	Engineering	Depreciation
10-10-815	Atlanta	Engineering	Insurance
10-10-825	Atlanta	Engineering	Office supplies
10-10-830	Atlanta	Engineering	Salaries and wages
10-10-835	Atlanta	Engineering	Telephones
10-10-840	Atlanta	Engineering	Training
10-10-845	Atlanta	Engineering	Travel and entertainment
10-10-850	Atlanta	Engineering	Utilities
10-10-855	Atlanta	Engineering	Other expenses
10-10-860	Atlanta	Engineering	Interest expense
10-20-800	Atlanta	Sales	Bank charges
10-20-805	Atlanta	Sales	Benefits
10-20-810	Atlanta	Sales	Depreciation
10-20-815	Atlanta	Sales	Insurance
10-20-825	Atlanta	Sales	Office supplies
10-20-830	Atlanta	Sales	Salaries and wages
10-20-835	Atlanta	Sales	Telephones
10-20-840	Atlanta	Sales	Training
10-20-845	Atlanta	Sales	Travel and entertainment
10-20-850	Atlanta	Sales	Utilities
10-20-855	Atlanta	Sales	Other expenses
10-20-860	Atlanta	Sales	Interest expense
10-00-900	Atlanta	xxx	Extraordinary items
20-00-010	Seattle	xxx	Cash
20-00-020	Seattle	xxx	Petty cash
20-00-030	Seattle	xxx	Accounts receivable
20-00-040	Seattle	xxx	Reserve for bad debts
20-00-050	Seattle	xxx	Marketable securities
20-00-060	Seattle	xxx	Raw materials inventory
20-00-070	Seattle	xxx	Work-in-process inventory

(Continued)

Account No.	Division	Department	Description
20-00-080	Seattle	xxx	Finished goods inventory
20-00-090	Seattle	xxx	Reserve for obsolete inventory
20-00-100	Seattle	xxx	Fixed assets—Computer equipment
20-00-110	Seattle	xxx	Fixed assets—Computer software
20-00-120	Seattle	xxx	Fixed assets—Furniture and fixtures
20-00-130	Seattle	xxx	Fixed assets—Leasehold improvements
20-00-140	Seattle	xxx	Fixed assets—Machinery
20-00-150	Seattle	xxx	Accumulated depreciation—Computer equipment
20-00-160	Seattle	xxx	Accumulated depreciation—Computer software
20-00-170	Seattle	xxx	Accumulated depreciation—Furniture and fixtures
20-00-180	Seattle	xxx	Accumulated depreciation—Leasehold improvements
20-00-190	Seattle	xxx	Accumulated depreciation—Machinery
20-00-200	Seattle	xxx	Other assets
20-00-300	Seattle	xxx	Accounts payable
20-00-310	Seattle	xxx	Accrued payroll liability
20-00-320	Seattle	xxx	Accrued vacation liability
20-00-330	Seattle	xxx	Accrued expenses liability—other
20-00-340	Seattle	xxx	Unremitted sales taxes
20-00-350	Seattle	xxx	Unremitted pension payments
20-00-360	Seattle	xxx	Short-term notes payable
20-00-370	Seattle	xxx	Other short-term liabilities
20-00-400	Seattle	xxx	Long-term notes payable
20-00-500	Seattle	xxx	Capital stock
20-00-510	Seattle	xxx	Retained earnings
20-00-600	Seattle	xxx	Revenue
20-00-700	Seattle	xxx	Cost of goods sold—Materials
20-00-710	Seattle	xxx	Cost of goods sold—Direct labor
20-00-720	Seattle	xxx	Cost of goods sold—Manufacturing supplies
20-00-730	Seattle	xxx	Cost of goods sold—Applied overhead
20-10-800	Seattle	Engineering	Engineering—Bank charges
20-10-805	Seattle	Engineering	Engineering—Benefits
20-10-810	Seattle	Engineering	Engineering—Depreciation
20-10-815	Seattle	Engineering	Engineering—Insurance
20-10-825	Seattle	Engineering	Engineering—Office supplies
20-10-830	Seattle	Engineering	Engineering—Salaries and wages
20-10-835	Seattle	Engineering	Engineering—Telephones
20-10-840	Seattle	Engineering	Engineering—Training
20-10-845	Seattle	Engineering	Engineering—Travel and entertainment
20-10-850	Seattle	Engineering	Engineering—Utilities
20-10-855	Seattle	Engineering	Engineering—Other expenses
20-10-860	Seattle	Engineering	Engineering—Interest expense
20-20-800	Seattle	Sales	Sales—Bank charges
20-20-805	Seattle	Sales	Sales—Benefits
20-20-810	Seattle	Sales	Sales—Depreciation
20-20-815	Seattle	Sales	Sales—Insurance
20-20-825	Seattle	Sales	Sales—Office supplies
20-20-830	Seattle	Sales	Sales—Salaries and wages
20-20-835	Seattle	Sales	Sales—Telephones
20-20-840	Seattle	Sales	Sales—Training
20-20-845	Seattle	Sales	Sales—Travel and entertainment
20-20-850	Seattle	Sales	Sales—Utilities
20-20-855	Seattle	Sales	Sales—Other expenses
20-20-860	Seattle	Sales	Sales—Interest expense
20-00-900	Seattle	xxx	Extraordinary items

JOURNAL ENTRIES

This appendix contains a comprehensive list of every journal entry that an accountant is likely to deal with. The entries are listed in alphabetical order, and include explanatory text. This text may be sufficient for one to copy into actual journal entry descriptions, with slight modifications. The text makes additional explanatory notations where necessary, but the main focus is on presenting a brief summary of each entry. The journal entries are listed under general topic headings, which are as follows:

- Acquisitions
- Bill and hold transactions

- Bank reconciliation
- Current liabilities
- Debt, convertible
- Debt extinguishment
- Debt issued with stock warrants
- Debt security transfers among portfolios
- Dividends
- Effective interest method
- Employee stock ownership plan (ESOP)
- Equity method of accounting for investments
- Equity security transfers between available-for-sale and trading portfolios
- Fixed assets
- Foreign currency
- Intangible assets
- Inventory adjustments
- Inventory in transit
- Inventory valuation
- Investments in debt securities
- Leases—lessee accounting
- Leases—lessor accounting
- Long-term construction contracts
- Marketable equity securities
- Notes and bonds
- Options
- Pensions
- Receivables
- Revenue recognition when right of return exists
- Revenue, installment
- Revenue, service
- Sale-leaseback transactions
- Stock
- Stock appreciation rights
- Stock subscriptions
- Taxes
- Treasury stock
- Warrants

A set of accounts is listed for each sample journal entry, which may vary somewhat from the titles of accounts used in one's company. If there are a wide range of possible entries to different accounts, then this is noted with an entry in brackets, such as "[Salaries—itemize by department]." A triple "x" is noted under the debit or credit heading for each entry, denoting the most likely entry that would be made. If there is a reasonable chance that either a debit or credit entry would be made, then this is noted in the description.

There are a few instances where journal entries should be reversed in the following accounting period. When this is necessary, a warning note is attached to the bottom of the relevant journal entries.

B.1   ACQUISITIONS

To record an acquisition using the fair market value of assets and liabilities, with an entry to goodwill that records the difference between this total and the price paid.

	Debit	Credit
Accounts receivable	xxx	
Marketable securities (current market value)	xxx	
Inventory (lower of cost or market)	xxx	
Computer equipment (appraised value)	xxx	
Computer software (appraised value)	xxx	
Furniture & fixtures (appraised value)	xxx	
Manufacturing equipment (appraised value)	xxx	
Goodwill	xxx	
Accounts payable		xxx
Debt (book value)		xxx
Common stock		xxx
Additional paid-in capital		xxx

Negative Goodwill Offset

To record the offsetting of negative goodwill against accounts that do not have to be carried at fair value. Since the accounts that must be carried at fair value include cash, receivables, and inventory, the primary asset left for offsetting purposes is usually fixed assets.

	Debit	Credit
Negative goodwill	xxx	
Fixed assets		xxx

If there are not sufficient assets available for the complete offsetting of negative goodwill, then the remaining balance of negative goodwill is recognized as an extraordinary item, as shown next.

	Debit	Credit
Negative goodwill	xxx	
Fixed assets		xxx
Extraordinary item—gain on purchase		xxx

Write-off of Impaired Goodwill

If the fair value of a reporting unit is less than its book value, then some portion of the goodwill asset originally created as part of the acquisition of that reporting unit must be charged to expense in the current period. The entry is shown next.

	Debit	Credit
Impaired goodwill expense	xxx	
Goodwill		xxx

Increased Investment in Subsidiary

If the acquiring entity does not initially purchase all outstanding shares of an acquiree but later purchases additional shares, then the additional payment is recorded as an increase in the investment in the subsidiary. The entry is shown next.

	Debit	Credit
Investment in subsidiary	xxx	
Cash		xxx

Spin-off of Subsidiary

When a parent company spins off a subsidiary to its shareholders in which it held a majority ownership interest, it must remove the book value of the subsidiary's assets and liabilities from its books. If the net book value of the subsidiary is positive, the parent company records this as a retained earnings reduction, as shown next.

	Debit	Credit
Accounts payable	xxx	
Debt	xxx	
Other liabilities	xxx	
Retained earnings	xxx	
Cash		xxx
Accounts receivable		xxx
Inventory		xxx
Fixed assets		xxx
Other assets		xxx

If the net book value of the subsidiary is negative, the parent company records this as an addition to the additional paid-in capital account, as shown next.

	Debit	Credit
Accounts payable	xxx	
Debt	xxx	
Other liabilities	xxx	
Cash		xxx
Accounts receivable		xxx
Inventory		xxx
Fixed assets		xxx
Other assets		xxx
Additional paid-in capital		xxx

B.2   BILL AND HOLD TRANSACTIONS

A common problem with bill and hold transactions is that the sale is recorded, but the subtraction from inventory of the items sold is not, resulting in a sale with a 100% gross margin. To avoid this, use the second part of the following journal entry to shift the sold inventory items into a special cost of goods sold account that clearly identifies the items sold. When the items are eventually shipped to the customer, the third journal entry is used to shift the expense into the regular cost of goods sold account. By using this approach, one can monitor the "Cost of Goods Sold—Bill and Hold" account to determine which billed inventory items have not yet been shipped.

	Debit	Credit
Accounts receivable	xxx	
Sales		xxx
Cost of goods sold—bill and hold	xxx	
Inventory		xxx
Cost of goods sold	xxx	
Cost of goods sold—bill and hold		xxx

B.3   BANK RECONCILIATION

To adjust the accounting records to reflect differences between the book and bank records. The cash entry is listed as a credit, on the assumption that bank-related expenses outweigh the interest income.

	Debit	Credit
Bank charges	xxx	
Credit card charges	xxx	
Interest income		xxx
Cash		xxx

B.4   CURRENT LIABILITIES

Accrue benefits. To accrue for all employee benefit expenses incurred during the month, for which an associated payable entry has not yet been made.

	Debit	Credit
Medical insurance expense	xxx	
Dental insurance expense	xxx	
Disability insurance expense	xxx	
Life insurance expense	xxx	
Accrued benefits		xxx

This entry should be *reversed* in the following accounting period.

Accrue bonuses. To record an estimated bonus amount. This entry assumes that a separate bonus expense account is charged, though it is also common practice to charge a salaries expense account. The accrual is reversed when the bonus is actually paid.

	Debit	Credit
Bonus expense	xxx	
Accrued salaries		xxx

Accrue commissions. To accrue the estimated commission expense prior to payment. The liability is recorded in an accrued salaries account in order to conserve the number of liability accounts, but can also be recorded in a separate accrued commissions account. This entry is typically reversed in the following accounting period to offset the actual commission payment.

	Debit	Credit
Commission expense	xxx	
Accrued salaries		xxx

Accrue property taxes. To accrue for the property tax liability incurred during the accounting period based on the known base of fixed assets.

	Debit	Credit
Property tax expense	xxx	
Property tax payable		xxx

This entry *should not be reversed* in the following accounting period, since the tax payment will not normally occur in the following period, but instead only once or twice per year. The actual payment should be charged directly against the accrual account with the following entry:

	Debit	Credit
Property tax payable	xxx	
Cash		xxx

Accrue royalties. To accrue the amount of royalties due to a supplier that have been earned but are not yet due for payment. This entry is reversed when the royalty payment is made.

	Debit	Credit
Royalty expense	xxx	
Accrued royalty liability		xxx

Accrue salaries and wages. To accrue for salaries and wages earned through the end of the accounting period, but not yet paid to employees as of the end of the accounting period.

	Debit	Credit
Direct labor expense	xxx	
[Salaries—itemize by department]	xxx	
Payroll tax expense	xxx	
Accrued salaries		xxx
Accrued payroll taxes		xxx

This entry should be *reversed* in the following accounting period.

Accrue vacation pay. To accrue vacation pay earned by employees, but not yet used by them, subject to the year-end maximum vacation carryforward limitation. The same entry can be used to record accrued sick time.

	Debit	Credit
Payroll taxes	xxx	
[Salaries—itemize by department]	xxx	
Accrued vacation pay		xxx

This entry *should not be reversed* in the following accounting period, since the vacation time may not be used in the following period. Instead, the actual vacation-related payment should be charged directly against the accrual account.

Accrue warranty claims. To accrue a reserve for warranty claims when a sale is made.

	Debit	Credit
Warranty expense	xxx	
Accrued warranty liability		xxx

Record customer advances. To record the liability associated with a customer advance prior to completion of services or delivery of goods to the customer. The second entry assumes that an advance is actually a deposit on the use of a company asset and will be returned once the usage period is completed.

	Debit	Credit
Cash	xxx	
Customer advances		xxx
Cash	xxx	
Customer deposits		xxx

B.5 DEBT, CONVERTIBLE

Record conversion of convertible debt to equity, book value method. If bondholders wish to convert their bonds into company stock, the following entry is used, on the assumption that the remaining balance of the bonds represents the value of the resulting equity.

	Debit	Credit
Bonds payable	xxx	
Premium on bonds payable [if premium existed]	xxx	
Discount on bonds payable [if discount existed]		xxx
Capital stock at par value		xxx
Additional paid-in capital		xxx

Record conversion of convertible debt to equity, market value method. This is a less-used alternative to the preceding book value method, under which any new stock issuance is valued at the market rate. The entry includes a gain or loss to reflect the difference between the market price of the equity and the book value of the bonds being converted, with the offset to the gain or loss being recorded in the Additional paid-in capital account.

	Debit	Credit
Bonds payable	xxx	
Loss on bond conversion [if any]	xxx	
Premium on bonds payable [if premium existed]	xxx	
Gain on bond redemption [if any]		xxx
Discount on bonds payable [if discount existed]		xxx
Capital stock at par value		xxx
Additional paid-in capital		xxx

Record issuance of convertible debt with strike price already in the money. This entry is used to record the intrinsic value of the conversion feature at the time of bond issuance, which is based on the difference between the strike price and the fair market value of the stock, multiplied by the number of shares into which the debt can be converted. This intrinsic value is added to the Additional paid-in capital account.

	Debit	Credit
Cash	xxx	
Discount on bonds payable [if applicable]	xxx	
Premium on bonds payable [if applicable]		xxx
Bonds payable		xxx
Additional paid-in capital		xxx

Record issuance of convertible debt with strike price already in the money but contingent upon a future event. The calculation is the same as for the last journal entry but only after the contingent event has occurred. In the meantime, the strike price issue is ignored, as shown in the first entry. Once the contingent event has occurred, the second journal entry shows a shift in funds to the Additional paid-in capital account, with the offset to a discount account.

	Debit	Credit
Cash	xxx	
Bonds payable		xxx
Discount on bonds payable	xxx	
Additional paid-in capital		xxx

Record conversion to equity with accrued but unpaid interest expense. If the terms of a convertible debt agreement require bondholders to forgo any accrued interest expense at the time they convert bonds to company stock, the related journal entry should include the recognition of that expense, as well as an offset to the capital account, as noted in the following journal entry:

	Debit	Credit
Interest expense	xxx	
Long-term debt	xxx	
Capital, par value [various stock accounts]		xxx
Capital [various stock accounts]		xxx

Record conversion to equity following a sweetening of conversion feature. If a company induces its bondholders to convert their holdings to equity by subsequently improving the conversion feature of the bond agreement, it must record an expense for the difference between the consideration given to induce the conversion and the consideration originally noted in the bond agreement. The entry is as follows:

	Debit	Credit
Bonds payable	xxx	
Debt conversion expense	xxx	
Capital account, par value		xxx
Additional paid-in capital		xxx

B.6   DEBT EXTINGUISHMENT

Repurchase of debt. This entry is used when a company elects to buy back issued debt ahead of its expiration date. There is usually a loss on the retirement to reflect the premium usually paid to investors to give up their bonds, while any remaining discount or premium on the debt must also be recognized at this time.

	Debit	Credit
Bonds payable	xxx	
Loss on bond retirement	xxx	
Premium on bonds payable [if applicable]	xxx	
Discount on bonds payable [if applicable]		xxx
Cash		xxx

Repurchase of debt with subsequent gain in intrinsic equity value. When convertible debt is retired for which the intrinsic value of its equity component has already been recorded, the intrinsic value must be determined again at the repurchase date and removed from the Additional paid-in capital account. If the value of the equity component has *risen* since the initial entry, then the entry is as follows:

	Debit	Credit
Bonds payable	xxx	
Additional paid-in capital	xxx	
Cash		xxx
Discount on bonds payable		xxx
Gain on debt extinguishment		xxx

Repurchase of debt with subsequent loss in intrinsic equity value. When convertible debt is retired for which the intrinsic value of its equity component has already been recorded, the intrinsic value must be determined again at the repurchase date and removed from the Additional paid-in capital account. If the value of the equity component has *fallen* since the initial entry, then the entry is as follows:

	Debit	Credit
Bonds payable	xxx	
Additional paid-in capital	xxx	
Loss on debt extinguishment	xxx	
Cash		xxx
Discount on bonds payable		xxx

Asset transfer to eliminate debt. When a company exchanges an asset with a lender to eliminate a debt, the value of the transferred asset is first written up or down to match its book value to its fair market value, as shown in the first entry. Its fair market value, as well as any accrued and unpaid interest expense, is then netted against the remaining debt, as shown in the second entry. Both entries assume a gain on the transaction, though the entry can be reversed to record a loss.

	Debit	Credit
Asset account	xxx	
Gain on asset transfer		xxx
Note payable	xxx	
Interest payable	xxx	
Asset account		xxx
Gain on debt settlement		xxx

B.7   DEBT ISSUED WITH STOCK WARRANTS

Initial entry of bonds sale with attached warrants. The first entry is used to assign a value to the warrants attached to the sale of bonds, based on the relative values of the warrants and bonds. The entry includes a provision for any discount or premium on bonds sold. The second entry shifts funds into an expired warrants account, on the assumption that the warrants are never exercised by the holder.

	Debit	Credit
Cash	xxx	
Discount on bonds payable [if applicable]	xxx	
Premium on bonds payable [if applicable]		xxx
Bonds payable		xxx
Additional paid-in capital		xxx
Additional paid-in capital	xxx	
Additional paid-in capital—expired warrants		xxx

B.8   DEBT SECURITY TRANSFERS AMONG PORTFOLIOS

Shift investment designation from the available-for-sale debt security portfolio to the trading debt security portfolio. Any debt security shifted from the available-for-sale portfolio to the trading portfolio must be recorded at its fair market value on the date of the transfer. The first journal entry records the recognition of a loss on the transfer date, while the second entry records a gain.

	Debit	Credit
Investment in debt securities—held for trading	xxx	
Loss on debt securities	xxx	
Investment in debt securities—available for sale		xxx
Unrealized loss on debt securities—available for sale		xxx
Investment in debt securities—held for trading	xxx	
Unrealized gain on debt securities—available for sale	xxx	
Investment in debt securities—available for sale		xxx
Gain on holding debt securities		xxx

Shift investment designation from the available-for-sale debt security portfolio to the held-to-maturity debt security portfolio. Any debt security shifted from the available-for-sale portfolio to the held-to-maturity portfolio must be recorded at its fair market value on the date of the transfer. The first journal entry records the recognition of a loss on the transfer date, while the second entry records a gain.

	Debit	Credit
Investment in debt securities—held to maturity	xxx	
Loss on debt securities	xxx	
Investment in debt securities—available for sale		xxx
Unrealized loss on debt securities—available for sale		xxx
Investment in debt securities—held to maturity	xxx	
Unrealized gain on debt securities—available for sale	xxx	
Investment in debt securities—available for sale		xxx
Gain on holding debt securities		xxx

Shift investment designation from the held-to-maturity debt security portfolio to the available-for-sale debt security portfolio. To record any accumulated gain or loss on a held-to-maturity debt security being transferred into the available-for-sale portfolio, which is recorded in other comprehensive income. The first entry records a loss on the transaction, while the second entry records a gain.

	Debit	Credit
Investment in debt securities—available for sale	xxx	
Unrealized loss on holding debt securities	xxx	
Investment in debt securities—held to maturity		xxx
Investment in debt securities—available for sale	xxx	
Investment in debt securities—held to maturity		xxx
Unrealized gain on holding debt securities		xxx

Shift investment designation from the held-to-maturity debt security portfolio to the held-for-trading debt security portfolio. To record any accumulated gain or loss on a held-to-maturity debt security being transferred into the held-for-trading portfolio, which is recorded in earnings. The first entry records a loss on the transaction, while the second entry records a gain. There are no unrealized gains or losses to recognize, since no gains or losses are recognized for held-to-maturity debt investments.

	Debit	Credit
Investment in debt securities—held for trading	xxx	
Loss on holding debt securities	xxx	
Investment in debt securities—held to maturity		xxx
Investment in debt securities—held for trading	xxx	
Investment in debt securities—held to maturity		xxx
Gain on holding debt securities		xxx

B.9   DIVIDENDS

Dividend declaration, cash payment. To separate the sum total of all declared dividends from retained earnings once dividends have been approved by the board of directors.

	Debit	Credit
Retained earnings	xxx	
Dividends payable		xxx

Dividend declaration, property dividend. To record the gain or loss on any property to be distributed as a dividend to shareholders, based on the fair value of the asset to be distributed on the date of declaration.

	Debit	Credit
Retained earnings [asset fair value]	xxx	
Loss on property disposal [if applicable]	xxx	
Gain on property disposal [if applicable]		xxx
Dividends payable [asset net book value]		xxx

Dividend payment, property dividend. To eliminate the dividend payable obligation and remove the asset being distributed from the company's records, including all related accumulated depreciation or amortization.

	Debit	Credit
Dividend payable	xxx	
Accumulated amortization [if needed]	xxx	
Accumulated depreciation [if needed]	xxx	
Asset		xxx

Dividend declaration, small stock dividend. To record a small stock dividend, record the fair value of the issued shares on the declaration date by removing the funds from the Retained earnings account and shifting them to the Stock and Additional paid-in capital accounts.

	Debit	Credit
Retained earnings	xxx	
Stock—par value		xxx
Stock—additional paid-in capital		xxx

Dividend declaration, large stock dividend. To record a large stock dividend, record the par value of the issued shares on the declaration date by removing the funds from the Retained earnings account and shifting them to the Stock account.

	Debit	Credit
Retained earnings	xxx	
Stock—par value		xxx

Dividend declaration, scrip dividend. To record the creation of a note payable to shareholders instead of the usual cash dividend.

	Debit	Credit
Retained earnings	xxx	
Notes payable		xxx

Dividend declaration, liquidating. To record a return of capital to investors, rather than a more traditional dividend that is theoretically based on a distribution of profits.

	Debit	Credit
Additional paid-in capital	xxx	
Dividends payable		xxx

Dividend payment in cash. To issue cash payment to shareholders for dividends declared by the board of directors. The first entry shows the payment of a traditional cash dividend, while the second entry shows the payment of a scrip dividend.

	Debit	Credit
Dividends payable	xxx	
Cash		xxx
Dividends payable	xxx	
Notes payable		xxx

B.10   EFFECTIVE INTEREST METHOD

Interest, imputed. To recognize the additional interest expense on a bond after it has been issued with a stated rate below the market rate (first entry), or to recognize a *reduced* level of interest expense on a bond after it has been issued with a stated rate higher than the market rate (second entry).

	Debit	Credit
Interest expense	xxx	
Discount on bonds payable		xxx
Cash		xxx
Interest expense	xxx	
Premium on bonds payable	xxx	
Cash		xxx

B.11   EMPLOYEE STOCK OWNERSHIP PLAN (ESOP)

Incurrence of loan to purchase shares. To record a loan on the company books when either it or its ESOP obtains a loan with a third-party lender in order to purchase shares from the company.

	Debit	Credit
Cash	xxx	
Notes payable		xxx

Purchase of shares by ESOP from sponsoring company. To record the transfer of company shares to the ESOP entity when it purchases the shares from the company. The shares have not yet been allocated to employees.

	Debit	Credit
Unearned ESOP shares	xxx	
Common stock		xxx

Payments against note payable by ESOP. To record a reduction in the note payable incurred by the ESOP or the company on its behalf. The second entry records the allocation of shares to plan participants, as triggered by the reduction in the note payable.

	Debit	Credit
Interest expense	xxx	
Notes payable	xxx	
Cash		xxx
Compensation expense	xxx	
Additional paid-in capital		xxx
Unearned ESOP shares		xxx

Dividends declared on shares held by ESOP. To record either a reduction in retained earnings (for shares allocated to employees by the ESOP) or compensation expense (for shares held by the ESOP) at the time of a dividend declaration.

	Debit	Credit
Retained earnings [for allocated shares in ESOP]	xxx	
Compensation expense [for unallocated shares in ESOP]	xxx	
Dividends payable		xxx

B.12 EQUITY METHOD OF ACCOUNTING FOR INVESTMENTS

Investment (equity method). To record the company's cash or loan investment in another business entity.

	Debit	Credit
Investment in [company name]	xxx	
Cash		xxx
Notes payable		xxx

Investment (equity method), record share of investee income. To record the company's proportional share of the income reported by [name of company in which investment was made]. The second entry records in a Deferred taxes account the amount of income taxes related to the investor's share of investee income.

	Debit	Credit
Investment in [company name]	xxx	
Income from equity share in investment	xxx	
Income tax expense	xxx	
Deferred tax liability		xxx

Investment (equity method), record dividends from investee. To reduce the amount of the original investment by the cash value of dividends received. In the second entry, we assume that deferred income tax was already recognized when the investor recorded a share of investee income, and now shift the portion of the deferred taxes related to dividends received to the Taxes payable account.

	Debit	Credit
Cash	xxx	
Investment in [company name]		xxx
Deferred tax liability	xxx	
Taxes payable		xxx

Investment (equity method), record periodic amortization of incremental increase in investee assets due to allocation of excess purchase price. To reduce the equity in the investee's income as recorded by the investor, based upon the periodic amortization of any investee assets to which value was assigned as a result of the apportionment of an investment exceeding the book value of the investee.

	Debit	Credit
Equity in [company name] income	xxx	
Investment in [company name]		xxx

Investment (equity method), sale of investment at a gain. To record a cash payment in exchange for liquidation of an investment, including the recording of a gain on the transaction. The second entry recognizes an income tax on the investment gain above any income tax previously deferred, and also shifts any previously deferred income tax into a current Taxes payable account.

	Debit	Credit
Cash	xxx	
Investment in [company name]		xxx
Gain on sale of investment		xxx
Income tax expense	xxx	
Deferred tax liability	xxx	
Taxes payable		xxx

Investment (equity method), sale of investment at a loss. To record a cash payment in exchange for liquidation of an investment, including the recording of a loss on the transaction. The second entry eliminates any previously deferred income tax.

	Debit	Credit
Cash	xxx	
Loss on sale of investment		xxx
Investment in [company name]		xxx
Deferred tax liability	xxx	
Income tax expense		xxx

B.13   EQUITY SECURITY TRANSFERS BETWEEN AVAILABLE-FOR-SALE AND TRADING PORTFOLIOS

Shift investment designation from a trading security to an available-for-sale security. To shift the designation of a security currently recorded as a trading security to that of an available-for-sale security. The journal entry includes provisions for the recognition of any gains or losses on the fair value of the securities transferred since they were last marked to market.

	Debit	Credit
Investments—available for sale	xxx	
Loss on equity securities	xxx	
Investments—held for trading		xxx
Gain on equity securities		xxx

Shift investment designation from an available-for-sale security to a trading security. To shift the designation of a security currently recorded as an available-for-sale security to that of a trading security, which requires the recognition of all unrealized gains or losses. The first entry assumes the recognition of unrealized losses on securities, while the second entry assumes the recognition of unrealized gains.

	Debit	Credit
Investments—held for trading	xxx	
Loss on equity securities	xxx	
Investments—available for sale		xxx
Unrealized loss on available-for-sale securities		xxx
Investments—held for trading	xxx	
Unrealized gain on available-for-sale securities	xxx	
Investments—available for sale		xxx
Gain on equity securities		xxx

B.14   FIXED ASSETS

Depreciation. To record the depreciation incurred during the month. The amortization account is used to write off intangible assets.

	Debit	Credit
Depreciation, computer equipment	xxx	
Depreciation, computer software	xxx	
Depreciation, furniture & fixtures	xxx	
Depreciation, leasehold improvements	xxx	
Depreciation, manufacturing equipment	xxx	
Amortization expense	xxx	
Accum. depreciation, computer equipment		xxx
Accum. depreciation, computer software		xxx
Accum. depreciation, furniture & fixtures		xxx
Accum. depreciation, leasehold improvements		xxx
Accum. depreciation, manufacturing equipment		xxx
Intangible assets		xxx

Fixed asset (capitalization of interest). To capitalize interest expense associated with the construction of a qualified asset.

	Debit	Credit
Asset account	xxx	
Interest expense		xxx

Fixed asset (impairment of). To record the reduction in book value when an asset's fair value is less than its book value.

	Debit	Credit
Impairment loss	xxx	
Accumulated depreciation		xxx

Fixed asset (retirement obligation). To record legally mandated asset retirement costs. The *first* entry records the initial ARO liability, while the *second* entry shows ongoing adjustments to the present value of the ARO liability as the termination date of the liability approaches and its present value increases. The *third* entry records a gradual reduction in the asset retirement liability account as actual expenses are incurred to remove an asset. The *fourth* entry records the final settlement of the liability; a loss will be incurred if the actual expense exceeds the amount of the initial liability, while a gain will be recorded if the reverse is true.

	Debit	Credit
Asset account	xxx	
Asset retirement obligation		xxx
Accretion expense	xxx	
Asset retirement obligation		xxx
Asset retirement obligation	xxx	
Accounts payable		xxx
Asset retirement obligation	xxx	
Loss on settlement of ARO liability	xxx	
Gain on settlement of ARO liability		xxx

Fixed asset (sale of). To record the cash received from the sale of an asset, as well as any gain or loss in its sale. This entry also eliminates all associated accumulated depreciation that has built up over the term of the company's ownership of the asset.

	Debit	Credit
Cash	xxx	
Accumulated depreciation	xxx	
Loss on sale of assets	xxx	
[various fixed asset accounts]		xxx
Gain on sale of assets		xxx

Fixed asset (outbound donation). To record the donation of a company asset to a charitable organization. This entry clears the original asset and depreciation entries from the company's records, and also records a gain or loss on the transaction in relation to the asset's fair market value after being netted against the asset's net book value.

	Debit	Credit
Charitable donations	xxx	
Accumulated depreciation	xxx	
Loss on property donation	xxx	
Gain on property donation		xxx
Asset account		xxx

Fixed asset (purchase with stock). To record the acquisition of an asset with company stock. The amount of the stock paid out must be split between the Par value and Paid-in capital accounts, depending upon the predetermined par value of each share issued.

	Debit	Credit
Asset account	xxx	
Stock, par value		xxx
Stock, additional paid-in capital		xxx

Fixed asset (exchange for a dissimilar asset). To record the trade of a company asset for a different type of asset, including a cash payment. Any loss on this transaction is caused by the remaining net book value of the asset being relinquished being higher than its fair value, with the reverse being true for a gain. The debit to the Accumulated depreciation account is used to clear from the accounting records the accumulated depreciation associated with the asset being traded away.

	Debit	Credit
Asset account for new asset	xxx	
Accumulated depreciation	xxx	
Loss on asset exchange	xxx	
Gain on asset exchange		xxx
Asset account for asset traded away		xxx
Cash		xxx

Fixed asset (write-off). To record the unreimbursed disposal of an asset. This entry also eliminates all associated accumulated depreciation that has built up over the term of the company's ownership of the asset.

	Debit	Credit
Accumulated depreciation	xxx	
Loss on disposal of assets	xxx	
[various fixed asset accounts]		xxx

B.15   FOREIGN CURRENCY

Financial statement translation adjustment. To record the difference between the exchange rate at the end of the reporting period and the exchange rate applicable to individual transactions. The sample entry shows credit adjustments to several accounts, but these entries could easily be debits instead, depending on changes in applicable exchange rates during the reporting period.

	Debit	Credit
Accumulated translation adjustments	xxx	
Various noncash asset accounts		xxx
Net income		xxx
Dividends declared		xxx

Translation of foreign currency transactions. To record any changes in the spot rate of exchange at which transactions denominated in a foreign currency will be recorded at the date when financial statements are issued. The *first journal entry* records a loss on a decline in the spot rate on an account receivable (resulting in a reduction in the amount of the receivable in U.S. dollars), while the *second entry* does the same for an account payable (resulting in an increase in the payable in U.S. dollars), and the *third entry* does this for an outstanding loan payable (resulting in an increase in the loan payable in U.S. dollars). For gains on these transactions, the second line of each entry would be reversed, and a credit to a gain account would be substituted for the loss account.

	Debit	Credit
Loss on foreign exchange transaction	xxx	
Accounts receivable		xxx
Loss on foreign exchange transaction	xxx	
Accounts payable		xxx
Loss on foreign exchange transaction	xxx	
Loans payable		xxx

Recognition of the sale of a foreign subsidiary. To recognize any accumulated translation gains or losses as the result of the sale or write-down of a company's investment in a foreign subsidiary. The entry can be reversed if a gain is to be recognized.

	Debit	Credit
Loss on sale of business entity	xxx	
Accumulated translation adjustments		xxx

B.16 INTANGIBLE ASSETS

Acquisition of intangible asset. To record the purchase of an intangible asset (shown here as a customer list). The second entry shows amortization of the intangible asset.

	Debit	Credit
Customer list	xxx	
Cash		xxx

	Debit	Credit
Customer list amortization expense	xxx	
Accumulated customer list amortization		xxx

Impairment of intangible asset. To record a decline in the fair value of an intangible asset (shown here as a customer list) below its net book value.

	Debit	Credit
Loss on impairment	xxx	
Customer list		xxx

B.17   INVENTORY ADJUSTMENTS

Adjust inventory for obsolete items. To charge an ongoing expense to the cost of goods sold that increases the balance in a reserve against which obsolete inventory can be charged (*first entry*). The *second entry* charges off specific inventory items against the reserve.

	Debit	Credit
Cost of goods sold	xxx	
Obsolescence reserve		xxx
Obsolescence reserve	xxx	
Raw materials inventory		xxx
Work-in-process inventory		xxx
Finished goods inventory		xxx

Adjust inventory to lower of cost or market. To reduce the value of inventory to a market price that is lower than the cost at which it is recorded in the company records.

	Debit	Credit
Loss on inventory valuation	xxx	
Raw materials inventory		xxx
Work-in-process inventory		xxx
Finished goods inventory		xxx

Adjust inventory to physical count. To adjust inventory balances, either up or down, as a result of changes in the inventory quantities that are noted during a physical count. The following entries assume that there are increases in inventory balances. If there are declines in the inventory balances, then the debits and credits are reversed.

	Debit	Credit
Raw materials inventory	xxx	
Work-in-process inventory	xxx	
Finished goods inventory	xxx	
Cost of goods sold		xxx

Write off abnormal scrap/spoilage. To shift unexpected, one-time scrap or spoilage costs directly to the cost of goods sold, effectively writing off this amount in the current period.

	Debit	Credit
Cost of goods sold	xxx	
Work-in-process inventory		xxx

B.18 INVENTORY IN TRANSIT

Record received goods. To increase inventory levels as a result of a supplier delivery.

	Debit	Credit
Raw materials inventory	xxx	
Accounts payable		xxx

Move inventory to work-in-process. To shift the cost of inventory to the work-in-process category once production work begins on converting it from raw materials to finished goods.

	Debit	Credit
Work-in-process inventory	xxx	
Raw materials inventory		xxx

Move inventory to finished goods. To shift the cost of completed inventory from work-in-process inventory to finished goods inventory.

	Debit	Credit
Finished goods inventory	xxx	
Work-in-process inventory		xxx

Sell inventory. To record the elimination of the inventory asset as a result of a product sale, shifting the asset to an expense and also recording the creation of an accounts receivable asset to reflect an unpaid balance from the customer on sale of the product.

	Debit	Credit
Cost of goods sold	xxx	
Finished goods inventory		xxx
Accounts receivable	xxx	
Revenues		xxx
Overhead cost pool		xxx

B.19   INVENTORY VALUATION

Record indirect expenses incurred. To add to the overhead cost pool the amount of indirect expenses related to the production process.

	Debit	Credit
Overhead cost pool	xxx	
Accounts payable		xxx

Record indirect wages incurred. To add to the overhead cost pool the amount of indirect wages related to the production process.

	Debit	Credit
Overhead cost pool	xxx	
Wages payable		xxx

Record receipt of supplies. To add the cost of incidental manufacturing supplies to the overhead cost pool for eventual allocation to inventory.

	Debit	Credit
Overhead cost pool	xxx	
Accounts payable		xxx

Record normal scrap/spoilage. To shift the normal, expected amount of scrap or spoilage cost to the overhead cost pool, from whence it is allocated as a part of overhead to inventory.

	Debit	Credit
Overhead cost pool	xxx	
Work-in-process inventory		xxx

Allocate overhead costs to inventory. To shift the amount of costs built up in the overhead cost pool to the work-in-process and finished goods inventory categories, as well as to the cost of goods sold for any inventory sold during the period.

	Debit	Credit
Cost of goods sold	xxx	
Work-in-process inventory	xxx	
Finished goods inventory	xxx	

B.20   INVESTMENTS IN DEBT SECURITIES

Initial investment designated as held for trading. To record an investment in debt securities that management intends to trade for a profit in the short term.

	Debit	Credit
Investment in debt securities—held for trading	xxx	
Cash		xxx

Initial investment designated as available-for-sale. To record an investment in debt securities that management intends to hold as a long-term investment.

	Debit	Credit
Investment in debt securities—available-for-sale	xxx	
Cash		xxx

Initial investment designated as held-to-maturity. To record an investment in debt securities that management has the intent and ability to hold to the debt maturity date.

	Debit	Credit
Investment in debt securities—held-to-maturity	xxx	
Cash		xxx

Gain or loss on debt investment designated as held for trading. The first journal entry records the immediate recognition in the current period of a loss due to a drop in the value of a debt investment designated as a trading security. The second journal entry records the immediate recognition of a gain due to an increase in the value of a debt investment designated as a trading security.

	Debit	Credit
Loss on debt security investment	xxx	
Investment in debt securities—held for trading		xxx
Investment in debt securities—held for trading	xxx	
Gain on debt securities—held for trading		xxx

Gain or loss on debt investment designated as available for sale. The first journal entry records the immediate recognition in the current period of a loss due to a drop in the value of a debt investment designated as an available-for-sale security, which is reported in the Other Comprehensive Income section of the income statement. The second journal entry records the immediate recognition of a gain due to an increase in the value of a debt investment designated as an available-for-sale security.

	Debit	Credit
Unrealized loss on debt security investment	xxx	
Deferred tax benefit	xxx	
Investment in debt securities—available-for-sale		xxx
Investment in debt securities—available-for-sale	xxx	
Unrealized gain on debt security investment		xxx
Deferred tax liability		xxx

Impairment in value of debt investments classified as held to maturity. To record a loss on a held-to-maturity debt investment, which only occurs when management considers a drop in value to be permanent in nature.

	Debit	Credit
Loss on debt investment	xxx	
Investment in debt securities—held-to-maturity		xxx

B.21   LEASES—LESSEE ACCOUNTING

Lease, capital (initial record by lessee). To record the initial capitalization of a lease, including imputed interest that is associated with the transaction and both the short-term and long-term portions of the associated account payable. A *second entry* records the interest expense associated with each periodic payment on the capital lease. A *third entry* records the depreciation expense associated with the capital lease in each accounting period.

	Debit	Credit
Capital leases	xxx	
Unamortized discount on notes payable	xxx	
Short-term liabilities		xxx
Long-term liabilities		xxx
Interest expense	xxx	
Unamortized discount on notes payable		xxx
Depreciation expense	xxx	
Accumulated depreciation—capital leases		xxx

B.22   LEASES—LESSOR ACCOUNTING

Initial lease record by lessor (sales-type lease). To record the initial lease transaction by the lessor, including the recognition of a sale, recording of an unearned interest liability, incurrence of a liability for any initial direct costs, and the transfer of the leased asset out of inventory.

	Debit	Credit
Lease receivable	xxx	
Cost of goods sold	xxx	
Sales		xxx
Inventory		xxx
Accounts payable [any initial direct costs]		xxx
Unearned interest		xxx

Receipt of cash payments by lessor (sales-type lease). To record the receipt of cash and the offsetting reduction in the lease receivable when periodic lease payments are made by the lessee to the lessor.

	Debit	Credit
Cash	xxx	
Lease receivable		xxx

Recording of periodic interest revenue by lessor (sales-type lease). To periodically record earned interest by shifting interest from the Unearned interest account into the Interest revenue account.

	Debit	Credit
Unearned interest	xxx	
Interest revenue		xxx

Return of asset to lessor at end of lease (sales-type lease). To record the receipt of a leased asset back into inventory upon its return by a lessee who has completed a lease term.

	Debit	Credit
Inventory	xxx	
Lease receivable		xxx

Initial lease record by lessor (direct financing lease). To record the initial lease transaction by the lessor, including the recording of an unearned interest liability, the incurrence of a liability for any initial direct costs, and the transfer of the leased asset out of inventory.

	Debit	Credit
Lease receivable	xxx	
Initial direct costs	xxx	
Asset [specify account]		xxx
Unearned interest		xxx
Cash		xxx

Receipt of cash payments by lessor (direct financing lease). To record the receipt of cash and the offsetting reduction in the lease receivable when periodic lease payments are made by the lessee to the lessor.

	Debit	Credit
Cash	xxx	
Lease receivable		xxx

Recording of periodic interest revenue by lessor (direct financing lease). To periodically record earned interest by shifting interest from the Unearned interest account into the Interest revenue account, with a portion of the unearned interest being allocated to an offset of initial direct costs.

	Debit	Credit
Unearned interest	xxx	
Interest revenue		xxx
Initial direct costs		xxx

Return of asset to lessor at end of lease (direct financing lease). To record the receipt of a leased asset upon its return by a lessee who has completed a lease term.

	Debit	Credit
Asset [specify account]	xxx	
Lease receivable		xxx

B.23   LONG-TERM CONSTRUCTION CONTRACTS

Record additional revenues under percentage of completion method. To record the amount of extra revenues thus far not recognized, comprising the difference between project expenses and the estimated gross profit margin, less prior billings. The second entry is the recording of a proportional amount of offsetting cost of goods sold, so that the principle of matching revenues to expenses is observed.

	Debit	Credit
Unbilled contract receivables	xxx	
Contract revenues earned		xxx
Cost of recognized revenues	xxx	
Construction in progress		xxx

Record excessive billings under percentage of completion method in a liability account. To record the amount of excess billings over the amount of project expenses and the estimated gross profit margin in a liability account.

	Debit	Credit
Contract revenues earned	xxx	
Billings exceeding project costs and margin		xxx

Record amount of costs exceeding the total project billing. To record the estimated amount of expenses incurred on a project that will exceed the total billable amount of the contract. This is a loss recognizable in the current period.

	Debit	Credit
Loss on uncompleted project	xxx	
Estimated loss on uncompleted contract		xxx

B.24   MARKETABLE EQUITY SECURITIES

Initial investment designated as held for trading. To record an investment that management intends to trade for a profit in the short term.

	Debit	Credit
Investment in equity securities—held for trading	xxx	
Cash		xxx

Initial investment designated as available for sale. To record an investment that management intends to hold as a long-term investment.

	Debit	Credit
Investment in equity securities—available for sale	xxx	
Cash		xxx

Gain or loss on investment designated as held for trading. The first entry shows the immediate recognition in the current period of a loss due to a drop in the value of an investment designated as a trading security, as well as the related tax effect. The second entry shows the immediate recognition in the current period of a gain due to an increase in the value of an investment designated as a trading security, as well as the related tax effect.

	Debit	Credit
Loss on equity security investment	xxx	
Deferred tax benefit	xxx	
Investment in equity securities—held for trading		xxx
Provision for income taxes		xxx
Investment in equity securities—held for trading	xxx	
Provision for income taxes	xxx	
Gain on equity security investments		xxx
Deferred tax liability		xxx

Gain or loss on investment designated as available for sale. The first entry shows an unrealized loss in the Other comprehensive income account on an investment designated as available for sale, as well as the related tax effect. The second entry shows an unrealized gain in the Other comprehensive income account on an investment designated as available for sale, as well as the related tax effect. In both cases, the tax effect is netted against the Investment account, rather than a Provision for income taxes account.

	Debit	Credit
Unrealized loss on equity security investment	xxx	
Deferred tax benefit	xxx	
Investment in equity securities—available for sale		xxx
Investment in equity securities—available for sale	xxx	
Unrealized gain on equity security investment	xxx	
Deferred tax liability		xxx

Impairment in value of equity investments classified as available for sale. When a drop in the value of an available-for-sale investment is judged to be other than temporary, the first journal entry should be used to recognize the drop in value. The entry includes the initial recognition of a related income tax benefit on the transaction. If one had previously recognized an income tax benefit associated with the loss but prior to its classification as a permanent decline in value, the offset to the deferred tax benefit would have been the investment account itself. If so, one should shift the offset from the investment account to an income tax liability account, as shown in the second journal entry.

	Debit	Credit
Loss on equity securities	xxx	
Deferred tax benefit	xxx	
Unrealized loss on available-for-sale securities		xxx
Provision for income taxes		xxx
Loss on equity securities	xxx	
Unrealized loss on available-for-sale securities		xxx
Provision for income taxes		xxx

B.25   NOTES AND BONDS

Sale of bonds at a discount. The first entry is made when bonds are sold at a discount from their face value, thereby increasing the effective interest rate. The second entry is made periodically to gradually reduce the discount, charging the offsetting debit to the interest expense account.

	Debit	Credit
Cash	xxx	
Discount on bonds payable	xxx	
Bonds payable		xxx
Interest expense	xxx	
Discount on bonds payable		xxx

Sale of bonds at a premium. The first entry is made when bonds are sold at a premium from their face value, thereby reducing the effective interest rate. The second entry is made periodically to gradually reduce the premium, charging the offsetting credit to the interest expense account.

	Debit	Credit
Cash	xxx	
Premium on bonds payable		xxx
Bonds payable		xxx
Premium on bonds payable	xxx	
Interest expense		xxx

Sale of debt issued with no stated interest rate. When there is no stated interest rate on a debt instrument, one must record the present value of the note using the market rate of interest at the time of the issuance. The first entry shows the initial recording of the debt sale, while the second entry shows the periodic reduction in interest expense payable.

	Debit	Credit
Cash	xxx	
Discount on note payable	xxx	
Note payable		xxx
Interest expense	xxx	
Discount on note payable		xxx

Issuance of debt for cash and other rights. When debt is issued in exchange for cash and some other form of consideration, the difference between the present value and face value of the debt is recorded as unearned consideration, to be recognized as the consideration is earned by the issuer. The first entry shows the initial recording of such a transaction, while the second entry shows the gradual reduction in unearned revenue.

	Debit	Credit
Cash	xxx	
Discount on note payable	xxx	
Note payable		xxx
Unearned revenue		xxx
Unearned revenue	xxx	
Revenue		xxx

Capitalization of debt issuance costs. Costs associated with the issuance of debt should be capitalized when the related debt is issued, as noted in the first journal entry. This amount should be ratably recognized over the term of the debt on a straight-line basis, as is shown in the second journal entry.

	Debit	Credit
Bond issuance costs	xxx	
Cash		xxx
Bond issuance expense	xxx	
Bond issuance costs		xxx

Notes issued for property. When a company issues debt in exchange for property, it discounts the note at either the stated interest rate on the debt or at the market rate (if the stated rate is not considered to be a fair rate). In either case, the value of the property acquired shall be debited, usually along with a discount on the note payable. The first entry shows this initial transaction, while the second entry shows the periodic reduction in the discount and corresponding recognition of interest expense.

	Debit	Credit
Property [various accounts]	xxx	
Discount on note payable	xxx	
Note payable		xxx
Interest expense	xxx	
Discount on note payable		xxx

B.26   OPTIONS

Options issued with strike price below the market price. If stock options are issued at a strike price that is already below the market price on the date of issuance, then the difference between the two prices must be immediately recognized as deferred compensation. The entry is as follows:

	Debit	Credit
Deferred compensation expense	xxx	
Options—additional paid-in capital		xxx

Options earned over time. Options are typically earned over time as services are performed for a company or vesting periods are completed. The periodic entry to recognize the Deferred compensation expense account is as follows:

	Debit	Credit
Compensation expense	xxx	
Deferred compensation expense		xxx

Options used to purchase shares. When an option holder exercises the option to purchase shares, the journal entry is identical to the simple purchase of shares without the presence of an option. This transaction is shown in the first entry. However, if some deferred compensation was recognized at the time of the initial stock grant, then the Options—additional paid-in capital account is reversed as part of the entry. This transaction is shown in the second journal entry.

	Debit	Credit
Cash	xxx	
Common stock—par value		xxx
Common stock—additional paid-in capital		xxx
Cash	xxx	
Options—additional paid-in capital	xxx	
Common stock—par value		xxx
Common stock—additional paid-in capital		xxx

Options lapsed (SFAS 123 approach). If an option holder elects to let a *fully vested* option lapse, the following entry does not reverse the associated compensation expense (as is the case under APB 25), but rather shifts the related equity into a different account.

	Debit	Credit
Options—additional paid-in capital	xxx	
Capital—unexercised options		xxx

Options purchased by the company (SFAS 123 approach). To recognize any compensation expense associated with unvested shares that are being purchased by a company, to the extent that the price paid is higher than the value of the options as measured under the fair value approach. All deferred compensation expense associated with the unvested portion of the options is accelerated and recognized at the time of the purchase.

	Debit	Credit
Compensation expense	xxx	
Deferred compensation expense		xxx
Cash		xxx

B.27 PENSIONS

Record net pension cost. The basic entry needed to record changes in the net pension cost is to itemize changes in the service cost, interest cost, and amortization of unrecognized prior service costs. The entry is shown next.

	Debit	Credit
Net periodic pension cost	xxx	
Accrued/prepaid pension cost		xxx

Contribution to pension plan. Whenever a company pays cash into its pension plan, this reduces the amount of its accrued/prepaid pension cost. The entry is shown next.

	Debit	Credit
Accrued/prepaid pension cost	xxx	
Cash		xxx

Record required minimum liability. A company may find it necessary to record a minimum pension liability if the unrecognized net gain or loss exceeds a band of 10% of the greater of the beginning balances of the market-related value of plan assets or the projected benefit obligation. The entry is shown next.

	Debit	Credit
Intangible asset—deferred pension cost	xxx	
Additional pension liability		xxx

The following entry is used if the existing balance of the required minimum pension liability must be subsequently adjusted downward.

	Debit	Credit
Additional pension liability	xxx	
Intangible asset—deferred pension cost		xxx
Excess of additional pension liability over unrecognized prior service cost		xxx

Record postretirement benefits. The recording of postretirement benefits besides those contained within a pension plan is very similar to the entry used for a pension plan. Only the name of the expense and related cost change, as noted in the following entry.

	Debit	Credit
Postretirement expense	xxx	
Cash		xxx
Accrued/prepaid postretirement cost		xxx

B.28 RECEIVABLES

Accounts receivable, initial entry. To record the creation of a receivable at the point when a sale is made. The entry includes the creation of a liability account for a sales tax. The second entry records the elimination of the account receivable when cash is received from the customer, while the third entry records the payment of sales taxes payable to the relevant government authority.

	Debit	Credit
Accounts receivable	xxx	
Sales		xxx
Sales taxes payable		xxx
Cash	xxx	
Accounts receivable		xxx
Sales taxes payable	xxx	
Cash		xxx

Accounts receivable, recording of long-term payment terms. To record any accounts receivable not due for payment for at least one year. The receivable is discounted at no less than the market rate of interest. The first journal entry shows the initial record of sale, while the second entry shows the gradual recognition of interest income associated with the receivable.

	Debit	Credit
Notes receivable	xxx	
Revenue		xxx
Discount on notes receivable		xxx
Discount on notes receivable	xxx	
Interest income		xxx

Accounts receivable, sale of. To record the outright sale of an account receivable, including the recognition of interest expense and any loss on the transaction due to the expected incurrence of bad debt losses by the factor on the purchased receivables.

	Debit	Credit
Cash	xxx	
Factoring expense	xxx	
Loss on sale of receivables	xxx	
Interest expense	xxx	
Accounts receivable		xxx

Accounts receivable, payment due from factor. To record the outright sale of accounts receivable to a factor, but without taking payment until the due date of the underlying receivables, thereby avoiding interest expenses. The second entry records the eventual payment by the factor for the transferred receivables.

	Debit	Credit
Receivable due from factor	xxx	
Factoring expense	xxx	
Loss on sale of receivables	xxx	
Accounts receivable		xxx
Cash	xxx	
Receivable due from factor		xxx

Accounts receivable, establishment of recourse obligation. To record an obligation to pay back a factor for any bad debts experienced as part of a receivable sale to the factor, for which the company is liable under a factoring with recourse arrangement. The second entry shows the recourse obligation being reduced as bad debts are incurred and the company pays back the factor for the receivables written off as bad debts.

	Debit	Credit
Allowance for bad debts	xxx	
Recourse obligation		xxx
Recourse obligation	xxx	
Cash		xxx

Accounts receivable, write-off. To cancel an account receivable by offsetting it against the reserve for bad debts located in the bad debt accrual account.

	Debit	Credit
Bad debt accrual	xxx	
Accounts receivable		xxx

Accrue bad debt expense. To accrue for projected bad debts, based on historical experience.

	Debit	Credit
Bad debt expense	xxx	
Bad debt accrual		xxx

Account for receipt of written-off receivable. To record the receipt of cash on a sale that had previously been written off as uncollectible.

	Debit	Credit
Cash	xxx	
Bad debt accrual		xxx

Accrue for sales returns. To accrue for expected sales returns from sales made on approval, based on historical experience.

	Debit	Credit
Sale returns expense	xxx	
Reserve for sales returns		xxx

Early payment discounts, record receipt of. To record the amount of early payment discounts taken by customers as part of their payments for accounts receivable.

	Debit	Credit
Cash	xxx	
Sales: Discounts taken	xxx	
Accounts receivable		xxx

B.29 REVENUE RECOGNITION WHEN RIGHT OF RETURN EXISTS

To record predictable amounts of sales returns. When the amount of sales returns can be reasonably estimated, one should record an estimate of returns, which is noted in the first journal entry. The second entry notes the offsetting of an actual return against the sales return reserve, while the third entry notes the elimination of any remaining amount left in the reserve after the right of return has expired.

Note:

In the case of sales where the amount of sales returns is not predictable, the same entries are used, but they will apply to the entire amount of sales made, rather than just an estimated amount of returns.

	Debit	Credit
Revenue	xxx	
Cost of goods sold		xxx
Deferred gross profit		xxx
Finished goods inventory	xxx	
Deferred gross profit	xxx	
Loss on returned inventory	xxx	
Accounts receivable		xxx
Cost of goods sold	xxx	
Deferred gross profit	xxx	
Revenue		xxx

B.30 REVENUE, INSTALLMENT

Revenue (installment basis). To record the initial installment sale, as noted in the *first entry*. As cash is received over time in payment of installment accounts receivable, the *second entry* is used to recognize portions of the gross profit and interest income from the installment sale.

	Debit	Credit
Installment receivables collectible in [year]	xxx	
Inventory		xxx
Deferred gross profit		xxx
Cash	xxx	
Deferred gross profit	xxx	
Installment receivables collectible in [year]		xxx
Interest income		xxx
Recognized gross profit		xxx

Repossession of goods sold under installment plans. When goods are repossessed due to lack of payment under an installment sales plan, the deferred gross profit associated with the initial sale must be reversed, while the repossessed goods should be transferred back into inventory at their fair market value. If there is a difference between the book value and fair value of the goods, then a gain or loss should be recognized on the difference. The following entry illustrates the transaction.

	Debit	Credit
Finished goods inventory	xxx	
Loss on repossessed inventory	xxx	
Deferred gross profit	xxx	
Accounts receivable		xxx

B.31   REVENUE, SERVICE

Record unearned service revenue. To record a liability when a sales transaction for unearned services work is recorded. The first entry records the offset to an account receivable in a liability account, while the second entry records incremental revenue recognition from the liability account as services are completed.

	Debit	Credit
Accounts receivable	xxx	
Unearned service contracts		xxx
Unearned service contracts	xxx	
Service revenue		xxx

Record earned revenue under the proportional performance method. Under the proportional performance method, one can recognize revenue in proportion to the amount of direct cost incurred on a service job. The first entry is the simplest, showing a basic sale transaction under which the customer is billed for the same amount of proportional revenue recognized by the company. The second entry assumes that there is no customer billing yet to match the revenue recognized, so the sales offset is stored in an asset account. The third entry shows the reduction of the asset account when a customer billing eventually occurs.

	Debit	Credit
Accounts receivable	xxx	
Sales		xxx
Earned revenue asset account	xxx	
Sales		xxx
Accounts receivable	xxx	
Earned revenue asset account		xxx

Recognize a loss on a service contract. This entry is used when it becomes apparent that actual and estimated expenses on a service contract will exceed related revenue. An estimated loss is recognized, while the offsetting credit is first used to eliminate any unrecognized contract costs, with the remainder being credited to an estimated loss account that is later drawn down as actual losses are incurred.

	Debit	Credit
Loss on service contract	xxx	
Unrecognized contract costs		xxx
Estimated loss on service contracts		xxx

B.32   SALE-LEASEBACK TRANSACTIONS

Sale-leaseback transactions for the lessee (capital lease). The first entry records the initial sale of an asset by the eventual lessee to the lessor, while the second entry records the coincident incurrence of a lease obligation for the same asset. The third entry records any lease payment by the lessee to the lessor, while the fourth entry records depreciation on the leased asset (on the assumption that this is a capital lease). The fifth entry records the periodic recognition of portions of the unearned profit on the initial asset sale.

	Debit	Credit
Cash	xxx	
Asset [variety of possible accounts]		xxx
Unearned profit on sale-leaseback		xxx
Leased asset [variety of possible accounts]	xxx	
Lease obligation		xxx
Lease obligation	xxx	
Cash		xxx
Amortization expense	xxx	
Accumulated amortization		xxx
Unearned profit on sale-leaseback	xxx	
Amortization expense		xxx

B.33   STOCK

Initial sale of stock. When a company sells shares to an investor, it allocates a portion of the sale price to a par value account matching the stated par value of each share sold, with the remainder being credited to an Additional paid-in capital account, as noted in the following entry.

	Debit	Credit
Cash	xxx	
Stock—par value		xxx
Stock—additional paid-in capital		xxx

Netting of stock issuance costs against sale proceeds. To net stock issuance costs, such as legal, underwriting, certificate printing, and security registration fees, against the proceeds of a stock sale.

	Debit	Credit
Additional paid-in capital	xxx	
Stock issuance expenses		xxx

Stock issued for services rendered or goods received. To record the fair value of services or goods received in exchange for stock.

	Debit	Credit
Expense [reflecting specific services or goods received]	xxx	
Stock—par value		xxx
Additional paid-in capital		xxx

Conversion of preferred stock to common stock. To record the conversion of preferred stock to common stock under a conversion option. The second entry shows this conversion when the par value of the common stock is greater than the entire purchase price of the preferred stock, requiring an additional contribution from the retained earnings account.

	Debit	Credit
Preferred stock—par value	xxx	
Preferred stock—additional paid-in capital	xxx	
Common stock—par value		xxx
Common stock—additional paid-in capital		xxx
Preferred stock—par value	xxx	
Preferred stock—additional paid-in capital	xxx	
Retained earnings	xxx	
Common stock—par value		xxx

Stock split with no change in par value. To record a stock split where the par value of the stock is not proportionately reduced to match the number of new shares issued. This requires a transfer from the Additional paid-in capital account to fund the additional amount of par value required for the new shares.

	Debit	Credit
Stock–additional paid-in capital	xxx	
Stock—par value		xxx

B.34   STOCK APPRECIATION RIGHTS (SAR)

Record increase in value of SAR grant payable in cash. When an initial SAR grant is made, no entry is required. When there is an increase in value of the underlying share value over the stock price at which the SAR was granted, the difference is recorded as compensation expense. The entry is as follows:

	Debit	Credit
Compensation expense	xxx	
SAR liability		xxx

Record increase in SAR grant payable in stock. When there is an increase in value of the underlying share value over the stock price at which the SAR was granted, the difference is recorded as compensation expense, while the offsetting credit is to a Stock rights outstanding equity account.

	Debit	Credit
Compensation expense	xxx	
Stock rights outstanding		xxx

Record exercise of SAR grant payable in cash. When the holder of a SAR wishes to exercise it and the payment is in cash, the amount of the accumulated SAR liability is reversed, with the difference being credited to cash, representing the payment to the SAR holder. The entry is as follows:

	Debit	Credit
SAR liability	xxx	
Cash		xxx

Record exercise of SAR grant payable in stock. When the holder of a SAR wishes to exercise it and the payment is in stock, the amount of the accumulated stock rights outstanding is reversed, with the difference being credited to the par value account and additional paid-in capital account, representing the payment to the SAR holder. The entry is as follows:

	Debit	Credit
Stock rights outstanding	xxx	
Stock—par value		xxx
Stock—additional paid-in capital		xxx

B.35 STOCK SUBSCRIPTIONS

Stock subscription, initial entry. To record the initial commitment by potential investors to purchase shares of company stock, with no cash yet received.

	Debit	Credit
Stock subscriptions receivable	xxx	
Common stock subscribed		xxx
Additional paid-in capital		xxx

Stock subscription, payment of. To record the receipt of cash from investors to fulfill their earlier commitments to purchase stock under a stock subscription agreement.

	Debit	Credit
Cash	xxx	
Stock subscriptions receivable		xxx
Common stock subscribed	xxx	
Common stock		xxx

B.36 TAXES

Income tax expense. To record income taxes, which includes taxes payable in the current period (income tax expense), taxes payable in a future period (deferred tax liability), and taxes payable in the current period (income tax payable).

	Debit	Credit
Income tax expense	xxx	
Deferred tax liability		xxx
Income tax payable		xxx

Tax loss carryback. To record a receivable due from the government in the amount of a tax loss that can be carried back to a previous period. The benefit due to the loss carryback is a contra income tax expense, and is recognizable in the period when the loss is incurred.

	Debit	Credit
Accounts receivable – Income taxes	xxx	
Benefit due to loss carryback		xxx

Tax loss carryforward. To record an asset associated with the carryforward of a net operating loss into a future period. The benefit due to the loss carryforward is a contra income tax expense, and is recognizable in the period when the loss is incurred. The second entry shows the use of the deferred tax asset in a subsequent period, when there is sufficient net income to use a portion or all of the tax loss carryforward.

	Debit	Credit
Deferred tax asset	xxx	
Benefit due to loss carryback		xxx

	Debit	Credit
Income tax expense	xxx	
Deferred tax asset		xxx
Income tax payable		xxx

Tax valuation allowance. To record a valuation allowance if it is more likely than not that a portion of a deferred tax asset will not be realized. The entry increases income tax expense in the current period, while creating a contra account to offset the valuation allowance. The second entry shows a reversal of the allowance account to reflect a reduction in the estimated amount of the valuation.

	Debit	Credit
Income tax expense	xxx	
Allowance to reduce		xxx
deferred tax asset to		
expected realizable value		

	Debit	Credit
Allowance to reduce deferred tax	xxx	
asset to expected realizable		
value		
Income tax expense		xxx

B.37 TREASURY STOCK

Treasury stock, purchase under the cost method. To record the acquisition by a company of its own stock.

	Debit	Credit
Treasury stock	xxx	
Cash		xxx

Treasury stock, retirement under the cost method. This method is used when there is an assumption that repurchased shares will be permanently retired. The original Common stock and Additional paid-in capital accounts are reversed with any loss on the purchase being charged to the Retained earnings account, and any gain being credited to the Additional paid-in capital account.

	Debit	Credit
Common stock—par value	xxx	
Additional paid-in capital	xxx	
Retained earnings		xxx
Cash		xxx

Treasury stock, sale at price higher than acquisition price. To record the sale of treasury stock to investors by the company at a price higher than the price at which the company acquired the shares, with payments in excess of treasury stock cost being credited to the Additional paid-in capital account. This entry uses the cost method of accounting for treasury stock.

	Debit	Credit
Cash	xxx	
Treasury stock		xxx
Additional paid-in capital—treasury stock		xxx

Treasury stock, sale at price lower than acquisition price. To record the sale of treasury stock to investors by the company at a price lower than the price at which the company acquired the shares, with the loss on the sale being charged to the Additional paid-in capital account until that account is emptied, with any remaining loss being charged to the retained earnings account. This entry uses the cost method of accounting for treasury stock.

	Debit	Credit
Cash	xxx	
Additional paid-in capital—treasury stock	xxx	
Retained earnings	xxx	
Treasury stock		xxx

Treasury stock, purchase under the constructive retirement method. This method is used when there is an assumption that the repurchased shares will be permanently retired or when mandated by state law. The original Common stock and Additional paid-in capital accounts are reversed with any loss on the purchase being charged to the retained earnings account, and any gain being credited to the Additional paid-in capital account.

	Debit	Credit
Common stock—par value	xxx	
Additional paid-in capital	xxx	
Retained earnings	xxx	
Cash		xxx

Treasury stock, repurchase under a greenmail agreement. When a company is forced to buy back shares at above-market prices under the threat of a corporate takeover, the difference between the repurchase price and the market price must be charged to expense, as noted in the following entry.

	Debit	Credit
Treasury stock	xxx	
Excess stock repurchase expense	xxx	
Cash		xxx

B.38   WARRANTS

Initial entry of bonds sale with attached warrants. The first entry is used to assign a value to the warrants attached to the sale of bonds, based on the relative values of the warrants and bonds. The entry includes a provision for any discount or premium on bonds sold. The second entry shifts funds into an expired warrants account, on the assumption that the warrants are never exercised by the holder. The third entry shows the proper treatment of a warrant that is converted to stock with an additional cash payment included.

	Debit	Credit
Cash	xxx	
Discount on bonds payable [if applicable]	xxx	
Premium on bonds payable [if applicable]		xxx
Bonds payable		xxx
Additional paid-in capital–warrants		xxx
Additional paid-in capital–warrants	xxx	
Additional paid-in capital—expired warrants		xxx
Cash	xxx	
Additional paid-in capital—warrants	xxx	
Common stock—par value		xxx
Common stock—additional paid-in capital		xxx

APPENDIX C

INTEREST TABLES

There are five tables in this appendix that relate to the most common calculations used for interest rate analyses. Each one uses a standard format that lists the interest rate, from 1% to 13%, across the top and the number of years, from 1 to 30, down the left side. The underlying calculation for each one is noted below, as well as a brief example describing how to use each one.

C.1 SIMPLE INTEREST TABLE

The simple interest table in Exhibit C.1 is used to find the total interest expense on an investment or debt that is to be completed in some future period, without factoring in the impact of any compounding of interest. The calculation is:

$$(\text{Interest rate} \times \text{Number of years that interest accrues})$$

For example, to determine the total amount of an investment of $50,000 at the end of seven years, using an interest rate of 9%, go to the simple interest table. Next, move down to the row that contains interest rate factors for seven years, and move across to find the cell for the 9% interest rate, which contains a factor of 1.63. Then, multiply this by $50,000 to arrive at $81,500.

C.2 COMPOUND INTEREST (FUTURE AMOUNT OF 1 AT COMPOUND INTEREST DUE IN *N* PERIODS)

The table in Exhibit C.2 is used to find the total interest expense on an investment or debt that is to be completed in some future period, including the impact of any compounding of interest. The calculation is:

$$(1 + \text{Interest rate})^{\text{Number of years}}$$

For example, to determine the total amount of an investment of $50,000 at the end of 11 years, using an interest rate of 8%, go to the compound interest table for future amounts, move down to the row that contains interest rate factors for 11 years, and move across to

Number of Years	Interest Rate												
	1%	2%	3%	4%	5%	6%	7%	8%	9%	10%	11%	12%	13%
1	1.01	1.02	1.03	1.04	1.05	1.06	1.07	1.08	1.09	1.10	1.11	1.12	1.13
2	1.02	1.04	1.06	1.08	1.10	1.12	1.14	1.16	1.18	1.20	1.22	1.24	1.26
3	1.03	1.06	1.09	1.12	1.15	1.18	1.21	1.24	1.27	1.30	1.33	1.36	1.39
4	1.04	1.08	1.12	1.16	1.20	1.24	1.28	1.32	1.36	1.40	1.44	1.48	1.52
5	1.05	1.10	1.15	1.20	1.25	1.30	1.35	1.40	1.45	1.50	1.55	1.60	1.65
6	1.06	1.12	1.18	1.24	1.30	1.36	1.42	1.48	1.54	1.60	1.66	1.72	1.78
7	1.07	1.14	1.21	1.28	1.35	1.42	1.49	1.56	1.63	1.70	1.77	1.84	1.91
8	1.08	1.16	1.24	1.32	1.40	1.48	1.56	1.64	1.72	1.80	1.88	1.96	2.04
9	1.09	1.18	1.27	1.36	1.45	1.54	1.63	1.72	1.81	1.90	1.99	2.08	2.17
10	1.10	1.20	1.30	1.40	1.50	1.60	1.70	1.80	1.90	2.00	2.10	2.20	2.30
11	1.11	1.22	1.33	1.44	1.55	1.66	1.77	1.88	1.99	2.10	2.21	2.32	2.43
12	1.12	1.24	1.36	1.48	1.60	1.72	1.84	1.96	2.08	2.20	2.32	2.44	2.56
13	1.13	1.26	1.39	1.52	1.65	1.78	1.91	2.04	2.17	2.30	2.43	2.56	2.69
14	1.14	1.28	1.42	1.56	1.70	1.84	1.98	2.12	2.26	2.40	2.54	2.68	2.82
15	1.15	1.30	1.45	1.60	1.75	1.90	2.05	2.20	2.35	2.50	2.65	2.80	2.95
16	1.16	1.32	1.48	1.64	1.80	1.96	2.12	2.28	2.44	2.60	2.76	2.92	3.08
17	1.17	1.34	1.51	1.68	1.85	2.02	2.19	2.36	2.53	2.70	2.87	3.04	3.21
18	1.18	1.36	1.54	1.72	1.90	2.08	2.26	2.44	2.62	2.80	2.98	3.16	3.34
19	1.19	1.38	1.57	1.76	1.95	2.14	2.33	2.52	2.71	2.90	3.09	3.28	3.47
20	1.20	1.40	1.60	1.80	2.00	2.20	2.40	2.60	2.80	3.00	3.10	3.40	3.60
21	1.21	1.42	1.63	1.84	2.05	2.26	2.47	2.68	2.89	3.10	3.31	3.52	3.73
22	1.22	1.44	1.66	1.88	2.10	2.32	2.54	2.76	2.98	3.20	3.42	3.64	3.86
23	1.23	1.46	1.69	1.92	2.15	2.38	2.61	2.84	3.07	3.30	3.53	3.76	3.99
24	1.24	1.48	1.72	1.96	2.20	2.44	2.68	2.92	3.16	3.40	3.64	3.88	4.12
25	1.25	1.50	1.75	2.00	2.25	2.50	2.75	3.00	3.25	3.50	3.75	4.00	4.25
26	1.26	1.52	1.78	2.04	2.30	2.56	2.82	3.08	3.34	3.60	3.86	4.12	4.38
27	1.27	1.54	1.81	2.08	2.35	2.62	2.89	3.16	3.43	3.70	3.97	4.24	4.51
28	1.28	1.56	1.84	2.12	2.40	2.68	2.96	3.24	3.52	3.80	4.08	4.36	4.64
29	1.29	1.58	1.87	2.16	2.45	2.74	3.03	3.32	3.61	3.90	4.19	4.48	4.77
30	1.30	1.60	1.90	2.20	2.50	2.80	3.10	3.40	3.70	4.00	4.30	4.60	4.90

EXHIBIT C.1   SIMPLE INTEREST TABLE

find the cell for an 8% interest rate, which contains a factor of 2.3316. Then, multiply this by $50,000 to arrive at $116,580.

C.3   COMPOUND INTEREST (PRESENT VALUE OF 1 DUE IN N PERIODS)

The table in Exhibit C.3 is used to determine the discounted current value of an investment that will be payable in a fixed amount at some point in the future. The calculation is:

$$\frac{1}{(1 + \text{Interest rate})^{\text{Number of years}}}$$

For example, to determine the discounted current value of a payment of $50,000 that will occur in 17 years, assuming a compounded rate of investment in the interim of 7%, go to the compound interest table for the present value of money due in future periods. Move

Interest Rate

Number of Years	1%	2%	3%	4%	5%	6%	7%	8%	9%	10%	11%	12%	13%
1	1.01000	1.02000	1.03000	1.04000	1.05000	1.06000	1.07000	1.08000	1.09000	1.10000	1.11000	1.12000	1.13000
2	1.02010	1.04040	1.06090	1.08160	1.10250	1.12360	1.14490	1.16640	1.18810	1.21000	1.23210	1.25440	1.27690
3	1.03030	1.06121	1.09273	1.12486	1.15763	1.19102	1.22504	1.25971	1.29503	1.33100	1.36763	1.40493	1.44290
4	1.04060	1.08243	1.12551	1.16986	1.21551	1.26248	1.31080	1.36049	1.41158	1.46410	1.51807	1.57352	1.63047
5	1.05101	1.10408	1.15927	1.21665	1.27628	1.33823	1.40255	1.46933	1.53862	1.61051	1.68506	1.76234	1.84244
6	1.06152	1.12616	1.19405	1.26532	1.34010	1.41852	1.50073	1.58687	1.67710	1.77156	1.87041	1.97382	2.08195
7	1.07214	1.14869	1.22987	1.31593	1.40710	1.50363	1.60578	1.71382	1.82804	1.94872	2.07616	2.21068	2.35261
8	1.08286	1.17166	1.26677	1.36857	1.47746	1.59385	1.71819	1.85093	1.99256	2.14359	2.30454	2.47596	2.65844
9	1.09369	1.19509	1.30477	1.42331	1.55133	1.68948	1.83846	1.99900	2.17189	2.35795	2.55804	2.77308	3.00404
10	1.10462	1.21899	1.34392	1.48024	1.62889	1.79085	1.96715	2.15892	2.36736	2.59374	2.83942	3.10585	3.39457
11	1.11567	1.24337	1.38423	1.53945	1.71034	1.89830	2.10485	2.33164	2.58043	2.85312	3.15176	3.47855	3.83586
12	1.12683	1.26824	1.42576	1.60103	1.79586	2.01220	2.25219	2.51817	2.81266	3.13843	3.49845	3.89598	4.33452
13	1.13809	1.29361	1.46853	1.66507	1.88565	2.13293	2.40985	2.71962	3.06580	3.45227	3.88328	4.36349	4.89801
14	1.14947	1.31948	1.51259	1.73168	1.97993	2.26090	2.57853	2.93719	3.34173	3.79750	4.31044	4.88711	5.53475
15	1.16097	1.34587	1.55797	1.80094	2.07893	2.39656	2.75903	3.17217	3.64248	4.17725	4.78459	5.47357	6.25427
16	1.17258	1.37279	1.60471	1.87298	2.18287	2.54035	2.95216	3.42594	3.97031	4.59497	5.31089	6.13039	7.06733
17	1.18430	1.40024	1.65285	1.94790	2.29202	2.69277	3.15882	3.70002	4.32763	5.05447	5.89509	6.86604	7.98608
18	1.19615	1.42825	1.70243	2.02582	2.40662	2.85434	3.37993	3.99602	4.71712	5.55992	6.54355	7.68997	9.02427
19	1.20811	1.45681	1.75351	2.10685	2.52695	3.02560	3.61653	4.31570	5.14166	6.11591	7.26334	8.61276	10.19742
20	1.22019	1.48595	1.80611	2.19112	2.65330	3.20714	3.86968	4.66096	5.60441	6.72750	8.06231	9.64629	11.52309
21	1.23239	1.51567	1.86029	2.27877	2.78596	3.39956	4.14056	5.03383	6.10881	7.40025	8.94917	10.80385	13.02109
22	1.24472	1.54598	1.91610	2.36992	2.92526	3.60354	4.43040	5.43654	6.65860	8.14027	9.93357	12.10031	14.71383
23	1.25716	1.57690	1.97359	2.46472	3.07152	3.81975	4.74053	5.87146	7.25787	8.95430	11.02627	13.55235	16.62663
24	1.26973	1.60844	2.03279	2.56330	3.22510	4.04893	5.07237	6.34118	7.91108	9.84973	12.23916	15.17863	18.78809
25	1.28243	1.64061	2.09378	2.66584	3.38635	4.29187	5.42743	6.84848	8.62308	10.83471	13.58546	17.00006	21.23054
26	1.29526	1.67342	2.15659	2.77247	3.55567	4.54938	5.80735	7.39635	9.39916	11.91818	15.07986	19.04007	23.99051
27	1.30821	1.70689	2.22129	2.88337	3.73346	4.82235	6.21387	7.98806	10.24508	13.10999	16.73865	21.32488	27.10928
28	1.32129	1.74102	2.28793	2.99870	3.92013	5.11169	6.64884	8.62711	11.16714	14.42099	18.57990	23.88387	30.63349
29	1.33450	1.77584	2.35657	3.11865	4.11614	5.41839	7.11426	9.31727	12.17218	15.86309	20.62369	26.74993	34.61584
30	1.34785	1.81136	2.42726	3.24340	4.32194	5.74349	7.61226	10.06266	13.26768	17.44940	22.89230	29.95992	39.11590

EXHIBIT C.2 COMPOUND INTEREST TABLE (FUTURE AMOUNT OF 1 AT COMPOUND INTEREST DUE IN N PERIODS)

Interest Rate

Number of Years	1%	2%	3%	4%	5%	6%	7%	8%	9%	10%	11%	12%	13%
1	0.99010	0.98039	0.97087	0.96154	0.95238	0.94340	0.93458	0.92593	0.91743	0.90909	0.90090	0.89286	0.88496
2	0.98030	0.96117	0.94260	0.92456	0.90703	0.89000	0.87344	0.85734	0.84168	0.82645	0.81162	0.79719	0.78315
3	0.97059	0.94232	0.91514	0.88900	0.86384	0.83962	0.81630	0.79383	0.77218	0.75131	0.73119	0.71178	0.69305
4	0.96098	0.92385	0.88849	0.85480	0.82270	0.79209	0.76290	0.73503	0.70843	0.68301	0.65873	0.63552	0.61332
5	0.95147	0.90573	0.86261	0.82193	0.78353	0.74726	0.71299	0.68058	0.64993	0.62092	0.59345	0.56743	0.54276
6	0.94205	0.88797	0.83748	0.79031	0.74622	0.70496	0.66634	0.63017	0.59627	0.56447	0.53464	0.50663	0.48032
7	0.93272	0.87056	0.81309	0.75992	0.71068	0.66506	0.62275	0.58349	0.54703	0.51316	0.48166	0.45235	0.42506
8	0.92348	0.85349	0.78941	0.73069	0.67684	0.62741	0.58201	0.54027	0.50187	0.46651	0.43393	0.40388	0.37616
9	0.91434	0.83676	0.76642	0.70259	0.64461	0.59190	0.54393	0.50025	0.46043	0.42410	0.39092	0.36061	0.33288
10	0.90529	0.82035	0.74409	0.67556	0.61391	0.55839	0.50835	0.46319	0.42241	0.38554	0.35218	0.32197	0.29459
11	0.89632	0.80426	0.72242	0.64958	0.58468	0.52679	0.47509	0.42888	0.38753	0.35049	0.31728	0.28748	0.26070
12	0.88745	0.78849	0.70138	0.62460	0.55684	0.49697	0.44401	0.39711	0.35553	0.31863	0.28584	0.25668	0.23071
13	0.87866	0.77303	0.68095	0.60057	0.53032	0.46884	0.41496	0.36770	0.32618	0.28966	0.25751	0.22917	0.20416
14	0.86996	0.75788	0.66112	0.57748	0.50507	0.44230	0.38782	0.34046	0.29925	0.26333	0.23199	0.20462	0.18068
15	0.86135	0.74301	0.64186	0.55526	0.48102	0.41727	0.36245	0.31524	0.27454	0.23939	0.20900	0.18270	0.15989
16	0.85282	0.72845	0.62317	0.53391	0.45811	0.39365	0.33873	0.29189	0.25187	0.21763	0.18829	0.16312	0.14150
17	0.84438	0.71416	0.60502	0.51337	0.43630	0.37136	0.31657	0.27027	0.23107	0.19784	0.16963	0.14564	0.12522
18	0.83602	0.70016	0.58739	0.49363	0.41552	0.35034	0.29586	0.25025	0.21199	0.17986	0.15282	0.13004	0.11081
19	0.82774	0.68643	0.57029	0.47464	0.39573	0.33051	0.27651	0.23171	0.19449	0.16351	0.13768	0.11611	0.09806
20	0.81954	0.67297	0.55368	0.45639	0.37689	0.31180	0.25842	0.21455	0.17843	0.14864	0.12403	0.10367	0.08678
21	0.81143	0.65978	0.53755	0.43883	0.35894	0.29416	0.24151	0.19866	0.16370	0.13513	0.11174	0.09256	0.07680
22	0.80340	0.64684	0.52189	0.42196	0.34185	0.27751	0.22571	0.18394	0.15018	0.12285	0.10067	0.08264	0.06796
23	0.79544	0.63416	0.50669	0.40573	0.32557	0.26180	0.21095	0.17032	0.13778	0.11168	0.09069	0.07379	0.06014
24	0.78757	0.62172	0.49193	0.39012	0.31007	0.24698	0.19715	0.15770	0.12640	0.10153	0.08170	0.06588	0.05323
25	0.77977	0.60953	0.47761	0.37512	0.29530	0.23300	0.18425	0.14602	0.11597	0.09230	0.07361	0.05882	0.04710
26	0.77205	0.59758	0.46369	0.36069	0.28124	0.21981	0.17220	0.13520	0.10639	0.08391	0.06631	0.05252	0.04168
27	0.76440	0.58586	0.45019	0.34682	0.26785	0.20737	0.16093	0.12519	0.09761	0.07628	0.05974	0.04689	0.03689
28	0.75684	0.57437	0.43708	0.33348	0.25509	0.19563	0.15040	0.11591	0.08955	0.06934	0.05382	0.04187	0.03264
29	0.74934	0.56311	0.42435	0.32065	0.24295	0.18456	0.14056	0.10733	0.08215	0.06304	0.04849	0.03738	0.02889
30	0.74192	0.55207	0.41199	0.30832	0.23138	0.17411	0.13137	0.09938	0.07537	0.05731	0.04368	0.03338	0.02557

EXHIBIT C.3 COMPOUND INTEREST TABLE (PRESENT VALUE OF 1 DUE IN N PERIODS)

Number of Years	Interest Rate												
	1%	2%	3%	4%	5%	6%	7%	8%	9%	10%	11%	12%	13%
1	0.99010	0.98039	0.97087	0.96154	0.95238	0.94340	0.93458	0.92593	0.91743	0.90909	0.90090	0.89286	0.88496
2	1.97040	1.94156	1.91347	1.88609	1.85941	1.83339	1.80802	1.78326	1.75911	1.73554	1.71252	1.69005	1.66810
3	2.94099	2.88388	2.82861	2.77509	2.72325	2.67301	2.62432	2.57710	2.53129	2.48685	2.44371	2.40183	2.36115
4	3.90197	3.80773	3.71710	3.62990	3.54595	3.46511	3.38721	3.31213	3.23972	3.16987	3.10245	3.03735	2.97447
5	4.85343	4.71346	4.57971	4.45182	4.32948	4.21236	4.10020	3.99271	3.88965	3.79079	3.69590	3.60478	3.51723
6	5.79548	5.60143	5.41719	5.24214	5.07569	4.91732	4.76654	4.62288	4.48592	4.35526	4.23054	4.11141	3.99755
7	6.72819	6.47199	6.23028	6.00205	5.78637	5.58238	5.38929	5.20637	5.03295	4.86842	4.71220	4.56376	4.42261
8	7.65168	7.32548	7.01969	6.73274	6.46321	6.20979	5.97130	5.74664	5.53482	5.33493	5.14612	4.96764	4.79877
9	8.56602	8.16224	7.78611	7.43533	7.10782	6.80169	6.51523	6.24689	5.99525	5.75902	5.53705	5.32825	5.13166
10	9.47130	8.98259	8.53020	8.11090	7.72174	7.36009	7.02358	6.71008	6.41766	6.14457	5.88923	5.65022	5.42624
11	10.36763	9.78685	9.25262	8.76048	8.30641	7.88687	7.49867	7.13896	6.80519	6.49506	6.20652	5.93770	5.68694
12	11.25508	10.57534	9.95400	9.38507	8.86325	8.38384	7.94269	7.53608	7.16073	6.81369	6.49236	6.19437	5.91765
13	12.13374	11.34837	10.63496	9.98565	9.39357	8.85268	8.35765	7.90378	7.48690	7.10336	6.74987	6.42355	6.12181
14	13.00370	12.10625	11.29607	10.56312	9.89864	9.29498	8.74547	8.24424	7.78615	7.36669	6.98187	6.62817	6.30249
15	13.86505	12.84926	11.93794	11.11839	10.37966	9.71225	9.10791	8.55948	8.06069	7.60608	7.19087	6.81086	6.46238
16	14.71787	13.57771	12.56110	11.65230	10.83777	10.10590	9.44665	8.85137	8.31256	7.82371	7.37916	6.97399	6.60388
17	15.56225	14.29187	13.16612	12.16567	11.27407	10.47726	9.76322	9.12164	8.54363	8.02155	7.54879	7.11963	6.72909
18	16.39827	14.99203	13.75351	12.65930	11.68959	10.82760	10.05909	9.37189	8.75563	8.20141	7.70162	7.24967	6.83991
19	17.22601	15.67846	14.32380	13.13394	12.08532	11.15812	10.33560	9.60360	8.95011	8.36492	7.83929	7.36578	6.93797
20	18.04555	16.35143	14.87747	13.59033	12.46221	11.46992	10.59401	9.81815	9.12855	8.51356	7.96333	7.46944	7.02475
21	18.85698	17.01121	15.41502	14.02916	12.82115	11.76408	10.83553	10.01680	9.29224	8.64869	8.07507	7.56200	7.10155
22	19.66038	17.65805	15.93692	14.45112	13.16300	12.04158	11.06124	10.20074	9.44243	8.77154	8.17574	7.64465	7.16951
23	20.45582	18.29220	16.44361	14.85684	13.48857	12.30338	11.27219	10.37106	9.58021	8.88322	8.26643	7.71843	7.22966
24	21.24339	18.91393	16.93554	15.24696	13.79864	12.55036	11.46933	10.52876	9.70661	8.98474	8.34814	7.78432	7.28288
25	22.02316	19.52346	17.41315	15.62208	14.09394	12.78336	11.65358	10.67478	9.82258	9.07704	8.42174	7.84314	7.32999
26	22.79520	20.12104	17.87684	15.98277	14.37519	13.00317	11.82578	10.80998	9.92897	9.16095	8.48806	7.89566	7.37167
27	23.55961	20.70690	18.32703	16.32959	14.64303	13.21053	11.98671	10.93516	10.02658	9.23722	8.54780	7.94255	7.40856
28	24.31644	21.28127	18.76411	16.66306	14.89813	13.40616	12.13711	11.05108	10.11613	9.30657	8.60162	7.98442	7.44120
29	25.06579	21.84438	19.18845	16.98371	15.14107	13.59072	12.27767	11.15841	10.19828	9.36961	8.65011	8.02181	7.47009
30	25.80771	22.39646	19.60044	17.29203	15.37245	13.76483	12.40904	11.25778	10.27365	9.42691	8.69379	8.05518	7.49565

Exhibit C.4 Present Value of Ordinary Annuity of 1 per Period

Interest Rate

Number of Years	1%	2%	3%	4%	5%	6%	7%	8%	9%	10%	11%	12%	13%
1	1.00000	1.00000	1.00000	1.00000	1.00000	1.00000	1.00000	1.00000	1.00000	1.00000	1.00000	1.00000	1.00000
2	2.01000	2.02000	2.03000	2.04000	2.05000	2.06000	2.07000	2.08000	2.09000	2.10000	2.11000	2.12000	2.13000
3	3.03010	3.06040	3.09090	3.12160	3.15250	3.18360	3.21490	3.24640	3.27810	3.31000	3.34210	3.37440	3.40690
4	4.06040	4.12161	4.18363	4.24646	4.31013	4.37462	4.43994	4.50611	4.57313	4.64100	4.70973	4.77933	4.84980
5	5.10101	5.20404	5.30914	5.41632	5.52563	5.63709	5.75074	5.86660	5.98471	6.10510	6.22780	6.35285	6.48027
6	6.15202	6.30812	6.46841	6.63298	6.80191	6.97532	7.15329	7.33593	7.52333	7.71561	7.91286	8.11519	8.32271
7	7.21354	7.43428	7.66246	7.89829	8.14201	8.39384	8.65402	8.92280	9.20043	9.48717	9.78327	10.08901	10.40466
8	8.28567	8.58297	8.89234	9.21423	9.54911	9.89747	10.25980	10.63663	11.02847	11.43589	11.85943	12.29969	12.75726
9	9.36853	9.75463	10.15911	10.58280	11.02656	11.49132	11.97799	12.48756	13.02104	13.57948	14.16397	14.77566	15.41571
10	10.46221	10.94972	11.46388	12.00611	12.57789	13.18079	13.81645	14.48656	15.19293	15.93742	16.72201	17.54874	18.41975
11	11.56683	12.16872	12.80780	13.48635	14.20679	14.97164	15.78360	16.64549	17.56029	18.53117	19.56143	20.65458	21.81432
12	12.68250	13.41209	14.19203	15.02581	15.91713	16.86994	17.88845	18.97713	20.14072	21.38428	22.71319	24.13313	25.65018
13	13.80933	14.68033	15.61779	16.62684	17.71298	18.88214	20.14064	21.49530	22.95338	24.52271	26.21164	28.02911	29.98470
14	14.94742	15.97394	17.08632	18.29191	19.59863	21.01507	22.55049	24.21492	26.01919	27.97498	30.09492	32.39260	34.88271
15	16.09690	17.29342	18.59891	20.02359	21.57856	23.27597	25.12902	27.15211	29.36092	31.77248	34.40536	37.27971	40.41746
16	17.25786	18.63929	20.15688	21.82453	23.65749	25.67253	27.88805	30.32428	33.00340	35.94973	39.18995	42.75328	46.67173
17	18.43044	20.01207	21.76159	23.69751	25.84037	28.21288	30.84022	33.75023	36.97370	40.54470	44.50084	48.88367	53.73906
18	19.61475	21.41231	23.41444	25.64541	28.13238	30.90565	33.99903	37.45024	41.30134	45.59917	50.39594	55.74971	61.72514
19	20.81090	22.84056	25.11687	27.67123	30.53900	33.75999	37.37896	41.44626	46.01846	51.15909	56.93949	63.43968	70.74941
20	22.01900	24.29737	26.87037	29.77808	33.06595	36.78559	40.99549	45.76196	51.16012	57.27500	64.20283	72.05244	80.94683
21	23.23919	25.78332	28.67649	31.96920	35.71925	39.99273	44.86518	50.42292	56.76453	64.00250	72.26514	81.69874	92.46992
22	24.47159	27.29898	30.53678	34.24797	38.50521	43.39229	49.00574	55.45676	62.87334	71.40275	81.21431	92.50258	105.49101
23	25.71630	28.84496	32.45288	36.61789	41.43048	46.99583	53.43614	60.89330	69.53194	79.54302	91.14788	104.60289	120.20484
24	26.97346	30.42186	34.42647	39.08260	44.50200	50.81558	58.17667	66.76476	76.78981	88.49733	102.17415	118.15524	136.83147
25	28.24320	32.03030	36.45926	41.64591	47.72710	54.86451	63.24904	73.10594	84.70090	98.34706	114.41331	133.33387	155.61956
26	29.52563	33.67091	38.55304	44.31174	51.11345	59.15638	68.67647	79.95442	93.32398	109.18177	127.99877	150.33393	176.85010
27	30.82089	35.34432	40.70963	47.08421	54.66913	63.70577	74.48382	87.35077	102.72313	121.09994	143.07864	169.37401	200.84061
28	32.12910	37.05121	42.93092	49.96758	58.40258	68.52811	80.69769	95.33883	112.96822	134.20994	159.81729	190.69889	227.94989
29	33.45039	38.79223	45.21885	52.96629	62.32271	73.63980	87.34653	103.96594	124.13536	148.63093	178.39719	214.58275	258.58338
30	34.78489	40.56808	47.57542	56.08494	66.43885	79.05819	94.46079	113.28321	136.30754	164.49402	199.02088	241.33268	293.19922

EXHIBIT C.5 FUTURE AMOUNT OF ORDINARY ANNUITY OF 1 PER PERIOD

down to the row that contains discounting factors for 17 years, and move across to find the cell for a 7% interest rate, which contains a factor of 0.3166. Then, multiply this by $50,000 to arrive at $15,830.

C.4   PRESENT VALUE OF ORDINARY ANNUITY OF 1 PER PERIOD

The table in Exhibit C.4 is used to find the present value of a fixed number of payments in the future. The calculation is:

$$\frac{1 - \dfrac{1}{(1 + \text{Interest rate})^{\text{Number of years}}}}{\text{Interest rate}}$$

For example, to determine the present value of a series of annual payments of $2,500 for the next 22 years at a discount rate of 13%, go to the table for the present value of an ordinary annuity of 1 per period. Move down to the row that contains discounting factors for 22 years, and move across to find the cell for a 13% interest rate, which contains a discount factor of 7.1695. Then, multiply this by $2,500 to arrive at a present value of $17,923.75.

C.5   FUTURE AMOUNT OF ORDINARY ANNUITY OF 1 PER PERIOD

The table in Exhibit C.5 is used to determine the future value of a series of fixed payments. The calculation is:

$$\frac{(1 + \text{Interest rate})^{\text{Number of years}} - 1}{\text{Interest rate}}$$

For example, to determine the future value of a series of 10 $5,000 annual payments at an interest rate of 5%, go to the table for the future amount of an ordinary annuity. Move down to the row that contains compounding factors for 10 years, and move across to find the cell for a 5% interest rate, which contains a discount factor of 12.5779. Then, multiply this by $5,000 to arrive at a future value of $62,889.50.

RATIOS

This appendix contains the formulas needed to calculate many of the most common accounting ratios, as well as brief explanations for each one. They are listed in alphabetical order.

- *Accounts payable days*. This formula is similar to the accounts payable turnover calculation, except that it converts the amount of outstanding payables into the average number of days of purchases that are currently unpaid. The formula is:

$$\frac{\text{Ending accounts payable}}{\text{Annual purchases}/365}$$

- *Accounts payable turnover*. This formula reveals the speed with which a company is paying its accounts payable, and is a particularly effective way to determine company liquidity levels when tracked on a time line, so that changes in payment patterns are readily apparent. The formula is:

$$\frac{\text{Total purchases}}{\text{Average level of accounts payable}}$$

- *Accounts receivable days*. This formula is similar to the accounts receivable turnover calculation, except that it converts the amount of outstanding receivables into the average number of days it will take to collect them. The formula is:

$$\frac{(\text{Beginning accounts receivable} + \text{Ending accounts receivable})/2}{\text{Annualized revenue}/365}$$

- *Accounts receivable turnover*. This formula is used to determine the number of days over which the average account receivable is outstanding. It is best used when plotted on a trend line, in order to spot and act upon any unfavorable changes. The formula is:

$$\frac{\text{Annualized credit sales}}{(\text{Beginning accounts receivable} + \text{Ending accounts receivable})/2}$$

- *Backlog to sales ratio*. This formula is a good way to determine if there will be trouble achieving sales goals in the near term, since a low proportion of backlog to sales reveals that only some last-minute orders will allow a company to reach its sales targets. However, the ratio can be misleading if sales are highly seasonal, since the backlog will drop significantly once the prime sales season is over. The formula is:

$$\frac{\text{Dollar total of all orders not yet in production}}{\text{Average monthly revenue}}$$

- *Backlog days ratio*. This formula is similar to the backlog to sales ratio, except that it converts the backlog amount into the number of days sales that they represent. The formula is:

$$\frac{\text{Total backlog}}{\text{Annualized revenue}/365}$$

- *Bill of material accuracy*. This formula reveals the percentage of line items on a company's bills of material that contain accurate part numbers, quantities, and units of measure. Though this is not strictly an accounting measure, the accuracy of a company's bill of material records has a major impact on the accuracy of its finished goods and work-in-process inventory, and so is of concern to the accountant. The formula is:

$$\frac{\text{Number of accurate parts itemized on a bill of material}}{\text{Total number of parts itemized on a bill of material}}$$

- *Book value*. This formula results in a price per share that should theoretically be realized if a company were to liquidate, paying off all liabilities. It is strictly theoretical, for it presumes that the liquidation value of all assets and liabilities on the books exactly matches the amounts shown on the balance sheet. The formula is:

$$\frac{\text{Stockholder's equity}}{\text{Number of common shares outstanding}}$$

- *Breakeven plant capacity*. This formula reveals the manufacturing capacity level at which a company will break even. This formula must be used with some caution, for the fixed expense level used in its calculation is assumed to be constant through a wide range of capacity levels (which is not always true), while it also assumes that the current level of capacity usage is known (which may be difficult to determine). Consequently, the results may not be precise. The formula is:

$$\frac{\text{Fixed expenses} \times \text{Current percent of plant usage}}{\text{Revenue} - \text{Variable expenses}}$$

- *Breakeven point*. This formula is used to determine the minimum sales level at which a company or some smaller business unit will generate a profit of exactly zero. It is particularly useful when compared to production capacity, since it can reveal that a company may use nearly all of its capacity just to reach breakeven, and so has no chance to earn more than a small profit even at full capacity. The formula is:

$$\frac{\text{Total operating expenses}}{\text{Average gross margin}}$$

Total operating expenses are defined as all expenses related to the business unit that are not part of the cost of goods sold.

- *Capital employed ratio*. This formula is used to determine how efficiently capital is being used to generate sales. It subtracts all assets not directly associated with operations, such as investments, and divides the remainder into annual sales. The formula is:

$$\frac{\text{Annualized revenue}}{\text{Capital} - \text{Assets not directly related to operations}}$$

- *Cash flow adequacy.* This formula is the most comprehensive one for determining if a company's cash flows are sufficient to meet all ongoing commitments outside of standard operations, such as asset purchases, dividend payouts, and debt payments. A ratio of more than one indicates a sufficient level of cash flow. The formula is:

$$\frac{\text{Cash flow from operations}}{\text{All budgeted payments for asset purchases, debt, and dividend payments}}$$

- *Cash ratio.* This formula is more restrictive than the quick ratio, because it compares only those assets that can be immediately converted to cash to any current liabilities (for example, it excludes accounts receivable from the calculation). This gives the best picture of extremely short-term liquidity for an organization. The formula is:

$$\frac{\text{Cash} + \text{Marketable securities}}{\text{Current liabilities}}$$

- *Cash turnover ratio.* This formula is used to determine the level of efficient use that management is making of its cash. Ideally, there should be only the minimum amount of cash on hand to deal with operating needs, while all other cash is shifted to investments. The formula is:

$$\frac{\text{Total sales}}{\text{Total period} - \text{end cash}}$$

- *Collection period.* This formula is used to determine the average number of days that invoices are outstanding. Any changes in the collection period over time are indicative of either changes in the level of collection effort or in the credit policies being extended to customers. The formula is:

$$\frac{\text{Average annualized accounts receivable}}{\text{Average daily credit sales}}$$

- *Current ratio.* This is a simple means for determining a company's level of liquidity. If the ratio of current assets to current liabilities is substantially greater than one, then the company can be said to have good liquidity. However, since a component of this calculation is inventory (which may not be readily convertible to cash), it can be misleading. A better calculation for the purposes of determining liquidity is the quick ratio. The formula for the current ratio is:

$$\frac{\text{Cash} + \text{Accounts receivable} + \text{Marketable securities} + \text{Inventory}}{\text{Accounts payable} + \text{Other short} - \text{term liabilities}}$$

- *Debt/equity ratio.* This formula is used by lenders to determine the degree of leverage that a management team has created. Though this measure will vary widely by industry, a debt level that is higher than the amount of equity will generally be an indication of excessive leverage. The formula is:

$$\frac{\text{Long-term debt} + \text{Short-term debt}}{\text{Total equity}}$$

- *Dividend payout ratio.* This formula is used to determine the proportion of cash flow that is being consumed by dividend payments. It is most useful when tracked on a time line, so that one can see if there is a trend that may result in a company's inability to pay dividends. The formula is:

$$\frac{\text{Total dividend payments}}{\text{Cash flow from operations}}$$

- *Economic value added.* This formula is used to determine if a company is earning a return on capital that is higher than its cost of capital, and is useful for tracking a company's ability to provide good returns on invested capital to its investors. The formula is:

$$(\text{Net investment}) \times (\text{Actual return on assets} - \text{Required minimum rate of return})$$

- *Fixed asset turnover.* This formula is used to determine the amount of fixed assets needed to obtain a specified sales level. It should not be relied upon for precise predictions of asset investments that will be needed to support increased sales levels, but can be a reasonable method for cross-checking the adequacy of budgeted capital purchases at various levels of sales activity. The formula is:

$$\frac{\text{Net sales}}{(\text{Beginning fixed assets} + \text{Ending fixed assets})/2}$$

- *Fixed assets to total assets ratio.* This formula is used to determine the proportion of fixed assets that are likely to be required as other asset levels change. It is most often used as a cross-check when developing budgets, in order to verify if budgeted capital expenditure levels are in line with historical experience. The formula is:

$$\frac{\text{Total fixed assets prior to depreciation}}{\text{Total assets}}$$

- *Fixed assets to debt ratio.* This formula is of most use to a company's lenders, who may have collateralized their lending with its fixed assets. Lenders will have some assurance that they can offset unpaid debts with the sale of company assets if this ratio is less than one. However, the ratio uses the original book value of the fixed assets, rather than their current fair market value, so the ratio can be misleading. The formula is:

$$\frac{\text{Total fixed assets}}{\text{Total collateralized debt}}$$

- *Fringe benefits to direct labor ratio.* This formula is used to determine if a company's benefits expenditures are in line with those of its competitors. It can also be compared to the same ratio for specific departments of companies within other industries, in order to verify that benefit levels are sufficient for specific job categories, as well as industries. The formula is:

$$\frac{\text{Total fringe benefit expense}}{\text{Total labor salary and wage expense}}$$

- *General and administrative productivity.* This formula is used to compare the overhead costs in the selling, general and administrative expense categories to overall sales activity. It can be used for benchmarking purposes to see if a company's expenses in these areas are in line with those of similar companies. The formula is:

$$\frac{\text{Selling, general \& administrative expenses}}{\text{Annualized revenue}}$$

- *Indirect to direct labor ratio.* This formula is used to determine the level of efficiency a company has achieved in keeping its supporting staff of indirect labor personnel as small as possible. The formula is:

$$\frac{\text{Number of indirect labor full-time equivalents}}{\text{Number of direct labor full-time equivalents}}$$

- *Inventory accuracy.* This formula is used to determine the record accuracy within the inventory database. It requires one to compare a detailed list of booked inventory items to the inventory physically in the warehouse, and record as errors anything that has an inaccurate part or product description, location, quantity, or unit of measure. This information is critical to the accountant, who relies on accurate inventory records to create the financial statements. The formula is:

$$\frac{\text{Number of accurate inventory test items}}{\text{Total number of inventory items sampled}}$$

- *Inventory days on hand.* This formula is used to determine the number of days it would take to use up all of the inventory on hand, given an average level of sales to do so. The formula is:

$$365 \text{ days} \times \frac{\text{Ending inventory}}{\text{Annualized cost of goods sold}}$$

- *Inventory turnover ratio.* This formula is frequently used to compare the proportion of inventory on hand to the level of sales. It can be compared to industry averages to see if there is too much inventory in stock. However, it can be misleading if sales levels fluctuate considerably during the year, resulting in wide fluctuations in the measurement. The formula is:

$$\frac{\text{Annualized cost of goods sold}}{\text{Average inventory}}$$

- *Net income to capital ratio.* This formula is used to determine the return, free and clear of all expenses, that investors are receiving on their invested equity. Though this provides some information to investors, the gain or loss on an investor's equity is also influenced by the perception of the future value of the company, which may be quite unrelated to the net income figure used in the calculation of this ratio. The formula is:

$$\frac{\text{Net income}}{\text{Stockholders' equity}}$$

- *Number of times interest earned.* This formula is used to determine the amount of excess cash that a company has available to cover its debt payments. If there is barely enough cash available to do so, then the organization has reached the practical limit of its borrowing capacity. The formula is:

$$\frac{\text{Average interest expense}}{\text{Total excess cash flow before interest payments}}$$

- *Obsolete inventory percentage.* This formula is used to determine the proportion of inventory that may require an obsolescence reserve. It is a highly judgmental calculation, since the "no recent usage" part of the calculation can refer to any time period that one may choose. The formula is:

$$\frac{\text{Cost of inventory items with no recent usage}}{\text{Total inventory cost}}$$

- *Operating cash flow.* This formula is used to strip away all impacts on reported cash flows that are caused by financing activities, so that one can see how much cash flow (if any) is being created by operations on an ongoing basis. The formula is:

$$\text{Profit} + \text{Noncash expenses} +/- \text{Changes in working capital}$$

- *Overhead to direct cost ratio.* This formula may be of interest when a company is deciding whether to use an activity-based costing (ABC) system. If this ratio is greater than one, then a strong case can be made to switch to ABC, because the company's cost structure leans so heavily toward overhead costs that it is necessary to take the greatest possible care in allocating it properly. The formula is:

$$\frac{\text{Total overhead costs}}{\text{Total direct material} + \text{Total direct labor costs}}$$

- *Price-earnings ratio.* This formula is used by investors to compare the relative price of a company's stock in relation to that of other companies in the same industry. If the ratio is low relative to the industry, then it may be worth buying, on the grounds that the market price of the stock should eventually return to the mean by rising. Also, a high ratio shows that investors have high expectations for the company, and so have bid up its price. The formula is:

$$\frac{\text{Current market price per share}}{\text{Earnings per share}}$$

- *Purchase discounts proportion of total payments.* This formula is used to determine the percentage of accounts payable for which discounts are being taken, and is most useful when tracked on a time line, in order to see if there are changes in the percentage that are indicative of missed discounts. The formula is:

$$\frac{\text{Total number of purchase discounts taken}}{\text{Total number of supplier invoices paid}}$$

- *Quick ratio.* This formula is used to determine a company's liquidity. It is better than the current ratio, because it excludes the impact of inventory (which may not be easily liquidated). A quick ratio of greater than one is indicative of a reasonable level of liquidity. The formula is:

$$\frac{\text{Cash} + \text{Accounts receivable} + \text{Marketable securities}}{\text{Accounts payable} + \text{Other short-term liabilities}}$$

- *Retained earnings to capital ratio.* This formula is useful for determining the proportion of a company's capital that is composed of retained profits. A high ratio reveals that a company has not only brought in a large amount of funds through profits, but also that it has retained the funds, rather than paid them out through dividends. The formula is:

$$\frac{\text{Retained earnings}}{\text{Stockholders' equity}}$$

- *Return on assets.* This formula is used to determine if company assets are being efficiently utilized to create profits. It focuses attention on the amount of assets used within a company, and frequently leads to tighter management of the capital budgeting process. Be aware that the "total assets" part of the equation includes all assets, such as cash, accounts receivable, inventory, and fixed assets. A common misconception is to only include fixed assets in the calculation. The formula is:

$$\frac{\text{Net income}}{\text{Total assets}}$$

- *Sales per person.* This formula gives an indication of the efficiency of a company in generating sales and manufacturing products or services. It should be compared to industry averages, since this measure varies widely by industry. The formula is:

$$\frac{\text{Revenue}}{\text{Total number of full-time equivalent employees}}$$

- *Scrap percentage.* This formula tracks the proportion of scrap that is spun off by a production operation. It is most useful when calculated for specific production lines or machines, so that problem areas can be more quickly identified and corrected. The formula is:

$$\frac{(\text{Actual cost of goods sold}) - (\text{Standard cost of goods sold})}{\text{Standard cost of goods sold}}$$

- *Work-in-process turnover.* This formula is useful for determining the proportion of work-in-process inventory that is required to produce a specific amount of product. It is closely watched by those companies installing accelerated production systems, such as just-in-time systems, that should result in reduced inventory levels in this area. The formula is:

$$\frac{\text{Total work-in-process inventory}}{\text{Annual cost of goods sold}}$$

- *Working capital productivity.* This formula is used to determine changes in the proportion of working capital to sales; a reduction in the proportion of working capital is evidence of enhanced levels of operational improvement. The formula is:

$$\frac{\text{Annual net sales}}{(\text{Beginning working capital} + \text{Ending working capital})/2}$$

DUE DILIGENCE CHECKLIST

The general topic of mergers and acquisitions was covered in Chapter 39, including a lengthy discussion of the key topics to address in a due diligence proceeding. This appendix includes a more detailed checklist that one can use as a master list, picking only those topics that appear to be relevant to the due diligence tasks at hand. They are as follows.

E.1 INDUSTRY OVERVIEW

- What is the size of the industry?
- How is the industry segmented?
- What is the industry's projected growth and profitability?
- What are the factors affecting growth and profitability?
- What are the trends in the number of competitors and their size, product innovation, distribution, finances, regulation, and product liability?

E.2 CORPORATE OVERVIEW

- When and where was the company founded, and by whom?
- What is its history of product development?
- What is the history of the management team?
- Has the corporate location changed?
- Have there been ownership changes?
- Have there been acquisitions or divestitures?
- What is its financial history?

E.3   ORGANIZATION AND GENERAL CORPORATE ISSUES

- Obtain the articles of incorporation and bylaws. Review for the existence of preemptive rights, rights of first refusal, registration rights, or any other rights related to the issuance or registration of securities.
- Review the bylaws for any unusual provisions affecting shareholder rights or restrictions on ownership, transfer, or voting of shares.
- Review the terms associated with any preferred stock or unexercised warrants.
- Describe any antitakeover provisions.
- Obtain certificates of good standing for the company and all significant subsidiaries.
- Obtain the minutes from all shareholder meetings for the past five years. Review them for proper notice prior to meetings, the existence of a quorum, and proper voting procedures; verify that stock issuances have been authorized; verify that insider transactions have been approved; verify that officers have been properly elected; verify that shares are properly approved and reserved for stock option and purchase plans.
- Obtain the minutes of the Executive Committee and Audit Committee for the past five years, as well as the minutes of any other special board committees. Review all documents.
- If the company is publicly held, obtain all periodic filings for the past five years, including the 10-K, 10-Q, 8-K, and Schedule 13D.
- Review all annual and quarterly reports to shareholders.
- Obtain a list of all states in which the company is qualified to do business and a list of those states in which it maintains significant operations. Determine if there is any state where the company is not qualified but should be qualified to do business.
- Review the articles of incorporation and bylaws of each significant subsidiary. Determine if there are restriction on dividends to the company. For each subsidiary, review the minutes of the board of directors for matters requiring disclosure. Also review each subsidiary's legal right to do business in each state in which it operates.
- Review the company's correspondence with the SEC, any national exchange, or state securities commission, other than routine transmittals, for the past five years. Determine if there are or were any enforcement or disciplinary actions or any ongoing investigations or suggestions of violations by any of these entities.
- Review all corporate insurance, using a schedule from the company's insurance agency. If there is material pending litigation, determine the extent of insurance coverage and obtain insurance company confirmation.
- Review all pending and threatened legal proceedings to which the company or any of its subsidiaries is a party. Describe principal parties, allegations, and relief sought. This includes any governmental or environmental proceedings. Obtain copies of existing consent decrees or significant settlement agreements relating to the company or its subsidiaries.
- Review the auditor's letter to management concerning internal accounting controls and procedures, as well as any management responses.
- If there has been a change in accountants during the past five years, find out why.
- Review any reports of outside consultants or analysts concerning the company.

- Review any correspondence during the past five years with the EPA, FTC, OSHA, EEOC, or IRS. Determine if there are any ongoing investigations or suggestions of violations by any of these agencies.
- Research any press releases or articles about the company within the past year (see Bloomberg.com, NEXIS, Equifax, etc.).
- Review all contracts that are important to operations. Also review any contracts with shareholders or officers. In particular, look for the following provisions:
  - Default or termination provisions.
  - Restrictions on company action.
  - Consent requirements.
  - Termination provisions in employment contracts.
  - Ownership of technology.
  - Cancellation provisions in major supply and customer contracts.
  - Unusual warranties or the absence of protective provisions.
- Review any required regulatory compliance and verify that necessary licenses and permits have been maintained, as well as ongoing filings and reports.
- Review all current patent, trademark, service mark, trade name, and copyright agreements, and note renewal dates.
- Project sales for the next five years for copyrighted works and products using the trademarked names.
- Obtain a list of all trademark applications currently in process, as well as those submitted following rejection by the Patent and Trademark Office.
- Estimate future revenue for the next five years for both current and expected patents.
- Review all related party transactions for the past three years.
- Review the terms of any outbound or inbound royalty agreements.
- Establish if any company software (either used internally or resold) was obtained from another company. If so, what are the terms under which the code is licensed? Are there any associated royalty payments?
- Review all legal invoices for the past two years.
- Obtain a copy of any factoring agreements.
- Obtain copies of all outsourcing agreements.

E.4   CAPITALIZATION AND SIGNIFICANT SUBSIDIARIES

- Review all board resolutions authorizing the issuance of stock to ensure that all shares are validly issued.
- Review debt agreements to which the company or any subsidiary is a party, as well as all debt guarantees. Note any restrictions on dividends, on incurring extra debt, and on issuing additional capital stock. Note any unusual consent or default provisions. If subordinated debt securities are being issued, compare new subordination provisions with the provisions for other agreements for compatibility. Review the latest borrowing base certificates. Inquire whether there are any defaults or potential defaults.

- Review any disclosure documents used in the private placement of securities or loan applications during the preceding five years.
- Review all documents affecting ownership, voting, or rights to acquire the company's stock for required disclosure and significance to the purchase transactions, such as warrants, options, security holder agreements, registration rights agreements, shareholder rights, or poison pill plans.

E.5   CULTURAL ISSUES—GENERAL

- Determine the general flow of decision-making processes.
- Determine the most common problem-solving systems used.
- Ascertain the types of conflict resolution used.
- Determine the general level of adherence to corporate policies.
- Ascertain formal and information communication systems.
- Itemize the performance monitoring systems used and the impact of these systems on employee behavior.
- Review documentation regarding previous ethical lapses by employees.

E.6   CULTURAL ISSUES—MANAGEMENT

- Determine the management style used.
- Ascertain the relationships among the management team.
- Determine the level and type of communication used prior to reaching decisions.
- Determine likely areas of interaction difficulty between the current management team and the company.

E.7   EMPLOYEES

- Obtain copies of any employment agreements.
- Obtain copies of any noncompete agreements.
- Obtain copies of any salesperson compensation agreements.
- Obtain copies of any director compensation agreements.
- Obtain copies of any option plans.
- Summarize any loan amounts and terms to officers, directors, or employees.
- Obtain any union labor agreements.
- Determine the number of states to which payroll taxes must be paid.
- Obtain a copy of the employee manual.
- Obtain a list of all employees, their current compensation, and compensation for the prior year.
- Summarize the names, ages, titles, education, experience, and professional biographies of the senior management team.
- Obtain copies of employee resumes.
- Establish the employee turnover rate for the past two years.
- Obtain a copy of the organization chart.

E.8 REVENUE

- Summarize sales by customer for the current and past year.
- Obtain a list of new customers gained in each of the last three years, along with sales by year.
- Obtain a list of all existing customers for whom there were minimal sales in the following year, for each of the last three years, showing sales in the year.
- Summarize sales by product for the current and past year.
- Summarize the backlog by customer.
- Summarize the backlog by custom work and standard products.
- Determine how much staffing is required to complete the existing backlog of custom work.
- Determine the seasonality of revenue.
- Determine the amount of ongoing maintenance revenue from standard software products.
- Obtain copies of all outstanding proposals, bids, and offers pending award.
- Obtain copies of all existing contracts for products or services, including warranty and guarantee work.

E.9 ASSETS

- Obtain copies of all asset leases, and review them for term, early payment, and bargain purchase clauses.
- Obtain copies of all office space lease agreements, and review them for term and renewal provisions.
- Review the title insurance for any significant land parcels owned by the company.
- Obtain current detail of accounts receivable.
- Obtain a list of all accounts and notes receivable from employees.
- Obtain a list of all inventory items, and discuss the obsolescence reserve.
- Obtain the current fixed asset listing, as well as depreciation calculations.
- Review the bad debt reserve calculation.
- Obtain an itemized list of all assets that are not receivables or fixed assets.
- Obtain any maintenance agreements on company equipment.
- Is there an upcoming need to replace assets?
- Discuss whether there are any plans to close, relocate, or expand any facilities.
- Itemize all capitalized R&D or software development expenses.

E.10 LIABILITIES

- Verify wage and tax remittances to all government entities, and that there are no unpaid amounts.
- Obtain a list of all accounts payable to employees.
- Review the sufficiency of accruals for wages, vacation time, legal expenses, insurance, property taxes, and commissions.
- Review the terms of any lines of credit.

- Review the amount and terms of any other debt agreements.
- Review the current accounts payable listing.
- Obtain copies of all unexpired purchasing commitments (purchase orders, etc.).

E.11   FINANCIAL STATEMENTS

- Obtain audited financial statements for the last three years.
- Obtain monthly financial statements for the current year.
- Establish the revenues and profits per employee.
- Establish the direct labor expense as a percentage of revenue.
- Obtain copies of federal tax returns for the last three years.
- Verify the most recent bank reconciliation.
- Determine profitability by product, by customer, and by segment.
- Obtain a copy of the business plan and budget.

E.12   INTERNET

- Does the company use the Internet for internal use as an interactive part of operations? What functions are used in this manner?
- Has the company's firewall ever been penetrated, and how sensitive is the information stored on the company network's publicly available segments?
- Does the company provide technical support information through its Web site?
- Are Web site usage statistics tracked? If so, how are they used for management decisions?
- In what way could operational costs decrease if the company's customers interacted with it through the Internet?

E.13   SOFTWARE DEVELOPMENT

- Who are the key development personnel involved with the creation, coding, and evaluation of software products? What is their tenure and educational background?
- How much money is invested annually in development? As a proportion of sales?
- What is the strategic plan for the development of new products? What is the timeline for their introduction? To what markets are they targeted?
- How many patches were required to make the last major software release stable and commercially viable?
- What was the average time required to resolve customer software problems?
- How many customer accounts have been lost due to a software upgrade? What reasons did they give for dropping maintenance?
- What operating system platforms are the target for the company's software products? Is there a plan to port any company products to other platforms? For what proportion of existing products has this been done?
- Does the company use structured programming techniques that allow for easy software updating, maintenance, and enhancement?

- What development languages and tools does the development staff use now? Are there plans to change to other languages and tools?
- What are the attributes that make the company's products unique?
- What is the company's strategy in designing new products (e.g., quality, support, special features).

E.14   PRODUCT DEVELOPMENT

- Itemize all current research and development activities, including projected time and costs to complete, and expected five-year revenue projections from each one.
- Identify the key staff required to complete each project.
- Identify likely patents to be obtained from existing research and development efforts.

E.15   MARKETING

- What types of advertising and promotion are used?
- Does the company have a Web site? Who owns the site and how is it hosted?
- Does the company use e-mail for marketing notifications to customers?
- What are the proportions of sales by distribution channel?
- How many customers can the company potentially market its products to? What would be the volume by customer?
- What is the company's market share? What is the trend?
- Are there new markets in which the products can be sold?

E.16   SALES

- What is the sales strategy (e.g., add customers, increase support, increase penetration into existing customer base, pricing, etc.)?
- What is the structure of the sales organization? Are there independent sales representatives?
- Obtain the sales organization chart.
- How many sales personnel are in each sales position?
- What is the sales force's geographic coverage?
- What is the sales force's compensation, split by base pay and commission?
- What was the sales per salesperson for the past year?
- What was the sales expense per salesperson for the past year?
- What is the sales projection by product for the next 12 months?
- Into what category do customers fall—end users, retailers, OEMs, wholesalers, and/or distributors?
- Who are the top 10 customers, based on sales volume?
- What is the historical sales volume to all customers for the past three years?
- How many customers are there for each product, industry, and geographic region?
- What is the average order size?

- Does the company have an Internet store? Does the site accept online payments and orders? What percentage of total sales come through this medium?
- How many customers have current subscriptions or maintenance for the company's software? What is the dollar amount per customer? What is the growth rate in the number of customers?
- What is the structure of the technical support group? How many people are in it, and what is their compensation?
- Obtain a list of all customers who have stopped doing business with the company in the last three years.

E.17   OTHER

- Discuss revenue recognition policies.
- Construct a cash forecast through the end of the year.
- Obtain a copy of the chart of accounts.
- Determine risk management strategies and insurance coverage.
- Is there a 401(k) plan? Any company contribution? Who manages it? Are contribution payments current?
- Evaluate the company benefit plan to determine its cost, as well as the amount of employee participation.
- Obtain a list of all significant accounting policies.

INDEX